THE EMC MASTERPIECE SERIES

Literature

and the Language Arts

GRADES 6–12

Discovering Literature
Grade 6

Exploring Literature
Grade 7

Responding to Literature
Grade 8

Experiencing Literature
Grade 9

Understanding Literature
Grade 10

The American Tradition
Grade 11

The British Tradition
Grade 12

World Literature

Imagine the Possibilities...

Literature
and the Language Arts

GRADES 6–12

MIDDLE SCHOOL PROGRAM SAMPLER

Why Choose *The EMC Masterpiece Series*?
1. Quality of literature
2. Diversity of literature selections
3. Reading strategies that provide access for all students
4. Direct writing instruction integrated with grammar development
5. In-depth coverage of language arts skills
6. Comprehensive support materials

Six Reasons to Choose *The EMC Masterpiece Series*

1. Quality of Literature

Clockwise from left: Chaim Potok, Gary Soto, Zora Neale Hurston

The EMC Masterpiece Series:
- Provides you and your students with a **comprehensive collection of classic literary works** as well as compelling **contemporary and multicultural selections**.

Award-Winning Authors:
- Maya Angelou, "Caged Bird"
- Chaim Potok, "Zebra"
- Gary Soto, "Born Worker"
- Frances Goodrich and Albert Hackett, *The Diary of Anne Frank*
- Seamus Heaney, "Digging"
- Zora Neale Hurston, "How the Snake Got Poison"
- Patricia McKissack, "The 11:59"

2. Diversity of Literature Selections

Clockwise from left: Sandra Cisneros, Joseph Bruchac, Cherylene Lee

- **Expands students' imaginative abilities and sympathies** by exposing them to points of view and cultural experiences unlike their own.
- Provides selections representative of the **cultural and ethnic diversity** of our literary heritage.
- Contains an unequaled representation of works by **authors from various cultural backgrounds**.

Diversity of Literature:
- Sandra Cisneros, "Good Hot Dogs"
- Joseph Bruchac, "Jed's Grandfather"
- Toni Cade Bambara, "The War of the Wall"
- Cherylene Lee, "Hollywood and the Pits"
- Li-Young Lee, "I Ask My Mother to Sing"
- Oscar Hijuelos, "Nothing but Drums"

3. Reading Strategies Provide Access for All Students

The EMC Masterpiece Series:
- Provides step-by-step study strategies to ensure the careful development of student understanding.
- Features a **reader response** emphasis that motivates students through high-interest affective and cognitive activities to relate literature to students' experiences, followed by teacher-directed activities to ensure cultural transmission.

The EMC Masterpiece Series helps students before, during, and after their reading of the selection with its **Guided Reading** program.

Before Reading

During Reading

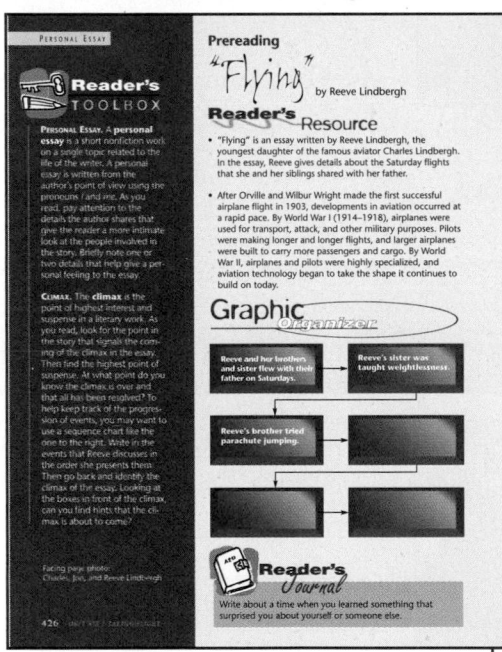

- **Reader's Resource** provides cross-curricular and contextual information.
- **Reader's Toolbox** introduces literary techniques or concepts that will help the reader understand the selection. The same concepts are reinforced in the Understanding Literature section of the Post-Reading materials.
- A **Graphic Organizer** or other visual literacy piece is provided for visual learners.
- **Reader's Journal** activities help create the anticipatory set by relating the literature to students' experiences.
- **Guided Reading Questions** help students gather facts about the selection that will help in their response to higher-level thinking skills.
- **Words for Everyday Use** provide pronunciations, parts of speech, definitions, and contextual sentences for vocabulary underlined in the selection.
- **Footnotes** explain obscure references, unusual usage, and terms meant to enter students' passive vocabularies.
- **ArtSmart** notes provide historical, cultural, or artistic information about fine art.

- **Respond to the Selection** activities relate the literature to students' lives.
- **Investigate, Inquire, and Imagine** questions base literature interpretation on textual evidence.
  - **Recall** questions address comprehension. **Interpret** questions use facts from the Recall question as a basis for valid interpretation.
  - **Analyze** questions ask readers to classify, compare and contrast, and identify relationships between ideas. **Synthesize** questions ask readers to integrate, restructure, predict, elaborate, and summarize.
  - **Evaluate** questions ask students to appraise, assess, critique, and justify certain aspects of a selection. **Extend** questions allow readers to try out their understanding in different situations.
  - **Perspective** questions encourage students to look for and value alternative perspectives. **Empathy** questions ask the student to demonstrate understanding of another person's worldview.

- **Understanding Literature** questions reinforce the literary concepts and techniques that were introduced on the Prereading page in the Reader's Toolbox feature.

- **Writer's Journal** includes three quick-writing prompts that are graded as simple, moderate, and challenging.

- **Language Arts Skill Builders** provide integrated activities in the following language arts areas, tying language arts instruction to the literature selection:

  - Language, Grammar, and Style
  - Speaking and Listening
  - Study and Research
  - Applied English
  - Collaborative Learning
  - Media Literacy
  - Vocabulary
  - Critical Thinking

After Reading

4. Direct Writing Instruction Integrated with Grammar Development

The **Guided Writing Program** provides direct writing instruction for each literature unit and pairs the writing process with an integrated **Language, Grammar, and Style** lesson. The Guided Writing lesson includes professional and student models, graphic organizers, questions that allow students to link their reading experience to the writing assignment, and an integrated grammar lesson. Additional support is provided by:

Writer's Resource. This ancillary provides general and mode-specific writing rubrics, student-friendly checklists, student models for each assignment, graphic organizers, and student handouts.

Electronic Guided Writing Software. The Guided Writing Software provides extended lessons that deliver print content and extensions electronically.

Language Arts Survey

The **Language Arts Survey** in *The EMC Masterpiece Series* has the most extensive language arts skills coverage of any program. The coverage of English skills is so comprehensive that an additional English skills textbook is not necessary. The Language Arts Survey sections may be taught as separate units, using the student textbook and ancillary worksheets, or may be taught in conjunction with study of the literature.

There are six sections in the Language Arts Survey:

1. The **Reading Resource** surveys and enhances the reading process.

2. The **Writing Resource** surveys the entire process of writing. It includes computer-assisted composition and portfolio writing.

3. The **Language, Grammar, and Style Resource** surveys key concepts in grammar, usage, mechanics, spelling, vocabulary development, and language variety. Grammar, usage, and mechanics instruction focus on editing and proofreading applications.

4. The **Speaking and Listening Resource** surveys verbal and nonverbal communication, active listening, interpersonal communication, discussion, public speaking, and oral interpretation.

5. The **Study and Research Resource** surveys thinking, reading, research, and test-taking skills, including skills for taking standardized tests.

6. The **Applied English Resource** surveys applications of English skills to the world of work.

Language Arts Survey: Writing

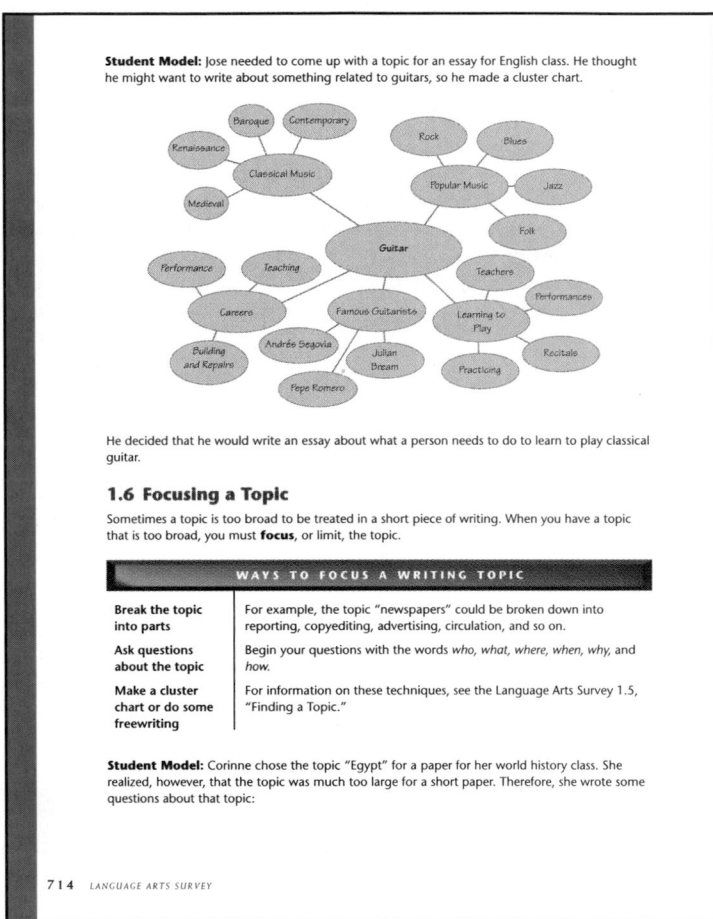

Student Model: Jose needed to come up with a topic for an essay for English class. He thought he might want to write about something related to guitars, so he made a cluster chart.

He decided that he would write an essay about what a person needs to do to learn to play classical guitar.

1.6 Focusing a Topic

Sometimes a topic is too broad to be treated in a short piece of writing. When you have a topic that is too broad, you must **focus**, or limit, the topic.

WAYS TO FOCUS A WRITING TOPIC	
Break the topic into parts	For example, the topic "newspapers" could be broken down into reporting, copyediting, advertising, circulation, and so on.
Ask questions about the topic	Begin your questions with the words *who, what, where, when, why,* and *how.*
Make a cluster chart or do some freewriting	For information on these techniques, see the Language Arts Survey 1.5, "Finding a Topic."

Student Model: Corinne chose the topic "Egypt" for a paper for her world history class. She realized, however, that the topic was much too large for a short paper. Therefore, she wrote some questions about that topic:

6. Comprehensive Support Materials

Literature
and the Language Arts
MIDDLE SCHOOL PROGRAM

Supplementary and Multimedia Components
The EMC Masterpiece Series provides a wide array of ancillary tools to offer teachers many options to help students connect with the literature.

Each level in the middle school program includes the following materials:
- Pupil's Edition with Language Arts Survey
- Annotated Teacher's Edition
- Annotated Teacher's Edition on CD-ROM (with links to Language Arts Survey and ancillaries)
- Teacher's Resource Kit
  - Program Manager with Scope and Sequence / Lesson Planning Guide
  - Parent and Community Involvement Handbook
  - 12 Unit Resource Books
    - Guided Reading Resource (Selection Worksheets and Graphic Organizers for Reader's Toolbox / Literary Tools, Post-Reading, and Understanding Literature)
    - Vocabulary SkillBuilders / Daily Oral Language Activities
    - Selection Check Tests and Selection Tests
    - Unit Tests
    - Answer Keys
    - Reading Logs
    - Research Journal
    - Language, Grammar and Style; Speaking and Listening; Study and Research; and Applied English worksheets related to unit
  - Guided Reading Resource
  - Guided Writing Resource
  - Language, Grammar, and Style Resource
  - Speaking and Listening Resource
  - Study and Research Resource
  - Applied English Resource
  - Transparency and Visual Literacy Resource
  - Assessment Resource

Additional components:
- Guided Writing Interactive Software
- Test Generator
- Audio Library on Audiocassette and Audio CD
- Electronic Library on CD-ROM
- Access Edition Supplemental Novels and Plays
- Assessment Manuals for Access Editions

TEXT SUPPORT TOOLS

- Annotated Teacher's Edition

- Annotated Teacher's Edition on CD-ROM

Teacher's Resource Kit for each level:
- Program Manager
- Parent and Community Involvement Handbook

- Unit Resource Books with ancillary materials for each unit:
    - Guided Reading Resource
    - Vocabulary Skillbuilders / Daily Oral Language Activities
    - Selection Check Tests and Selection Tests
    - Unit Tests
    - Answer Keys
    - Reading Logs
    - Research Journal
    - Integrated Language Arts Worksheets

- Assessment Resource

- Resource workbooks in these subject areas:
    - Guided Reading
    - Guided Writing
    - Language, Grammar, and Style
    - Speaking and Listening
    - Thinking, Study, and Research
    - Applied English
    - Visual Literacy / Transparency Resource

ADDITIONAL COMPONENTS FOR EACH LEVEL INCLUDE:

- Guided Writing Interactive Software

- Assessment Resource Test Generator

- Audio Library on Audiocassette and Audio CD

Other Supplementary Materials:

- Electronic Library on CD-ROM

- Access Editions

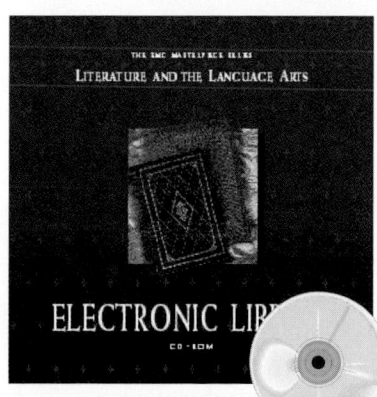

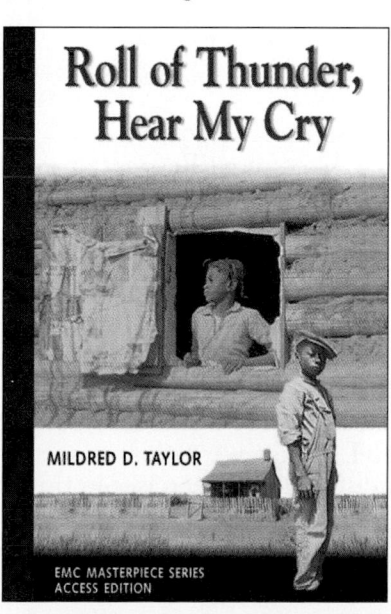

TEACHER'S RESOURCE KIT

The Teacher's Resource Kit for each level includes the following components:

Program Manager
The Program Manager provides thorough scope and sequence charts and clear, simple, ready-to-use lesson plans. Timed activities allow for a variety of approaches and scheduling options (including block scheduling) tailored to your classroom needs.

Parent and Community Involvement Handbook
The Parent and Community Involvement Handbook, featuring an introductory letter to parents written in both Spanish and English, helps parents assist their children with their studies through study log blackline masters, parent guides, activity lists, suggested reading lists, and additional resource references.

Unit Resource Books with ancillary materials for each unit:
Unit Resource Books pull together ancillary materials from a variety of sources that are used in each unit. They include the following:
- Guided Reading Resource
- Vocabulary Skillbuilders/Daily Oral Language
- Selection Check Tests and Selection Tests
- Unit Tests
- Answer Keys
- Reading Logs
- Research Journal
- Integrated Language Arts Worksheets

Assessment Resource
The Assessment Resource provides blackline master materials for:
- Unit study guides and tests, including vocabulary worksheets
- Selection check tests and comprehensive tests
- Language arts study guides, pre-tests, and post-tests
- Worksheets and forms for portfolio assessment
- Answer keys

Resource Workbooks
The Resource workbooks contain blackline masters of exercises keyed to the Language Arts Survey sections of the student textbooks. They provide additional skill exercises in these language arts subject areas:
- Guided Reading
- Guided Writing
- Language, Grammar, and Style
- Speaking and Listening
- Thinking, Study, and Research
- Applied English

ADDITIONAL COMPONENTS FOR EACH LEVEL INCLUDE:

Annotated Teacher's Edition on CD-ROM
- Annotated Teacher's Edition on CD-ROM, compatible with Macintosh and Windows systems, provides easy access to the selections.
- Teachers can view on screen or print selections into a more portable form instead of carrying the textbook home to plan classes.
- Teachers can preview blackline masters from Resource workbooks and other supplemental materials via hyperlinks.

Guided Writing Interactive Software
The Guided Writing Interactive Software builds on the Guided Writing and Integrated Language, Grammar, and Style lessons in the textbook. The "writer-friendly" word processor includes:
- Capacity for self-, peer, and teacher evaluation notes
- Spelling and grammar utilities
- Hypertext links providing help specific to the writing task
- Printable graphic organizers, checklists, and student handouts
- Portfolio management system for teachers
- Windows and Macintosh compatibility

Assessment Resource Test Generator
The Assessment Resource is available in electronic form, running on Windows and Macintosh formats. Teachers can generate customized true/false, multiple choice, short answer, and essay tests based on literature selections in each unit.

Audio Library on Audiocassette and Audio CD
- Includes 10 to 12 hours of audio recordings for each grade level in the program.
- Features authentic, dramatic interpretations by professional actors and academic scholars with a balance of multicultural male and female voices.
- Readings are geared toward English language and auditory learners.
- Available on audiocassette and audio compact disc.
- Accompanying Audio Library Booklet describes each performance and offers creative ideas on how to use the audio component selection in the classroom.

OTHER SUPPLEMENTARY MATERIALS

Electronic Library on CD-ROM
- Over 20,000 pages of literary classics
- Contains 120 long selections, including epic poems, novels, plays, nonfiction, and verse; as well as 194 short selections, which include poetry and excerpts.
- Can view on screen or print out individual selections instead of carrying multiple texts home to plan classes.
- Electronic Library Guide provides teaching suggestions, enrichment activities, and Guided Reading blackline masters.
- Available for Windows and Macintosh.

Access Editions
Each **Access Edition** contains the following materials:
- The complete literary work
- A historical introduction including an explanation of literary or philosophical movements relevant to the work
- A biographical introduction with a time line of the author's life
- Art, including explanatory illustrations, maps, genealogies and plot diagrams, as appropriate to the text
- Study apparatus for each chapter or section, including:
  - Guided Reading Questions
  - Words for Everyday Use entries for point-of-use vocabulary development
  - Footnotes
  - Responding to the Selection questions
  - Reviewing the Selection questions (with recalling, interpreting, and high-level questions to assure your students a close and accessible reading of the text)
  - Understanding Literature questions
- A list of topics for creative writing, critical writing, and research projects
- A glossary of Words for Everyday Use
- A Handbook of Literary Terms

Each Access Edition title is supplemented with an **Assessment Manual** that provides a full assessment program. The Assessment Manual is divided into five parts:
1. **Answer Key**—provides answers to the Reviewing the Selection and Understanding Literature questions in the text.
2. **Graphic Organizers**—enhances students' comprehension of the selection.
3. **Vocabulary and Literary Terms Review**—tests students' knowledge of the Words for Everyday Use and literary terms defined in the work.
4. **Exam Masters**—contain complete exams that test students' overall comprehension of the work through both creative writing, critical writing, and research projects.
5. **Evaluation Forms**—provide tools for self-, peer-, and teacher assessment of creative writing, critical thinking and research projects.

Contents

Overview

The editors and authors of *The EMC Masterpiece Series, Literature and the Language Arts* have designed the middle school program to be as student- and teacher-friendly as possible. The course is divided into twelve units, offering flexibility for a variety of scheduling options. *Literature and the Language Arts* takes both a theme-based and genre-based approach to the teaching of literature: Part One presents six theme-based units, and Part Two presents six genre-based units. Teachers who wish to take a theme-based approach further should consult the Thematic Organization Chart on page T32. Teachers who wish to emphasize a genre approach should consult the Selections by Genre pages starting on page T35.

Part One: Themes in Literature presents literature using a thematic approach. This section begins with the premise that the middle school student's primary concern is him- or herself. From there, the themes move outward. Themes are Unit 1, Finding Your Place in the World; Unit 2, The World Around Us; Unit 3, From One World to Another; Unit 4, A Sporting Life; Unit 5, Chills and Thrills; and Unit 6, Taking Flight.

Part Two: Genres in Literature starts with Unit 7, The Oral Tradition. In Grade 7, The Oral Tradition unit focuses on World Mythology, with an emphasis on myths from Greece, Mesopotamia, Egypt, Africa, India, and Japan. (This is developed as part of a broader middle school oral tradition

scope and sequence in which Grade 6: Discovering Literature emphasizes different types of works, including myths, legends, fairy tales, and folk tales; and Grade 8: Responding to Literature provides an in-depth look at Folklore of the Americas.) The genre approach continues in Grade 7 with Unit 8, Stories to Tell: Fiction; Unit 9, Words in Motion: Poetry; Unit 10, Turning Words into Action: Drama; Unit 11, Telling It As It Is: Nonfiction; and Unit 12: Reading Between the Lines: Informational and Visual Media. Unit 12 approaches works that require a new type of visual and informational literacy and helps students extend the literacy they have developed in reading great works of literature throughout the *Literature and the Language Arts* program. Non-literary visual and informational media selections are frequently followed by literary texts in this unit. For example, Variations in Vital Signs by Age and Temperature Conversions charts work a student's ability to interpret numeric data and graphic organization. These selections are followed by the Related Reading "A Day's Wait" by Ernest Hemingway, in which a boy believes he is going to die because he confuses a Celsius and Fahrenheit thermometer. Historical photographs of the Oklahoma Dust Bowl by Arthur Rothstein are paired with passages from Karen Hesse's Newbery Award-winning novel *Out of the Dust*.

Each unit teaches English vocabulary with **Words for Everyday Use** and concludes with a **Unit Review** that offers a review of vocabulary and literary terms and **Reflecting on Your Reading** ques-

tions for discussion or writing. Each unit includes a **Guided Writing** lesson that integrates a lesson in language, grammar, and style.

Part Three: Language Arts Survey contains six sections. It offers comprehensive instruction in the complete range of language arts skills—Reading; Writing; Language, Grammar, and Style; Speaking and Listening; Study and Research; and Applied English. (Each lesson in the Language Arts Survey is keyed to a worksheet in one of the Resource Books in the Teacher's Resource Kit.)

The **Handbook of Literary Terms** defines and provides examples of terms for literary concepts, techniques, and genres of literature. The **Glossary** collects all the Words for Everyday Use and provides both pronunciations and definitions. The text ends with **indexes** of titles and authors, skills, Internet sites, and fine art.

Part One: Themes in Literature presents literature using a thematic approach. It consists of six units organized by themes designed to appeal to middle school readers.

Part Two: Genres in Literature contains six units building understanding in the five major literary genres—the oral tradition, fiction, poetry, drama, and nonfiction, as well as in informational and visual media.

An **Echoes** feature starts each theme-based unit with several quotations geared to get students thinking about the theme.

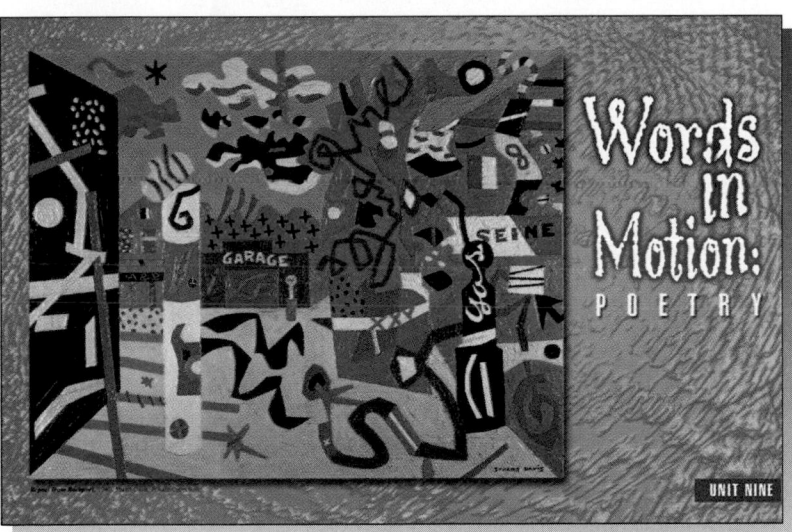

An **Elements of Genre** feature begins each genre-based unit with information about key literary concepts.

**Part Three: Language
Arts Survey** *is a comprehensive guide
containing the following six parts:*

*(1) The **Reading Resource** shows
students how to strategize and improve
their reading abilities. It emphasizes
adapting reading strategies depending on
purpose: reading for experience (literature), reading to learn (textbooks and
nonfiction), and reading for information
(Internet materials, reference works, and
visuals). It also includes a section on
vocabulary development. The Reading
Resource is used in Post-Reading activities and is referenced in the Individual
Learning Strategies feature in the
Annotated Teacher's Edition.*

*(2) The **Writing Resource** provides an
overview of the writing process and then
takes students step by step through that
process. The Writing Resource is used in
Post-Reading activities and extensively in
the Guided Writing lessons at the end of
each of the twelve literature units.*

*(3) The **Language, Grammar, and
Style Resource** provides a Language
Handbook, Grammar Handbook, and
Style Handbook to help students master
their use of the English language. The
Language Handbook explores appropriate
uses of English, including choices regarding formal and informal English; register, tone, and voice; irony, sarcasm, and
rudeness; and dialects. The Grammar
Handbook has been designed with the
understanding that the basic unit of
English meaning is the English sentence
and takes a sentence-based approach in
its instruction and all integrated grammar exercises. The Style Handbook is a
capitalization, punctuation, and spelling
reference.*

*(4) The **Speaking and Listening
Resource** provides instruction in the
power of communication, listening skills,
communicating with others, communica-*

*tion styles and cultural barriers, and
public speaking. The Speaking and
Listening Resource is used in Post-
Reading activities and in the Guided
Writing lessons.*

*(5) The **Study and Research
Resource** includes sections on thinking
skills, study skills, research skills, and
test-taking skills. It is used extensively in
Post-Reading activities and in Guided
Writing lessons. Particular attention is
given to conducting research online and
evaluating the reliability of Internet
sources.*

*(6) The **Applied English Resource**
includes instruction on applications of
English skills to the world of work. Topics
include following and giving directions,
writing step-by-step procedures, writing
personal and business letters, memos, proposals, public service announcements, and
displaying effective visual information.
These and other topics are integrated in
the Post-Reading activities throughout
the textbook.*

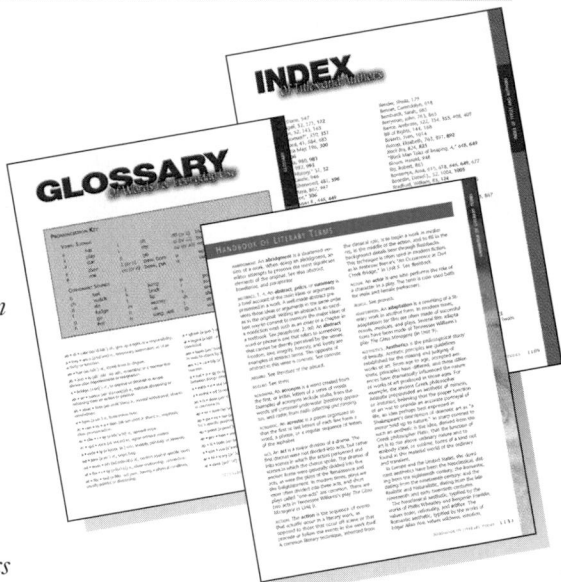

The textbook also contains

- *A thorough **Handbook of Literary
  Terms***

- *A **Glossary** of Words for
  Everyday Use*

- ***Indexes** of Titles and Authors,
  Skills, Internet Sites, and Fine Art*

Literature Instruction

Each lesson in *Literature and the Language Arts* contains materials for two phases of instruction, the Reader Response phase and the Teacher-Assisted phase.

The Reader Response Phase. Cognitive theory and common sense tell us that learning is more likely to occur when students are first provided with a context for what they are to learn. Each lesson in this book begins with a **Prereading** page that provides essential background information that connects the literary work to one or more other curricular areas and that gives the student an active reading strategy to carry out while reading the selection. This strategy often includes a **Graphic Organizer** to accommodate visual learning styles. The Cross-Curricular Connections identified in the **Reader's Resource** explore a wide variety of topics across the middle school curriculum. The precise content of the Reader's Resource entries varies according to the demands of the work to be read. If basic comprehension of the work requires understanding of a historical allusion, then that allusion is explained. If comprehension requires understanding of a literary technique, then that technique is described. In addition, the Prereading page provides information about the author and selection designed to arouse student interest. Each Prereading page also contains a **Reader's Toolbox** feature which introduces literary techniques or concepts that will help the reader understand the selection. The same concepts are reinforced in the Understanding Literature section of the Post-Reading material.

The Prereading page also includes a **Reader's Journal** activity that raises a central theme from the selection and asks the student to relate that theme to his or her own life. If, for example, a selection presents a character who fails to exhibit courage, the student might be asked to write about a time when he or she acted courageously or wanted to act courageously

Sample Prereading Page

Reader's Toolbox introduces literary techniques or concepts that will help the reader understand the selection. These same items will be developed further at the Post-Reading stage.

*A **Graphic Organizer** is provided in Prereading or Post-Reading for visual learners.*

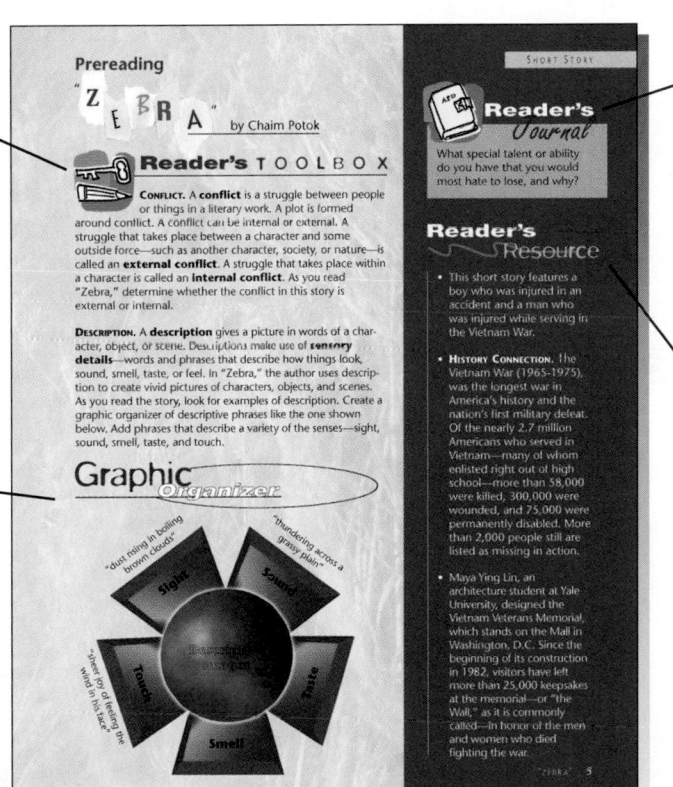

Reader's Journal activities help create the anticipatory set by relating the literature to students' own lives.

Reader's Resource provides cross-curricular and contextual information designed to help the student prepare for the literature selection.

but could not. After completing this exercise, students will be thinking of courage in terms of their own lives and will be more likely to relate personally to the selection and become emotionally invested in it. Emotional investment in the work is key to the reading of literature, and that is why the Reader's Journal activities are primarily affective in nature. Responses to these Reader's Journal activities can be made on the **Selection Worksheets** found in the **Unit Resource Books,** or they can be made in the student's notebook.

Once the student begins reading the selection, he or she can then take advantage of the **Guided Reading Questions** that appear within the literature selection. These comprehension questions are designed to bring to the student's attention key passages in the selection and issues raised by those passages. These

Guided Reading questions take the student through the selection, ensuring that the most important or interesting aspects of the selection will not be missed. (It would be wonderful if every student could have his or her own private tutor while reading the literature. These questions provide the next best thing.) The student can answer these questions on the Selection Worksheets or in his or her notebook.

After reading the selection, students can meet in small collaborative learning groups to share responses to the Reader's Journal activity and Guided Reading Questions. In these groups, students can also discuss the questions raised in the **Respond to the Selection** feature that follows the selection. Again, this is an affective-response prompt designed to connect the student emotionally to the literature.

These three components of the instructional apparatus, the Reader's Journal activity, the Guided Reading questions, and the Respond to the Selection activity, connect the student to the selection, guide him or her through it, and then make it possible for the student to share his or her responses with others. Together, these activities ensure that once the teacher-assisted phase of the instruction begins, the student will have a wealth of responses to share in discussions with the whole class.

Additional teaching suggestions for the Reader's Journal and Respond to the Selection activities are provided in the Annotated Teacher's Edition. Answers to Guided Reading Questions appear on the corresponding page of the Annotated Teacher's Edition.

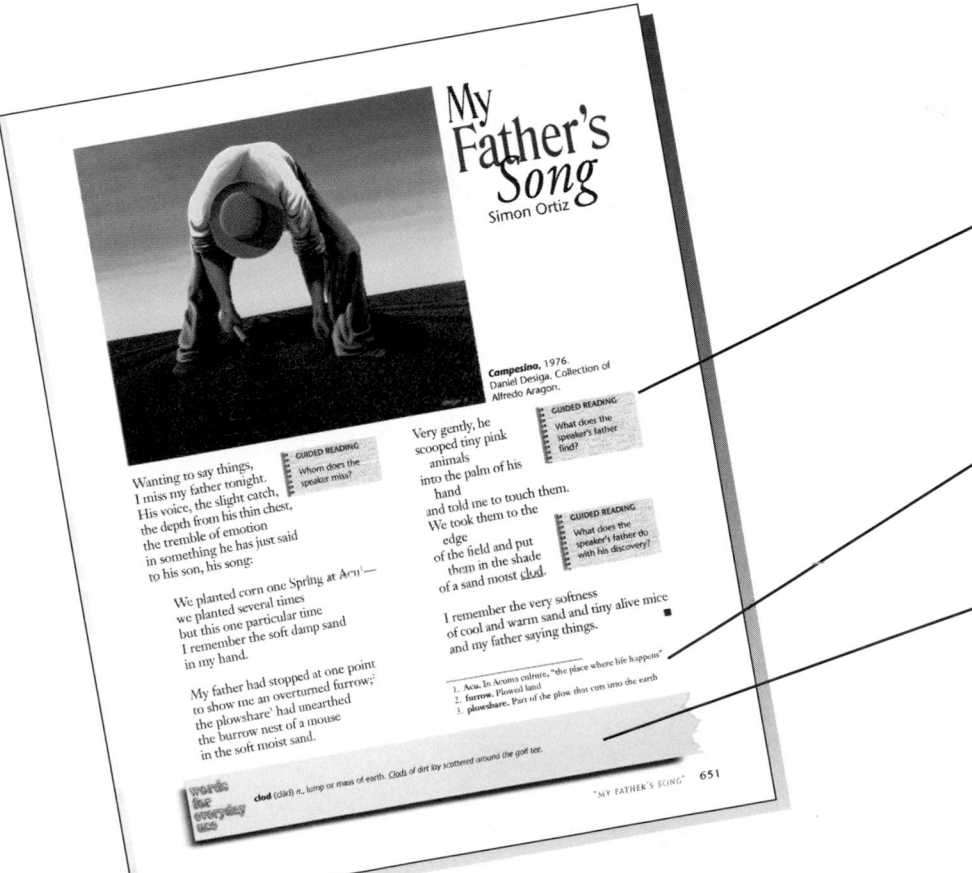

Sample Selection Page

Guided Reading Questions *guide students through the selection and help them to recognize and understand important ideas and key points. The questions help all students reach a basic understanding of the selection.*

Footnotes *explain obscure references, unusual usages, and terms meant to enter students' passive vocabularies and are defined separately from active vocabulary.*

The *Words for Everyday Use* *feature, included in selections at point of use, defines and gives pronunciations for difficult terms meant to enter students' active vocabularies, and includes a contextual sentence to increase vocabulary development.*

The Teacher-Assisted Phase. The **Investigate, Inquire, and Imagine** questions that follow the Respond to the Selection feature are designed to take the student through the selection step by step, building upon his or her responses and refining them through questions of successive complexity. These questions are paired to complement each other and increase in complexity and sophistication to develop higher-level thinking skills. The most basic pairing, **Recall/Interpret**, is followed by **Analyze/Synthesize**, and may conclude with either an **Evaluate/Extend** or **Perspective/Empathy** pairing.

These question sets are structured to develop different levels of cognitive thinking skills, based on *Bloom's Taxonomy of Educational Objectives*. Bloom's taxonomy has been the most widely employed system for labeling and understanding levels of cognitive processing used in test construction since its publication in 1956. It is commonly used in variously modified forms by many educational test developers. The primary categories of cognitive thinking levels in Bloom's taxonomy include the following six levels:

1. Knowledge: involves the recall of specifics, methods, and processes
2. Comprehension: represents the lowest level of understanding
3. Application: uses abstractions in particular and concrete situations
4. Analysis: breaks down communication into its elements or parts
5. Synthesis: brings together elements and parts to form a whole
6. Evaluation: makes judgments about the value of material and methods

The questions in Investigate, Inquire, and Imagine take the students through these six levels of the cognitive domain, as well as taking them a step further by developing their appreciation of other perspectives and empathy for others.

- Recall questions ensure that students remember the basic key facts from the selections (knowledge).
- Interpret questions use facts from Recall questions as a basis for valid interpretation (comprehension).
- Analyze questions ask readers to classify, compare and contrast, and identify relationships between ideas (analysis).
- Synthesize questions are linked to Analyze questions and ask readers to integrate, restructure, predict, elaborate, and summarize (synthesis).
- Evaluate questions ask students to appraise, assess, critique, and make judgments about certain aspects of a selection (evaluation).
- Extend questions are paired with Evaluate questions, and allow readers to try out their understanding in a different context that may link to a student's own experience, to a contemporary real world situation, or to another literary or artistic work (application).
- Perspective questions develop insight and self-knowledge by encouraging students to look for and value alternative perspectives.
- Empathy questions complement Perspective questions and facilitate knowledge of others by asking students to demonstrate understanding of another person's worldview. See table below.

Because students are frequently unfamiliar with literary terminology and its applications, such terminology does not appear in the questions for Investigate, Inquire, and Imagine. Literary terminology and techniques are covered in the

next part of the instructional apparatus, which is called **Understanding Literature.** Reinforcing the terms defined in the Reader's Toolbox feature on the Prereading page, each Understanding Literature activity begins with a bold-faced term that identifies a literary movement, genre, or technique. The term is followed by its definition and by one or more questions that apply the concept to the selection. Having responded to the selection and having reviewed it in detail, the student can now learn some of the technical details about how the selection worked to achieve its effects. Students needing or desiring additional information about a term introduced in the Reader's Toolbox and Understanding Literature sections can refer to the discussion of that term in the **Handbook of Literary Terms** at the back of the book.

Approaches to the teacher-assisted phase of the literature instruction can vary, depending on your teaching style and your students' needs. Some teachers will prefer to have students answer the Investigate, Inquire, and Imagine and Understanding Literature questions individually or in small groups and will then hold whole-class discussions of these questions. Others will prefer to treat these questions as prompts for whole-class, teacher-directed discussions. Another alternative, especially appropriate in advanced classes, is to assign students to lead small group or whole-class discussions of these questions.

Inquire, Investigate, Imagine	Bloom's Taxonomy
Recall	Knowledge
Interpret	Comprehension
Analyze	Analysis
Synthesize	Synthesis
Evaluate	Evaluation
Extend	Application
Alternate Question Set	
Perspective	Insight and self-knowledge
Empathy	Knowledge of others

Gains in Critical Thinking

Instruction in Other Language Arts Skills: An Integrated Approach

It has been shown that a student may demonstrate knowledge in a classroom but be unable to use that knowledge in "real-life" situations. Grammar, usage, mechanics, spelling, and vocabulary skills have traditionally been taught in isolation as independent skills but, just as instruction in the separate concepts of physiology does not make us healthier, neither does instruction in the abstract concepts of speech or grammar make us speak or write better (Hillocks; Braddock). Skills must be taught in ways that enable students to "transfer" them to real contexts, i.e., to use them in their lives. The transferability of knowledge is a function of meaningfulness (Prawat). Teachers can promote meaningfulness by providing (1) a wide variety of examples, (2) practice in a wide variety of contexts, (3) an explanation of the value or uses of the lesson, (4) an advance organizer at the beginning of the lesson, and (5) reviews. These five tasks have served as guideposts in the planning and writing of *Literature and the Language Arts*.

The exercises in this text are organized so that instruction in essential skills—reading; writing; language, grammar and style; speaking and listening; media literacy; study and research; critical thinking;

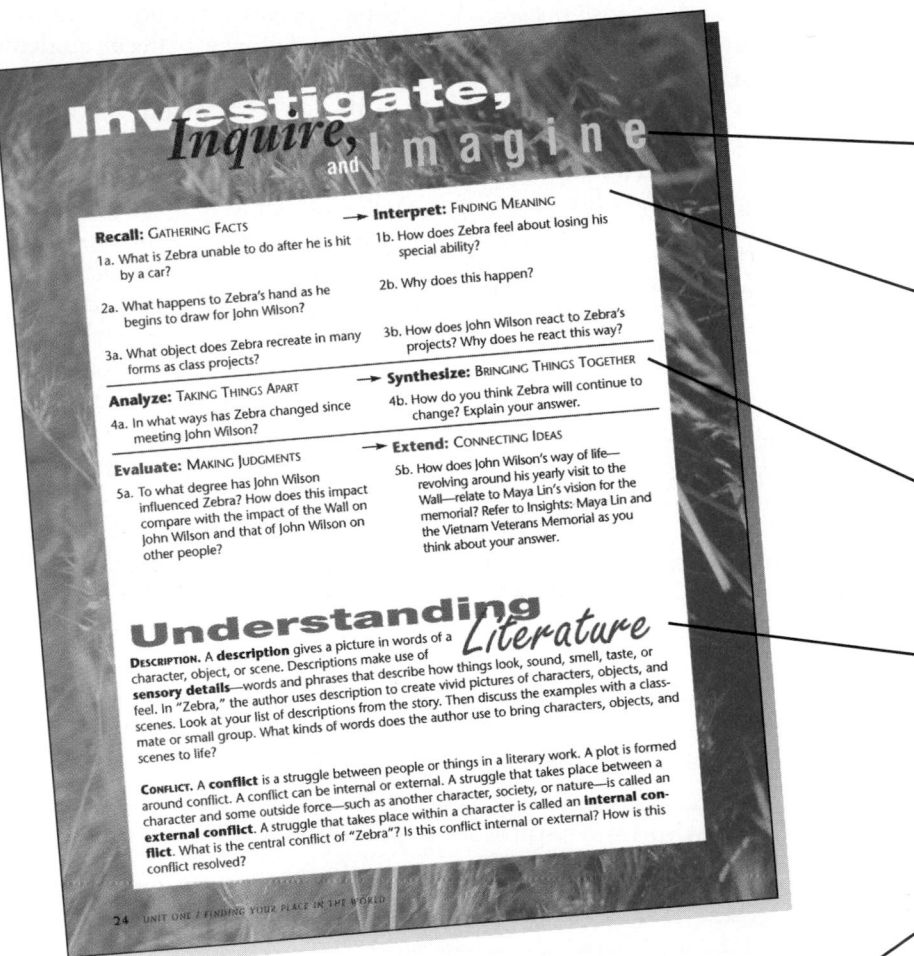

Sample Post-Reading Page

Investigate, Inquire, and Imagine takes students through the work step by step, building from their individual responses a complete interpretation of the selection.

Recall questions address comprehension of key facts from the selection. *Interpret* questions, keyed to the Recall questions by arrows, evoke interpretations based on evidence from the selection.

Paired questions such as *Analyze / Synthesize*, *Evaluate / Extend*, and *Perspective / Empathy* lead students to higher-level thinking.

Understanding Literature questions reinforce the Reader's Toolbox concepts introduced in Prereading.

Respond to the Selection is a reader response activity designed to elicit an affective response to the selection.

About the Author includes firsthand interview material or extensive biographical material.

test-taking; vocabulary development; and applied English—develops in the context of activities integrated with the study of literature. The connection to engaging literature can provide motivation and context for teaching these practical skills.

The **Writer's Journal** activities in the Post-Reading section of the lesson use the selection as a springboard for creative and critical quick-writing assignments. Several **Skill Builders** activities follow the Writer's Journal. These help students develp proficiency in language arts areas,

including language, grammar, and style; speaking and listening; study and research; applied English; collaborative learning; media literacy; vocabulary development; and critical thinking.

A typical Skill Builder asks students to read a section of the Language Arts Survey and then complete an exercise. Each exercise relates to the work of literature that students have just studied. For example, a Skill Builder exercise on page 196 teaches students how to understand base works and prefixes to develop

vocabulary based on Joan Aiken's "The Serial Garden" in Unit 3. A media literacy activity on page 596 asks students to use and create maps based on the setting of Paul Gallico's novella *The Snow Goose* in Unit 8.

Many literary selections are followed by a **Related Reading** or **Insights** feature. These features enrich the reading experience by allowing students to connect selections they have read to a larger context.

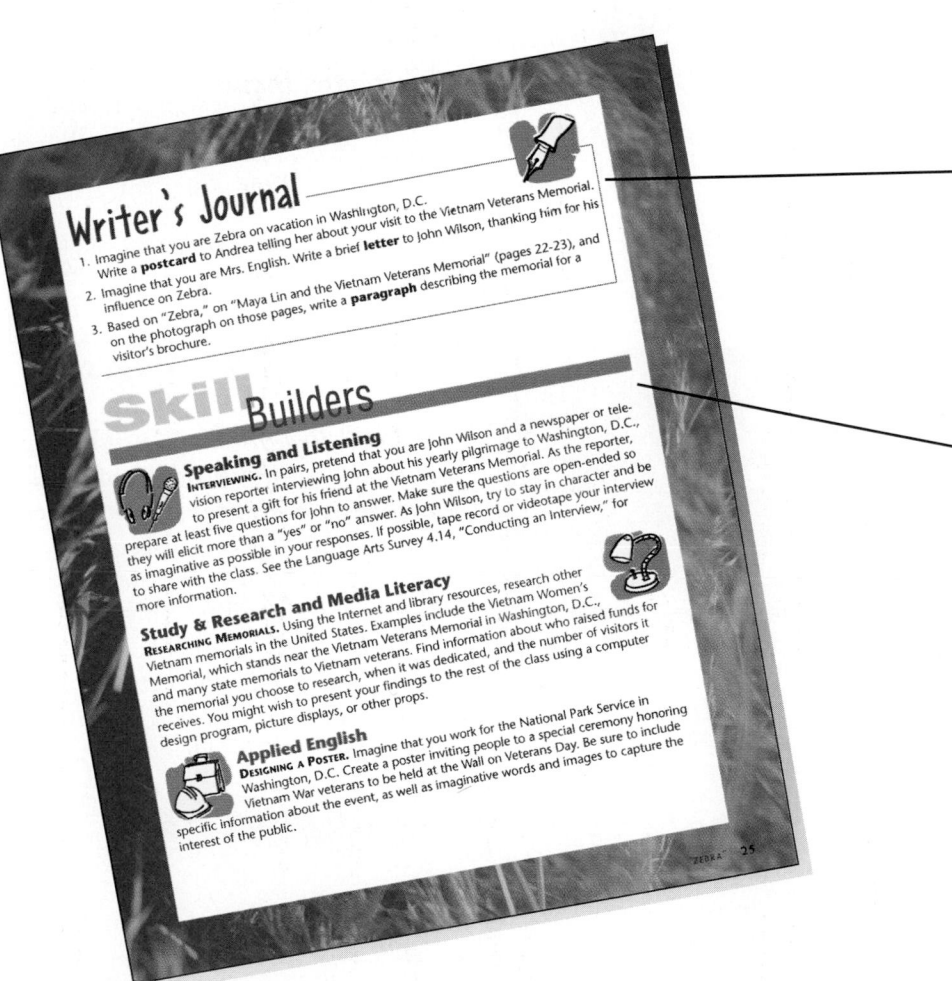

Sample Post-Reading Page

Writer's Journal activities use the selection as a springboard for engaging writing assignments that require both creative and critical thinking skills. Every literary selection includes three writing prompts that are graded as simple, moderate, and challenging.

Skill Builders activities provide integrated activities in language arts areas, including language, grammar, and style; speaking and listening; study and research; applied English; collaborative learning; media literacy; vocabulary development; and critical thinking.

The **Language Arts Survey** at the back of the book provides a comprehensive overview of the complete range of language arts skills. The survey is divided into six sections, as follows:

- Reading Resource
- Writing Resource
- Language, Grammar, and Style Resource
- Speaking and Listening Resource
- Study and Research Resource
- Applied English Resource

Students are asked to refer to these sections when doing writing or language arts skills activities. Teachers wishing to give their students additional practice in any of these skills areas will find, for each lesson in the Language Arts Survey, a corresponding worksheet in one of the **Resource Books** found in the Teacher's Resource Kit. Teachers wishing to present whole units related to specific language arts skills can have students work through parts of the Language Arts Survey, doing the activities found in the Resource Books.

Partial Bibliography

Ausubel, D. *Educational Psychology.* 2nd ed. New York: Holt, 1978.

Bloom, B., et al. *Taxonomy of Educational Objectives, Handbook I, Cognitive Domain,* New York, NY: David McKay Company, Inc., 1956.

Braddock, R., R. Lloyd-Jones, and L. Schoer. *Research in Written Composition.* Champaign, IL: NCTE, 1963.

Bruner, J. *Toward a Theory of Instruction.* New York: Norton, 1966.

Eggen, P., and D. Kauchak. *Educational Psychology: Classroom Connections.* 2nd ed. New York: Merrill, 1994.

Eisner, E. *The Educational Imagination.* 2nd ed. New York: Macmillan, 1985.

Hillocks, G., Jr. *Research on Written Composition: New Directions for Teaching.* Urbana, IL: Natl. Conference on Research in English and ERIC/CRCS, 1986.

Novak, J. D. *A Theory of Education.* Ithaca, NY: Cornell UP, 1984.

Prawat, R. "Promoting Access to Knowledge, Strategy, and Disposition in Students: A Research Synthesis." *Review of Educational Research* 59 (1989): 1–41.

Sample Insights Pages

Related Reading and **Insights** *features follow some selections and provide enrichment by expanding upon a theme, genre, historical period or event, or other idea relevant to the literary work. For example,* Insights: Maya Lin and the Vietnam Veterans Memorial *follows Chaim Potok's short story,* "Zebra," *about a Vietnam veteran and artist who visits the Memorial each year.*

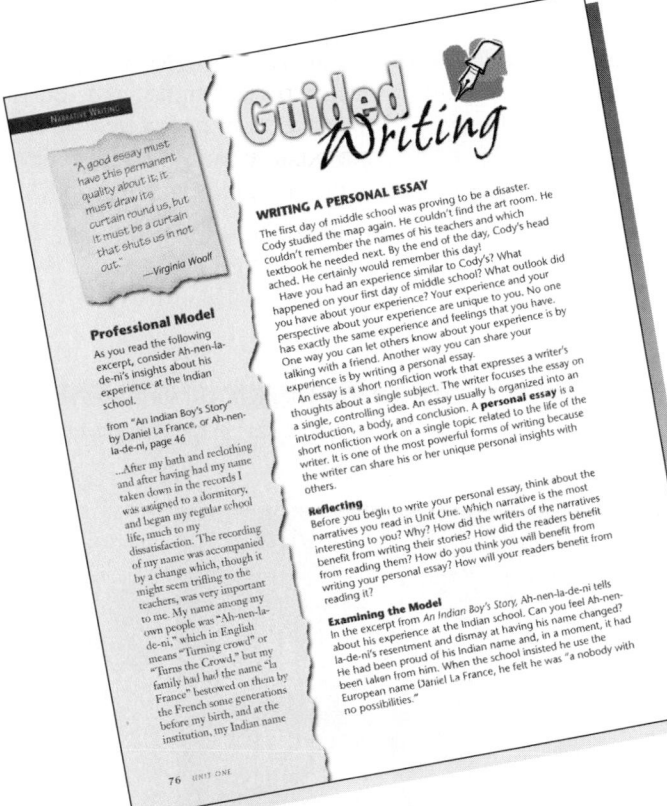

Guided Writing lessons at the end of each unit of the student edition provide direct writing instruction that covers a variety of purposes and different approaches to the writing process. Each Guided Writing lesson includes integrated Language, Grammar, and Style instruction to teach key language arts concepts in the context of writing.

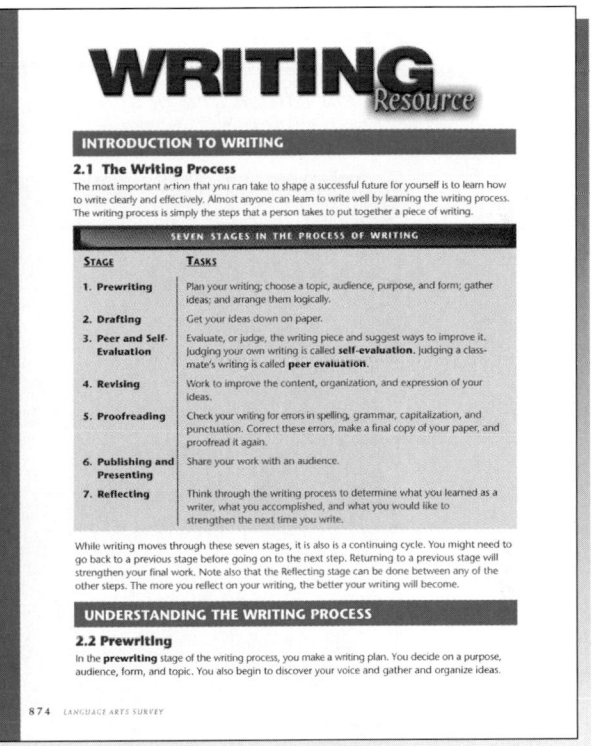

The Writing Resource in the **Language Arts Survey** at the end of the student edition provides a comprehensive overview of the complete range of language arts skills.

Language Arts **Resource Books** found in the Teacher's Resource Kit provide activities keyed to each lesson in the Language Arts Survey.

The **Annotated Teacher's Edition** is designed to be as "teacher-friendly" as possible. Answers for exercises are usually provided on the same pages as the exercises themselves. All items are color-coded:

- white backgrounds: answers to student edition questions, exercises, and selection check tests
- green backgrounds: supplementary notes and background information

- pink backgrounds: cross-curricular connections and activities, and quotes
- blue backgrounds: additional resources and questions and activities

Sample Unit Opening Pages

The **Unit Skills Outline** lists the skills taught in the student edition and in additional activities in this Annotated Teacher's Edition.

Connections Across the Curriculum lists the cross-curricular activities from the unit.

A list of **Goals/Objectives** helps you plan overall intended learning outcomes for the unit. Affective goals are consistent with the philosophy of the program and its emphasis on reader involvement. Cognitive goals stress the understanding of literary techniques and development of skills taught in the Guided Writing lesson at the end of the unit.

Teaching the Multiple Intelligences lists activities from the unit that call for the exercise of students' multiple intelligences.

Sample Unit Review Pages

Vocabulary Development *provides an activity for students to use to reinforce vocabulary acquisition as they prepare for the unit test. Additional vocabulary development work is available in the Vocabulary Resource, which is part of the Teacher's Resource Kit.*

Additional Resources *notes identify assessment materials for the unit and study guides and worksheets for student review and practice.*

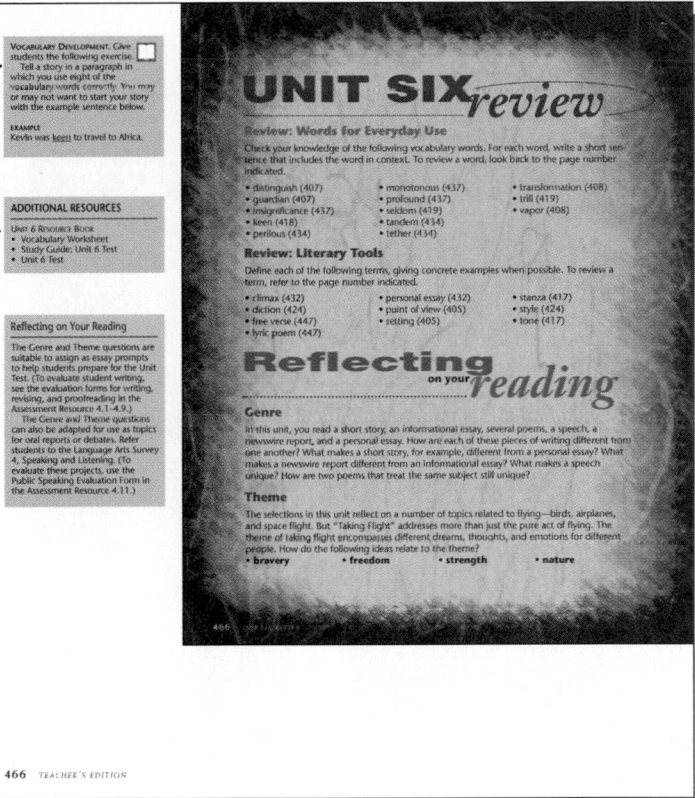

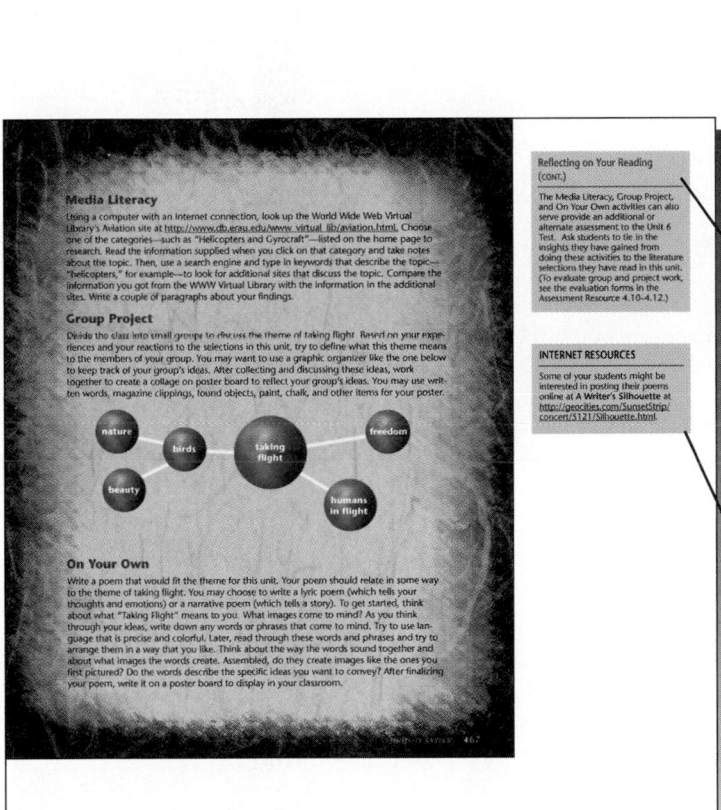

Reflecting on Your Reading *questions extend the ideas presented throughout the unit. These questions, which are appropriate prompts for writing, research, or discussion, cover genres, themes, and historical and biographical issues and allow students to synthesize the material from the unit.*

*Other features, such as **Internet Resources** and **Art Smart**, provide additional ways to extend and summarize the concepts learned throughout the unit.*

Sample Prereading Page

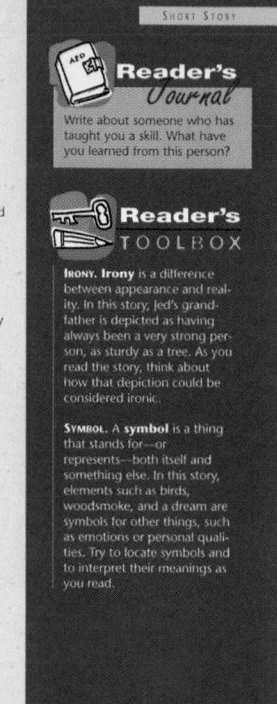

Prereading

SHORT STORY

"Jed's Grandfather"
by Joseph Bruchac

Reader's Resource

- The main character in this story has a disturbing dream related to what is happening in his life. Dreams have played an important role in ancient and primitive cultures. Throughout time, many people have believed that dreams were visits from a supreme being, predictions of the future, or the activities of human souls freed by sleep.

- **SCIENCE CONNECTION.** Austrian psychiatrist Sigmund Freud (1856–1939) was one of the first modern scientists to study dreams. He believed that dreams were keys to the makeup of each person. He also believed that dreams had symbolic meaning. Another modern psychiatrist, Swiss researcher Carl Gustav Jung (1875–1961), added to Freud's ideas. Jung believed that dreams express the thoughts people are not conscious of, including their worries about the future.

- This story takes place in a rural area on Indian Lake, probably in the Adirondack Mountains in New York. The Sabael family in the story lives much as Jed's ancestors did, relying little on outsiders to provide the necessities of life. Instead, they rely on their own abilities to gather food and water, to supply shelter and warmth, and to cope with hardship.

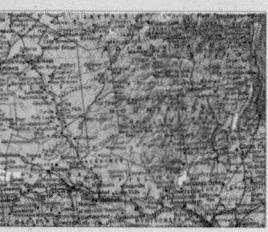

Reader's Journal

Write about someone who has taught you a skill. What have you learned from this person?

Reader's TOOLBOX

IRONY. Irony is a difference between appearance and reality. In this story, Jed's grandfather is depicted as having always been a very strong person, as sturdy as a tree. As you read the story, think about how that depiction could be considered ironic.

SYMBOL. A **symbol** is a thing that stands for—or represents—both itself and something else. In this story, elements such as birds, woodsmoke, and a dream are symbols for other things, such as emotions or personal qualities. Try to locate symbols and to interpret their meanings as you read.

"JED'S GRANDFATHER" **95**

GOALS/OBJECTIVES

Studying this lesson will enable students to
- relate to a character's feelings about his dying grandfather
- briefly describe some different opinions about dreams and their meaning
- define *irony* and recognize the use of irony in their reading

- define *symbolism* and identify symbols in literature
- edit for capitalization errors
- work in groups to research a Native American language
- take notes and document sources to prepare a report on dreams

ADDITIONAL RESOURCES

UNIT 2 RESOURCE BOOK
- Selection Worksheet 2.3
- Selection Check Test 4.2.5
- Selection Test 4.2.6
- Language, Grammar, and Style Resource 3.86, 3.89, 3.91

READER'S JOURNAL

As an alternate activity, encourage students to write their thoughts and feelings about one of their grandparents or about another elderly person they know.

CROSS-CURRICULAR CONNECTION

SCIENCE
- Whereas Freud thought that dreams revealed our hidden desires, Jung felt that dreams could reveal a whole variety of thoughts, not only desires but also fears and worries. He also believed that certain symbols found in people's dreams can be considered archetypes, or symbols that are shared by all human beings and passed down from generation to generation. Freud wrote about his ideas in his book *Interpretation of Dreams* (1900), and Jung discussed his in *Psychology of the Unconscious* (1916).
- Dreams occur during the rapid-eye-movement (REM) stage of sleep. Often the movement of a dreamer's eyes during this stage reflects what he or she is dreaming about. For example, a dreamer may cast his or her eyes upward if dreaming about a bird in the sky. Dreaming is necessary for mental health. Studies show that adults dream an average of 1½ to 2 hours for every 8 hours of sleep. If deprived of dream-sleep, people tend to become anxious, irritable, and less physically coordinated.

TEACHER'S EDITION **95**

Additional Resources notes identify materials from the Teacher's Resource Kit to use in teaching the selection: worksheets from the Reader's Guide and from the Language Arts Resource Books, and selection check tests and tests from the Assessment Resource.

Reader's Journal notes give suggestions for helping students relate the topic to their experience, anticipate questions or difficulties students may have, or provide additional prompts for students who have trouble starting. Special attention is given to problems that may arise from student diversity.

Cross-Curricular Connections and *Historical, Literary, Bibliography,* and *Biographical Notes* provide additional information to enhance the reading of the selections.

Cross-references (not shown) to additional instruction, worksheets, and assessment materials are provided throughout the annotations.

A list of **Goals/Objectives** *helps you plan intended learning outcomes for the selection. Affective goals are consistent with the philosophy of the program and its emphasis on reader involvement. Cognitive goals encompass content, literary technique, interpretation of the selection in historical context, and language arts skills taught in the student text.*

Sample Selection Pages

Answers to Guided Reading Questions *are keyed to questions in the student edition.*

*Color-coded **icons** identify at a glance **cross-curricular** activities (brown), **multiple intelligences** activities (green), and **SCANS** activities (blue). A key to these icons is provided on page T29 of this Annotated Teacher's Edition.*

Individual Learning Strategies *provide additional lesson plans for individual instruction in the following areas:*

- **Motivation** *strategies encourage students to take an interest in the selection and relate it to their own lives.*
- **Reading Proficiency** *activities focus on developing reading skills and present reading strategies to help students with reading difficulties.*
- **English Language Learning** *activities provide support for students whose native language is not English, including **Additional Vocabulary** to help you offer instruction before students encounter difficulty in reading.*
- **Special Needs** *activities offer assistance in planning instruction for students with learning disabilities and mentally challenged students to help them succeed in your classroom.*
- **Enrichment** *activities to challenge students with special academic gifts and talents and provide opportunities for independent study and self-guided research.*

Cross Curricular Activities *involve knowledge, skills, research, and resources from disciplines other than language arts.*

Quotables *further discussion by tying the reading to a broader context.*

Internet Resources *(not shown) provide a wealth of online resources and information on authors and literary selections, links to related readings, and Internet activities.*

*The **Art Smart** feature (not shown) provides a visual literacy component that connects fine art to the literature studied.*

Vocabulary from the Selection *provides a comprehensive list of the Words for Everyday Use from the selection.*

Sample Selection
Post-Reading Pages

*Notes on the **Respond to the Selection** questions help you help students relate the topic to their experience, anticipate questions or difficulties students might have, or suggest alternative formats (such as large or small group discussion or role playing). These notes give special attention to concerns of diversity.*

*▬ **Selection Check Test with Answers** includes the questions with answers and appears on or near the last page of each selection. You can photocopy the test from the Assessment Resource and distribute it, or you can present the questions orally.*

Answers to Inquire, Investigate, Imagine gives sample responses to Recall/Interpret, Analyze/Synthesize, Evaluate/Extend, and Perspective/Empathy question sets.

Answers to Understanding Literature provides possible answers for these discussion questions.

Respond to the SELECTION

What things do you treasure? Why are they meaningful to you?

About the AUTHOR

"When I was a kid—12, 14, around there—I would much rather have been a good baseball player or a hit with the girls. But I couldn't play ball, I couldn't dance."

Instead, **Shel Silverstein**—author, poet, cartoonist, composer, lyricist, screenwriter, playwright—started writing and drawing at a young age, developing early his unique style and voice. Silverstein was born in Chicago, Illinois in 1932. In the 1950s, he served in the military in Japan and Korea, and he was the cartoonist for the military newsletter. In 1952, he began his professional career as a magazine writer and cartoonist. Although he is perhaps most widely known for his children's books, Silverstein didn't start out writing for children. One day a friend of his brought him to talk to an editor who convinced him to write for children. He agreed, and went on to publish many books, including *The Giving Tree*, *A Light in the Attic*, and *Where the Sidewalk Ends*. Shel Silverstein died on May 10, 1999. In a National Public Radio interview on May 11, 1999, children's book critic Leonard Marcus said about Silverstein, "I think you could say that he was the troubadour king of American children's books...I think adults as well as children identify with a lot of his poems, because he was always pointing out what the little, single person, up against a much bigger world, has to contend with."

"FORGOTTEN LANGUAGE" AND "HECTOR THE C...

RESPOND TO THE SELECTION

Ask students to consider whether other people would find these objects as meaningful as they do or whether outsiders might consider their treasures junk. What might these say to someone to explain why their items is a treasure.

SELECTION CHECK TEST 4.9.11 WITH ANSWERS

Check Your Reading
SHORT ANSWER
1. In "Forgotten Language," what language did the speaker once speak? **The speaker once spoke the language of the flowers.**
2. In "Forgotten Language," who gossips? **The starlings gossip.**
3. Name two things that Hector collects. **Responses will vary.**
4. In "Hector the Collector," how does Hector feel about his collection? **He loves it very much.**
5. In "Hector the Collector," what do the people call his collection? **The people call it junk.**

Reader's Toolbox
SENTENCE COMPLETION
Fill in the blanks using the following terms. You may not use every term, and you may use some terms more than once.

repetition rhyme end rhyme
internal rhyme alliteration assonance

1. _____ is demonstrated in the following line: "and all the silly sightless people." **Alliteration**
2. _____ is demonstrated in the

ANSWERS TO INVESTIGATE, INQUIRE, IMAGINE

RECALL
1a. The speaker used to speak the language of flowers, caterpillars, starlings, houseflies, crickets, and the snow.
2a. All Hector's treasures are broken or useless items that most people would consider to be junk.
3a. Hector calls out to them, "Come and share my treasure trunk!" They call his things junk.

INTERPRET
1b. *Responses will vary.*
2b. Students may say that Hector has fun collecting these items and finds them to be interesting so he places value on them.
3b. Hector may call out to the people because he wants to share with them his love and enthusiasm for these objects. The people respond in this way because they do not share Hector's feelings about his treasures and have different values.

ANALYZE
4a. The speaker communicated with nature by speaking to flowers, understanding the words of the caterpillar, smiling at the gossip of starlings, sharing a conversation with the housefly, answering the questions of crickets, and joining in the crying of falling dying snowflakes.

SYNTHESIZE
4b. The "forgotten" language may signify a close connection to nature and its creatures and an innocence that the speaker has lost as he or she has grown up.

PERSPECTIVE
5a. Students may say that Hector loves his things because they are an expression of his personality and interests; he has spent much time assembling his unique collection of things and he loves them, so to him they are more precious than gold and diamonds.

EMPATHY
5b. Students may say that Hector was probably hurt by the people's response because he may have been hoping they would share his interest and love in his unique collection of junk. Hector might deny that his collection is junk. Hector might change his thinking if people express negative attitudes toward his collection for long enough.

642 TEACHER'S EDITION

Investigate, *Inquire,* and Imagine

Recall: GATHERING FACTS
1a. In "Forgotten Language," what language did the speaker used to know?

2a. What do all of Hector's treasures have in common?

3a. What does Hector call to the people? What do they say in response?

Interpret: FINDING MEANING
1b. How might the speaker have forgotten the language?

2b. Why might these things be valuable to Hector?

3b. Why does Hector do this? Why do the people respond this way?

Analyze: TAKING THINGS APART
4a. In what ways did the speaker of "Forgotten Language" once communicate with the different elements in nature?

Synthesize: BRINGING THINGS TOGETHER
4b. What might "forgotten language" signify?

Perspective: LOOKING AT OTHER VIEWS
5a. Why does Hector love his things more than obviously valuable things?

Empathy: SEEING FROM INSIDE
5b. How might Hector have reacted to the people's response? What might he say to the people? How might he one day change his thinking?

Understanding *Literature*

REPETITION. Repetition is more than one use of a sound, word, or group of words. Repetition is a tool that works to create or enhance rhythm. It also gives the sense that the speaker is "dwelling on" the repeated idea. What does the repetition in "Forgotten Language" indicate about the speaker's focus? What is the speaker dwelling on? Explain whether repetition makes the poem more meaningful. How does repetition enhance the rhythm of "Hector the Collector"?

RHYME. Rhyme is the repetition of sounds at the ends of words. Rhyme can enhance the musical quality of a poem. Many poems reveal a pattern of rhyming words that appear at the ends of lines. These are called *end rhymes. Internal rhymes* are rhymes within the line. How do internal rhymes help tighten the poem "Hector the Collector"? In what ways do end rhymes help weave the poem?

642 UNIT NINE / POETRY

ANSWERS TO UNDERSTANDING LITERATURE

REPETITION. The speaker repeats the lines, "Once I spike the language of the flowers" and "How did it go?" The speaker also repeats the "Once I [verb]" format for the beginnings of many of the lines. This repetition indicates that the speaker is focusing on the loss he or she feels about his or her connection to nature. The speaker is dwelling on what he or she could once do and is wondering how he or she lost this ability. Students may say repetition makes this poem more meaningful because it emphasizes the speaker's sadness and sense of loss. Repetition helps give "Hector the Collector" helps give the poem a quick, playful rhythm. **RHYME.** Internal rhyme in select lines helps to tighten the poem because the poem is essentially a long list of things. The internal rhyme also provides "surprises" of sound in certain lines to help maintain the reader's interest. End rhymes also help give cohesiveness and help the reader to move with interest through the list of things this poem presents. It also gives this poem a light and playful rhythm.

T16

Sample Selection Post-Reading Page

Answers to Skill Builders *provides model answers for Language Grammar, and Style, Speaking and Listening, Critical Thinking, Study and Research, Media Literacy, Collaborative Learning, Vocabulary, and Applied English activities.*

Writer's Journal

1. Choose one of the poems in this unit and make a **comic strip** to illustrate it. Submit the poem and your comic strip to your school newspaper or to a different publication.

2. Suppose you are writing an editorial about airplane noise in your neighborhood. In your editorial, create an **onomatopoeia** for the sound a low-flying airplane makes.

3. Imagine that you are Hector the Collector as an adult and that you are opening a business to buy and sell antiques and collectors' items. Write a **jingle** advertising your store.

Skill Builders

Language, Grammar, and Style

TECHNIQUES OF SOUND. Write a poem on a subject you find appealing and use at least three of the sound techniques highlighted in this unit. Try to incorporate aspects of rhyme, rhythm, alliteration, assonance, onomatopoeia, and repetition. You may want to begin your poem by freewriting. Write down words and phrases that you like and that create interesting sound combinations. Then work the phrases together into a poem.

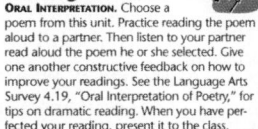

Vocabulary

BLENDS. Blends are new words created by joining together two existing words. Look at the following list of words and try to figure out what two words were combined to make each blend. Then, create five new blends of your own. Write them in contextual sentences on the board in your classroom to see if your classmates can guess what two words each blend was derived from.

1. glimmer   3. squiggle   5. mingy
2. smash   4. motel

Study and Research

THESIS STATEMENTS. Choose one of the following topics to research. Then write a thesis about the topic

you choose. A thesis is a main idea in a work of nonfiction such as an essay. For example, if your topic is "rhyme in poetry," your thesis might be "rhyme makes poetry more pleasing for most people." After formulating your thesis, use library resources and the Internet to investigate the topic. Find data that supports your thesis and also data that disputes it. After you have exhausted a number of resources, look critically at the information you have pulled together. What can you conclude from your research? Do your findings support or negate your thesis? How would you modify your thesis to fit your findings?

Topics: Rhyme in poetry
Shel Silverstein's poems and pictures
Poetry and song
Uses of alliteration

Speaking and Listening & Collaborative Learning

ORAL INTERPRETATION. Choose a poem from this unit. Practice reading the poem aloud to a partner. Then listen to your partner read aloud the poem he or she selected. Give one another constructive feedback on how to improve your readings. See the Language Arts Survey 4.19, "Oral Interpretation of Poetry," for tips on dramatic reading. When you have perfected your reading, present it to the class.

ANSWERS TO SKILL BUILDERS

Language, Grammar, and Style
TECHNIQUES OF SOUND. Responses will vary, but make sure that students identify their use of the sound techniques listed in the Skill Builder activity on page 643. You may want to challenge students to form teams and write a group poem. The team whose poem includes the most techniques wins.

Vocabulary
BLENDS. For the blends listed, you may need to have students consult a dictionary. See the Language Arts Survey 1.17, "Using a Dictionary." Responses may include the following:

1. glimmer
   blend of *gleam + shimmer*

2. smash
   blend of *smack + mash*

3. squiggle
   blend of *squirm + wiggle*

4. motel
   blend of *motor + hotel*

5. mingy
   blend of *mean + stingy*

Study and Research
THESIS STATEMENTS. Refer students to the Language Arts Survey 2.25, "Writing a Thesis Statement" and 2.26, "Writing Main Ideas and Supporting Details" for the writing part of this activity. Refer them to the Language Arts Survey, 5.17–5.29, for help in locating and evaluating sources.

Speaking and Listening & Collaborative Learning
ORAL INTERPRETATION. See the Assessment Resource 4.10, "Collaborative Learning Evaluation Form" and 4.11, "Public Speaking Evaluation Form" to evaluate student performance in this activity.

"FORGOTTEN LANGUAGE" AND "HECTOR THE COLLECTOR"   **643**

Using Literature and the Language Arts *for Writing Instruction*

Recent Advances in the Theory of Writing Instruction

One of the most exciting things that has happened in English education in the past few years is that a new model of writing instruction that respects the student's voice and effort has emerged. That model is the process and portfolio approach. Process and portfolio instruction breaks individual acts of writing and the overall business of learning to write into manageable steps, with guidance and feedback at each step. When students are given writing assignments today, they no longer have to figure out on their own how to get from the assignment to the completed piece of writing. Instead, they are trained in techniques for prewriting, drafting, evaluating their drafts by themselves and with peers, revising, and publishing. They are also given opportunities to reflect on this process. Writing portfolios and evaluation forms are used to track development of pieces of writing over time. Assessment has been expanded from simple marking of papers to include self-evaluation, peer evaluation, and a variety of approaches that avoid turning teachers into copyeditors. The result of these changes in writing instruction has been that student writing has improved dramatically in recent years.

Literature and the Language Arts contains comprehensive materials for integrated instruction in the writing process and for the management of writing portfolios. Through its **Guided Writing** program, students experience direct writing instruction that is integrated with the study of literature as well as with other key language arts areas, especially language, grammar, and style.

The **Writer's Journal** activities following each selection use the literature as a springboard for engaging quick-writing assignments that require both creative and critical thinking skills. Every literary selection includes three writing prompts that are graded 1) simple, 2) moderate, and 3) challenging.

Pre-testing and Assessment

Before beginning instruction in the writing process, you may wish to have students take the Writing Skills Comprehensive Test 3.1 in the Assessment Resource Book contained in the Teacher's Resource Kit. This test is designed to assess students' familiarity with basic writing concepts and skills. The test may be used to assess which techniques and skills students need to focus on during the course, or it may be used at the end of the course to assess students' understanding of basic writing skills and concepts. Beyond this, however, assessing individual pieces of student writing is the most critical step to knowing each student's strengths and weaknesses. See "Process for Writing Assignments," "Using Writing Portfolios," and "Assessing Student Writing" below.

The Guided Writing Program

Literature and the Language Arts offers complete, direct writing instruction that integrates the writing process with the study of literature and the development of other key language arts skills. At the end of each of twelve literature units, a Guided Writing lesson provides direct, step-by-step instruction in the process of writing. This lesson is integrated with the following:
(1) the literature in the unit
(2) a Language, Grammar, and Style lesson that teaches key concepts in the context of writing
(3) the Language Arts Survey in the textbook
(4) the Resource Books in the Teacher's Resource Kit
(5) the Guided Writing software that provides extended lessons and a writer-friendly word processor that allows self-, peer, and teacher evaluation comments to be delivered electronically.

Before starting the actual assignment, students are asked to consider the mode and purpose of the writing they are about to do, and to adapt their skills accordingly. The Language Arts Survey 2.3, "Identifying Your Purpose," outlines and explains the purpose of the following modes: expository/informative, imaginative, narrative, personal/expressive, and persuasive/argumentative. Many writing assignments work with a combination of modes.

The writing assignment ties directly to the literature unit studied, frequently using a passage from literature in that unit as a Professional Model that students are invited to examine as they prepare themselves to write. In some cases, a Student Model introduces the writing assignment. At other times, a Student Model appears later in the lesson to show the stages of drafting and revision.

As students enter the Prewriting stage, they are asked to consider voice, audience, and strategy in the Finding Your Voice, Identifying Your Audience, and Writing with a Plan sections. A Student Model Graphic Organizer shows prewriting work especially helpful to visual learners; from here students enter the Drafting stage, where they are coached through the process of organizing their words and getting them down on paper. From here, students are

Students examine a Professional Model as they prepare to write.

In Prewriting, students are taken through the steps of Identifying Your Audience, Finding Your Voice, and Writing with a Plan.

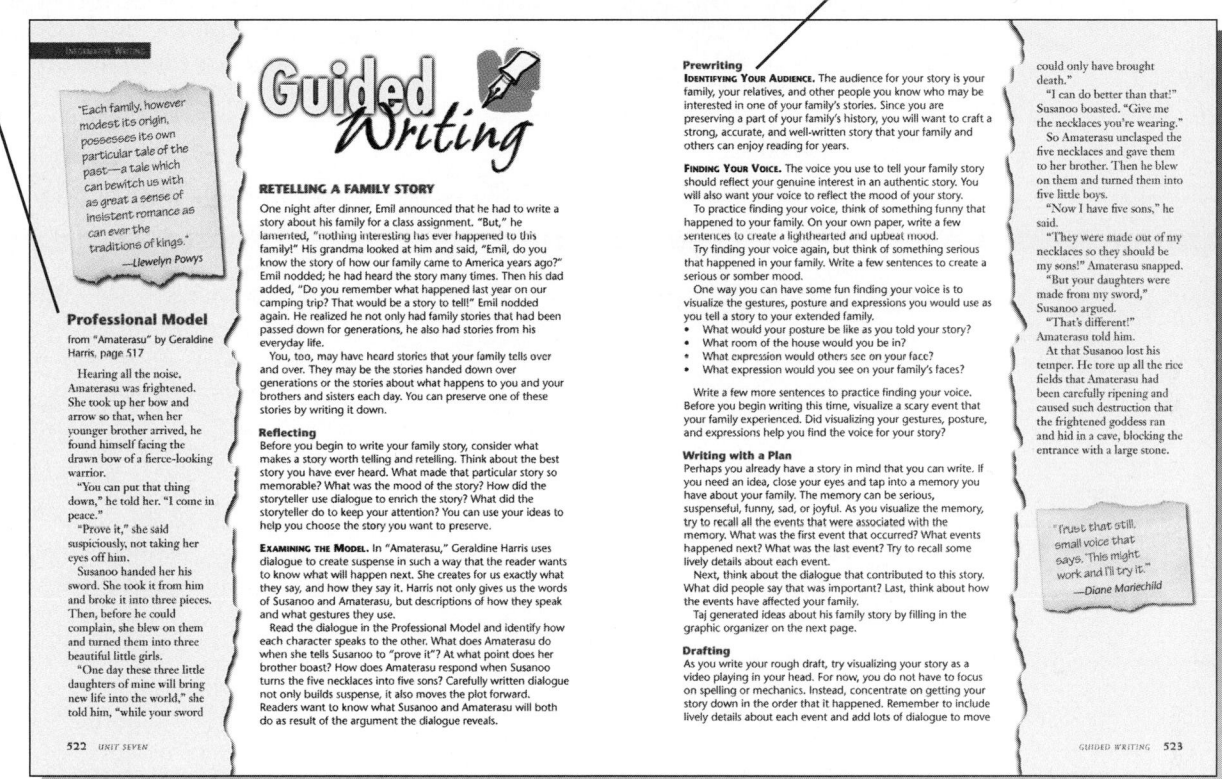

INFORMATIVE WRITING

"Each family, however modest its origin, possesses its own particular tale of the past—a tale which can bewitch us with as great a sense of insistent romance as can ever the traditions of kings."
—Llewelyn Powys

Professional Model

from "Amaterasu" by Geraldine Harris, page 517

Hearing all the noise, Amaterasu was frightened. She took up her bow and arrow so that, when her younger brother arrived, he found himself facing the drawn bow of a fierce-looking warrior.

"You can put that thing down," he told her. "I come in peace."

"Prove it," she said suspiciously, not taking her eyes off him.

Susanoo handed her his sword. She took it from him and broke it into three pieces. Then, before he could complain, she blew on them and turned them into three beautiful little girls.

"One day these three little daughters of mine will bring new life into the world," she told him, "while your sword

522 UNIT SEVEN

Guided Writing

RETELLING A FAMILY STORY

One night after dinner, Emil announced that he had to write a story about his family for a class assignment. "But," he lamented, "nothing interesting has ever happened to this family!" His grandma looked at him and said, "Emil, do you know the story of how our family came to America years ago?" Emil nodded; he had heard the story many times. Then his dad added, "Do you remember what happened last year on our camping trip? That would be a story to tell!" Emil nodded again. He realized he not only had family stories that had been passed down for generations, he also had stories from his everyday life.

You, too, may have heard stories that your family tells over and over. They may be the stories handed down over generations or the stories about what happens to you and your brothers and sisters each day. You can preserve one of these stories by writing it down.

Reflecting

Before you begin to write your family story, consider what makes a story worth telling and retelling. Think about the best story you have ever heard. What made that particular story so memorable? What was the mood of the story? How did the storyteller use dialogue to enrich the story? What did the storyteller do to keep your attention? You can use your ideas to help you choose the story you want to preserve.

Examining the Model

In "Amaterasu," Geraldine Harris uses dialogue to create suspense in such a way that the reader wants to know what will happen next. She creates for us exactly what they say, and how they say it. Harris not only gives us the words of Susanoo and Amaterasu, but descriptions of how they speak and what gestures they use.

Read the dialogue in the Professional Model and identify how each character speaks to the other. What does Amaterasu do when she tells Susanoo to "prove it"? At what point does her brother boast? How does Amaterasu respond when Susanoo turns the five necklaces into five sons? Carefully written dialogue not only builds suspense, it also moves the plot forward. Readers want to know what Susanoo and Amaterasu will both do as result of the argument the dialogue reveals.

Prewriting

Identifying Your Audience. The audience for your story is your family, your relatives, and other people you know who may be interested in one of your family's stories. Since you are preserving a part of your family's history, you will want to craft a strong, accurate, and well-written story that your family and others can enjoy reading for years.

Finding Your Voice. The voice you use to tell your family story should reflect your genuine interest in an authentic story. You will also want your voice to reflect the mood of your story.

To practice finding your voice, think of something funny that happened to your family. On your own paper, write a few sentences to create a lighthearted and upbeat mood.

Try finding your voice again, but think of something serious that happened in your family. Write a few sentences to create a serious or somber mood.

One way you can have some fun finding your voice is to visualize the gestures, posture and expressions you would use as you tell a story to your extended family.

* What would your posture be like as you told your story?
* What room of the house would you be in?
* What expression would others see on your face?
* What expression would you see on your family's faces?

Write a few more sentences to practice finding your voice. Before you begin writing this time, visualize a scary event that your family experienced. Did visualizing your gestures, posture, and expressions help you find the voice for your story?

Writing with a Plan

Perhaps you already have a story in mind that you can write. If you need an idea, close your eyes and tap into a memory you have about your family. The memory can be serious, suspenseful, funny, sad, or joyful. As you visualize the memory, try to recall all the events that were associated with the memory. What was the first event that occurred? What events happened next? What was the last event? Try to recall some lively details about each event.

Next, think about the dialogue that contributed to this story. What did people say that was important? Last, think about how the events have affected your family.

Taj generated ideas about his family story by filling in the graphic organizer on the next page.

Drafting

As you write your rough draft, try visualizing your story as a video playing in your head. For now, you do not have to focus on spelling or mechanics. Instead, concentrate on getting your story down in the order that it happened. Remember to include lively details about each event and add lots of dialogue to move

could only have brought death."

"I can do better than that!" Susanoo boasted. "Give me the necklaces you're wearing."

So Amaterasu unclasped the five necklaces and gave them to her brother. Then he blew on them and turned them into five little boys.

"Now I have five sons," he said.

"They were made out of my necklaces so they should be my sons!" Amaterasu snapped.

"But your daughters were made from my sword," Susanoo argued.

"That's different!" Amaterasu told him.

At that Susanoo lost his temper. He tore up all the rice fields that Amaterasu had been carefully ripening and caused such destruction that the frightened goddess ran and hid in a cave, blocking the entrance with a large stone.

"Trust that still, small voice that says, 'This might work and I'll try it.'"
—Diane Mariechild

GUIDED WRITING 523

shown a Student Model in draft form that contains self- and peer evaluation comments. A student-friendly evaluation checklist provides a rubric for students to use in the Self- and Peer Evaluation stage. Students are then led through the Revising, Proofreading, Publishing and Presenting, and Reflecting stages.

While the Guided Writing lesson takes students through these stages, it reminds them that writing is a continuing cycle and that they may need to go back to a previous stage before proceeding to the next step. It also shows how Reflecting, while always useful to bring closure to a writing assignment, can be done at any stage and at several times throughout the writing process. (For more information, see the Language Arts Survey 2.1, "The Writing Process," on page 874 of this textbook.)

Students are also introduced to a key Language, Grammar, and Style concept within the Guided Writing lesson. Designed with the idea that grammar is best taught in the context of writing rather than in isolation, the Language, Grammar, and Style lesson offers solid instruction by helping students to 1) identify correct grammatical usage in the Professional Model, 2) revise incorrect grammatical usage in the Student Model and examples, and 3) demonstrate correct grammatical usage in their own work. Throughout this lesson, students can refer to the Language, Grammar, and Style Resource of the Language Arts Survey for additional support.

The Language Arts Survey further integrates language arts instruction with the Guided Writing lesson. Section 2 of the Language Arts Survey, the Writing Resource, begins on page 874 and surveys the entire writing process from prewriting through drafting, self- and peer evaluation, revising, proofreading, publishing and presenting, and reflecting on the process. This section of the

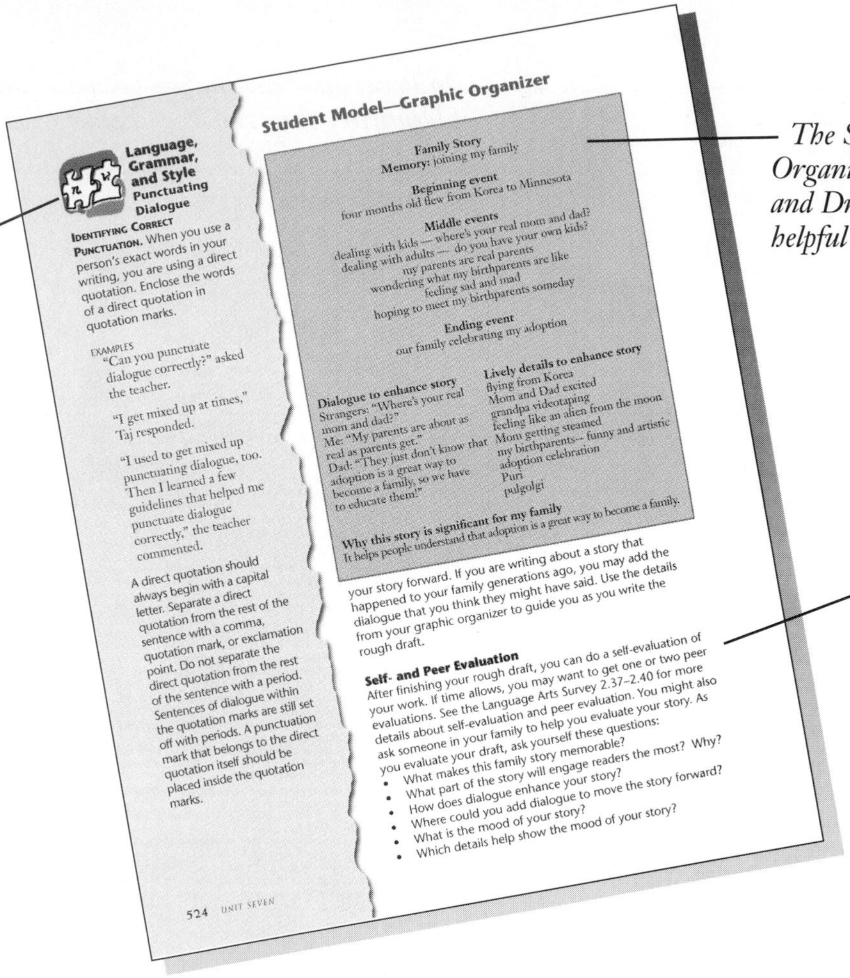

A Language, Grammar, and Style lesson is integrated with the Guided Writing lesson. It links directly to the Language Arts Survey at the back of the textbook.

The Student Model—Graphic Organizer shows Prewriting and Drafting work especially helpful to visual learners.

A student-friendly evaluation checklist provides a rubric for students to use in the Self- and Peer Evaluation stage.

Language, Grammar, and Style
Punctuating Dialogue

IDENTIFYING CORRECT PUNCTUATION. When you use a person's exact words in your writing, you are using a direct quotation. Enclose the words of a direct quotation in quotation marks.

EXAMPLES

"Can you punctuate dialogue correctly?" asked the teacher.

"I get mixed up at times," Taj responded.

"I used to get mixed up punctuating dialogue, too. Then I learned a few guidelines that helped me punctuate dialogue correctly," the teacher commented.

A direct quotation should always begin with a capital letter. Separate a direct quotation from the rest of the sentence with a comma, quotation mark, or exclamation point. Do not separate the direct quotation from the rest of the sentence with a period. Sentences of dialogue within the quotation marks are still set off with periods. A punctuation mark that belongs to the direct quotation itself should be placed inside the quotation marks.

Student Model—Graphic Organizer

Family Story
Memory: joining my family

Beginning event
four months old flew from Korea to Minnesota

Middle events
dealing with kids — where's your real mom and dad?
dealing with adults — do you have your own kids?
my parents are real parents
wondering what my birthparents are like
feeling sad and mad
hoping to meet my birthparents someday

Ending event
our family celebrating my adoption

Dialogue to enhance story
Strangers: "Where's your real mom and dad?"
Me: "My parents are about as real as parents get."
Dad: "They just don't know that adoption is a great way to become a family, so we have to educate them!"

Lively details to enhance story
flying from Korea
Mom and Dad excited
grandpa videotaping
feeling like an alien from the moon
Mom getting steamed
my birthparents— funny and artistic
adoption celebration
Puri
pulgogli

Why this story is significant for my family
It helps people understand that adoption is a great way to become a family.

your story forward. If you are writing about a story that happened to your family generations ago, you may add the dialogue that you think they might have said. Use the details from your graphic organizer to guide you as you write the rough draft.

Self- and Peer Evaluation
After finishing your rough draft, you can do a self-evaluation of your work. If time allows, you may want to get one or two peer evaluations. See the Language Arts Survey 2.37–2.40 for more details about self-evaluation and peer evaluation. You might also ask someone in your family to help you evaluate your story. As you evaluate your draft, ask yourself these questions:

- What makes this family story memorable?
- What part of the story will engage readers the most? Why?
- How does dialogue enhance your story?
- Where could you add dialogue to move the story forward?
- What is the mood of your story?
- Which details help show the mood of your story?

524 UNIT SEVEN

Survey is divided into fifty lessons. Additional practice activities for each lesson in the Language Arts Survey can be found in the Guided Writing Resource Book in the Teacher's Resource Kit. Other Language Arts Survey sections offer similar support, especially Section 3, the Language, Grammar, and Style Resource, and Section 5, the Study and Research Resource. Section 1, the Reading Resource, is frequently referenced in the Individual Learning Strategies feature of the Annotated Teacher's Edition as a way to offer students struggling with reading proficiency extra help as they work through the lessons. Section 3, the

Speaking and Listening Resource, provides direct instruction for writing assignments that require oral communication; and Section 6, the Applied English Resource, provides direct instruction in technical writing and school-to-work applications.

Corresponding Resource Books in the Teacher's Resource Kit provide blackline masters with exercises keyed to each numbered section of the Language Arts Survey. This offers teachers a way to make sure students are mastering basic concepts.

Finally, the Guided Writing Interactive Software provides extended lessons and a writer-friendly word processor that allows

self-, peer, and teacher evaluation comments to be delivered electronically. While the print lessons do not depend on software for students to complete the assignments, the electronic version of the Guided Writing program provides printable worksheets, graphic organizers, checklists, and student models to use as handouts; spelling and grammar utilities; hypertext links providing help specific to the writing task; and a portfolio management system for teachers. The Guided Writing Interactive Software is compatible with Windows and Macintosh computers.

Note: Teachers who wish to do so can teach the Guided Writing program as a

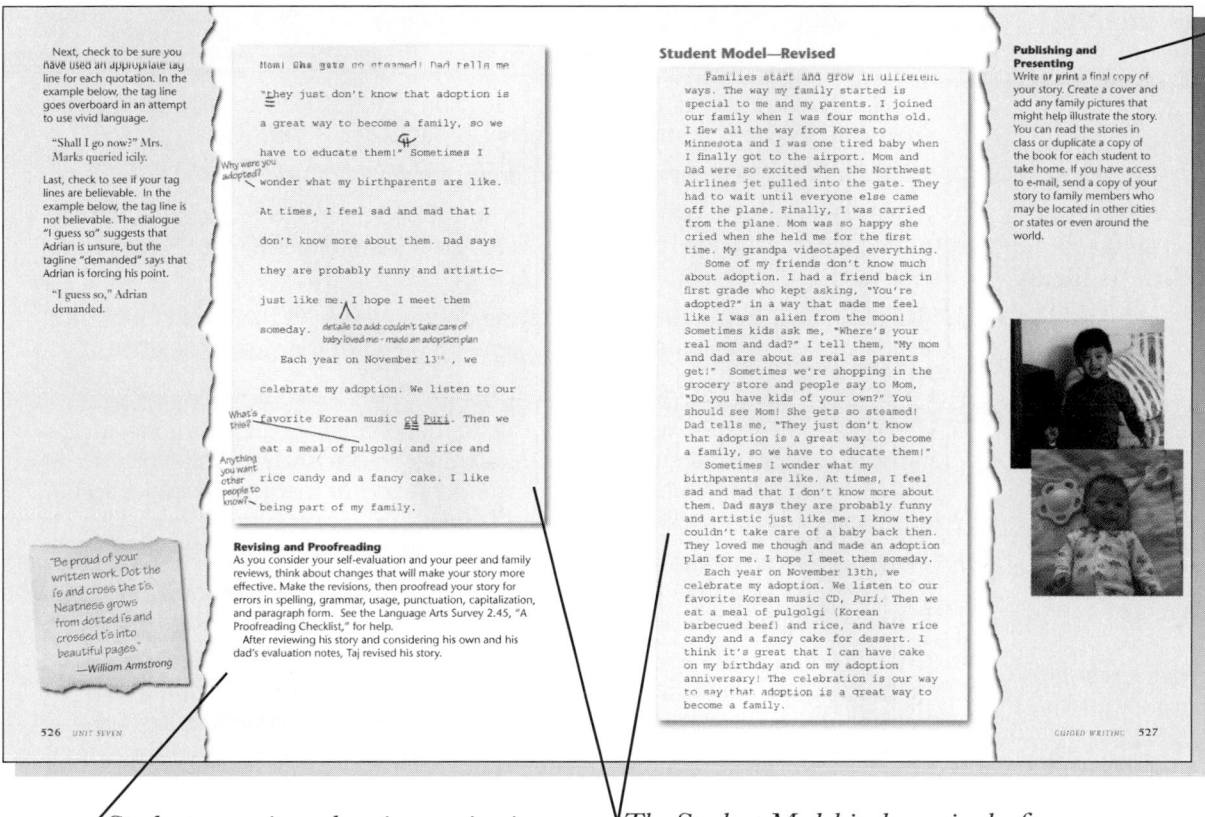

In Publishing and Presenting, students are given different options for presenting their work to an audience.

Students are given clear instruction in the Revising and Proofreading stages.

The Student Model is shown in draft and revised versions whenever possible.

separate composition course by using the Guided Writing lessons at the end of each of the twelve literature units, the Writing Resource in the Language Arts Survey in its entirety, the Guided Writing Resource Books, and the Guided Writing Interactive Software.

Process for Writing Assignments

The editors and authors recommend the sequence of activities in the chart on page T22 for the writing assignments at the end of each unit. Steps 1–11 may be repeated for each writing assignment. Then, periodically, step 12 should also be completed.

Using Writing Portfolios

The student's **Writing Portfolio** is a folder in which he or she stores drafts and finished pieces of writing. You can ask your students to keep a portfolio to enable you and the students to assess their progress over time. Portfolios show students' capabilities and progress better than any test or single writing assignment can.

You may wish to ask your students to keep **comprehensive portfolios** that contain all the writing that they do for class, along with Writing Summary Forms and/or evaluation forms for each piece of writing. Alternatively, you can ask your students to keep **selected portfolios** that contain pieces of writ-

ing chosen by the students as representative of their best work. Students should be encouraged to choose for their selected portfolios pieces that show the various skills they have developed and the various types of writing that they have done (informative, persuasive, creative, etc.). When students place works in their portfolios, make sure that they attach their notes and drafts behind the finished works so that you will be able to see at a glance how each piece of writing was developed. Also have students attach to their works any evaluation forms they have used.

From time to time, you will want to do a comprehensive evaluation of the students' portfolios. A Comprehensive Portfolio Evaluation Form: Teacher

4.7, in the Assessment Resource, has been provided for this purpose. You should also have each student do his or her own comprehensive evaluation using the Comprehensive Portfolio Evaluation Form: Student 4.8 in the Assessment Resource. Once these evaluations are complete, you can meet in a conference with each student to discuss his or her progress, provide praise for work well done, and make plans for improvement in the future.

Assessing Student Writing

(For a more complete treatment of assessment, see the introduction to the Guided Writing and Assessment Resource Books in the Teacher's Resource Kit.)

Assessment of student writing should not have as its primary purpose meting out rewards or punishments. Instead, assessment should be seen as a development tool allowing the teacher and the student, working in collaboration, to monitor the student's progress toward achieving his or her goals.

Approaches to assessment vary. Two common approaches to assessing writing are analytic evaluation and holistic evaluation.

Analytic Evaluation. An analytic evaluation of a piece of writing begins with an analysis of the several features or qualities desired in the writing. These desired features or qualities are then used as standards or criteria against which the piece is compared. The evaluator merely goes down the list of criteria, giving the piece of writing a score for each criterion. A summary evaluation of the writing is obtained by combining these several scores.

Analytic evaluation is particularly valuable for formative evaluation. A general

PROCESS FOR WRITING ASSIGNMENTS

1. WHOLE CLASS: Study of the literature selection in the student edition textbook, along with its corresponding instructional apparatus

2. TEACHER: Introduction of the writing prompt from the student text

3. STUDENT: Prewriting (with reference to any applicable prewriting lessons in the Writing Resource section of the Language Arts Survey, pages 874–883 of the student text)

4. STUDENT: Drafting (with reference to the drafting lesson in the Writing Resource section of the Language Arts Survey, pages 883–885 of the student text)

5. STUDENT: Sharing of draft with one or more peers

6. STUDENT and PEER(S): Evaluation of the draft and conferencing with one another and with the teacher if necessary (with reference to the Analytic Scale for Evaluation from the Annotated Teacher's Edition and/or the general evaluation forms and revision checklists 4.1–4.8 in the Assessment Resource)

7. STUDENT: Revising (with reference to the Revision and Proofreading Checklists 7.7 and 7.8 in the Assessment Resource, and to the revision section of the Writing Resource section of the Language Arts Survey on pages 886–887 of the student text)

8. STUDENT: Proofreading and preparation of the final manuscript (with reference to the Revising and Proofreading Checklists 4.9 in the Assessment Resource, and to the proofreading and manuscript preparation sections of the Writing Resource section of the Language Arts Survey, pages 887–889 of the student text) and completion of the Writing Summary Form 6.6 in the Assessment Resource

9. STUDENT and PEER(S): Publishing and/or presenting of the completed draft (with reference to the lesson on publishing and presenting in the Writing Resource section of the Language Arts Survey, page 889 of the student text)

10. STUDENT and TEACHER: Assessment and/or conferencing with regard to the completed work

11. STUDENT: Decision as to whether to place the completed work in the student's Writing Portfolio

12. STUDENT and TEACHER: Evaluate the student's Writing Portfolio (using the Comprehensive Portfolio Evaluation Form: Teacher 4.7 and the Comprehensive Portfolio Evaluation Form: Student 4.8 in the Assessment Resource) and hold a teacher-student conference to discuss the evaluation and to set goals for future writing improvement.

judgment of a student's work may be daunting, especially for students who do not do as well as they expect to do. Likewise, students who perform well, if given general comments about the writing, find in such general judgments little specific guidance telling them what they

might do to write better. An analytic evaluation can show students exactly what their strengths and weaknesses are and where they should concentrate their efforts.

Analytic evaluation is valuable as a measure of either progress or achieve-

ment. To evaluate progress, you can evaluate the student's progress in each area by comparing the current work with previous similar writing assignments. To measure raw achievement, you can compare the student's product against some imagined ideal. Of course, in either case you must make sure that your students are aware of the criteria on which they are being graded.

The Analytic Evaluation Scales provided in the Assessment Resource include lists of appropriate criteria for analytic evaluation, along with simple procedures for scoring. In addition, a general Writing Evaluation Form: Analytic Scale is provided as item 4.4 of the Assessment Resource.

Holistic Evaluation. Holistic evaluation of a piece of writing calls for an overall judgment. Holistic evaluation is most useful as a measure of achievement. It is difficult to score holistic evaluations according to a student's progress. To do a holistic evaluation, simply look over the general analytic criteria and then assign a score that reflects how well the student met those criteria taken as a whole.

Holistic evaluation takes less time than analytic evaluation and in most cases results in the same score. The saved time can be used to make encouraging written comments to the student, pointing out features of the writing that you admire and features of the writing that you would like to see improve in the student's future work. A general Self- and Peer Evaluation Form: Holistic Response is provided in the Assessment Resource 4.5.

Grading. Some teachers prefer to grade each writing assignment. Others feel that grading selected assignments chosen by the teacher and student to reflect the student's best work provides a more realistic assessment of the student's optimal capabilities. If the latter option is chosen, you may wish to provide credit for completion of assignments that are not graded.

Marking Student Papers. A student who receives from a teacher a returned paper covered with corrections in red ink is not likely to be encouraged to do more and better writing. Furthermore, such marking of student papers is enormously time consuming and discourages frequent writing practice. A more encouraging approach is to mark one or two consistent problems and to mark three or four successes in each paper or, better yet, to allow students and their peers to do such marking and then to review these evaluations in conferences. Such marking can be done in conjunction with the completion of evaluation forms and/or analytic scales.

Reports and Research Papers

Literature and the Language Arts contains complete materials for instruction in the preparation of reports and research papers. The Research Skills section of the Study and Research Resource in the Language Arts Survey, pages 929–936 of the student text, contains a complete overview of research procedures, from using the library to documenting print and Internet sources. The Reflecting on Your Reading questions that appear at the end of each Unit Review make excellent topics for extended reports or research papers. Further instruction on preparing longer papers can be found in the sections on organizing ideas, outlining, and drafting in the Writing Resource in the Language Arts Survey, pages 880–885 of the student text. These sections of the Language Arts Survey are accompanied by worksheets in the corresponding Resource Books in the Teacher's Resource Kit.

Remedial Exercises in Specific Writing Skills

As you evaluate your students' writing, you will discover consistent areas of weakness. One student may have trouble making transitions, another may consistently use serial commas incorrectly, and another may rely too heavily on the passive voice. The Language Arts Survey in the student edition and the accompanying Resource Book worksheets provide ample activities for remediation of particular recurring problems. Most of the instruction and activities in the Writing and Language, Grammar, and Style sections of the Language Arts Survey are useful for this purpose. Thus, if a student has a tendency to write sentence fragments, you can have him or her read the Language Arts Survey 3.31, "Correcting Sentence Fragments," on page 898 of the student text. That student can then do corresponding worksheet 3.31 in the Language, Grammar, and Style Resource Book. If a student has problems organizing his or her ideas, you can have him or her read the Language Arts Survey 2.24, "Organizing Ideas"on page 880 and complete corresponding worksheet 2.24 in the Guided Writing Resource Book. Thus, you can use the Language Arts Survey and the Resource Books to individualize your writing instruction and to target it to remediate particular writing problems your students encounter.

Instructional Options

Literature and the Language Arts contains a number of features that allow you the flexibility to organize your instruction to best suit you and your district's requirements. The following chart offers some tips for using your chosen approach to the text.

FEATURES OF THE PROGRAM, BY APPROACH

Thematic Approach

- Units 1-6 provide selections organized by theme.
- The Thematic Organization Chart chart on pages T32–T34 lists all the selections in the book under forty-seven major themes.
- Writer's Journal prompts following selections ask students to explore and develop their thoughts about thematic topics.
- Reflecting on Your Reading questions in the Theme, Group Project, and On Your Own sections of the Unit Review help students explore thematic relations among the selections.

Writing Approach

- Writer's Journal activities following each selection use the literature as a springboard for engaging writing assignments that require both creative and critical thinking skills.
- Guided Writing lessons at the end of each unit provide direct instruction that integrates the writing process with the study of literature and the development of other language arts skills.
- The Selections by Genre pages beginning on page T35 list all the selections in the book under six genres of writing. Use the chart to find examples of the types of writing you wish to teach.
- The Language Arts Survey Writing Resource provides instruction in all phases of writing, editing, and proofreading, student and peer evaluation, publishing and presenting, and reflecting on the writing process.
- The *Writing Resource* book provides guided exercises in all writing phases. These worksheets are keyed to the instructional text in the Language Arts Survey.

Genre Approach

- Units 7-11 provide an overview of the five traditional literary genres (the oral tradition, fiction, poetry, drama, and nonfiction). Unit 12 helps students to extend their literacy skills to explore informational and visual media.

- The Selections by Genre pages beginning on page T35 list all the selections in the book by genre. Use the chart to find examples of the types of literature you wish to teach.
- The Guided Writing lessons at the end of each unit and the Writing Resource in the Language Arts Survey provide instruction in techniques that are characteristic of the various genres of writing.
- Questions for Understanding Literature following selections help students understand the use of literary techniques.
- Reflecting on Your Reading questions in the Genre, Group Project, and On Your Own sections of the Unit Review relate matters of genre and literary technique to thematic issues.

Skills Approach

- The Language Arts Survey following Unit 12 provides instruction in the range of language arts skills and concepts, including reading, writing, language, grammar and style, speaking and listening, study and research, and applied English.
- Use the Scope and Sequence Charts in the *Program Manager* to locate additional exercises in specific language arts skills.
- The Resource Books in the Teacher's Resource Kit provide guided exercises in the range of language arts skills: reading, writing, language, grammar and style, speaking and listening, study and research, applied English, critical thinking, and testing. These worksheets are coordinated with the instructional text in the Language Arts Survey.
- The *Assessment Resource* contains tests for language arts skills in reading, writing, language, grammar and style, speaking and listening, study and research, applied English, critical thinking, and testing. These materials are coordinated with the instructional text in the Language Arts Survey and with the worksheets in the Resource Books.

Teaching to Develop Students' Multiple Intelligences and to Accommodate Diverse Learning Styles

Activities using multiple intelligences are identified by green icons. See the legend on page T29.

Use the techniques in the chart at right to teach and encourage students with diverse intellectual strengths and learning styles and to help all students use and develop the full range of their abilities.

Teaching English Language Learners

Use the techniques in the chart at right to facilitate learning and participation for students whose native language is not English.

Teaching Students with Diverse Cultural Backgrounds

Use the techniques in the chart at right to facilitate learning and participation for students with diverse cultural backgrounds.

TEACHING MULTIPLE INTELLIGENCES

- Use multiple modes of expression: e.g., read selections aloud; read questions aloud; use visual aids—charts, graphs, tables, or other graphics, art, and films; play songs; and perform demonstrations.
- Encourage students to use multiple modes of expression, including nonverbal expressions and performances such as drawing, painting, collage, sculpture, dance and choreography, acting and oral interpretation, photography, filmmaking, video production, and musicianship and singing.
- Ask students to read aloud.
- Precede written work with a related oral activity.
- Teach students to use graphic aids for understanding and for studying.
- Facilitate group work.
- Use cooperative learning.
- Allow students ample thinking time.

TEACHING ENGLISH LANGUAGE LEARNERS

- Ask students to read aloud.
- Precede written work with a related oral activity.
- Use cooperative learning.
- Allow ample thinking time.
- When using small groups, pair with English-proficient students.
- Provide ample opportunity for nongraded, even nonevaluated, writing in English.
- Use multiple modes of expression: e.g., read selections aloud; read questions aloud; use visual aids—charts, graphs, tables, or other graphics, art, and films; play songs; and perform demonstrations.
- Encourage students to use multiple modes of expression, including nonverbal expressions and performances such as drawing, painting, collage, sculpture, dance and choreography, acting and oral interpretation, photography, filmmaking, video production, and musicianship and singing.

TEACHING STUDENTS WITH DIVERSE CULTURAL BACKGROUNDS

- Encourage discussion of cultural differences; invite students to share contrasting experiences; invite them to discuss events and characters from the selections that strike them as odd. Rely on students for your cultural information; be aware that you are liable to overlook differences unless you can take a different point of view.
- Use multiple modes of expression: e.g., read selections aloud; read questions aloud; use visual aids—charts, graphs, tables, or other graphics, art, and films; play songs; and perform demonstrations.
- Encourage students to use multiple modes of expression, including nonverbal expressions and performances such as drawing, painting, collage, sculpture, dance and choreography, acting and oral interpretation, photography, filmmaking, video production, and musicianship and singing.
- Precede written work with a related oral activity.
- Use cooperative learning.
- Allow ample thinking time.
- When using small groups, pair with English-proficient students.
- Preview/explain culturally loaded terms and names.
- Discuss idioms and word origins.
- Discuss topics with universal appeal and relevance—for instance, independence versus family ties, independence versus friendship, or identity.
- Discuss literature from both an "insider" and an "outsider" perspective.

Teaching Students with Special Needs

Students with special needs may include student with learning disabilities or students who are mentally challenged. Learning disabilities are physical conditions that make it difficult to complete certain types of tasks. Students with learning disabilities are often highly intelligent but lack specific abilities; for instance, one person may lack the ability to discriminate certain sounds, while another person may be able to discriminate among sounds but be unable to remember certain auditory messages. Mentally challenged students are often eager to learn but need lessons adapted to make learning meaningful to them. Use the techniques in the chart at right to help students with special needs succeed in your classroom.

TEACHING STUDENTS WITH SPECIAL NEEDS

- Discover the particular effects of each individual's disability and try to fill gaps.
- Allow ample thinking time.
- Seat students in front.
- Repeat important ideas frequently.
- Summarize and check students' bearings frequently.
- Monitor progress frequently.
- On larger projects, provide step-by-step guidance.
- Precede written work with a related oral activity.
- Use cooperative learning.

- Use multiple modes of expression: e.g., read selections aloud; read questions aloud; use visual aids—charts, graphs, tables, or other graphics, art, and films; play songs; and perform demonstrations.
- Encourage students to use multiple modes of expression, including nonverbal expressions and performances such as drawing, painting, collage, sculpture, dance and choreography, acting and oral interpretation, photography, filmmaking, video production, and musicianship and singing.

Teaching Students with Special Academic Gifts and Talents

Just as students who work below grade level may lose interest because tasks are too difficult, students with special academic gifts and talents may lose interest because they complete work quickly or because they are not sufficiently challenged.

Activities involving other curricular areas are identified by red icons. See the legend on page T31.

TEACHING STUDENTS WITH SPECIAL ACADEMIC GIFTS AND TALENTS

- Encourage students to use multiple modes of expression, including nonverbal expressions and performances such as drawing, painting, collage, sculpture, dance and choreography, acting and oral interpretation, photography, filmmaking, video production, and musicianship and singing.
- Use cooperative learning.

- Allow ample thinking time.
- Involve students in the planning, preparation, and presentation or conduct of lessons.
- Provide or encourage extension activities once mastery is demonstrated.
- Provide or encourage self-guided activities and independent research.

66[C]hildren come to school with misconceptions about outside ethnic groups and with a white bias. However, . . . students' racial attitudes can be modified and made more democratic and . . . the racial attitudes of young children are much more easily modified than the attitudes of older students and adults. . . . If we are to help students acquire the attitudes needed to survive in a multicultural and diverse world, we must start early. . . .

"A school experience that is multicultural includes content, examples, and realistic images of diverse racial and ethnic groups. Cooperative learning activities in which students from diverse groups work to attain shared goals is also a feature of the school, as well as simulated images of ethnic groups that present them in positive and realistic ways. Also essential within such a school are adults who model the attitudes and behaviors they are trying to teach. Actions speak much louder than words.99

—James A. Banks
"Multicultural Education:
Historical Development, Dimensions, and Practice"
Review of Research in Education
19 (1993): 37–38

Achieving Gender Equity

Sexism cannot be combatted subtly (Sadker and Sadker 123). In addition to using the techniques listed at right, make a directed effort to combat gender stereotypes and to treat all students as valued learners.

Facts: Boys call out answers eight times as frequently as do girls (Sadker and Sadker 43). Boys receive more evaluative feedback—both positive and negative (Sadker, Sadker, and Klein 300; Sadker and Sadker 55).

Responses:
- Make a special effort to call on girls and to give them specific feedback, both positive and negative. (Sadker and Sadker 266–267.)
- When intervening in student-student interactions, concentrate on raising girls' confidence rather than criticizing boys' behavior.

Fact: Exposure to gender-biased materials appears to increase gender stereotypes (Sadker, Sadker, and Klein 279; Sadker and Sadker 73–75, 128–135, 266).

Responses:
- Be aware of biases in literature and point them out.
- When appropriate, provide historical context for stereotyping by explaining older attitudes and practices.
- Provide direct lessons about gender stereotypes and gender-related communication styles.

Facts: Girls are more likely than boys to attribute their successes to luck and less likely than boys to attribute their successes to ability (Sadker, Sadker, and Klein 303). Girls are more likely than boys to attribute their failures to lack of ability and less likely than boys to attribute their failures to lack of effort (303). Teachers are more likely to comment on girls' appearance and the neatness of their work, and more likely to comment on the intellectual qualities of boys' work (Sadker and Sadker 57).

Responses:
- Make an effort to avoid commenting on students', especially girls', appearance.
- Make an effort to attribute all success to effort and ability.
- Make an effort to rebut forcefully students' self-deprecating comments.

Facts: Girls have lower expectations of success (Sadker, Sadker, and Klein 302) and are more likely to display signs of "learned helplessness" (303). Teachers are more likely to help boys solve their own problems, but to solve problems for girls (Sadker and Sadker 81–83).

Responses:
- Fear of being "too tough" on girls is patronizing and hinders them from developing independence and confidence. Don't be afraid to criticize girls' work and don't let them off easy (Holt; Sizer).
- Make an effort to rebut forcefully students' self-deprecating comments.

Teaching Students to Work Cooperatively

Prepare your students for work in cooperative learning groups by teaching them how to listen actively, how to participate fully in discussions, and how to give one another positive feedback. Refer students to the lessons on listening, interpersonal communication, and discussion, sections 4.1–4.13 of the Language Arts Survey.

Uses for Small Groups. Use these task and project ideas to direct the work of collaborative learning groups.

- brainstorming
- peer tutorial sessions
- learning partners for practice or review and for all stages of the writing process
- inquiry-based concept learning
- multimedia and community-based projects
- topical symposia
- panel discussions
- mock jury trials
- role playing
- dramatizations
- simulations
- reader's theater

TEACHING STUDENTS TO WORK COOPERATIVELY

PREPARING STUDENTS FOR SMALL GROUP WORK

PARTICIPATION

- Review/preteach vocabulary and cultural concepts for nonnative speakers.
- Begin with a nongraded, fun, get-to-know-one-another activity.
- Take steps to ensure that group members know each other's names.
- Assign tasks that call on multiple intelligences.
- Ask questions that call for personal response and interpretation.
- Value interpretations that differ from your own.
- Have students determine the wording of their topics or questions.
- Don't talk too much.
- Model tentativeness and openness.
- Model courtesy and respect for all.
- Respond only holistically and orally to early drafts and initial products.
- Avoid judging early drafts; discuss ideas rather than expression.
- Discuss anonymous samples.
- Praise students for taking risks.
- Require (only) positive feedback from peers.
- Use joint grading for group work: (1) everyone in the group receives the average among the group; (2) everyone receives the lowest grade among the group; (3) a final product is graded and everyone receives that grade.

LEADERSHIP

- Ask students to conduct lessons.
- Rotate leadership assignments in groups.

- Appoint two group leaders—one to learn from the other.
- Model and give direct instruction and practice in asking questions.
- Model and give direct instruction and practice in reporting a summary.
- Model and give direct instruction and practice in involving nonparticipants.
- Model and give direct instruction and practice in restraining dominators.
- Model and give direct instruction and practice in providing positive feedback.
- Model and give direct instruction and practice in providing constructive feedback.

LISTENING/DISCUSSING

- Model, explain, and encourage attentive listening, eye contact, and not interrupting.
- Give practice in paraphrasing students' words and your own.
- Ask students to identify good speaking and listening habits and skills.
- Ask students to evaluate group processes and their roles in their groups (use *Assessment Resource* form 4.10).

FORMING GROUPS

- Groups should contain a maximum of six students for a complex task, a maximum of four otherwise.
- For peer writing groups, two may be the ideal size. Require periodically that students change partners.
- In the prewriting stage, it can be helpful to match those who share a primary language other than English.

- Working groups should contain students of varied abilities.
- Allow groups to vary their seating arrangements (suggest possibilities).

GUIDING AND MONITORING

- Give specific tasks.
- Explain criteria for success.
- Assign roles in groups, or assign groups to distribute roles.
- When assigning roles in groups, divide responsibilities to assure interdependence and cooperation. One workable division of responsibilities includes (1) a discussion leader/facilitator; (2) a recorder; (3) a reporter; (4) a materials manager.
- Specify desired behaviors (see "Preparing Students for Small Group Work," above).
- Monitor group interactions and advise when appropriate.
- Intervene to diffuse conflict and to foster collaborative skills.
- When intervening in group work, ask a question rather than giving advice directly.
- If multiple groups have the same problem, interrupt the process and clarify or reteach.

CLOSURE AND ASSESSMENT

- Ask for sharing of a product.
- Both students and teacher should assess the quality of the product. Assessment can be among the entire class or only within groups.
- Both students and teacher should assess the quality of the group processes and communication.

Planning for Conferences and Portfolio Evaluation

As a teacher you have a number of distinguishable evaluative roles as outlined in the charts at right. Of course, you will not take on all of these roles at once. Make sure that students know which role to expect *before* they receive feedback.

References

Herman, J., P. Aschbacher, and L. Winters. *A Practical Guide to Alternative Assessment.* Alexandria, VA: ASCD, 1992.

Eggen, P., and D. Kauchak. *Educational Psychology.* 2nd ed. New York: Merrill, 1994.

Gardner, H. *Frames of Mind: The Theory of Multiple Intelligences.* New York: Basic, 1985.

———. *The Unschooled Mind: How Children Think and How Schools Should Teach.* New York: Basic, 1991.

Holt, J. *How Children Learn.* New York: Putnam, 1967.

Ohrlich, D., et al. *Teaching Strategies.* 4th ed. Lexington, MA: Heath, 1994.

Sadker, M., and D. Sadker. *Failing at Fairness.* New York: Scribner's, 1993.

Sadker, M., D. Sadker, and S. Klein. "The Issue of Gender in Elementary and Secondary Education." *Review of Research in Education* 17 (1991): 269–334.

Sizer, T. *Horace's Compromise.* Boston: Houghton, 1984.

Slavin, R. *Cooperative Learning: Theory, Research, and Practice.* Englewood Cliffs, NJ: Prentice, 1990.

———. *Educational Psychology.* 3rd ed. Englewood Cliffs, NJ: Prentice, 1991.

UNDERSTANDING THE ROLES OF EVALUATORS

ROLE	FUNCTION
AUDIENCE	to listen to ideas, to challenge, to question, to enlarge perspective
PROOFREADER	to correct grammar, usage, and mechanics
GRADER	to judge against external, more or less objective, and more or less arbitrary standards
ADVISOR	to prod for problem soutions, to encourage, to give suggestions, to remind of objectives

ROLE	TEACHING TIPS
AUDIENCE	Act exclusively as an audience when you read and comment on drafts. Comments on drafts should avoid direct criticism and should aim at raising students' excitement about further writing and revising.
PROOFREADER	Overemphasis on proofreading and points of grammar, usage, and mechanics can drain students' interest in and enthusiasm for writing as well as their self-confidence. Use proofreading as a peer function, and allow students to learn from reading and proofreading each other's papers.
GRADER	Avoiding grading as much as possible allows both you and students to concentrate on clear and honest expression and to preserve intrinsic motivation.
ADVISOR	Because the advising function requires one-on-one interchange, you should reserve for it as much of the precious evaluation time as you can.

CONDUCTING CONFERENCES

- Examine the portfolio before conferencing with the student. Make sure it contains all required material, including the student's evaluations of each piece of writing (*Assessment Resource* 4.1–4.6 and of the portfolio as a whole (*Assessment Resource* 4.8).
- Evaluate the portfolio before conferencing. Complete the portfolio evaluation form (*Assessment Resource* 4.7), making special note of any discrepancies between your evaluaiton and the student's.
- Do not attempt to discuss all aspects of the portfolio or the student's class performance. Choose two or three broad, major points and one or two specific problems to focus on in the conference.
- As an alternative to conferencing, you may sometimes complete and hand to students a Portfolio Evaluation Form and additional writing evaluation forms (*Assessment Resource* 4.1–4.6). You will still need to allow time for students to respond to and ask questions about their evaluations, and to hold conferences with students who need special help or encouragement.
- To allow ample class time for conferences, you must assign sufficient work that students can do independently to keep them busy on conference days. Thus, you must establish the writing process and the peer groups early in the term.
- In addition, to allow yourself ample time to evaluate portfolios you must involve students in ongoing self- and peer evaluation.

Additional Resources for Language Arts Teachers

TEACHING LITERATURE

Applebee, A. N. *Tradition and Reform in the Teaching of English: A History.* Urbana, IL: NCTE, 1974.

Atwell, N. *In the Middle: Writing, Reading, and Learning with Adolescents.* Portsmouth, NH: Heinemann, 1987.

Beach, R., and J. Marshall. *Teaching Literature in the Secondary School.* Orlando, FL: Harcourt, 1991.

Becoming a Nation of Readers: The Report of the Commission on Reading. Washington, DC: NIE, 1984.

Buck, C., ed. *The Bloomsbury Guide to Women's Literature.* New York: Prentice, 1992.

Bushman, J., and K. Bushman. *Using Young Adult Literature in the Classroom.* New York: Macmillan, 1992.

Cooper, C. R., ed. *Researching Response to Literature and the Teaching of Literature.* Norwood, NJ: Ablex, 1988.

Farrell, E. J., and J. Squire, eds. *Transactions with Literature: A Fifty-Year Perspective.* Urbana, IL: NCTE, 1990.

Flood, J., et al., eds. *Handbook of Research on Teaching the English Language Arts.* New York: Macmillan, 1991.

Glazer, S. *Reading Comprehension: Self-monitoring Strategies That Create Independent Readers.* New York: Scholastic, 1992.

Langer, J. A., ed. *Literature Instruction: A Focus on Student Response.* Urbana, IL: NCTE, 1992.

Lee, C., and T. Gura. *Oral Interpretation.* 8th ed. Boston: Houghton, 1992.

Marzano, R. *Cultivating Thinking English and the Language Arts.* Urbana, IL: NCTE, 1991.

Newell, G. E., and R. K. Durst. *Exploring Texts: The Roles of Discussion and Writing in the Teaching and Learning of Literature.* Norwood, MA: Christopher-Gorden, 1993.

Probst, R. E. *Response and Analysis: Teaching Literature in Junior and Senior High School.* Portsmouth, NH: Boynton/Cook, 1988.

Rosenblatt, L. *Literature as Exploration.* 4th ed. New York: MLA, 1983.

———. *The Reader, the Text, the Poem: The Transactional Theory of the Literary Work.* Carbondale, IL: Southern Illinois UP, 1978.

Wagner, B. J., and M. Larson. *Situations: A Casebook of Virtual Realities for the English Teacher.* Portsmouth, NH: Boynton/Cook, 1994.

Widdowson, P., ed. *Re-reading English.* London: Routledge, 1982.

TEACHING WRITING

Bogel, F. V., and K. K. Gottschalk, eds. *Teaching Prose.* New York: Norton, 1988.

Dellinger, D. G. *Out of the Heart: How to Design Writing Assignments for High School Courses.* Berkeley, CA: Bay Area Writing Project.

Elbow, P. *Writing with Power: Techniques for Mastering the Writing Process.* New York: Oxford UP, 1981.

Flower, L. S. *Problem-Solving Strategies in Writing.* 2nd ed. Orlando, FL: Harcourt, 1985.

Fulwiler, T., ed. *The Journal Book.* Portsmouth, NH: Heinemann, 1987.

Handa, C., ed. *Computers and Community: Teaching Composition in the Twenty-First Century.* Portsmouth, NH: Boynton/Cook, 1990.

Harris, M. *Teaching One-to-One: The Writing Conference.* Urbana, IL: NCTE, 1986.

Hawisher, G. E. "Research and Recommendations for Computers and Composition." *Critical Perspectives on Computers and Composition Instruction.* Ed. G. E. Hawisher and C. L. Selfe. New York: Teacher's Coll. P, 1989: 44–69.

Irmscher, W. *Teaching Expository Writing.* New York: Holt, 1979.

Kirby, D., and T. Liner. *Inside Out: Developmental Strategies for Teaching Writing.* Upper Montclair, NJ: Boynton/Cook, 1981.

Langer, J. A., and A. N. Applebee. *How Writing Shapes Thinking: A Study of Teaching and Learning.* NCTE Research Rept. No. 22. Urbana, IL: NCTE, 1987.

Lindemann, E. *A Rhetoric for Writing Teachers.* New York: Oxford UP, 1982.

Moffett, J., and B. J. Wagner. *Student-Centered Language Arts, K–12.* 4th ed. Portsmouth, NH: Boynton/Cook, 1992.

Murray, D. *Write to Learn.* New York: Holt, 1984.

Rodrigues, D., and R. Rodrigues. *Teaching Writing with Word Processors, Grades 1–13.* Urbana, IL: NCTE, 1987.

Romano, T. *Clearing the Way: Working with Teenage Writers.* Portsmouth, NH: Heinemann, 1987.

Ross, M., D. Brackett, and A. Maxon. *Assessment and Management of Mainstreamed Hearing-Impaired Children.* Austin, TX: Pro-Ed, 1991.

Shaughnessy, M. *Errors and Expectations.* New York: Oxford UP, 1977.

Spear, K. *Sharing Writing.* Upper Montclair, NJ: Boynton/Cook, 1988.

Tate, G., and E. Corbett, eds. *The Writing Teacher's Sourcebook.* New York: Oxford UP, 1981.

Weaver, Constance. *Grammar for Teachers.* Urbana, IL: NCTE, 1979.

TEACHING GRAMMAR

Elley, W. B., et al. "The Role of Grammar in a Secondary School English Curriculum." *Research in the Teaching of English* 10 (1976): 5–21.

Hillocks, G., Jr. *Research on Written Composition.* Urbana, IL: Natl. Conference on Research in English and ERIC/CRCS, 1986.

TEACHING THINKING SKILLS

Ausubel, D. P. *Educational Psychology.* 2nd ed. New York: Holt, 1978.

Chance, P. *Thinking in the Classroom: A Survey of Programs.* New York: Teacher's Coll. P, 1986.

Costa, A. L. *Developing Minds: A Resource Book for Teaching Thinking.* Rev. ed. 2 Vols. Alexandria, VA: ASCD, 1991.

Gardner, H. *The Unschooled Mind.* New York: Basic, 1991.

Horton, S. *Thinking through Writing.* Baltimore: Johns Hopkins UP, 1982.

Lazear, D. G. *Teaching for Multiple Intelligences.* Fastback No. 342. Bloomington, IN: Phi Delta Kappa Educ. Foundation, 1992.

Nickerson, R. S., D. N. Perkins, and E. E. Smith. *The Teaching of Thinking.* Hillsdale, NJ: Erlbaum, 1985.

Novak, J. D., and D. B. Gowin. *Learning How to Learn.* New York: Cambridge UP, 1984.

Pressley, M., et al. *Cognitive Strategy Instruction That Really Improves Children's Academic Performance.* Cambridge, MA: Brookline, 1990.

Resnick, L. B. *Education and Learning to Think.* Washington, DC: Natl. Academy P, 1987.

Resnick, L. B., and L. E. Klopfer, eds. *Toward the Thinking Curriculum: Current Cognitive Research.* Alexandria, VA: ASCD, 1989.

Rogoff, B. *Apprenticeship in Thinking.* New York: Cambridge UP, 1989.

Sternberg, R. J. "How Can We Teach Intelligence?" *Educational Leadership* 42 (1984): 38–50.

Sternberg, R. J., and T. I. Lubart. "Creating Creative Minds." *Phi Delta Kappan* 72 (1991): 608–614.

Sternberg, R. J., and R. Wagner. *Practical Intelligence.* New York: Cambridge UP, 1985.

ASSESSMENT

California Assessment Program. *The California Assessment Program: A Position Paper on Testing and Instruction.* Sacramento, CA: CAP, 1990.

Cambourne, B., and J. Turbil. "Assessment in Whole-Language Classrooms: Theory into Practice." *Elementary School Journal* 90 (1991): 337–349.

García, G. E., and P. D. Pearson. "Assessment and Diversity." *Review of Research in Education* 20 (1994): 337–391.

Gronlund, N. E., and R. L. Linn. *Measurement and Evaluation in Teaching.* 6th ed. New York: Macmillan, 1990.

Herman, J. L., P. R. Aschbacher, and L. Winters. *A Practical Guide to Alternative Assessment.* Alexandria, VA: ASCD, 1992.

Johnston, P. H. *Constructive Evaluation of Literate Activity.* White Plains, NY: Longman, 1992.

Smith, M. A., and M. Ylvisaker, eds. *Teacher's Voices: Portfolios in the Classroom.* Berkeley, CA: Natl. Writing Project, 1994.

Wolf, D., et al. "To Use Their Minds Well: Investigating New Forms of Student Assessment." *Review of Research in Education* 17 (1991): 31–74.

Yancey, K. B., ed. *Portfolios in the Writing Classroom.* Urbana, IL: NCTE, 1992

TEACHING SPECIAL POPULATIONS

Banks, J., and C. M. Banks, eds. *Multicultural Education: Issues and Perspectives.* 2nd ed. Boston: Allyn, 1993.

Brooks, C., ed. *Tapping Potential: English and the Language Arts for the Black Learner.* Urbana, IL: NCTE, 1985.

Cummins, J. *Empowering Minority Students.* Sacramento, CA: CA Assoc. for Bilingual Education, 1989.

Farr, M., and H. Daniels. *Language Diversity and Writing Instruction.* New York: ERIC Clearinghouse on Urban Education/Columbia UP, 1986.

Garcia, E. E. "Language, Culture, and Education." *Review of Research in Education* 19 (1993): 51–98.

Haberman, M. "The Pedagogy of Poverty versus Good Teaching." *Phi Delta Kappan* (1991): 290–294.

Hernandez, H. *Multicultural Education: A Teacher's Guide to Content and Process.* Columbus, OH: Merrill, 1989.

Kronick, D. *New Approaches to Learning Disabilities.* Philadelphia, PA: Grune & Stratton, 1988.

Marik, R. *Special Education Students Write: Classroom Activities and Assignments.* Berkeley, CA: Bay Area Writing Project, 1982.

Shade, B. J. *Culture, Style, and the Educative Process.* Springfield, IL: Charles Thomas, 1989.

Slavin, R., N. Karweit, and N. Madden, eds. *Effective Programs for Students at Risk.* Boston: Allyn, 1989.

West, W. W. *Teaching the Gifted and Talented in the English Classroom.* Washington, DC: NEA, 1980.

GENDER ISSUES

Brown, L. M., and C. Gilligan. *Meeting at the Crossroads: Women's Psychology and Girls' Development.* Cambridge: Harvard UP, 1992.

Gilbert, P. *Gender, Literacy, and the Classroom.* Carlton South, Victoria: Austral. Reading Assn., 1989.

Sadker, M., and D. Sadker. *Failing at Fairness: How Schools Cheat Girls.* New York: Scribner's, 1994.

Sadker, M., D. Sadker, and S. Klein. "The Issue of Gender in Elementary and Secondary Education." *Review of Research in Education* 17 (1991): 269–334.

Wellesley College Center for Research on Women. *How Schools Shortchange Girls: The AAUW Report.* Washington, DC: American Assn. of Univ. Women, 1992.

TEACHING HIGH SCHOOL-AGE STUDENTS

Applebee, A. N. *The Child's Concept of Story: Ages Two to Seventeen.* Chicago: U of Chicago P, 1978.

Flavell, J. *Cognitive Development.* 2nd ed. Englewood Cliffs, NJ: Prentice, 1985.

Kohlberg, L. "Education for Justice: A Modern Statement of the Platonic View." *Five Lectures on Moral Education.* Ed. N. F. Sizer and T. R. Sizer. Cambridge: Harvard UP, 1970.

KEY TO ICONS

Cross-curriculum Icons

 Arts and Humanities

 Mathematics and Sciences

 Social Studies

 Applied Arts

Multiple Intelligence Icons

 Musical Intelligence
Ability to produce and to appreciate forms of musical expression

 Logical-Mathematical Intelligence
Ability to reason and to discern logical or numerical patterns

 Spatial Intelligence
Ability to configure space to pose and solve problems

 Kinesthetic Intelligence
Ability to use the body effectively to solve problems

 Interpersonal/ Intrapersonal Intelligence
Ability to respond to the needs of others, self

 Naturalist Intelligence
Ability to respond to surrounding environment

SCANS Icons

 Managing Resources
Identifies, organizes, plans, allocates time, money, materials, space, human resources

 Interpersonal Skills
Works with others as member of team

 Information Skills
Acquires, evaluates, organizes, maintains, interprets, communicates, and processes information

 Systems Skills
Understands complex inter-relationships

 Technology Skills
Selects, applies, and maintains appropriate technology to perform tasks and solve problems

 Basic Skills
Reads, writes, performs arithmetic and mathematical operations, and listens and speaks well

 Thinking Skills
Thinks creatively, makes decisions, solves problems, visualizes, knows how to learn, and reasons

 Personal Qualities
Displays responsibility, self-esteem, sociability, self-management, and integrity and honesty

Thematic Organization Chart

The chart on these pages lists forty-seven common literary themes and identifies the selections in this book that deal with these themes. Choose the themes you wish to teach in your course, and use the chart to identify selections that deal with those themes.

Selection	AGE	ALIENATION	ART AND ARTISTRY	BEAUTY	BIRTH	CONFUSION	COURAGE AND FEAR	DEATH	DISCOVERING AND LEARNING	DIVERSITY AND PLURALISM	DRAMA AND ACTING	EXILE	FAITH	FAMILY	FREEDOM	FRIENDSHIP	THE FUTURE	GIVING	GOD	GREED AND AMBITION	GROWTH/GROWING UP	HERO/HEROISM	HOME AND COUNTRY	HONESTY	HOPE	IDENTITY	IMAGINATION	INDEPENDENCE	JUSTICE	KNOWLEDGE/WISDOM	LAW AND CUSTOM	LEADERSHIP AND AUTHORITY	LOSS AND REMEMBRANCE	LOVE	NATURE	ORDER/DISORDER	PARENTS AND CHILDREN	PEACE	PRIDE AND VANITY	RELIGION	SCIENCE	STRUGGLE	TECHNOLOGY	TRUTH/REALITY	WAR	WORK	WRITING AND BOOKS
UNIT 1																																															
"Zebra," 6			•	•			•		•							•	•								•	•																					
"Be-ers and Doers," 29														•												•													•								
"Name Giveaway," 44		•																								•						•															
from *An Indian Boy's Story*, 46		•																								•						•															
"The Fan Club," 50		•					•		•						•									•																				•			
"Two People I Want to Be Like," 57																									•	•				•																	
"Destroy the Four Olds!" from *Red Scarf Girl*, 63		•					•	•						•	•								•			•			•	•						•						•					
UNIT 2																																															
"in the inner city," 90																									•	•																					
"The City Is So Big," 91		•					•																																								
"Jed's Grandfather," 96	•							•						•		•			•							•											•										
"Birdfoot's Grampa," 101																				•										•					•												
"Under the Harvest Moon," 106				•																															•												
"Theme in Yellow," 107				•																															•												
"A Letter to God," 109													•						•	•																						•					
"The Green Mamba," 115							•																												•							•					
"How the Snake Got Poison," 121									•																					•					•												
"Dinner Party," 122		•					•																												•							•					
"Ships in the Desert," 128																				•										•					•	•					•		•				
"Song of Thunders," 140				•																															•												
"Song of the Crows," 141				•																															•												
UNIT 3																																															
"Hollywood and the Pits," 159									•		•									•						•		•									•			•							•
"The Serial Garden," 177				•													•																•											•			
"An Unforgettable Journey," 199		•					•					•	•										•										•				•					•					
Hmong Storycloth, 205		•	•				•					•	•										•										•									•					
"The Inn of Lost Time," 211								•																						•			•		•									•			
"The Listeners," 224								•																			•								•												
UNIT 4																																															
"400-Meter Freestyle," 232				•																																						•					•
How She Played the Game, 242							•		•	•										•						•						•										•					
"First Love," 263									•																									•													
"Point Guard," 264				•																																						•					
"The Women's 400 Meters," 273				•																																						•			•		
from *Off the Court*, 277		•							•																	•																•					•
"Tennis in the City: for Arthur Ashe," 290		•							•				•												•																	•					
"A Black Athlete Looks at Education," 291									•	•																•													•								

	AGE	ALIENATION	ART AND ARTISTRY	BEAUTY	BIRTH	CONFUSION	COURAGE AND FEAR	DEATH	DISCOVERING AND LEARNING	DIVERSITY AND PLURALISM	DRAMA AND ACTING	EXILE	FAITH	FAMILY	FREEDOM	FRIENDSHIP	THE FUTURE	GIVING	GOD	GREED AND AMBITION	GROWTH/GROWING UP	HERO/HEROISM	HOME AND COUNTRY	HONESTY	HOPE	IDENTITY	IMAGINATION	INDEPENDENCE	JUSTICE	KNOWLEDGE/WISDOM	LAW AND CUSTOM	LEADERSHIP AND AUTHORITY	LOSS AND REMEMBRANCE	LOVE	NATURE	ORDER/DISORDER	PARENTS AND CHILDREN	PEACE	PRIDE AND VANITY	RELIGION	SCIENCE	STRUGGLE	TECHNOLOGY	TRUTH/REALITY	WAR	WORK	WRITING AND BOOKS
"Roberto Clemente: A Bittersweet Memoir," 296			●				●	●	●								●					●	●										●														
"Searching for January," 308																					●				●								●								●						
UNIT 5																																															
"The 11:59," 328							●	●									●																●													●	
"Pets," 343		●			●		●	●																									●								●						
"Qwertyuiop," 358		●					●																										●								●					●
"The Foghorn," 371		●					●								●																		●														
"Once by the Pacific," 380		●		●			●																												●	●											
"The Tell-Tale Heart," 386		●						●					●																●				●														
UNIT 6																																															
"The Hummingbird That Lived through Winter," 406	●		●					●							●										●										●	●											
"Mute Dancers: How to Watch a Hummingbird," 410			●						●																								●						●								
"Humming Bird," 413			●																																●												
"Sympathy," 418		●								●					●											●							●									●					
"Caged Bird," 419		●								●					●											●							●									●					
"The *Challenger* Disaster," 425							●														●												●														
"Something Dreadfully Wrong in What Appeared to Be Picture-Perfect Launch," 427						●		●																																		●					
"High Flight," 428								●							●				●				●																			●					
"Flying," 433		●					●		●			●																										●									
"The Spirit of Charles Lindbergh," 440									●												●																										
"Feel Like a Bird," 448			●																																●												
"Freedom," 450															●																																
UNIT 7																																															
"Persephone and Demeter," 474			●				●	●				●		●																					●	●	●										
"The Epic of Gilgamesh," 482	●						●	●						●		●						●			●					●			●	●	●				●			●	●				
"The Secret Name of Ra," 492								●											●										●		●				●							●					
"Why the Sky Is Far Away from the Earth," 501																			●											●																	
"The Instruction of Indra," 508								●											●										●					●			●		●					●		●	
"Amaterasu," 516																																			●	●		●		●							
UNIT 8																																															
"The Ground Is Always Damp," 535		●	●							●												●											●						●			●					
"Luke Baldwin's Vow," 542						●	●												●	●								●		●			●	●	●	●											
"Getting the Facts of Life," 557							●							●						●																				●		●	●				
"A Secret for Two," 570	●						●	●							●																				●	●										●	
The Snow Goose, 579	●	●		●			●	●	●						●	●		●				●											●	●	●						●			●		
"Investment in the Future," 597															●												●	●					●														
UNIT 9																																															
"Poetry," 614		●	●	●				●																																							●
"How to Eat a Poem," 615			●																											●																	●
"Filling Station," 620			●					●																									●													●	

Title	AGE	ALIENATION	ART AND ARTISTRY	BEAUTY	BIRTH	CONFUSION	COURAGE AND FEAR	DEATH	DISCOVERING AND LEARNING	DIVERSITY AND PLURALISM	DRAMA AND ACTING	EXILE	FAITH	FAMILY	FREEDOM	FRIENDSHIP	THE FUTURE	GIVING	GOD	GREED AND AMBITION	GROWTH/GROWING UP	HERO/HEROISM	HOME AND COUNTRY	HONESTY	HOPE	IDENTITY	IMAGINATION	INDEPENDENCE	JUSTICE	KNOWLEDGE/WISDOM	LAW AND CUSTOM	LEADERSHIP AND AUTHORITY	LOSS AND REMEMBRANCE	LOVE	NATURE	ORDER/DISORDER	PARENTS AND CHILDREN	PEACE	PRIDE AND VANITY	RELIGION	SCIENCE	STRUGGLE	TECHNOLOGY	TRUTH/REALITY	WAR	WORK	WRITING AND BOOKS
"A Deserted Barn," 622	•							•				•																					•														
"the / sky / was," 626			•	•																						•									•												
"I to My Perils," 631							•																																			•		•			
"Blackberry Eating," 635				•				•																											•												
"Forgotten Language," 639	•							•																										•	•												
"Hector the Collector," 640			•	•																													•														
"Lost Parrot," 646																																	•														•
"My Father's Song," 651						•		•						•																			•	•	•		•										
"The Charge of the Light Brigade," 657							•	•	•											•												•				•						•			•		
"Corners on the Curving Sky," 662				•																										•					•									•			
"Under the Apple Tree," 665				•																															•												
"The old pond...," 670																																			•	•		•						•			
"Misty grasses...," 670																																			•	•		•						•			
"Summer night...," 670																																			•	•		•						•			
"Lost in Translation," 672									•	•																																					•
UNIT 10																																															
The Miracle Worker, 688								•	•	•	•			•	•	•			•		•	•		•									•				•			•						•
"If You Could Write One Great Poem, What Would You Want It to Be About?", 750			•	•				•																			•																				•
UNIT 11																																															
"Elizabeth I" from *Ten Queens: Portraits of Women in Power*, 770																				•		•		•						•	•	•			•		•										
"Caesar the Giant" from *My Life in Dog Years*, 781											•																							•	•												
"Appearances Are Destructive," 792		•						•																		•									•												
"The Size of Things" from *Red Giants and White Dwarfs*, 800								•																											•						•		•				
"The Price of Freedom," 810															•			•		•		•											•												•		
UNIT 12																																															
Variations in Vital Signs by Age / Temperature Conversions, 832																																									•						
"A Day's Wait," 833							•	•	•					•																•				•			•					•					
Historical Photographs, 838																							•										•		•							•					
from *Out of the Dust*, 841						•	•																•										•		•		•					•					
from *The New Way Things Work*, 845									•																																•		•				
"How to Chop an Onion" from *The Old Farmer's Almanac*, 851									•																																						

Selections by Genre

These pages list all the selections in this book, organized by genre. Choose the genres you wish to teach in your course, and use the list to identify selections that represent those genres.

VISUAL AND INFORMATIONAL MEDIA

Literature

and the Language Arts

Exploring Literature

THE EMC MASTERPIECE SERIES

SECOND EDITION

EMCParadigm Publishing Saint Paul, Minnesota

Staff Credits

Editorial

Laurie Skiba
Editor

Lori Ann Coleman
Associate Editor

Brenda Owens
Associate Editor

Diana Moen
Associate Editor

Gia Marie Garbinsky
Assistant Editor

Jennifer Anderson
Assistant Editor

Janice Johnson
Curriculum Specialist

Paul Spencer
Art and Photo Researcher

Chris Bohen
Editorial Assistant

Chris Nelson
Editorial Assistant

Design

Shelley Clubb
Production Manager

Karen Michels
Design Manager

C. Vern Johnson
Senior Designer

Jennifer Wreisner
Senior Designer

Michelle Lewis
Design Specialist

Julie L. Hansen
Design Specialist

Cover Credits

Cover Designer: C. Vern Johnson

Utsu Mountain at Okabe **[Detail]**, 1833. Utagawa Hiroshige.

Extinguished Sun and Moon and Fallen Stars **[Detail]**, 1476. Cristoforo de Predis.

The Library **[Detail]**, 1960. Jacob Lawrence.

People at Night, Guided by Phosphorus Traces of Snails **[Detail]**, 1940. Joan Miro.

ISBN 0-8219-2048-0 (Student Edition)   ISBN 0-8219-2049-9 (Annotated Teacher's Edition)

©2001 by EMC Corporation

Published by EMC/Paradigm Publishing
875 Montreal Way
St. Paul, Minnesota 55102
800-328-1452
www.emcp.com
E-mail: educate@emcp.com

Printed in the United States of America.
10 9 8 7 6 5 4 3 2 1   XXX 06 05 04 03 02 01

Literature
and the Language Arts
SECOND EDITION

REDWOOD LEVEL
DISCOVERING LITERATURE

WILLOW LEVEL
UNDERSTANDING LITERATURE

CEDAR LEVEL
EXPLORING LITERATURE

PINE LEVEL
THE AMERICAN TRADITION

OAK LEVEL
RESPONDING TO LITERATURE

MAPLE LEVEL
THE BRITISH TRADITION

BIRCH LEVEL
EXPERIENCING LITERATURE

CYPRESS LEVEL
WORLD LITERATURE

Consultants and Writers

Senior Consultant
Dr. Edmund J. Farrell
Emeritus Professor of English Education
University of Texas at Austin
Austin, Texas

Maria Backus
Educational Writer
Arvada, Colorado

Amy Bergstrom
Instructor
Education Department
University of Minnesota
Duluth, Minnesota

Diana Blythe
Senior Content Manager
Humanities Software, a division
of Advantage Learning
    Systems, Inc.
Hood River, Oregon

Cherie Boen
National Board Certified
    Teacher
Educational Consultant
Minneapolis, Minnesota

Jamy Bond
Educational Writer
Washington, D. C.

Walker Brents, III
Instructor
Berkwood-Hedge School
Berkeley, California

Nancy Campbell
Educational Writer
Richfield, Minnesota

Linda Christopherson
Educational Writer
Charlotte, North Carolina

Dr. Mary Curfman
Language Arts Supervisor
Department of Curriculum and
    Professional Development
Clark County Schools
Las Vegas, Nevada

Lisa De Leon
Educational Writer
Northfield, Minnesota

Rebecca Gander
Educational Consultant
Anoka, Minnesota

Sara Hyry
Educational Writer
Easthampton, Massachusetts

Christina Kolb
Educational Writer
Newton, Massachusetts

Sharon Kremer
English Department Chair
A. O. Calhoun Middle School
Denton, Texas

Jon Madian
Senior Instructional Designer
Humanities Software, a division
of Advantage Learning
    Systems, Inc.
Hood River, Oregon

Beverly Martin
Managing Editor
Humanities Software, a division
of Advantage Learning
    Systems, Inc.
Hood River, Oregon

Mertys Mrvos
Language Arts/Reading
    Instructor
South View Middle School
Edina, Minnesota

Carol Satz
Clinician
Center for Reading and
    Writing
Rider University
Lawrenceville, New Jersey

Karen Schwabach
Itinerant Literacy Leader
Lower Kuskokwim School
District
Bethel, Alaska

Elnora Shields
Educational Consultant
Durham, North Carolina

Dr. Jane Shoaf
Educational Consultant
Edenton, North Carolina

Kendra Sisserson
Research Associate
University of Chicago
Chicago, Illinois

Jim Swanson
Educational Consultant
Minneapolis, Minnesota

Shannon Taylor
Educational Writer
Eagan, Minnesota

Anne Todd
Educational Writer
Walnut Creek, California

Jan Toth
Language Arts Instructor
Whitman Middle School
Seattle, Washington

Geraldine Troutman
Reading Mentor
Hollywood Beach Elementary
    School
Advisor, Curriculum Council
    Advisory Committee
Hueneme School District
Oxnard, California

Anita Usmiani
Language Arts Supervisor
Hamilton Township School
    District
Hamilton, New Jersey

Red Lake Fishermen, 1946–1961. Patrick Des Jarlait.

The Vinery, 1816. Humphry Repton.

Charles Lindbergh

Amaterasu Appearing from the Cave,
1882. Taiso Yoshitoshi.

Campesino, 1976. Daniel Desiga.

The Procession of Queen Elizabeth I, c.1500s. English Artist.

Fishermen of the North, 1965. Patrick Des Jarlait.

The Miracle Worker. Produced by Stages Theatre Company

3   LANGUAGE, GRAMMAR, AND STYLE

To the Student

Features of Your Textbook

A Guide for Reading

When you open your *EMC Masterpiece Series* textbook, you will find great literature, both classic and contemporary, by a wide variety of authors. You will also find useful step-by-step study strategies for each selection, helpful background information, and activities that allow you to relate the literature to your own experiences and share your point of view.

The **Guided Reading** program in this *EMC Masterpiece Series* book gives you tips before, during, and after you read each selection. Read on for a description of the features you will find in your textbook.

- **Reader's Resource** gives you background and other information you'll need for the reading.

- **Reader's Toolbox** features point out and explain literary techniques that are used in the selection.

- A **Graphic Organizer** is provided to help you sort out the important points on paper.

- **Guided Reading Questions** within the selection help you check your understanding of the reading.

- **Words for Everyday Use** includes the definition and pronunciation for new vocabulary. A sample sentence demonstrates the use of the word in context.

- **Footnotes** explain unfamiliar terms or unusual words.

- **Art Smart** features provide information about the history, culture, or artistic technique of the fine art throughout the textbook and foster critical viewing of the art.

- **Respond to the Selection** allows you to relate the literature to your own experiences.

- **Investigate, Inquire, and Imagine** contains questions you need to perfect your understanding of the reading, from basic recalling and interpreting questions to ones that ask you to analyze, synthesize, evaluate, and extend your ideas. Some questions also ask you to look at a specific point of view, or examine a different perspective.

- **Understanding Literature** follows up on the literary techniques introduced in Reader's Toolbox and asks you questions to further your understanding.

- **Writer's Journal** gives you three quick-writing options to help you build writing skills.

- **Skill Builders** contain creative activities that tie literature to other language arts areas such as grammar, vocabulary development, public speaking, study and research, collaborative learning, media literacy, and applied English.

A Guide for Writing

At the end of each unit of your textbook you will find a **Guided Writing** activity that takes you through the steps of the writing process. The lesson includes models from professional writers and students. Also included are graphic organizers, questions to get you thinking, and an integrated **Language, Grammar, and Style** lesson to help you brush up on grammar points.

A Guide for Language Arts Skills

The **Language Arts Survey** in the back of your textbook is your resource for information about how to use the English language effectively. It includes tips on what you need to know to write, speak, and read effectively. There are six sections in the Language Arts Survey: the **Reading Resource**, the **Writing Resource**, the **Language, Grammar, and Style Resource**, the **Speaking and Listening Resource**, the **Study and Research Resource**, and the **Applied English Resource**. Do you need to correct a passive sentence? include an Internet site in a research paper? interview someone in the community? write a letter? It's all here for you.

Themes in Literature

PART ONE

GOALS/OBJECTIVES

Studying this unit will enable students to
- enjoy fiction, nonfiction, and poems exploring the theme of finding your place in the world
- define and identify examples of *character, conflict, description, dialogue, image, imagery, memoir, motive, plot,* and *speaker.*
- engage in a meaningful book club or literature circle experience
- write a personal essay
- recognize the parts of a sentence and demonstrate an ability to write in complete sentences

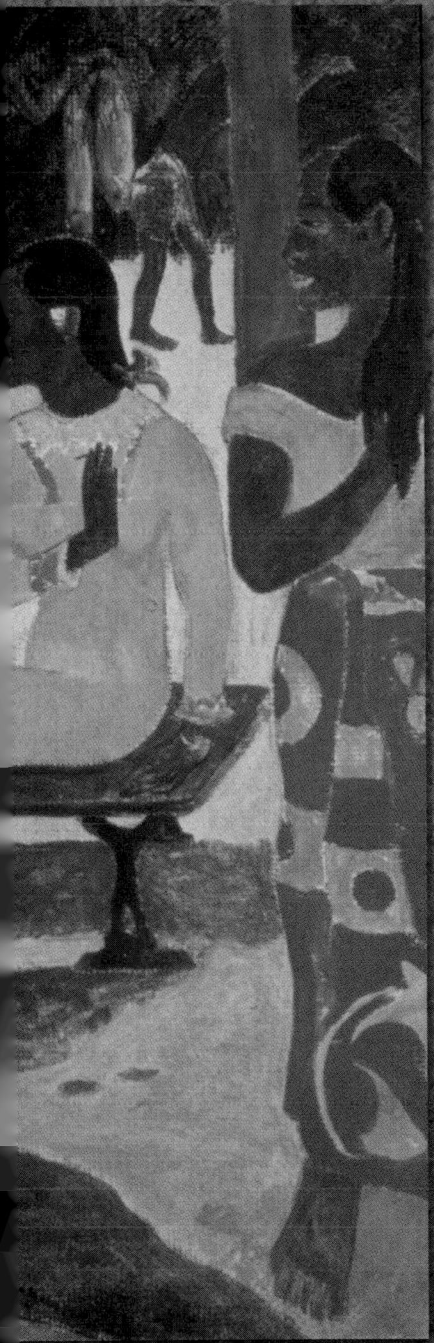

Finding Your PLACE in the WORLD

The Market, 1892. Paul Gauguin.

UNIT ONE

TEACHING THE MULTIPLE INTELLIGENCES

(Continued on page 4)

Begin a class discussion by having students read the quotations in the Echoes feature. Ask them the following:

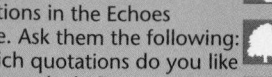

- Which quotations do you like best, and why?
- Do you look at finding your own place in the world as an exciting prospect or something that frightens you?
- Which speakers quoted see the world as a friendly, inviting place? Which see it as hostile?
- Is it possible, as Mahatma Gandhi says, to "be the change you wish to see in the world"?
- Do you agree with E. E. Cummings that the world is trying its best "to make you like everybody else"? What examples can you think of that support or argue against this statement?

As an alternate activity, you may want to have students freewrite about one or two of the questions above.

TEACHING THE MULTIPLE INTELLIGENCES (CONT.)

echoes

Tell me, what is it you plan to do with your one wild and precious life?
—*Mary Oliver*

You must be the change you wish to see in the world.
—*Mahatma Gandhi*

How does it feel
To be on your own
With no direction home
Like a complete unknown
Like a rolling stone?
—*Bob Dylan*

The real voyage of discovery lies not in seeking new landscapes but in having new eyes.
—*Marcel Proust*

Far away there in the sunshine are my highest aspirations. I may not reach them, but I can look up and see their beauty, believe in them, and try to follow where they lead.
—*Louisa May Alcott*

Wherever you are it is your own friends who make your world.
—*William James*

Life loves to be taken by the lapel and be told: "I am with you, kid. Let's go."
—*Maya Angelou*

The hardest battle is to be nobody but yourself in a world that is doing its best, night and day, to make you like everybody else.
—*E. E. Cummings*

4 *UNIT ONE*

TEACHING THE MULTIPLE INTELLIGENCES (CONT.)

Prereading

"ZEBRA"
by Chaim Potok

Reader's TOOLBOX

CONFLICT. A **conflict** is a struggle between people or things in a literary work. A plot is formed around conflict. A conflict can be internal or external. A struggle that takes place between a character and some outside force—such as another character, society, or nature—is called an **external conflict**. A struggle that takes place within a character is called an **internal conflict**. As you read "Zebra," determine whether the conflict in this story is external or internal.

DESCRIPTION. A **description** gives a picture in words of a character, object, or scene. Descriptions make use of **sensory details**—words and phrases that describe how things look, sound, smell, taste, or feel. In "Zebra," the author uses description to create vivid pictures of characters, objects, and scenes. As you read the story, look for examples of description. Create a graphic organizer of descriptive phrases like the one shown below. Add phrases that describe a variety of the senses—sight, sound, smell, taste, and touch.

Graphic Organizer

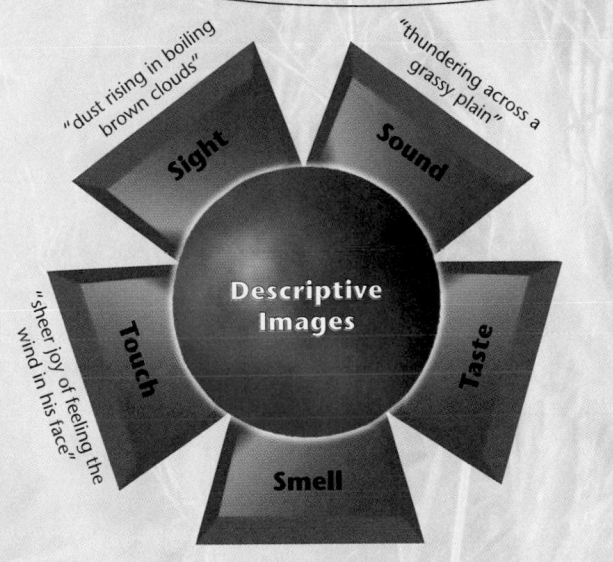

"dust rising in boiling brown clouds"

"thundering across a grassy plain"

Sight

Sound

Descriptive Images

Touch

Taste

"sheer joy of feeling the wind in his face"

Smell

Reader's Journal

What special talent or ability do you have that you would most hate to lose, and why?

Reader's Resource

- This short story features a boy who was injured in an accident and a man who was injured while serving in the Vietnam War.

- **HISTORY CONNECTION.** The Vietnam War (1965-1975), was the longest war in America's history and the nation's first military defeat. Of the nearly 2.7 million Americans who served in Vietnam—many of whom enlisted right out of high school—more than 58,000 were killed, 300,000 were wounded, and 75,000 were permanently disabled. More than 2,000 people still are listed as missing in action.

- Maya Ying Lin, an architecture student at Yale University, designed the Vietnam Veterans Memorial, which stands on the Mall in Washington, D.C. Since the beginning of its construction in 1982, visitors have left more than 25,000 keepsakes at the memorial—or "the Wall," as it is commonly called—in honor of the men and women who died fighting the war.

ADDITIONAL RESOURCES

UNIT 1 RESOURCE BOOK
- Selection Worksheet 1.1
- Selection Check Test 4.1.1
- Selection Test 4.1.2
- Language, Grammar, and Style Resource 3.15, 3.66
- Speaking and Listening Resource 4.14

ANSWERS TO READER'S TOOLBOX

CONFLICT. See Understanding Literature on page 24 for further questions and answers about conflict.

DESCRIPTION. Students may include some of the following phrases from the story in their graphic organizers.

Sight: "a huge rushing shadow appeared"; "long brown hair spilled out below his dark-blue farmer's cap"; "a valley filled with yellow stones and surrounded by red mountains...an army of green shadows...an army of purple shadows"; "intricate spidery webs in the skin below his gray eyes"; "his hand—how dirty it was, the fingers and palm smudged with black ink and encrusted with colors"

Sound: "shouting and laughing with full voices"; "joyous sounds went ringing through the quiet street"; "low, friendly, shy voice"; "Kevin talked in blurred, high-pitched tones"; "tiny clickings of its hooves"

Touch: "he loved to feel the wind rushing across his neck"; "the cool wind caressing his arms and legs and neck"; "Zebra's hand began to tingle and throb"; "the sling chafed his neck and felt warm and clumsy on his bare arm"

READER'S JOURNAL

As an alternative activity, ask students to name a special talent or ability they would like to have. Why would they want this talent or ability? Is this talent or ability something people are born with, or is something than can be learned? If it can be learned, how would students go about learning it?

GOALS/OBJECTIVES

Studying this lesson will enable students to
- appreciate a short story featuring people with physical disabilities
- briefly describe the Vietnam War
- briefly explain the history of the Vietnam Veterans Memorial

- define and give examples of *external* and *internal* conflict
- understand the role of description in writing

INDIVIDUAL LEARNING STRATEGIES

MOTIVATION
"Zebra" features an artist named John Wilson who teaches students to "see" in new ways. Encourage students to focus on the parts of the story that take place in the summer art class. After they have read the story, ask students to draw or create a piece of art using Wilson's methods. You may also wish to explore the kinesthetic activities on pages 8 and 9 of the Teacher's Edition.

READING PROFICIENCY
Some students might be confused by the title "Zebra," and think the story is actually about a zebra and takes place in a zoo or in Africa. Encourage students to read the Prereading page, especially the Reader's Resource, for background information about "Zebra." You might wish to ask students to predict what the story will be about based on the title.

ENGLISH LANGUAGE LEARNING
Point out the following vocabulary words and expressions.
in vain—without force or effect
you-all—Southern colloquialism used primarily as plural form of address
Tylenols—pain medication
space cadet—often used as a derogatory label, in this instance literally a student in a futuristic world
Mediterranean—large sea surrounded by Europe, Africa, and Asia
studio—room where an artist works

SPECIAL NEEDS
Students will find it helpful to listen to the selection on audiocassette. Make sure students focus on the Guided Reading questions and the Recall questions in the Investigate, Inquire, and Imagine section.

ENRICHMENT
Suggest that students work in small groups to compare and contrast the Vietnam War with the Gulf War, the conflicts in Kosovo or Somalia, or another war, and prepare a presentation about their findings for the class. Ask students the following questions to help them get started: What caused the conflict? What role, if any, did the United States play in the conflict? What was the result of the conflict? What was or is the American public's perception of the conflict?

ZEBRA

Chaim Potok

His name was Adam Martin Zebrin, but everyone in his neighborhood knew him as Zebra.

He couldn't remember when he began to be called by that name. Perhaps they started to call him Zebra when he first began running. Or maybe he began running when they started to call him Zebra.

He loved the name and he loved to run.

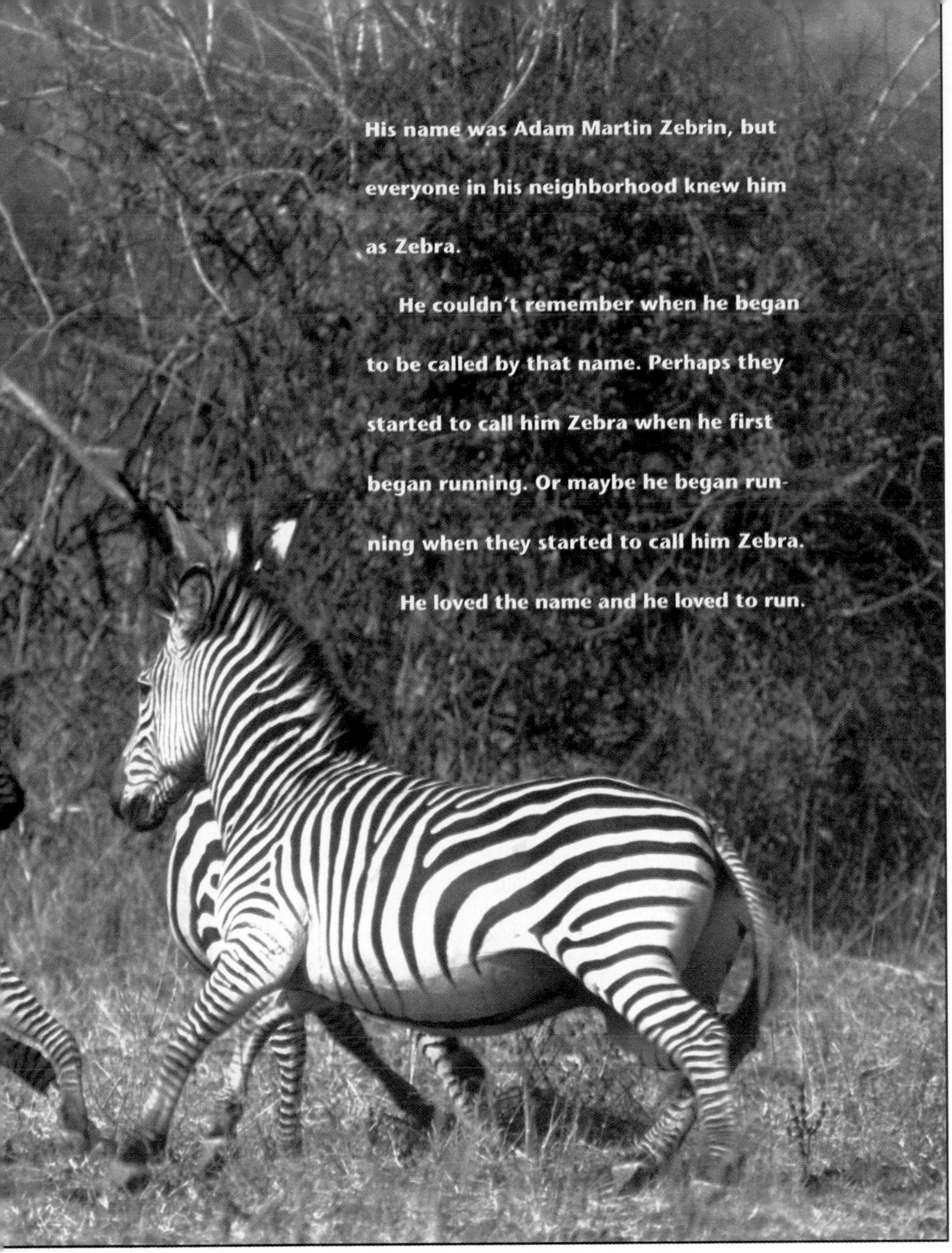

VOCABULARY FROM THE SELECTION

batter
contour
dapper
discipline
exuberant
gaunt
jaunty
laden
menace
peer
poised
quaver
ruddy
somber
tendon
wince
wondrous

HISTORICAL NOTE

You may wish to share with students the following background information about the Vietnam War: The conflict known as the Vietnam War began when Communist militants in South Vietnam, known as the Vietcong, tried to overthrow the government of South Vietnam with the help of their Communist neighbor—North Vietnam. This struggle then developed into a war between North and South Vietnam. Over forty countries, including the Unites States, supported South Vietnam with weapons and troops, while the country that was then known as the Soviet Union and the People's Republic of China—two Communist nations—supported North Vietnam. The war also spilled over into Vietnam's neighboring countries of Laos and Cambodia.

The war became increasingly unpopular in the United States as it dragged on, and many people protested U.S. involvement. U.S. intervention did not prove successful and the North Vietnamese toppled the government of South Vietnam, forming a unified Vietnam. While the loss of American lives, as described on the Prereading page, was quite high, the cost in Vietnam was much, much higher. In this bloody conflict about 2 million Vietnamese were killed, 3 million wounded, and about 12 million people in this region of the world (known as Indochina) became refugees.

**ANSWERS TO GUIDED
READING QUESTIONS**

1. Zebra imagines that he would change into an eagle.
2. Zebra was hit by a car.
3. Zebra hurts his leg and his hand.

**ADDITIONAL QUESTIONS
AND ACTIVITIES**

Encourage students to discuss physical activities they enjoy. What type of exercise makes them feel their best? What is it they enjoy about these activities?

CROSS-CURRICULAR ACTIVITIES

PHYSICAL FITNESS. Encourage students to plan their own physical fitness regimen that includes exercise and a healthy diet. They should do some research in the library, on the Internet, or by talking to gym teachers, nutritionists or trainers, and then write up a physical fitness plan. Students should keep track over a course of a week how well they keep up with their plan. Students then should write a brief paragraph describing how their physical fitness regimen felt and whether they plan to continue it.

When he was very young, his parents took him to a zoo, where he saw zebras for the first time. They were odd-looking creatures, like stubby horses, short-legged, thick-necked, with dark and white stripes.

Then one day he went with his parents to a movie about Africa, and he saw zebras, hundreds of them, thundering across a grassy plain, dust rising in boiling brown clouds.

Was he already running before he saw that movie, or did he begin to run afterward? No one seemed able to remember.

He would go running through the neighborhood for the sheer joy of feeling the wind on his face. People said that when he ran he arched his head up and back, and his face kind of flattened out. One of his teachers told him it was clever to run that way, his balance was better. But the truth was he ran that way, his head thrown back, because he loved to feel the wind rushing across his neck.

Each time, after only a few minutes of running, his legs would begin to feel <u>wondrously</u> light. He would run past the school and the homes on the street beyond the church. All the neighbors knew him and would wave and call out, "Go, Zebra!" And sometimes one or two of their dogs would run with him awhile, barking.

He would imagine himself a zebra on the African plain. Running.

There was a hill on Franklin Avenue, a steep hill. By the time he reached that hill, he would feel his legs so light it was as if he had no legs at all and was flying. He would begin to descend the hill, certain as he ran that he needed only to give himself the slightest push and off he would go, and instead of a zebra he would become the bird he had once seen in a movie about Alaska, he would swiftly change into an eagle, soaring higher and higher, as light as the gentlest breeze, the cool wind caressing his arms and legs and neck.

Then, a year ago, racing down Franklin Avenue, he had given himself that push and had begun to turn into an eagle, when a huge rushing shadow appeared in his line of vision and crashed into him and plunged him into a darkness from which he emerged very, very slowly. . . .

"Never, never, *never* run down that hill so fast that you can't stop at the corner," his mother had warned him again and again.

His schoolmates and friends kept calling him Zebra even after they all knew that the doctors had told him he would never be able to run like that again.

His leg would heal in time, the doctors said, and perhaps in a year or so the brace should come off. But they were not at all certain about his hand. From time to time his injured hand, which he still wore in a sling, would begin to hurt. The doctors said they could find no cause for the pain.

One morning, during Mr. Morgan's geography class, Zebra's hand began to hurt badly. He sat staring out the window at the sky. Mr. Morgan, a stiff-mannered person in his early fifties, given to smart suits and <u>dapper</u> bow ties, called on him to respond to a question. Zebra stumbled about in vain for the answer. Mr. Morgan told him to pay

> **GUIDED READING**
> What does Zebra imagine would happen if he gave himself an extra push as he ran down the hill on Franklin Avenue?

> **GUIDED READING**
> What happened to Zebra a year ago?

> **GUIDED READING**
> What injuries does Zebra have as a result of his accident?

---

words for everyday use

won • drous (wən' drəs) *adj.*, extraordinary, remarkable. *We spent a <u>wondrous</u> week on vacation by the sea.*
wondrously *adv.*

dap • per (dap ´ər) *adj.*, neat and trim; stylish. *The young twins were <u>dapper</u> in their matching holiday outfits.*

attention to the geography *inside* the classroom and not to the geography outside.

"In this class, young man, you will concentrate your attention upon the earth, not upon the sky," Mr. Morgan said.

Later, in the schoolyard during the midmorning recess, Zebra stood near the tall fence, looking out at the street and listening to the noises behind him.

GUIDED READING

Where does Zebra stand during recess?

His schoolmates were racing about, playing exuberantly, shouting and laughing with full voices. Their joyous sounds went ringing through the quiet street.

Most times Zebra would stand alongside the basketball court or behind the wire screen at home plate and watch the games. That day, because his hand hurt so badly, he stood alone behind the chain-link fence of the schoolyard.

That's how he happened to see the man. And that's how the man happened to see him.

One minute the side street on which the school stood was strangely empty, without people or traffic, without even any of the dogs that often roamed about the neighborhood—vacant and silent, as if it were already in the full heat of summer. The red-brick ranch house that belonged to Mr. Morgan, and the white clapboard[1] two-story house in which Mrs. English lived, and the other homes on the street, with their columned front porches and their back patios, and the tall oaks—all stood curiously still in the warm golden light of the mid-morning sun.

> He would imagine himself a zebra on the African plain. Running.

Then a man emerged from wide and busy Franklin Avenue at the far end of the street.

Zebra saw the man stop at the corner and stand looking at a public trash can. He watched as the man poked his hand into the can and fished about but seemed to find nothing he wanted. He withdrew the hand and, raising it to shield his eyes from the sunlight, glanced at the street sign on the lamppost.

GUIDED READING

What does Zebra see the man do?

He started to walk up the street in the direction of the school.

He was tall and wiry, and looked to be about forty years old. In his right hand he carried a bulging brown plastic bag. He wore a khaki army jacket, a blue denim shirt, blue jeans, and brown cowboy boots. His gaunt face and muscular neck were reddened by exposure to the sun. Long brown hair spilled out below his dark-blue farmer's cap. On the front of the cap, in large orange letters, were the words LAND ROVER.

He walked with his eyes on the sidewalk and curb, as if looking for something, and he went right past Zebra without noticing him.

Zebra's hand hurt very much. He was about to turn away when he saw the man stop and look around and peer up at the red-brick wall of the school. The man set down the bag and took off his cap and stuffed it into a pocket of his jacket. From one of his jeans pockets he

---

1. **clapboard.** Type of board used for siding

---

words for everyday use

ex • u • ber • ant (ig zü' bə rənt) *adj.*, with joy and enthusiasm. *She was exuberant about the good news.* **exuberantly** *adv.*

gaunt (gänt) *adj.*, lean, thin, angular. *The gaunt young man looked even skinnier in a suit.*

ANSWERS TO GUIDED READING QUESTIONS

1. Zebra stands near the fence during recess.
2. Zebra sees the man poke into a public trash can.

CROSS-CURRICULAR ACTIVITIES

SCIENCE. Inform students that almost twenty percent of the U.S. population has some form of disability. Disabilities can be temporary, such as a broken arm, or easily corrected, such as poor eyesight which can be corrected by using glasses. About 24 million Americans have a more severe disability. Most people who have a disability object to the term *handicap* because many people with a seemingly severe disability, such as having lost the use of their legs, lead lives equal to those of the non-disabled. People with disabilities have made much headway in the twentieth century in overcoming stereotypes. Encourage students to do some research on the life of a person who has or had a disability. Possible subjects include Helen Keller or Franklin Delano Roosevelt. Students should describe what this person's disability was, how the person coped with it, and what the person achieved.

removed a handkerchief, with which he then wiped his face. He shoved the handkerchief back into the pocket and put the cap back on his head.

Then he turned and saw Zebra.

He picked up the bag and started down the street to where Zebra was standing. When the man was about ten feet away, Zebra noticed that the left sleeve of his jacket was empty.

The man came up to Zebra and said in a low, friendly, shy voice, "Hello."

Zebra answered with a cautious "Hello," trying not to look at the empty sleeve, which had been tucked into the man's jacket pocket.

The man asked, with a distinct Southern accent, "What's your name, son?"

Zebra said, "Adam."

"What kind of school is this here school, Adam?"

"It's a good school," Zebra answered.

"How long before you-all begin your summer vacation?"

"Three days," Zebra said.

"Anything special happen here during the summer?"

"During the summer? Nothing goes on here. There are no classes."

"What do you-all do during the summer?"

"Some of us go to camp. Some of us hang around. We find things to do."

Zebra's hand had begun to tingle and throb. Why was the man asking all those questions? Zebra thought maybe he shouldn't be talking to him at all. He seemed vaguely <u>menacing</u> in that army jacket, the dark-blue cap with the words LAND ROVER on it in orange letters, and the empty sleeve. Yet there was kindness in his gray eyes and <u>ruddy</u> features.

The man gazed past Zebra at the students playing in the yard. "Adam, do you think

Citröen, 1989. Jerry Barrish. Private Collection.

art smart

Like the fictional John Wilson in "Zebra," real-life artist Jerry Barrish makes sculptures from found objects. The idea came to him when he noticed a lot of trash on the beach near his home in California. "I was frustrated by all the plastic, and I decided to collect it and make a Christmas tree," Barrish says. "Then I made Christmas ornaments." How does the sculpture and the one on page 15 compare to the images you have of the art described in this story?

words for everyday use

men • a • ce (men' əs) *v.,* act threatening. *The bear's <u>menacing</u> growl scared off the tourist.* **menacing** *adj.*

rud • dy (rəd' ə) *adj.,* reddish. *The toddler's <u>ruddy</u> complexion matched the bright roses.*

your school would be interested in having someone teach an art class during the summer?"

That took Zebra by surprise. "An *art* class?"

"Drawing, sculpting, things like that."

Zebra was trying *very hard* not to look at the man's empty sleeve. "I don't know. . . ."

"Where's the school office, Adam?"

"On Washington Avenue. Go to the end of the street and turn right."

"Thanks," the man said. He hesitated a moment. Then he asked, in a quiet voice, "What happened to you, Adam?"

"A car hit me," Zebra said. "It was my fault." The man seemed to <u>wince</u>.

For a flash of a second, Zebra thought to ask the man what had happened to *him*. The words were on his tongue. But he kept himself from saying anything.

The man started back up the street, carrying the brown plastic bag.

Zebra suddenly called, "Hey, mister."

The man stopped and turned. "My name is John Wilson," he said softly.

"Mr. Wilson, when you go into the school office, you'll see signs on two doors. One says 'Dr. Winter,' and the other says 'Mrs. English.' Ask for Mrs. English."

Dr. Winter, the principal, was a <u>disciplinarian</u> and a grump. Mrs. English, the assistant principal, was generous and kind. Dr. Winter would probably tell the man to call his secretary for an appointment. Mrs. English might invite him into her office and offer him a cup of coffee and listen to what he had to say.

The man hesitated, looking at Zebra.

"Appreciate the advice," he said.

Zebra watched him walk to the corner.

Under the lamppost was a trash can. Zebra saw the man set down the plastic bag and stick his hand into the can and haul out a <u>battered</u> umbrella.

The man tried to open the umbrella, but its metal ribs were broken. The black fabric dangled flat and limp from the pole. He put the umbrella into the plastic bag and headed for the entrance to the school.

A moment later, Zebra heard the whistle that signaled the end of recess. He followed his classmates at a distance, careful to avoid anyone's bumping against his hand.

He sat through his algebra class, copying the problems on the blackboard while holding down his notebook with his left elbow. The sling chafed his neck and felt warm and clumsy on his bare arm. There were sharp pains now in the two curled fingers of his hand.

GUIDED READING

What sensations does Zebra feel as he sits in his algebra class?

Right after the class he went downstairs to the office of Mrs. Walsh, a cheerful, gray-haired woman in a white nurse's uniform.

She said, "I'm sorry I can't do very much for you, Adam, except give you two Tylenols."

He swallowed the Tylenols down with water.

On his way back up to the second floor, he saw the man with the dark-blue cap emerge from the school office with Mrs. English. He stopped on the stairs and watched as the man and Mrs. English stood talking together. Mrs. English nodded and smiled and shook the man's hand.

The man walked down the corridor, carrying the plastic bag, and left the school building.

ANSWER TO GUIDED READING QUESTION

1. Zebra's neck is chafed by the sling and he has sharp pains in his left hand.

ADDITIONAL QUESTIONS AND ACTIVITIES

Ask students the following questions:
1. What does the man ask Zebra in a "quiet voice"?
2. Why do you think the man asks this question in a quiet voice?
3. What is Zebra's response to this question?
4. What is the man's reaction to Zebra's statement?
5. Why do you think that the man reacts in this way?

Answers
1. The man asks Zebra how he was hurt.
2. Students may say the man asks it in a quiet voice because he knows that it is probably a sensitive issue for Zebra.
3. Zebra says that a car hit him and that it was his own fault.
4. The man winces.
5. Students may say that the man winces because of Zebra's terrible accident and also because Zebra blames himself for it.

---

words for everyday use

wince (wins) *v.*, flinch, shrink back. *He <u>winced</u> when the doctor removed the deep splinter.*

dis • ci • pli • nar • i • an (dis ə pli ner' ē ən) *n.*, one who enforces order. *Of all the tennis coaches, Mrs. Lee was the strictest <u>disciplinarian</u>.*

bat • ter (bat' ər) *v.*, wear out, damage, beat. *He insisted on using the old, <u>battered</u> baseball glove.* **battered** *adj.*

LITERARY NOTE

Fiction is prose writing about imaginary events or characters. One type of fiction is the short story, which is a brief work of fiction. On this page of the short story "Zebra," some of the characters tell their own fictional short stories. Ask students to explain what each story reveals about the person who tells it. *Answers.* Students may say that Andrea's story about the woman scientist who heals trees reveals that Andrea probably enjoys nature and may hope to be a scientists one day. Students may say that Mark's story about space cadets and time travel reveals that he is probably a fan of science fiction. Kevin's story about the shadows of different colors fighting reveals that he is probably a sensitive boy who thinks about the world in a highly imaginative way. Zebra's story about the bird that breaks a wing and dies reveals Zebra's preoccupation with his injured hand and his state of sadness.

Zebra went slowly to his next class.

The class was taught by Mrs. English, who came hurrying into the room some minutes after the bell had rung.

"I apologize for being late," she said, sounding a little out of breath. "There was an important matter I had to attend to."

Mrs. English was a tall, gracious woman in her forties. It was common knowledge that early in her life she had been a journalist on a Chicago newspaper and had written short stories, which she could not get published. Soon after her marriage to a doctor, she had become a teacher.

This was the only class Mrs. English taught.

Ten students from the upper school—seventh and eighth grades—were chosen every year for this class. They met for an hour three times a week and told one another stories. Each story would be discussed and analyzed by Mrs. English and the class.

> **GUIDED READING**
> What do the students do in Mrs. English's class?

Mrs. English called it a class in the *imagination*.

Zebra was grateful he did not have to take notes in this class. He had only to listen to the stories.

That day, Andrea, the freckle-faced, redheaded girl with very thick glasses who sat next to Zebra, told about a woman scientist who discovered a method of healing trees that had been blasted apart by lightning.

Mark, who had something wrong with his upper lip, told in his quavery voice about a selfish space cadet who stepped into a time machine and met his future self, who turned out to be a hateful person, and how the cadet then returned to the present and changed himself.

Kevin talked in blurred, high-pitched tones and often related parts of his stories with his hands. Mrs. English would quietly repeat many of his sentences. Today he told about an explorer who set out on a journey through a valley filled with yellow stones and surrounded by red mountains, where he encountered an army of green shadows that had been at war for hundreds of years with an army of purple shadows. The explorer showed them how to make peace.

When it was Zebra's turn, he told a story about a bird that one day crashed against a closed windowpane and broke a wing. A boy tried to heal the wing but couldn't. The bird died, and the boy buried it under a tree on his lawn.

When he had finished, there was silence. Everyone in the class was looking at him.

"You always tell such sad stories," Andrea said.

The bell rang. Mrs. English dismissed the class.

In the hallway, Andrea said to Zebra, "You know, you are a very gloomy life form."

> **GUIDED READING**
> What does Andrea tell Zebra after class?

"Andrea, get off my case," Zebra said.

He went out to the schoolyard for the midafternoon recess. On the other side of the chain-link fence was the man in the dark-blue cap.

Zebra went over to him.

"Hello again, Adam," the man said. "I've been waiting for you."

"Hello," said Zebra.

"Thanks much for suggesting I talk to Mrs. English."

"You're welcome."

"Adam, you at all interested in art?"

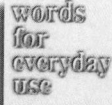 **words for everyday use**

qua • ver (kwā′ vər) v., shake, tremble. *The old woman's hand quavers when she waves.* **quavery** adj.

"No."

"You ever try your hand at it?"

"I've made drawings for class. I don't like it."

"Well, just in case you change your mind, I'm giving an art class in your school during the summer."

"I'm going to camp in August," Zebra said.

"There's the big long month of July."

"I don't think so," Zebra said.

"Well, okay, suit yourself. I'd like to give you something, a little thank-you gift."

He reached into an inside pocket and drew out a small pad and a pen. He placed the pad against the fence.

"Adam, you want to help me out a little bit here? Put your fingers through the fence and grab hold of the pad."

Extending the fingers of his right hand, Zebra held the pad to the fence and watched as the man began to work with the pen. He felt the pad move slightly.

"I need you to hold it real still," the man said.

He was standing bent over, very close to Zebra. The words LAND ROVER on his cap shone in the afternoon sunlight. As he worked, he glanced often at Zebra. His tongue kept pushing up against the insides of his cheeks, making tiny hills rise and fall on his face. Wrinkles formed intricate spidery webs in the skin below his gray eyes. On his smooth forehead, in the blue and purple shadows beneath the peak of his cap, lay glistening beads of sweat. And his hand—how dirty it was, the fingers and palm smudged with black ink and encrusted with colors.

Then Zebra glanced down and noticed the plastic bag near the man's feet. It lay partly open. Zebra was able to see a large pink armless doll, a dull metallic object that looked like a dented frying pan, old newspapers, strings of cord, crumpled pieces of red and blue cloth, and the broken umbrella.

"One more minute is all I need," the man said.

He stepped back, looked at the pad, and nodded slowly. He put the pen back into his pocket and tore the top page from the pad. He rolled up the page and pushed it through the fence. Then he took the pad from Zebra.

"See you around, Adam," the man said, picking up the plastic bag.

Zebra unrolled the sheet of paper and saw a line drawing, a perfect image of his face.

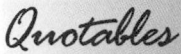

GUIDED READING

What does John Wilson give Zebra?

He was looking at himself as if in a mirror. His long straight nose and thin lips and sad eyes and gaunt face; his dark hair and smallish ears and the scar on his forehead where he had hurt himself years before while roller skating.

In the lower right-hand corner of the page the man had written: "To ADAM, with thanks. John Wilson."

Zebra raised his eyes from the drawing. The man was walking away.

Zebra called out, "Mr. Wilson, all my friends call me Zebra."

The man turned, looking surprised.

"From my last name," Adam said. "Zebrin. Adam Martin Zebrin. They call me Zebra."

"Is that right?" the man said, starting back toward the fence. "Well, in that case you want to give me back that piece of paper."

He took the pad and pen from his pocket, placed the page on the pad, and, with Zebra holding the pad to the fence, did something to the page and then handed it back.

"You take real good care of yourself, Zebra," the man said.

He went off toward Franklin Avenue.

Zebra looked at the drawing. The man had crossed out ADAM and over it had drawn an animal with a stubby neck and short legs and a striped body.

A zebra!

Its legs were in full gallop. It seemed as if it would gallop right off the page.

1. John Wilson gives Zebra a drawing he has made of him.

Quotables

"Art is not a handicraft, it is the transmission of feeling the artist has experienced."

—Leo Tolstoy

ADDITIONAL QUESTIONS AND ACTIVITIES

Ask students to discuss how they feel about the Tolstoy quote above. Have them explain why they agree or disagree with this definition of art. You may wish to define *handicraft* for them as a skill practiced with the hands. Then ask students the following questions about this quote in relation to the action in "Zebra."

1. Explain whether you would define the work Mr. Wilson does in sketching Zebra a handicraft.

2. In what way is the drawing an expression of the artist's feelings? In what way does the drawing affect Zebra's feelings?

Answers

1. Responses will vary, but students may suggest that it does seem to be a handicraft because Mr. Wilson works hard with his one hand to create the picture and must focus all his concentration, as shown by the physical expressions he makes while drawing.

2. Students may say that the drawing is an expression of the artist's thankfulness to Zebra for telling him to whom he should talk about a summer art class, as well as his sympathy and empathy for Zebra's injured hand. The drawing thrills Zebra so much that the zebra over his name seems to gallop to him, reminding him of the time when he too ran swiftly.

1. The zebra seems to have moved. Zebra thinks he has a fever.

CROSS-CURRICULAR CONNECTION

MATHEMATICS AND SCIENCES. The normal temperature for the human body is 98.6 degrees Fahrenheit, or 37 degrees Celsius. Fever occurs when the body's heat-regulating system is not working properly, and the body's temperature increases. Increased body temperature can cause headaches and increased pulse and breathing rates. There are three stages to most fevers. First, the person feels cold and shivers. Then, as the body's temperature reaches its highest point, the person feels quite hot. The person's temperature then begins to fall gradually, the person sweats a lot, and slowly feels better. Because fever is very hard on the body and causes dehydration, people often have strange thoughts and dreams when they have a fever.

A strong breeze rippled across the drawing, causing it to flutter like a flag in Zebra's hand. He looked out at the street.

The man was walking slowly in the shadows of the tall oaks. Zebra had the odd sensation that all the houses on the street had turned toward the man and were watching him as he walked along. How strange that was: the windows and porches and columns and front doors following intently the slow walk of that tall, one-armed man—until he turned into Franklin Avenue and was gone.

The whistle blew, and Zebra went inside. Seated at his desk, he slipped the drawing carefully into one of his notebooks.

From time to time he glanced at it.

Just before the bell signaled the end of the school day, he looked at it again.

Now *that* was strange!

He thought he remembered that the zebra had been drawn directly over his name: the head over the A and the tail over the M. Didn't it seem now to have moved a little beyond the A?

Probably he was running a fever again. He would run mysterious fevers off and on for about three weeks after each operation on his hand. Fevers sometimes did that to him: excited his imagination.

> **GUIDED READING**
>
> What seems to have happened to the zebra in the drawing? What does Zebra thinks caused this?

He lived four blocks from the school. The school bus dropped him off at his corner. In his schoolbag he carried his books and the notebook with the drawing.

His mother offered him a snack, but he said he wasn't hungry. Up in his room, he looked again at the drawing and was astonished to discover that the zebra had reached the edge of his name and appeared <u>poised</u> to leap off.

It *had* to be a fever that was causing him to see the zebra that way. And sure enough, when his mother took his temperature, the thermometer registered 102.6 degrees.

She gave him his medicine, but it didn't seem to have much effect, because when he woke at night and switched on his desk light and peered at the drawing, he saw the little zebra galloping across the page, along the <u>contours</u> of his face, over the hills and valleys of his eyes and nose and mouth, and he heard the tiny clickings of its hooves as cloudlets of dust rose in its wake.

He knew he was asleep. He knew it was the fever working upon his imagination.

But it was so real.

The little zebra running . . . .

When he awoke in the morning the fever was gone, and the zebra was quietly in its place over ADAM.

Later, as he entered the school, he noticed a large sign on the bulletin board in the hallway:

SUMMER ART CLASS

The well-known American artist Mr. John Wilson will conduct an art class during the summer for students in 7th and 8th grades. For details, speak to Mrs. English. There will be no tuition fee for this class.

During the morning, between classes, Zebra ran into Mrs. English in the second-floor hallway.

"Mrs. English, about the summer art class . . . is it okay to ask where—um—where Mr. Wilson is from?"

"He is from a small town in Virginia. Are you thinking of signing up for his class?"

"I can't draw," Zebra said.

---

words for everyday use

poised (poizd) *adj.*, composed or ready; marked by balance. *The young man's fingers were <u>poised</u> to begin typing.*

con • tour (kän' tur) *n.*, the outline of a curve or shape. *In the dark, she could make out only the <u>contours</u> of the car on the street.*

Calico, 1990. Jerry Barrish. Private Collection.

1. According to Mrs. English, John Wilson was wounded in the war in Vietnam.

ART SMART

"Found art" is art that is created from objects the artist finds, often objects that have been thrown away. Encourage students to analyze *Calico* and determine what parts or objects were used to create this sculpture. Inform students that in galleries and museums, art is frequently displayed with a card that lists the work's title, its author, the date it was created, and the media used to create it. *Media* refers to the materials, such as oil paint or canvas, used to create a work of art. Students should create such a card for the sculpture on this page.

"Drawing is something you can learn."

"Mrs. English, is it okay to ask how did Mr. Wilson—um—get hurt?"

The school corridors were always crowded between classes. Zebra and Mrs. English formed a little island in the bustling, student-jammed hallway.

"Mr. Wilson was wounded in the war in Vietnam," Mrs. English said. "I would urge you to join his class. You will get to use your imagination."

> **GUIDED READING**
>
> According to Mrs. English, how did John Wilson lose his arm?

For the next hour, Zebra sat impatiently through Mr. Morgan's geography class, and afterward he went up to the teacher.

"Mr. Morgan, could I—um—ask where is Vietnam?"

Mr. Morgan smoothed down the jacket of his beige summer suit, touched his bow tie, rolled down a wall map, picked up his pointer, and cleared his throat.

"Vietnam is this long, narrow country in southeast Asia, bordered by China, Laos, and Cambodia. It is a land of valleys in the north, coastal plains[2] in the center, and marshes[3] in the south. There are barren mountains and tropical rain forests. Its chief crops are rice, rubber, fruits, and vegetables. The population numbers close to seventy million people. Between 1962 and 1973, America fought a terrible war there to prevent the south from falling into the hands of the communist north. We lost the war."

"Thank you."

"I am impressed by your suddenly awakened interest in geography, young man, though I

---

2. **coastal plains.** Low, flat land near a coastline
3. **marshes.** Soft, wet land

1. Zebra is afraid of his hand and finds it mysterious.
2. John Wilson was a helicopter pilot in Vietnam.

ADDITIONAL QUESTIONS AND ACTIVITIES

Zebra's dad says that maybe Zebra will become "a Matisse instead of a lawyer like his dad." Ask students to write a personal essay about where their own career interests lie. They should also write about the careers of their family members and explain how their family's careers affect their own future plans. For example, do they hope to follow in the footsteps of a family member, or have they learned that they would not enjoy a certain career because of a family member's experiences?

must remind you that your class is studying the Mediterranean,"[4] said Mr. Morgan.

During the afternoon recess, Zebra was watching a heated basketball game, when he looked across the yard and saw John Wilson walk by, carrying a <u>laden</u> plastic bag. Some while later, he came back along the street, empty-handed.

Over supper that evening, Zebra told his parents he was thinking of taking a summer art class offered by the school.

His father said, "Well, I think that's a fine idea."

"Wait a minute. I'm not so sure," his mother said.

"It'll get him off the streets," his father said. "He'll become a Matisse[5] instead of a lawyer like his dad. Right, Adam?"

"Just you be very careful," his mother said to Adam. "Don't do anything that might injure your hand."

"How can drawing hurt his left hand, for heaven's sake?" said his father.

That night, Zebra lay in bed looking at his hand. It was a dread and a mystery to him, his own hand. The fingers were all there, but like dead leaves that never fell, the

> **GUIDED READING**
> How does Zebra feel about his hand?

ring and little fingers were rigid and curled, the others barely moved. The doctors said it would take time to bring them back to life. So many broken bones. So many torn muscles and <u>tendons</u>. So many injured nerves. The dark shadow had sprung upon him so suddenly. How stupid, stupid, *stupid* he had been!

He couldn't sleep. He went over to his desk and looked at John Wilson's drawing. The galloping little zebra stood very still over ADAM.

Early the following afternoon, on the last day of school, Zebra went to Mrs. English's

office and signed up for John Wilson's summer art class.

"The class will meet every weekday from ten in the morning until one," said Mrs. English. "Starting Monday."

Zebra noticed the three plastic bags in a corner of the office.

"Mrs. English, is it okay to ask what Mr. Wilson—um—did in Vietnam?"

"He told me he was a helicopter pilot," Mrs. English said. "Oh, I neglected to mention that

> **GUIDED READING**
> What did John Wilson do in Vietnam?

you are to bring an unlined notebook and a pencil to the class."

"That's all? A notebook and a pencil?"

Mrs. English smiled. "And your imagination."

When Zebra entered the art class the next Monday morning, he found about fifteen students there—including Andrea from his class with Mrs. English.

The walls of the room were bare. Everything had been removed for the summer. Zebra noticed two plastic bags on the floor beneath the blackboard.

He sat down at the desk next to Andrea's.

She wore blue jeans and a yellow summer blouse with blue stripes. Her long red hair was tied behind her head with a dark-blue ribbon. She gazed at Zebra through her thick glasses, leaned over, and said, "Are you going to make gloomy drawings, too?"

Just then John Wilson walked in, carrying a plastic bag, which he put down on the floor next to the two others.

He stood alongside the front desk, wearing a light-blue long-sleeved shirt and jeans. The

---

4. **Mediterranean.** Region surrounding the Mediterranean Sea and including parts of southern Europe and northern Africa
5. **Matisse.** Henri-Émile-Benoit Matisse. French painter

---

words for everyday use

la • den (lād' ən) *adj.*, carrying a load or burden. *Our suitcases were <u>laden</u> with souvenirs from the vacation.*

ten • don (ten' dan) *n.*, connective tissue attaching muscle to bone. *The basketball player needed surgery after injuring a <u>tendon</u> in her knee.*

left shirtsleeve had been folded back and pinned to the shirt. The dark-blue cap with the words LAND ROVER sat <u>jauntily</u> on his head.

"Good morning to you-all," he said, with a shy smile. "Mighty glad you're here. We're going to do two things this summer. We're going to make paper into faces and garbage into people. I can see by your expressions that you don't know what I'm talking about, right? Well, I'm about to show you."

He asked everyone to draw the face of someone sitting nearby.

Zebra hesitated, looked around, then made a drawing of Andrea. Andrea carefully drew Zebra.

He showed Andrea his drawing.

"It's awful." She grimaced. "I look like a mouse."

Her drawing of him was good. But was his face really so sad?

GUIDED READING

What emotion does Andrea portray on Zebra's face?

John Wilson went from desk to desk, <u>peering</u> intently at the drawings. He paused a long moment over Zebra's drawing. Then he spent more than an hour demonstrating with chalk on the blackboard how they should not be thinking *eyes* or *lips* or *hands* while drawing, but should think only *lines* and *curves* and *shapes*; how they should be looking at where everything was situated in relation to the edge of the paper; and how they should not be looking *directly* at the edges of what they were drawing but at the space *outside* the edges.

Zebra stared in wonder at how fast John Wilson's hand raced across the blackboard, and at the empty sleeve rising and falling lightly against the shirt.

"You-all are going to learn how to *see* in a new way," John Wilson said.

They made another drawing of the same face.

"Now I look like a horse," Andrea said. "Are you going to add stripes?"

"You are one big pain, Andrea," Zebra said.

Shortly before noon, John Wilson laid out on his desk the contents of the plastic bags: a clutter of junked broken objects, including the doll and the umbrella.

Using strips of cloth, some lengths of string, crumpled newspaper, his pen, and his one hand, he swiftly transformed the battered doll into a red-nosed, umbrella-carrying clown, with baggy pants, a tattered coat, a derby hat, and a <u>somber</u> smile. Turning over the battered frying pan, he made it into a pedestal, on which he placed the clown.

"That's a sculpture," John Wilson said, with his shy smile. "Garbage into people."

The class burst into applause. The clown on the frying pan looked as if it might take a bow.

"You-all will be doing that, too, before we're done," John Wilson said. "Now I would like you to sign and date your drawings and give them to me."

When they returned the next morning the drawings were on a wall.

Gradually, in the days that followed, the walls began to fill with drawings. Sculptures made by the students were looked at with care, discussed by John Wilson and the class, and then placed on shelves along the walls: a miniature bicycle made of wire; a parrot made of an old sofa cushion; a cowboy made of rope and string; a fat lady made of a dented metal pitcher; a zebra made of glued-together scraps of cardboard.

"I like your zebra," Andrea said.

"Thanks," Zebra said. "I like your parrot."

---

words for everyday use

jaun • ty (jän' tē) *adj.*, spright, lively. *The jaunty old dog wagged its tail and leaped into my lap.* **jauntily** *adv.*

peer (pēr') *v.*, look closely. *Elena peered at the old family photos, trying to recognize her aunt.*

som • ber (säm bər) *adj.*, dark and depressing; gloomy. *The somber old house stood empty for years.*

---

1. Andrea portrays sadness on Zebra's face.

ART SMART

Share the following information with students: The first step professional artists take in producing any drawing is to observe and sketch the lines and contours of their subject. Important details are added and corrected and minor techniques are left until last. John Wilson's instructions are good advice for beginning artists. Artists must train themselves to think in term of shape and form rather than in terms of stock things like *eyes* and *lips*. Tell students that if they are interested in learning to draw in this way, they should talk to your school art teacher about learning to draw by contour. He or she may have good tips for them.

CROSS-CURRICULAR ACTIVITIES

ARTS AND HUMANITIES. Encourage students to create their own examples of "found art." For supplies, students may ask their families if they can rummage through attics or garages or basements for items the family no longer wants. Tell students that they should let the shape and form of the objects they find inspire what they create. Students should have adult supervision in joining their found objects together, using materials such as glue or staples. Students may wish to bring their found art in to share with classmates. You might create a classroom display of found art to display students' efforts.

One morning John Wilson asked the class members to make a contour drawing of their right or left hand. Zebra felt himself sweating and trembling as he worked.

> **GUIDED READING**
> What does John Wilson ask the class to draw? How does Zebra react?

"That's real nice," John Wilson said, when he saw Andrea's drawing.

He gazed at the drawing made by Zebra.

"You-all were looking at your hand," he said. "You ought to have been looking at the edge of your hand and at the space outside."

Zebra drew his hand again. Strange and ugly, the two fingers lay rigid and curled. But astonishingly, it looked like a hand this time.

One day, a few minutes before the end of class, John Wilson gave everyone an assignment: draw or make something at home, something very special that each person *felt deeply* about. And bring it to class.

Zebra remembered seeing a book entitled *Incredible Cross-Sections* on a shelf in the family room at home. He found the book and took it into his room.

There was a color drawing of a rescue helicopter on one of the Contents pages. On pages 30 and 31, the helicopter was shown in pieces, its complicated insides displayed in detailed drawings. Rotor blades, control rods, electronics equipment, radar scanner, tail rotor, engine, lifeline, winch—all its many parts.

Zebra sat at his desk, gazing intently at the space outside the edges of the helicopter on the Contents page.

> **GUIDED READING**
> What does Zebra's drawing for John Wilson include?

He made an outline drawing and brought it to class the next morning.

John Wilson looked at it. Was there a stiffening of his muscular neck, a sudden tensing of the hand that held the drawing?

He took the drawing and tacked it to the wall.

The next day he gave them all the same home assignment: draw or make something they *felt very deeply* about.

That afternoon, Zebra went rummaging about the trash bin in his kitchen and the garbage cans that stood near the back door of his home. He found some sardine cans, a broken eggbeater, pieces of cardboard, chipped buttons, bent bobby pins, and other odds and ends.

With the help of epoxy glue,[6] he began to make of those bits of garbage a kind of helicopter. For support, he used his desktop, the floor, his knees, the elbow of his left arm, at one point even his chin. Struggling with the last piece—a button he wanted to position as a wheel—he realized that without thinking he had been using his left hand, and the two curled fingers had straightened slightly to his needs.

> **GUIDED READING**
> What does Zebra realize he has done without thinking?

His heart beat thunderously. There had been so many hope-filled moments before, all of them ending in bitter disappointment. He would say nothing. Let the therapist or the doctors tell him. . . .

The following morning, he brought the helicopter to the class.

"Eeewwww, what is *that*?" Andrea grimaced.

"Something to eat you with," Zebra said.

"Get human, Zebra. Mr. Wilson will have a laughing fit over that."

But John Wilson didn't laugh. He held the helicopter in his hand a long moment, turning it this way and that, nodded at Zebra, and placed it on a windowsill, where it shimmered in the summer sunlight.

The next day, John Wilson informed everyone that three students would be leaving the class at the end of July. He asked each of those students to make a drawing for him that he would get to keep. Something to remember them by. All their other drawings and sculptures they could take home.

---

6. **epoxy glue.** Type of flexible glue

Zebra lay awake a long time that night, staring into the darkness of his room. He could think of nothing to draw for John Wilson.

In the morning, he sat gazing out the classroom window at the sky and at the helicopter on the sill.

"What are you going to draw for him?" Andrea asked.

Zebra shrugged and said he didn't know.

"Use your imagination," she said. Then she said, "Wait, what am I seeing here? Are you able to move those fingers?"

"I think so."

"You *think* so?"

"The doctors said there was some improvement."

Her eyes glistened behind the thick lenses. She seemed genuinely happy.

He sat looking out the window. Dark birds wheeled and soared. There was the sound of traffic. The helicopter sat on the windowsill, its eggbeater rotor blades ready to move to full throttle.

Later that day, Zebra sat at his desk at home, working on a drawing. He held the large sheet of paper in place by pressing down on it with the palm and fingers of his left hand. He drew a landscape: hills and valleys, forests and flatlands, rivers and plateaus.[7] Oddly, it all seemed to resemble a face.

Racing together over that landscape were a helicopter and a zebra.

It was all he could think to draw. It was not a very good drawing. He signed it: "To JOHN WILSON, with thanks. Zebra."

The next morning, John Wilson looked at the drawing and asked Zebra to write on top of the name "John Wilson" the name "Leon."

"He was an old buddy of mine, an artist. We were in Vietnam together.

> **GUIDED READING**
> Who is Leon?

Would've been a much better artist than I'll ever be."

Zebra wrote in the new name.

"Thank you kindly," John Wilson said, taking the drawing. "Zebra, you have yourself a good time in camp and a good life. It was real nice knowing you."

He shook Zebra's hand. How strong his fingers felt!

"I think I'm going to miss you a little," Andrea said to Zebra after the class.

"I'll only be away a month."

"Can I help you carry some of those drawings?"

"Sure. I'll carry the helicopter."

Zebra went off to a camp in the Adirondack Mountains[8]. He hiked and read and watched others playing ball. In the arts and crafts program he made some good drawings and even got to learn a little bit about watercolors. He put together clowns and airplanes and helicopters out of discarded cardboard and wood and clothing. From time to time his hand hurt, but the fingers seemed slowly to be coming back to life.

"Patience, young man," the doctors told him when he returned to the city. "You're getting there."

One or two additional operations were still necessary. But there was no urgency. And he no longer needed the leg brace.

> **GUIDED READING**
> What is happening to Zebra's hand? What does he no longer need?

On the first day of school, one of the secretaries found him in the hallway and told him to report to Mrs. English.

---

7. **plateaus.** High, flat lands
8. **Adirondack Mountains.** Group of mountains in northeastern New York

"ZEBRA" **19**

Racing together over that landscape were a helicopter and a zebra.

ANSWERS TO GUIDED READING QUESTIONS

1. Zebra draws a landscape that resembles a face, with a zebra and a helicopter racing across it.
2. Leon was an artist and John Wilson's friend. They were in Vietnam together.
3. Zebra's hand is coming back to life. He no longer needs the leg brace.

ADDITIONAL QUESTIONS AND ACTIVITIES

Ask students the following questions:
1. What does Andrea note about Zebra?
2. What is Andrea's reaction when Zebra says that the doctors say there has been some improvement? How does Andrea feel about what Zebra is now able to do?
3. What does Andrea say to Zebra on the last day of art class before he heads to camp?
4. If you had to make a prediction about Andrea and Zebra, what might you say about the way their relationship might change?
5. Describe the drawing that Zebra creates for Mr. Wilson to keep.
6. What does Mr. Wilson ask Zebra to write on the drawing? Why do you think Mr. Wilson asks him to do this?

Answers
1. Andrea notes that Zebra can move the fingers in his injured hand.
2. Andrea's eyes glisten (with tears) behind her glasses. She seems to feel moved and relieved that Zebra is finally healing.
3. Andrea says she will miss Zebra a little.
4. Students may suggest that Zebra and Andrea may become friends.
5. Zebra draws a landscape that resembles a human face with a helicopter and a zebra racing over it.
6. Mr. Wilson asks Zebra to write "To Leon" over where he had written "To John Wilson, with thanks. Zebra." Students may say that Zebra's drawing makes John Wilson think of his friend who was in Vietnam with him and was an artist who probably died.

TEACHER'S EDITION **19**

1. Each year John Wilson visits the Vietnam Veterans Memorial and, next to his friend'd name on the wall, he leaves a gift that someone creates.
2. Zebra decides to walk along Franklin Avenue to the corner where he was hit by a car.
3. Andrea tells Zebra he is becoming a pleasant life form.

LITERARY NOTE

THEME. A **theme** is a central idea in a literary work. Tell students that one of the themes in "Zebra" is healing. Ask students to discuss how the characters in this story heal, both emotionally and physically.
Answers. Students may suggest that Zebra heals physically as his leg and hand heal, and emotionally as he loses his sadness, gains confidence, and makes friends under Mr. Wilson's instruction. Mr. Wilson also seems to heal emotionally as he reveals his gratitude and thanks for Zebra's gift for his departed friend; such gifts seem to be Mr. Wilson's way of getting over his feelings of sadness at his friend's loss of life.

"Did you have a good summer?" Mrs. English asked.

"It was okay," Zebra said.

"This came for you in the mail."

She handed him a large brown envelope. It was addressed to Adam Zebrin, Eighth Grade, at the school. The sender was John Wilson, with a return address in Virginia.

"Adam, I admit I'm very curious to see what's inside," Mrs. English said.

She helped Zebra open the envelope.

Between two pieces of cardboard were a letter and a large color photograph.

The photograph showed John Wilson down on his right knee before a glistening dark wall. He wore his army jacket and blue jeans and boots, and the cap with the words LAND ROVER. Leaning against the wall to his right was Zebra's drawing of the helicopter and the zebra racing together across a facelike landscape. The drawing was enclosed in a narrow frame.

The wall behind John Wilson seemed to glitter with a strange black light.

Zebra read the letter and showed it to Mrs. English.

Dear Zebra,

One of the people whose names are on this wall was among my very closest friends. He was an artist named Leon Kellner. Each year I visit him and leave a gift—something very special that someone creates and gives me. I leave it near his name for a few hours, and then I take it to my studio in Virginia, where I keep a collection of those gifts. All year long I work in my studio, but come summer I go looking for another gift to give him.

Thank you for your gift.

> Your friend,
> John Wilson

P.S. I hope your hand is healing.

> **GUIDED READING**
> What does John Wilson do each year?

Mrs. English stood staring awhile at the letter. She turned away and touched her eyes. Then she went to a shelf on the wall behind her, took down a large book, leafed through it quickly, found what she was searching for, and held it out for Zebra to see.

Zebra found himself looking at the glistening black wall of the Vietnam Memorial in Washington, D.C. And at the names on it, the thousands of names. . . .

Later, in the schoolyard during recess, Zebra stood alone at the chain-link fence and gazed down the street toward Franklin Avenue. He thought how strange it was that all the houses on this street had seemed to turn toward John Wilson that day, the windows and porches and columns and doors, as if saluting him.

Had that been only his imagination?

Maybe, Zebra thought, just maybe he could go for a walk to Franklin Avenue on Saturday or Sunday. He had not walked along Franklin Avenue since the accident; had not gone down that steep hill. Yes, he would walk carefully down that hill to the corner and walk back up and past the school and then the four blocks home.

Andrea came over to him.

> **GUIDED READING**
> What does Zebra decide to do?

"We didn't get picked for the story class with Mrs. English," she said. "I won't have to listen to any more of your gloomy stories."

Zebra said nothing.

"You know, I think I'll walk home today instead of taking the school bus," Andrea said.

"Actually, I think I'll walk, too," Zebra said. "I was thinking maybe I could pick up some really neat stuff in the street."

"You are becoming a pleasant life form," Andrea said. ∎

> **GUIDED READING**
> What does Andrea tell Zebra he is becoming?

Respond *to the* SELECTION

How has John Wilson changed Zebra's life? How has Zebra changed John Wilson's life?

About *the* AUTHOR

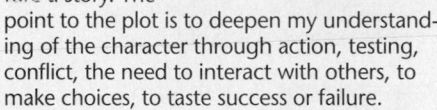

Chaim Potok, born in New York City in 1929, began writing fiction at the age of 16. Since then, he has written essays, plays, short stories, articles, children's books, and novels—including his most famous work, the novel *The Chosen*. Below, Potok answers some questions about this story and about his work.

Zebra is such an intriguing character. How did you create him?
When I was nine or ten years old, I suffered a serious eye injury in a snowball fight. Months later, near the end of the spring term, a man suddenly appeared in my school and offered to teach drawing during the summer to anyone interested. I took his class and discovered that I could draw and paint. These two elements—the injury and the man—came together in "Zebra" and were brought up to the present, because I needed to add a third element—Vietnam—to the story. I should add that, like Zebra, I was a good runner. For the sake of the story, I gave Zebra a hand injury to connect him to drawing and to the wound suffered by John Wilson in Vietnam.

How did you decide to incorporate John Wilson into this story?
John Wilson was in the story from the start. He is modeled, in part, after a very good friend of mine, who was a major with Special Forces (Green Berets) in Vietnam.

When you begin writing a story or novel, what comes first—the plot or the characters?
I always begin with characters. People are, for me, the heart of any story I write. I must know my characters, their conflicts, their hopes, dreams, angers, frustrations, loves, hates. I must see them, hear them. Often I dream about them, sense them near me. It is only when I feel I truly know a character, or characters, that I begin to structure a story. The point to the plot is to deepen my understanding of the character through action, testing, conflict, the need to interact with others, to make choices, to taste success or failure.

What besides writing do you enjoy doing? How does your life influence what you write?
I love being with my family. I enjoy the company of my friends. I travel. Everything I see and hear influences my writing. How can it be otherwise? Writers are like giant receptacles, scooping up everything on the way to their desks.

What do you hope young people will gain from reading your work?
First, I hope they will read "Zebra" as a good story, enjoying it for the sheer pleasure of its storytelling. Then, I would want them to recognize that it is more than an entertainment, that there are serious issues in it that touch their lives. Finally, I would like to believe that there is enough in the story for it to linger in memory as an experience that most young people go through on the journey to adulthood: not letting yourself be broken by the really difficult moments in life, but getting through them and growing up.

"ZEBRA" **21**

SELECTION CHECK TEST 4.1.1 WITH ANSWERS (CONT.)

2. Which character changes his or her feelings toward Zebra during the story?
   a. Mrs. English
   b. John Wilson
   c. Andrea
   d. Kevin
3. During their first conversation at the schoolyard fence, John Wilson asks Zebra about his school's summer schedule. This conversation hints at what we learn later in the story—that Mr. Wilson will teach art at the school over the summer. This is an example of what literary technique?
   a. foreshadowing
   b. description
   c. conflict
   d. characterization

RESPOND TO THE SELECTION

Encourage students to discuss special relationships they have had that have changed the paths of their lines for the better.

SELECTION CHECK TEST 4.1.1 WITH ANSWERS

Checking Your Reading
1. Why did Zebra stop running? **Zebra was injured when he was hit by a car.**
2. What part of Zebra's body continues to hurt even though the doctors cannot find a reason for the pain? **His hand continues to hurt.**
3. Where is Zebra when he first sees John Wilson? **Zebra is standing in the schoolyard, looking out at the street.**
4. What was John Wilson's job before he was injured? **John Wilson was a helicopter pilot in the military.**
5. Why does Zebra leave the art class at the end of July? **He leaves to attend summer camp.**

Vocabulary in Context
Fill in each blank below with the most appropriate vocabulary word from "Zebra." You may have to change the tense of the word.

ruddy   wince   poised   gaunt
quavery   dapper   menacing

1. After studying hard and earning good grades, Adam seemed **poised** to attend a good college.
2. The doctor's rough manipulation of his broken ankle made the injured climber **wince.**
3. The snake's **menacing** rattle warned the hikers away from the bush.
4. My grandmother's eyes twinkled at the **dapper** sight of grandfather in his new suit and hat.
5. Since Alice took up marathon running, no matter how much she eats she maintains a **gaunt** appearance.

Reader's Toolbox
1. What is the primary conflict in the story?
   a. Zebra vs. John Wilson
   b. Zebra vs. Andrea
   c. Zebra vs. himself
   d. Zebra vs. Mrs. English

Ask students the following questions about Insights: Maya Lin and the Vietnam Veterans Memorial.

1. Why did Lin originally design the memorial?
2. What does Lin think a war memorial should be? What shouldn't it be?
3. What are the walls of the memorial made of? What does this substance mean to Lin?
4. What is carved on the walls of the memorial?

Answers

1. She designed it for a seminar on funerary architecture when she and members of her class were questioning the purposes and responsibilities of war memorials.
2. Lin thinks a war memorial should be honest about the reality of war and be for those who lost their lives in the war. She does not think that a war memorial should be a static object that people just look at, but something people can relate to like a journey and form their own conclusion about.
3. The walls are made of polished black granite that reflects people's faces and their environment. Lin thinks of the dark wall as being a "rift in the earth" that creates "an interface between the sunny world and the quiet dark world beyond."
4. The names of the dead are carved there.

Maya Lin and the Vietnam Veterans Memorial

Jan C. Scruggs, a former infantryman who fought in Vietnam, led a movement to build a monument to the men and women who had died fighting in the Vietnam War. Scruggs was moved not only by his experiences during the war, but also by the harsh reality that veterans who had served in Vietnam had received little recognition for their contributions. This happened because of the controversy raging over the United States' involvement in the war.

In October of 1980, the Vietnam Veterans Memorial Fund, headed by Scruggs, announced a national design competition open to any United States citizen, 17 years of age or older. From the competition's entries, judges would select a design for the memorial. More than 1,400 design entries were submitted and reviewed anonymously by a jury of eight internationally recognized artists and designers. On May 1, 1981, the jury unanimously selected #1026 by Maya Ying Lin, a 21-year-old Asian American woman from Athens, Ohio, as the winning entry. At the time, Lin was a student at Yale University. She explained her entry:

Maya Lin, 1987.

I had designed the memorial for a seminar on funerary architecture.... We had already been questioning what a war memorial is, its purpose, its responsibility.... I felt a memorial should be honest about the reality of war and be for the people who gave their lives.... I didn't want a static object that people would just look at, but something they could relate to as on a journey, or passage, that would bring each to his own conclusions.... I had an impulse to cut open the earth...an initial violence that in time would heal.... It was as if the black-brown earth were polished and made into an interface between the sunny world and the quiet dark world beyond, that we can't enter.... The names would become the memorial. There was no need to embellish.

The Vietnam Veterans Memorial is formed by two walls that are each 246 feet and 8 inches long. The walls meet at an angle of 125.12 degrees and point to the Washington Monument and the Lincoln Memorial, joining the memorial to other important symbols of United States history. The walls are made from black granite that has been polished to reflect the sky and the ground, as well as the faces of visitors as they read the names. In her design competition submission, Lin described her vision for the Memorial:

Walking through this park, the Memorial appears as a rift in the earth. A long, polished, black stone wall, emerging from and receding into the earth. Approaching the Memorial, the ground slopes gently downward and the low walls emerging on either side, growing out of the earth, extend and converge at a point below and ahead. Walking into this grassy site con-

Night Patrol, 1995. Larry Powell. Collection of the Artist.

tained by the walls of the Memorial we can
barely make out the carved names upon the
Memorial's walls. These names, seemingly infinite in number, convey the sense of overwhelming numbers, while unifying these individuals
into a whole.

The Memorial is composed not as an unchang-
ing monument, but as a moving composition to
be understood as we move into and out of it.
The passage itself is gradual; the descent to the
origin slow, but it is at the origin that the
Memorial is to be fully understood. At the intersection of these walls, on the right side, is
carved the date of the first death. It is followed
by the names of those who died in the war, in
chronological order. These names continue on
this wall appearing to recede into the earth at
the wall's end. The names resume on the left
wall as the wall emerges from the earth, continuing back to the original where the date of the
last death is carved.

Some people voiced reservations about Lin's

memorial design. Opponents wanted something more
traditional, questioned her abilities, and voiced concern about her identity as a young Asian American
woman. When the committee stood firm in its decision, protesters argued for a flag to be included and
wanted the color of the memorial changed from
black to white. Amid all the controversy, the young
Maya Lin held her ground and defended her vision
and design. Lin said, "So what the Memorial's about
is honesty—all I was saying in this piece was the
cost of war is these individuals. And we have to
remember them first."

The Vietnam Veterans Memorial was dedicated on
the Mall in Washington, D.C., on November 13,
1982. More than 2.5 million people visit the Vietnam
Veterans Memorial each year. Many people leave
mementos and symbolic gifts, such as flowers,
poems, and photographs. The Memorial provides an
opportunity for people of all ages and backgrounds
to take an intimate look at the results of war and to
reflect upon the involvement of the United States in
the Vietnam War.

"ZEBRA" **23**

RECALL

1a. Zebra is no longer able to run after he is hit by a car.
2a. Zebra's hand begins to heal.
3a. Zebra recreates a helicopter in many forms as class projects.

INTERPRET

1b. Zebra is depressed and angry because he is no longer able to run.
2b. This happens because Zebra focuses on creating art, rather than thinking about his hand and what he cannot do. Students might also say that as Zebra becomes interested in John Wilson and his experiences in Vietnam, he begins to forget his own problems.
3b. John Wilson reacts emotionally to the helicopters Zebra creates. He is probably remembering his experiences in Vietnam as a helicopter pilot.

ANALYZE

4a. Since meeting John Wilson, Zebra has improved physically and mentally. He no longer needs a brace on his leg and he has begun to use his left hand again. When Zebra first met John, he felt that he no longer had a purpose because he could not run. But John teaches him to appreciate what he has and to succeed in areas other than running. Evidence that Zebra is changing includes his participation in John's class even though he usually remains separated from others, regaining use of his left hand, his interest in John's experiences in the Vietnam War, and his willingness to walk down Franklin Avenue for the first time since his accident.

SYNTHESIZE

4b. Zebra will probably continue to heal physically and will continue to draw and to create sculptures. He will probably try to become more involved in the world around him.

EVALUATE

5a. Students may say that John Wilson has greatly influenced Zebra, allowing Zebra to stop grieving over his accident and to focus on what he can do. Because John also has been injured, he is able to show Zebra by example that a person with a disability can still contribute to society. John inspires Zebra and others in his art class to dream, to imagine, and to accomplish things they never thought possible. The Wall is very important to Mr. Wilson—he visits it each year.

Investigate, Inquire, and Imagine

Recall: GATHERING FACTS

1a. What is Zebra unable to do after he is hit by a car?

2a. What happens to Zebra's hand as he begins to draw for John Wilson?

3a. What object does Zebra recreate in many forms as class projects?

Interpret: FINDING MEANING

1b. How does Zebra feel about losing his special ability?

2b. Why does this happen?

3b. How does John Wilson react to Zebra's projects? Why does he react this way?

Analyze: TAKING THINGS APART

4a. In what ways has Zebra changed since meeting John Wilson?

Synthesize: BRINGING THINGS TOGETHER

4b. How do you think Zebra will continue to change? Explain your answer.

Evaluate: MAKING JUDGMENTS

5a. To what degree has John Wilson influenced Zebra? How does this impact compare with the impact of the Wall on John Wilson and that of John Wilson on other people?

Extend: CONNECTING IDEAS

5b. How does John Wilson's way of life—revolving around his yearly visit to the Wall—relate to Maya Lin's vision for the memorial? Refer to Insights: Maya Lin and the Vietnam Veterans Memorial as you think about your answer.

Understanding Literature

DESCRIPTION. A **description** gives a picture in words of a character, object, or scene. Descriptions make use of **sensory details**—words and phrases that describe how things look, sound, smell, taste, or feel. In "Zebra," the author uses description to create vivid pictures of characters, objects, and scenes. Look at your list of descriptions from the story. Then discuss the examples with a classmate or small group. What kinds of words does the author use to bring characters, objects, and scenes to life?

CONFLICT. A **conflict** is a struggle between people or things in a literary work. A plot is formed around conflict. A conflict can be internal or external. A struggle that takes place between a character and some outside force—such as another character, society, or nature—is called an **external conflict**. A struggle that takes place within a character is called an **internal conflict**. What is the central conflict of "Zebra"? Is this conflict internal or external? How is this conflict resolved?

ANSWER TO INVESTIGATE, INQUIRE, IMAGINE (CONT.)

Wall has enabled him to come to terms with the loss of his friend and with the pain he suffered as a result of the Vietnam War. The Wall helps Mr. Wilson heal his grief just as Mr. Wilson helps Zebra heal his.

EXTEND

5b. Students might say that the Wall allows Mr. Wilson to take a journey out of his grief and pain and to reach out to others through art. Maya Lin says, "I didn't want a static object that people would just look at, but something they could relate to as on a journey, or passage, that would bring each to his own conclusions." By returning to the Wall every year with a gift for his friend Leon Kellner, John not only honors his friend but also inspires others to face their own problems.

Answers to Understanding Literature can be found on page 25.

Writer's Journal

1. Imagine that you are Zebra on vacation in Washington, D.C. Write a **postcard** to Andrea telling her about your visit to the Vietnam Veterans Memorial.
2. Imagine that you are Mrs. English. Write a brief **letter** to John Wilson, thanking him for his influence on Zebra.
3. Based on "Zebra," on "Maya Lin and the Vietnam Veterans Memorial" (pages 22-23), and on the photograph on those pages, write a **paragraph** describing the memorial for a visitor's brochure.

Skill Builders

Speaking and Listening

INTERVIEWING. In pairs, pretend that you are John Wilson and a newspaper or television reporter interviewing John about his yearly pilgrimage to Washington, D.C., to present a gift for his friend at the Vietnam Veterans Memorial. As the reporter, prepare at least five questions for John to answer. Make sure the questions are open-ended so they will elicit more than a "yes" or "no" answer. As John Wilson, try to stay in character and be as imaginative as possible in your responses. If possible, tape record or videotape your interview to share with the class. See the Language Arts Survey 4.14, "Conducting an Interview," for more information.

Study & Research and Media Literacy

RESEARCHING MEMORIALS. Using the Internet and library resources, research other Vietnam memorials in the United States. Examples include the Vietnam Women's Memorial, which stands near the Vietnam Veterans Memorial in Washington, D.C., and many state memorials to Vietnam veterans. Find information about who raised funds for the memorial you choose to research, when it was dedicated, and the number of visitors it receives. You might wish to present your findings to the rest of the class using a computer design program, picture displays, or other props.

Applied English

DESIGNING A POSTER. Imagine that you work for the National Park Service in Washington, D.C. Create a poster inviting people to a special ceremony honoring Vietnam War veterans to be held at the Wall on Veterans Day. Be sure to include specific information about the event, as well as imaginative words and images to capture the interest of the public.

Speaking and Listening
INTERVIEWING. Pairs of students might also change roles, so each student has the opportunity to practice being the interviewer and the person interviewed. refer students to the Language Arts Survey 4.10, "Asking and Answering Questions," for some guidelines on interpersonal communication.

Study and Research & Media Literacy
RESEARCHING MEMORIALS. A good starting point for students' research is the Internet. Students may find periodicals to be helpful as well. You may encourage students to find out whether there are any war memorials in their own city and town. If so, for what wars? How many people in their city or town died in a particular war?

Applied English
DESIGNING A POSTER. Tell students that their poster should provide all the information a person would need to attend the ceremony, including the day, time, place, and any other specific instructions.

(Continued on page 26)

ANSWERS TO UNDERSTANDING LITERATURE

Description. Responses will vary, but students might say that the author uses vivid verbs and adjectives to bring characters, objects, and scenes to life.

Conflict. The central conflict of "Zebra" is Zebra's struggle to recover both physically and mentally from his accident. This conflict is internal because it takes place within Zebra as he struggles with his limitations. The conflict is resolved through Zebra's relationship with John Wilson, who teaches Zebra that even though he can no longer run, there are many other things he can do.

Language, Grammar, and Style

FUNCTIONS OF SENTENCES. Four different kinds of sentences express four different kinds of thoughts and feelings:

- A **declarative sentence** gives facts and ends with a period.
- An **interrogative sentence** asks a question and ends with a question mark.
- An **imperative sentence** gives orders or makes a request and ends with a period or exclamation mark.
- An **exclamatory sentence** expresses strong feeling and ends with an exclamation mark.

Read the Language Arts Survey 3.15, "Functions of Sentences." On your own paper, identify whether each sentence below is declarative, interrogative, imperative, or exclamatory.

1. Zebra and Andrea are in Mrs. English's storytelling class.
2. Do you think John Wilson will come back next year?
3. Maya Lin designed the Vietnam Veterans Memorial.
4. Sign up for John Wilson's next class!
5. I really want to take that art class!

Collaborative Learning

DESIGNING A MEMORIAL. Imagine that your state is having a contest to design a memorial to the soldiers of the Vietnam War. Form committees and design a concept for the memorial. Be sure to include drawings and descriptions of your plan, as well as the ideas behind your plan.

Vocabulary

FORMING ADJECTIVES. *Menacing*, a Word for Everyday Use on page 10, is an adjective formed from the noun *menace* by adding the suffix *-ing*. When you add a suffix to a word ending with an *e*, the *e* is dropped. Create new words by adding the suffixes shown to the following words:

1. smile + -ing =
2. glare + -ing =
3. lose + -ing =
4. space + -ious =
5. love + -able =

For more help with adjectives, see the Language Arts Survey 3.66, "Adjectives."

Maya Lin's Vietnam Veterans Memorial has caused an outpouring of emotion unlike any other memorial. As soon as it opened, something happened that no one had anticipated—visitors began to leave messages and small gifts along the base of the wall. The practice resembles a tradition found in many cultures. On the Day of the Dead in Mexico, for example, people commonly make altars on which to leave gifts for the souls of departed family members. All types of objects are left at the Vietnam Veterans Memorial—photos, poems, food, combat boots, flags, military medals, and many unusual items that have secret, personal mean- ings. All the objects are collected each day and preserved by the National Park Service. Some were even displayed in a special exhibition by the Smithsonian Institution in 1995, when the number of objects had reached 30,000.

Night Patrol, 1995. Larry Powell. Collection of the Artist.

Prereading

"BE-ERS AND DOERS"

by Budge Wilson

Reader's Resource

- **SOCIAL STUDIES CONNECTION.** "Be-ers and Doers" revolves around the idea that every person is born with a certain personality type, causing him or her to behave in a particular way. Psychologists have developed a variety of ways to define different personality types. One of the most basic theories, developed by Friedman and Roseman, defines type A personalities and type B personalities. People with type A personalities typically are more competitive, more rushed, time oriented, and aggressive. People with type B personalities generally are more relaxed, more flexible, more passive, and less stressed. More recent studies have added a type C personality, which applies to people who seem patient and cooperative but not assertive. Type C people seem like type B people on the surface, but they tend to suppress feelings of stress and to put their own needs last. Researchers say that people with type A and type C personalities are at a higher risk for diseases such as cancer and heart disease.

- **GEOGRAPHY CONNECTION.** This story takes place in Nova Scotia, an eastern province of Canada. One of the Maritime provinces on Canada's Atlantic coast, Nova Scotia includes a peninsula that sprawls east from the Canadian mainland. Nova Scotia also includes all of Cape Breton Island. The province has more than 4,700 miles of coastline, ranging from fertile coastal lowlands in the north to the jagged, rocky, and barren southern shores. The Annapolis River Valley, in western Nova Scotia, is famous for its apple orchards and productive farmland.

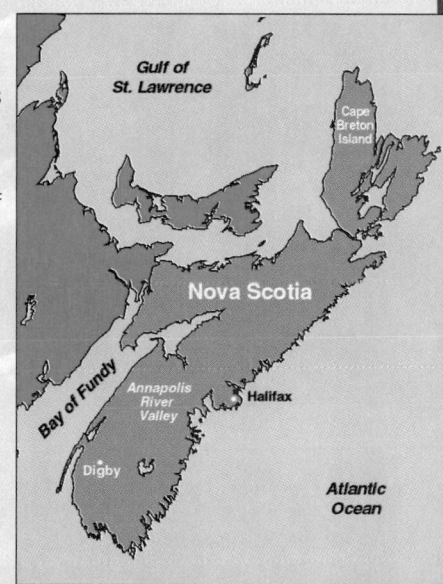

Reader's Journal

Are you a "be-er" or a "doer"?

Reader's TOOLBOX

CHARACTER. A **character** is a person (or sometimes an animal) who takes part in the action of a literary work. A character's human qualities, or character traits, are what bring that character to life for the reader. As you read the story, think about the qualities each individual has that make that person a "be-er" or a "doer."

PLOT. A **plot** is a series of events related to a central conflict, or struggle. The structure of a plot is based on an author's choice of events related to that conflict and the ordering of those events. As you read "Be-ers and Doers" think about the events and situations the author chooses to describe.

ADDITIONAL RESOURCES

UNIT 1 RESOURCE BOOK
- Selection Worksheet 1.2
- Selection Check Test 4.1.3
- Selection Test 4.1.4
- Language, Grammar, and Style Resource 3.17

READER'S JOURNAL

You might help students form their responses by asking the following questions: Do you find that you feel or act more like a be-er or a doer depending on the situation? For example, are you a be-er when it comes to hanging out with friends, but a doer when you have to clean your room or accomplish other tasks? As an alternate activity, ask students the following questions: Do you consider yourself a type A, B, or C personality, based on the descriptions in Reader's Resource? If none of the descriptions applies to you, write a new definition describing your "type D" personality.

GOALS/OBJECTIVES

Studying this lesson will enable students to
- enjoy a short story about members of a family with very different personalities
- briefly describe different personality types
- briefly explain the geography of Nova Scotia

- define *character* and recognize differences among characters
- understand the role of *plot* in a story

MOTIVATION
To spark students' interest in the story, have them complete the personality quiz on page 39. Have students discuss whether or not they agree with the assessment. After they have read the selection, students should decide which character would have scored closest to themselves if he or she had taken the same test.

READING PROFICIENCY
Some students might find the Nova Scotian dialect used in the selection difficult to understand. Have students read the Language, Grammar, and Style: Examining Dialect activity in the Skill Builders section on page 42. As they read the selection, students should create a chart containing examples of dialect and phrases "translating" the dialect into their own words.

ENGLISH LANGUAGE LEARNING
Point out the following vocabulary words and expressions.
stocks and bonds—capital invested in a company through the buying of shares that entitles the buyer to a share in the ownership, dividends, and voting rights
nerves—anxiety
embroidering and crocheting—types of needlework
storm (v.)—to attack in a vigorous or angry outburst
drum (v.)—to instill by continued repetition
scudding—to be driven or run before the wind
carol—a Christmas song
incendiary bomb—device used to start fires
table runners—a long, narrow, decorative cloth for the top of a table
second-degree burns—blistering as a result of fire damage
horizon—the line where the sky seems to meet the earth

SPECIAL NEEDS
Students will find it helpful to listen to the selection on audiocassette. Make sure students focus on the Guided Reading questions and the Recall questions in the Investigate, Inquire, and Imagine section.

ENRICHMENT
Students might enjoy researching other personality tests, such as the Meyers-Briggs

INDIVIDUAL LEARNING STRATEGIES (CONT.)

personality-type indicator, and selecting one to administer to the class. Some of these tests are available on the Internet. As part of their research, students should find out what kinds of careers are recommended for people with each personality type and share their findings with the class.

Be-ers and Doers

Budge Wilson

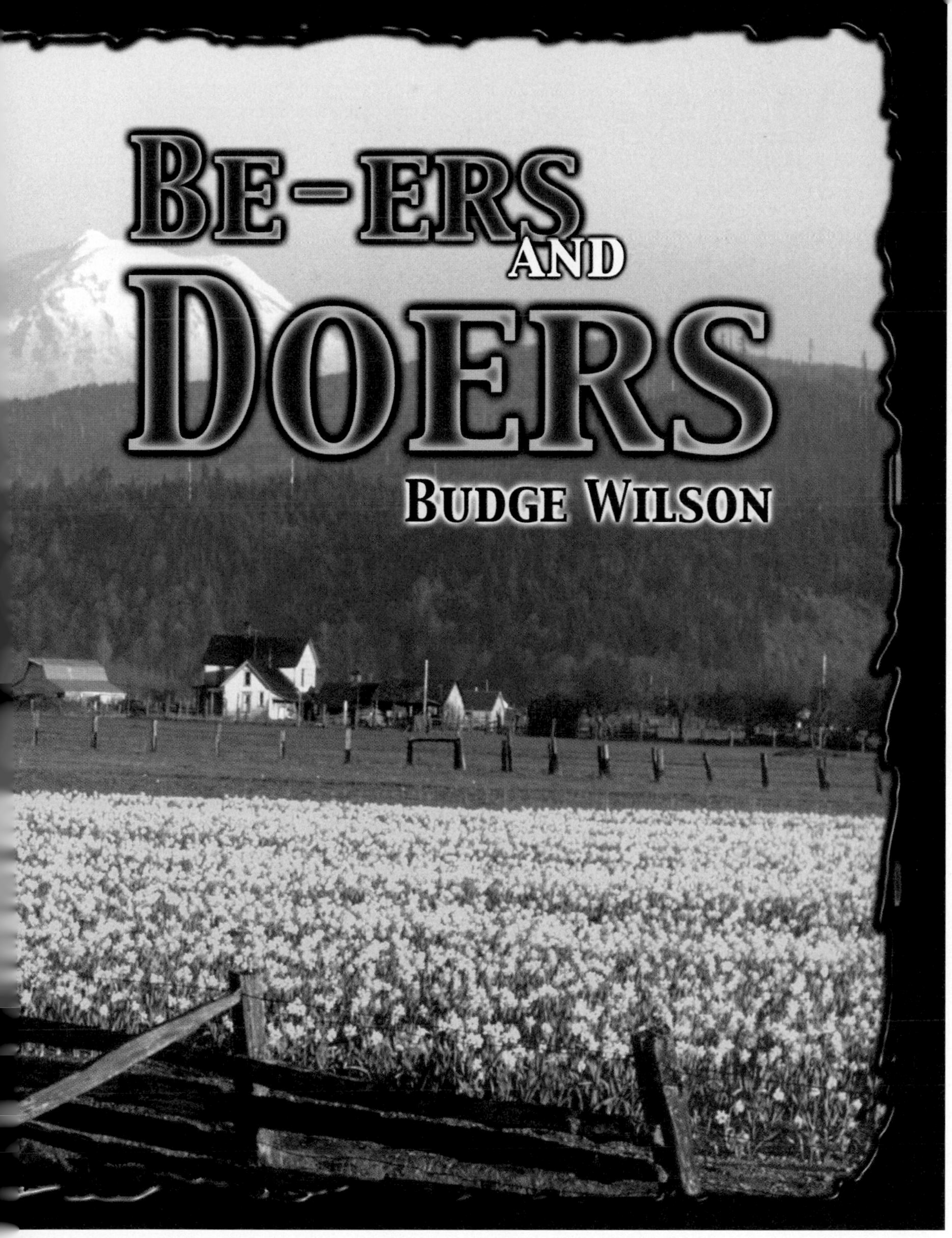

VOCABULARY FROM THE SELECTION

accelerate
conform
contrary
malleable
miser

ART SMART

Inform students that the beauty of farmland—as shown on this page—has inspired many artists. Jean François Millet (1814–1875) was a French painter. Many people interpreted his paintings of peasants working in the fields as a form of social protest. Winslow Homer (1836–1910) was an American painter whose work of the 1870s includes many scenes of farm life. Vincent van Gogh (1853–1890), the well-known Dutch Expressionist painter, depicted many scenes of rural peasant life. Encourage students to locate a reproduction of a painting showing farm life by one of these artists. Possible sources include the art books in your school or local library. Share the images of farm life with the class. Ask them to discuss how the artist portrays farm life in each painting. What attitudes toward the subject are conveyed in each piece?

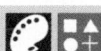

1. The first five years were peaceful because Adelaide was a conformist and did what her mother told her.
2. Adelaide's mother says she is a doer.
3. Adelaide's father likes to sit on the porch swing and watch the seasons change.

ADDITIONAL QUESTIONS AND ACTIVITIES

Ask students the following questions:
1. How would you describe the personality of Adelaide, the narrator?
2. What is Adelaide's mother's personality like?
3. What is Adelaide's father's personality like?
4. What evidence is there that Adelaide's father doesn't spend all his time being, but at least part of it doing?

Answers
1. Adelaide is a conformist and does whatever her mother tells her without question.
2. Adelaide's mother is a "doer," a person filled with incredible energy who is very concerned with getting things done and accomplishing things.
3. Adelaide's father is a "be-er," very calm and peaceful in temperament. He seems to enjoy just sitting and watching the landscape.
4. The fact that the father is able to do all the work of keeping the farm running is evidence that the father does spend some time doing, just at his own pace.

Mom was a little narrow wisp of a woman. You wouldn't have thought to look at her that she could move a card table; even for me it was sometimes hard to believe the ease with which she could shove around an entire family. Often I tried to explain her to myself. She had been brought up on the South Shore of Nova Scotia. I wondered sometimes if the scenery down there had rubbed off on her—all those granite rocks and fogs and screeching gulls, the slow, laboring springs, and the quick, grudging summers. And then the winters—grayer than doom, and endless.

I was the oldest. I was around that house for five years before Maudie came along. They were peaceful, those five years, and even now it's easy to remember how everything seemed calm and simple. But now I know why. I was a <u>conformist</u> and <u>malleable</u> as early as three years old; I didn't buck the system. If Mom said, "Hurry, Adelaide!" If she said to me, at five, "Fold that laundry, now, Adie, and don't let no grass grow under your feet," I folded it fast. So there were very few battles at first, and no major wars.

> **GUIDED READING**
> Why were the first five years peaceful?

Dad, now, he was peaceful just by nature. If a tornado had come whirling in the front door and lifted the roof clear off its hinges, he probably would have just scratched the back of his neck and said, with a kind of slow surprise, "Well! Oho! Just think o' that!" He had been born in the Annapolis Valley, where the hills are round and gentle, and the summers sunlit and very warm.

"Look at your father!" Mom would say to us later. "He thinks that all he's gotta do is *be*. Well, bein' ain't good enough. You gotta *do*, too. Me, I'm a doer." All the time she was talking, she'd be knitting up a storm, or mixing dough, or pushing a mop—hands forever and ever on the move.

> **GUIDED READING**
> What does Adelaide's mother say about herself?

Although Mom was fond of pointing out to us the things our father didn't do, he must have been doing something. Our farm was in the most fertile part of the valley, and it's true that we had the kind of soil that seemed to make things grow all of their own accord. Those beets and carrots and potatoes just came pushing up into the sunshine with an effortless grace, and they kept us well fed, with plenty left over to sell. But there was weeding and harvesting to do, and all those ten cows to milk—not to mention the thirty apple trees in our orchard to be cared for. I think maybe he just did his work so slowly and quietly that she found it hard to believe he was doing anything at all. Besides, on the South Shore, nothing ever grew without a struggle. And when Dad was through all his chores, or in between times, he liked to just sit on our old porch swing and watch the spring unfold or the summer blossom. And in the fall, he sat there smiling, admiring the rows of

> **GUIDED READING**
> What does Adelaide's father like to do?

"He thinks that all he's gotta do is *be*. Well, bein' ain't good enough. You gotta *do*, too."

words for everyday use

con • form (kən fôrm′) *v.*, act obedient or compliant. *Ron <u>conforms</u> to all the rules.* **conformist** *n.*

mal • lea • ble (mal′ ē ə bəl) *adj.*, capable of being shaped or controlled by outside forces. *I squeezed and rolled the clay until it was <u>malleable</u>.*

vegetables, the giant sunflowers, the golden leaves gathering in the trees of North Mountain.

Maudie wasn't Maudie for the reasons a person is a Ginny or a Gertie or a Susie. She wasn't called Maudie because she was cute. She got that name because if you've got a terrible name like Maud, you have to do something to rescue it. She was called after Mom's aunt Maud, who was a <u>miser</u> and had the whole Bank of Nova Scotia under her mattress. But she was a crabby old thing who just sat around living on her dead husband's stocks and bonds. A be-er, not a doer. Mom really scorned Aunt Maud and hated her name, but she had high hopes that our family would sometime cash in on that gold mine under the mattress. She hadn't counted on Aunt Maud going to Florida one winter and leaving her house in the care of a dear old friend. The dear old friend emptied the contents of the mattress, located Aunt Maud's three diamond rings, and took off for Mexico, leaving the pipes to freeze and the cat to die of starvation. After that, old Aunt Maud couldn't have cared less if everybody in the whole district[1] had been named after her. She was that bitter.

Maudie was so like Mom that it was just as if she'd been cut out with a cookie cutter from the same dough. Raced around at top speed all through her growing-up time, full of projects and sports and hobbies and gossip and nerves. And mad at everyone who sang a different tune.

But this story's not about Maudie. I guess you could say it's mostly about Albert.

Albert was the baby. I was eight years old when he was born, and I often felt like he was my own child. He was special to all of us, I guess, except maybe to Maudie, and when Mom saw him for the first time, I watched a slow soft tenderness in her face that was a rare thing for any of us to see. I was okay because I was cooperative, and I knew she loved me. Maudie was her clone, and almost like a piece of herself, so they admired one another, although they were too similar to be at peace for very long. But Albert was something different. Right away, I knew she was going to pour into Albert something that didn't reach the rest of us, except in part. As time went on, this scared me. I could see that she'd made up her mind that Albert was going to be a perfect son. That meant, among other things, that he was going to be a fast-moving doer. And even when he was three or four, it wasn't hard for me to know that this wasn't going to be easy. Because Albert was a be-er. *Born* that way.

As the years went by, people around Wilmot used to say, "Just look at that family of Hortons. Mrs. Horton made one child—Maudie. Then there's Adelaide, who's her own self. But Albert, now. Mr. Horton made him all by himself. They're alike as two pine needles."

And just as nice, I could have added. But Mom wasn't either pleased or amused. "You're a bad influence on that boy, Stanley," she'd say to my dad. "How's he gonna get any ambition if all he sees is a father who can spend up to an hour leanin' on his hoe, starin' at the Mountain?" Mom had it all worked out that Albert was going

---

1. **district.** Administrative division in Canadian provinces; similiar to county

GUIDED READING

Who is Maudie like?

GUIDED READING

About what has Adelaide's mother made up her mind?

---

words for everyday use

mi • ser (mī′ zər) *n.*, a person who is extremely stingy with money. *Uncle Morris, a real <u>miser</u>, has sixty-two coffee cans full of quarters in his closet, but he never spends money for fun.*

1. Maudie is like her mother.
2. Adelaide's mother has made up her mind that Albert is going to be a perfect son.

ADDITIONAL QUESTIONS AND ACTIVITIES

Ask students the following questions:
1. Why is Adelaide's sister named after Aunt Maud? What happens to dash the mother's hopes?
2. How does Adelaide's mother feel about Aunt Maud? Why does she feel this way?
3. What is Maudie's personality like?
4. What is the relationship between Maudie and her mother like?
5. What does Adelaide's mother want to do with Albert? What does "perfect" mean to the mother? What is the problem with her plan?

Answers
1. She is named after Aunt Maud because her mother hoped the family could cash in on the fortune Aunt Maud kept under her mattress. However, her hopes are dashed when Aunt Maud's fortune is stolen by a "dear old friend."
2. Adelaide's mother despises Maud because she is a be-er who, until she was robbed, lived off her dead husband's money.
3. Maudie is just like her mother: she is a doer, an active whirlwind of energy, always busy with projects and activities.
4. They admire each other, but often argue because they are too much alike.
5. She wants to turn Albert into the perfect son. "Perfect," to the mother, means being a doer. The problem is that Albert is a born be-er.

Quotables

"My vegetable love should grow Vaster than empires, and more slow."

—Andrew Marvell, from "To His Coy Mistress"

---

to be a lawyer or a doctor or a Member of Parliament.[2]

GUIDED READING

What does Mrs. Horton want Albert to become?

My dad didn't argue with her, or at least not in an angry way, "Aw, c'mon now, Dorothy," he might say to her, real slow. "The vegetables are comin' along jest fine. No need to shove them more than necessary. It does a man good to look at them hills. You wanta try it sometime. They tell you things."

"Nothin' *I* need t'hear," she'd huff, and disappear into the house, clattering pans, thumping the mop, scraping the kitchen table across the floor to get at more dust. And Albert would just watch it all, saying not a word, chewing on a piece of grass.

Mom really loved my dad, even though he drove her nearly crazy. Lots more went on than just nagging and complaining. If you looked really hard, you could see that. If it hadn't been for Albert and wanting him to be a four-star son, she mightn't have bothered to make Dad look so useless. Even so, when they sat on the swing together at night, you could feel their closeness. They didn't hold hands or

GUIDED READING

What do Adelaide's parents do at night?

anything. Her hands were always too busy embroidering, crocheting, mending something, or just swatting mosquitoes. But they liked to be together. Personal chemistry, I thought as I grew older, is a mysterious and contrary thing.

One day, Albert brought his report card home from school, and Mom looked at it hard and anxious, eyebrows knotted. " 'Albert seems a nice child,' " she read aloud to all of us, more loudly than necessary, " 'but his marks could be better. He spends too much

---

time looking out the window, dreaming.' " She paused. No one spoke.

"Leanin' on his hoe," continued Mom testily. "Albert!" she snapped at him. "You pull up your socks by Easter or you're gonna be in deep trouble."

Dad stirred uneasily in his chair. "Aw, Dorothy," he mumbled. "Leave him be. He's a good kid."

"Or could be. *Maybe*," she threw back at him. "What he seems like to me is rock-bottom lazy. He sure is slow-moving, and could be he's slow in the head, too. Dumb."

GUIDED READING

What does Mrs. Horton say about Albert?

Albert's eyes flickered at that word, but that's all. He just stood there and watched, eyes level.

"But I love him a lot," continued Mom, "and unlike you, I don't plan t'just sit around and watch him grow dumber. If it's the last thing I do, I'm gonna light a fire under his feet."

Albert was twelve then, and the nagging began to accelerate in earnest.

"How come you got a low mark in your math test?"

"I don't like math. It seems like my head don't want it."

"But do you *work* at it?"

"Well, no. Not much. Can't see no sense in workin' hard at something I'll never use. I can add up our grocery bill. I pass. That's enough."

"Not for me, it ain't," she'd storm back at him. "No baseball practice for you until you get them sums perfect. Ask Maudie t'check them." Maudie used to drum that arithmetic into him night after night. She loved playing

---

2. **Parliament.** Canadian federal government system, composed of the Senate, the House of Commons, and the Governor General (representing the Queen of England)

---

words for everyday use

con • trar • y (kän' trer ē) *adj.*, not in agreement with what is usual or expected. *The manager's announcement was contrary to usual company policy.*

ac • cel • er • ate (ik sel' ə rāt) *v.*, to increase in speed. *The bicycle began to accelerate as it moved down the steep hill.*

ART SMART

Nova Scotia is known for its rocky coastline, as shown in the photograph on this page. Ask students to discuss how they would feel about growing up in such a place.

ADDITIONAL QUESTIONS AND ACTIVITIES

Remind students of the old saying, "opposites attract." Ask students to discuss how they feel about this idea personally. Does the saying fit Mr. and Mrs. Horton? What evidence can you point to that supports your opinion?
Answers. Most students will say that Mr. and Mrs. Horton's relationship does seem to be a good example of the old saying, "opposites attract." As evidence students may point to the fact that the two love each other even though they are so different, as can be seen when they sit together on the swing at night, just enjoying each other's company.

schoolteacher, and that's how she eventually ended up. And a cross one.

One thing Albert was good at, though, was English class. By the time

> **GUIDED READING**
> What is Albert good at?

he got to high school, he spent almost as much time reading as he did staring into space. His way of speaking changed. He stopped dropping his *g*'s. He said *isn't* instead of *ain't*. His tenses were all neated up. He wasn't putting on airs. I just think that all those people in his books started being more real to him than his own neighbors. He loved animals, too. He made friends with the calves and even the cows. Mutt and Jeff, our two gray cats, slept on his bed every night. Often you could see him out in the fields, talking to our dog, while he was working.

"Always messin' around with animals," complained Mom. "Sometimes I think he's three parts woman and one part child. He's fifteen years old, and last week I caught him bawlin' in the hayloft after we had to shoot that male calf. Couldn't understand why y' can't go on feedin' an animal that'll never produce milk."

"Nothing wrong with liking animals," I argued. I was home for the weekend from my secretarial job in Wolfville.

> **GUIDED READING**
> Where does Adelaide now live?

"Talkin' to dogs and cryin' over cattle is not what I'd call a shortcut to success. And the cats spend so much time with him that they've forgotten why we brought them into the house in the first place. For mice."

1. Albert and his father lay down to watch the sky.
2. Adelaide's husband and new baby, Jennifer, go home with her for Christmas.
3. Adelaide's father gives her mother a sapphire ring for Christmas.

ADDITIONAL QUESTIONS AND ACTIVITIES

Ask students the following questions:
1. Why is Adelaide more willing to defend Albert now that she is older?
2. What scene does Adelaide see her father and brother enjoying?
3. What do her brother and father do to better enjoy the scene?
4. How do you think Mrs. Horton would feel about the actions of her husband and son?
5. How do you think Adelaide feels about these actions?

Answers
1. Students may suggest that Adelaide is less interested now that she is older in conforming to please her mother and is more interested that Albert develop into the person he wants to be.
2. She sees them enjoying the geese flying across the blue sky in autumn.
3. They throw down their rakes and lie on their backs to better enjoy the scene.
4. Mrs. Horton would probably be scornful and angry that the men would put down their rakes to lie on their backs and watch the sky. Adelaide seems to appreciate the same natural beauty that father and son enjoy and does not judge their actions.

"Maybe there's more to life than success or mice," I said. I was twenty-three now, and more interested in Albert than in conformity.

Mom made a "huh" sound through her nose. "Adelaide Horton," she said, "when you're my age, you'll understand more about success and mice than you do now. Or the lack of them." She turned on her heel and went back in the house. "And if you can't see," she said through the screen door, "why I don't want Albert to end up exactly like your father, then you've got even less sense than I thought you had. I don't want any son of mine goin' through life just satisfied to *be*." Then I could hear her banging around in the kitchen.

I looked off the verandah[3] out at the front field, where Dad and Albert were raking up hay for the cattle, slowly, with lots of pauses for talk. All of a sudden they stopped, and Albert pointed up to the sky. It was fall, and four long wedges of geese were flying far above us, casting down their strange muffled cry. The sky was cornflower blue, and the wind was sending white clouds scudding across it. My breath was caught with the beauty of it all, and as I looked at Dad and Albert, they threw away their rakes and lay down flat on their backs, right there in the front pasture, in order to drink in the sky. And after all the geese had passed over, they stayed like that for maybe twenty minutes more.

> **GUIDED READING**
> Why do Albert and his father lay down?

We were all home for Christmas the year Albert turned eighteen. Maudie was having her Christmas break from teaching, and she was looking skinnier and more tight-lipped than I remembered her. I was there with my husband and my new baby, Jennifer, and Albert was even quieter than usual. But content, I

> **GUIDED READING**
> Who goes home with Adelaide for Christmas?

thought. Not making any waves. Mom had intensified her big campaign to have him go to Acadia University in the fall. "Pre-law," she said, "or maybe teacher training. Anyways, you gotta go. A man has to be successful." She avoided my father's eyes. "In the fall," she said. "For sure."

"It's Christmas," said Dad, without anger. "Let's just be happy and forget all them plans for a few days." He was sitting at the kitchen table breaking up the bread slowly, slowly, for the turkey stuffing. He chuckled. "I've decided to be a doer this Christmas."

"And if the doin's bein' done at that speed," she said, taking the bowl from him, "we'll be eatin' Christmas dinner on New Year's Day." She started to break up the bread so quickly that you could hardly focus on her flying fingers.

Christmas came and went. It was a pleasant time. The food was good; Jennifer slept right through dinner and didn't cry all day. We listened to the Queen's Christmas message; we opened presents. Dad gave Mom a ring with a tiny sapphire in it, although she'd asked for a new vacuum cleaner.

> **GUIDED READING**
> What does Adelaide's father give her mother for Christmas?

"I like this better," she said, and looked as though she might cry.

"We'll get the vacuum cleaner in January," he said, "That's no kind of gift to get for Christmas. It's a work thing."

She looked as if she might say something, but she didn't.

It was on December 26th that it happened. That was the day of the fire.

It was a lazy day. We all got up late, except me, of course, who had to feed the baby at two and at six. But when we were all up, we just sort of lazed around in our dressing

---

3. **verandah.** Open porch area, usually with a roof

gowns, drinking coffee, admiring one anothers' presents, talking about old times, singing a carol or two around the old organ. Dad had that look on him that he used to get when all his children were in his house at the same time. Like he was in temporary possession of the best that life had to offer. Even Mom was softened up, and she sat by the grate fire and talked a bit, although there was still a lot of jumping up and down and rushing out to the kitchen to check the stove or cut up vegetables. Me, I think that on the day after Christmas you should just eat up leftovers and enjoy a slow state of collapse. But you can't blame a person for feeding you. It's handy to have a Martha or two around a house that's already equipped with three Marys.[4]

Albert was the best one to watch, though. To me, anyway. He was sitting on the floor in his striped pajamas, holding Jennifer, rocking her, and singing songs to her in a low, crooning voice. Tender, I thought, the way I like a man to be.

Albert had just put the baby back in her carriage when a giant spark flew out of the fireplace. It hit the old nylon carpet like an incendiary bomb, and the rug burst into flames. Mom started waving an old afghan over it, as though she was blowing out a match, but all she was doing was fanning the fire.

> **GUIDED READING**
> How does Mrs. Horton react to the fire?

While most of us stood there in immovable fear, Albert had already grabbed Jennifer, carriage and all, and rushed out to the barn with her. He was back in a flash, just in time to see Maudie's dressing gown catch fire. He pushed her down on the floor and lay on top of her to smother the flames, and then he was up on his feet again, taking charge.

"Those four buckets in the summer kitchen!" he yelled. "Start filling them!" He pointed to Mom and Dad, who obeyed him like he was a general and they were the privates. To my husband he roared, "Get out to th' barn and keep that baby warm!"

> **GUIDED READING**
> How do Mr. and Mrs. Horton react to Albert's command?

"And you!" He pointed to me. "Call the fire department. It's 825-3131." In the meantime, the smoke was starting to fill the room and we were all coughing. Little spits of fire were crawling up the curtains, and Maudie was just standing there, shrieking.

Before Mom and Dad got back with the water, Albert was out in the back bedroom hauling up the carpet. Racing in with it over his shoulder, he bellowed, "Get out o' the way!" and we all moved. Then he slapped the carpet over the flames on the floor, and the fire just died without so much as a protest. Next he grabbed one of the big cushions off the sofa, and chased around after the little lapping flames on curtains and chairs and table runners, smothering them. When Mom and Dad appeared with a bucket in each hand, he shouted, "Stop! Don't use that stuff! No need t'have water damage too!"

Then Albert was suddenly still, hands hanging at his sides with the fingers spread. He smiled shyly.

"It's out," he said.

I rushed up and hugged him, wailing like a baby, loving him, thanking him. For protecting Jennifer—from smoke, from fire, from cold, from heaven knows what. Everyone opened windows and doors, and before too long, even the smoke was gone. It smelled pretty awful, but no one cared.

> **GUIDED READING**
> What does Adelaide do when the fire is out?

4. **Martha . . . Marys.** Reference to the Bible, Luke 10:38-42, in which Martha busily works while Mary sits and listens to Jesus

Albert was the best one to watch, though. To me, anyway.

1. Mrs. Horton waves an afghan over the fire, causing it to burn more intensely.
2. Mr. and Mrs. Horton quickly obey Albert's command, as if he were a general.
3. When the fire is out, Adelaide hugs Albert and thanks him for saving her baby.

HISTORICAL NOTE

Tell students that the first known firefighters were established by the Roman Emperor Augustus in 24 BC. The first firefighters had very few tools to use in combating blazes. Firefighters would stand in long lines and pass buckets of water from hand to hand to put out flames. They would also use axes to cut away brush and other plants to prevent fire from spreading.

1. Mrs. Horton has been looking for a sign that Albert is "one hundred percent alive."
2. Albert makes a sound like that of a dog before he leaps for the throat.
3. Albert is going to be himself.
4. Adelaide says that her father might have died because all his silent tensions finally burst.

LITERARY TECHNIQUE

CRISIS. The **crisis,** or **turning point,** is the point in a plot when something happens to determine the future course of events and the eventual fate of the main character or characters. Ask students to identify the crisis of this story. Ask them to explain the way this event changed the lives of the main characters. Why do they think Albert fainted after this crisis was past? What does he do when he recovers? *Answers.* Students may say that the crisis comes when after the fire, Mrs. Horton praises her son for acting like a doer, and he explodes at her, telling her that he is his own person. Students may say that this event nay have stopped Mrs. Horton's relentless pushing, and it gave Albert the courage to actually become his own person and live the life he wanted to live, without worrying about his mother. Albert may faint not only from the physical shock of his burns, but also from the emotional stress of at long last standing up to his mother. Albert leaves home as soon as he recovers.

When we all gathered again in the parlor to clear up the mess, and Jennifer was back in my bedroom asleep, Mom stood up and looked at Albert, her eyes ablaze with admiration—and with something else I couldn't put my finger on.

"Albert!" she breathed. "We all thank you! You've saved the house, the baby, all of us, even our Christmas presents. I'm proud, proud, *proud* of you."

Albert just stood there, smiling quietly, but very pale. His hands were getting red and sort of puckered looking.

Mom took a deep breath. "And *that*," she went on, "is what I've been looking for, all of your life. Some sort of a sign that you were one hundred percent alive. And now we all know you are. Maybe even a lick more alive than the rest of us. So!" She folded her arms, and her eyes bored into him. "I'll have no more excuses from you now. No one who can put out a house fire single-handed and rescue a niece and a sister and organize us all into a fire brigade is gonna sit around for the rest of his life gatherin' dust. No siree! Or leanin' against no hoe. Why, you even had the fire department number tucked away in your head. Just imagine what you're gonna be able to do with them kind o' brains! I'll never, never rest until I see you educated and successful. Doin' what you was meant to do. I'm just proud of you, Albert. So terrible proud!"

> **GUIDED READING**
> What has Mrs. Horton been looking for?

Members of the fire department were starting to arrive at the front door, but Albert ignored them. He was white now, like death, and he made a low terrible sound. He didn't exactly pull his lips back from his teeth and growl, but the result was similar. It was like the sound a dog makes before he leaps for the throat. And what he said was "*You jest leave me be, woman!*"

> **GUIDED READING**
> What sound does Albert make?

We'd never heard words like this coming out of Albert, and the parlor was as still as night as we all listened.

"You ain't proud o' me, Mom," he whispered, all his beautiful grammar gone. "Yer jest proud o' what you want me t'be. And I got some news for you. Things I shoulda tole you years gone by. *I ain't gonna be what you want.*" His voice was starting to quaver now, and he was trembling all over. "*I'm gonna be me*. And it seems like if that's ever gonna happen, it'll have t'be in some other place. And I plan t'do somethin' about that before the day is out."

> **GUIDED READING**
> What is Albert going to be?

Then he shut his eyes and fainted right down onto the charred carpet. The firemen carried him off to the hospital, where he was treated for shock and second-degree burns. He was there for three weeks.

M y dad died of a stroke[5] when he was sixty-six. "Not enough exercise," said Mom, after she'd got over the worst part of her grief. "Too much sittin' around watchin' the lilacs grow. No way for his blood to circulate good." Me, I ask myself if he just piled up his silent tensions until he burst wide open. Maybe he wasn't all that calm and peaceful after all. Could be he was just waiting, like Albert, for the moment when it would all come pouring out. Perhaps that wasn't the way it was; but all the same, I wonder.

> **GUIDED READING**
> What reason does Adelaide offer for her father's death?

Mom's still going strong at eighty-eight. Unlike Dad's, her blood must circulate like a racing stream, what with all that rushing around; she continues to move as if she's being chased. She's still knitting and preserving and scrubbing and mending and preaching. She'll never get one of those

---

5. **stroke.** Result of a rupture or clot of an artery in the brain

Family of Five. Diana Ong.

GUIDED READING

Why will Mrs. Horton never get cancer?

tension diseases like angina[6] or cancer or even arthritis, because she doesn't keep one single thing bottled up inside her for more than five minutes. Out it all comes like air out of a flat tire—with either a hiss or a bang.

Perhaps it wasn't growing up on the South Shore that made Mom the way she is. I live on that coast now, and I've learned that it's more than just gray and stormy. I know about the long sandy beaches and the peace that comes of a clear horizon. I've seen the razzle-dazzle colors of the low-lying scarlet bushes in the fall, blazing against the black of the spruce trees and the bluest sky in the world.

---

6. **angina.** Disease of the heart

ANSWER TO GUIDED READING QUESTION

1. Mrs. Horton will never get cancer because she doesn't keep anything bottled up inside her.

CROSS-CURRICULAR ACTIVITIES

MATHEMATICS AND SCIENCES. Students may enjoy taking the personality quiz on page 39 and doing the Critical Thinking & Applied English Skill Builder activity on page 42 to explore whether they are a "be-ers" or "doers." They may also like to consider whether they are introverts or extroverts. Inform students that some psychiatric experts believe that we are born one or the other—that this personality trait is the result of nature rather than nurture. Introverts interact with others less readily and may be shy and quiet, while extroverts talk to others easily and like to be the center of attention. Both personality types have their benefits and drawbacks, and one is not better than the other. Few people are complete extroverts and introverts, and their personality types fall somewhere in between, showing mild extroverted or mild introverted tendencies. Ask students to think about themselves and their own lives; write a paragraph labeling themselves as an introvert, an extrovert, or somewhere in between; and state the reasons behind their choice.

ART SMART

Ask students to discuss what is revealed about the family of five in Diana Ong's art. What words would they use to describe the relationships in this family?

ANSWERS TO GUIDED READING QUESTIONS

1. Adelaide thinks her mother never stopped long enough to notice things like the natural beauty in her surroundings.
2. At his new house, Albert has a cow, a beagle, four cats, and about five hundred books.

RESPOND TO THE SELECTION

You might also ask students what advice they would give Mrs. Horton about her relationships with her family or her behavior in general.

SELECTION CHECK TEST 4.1.3 WITH ANSWERS

Checking Your Reading
1. Where does the story take place? **The story takes place in Nova Scotia, Canada.**
2. What is the family's business? **The family's business is a farm.**
3. Which parent does Albert resemble more—his mother or his father? **Albert resembles his father.**
4. Why is Albert a hero on the day after Christmas? **Albert is a hero because he saves his family from a fire.**
5. How does Albert react to his mother's praise of his heroism? **Albert scorns his mother's praise.**

Vocabulary in Context
Fill in each blank below with the most appropriate vocabulary word from "Be-ers and Doers." You may have to change the tense of the word.
contrary   conformist   miser
accelerate
1. _____ to everyone's expectations, Marjorie Elkins won the election. **Contrary**
2. For years the old _____ had stuffed money under his mattress, in the rafters, and in every nook of the house. **miser**
3. The student driver found it difficult to _____ up the steep hill. **accelerate**

Reader's Toolbox
Write the letter of each line to put the following events in the correct plot order.
a. Mrs. Horton names Maud after her own aunt.
b. Albert moves into a small house with a view of the Bay of Fundy.

I'm familiar with the way one single radiant summer day can make you forget a whole fortnight of fog—like birth after a long labor. You might say that the breakers out on the reefs are angry or full of threats. To me, though, those waves are leaping and dancing, wild with freedom and joyfulness. But I think Mom was in a hurry from the moment she was born. I doubt if she ever stopped long enough to take notice of things like that.

> **GUIDED READING**
> What does Adelaide think about her mother?

Albert left home as soon as he got out of the hospital. He worked as a stevedore[7] in Halifax for a number of years, and when he got enough money saved, he bought a little run-down house close to Digby, with a view of the Bay of Fundy. He's got a small chunk of land that's so black and rich that it doesn't take any pushing at all to make the flowers and vegetables grow. He has a cow and a beagle and four cats—and about five hundred books. He fixes lawn mowers and boat engines for the people in his area, and he putters away at his funny little house. He writes pieces for the *Digby Courier* and the *Novascotian*, and last winter he confessed to me that he writes poetry. He's childless and wifeless, but he has the time of day for any kid who comes around to hear stories or to have a broken toy fixed. He keeps an old rocker out on the edge of the cliff, where he can sit and watch the tides of Fundy rise and fall. ∎

> **GUIDED READING**
> What does Albert have at his new house?

---

7. **stevedore.** Person who loads and unloads the cargo of a ship

Respond *to the* SELECTION

Do you think Adelaide's mother, at the age of eighty-eight, is satisfied with her life? Why, or why not? Do you think she is pleased with how her children have grown up? Why, or why not?

About *the* AUTHOR

Budge Wilson grew up in Nova Scotia, Canada, the setting for many of her stories. Wilson mainly writes fiction for and about young people, drawing on her own experiences and those of friends and family members. Many of her stories explore human relationships and the struggles people experience growing up. Wilson has won numerous awards for her work and travels widely to speak in schools and libraries. Her books include *The Leaving* and *The Dandelion Garden*, two collections of short stories, and the novels *Breakdown*, *Thirteen Never Changes*, and *Sharla*.

SELECTION CHECK TEST 4.1.3 WITH ANSWERS (CONT.)

c. Mrs. Horton is disappointed in the math grades on Albert's report card.
d. Albert saves the family from the fire.
e. Albert's mother tells Albert how proud she is of him.

Students should order the events as follows:
1. a, 2. c, 3. d, 4. e, 5. b

What is your *personality* **type**

1. Before going to bed on a school night, I:
   A. make sure my homework is done and my clothes are set out for the morning.
   B. watch my favorite show on television.
   C. spend an hour on the phone with a friend, planning a weekend outing.
2. I make my bed:
   A. perfectly—every day.
   B. in a passable way—most of the time.
   C. only when forced to do it.
3. During vacations, I prefer to:
   A. relax and enjoy the free time.
   B. get a job to make money.
   C. join a club or sports team, attend events, go on excursions with family or friends.
4. Given free time in class, I:
   A. spend it doing homework for other classes.
   B. work ahead in my textbook.
   C. read for fun, draw, or chat with friends.
5. I worry about having enough time in the day to accomplish all I need to do. (Circle one answer.)
   A. true
   B. false
6. After a great day, I feel as if I have:
   A. done something helpful.
   B. accomplished a lot of work.
   C. discovered something beautiful.
7. My favorite shoes:
   A. are comfortable.
   B. look great.
   C. are practical.
8. I would spend an unexpected inheritance on:
   A. a new sports car.
   B. a new pet.
   C. investments.
9. If a friend betrays my trust, I:
   A. never speak to him or her again.
   B. confront him or her immediately, expressing my anger.
   C. wait a day and then ask the friend why he or she did such a thing.
10. Which of the following situations would likely make you mad? (Check all that apply.)
    __ a waiter is rude to you.
    __ a teacher criticizes a paper on which you worked very hard.
    __ your brother borrows your bicycle without asking.
    __ a parent makes a negative remark about your clothes or hair.
    __ a friend cancels her plans with you to do something with another friend instead.
    __ the computer you are using malfunctions, causing you to lose your nearly completed research paper.

Scoring:

1. A=4, B=0, C=2	5. A=4, B=0	9. A=2, B=4, C=0
2. A=4, B=2, C=0	6. A=2, B=4, C=0	10. 2 points for each item
3. A=0, B=4, C=2	7. A=0, B=2, C=4	checked
4. A=2, B=4, C=0	8. A=2, B=2, C=4	Add your points.

Teaching Note

Refer students to the Skill Builders activity, Critical Thinking & Applied English, "Analyzing a Quiz" on page 42 for tips on how to evaluate their quiz results.

RECALL

1a. Albert's two greatest loves are books and animals.

2a. Adelaide eventually lives on the South Shore, the same coast where her mother grew up. Adelaide appreciates the beaches, the colors in the fall, radiant summer days, and the waves.

3a. Through her words, readers learn that Mrs. Horton is impatient, critical, quick-tempered, and stubborn. Mrs. Horton's actions reveal the same qualities, but they also reveal gentler qualities. For example, when Albert was born she showed a tenderness that Adelaide had never before seen in her mother, she enjoys sitting on the porch with her husband in the evenings, and she reacts emotionally when her husband gives her a sapphire ring for Christmas.

INTERPRET

1b. Albert likes books because the characters are more real to him than actual people he knows. Students might also say that Albert likes to read as a means of escape. Students might say that Albert likes animals because they accept him as he is.

2b. Adelaide views the South Shore differently than her mother because her mother probably never took time to notice and appreciate the natural beauty of the coast. Albert would probably see it the same way as Adelaide.

3b. Responses will vary, but students will probably say that despite her constant criticism and badgering, Mrs. Horton doesn't have much influence on her family members because they continue to think and act the same way. Apparently, she has not been able to change any of them.

ANALYZE

4a. Adelaide's descriptions of Albert include her own observations, such as the following: "He was special to all of us" and "Albert was a be-er. *Born* that way." Her descriptions also include Mrs. Horton's comments that Albert is lazy, slow, and dumb. Students will probably say that all of these observations are opinions, but that Adelaide's are based more on fact than her mother's are because Mrs. Horton wants to see Albert a certain way. Facts about Albert include that he is good at English, he likes animals, and he expertly handled the fire.

Investigate, Inquire, and Imagine

Recall: GATHERING FACTS

1a. By the time Albert reaches high school, what are his two greatest loves?

2a. Where does Adelaide eventually live? What does she appreciate about this place?

3a. What does the reader learn about Mrs. Horton through her words? through her actions?

Interpret: FINDING MEANING

1b. What about these two things is attractive to Albert, and why?

2b. Why does Adelaide view this place differently than her mother probably did? What would Albert think about it?

3b. How much influence does Mrs. Horton seem to have on her family members? Does she cause people to think or act differently than they otherwise would? Do people change as a result of her influence?

Analyze: TAKING THINGS APART

4a. Identify ways in which Adelaide describes her brother Albert. Categorize each example as fact or opinion.

Synthesize: BRINGING THINGS TOGETHER

4b. What does Adelaide think about be-ers and doers? Summarize her thoughts and the message you think she has in telling this story.

Evaluate: MAKING JUDGMENTS

5a. How well does Mrs. Horton assess the death of her husband? Is her reasoning logical? How does Adelaide's view differ from Mrs. Horton's?

Extend: CONNECTING IDEAS

5b. According to the Reader's Resource on page 27, an individual with a type C personality tends to keep things pent up inside without voicing his or her emotions. Based on this, label Mr. Horton, Mrs. Horton, Adelaide, Maudie, and Albert as personality types A, B, or C. Give reasons for your answer.

Perspective: LOOKING AT OTHER VIEWS

6a. How would Mr. Horton view Albert's adult life? Would he view Albert as successful? Why, or why not? Why would Mrs. Horton view things differently? How does Adelaide probably view Albert as an adult?

Empathy: SEEING FROM INSIDE

6b. Rewrite the final paragraph of the story from the point of view of Mrs. Horton, Mr. Horton, or Maudie.

ANSWERS TO INVESTIGATE, INQUIRE, IMAGINE (CONT.)

SYNTHESIZE

4b. Responses will vary, but students might say that Adelaide seems to prefer be-ers to doers because they are less judgmental, more relaxed, and more appreciative of nature. Students will probably say that Adelaide's message is that people should accept others as they are.

EVALUATE

5a. Mrs. Horton believes that her husband died because he sat around too much. Her reasoning is based on her opinion, not logic. Adelaide believes her father died because of all his pent-up tensions.

(Continued on page 41)

Understanding *Literature*

CHARACTER. A **character** is a person (or sometimes an animal) who takes part in the action of a literary work. A character's human qualities, or character traits, bring that character to life for the reader. Note the character traits of each person in the Horton family. Can each character be classified as either a "be-er" or a "doer"? Why do you think the author chose to make Adelaide the narrator of the story?

PLOT. A **plot** is a series of events related to a central conflict, or struggle. The structure of a plot is based on an author's choice of events to include in the story and the ordering of those events. A typical plot includes an **inciting incident**, which introduces the central conflict; a **climax**, which is the point of highest interest and suspense; and a **resolution**, which is the point at which the central conflict ends.

Not all plots are chronological, or arranged in the order of time. Nor do plots have to include all events that could or would have taken place within the time span of the story. Review "Be-ers and Doers" and use the following graphic organizer to identify important situations and events in the story. Then determine which of these episodes is the inciting incident, which is the climax, and which indicates resolution.

Graphic Organizer

Situation or event	Part of plot (label the inciting incident, the climax, and the resolution)
Adelaide describes her mother, her father, Maudie, and Albert.	
Although Albert is born a "be-er," Adelaide's mother decides he will be a "doer."	

Writer's Journal

1. Imagine that Adelaide's parents decided to sell their farm and home. Write a brief **real estate advertisement** for the estate.

2. Imagine that one of Albert's poems wins a contest, earning him a bit of fame in Nova Scotia. Write a **biographical paragraph** about Albert to accompany his winning poem in an upcoming edition of the *Digby Courier*.

3. List five **personality traits** belonging to someone close to you. Based on your list, decide whether you think that person is a "be-er" or a "doer." Share your findings with the person to see if he or she agrees.

Character. Most of the characters in "Be-ers and Doers" can be classified as either be-ers or doers. The author may have used Adelaide as the narrator because she has a more moderate disposition than the rest of her family—she is neither an extreme be-er nor a doer.

Plot. Responses will vary, but students' charts should include the following information:

Situations or events: Adelaide describes her mother, her father, Maudie, and Albert; Although Albert is born a "be-er," his mother decides he will be a "doer" (This is the inciting incident); Albert brings home his report card at age 12; Albert shows his love for books and animals in high school; The whole family comes home for Christmas the year Albert is 18; A fire starts in the house; Albert saves the house and the family (This is the climax); Albert confronts his mother (This is the resolution); Adelaide describes her father's death, her mother's life, her own life, and Albert's life.

ANSWERS TO INVESTIGATE, INQUIRE, IMAGINE (CONT.)

EXTEND
5b. Responses will vary, but may include the following: Mr. Horton, type B (or C if students believe Adelaide's theory that he died from holding in his tensions); Mrs. Horton, type A; Adelaide, type B; Maudie, type A; and Albert, type B (or C based on his outburst after the fire).

PERSPECTIVE
6a. Mr. Horton would probably view Albert as a success because he is content and doing what he wants to do. Mrs. Horton probably regards her son as a failure because he's not a doctor or a lawyer. She doesn't understand how someone could be happy living a quiet, unambitious life. Adelaide probably views Albert as successful.

EMPATHY
6b. Responses will vary.

Language, Grammar, and Style
Examining Dialect. Responses will vary, but students might include the following in their answers.
Dialect from the story: "Well! Oho! Just think o' that!"
Phrase you might hear or say: "Oh my gosh! Can you believe it?"
Dialect from the story: "You pull up your socks by Easter or you're gonna be in deep trouble." Phrases you might hear or say: "You better watch out or you're going to get it."
Dialect from the story: "Not for me, it ain't." Phrases you might hear or say: "Oh, no, it isn't."
Dialect from the story: "Let's just be happy and forget all them plans for a few days." Phrases you might hear or say: "Just leave it alone for now."
Dialect from the story: "Maybe even a lick more alive than the rest of us." Phrases you might hear or say: "Maybe even a step ahead of the rest of us."
Dialect from the story: "No siree!" Phrases you might hear or say: "No way!"
Dialect from the story: "Just imagine what you're gonna be able to do with them kind o' brains!" Phrases you might hear or say: "You'll go far with that head on your shoulders!"
Dialect from the story: "Doin' what you was meant to do." Phrases you might hear or say: "Following the road to success."

Language, Grammar, and Style
FINDING THE COMPLETE SUBJECT AND COMPLETE PREDICATE

1. Complete subject: Albert and Mr. Horton; Complete predicate: were be-ers, not doers.
2. Complete subject: Such an apple crop; Complete predicate: impressed everyone in the region.
3. Complete subject: All of the Hortons; Complete predicate: ate dinner at half past six.
4. Complete subject: Mrs. Horton; Complete predicate: wanted Albert to be more ambitious.
5. Complete subject: A cow, a beagle, and four cats; Complete predicate: live with Albert
6. Complete subject: Adelaide and her family; Complete predicate: came home for Christmas.
7. Complete subject: Maudie; Complete predicate: was named after Mom's aunt Maud.
8. Complete subject: The Horton family; Complete predicate: lives in Nova Scotia.

Skill Builders

Study and Research

GEOGRAPHICAL RESEARCH. Using resources from your school or public library, including the Internet, research the regions of Nova Scotia. Where would you want to live if you moved to that province? Where in the province would you want to take a vacation? What type of jobs are available that are attractive to you? What annual events take place in Nova Scotia? What types of recreation are most common?

Language, Grammar, and Style

EXAMINING DIALECT. Look at the dialogue in "Be-ers and Doers." What things do characters in the story say that seem different from the everyday language that you use? These words and phrases are examples of the use of **dialect**, or a version of language spoken by the people of a particular place, time, or social group. List examples of dialect in the story. Then write examples of phrases with similar meanings—as you would say them or as you have heard them said—next to the examples from the story. Your phrases may use either formal or informal English.

EXAMPLE "Well! Oho! Just think o' that!"
"Oh my gosh! Can you believe it?"

Critical Thinking & Applied English

ANALYZING A QUIZ. Look back at "What Is Your Personality Type," the Insights personality quiz on page 39. How many points did you tally? What do you think this indicates about your personality? How does your point total reflect whether you are a be-er or a doer? Write the answer key for this quiz, stating what each of the following ranges of point totals means:

40-48 points; 26-38 points; 10-24 points; 0-8 points. If you have time, you may want to add questions to the quiz and modify the answer key to reflect the new point totals.

Language, Grammar, and Style

FINDING THE COMPLETE SUBJECT AND COMPLETE PREDICATE. All simple English sentences can be divided into two parts: the subject and the predicate. Read the Language Arts Survey 3.17, "Finding the Complete Subject and Complete Predicate in a Sentence." Then copy the sentences below onto your own paper. Underline the complete subject once and the complete predicate twice.

EXAMPLE Everyone ignored Mrs. Horton's advice.

1. Albert and Mr. Horton were be-ers, not do-ers.
2. Such an apple crop impressed everyone in the region.
3. All of the Hortons ate dinner at half past six.
4. Mrs. Horton wanted Albert to be more ambitious.
5. A cow, a beagle, and four cats live with Albert.
6. Adelaide and her family came home for Christmas.
7. Maudie was named after Mom's aunt Maud.
8. The Horton family lives in Nova Scotia.
9. The crops, the cows, and the apple trees needed tending.
10. The countryside around North Mountain is beautiful.

9. Complete subject: The crops, the cows, and the apple trees; Complete predicate: needed tending.
10. Complete subject: The countryside around North Mountain; Complete predicate: is beautiful.

Prereading

"Name Giveaway"

by Phil George

Reader's TOOLBOX

SPEAKER. The **speaker** is the voice that speaks, or narrates, a poem or story. The speaker may or may not be the author. Poets, like writers of fiction, can create characters in their poems. As you read this poem, think about the speaker. Is the speaker the voice of the poet or that of a created character? Find reasons for your answer.

IMAGE AND IMAGERY. An **image** is language that creates a literal or concrete representation of an object or experience. An image is also the vivid mental picture created in the reader's mind by that language. The combination of images within a poem is the poem's **imagery**. What image or images stand out in this poem? Why?

Graphic Organizer

Fill in the outer circles with the different points the speaker makes in "Name Giveaway." Then, summarize briefly the meaning of the poem.

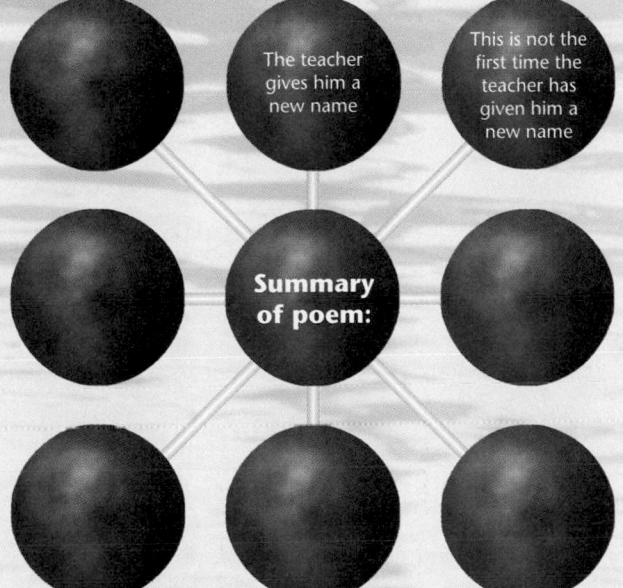

The teacher gives him a new name

This is not the first time the teacher has given him a new name

Summary of poem:

POEM

Reader's Journal

To what degree is your name part of who you are? Why?

Reader's Resource

• **HISTORY CONNECTION.** In the late 1800s and early 1900s, government agencies and churches set up boarding schools for Native American children. Government officials forced Native American parents to send their children to the boarding schools, where students were required to conform to the language, dress, and religion of white people.

• One of the customs Native Americans were forced to acquire was the use of English given names (first names) and surnames (last names). Even the English translations of Native Americans' traditional names were often forbidden. Instead, government or church officials within Native American communities were encouraged to assign everyone new names, such as James Peterson, Robert Jackson, and Mary James.

"NAME GIVEAWAY"   43

ADDITIONAL RESOURCES

UNIT 1 RESOURCE BOOK
• Selection Worksheet 1.3
• Selection Check Test 4.1.5
• Selection Test 4.1.6

ANSWERS TO READER'S TOOLBOX

GRAPHIC ORGANIZER. Students may include the following points from the poem in their graphic organizers:

The teacher didn't have a feast or a giveaway to mark the occasion of his new name; He does not know what "George" means; The teacher calls him "Phillip," too; The teacher must not be able to remember his real name, Two Swans Ascending From Still Waters.

Summary of poem: the speaker is upset and confused because the teacher has changed his name.

READER'S JOURNAL

You might also ask students the following questions: Have you ever asked your parents why they chose your name? Have you ever thought about giving yourself a different name? If you could pick any name for yourself, what would it be? Explain why you think this would be a better name. Write about these questions in your journal.

GOALS/OBJECTIVES

Studying this lesson will enable students to
• understand a brief poem that shows a person from one culture being forced to adapt to the culture of another
• relate to the experiences of a Native American boy in a government-run boarding school

• define and understand *speaker*
• define *image* and *imagery* and discover how images convey meaning to a reader

MOTIVATION
Students might be particularly interested in the Media Literacy activity on page 48. If students are not able to find actual references about famous people changing their names, encourage students to share anecdotal examples with the class.

READING PROFICIENCY
Some students might find it difficult to understand "Name Giveaway" because the events in the poem do not seem to happen in a clearly defined chronological order. Encourage students to complete the graphic organizer to help them understand the speaker's experiences, as well as the meaning of the poem.

ENGLISH LANGUAGE LEARNING
After they have read the poem, ask students if they have ever had an experience like the one described here. If so, how did they handle the situation? Have they had to modify their names at all? How did they feel about doing that?

SPECIAL NEEDS
Students will find it helpful to listen to the selection on audiocassette. Make sure students focus on the Guided Reading questions and the Recall questions in the Investigate, Inquire, and Imagine section.

ENRICHMENT
Suggest that students work in small groups to research Native American people. Students should choose a particular tribe or group from one particular area to study. In their research students might focus on language, daily life, art, or trade.

ANSWER TO GUIDED READING QUESTION

1. The speaker's name is Two Swans Ascending From Still Waters. According to the speaker, the teacher changes his name to something that's easier for her to remember.

Name Giveaway

Phil George

That teacher gave me a new name...again.
　　She never even had feasts or a giveaway!

Still I do not know what "George" means;
　　and now she calls me: "Phillip."

　　　　TWO SWANS <u>ASCENDING</u> FROM STILL WATERS
　　must be a name too hard to remember. ■

GUIDED READING
What is the speaker's name? Why does the teacher change the speaker's name?

words for everyday use
as • cend (ə send′) v., move upward, rise. *The child watched as her balloon <u>ascended</u> into the sky.* **ascending** *adj.*

VOCABULARY FROM THE SELECTION

ascend

Indian Blackboard Series, 1989. Jane Ash Poitras. Private Collection.

Respond *to the* SELECTION

How would you view a teacher who changed your name?

About *the* AUTHOR

Phil George is a Nez Percé-Tsimshian poet. His Native American name is Two Swans Ascending From Still Waters. He is the great-grandson of Chief Tawatoy. He loves grandmas, war-dancing, and frybread. George is a member of the Seven Drum religion.

art smart

Jane Ash Poitras is a Canadian artist and member of the Cree Nation. She was orphaned at age six and grew up in a foster home, separated from her Indigenous heritage. As an adult she researched her past, which led her to make artwork about the cultural disruption of Native people. The above work is part of her series of collages entitled "Indian Blackboard." What elements of this picture suggest alienation, confusion, and discomfort?

"NAME GIVEAWAY" **45**

SELECTION CHECK TEST 4.1.5 WITH ANSWERS

Checking Your Reading
SHORT ANSWER
1. Who has given the speaker his new name? **The teacher has given the speaker his new name.**
2. What did the speaker decide must be the reason for his being given a new name? **The speaker decides that he was given a new name because his original name must be too hard to remember.**
3. What did the speaker expect to happen in celebration of a new name? **The speaker expects feasting and a giveaway celebration.**
4. Why did the name "Phillip George" confuse the speaker? **He doesn't understand either name.**
5. What is the speaker's original name? **The speaker's original name is Two Swans Ascending From Still Water.**

Reader's Toolbox
MULTIPLE CHOICE
1. The speaker in "Name Giveaway" was most likely
   a. the poet
   b. a teacher
   c. a friend of the poet
   d. a classmate
2. Which of the following feelings or emotions was reflected in the poem?
   a. satisfaction
   b. terror
   c. confusion
   d. hope

RESPOND TO THE SELECTION

Encourage students to discuss how they feel about the ways in which Native American children were treated, as described in Reader's Resource on page 43.

ADDITIONAL QUESTIONS AND ACTIVITIES

EXAMPLE. What is the poet's name?
The poet's name is Phil George.

1. What did the teacher give the speaker again?
   The teacher gave the speaker a new name.
2. What did the teacher not do?
   The teacher did not have feasts or a giveaway.
3. What is the speaker's problem with the new names?
   The speaker does not know what the names mean.
4. What is the speaker's real name?
   The speaker's real name is Two Swans Ascending From Still Waters.

An Indian Boy's Story

ADDITIONAL QUESTIONS AND ACTIVITIES

ADDITIONAL QUESTIONS AND ACTIVITIES

Have students write a name (first and last) on an adhesive-backed name tag. Put all the finished name tags in a hat and have each student remove one. Ask the students to wear their new name tags for one day. The next day, students should discuss how they felt about wearing the name tag for a day. What did they like or not like about the name on the name tag?

LITERARY TECHNIQUE

SIMILE. A **simile** is a comparison using *like* or *as*. Ask students the following questions: What simile does the narrator of "An Indian Boy's Story" use to describe the children after their first bath at the school? In what way were the children like these things? Explain whether you found this simile to be effective. *Answers.* Students should point to the following: "Thereafter he [the new student] was released by the torturers, and could be seen sidling about the corridors like a lonely crab, silent, sulky, immaculately clean and most disconsolate." The children are like crabs in their careful sideways-way of moving after having been given a bath. Responses will vary.

CROSS-CURRICULAR CONNECTION

SOCIAL STUDIES. Inform students that throughout U.S. history, most American women have changed their surname (last name) to their husband's upon their marriage. For many American women today, this tradition is still an important one and they follow this practice. Other women feel, however, much like the speaker of this poem and the narrator of the related reading—that their given name is part of their identity—and they choose to keep their original last name. In some cultures, it is customary for the husband to take the wife's last name. Today some American couples also do this, or incorporate the wife's given surname as a part of a new, hyphenated surname. Today some couples even come up with a new

Ah-nen-la-de-ni

When I was thirteen a great change occurred, for the honey-tongued agent of a new Government contract Indian school appeared on the reservation, drumming up boys and girls for his institution. He made a great impression by going from house to house and describing, through an interpreter, all the glories and luxuries of the new place, the good food and teaching, the fine uniforms, the playground and its sports and toys.

All that a wild Indian boy had to do, according to the agent, was to attend this school for a year or two, and he was sure to emerge therefrom with all the knowledge and skill of the white man....

I had, up to this time, been leading a very happy life, helping with the planting, trapping, fishing, basket making and playing all the games of my tribe —which is famous at lacrosse—but the desire to travel and see new things and the hope of finding an easy way to much knowledge in the wonderful school outweighed my regard for my home and its joys, and so I was one of the twelve boys who in 1892 left our reservation to go to the Government contract school for Indians, situated in a large Pennsylvania city and known as the Institute.

Till I arrived at the school I had never heard that there were any other Indians in the country other than those of our reservation, and I did not know that our tribe was called Mohawk. My people called themselves "Ga-nien-ge-ha-ga," meaning "People of the Beacon Stone," and Indians generally they termed "On-give-hon-we," meaning "Real-men" or "Primitive People."

My surprise, therefore, was great when I found myself surrounded in the school yard by strange Indian boys belonging to tribes of which I had never heard, and when it was said that my people were only the "civilized Mohawks," I at first thought that "Mohawk" was a nickname and fought any boy who called me by it.

I had left home for the school with a great deal of hope, having said to my mother: "Do not worry. I shall soon return to you a better boy and with a good education!" Little did I dream that that was the last time I would ever see her kind face. She died two years later, and I was not allowed to go to her funeral.

The journey to Philadelphia had been very enjoyable and interesting. It was my first ride on the "great steel horse," as the Indians called the railway train, but my frame of mind changed as soon as my new home was reached.

The first thing that happened to me and to all other freshly caught young redskins when we arrived at the institution was a bath of a particularly disconcerting sort. We were used to baths of the swimming variety, for on the reservation we boys spent a good deal of our time in the water, but this first bath at the institution was different. For one thing, it was accompanied by plenty of soap, and for another thing, it was preceded by a haircut that is better described as a crop.

The little newcomer, thus cropped and delivered over to the untender mercies of larger Indian boys of tribes different from his own, who laughingly attacked his bare skin with very hot water and very hard scrubbing brushes, was likely to emerge from the encounter with a clean skin but perturbed mind. When, in addition, he was prevented from expressing his feelings in the only language he knew, what wonder if some rules of the school were broken.

After the astonishing bath the newcomer was freshly clothed from head to foot, while the raiment in which he came from the reservation was burned or buried.

Thereafter he was released by the torturers, and could be seen sidling about the corridors like a lonely crab, silent, sulky, immaculately clean and most disconsolate.

After my bath and reclothing and after having had my name taken down in the records I was assigned to a dormitory, and began my regular school life, much to my dissatisfaction. The recording of my name was accompanied by a change which, though it might seem trifling to the teachers, was very important to me. My name among my own people was "Ah-nen-la-de-ni," which in English means "Turning crowd" or "Turns the crowd," but my family had had the name "La France" bestowed on them by the French some generations before my birth, and at the institution my Indian name was discarded, and I was informed that I was henceforth to be known as Daniel La France.

It made me feel as if I had lost myself. I had been proud of myself and my possibilities as "Turns the crowd," for in spite of their civilized surroundings the Indians of our reservation in my time still looked back to the old warlike days when the Mohawks were great people, but Daniel La France was to me a stranger and a nobody with no possibilities. It seemed as if my prospect of a chiefship had vanished. I was very homesick for a long time.

ABOUT THE RELATED READING

Ah-nen-la-de-ni published in 1903 the story of his youth. This selection is an excerpt. Ah-nen-la-de-ni was born in 1879. His father, a medicine man—or doctor of traditional Native medicine—took the family frequently on trips away from their reservation home in New York. They traveled along the United States-Canada border, where Ah-nen-la-de-ni's father sold his medicines and treatments. After he finished school, Ah-nen-la-de-ni became a nurse.

CROSS-CURRICULAR CONNECTION (CONT.)

surname upon their marriage, perhaps an old family name important to them both. Encourage students to discuss their reactions to the choices people make with their married names. What do students envision themselves doing about their married name sometime in the future?

Investigate, Inquire, and Imagine

Recall: GATHERING FACTS

1a. In the poem, "Name Giveaway," what has the teacher done again?

2a. What is the speaker's original name?

→ **Interpret:** FINDING MEANING

1b. How does the speaker feel about what the teacher has done?

2b. How might the speaker's name reflect his identity and personality?

Analyze: TAKING THINGS APART

3a. What evidence can you find that demonstrates the teacher's understanding of and feelings toward the speaker and his culture?

→ **Synthesize:** BRINGING THINGS TOGETHER

3b. Why does the teacher act in this way? Do you agree with the reason the speaker offers? Why or why not? What might other possible reasons be?

Perspective: LOOKING AT OTHER VIEWS → **Empathy:** SEEING FROM INSIDE

4a. The speaker in this poem reacts after a teacher changes his name. Is the speaker's reaction understandable? Why or why not?

4b. Imagining yourself in the speaker's place, what might your next step be? Would you confront the teacher? Would you live with the new names? Explain your answer.

Evaluate: MAKING JUDGMENTS → **Extend:** CONNECTING IDEAS

5a. How well does "Name Giveaway" communicate the speaker's ideas and frustrations?

5b. Compare Ah-nen-la-de-ni's story in the Related Reading to that of the speaker of the poem. What thoughts and emotions do you think the young men shared?

Understanding Literature

SPEAKER. The **speaker** is the voice that speaks, or narrates, a poem or story. What can you learn about the speaker's emotions and thoughts by looking at his words and how he presents them? What tools does the speaker use for emphasis?

IMAGE. An **image** is language that describes something that can be seen, heard, touched, tasted, or smelled. The combination of images within a poem is the poem's *imagery*. Imagery conveys meaning to the reader. Images can also arouse emotions, such as sadness, frustration, anger, joy, or peace. What individual images can you find in the poem? What does the combination of images within the poem convey to you? What emotions are aroused by the poem's imagery?

ANSWERS TO UNDERSTANDING LITERATURE

Speaker. The speaker seems frustrated and angry. Evidence to support this claim includes the use of an exclamation point, the use of capital letters for his own name, and putting the new names in quotation marks. He also uses phrases such as "That teacher," "again," and "never even."

Image. The name Two Swans Ascending From Still Waters is an image in itself. The plainness of the rest of the poem suggests a sterile, staid, disdainful environment. Students may say that the poem evokes the emotions that the speaker feels. The speaker's name may evoke a sense of beauty, surprise, and wonder.

ANSWERS TO INVESTIGATE, INQUIRE, IMAGINE

RECALL

1a. The teacher has changed the speaker's name again.

2a. The speaker's original name is Two Swans Ascending From Still Waters.

INTERPRET

1b. The speaker is upset by what the teacher has done.

2b. Students may say that the speaker is a quiet and calm person, a person who respects beauty, or a person who respects nature.

ANALYZE

3a. Responses should include some of the following: the teacher did not have feasts or a giveaway for the naming, which would be expected in the speaker's culture; the teacher did not tell the speaker what George and Phillip mean or why she was using those names; the teacher does not understand the importance of the speaker's real name; the teacher shows no respect for the speaker's name.

SYNTHESIZE

3b. Students may say that the teacher gives the speaker new names out of convenience for herself, because she is uncomfortable with the speaker's culture, or because she is trying to "Americanize" the speaker. Students may say that the speaker's reason is plausible but probably not the only reason.

PERSPECTIVE

4a. Students may say that the speaker's reaction is understandable because a person's name is a part of his or her identity.

EMPATHY

4b. Students may say that they would tell the teacher that they prefer their original name, that they would do nothing, that they'd quit school, or that they would refuse to acknowledge the new names. They may say that they would confront the teacher to solve the problem or that they would not confront the teacher, believing that doing so would be futile.

EVALUATE

5a. *Responses will vary.*

EXTEND

5b. Responses will vary, but students might say that both young men were angry that their names were changed without their consent. Students might also say that both young men felt alienated and uncomfortable in the white schools.

Refer students to the Language Arts Survey 5.25, "Using the Internet," if they need help or additional instruction in using the Internet. You may wish to bring students to your school library or computer center to guide students through this research activity, showing them how to find the information they need. You might also ask them to read the Language Arts Survey 5.34, "How to Understand Internet Sites." Remind them that not every site they see on the Internet is a reliable source of information, but that such sources do exist. Give them some tips on distinguishing between the two. For example sites affiliated with a university or reliable organization may be more likely to have reliable information than individuals' Internet sites.

COLLABORATIVE LEARNING
Students might discuss in small groups how they feel about the meanings of their own names and whether or not the meanings fit their personalities. Many students, particularly if they no longer speak the language of their ancestors, may be surprised by the meaning of their name.

MEDIA LITERACY
Students might also discuss whether they prefer the celebrity's original name or his or her professional one. If students were to become involved in sports or entertainment, would they change their names? Why, or why not?

Writer's Journal

1. Write a **letter** from the speaker to the teacher, explaining why the name Two Swans Ascending From Still Waters is important to you.

2. Write a **memo** from a government official to teachers at boarding school for Native Americans. Stress in the memo the importance of introducing and using practical names with students.

3. For one of your friends, write a **name** that—like Two Swans Ascending From Still Waters—creates a vivid image and reflects the friend's personality.

Skill Builders

Study and Research

LOOKING AT HISTORY. Research Native American boarding schools of the late 1800s and early 1900s, looking for reasons behind the U.S. government's desire to change the names of Indian students. How did officials defend the campaign to change names? Did reasons vary from one official to the next? Did any reasons seem valid? Why or why not? Using the Internet, try the following resources, and others you may find, for information:
Texts by and about Native Americans from the Modern English Collection, Electronic Text Center, University of Virginia Library, at
http://etext.lib.virginia.edu/subjects/natam.html
Bureau of Indian Affairs, U.S. Department of the Interior, at
http://www.doi.gov/bureau-indian-affairs.html
Native American History Archive, Institute for Learning Technologies, Columbia University, at
http://www.ilt.columbia.edu/k12/naha/index.html

Collaborative Learning

RESEARCHING NAMES. Form a small group to research names. Together, list at least ten given, or first, names that interest members of the group. You may want to research your own names. Try to choose a variety of names—from different time periods, both common and uncommon, and from other parts of the world. Examples you may want to try include Sojourner, Mortimer, Emilio, Prudence, Dominique, Hanako, Ashanti, and Dolores. Using books and documents from the school library, the public library, or the Internet, find the meanings of the names on your list. After your group has finished, share your findings with your class.

Media Literacy

POP CULTURE. Many well-known figures in sports, entertainment, politics, and other areas have changed their names or use stage names. Using magazines such as *People*, *Biography*, *Sports Illustrated*, and *Entertainment Weekly*, look for articles that feature celebrities. How many references can you find about famous people who have modified or changed their names? What reasons do they give for doing so?

Prereading

"The Fan Club"

by Rona Maynard

Reader's TOOLBOX

IRONY. Irony is a difference between appearance and reality. A person saying one thing and doing the opposite is an example of an ironic situation. A person believing one thing will happen when something different is about to occur is another example. Look for examples of irony as you read the story.

THEME. A **theme** is a central idea in a literary work. As you read "The Fan Club," try to find the central ideas in the story. What important ideas does the story convey?

Graphic *Organizer*

Create a flow chart to keep track of the actions and events in "The Fan Club." At the end of the chart describe what you believe to be the main idea of the story.

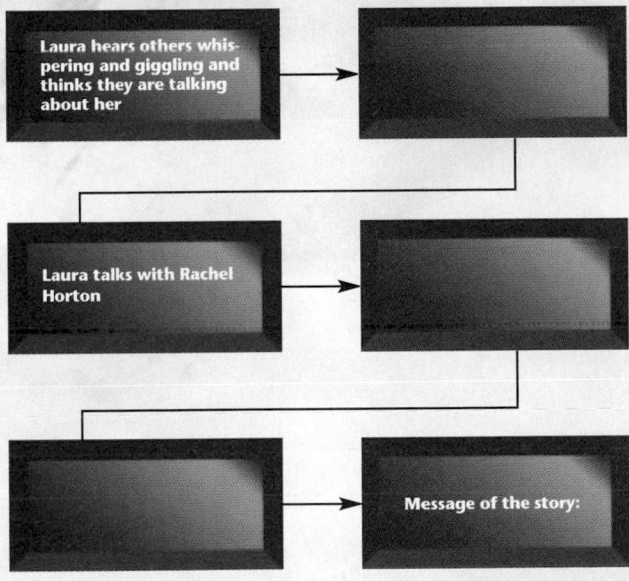

Laura hears others whispering and giggling and thinks they are talking about her

Laura talks with Rachel Horton

Message of the story:

Reader's Resource

- **SOCIAL STUDIES CONNECTION.** Social groups often cause feelings of peer pressure among individuals seeking or wanting to maintain acceptance in the group. When a person is highly motivated to belong to a group, he or she is more likely to conform to the group's standards of conduct. An individual's personality also may change in different social settings. A person might behave loudly and obnoxiously with one group but act quietly and timidly with another, for example.

- Intolerance, prejudice, and discrimination are words that describe hostile feelings and actions toward a person or persons based on unjustified opinions. What are some reasons people might act in this way? What reactions may occur among people who experience the effects of intolerance, prejudice, and discrimination?

Reader's Journal

What is more important belonging to a group or standing by your beliefs?

ADDITIONAL RESOURCES

UNIT 1 RESOURCE BOOK
- Selection Worksheet 1.4
- Selection Check Test 4.1.7
- Selection Test 4.1.8
- Language, Grammar, and Style Resource 3.18, 3.19
- Speaking and Listening Resource 4.18
- Study and Research Resource 5.29

ANSWERS TO READER'S TOOLBOX

GRAPHIC ORGANIZER. Responses may vary, but students might fill out their charts in the following way:

Laura hears whispering and giggling→Laura assumes people are laughing at her→Laura and Rachel chat→Rachel invites her to her home→Laura accepts reluctantly→Laura gives her speech about civil rights→Rachel gives a speech about shells→people laugh at Rachel→Laura breaks down and joins the nastiness.

Message or lesson of the story: It is easy to talk about civil rights in the abstract, but shunning a group to defend such rights takes courage and a strong character.

READER'S JOURNAL

You might also ask students the following questions: How important is it to you to belong to a group? Do you ever feel that there is too much pressure to belong to certain groups? To what groups do you belong? What do you think your life would be like if you did not belong to any group or groups?

CROSS-CURRICULAR ACTIVITIES

SCIENCE. In Reader's Resource on page 49, ideas about social groups are presented. Such ideas are the focus of the science of social psychology. Social psychologists examine social groups and how a person's place within a social group affects the way in which he or she perceives others. Social psychologists have conducted experiments that have given information about people's behavior in groups. One important factor in group behavior is called group cohesiveness. Group cohesiveness is the degree to which the members of a group are attracted to that group. Members of a cohesive group have higher morale and enthusiasm for the group and the group's activities. While group cohesiveness can be positive, it can also have negative consequences. When a group's standards involve making others feel inferior, as they do in "The Fan Club," group cohesiveness can encourage the members of a group to behave in intolerant, or unaccepting, ways.

GOALS/OBJECTIVES

Studying this lesson will enable students to
- appreciate a story about intolerance and group thinking
- explore the ideas of prejudice, peer pressure, and discrimination
- enjoy a poem about positive attitudes toward society
- identify the theme of a story
- define *irony* and recognize irony in a story

The FAN Club

Rona Maynard

*I*t was Monday again. It was Monday and the day was damp and cold. Rain splattered the cover of *Algebra I* as Laura heaved her books higher on her arm and sighed. School was such a bore.

School. It loomed before her now, massive and dark against the sky. In a few minutes, she would have to face them again—Diane Goddard with her sleek blond hair and Terri Pierce in her candy-pink sweater. And Carol and Steve and Bill and Nancy. . . . There were so many of them, so exclusive as they stood in their tight little groups laughing and joking.

◄ *Braids*, 1917. Amedeo Modigliani. Private Collection.

VOCABULARY FROM THE SELECTION

billow	jostle
cynical	malicious
gaudy	submerge
gesture	throng
irrational	

INDIVIDUAL LEARNING STRATEGIES

MOTIVATION
Encourage students to participate in the Rewriting Dialogue activity on page 55 of the Teacher's Edition. In addition to the scene featured in that activity, students could select any part of the story to rewrite and enact.

READING PROFICIENCY
Students will benefit from completing the graphic organizer on page 49 of the Pupil's Edition as they read. Students should make a chart like the one featured in the text in their journals and fill it in with actions and events from the story. After reading the story, students can meet in small groups to share what they consider to be the message or lesson of the story.

ENGLISH LANGUAGE LEARNING
Point out the following vocabulary words and expressions.
[use vocabulary and pronunciations from page 155 of old ATE (copy attached)]

SPECIAL NEEDS
Students will find it helpful to listen to the selection on audiocassette. Make sure students focus on the Guided Reading questions and the Recall questions in the Investigate, Inquire, and Imagine section.

ENRICHMENT
Share with students the information about social psychology found in the Cross-Curricular Connections box on page 49 of the Teacher's Edition. Ask students to conduct their own human observation experiment. They should go someplace where there is a crowd or more than a few people (school hallway, park, supermarket, or library). Students should simply

INDIVIDUAL LEARNING STRATEGIES (CONT.)

observe and take notes about people's behavior. Do they notice anything interesting? How do people behave with people they know? How do people behave with strangers? Can students make any generalizations based on their observations? Students should share their notes with the rest of the class.

1. Laura thinks that the group is
   whispering about her and staring
   at her.
2. Laura thinks that the group is
   exclusive, cold, and unkind. She
   also thinks that everyone in the
   group is alike.
3. Laura says she's glad that Rachel
   likes her poem.

CROSS-CURRICULAR ACTIVITIES

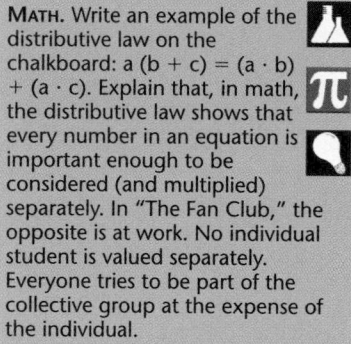

SCIENCE AND HEALTH. Ask students to find books and articles in the library that address issues of self-esteem in young people. How might Rachel's school experience affect her years from now? Ask them also to consider how the treatment of Rachel by her classmates reflects on the self-esteem of the victimizers.

MATH. Write an example of the distributive law on the chalkboard: $a(b + c) = (a \cdot b) + (a \cdot c)$. Explain that, in math, the distributive law shows that every number in an equation is important enough to be considered (and multiplied) separately. In "The Fan Club," the opposite is at work. No individual student is valued separately. Everyone tries to be part of the collective group at the expense of the individual.

Why were they so cold and unkind? Was it because her long stringy hair hung in her eyes instead of dipping in graceful curls? Was it because she wrote poetry in algebra class and got A's in Latin without really trying? Shivering, Laura remembered how they would sit at the back of English class, passing notes and whispering. She thought of their identical brown loafers, their plastic purses, their hostile stares as they passed her in the corridors. She didn't care. They were clods, the whole lot of them.

> **GUIDED READING**
>
> Laura thinks this group of students is whispering about and staring at whom?

She shoved her way through the door and there they were. They thronged the hall, streamed in and out of doors, clustered under red and yellow posters advertising the latest dance. Mohair sweaters, madras shirts, pea-green raincoats. They were all alike, all the same. And in the center of the group, as usual, Diane Goddard was saying, "It'll

> **GUIDED READING**
>
> What does Laura think about the group?

be a riot! I just can't wait to see her face when she finds out."

Laura flushed painfully. Were they talking about her?

"What a scream! Can't wait to hear what she says!"

Silently she hurried past and submerged herself in the stream of students heading for the lockers. It was then that she saw Rachel Horton—alone as always, her too-long skirt billowing over the white, heavy columns of her legs, her freckled face ringed with shapeless black curls. She called herself Horton, but everyone knew her father was Jacob Hortensky, the tailor. He ran that greasy little shop where you could always

smell the cooked cabbage from the back rooms where the family lived.

"Oh, Laura!" Rachel was calling her. Laura turned, startled.

"Hi, Rachel."

"Laura, did you watch *World of Nature* last night? On Channel 11?"

"No—no, I didn't." Laura hesitated. "I almost never watch that kind of program."

"Well, gee, you missed something— last night, I mean. It was a real good show. Laura, it showed this fly being born!" Rachel was smiling now; she waved her hands as she talked.

"First the feelers and then the wings. And they're sort of wet at first, the wings are. Gosh, it was a good show."

"I bet it was." Laura tried to sound interested. She turned to go, but Rachel still stood there, her mouth half open, her pale, moon-like face strangely urgent. It was as if an invisible hand tugged at Laura's sleeve.

"And Laura," Rachel continued, "that was an awful good poem you read yesterday in English."

Laura remembered how Terri and Diane had laughed and whispered. "You really think so? Well, thanks, Rachel. I mean, not too many people care about poetry."

"Yours was real nice though. I wish I could write like you. I always like those things you write."

Laura blushed. "I'm glad you do."

> **GUIDED READING**
>
> What does Laura say about Rachel's compliment?

"Laura, can you come over sometime after school? Tomorrow maybe? It's not very far and you can stay for dinner. I told my parents all about you!"

Laura thought of the narrow, dirty street and the tattered awning in front of the tailor

---

words for everyday use

throng (thrôŋ) *v.*, crowd; press upon in large numbers. *Fans throng the stadium on game days.*

sub • merge (sub mərj´) *v.*, to put or go into or under, as in water. *Ian took a deep breath and submerged to the sandy lake bottom.*

bil • low (bil´ō) *v.*, surge; swell. *The drying sheets billow in the wind.* **billowing** *adj.*

shop. An awful district, the kids said. But she couldn't let that matter. "Okay," she said. And then, faking enthusiasm, "I'd be glad to come."

She turned into the algebra room, sniffing at the smell of chalk and dusty erasers. In the back row, she saw the "in" group, laughing and joking and whispering.

"What a panic!"

"Here, you make the first one."

Diane and Terri had their heads together over a lot of little cards. You could see they were cooking up something.

Fumbling through the pages of her book, she tried to memorize the theorems[1] she hadn't looked at the night before. The laughter at the back of the room rang in her ears. Also those smiles—those heartless smiles. . . .

A bell buzzed in the corridors; students scrambled to their places. "We will now have the national anthem," said the voice on the loudspeaker. Laura shifted her weight from one foot to the other. It was so false, so pointless. How could they sing of the land of the free, when there was still discrimination. Smothered laughter behind her. Were they all looking at her?

And then it was over. Slumping in her seat, she shuffled through last week's half-finished homework papers and scribbled flowers in the margins.

In the back row, she saw the "in" group, laughing and joking and whispering.

GUIDED READING
How does Laura respond to Rachel's invitation?

GUIDED READING
What does Laura think about the national anthem? What does she hear?

"Now this one is just a direct application of the equation." The voice was hollow, distant, an echo beyond the sound of rustling papers and hushed whispers. Laura sketched a guitar on the cover of her notebook. Someday she would live in the Village[2] and there would be no more algebra classes and people would accept her.

She turned towards the back row. Diane was passing around one of her cards. Terri leaned over, smiling. "Hey, can I do the next one?"

". . . by using the distributive law." Would the class never end? Math was so dull, so painfully dull. They made you multiply and cancel and factor, multiply, cancel, and factor. Just like a machine. The steel sound of the bell shattered the silence. Scraping chairs, cries of "Hey, wait!" The crowd moved into the hallway now, a thronging, jostling mass.

Alone in the tide of faces, Laura felt someone nudge her. It was Ellen. "Hey, how's that for a smart outfit?" She pointed to the other side of the hall.

GUIDED READING
How do the other students behave toward Rachel?

The gaudy flowers of Rachel Horton's blouse stood out among the fluffy sweaters and pleated skirts. What a lumpish, awkward creature Rachel was. Did she have to dress like that? Her socks had fallen untidily around her heavy ankles, and her slip showed a raggedy edge of lace. As she moved into the English room, shoelaces trailing, her books tumbled to the floor.

1. **theorem.** Mathematical formula
2. **Village.** Greenwich Village, a section of New York City

words for everyday use

jos • tle (jäs´l) v., push roughly. *The students jostle one another as they board the bus.* **jostling** adj.
gau • dy (gôd´ē) adj., bright and showy, but lacking in good taste. *Everyone noticed Aunt Edna's gaudy hat pin.*

ANSWERS TO GUIDED READING QUESTIONS

1. Laura fakes enthusiasm about Rachel's invitation.
2. Laura thinks it is false and pointless to sing of the land of the free when there is still discrimination. She hears smothered laughter behind her.
3. The other students make fun of Rachel and her clothing.

ADDITIONAL QUESTIONS AND ACTIVITIES

Ask students to answer the following questions:
- Why does Laura not seem excited to have Rachel for a friend?
- How might Rachel feel if she knew what Laura was thinking when Rachel invited her to her house?

Answers. Responses will vary. Students might say that Laura is so caught up in the idea that Rachel is unpopular that she does not feel comfortable with her as a friend. She is afraid of being teased.

Students might recognize that Rachel would probably feel hurt and disappointed if she knew what Laura was thinking.

ANSWER TO GUIDED READING QUESTION

1. Laura says that lots of people sit back and wait for someone else to take care of discrimination and violence.

ADDITIONAL QUESTIONS AND ACTIVITIES

Ask students to discuss the ideas expressed in Laura's speech. Do they agree with them? What is the best point that she makes? Do they think that Laura will hold true to these ideals?

ART SMART

Encourage students to observe the girl in the photograph on page 54. They should then write about what the girl seems to be thinking and feeling. What nonverbal cues let students know she is feeling this way?

"Isn't that something?" Terri said. Little waves of mocking laughter swept through the crowd.

The bell rang; the laughter died away. As they hurried to their seats, Diane and Terri exchanged last-minute whispers. "Make one for Steve. He wants one too!"

Then Miss Merrill pushed aside the book she was holding, folded her hands, and beamed. "All right, people, that will be enough. Now, today we have our speeches. Laura, would you begin please?"

So it was her turn. Her throat tightened as she thought of Diane and Carol and Steve grinning and waiting for her to stumble. Perhaps if she was careful they'd never know she hadn't thought out everything beforehand. Careful, careful, she thought. Look confident.

"Let's try to be prompt." Miss Merrill tapped the cover of her book with her fountain pen.

Laura pushed her way to the front of the class. Before her, the room was large and still. Twenty-five round, blurred faces stared blankly. Was that Diane's laughter? She folded her hands and looked at the wall, strangely distant now, its brown paint cracked and peeling. A dusty portrait of Robert Frost, a card with the seven rules for better paragraphs, last year's calendar, and the steady, hollow ticking of the clock.

Laura cleared her throat. "Well," she began, "my speech is on civil rights." A chorus of snickers rose from the back of the room.

"Most people," Laura continued, "most people don't care enough about others. Here in New England, they think they're pretty far removed from discrimination and violence. Lots of people sit back and fold their hands and wait for

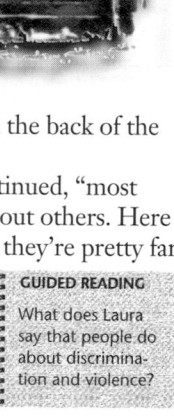

GUIDED READING

What does Laura say that people do about discrimination and violence?

somebody else to do the work. But I think we're all responsible for people that haven't had some of the advantages. . . ."

Diane was giggling and <u>gesturing</u> at Steve Becker. All she ever thought about was parties and dates—and such dates! Always the president of the student council or the captain of the football team.

"A lot of people think that race prejudice is limited to the South. But most of us are prejudiced—whether we know it or not. It's not just that we don't give other people a chance; we don't give ourselves a chance either. We form narrow opinions and then we don't see the truth. We keep right on believing that we're open-minded liberals when all we're doing is deceiving ourselves."

How many of them cared about truth? Laura looked past the rows of blank, empty faces, past the bored stares and <u>cynical</u> grins.

> **GUIDED READING**
> What does Laura think about during her speech?

"But I think we should try to forget our prejudices. We must realize now that we've done too little for too long. We must accept the fact that one person's misfortune is everyone's responsibility. We must defend the natural dignity of people—a dignity that thousands are denied."

> **GUIDED READING**
> What does Laura say about responsibility? about dignity?

None of them knew what it was like to be unwanted, unaccepted. Did Steve know? Did Diane?

> **GUIDED READING**
> What does Laura wonder about the "in" group?

"Most of us are proud to say that we live in a free country. But is this really true? Can we call the United States a free country when millions of people face prejudice and discrimination? As long as one person is forbidden to share the basic rights we take for granted, as long as we are still the victims of <u>irrational</u> hatreds, there can be no freedom. Only when every American learns to respect the dignity of every other American can we truly call our country free."

The class was silent. "Very nice, Laura." Things remained quiet as other students droned through their speeches. Then Miss Merrill looked briskly around the room. "Now, Rachel, I believe you're next."

There was a ripple of dry, humorless laughter—almost, Laura thought, like the sound of a rattlesnake. Rachel stood before the class now, her face red, her heavy arms piled with boxes.

Diane Goddard tossed back her head and winked at Steve.

"Well, well, don't we have lots of things to show," said Miss Merrill. "But aren't you going to put those boxes down, Rachel? No, no, not there!"

"Man, that kid's dumb," Steve muttered, and his voice could be clearly heard all through the room.

With a brisk rattle, Miss Merrill's pen tapped the desk for silence.

Rachel's slow smile twitched at the corners. She looked frightened. There was a crash and a clatter as the tower of boxes slid to the floor. Now everyone was giggling.

"Hurry and pick them up," said Miss Merrill sharply.

Rachel crouched on her knees and began very clumsily to gather her scattered treasures. Papers and boxes lay all about, and some of the boxes had broken open, spilling their contents in wild confusion. No one

---

words for everyday use

ges • ture (jes´chər) v., express or emphasize ideas and emotions with physical movement. *The politician <u>gestures</u> wildly with his arms to make a point.*

cy • ni • cal (sin´i kəl) adj., sarcastic; sneering. *The mean boy wore a <u>cynical</u> smirk.*

ir • ra • tion • al (ir rash´ə nəl) adj., lacking reason; absurd. *Because Emma had never tried squash, her dislike of the vegetable was <u>irrational</u>.*

ANSWERS TO GUIDED READING QUESTIONS

1. Laura wonders how many of her classmates care about truth.
2. Laura says that one person's misfortune is everyone's responsibility, and that the natural dignity of people must be defended.
3. Laura wonders if anyone in the popular group knows what it is like to be unwanted or unaccepted.

CROSS-CURRICULAR ACTIVITIES

REWRITING DIALOGUE. Read the following line from the story: "With a brisk rattle, Miss Merrill's pen tapped the desk for silence." Then ask students to imagine that that line is eliminated from the story. Have them work in groups of four to brainstorm how Miss Merrill could have reacted to the situation in a way that would show sensitivity and respect for Rachel. Students should then write dialogue that shows how Miss Merrill's actions change the outcome of the story for Diane, Laura, and Rachel. Have student groups act out their scenes. Discuss in class whether this is a problem that the students should have worked out themselves or whether teacher involvement would have made a difference.

ADDITIONAL QUESTIONS AND ACTIVITIES

EXAMPLE. Where is Laura going on Monday morning? **Laura is going to school.**

1. Which people does Laura dread seeing? **She dreads seeing the popular kids in her class.**
2. About whom does Laura think the popular kids whisper? **Laura thinks the popular kids whisper about her.**
3. Who invites Laura to come to her house after school? **Rachel invites Laura to her house.**
4. What is the subject of Laura's speech? **Civil rights is the subject of Laura's speech.**
5. What does the class do when Rachel gives her speech? **The class laughs and makes fun of Rachel.**

1. Laura realizes that the whispering all morning has been about Rachel, not herself.

SELECTION CHECK TEST 4.1.7 WITH ANSWERS

Checking Your Reading

1. Against whom does Laura think the members of the "in" group are plotting when she hears them giggling in the hallway at school? **Laura thinks the "in" group are plotting against her.**
2. Who invites Laura to come over after school? **Rachel invites Laura to come over to her house after school.**
3. What is the subject of Laura's speech? **Laura's speech is about civil rights.**
4. What is Miss Merrill's reaction to Rachel's speech? **Miss Merrill is impatient and cross with Rachel.**
5. What is written on the card that Diane gives to Laura? **"Hortensky Fan Club" is written on the card.**

Vocabulary in Context

Fill in each blank below with the most appropriate vocabulary word from "The Fan Club." You may have to change the tense of the word.

malicious throng gaudy jostling
cynical billow irrational

1. My grandmother's taste has always included loud, bright colors and _____ jewelry. **gaudy**
2. Rebecca held her daughter's hand tightly as they maneuvered through the _____ crowd of holiday shoppers. **jostling**
3. Pointing to the damage, Mr. Nichols said, "That wasn't just a prank. **That was _____."** **malicious**
4. Before the parade, the beauty queen sewed tiny weights into her hem so her skirt would not _____ in the wind. **billow**
5. The singer bounded onstage to the delight of the screaming _____. **throng**

Reader's Toolbox

1. Often in a story, a character must decide whether to do what she knows is right or to follow the crowd. How does the reader know that Laura chooses to follow the crowd?
   a. she goes to Rachel's house for dinner
   b. she accepts Terri's party invitation

---

went to help. At last she scrambled to her feet and began fumbling with her notes.

"My—my speech is on shells."

A cold and stony silence had settled upon the room.

"Lots of people collect shells, because they're kind of pretty—sort of, and you just find them on the beach."

"Well, whaddaya know!" It was Steve's voice, softer this time, but all mock amazement. Laura jabbed her notebook with her pencil. Why were they so cruel, so thoughtless? Why did they have to laugh?

"This one," Rachel was saying as she opened one of the boxes, "it's one of the best." Off came the layers of paper and there, at last, smooth and pearly and shimmering, was the shell. Rachel turned it over lovingly in her hands. White, fluted sides, like the closecurled petals of a flower; a scrolled coral back. Laura held her breath. It was beautiful. At the back of the room snickers had begun again.

"Bet she got it at Woolworth's," somebody whispered.

"Or in a trash dump." That was Diane. Rachel pretended not to hear, but her face was getting very red and Laura could see she was flustered.

"Here's another that's kind of pretty. I found it last summer at Ogunquit."[3] In her outstretched hand there was a small, drab, brownish object. A common snail shell. "It's called a . . . It's called. . . ."

Rachel rustled through her notes. "I—I can't find it. But it was here. It was in here somewhere. I know it was." Her broad face had turned bright pink again. "Just can't find it. . . ." Miss Merrill stood up and strode toward her. "Rachel," she said sharply, "we are supposed to be prepared when we make a

speech. Now, I'm sure you remember those rules on page twenty-one. I expect you to know these things. Next time you must have your material organized."

The bell sounded, ending the period. Miss Merrill collected her books.

Then, suddenly, chairs were shoved aside at the back of the room and there was the sound of many voices whispering. They were standing now, whole rows of them, their faces grinning with delight. Choked giggles, shuffling feet—and then applause—wild, sarcastic, <u>malicious</u> applause. That was when Laura saw that they were all wearing little white cards with a fat, frizzy-haired figure drawn on the front. What did it mean? She looked more closely. "HORTENSKY FAN CLUB," said the bright-red letters.

So that was what the whispering had been about all morning. She'd been wrong. They weren't out to get her after all. It was only Rachel.

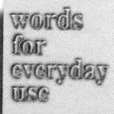

GUIDED READING
What does Laura realize?

Diane was nudging her and holding out a card. "Hey, Laura, here's one for you to wear."

For a moment Laura stared at the card. She looked from Rachel's red, frightened face to Diane's mocking smile, and she heard the pulsing, frenzied rhythm of the claps and the stamping, faster and faster. Her hands trembled as she picked up the card and pinned it to her sweater. And as she turned, she saw Rachel's stricken look.

"She's a creep, isn't she?" Diane's voice was soft and intimate.

And Laura began to clap. ∎

---

3. **Ogunquit.** Resort town in southern Maine

---

words for everyday use

ma • li • cious (mə li′ shəs) *adj.*, marked by a desire to cause pain or distress. *The bombing was a <u>malicious</u> attack.*

SELECTION CHECK TEST 4.1.7 WITH ANSWERS (CONT.)

c. he gives her homework answers to Steve
d. she pins on the card given to her by Diane
2. When a character says or seems to believe one thing, but does the opposite, this is an example of
a. sarcasm b. plot **c. irony** d. metaphor
3. A *theme* in a literary work is
a. the emotional tone   b. another word for its plot
c. a central idea that the work conveys
d. a subtitle

4. When Laura stands up to give her speech, she feels
a. confident **b. nervous** c. angry d. bored
5. "The Fan Club" is told from what point of view?
a. first person b. second person **c. third person limited** d. third person all knowing

Respond *to the* SELECTION

If you were Rachel, how would you have reacted to the students in the last scene of the story?

RELATED READING

TWO people
I Want to Be Like

Eve Merriam

That man
    stuck in traffic
        not pounding his fists against the steering wheel
          not trying to shift to the next lane
          just
            using the time
              for a slow steady grin
              of remembering
              all the good unstuck times

        and that woman
          clerking in the supermarket
        at rush hour
          bagging bottles and cartons and boxes and jars and
         cans
          punching it all out
         slapping it all along
          and leveling a smile
         at everyone in the line.

      I wish they were married to each other.

      Maybe it's better they're not,
      so they can pass their sweet harmony
      around.

ABOUT THE RELATED READING:
Eve Merriam was an award-winning poet and playwright who wrote more than thirty books. Among her poetry collections are *Family Circle, It Doesn't Have to Rhyme,* and *If Only I Could Tell You,* from which "Two People I Want to Be Like" was selected.

"THE FAN CLUB" **57**

RECALL

1a. Laura writes poetry in algebra class and gets *A*'s in Latin without really trying.

2a. Rachel Horton's real name is Rachel Hortensky.

3a. Laura's speech is about civil rights.

4a. Laura realizes that the whispering all morning had been about Rachel, not herself.

INTERPRET

1b. Laura fears that the ease with which she accomplishes her work and achieves good grades is looked upon with disdain by the popular crowd. She may fear being labeled as a brain, a bookworm, or a teacher's pet.

2b. Rachel may have changed her last name so that no one would think she is Polish (Polish names often end in -sky or -ski). Discrimination against Polish immigrants was common earlier in the twentieth century.

3b. Laura's speech reveals that she feels strongly about civil rights. She thinks that it is wrong to discriminate against people or to hold prejudices against anyone.

4b. Laura feels relieved when she realizes that the popular group has been plotting against Rachel and not against herself.

ANALYZE

5a. Responses will vary. About Laura's feelings toward Rachel, students should include that Laura has mixed feelings. Although she does not necessarily dislike Rachel, she feels that associating with Rachel will make her a target for the laughs and whispers of the popular crowd. Regarding the popular students, students should recognize that Laura thinks they are cold and unkind, that they are clods, that they are all alike, that they are shallow, and that they are cruel, thoughtless, and malicious. In her speech, Laura reflects on society when she says that people don't care enough about others, that people form narrow opinions about others, and that everyone needs to work to rid society of discrimination and prejudice.

SYNTHESIZE

5b. Although Laura's speech reveals her convictions about civil rights and the evils of discrimination and prejudice, her actions reveal different attitudes. Laura does not

Investigate, Inquire, and Imagine

Recall: GATHERING FACTS

1a. What does Laura do in algebra class? What does she do in Latin class?

2a. What is Rachel Horton's real name?

3a. What is the subject of Laura's speech?

4a. What does Laura realize when she sees the writing on one of the white cards?

Interpret: FINDING MEANING

1b. Why might this behavior cause other students to act coldly toward her?

2b. What reasons might Rachel have for changing her last name at school?

3b. What does Laura's speech reveal about her character? How does she later contradict herself?

4b. How does Laura feel when she realizes what the group had been plotting? Why does she join the "fan club"?

Analyze: TAKING THINGS APART

5a. Examining Laura's thoughts, words, and actions, identify her feelings toward the people around her. Categorize your findings. How does she feel about Rachel? What are her feelings toward the group of popular students? How does she feel about society?

Synthesize: BRINGING THINGS TOGETHER

5b. How do Laura's attitudes toward others reflect her personal character?

Evaluate: MAKING JUDGMENTS

6a. How effectively does "The Fan Club" deliver important ideas about human character and individual attitudes toward society?

Extend: CONNECTING IDEAS

6b. The poem "Two People I Want to Be Like" also deals with human character and attitudes toward society but takes a different approach in delivering its main idea. How is the approach different from that of "The Fan Club"? How are the people in the poem different from or similar to the characters in "The Fan Club"?

Understanding Literature

THEME. A **theme** is a central idea in a literary work. What theme or themes are central to "The Fan Club"? Which parts of the story convey the theme or themes most strongly?

ANSWERS TO INVESTIGATE, INQUIRE, IMAGINE (CONT.)

act upon her convictions but chooses to join in with the popular group's discriminatory, unkind, malicious behavior. Students may say she has weak personal character. Students might also note that Laura is so preoccupied with how she is viewed by the "popular" crowd that she doesn't see them as individuals who might have problems and insecurities of their own.

EVALUATE

6a. "The Fan Club" contains powerful messages about human character and individual attitudes toward society. Students may say that the story delivers messages about human character and individual attitudes toward society very effectively by demonstrating how Laura thinks and speaks about

(Continued on page 59)

IRONY. **Irony** is a difference between appearance and reality. What does Laura say and do that makes her decision at the end of the story ironic? What might Laura have found to be ironic about the labels on the white cards?

Writer's Journal

1. Write a **note** to Miss Merrill, the teacher in "The Fan Club," posing as the parent of one of the students in the class. Inform her of your feelings about the speech assignment.

2. Imagine that your best friend is running for class president. Write a short **editorial letter** to the school newspaper, describing the characteristics of your friend that make him or her the best candidate for president.

3. Imagine you are the coach of a soccer team made up of five- and six-year-olds. Write a short **speech** for an end-of-season picnic, stating why you enjoyed working with your team.

Skill Builders

Language, Grammar, and Style
FINDING THE SIMPLE SUBJECT AND VERB

To find basic meaning in a sentence, you need to get down to the most basic sentence units. These are the **simple subject** and the **simple predicate.** Most people call the simple predicate the **verb.** Read the Language Arts Survey 3.18, "Finding the Simple Subject and Simple Predicate in a Sentence" and 3.19, "How to Find the Simple Subject and Verb." Then copy the sentences below onto your own paper. Underline the simple subject once and the verb twice.

EXAMPLE The popular <u>girls</u> <u>treated</u> Rachel badly.
1. The group laughed when Laura gave her speech about seashells.
2. Everyone has joined the Hortensky Fan Club.
3. Laura might have been rehearsing her speech for hours.
4. The nervous girl sometimes stutters in front of a crowd.
5. The unpopular girl did not dress in the right clothes.

Speaking and Listening
PERSUASIVE SPEECH. In "The Fan Club," Laura gives a speech on civil rights, stating her reasons why people should not discriminate against others. Choose a topic about which you believe people have narrow opinions. Write and present a persuasive speech to try to convince others to accept what you understand to be the truth. After you have presented your speech, poll your classmates to see if their opinions have changed as a result of your speech. For more information, see the Language Arts Survey 4.18, "Guidelines for Giving a Speech."

**Language, Grammar, and Style:
Subject-Verb Agreement**
1. The <u>group</u> <u>laughed</u> when Rachel gave her speech about seashells.
2. <u>Everyone</u> <u>has joined</u> the Hortensky Fan Club.
3. <u>Laura</u> <u>might have been rehearsing</u> her speech for hours.
4. The nervous <u>girl</u> sometimes <u>stutters</u> in front of a crowd.
5. The unpopular <u>girl</u> <u>did</u> not <u>dress</u> in the right clothes.

**Speaking and Listening:
Persuasive Speech**
For instruction on preparing a speech, refer students to the Language Arts Survey 4.15, "Giving a Speech." You may suggest the following as possible topics to your students if they are having trouble getting started: whether the driving age should be increased to 19, whether dress codes should be enforced in schools, freedom of speech, religious tolerance, and any other topic you think it might be worthwhile for your students to discuss.

(Continued on page 60)

ANSWERS TO INVESTIGATE, INQUIRE, IMAGINE (CONT.)

discrimination but still acts in an opposite way. Laura herself can be symbolic of a society that feels that discrimination is wrong but acts in a way that perpetuates discrimination.

EXTEND
6b. "The Fan Club" makes a negative statement about human character, but "Two People I Want to Be Like" makes a positive statement about human character. The people in the poem deal with adversity in a way that demonstrates patience, dignity, a positive attitude, and respect for others. Besides Rachel, the characters in "The Fan Club" show no respect for others, act impatiently, and demonstrate a negative attitude toward society.

ANSWERS TO UNDERSTANDING LITERATURE

Theme. The main theme of "The Fan Club" is that beliefs must be backed by action to be truly effective and meaningful. (As the saying goes, if you're gonna talk the talk, you gotta walk the walk.) The parts of the story that convey this theme most strongly include the conversation between Laura and Rachel in the hall when Laura can barely conceal her discomfort at being associated with Rachel and the scene at the end of the story when Laura joins in the taunting of Rachel because she is too afraid of her classmates' opinions to defend Rachel despite her earlier speech against discrimination.

Irony. Despite the fact that she gives a speech entreating her classmates to be more accepting of those who are different than themselves and to protect the dignity of others, Laura takes part in the ridicule of Rachel. The labels reading "Hortensky Fan Club" are ironic because the students are anything but fans of Rachel.

Vocabulary

ANTONYMS. Responses will vary, but may include the following:

1. friendly
2. wide
3. kind
4. dull
5. full
6. interested
7. tame
8. rough
9. colorful
10. distant

Vocabulary

ANTONYMS. An antonym is a word that means the opposite of another word. Find an antonym (or near-antonym) for each of the following adjectives, or description words, from "The Fan Club." Use a dictionary or a thesaurus to check your answers or to help lead you to the answers.

EXAMPLE common _____rare_____

1. hostile
2. narrow
3. heartless
4. gaudy
5. hollow
6. bored
7. wild
8. smooth
9. drab
10. intimate

Applied English & Study and Research

WRITING COMPANY POLICY. Laws in the United States prohibit discrimination in the workplace. For example, Title VII of the Civil Rights Act of 1964 outlaws discrimination in hiring, firing, compensation, apprenticeships, training, terms, conditions, or privileges of employment based on race, religion, creed, sex, or national origin. In 1967 it became illegal to discriminate based on a person's age. In 1972 the Equal Employment Opportunity Act created a commission to regulate and enforce anti-discrimination laws in the workplace. Later amendments to the Civil Rights Act added marital status, national origin, and disability to the list of reasons for which an employee or potential employee could not be discriminated against.

To further explore the Civil Rights Act and its amendments, conduct a search on the Internet or look for materials in your library. You may want to read your school district's policy or that of a company employing a friend or family member. Most U.S. companies develop their own written statements about equal opportunity based on the laws.

After comparing and contrasting several policies, write an equal opportunity and anti-discrimination policy for your own school. Think about the ways in which to ensure that each student would be treated equally by administrators, teachers, and fellow students. Check your policy to make sure it sets the right tone, is clearly understandable, and outlines your beliefs.

Media Literacy and Collaborative Learning

ANALYZING THE MEDIA. Form small groups and briefly discuss the topics of conformity and individuality. How often do your group members feel they have to choose between conforming to the standards of others and asserting their individuality? What situations call for this choice? Which choice do members of your group usually make? Why? Are there times when it's better to conform? Are there times when it's better to stand on your own? Explain. Next, as a group, think about how these topics are portrayed in the media. Can you call to mind television or radio commercials, magazine ads, books, billboards, or other media that deal either with being yourself or with following the group? Gather as many examples as you can of these topics in the media. As a group, share your examples. Analyze each example and draw some conclusions about the media and about conformity vs. individuality. What messages do your examples send about conformity or individuality? How persuasive would people your age find each example? Why? What elements of each example make it persuasive or compelling? For more Information, see the Language Arts Survey 5.29, "Evaluating Information and Media Sources."

Prereading

"Destroy the Four Olds!"

by Ji-li Jiang

Reader's TOOLBOX

MEMOIR. A **memoir** is a nonfiction narration that tells a story. A memoir can be autobiographical (about one's own life) or biographical (about someone else's life). Memoirs are based on a person's experiences and reactions to historical events. Ji-li Jiang wrote *Red Scarf Girl* to relate her experiences during China's Cultural Revolution (1966–1976). "Destroy the Four Olds!" is a chapter from her memoir.

MOTIVE. A **motive** is a reason for acting in a certain way. In this selection, many of the motives are explained by the narrator, Ji-li, or are revealed in dialogue. When motives are not revealed, try to use contextual clues to figure out the reasons people act in a particular way.

DIALOGUE. Dialogue is conversation involving two or more characters. Through dialogue, a reader learns a lot about the characters. As you read, closely examine the dialogue to understand more about the characters and their beliefs. Use the graphic organizer below to arrange your ideas.

Graphic Organizer

Character	Statement	What the statement reveals
Ji-li	"After all, without revolution, how can we have peace?"	Ji-li is enthusiastic about the Cultural Revolution.

Reader's Journal

How do you respond to new rules that seem harsh or extreme?

Reader's Resource

- **HISTORY CONNECTION.** In 1949 China became a communist country called the People's Republic of China. In communism, everyone is supposed to work toward the common good, and material goods and services are supposed to be distributed fairly. Mao Ze-dong was chairman of the Chinese Communist Party until his death in 1976. ("Ze-dong" was commonly spelled "Tse-tung" in the past.)

- From 1966 to 1976, Chairman Mao led a large-scale political campaign called the Cultural Revolution. Because of political unrest within the Communist Party leadership, Mao turned to new leaders— students—in promoting the Cultural Revolution. Many older students became members of the Red Guard, which took responsibility for enforcing the rules of the Cultural Revolution.

- Younger students were also called upon to promote the ideas of the Cultural Revolution. Elementary and middle-school students like Ji-li Jiang became members of the Young Pioneers, an organization considered the first step toward membership in the Communist Party. Members wore red scarves as emblems of the Young Pioneers.

GOALS/OBJECTIVES

Studying this lesson will enable students to
- appreciate an excerpt from an autobiographical memoir
- briefly describe the Chinese Cultural Revolution
- define *motive* and identify the motives of various characters
- define *dialogue* and understand how dialogue contributes to characterization

---

ADDITIONAL RESOURCES

UNIT 1 RESOURCE BOOK
- Selection Worksheet 1.5
- Selection Check Test 4.1.9
- Selection Test 4.1.10
- Speaking and Listening Resource 4.21

ANSWERS TO READER'S TOOLBOX

GRAPHIC ORGANIZER. Students may include some of the following phrases from the story in their graphic organizers.

Grandma: "That sign cost the owner a fortune. ...What a shame! What a shame!" Grandma isn't completely supportive of the revolution.

Ji-yong: "That's superstition, and superstition is fourolds." Ji-yong is eager to get rid of the old ways.

Ji-li: "You really embarrass me." Ji-li cares what other think about her and her family.

Male high school student: "What's more, they are detrimental to the revolution, so we must oppose them resolutely." This student, like many others, is a fervent supporter of the revolution.

Yang Fan: "An Yi, you're spreading the fourolds." Yang Fan doesn't usually express her own opinions, so perhaps this is her attempt to be more assertive.

Du Hai: "You two are typical 'teachers' obedient little lambs,' do you know that?" Du Hai is trying to impress the other students with his knowledge about the revolution.

READER'S JOURNAL

You might ask students to write about a specific situation in which they were faced with a rule they felt was unfair. Did they obey the rule? Why, or why not? What were the consequences for disobeying the rule? If they chose to disobey the rule, why did they feel justified in doing so? Would they react the same way again?

INDIVIDUAL LEARNING STRATEGIES

MOTIVATION
Encourage students to find poems, stories, song lyrics, or novels about revolution. Students can present the work to the class and explain how it reflects the idea of revolution.

READING PROFICIENCY
Introduce the concept of "fourolds" to students before they begin reading the selection. Explain to students that fourolds was a term coined in China to label the four main components supporters of the Cultural Revolution wished to change: old ideas, old culture, old customs, and old habits.

ENGLISH LANGUAGE LEARNING
Some students might have difficulty with the names of the characters in this selection. Explain to students that in Chinese culture, the family name, or surname, is used first, followed by the person's given name. For example, the character Du Hai refers to Ji-li as Jiang Ji-li. Encourage students to make a list of the characters' names as they read, accompanied by a brief description. For example: Ji-li Jiang: main character; Ji-yong: her brother; Ji-yun: her younger sister; An Yi: Ji-li's friend.

SPECIAL NEEDS
Students will find it helpful to listen to the selection on audiocassette. Make sure students focus on the Guided Reading questions and the Recall questions in the Investigate, Inquire, and Imagine section.

ENRICHMENT
After reading the selection, students should research the effects of the Cultural Revolution in China. How and why did the revolution end? Was it considered a success? Why, or why not? What lasting effects, if any, did the revolution have?

Destroy the FOUR OLDS!

Ji-li Jiang

Almost every Sunday afternoon Dad wanted to take a long nap in peace, and so he gave us thirty fen to rent picture books. Hand in hand, Ji-yong, Ji-yun, and I would walk down the alley to Grandpa Hong's bookstall.

The alley on which he lived was famous for its handsome buildings, and it was wide enough for two cars to pass abreast. Like a tree with only one trunk, our alley had only one exit to the busy street. Five smaller alleys branched off the main alley on both sides, and each of these small alleys was lined with brownstone town houses. The houses were three stories tall and exactly alike, with square, smiling courtyards hidden behind their front

CROSS-CURRICULAR CONNECTION

HISTORY. After China became a communist country called the People's Republic of China in 1949, the government immediately began to try to transform China into a socialist society. The government controlled what forms of religion people could practice, children were told to look to the state rather than their parents for guidance, and party members tried to "reform" the thoughts of any person who opposed the changes taking place in communist China. In the first few years after communism became the official form of government, between one and two million people were executed for supposedly being "counterrevolutionaries," or people who did not support the communist party.

As time passed, however, more and more intellectuals and professionals wanted a more moderate form of communism. In 1956, Chairman Mao encouraged people to express their dissatisfaction with government policies. So much criticism followed that in 1957 Mao abandoned this experiment with freedom of speech, and it was again dangerous to speak against the government and the communist party. In 1958 Mao stepped down as head of state, and he was succeeded by as leader with more moderate beliefs. Mao remained the Chairman of the communist party—a position of great power. In 1966, Mao launched the Cultural Revolution. He hoped to renew the revolutionary enthusiasm for communism that existed back in 1949. He also hoped to crush the more moderate elements of the party and eliminate any hint of "bourgeois" privilege. Student leaders who called themselves the Red Guard began sometimes-violent protests in support of Mao and against moderate party members, officials, and intellectuals. They purged the government of many moderate leaders, including the head of state.

VOCABULARY FROM THE SELECTION

aggressor	pernicious
auspicious	prosperity
chortle	quiver
detrimental	resolute
indignant	revel
mutilate	ruthless
oppose	submissive
oppress	

1. The single-family homes are now
shared by several families.
2. It costs children thirty fen to rent
sixty picture books.
3. The "Four Olds" are old ideas, old
culture, old customs, and old
habits.
4. People break the signs because the
names of the shops are associated
with the "old culture."

ADDITIONAL QUESTIONS AND ACTIVITIES

Inform students that **propaganda** is the intentional use of false arguments to persuade others. Propaganda was a tool people who supported the Cultural Revolution used to sway others to join them and to denounce anything that was not strictly socialist and revolutionary. Based on what students have read so far, how well is the propaganda working? Do the children in this story accept what they have been told as fact or recognize that it is propaganda? Encourage students to question as they read, trying to identify elements of propaganda. *Answers.* Students may say that the propaganda is working well—Chairman Mao is called "beloved" by the children and they accept what they hear on the radio—that they must destroy old ideas, old culture, old customs, and old habits. The children accept what they hear as fact and do not question it as possible propaganda.

LITERARY TECHNIQUE

COINED WORDS. Coined words are ones that are intentionally created, often from already existing words or word parts. Ask students to identify the word that is coined on this page. From what is this new word created? *Answers.* Students should recognize that the term *fourolds* is coined. It is created from *four,* for the number of things that have to be destroyed, and *olds,* which modifies each of the things that has to be destroyed.

---

gates, and small kitchen courtyards in the back. Once these had been town houses for wealthy families. Many of the original inhabitants still lived there, although now each building was shared by several families.

> **GUIDED READING**
> How have the homes changed?

Grandpa Hong's bookstall was on the corner at the entrance of our alley. All the children in the neighborhood loved the stall and Grandpa Hong, with his gray hair and wispy beard. He would look at us through his old yellowed glasses and smile. He knew just which books each of us liked best and that I would choose fairy tales, Ji-yong would get adventure stories, and Ji-yun would want animal stories. If you read the books at Grandpa Hong's bookstall, you could rent sixty picture books for thirty fen.[1] Two books for a fen! What a deal! After helping us with our choices, Grandpa Hong always gave us each an extra book for free.

Against the walls in the place were hard wooden benches that rocked on the uneven mud floor. We

> **GUIDED READING**
> How much does it cost children to rent books?

would sit in a row on one of these benches, each of us with a pile of twenty-one picture books, and read them, one after another. Then we would trade piles and read again. This was how I met many beloved friends: the Monkey King, the River Snail Lady, Snow White, Aladdin, and many others. Inside the bookstall I traveled to mysterious places to meet ancient beauties or terrible monsters. Often I forgot where I was. When

the sky was almost dark, the three of us would have finished all sixty-three books, and Dad would have finished his nap.

This Sunday there were no other children at the stall when we arrived. We had just settled down to read when An Yi rushed in. An Yi and I had known each other ever since we were babies. She came to the bookstall quite often and knew just where to find me on a Sunday afternoon.

"Come on, you guys!" she wheezed. An Yi had severe asthma. "They're breaking the sign at the Great <u>Prosperity</u> Market!"

We dropped our books and rushed out with her. This was our first chance to watch the campaign to "Destroy the Four Olds" in action.

This was our first chance to watch the campaign to "Destroy the Four Olds" in action.

Our beloved Chairman Mao had started the Cultural Revolution in May. Every day since then on the radio we heard about the need to end the evil and <u>pernicious</u> influences of the "Four Olds": old ideas, old culture, old customs, and old habits. Chairman Mao told us we would never succeed at building a strong socialist[2] country until we destroyed the "Four Olds" and established the "Four News." The names of many shops still stank of old culture, so the signs had to be smashed to make way for the coming of new ideas.

> **GUIDED READING**
> What are the "Four Olds"?

> **GUIDED READING**
> Why do people break the signs?

---

1. **fen.** Chinese "penny," worth 1/100 of a yuan
2. **socialist.** Based on socialism, an economic system in which the government controls resources and distributes wealth evenly among everyone

words for everyday use

pros • per • i • ty (prä spər′ ə tē) *n.,* economic well-being. *The farmers enjoyed <u>prosperity</u> after a bountiful harvest.*
per • ni • cious (pər ni′ shəs) *adj.,* destructive. *The <u>pernicious</u> effects of water pollution could destroy the fish in the river.*

The Great Prosperity Market was on Nanjing Road, Shanghai's busiest shopping street, only two blocks from our alley. Nanjing Road was lined with big stores, and always bustled with activity. The street was full of bicycles and pedicabs[3] and trolleys, and the sidewalks were so crowded with shoppers, they spilled off the sidewalk into the street. We were still quite a distance away when we heard the hubbub and ran faster.

A big crowd had gathered outside the Great Prosperity Market, one of the most successful food stores in the city. It was full of good things to eat, with rare delicacies from other provinces and delicious items like dried duck gizzards strung up in its window. But today the window was bare. The store was deserted. All eyes were riveted on a dense ring of people in the street. Some young men were cheering excitedly for the people inside the circle, but half the crowd were merely craning their necks and watching.

We wriggled our way between the bodies.

Lying on the dirty ground inside the circle was a huge wooden sign, at least twelve feet long. It was still impressive, although the large golden characters GREAT PROSPERITY MARKET had lost their usual shine and looked dull and lifeless on the red background.

> **GUIDED READING**
> What is the crowd observing?

Two muscular young men in undershirts, probably salesmen from the store, were gasping next to it.

"Come on. Try again!" shouted the taller of the two.

He spat into his palms and rubbed them together. Then, with the help of the other, he lifted the board to shoulder height. "One, two, three!" They threw the board to the ground.

The board bounced twice but did not break. The two men threw the board again. Nothing happened.

"Put one end on the curb. Stamp on it. That's bound to work," someone suggested.

"Good idea!"

"Come on! Try it!"

Amid a clamor of support, the two men moved the board half onto the sidewalk. Then they jumped onto it. "One . . . two . . . three . . ." We heard their shoes strike the hard wood. But the board did not yield.

"This fourolds is really hard. Hey! Come on. Let's do it together!" the tall fellow shouted at the crowd.

I looked at An Yi to see if she would like to join me, but while I was hesitating,

> **GUIDED READING**
> What does the man invite the spectators to do?

the board became fully occupied. Ji-yong had moved faster and was one of the dozen people on it. They stamped, bounced, and jumped with excitement. One stepped on another's shoes. Hips and shoulders bumped. We all laughed.

The board refused to break. Even under a thousand pounds it did not give way. The crowd became irritated and started shouting suggestions.

"Take it to a carpenter and let him use it for something!"

"Let's get a truck and drive over it!"

Someone started pushing through the circle.

"Hey, I've got an ax. Let me through! I've got an ax!"

We stood back to give the man room. He lifted the ax to his shoulder and paused. The blade flashed in the sunlight as it began to move faster and faster in a shining arc until it crashed into the sign. The wood groaned with the impact, and we all cheered. The man gave the sign another blow, and another. At last the sign gave way. With another groan and a crack it broke in two.

Everyone cheered. People rushed forward to stamp on what remained of the sign. An Yi and I had found a few classmates in the crowd, and we all embraced, jumped, and shouted. Although what we had smashed was no

> **GUIDED READING**
> How does the crowd react when the sign breaks?

---

3. **pedicab.** Tricycle that carries the driver and two passengers

ANSWERS TO GUIDED READING QUESTIONS

1. The crowd is observing two young men trying to smash a wooden sign.
2. The man invites the spectators to help him break the sign.
3. The crowd cheers when the sign breaks.

Quotables

"'It's always best on these occasions to do what the mob do.'

'But suppose there are two mobs?' suggested Mr. Snodgrass.

'Shout with the largest,' replied Mr. Pickwick."

—Charles Dickens, from *The Pickwick Papers*

ADDITIONAL QUESTIONS AND ACTIVITIES

Inform students that both the above quotation and what occurs on this page are good examples of mob mentality—people behaving in ways they would not act ordinarily because they are part of a large group and want to go along with what the group is doing. Ask students to point to examples of the way the crowd members encourage one another to act destructively. *Answers.* Students may point to the people clapping as the men jump on the sign to break it, one of the men shouting to the crowd to help him break the sign, the crowd rushing to jump on the sign, and the crowd cheering as a man strikes the sign with an ax.

1. Ji-li and the other young people feel proud because they are bringing new life to China by changing the names of shops they pass.
2. Ji-li's grandma thinks it is a shame that people smashed the sign.
3. The name Great Prosperity is bad because it means to make a fortune, or a lot of money, which, according to the doctrine of the Revolution, is "what bad people do."

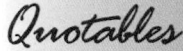

Quotables

"What's in a name? that which we call a rose

By any other name would smell as sweet."

—William Shakespeare, from *The Tragedy of Romeo and Juliet*

ADDITIONAL QUESTIONS AND ACTIVITIES

Share with students the quotation above. Then ask them to discuss how the attitude in the quotation compares and contrasts with the attitude about names shown by those who support the Cultural Revolution. Have them begin their comparison by identifying each attitude. Would Ji-li and her siblings and friends agree that "a rose / By any other name would smell as sweet"?
Answers. Students should recognize that the attitude in the quotation—that the essence of something rather than the name matters—stands in direct opposition to the attitude of those who support the Cultural Revolution—that names do matter and that any name that does not reflect the revolutionary socialist cause must be changed.

ADDITIONAL QUESTIONS AND ACTIVITIES

Ask students the following questions:
1. What is Grandma's reaction when the children proudly describe the destruction of the "Great Prosperity" sign?
2. What do the children tell their grandmother they must destroy?

---

more than a piece of wood, we felt we had won a victory in a real battle.

Bathed in the evening's glow, we jumped and giggled all the way home. Inspired by what we'd seen, we noticed that other stores we passed also needed to change their names.

"Look. This is called the Good Fortune Photo Studio. Doesn't that mean to make a lot of money, just like Great Prosperity? Chairman Mao told us that was exploitation.[4] Don't you think this is fourolds?" Ji-yong asked enthusiastically.

"Right. We should change it to the Proletarian[5] Photo Studio."

"Here's another one. The Innocent Child Toy Shop," An Yi exclaimed. "*Innocent* is a neutral word. It shows a lack of class awareness.[6] What should we change it to?"

"How about the Red Child Toy Shop?"

"That's great," I said. "And we should change the Peace Theater to the Revolution Theater. After all, without revolution, how can we have peace?"

We felt proud of ourselves. We were certain that we were bringing a new life to China.

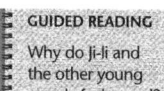
GUIDED READING
Why do Ji-li and the other young people feel proud?

So Grandma's reaction was a surprise to me. At dinner I told her and my parents all about what had happened.

"My goodness!" she blurted out. "That sign cost the owner a fortune. They always said that since an especially <u>auspicious</u> date was chosen to hang the sign, the store has been prosperous for more than thirty years. What a shame! What a shame!"

GUIDED READING
What does Ji-li's grandma think about smashing the sign?

"But Grandma, we have to get rid of those old ideas, old culture, old customs, and old habits. Chairman Mao said they're holding us back," I informed her.

"Besides, Grandma, there's no such thing as an auspicious date. That's superstition, and superstition is fourolds. And the name Great Prosperity is very bad. Great Prosperity means to make a fortune, and making a fortune is what bad people do. Right?" Ji-yong tilted his head toward Mom and Dad.

GUIDED READING
Why is the name Great Prosperity bad?

Mom and Dad looked at each other and then turned to Grandma.

"Yes, Ji-yong is right," Mom said, and shook her head.

Even my little sister, Ji-yun, knew that the old superstitions were silly. Like not sweeping the floor on New Year's Day so you would not sweep the god of wealth out of the house, or eating a spring roll so you would roll the money in. I told Grandma what I had heard from my classmates. "An Yi said her uncle knew a family who spent a lot of money when their grandma died. First they had to keep vigil by the coffin for a week. Then after the burial they had to have a banquet and serve bean curd to the relatives every seventh day for seven weeks, and on the forty-ninth day they had the last banquet, all just so the soul could get into heaven. Then they burned spirit money so that the dead person would have money in heaven. What good does all that do? Besides, there is no such thing as

---

4. **exploitation.** Unfair use of someone's labor or resources
5. **proletarian.** Member of the working class
6. **class awareness.** Recognition of a family's status as "red," or revolutionary, versus "black," or unreliable. This distinction became particularly important during the Cultural Revolution.

---

words for everyday use

aus • pi • cious (ô spiʹ shəs) *adj.,* favorable; indicative of future success. *Because of the child's <u>auspicious</u> birth date, people predicted he would be famous one day.*

ADDITIONAL QUESTIONS AND ACTIVITIES (CONT.)

3. How do you think the children's words make the grandmother feel? Why might she not share in her grandchildren's enthusiasm to destroy the fourolds?
Answers
1. Grandma reveals her shock and dismay, pointing out that the sign was expensive and meaningful to the shop owners and that destroying it is "a shame."

2. They tell their grandmother that they must destroy "old ideas, old culture, old customs, and old habits."
3. Students may say that the grandmother may feel saddened to hear these words. She probably does not share in the children's enthusiasm to destroy the fourolds because she is part of the generation and culture that Mao is saying must be destroyed.

heaven. It's these old ideas that are holding the country back."

Ji-yong and Ji-yun and I talked about the new shop names we had thought of. Mom and Dad did not say anything. They did not seem very enthusiastic about the new campaign. That was surprising,

GUIDED READING
What surprises Ji-li?

because they had been very enthusiastic about previous movements. When I was little, Chairman Mao had challenged the nation to catch up with England and America in steel production. Mom had helped me collect scrap iron to make steel, and even let me donate our cast-iron kettle to the cause. When natural disasters had caused food shortages, Chairman Mao had urged us all to produce food. Mom had helped me grow pots of seaweed on the balcony, as all my classmates did. Chairman Mao's campaign to "Destroy the Four Olds" was even more important than the others. The newspapers and the radio said so. I knew the movement was vital to our country's future, and I did not understand how Mom and Dad could not be interested in it.

★   ★   ★   ★   ★

It was almost unbelievable. Within a couple of days almost all the fourolds shop signs had been removed. The stores we had talked about had all been renamed. Red banners now hung over the doorways as temporary

GUIDED READING
What has happened to the old shop signs?

signs, with the new names painted in black or white. The red cloths were not as nice as the old signs, but their revolutionary spirit brought a new energy to the whole city. It seemed to me that the very air had become purer with the change.

What excited me and my friends most, though, was that the Peace Theater really did become the Revolution Theater, as we had said it should. We felt like real revolutionaries at last.

My friends and I had grown up with the stories of the brave revolutionaries who had saved China. We were proud of our precious red scarves, which, like the national flag, were dyed red with the blood of our revolutionary martyrs. We had often been sorry that we were too young to have fought with Chairman Mao against the Japanese invaders, who tried to conquer China; against

GUIDED READING
What do the young people regret?

the dictator Chiang Kai-shek, who <u>ruthlessly</u> <u>oppressed</u> the Chinese people; and against the American <u>aggressors</u> in Korea. We had missed our chance to become national heroes by helping our motherland.

GUIDED READING
Why is destroying the fourolds important? Why is this battle so difficult?

Now our chance had come. Destroying the fourolds was a new battle, and an important one: It would keep China from losing her Communist ideals. Though we were not facing real guns or real tanks, this battle would be even harder, because our enemies, the rotten ideas and customs we were so used to, were inside ourselves.

I was so excited that I forgot my sadness about the audition.[7] There were many more important missions waiting for me. I felt I was already a Liberation Army soldier who was ready to go out for battle.

---

7. **audition.** Refers to an event in an earlier chapter of *Red Scarf Girl*

ruth • less (rüth' ləs) *adj.*, cruel; without mercy. *The <u>ruthless</u> dog attacked the intruder.* **ruthlessly** *adv.*

op • press (ə pres') *v.*, to crush or burden by abuse of power. *The king will <u>oppress</u> those who disagree with his ideas.*

ag • gres • sor (ə gres' ər) *n.*, attacker. *The ordinarily mild-mannered boy became an <u>aggressor</u> on the football field.*

"DESTROY THE FOUR OLDS!"   **67**

ANSWERS TO GUIDED READING QUESTIONS

1. Ji-li is surprised that her parents aren't enthusiastic about the new campaign.
2. The old shop signs have been replaced by red banners with new names printed on them.
3. The young people regret that they weren't able to fight for their country.
4. Destroying the fourolds is important because it will keep China from losing its Communist ideals. This battle is difficult because the enemies are inside the people.

CROSS-CURRICULAR CONNECTION

HISTORY. Inform students that several historical events are mentioned on this page and share the following information with them.

When the narrator mentions the Japanese invaders, she is referring to a struggle between China and Japan that began in the 1930s when Japan invaded Manchuria and Northern China. Once the Japanese had control of Manchuria, they renamed it Manchukuo. In 1937, Japan and China battled each other as part of a global conflict known as World War II. At the end of the war, Japan was utterly defeated and China reclaimed Manchuria.

When the narrator mentions the dictator Chiang Kai-shek she is referring to a Chinese politician and military leader. Chiang Kai-shek (1887–1975) helped unify China in the late 1920s and was the military leader of China throughout World War II. Although he was opposed to Communism and Communist Party head Mao Zedong, Chiang moderated his anticommunist position so that China would stop its domestic fighting and unite against the Japanese invaders. After World War II, however, the two leaders and their parties' clash for political power led to years of civil war and Mao's eventual victory. Chiang fled to Taiwan, became the leader there, and helped the Taiwanese economy to flourish.

When the narrator mentions the American aggressors in Korea, she is referring to U.S. involvement in the Korean War (1950–1953). The Korean War began as a struggle between North and South Korea.

CROSS-CURRICULAR CONNECTION (CONT.)

North Korea, a communist nation, invaded South Korea. China and the former Soviet Union supported North Korea, while the United States and members of the United Nations supported South Korea. When the tide of the war turned, UN troops actually invaded North Korea and captured its capital. The UN troops sought to push North Korean forces up beyond the Yalu River, which separates North Korea from China. China warned they would attack UN troops who approached the Yalu River. Fighting broke out between China and UN Troops, and communists pushed UN forces out of North Korea. Eventually the war ended in a truce between North and South Korea.

1. The high-school students are looking at people's pants and shoes.
2. Tight pants and pointed shoes are considered unacceptable.

LITERARY TECHNIQUE

SYMBOL. A **symbol** is a thing that stands for or represents both itself and something else. Inform students that anything "Western" in appearance was not tolerated because it was seen as representing capitalism and as a threat to communism. Share the definition of symbol with students, then ask them the following questions: What are the young people doing in the crowd? What about the appearance of the man whom they target stands out? What do the young people see his shoes as? Of what are they symbolic? What does the man point out about the shoes? Do the young people accept the man's logic? Why, or why not? What is your opinion of the situation? Is the attempt to eliminate all symbols of fourolds out of control?

Answers. The young people are inspecting people's clothes to make sure that they do not reflect any fourolds. The man they target is a well-dressed handsome man, wearing sharply creased pants and two-tone shoes. The young people see his shoes as symbolizing Western culture, capitalism, and the fourolds that must be destroyed. The man points out he bought the shoes in a department store run by the Chinese government and that they therefore cannot be fourolds. The young people do not accept his logic, saying that even government-run stores aren't free of fourolds. Students may suggest that it is ridiculous for the young people to categorize the man's shoes as Western when they were sold in a Chinese government-run store. They may say that the attempt to rid China of anything symbolic of fourolds is getting out of control.

Ji-yun and I were walking home. The street was crowded with the bicycles of people coming home from work and with electric trolley buses blowing horns and crammed with passengers.

As usual, Ji-yun had not done very well at her piano lesson. "You have to pay attention to your teacher," I was telling her. "He told you to slow down when you got to the end of the last verse, but you sped up. I don't know what's wrong with you. Now, what did he say about the new piece? What kind of mood is it?"

"Happy?" Ji-yun guessed.

I sighed. "He said it was stirring. That's a lot more than just happy. You have to pay attention. You really embarrass me. You—"

The sight of some high school students distracted me. Two boys and a pigtailed girl were walking toward us. They were young, no more than three or four years older than me. They walked slowly through the bustling crowd, looking closely at people's pants and shoes. My sister and I stared at them with admiration. We knew they must be student inspectors. The newspapers had pointed out that the fourolds were also reflected in clothing, and now high school students had taken responsibility for eliminating such dress. For example, any pants with a leg narrower than eight inches for women or nine inches for men would be considered fourolds.

> **GUIDED READING**
>
> What are the high school students looking at?

> **GUIDED READING**
>
> What clothing is considered unacceptable?

A bus pulled up at the bus stop behind us. Quite a few people got on and off. As the bus pulled away, we saw a crowd gathered at the curb. "Oh boy, they found a target." I took Ji-yun by the hand and dashed over.

". . . tight pants and pointed shoes are what the Western bourgeoisie[8] admire. For us proletarians they are neither good-looking nor comfortable. What's more, they are <u>detrimental</u> to the revolution, so we must <u>oppose</u> them <u>resolutely</u>." One of the boys, the one who was wearing glasses, was just finishing his speech.

The guilty person was a very handsome man in his early thirties. He wore dark-framed glasses, a cream-colored jacket with the zipper half open, and a pair of sharply creased light-brown pants. He had also been wearing fashionable two-tone shoes, "champagne shoes" we called them, of cream and light-brown leather. They were lying on the ground next to him as he stood with one foot on the ground and the other resting in the lap of the student measuring his pants.

The man kept arching his foot as if the pebbles on the sidewalk hurt him. He looked nervous, standing in his white socks while the inspectors surrounded him, holding his hands <u>submissively</u> along his trouser seams. Occasionally he raised his hands a little to balance himself. His handsome face blushed scarlet, then turned pale. A few times he bit his lips.

One of the boys was trying to squeeze an empty beer bottle up the man's trouser leg. This was a newly invented measurement. If the bottle could not be stuffed into the trouser leg, the pants were considered fourolds and

---

8. **bourgeoisie.** Member of the middle class; during the Cultural Revolution, used to describe people accused of enjoying a "capitalist" lifestyle

det • ri • men • tal (de trə men′ təl) *adj.,* damaging. *The girl's negative remarks were <u>detrimental</u> to school spirit.*

op • pose (ə pōz′) *v.,* to be opposite or against something; to resist. *I know my father will <u>oppose</u> this risky plan.*

res • o • lute (re zə lüt′) *adj.,* firmly; decisively. *She was <u>resolute</u> about leaving at noon no matter what.* **resolutely** *adv.*

sub • mis • sive (səb mi′ siv) *adj.,* obedient; passive. *The <u>submissive</u> young fox followed its mother to the den.* **submissively** *adv.*

68   UNIT ONE / *FINDING YOUR PLACE IN THE WORLD*

treated with "revolutionary operations"—cut open.

The boy tried twice. The girl waved her scissors with unconcealed delight. "Look! Another pair of too-tight pants. Now let's get rid of the fourolds!" She raised the scissors and deftly cut the pants leg open. Then, with both hands, she tore the pants to the knee so the man's pale calf was exposed.

The crowd stirred. Some people pushed forward to have a closer look, some nervously left the circle when they saw the scissors used, and some glanced at their own pants. As the girl started on the other leg of the trousers, the boy with the glasses picked up the man's shoes and waved them to the crowd. "Pointed shoes! Fourolds!" he shouted.

"But I bought them in the Number One Department Store here. It's run by the government. How can they be fourolds?" the man cried out in despair.

"What makes you think that government-owned stores are free of fourolds? That statement itself is fourolds. Didn't you see all the shop signs that were knocked down? Most of those stores belonged to the government." With a snort the boy dropped the man's foot and stood up. The man lost his balance and nearly fell over.

The crowd gave a burst of appreciative laughter.

Encouraged, the three students enthusiastically began cutting open the shoes. All eyes were focused on them. No one paid any attention to their owner. I looked at the man.

He stood on the sidewalk, awkward and humiliated, trouser legs flapping around his ankles, socks falling down. A tuft of hair hung over his forehead. He looked at his pants, pushed up his glasses nervously, and quickly glanced around. Our eyes met. Immediately he turned away.

The students cheered and triumphantly threw the mutilated shoes into the air.

The man quivered. Suddenly he turned around and began to walk away.

"Wait." One boy picked up the shoes and threw them at the man. "Take your fourolds with you. Go home and thoroughly remold your ideology."[9]

The man took his broken shoes in hand and made his way out of the crowd, his cut pants flapping.

Someone chortled. "He'll have holes in his socks when he gets home."

I watched the spectators disperse. The students strutted proudly down the street.

Ji-yun tugged on my arm. "Come on. It's over."

I took her hand and we headed home in silence. "That poor guy," I finally said. "He should know better than to dress that way, but I'd just die if somebody cut my pants open in front of everybody like that."

School had just let out. No sooner had we left the classroom than the rain began to pour down in huge drops. Those of us who hadn't brought umbrellas scurried back into the classroom.

---

9. **remold your ideology.** A phrase meaning to change or correct one's belief to match communist ideals

---

GUIDED READING

What do the inspectors do to pants that fail the test?

GUIDED READING

How does the man defend his shoes?

GUIDED READING

How did Ji-li react after the man and the spectators leave?

---

words for everyday use

mu • ti • late (myü' təl āt) v., break; ruin; destroy. *I mutilated my book when I dropped it down three flights of stairs.* **mutilated** adj.

quiv • er (kwi' vər) v., tremble; shake. *My cat will quiver in fear at the first sight of a dog.*

chor • tle (chŏr təl) v., laugh; chuckle. *The clown's antics caused the boy to chortle with glee.*

ANSWERS TO GUIDED READING QUESTIONS

1. The inspectors cut open pants legs that fail the test.
2. The man defends his shoes by saying he bought them in a government-run department store.
3. Ji-li feels sorry for the man.

LITERARY TECHNIQUE

CRISIS. The **crisis,** or **turning point,** is the point in a plot when something happens to determine the future course of events and the eventual fate of the main character. Ask students to explain why Ji-li's reaction to what she witnesses the young people doing to the man might be a crisis or turning point for her. *Answers.* Students may suggest that her sympathy with the man who has been humiliated is a turning point because she is no longer blindly accepting all the Cultural Revolution's propaganda and is questioning the justice of things on her own.

1. Yang Fan's classmates call her Echo because she is hesitant to express opinions of her own.
2. No one wants to offend Du Hai because his mother is the Neighborhood Party Committee Secretary.
3. Du Hai says that it is nonsense to respect teachers.

ADDITIONAL QUESTIONS AND ACTIVITIES

Inform students that on this page, the children argue about the etymology, or origin, of a word. Have students review the Language Arts Survey 1.17, "Using a Dictionary." Then have them answer the following questions.

1. What is the etymology of the word *panda*?
2. What is the etymology of the word *tiger*?
3. What do these two etymologies reveal about the ways that words enter a language?

Answers

1. *Panda* comes from a native word in Nepal.
2. *Tiger* comes from a middle English word *tygre,* derived from an Old English and Old French term *tigre,* both of which came from a Latin word *tigris*. The Latin word itself comes from a Greek word, which came from an Iranian word *tigra,* meaning sharp. This Iranian term comes from an Indo-European word *(s)teig,* meaning stick.
3. Students may say that they reveal that words can enter a language either very directly or in a very roundabout way, as meanings, spellings, and pronunciations change over the centuries.

"Gosh! I should have brought my *yang-san* like Mom told me to." An Yi gasped for breath while brushing the rain off her clothes.

"An Yi, you're spreading the fourolds." Yang Fan popped up behind her and spoke half jokingly. I was surprised. Yang Fan was usually so hesitant to express an opinion of her own that we called her Echo.

> **GUIDED READING**
> Why do Yang Fan's classmates call her Echo?

"What? What do you mean?" An Yi asked indignantly.

"You just said *yang-san* for 'umbrella.' Isn't that spreading the fourolds?"

"Are you kidding? If *yang-san* is fourolds, then what about 'raincoat'?"

Several other classmates laughed and gathered around An Yi and Yang Fan.

Yang Fan's smile faded into embarrassment.

"What's so funny? That *is* fourolds." Du Hai stepped onto a chair and sat heavily on a desk. "*Yang* means foreign. *Yang-san* means foreign umbrella. They were called that because before Liberation[10] we had to import them. Now we make them in China. So why do you still call it a *yang-san*? Doesn't that show that you're a xenophile[11] who worships anything foreign?" Du Hai reveled in the new phrase he had learned from the newspaper.

Du Hai was trouble. He was mischievous and a terrible student, but he was hard to beat in an argument. Most important of all, his mother was the Neighborhood Party Committee Secretary, and so no one wanted to offend him.

> **GUIDED READING**
> Why does no one want to offend Du Hai?

He looked at us and we looked at him.

"First of all, this *yang* means sun, not foreign. And this *yang-san* means sun umbrella, parasol, not foreign umbrella." I didn't even look at Du Hai while I corrected his mistake. "If you want to talk about fourolds, Yang Fan, you always say *yang-huo* for matches. That really does mean foreign fire. So aren't you spreading the fourolds too?" I sneaked a glance at Du Hai as I supported An Yi. Everyone laughed.

Yang Fan did not expect my attack and was caught short. She looked to Du Hai for help.

"Well, you always say good morning and good afternoon to the teachers." Du Hai struck back. "That's fourolds too, don't you know that?"

"What's wrong with saying good morning to the teachers? They teach you and you should respect them," An Yi fired back before I could stop her.

"Respect the teachers? That's the nonsense of 'teachers' dignity.' You two are typical 'teachers' obedient little lambs,' do you know that?" Du Hai recited more phrases from the newspaper.

> **GUIDED READING**
> What does Du Hai say is nonsense?

The world had turned upside down. Now it was a crime for students to respect teachers. I couldn't keep calm.

"We're 'teachers' obedient little lambs,' are we? Well, what about you, Du Hai? You're full of the fourolds. On the last arithmetic test you only got twenty-six out of a hundred, and you said that your stupidity was due to your sins in a former life. Isn't that what you said? Isn't reincarnation[12] a superstition?" I raised my voice.

---

10. **Liberation.** Establishment of the Chinese Communist government in 1949
11. **xenophile.** Person attracted to anything foreign
12. **reincarnation.** Rebirth of a soul in a new body after death

---

words for everyday use

in • dig • nant (in dig′ nənt) *adj.,* angry about something perceived as unfair or mean. *The indignant student replied firmly to the accusation.* **indignantly** *adv.*

rev • el (re′ vəl) *v.,* take immense pleasure. *He reveled in the news that his science project had won the contest.*

读毛主席的书 听毛主席的话

Read Chairman Mao's Books and Listen to His Words, 1965. Huang Dijan.

"And you also said that the fortune-teller told you 'small eyes, large fortune.' Isn't that fourolds too?" An Yi kept pressing hard.

Du Hai's tiny, squinty eyes got even smaller. "That . . . that was just a joke. Anyway, I'm not as full of the fourolds as you are. You always say, 'Listen to the teachers, listen to your parents.'" He wheezed in an expert imitation of An Yi, and all of our classmates burst into laughter. Du Hai and Yang Fan looked immensely pleased with themselves.

GUIDED READING

How does Du Hai imitate An Yi?

"Jiang Ji-li, your family has a housekeeper. That is exploitation. You're a capitalist."[13]

"An Yi, you use facial cream every day. That is bourgeois ideology. And your long hair is,

This kind of poster would have appeared by the thousands all over China at the time of the Cultural Revolution. It represents Mao as a cheerful god-like figure, and the caption instructs, "Read Chairman Mao's books and listen to his words." Propaganda posters use the same techniques that are used to sell products in capitalist countries. The bright colors grab attention, and the message is simple and uplifting. Here the product is communism, which seems to make the people as happy as they would be if they were drinking a soft drink in an American billboard.

too. Shame on you. Why don't you get your hair cut short in a revolutionary style?"

Du Hai and Yang Fan took turns attacking us, so quickly and fiercely that An Yi and I did not have a chance to reply. Everyone laughed at our helplessness.

"Well, the rain's stopped. Let's go home." Feeling they had the upper hand and wanting to quit while they were ahead, Du Hai and Yang Fan picked up their schoolbags and swaggered off. The rest of the crowd followed them out, still shouting with laughter.

We two were left alone, angry and helpless.

GUIDED READING

How do the two girls feel?

"What's wrong with using skin cream and wearing a braid?" said An Yi, stamping hard on the ground.

"But maybe they're right about the housekeeper," I admitted as we slung our schoolbags over our shoulders. "I guess I'll have to tell Mom what they said about Song Po-po." ■

13. **capitalist.** Person embracing capitalism, an economic system defined by private ownership, free competition, and business for profit

Respond *to the* **SELECTION**

What would happen if your community held a "destroy the four olds" campaign?

Checking Your Reading

1. Nearly every Sunday, what does the girls' father give them money to rent? **Nearly every Sunday, the girls' father gives them money to rent picture books.**
2. What are the Four Olds? **The "Four Olds" are old ideas, old culture, old customs, and old habits.**
3. What new name is given to the Peace Theater? **The Peace Theater is given the new name of "Revolution Theater."**
4. What do the crowds do to the shop signs? **The crowds knock down the shop signs and replace them with signs that reflect the ideals of the Cultural Revolution.**
5. What do the students do to the well-dressed man? **They mock him and cut his pants and shoes.**

Vocabulary in Context

Fill in each blank below with the most appropriate vocabulary word from "Destroy the Four Olds!" You may have to change the tense of the word.

> detrimental   quiver   revel
> submissively   prosperity   oppose
> resolutely

1. Jake's dog is not afraid of much, but whenever there's a storm he hides under the bed and _____. **quivers**
2. Once Leticia graduated from college and got her first job, she enjoyed her new _____. **prosperity**
3. Many people do not realize the _____ effect that even one cigarette can have. **detrimental**
4. The firefighters _____ fought the blaze for hours. **resolutely**
5. When his mother called him in for dinner, Danny _____ climbed off the jungle gym and headed home. **submissively**

Reader's Toolbox

1. According to the selection, during the Cultural Revolution Chairman Mao largely relied on the support of
   a. students
   b. tourists
   c. older people who remembered the War
   d. foreign governments
2. A reason for acting in a certain way is known as
   a. plot device
   b. motive
   c. inciting incident
   d. metaphor
3. A nonfiction narration that tells a story based on a person's

---

About the AUTHOR

Ji-li Jiang was born in Shanghai, China, in 1954. Haunted by the years she lived under the Cultural Revolution, she moved to the United States in 1984. During her first years in the country, she was constantly astonished by the freedoms Americans enjoyed. After making it through college and embarking on a successful career, Jiang found she still could not forget China. In 1992 she started her own company, East West Exchange, to promote cultural exchange between the United States and China. She also wrote *Red Scarf Girl*, which was published in 1997. Jiang speaks about her experiences and her writing:

Why did you want to write this story for young readers instead of for adults?
To tell the truth, I didn't plan to write a children's book when I started. I was inspired by *The Diary of Anne Frank*, and I decided to write my story through a little girl's innocent eyes instead of as an adult looking back. Before I even started, I was very clear that I wanted to limit the story to what a child might have been aware of at that time, without an adult's analysis, without judgment. I guess that's the main reason this became a book for young adults. I am very happy with the result. I used to be a teacher myself, and I feel very rewarded to be able to reach so many children with my story. When I first came to America, I was amazed by the beautiful lives American children have. Wow, I thought, they have everything, big houses, nice cars, tons of toys, countless books. They even have school buses to pick them up every day. They really have everything you can imagine. But gradually, I learned that American kids also have a lot of difficulties in their lives, although different from mine. At home, some kids have a single parent or even abusive parents; at school, they have to deal with peer pressure related to drugs, sex, gangs, violence, etc. I realized that all of us, little Ji-li in China in the 60s, or little Mary or David in America in the 90s, have to deal with difficulties in our lives. If they can gain a little courage from reading my book, and learn to follow their own hearts and use their own brains to make decisions instead of yielding to pressure, I will feel extremely gratified.

What was it like to write about a time in your life that was confusing, scary, and sometimes sad?
It was very painful to relive this dark time. Many times, I couldn't continue. I had to drive to the beach to recover myself. I stared across the Pacific Ocean, seeing that little girl, frightened, suffering and struggling. I cried.

How did your experiences during this time shape who you are today? How have they contributed to your beliefs and to your way of viewing the world around you?
Before the Cultural Revolution, I was a very happy and innocent girl. The world seemed perfect to me. The Cultural Revolution was the first time that I experienced constant humiliation, horror and despair. Since I didn't have older brothers or sisters, I had no choice but to face them myself. As a little girl, I dried my tears and plucked up the courage to deal with one difficulty after another. To survive I had to become stronger and tougher. The Cultural Revolution taught me to never give up. The Cultural Revolution made me more mature politically. I understood how evil the greed for power and money can be and I learned not to blindly trust and worship anyone. Instead of being bitter, I realize I can do something, even if in a very small way, to prevent this from happening again. That's the reason I wrote this book. I don't think we will ever make evil disappear entirely, but we can make a difference by doing what we can where we are. I do believe a better understanding will make the world more peaceful and better.

SELECTION CHECK TEST 4.1.9 WITH ANSWERS (CONT.)

experiences is known as
a. monologue
b. memoir
c. dialogue
d. journal

4. "Destroy the Four Olds" was told from what point of view?
   a. first person
   b. second person
   c. third person limited
   d. third person all knowing

5. Throughout the story, Ji-li and her friends tried to see who could
   a. be most loyal to Chairman Mao
   b. be most obedient to their parents
   c. break rules without getting caught
   d. earn the best grades in school

Investigate, *Inquire,* and Imagine

Recall: GATHERING FACTS

1a. What name was on the sign lying on Nanjing Road?

2a. How did the crowd react when the student inspectors cut open the man's pants leg?

3a. According to Du Hai, why was greeting your teachers a fourold?

Interpret: FINDING MEANING

1b. Why were people trying to break the sign?

2b. Why did some people seem nervous?

3b. How did Du Hai feel about teachers?

Evaluate: MAKING JUDGMENTS

4a. How effective did the "destroy the four olds" campaign seem to be in creating a sense of unity and strength among the people?

Extend: CONNECTING IDEAS

4b. In what ways might the campaign have backfired? For example, imagine that the crowd turned on the student inspectors. How might that have happened? Rewrite that scene based on your ideas.

Analyze: TAKING THINGS APART

5a. In which ways did Du Hai and Yang Fan accuse An Yi and Ji-li of spreading the four olds?

Synthesize: BRINGING THINGS TOGETHER

5b. Consider how the "destroy the four olds" campaign influenced people's thinking. What might Du Hai have said about Grandpa Hong's bookstall?

Perspective: LOOKING AT OTHER VIEWS

6a. Why does Ji-li respond to the campaign and the Cultural Revolution the way she does?

Empathy: SEEING FROM INSIDE

6b. How would you have responded to these restrictions? Why?

Understanding *Literature*

MEMOIR. A **memoir** is a nonfiction narration, which tells a story. Memoirs focus on a person's experiences and reactions to historical events. Although memoirs can be autobiographical (about one's own life) or biographical (about someone else's life), they differ from strict autobiography or biography by stressing experiences and events rather than an individual's life. Look back at "Destroy the Four Olds." Do you learn more about Ji-li or about the Cultural Revolution? Explain your answer.

ANSWERS TO INVESTIGATE, INQUIRE, IMAGINE (CONT.)

Grandpa Hong charged money for lending out books. In fact, in the chapter following "Destroy the Four Olds!" the door of Grandpa Hong's bookstall is sealed shut with political posters. The posters flash phrases such as "Propagating Feudal, Capitalistic, and Revisionist Ideals" and "Poisoning our Youth."

PERSPECTIVE
6a. Students may suggest that Ji-li is influenced by the

pervasive propaganda of the Cultural Revolution and by her peers to unquestioningly accept its values. Toward the end she begins to question things more closely.

EMPATHY
6b. *Responses will vary.*

Answers to Understanding Literature can be found on page 74.

ANSWERS TO INVESTIGATE, INQUIRE, IMAGINE

RECALL
1a. The name on the sign was Great Prosperity Market.
2a. When the student inspectors cut open the man's pants leg, some people push forward to have a closer look, but some people leave nervously and others glance at their own pants legs.
3a. Du Hai says that respecting one's teachers is based on the "nonsense of 'teachers' dignity."

INTERPRET
1b. The people were trying to break the sign because the name of the store, Great Prosperity Market, meant to make a fortune, which is a bad thing according to the philosophy of the Communist Party.
2b. Students may say that some people are nervous because they feel uncomfortable about the inspectors' actions. Students may also say that some people may be worried that their own pants would not pass the test.
3b. Du Hai does not respect teachers. He feels that their assumed "dignity" is a thing of the past.

EVALUATE
4a. Students may say that the campaign seems effective in creating a sense of unity and strength because it brings people together to join in the same causes. Students may also say that it was ineffective in creating a sense of unity and strength because it caused people to accuse one another.

EXTEND
4b. Because the Cultural Revolution enforced such rigid rules and guidelines, nearly everyone deviated from the ideal behaviors in one way or another. No one was perfect.
   In the scene with the student inspectors, someone in the crowd might have noticed some deviation from the established rules of conduct on the part of the inspectors themselves, starting a confrontation.

ANALYZE
5a. Du Hai and Yang Fan accuse An Yi and Ji-li of spreading the four olds by using old terms, greeting teachers, listening to parents and teachers, having a housekeeper, using facial cream, and having long hair.

SYNTHESIZE
5b. Du Hai might have said that the bookstall was capitalist, because

Study and Research & Media Literacy
TRACKING HISTORY. For more information on using these resources, refer students to the Language Arts Survey 5.18, "How to Locate Library Materials" and 5.23, "Using Biographical References, Encyclopedias, and Periodicals." This lesson may be a good opportunity for you to take students to your school library and show them where reference material is kept.

Speaking and Listening & Collaborative Learning
DEBATING. Inform students that when they are given a side to support in a debate, they should put personal convictions aside if their own feelings do not align with the argument they must make. They should do their best to come up with reasons to support their assigned position.

MOTIVE. A **motive** is a reason for acting in a certain way. What is the student inspectors' motive in responding to the Cultural Revolution? Do you think Ji-li's parents and grandmother share this motive? Why or why not?

DIALOGUE. Dialogue is conversation involving two or more characters. Through dialogue, a reader learns a lot about the characters. What does dialogue reveal about Ji-li? Du Hai? What does dialogue fail to reveal?

Writer's Journal

1. Write a **paragraph** or two in the form of a memoir, telling a story about an event you participated in or witnessed.
2. Write a few of lines of **dialogue** between two students arguing over a seat on the bus. Imagine the dialogue is for a role-playing exercise in conflict management.
3. Write a **memo** to Ji-li Jiang from one of her teachers, either encouraging her to participate in the "destroy the four olds" campaign or discouraging her from doing so.

Skill Builders

Study & Research and Media Literacy

TRACKING HISTORY. Using an encyclopedia or a history book on China, create a timeline outlining the history of the country. Pay attention to major changes in China's leadership, culture, and economy. Look for parallel movements in these three areas through time.

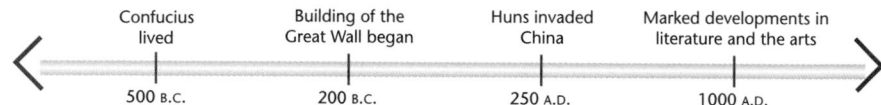

Confucius lived	Building of the Great Wall began	Huns invaded China	Marked developments in literature and the arts
500 B.C.	200 B.C.	250 A.D.	1000 A.D.

Speaking and Listening & Collaborative Learning
DEBATING. Organize in small groups of six to eight students. Divide your group in half, creating opposing sides for a debate. Side one favors strict rules and harsh consequences for breaking the rules. Side two feels that people can monitor their own behavior and believes in few restrictions. Together, jot down some specific points supporting your side's position. Then regroup to debate the issue, with the goal of reaching an agreement. For more assistance in holding a debate, see the Language Arts Survey 4.21, "Participating in a Debate."

ANSWERS TO UNDERSTANDING LITERATURE

Memoir. Responses will vary, but students will probably say that they learn more about the Cultural Revolution than about Ji-li.
Motive. The student inspectors seem eager for an opportunity to protect the communist ideals of their country. They are young and are not particularly attached to the "fourolds." Ji-li's parents and

grandmother do not share this motive. Students might say that they are reluctant to get go of the ideas, culture, customs, and habits that have been part of their lives.
Dialogue. Dialogue reveals that Ji-li and Du Hai are both enthusiastic about the revolution. Dialogue fails to reveal what Du Hai is thinking.

for your READING LIST

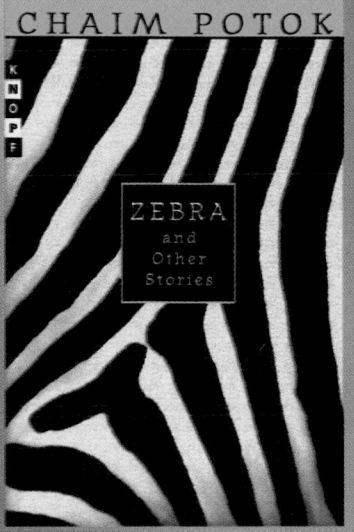

Zebra and Other Stories, by Chaim Potok, is a collection of six stories about young people and the issues they face as they grow up. These glimpses into the lives of ordinary kids reveal intense yet very real situations. Potok's wonderful storytelling ability demonstrates a respect for young people and an understanding of the impact that family, peers, grief, hope, and self-confidence can have on a person's life. In addition to Zebra, you will meet B.B., who learns to cope with change in her family. Moon must come to terms with events outside his comfortable lifestyle that nevertheless affect him directly. In "Isabel," a lonely girl struggles to find her place in a changing family. Nava gathers the confidence to stand up for herself. In "Max," a girl named Emmie forces her family to see her as the person she is. Mostly known for adult novels, Potok offers here a collection of thoughtful, respectful stories that young people can appreciate.

BOOK CLUB

DISCUSSION PROMPTS. After everyone in the group has finished reading the book, decide on a time to meet for discussion. You may find it helpful to use these questions as you get started. Read a question aloud and make sure each student has the opportunity to respond. Then ask one another further questions based on their responses.

- Which story in the collection did you like best? What made that story stand out for you?
- Who was your favorite character, and why?
- Did all the issues in the stories seem believable? Why, or why not?
- To whom would you recommend this book?
- How would you have handled your discovery if you had been in B.B.'s place?
- Why does Moon play the drums? How might Moon reply to the question?
- How does Nava learn about who she is? How does she use that knowledge?
- Why does Isabel have such a hard time coping with the changes in her family?
- How is Maxie like Max? How is Emmie like Max? How does Emmie convince her family of what she is and what she wants?

Other books you may want to read:
The Leaving and Other Stories by Budge Wilson
Red Scarf Girl by Ji-li Jiang
If Only I Could Tell You: Poems for Young Lovers and Dreamers by Eve Merriam

For Your Reading List
Zebra and Other Stories has received several favorable reviews which have appeared in *Booklist*, the *Kirkus Review*, and the *Horn Book Magazine*. Chaim Potok's short story collection provides an excellent starting point for students as they begin forming a book club or literature circle. Students can read all of the stories in this collection, as For Your Reading List suggests, or read only one or two if time is limited.

Book Club
DISCUSSION PROMPTS. Use this as an opportunity to introduce students to the Language Arts Survey Reading Resource on page 866. Have them read the following sections as they prepare for their book clubs: 1.3, "Reading Literature: Educating Your Imagination," 1.4, "Educating Your Imagination as an Active Reader," 1.5 "Keeping a Reader's Journal," 1.6, "Reading Silently versus Reading Out Loud," 1.7, "Reading with a Book Club or Literature Circle," and 1.8, "Guidelines for Discussing Literature in a Book Club." See the Guided Reading Resource 1.3–1.8 in the Teacher's Resource Kit for blackline masters of worksheets that will help students work these concepts more thoroughly.

NARRATIVE WRITING

Examining the Model

REFLECTING. Encourage students to think about a feeling or an attitude they would like to explore more. In what incident in their life did that feeling or attitude manifest itself?

EXAMINING THE MODEL. Ask students how Ah-nen-la-de-ni changed due to the experience he described. Ask the Native American students in your class to share their experiences of living between two cultures. Why do they understand Ah-nen-la-de-ni's experience? Students might benefit from reading the Language Arts Survey 2.10, "Learning from Professional Models."

GUIDED WRITING
Software

See the Guided Writing Software for an extended version of this lesson that includes printable graphic organizers, extensive student models and student-friendly checklists, and self-, peer, and teacher evaluation features.

"A good essay must have this permanent quality about it; it must draw its curtain round us, but it must be a curtain that shuts us in not out."

—Virginia Woolf

Professional Model

As you read the following excerpt, consider Ah-nen-la-de-ni's insights about his experience at the Indian school.

from "An Indian Boy's Story" by Daniel La France, or Ah-nen-la-de-ni, page 46

...After my bath and reclothing and after having had my name taken down in the records I was assigned to a dormitory, and began my regular school life, much to my dissatisfaction. The recording of my name was accompanied by a change which, though it might seem trifling to the teachers, was very important to me. My name among my own people was "Ah-nen-la-de-ni," which in English means "Turning crowd" or "Turns the Crowd," but my family had had the name "la France" bestowed on them by the French some generations before my birth, and at the institution, my Indian name

Guided Writing

WRITING A PERSONAL ESSAY

The first day of middle school was proving to be a disaster. Cody studied the map again. He couldn't find the art room. He couldn't remember the names of his teachers and which textbook he needed next. By the end of the day, Cody's head ached. He certainly would remember this day!

Have you had an experience similar to Cody's? What happened on your first day of middle school? What outlook did you have about your experience? Your experience and your perspective about your experience are unique to you. No one has exactly the same experience and feelings that you have. One way you can let others know about your experience is by talking with a friend. Another way you can share your experience is by writing a personal essay.

An essay is a short nonfiction work that expresses a writer's thoughts about a single subject. The writer focuses the essay on a single, controlling idea. An essay usually is organized into an introduction, a body, and conclusion. A **personal essay** is a short nonfiction work on a single topic related to the life of the writer. It is one of the most powerful forms of writing because the writer can share his or her unique personal insights with others.

Reflecting

Before you begin to write your personal essay, think about the narratives you read in Unit One. Which narrative is the most interesting to you? Why? How did the writers of the narratives benefit from writing their stories? How did the readers benefit from reading them? How do you think you will benefit from writing your personal essay? How will your readers benefit from reading it?

Examining the Model

In the excerpt from *An Indian Boy's Story,* Ah-nen-la-de-ni tells about his experience at the Indian school. Can you feel Ah-nen-la-de-ni's resentment and dismay at having his name changed? He had been proud of his Indian name and, in a moment, it had been taken from him. When the school insisted he use the European name Daniel La France, he felt he was "a nobody with no possibilities."

Prewriting

FINDING YOUR VOICE. You can make your essay inviting to read by using your natural, personal voice as you share your experience and perspective. Think of your reader as an attentive friend with whom you are having a conversation. Allow your memory to recall the vivid details and drama of your experiences and then, just write.

To help you practice using your natural, personal voice, imagine that you have just experienced each situation below. On your own piece of paper, write four or five sentences of dialog that express your personal response to each situation.

- Your team just won the soccer tournament.
- It is the first day of summer, and you will be working at a job.
- The postal service just delivered a huge package addressed to you.

IDENTIFYING YOUR AUDIENCE. Your peers would be a good audience for this piece of writing since they may have had experiences similar to yours. They will want to hear your perspective and think about how it is similar to or different from their own. You could also share your experience and perspective with your family and adults who are important to you.

As you write, consider the information and details that will be important to your audience, keep their interest, and help them see the value in what you have to say.

WRITING WITH A PLAN. You might know what you want to write about already. Cody wanted to write about his first day of middle school. Tamara wanted to write about her experience taking care of two-year old twins. Sean wasn't sure what to write about, so he took some time to brainstorm ideas. His list of ideas is shown below.

Experiences I Could Write About
summer camp in the Rockies
getting through math last year
visiting grandma in the nursing home
my first time skiing
taking care of my brother during the summer

On your own paper, **brainstorm** a list of several of your experiences. As you review your list, contemplate what you would share about each experience, your unique perspective on the experience, and why others could find it interesting. Then select the one you will write about in your personal essay.

Sean decided to write about his experience at summer camp in the Rocky Mountains. To get his thoughts flowing, he did some freewriting about hiking up the long mountain trails. He also wrote about his perspective of the experience as well: it was fun but exhausting.

was discarded, and I was informed that I was henceforth to be known as Daniel La France.

It made me feel as if I had lost myself. I had been proud of myself and my possibilities as "Turns the crowd," for in spite of their civilized surrounding the Indians of our reservation in my time still looked back to the old warlike days when the Mohawks were great people, but Daniel La France was to me a stranger and a nobody with no possibilities. It seemed as if my prospect of a chiefship had vanished. I was very homesick for a long time....

"I always tell would-be writers to search their own memories for a time when they experienced a strong emotion: fear, anger, joy, sorrow, guilt. How, as a result of the experience that created that emotion, did they change? There is where the story lies."

—Lois Lowry

Prewriting

FINDING YOUR VOICE. Encourage students to read the Language Arts Survey 2.5, "Finding Your Voice," and 3.3, "Register, Tone, and Voice."

IDENTIFYING YOUR AUDIENCE. Ask students for whom, besides themselves, the message of their personal essay is intended. Tell students to focus on expressing themselves for that particular person or persons. Have students read the Language Arts Survey 2.4, "Identifying Your Audience." Encourage students to use vocabulary with which their audience will be familiar.

WRITING WITH A PLAN. Have the class brainstorm possible topics for a personal essay before they brainstorm for their own topic. Discuss why certain topics will not work. Encourage students to minimize the scope of their personal essay. Students might make two lists: "Good Things that Happened to Me" and "Bad Things that Happened to Me." Students might choose to write about whichever topic they feel strongest about.

INDIVIDUAL LEARNING STRATEGIES

MOTIVATION
Tell the class topics that you have written personal essays about or would like to write. Mention memorable essays students in past years have written and read one to the class. Ask students to share what they learned about the writer by hearing his or her essay.

READING PROFICIENCY
Ask students to read each heading and subheading and speculate on what each section will be about. Have them identify the author's purpose in writing the Professional Model.

ENGLISH LANGUAGE LEARNING
See strategies for Reading Proficiency above that will also benefit students who are English language learners. Encourage non-native speakers to find a personal essay written in their native language. This might give them an idea about writing about something that happened in their own culture. If they choose to write such an essay,

INDIVIDUAL LEARNING STRATEGIES (CONT.)

explain that it may be necessary for them to explain cultural elements with which Americans may not be familiar.

SPECIAL NEEDS
Students with special needs may need help understanding the Graphic Organizer and making one of their own. Suggest possible topics so that they understand the possibilities. They may need help in

choosing a suitable topic. Help them by asking questions about their experiences.

ENRICHMENT
Have students find several personal essays in the library and report back on the topics they covered. Students might discuss how adults' personal essays differ from students'.

Writing Complete Sentences
LESSON OVERVIEW
In this lesson, students will be asked to do the following:
• Identify Complete Sentences, 79
• Fix Fragment Sentences, 79
• Use Complete Sentences, 79

INTRODUCING THE SKILL. Explain to students that being able to write complete sentences will help them in all their classes, not just English.

PREVIEWING THE SKILL. Students will benefit from reading the Language Arts Survey 3.31, "Correcting Sentence Fragments." You might make a list of sentence fragments that students have used in their writing for class and explain how to make each example a complete sentence.

PRACTICING THE SKILL. For additional practice, have students work through the exercise in the following section of the Language, Grammar, and Style Resource located in the Teacher's Resource Kit: 3.31, "Correcting Sentence Fragments."

Language, Grammar, and Style
Writing Complete Sentences

When you speak, you often express yourself using fragments. Using fragments in speech is often acceptable. You can convey a great deal of information from tone of voice, body language, and facial expression. Your listener can also ask about something he or she may not have understood.

When you write, however, the extra ways to communicate are not available for readers, so you have to do it all with words. That's why sentences are so important. They are the basic units of thought. To communicate clearly in your writing, you must use **complete sentences**.

These are only pieces of complete thoughts:

To the store.
With my friend after school.
The girl in the green jeans.

Because they are only pieces of complete thoughts, they are called **fragments**. Each fragment needs more material to make it into a complete sentence:

My mother sent me to the store for milk.
I play catch with my friend after school.
In math I sit in front of the girl in the green jeans.

On your own paper, freewrite for a few minutes to tell the story about what happened to you. Write about your experience, your reaction to the experience, and what you learned from your experience.

After you freewrite, step back and think about what you have learned. Cody, for example, had a terrible start to middle school. He felt overwhelmed. When he stepped back and thought about his experience, he realized that it might help if the school paired up new students with older students during the first few days of school.

What did you learn from your experience? What do you know now that you did not know at the time? What would you like others to know? You can use your thoughts to come up with a single, controlling idea to develop in your personal essay.

The single, controlling idea in the Professional Model is that the school tried to get rid of Ah-nen-la-de-ni's Indian identity. Each sentence in the excerpt contributes to that single, controlling idea.

Read the following two sentences. Which one would contribute to the controlling idea in the excerpt? Why?

I was unsure of this new person that I was supposed to become.
The teachers encouraged us to express our ideas.

Sean used the graphic organizer below to help him determine the controlling idea he wanted to express in his personal essay. Copy the graphic organizer onto your own paper. First, list details about your experience and your perspective on it. From this information, identify the controlling idea—the main point—that you want to use in your personal essay.

Student Model—Graphic Organizer

TOPIC: SUMMER CAMP IN THE ROCKIES

Experience
outdoor lab
steep trails
geology trail—almost straight up
switchbacks
large slippery rocks
dinner
bed

Perspective
really hard work to climb
tired when we got to the top
fun to climb
learned a lot

Controlling Idea
Hiking in the outdoor lab was great fun, but you really have to work hard to do it.

Drafting

Since your personal essay tells a narrative, or a story about your experience, you can use **chronological order** to organize your essay. Start with an introduction that includes your controlling idea. In the body paragraphs, relate what happened and explain how the experience helped you develop your perspective. In the conclusion, summarize what you learned from your experience and perspective. Also provide some direction for your audience about the experience. Should they experience this, too? Should they approach this experience in a different manner? Should they avoid the experience altogether?

You do not need to focus on the mechanics, grammar, or spelling at this writing stage. You can go back later and check for errors. For now, focus on the big picture—the single controlling idea that you have in mind. Each sentence that you write should contribute to your controlling idea.

Use a first person point of view since you are telling about your own experience and perspective. Use words like *I, my, me,* and *mine.* Your readers want to hear about what happened to you and your insight about it.

To start your draft, you might begin by stating your controlling idea. For example, Sean started by writing:

> Hiking in the mountains is great fun, but you really have to work hard. I found this out last summer when I went to a camp in the Rocky Mountains.

You can refer to your freewriting notes and graphic organizer as you continue writing your rough draft. For more information, see the Language Arts Survey 2.31, "Drafting."

Self- and Peer Evaluation

After you finish your first draft, complete a self-evaluation of your writing. You may also want to get one or two peer evaluations if you have time. See the Language Arts Survey 2.37 for more details about self-evaluation and peer evaluation.

As you evaluate your essay or that of a classmate, answer the following questions.

- What personal experience does the essay relate? What insight or perspective does the author have about the experience? What could be added to clarify the perspective?
- What technique does the essay use to hook the reader in the introduction? How effectively is it used?
- How thoroughly does the essay elaborate on the controlling idea? What additional information might be included to further develop the author's perspective? What might be deleted?
- How does the information in each paragraph contribute to the controlling idea?

These are complete sentences because they express complete thoughts.

IDENTIFYING COMPLETE SENTENCES. In the sentences below, identify which are the complete sentences and which are fragments. Underline the complete subject once and underline the complete predicate twice. For more information, see the Language Arts Survey 3.17, "Finding The Complete Subject and Complete Predicate in a Sentence."

Ah-nen-la-de-ni disliked the Indian school.
Because his name was changed. He was at the school.
For a long time.
Despite his protests.
His name was changed.

FIXING FRAGMENT SENTENCES. Look at the fragments that you identified above. Change them to complete sentences by adding a subject or predicate where necessary. Also look for fragments in Sean's personal essay. Explain whether a subject or predicate is missing. Then edit the sentences to make them complete.

USING COMPLETE SENTENCES. Look at each sentence in your personal essay. Underline the complete subject once and underline the complete predicate twice. Correct any fragments you find and change them to complete sentences.

Drafting

Review with students the definition for chronological order. Chronological order is the arrangement of details in order of their occurrence. You might also review a first-person point of view. Students might need help expressing their controlling idea. You might put students in pairs so that they can help each other write their controlling idea down. Encourage students to use their completed Graphic Organizer modeled on page 78 to help them make sure they are following their plan for their personal essay. Have students write a discovery draft in which they do not focus on spelling, grammar, usage, and mechanics.

Self- and Peer Evaluation

Have students use the checklist on page 79 for self- and peer evaluation. See the Guided Writing Resource located in the Teacher's Resource Kit for a blackline master of the checklist. The checklist is intended to act as a student-friendly rubric that should help students identify specific evidence of writing strengths and areas needing improvement. Make sure students provide concrete suggestions for improvement or specific evidence of the effectiveness of their personal essay. Students might benefit from reading the Language Arts Survey 2.37–2.40 for more details about self- and peer evaluation.

Teacher's Note

Have students compare the Student Model—Draft on page 80 with the final version presented on page 82. What improvements did Sean make? In what ways could the Student Model—Revised be further improved?

> "Writing is like anything—baseball playing, piano playing, sewing, hammering nails. The more you work at it, the better you get. But it seems to take a longer time to get better at writing than hammering nails."
>
> —Betsy Byars

> "A writer needs three things: experience, observation, and imagination."
>
> —William Faulkner

- What descriptive words and specific details could be added to make the essay more interesting to the reader?
- What changes in sentence structure—such as a greater variety of sentence structures or correction of run-on sentences and fragments—might improve the writing?
- What type of information does the conclusion provide for the reader? What might be added or deleted?

Sean did a self-evaluation of his personal essay about his experience at a summer camp in the Rocky Mountains. He also compared his essay to his graphic organizer to make sure that the information in his essay related to his controlling idea.

Student Model—Draft

Hiking in the mountains is great fun, I found this out last summer when I went to a camp in the Rocky Mountains. For the first few days, my ~~Outdoor lab is interesting~~ but you

Be more specific

friends and I hiked through really have to work hard. ~~All of the~~ several very steep trails which were hard to climb. Then one morning, our

Add more to introduction

~~trails are very steep and hard to~~ teacher announced that we would be taking the Geology Trail.

that ~~climb.~~ On ~~the Geology~~ trail, we had to

climb almost straight up! There are a

lot of switchbacks and turns on it. My

friends and I tripped over large rocks,

but we helped each other until ~~After~~ we finally got to the top, ~~we were~~

~~very tired! But it was fun to climb. On~~

~~the large rocks up there. Then the~~

80   UNIT ONE

80   TEACHER'S EDITION

teacher scolded us for it. On the way

down, it was so slippery I probably

fell six times! ~~It reminded me of the~~

~~time that I fell on some slippery rocks~~

~~and landed in the creek by~~ our ~~house.~~

~~When we got down we ate dinner and went~~
By the end of the day, we
were so tired we couldn't
~~to bed I could not get~~ to sleep. When ~~I~~ for a long time.
we
did get
finally ~~got~~ to sleep, ~~I did not wake up~~

nothing could wake us up!   Add a conclusion
~~until the next morning.~~

Hiking in the mountains with my friend was an experience I'll never
forget. It was hard work, but I learned to climb steep trails and
depend on my friends.

Revising and Proofreading

If possible, give yourself some "wait time" after you complete your self- and peer evaluations. Then you will be able to look at your essay in a new light. Review your notes from your evaluations, then revise your essay. Concentrate on improving the organization of the essay. Be sure you have an introduction, a body, and a conclusion to your essay. Let your readers understand your controlling idea by focusing on your experience, your perspective, and the story you tell.

Proofread your revised draft for errors in sentence construction. Read each sentence carefully and make sure each sentence is complete and not a fragment.

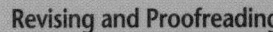

Revising and Proofreading

Remind students that revising includes adding or expanding, cutting or condensing, replacing, and moving text. Have students read the Language Arts Survey 2.41, "Revising." A handout of the proofreading checklist found in the Language Arts Survey on page 888 is available in the Teacher's Resource Kit, Guided Writing Resource book 2.45. Students may be interested in using common proofreader's symbols, which are found in the Language Arts Survey 2.44, "Using Proofreader's Marks."

Publishing and Presenting

Publishing and Presenting

Rewrite your final copy in ink or print it from a computer. You may want to create a cover that illustrates part of your story or that you personalize in some other way. Decide how you will present your personal essay to other students. You may want to meet in small reading groups and read the essays aloud. Or you may want to prepare a class book of all the essays.

If you have written your essay for your family or other adults, decide how you will pass the essay along from one person to the next. You might send a photocopy or an e-mail with your essay included.

To make sharing your essay more interesting, try a round robin reading. Make a list of the people that you would like to read your essay. Include each person's street or e-mail address. Send one photocopy or one e-mail of your essay along with your list of readers to the first person on your list. Ask the first person to read your essay, make a brief comment about it, and then send the essay and comment to the next person on the list. Be sure that you are the last person on the list, so you can receive all of your readers' comments.

Student Model—Revised

Mountains are exciting to me, so when I heard about a summer outdoor lab camp in the Rocky Mountains, I was ready to go. That's when I found out that hiking in the mountains is great fun, but you really have to work hard to do it.

For the first few days, my friends and I hiked through several very steep trails which were hard to climb. Then one morning, our teacher announced that we would be taking Geology Trail. On that trail, we had to climb almost straight up! There are a lot of switchbacks and turns on it. My friends and I tripped over large rocks, but we helped each other until we finally got to the top.

On the way down, it was so slippery I probably fell at least six times! By the end of the day, we were so tired we couldn't get to sleep for a long time. When we finally did get to sleep, nothing could wake us!

Hiking in the mountains with my friends was an experience I'll never forget. It was hard work, but I learned to climb steep trails and depend on my friends.

UNIT ONE *review*

Review: Words for Everyday Use

Check your knowledge of the following vocabulary words. Choose ten of these words that you would like to incorporate into your own daily language. For each word, write a short sentence that includes the word in context. To review a word, look back to the page number indicated.

- accelerate (32)
- aggressor (67)
- ascend (44)
- auspicious (66)
- batter (11)
- billow (52)
- chortle (69)
- conform (30)
- contour (14)
- contrary (32)
- cynical (55)
- dapper (8)
- detrimental (68)
- disciplinarian (11)
- exuberant (9)
- gaudy (53)

- gaunt (9)
- gesture (55)
- indignant (70)
- irrational (55)
- jaunty (17)
- jostle (53)
- laden (16)
- malicious (56)
- malleable (30)
- menace (10)
- miser (31)
- mutilate (69)
- oppose (68)
- oppress (67)
- peer (17)
- pernicious (64)

- poised (14)
- prosperity (64)
- quaver (12)
- quiver (69)
- resolute (68)
- revel (70)
- ruddy (10)
- ruthless (67)
- somber (17)
- submerge (52)
- submissive (68)
- tendon (16)
- throng (52)
- wince (11)
- wondrous (8)

Review: Literary Tools

Be prepared to define each of the following terms, giving concrete examples when possible. To review a term, refer to the page number indicated.

- character (27)
- conflict (5)
- description (5)
- dialogue (61)

- image (43)
- imagery (43)
- irony (49)
- memoir (61)

- motive (61)
- plot (27)
- speaker (43)
- theme (49)

 **art** s m a r t

Look back at the painting on pages 2–3. Artists often borrow from cultures not their own. Paul Gauguin (1848–1903) was a French artist who was influenced by many cultures. Late in his life he moved to Tahiti, where this painting was made. Although 19th century Tahiti and ancient Egypt are thousands of miles and thousands of years apart, what similarities can you find between this painting of Isis on page 492?

VOCABULARY DEVELOPMENT. Give students the following exercise.

Read the Language Arts Survey 1.16, "Using Context Clues to Estimate Word Meaning." Then choose twenty words from the list on page 83 that you would like to incorporate into your everyday vocabulary. Write a sentence containing a context clue for each word you chose. Use more than one type of context clue in your sentences.

EXAMPLE
auspicious
The girl's future looked especially **auspicious**, and everyone expected good things for her.

ADDITIONAL RESOURCES

UNIT 1 RESOURCE BOOK
- Vocabulary Worksheet
- Study Guide: Unit 1 Test
- Unit 1 Test

Reflecting on your reading

Theme

The selections in this unit explore the theme of finding your place in the world. The main characters in each selection are struggling to find where they as individuals belong in the world around them. For example, in "Destroy the Four Olds" Ji-li is a Chinese girl, a Young Patriot, and a member of the Jiang family, yet she is unsure how she should act and which guidelines she should follow during the political campaign. In "The Fan Club," Laura's desire to be accepted conflicts with her beliefs about how people should treat others. The main character in "Zebra" struggles with his physical impairments as he distances himself from people.

Group Project

Discuss in small groups the theme of finding your place in the world. In what different ways do the characters in the selections in this unit approach the issues of identity and fitting in with others? How do they realize or maintain their beliefs and ideals? How do they adapt to the situations that confront them? Do you consider their adaptations to be successful? Why, or why not? You may want to use the graphic organizer on the facing page to order your thoughts as you develop ideas for the group project.

With members of your group, create a collage or poster around that reflect the theme of finding your place in the world. Focus on a character's thoughts and views about identity and fitting in with others. The collage or poster could address feelings of self-confidence, peer pressure, worries, hopes, relationships, and other issues you discussed. Share your group's project with the class.

Critical Thinking

You already have studied the thought processes of the characters in the selections in this unit. While working with the group, you will need to follow your own thought process and express your thoughts to others. Keep the following questions in mind as you work.
- What is the best way to put your thoughts into words and vocalize them?
- How can you make sure everyone in the group has the opportunity to share his or her opinion?
- When is it possible for differing opinions to be equally valid?

Graphic Organizer

	Zebra	Albert	Victor	Phil	Laura	Ji-li	Group discussion notes
Identity							
Environment							
Struggles							
Thoughts and views about "finding your place in the world"							

On Your Own

Write an essay about finding your place in the world.
As you plan your essay, think about the following questions.

- When is it most difficult to figure out how you fit in with others?
- What kinds of things cause you to worry about fitting in?
- When do you feel most confident about your identity and your place in the world?
- What can difficult situations teach you about yourself?

On Your Own

To get students started with the essay prompts in On Your Own, have them review the responses they made in the Reader's Journal and Respond to the Selection activities as they read the selections in this unit.

UNIT SKILLS OUTLINE

Literary Skills and Concepts

Writing Skills and Concepts

Language, Grammar, and Style

Christina's World, 1948. Andrew Wyeth. The Museum of Modern Art, New York.

GOALS/OBJECTIVES

Studying this unit will enable students to
- enjoy fiction, nonfiction, and poems exploring the theme of the world around us
- define and identify examples of *characterization, figurative language, imagery, irony, irony of situation, oral tradition, personification, setting, suspense,* and *symbol.*

- read independently to explore other cultures
- write a comparison-contrast essay
- recognize action and state of being verbs and different verb tenses; demonstrate an ability to use tenses consistently

The World around US

UNIT TWO

CROSS-CURRICULAR CONNECTIONS

Arts and Humanities
Documentary on Our Vanishing Wilderness, 130
Environmental Poster Contest, 132
Extinct Species, 133
Favorite Things, 97
Four Seasons and Human Emotions, 106
Habitat for Humanity, 90
Orphism, 107
Poem about Death and Dying, 96
Portraying a Snake, 114
Pumpkin-Decorating Contest, 107
Researching Cities, 90
Singing and Playing Dream Songs, 141
Urban Lifestyle, 90
Writing Dream Songs, 140

Mathematics and Sciences
Coral Reefs, 134
Extinct Species, 133
Freud's and Jung's Theories on Dreaming, 95
Human Actions and the Environment, 129
Paired Research, 115
Report on Hail, 109
Report on Locusts, 109
Researching Cancer, 99
Researching Sparrows, 98
Role-Playing an Environmentalist, 128
Television Documentary on Snakes, 114

Social Studies
Cultural Significance of Snakes, 118
Freud's and Jung's Theories on Dreaming, 95
Habitat for Humanity, 90
History of India, 122
Human Actions and the Environment, 129
Impact of the Industrial Revolution on the Environment, 131
Living in an Opposite Place, 91
Researching Cities, 90
The Abenaki, 100
Urban Lifestyle, 90

Applied Arts
Pumpkin-Decorating Contest, 107

TEACHING THE MULTIPLE INTELLIGENCES

Musical
Favorite Things, 97
Portraying a Snake, 114
Singing and Playing Dream Songs, 141
Writing Dream Songs, 140

Logical-Mathematical
City versus Country Living Chart, 90
Coral Reefs, 134
Extinct Species, 133
Human Actions and the Environment, 129
Paired Research, 115
Perils of Modern Life, 91
Poem about Death and Dying, 96
Report on Hail, 109
Report on Locusts, 109
Researching Cities, 90
Urban Lifestyle, 90

Spatial
Bettering the Environment, 128
Documentary on Our Vanishing Wilderness, 130
Environmental Poster Contest, 132
Extinct Species, 133

(Continued on page 88)

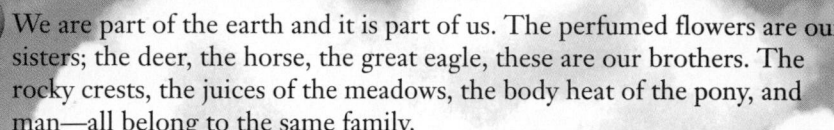
ADDITIONAL QUESTIONS AND ACTIVITIES

Begin a class discussion by having students read the quotations in the Echoes feature. Ask them the following:

- Which quotations, if any, have you read or heard before? Which are new to you?
- Which people quoted favor wilderness over urban areas? Which people quoted favor cities?
- Which quotations do you agree with most? Do you agree with Henry Beston's or Michelangelo Antonioni's words more? Why?
- If you decided to follow the words of Dolores Huerta or Rachel Carson, what would your plan of action be?

As an alternate activity, you may want to have students freewrite about one or two of the questions above.

TEACHING THE MULTIPLE INTELLIGENCES (CONT.)

We are part of the earth and it is part of us. The perfumed flowers are our sisters; the deer, the horse, the great eagle, these are our brothers. The rocky crests, the juices of the meadows, the body heat of the pony, and man—all belong to the same family.

—*Chief Seattle*

To make a prairie it takes a clover and one bee,
One clover, and a bee,
And revery.
The revery alone will do,
If bees are few.

—*Emily Dickinson*

Touch the earth, love the earth, honor the earth, her plains, her valleys, her hills, and her seas; rest your spirit in her solitary places.

—*Henry Beston*

I have never felt salvation in nature. I love cities above all.

—*Michelangelo Antonioni*

We must use our lives to make the world a better place, not just to acquire things. That is what we are put on earth for.

—*Dolores Huerta*

To one who has been long in city pent,
'Tis very sweet to look into the fair
And open face of heaven . . .

—*John Keats*

All cities are mad, but the madness is gallant. All cities are beautiful, but the beauty is grim.

—*Christopher Morley*

I believe that whenever we destroy beauty, or substitute something man-made and artificial for a natural feature of the earth, we have retarded some part of man's spiritual growth.

—*Rachel Carson*

TEACHING THE MULTIPLE INTELLIGENCES (CONT.)

Prereading

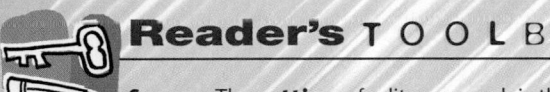

"in the inner city" by Lucille Clifton
and **"The City is so Big"** by Richard Garcia

Reader's T O O L B O X

SETTING. The **setting** of a literary work is the time and place in which it happens. Writers create settings in many different ways, using details to create a sense of a particular time and place. As you read, look for the ways the speaker in each poem conveys a sense of setting.

IMAGERY. Taken together, the images in a poem or passage are called its **imagery**. Images are created from language that describes things that can be seen, heard, touched, tasted, or smelled. What does the imagery of "in the inner city" leave you thinking about? How does it differ from the imagery in "The City Is So Big"? You may want to use the graphic organizers below to sort your thoughts.

Graphic *Organizer*

"in the inner city"

Image	What the image suggests
pastel lights	sterile

"The City Is So Big"

Image	What the image suggests
bridges quake with fear	rumbling, loud noises and traffic jams

Reader's *Journal*

Describe what for you would make the perfect city.

Reader's *Resource*

- **SOCIAL STUDIES CONNECTION.** For many decades, people in the United States have been concerned about deteriorating urban—or inner city—areas. In the 1930s, officials developed programs to tackle problems of urban deterioration. Today, these urban renewal programs differ greatly in their approach to these problems. In some, inner cities are completely demolished and rebuilt. In others, people work to restore and rehabilitate buildings and neighborhoods. Some urban renewal programs strive to preserve residential areas, public housing, parks, and playgrounds. Others focus on commercial and industrial development.

89

ADDITIONAL RESOURCES

UNIT 2 RESOURCE BOOK
"in the inner city"
- Selection Worksheet 2.1
- Selection Check Test 4.2.1
- Selection Test 4.2.2

"The City is so Big"
- Selection Worksheet 2.2
- Selection Check Test 4.2.3
- Selection Test 4.2.4
- Speaking and Listening Resource 4.19
- Study and Research Resource 5.17–5.44

GRAPHIC ORGANIZER

Students may include the following points from the poems in their graphic organizers:
For "in the inner city": silent nights—emptiness, lifelessness; houses straight as dead men—orderly, but lifeless; pastel lights—seems wimpy, spiritless.
For "The City Is So Big": lights slide from house to house—sounds scary, slowly moving headlights; trains passing windows shining like a smile full of teeth—sounds threatening as if it might bite; machines eating houses—sounds like a science fiction story; stairways walking by themselves—sounds creepy and unnatural; elevators making people disappear—sounds scary and lonely, a world where machines rule.

READER'S JOURNAL

Ask students to write about whether they feel they are "city" people or "country" people. Do they enjoy living where they live, or would they prefer to live in a different neighborhood or area? As an alternative activity, students might write about what frightened them when they were younger. Did they ever imagine monsters under their bed or in their closet? Have students describe their childhood fears and how they conquered them.

GOALS/OBJECTIVES

Studying this lesson will enable students to
- understand the feelings the speaker of a poem has about his or her home
- appreciate a poem that imaginatively describes a city
- contrast two places
- define and understand *setting*
- define and identify *imagery* in poetry

INDIVIDUAL LEARNING STRATEGIES

MOTIVATION
Encourage students to make pro and con charts listing the benefits and drawbacks of living in the city and living in the country. Students might then share the pros and cons they have listed in their charts. Encourage them to discuss where they would prefer to live when they are older and why.

READING PROFICIENCY
While both selections contain fairly simple vocabulary, students may have trouble reading them since they are not punctuated or divided into sentences. Read the poems aloud for them or have them listen to the audiocassette so they can hear the pauses. Then have them read the poems aloud or softly to themselves.

ENGLISH LANGUAGE LEARNING
elevator—device for moving people or things from floor to floor in a building
inner city—the interior of a city as opposed to the borders or outskirts
pastel—soft and pale
quake—shake or vibrate
uptown—residential area away from the main business area of a city

SPECIAL NEEDS
Students will find it helpful to listen to the selection on audiocassette. Make sure students focus on the Guided Reading questions and the Recall questions in the Investigate, Inquire, and Imagine section.

ENRICHMENT
Have students research cities. Possible subjects might include the rise of cities; differences between city life and country, suburban, or small town life; or the history, cultural offerings, technological and artistic developments, and other aspects of specific cities such as New York, Tokyo, Rome, or Buenos Aires. Students might also research Habitat for Humanity and other organizations whose purpose includes revitalizing urban areas.

ANSWER TO GUIDED READING QUESTION

1. The speaker is happy to be alive and in the inner city.

in the inner city

Lucille Clifton

in the inner city
or
like we call it
home
5   we think a lot about uptown
and the silent nights
and the houses straight as
dead men
and the pastel lights
10   and we hang on to our no place
happy to be alive
and in the inner city
or
like we call it
15   home

GUIDED READING
What is the speaker happy about?

The City is so BIG

Richard Garcia

The city is so big
Its bridges quake with fear
I know, I have seen at night

The lights sliding from house to house
5   And trains pass with windows shining
Like a smile full of teeth

I have seen machines eating houses
And stairways walk all by themselves
And elevator doors opening and closing
10 And people disappear.

GUIDED READING

Why do the city's bridges quake?

Quotables

"City Life. Millions of people being lonesome together."

—Henry David Thoreau

"Cities, like cats, will reveal themselves at night."

—Rupert Brooke

ANSWER TO GUIDED READING QUESTION

1. The bridges quake because the city is so big it scares them.

CROSS-CURRICULAR ACTIVITIES

LIVING IN AN OPPOSITE PLACE. Divide the class into pairs of students. Explain that people from cities often dream of living in the country and vice versa. Ask students, "Which group of people do you think longs to change the most? Why? Pretend that your home could magically become the exact opposite of where you are living now—apartment to huge home, prairie to mountains, hot weather to cold weather, etc. Could you ever feel at home in this new place? Why, or why not?" Have the student pairs discuss these questions. You might then want to extend the discussion as a class.

PERILS OF MODERN LIFE. Garcia's poem could be interpreted as a child's or a pet's view of the city. Some might even see it as an alien's view. Make a list on an overhead transparency or on the chalkboard of student-generated responses to the question: "What things in a house or community could frighten someone unfamiliar with our way of life?"

Get students started with these suggestions:
Freezer—turns food into "stones"
TV—makes people tiny and two-dimensional, and traps them inside a box
Telephone—makes voices even when no one is there
Vacuum—makes things disappear
Airplane—huge bird that brings people high in the air and then disappears into the clouds

As a culminating activity, you can show parts of the movie *Crocodile Dundee,* in which a man from the Australian Outback tries to understand modern life in New York City.

SELECTION CHECK TEST 4.2.1 WITH ANSWERS

Checking Your Reading
"IN THE INNER CITY"
1. What does the speaker like to call the inner city? **The speaker likes to call the inner city "home."**
2. What are the nights like in uptown? **The nights are silent.**
3. What do the people of the inner city think about a lot? **They think about uptown.**
4. What are the houses like in uptown? **They are straight as dead men.**
5. What word describes the lights uptown? **The lights are pastel.**

SELECTION CHECK TEST 4.2.3 WITH ANSWERS

Checking Your Reading
"THE CITY IS SO BIG"
1. What do the bridges in the city do? **The bridges quake with fear.**
2. When does the speaker observe these scary images of the city? **The speaker says that he or she has seen these things at night.**
3. What do the shining train windows look like? **They look like "a smile full of teeth."**
4. What do the machines and stairways do? **The machines eat houses and the stairways walk by themselves.**
5. What happens when the elevator doors open and close? **People disappear.**

Respond to the SELECTION

Which of the two poems better describes your ideas about city life? Why?

About the AUTHORS

Lucille Clifton is a self-taught poet who teaches at Columbia University and at St. Mary's College of Maryland. She has also served as the poet laureate for Maryland. Clifton was born near Buffalo, New York, in 1936. Her first book of poetry, *Good Times*, was published in 1969. Since then she has published a number of poetry collections, including *Quilting: Poems 1987–1990* and *The Terrible Stories*. Clifton has also written many children's books. They include *My Friend Jacob*, *Three Wishes*, and a series of books based on the character Everett Anderson. Clifton's six children have inspired much of her poetry.

Richard Garcia was born in San Francisco, California, in 1941. Besides California, he has lived in Mexico and in Israel. Garcia has served as the director of the Poets in the Schools program in Marin County, California. He writes poetry for both adults and young people. If you like "The City Is So Big," you may want to read his collection *Selected Poetry* (1973.)

92   UNIT TWO / THE WORLD AROUND US

ANSWERS TO INVESTIGATE, INQUIRE, IMAGINE (CONT.)

EXTEND
6b. *Responses will vary.* The speakers of the two poems would both probably like to see cities become friendlier places. The speaker of "in the inner city" dislikes the sterile, lifeless atmosphere of uptown, while the speaker of "The City Is So Big" feels that individual people get swallowed up by the hugeness of the city. Both speakers may find some aspects of cities frightening. However, the speaker of "in the inner city" has a much more positive view of the city. He or she argues that while an outsider might find the city impersonal or scary, many people feel at home there.

Investigate, Inquire, and Imagine

Recall: GATHERING FACTS

1a. What two things does the speaker in "in the inner city" call the inner city?

2a. In Lucille Clifton's poem, what do people in the inner city think about a lot?

3a. What does the speaker say about the bridges in "The City Is So Big"?

4a. In Richard Garcia's poem, what has the speaker seen machines do?

→ Interpret: FINDING MEANING

1b. By referring to the inner city in those terms, what does the speaker reveal about his or her feelings about the inner city?

2b. Why might residents think about this place so much?

3b. What might cause the bridges to do this?

4b. In what way might machines actually do this? What might the speaker be saying about the role of machines in city life?

Analyze: TAKING THINGS APART

5a. Compare and contrast the speaker's feelings about the city in "in the inner city" with those of the speaker in "The City Is So Big." How does each speaker feel about the city? How are the speakers' views similar? How are they different?

→ Synthesize: BRINGING THINGS TOGETHER

5b. In Clifton's poem, what do the speaker's thoughts reveal about him or her? What do the speaker's thoughts in Garcia's poem reveal about that person? What generalizations can you make about each speaker?

Evaluate: MAKING JUDGMENTS

6a. Do you agree with the speaker's ideas in "in the inner city"? Why, or why not? Do you agree with the thoughts expressed by the speaker in "The City Is So Big"? Why, or why not?

→ Extend: CONNECTING IDEAS

6b. What might the speaker in "in the inner city" have in common with the speaker in "The City Is So Big"? About what might they disagree?

Understanding Literature

SETTING. The **setting** of a literary work is the time and place in which it happens. How is the inner city described in "In the Inner city"? How is uptown described in "in the inner city"? How is the setting described in "The City Is So Big"?

RECALL

1a. The speaker calls the inner city "home" and "no place."

2a. The people in the inner city think about uptown a lot.

3a. The speaker says the bridges "quake with fear."

4a. The speaker has seen "machines eating houses."

INTERPRET

1b. The speaker reveals mixed feelings about the inner city. The word "home" suggests that the inner city is a place where the speaker feels comfortable and accepted. By using the term "no place," the speaker shows some negative feelings about the inner city.

2b. The residents of the inner city may think about uptown a lot because it contrasts sharply with where they live. People in the inner city may wish they had more money and luxurious homes, as those living uptown probably do.

3b. Students may say that literally speaking, the traffic on the bridges causes the bridges to shake or quake; and that figuratively the tall bridges quake with fear because they see how big the city is and are overwhelmed by it.

4b. The machines could be demolishing old or broken-down buildings to make way for new or bigger buildings. The speaker may be voicing a concern that tearing down houses with little thought or effort can be destructive to people.

ANALYZE

5a. Although both speakers reveal negative feelings about the city, the speaker in "in the inner city" has mixed feelings, calling the inner city both "home" and "no place." The speaker in "The City Is So Big" reveals fear and powerlessness. Here the speaker seems to dislike the ideals of "progress" as they relate to rebuilding, technological changes, and overdevelopment.

SYNTHESIZE

5b. The speaker in Clifton's poem might feel as if his or her life is more unstable than the lives of those who live uptown, but the speaker is "happy to be alive / and in the inner city." In spite of its shortcomings, it is home to the speaker. Students may say that this person seems content despite living in imperfect conditions. Because of the fear the speaker expresses in Garcia's poem, this

---

ANSWERS TO INVESTIGATE, INQUIRE, IMAGINE (CONT.)

person might prefer to live in a rural environment, one that is more personal and less anonymous. Students may say that the speaker could be a young child or a person new to the city.

EVALUATE

6a. *Responses will vary.* Students may agree with the speaker's ideas "in the inner city," arguing points for staying there. If they disagree, they might cite reasons for moving to uptown or elsewhere.

Students may agree with the speaker in "The City Is So Big," stating that so-called progress is not always in the best interest of people. Others may disagree, saying that redevelopment and technological advances are necessary and desired. Students might find the elements in Garcia's poem exciting instead of frightening.

(Continued on page 92)

Collaborative Learning
URBAN PLANNING. Students who like this activity might like to try the urban planning computer game SimCity. Information is available on the Internet at www. simcity.com. Teacher's guides for this computer game are also available.

ANSWERS TO UNDERSTANDING LITERATURE

SETTING. In "in the inner city," the inner city is contrasted with uptown. The setting of uptown is described more fully than that of the inner city. The speaker conveys a contrast between what he or she calls home and the uptown setting, which is silent, lifeless with its houses "straight as / dead men," and pale pastel lights. Students may infer that the inner city may be noisy and full of life; they may guess that, instead of pastel lights, it might be dark or filled with bright lights. Despite the fact that the inner city is "no place," people hang onto it, "happy to be alive." In "The City Is So Big," the setting is conveyed through the speaker's direct description of quaking bridges, "lights sliding," trains passing, "machines eating houses," escalators that "walk all by themselves," and elevators into which "people disappear." The overall setting conveyed is an unfriendly place—one of metal, concrete, and glass.

IMAGERY. The imagery in "in the inner city" conveys a contrast between downtown and uptown. Uptown seems quiet, tranquil, well-lit, and ordinary. Downtown seems very different. In "The City Is So Big," the imagery, including visuals such as sliding lights, trains with teethlike windows, machines like monsters "eating houses," and the loud noise the trains and machines make, is eerie and frightening.

IMAGERY. Taken together, the images in a poem or passage are called its **imagery**. Images are created from language that describes things that can be seen, heard, touched, tasted, or smelled. What does the imagery convey in "in the inner city"? What does the imagery convey in "The City Is So Big"?

Writer's Journal

1. Write **dictionary entries** for a children's dictionary, defining the following terms: city, downtown, and uptown. Imagine the dictionary is for elementary-age students.

2. Write a **slogan** attracting people to visit a freshly renovated or historically preserved downtown area.

3. Imagine that you are running for mayor. Write a **list of goals** you would propose to make the city a better place.

Skill Builders

Collaborative Learning

URBAN PLANNING. In small groups, brainstorm ideas for creating an ideal city. Using large sheets of paper or posterboard, map out your city. Your group should keep in mind the following elements: commercial, industrial, and residential areas; public places such as government buildings, libraries, schools, police and fire departments, hospitals, and parks; transportation; natural resources; and utilities such as water, electricity, and gas. Use different colors, patterns, and icons to identify parts of your city. If possible, use a computer printer to create labels for the elements. After you finish, share your group's city plan with the class.

Study and Research

RESEARCHING A CITY. At your school or local public library, research an urban area in the United States. Work with encyclopedias, books, magazines, computer Internet sites, and other resources to find information. You may choose to focus on the city's history, landmarks, downtown area, transportation systems, population, economy, or geography. Keep a research journal as you gather information. Present your findings to your class. For help with research, you may want to review the Language Arts Survey 5.17–5.44, "Research Skills."

Speaking and Listening

READING POETRY ALOUD. As a class, find other poems about cities. Each person in the class should select a poem to read aloud to the class. Rehearse your poem before you present it, memorizing it if possible. You might want to review the Language Arts Survey 4.19, "Oral Interpretation of Poetry," for tips on preparing and presenting your selection.

Prereading

"Jed's Grandfather"

by Joseph Bruchac

Reader's Resource

- The main character in this story has a disturbing dream related to what is happening in his life. Dreams have played an important role in ancient and primitive cultures. Throughout time, many people have believed that dreams were visits from a supreme being, predictions of the future, or the activities of human souls freed by sleep.

- **SCIENCE CONNECTION.** Austrian psychiatrist Sigmund Freud (1856–1939) was one of the first modern scientists to study dreams. He believed that dreams were keys to the makeup of each person. He also believed that dreams had symbolic meaning. Another modern psychiatrist, Swiss researcher Carl Gustav Jung (1875–1961), added to Freud's ideas. Jung believed that dreams express the thoughts people are not conscious of, including their worries about the future.

- This story takes place in a rural area on Indian Lake, probably in the Adirondack Mountains in New York. The Sabael family in the story lives much as Jed's ancestors did, relying little on outsiders to provide the necessities of life. Instead, they rely on their own abilities to gather food and water, to supply shelter and warmth, and to cope with hardship.

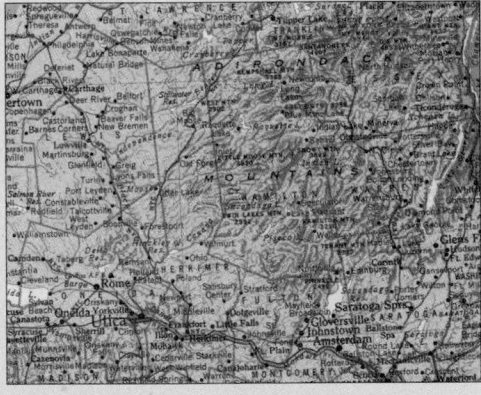

Reader's Journal

Write about someone who has taught you a skill. What have you learned from this person?

Reader's TOOLBOX

IRONY. Irony is a difference between appearance and reality. In this story, Jed's grandfather is depicted as having always been a very strong person, as sturdy as a tree. As you read the story, think about how that depiction could be considered ironic.

SYMBOL. A symbol is a thing that stands for—or represents—both itself and something else. In this story, elements such as birds, woodsmoke, and a dream are symbols for other things, such as emotions or personal qualities. Try to locate symbols and to interpret their meanings as you read.

ADDITIONAL RESOURCES

UNIT 2 RESOURCE BOOK
- Selection Worksheet 2.3
- Selection Check Test 4.2.5
- Selection Test 4.2.6
- Language, Grammar, and Style Resource 3.86, 3.89, 3.91

READER'S JOURNAL

As an alternate activity, encourage students to write their thoughts and feelings about one of their grandparents or about another elderly person they know.

CROSS-CURRICULAR CONNECTION

SCIENCE
- Whereas Freud thought that dreams revealed our hidden desires, Jung felt that dreams could reveal a whole variety of thoughts, not only desires but also fears and worries. He also believed that certain symbols found in people's dreams can be considered archetypes, or symbols that are shared by all human beings and passed down from generation to generation. Freud wrote about his ideas in his book *Interpretation of Dreams* (1900), and Jung discussed his in *Psychology of the Unconscious* (1916).
- Dreams occur during the rapid-eye-movement (REM) stage of sleep. Often the movement of a dreamer's eyes during this stage reflects what he or she is dreaming about. For example, a dreamer may cast his or her eyes upward if dreaming about a bird in the sky. Dreaming is necessary for mental health. Studies show that adults dream an average of 1½ to 2 hours for every 8 hours of sleep. If deprived of dream-sleep, people tend to become anxious, irritable, and less physically coordinated.

GOALS/OBJECTIVES

Studying this lesson will enable students to
- relate to a character's feelings about his dying grandfather
- briefly describe some different opinions about dreams and their meaning
- define *irony* and recognize the use of irony in their reading
- define *symbolism* and identify symbols in literature
- edit for capitalization errors
- work in groups to research a Native American language
- take notes and document sources to prepare a report on dreams

1. Jed remembers last night's dream.
2. The swallows fly by themselves rather than fluttering in groups.

INDIVIDUAL LEARNING STRATEGIES

MOTIVATION
The Adirondack region, where this story takes place, is a popular vacation area because of the natural beauty of its many lakes, mountainous areas, and pristine woods. Encourage students to plan an imaginary trip to the Adirondack mountains in both summer and in winter. What activities might they enjoy in each of these seasons?

READING PROFICIENCY
Identify for students who the characters are in this story and how they are related to one another. Create an outline of the action of the story. Tell students to use this outline to help guide them through the story, and to think about not only the events that occur but how characters feel about these events.

ENGLISH LANGUAGE LEARNING
Point out the following words and expressions.
cobwebs—anything flimsy or entrapping, like a spider's web
ye—you
coffee mill—machine for grinding roast coffee beans
bull's-eye pane of glass—round and curved piece of glass that focuses light like a lens
ash—a type of tree
locust post—post made from the wood of a locust tree, known for its very hard, durable wood
woodlot—piece of land on which trees are grown for firewood or lumber
squabbling—fighting noisily over a small matter

SPECIAL NEEDS
Encourage students to write their answers to the Guided Reading questions because these will point them to key events in the story. Students may also find it helpful to participate in or view a role-playing session in which one student plays Jed and the other student plays Jed's grandfather.

Jed's Grandfather
Joseph Bruchac

Jed slowly worked the handle of the backyard pitcher pump. He watched the water lap from side to side in waves as he tilted the bucket back and forth. The patterns of the dream were still going through his head. They hadn't been washed away with the first splash of water from the trough, water so cold that a paper-thin layer of ice still had to be brushed away these early spring mornings. Washing his face usually cleared whatever cobwebs of sleep still clung to his face and his thoughts, but it hadn't happened this morning. The dream was still with him.

> **GUIDED READING**
> What does Jed remember while he fills the bucket of water?

The swallows had flown up now. The red sun was a finger's width above the hill. He looked up and watched the swallows darting, stitching the face of the sky the way his mother's needle covered a piece of cloth. The other birds, shorter-winged, fluttered in groups, as if afraid to fly by themselves the way the swallows did. The swallows were the adventurous ones. He remembered how his grandfather first pointed out to him the way a swallow can dart down to the surface of a lake and scoop up a mouthful of water without landing. They had watched swallows doing

> **GUIDED READING**
> What makes the swallows different from other birds?

words for everyday use   **trough** (träf') *n.*, a long shallow container for water or animal feed. *The pigs shoved each other as they hungrily ate corn from the long wooden trough.*

INDIVIDUAL LEARNING STRATEGIES (CONT.)

ENRICHMENT
Encourage students to share their own feelings about death and dying in a poem, short story, or personal essay. Students might wish to write about their own experiences with losing a loved one, but if they find writing about such a topic too painful, they might write about death in a more abstract, impersonal way.

that, drinking from the pond below the house that day last blueberry season when Grandfather rowed him out to The Island.

Usually the sight of the swallows in the morning sky would drive everything else out of his thoughts. He'd arch his back, lift his chin, hold out his arms, hearing his Grandfather's soft voice guiding him. "You want to be a swallow, Jeddy? You can do it. Just feel the wind under ye. That's it."

That wouldn't work this morning. The dream was too strong. He was in the boat, dark water widening between them. The old man stood there on The Island, unaware of the great dark wave coming at him from behind. His eyes were on Jed, but Jed couldn't call out. He couldn't move his arms. He wanted to turn into a swallow, fly out and rescue him, but he was paralyzed. Then the water between them began to open like a crack in the earth . . .

GUIDED READING
Who appears in Jed's dream?

"Jed!" It was his mother's voice. Jed looked up. The bucket was filled and overflowing around his feet. A chicken was scurrying around the edge of the spreading water, now and then lifting a foot and shaking it as the water touched it. Jed carried the bucket into the kitchen.

His parents were at the table. Jed bent his arms and arched his back, hefting the bucket up onto the sink shelf.

"You're getting stronger ever day, son," his father said, thin hand around a steaming mug. Behind him the wood stove crackled, a sound Jed had always loved. The steam from his father's coffee rose through the cold morning air of the kitchen. Jed could smell the coffee. It was a good smell, just as good but not quite the same as that smell when he ground the

beans in the coffee mill with its blue enamel[1] sides. But even the good smell of the coffee couldn't drive away the dream. It was there, between him and the things which were good and pleasant in his life, there the way a thick fog comes between a boat and the land. He was on the boat. He didn't know which way was home.

GUIDED READING
What comes between Jed and the pleasant things in his life?

Jed's mother smiled at him, wiped her hands on her apron. It was the first time he had really noticed the way his mother always wiped her hands on her apron before she spoke when they were at the table. She used the same care with her words that she did in making their food. All around Jed were familiar things, things known and loved, but he was seeing them for the first time . . . the small crystal dog in the east window where a bull's-eye pane of glass split the sun like a <u>prism</u> and painted a rainbow on the wall near the stairs . . . the woodbox with its splintery top which sometimes snagged his left thumb when he went for an armful of <u>kindling</u> . . . the rocking chair which always caught the last rays of the setting sun, the chair which was empty now . . .

"He just takes after his . . ." his mother was saying. She stopped in mid-sentence. Jed finished the sentence in his own mind. He takes after his grandfather. Jed's father was a good man, hard-working, but he never had the strength of his wife's people, the Sabaels. That was why he worked as a clerk at the store in town three miles from the farm. It was Jed's grandfather, straight as an ash, who

---

1. **enamel.** Hard, glossy coating applied to the surface of metal, glass, or pottery

words for everyday use

prism (pri' zəm) *n.*, a transparent crystal form that distorts light which passes through it. *The small crystal prism that hung in my window threw beautiful patterns of light all around the room.*

kin • dling (kin' liŋ) *n.*, small sticks of wood or other materials used for starting a fire. *The campers gathered newspaper and twigs to use as kindling for the campfire.*

ANSWERS TO GUIDED READING QUESTIONS

1. The "old man," Jed's grandfather, appears in the dream.
2. The dream comes between Jed and the pleasant things in his life.

CROSS-CURRICULAR ACTIVITIES

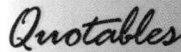

ARTS AND HUMANITIES. The narrator of this story vividly describes the familiar things that Jed knows and loves. Encourage students to write a brief description of some of the things they know and love. After students have written their descriptions, have students portray artistically—in a drawing or painting—the things they know and love.

You may also wish to play for students one of the most enduring songs about favorite things, Rodgers and Hammerstein's "My Favorite Things." Some of the lyrics to this song appear below. You might encourage students to discuss how their lists are similar to or different from the lists of the speaker in "My Favorite Things."

Quotables

"Raindrops on roses and whiskers on kittens
Bright copper kettles and warm woolen mittens
Brown paper packages tied up with strings
These are a few of my favorite things."

—Oscar Hammerstein

VOCABULARY FROM THE SELECTION

trough	prism
kindling	social
tether	sinewy

1. Jed is like his grandfather because they are both strong.
2. Jed's grandfather has shown him how to weave baskets.

CROSS-CURRICULAR ACTIVITIES

MATHEMATICS AND SCIENCES. The above quotation is probably one of the most famous about a sparrow. Share this quote with students and point out both the image of sparrows in flight on this page and the paragraph on sparrows in this short story. Encourage students to prepare a brief report on sparrows answering questions such as the following: What characteristics are distinctive to the sparrow? What are some different types of sparrow? Why do you think both artists and authors have been inspired by the sparrow?

GUIDED READING
In what way is Jed like his grandfather?

always did the work around the farm. Jed was only ten, but he was already as strong as his father.

"Jed," his mother said, her hands smoothing her apron, "you aren't eating."

The pancakes were dry in his mouth. He knew they were good. They were the pancakes his mother was famous for at church <u>socials</u>. They were light and smelled of the goodness of a summer wheatfield, but he couldn't taste them. Instead he tasted the moist air within the fog, felt the pressure of the building storm throb around his temples as the great dark wave lifted.

Jed's father was saying something to his mother. What was it? Starving himself? Jed hadn't heard the words for sure over the roaring of the wave.

"Are you sure?" his mother said.

"You're his daughter," Jed's father answered. He spoke in the same quiet voice Jed heard him use when he answered a customer who asked what to buy to get rid of potato bugs or whether the percale[2] was what she really wanted for her money's worth.

Jed's mother rose and walked over to the stove. She took the plate which had been

Flight of the Swallows, 1913. Giacomo Balla. Private Collection.

warming there and covered it with a cloth. She put the cloth-covered plate, some silverware and a stoppered[3] bottle into a basket. Jed recognized the basket. It was one Grandfather made. He remembered the sounds of the mallet as his grandfather pounded the side of the felled ash tree to break loose the withes[4] he'd trim to size. His grandfather had shown him the steps many times, shown him by doing. He felt as if the way of making a basket was woven into him the way the pattern of a web is woven into a spider's limbs. It was a craft passed down for more generations than the Sabaels could count, passed down before Jed's father's people had stepped from their ships onto these shores. For

GUIDED READING
What skill had Jed's grandfather shown him?

---

2. **percale.** Type of cotton cloth
3. **stoppered.** Plugged with a stopper such as a cork
4. **withes.** Thin, flexible twigs or sticks

---

words for everyday use

so • cial (sō shəl) *n.*, a party or gathering, especially when held by members of a group. *Each year, the student council organized an ice-cream <u>social</u> for all the students.*

a moment the thought of Grandfather's sure hands weaving a basket drove away the dream. Then the pounding of the mallet became the pounding of whitecaps[5] against the side of the boat and he saw the old man's figure made small by the lifting darkness.

"Take this down to the Little House, Jed," his mother said. She was holding the basket out to him. Jed looked up into her eyes for a moment and then reached out his hand.

> **GUIDED READING**
>
> What does Jed's mother ask him to do with the basket of food?

No smoke was rising from the chimney. Had it been rising it would have traced a perfect line up the face of the mountains and sky above Indian Lake. That was the way smoke rose on spring mornings such as this from the small one-roomed house his grandfather had built where the field fell away, green becoming the grey of stone, then the blue of water. A small boat was tied to a pole that jutted out of the water. The boat moved with the water the way a horse moves when tied to a rail . . . not pulling hard enough to break free, hardly even putting a strain on its <u>tether</u>, but showing in its motion how anxious it is to be on its way. The boat was still there. But there was no smoke.

Jed drew in a breath, feeling it catch in his stiff throat. But before he could speak he heard his grandfather's voice.

"Come," the old man called out, making that simple word one of many meanings. It meant he knew who was there. It meant Jed was welcome. It meant something else, too. It was like the words in the old language his grandfather seldom spoke, the language few people knew he knew. Jed pulled gently at the locust post which held up the small open gate. It creaked as he pulled at it, but the old wood was still firm. A locust post can stay in the ground a hundred years and still bend any nail you're fool enough to try to drive into it. A hundred years.

Jed went in. Joseph Sabael was sitting on the edge of his cot. There was a blanket around his shoulders and he was wearing his woolens, but his feet were bare. There was no rug on the floor, no fire in the stove. It was cold in the Little House, but not as cold as Jed had thought it would be. There was a faint odor in the air, one Jed had not really noticed before. It confused him.

"That's just how the cancer smells, Jeddy," his grandfather said. "Don't pay it no mind. It's just as natural as anything else."

> **GUIDED READING**
>
> What does Jed's grandfather say causes the strange odor?

Jed looked at him. Joseph Sabael had always been a tall man, but never one whose frame put on bulk. His shoulders had been broad, but not heavy. His arms had always been long and <u>sinewy</u> like the others in the town who worked the land or the big woods, not the ham-thick sort of arm which turned to softness with age. Like an ash tree's limbs, that was how his grandfather's arms had seemed. But now there was a different look to the old man. His eyes had fallen back into their sockets and one could see the bones beneath the skin in his arms. As he sat hands clasping the blanket about him, it seemed as if his shoulders were folding in around his chest. Jed held out the basket.

"Mama sent you this," he said.

"I be glad she let you come," Grandfather said. He didn't reach out his hands for the basket.

---

5. **whitecaps.** Waves breaking into white foam

---

words for everyday use

teth • er (te′ thər) *n.,* a rope, chain, or other restraint used to tie an animal so that it cannot move beyond a certain point. *Our family dog is tied by a <u>tether</u> to the fence during the day.*

sin • ewy (sin yə wē) *adj.,* strong with cordlike muscles. *Marisa had a runner's legs, tough and <u>sinewy</u>, not thin and bony.*

1. Jed's mother asks him to take the basket down to "the Little House."
2. Jed's grandfather says that his cancer causes the strange odor.

CROSS-CURRICULAR ACTIVITIES

MATHEMATICS AND SCIENCE. In this story, Jed's grandfather is dying of cancer. Share with students that cancer is a disease characterized by the uncontrolled growth of cells that disrupt body tissue. There are many different types of cancer, and all types of cancer can be fatal. Encourage students to work in small groups to research one of the following types of cancer: lung cancer, skin cancer, bone cancer, breast cancer, or any other type of cancer in which students are interested. Each group should then work to prepare a report on their chosen type of cancer. Students should focus their reports on the following questions: How many people are affected by this form of cancer? What causes this type of cancer? What are the effects of this type of cancer? What are the chances for surviving this type of cancer with proper treatment? What are some of the ways this cancer is treated? What, if anything, can be done to avoid getting this type of cancer?

CROSS-CURRICULAR CONNECTION

HISTORY. Inform students that the Abenaki are a group of Native Americans who all once spoke the Algonquian language. The Penobscot, Malecite, and Passamaquoddy, among others, were all part of the Abenaki confederacy, or alliance. The Abenaki people once lived in Maine and in Canada, and sided with the French against the British when these two European powers were struggling over control of North America. The Abenaki lost to the British in 1725, and their confederacy was destroyed.

100

"I wasn't sure I wanted to until now," Jed said. He heard his own voice as if it were the voice of a stranger.

His grandfather nodded. Very slowly, he got up from the bed. It seemed to Jed as if he were watching something happen as strange and wonderful, as magical as a tree uprooting itself and stepping across the woodlot. Joseph Sabael walked very slowly to the back door of the Little House. Jed opened it for him. Together they stepped out into the light from the open water, a light which made Jed's eyes squint against the brightness of it all. His grandfather sat down carefully in the rough wooden chair which faced The Island. Again Jed smelled that strange odor, but now he knew what it was and he was not confused. It was his grandfather's death.

Gulls began swooping down in front of them. They were grey and white. From their yellow beaks came those raucous[6] squawks which seemed to Jed to be the one thing which linked them to the rock they flew up from. Those voices, rough and filled with the earth, were all that kept the gulls from flying up and up forever until they blended with the sky.

His grandfather made a small motion with his hand and Jed opened the basket. He removed the cloth from the plate. The heat rose up to touch the back of his hand. With his fingers he broke the pancakes up into small pieces. Then, piece by piece, he tossed them up into the air. Swooping, diving, squabbling in mid-air, the gulls caught them all. Not one piece touched the waveless lake. ∎

---

6. **raucous.** Disorderly; rowdy

Respond *to the* SELECTION

Have you ever been so anxious about something that it made it hard for you to think or eat? Write about this experience in your journal.

About *the* AUTHOR

Joseph Bruchac is an Abenaki poet and writer who often draws on his heritage in developing his stories and poems. Many of his writings and retellings are for children and teens.

Bruchac was born in 1942 and grew up in the foothills of the Adirondack Mountains in New York. As a young adult, he began to seek out Native American stories, which he has retold in collections such as *Flying with the Eagle, Racing the Great Bear: Stories from Native North America, The Girl Who Married the Moon: Tales from Native North America,* and *Lasting Echoes, An Oral History of Native American People.* Bruchac also enjoys storytelling and has traveled around the country to share Native American stories with many audiences.

Bruchac has also written poetry, such as in his collection *No Borders,* and novels, including *Dawn Land* and *Heart of a Chief.*

Natterjack Toad, 1897. French Artist.
Natural History Museum, London.

BIRD foot's Grampa

Joseph Bruchac

The Old Man
must have stopped our car
two dozen times to climb out
and gather into his hands
the small toads blinded
by our lights and leaping
like live drops of rain.

The rain was falling,
a mist around his white hair,
and I kept saying,
"You can't save them all,
accept it, get in,
we've got places to go."

But, leathery hands full
of wet brown life,
knee deep in the summer
roadside grass,
he just smiled and said,
"They have places to go, too." ■

"JED'S GRANDFATHER" **101**

RECALL

1a. Jed dreams he is in a boat while an old man, probably his grandfather, stands on the shore of an island. A wave is coming up from behind threatening to wash the old man away, but Jed is paralyzed, unable to call out to the old man or help him.

2a. Jed has his grandfather's physical strength. Jed remembers that his grandfather made the basket, showing Jed the craft of basket weaving.

3a. Jed's grandfather says the smell of cancer is "as natural as anything else." Jed's grandfather wants Jed to throw the food to the gulls.

INTERPRET

Responses will vary. Possible responses are given.

1b. Students mat say that Jed has this dream because he is worried about his grandfather who is dying of cancer. The dream reveals that Jed feels powerless because he cannot save his grandfather.

2b. Jed's grandfather has passed on his strength, and in a more direct way, he has passed on his knowledge of crafts such as basket-making, which have been passed down for generations.

3b. Jed's grandfather seems to view the cancer as a natural part of life. He has accepted the fact that he is going to die and therefore does not eat the food Jed brings him.

ANALYZE

4a. The swallows and gulls are different from humans in that they are not as connected to the earth—they can soar above it. Jed's grandfather says that humans can be more like swallows if they try to "feel the wind" under themselves.

SYNTHESIZE

4b. Students may say that Jed's grandfather was trying to teach him not to be afraid to fly on his own, like the swallows. In order to be free, like the gulls and swallows, we must let go of our fear and accept death and let go of the people we love.

PERSPECTIVE

5a. *Responses will vary.* Students may suggest that Jed is saddened by the changes in his grandfather and does not want to accept them. This is revealed in Jed's uncertainty about visiting his grandfather. He also has trouble thinking, eating, and enjoying the pleasant parts of

Investigate, *Inquire,* and Imagine

Recall: GATHERING FACTS

1a. What dream does Jed have?

2a. In what way is Jed like his grandfather? What does Jed remember about the woven basket his mother asks him to take to his grandfather?

3a. What does Jed's grandfather say about the smell of cancer? What does he want Jed to do with the food Jed brings him?

→ **Interpret:** FINDING MEANING

1b. Why do you think Jed has this dream? What do you think the dream reveals about the way Jed is feeling?

2b. What has Jed's grandfather passed on to Jed?

3b. How does Jed's grandfather seem to view his illness? Why doesn't he want to eat? Explain.

Analyze: TAKING THINGS APART

4a. What makes the swallows and the gulls different from humans? According to Jed's grandfather, how can humans be more like swallows?

→ **Synthesize:** BRINGING THINGS TOGETHER

4b. What do you think Jed's grandfather was trying to teach Jed about the swallows and about life? What must a person let go of in order to be free?

Perspective: LOOKING AT OTHER VIEWS

5a. How does Jed feel about his grandfather's illness, and how does it affect Jed's daily life? Explain, giving examples from the story. How do you think Jed was feeling as he threw his grandfather's food to the gulls?

→ **Empathy:** SEEING FROM INSIDE

5b. If you were Jed and your grandfather wanted you to throw his food to the gulls, how would you react? Would you do what he wanted? Explain.

Understanding *Literature*

IRONY. Irony is a difference between appearance and reality. Irony is used in several places in this story. Why might it be considered ironic that Jed's grandfather has become weak and frail, given the description of how he was in the past? What might be ironic about the fact that the locust post outside Jed's grandfather's cabin will last "a hundred years"?

SYMBOL. A symbol is a thing that stands for or represents both itself and something else. Symbols in this story include swallows, gulls, ash trees, woodsmoke, the wave in Jed's dream, and the strange odor. Think of the ways in which each of these items is presented in the story. For example, the swallows are described as adventurous, not afraid to fly by themselves, and

---

ANSWERS TO INVESTIGATE, INQUIRE, IMAGINE (CONT.)

his life because he is so worried about his grandfather. Jed also feels confused by the presence of a strange smell, which he recognizes as the smell, or sense, of his grandfather's approaching death. When Jed throws his grandfather's food to the gulls, he probably feels pain and sadness because he knows this means his grandfather is starving himself or is unable to eat because of his illness. At the same time, Jed is probably feeling as sense of

letting go of his grandfather and accepting his death.

EMPATHY

5b. *Responses will vary.*

Answers to Understanding Literature can be found on page 103.

being able to drink water without ever landing on ground. Jed's grandfather tells Jed that he can be a swallow if he tries. To Jed's grandfather, they might symbolize, or represent, the ability to be free in life, to not be afraid to go out on one's own, and to not be attached to earthly things. Use the graphic organizer below as a model to explore the use of symbols in this story.

Graphic *Organizer*

The story "Jed's Grandfather" makes use of symbolism to communicate feelings and ideas. Explore one or two of the symbolic elements of the story through a cluster chart. In the center circle, write one of the symbols from the story. Possible symbols to explore include: swallows, gulls, ash trees, woodsmoke, a wave, and the strange odor. Branching out from the center, write the different ways the object is described in the story. An example is shown below.

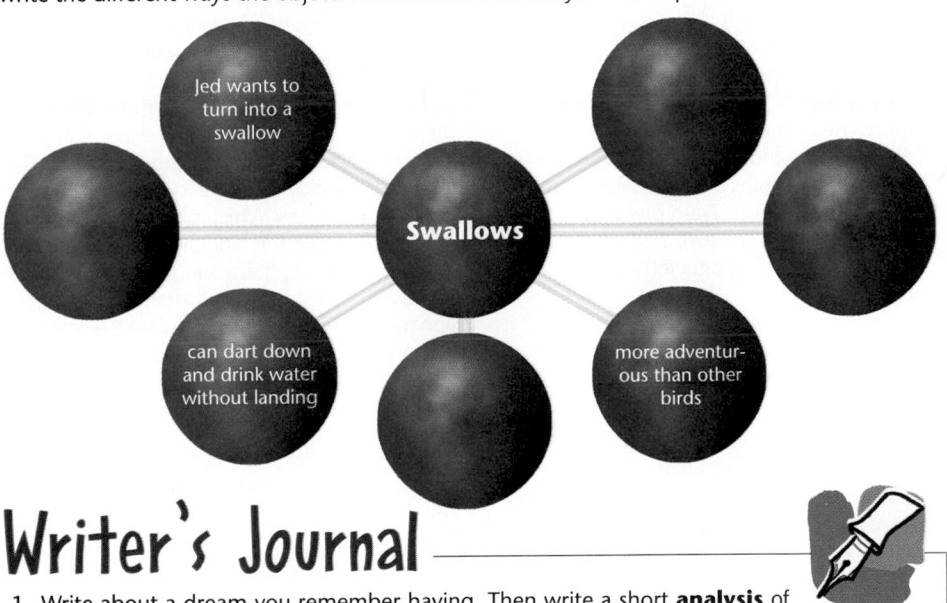

- Jed wants to turn into a swallow
- Swallows
- can dart down and drink water without landing
- more adventurous than other birds

Writer's Journal

1. Write about a dream you remember having. Then write a short **analysis** of your dream. What do you think the dream means, or symbolizes, about your feelings or thoughts?

2. In his own way, Jed's grandfather helps Jed to understand and deal with his oncoming death. Write some additional **dialogue** between Jed and his grandfather in which Grandfather talks to Jed directly about death. Refer to the Language Arts Survey 3.86, "Quotation Marks," for help in punctuating your dialogue.

3. Imagine that you are Jed and want to share with others what your grandfather is like and what he has taught you. Write a **tribute** to Jed's grandfather, using information you learned in the story. You may use informal language.

ANSWERS TO UNDERSTANDING LITERATURE

IRONY. It is ironic that Jed's grandfather is so weak and frail because he always seemed to Jed to be strong and "straight as an ash." His strength and endurance seemed permanent as a tree to Jed, but in reality these qualities are not permanent. The fact that the locust post will last a hundred years is ironic because it will be around long after Jed's grandfather is dead and one would think a person is more significant and enduring than something as trivial as a fence post.

SYMBOLISM. Students might say that similar to the swallows, the gulls also symbolize freedom from earthy cares and concerns. The ash tree might symbolize strength. The ash tree is strong but not indestructible. just as the ash tree can fall and be stripped to make baskets, Jed's grandfather is losing his strength and approaching death. Woodsmoke coming from his grandfather's house might symbolize life because Jed knows that when it is not present that his grandfather is either dead or very close to death. The wave in Jed's dream symbolizes death, which Jed is powerless to prevent. The strange odor symbolizes the presence of cancer and death.

GRAPHIC ORGANIZER

Students may point to the following words and phrases for swallows: "fly by themselves," the grandfather tells Jed he can be a swallow if he tries to "feel the wind under ye"; for gulls: "gray and white," swooping, diving, and squabbling in mid-air, make "raucous squawks," which are "all that kept the gull from flying up and up forever"; for ash trees: "Jed's grandfather is "straight as an ash," Jed's grandfather strips the twigs from a felled ash to make baskets, and his grandfather standing like "a tree uprooting itself"; for woodsmoke: "No smoke was rising from the chimney," the perfect line of smoke rising from the grandfather's one-room house in the past, Jed catching his breath when he realizes there is no smoke, and there being no fire in the stove when Jed enters his grandfather's house; for

GRAPHIC ORGANIZER (CONT.)

waves: the pattern of waves in a bucket reminding Jed of his dream, "the great dark wave coming at him [the grandfather] from behind," the whitecaps pounding on the boat, waves moving the boat tethered by the grandfather's cabin, and the description of the waveless lake at the end of the story; for odor: faint and confusing, smell of cancer, and Jed no longer being confused by the scent of his grandfather's death.

Language Grammar, and Style
EDITING FOR CAPITALIZATION ERRORS. Students may be confused by some of the capitalization in the story. For example, places such as "The Island" and the "Little House," which would normally use all lowercase letters, are capitalized because they are special nicknames used by the family. Explain that these terms, found in sentences 1 and 4, should be capitalized because they are used as specific place names, but ordinarily they should be lowercased.

1. Jed remembered the day when Grandfather rowed him out to what the Sabaels called The Island.
2. Jed's mother made pancakes that smelled like a summer wheatfield.
3. Father worked as a clerk in a store called Groceries and More.
4. They called the small house where his grandfather lived the Little House.
5. The house where Joseph Sabael lived was near Indian Lake.

Collaborative Learning
STUDYING NATIVE LANGUAGES. If there is a Native American community in your area, students could contact a community leader and learn what language programs are being conducted. You may wish to refer students to the following Web sites that have information about Native American languages: Native American Language Links, http://www.mcn.net/~wleman/langlimks.htm
Native Languages Page, http://www.pitt.edu/~lmitten/natlang.htm

Study and Research
THE IMPORTANCE OF DREAMS. To evaluate students' reports, use the Assessment Resource 4.12, Project Evaluation Form.

Skill Builders

Language, Grammar, and Style
EDITING FOR CAPITALIZATION ERRORS. You may notice in the story "Jed's Grandfather" that at times "Grandfather" is capitalized and that other times it is not. Any word for a family relation, such as *Mom, Dad,* or *Grandpa,* should be capitalized unless a modifier such as *the, a, my,* or *your* comes before it. Other words that should be capitalized include the first word of every sentence, the word *I,* and **proper nouns** such as the names of specific people, places, and pets. Refer to the Language Arts Survey 3.89, "Proper Nouns and Adjectives," and 3.91, "Family Relationships and Titles of Persons," for more information. Then rewrite the following sentences on your own paper, changing lowercase letters to capital letters whenever necessary.

1. Jed remembered the day when grandfather rowed him out to what the sabaels called the island.
2. jed's mother made pancakes that smelled like a summer wheatfield.
3. father worked as a clerk in a store called groceries and more.
4. they called the small house where his grandfather lived the little house.
5. the house where joseph sabael lived was near indian lake.

Collaborative Learning
STUDYING NATIVE LANGUAGES. In this selection, the reader learns that Jed's grandfather knows the old language but seldom speaks it. The old language is a Native American language which the grandfather spoke as a boy but never passed on to his children or grandchildren. At one time more than 500 Native American languages existed in the United States., but at present only 209 are still being used. Many of these are in danger of dying out as young people no longer learn them. Form groups of four or five students and research a Native American language, using the Internet, a local library, or a local college or university as resources. Which group of Native Americans speaks this language? In what region is it spoken? What, if anything, is being done to preserve the language? Put together a mini dictionary for the language, including a few words and phrases and their English equivalents. When you have completed your research, present your findings to the class.

Study and Research
THE IMPORTANCE OF DREAMS. Dreams are highly significant to Native American culture. Find evidence of this by going online or to the library to find Native American myths and stories where dreams are a part of the literature. You may want to start with other works Joseph Bruchac has written or edited. See For Your Reading List on page 145 for a title to help you get started. As you find dreams in the literature, summarize their significance and how the people in the stories respond to them. Report your findings in small groups.

Prereading

"UNDER THE HARVEST MOON"
and
"Theme in Yellow" by Carl Sandburg

Reader's TOOLBOX

PERSONIFICATION. Personification is a figure of speech in which an idea, animal, or thing is described as if it were a person. Look for examples of personification as you read these two poems.

SYMBOL. A symbol is a thing that stands for, or represents, both itself and something else. Most symbols are concrete words or phrases that name something we can see, hear, touch, taste, or smell. Symbols often represent abstract concepts—such as happiness, freedom, or honesty—that cannot be perceived by the five senses.

There are a number of traditional symbols that have widely recognized associations. Examples of these include doves for peace, the color green for jealousy, spring for youth, wind for change, rainbows for hope, roses for beauty, and roads for the journey through life. In "Under the Harvest Moon," Sandburg tells the reader what the abstract concept is and ties it to concrete details. As you read this poem, look at the links between the abstract concepts of death and love and the concrete details used to describe each concept. Below is a chart you can use to organize your ideas.

Graphic Organizer

Symbol	What does it do?	How is it described?	When, where, and with what does it come?
Death			
Love			

Reader's Journal

What do you think of when you hear the word "autumn"?

Reader's Resource

- **SCIENCE CONNECTION.** The harvest moon is the full moon of September and that which occurs nearest the autumn equinox—the time when fall begins in the northern hemisphere and spring begins in the southern hemisphere. The harvest moon rises early and is full or nearly full for several days in a row. It often appears bigger and brighter than other full moons because it is close to the horizon. The harvest moon got its name because in the past farmers often depended on its light to finish bringing in their crops.

- **HISTORY CONNECTION.** Halloween began thousands of years ago with the Celtic peoples of Ireland, England, and France. The ancient celebration *Samhain* was one of four major high days, or holidays, celebrated by the Celts. These major high days were referred to as fire festivals, because the Celts regarded fire as a symbol of divinity, holiness, truth, and beauty. Samhain was the most important fire festival because it marked the Celtic new year.

105

ADDITIONAL RESOURCES

UNIT 2 RESOURCE BOOK
- Selection Worksheet 2.4
- Selection Check Test 4.2.7
- Selection Test 4.2.8
- Language, Grammar, and Style Resource 3.20
- Applied English Resource 6.9

GRAPHIC ORGANIZER

For *death*, students might write the following:
What does it do?— "Comes and whispers to you"; How is it described—"Death, the gray mocker," and "As a beautiful friend / Who remembers"; When, where, and with what does it come?— "Under the harvest moon / When the soft silver / Drips shimmering / Over the garden nights."

For *love*, students might write the following:
What does it do?—"Comes and touches you/With a thousand memories,/And asks you/Beautiful, unanswerable questions"; How is it described?—"with little hands"; When, where, and with what does it come?— "Under the summer roses / When the flagrant crimson / Lurks in the dusk / Of the wild red leaves."

READER'S JOURNAL

Encourage students to list details about autumn that appeal to each of the five senses—sight, sound, smell, taste, and touch.

GOALS/OBJECTIVES

Studying this lesson will enable students to
- appreciate two poems that depict seasons vividly
- briefly describe what a harvest moon is and the origin of Halloween
- define *personification* and point to examples of personification in literature
- define *symbolism* and explain how the symbol and the thing its stands for are related
- create publicity for a harvest festival
- use an almanac to find information

MOTIVATION
Encourage students to hold a class discussion on fall and the things they associate with this time of year. Encourage them to come up with as large a list of fall things as possible, as you jot their ideas on the board.

READING PROFICIENCY
Students may benefit from hearing you read the poems aloud or play them on audiocassette. Encourage them to close their eyes and try to imagine the pictures the words create as they hear the poem read aloud.

ENGLISH LANGUAGE LEARNING
Point out the following words and expressions.
shimmering—shining with a soft trembling light
mocker—one who mocks, or makes fun of, others
crimson—red
lurks—sneaks; lies in wait
dusk—semidark period between sunset and night or between night and sunrise
jack-o'-lantern—lantern or light made of a pumpkin cut to look like a human face

SPECIAL NEEDS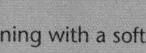
Students may benefit from the following explanation before they begin reading the selections: In "Under the Harvest Moon," the speaker describes two different seasons—fall and late summer—one in each stanza, or group of lines. The speaker then tells what he or she associates with each of these seasons. Tell students to jot down what season is described in each stanza and what is associated with each season. In "Theme in Yellow," the speaker of the poem is a pumpkin. When the speaker says, "I spot the hills/With yellow balls in autumn," the speaker is talking about pumpkins collectively, or as a group of which the speaker is a part.

ENRICHMENT
Encourage students to write a brief poem or personal essay in which they associate a different human emotion with each of the four seasons.

Under the HARVEST MOON

Carl Sandburg

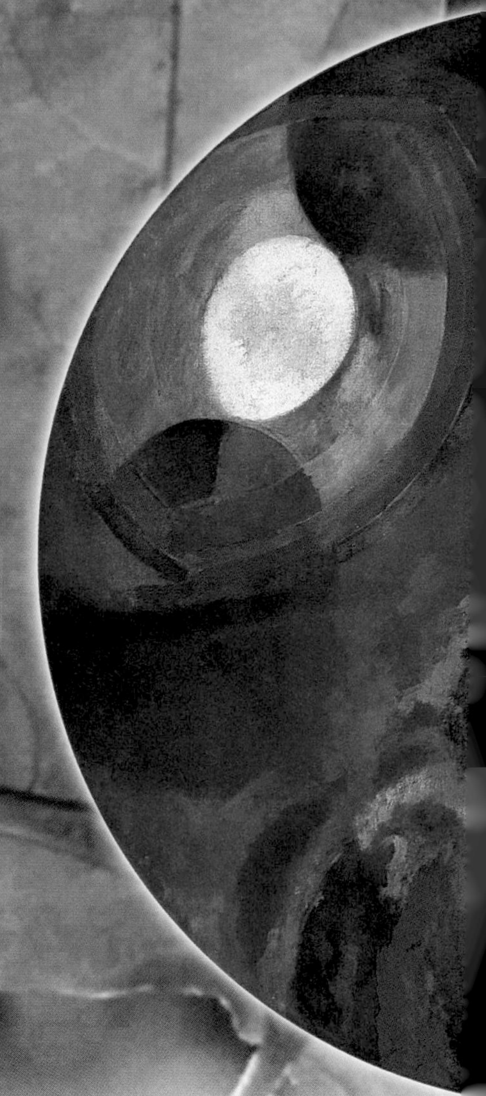

Under the harvest moon,
When the soft silver
Drips shimmering
Over the garden nights,
5 Death, the gray mocker,
Comes and whispers to you
As a beautiful friend
Who remembers.

> **GUIDED READING**
> Who comes and whispers to you?

Under the summer roses
10 When the flagrant crimson
Lurks in the dusk
Of the wild red leaves,
Love, with little hands,
Comes and touches you
15 With a thousand memories,
And asks you
Beautiful, unanswerable questions. ■

> **GUIDED READING**
> What does love do?

---

1. **flagrant.** Fiery hot, burning

ANSWERS TO GUIDED READING QUESTIONS

1. "Death, the gray mocker," comes and whispers to you.
2. Love touches you with a thousand memories and asks you beautiful, unanswerable questions.

THEME in *yellow*

Carl Sandburg

I spot the hills

With yellow balls in autumn.

I light the prairie cornfields

Orange and <u>tawny</u> gold clusters

5 And I am called pumpkins.

On the last of October

When dusk is fallen

Children join hands

And circle round me

10 Singing ghost songs

And love to the harvest moon;

I am a jack-o'-lantern

With terrible teeth

And the children know

15 I am fooling. ■

Simultaneous Contrasts: Sun and Moon, 1912.
Robert Delaunay. Museum of Modern Art, New York.

> **GUIDED READING**
>
> What happens on the last day of October?

words for everyday use

taw • ny (tä nē) *adj.*, of a warm sandy color. *Maria's <u>tawny</u> skin glowed in the afternoon sun.*

ANSWER TO GUIDED READING QUESTION

1. At dusk, children join hands and circle around the pumpkin, singing ghost songs.

CROSS-CURRICULAR ACTIVITIES

ART AND HUMANITIES AND APPLIED ARTS. Encourage students to hold a pumpkin-decorating contest. Students can buy pumpkins and then decorate them using paint, yarn, paper, glue, markers, and other inexpensive items, such as toy sunglasses or fake noses. While students can make their pumpkins look like people, they can also explore other ideas such as pumpkin animals, aliens, or objects. Tell students not to carve their pumpkins unless they have adult supervision, and under no circumstances should they use candles to light their pumpkins. Have those students who have adults help them carve a pumpkin use miniature flashlights instead. Students should create their pumpkins at home and then bring them in to share with classmates. Students may wish to vote on the funniest pumpkin, the scariest pumpkin, and the most creative pumpkin.

ART SMART

Inform students that Robert Delaunay (1885–1941) was a French painter and one of the first abstract painters. He began an original style of painting called Orphism. Orphists, like Delaunay, used vivid colors and round shapes in their work. Ask students what elements of Orphism they see in *Simultaneous Contrasts: Sun and Moon*.

Respond to the SELECTION

What is your favorite thing about autumn? What do you least like about autumn? Explain your answers.

About the AUTHOR

Carl Sandburg (1878–1967), a son of Swedish immigrants, grew up in Galesburg, Illinois. He attended school until age thirteen, then traveled from job to job throughout the Midwest, working as a brick maker, a carpenter's helper, a house painter, and a milk wagon driver. Sandburg's experiences gave him a close look at the lives of ordinary working people, with whom he felt a deep kinship. He later served as a soldier during the Spanish–American War (1898), briefly attended college, worked as an advertising writer and journalist, and became involved in politics.

In his poetry, Sandburg often wrote about ordinary people and everyday life—"simple poems for simple people." His poems are collected in books such as *Chicago Poems* (1918), *Cornhuskers* (1918), *Smoke and Steel* (1920), and *The People, Yes* (1936). Sandburg often traveled around the country, reading his poetry and performing folk songs. He is also known for the biographies *Abraham Lincoln: The Prairie Years* (1926) and *Abraham Lincoln: The War Years* (1939).

ABOUT THE RELATED READING ➤
Gregorio López y Fuentes was a Mexican writer born in 1895. In his best-known novel, *El Indio,* he wrote about the lives of Mexico's native peoples and of the injustices that they faced in the early 1900s. López y Fuentes set his other novels, *Campamento* and *Tierra,* during the Mexican Revolution (1910–1940). He died in 1966.

LITERARY TECHNIQUE

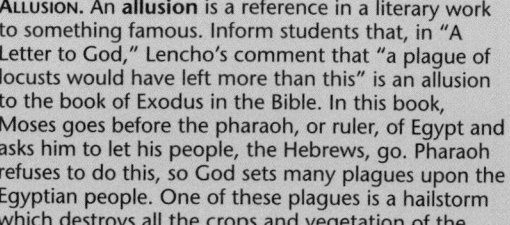

ALLUSION. An **allusion** is a reference in a literary work to something famous. Inform students that, in "A Letter to God," Lencho's comment that "a plague of locusts would have left more than this" is an allusion to the book of Exodus in the Bible. In this book, Moses goes before the pharaoh, or ruler, of Egypt and asks him to let his people, the Hebrews, go. Pharaoh refuses to do this, so God sets many plagues upon the Egyptian people. One of these plagues is a hailstorm which destroys all the crops and vegetation of the Egyptians. This plague is followed by a plague of locusts which eat the remainder of the crops in Egypt. Ask students why this allusion is appropriate to Lencho's situation. What does this allusion indicate about Lencho's character?
Answers. Students may say that the hailstorm seems as devastating to Lencho as the plagues did to the Egyptians. Students may say that the allusion reveals that Lencho is a faithful and religious person who knows the Bible well.

A Letter to GOD

Gregorio López y Fuentes, translation by
Donald A. Yates

The house—the only one in the entire valley—sat on the crest of a low hill. From this height one could see the river and, next to the corral, the field of ripe corn dotted with the kidney bean flowers that always promised a good harvest.

The only thing the earth needed was a rainfall, or at least a shower. Throughout the morning Lencho—who knew his fields intimately—had done nothing else but scan the sky toward the northeast.

"Now we're really going to get some water, woman."

The woman, who was preparing supper, replied: "Yes, God willing."

The oldest boys were working in the field, while the smaller ones were playing near the house, until the woman called them all, "Come for dinner . . ."

It was during the meal that, just as Lencho had predicted, big drops of rain began to fall. In the northeast huge mountains of clouds could be seen approaching. The air was fresh and sweet.

The man went out to look for something in the corral for no other reason than to allow himself the pleasure of feeling the rain on his body, and when he returned he exclaimed, "Those aren't raindrops falling from the sky, they're new coins. The big drops are ten-centavo pieces and the little ones are fives . . ."

With a satisfied expression he regarded the field of ripe corn with its kidney bean flowers, draped in a curtain of rain. But suddenly a strong wind began to blow and, together with the rain, very large hailstones began to fall. These truly did resemble new silver coins. The boys, exposing themselves to the rain, ran out to collect the frozen pearls.

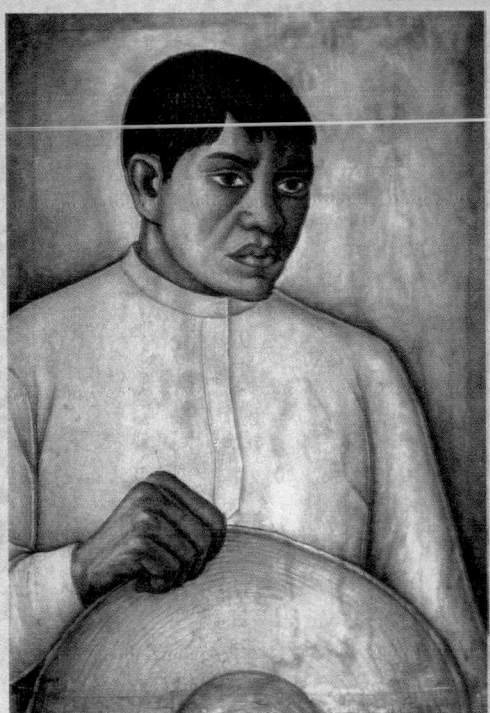

Campesino Sombrero, 1926. Diego Rivera.

"It's really getting bad now," exclaimed the man, mortified. "I hope it passes quickly."

It did not pass quickly. For an hour the hail rained on the house, the garden, the hillside, the cornfield, on the whole valley. The field was white, as if covered with salt. Not a leaf remained on the trees. The corn was totally destroyed. The flowers were gone from the kidney bean plants. Lencho's soul was filled with sadness. When the storm had passed, he stood in the middle of the field and said to his sons, "A plague of locusts would have left more than this . . . The hail has left nothing; this year we will have no corn or beans. . . ."

That night was a sorrowful one: "All our work, for nothing! There's no one who can help us!"

"We'll all go hungry this year . . ."

CROSS-CURRICULAR ACTIVITIES

SCIENCE AND MATHEMATICS. Encourage students to work in pairs to prepare a report on hail, explaining what it is, how it forms, its size, and its effects. As an alternate activity, students might work in pairs to prepare reports on locusts, describing the physical characteristics of locusts, how they differ in their gregarious and solitary phases, why plagues of locusts occur, and what can be done to stop plagues of locusts. Each pair of students should work together to prepare a brief research report (no more than a page).

ADDITIONAL QUESTIONS AND ACTIVITIES

1. Ask students the following questions once they have read "A Letter to God":
2. What are Lencho and his wife waiting for at the beginning of the story? What happens when it arrives?
3. How does Lencho feel when his crops are destroyed?
4. Whom does Lencho ask for help after the disaster? In what way does he ask for help?
5. Does Lencho expect his request to be met? Why, or why not?
6. Who responds to Lencho's letter? In what way does this person go about answering Lencho's letter?
7. Why does this person decide to help Lencho? What does this action say about this person?
8. How does Lencho feel when he receives the response to his letter? What does he do?
9. Why does Lencho react this way? Why is his reaction ironic?

Answers
1. Lencho and his wife are waiting for rain for their crops. When the rain arrives, it turns into a hailstorm, destroying Lencho's crops.
2. Lencho is saddened and worried when his crops are destroyed.
3. Lencho asks God for help. He writes a letter to God, asking for one hundred pesos to resow his fields.
4. Lencho expects that his request will be met because he has extraordinary faith in God.
5. The postmaster responds to Lencho's letter. He answers the letter by giving some of his own

---

ADDITIONAL QUESTIONS AND ACTIVITIES (CONT.)

money and gathering contributions from his workers and friends to help Lencho.
6. The postmaster decides to help Lencho because he is impressed by the farmer's faith. His actions reveal that he is a compassionate and caring person.
7. Lencho is angry when he receives the response and writes a letter back to God asking for the rest of his money and calling the post office employees "a bunch of crooks."

8. Lencho reacts this way because he cannot believe that God would only partially fulfill his request, so he assumes that the postal workers have stolen some of the money. His reaction is ironic because he is accusing the very people who raised the money of having stolen some of it. We would expect Lencho to be grateful for the good deed, but the opposite happens.

RECALL

1a. The "soft silver" is dripping over the "garden night."
2a. Love comes with "little hands" that touch you with "a thousand memories."
3a. In "Theme in Yellow" the speaker is a pumpkin.
4a. The speaker is changed into a jack-o'-lantern.

INTERPRET

1b. The light of the harvest moon casts a soft silver light over the garden.
2b. Love comes with little hands that touch you with a thousand memories because people tend to cherish their memories of loved ones.
3b. The speaker describes October because that is the time when pumpkins are harvested.
4b. Students may say that the children know a jack-o'-lantern cannot harm them and that its frightening face is just for show and for fun.

ANALYZE

5a. Students may suggest that the two poems are similar in that they both describe autumn when the harvest moon shines at night. Both poems also create vivid images of a particular time and place. The speaker in "Under the Harvest Moon" seems to be human, while the speaker in "Theme in Yellow" is a pumpkin. The mood of "Under the Harvest Moon," is a bit melancholy and wistful while the mood of "Theme in Yellow" is lighthearted.

SYNTHESIZE

5b. In "Under the Harvest Moon," autumn images include soft silver shimmering over the garden at night and death coming as a "gray mocker." Other autumn images include the last of the summer roses and the wild red leaves lurking in the dusk. The feeling is one of beauty but of impending death. There is also the feeling of fondly remembering people and times you have loved. In "Theme in Yellow," autumn images include yellow pumpkins spotting the hills, pumpkins lighting up the prairie cornfields, and children circling around a terrible-toothed jack-o'-lantern while singing ghost songs. The feeling this poem evokes is one of beauty, cheer, and togetherness. Students may suggest that the poet could feel that fall is beautiful time for celebrating the harvest and Halloween but also recognize that fall brings death because it is the end of the growing season and the herald of winter.

But in the hearts of all who lived in that solitary house in the middle of the valley, there was a single hope: help from God.

"Don't be so upset, even though this seems like a total loss. Remember, no one dies of hunger!"

"That's what they say; no one dies of hunger . . ."

All through the night, Lencho thought only of his one hope, the help of God, whose eyes, as he had been instructed, see everything, even what is deep in one's conscience.

Lencho was an ox of a man, working like an animal in the fields, but still he knew how to write. The following Sunday, at daybreak, after having convinced himself that there is a protecting spirit, he began to write a letter which he himself would carry to town and place in the mail.

It was nothing less than a letter to God.

"God," he wrote, "if you don't help me, my family and I will go hungry this year. I need a hundred pesos in order to resow the field and to live until the crop comes, because of the hailstorm. . . ."

He wrote "To God" on the envelope, put the letter inside, and, still troubled, went to town. At the post office he placed a stamp on the letter and dropped it into the mailbox.

One of the employees, who was a postman and also helped at the post office, went to his boss, laughing heartily, and showed him the letter to God. Never in his career as a postman had he known that address. The postmaster—a fat, amiable fellow—also broke out laughing, but almost immediately he turned serious and, tapping the letter on his desk, commented: "What faith! I wish I had the faith of the man who wrote this letter. To believe the way he believes. To hope with the confidence that he knows how to hope with. Starting up a correspondence with God!"

So, in order not to disillusion that prodigy of faith, revealed by a letter that could not be delivered, the postmaster came up with an idea: answer the letter. But when he opened it, it was evident that to answer it he needed something more than good will, ink, and paper. But he stuck to his resolution. He asked for money from his employee, he himself gave part of his salary, and several friends of his were obliged to give something "for an act of charity."

It was impossible for him to gather together the hundred pesos requested by Lencho, so he was able to send the farmer only a little more than half. He put the bills in an envelope addressed to Lencho and with them a letter containing only a single word as a signature:

GOD

The following Sunday Lencho came a bit earlier than usual to ask if there was a letter for him. It was the postman himself who handed the letter to him, while the postmaster, experiencing the contentment of a man who has performed a good deed, looked on from the doorway of his office.

Lencho showed not the slightest surprise on seeing the bills—such was his confidence—but he became angry when he counted the money. God could not have made a mistake, nor could he have denied Lencho what he had requested!

Immediately, Lencho went up to the window to ask for paper and ink. On the public writing table, he started in to write, with much wrinkling of his brow, caused by the effort he had to make to express his ideas. When he finished, he went to the window to buy a stamp, which he licked and then affixed to the envelope with a blow of his fist.

The moment that the letter fell into the mailbox the postmaster went to open it. It said:

"God: Of the money that I asked for, only seventy pesos reached me. Send me the rest, since I need it very much. But don't send it to me through the mail, because the post office employees are a bunch of crooks. Lencho." ■

ANSWERS TO INVESTIGATE, INQUIRE, IMAGINE (CONT.)

EVALUATE

6a. *Responses will vary.* Students may say that "Under the Harvest Moon" does reveal the content of the poem very well because it describes an autumnal moonlit scene, while the second half of the poem describes dusk under the remaining summer roses after the leaves have already turned red. Students may have mixed feelings about "Theme in Yellow" as the title for the second poem. Some may say that they found it misleading because it only explored one yellow thing—pumpkins, which are mostly orange. Other students may say the poet was describing the way pumpkins and the whole fall season are filled with glowing color. Students may be surprised that the speaker calls death "a beautiful friend" and that the speaker of "Theme in Yellow" is a pumpkin.

EXTEND

6b. *Responses will vary.*

Investigate, *Inquire,* and Imagine

Recall: GATHERING FACTS   → **Interpret:** FINDING MEANING

1a. In "Under the Harvest Moon," what is happening when "Death, the gray mocker, / Comes and whispers to you"?

1b. What causes this to happen?

2a. What does "Love" do?

2b. Why does "Love" do this?

3a. In "Theme in Yellow," who is the speaker?

3b. Why does the speaker describe this time of year?

4a. How is the speaker changed by the end of "Theme in Yellow"?

4b. How do the children know the speaker is fooling?

Analyze: TAKING THINGS APART   → **Synthesize:** BRINGING THINGS TOGETHER

5a. In what ways are these two poems similar? How are they different?

5b. Each poem offers a unique image of autumn and conveys a distinct feeling about the season. Describe the image of autumn and the feeling it evokes in "Under the Harvest Moon." Do the same for "Theme in Yellow." How might the poet's feelings about autumn incorporate these different images and feelings?

Evaluate: MAKING JUDGMENTS   → **Extend:** CONNECTING IDEAS

6a. How well does the title "Under the Harvest Moon" reveal the poem's content? How well does the title "Theme in Yellow" reveal that poem's content? Did the content of either poem surprise you? Explain your answer.

6b. Which poem comes closer to representing autumn as you would represent it? Why? How do these poems link the ideas of fall and harvest with the spiritual world? How does the Related Reading link those ideas?

Understanding *Literature*

PERSONIFICATION. Personification is a figure of speech in which an idea, animal, or thing is described as if it were a person. What is personified in "Under the Harvest Moon"? How do you know? What is personified in "Theme in Yellow"? How do you know? How does personification affect the objects being described? How might each poem be different if these objects were not personified?

ANSWERS TO UNDERSTANDING LITERATURE

PERSONIFICATION. Death is personified. Death is called a mocker and compared to a beautiful friend, which implies that death is human. Pumpkins are personified in this poem as being aware and able to see and think. The fact that the poem is written from a pumpkin's point of view and that the pumpkin uses the word *I* is evidence of personification. Students may say that the personification of death as a beautiful friend makes it seem less frightening and strange, while the personifi-cation of pumpkins focuses the reader's attention on pumpkins as a symbol of autumn. Students may say that each poem would be less striking without personi-fication.

SYMBOLISM. Students may say that death is linked to autumn because the time of year marks the end of the growing season before a barren winter. Students may say that love is linked to autumn because it is a time of wild beauty and of fondly remembering the past.

Applied English

PUBLICITY. Evaluate students' newspaper advertisements, posters, and press releases using the guidelines for assessing projects in the Assessment Resource 4.12. Students might find this project more enjoyable if they work in groups of five or six. They can then decide on what occurs at their Harvest Festival and create all the forms of publicity listed to draw attention to their festival.

Language, Grammar, and Style

DIRECT OBJECTS

1. *verb:* wanted; *direct object:* company
2. *verb:* are flying; the sentence has no direct object—"south" is an adverb
3. *verb:* remember; *direct object:* dreams
4. *verb:* saved; *direct object:* frogs
5. *verb:* waited; the sentence has no direct object—"me" is an indirect object

Study and Research

USING AN ALMANAC. As an alternative, you could have students look up the definition of a blue moon. Also, share with students the names of some of the other moons of the year. They are as follows.

January: Wolf Moon
February: Ice or Snow Moon
March: Storm or Worm Moon
April: Growing or Pink Moon
May: Hare or Flower Moon
June: Mead or Strawberry Moon
July: Hay or Buck Moon
August: Corn or Sturgeon Moon
September: Harvest Moon
October: Blood or Hunter's Moon
November: Snow or Beaver Moon
December: Cold Moon. The Cherokee also had traditional names for the moons. They are as follows:
Cherokee Moons
January: Month of the Cold Moon
February: Month of the Bony Moon
March: Month of the Windy Moon
April: Month of the Flower Moon
May: Month of the Planting Moon
June: Month of the Green Corn Moon
July: Month of the Ripe Corn Moon
August: Month of the end of the Fruit Moon
September: Month of the Nut Moon
October: Month of the Harvest Moon
November: Month of the Trading Moon
December: Month of the Snow

SYMBOL. A **symbol** is a thing that stands for or represents both itself and something else. In "Under the Harvest Moon," Sandburg tells the reader what the abstract concept is and ties it to concrete details. Look at the chart you created for "Death" and "Love." What did you write about "Death"? about "Love"? How is "Death" linked to autumn? How is "Love" linked to autumn?

Writer's Journal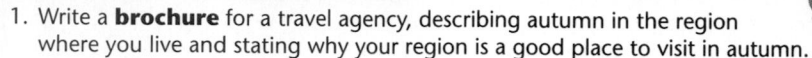

1. Write a **brochure** for a travel agency, describing autumn in the region where you live and stating why your region is a good place to visit in autumn.
2. Imagine you have a new neighbor from a different country who wants to learn about autumn traditions in the United States. Write **directions** for one of the following: carving a jack-o'-lantern, baking a pumpkin or an apple pie, wild ricing, or making a cornucopia.
3. Write a **free verse poem** about your favorite season and share it with your class.

Skill Builders

Applied English

PUBLICITY. Imagine that you are in charge of a town's annual Harvest Festival, in which different locally-grown fruits and vegetables are judged for size and quality. The festival also features hay rides, pony rides, games, and bonfire cookouts. Design a newspaper advertisement, a poster, or a press release to inform people of the event. Be sure to include all key information, including the date, time, and location of the festival. For more information, see the Language Arts Survey 6.9, "Delivering a Press Release."

Language, Grammar, and Style

DIRECT OBJECTS. A sentence must have a subject and a verb, but sometimes a sentence has other parts that complete the meaning—such as **direct objects** and *indirect objects*. Underline the verb and identify the direct object for each of the sentences below. For more information, see the Language Arts Survey 3.20, "Completers for Action Verbs: Direct and Indirect Objects."

example: I <u>brought</u> him lunch.   *brought what?* lunch   *verb:* brought   *direct object:* lunch

1. My grandfather wanted company.
2. The geese are flying south.
3. Remember your dreams.
4. We saved the frogs from being run over.
5. My mother waited for me to return to the house.

Study and Research

USING AN ALMANAC. Look for a current copy of *The Old Farmer's Almanac* in your local library. Use the almanac to answer the following questions. On what day does the harvest moon appear? When is the next full moon? What is it called? What kind of weather does the Alamanac forecest for the month you are currently in? How accurate is the forecast? Read an article in the *Almanac* and report on it to your class.

Prereading

"The Green Mamba"
by Roald Dahl

Reader's Resource

- "The Green Mamba" comes from a book of essays called *Going Solo*. The book is about author Roald Dahl's experiences while serving as a fighter pilot in Africa during World War II (1939–1945).

- **HISTORY CONNECTION.** This story takes place in Dar es Salaam in what is now known as Tanzania, a country that lies just south of the equator in East Africa. From 1922 to 1961, Tanzania was ruled by the British and was called Tanganyika, the name used in this story. Dar es Salaam is the nation's largest city. It has served as the capital for many decades.

- **SCIENCE CONNECTION.** About 2,700 species of snakes exist on the earth. Of these, only about 375 are venomous—their bites deliver poison—or venom—to the blood of the victim. Scientists today know much more about snake venom than they did in previous decades, and the chance of successfully treating a venomous snake bite is better than ever. Mambas are poisonous African tree snakes known for their beauty, their length (up to fourteen feet), their speed (up to twenty miles per hour), and their fighting nature. Capable of injecting more venom per bite than cobras, mambas can produce bites that are deadly if not treated in time.

- As a result of human activities that threaten snakes, their populations are declining. Yet few people have even noticed. In part, snakes lead secretive lives and are hard to monitor. But another reason is that people are more apt to help conserve warm, furry animals than the less cuddly ones. By keeping rats and mice in check, snakes help keep pests out of the world's grain supplies and help control the diseases—sometimes deadly—that rodents transmit to humans. Furthermore, medical researchers have found that certain snake venoms can help in the treatment of many serious conditions, including cancer, heart disease, and epilepsy. Because of its healing qualities, snake venom is more expensive than gold.

Reader's Journal

What would you do if someone told you a deadly snake had just entered your house?

Reader's TOOLBOX

SUSPENSE. Suspense is a feeling of expectation, anxiety, or curiosity created by questions raised in the mind of a reader. As this story unfolds, readers fear that someone will be bitten by the green mamba. This fear is reinforced by the author's attention to *concrete details*, which carefully describe things that can be seen, tasted, touched, heard, or smelled. How do these concrete descriptions draw the story out, create a strong emotional response in readers, and add to the suspense?

CHARACTERIZATION. Characterization is the act of creating or describing a character. In "The Green Mamba," Dahl conveys the thoughts and feelings of the characters as we see how they react to the action. As you read the story, make a list of the words and phrases that characterize the snake-man. Be sure to include details about how he dresses, moves, and arms himself to deal with the deadly snake. Circle or bracket items on your list that use concrete words.

ADDITIONAL RESOURCES

UNIT 2 RESOURCE BOOK
- Selection Worksheet 2.5
- Selection Check Test 4.2.9
- Selection Test 4.2.10
- Language, Grammar, and Style Resource 3.20
- Applied English Resource 6.11

READER'S JOURNAL

Ask students to work in pairs to role-play such a confrontation. One students should play the person being the news that a snake was just seen entering the other student's house, while the other student should play the person who has just heard this news. The students should then switch roles. Encourage students to come up with a variety of possible responses from the terrified to the outraged to the matter-of-fact.

GRAPHIC ORGANIZER

Explain to students that a **concrete** word names something that can be directly seen, tasted, touched, heard, or smelled. They may include the following phrases in their list: old Englishman; likes snakes; [wears leather boots made of thick cowhide]; [small]; impressive looking; [pale-blue eyes]; [moves like a leopard]

GOALS/OBJECTIVES

Studying this lesson will enable students to
- enjoy suspenseful writing about poisonous snakes
- briefly describe some basic facts about snakes
- define *suspense* and identify the details that help create suspense in a piece of writing
- define *characterization* and identify the details, both concrete and abstract, used to create a character
- identify dialect and understand how it contributes to writing
- conduct an interview
- research a topic using the library or the Internet
- create a map

INDIVIDUAL LEARNING STRATEGIES

MOTIVATION
Find a television documentary on snakes to show to your class before they read "The Green Mamba." The Discovery Channel, The Learning Channel, and public television are all great resources to explore for finding documentaries on snakes.

READING PROFICIENCY
Tell students to make sure they read the Prereading page which provides background on where the story is set and on one of its main characters—a snake. Students may have more confidence if they form reading pairs, so that they can discuss their answers to Guided Reading questions and their thoughts about what happens in "The Green Mamba" before answering the questions in Investigate, Inquire, and Imagine.

ENGLISH LANGUAGE LEARNING
Point out the following words and expressions.
cobras—very poisonous snakes of Africa and Asia with loose skin around the neck that raises into a hood when the animal is threatened
puff adders—type of poisonous snake found in Africa
dumbfounded—made speechless with shock
implement—any device used in an activity
Airedale—type of small and usually aggressive dog with a hard and wiry tan coat with black markings
swivel—cause to turn or rotate
moccasins—slippers of soft, flexible leather
flailing—swinging in a wide motion

SPECIAL NEEDS
Students may have a hard time visualizing the green mamba, especially if they live in an urban environment and have never seen a snake. Bring in pictures of snakes from encyclopedias, the Internet, or nature magazines. You might also measure a distance of fourteen feet against one of your classroom walls, so students can visualize how long mambas can grow.

ENRICHMENT
People throughout the ages have been fascinated by the appearance and movement of

snakes and have tried to capture snakes artistically in drawing, painting, sculpture, music, and dance. Encourage students to choose an artistic medium they enjoy, from those listed above, and use it to vividly portray a snake to their classmates.

INDIVIDUAL LEARNING STRATEGIES (CONT.)

The GREEN Mamba

Roald Dahl

OH, THOSE SNAKES! How I hated them! They were the only fearful thing about Tanganyika, and a newcomer very quickly learnt to identify most of them and to know which were deadly and which were simply poisonous. The killers, apart from the black mambas, were the green mambas, the cobras and the tiny little puff adders that looked very much like small sticks lying motionless in the middle of a dusty path, and so easy to step on.

GUIDED READING

Which snakes in Tanganyika are deadly?

One Sunday evening I was invited to go and have a sundowner[1] at the house of an Englishman called Fuller who worked in the Customs office[2] in Dar es Salaam. He lived with his wife and two small children in a plain white wooden house that stood alone some way back from the road in a rough grassy piece of ground with coconut trees scattered about. I was walking across the grass towards the house and was about twenty yards away when I saw a large green snake go gliding straight up the veranda[3] steps of Fuller's house and in through the open front door. The brilliant yellow-green skin and its great size made me certain it was a green mamba, a creature almost as deadly as the black mamba, and for a few seconds I was so startled and dumbfounded and horrified that I froze to the spot. Then I pulled myself together and ran round to the back of the house shouting, "Mr Fuller! Mr Fuller!"

GUIDED READING

Why is the narrator horrified?

Mrs Fuller popped her head out of an upstairs window. "What on earth's the matter?" she said.

"You've got a large green mamba in your front room!" I shouted. "I saw it go up the veranda steps and right in through the door!"

"Fred!" Mrs Fuller shouted, turning round. "Fred! Come here!"

Freddy Fuller's round red face appeared at the window beside his wife. "What's up" he asked.

"There's a green mamba in your living-room!" I shouted.

Without hesitation and without wasting time with more questions, he said to me, "Stay there. I'm going to lower the children down to you one at a time." He was completely cool and unruffled. He didn't even raise his voice.

GUIDED READING

What does Mr. Fuller do?

---

1. **sundowner.** An evening refreshment
2. **customs office.** Government agency that controls taxes on imports and exports
3. **veranda.** Open air porch area, usually with a roof

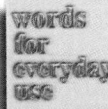

words for everyday use

un·ruf·fled (un ru' fəld) adj., poised; cool. *Despite the hubbub, our teacher remained unruffled.*

◄ *Danger on the Stairs*, 1927. Pierre Roy. The Museum of Modern Art, New York.

ANSWERS TO GUIDED READING QUESTIONS

1. Black mambas, green mambas, cobras, and puff adders are deadly snakes in Tanganyika.
2. The narrator is horrifies because he sees a snake enter the Fullers' house.
3. Mr. Fuller remains calm and says he will lower the children down

VOCABULARY FROM THE SELECTION

forlorn malevolent
manipulate unruffled
wheedling

CROSS-CURRICULAR ACTIVITIES

MATHEMATICS AND SCIENCES. Encourage students to work in pairs to find answers to the following questions about snakes. Students should use the resources in their school or local library to answer these questions.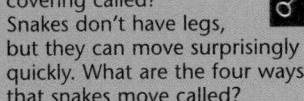

1. When snakes shed their skin, they also shed a hard, transparent covering over their eyes. What is this covering called?
2. Snakes don't have legs, but they can move surprisingly quickly. What are the four ways that snakes move called?
3. Can snakes spit poison?
4. Can snakes hear like we do?
5. When snakes flick their tongues, what sense are they using?

Answers
1. It is called a spectacle.
2. Snakes move by the serpentine method in which the snake pushes against the ground; the caterpillar (or rectilinear) method in which large snakes' strong muscles move their skin forward, dragging them along; desert snakes move by sidewinding or moving their bodies in sideways looping motions in the sand; and by the concertina method in which the snake stretches and pulls together its body.
3. Three types of snakes can spit poison, which can blind their attacker.
4. No, snakes are deaf, but can feel vibrations through the ground and use this sensation as their form of hearing.
5. Snakes have strong senses of smell and use their tongues to pick up odors.

1. The snake-man is an Englishman who has lived in Africa for years and who likes, understands, and never kills snakes. Instead he sells snakes to zoos and laboratories.
2. The children are worried about Jack, their dog.

ADDITIONAL QUESTIONS AND ACTIVITIES

Encourage students to discuss the snake-man's attitude toward the snake. How would they define the snake-man's attitude toward nature and the environment? What evidence can they point to in support of their opinions?

ANSWERS. Students may suggest that the snake-man is respectful and as gentle as possible with the snake, seeking to soothe it with his voice and assuring it that he won't kill it. The students may say that the snake-man is respectful of nature and the environment, seeking to minimize the negative effect humans can have on nature. As evidence students may point to the fact that the snake-man seeks to understand snakes and never kills them, selling them instead to zoos or laboratories. Students may also say that he stops buying snakes from the natives when he sees that this practice encourages the natives to risk their lives trying to catch the deadly snakes. Other students may point out that laboratories may perform cruel research or even kill snakes to study them. Encourage students to be respectful and listen to one another's opinions because animal testing in laboratories is a sensitive issue for many. Point out to students that it was less of an issue at the time when the story was written, so neither the narrator nor the snake-man probably interpreted selling snakes to laboratories as harmful.

A small girl was lowered down to me by her wrists and I was able to catch her easily by the legs. Then came a small boy. Then Freddy Fuller lowered his wife and I caught her by the waist and put her on the ground. Then came Fuller himself. He hung by his hands from the window-sill and when he let go he landed neatly on his two feet.

We stood in a little group on the grass at the back of the house and I told Fuller exactly what I had seen.

The mother was holding the two children by the hand, one on each side of her. They didn't seem to be particularly alarmed.

"What happens now?" I asked.

"Go down to the road, all of you," Fuller said. "I'm off to fetch the snake-man." He trotted away and got into his small ancient black car and drove off. Mrs Fuller and the two small children and I went down to the road and sat in the shade of a large mango tree.

"Who is this snake-man?" I asked Mrs Fuller.

"He is an old Englishman who has been out here for years," Mrs Fuller said. "He actually *likes* snakes. He understands them and never kills them.

> **GUIDED READING**
> Who is the snake-man?

He catches them and sells them to zoos and laboratories all over the world. Every native for miles around knows about him and whenever one of them sees a snake, he marks its hiding place and runs, often for great distances, to tell the snake-man. Then the snake-man comes along and captures it. The snake-man's strict rule is that he will never buy a captured snake from the natives."

"Why not?" I asked.

"To discourage them from trying to catch snakes themselves," Mrs Fuller said. "In his early days he used to buy caught snakes, but so many natives got bitten trying to catch them, and so many died, that he decided to put a stop to it. Now any native who brings in a caught snake, no matter how rare, gets turned away."

"That's good," I said.

"What is the snake-man's name?" I asked.

"Donald Macfarlane," she said. "I believe he's Scottish."

"Is the snake in the house, Mummy?" the small girl asked.

"Yes, darling. But the snake-man is going to get it out."

"He'll bite Jack," the girl said.

"Oh, my God!" Mrs Fuller cried, jumping to her feet. "I forgot about Jack!" She began calling out, "Jack! Come here, Jack! Jack! . . . Jack! . . . Jack!"

> **GUIDED READING**
> What are the children worried about?

The children jumped up as well and all of them started calling to the dog. But no dog came out of the open front door.

"He's bitten Jack!" the small girl cried out. "He must have bitten him!" She began to cry and so did her brother, who was a year or so younger than she was. Mrs Fuller looked grim.

"Jack's probably hiding upstairs," she said. "You know how clever he is."

Mrs Fuller and I seated ourselves again on the grass, but the children remained standing.

In between their tears they went on calling to the dog.

"Would you like me to take you down to the Maddens' house?" their mother asked.

"No!" they cried. "No, no, no! We want Jack!"

"Here's Daddy!" Mrs Fuller cried, pointing at the tiny black car coming up the road in a swirl of dust. I noticed a long wooden pole sticking out through one of the car windows.

The children ran to meet the car. "Jack's inside the house and he's been bitten by the snake!" they wailed. "We know he's been bitten! He doesn't come when we call him!"

Mr Fuller and the snake-man got out of the car. The snake-man was small and very old, probably over seventy. He wore leather boots made of thick cowhide and he had long gauntlet-type gloves[4] on his hands made of the same stuff. The gloves reached above his elbows. In his right hand he carried an extraordinary implement, an eight-foot-long wooden pole with a forked end. The two prongs of the fork were made, so it seemed, of black rubber, about an inch thick and quite flexible, and it was clear that if the fork was pressed against the ground the two prongs would bend outwards, allowing the neck of the fork to go down as close to the ground as necessary. In his left hand he carried an ordinary brown sack.

Donald Macfarlane, the snake-man, may have been old and small but he was an impressive-looking character. His eyes were pale blue, deep-set in a face round and dark and wrinkled as a walnut. Above the blue eyes, the eyebrows were thick and startlingly white, but the hair on his head was almost black. In spite of the thick leather boots, he moved like a leopard, with soft slow cat-like

strides, and he came straight up to me and said, "Who are you?"

"He's with Shell[5]," Fuller said. "He hasn't been here long."

"You want to watch?" the snake-man said to me.

"Watch?" I said, wavering. "Watch? How do you mean watch? I mean where from? Not in the house?"

"You can stand out on the veranda and look through the window," the snake-man said.

"Come on," Fuller said. "We'll both watch."

"Now don't do anything silly," Mrs Fuller said.

The two children stood there <u>forlorn</u> and miserable, with tears all over their cheeks.

The snake-man and Fuller and I walked over the grass towards the house, and as we approached the veranda steps the snake-man whispered, "Tread softly on the wooden boards or he'll pick up the vibration. Wait until I've gone in, then walk up quietly and stand by the window."

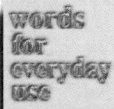

GUIDED READING

Why does the snake-man tell the men to tread softly on the veranda?

The snake-man went up the steps first and he made absolutely no sound at all with his feet. He moved soft and catlike on to the veranda and straight through the front door and then he quickly but very quietly closed the door behind him.

I felt better with the door closed. What I mean is I felt better for myself. I certainly didn't feel better for the snake-man. I figured he was committing suicide. I followed Fuller on to the veranda and we both crept over to the window. The window was open, but it had a fine mesh mosquito-netting all over it.

---

4. **gauntlet-type gloves.** Protective gloves
5. **Shell.** Shell Oil, the company Dahl flew for

1. The snake-man tells them to tread softly or the snake will pick up on the vibration of their steps.

LITERARY TECHNIQUE

PERSONAL ESSAY. A **personal essay** is a short nonfiction work on a single topic related to the life of the writer. Inform students that "The Green Mamba" is a personal essay and a work of nonfiction. Ask them to identify the single topic it explores. Encourage them to explain whether it surprises them that "The Green Mamba" is a work of nonfiction. Ask them to identify elements of the story that make it seem fictional or nonfictional.

Answers. Students should be able to identify the single topic as the narrator's experience of seeing a snake-man retrieve a deadly green mamba from the home of an English family. Some students may feel that the exotic location, the surprise of a deadly snake in a house, and the suspense made this seem like a work of fiction. Other students may say that the vivid detail and the realistic descriptions made the story seem very much like a work of nonfiction.

CROSS-CURRICULAR CONNECTION

HISTORY. Not all cultures view serpents in a negative light. These reptiles play a role in the mythology and folklore of many lands, and some cultures actually revere snakes. In ancient Egypt, snakes were kin to gods. The Greeks and Romans believed serpents brought good luck. The West African kingdom of Dahomey worshipped a python god. In India, cobras are thought to protect the earth from evil. Similarly, in China and Japan snakes were said to guard volcanoes. In Central America, the Aztecs worshipped a god that was part rattlesnake and part bird, and emperors were considered to be descendants of serpents. Many North American tribes also honored the rattlesnake, sometimes calling it Great Father, and some groups constructed huge earthen mounds, some in the form of snakes. The monuments were used for burial and for temples.

The ancient Hebrews, however, thought snakes were evil since they were worshipped by the Egyptians—enemies of the Hebrews. In the Bible, a serpent tempts Eve to eat the forbidden fruit in the Garden of Eden. Christian artists in the Middle Ages carried this negative image even further, depicting the serpent as Satan. The hatred that evolved continues around the world to this day. People chop up snakes on sight, crush them with tires on roadways, skin them to make belts and boots, get paid bounties for their carcasses, sell their fat and venom for use in a variety of products, destroy their habitats, and eat their flesh.

That made me feel better still. We peered through the netting.

The living-room was simple and ordinary, coconut matting on the floor, a red sofa, a coffee-table and a couple of armchairs. The dog was sprawled on the matting under the coffee-table, a large Airedale with curly brown and black hair. He was stone dead.

The snake-man was standing absolutely still just inside the door of the living-room. The brown sack was now slung over his left shoulder and he was grasping the long pole with both hands, holding it out in front of him, parallel to the ground. I couldn't see the snake. I didn't think the snake-man had seen it yet either.

A minute went by . . . two minutes . . . three . . four . . . five. Nobody moved. There was death in that room. The air was heavy with death and the snake-man stood as motionless as a pillar of stone, with the long rod held out in front of him.

And still he waited. Another minute . . . and another . . . and another.

And now I saw the snake-man beginning to bend his knees. Very slowly he bent his knees until he was almost squatting on the floor, and from that position he tried to peer under the sofa and the armchairs.

And still it didn't look as though he was seeing anything.

Slowly he straightened his legs again, and then his head began to swivel around the room. Over to the right, in the far corner, a staircase led up to the floor above. The snake-man looked at the stairs, and I knew very well what was going through his head. Quite abruptly, he took one step forward and stopped.

Nothing happened.

A moment later I caught sight of the snake. It was lying full-length along the

> *It lay there like a long, beautiful, deadly shaft of green glass, quite motionless, perhaps asleep.*

skirting[6] of the right-hand wall, but hidden from the snake-man's view by the back of the sofa. It lay there like a long, beautiful, deadly shaft of green glass, quite motionless, perhaps asleep. It was facing away from us who were at the window, with its small triangular head resting on the matting near the foot of the stairs.

GUIDED READING

Who sees the snake first? What does he do?

I nudged Fuller and whispered, "It's over there against the wall." I pointed and Fuller saw the snake. At once, he started waving both hands, palms outward, back and forth across the window, hoping to get the snake-man's attention. The snakeman didn't see him. Very softly, Fuller said, "Pssst!" and the snake-man looked up sharply. Fuller pointed. The snake-man understood and gave a nod.

Now the snake-man began working his way very very slowly to the back wall of the room so as to get a view of the snake behind the sofa. He never walked on his toes as you or I would have done. His feet remained flat on the ground all the time. The cowhide boots were like moccasins, with neither soles nor heels. Gradually, he worked his way over to the back wall, and from there he was able to see at least the head and two or three feet of the snake itself.

But the snake also saw him. With a movement so fast it was invisible, the snake's head came up about two feet off the floor and the front of the body arched backwards, ready to strike. Almost simultaneously, it bunched its whole body into a series of curves, ready to flash forward.

6. **skirting.** Baseboard

The snake-man was just a bit too far away from the snake to reach it with the end of his pole. He waited, staring at the snake, and the snake stared back at him with two small malevolent black eyes.

Then the snake-man started speaking to the snake. "Come along, my pretty," he whispered in a soft wheedling voice. "There's a good boy. Nobody's going to hurt you. Nobody's going to harm you, my pretty little thing. Just lie still and relax . . ." He took a step forward towards the snake, holding the pole out in front of him.

What the snake did next was so fast that the whole movement couldn't have taken more than a hundredth of a second, like the flick of a camera shutter. There was a green flash as the snake darted forward at least ten feet and struck at the snake-man's leg. Nobody could have got out of the way of that one. I heard the snake's head strike against the thick cowhide boot with a sharp little crack, and then at once the head was back in that same deadly backward-curving position, ready to strike again.

"There's a good boy," the snake-man said softly. "There's a clever boy. There's a lovely fellow. You mustn't get excited. Keep calm and everything's going to be all right." As he was speaking, he was slowly lowering the end of the pole until the forked prongs were about twelve inches above the middle of the snake's body. "There's a lovely fellow," he whispered. "There's a good kind little chap. Keep still now, my beauty. Keep still, my pretty. Keep quite still. Daddy's not going to hurt you."

I could see a thin dark trickle of venom running down the snake-man's right boot where the snake had struck.

The snake, head raised and arcing backwards, was as tense as a tight-wound spring and ready to strike again. "Keep still, my lovely," the snake-man whispered. "Don't move now. Keep still. No one's going to hurt you."

Then *wham*, the rubber prongs came down right across the snake's body, about midway along its length, and pinned it to the floor. All I could see was a green blur as the snake thrashed around furiously in an effort to free itself. But the snake-man kept up the pressure on the prongs and the snake was trapped.

What happens next? I wondered. There was no way he could catch hold of that madly twisting flailing length of green muscle with his hands, and even if he could have done so, the head would surely have flashed around and bitten him in the face.

Holding the very end of the eight-foot pole, the snake-man began to work his way round the room until he was at the tail end of the snake. Then, in spite of the flailing and the thrashing, he started pushing the prongs forward along the snake's body towards the head. Very very slowly he did it, pushing the rubber prongs forward over the snake's flailing body, keeping the snake pinned down all the time and pushing, pushing, pushing the long wooden rod forward millimetre[7] by millimetre. It was a fascinating and frightening thing to watch, the little man with white eyebrows and black hair carefully manipulating his long implement and sliding the fork ever so slowly along the length of the twisting snake towards the head. The snake's

GUIDED READING
What happens when the snake strikes?

GUIDED READING
What does the snake-man do with the pronged pole?

---

7. **millimetre.** British spelling of millimeter, a Metric unit of measure

---

words for everyday use

ma • lev • o • lent (mə le′ və lənt) *adj.,* having or showing hatred. *The young man's malevolent gesture revealed his anger.*

whee • dling (hwēd liŋ) *adj.,* coaxing; flattering. *The girl spoke with a pleading, wheedling tone when she wanted a treat.*

arc (ärk′) *v.,* to follow a curved course. *The rainbow arced over the horizon.*

ma • nip • u • late (mə ni′ pyə lāt) *v.,* to treat or operate with the hands in a skillful manner. *Gina carefully manipulated the tangled necklaces until she go them apart.*

ANSWERS TO GUIDED READING QUESTIONS

1. The snake strikes the snake-man's boot, so quickly that it takes only a hundredth of a second before the snake is poised and ready to strike again.
2. The snake-man pins the snake to the floor with the pronged pole.

ADDITIONAL QUESTIONS AND ACTIVITIES

If students enjoyed "The Green Mamba" and the related readings, encourage them to read another work about snakes, this one a poem called "Snake," by D. H. Lawrence. This poem might generate a discussion on how the speaker's attitude toward the snake compares and contrasts with that of the narrator and the snake-man in "The Green Mamba" and that of the dinner guests in "The Dinner Party." A few lines from this poem appear below.

Quotables

"The voice of my education said to me He must be killed, For in Sicily the black snakes are innocent, the gold are venomous.

And voices in me said, If you were a man You would take a stick and break him now, and finish him off.

But must I confess how I liked him, How glad I was he had come as a guest in quiet, to drink at my water trough"

—from D. H. Lawrence's *"Snake"*

1. When the prongs are just behind the snake's head, the snake-man grabs the snake firmly by the neck and lowers it headfirst into the sack.
2. The snake-man's final instructions are to move the dead dog before the children see it.

RESPOND TO THE SELECTION

Encourage students to discuss in small groups why many people enjoy frightening or suspenseful things, such as roller coaster rides and scary movies.

SELECTION CHECK TEST 4.2.9 WITH ANSWERS

Checking Your Reading
1. On what continent does the story take place? **The story takes place in Africa.**
2. How do the Fullers discover that a green mamba has entered their house? **The narrator, a guest of the Fullers, sees it and hurries to warn the family.**
3. Why is everyone so concerned about the green mamba? **Green mambas are extremely poisonous and dangerous.**
4. How do the children escape danger? **The children are lowered from an upstairs window to safety.**
5. What eventually happens to the green mamba? **The snake-man captures the green mamba.**

Vocabulary in Context
Fill in each blank below with the most appropriate vocabulary word from "The Green Mamba." You may have to change the tense of the word.

unruffled   forlorn   malevolent
wheedling   arc   manipulating

1. Ignoring his students' _____ voices begging him to put the test off to another day, Mr. Atkinson called for silence and distributed the semester exam. **wheedling**
2. When the thunderstorm struck, the _____ campers huddled miserably in their tents. **forlorn**
3. When the boat began to take on water, the _____ guide calmly directed everyone to put on life preservers and bail. **unruffled**
4. The balloonist easily _____

---

body was thumping against the coconut matting with such a noise that if you had been upstairs you might have thought two big men were wrestling on the floor.

Then at last the prongs were right behind the head itself, pinning it down, and at that point the snake-man reached forward with one gloved hand and grasped the snake very firmly by the neck. He threw away the pole. He took the sack off his shoulder with his free hand. He lifted the great, still twisting length of the deadly green snake and pushed the head into the sack. Then he let go the head and bundled the rest of the creature in and closed the sack. The sack started jumping about as though there were fifty angry rats inside it, but the snake-man was now totally relaxed and he held the sack casually in one hand as if it contained no more than a few pounds of potatoes. He stooped and picked up his pole from the floor, then he turned and looked towards the window where we were peering in.

"Pity about the dog," he said. "You'd better get it out of the way before the children see it." ∎

> **GUIDED READING**
> What does the snake-man do once the prongs are just behind the snake's head?

> **GUIDED READING**
> What are the snake-man's final instructions to the two men watching him?

Respond *to the* SELECTION

If you were the narrator, would you want to watch the snake-man? Why, or why not?

About *the* AUTHOR

Roald Dahl (1916–1990) lived a life of adventure before becoming a writer. Born in Llandaff, South Wales, he was educated in English schools, where he did poorly. His first job involved travel across Tanganyika (now Tanzania) in Africa. During World War II, he was a fighter pilot with the Royal Air Force until injuries forced him to take a desk job in Washington, DC. There he began writing stories for American magazines. He wrote one book for children during the war but did not concentrate on writing for young readers until he began writing for his own children. Dahl was married twice and had five children. His books include *James and the Giant Peach* and *Charlie and the Chocolate Factory*.

SELECTION CHECK TEST 4.2.9 WITH ANSWERS (CONT.)

the ropes and valves to guide the hot-air balloon over the green fields and low hills. **manipulated**
5. The mob boss faced his enemy with a(n) _____ stare. **malevolent**

How the Snake Got Poison

Zora Neale Hurston

Well, when God made de snake he put him in de bushes to ornament de ground. But things didn't suit de snake so one day he got on de ladder and went up to see God. "Good mawnin', God."

"How do you do, Snake?"

"Ah ain't so many, God, you put me down there on my belly in de dust and everything trods upon me and kills off my generations. Ah ain't got no kind of protection at all."

God looked off towards immensity and thought about de subject for awhile, then he said, "Ah didn't mean for nothin' to be stompin' you snakes lak dat.

"You got to have some kind of a protection. Here, take dis poison and put it in yo' mouf and when they tromps on you, protect yo' self."

So de snake took de poison in his mouf and went on back.

So after awhile all de other varmints went up to God.

"Good evenin', God."

"How you makin' it, varmints?"

"God, please do somethin' 'bout dat snake. He' layin' in de bushes there wid poison in his mouf and he's strikin' everything dat shakes de bush. He's killin' up our generations. Wese skeered to walk de earth."

So God sent for de snake and tole him:

"Snake, when Ah give you dat poison, Ah didn't mean for you to be hittin' and killin' everything dat shake de bush. I give you dat poison and tole you to protect yo'self when they tromples on you. But you killin' everything dat moves. Ah didn't mean for you to do dat."

De snake say, "Lawd, you know Ah'm down here in de dust. Ah ain't got no claws to fight wid, and Ah ain't got no feets to git me out de way. All Ah kin see is feets comin' to tromple me. Ah can't tell who my enemy is and who is my friend. You gimme dis protection in my mouf and Ah uses it."

God thought it over for a while then he says:

"Well, snake, I don't want yo' generations all stomped out and I don't want you killin' everything else dat moves. Here take dis bell and tie it to yo' tail. When you hear feets comin' you ring yo' bell and if it's yo' friend, he'll be keerful. If it's yo' enemy, it's you and him."

So dat's how de snake got his poison and dat's how come he got rattles.

Biddy, biddy, bend my story is end.

Turn loose de rooster and hold de hen. ■

ABOUT THE RELATED READING

"How the Snake Got Poison" is a traditional African American folk tale. **Zora Neale Hurston** (1891–1960) has retold a number of such tales in books such as *Of Mules and Men* and *Go Gator and Muddy the Water.* Hurston also wrote many other works, including short stories, novels, plays, and essays.

The *Dinner* PARTY

Mona Gardner

The country is India. A colonial official and his wife are giving a large dinner party. They are seated with their guests—army officers and government attachés and their wives, and a visiting American naturalist—in their spacious dining room, which has a bare marble floor, open rafters and wide glass doors opening onto a veranda.

A spirited discussion springs up between a young girl who insists that women have outgrown the jumping-on-a-chair-at-the-sight-of-a-mouse era and a colonel who says that they haven't.

"A woman's unfailing reaction in any crisis," the colonel says, "is to scream. And while a man may feel like it, he has that ounce more of nerve control than a woman has. And that last ounce is what counts."

The American does not join in the argument but watches the other guests. As he looks, he sees a strange expression come over the face of the hostess. She is staring straight ahead, her muscles contracting slightly. With a slight gesture she summons the native boy standing behind her chair and whispers to him. The boy's eyes widen: he quickly leaves the room.

Of the guests, none except the American notices this or sees the boy place a bowl of milk on the veranda just outside the open doors.

The American comes to with a start. In India, milk in a bowl means only one thing—bait for a snake. He realizes there must be a cobra in the room. He looks up at the rafters—the likeliest place—but they are bare. Three corners of the room are empty, and in the fourth the servants are waiting to serve the next course. There is only one place left—under the table.

His first impulse is to jump back and warn the others, but he knows the commotion would frighten the cobra into striking. He speaks quickly, the tone of his voice so arresting that it sobers everyone.

"I want to know just what control everyone at this table has. I will count to three hundred—that's five minutes—and not one of you is to move a muscle. Those who move will forfeit fifty rupees. Ready!"

The twenty people sit like stone images while he counts. He is saying, ". . . two hundred and eighty. . ." when, out of the corner of his eye, he sees the cobra emerge and make for the bowl of milk. Screams ring out as he jumps to slam the veranda doors safely shut.

"You were right, Colonel!" the host exclaims. "A man has just shown us an example of perfect control."

"Just a minute," the American says, turning to his hostess. "Mrs. Wynnes, how did you know that cobra was in the room?"

A faint smile lights up the woman's face as she replies: "Because it was crawling across my foot." ∎

Colonial house in Gujaret, India. Hans Georg Roth.

ABOUT THE RELATED READING

Mona Gardner wrote short stories and novels during her lifetime (1900–1981). She collected much of the material for her stories during her extensive travels around the world. "The Dinner Party" examines people's attitudes about gender in colonial India. (India was under British rule from 1757 to 1947.) Many of Gardner's stories were published in magazines such as *The New Yorker, Saturday Review of Literature*, and *Reader's Digest*.

art smart.

Examine the architecture, furniture, rugs, and artwork adorning this room. What does this tell you about the people who lived there? Using what you already know about living conditions in India, propose a theory about how British and American people fared in colonial India and about how Indian people fared.

"THE GREEN MAMBA" **123**

ADDITIONAL QUESTIONS AND ACTIVITIES

Have students discuss the following questions about "The Dinner Party":
1. What "spirited" discussion occurs at the dinner party?
2. What does one American note about his hostess's expression? What does the hostess then do?
3. What does the American see the boy do? In what way does the American interpret this action?
4. What does the American do when he realizes the cobra is under the table?
5. What does the host say once the snake emerges and heads for the bowl and is shut outside?
6. What does the American ask the hostess, Mrs. Wynnes? What is her response? What do her words reveal about her character and the topic that was under discussion?

Answers
1. A girl says that women have outgrown the "jumping-on-a-chair-at-the-sight-of-a-mouse era," but a colonel says women still scream at any crisis and that men have more control over their nerves.
2. An American notes that his hostess is staring straight ahead, her muscles contracted. The hostess then whispers to a servant boy.
3. The American sees the boy put a bowl of milk on the veranda outside. The American knows that this means there must be a cobra in the room.
4. The American orders everyone to test their self-control by holding still while he counts to three hundred.
5. The host says a man has shown an example of perfect control.
6. The American asks the hostess how she knew a cobra was in the room. She says she knew because it was crawling across her foot. Her response reveals that women can have nerves of steel, contrary to what the colonel suggested.

LITERARY TECHNIQUE

IRONY OF SITUATION. An event that contradicts the expectations of the characters, the reader, or the audience of a literary work is an example of **irony of situation**. Ask students to explain why the last line of the story might be considered an example of irony of situation.

Answers. Students may suggest that this line is ironic because it contradicts the expectations of those male members of the room who assumed that women could not control their nerves.

RECALL

1a. Without further questioning, he carefully lowers his wife and children down from the second-story window and then climbs down himself. He is completely cool and unruffled and does not even raise his voice.

2a. All three are very worried about Jack and call frantically for him. They understand the danger Jack is in. When the dog doesn't come, Mrs. Fuller tries to calm her children by suggesting he is simply hiding.

3a. He whispers in a soft, wheedling voice, trying to entice and flatter the snake. He tells the snake he's a good boy, nobody is going to hurt him, he shouldn't get excited, just keep calm and everything will be all right.

INTERPRET

1b. He understands the danger and recognizes the need to act quickly and without fuss so the snake won't be provoked to strike. His cool manner suggests that he has dealt with deadly snakes before and feels confident that he can control the situation.

2b. Mrs. Fuller and the children are very fond of Jack, and he seems to be an object on which they can project their own emotions. They know they can't show any alarm when they themselves are at risk, yet their worrying about the dog suggests they are really very afraid of the snake.

3b. He seems to respect the snake because he moves so carefully and says he won't hurt it. He treats it very cautiously, trying to entice and flatter the snake into cooperating by keeping still. He clearly does not want to harm the snake, yet his wheedling tone and manner also suggest he does not trust it. The snake-man is aware of the power of the deadly snake and knows that he must respect such power.

ANALYZE

4a. The snake-man is described as an old Englishman who likes snakes, as never buying snakes from natives because he does not want natives to harm themselves by attempting to catch snakes, as being small old and over seventy, as wearing the right clothes and carrying the right tools for his job, as walking soundlessly on his moccasins, as speaking softly and in a wheedling manner to the

Investigate, Inquire, and Imagine

Recall: GATHERING FACTS

1a. How does Mr. Fuller respond to the news that a green mamba has entered his living room? What does he do? How does he act?

2a. How do the children and Mrs. Fuller respond when they realize the dog is still in the house? What are they each thinking and feeling?

3a. How does the snake-man talk to the snake? What tone and volume does he use? What does he say?

Interpret: FINDING MEANING

1b. Based on Mr. Fuller's actions and reactions, how do you think he feels about the snake?

2b. What role does the dog play in this story?

3b. How would you say the snake-man feels about the snake? How does he treat the snake? What is his attitude toward the snake?

Analyze: TAKING THINGS APART

4a. What words and phrases does the narrator use to describe the green mamba and its actions? What words and phrases does he use to describe the snake-man and his actions?

Synthesize: BRINGING THINGS TOGETHER

4b. In your own words, summarize the narrator's characterization of both the green mamba and the snake-man.

Evaluate: MAKING JUDGMENTS

5a. How effective is the snake-man's method of dealing with the green mamba? How else might he handle the situation?

Extend: CONNECTING IDEAS

5b. What would the snake-man tell the guests in Mona Gardner's story "The Dinner Party"? How are the responses of the hostess and of the American to the cobra similar to those of the snake-man? How are they different?

Understanding Literature

SUSPENSE. Examine how Roald Dahl builds **suspense** in "The Green Mamba." Compare with your classmates your experiences as you read the story. In what ways did you question what would happen next? Were you shocked or sickened by the action? Were you attracted to the danger? When did you first begin feel a little anxious, and why? Note the points in the story where you felt the suspense increase. At what point in the story did you feel the most suspense—the most fear about what would happen next?

ANSWERS TO INVESTIGATE, INQUIRE, IMAGINE (CONT.)

snake, and as giving matter-of-fact advice about the dead dog. Students may say the snake is portrayed as having "brilliant yellowy-green skin," as being "death in that room," as being "a long, beautiful, deadly shaft of green glass," as being "malevolent," and as being able to move as fast as a camera's shutter.

SYNTHESIZE

4b. Responses will vary, but students may say the snake-man is portrayed as being knowledgeable and good at his job. The snake is portrayed as beautiful, powerful, and deadly.

EVALUATE

5a. Students may say the snake-man's method is extremely effective. Students might say the snake-man could simply kill the snake, but then this story would lose its quality of reverence for even the deadly things of nature.

(Continued on page 126)

Characterization. Look at the list you made that shows the **characterization** of the snake-man. In a small group, discuss which things on the list added to the suspense you felt as you read the story. Which *concrete details* were used to develop characterization? Make characterization lists for other characters—Mr. Fuller, the narrator, Mrs. Fuller, the children, and the green mamba. Compare and contrast the characterizations. Which are the most concrete? Which characters are described most fully? How are the reactions of each character to the snake similar? How are they different? How do the reactions of the characters add to the story's suspense?

Writer's Journal

1. Imagine that you are the narrator of this story. Write a **letter** home describing the encounter you had with the green mamba while visiting a friend in Tanganyika.

2. Write a **paragraph** describing something that happened recently, such as a party you went to, a movie you saw, a game you played, or a trip you went on. Use as many concrete words as possible in your description.

3. Write a **short story** about something scary that once happened. As you write, try to stretch the story out and build suspense as much as you can. Use concrete descriptions of sights, sounds, smells, tastes, and touch. Show the reactions of your characters as each new concrete experience builds upon the previous ones.

Skill Builders

Language, Grammar, and Style

UNDERSTANDING DIALECT. Dialect (a version of language spoken by people of a particular place, time, or group) is an important part of Zora Neale Hurston's story "How the Snake Got Poison." Hurston tells this folk tale in the African American dialect of the South. Read the story aloud or listen to an audiotape. What does dialect add to the story? Translate the first few paragraphs of the story into standard English and read this aloud. Which version do you find the most interesting to listen to? Why?

Speaking and Listening & Collaborative Learning

INTERVIEWING AND REPORTING. In a small group, have each member take a role from "The Green Mamba," leaving one person to be a newspaper reporter. The newspaper reporter should draw up a list of questions to ask witnesses (the characters in "The Green Mamba") about their thoughts, feelings, and observations while the green mamba was in the house. While the reporter is conducting the interviews, each group member should listen carefully and record (either on cassette tape or on paper) the responses. Then, working together, write an article that will appear in the local newspaper. Be sure to include a headline, or title, for the article. Using notes from your interviews, include quotes from people who were on the scene about their observations and reactions to the incident.

ANSWERS TO INVESTIGATE, INQUIRE, IMAGINE (CONT.)

EXTEND

5b. The snake-man would probably tell the guests that there is a cobra under the table and that everyone should remain motionless until it leaves. Like the snake-man, both the hostess and the American recognize the need to stay calm and still. But the hostess handles the situation by enticing the snake to leave rather than by trying to capture it. The American, rather than focusing intensely on the snake the way the snake-man does, instead comes up with a creative and playful ploy to divert attention from a tense situation.

ANSWERS TO UNDERSTANDING LITERATURE

SUSPENSE. As this story unfolds, readers fear that the green mamba will bite someone. This fear is reinforced by the author's attention to concrete details, carefully describing things that can be seen, tasted, touched, heard, or smelled. Readers question what will happen next. They want to read on and learn the answer, but at the same time they may also feel afraid to find out. Students might point to a peak of suspense when the snake-man is inside the house but cannot see the snake and when the snake darts out and bites him.

CHARACTERIZATION. Most students will say that the characterization that built suspense was concrete. Students' characterization lists will vary, but may include details such as Mr. Fuller being cool and unruffled and being bold enough to get the snake-man's attention. Students may point to the narrator's horror in seeing the snake enter the house, his running to tell the Fullers about the snake, and his not being sure whether he wants to watch its capture. Students may point to Mrs. Fuller not seeming to be alarmed, her looking grim when she learns about the dog being in the house, and her trying to protect her children from fear by trying to take them to a neighbor's house. For the children, students might point out that they are not "particularly alarmed" until they remember Jack. The mamba is described as deadly and beautiful as a shaft of green glass. Students may say that the characterization of the snake-man and the snake are the fullest. All the characters are not surprised to see the snake, but do fear its deadly power. Mr. Fuller and his wife react with more control than the narrator and the children. The snake-man reacts calmly, confident in his own ability to handle snakes. The contrasting reactions of coolness, terror, and confidence make the reader uncertain about the outcome of the events.

Language, Grammar, and Style
Most students will say that the dialect adds a realistic flavor to the story, as well as making it seem more like someone is speaking to them directly. Most students will find the version with dialect to be more interesting.

Speaking and Listening & Collaborative Learning
Make sure that students assign roles to all the major characters in the story—the narrator, Mr. Fuller, Mrs. Fuller, the young girl, the young boy, and the snake-man. For fun, the students might also assign the role of the snake to one student. Tell students that even though the reporter is in charge of coming up with the questions (just as the students who are assigned roles must come up with their own answers), the students must write the article together, as a group.

Study and Research
Encourage students to refer to the Language Arts Survey 5.23, "Using Biographical References, Encyclopedias, and Periodicals" and 5.25, "Using the Internet" for information on how to use these resources to gather information. Students should write their responses in the form of a very brief (one- or two-paragraph) essay on their chosen type of snake.

Media Literacy
Encourage students to base their maps on facts about Tanzania that they gather from an atlas or almanac. Refer them to the Language Arts Survey 5.22, "Using Almanacs, Yearbooks, and Atlases." When students are done with their maps, display them on a bulletin board.

Critical Thinking
Students' theme statements should clearly identify the character with whose reaction they can most identify. Students may admire the snake-man's reaction, but say they don't have his experience, so would find it hard to be so matter-of-fact in his situation. Students' ideas about confronting fear will vary.

Study and Research
RESEARCHING POISONOUS SNAKES. Using the library or the Internet, look up information on the green mamba, the black mamba, the cobra, the puff adder, or another poisonous snake. Research the snake's physical description, habitat, diet, and population status (is it endangered?). Try to answer most of the following questions about the snake. Where does it live? Is it extremely venomous? What does it eat? Does its venom have medical uses? Report your findings to the class.

Language, Grammar, and Style
INDIRECT OBJECTS. If a sentence has a direct object completing the action of the verb, it is sometimes received by someone or something. This receiver is called the **indirect object**.

EXAMPLE   The man showed us the snake.
What is the action? (the verb)
showed
Who showed? (the subject)
The man
The man showed what? (the direct object) snake

To find the **indirect object**, check to see if the direct object has a receiver. Who got the *direct object*? In this sentence we ask, "The man showed the snake to whom?" The answer is <u>us</u>. On your own sheet of paper, identify the verb, the subject, the direct object, and the indirect object for each of the sentences below. If the sentence has no direct or indirect object, indicate that as well. For more information, see the Language Arts Survey 3.20, "Completers for Action Verbs: Direct and Indirect Objects."

1. The snake gave the children a fright.
2. The snake-man came quickly.
3. A deadly cobra bit my leg.
4. It gave me poison.
5. Snake venom actually heals many people each year.

Critical Thinking
LINKING THEMES. Consider how characters in "The Green Mamba," "How the Snake Got Poison," and "The Dinner Party" confront danger. What statements about life do these selections make? How do those statements differ? In your own words, describe the theme of each selection.

Whose response in these selections is most like your own would be? Whose response do you most admire? What suggestions would you make about confronting fear? Form you own theme statement about this subject.

Media Literacy
CREATING A MAP. Use the map below as a base. Add to the map additional features, such as mountains, rivers, cities, regions and label the features. To keep the map easy to read, you may need to use colors and symbols for certain features. You may also want to label neighboring countries. If necessary, create a key that shows what different symbols you may have used stand for. For more information, see the Language Arts Survey 6.11, "Displaying Effective Visual Information."

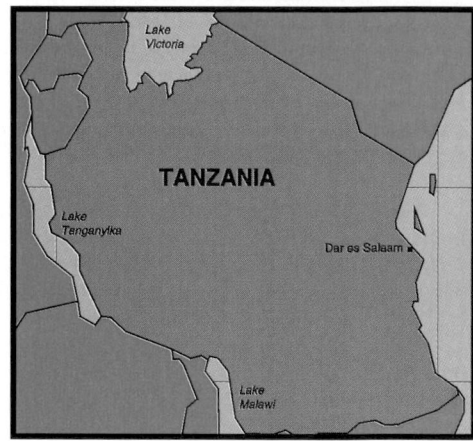

Prereading

"Ships in the Desert" by Al Gore

Reader's Resource

- This selection is from *Earth in the Balance: Ecology and the Human Spirit*. Al Gore wrote the book as a U.S. senator, hoping to inform people about the environment, its problems, and possible solutions.

- **SCIENCE CONNECTION.** In a healthy environment, things are balanced—they have adjusted to one another and to the surrounding conditions. If plants, animals, air, soil, and water are in a balanced relationship, an environment can stay the same for hundreds of years. Environmental change occurs when a new element appears and upsets the balance.

- Nature sometimes causes environmental change through such things as a disease that wipes out a group of living things, a forest fire that destroys animal and plant habitats, or a climate change to which living things are unable to adapt. Humans may cause environmental change through such things as urban expansion that destroys natural habitats, chemical and industrial wastes that pollute natural resources, and fuel emissions that poison the air. Sometimes people make such errors because they are not aware of the long-term effects of their actions. Other times, they ignore the long-term effects for short-term gain.

Graphic Organizer

This selection discusses a number of environmental problems and their possible causes. In your journal, make a chart like the one

Environmental Problem	Possible Cause
several million starfish killed	radioactive military waste in White Sea

started at right. As you read, make note of each environmental problem and its possible causes.

Reader's Journal

What local issues and problems concern you? How did you learn of them? What is your stance?

Reader's TOOLBOX

IRONY OF SITUATION. Irony is a difference between appearance and reality. An event that contradicts the expectations of the characters, the reader, or the audience of a literary work is an example of **irony of situation**. In this selection, there are several examples of irony of situation as the narrator encounters strange circumstances in the natural world. As you read, find where irony of situation occurs.

FIGURES OF SPEECH. A **figure of speech** is writing or speech that has more than a straightforward, literal meaning. This language is meant to be understood imaginatively instead of literally. Many writers, such as the writer of this selection, sometimes use figures of speech to describe a situation in a new way.

Image on following page: Fishing ships sit stranded in a desert that once was part of the Aral Sea. Formerly the fourth-largest inland sea in the world and the biggest producer of fish in north central Asia, the Aral Sea is drying up because of human intervention. The groove in the sand is from a canal dug by owners of fishing boats trying to reach the sea as the water steadily retreated.

GRAPHIC ORGANIZER

Students might include the following problems and possible causes in their charts: Aral Sea is dead/water is diverted for irrigation of cotton crops in the desert; dead dolphins washing up on the Riviera, dead dolphins along gulf coast in Texas/accumulated environmental stress, which made dolphins too weak to fight off a virus; millions of dead starfish/radioactive waste; dead birds and otters washing up on Prince William Sound/oil spill; polar ice cap might be thinning/global warming caused by rising levels of CO_2, which result from increased burning of coal and oil.

READER'S JOURNAL

As an alternate activity, ask students to imagine the way their lives would change if the climate in their town or city changed very suddenly, becoming hotter or colder, dryer or wetter.

GOALS/OBJECTIVES

Studying this lesson will enable students to
- analyze and appreciate an environmental essay
- understand the importance of a balanced environment
- define *irony of situation* and identify this type of irony in their reading
- define *figurative language* and point to examples of figurative language in their reading
- work as part of a group to research an environmental issue
- write a press release on an environmental issue
- use hyphens and dashes properly

MOTIVATION
Students might enjoy playing the role of environmentalist themselves and report on the state of the environment in their own town or city. Encourage them to work in groups of four or five to discover a local environmental issue. Each group can then report on their findings to the class. Students may find their issue in a local paper or learn of it through fellow townspeople, or they may already know of issues through their own observation.

READING PROFICIENCY Help students to make an outline of "Ships of the Desert" by identifying the main idea in each of its paragraphs, so students have a general overview of this essay. Ask them to identify at least one idea in each paragraph that supports the main idea.

ENGLISH LANGUAGE LEARNING
Point out the following vocabulary words and expressions.
hip boots—waterproof boots that come up to the hips, used for wading in water without getting wet
Siberia—region in North Asia
radioactive—giving off energy that can be harmful or fatal to living creatures
Riviera—coastline of the Mediterranean sea stretching from France to Italy
hypodermic needle—medical needle that doctors use for injections
billowing—forming a large, swelling mass
poachers—people who hunt animals illegally
ivory—hard white substance that comes from the tusks of elephants and walruses. Once used for making jewelry and other items, it is extremely valuable but illegal to sell in most countries.
hostile—unfriendly, as an enemy

SPECIAL NEEDS
Students may benefit from listening to the selection on audiocassette or hearing you read the selection aloud. Then tell students to read the essay to themselves, stopping to answer the Guided Reading questions as they read.

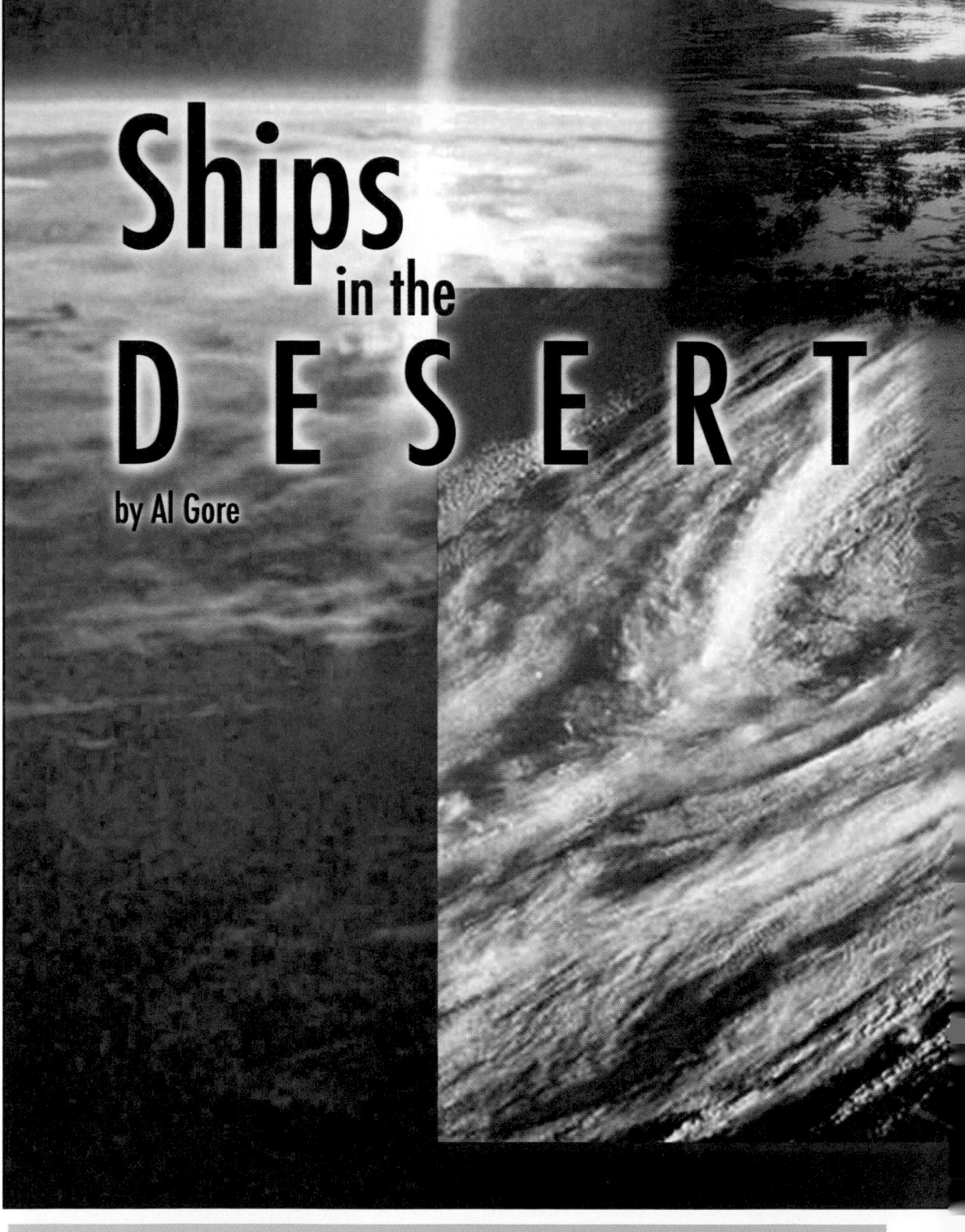

Ships
in the
DESERT

by Al Gore

INDIVIDUAL LEARNING STRATEGIES (CONT.)

ENRICHMENT
Encourage students to actually take part in helping to better our environment. You might encourage them to organize a recycling drive, to clean up a local park, to make an effort to use less electricity and more public transportation, to write their congress representatives on environmental issues, and to write to the owners of companies that pollute the environment to urge them to clean up their factories. Tell students to turn what upsets them about the state of the environment into positive action. As a class, you might brainstorm ways that students can help become part of the solution by helping to conserve and protect planet Earth.

CROSS-CURRICULAR ACTIVITIES

SOCIAL STUDIES AND SCIENCE. The author of this selection visits many places to witness the toll human actions are taking on the environment. Have students use a map or a globe to locate the different places the narrator describes. You might combine this activity with a lesson on how to use an atlas. Refer students to the Language Arts Survey 5.22, "Using Almanacs, Yearbooks, and Atlases."

Have each student find a newspaper or magazine article about an environmental problem and then mark its area of origin on a large wall map. Students could add to the map a notecard summarizing each environmental problem.

I was standing in the sun on the hot steel deck of a fishing ship capable of processing a fifty-ton catch on a good day. But it wasn't a good day. We were anchored in what used to be the most productive fishing site in all of central Asia, but as I looked out over the bow, the prospects of a good catch looked <u>bleak</u>. Where there should have been gentle blue-green waves lapping against the side of the ship, there was nothing but hot dry sand—as far as I could see in all directions. The other ships of the fleet were also at rest in the sand, scattered in the dunes that stretched all the way to the horizon.

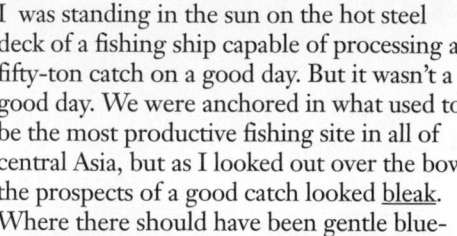

GUIDED READING

Why is it a bad fishing day? What is unusual about the location of the ship?

Oddly enough, it made me think of a fried egg I had seen back in the United States on television the week before. It was sizzling and popping the way a fried egg should in a pan, but it was in the middle of a sidewalk in downtown Phoenix. I guess it sprang to mind because, like the ship on which I was standing, there was nothing wrong with the egg itself. Instead, the world beneath it had changed in an unexpected way that made the egg seem—through no fault of its own—out of place. It was illustrating the newsworthy point that at the time Arizona wasn't having an especially good day, either, because for the second day in a row temperatures had reached a record 122 degrees.

As a camel walked by on the dead bottom of the Aral Sea, my thoughts returned to the unlikely ship of the desert on which I stood, which also seemed to be illustrating the point that its world had changed out from underneath it with sudden cruelty. Ten years ago the Aral was the fourth-largest inland sea in the world, comparable to the largest of North America's Great Lakes. Now it is disappearing because the water that used to feed it has been <u>diverted</u> in an ill-considered irrigation scheme to grow cotton in the desert. The new shoreline was almost forty kilometers across the sand from where the fishing fleet was now permanently docked. Meanwhile, in the nearby town of Muynak the people were still canning fish—brought not from the Aral Sea but shipped by rail through Siberia from the Pacific Ocean, more than a thousand miles away.

GUIDED READING

What has caused the change in the fishing industry?

I had come to the Aral Sea in August 1990 to witness at first hand the destruction taking place there on an almost biblical scale. But during the trip I encountered other images that also alarmed me. For example, the day I returned to Moscow from Muynak, my friend Alexei Yablokov, possibly the leading environmentalist in the Soviet Union, was returning from an emergency expedition to the White Sea, where he had investigated the mysterious and <u>unprecedented</u> death of several *million* starfish, washed up into a knee-deep mass covering many miles of beach. That night, in his apartment, he talked of what it was like for the residents to wade through the starfish in hip boots, trying to explain their death.

Later investigations identified radioactive military waste as the likely culprit in the White Sea deaths. But what about all of the other mysterious mass deaths washing up on beaches around the world? French scientists recently concluded that the explanation for the growing number of dead dolphins washing up along the Riviera was accumulated

words for everyday use

bleak (blēk) *adj.,* not promising or hopeful. *Our future will be <u>bleak</u> if we do not take care of serious problems now.*

di • vert (dī vurt') *v.,* turn aside from a course or direction. *We must <u>divert</u> the coming disaster.*

un • prec • e • dent • ed (un pres' ə den'tid) *adj.,* unheard of; new. *A seventh grade student playing for the varsity high school team was <u>unprecedented</u>.*

environmental stress, which, over time, rendered the animals too weak to fight off a virus. This same <u>phenomenon</u>

GUIDED READING

What explanations are offered for the dead starfish, dolphins, otters, and sea birds?

may also explain the sudden increase in dolphin deaths along the Gulf Coast in Texas as well as the mysterious deaths of 12,000 seals whose corpses washed up on the shores of the North Sea in the summer of 1988. Of course, the oil-covered otters and seabirds of Prince William Sound a year[1] later presented less of a mystery to science, if no less an <u>indictment</u> of our civilization.

As soon as one of these troubling images fades, another takes its place, provoking new questions. What does it mean, for example, that children playing in the morning surf must now dodge not only the occasional jellyfish but the occasional hypodermic needle washing in with the waves? Needles, dead dolphins, and oil-soaked birds—are all these signs that the shores of our familiar world are fast eroding, that we are now standing on some new beach, facing dangers beyond the edge of what we are capable of imagining?

With our backs turned to the place in nature from which we came, we sense an unfamiliar tide rising and swirling around our ankles, pulling at the sand beneath our feet. Each time this strange new tide goes out, it leaves behind the flotsam and jetsam[2] of some giant shipwreck far out at sea, startling images washed up on the sands of our time, each a fresh warning of hidden dangers that lie ahead if we continue on our present course.

My search for the underlying causes of the environmental crisis has led me to travel around the world to examine and study many of these images of destruction. At the very bottom of the earth, high in the Trans-Antarctic Mountains, with the sun glaring at midnight through a hole in the sky, I stood in the unbelievable coldness and talked with a scientist in the late fall of 1988 about the tunnel he was digging through time. Slipping his parka back to reveal a badly burned face that was cracked and peeling, he pointed to the annual layers of ice in a core sample dug from the glacier on which we were standing. He moved his finger back in time to the ice of two decades ago. "Here's where the U.S. Congress passed the Clean Air Act," he said. At the bottom of the world, two continents away from Washington, D.C., even a small reduction in one country's emissions had changed the amount of pollution found in the remotest and least accessible place on earth.

But the most significant change thus far in the earth's atmosphere is the one that began with the industrial revolution early in the last century and has picked up speed ever since. Industry meant coal, and later oil, and we began to burn lots of it—bringing rising levels of carbon dioxide (CO_2), with its ability to trap more heat in the atmosphere and slowly warm the earth. Fewer than a hundred yards from the South Pole, upwind from the ice

---

1. **oil-covered otters . . . a year later.** Refers to the Exxon-Valdez oil spill of 11 million gallons in Prince William Sound, Alaska, in 1989
2. **flotsam and jetsam.** Floating debris

---

words for everyday use

phe • nom • e • non (fə näm′ ə nən′) *n.*, extremely unusual or extraordinary thing or occurrence. *The aurora borealis is an amazing <u>phenomenon</u>.*

in • dict • ment (in dīt′ mənt) *n.*, accusation of wrongdoing, criminal charge. *Joe received an <u>indictment</u>, but he was never found guilty of the crime.*

ANSWER TO GUIDED READING QUESTION

1. The dead starfish were likely killed by radioactive military wastes. The dead dolphins probably suffered accumulated environmental stress that caused an immune deficiency. The otters and seabirds were killed by an oil spill.

CROSS-CURRICULAR CONNECTION

HISTORY. The Industrial Revolution began in England in the 1700s with the invention of machines for weaving. Over the following centuries the environment was affected by the world's increasing reliance on industry. For example, polluting energy sources such as coal and petroleum were used in greater and greater quantities; factories were developed and began dumping waste products into the air, soil, and water; and new methods of transportation, such as trains, cars, and airplanes, added to the environmental stress.

ADDITIONAL QUESTIONS AND ACTIVITIES

Encourage students to hold a class discussion on the benefits and drawbacks of the Industrial Revolution. You might divide the board into two columns and list the ideas that students come up with. Ask them to think about the ways industry has changed their lives for the better? In what ways has it changed their lives and the environment for the worse?

1. The rising levels of CO₂ cause
temperatures to rise. As
temperatures rise in the polar
regions, the ice of the polar ice
caps melt. This could have a
disastrous effect on weather
patterns around the globe.

CROSS-CURRICULAR ACTIVITIES

ARTS AND HUMANITIES.
Encourage students to hold a
class-wide environmental
poster contest. Each student
should create a poster about
an environmental issue about
which they feel strongly.
Possible topics include
pollution, rainforest
conservation, and saving an
endangered species of animal. Each
student's poster should have a
slogan that helps portray the
student's cause. For example, for
pollution, a student might write,
"Mother Nature Can't Keep Going If
We Don't Stop Polluting," and paint
a picture of planet Earth with a
crying human face and factories
billowing smoke around the earth's
circumference. Encourage students
to use their imaginations to come
up with images that vividly portray
the issue they have chosen.
Students might then vote on the
most effective poster.

runway where the ski plane lands and keeps its engines running to prevent the metal parts from freeze-locking together, scientists monitor the air several times every day to chart the course of that <u>inexorable</u> change. During my visit, I watched one scientist draw the results of that day's measurements, pushing the end of a steep line still higher on the graph. He told me how easy it is—there at the end of the earth—to see that this enormous change in the global atmosphere is still picking up speed.

Two and a half years later I slept under the midnight sun at the other end of our planet, in a small tent pitched on a twelve-foot-thick slab of ice floating in the frigid Arctic Ocean. After a hearty breakfast, my companions and I traveled by snowmobiles a few miles farther north to a <u>rendezvous</u> point where the ice was thinner—only three and a half feet thick—and a nuclear submarine hovered in the water below. After it crashed through the ice, took on its new passengers, and resubmerged, I talked with scientists who were trying to measure more accurately the thickness of the polar ice cap, which many believe is thinning as a result of global warming. I had just negotiated an agreement between ice scientists and the U.S. Navy to secure the release of previously top secret data from submarine sonar tracks, data that could help them learn what is happening to the north polar cap. Now, I wanted to see the pole itself, and some eight hours after we met the submarine, we were crashing through that ice, surfacing, and then I was standing in an eerily beautiful snowscape, windswept and sparkling white, with the horizon defined by little hummocks, or

"pressure ridges" of ice that are pushed up like tiny mountain ranges when separate sheets collide. But here too, CO₂ levels are rising just as rapidly, and ultimately temperatures will rise with them—indeed, global warming is expected to push temperatures up much more rapidly in the polar regions than in the rest of the world. As the polar air warms, the ice here will thin; and since the polar cap plays such a crucial role in the world's weather system, the consequences of a thinning cap could be disastrous.

> **GUIDED READING**
> What effects might rising levels of CO₂ have?

Considering such scenarios is not a purely <u>speculative</u> exercise. Six months after I returned from the North Pole, a team of scientists reported dramatic changes in the pattern of ice distribution in the Arctic, and a second team reported a still controversial claim (which a variety of data now suggest) that, overall, the north polar cap has thinned by 2 percent in just the last decade. Moreover, scientists established several years ago that in many land areas north of the Arctic Circle, the spring snowmelt now comes earlier every year, and deep in the tundra[3] below, the temperature of the earth is steadily rising.

As it happens, some of the most disturbing images of environmental destruction can be found exactly halfway between the North and South poles—precisely at the equator in Brazil—where billowing clouds of smoke regularly blacken the sky above the immense but now threatened Amazon rain forest. Acre

---

3. **tundra.** Flat, frozen, treeless land

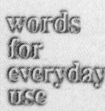
words for everyday use

in • ex • o • ra • ble (in eks' ə rə bəl) *adj.*, that cannot be altered or checked. *Li believes we can change our fate, but I believe our fate is <u>inexorable</u>.*

ren • dez • vous (rän' dā voo') *n.*, place designated for meeting or assembly. *The <u>rendezvous</u> site for the student council meeting will be the library.*

spec • u • la • tive (speculative) *adj.*, theoretical, not practical. *Your <u>speculative</u> ideas are interesting, but they will not solve the problem.*

Number of Species Lost Each Year

100,000
10,000
1,000
100
10
1

1700   1800   1900   2000

This graph portrays the estimated loss of living species from 1700 and 1992. The normal rate of extinction remained essentially unchanged for the last 65 million years—from the disappearance of dinosaurs and other prehistoric animals until the present century. Since the mid-1900s, extinction rates have exploded.

by acre, the rain forest is being burned to create fast pasture for fast-food beef; as I learned when I went there in early 1989, the fires are set earlier and earlier in the dry season now, with more than one Tennessee's worth of rain forest being slashed and burned each year. According to our guide, the biologist Tom Lovejoy, there are more different species of birds in each square mile of the Amazon than exist in all of North America—which means we are silencing thousands of songs we have never even heard.

But for most of us the Amazon is a distant place, and we scarcely notice the disappearance of these and other vulnerable species. We ignore these losses at our <u>peril</u>, however. They're like the <u>proverbial</u> miners' canaries, silent alarms whose message in this case is that living species of animals and plants are now vanishing around the world

> **GUIDED READING**
> Why is it easy to ignore the plight of the Amazon rainforest?

words for everyday use

per • il (per' əl) *n.*, danger, exposure to harm. *Maya put herself in great <u>peril</u> to save her cat from the rising floodwaters.*

pro • ver • bi • al (prō vər' bē əl) *adj.*, well known because commonly referred to. *Isabelle was drawn to Walter like the <u>proverbial</u> moth to the flame.*

ANSWERS TO GUIDED READING QUESTIONS

1. The bleaching of coral reefs indicates warmer ocean temperatures. The warmer temperatures put stress on the organisms that live in the coral and give it its color. The fact that bleaching is becoming more and more common suggests that ocean temperatures are rising more rapidly.
2. The author sees acres of untouched forest being bulldozed to make room for buildings, parking lots, and streets. Wild creatures are forced to flee. In the process, deer are hit by cars and pheasants dart into yards.

CROSS-CURRICULAR ACTIVITIES

MATHEMATICS AND SCIENCE. Encourage students to prepare brief written reports (no more than three paragraphs) on coral reefs. Students reports should answer the following questions: What is a coral reef, and what is coral? What are some of the world's great coral reefs? What types of creatures, other than coral, make their homes in coral reefs? What is an artificial coral reef, and how is one created? Encourage students to include pictures, drawings, or maps in their reports.

one thousand times faster than at any time in the past 65 million years (see graph on page 143).

To be sure, the deaths of some of the larger and more spectacular animal species now under siege do occasionally capture our attention. I have also visited another place along the equator, East Africa, where I encountered the grotesquely horrible image of a dead elephant, its head mutilated by poachers who had dug out its valuable tusks with chain saws. Clearly, we need to change our purely <u>aesthetic</u> consideration of ivory, since its source is now so threatened. To me, its <u>translucent</u> whiteness seems different now, like evidence of the ghostly presence of a troubled spirit, a beautiful but chill <u>apparition</u>, inspiring both wonder and dread.

A similar apparition lies just beneath the ocean. While scuba diving in the Caribbean, I have seen and touched the white bones of a dead coral reef. All over the earth, coral reefs have suddenly started to "bleach" as warmer ocean temperatures put unaccustomed stress on the tiny organisms that normally live in the skin of the coral and give the reef its natural coloration. As these organisms—nicknamed "zooks"—leave the membrane of the coral, the coral itself becomes transparent, allowing its white limestone skeleton to shine through—hence its bleached appearance. In the past, bleaching was almost always an occasional and temporary phenomenon, but repeated episodes can exhaust the coral. In the last few years, scientists have been shocked at the sudden occurrence of extensive worldwide bleaching episodes from which increasing numbers of coral

> **GUIDED READING**
> What problem does the bleaching of coral reefs indicate?

reefs have failed to recover. Though dead, they shine more brightly than before, haunted perhaps by the same ghost that gives spectral light to an elephant's tusk.

But one doesn't have to travel around the world to witness humankind's assault on the earth. Images that signal the distress of our global environment are now commonly seen almost anywhere. A few miles from the Capitol, for example, I encountered another startling image of nature out of place. Driving in the Arlington, Virginia, neighborhood where my family and I live when the Senate is in session, I stepped on the brake to avoid hitting a large pheasant walking across the street. It darted between the parked cars, across the sidewalk, and into a neighbor's backyard. Then it was gone. But this apparition of wildness persisted in my memory as a puzzle: Why would a pheasant, let alone such a large and beautiful mature specimen, be out for a walk in my neighborhood? Was it a much wilder place than I had noticed? Were pheasants, like the trendy Vietnamese potbellied pigs, becoming the latest fashion in unusual pets? I didn't solve the mystery until weeks later, when I remembered that about three miles away, along the edge of the river, developers were bulldozing the last hundred acres of untouched forest in the entire area. As the woods fell to make way for more concrete, more buildings, parking lots, and streets, the wild things that lived there were forced to flee. Most of the deer were hit by cars; other creatures—like the pheasant that

> **GUIDED READING**
> What destruction of nature does the author find close to home? What effect of this destruction does he see?

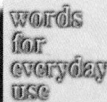 **words for everyday use**

aes • thet • ic (es thet' ik) *adj.*, referring to beauty. *Although it was severely cold, Kyle chose not to wear a hat for <u>aesthetic</u> reasons.*

trans • lu • cent (trans loo' sant) *adj.*, partially transparent. *The <u>translucent</u> curtains allowed light into the room but blocked the view from outside.*

ap • pa • ri • tion (ap' ə rish' ən) *n.*, anything that appears unexpectedly or in an extraordinary way; ghost. *Fay was startled by the <u>apparition</u> as she walked down the lonely street.*

darted into my neighbor's backyard—made it a little farther.

Ironically, before I understood the mystery, I felt vaguely comforted to imagine that perhaps this urban environment, so similar to the one in which many Americans live, was not so hostile to wild things after all. I briefly supposed that, like the resourceful raccoons and possums and squirrels and pigeons, all of whom have adapted to life in the suburbs, creatures as wild as pheasants might have a fighting chance. Now I remember that pheasant when I take my children to the zoo and see an elephant or a rhinoceros. They too inspire wonder and sadness. They too remind me that we are creating a world that is hostile to wildness, that seems to prefer concrete to natural landscapes. We are encountering these creatures on a path we have paved—one that ultimately leads to their extinction. ∎

GUIDED READING

What feelings do the animals in a zoo inspire in the author?

Respond to the SELECTION

Do you agree or disagree with the statement "We are creating a world that is hostile to wildness, that seems to prefer concrete to natural landscapes." Explain, using examples from your own life.

About the AUTHOR

Al Gore (b. 1948) became the vice president of the United States in 1992, when William Clinton was elected the 42nd president. That same year, he published the book *Earth in the Balance: Ecology and the Human Spirit*, from which this selection was taken. Before beginning a career in politics, Gore worked as a journalist for seven years. He then spent many years representing Tennessee in Congress. In 1976, he won a seat in the House of Representatives, and in 1984 he was elected to the Senate. Gore was a leader of environmental awareness in Congress, and he has spent many years studying the global environment. As vice president, Gore worked with the president to preserve natural resources, protect people from toxic wastes, and fight threats such as global warming.

"SHIPS IN THE DESERT" **135**

ANSWER TO GUIDED READING QUESTION

1. The animals inspire wonder and sadness in the author. They remind him that humans are creating a world that is hostile to wildness.

RESPOND TO THE SELECTION

Encourage students to hold a class debate. Assign some students to support the environmentalists' cause. Assign others to support the position of industrialists and developers.

SELECTION CHECK TEST 4.2.11 WITH ANSWERS

Note: See the Assessment Resource for the complete Selection Check Test.

Checking Your Reading
1. According to the selection, why do poachers kill elephants? **Poachers kill elephants for their ivory tusks.**
2. According to the selection, the rainforest is being chopped down to make room for what? **The rainforest is being chopped down to make room for pastures for fast-food beef.**
3. What environmental stress began with the Industrial Revolution? **The Industrial Revolution contributed to global warming.**
4. Where was Gore when he was startled by the sight of a pheasant? **Gore was startled by the sight of a pheasant in his neighborhood in Virginia.**
5. Is the earth's temperature rising or falling? **The earth's temperature is rising.**

Vocabulary in Context
Fill in each blank below with the most appropriate vocabulary word. You may have to change the tense of the word.

inexorable   rendezvous   peril
apparition   divert   bleak   indictment

1. Mabel's first job as a police officer was to _____ traffic away from the scene of the crime. **divert**
2. Half the class got lost on our field trip because no one was exactly sure where and when to _____. **rendezvous**
3. When the storm finally passed, the family emerged from the storm cellar to observe the _____ landscape left in the storm's path. **bleak**

Reader's Toolbox
1. Gore enhanced his credibility in reporting on these events by letting the reader know that

TEACHER'S EDITION **135**

SELECTION CHECK TEST 4.2.11 WITH ANSWERS (CONT.)

a. he was a senator before he was vice president.
b. he had visited the places he describes.
c. he lived in a neighborhood located near woods.
d. he had donated a lot of money to environmental causes.
2. Irony of situation occurs when
a. a character says one thing but does another.
b. a character speaks directly to the audience to explain a situation.
c. an event predicts future events in the story.
d. an event contradicts the expectations of the characters, the reader, or the audience.
3. Figurative language is language that
a. has more than a straight-forward, literal meaning.
b. uses strong concrete details.
c. can be understood in more than one language.
d. helps the reader understand a character's motivation.

ANSWERS TO INVESTIGATE,
INQUIRE, IMAGINE

RECALL

1a. An ill-advised irrigation scheme drained the Aral Sea.
2a. The ice samples show lesser amounts of air pollution after the passage of the Act.
3a. In the Amazon rainforest, an area the size of Tennessee was burned each year.

INTERPRET

1b. This examples shows that in many cases humans plan projects without analyzing the effects they will have on the environment.
2b. You can conclude that air pollution is a global problem because the lessening of pollution in the United States led to a lessening of pollution in the remote Arctic.
3b. The burning of vast tracts of land has made thousands of species extinct.

ANALYZE

4a. Irrigating without considering what will happen to the body of water used as a source; polluting the air and the oceans with radioactive carbon dioxide, radioactive waste, oil, and other pollutants; and cutting down vast tracts of wilderness to build new developments without considering the forms of life that call this habitat home are all human actions that lead to the disasters the author describes.

SYNTHESIZE

4b. The examples show that humans can have a destructive effect on nature and that humans often fail to appreciate the complex natural world in which they live. If the rate of loss of species continues, the ecosystem could collapse from the destruction of food chains.

EVALUATE

5a. Responses will vary, but students may suggest that individual actions such as recycling, making an effort to take public transportation, and cutting down on energy consumption may help the environment, as will group efforts such as petitioning governments to conserve land and stop the destruction of the rainforests and to place stricter regulations on industrial polluters. The fact that human population is booming and that people need to find new places to live, new energy sources, and new ways to support

Investigate, Inquire, and Imagine

Recall: GATHERING FACTS

1a. What has caused the disappearing of the Aral Sea?

2a. What effect did passage of the Clean Air Act by the United States Congress have on ice core samples dug from polar glaciers?

3a. In early 1989, the author discovered that the Amazon rain forest was being destroyed at a rapid rate. How much of the rain forest was being burned each year?

Interpret: FINDING MEANING

1b. What impression of human planning does this create?

2b. What conclusions about air pollution can you draw from this evidence?

3b. Why is it a bad policy to destroy the rain forest in this way?

Analyze: TAKING THINGS APART

4a. What are the human actions which cause the various environmental disasters the author describes?

Synthesize: BRINGING THINGS TOGETHER

4b. From the examples given by the author, what conclusions can you draw about human beings' relationship with nature? What do you think will happen if the number of species lost each year continues at the current rate?

Evaluate: MAKING JUDGMENTS

5a. What can humans do to lessen or reverse their negative effects on the environment? What could make it difficult to stop humans from hurting the environment? In your opinion, what will be the most difficult thing to change, and why?

Extend: CONNECTING IDEAS

5b. Thinking about ecological issues in your own community, consider how you could help save the environment. In groups of four, brainstorm ideas for helping, volunteer opportunities and fundraising plans you could participate in as a class.

Understanding Literature

IRONY OF SITUATION. An event that contradicts the expectations of the characters or narrators, the reader, or the audience of a literary work is an example of **irony of situation**. The Aral Sea problem that the author describes involves an irony of situation. So does the sighting of the pheasant. What in these two anecdotes contradicts your expectations as a reader? What is the author's purpose in using these ironic situations?

ANSWERS TO INVESTIGATE, INQUIRE, IMAGINE (CONT.)

themselves may make it difficult to stop environmental destruction. Responses will vary, but students should present reasons to support their opinions.

EXTEND
5b. *Responses will vary.*

FIGURES OF SPEECH. A **figure of speech** is language that has more than a straightforward, literal meaning. In paragraph 7 of this selection, what examples of figures of speech can you identify? What words might the author have used to describe the situation literally? What effect does the use of figures of speech have on the description?

Writer's Journal

1. Imagine you are a news reporter writing a story about one of the environmental disasters described in this selection. Write the **news headline** for your story. Remember that it must be short, excluding any articles such as *a, an,* or *the,* and that it must be attention-grabbing.

2. Write a **narrative paragraph** containing an example of *irony of situation.* For example, your paragraph could be about a criminal who spends hours breaking into a bank vault only to find that the vault is empty and has not been used for years.

3. Select one of the environmental disasters described in the selection and write a **letter** to the editor of your local paper calling attention to the problem and stressing why, in your opinion, the problem needs to be resolved. Include in your letter one suggestion as to what your community can do to help.

Skill Builders

Study and Research & Collaborative Learning
ENVIRONMENTAL CONCERNS. In groups of four or five students, research one of the environmental issues that Al Gore discusses in the essay you just read. Use resources from your local library, including periodicals, and search the Internet for the most updated information. For example, you might find out what has been done to protect the Brazilian rain forest in the years since this essay was written, or you might discover what is currently being done to protect the elephants from poachers in East Africa. Write a report summarizing what you have learned. Include any charts or graphs you encounter in your research. Also include the names, addresses, and web site names of any organizations which are currently working to resolve the environmental problem.

Media Literacy & Collaborative Learning
WRITING A PROPOSAL. Form a group of five students and select an environmental cause that interests you. Imagine that you are going to form a student group working for that cause. Write a proposal to an organization that might be willing to fund your cause, or write a proposal to your school, asking for permission to hold a fundraiser. See the Language Arts Survey 6.8, "Writing a Proposal," for more information. When you have finished, share your ideas with the class. You could then agree on volunteer activities to participate in as a class.

Study and Research & Collaborative Learning
ENVIRONMENTAL CONCERNS. Make sure that students form a research plan. They should plan to find sources, take notes from these sources and attribute the sources properly, create a rough outline of their report, refine their outline, create a rough draft, and then finally after peer review write their final draft. Students may find the following Language Arts Survey sections helpful: 2.37, "Self- and Peer Evaluation," 5.19, "Using Reference Works," and 5.35, "Documenting Sources."

Media Literacy & Collaborative Learning
WRITING A PROPOSAL. Encourage students to review the guidelines in the Language Arts Survey 4.13, "Collaborative Learning and Communication." Encourage students to plan a group that supports a cause they find meaningful, and then actually carry through with their plans.

ANSWERS TO UNDERSTANDING LITERATURE

IRONY OF SITUATION. The images of a ship in the desert and a large pheasant walking across a suburban street contradict the reader's expectations because both the ship and the pheasant are in strange, uncharacteristic settings. The author uses these ironic examples because he wants to stress how disturbed the ecosystem has become.

FIGURATIVE LANGUAGE. The author uses the phrases "we sense and unfamiliar tide rising and swirling" and "it leaves behind the flotsam and jetsam of some giant shipwreck far out at sea." the author is using the language of the sea and of a shipwreck to describe the many environmental disasters we face.

Language, Grammar, and Style
HYPHENS AND DASHES

1. I was standing in the bottom of the Aral Sea—which had been dried up by an irrigation scheme—when a camel walked by.
2. The Aral Sea was once the fourth-largest inland sea in the world.
3. Dolphins lay dead in the ankle-deep water along the shores of the Riviera.
4. Oil-soaked birds and otters—victims of the oil spill in Prince William Sound—were shown on television.
5. The Clean Air Act—an act that passed in the United States Congress in the 1960s—reduced air pollution worldwide.
6. I watched one scientist—nicknamed Frosty—work on a core sample of ice dug from the freezing cold glacier.
7. If the polar cap thins—and many scientists believe it is thinning—there could be disastrous climate changes on earth.
8. The Amazon rain forest—a treasure chest of never-before-seen species of animals and plants—is being burned for use by cattle ranchers.
9. The ghostly-looking whiteness of ivory haunted me after I saw pictures of elephants murdered by poachers.
10. The pheasant—a wild bird very popular with game hunters—is rarely found in traffic-clogged city neighborhoods.

Language, Grammar, and Style

HYPHENS AND DASHES. A **hyphen** is used to make a compound word. Examples from this selection include "blue-green waves" or "a twelve-foot-thick slab of ice." A **dash** is used to show a sudden break or change of thought. An example from the selection is "the world beneath it had changed in an unexpected way that made the egg seem—through no fault of its own—out of place." Refer to the Language Arts Survey 3.87 for more examples. Then, on your own paper, rewrite the sentences below, inserting hyphens and dashes where they are needed.

1. I was standing on the bottom of the Aral Sea which had been dried up by an irrigation scheme when a camel walked by.
2. The Aral Sea was once the fourth largest inland sea in the world.
3. Dolphins lay dead in the ankle deep water along the shores of the Riviera.
4. Oil soaked birds and otters victims of the oil spill on Prince William Sound were shown on television.
5. The Clean Air Act an act that passed in the United States Congress in the 1960s reduced air pollution worldwide.
6. I watched one scientist nicknamed Frosty work on a core sample of ice dug from the freezing cold glacier.
7. If the polar ice cap thins and many scientists believe it is thinning there could be disastrous climate changes on earth.
8. The Amazon rain forest a treasure chest of never before seen species of animals and plants is being burned for use by cattle ranchers.
9. The ghostly looking whiteness of ivory haunted me after I saw pictures of elephants murdered by poachers.
10. The pheasant a wild bird very popular with game hunters is rarely found in traffic clogged city neighborhoods.

Vocabulary Development

WORDS IN CONTEXT. Each underlined word in the sentences below is a Word for Everyday Use from "Ships in the Desert." Review each sentence and determine whether the underlined word is used correctly within the sentence. If it is, leave the sentence alone. If the word is used incorrectly, use the word correctly in a sentence of your own. For more information, see the Language Arts Survey 1.16, "Using Context Clues to Estimate Word Meaning."

1. Because the detective's theory was <u>speculative</u>, the police force considered the case solved.
2. As she purchased the jacket, Lani realized she was committing an <u>inexorable</u> act.
3. Leon's heart began to pound as he became aware of the <u>peril</u> he was in.
4. Iman's unique and original tellings of stories always included many <u>proverbial</u> phrases.
5. The new owners greatly improved the <u>aesthetic</u> appeal of the house by repainting and planting trees, shrubs, and flowers.
6. The puppy nudged and nipped but could not <u>divert</u> Nina from the suspenseful book she was reading.
7. The arrival of winter is an <u>unprecedented</u> event.

Prereading

"SONG OF THE THUNDERS" and "SONG OF THE CROWS"
from *Chippewa Customs* by Frances Densmore

Reader's T O O L B O X

ORAL TRADITION. An **oral tradition** is a work, idea, or custom passed by word of mouth from generation to generation. Works found in the oral traditions of peoples around the world include folk tales, fables, fairy tales, tall tales, nursery rhymes, proverbs, legends, myths, parables, riddles, charms, spells, and ballads. "Song of the Thunders" and "Song of the Crows" come from the Anishinabe, or Ojibway, people. The Anishinabe are a group of American Indians who live primarily in Minnesota, Wisconsin, and Canada. It was almost the year 1900 before Anishinabe music was recorded and studied. Until that time, the Anishinabe preserved their songs by memory and passed them orally to each generation. At the time when Frances Densmore recorded and studied these songs, the Anishinabe people were called Chippewa by the government.

PERSONIFICATION. Personification is a figure of speech in which an idea, animal, or thing is described as if it were human. As you read, think about what is being personified in each song.

Graphic  *Organizer*

Look at the three diagrams below. Choose which you think would be the best setting in which to tell and hear a story, or arrange a setting of your own. List three reasons to support your decision.

1.

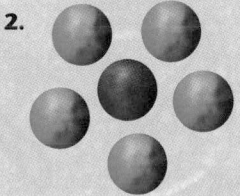

2.

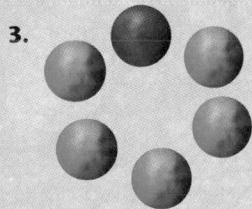

3.

Reader's *Journal*

Describe your dreams that have seemed the most vivid and have remained the most memorable.

Reader's *Resource*

- "Song of the Thunder" and "Song of the Crows" are Anishinabe dream songs that were later used as war songs. Dream songs are composed during a dream or on waking from a dream. Most are about animals or nature. The dreamer's *manido'*, or spirit, becomes the animal or natural occurrence.

- **CULTURAL CONNECTION.** Dreams are important in many religions throughout the world. For Anishinabe people, dreams have a spiritual meaning and are often used for guidance. Not every dream provides a person with guidance, however, and a person may wait years before fully understanding the meaning of their dreams

- In "Song of the Thunders," the singer wonders about and watches the mystery of a storm taking place until he feels himself become a part of the storm and sings its song. In the "Song of the Crows", the singer has the power to understand the language of the crows.

139

ADDITIONAL RESOURCES

Unit 2 Resource Book
- Selection Worksheet 2.7
- Selection Check Test 4.2.13
- Selection Test 4.2.14

ANSWERS TO READER'S TOOLBOX

GRAPHIC ORGANIZER. Responses will vary, but students should list at least three reasons to support their choice.

READER'S JOURNAL

If students cannot recall such dreams, tell them to write about an element of nature or an animal that captures their imagination.

GOALS/OBJECTIVES

Studying this lesson will enable students to
- enjoy two Native American dream songs
- briefly explain what dream songs are and explain a little of their history
- define *oral tradition* and appreciate works from the oral tradition
- define *personification* and identify examples of personification
- locate Native American songs through research
- rewrite a new article from a different point of view
- share an example of their own oral tradition with other students

MOTIVATION

Encourage students to work in groups of three or four to enact either what thunder clouds might look like, sound like, and act like as they are blown across the sky or what sights, sounds, and actions they associate with crows bringing the rain.

READING PROFICIENCY

Even though both songs are composed of short, simple words, students may have trouble deciphering their meaning. Encourage students to read each line of the songs, including their titles, which hold clues to what the poems are saying. Students should also carefully read the Reader's Resource on the Prereading page because this section spells out what occurs in each of the songs.

ENGLISH LANGUAGE LEARNING

Point out the following vocabulary words and expressions.
thunders—loud, rumbling sounds that follow a flash of lightning

SPECIAL NEEDS

As both songs were originally passed through the oral tradition, students will benefit especially from hearing these songs aloud. You might pair students to work together reading the songs to each other, experimenting with different voices and gestures to convey what is said in each.

ENRICHMENT

Encourage students to write their own "dream songs." Students should write a few lines when they wake up after a vivid dream. Tell students not to worry about the form their words take or the images they describe. They should not worry about modeling their "dream songs" on those presented here, but instead focus on capturing in words the images in a dream.

ANSWER TO GUIDED READING QUESTION

1. The wind carries the thunder across the sky.

Chippewa Hoop Dancer, 1968. Patrick Des Jarlait.

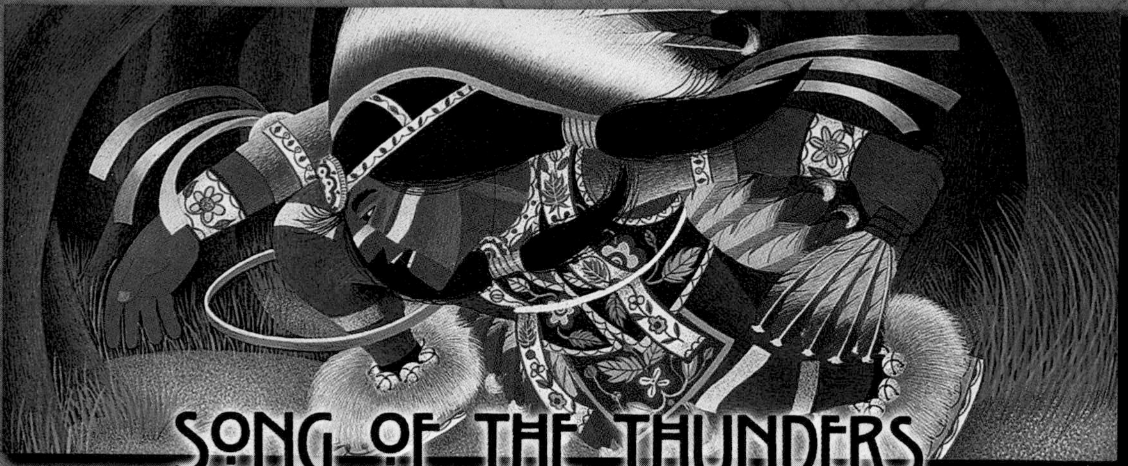

SONG OF THE THUNDERS

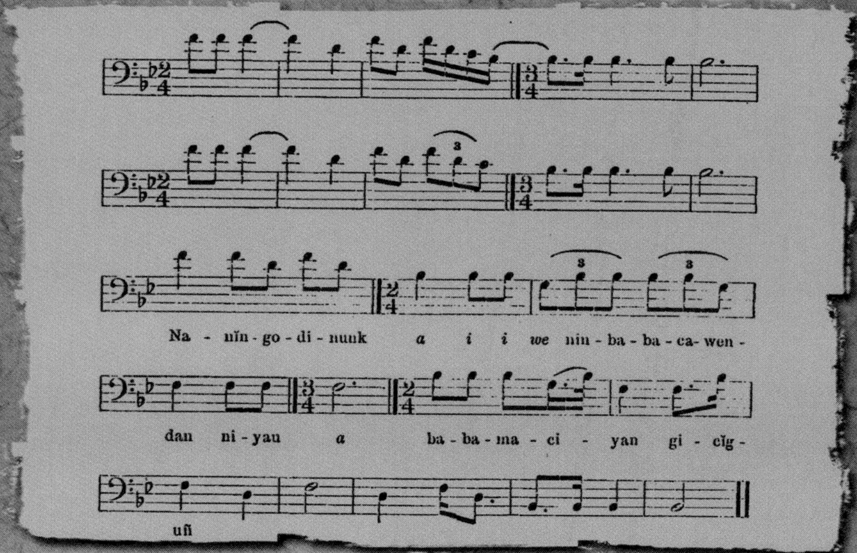

Sung by Gágandac´

Na´nĭngo´dinunk	....	Sometimes
ninbaba´cawen´dan	....	I go about <u>pitying</u>
Niyau´	....	Myself
Baba´maciyan´	....	While I am carried by the wind
Gicĭguñ´	....	Across the sky

GUIDED READING

Who carries the thunders across the sky?

words for everyday use

pity (pi´tē) v., to feel compassion or sympathy for (someone or something). *After Virginia lost her purse, my mother <u>pitied</u> her and bought her a new one.*

140   UNIT TWO / THE WORLD AROUND US

Fishermen of the North, 1965. Patrick Des Jarlait.

CROSS-CURRICULAR ACTIVITIES

ART AND HUMANITIES. Encourage students who can read music to share the melody of "Song of the Thunders" and "Song of The Crows" with their classmates. Musicians might play the music to these songs on the instrument of their choice. Singers might either hum the melody or try singing the Anishinabe words to these songs.

SONG OF THE CROWS

Be - ba - ni - ga - ni   hi   nin - di - gog . . bi -

ně - si - wûg ɛ   nin - wĕn - dji - gi - mi - wûñ an - deg - nin - di - go

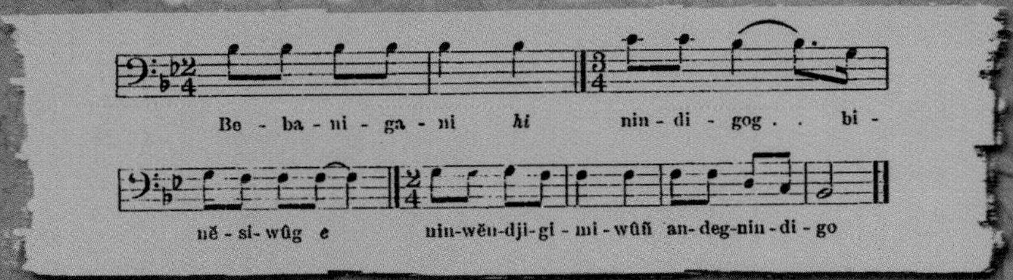

Sung by Henry Selkirk

Be´bani´gani´	The first to come
Nin´digog´	I am called
Binĕ´siwûg´	Among the birds
Nin´wĕndjigi´miw´ûñ´	I bring the rain
Andeg´nindigo´	Crow is my name

GUIDED READING

What does the crow bring?

Checking Your Reading
1. In "Song of the Thunders," what carries the speaker across the sky? **The wind carries the speaker across the sky.**
2. In "Song of the Thunders," how does the speaker sometimes feel? **The speaker sometimes pities himself or herself.**
3. In "Song of the Crows," what does the crow bring? **The crow brings the rain.**

Reader's Toolbox
1. From what point of view was each song written? **Each song is written from the first-person point of view.**
2. What is personification? **Personification is a figure of speech in which an animal, idea, thing, or emotion is given human characteristics.**
3. What is a dream song? **A dream song is a song composed during a dream or upon awaking from a dream.**

RESPOND TO THE SELECTION

As an alternate activity, you might encourage students to discuss their dreams and the images they see in them.

Red Lake Fishermen, 1946/1961. Patrick Des Jarlait. Minnesota Museum of American Art.

Patrick Des Jarlait (1921–1972), an Ojibway artist, was born and raised on Red Lake Indian Reservation in Minnesota. He began drawing and sketching at an early age and later developed a unique painting style using watercolors and tiny brush strokes. He carefully observed the traditions of his native culture, which he incorporated into much of his work. What do his paintings show about Ojibway life? What connections can you find between Des Jarlait's art and the songs recorded by Frances Densmore?

Respond *to the* SELECTION

Describe the thoughts and emotions you would have if you were a storm cloud.

About *the* AUTHOR

Frances Densmore was born in southern Minnesota in 1867. She grew up in a household that favored serious study and musical accomplishment over fun and free time. Densmore studied music and attended the Oberlin College Conservatory in Ohio. She went on to teach music and to play the church organ in Red Wing, Minnesota.

As a child, Densmore was curious about the Dakota encampment across the river from her home. Her mother explained that the Dakota "were people with different customs from our own." Densmore continued to think about Native American culture as an adult and devoted much of her life to studying the music of indigenous nations throughout the United States, including the Anishinabe in her own home state.

In working with the Anishinabe people, Densmore learned about the group's culture and traditions from stories and songs explained to her by tribal elders. Henry Selkirk, who sang "Song of the Crows," explained that song. "A young man was fasting where his father had taken him. It was in the fall, and the flocks of crows were getting ready to go south. The young man heard the crows in the trees and imagined that he learned this song from them. Afterward the crow was his manidó because it had given him the power to understand the language of the crows. The words of the song mean that the crows are the first birds to come in the spring, and so the old-time Indians thought that the crows brought the spring rains. This was first a dream song and afterward it was used as a war dance."

142 *UNIT TWO / THE WORLD AROUND US*

Investigate, *Inquire,* and Imagine

Recall: GATHERING FACTS

1a. In "Song of the Thunders," how does the storm feel?

2a. How often does the storm pity itself?

3a. In "Song of the Crows," who is the first to arrive?

→ **Interpret:** FINDING MEANING

1b. Why would a storm feel this way?

2b. What do you think the storm is doing when it is not pitying itself?

3b. What is the significance of this animal?

Analyze: TAKING THINGS APART

4a. Identify places in the songs where the dreamer has become something or someone else.

→ **Synthesize:** BRINGING THINGS TOGETHER

4b. How does this help the dreamer to understand nature better?

Evaluate: MAKING JUDGMENTS

5a. After listening to a recording of these songs, decide if the melody and rhythm suit the words. Explain your answer.

→ **Extend:** CONNECTING IDEAS

5b. Using the lyrics from these songs, compose your own music to suit the words. How does your choice differ from the originals?

Understanding *Literature*

ORAL TRADITION. An **oral tradition** is a work, idea, or custom passed by word of mouth from generation to generation. Works found in the oral traditions of peoples around the world include folk tales, fables, fairy tales, tall tales, nursery rhymes, proverbs, legends, myths, parables, riddles, charms, spells, and ballads. How does the fact that these Anishinabe oral traditions are songs influence the listener?

PERSONIFICATION. Personification is a figure of speech in which something not human is described as if it were human. Who does the dreamer become in each of the songs? How effective is the use of personification in the songs?

ANSWERS TO INVESTIGATE, INQUIRE, IMAGINE

RECALL

1a. The storm pities itself.

2a. The storm may feel sorry for itself because it is being carried along by the wind and cannot resist this force.

3a. The speaker, the crow, is first to arrive.

INTERPRET

1b. Students may suggest that a storm may feel this way because the creatures down on earth do not like storms, because the storm feels too heavy with rain, because it knows it is about to experience a thunder and lightning storm, or because it has no control over where it is carried by the wind.

2b. Students may suggest that the storm may be raining or causing lightning storms.

3b. This animal brings the spring rains.

ANALYZE

4a. Students may point to the speaker becoming a thunder storm in "Song of the Thunders" and a crow in "Song of the Crows."

SYNTHESIZE

4b. Responses will vary. Students may suggest that dreams of being something other than human—being a part of nature—may make a person more empathetic to nature and able to understand it. It is the old case of knowing someone by walking a mile in their shoes.

EVALUATE

5a. Responses will vary. Students should support their answers by describing the melody or rhythm and how these compare to the lyrics.

EXTEND

5b. *Responses will vary.*

ANSWERS TO UNDERSTANDING LITERATURE

ORAL TRADITION. Responses will vary but students may suggest that the fact that people shares these dream songs from generation to generation helps the reader to realize how connected the Anishinabe were to nature and their environment.

PERSONIFICATION. The speaker becomes a storm and a crow. The personification is very effective because the speaker is actually speaking from the point of view of the things he or she describes.

ANSWERS TO SKILL BUILDERS

Study and Research
RESEARCHING SONGS. Students might wish to begin their search on the Internet. Other possible sources include books on Native American life and traditions. Students should check out such resources from their school or local library.

Speaking and Listening
WRITING A SONG. Students who are uncomfortable singing or sharing a recording with the class can present their song aloud as a poem in a oral interpretation to their classmates. Encourage them to read the Language Arts Survey 4.19, "Oral Interpretation of Poetry."

Media Literacy
REWRITING AN ARTICLE. Students may find this exercise easier if they freewrite about storms, what they look like, and feel like as a prewriting exercise. Encourage them to have fun and be creative with this activity.

Collaborative Learning
SHARING STORIES. Have students review the Language Arts Survey 4.10, "Asking and Answering Questions," and 4.11, "Being Considerate of Other Cultures and Communication Styles." Encourage students to listen with an open mind and be respectful. They might write essays afterward on what elements of other people's cultures they might like to include as part of their own traditions one day.

Writer's Journal

1. Pretend you are a storm that pities itself. Write a **poem** that explains your feelings and your behavior.
2. Write four or five lines of a **song** about an element of nature.
3. You have just awakened from a dream about a blinding snowstorm. Describe your dream in a brief **journal entry**.

Skill Builders

Study and Research
RESEARCHING SONGS. Do some research about Native American songs. Find at least three examples of songs from different nations. Look for differences and similarities in songs from different areas in the United States. Are the subjects of the songs different from region to region? Do different Native American groups show unique qualities in their songs? Share your findings with the class.

Speaking and Listening
WRITING A SONG. In small groups, pretend you are an animal or an act of nature. Write a song that describes your feelings, your fears, and your hopes. What are the advantages or disadvantages of being you? If possible, tape record or videotape your song to share with the class.

Media Literacy
REWRITING AN ARTICLE. Find a newspaper or magazine article about a storm. Rewrite the article from the point of view of the storm. Compare your article with the original. How does the tone of the article change? What, if anything, has stayed the same?

Collaborative Learning
SHARING STORIES. Think about something that has been sung or retold many times in your family. In small groups of four or five, share the oral traditions that reflect each family's culture or beliefs. Make a tape recording of the stories or songs. As you listen to them, discuss what you can learn about each person's culture and traditions. How are the people in your family different from other groups? How are they the same?

for your READING LIST

Dawn Land, by Joseph Bruchac, is a novel about Native American life about 10,000 years ago in the northeastern United States. The main character of the novel, Young Hunter, is a member of the Only People and is called to defend his community against a great but unknown danger. In his quest, Young Hunter must rely on the strength of his spirit and character—gained from the teachings of his people, from his communion with the natural world, and from his own awakening spirituality. Bruchac, an Abenaki storyteller and poet, has woven Native American myth, folklore, and fiction together to craft a tale that explores the human soul while pulling the reader through an exciting chain of events.

EXPLORING OTHER CULTURES

Books are an entertaining and accessible way to explore other cultures in the world around us. Reading about another way of life makes us challenge our own ways of thinking and doing things. As you read books about people living in other times, places, circumstances, or communities, you might explore the following questions:

- What drew you to learning more about this people or culture? What intrigues you about this way of life? Does this subject relate to you personally, either in terms of ancestry, shared beliefs, or experience, or does it interest you for other reasons? Explain your answer.
- Is the author a reliable source for information about this subject matter? Does the author have personal experience with the culture he or she describes?
- Is the book fact, fiction, or a combination of the two? Before accepting information as fact, be sure to check other reliable sources on the subject.
- What have you learned about the culture you've read about? What have you learned about yourself in the process? What elements of the culture appeal to you? What don't you like about this specific way of life or way of thinking? Has this story or information changed your thinking in any way? Has this book made you want to know more about the subject?

You might choose to read several books about the same culture or way of life. How is the treatment of the subject matter similar or different? Is one approach more compelling than another? Explain your answer.

Other books you may want to read:
Native American Stories by Joseph Bruchac
Going Solo by Roald Dahl
Rootabaga Stories by Carl Sandburg

For Your Reading List

Dawn Land, Joseph Bruchac's first young adult novel, provides enough action and tight pacing to keep adolescent boys—and girls—reading. *Kirkus Reviews* has said that in the telling of this tale, Bruchac "finds an incantatory rhythm appropriate to this North American version of magical realism." If time is limited, you may want to assign the alternative selections listed on the Pupil's Edition page. *Native American Stories* by Joseph Bruchac and *Rootabaga Stories* by Carl Sandburg both offer shorter selections from which students can choose; *Going Solo* by Roald Dahl is a nonfiction narrative of Dahl's life between 1938–1941, when he was a pilot in the Navy. The nonfiction selection "The Green Mamba" in this unit is included in Dahl's memoir.

Exploring Other Cultures

Use this as an opportunity to continue introducing students to the Language Arts Survey Reading Resource. Have them read the following sections as they prepare for their book clubs: 1.3, "Reading Literature: Educating Your Imagination," 1.4, "Educating Your Imagination as an Active Reader," 1.5 "Keeping a Reader's Journal," 1.6, "Reading Silently versus Reading Out Loud," 1.7, "Reading with a Book Club or Literature Circle," and 1.8, "Guidelines for Discussing Literature in a Book Club." See the Guided Reading Resource 1.3–1.8 in the Teacher's Resource Kit for blackline masters of worksheets that will help students work these concepts more thoroughly.

GUIDED WRITING
Software

See the Guided Writing Software for an extended version of this lesson that includes printable graphic organizers, extensive student models and student-friendly checklists, and self-, peer, and teacher evaluation features.

Professional Model

In "Ships in the Desert," excerpted from his book *Earth in the Balance: Ecology and the Human Spirit*, Al Gore informed people about drastic environmental changes in the Aral Sea.

from "Ships in the Desert" by Al Gore, page 130

I was standing in the sun on the hot steel deck of a fishing ship capable of processing a fifty-ton catch on a good day. But it wasn't a good day. We were anchored in what used to be the most productive fishing site in all of central Asia, but as I looked out over the bow, the prospects of a good catch looked bleak. Where there should have been gentle blue-green waves lapping against the side of the ship, there was nothing but hot dry sand . . .

Oddly enough, it made me think of a fried egg I had seen back in the United States on television the week before. It was sizzling and popping the way a fried egg should in a pan, but it was in the middle of a sidewalk in downtown Phoenix. I guess it sprang to mind because, like the ship I was on, there was nothing wrong with the egg itself. Instead, the world beneath it had changed in an unexpected way that made the egg seem...out of place. It was illustrating the newsworthy point that at the time Arizona wasn't having an especially

Guided Writing

WRITING A COMPARISON-CONTRAST ESSAY

Trenton couldn't decide if he should ride the new "Twister" ride at the fair or not. He nabbed Karina as she got off the ride. "What's it like?" he asked. How could Karina describe "Twister" to someone who had never experienced the twists, reverses, and tumbles? One way that she could clearly inform Trenton would be to describe how "Twister" was similar to some rides and different from others that Trenton had ridden.

"It's not as fast as the roller coaster, but it has way more twists than even the 'Gyro Cycle,'" Karina explained. She accomplished her purpose. There was no question left in Trenton's mind – this ride was for him.

A writer's aim or purpose in writing is often to inform readers about unfamiliar topics, concepts, places, or problems. Like Karina, a writer can inform others by making comparisons—showing how something is similar or parallel to something else—and contrasts—showing how something is different from something else.

Examining the Model

As a U.S. senator, Al Gore wanted to inform people about the environment, its problems, and possible solutions. In "Ships in the Desert," Gore uses comparisons and contrasts to inform his readers about the disappearing Aral Sea, which was once the fourth-largest inland sea in the world.

Al Gore compares and contrasts the familiar and the unfamiliar to help people understand how the environment is changing. He compares the ship on the sand to the egg frying on the hot sidewalk. In what way is the ship similar to the egg? There was nothing wrong with the ship or the egg, but, for each, the world beneath it had changed in an unexpected way. The sidewalk beneath the egg had become so hot that it could fry the egg; the water that was once beneath the ship was now 40 kilometers away and the fishing ship was permanently docked on sand. Al Gore also contrasted the original size and condition of the Aral Sea with its reduced size and condition after the water from the sea was used to irrigate the desert.

Examining the Model

So that students can visualize what is being compared and contrasted in the professional model, make a Graphic Organizer modeled on the one on page 147.

Some students might benefit from reading the Language Arts Survey 2.10, "Learning from Professional Models."

Prewriting

WRITING WITH A PLAN. Before you begin your comparison-contrast essay, think about topics that you could compare and contrast. For example, you can compare and contrast two social activities (such as the state fair and a school carnival), two viewpoints (such as those of an environmentalist and those of an industrialist), two environments (such as oceans and deserts), two processes (such as traveling in an urban area and traveling in a rural area), two activities (such as swimming and school), two sports (such as soccer and basketball), or two places (such as Earth and Mars).

Number your own paper from one to ten. After each number, list a pair of topics, such as swimming and school, that you could compare and contrast. Review your list. Which paired topics offer the greatest opportunities for showing similarities and differences? Which topics appeal to you? Which topics do you have the most interest in? Answer these questions. Then select a pair of topics to compare and contrast.

Consider how your topics are alike and how they are different from each other. Then list the similarities and differences you have discovered. The graphic organizer below shows the similarities and differences Paul discovered about swimming and school. Copy the graphic organizer on your own paper and fill in the similarities and differences for your topics.

Student Model—Graphic Organizer

Similarities   **and**   Differences
school and swimming

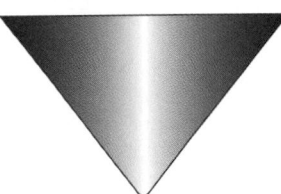

discipline
practice
keep at it

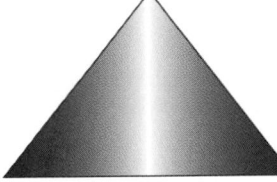

school	swimming
trains brain	trains body
work	fun
not active	active
keep up with	my own
classmates	pace

good day either, because for the second day in a row temperatures had reached a record 122 degrees . . .

Ten years ago the Aral was the fourth-largest inland sea in the world….Now it is disappearing because the water that used to feed it has been diverted in an ill-considered irrigation scheme to grow cotton in the desert. The new shoreline was almost forty kilometers across the sand from where the fishing fleet was now permanently docked.

• • • • •

"When a camel is at the foot of a mountain, then judge of his height."
—*Hindu Proverb*

WRITING WITH A PLAN. Students might understand this assignment better if they read the Language Arts Survey 2.27, "Choosing a Method of Organization." Make it clear that comparison-and-contrast order is just one method of organization. Students who find it difficult to select a topic might find it helpful to freewrite. Have them read the Language Arts Survey 2.12, "Freewriting."

INDIVIDUAL LEARNING STRATEGIES

MOTIVATION
Share with students when comparing and contrasting is valuable in your life. Give students a list of topics and have them discuss what aspects can be compared and contrasted.

READING PROFICIENCY
Have students read the Language Arts Survey 1.12, "Seeking Knowledge as an Active Reader."

ENGLISH LANGUAGE LEARNING
See strategies for Reading Proficiency above that will also benefit students who are English language learners. Students might be more comfortable comparing and contrasting something relevant to their own culture.

SPECIAL NEEDS
Students with special needs might need your help to come up with a topic and to complete their Graphic Organizer.

ENRICHMENT
Have students look for magazine articles that use comparison-and-contrast order for their method of Organization. Ask students to summarize what is being compared and contrasted. Have students share their results in small groups.

IDENTIFYING YOUR AUDIENCE. Have students read the Language Arts Survey 2.4, "Identifying Your Audience." Encourage students to use vocabulary with which their audience is familiar.

FINDING YOUR VOICE. Encourage students to read the Language Arts Survey 2.5, "Finding Your Voice," and 3.3, "Register, Tone, and Voice."

Drafting

Students with more ambitious topics might find it useful to use the second method of comparison-and-contrast order as described on page 882 in which both subjects are compared and contrasted with regard to one quality, then with regard to a second quality, and so on. Encourage students to use their completed Graphic Organizer modeled on page 147 to help them make sure they are including all their main points in their first draft. Have students write a discovery draft in which they do not focus on spelling, grammar, usage, and mechanics. Students might benefit from reading the Language Arts Survey 2.31, "Drafting."

IDENTIFYING YOUR AUDIENCE. The topics you have chosen can help you determine who your audience is. Paul decided to write his essay for his parents, who thought he spent too much time swimming. He wanted to let his parents know that swimming, like school, had many benefits, but also that swimming had some rewards that school did not have.

Think about the following questions as you decide on an audience.

- Who is most interested in the topics you have chosen?
- Why are they interested?
- Which comparisons and contrasts would they find most interesting?
- What information will they find most beneficial?

After you determine your audience, place a star next to ideas in your graphic organizer that you especially want to include for your audience.

> "By the law of averages, one would think there would be a certain percentage of sentences that would turn out right the first time. None of mine seem to, though."
>
> —Jean Fritz

Review the comparisons and contrasts you are beginning to develop. Let your imagination roll these ideas around. Is there some unique, intriguing, or remarkable way that your topics relate to each other? For example, the ship anchored in sand reminded Gore of the egg frying on a sidewalk. Write down any intriguing ideas that you might develop further.

FINDING YOUR VOICE. Voice is the way a writer uses language to reflect his or her unique personality and attitude toward topic, form, and audience. A writer expresses voice through tone, word choice, and sentence structure. Al Gore's voice is deliberate and reflective. He wanted his reader to be informed about his environmental concerns. Before you write your essay, consider the voice that you will use. First, answer these questions:

- What do you think about the similarities and differences in your topics?
- What matters to you about these similarities and differences?
- What doesn't matter to you about these similarities and differences?
- What message would you like to convey?
- How would you like to convey the message—with a sense of urgency, a sense of humor, or a sense of revelation?

On your own paper, write down one similarity or difference that you realized when comparing and contrasting your paired topics. Rewrite the sentence as if it were urgent that everyone knew about your realization. Now rewrite it as if your realization as if you wanted to share it with friends to make them laugh. Finally, rewrite the sentence to create a sense of discovery or revelation. Notice how your voice changes in each of these sentences. Decide on a voice that you will use.

Drafting

Write a rough draft of your comparison-contrast essay. Concentrate on getting your ideas down on paper in a fairly logical order. Start by providing a brief introduction to your topics. Then describe in the next paragraph how your topics are alike. In the following paragraph, explain how your topics are different. Add a brief conclusion to your essay. Remember that your purpose is to inform your readers. Do not focus on mechanics or spelling now. For more information, see the Language Arts Survey 2.31, "Drafting."

Peer and Self-Evaluation

After you finish your first draft, complete a self-evaluation of your writing. If time allows, you may want to get one or two peer evaluations. For more information, see the Language Arts Survey 2.37, "Self- and Peer Evaluation."

Peer and Self-Evaluation

Have students use the checklist on page 149 for self- and peer evaluation. See the Guided Writing Resource located in the Teacher's Resource Kit for a blackline master of the checklist. The checklist is intended to act as a student-friendly rubric that should help students identify specific evidence of writing strengths and areas needing improvement. Make sure students provide concrete suggestions for improvement or specific evidence of the effectiveness of their comparison-and-contrast essay. Students might benefit from reading the Language Arts Survey 2.37–2.40 for more details about self-evaluation and peer evaluation.

As you evaluate your draft, ask yourself the following questions:

- Does the essay have a good opening sentence, or hook, to make the reader want to keep reading?
- Does the opening paragraph identify the essay's topics and purpose?
- Is an interesting and informative comparison developed?
- Is an interesting and informative contrast developed?
- Is there enough information to interest the audience? What details could be added for the audience? Which details could be deleted?
- Does the essay tell about a unique, intriguing, or remarkable relationship between the topics? What might the essay suggest?
- Does the essay have a conclusion?
- Are there problems in flow, sound, or word choice? How can these be improved?

Look at Paul's self-evaluation of his rough draft, in which he compared and contrasted swimming and school.

Student Model—Draft

Is there any relationship between swimming and school? At first glance, there didn't seem to be any. Isn't school just plain work and swimming just plain fun?

Shouldn't this paragraph tell that you're going to show how they are alike and different?

good line!

Yet, school and swimming were alike in many ways. If you want to do well at either one, you have to be disciplined. You have got to keep at it and do your best. If you swim on a team, you have to practice together and show up for the meets, too.

How is this like school?

Swimming and school are in many ways different. School pretty much trained our brains and swimming trained our bodies. I'm not very active at school, but swimming gives me great exercise. I

Language, Grammar, and Style
Using State of Being and Action Verbs; Keeping Verb Tense Consistent. To write effectively, you should know the difference between action and state of being verbs, and how to be consistent with verb tenses.

USING STATE OF BEING AND ACTION VERBS. A verb can express **action**.

The ship now *docks* in the sand.

The water *begins* 40 kilometers away.

A verb can also express a **state of being.**

The Aral Sea *was* beautiful.

There once *were* many fishing boats on this sea.

Identify the verbs in the following sentences. Tell whether they express action or state of being.

He stood in the sun on the hot steel deck of the ship.

continued on page 150

GUIDED WRITING   **149**

Using State of Being and Action Verbs; Keeping Verb Tense Consistent
LESSON OVERVIEW
In this lesson, students will be asked to do the following:

- Use State of Being and Action Verbs, 149
- Keep Verb Tense Consistent, 150
- Fix Inconsistent Verb Tense, 152
- Use Consistent Verb Tense, 152

INTRODUCING THE SKILL. Tell students that using state of being and action verbs and keeping verb tense consistent will improve their writing in all their classes.

PREVIEWING THE SKILL. Refer students to the Language Arts Survey 3.58, "Action Verbs," 3.59, "State of Being Verbs," and 3.62–3.64, "Verb Tenses," "Simple Tenses," and "Perfect Tenses."

PRACTICING THE SKILL. For additional practice, have students work through the exercises in the following sections of the Language, Grammar, and Style Resource located in the Teacher's Resource Kit: 3.58, "Action Verbs," 3.59, "State of Being Verbs," and 3.62–3.64 ("Verb Tenses," "Simple Tenses," "Perfect Tenses."

Revising and Proofreading

Remind students that revising includes adding or expanding, cutting or condensing, replacing, and moving text. Have students read the Language Arts Survey 2.41, "Revising." A handout of the proofreading checklist found in the Language Arts Survey on page 888 is available in the Teacher's Resource Kit, Guided Writing Resource Book 2.45. Students may want to use proofreader's marks when correcting their work; refer them to the Language Arts Survey 2.44, "Using Proofreader's Marks." Tell students the revising stage is the perfect place to include transitions such as *likewise, similarly,* and *in contrast;* have them read the Language Arts Survey 2.35, "Using Transitions Effectively." As students prepare their final manuscript they may find it useful to read the Language Arts Survey 2.46, "Proper Manuscript Form."

The blue-green waves of the Aral Sea no longer lap against the ship.

Now there is sand where once there was water.

While such writing is effective, too many state of being verbs can make your writing dull. Go through Paul's essay in this lesson and your own writing and circle the state of being verbs. Then see whether you can replace them with active verbs. When is it better to use state of being verbs? When is it better to use active verbs?

For more information, see the Language Arts Survey 3.58, "Action Verbs and State of Being Verbs."

KEEPING VERB TENSE CONSISTENT. Verbs carry a concept of time, called **tense**. Two kinds of tenses are the simple tenses—these express simple past, present, and future—and the perfect tenses that give information about actions that took place over time.

SIMPLE TENSES

Present tense verbs shows that something is happening now. **Past tense** verbs talk about something that happened before now, and **future tense** verbs talk about something that will happen in the future.

Present tense
  Today I <u>eat</u> ice cream.
  I <u>do eat</u> ice cream.
  I <u>am eating</u> ice cream.

can train at my own pace insted of
keeping up with my classmates the way I
have to at school.

Can you explain this more?

     I think school and swimming are
both important. They helped us prepare
both our minds and our bodies to be
strong now and in the future, too.

Revising and Proofreading

As you consider your essay and your self-evaluation and peer reviews, think about the changes that are suggested. Which changes are needed for your essay to be clearly understood by your reader? Which changes will help your essay stand out as an interesting and informative piece of writing? Which changes will tailor your essay to your audience? Make your revisions according to your decisions.

   Proofread your essay for errors in spelling, grammar, punctuation, capitalization, and other details. Circle any words that you think might be misspelled and check them in a dictionary. Check to see if you have been consistent in your use of verb tense.

   After reviewing his essay and considering his self- and peer evaluation notes, Paul revised his essay. Notice his improvements.

Student Model—Revised

     Gliding through the water in the pool.
Sitting in a desk at school. School and
swimming are different in many ways,
but are there any similarities? At first
glance, there don't seem to be any.
Isn't school just plain work and
swimming just plain fun?

Yet, school and swimming are alike in many ways. If you want to do well at either one, you have to be disciplined. You have got to keep at it and do your best. If you swim on a team, you have to practice together and show up for the meets, too. If you are in a group at school, you have to work with them and be there for all of your classes.

Swimming and school are in many ways different. School pretty much trains our brains and swimming trains our bodies. I'm not very active at school because in most of my classes I sit at a desk, but swimming gives me great exercise. When I'm swimming, I can train at my own pace, because I'm not on a team. In school, though, I can't go at my own pace because I need to keep up with my teachers and my classmates.

Even though swimming and school have their differences, I think they are both important. They help us prepare both our minds and our bodies to be strong now and in the future, too.

Past tense

Yesterday I <u>ate</u> ice cream.
Yesterday I <u>did eat</u> ice cream.
Yesterday I <u>was eating</u> ice cream.

Future tense

Tomorrow I <u>will eat</u> ice cream.
Tomorrow I <u>will be eating</u> ice cream.

Note that there are only two future tense forms.

PERFECT TENSES

Another group, called **perfect tenses**, also express past, present and future, but they add information about actions that continued over a period of time and were completed in the past or will be completed in the present or future. All perfect tenses use some form of the helping verb <u>to have.</u>

Present perfect tense

Today I <u>have eaten</u> ice cream.
Today I <u>have been eating</u> ice cream.

Past perfect tense

Yesterday I <u>had eaten</u> ice cream.
Yesterday I <u>had been eating</u> ice cream.

Future perfect tense

Tomorrow I <u>will have eaten</u> ice cream.
Tomorrow I <u>will have been eating</u> ice cream.

One error that student writers make is to shift tense in the middle of a piece of writing. Each piece of writing needs to maintain a consistent tense.

continued on page 152

Reflecting

You may want to have students write a journal entry reflecting on what they learned from writing a comparison-and-contrast essay. Have students read the Language Arts Survey 2.50, "Reflecting on Your Writing."

Publishing and Presenting

Have students share the comparison-and-contrast essay they wrote with the audience they selected and ask for feedback. Have students record their feedback in a journal entry. Was their essay a success? Did they get the reaction they expected? What strengths and weaknesses did the reader(s) point out?

IDENTIFYING CONSISTENT VERB TENSE. Reread the following passages from the opening paragraph of Al Gore's "Ships in the Desert." Identify the verb tenses for the verbs or verb forms that are underlined. How does the author use verb tense consistently and to convey action happening over time?

1. I <u>was standing</u> in the sun on the hot steel deck of a fishing ship...

2. But it <u>wasn't</u> a good day.

3. We <u>were anchored</u> in what used to be the most productive fishing site in all of central Asia...

4. ... as I <u>looked</u> out over the bow, the prospects of a good catch <u>looked</u> bleak.

5. Where there <u>should have been</u> gentle blue-green waves lapping against the side of the ship, there <u>was</u> nothing but hot dry sand ...

FIXING INCONSISTENT VERB TENSE. Read through the draft of Paul's comparison-contrast essay. Where does he use verb tense correctly? What sentences need to be revised to make the verb tense consistent? On your own piece of paper, rework Paul's draft, making the verb tenses consistent.

USING CONSISTENT VERB TENSE. Look at each sentence in your comparison-contrast essay. Underline the verbs and identify which tense they use. Correct any improper verb tenses and make the verbs reflect consistent tense. Make sure your verbs accurately depict the passage of time. For more information, see the Language Arts Survey 3.62, "Verb Tenses."

Reflecting

Training yourself to think about comparisons and contrasts has benefits beyond writing an essay. As you learn to compare and contrast, you are developing a more complex thinking process. After writing his essay, Paul realized how valuable swimming and school both are, and how each enriched the other. What new realizations came to you as you wrote about your topics? What different views did you see? How else can comparing and contrasting different topics and events in your life help you to grow as a thinker, as a writer, and as a person?

The Final Product

Consider your audience as you prepare the final draft of your essay. Since Paul wrote for his parents, he decided to use a letter format. Another idea might be to create a picture or collage that shows how your topics compare and contrast to one another. Then attach your final copy to the picture. Whichever method you choose, decide how it fits your audience and how it showcases the writing you have completed.

UNIT TWO *review*

Review: Words for Everyday Use

Check your knowledge of the following vocabulary words. For each word, write a short sentence that includes the word in context. To review a word, look back to the page number indicated.

- aesthetic (134)
- apparition (134)
- arc (119)
- bleak (130)
- divert (130)
- forlorn (117)
- indictment (131)
- inexorable (132)
- kindling (97)

- malevolent (119)
- manipulate (119)
- peril (133)
- phenomenon (131)
- prism (97)
- proverbial (133)
- rendezvous (132)
- sinewy (99)
- social (98)

- speculative (132)
- tawny (107)
- tether (99)
- translucent (134)
- trough (96)
- unprecedented (130)
- unruffled (115)
- wheedling (119)

Review: Literary Tools

Define each of the following terms, giving concrete examples when possible. To review a term, refer to the page number indicated.

- characterization (113)
- figurative language (127)
- imagery (89)
- irony (95)

- irony of situation (127)
- oral tradition (139)
- personification (105, 139)
- setting (89)

- suspense (113)
- symbol (95, 105)

Reflecting *on your reading*

Genre

In this unit you have read poems, short stories, lyrics, and works of nonfiction. Which selections appealed to you the most? Why? What unique elements does poetry bring to the topic of "The World Around Us"? In what ways do stories touch on the topic differently? How does nonfiction deal with the topic? What do the song lyrics recorded by Frances Densmore indicate about a culture's relationship with nature?

Theme

The poems, essays, and literary excerpts in this unit all reflect human interactions with or impressions about the world. Most of the readings deal with the natural world and how

---

VOCABULARY DEVELOPMENT. Give students the following exercise.

Use a dictionary to write the part of speech, a brief definition, and a contextual sentence for each of ten vocabulary words from Review: Words for Everyday Use on page 153. Then write a different form of the word, its part of speech, a brief definition, and a contextual sentence. For more information, see the Language Arts Survey 1.16, "Using Context Clues to Estimate Word Meaning" and 1.17, "Using a Dictionary."

EXAMPLE
phenomenon—n., extremely unusual or extraordinary thing or occurrence
The lunar eclipse last night was a **phenomenon** that was unusual; it won't occur for another two years.

phenomenal—adj., extraordinary, remarkable
The new music group is **phenomenal** for its extraordinary ability to write unforgettable songs.

As an alternative activity, you may want to have students use a dictionary to find as many forms of a vocabulary word as possible.

EXAMPLE
phenomenon
forms include *phenom, phenomena, phenomenal, phenomenalism, phenomenalistic, phenomenalistically,* and *phenomenology*

ADDITIONAL RESOURCES

UNIT 2 RESOURCE BOOK
- Vocabulary Worksheet
- Study Guide: Unit 2 Test
- Unit 2 Test

Reflecting on Your Reading

The Genre questions are suitable to assign as essay prompts to help students prepare for the Unit Test. Refer students to the Guided Writing lesson in this unit for guidance on writing a comparison-contrast essay. (To evaluate student writing, see the evaluation forms for writing, revising, and proofreading in the Assessment Resource 4.1–4.9.)

The questions in On Your Own and the Group Project can be adapted for use as topics for oral reports or debates. Refer students to the Language Arts Survey 4, Speaking and Listening. (To evaluate these projects, use the Public Speaking Evaluation Form in the Assessment Resource 4.11.)

The Group Project activity is intended to build collaborative learning and oral communication skills. Refer students to the Language Arts Survey 4.13, "Collaborative Learning and Communication." (To evaluate group work, see the evaluation forms in the Assessment Resource 4.10–4.12.)

human beings affect or are affected by elements of the natural world. In "Jed's Grandfather," Jed remembers watching the swallows with his grandfather and identifying with the birds' freedom and courage — this memory helps him come to terms with his grandfather's illness and how his grandfather views his own impending death. "The Green Mamba" and "The Dinner Party" are both stories that address how humans must sometimes coexist with fearful elements of nature — in both of these cases the fearful element of nature is a poisonous snake. And "Ships in the Desert" by Al Gore gives us several vivid examples of how the actions of humans in contemporary society have profoundly affected the environment. The two poems about cities, "in the inner city" and "The City is So Big," show us how far removed our industrial society is from nature and how people can impose natural, lifelike qualities on the concrete, metal, and artificial lights of our cities.

On Your Own

What issues in the news concern you as an individual? Write a letter to your U.S. senator about an environmental or global issue that you have strong views about. You may want to research the topic to become more informed before you write the letter. What information do you need to convey in the letter? What, specifically, are your concerns? What concrete advice, help, or resources could you ask for? Refer to the Language Arts Survey 6.6, "Writing a Business Letter" for more pointers.

Group Project

Discuss in small groups or as a class the various ways that our choices and actions affect the environment. Use the graphic organizer on the next page to organize your thoughts about actions that impact the environment. Are any of your activities harming the environment? Can you think of ways to pursue your activities while protecting the environment? Is there anything you can do to give back to nature something that you have taken away — e.g., planting a tree to "replace" some of the paper resources your class uses through the year? Are there any ways you can bring more of nature into our cities, buildings, or homes? What efforts can we make as individuals? What impact can we make when we combine out efforts as a group? Can we expect to see the difference our efforts might make in a week? a month? a year? several years? With members of your group or class, plan a project that would make some difference in the environment locally — in your home, a neighborhood, a park, your school. Create a written or pictorial outline showing the steps you would follow to realize your project. As you choose your project, think about what resources you would need and how your project would help the environment.

Here are some project ideas:
- Get permission to plant a tree or a butterfly garden in a park.
- Create a container garden to improve the air quality indoors.
- Find unusual ways to reuse or recycle large objects like used appliances, old tires, greatly worn and torn clothing, and discarded construction materials.
- Create a natural "view" where there are limited windows or where those windows look out onto other buildings or parking lots.
- Bring soothing or inspiring music to an environment that can be stressful or lonely.
- Clean up a roadside

Graphic *Organizer*

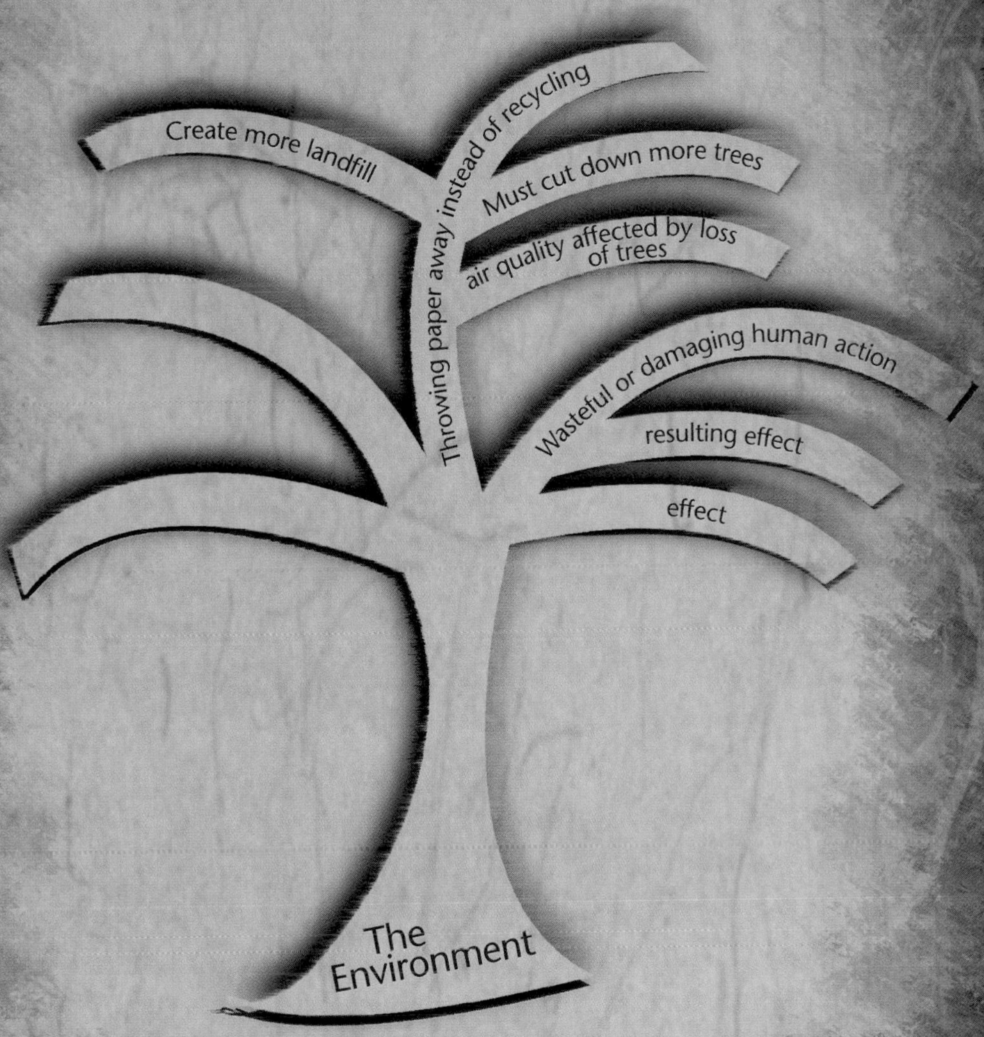

Create more landfill

Throwing paper away instead of recycling

Must cut down more trees

air quality affected by loss of trees

Wasteful or damaging human action

resulting effect

effect

The Environment

INTERNET RESOURCES

As students complete the Graphic Organizer on page 155 or brainstorm project ideas for the Group Project, you may want to have them consult the Wilderness Society's Earth Day Internet site at http://earthday.wilderness.org/ for more ideas. The site includes a link to "Kid's Stuff" that includes further listings for "cool sites," famous quotes, and "Listening to the Land," a link that provides successful actions people have taken to protect the world around them.

The False Mirror, 1928. Rene Magritte. The Museum of Modern Art, New York.

GOALS/OBJECTIVES

Studying this unit will enable students to
- enjoy fiction, nonfiction, and poems exploring the theme of going from one world to another
- define and identify examples of *autobiography, background information, chronological order, foreshadowing, frame story, homophones, internal conflict, irony of situation, point of view,* and *setting.*
- engage in a meaningful independent reading experience by writing an online book review
- write a personal letter
- identify colorful nouns, verbs, and modifiers and demonstrate an ability to use colorful language

From One WORLD to ANOTHER

UNIT THREE

(Continued on page 158)

Begin a class discussion by
having students read the
quotations in the Echoes
feature. Ask them the
following:
- Which quotations do you like
  best, and why?
- How do you approach new
  situations?
- What are the attitudes of the
  speakers quoted concerning new
  worlds?
- What other worlds do you think
  exist? What trip would you
  consider to be "the best of all
  journeys"?

As an alternate activity, you may
want to have students freewrite
about one or two of the questions
above.

TEACHING THE MULTIPLE
INTELLIGENCES (CONT.)

echoes

Two roads diverged in a wood, and I—
I took the one less traveled by,
And that has made all the difference.
—*Robert Frost*

One's destination is never a place but rather a new way of looking at things.
—*Henry Miller*

O brave new world / That has such people in 't!
—*William Shakespeare,* The Tempest

Space—the final frontier . . . These are the voyages of the Starship
Enterprise. Its five-year mission: to explore strange new worlds, to seek out
new life and new civilizations, to boldly go where no one has gone before.
—*Gene Roddenberry,* Star Trek

I hoped that the trip would be the best of all journeys; a journey into ourselves.
—*Shirley MacLaine*

We're not in Kansas anymore.
—*said by Dorothy in* The Wizard of Oz

Following the sun we left the old world.
—*Inscription on one of Christopher Columbus's ships*

But do you really mean . . . there could be other worlds—all over the
place, just around the corner—like that?
—*C.S. Lewis, said by Peter in* The Lion, the Witch, and the Wardrobe

I may not have gone where I intended to go, but I think I have ended up
where I intended to be.
—*Douglas Adams*

When one jumps over the edge, one is bound to land somewhere.
—*D. H. Lawrence*

158 UNIT THREE

TEACHING THE MULTIPLE INTELLIGENCES (CONT.)

Prereading

"HOLLYWOOD and the PITS"
by Cherylene Lee

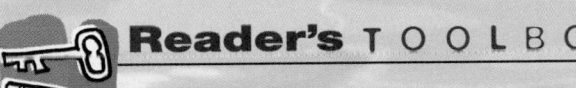

Reader's TOOLBOX

FIRST-PERSON POINT OF VIEW. The story "Hollywood and the Pits" is told from the **first-person point of view**, in which the narrator (the person telling the story) takes part in the action and refers to himself or herself in the first person, using pronouns such as *I, we, my, mine,* and *our.* This differs from the third-person point of view, in which the narrator is outside the action and uses words such as *he, she, it,* and *they.* In "Hollywood and the Pits," the narrator is the main character, so she tells the story from the point of view of the main character. As you read the story, look for details about the main character's point of view, as well as clues to the views of other characters in the story.

BACKGROUND INFORMATION. In "Hollywood and the Pits," the main story line is broken up several times by paragraphs that gives the reader **background information** about the factual history of the La Brea Tar Pits. How does this contribute to the story?

INTERNAL CONFLICT. Internal conflict is a struggle that takes place inside the mind of a character. The main character of this story is struggling with the changes she is experiencing. These changes spark an internal conflict that she sorts out as she shifts between two worlds—Hollywood and the La Brea Tar Pits. Look for signs of this internal conflict as you read the story. Use the chart below to track signs of inner conflict or struggle.

Graphic Organizer

Signs of internal conflict
"I grew up in Hollywood, a place where dreams and nightmares can often take the same shape."
Once the main character grew too tall, the Lee sister act didn't seem so cute anymore.

Reader's Journal

As you've grown older, what has changed about the things you like and dislike?

Reader's Resource

- This story takes place in Hollywood, a district in the city of Los Angeles, California. Hollywood is famous throughout the world for its entertainment industry. Many motion pictures and television shows are filmed there.

- For decades, parents have brought their aspiring actor children to Hollywood, where a very small percentage of auditioning actors ever get called back for a part in a commercial, TV program, or movie. In the 1930s, however, Shirley Temple became one of the most successful child stars in the history of film. The main character in "Hollywood and the Pits" is dubbed "The Chinese Shirley Temple."

- **SCIENCE CONNECTION.** The La Brea Tar Pits are located in Hollywood. Many thousands of years ago, during the Ice Age, some prehistoric animals became trapped and died in this pond of sticky asphalt. The asphalt, often popularly referred to as tar, preserved their bones, and archaeologists at the site are excavating (digging up) the fossils.

"HOLLYWOOD AND THE PITS" **159**

READER'S JOURNAL

You might also ask students to write about the ways in which adults' reactions to them have changed as they have grown older.

GRAPHIC ORGANIZER

Signs of internal conflict
1. "I grew up in Hollywood, a place where dreams and nightmares can often take the same shape."
2. "It sounded like every Oriental kid in Hollywood was working except me."
3. "I suppose a lot of my getting into show business in the first place was a matter of luck."
4. Once the main character grew too tall, the Lee sister act didn't seem so cute anymore.
5. "I never felt my mother pushed me to do something I didn't want to do. But I always knew if something I did pleased her."
6. "I took to performing easily."
7. "It never occurred to me that one day I wouldn't get parts or that I might not 'have what it takes.'"
8. "Before that summer my mother had always claimed she wanted me to be normal."
9. "I didn't know what I had had that I didn't seem to have anymore."

GOALS/OBJECTIVES

Studying this lesson will enable students to
- identify with a main character who is growing up and experiencing changes in her life
- briefly state what the La Brea Tar Pits are and cite some facts about them
- define *first-person point of view*
- define *background information* and identify background information in their reading
- define *internal conflict* and identify an internal conflict in a story
- answer critical questions on a nonfiction piece of writing
- research an archaeological site and write a business letter

INDIVIDUAL LEARNING STRATEGIES

MOTIVATION
Students may especially enjoy the Speaking and Listening: Auditioning activity. Tell students to not worry about overacting their role—they should throw themselves into it using gestures, facial expressions, and tone of voice. Students may even enjoy enacting commercials of their own creation in groups of two or three.

READING PROFICIENCY
Students may have difficulty shifting gears between the narrator's voice and the nonfictional information on the La Brea Tar Pits. Forewarn students that the writer of this story does make this shift in voice. Let them know that they will be able to tell when the writer is including a piece of nonfiction because the text is set off with fossil footprints and is in italic type. Students may benefit from hearing the story read aloud, with one person reading the narrator's voice and another person reading the pieces of nonfiction.

ENGLISH LANGUAGE LEARNING
Point out the following vocabulary words and expressions

archaeological—having to do with the scientific study of the life and culture of the past

plush—luxurious, as in furnishings

callbacks—invitation to return for a further round of auditions

studio—business that produces films or television shows

showbiz—show business, the entertainment industry

chauffeured—act as a chauffeur, drive people places

sass—talk rudely to

corny—unsophisticated, old-fashioned

shrimp or small fry—informal terms for a small person or child

Tootise Pop—type of lollipop or round candy on a stick

cascading—falling, like a waterfall

predators—animals that live by killings and eating other animals

City of Angels—another name for Los Angeles

SPECIAL NEEDS
Make sure students focus on answering the Guided Reading questions and writing out their

When I was fifteen, the pit opened its secret to me. I breathed, ate, slept, dreamed about the La Brea Tar Pits. I spent summer days working the archaeological dig, and in dreams saw the bones glistening, the broken pelvises[1], the skulls, the vertebrae[2] looped like a woman's pearls hanging on an invisible cord. I welcomed those dreams. I wanted to know where the next skeleton was, identify it, record its position, discover whether it was whole or not. I wanted to know where to dig in the coarse, black, gooey sand. I lost myself there and found something else.

1. **pelvis.** Skeletal structure at the end of the spine
2. **vertebrae.** Sections making up the spinal column

INDIVIDUAL LEARNING STRATEGIES (CONT.)

answers to the Recall questions at the selection's end. Check their comprehension with the Checking Your Reading portion of the Selection Check Test.

ENRICHMENT
Students may be interested in taking a trip to a local museum to see the fossils that archaeologists, like the ones who work in the La Brea Tar Pits, uncover. You may want to talk to the students' science teacher to see if you can arrange a joint trip. As students visit the museum, encourage them to take notes on the fossils they see. What do the fossils reveal about the creature who once lived?

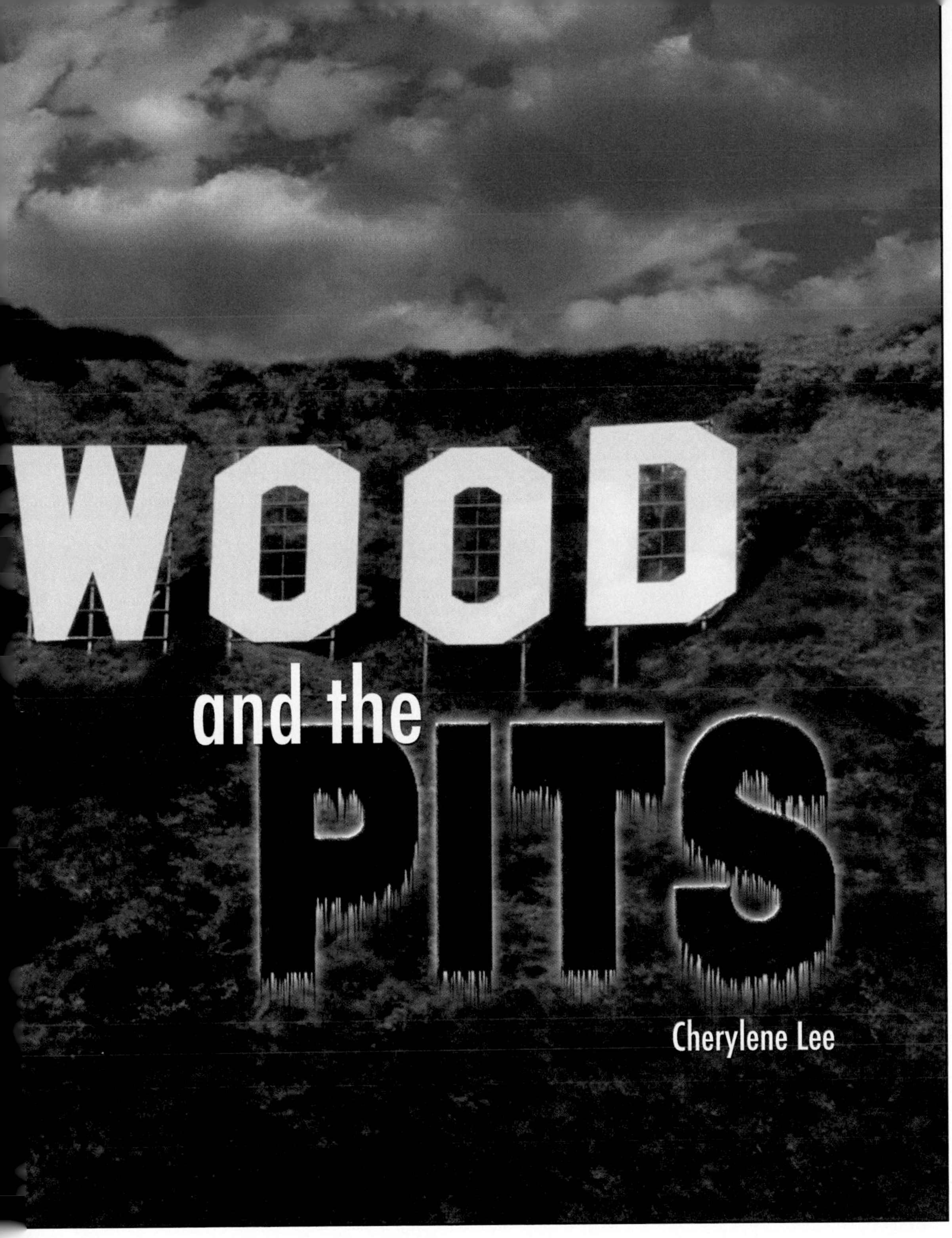
WOOD
and the
PITS
Cherylene Lee

ART SMART

Inform students that the image on this page, the Hollywood sign overlooking Hollywood, California, is probably one of the most familiar and well-known images around the world. To many people it represents fame, stardom, and the glamour of movies. Encourage students to brainstorm other extremely well-known images. What do these images represent?

GEOGRAPHICAL/ CULTURAL NOTE

Hollywood is a district of the city of Los Angeles, California. The town was planned in the 1880s, and it officially became part of Los Angeles in 1910. The first film studio was built there in 1911. Since then, Hollywood has become known to people around the world as a center of the film and television industries. Throughout the twentieth century and into the twenty-first, Hollywood has continued to draw young people searching for fame, stardom, power, and wealth. Sadly, very, very few of these young people ever see their dreams come true, and Hollywood is home to many homeless young people. Remind students that those who run away to Hollywood face many terrifying dangers because people who prey on those who are naïve and inexperienced also are drawn to Hollywood.

VOCABULARY FROM THE SELECTION

barrage	excavate
bewilder	herbivore
carnivorous	obsess
crescent	pore
deception	skew

My mother thought something was wrong with me. Was it good for a teenager to be fascinated by death? Especially animal death in the Pleistocene[3]? Was it normal to be so <u>obsessed</u> by a sticky brown hole in the ground in the center of Los Angeles? I don't know if it was normal or not, but it seemed perfectly logical to me. After all, I grew up in Hollywood, a place where dreams and nightmares can often take the same shape. What else would a child actor do?

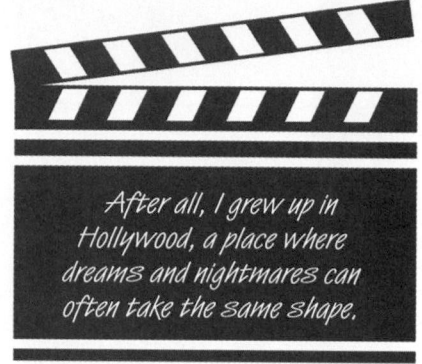

After all, I grew up in Hollywood, a place where dreams and nightmares can often take the same shape.

"Thank you very much, dear. We'll be letting you know."

I knew what that meant. It meant I would never hear from them again. I didn't get the job. I heard that phrase a lot that year.

I walked out of the plush office, leaving behind the casting director, producer, director, writer, and whoever else came to

> **GUIDED READING**
> What office is the narrator leaving? Why?

listen to my reading for a semiregular role on a family sitcom.[4] The carpet made no sound when I opened and shut the door.

I passed the other girls waiting in the reception room, each <u>poring</u> over her script.

The mothers were waiting in a separate room, chattering about their daughters' latest commercials, interviews, callbacks, jobs. It sounded like every Oriental kid in Hollywood was working except me.

My mother used to have a lot to say in those waiting rooms. Ever since I was three, when I started at the Meglin Kiddie Dance Studio, I was dubbed "The Chinese Shirley Temple"—always the one to be picked at auditions[5] and interviews, always the one to get the speaking lines, always called "the one-shot kid," because I could do my scenes in one take—even tight close-ups. My mother would

> **GUIDED READING**
> Why was she called "the one-shot kid"?

only talk about me behind my back because she didn't want me to hear her brag, but I knew that she was proud. In a way I was proud too, though I never dared admit it. I didn't want to be called a showoff. But I didn't exactly know what I did to be proud of either. I only knew that at fifteen I was now being passed over at all these interviews when before I would be chosen.

My mother looked at my face hopefully when I came into the room. I gave her a quick shake of the head. She looked <u>bewildered</u>. I felt bad for my mother then. How could I explain it to her? I didn't understand it myself. We

> **GUIDED READING**
> Why does the narrator give her mother a quick shake of the head? What does it mean?

left, saying polite good-byes to all the other mothers.

We didn't say anything until the studio parking lot, where we had to search for our

---

3. **Pleistocene.** Geological time period
4. **sitcom.** Situation comedy
5. **auditions.** Try outs

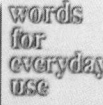

words for everyday use

ob • sess (əb ses') v., haunt or preoccupy the mind of. *Jack obsesses over his golf game and plays every day.* **obsessed,** adj.

pore (por') v., read studiously or attentively. *Jane pores over each month's issue of National Geographic.*

be • wil • der (bi wil' dər) v., confuse or puzzle. *The many rules of cribbage bewilder me.* **bewildered,** adj.

old blue Chevy among rows and rows of parked cars baking in the Hollywood heat.

"How did it go? Did you read clearly? Did you tell them you're available?"

"I don't think they care if I'm available or not, Ma."

"Didn't you read well? Did you remember to look up so they could see your eyes? Did they ask you if you could play the piano? Did you tell them you could learn?"

The barrage of questions stopped when we finally spotted our car. I didn't answer her. My mother asked about the piano because I lost out in an audition once to a Chinese girl who already knew how to play.

My mother took off the towel that shielded the steering wheel from the heat. "You're getting to be such a big girl," she said, starting the car in neutral. "But don't worry, there's always next time. You have what it takes. That's special." She put the car into forward and we drove through a parking lot that had an endless number of identical cars all facing the same direction. We drove back home in silence.

In the La Brea Tar Pits many of the <u>excavated</u> bones belong to juvenile mammals. Thousands of years ago thirsty young animals in the area were drawn to watering holes, not knowing they were traps. Those inviting pools had false bottoms made of sticky tar, which immobilized its victims and preserved their bones when they died. Innocence trapped by ignorance. The tar pits record that well.

> **GUIDED READING**
>
> Why did animals go to the tar pits? What happened there?

I suppose a lot of my getting into show business in the first place was a matter of luck—being in the right place at the right time. My sister, seven years older than me, was a member of the Meglin Kiddie Dance Studio long before I started lessons. Once during the annual recital held at the Shrine Auditorium, she was spotted by a Hollywood agent who handled only Oriental performers. The agent sent my sister out for a role in the *CBS Playhouse 90* television show *The Family Nobody Wanted*. The producer said she was too tall for the part. But true to my mother's training of always having a positive reply, my sister said to the producer, "But I have a younger sister…" which started my showbiz career at the tender age of three.

> **GUIDED READING**
>
> How did the main character get her start in showbiz? How old was she?

My sister and I were lucky. We enjoyed singing and dancing, we were natural hams, and our parents never discouraged us. In fact they were our biggest fans. My mother chauffeured us to all our dance lessons, lessons we begged to take. She drove us to interviews, took us to studios, went on location with us, drilled us on our lines, made sure we kept up our schoolwork and didn't sass back the tutors hired by studios to teach us for three hours a day. She never complained about being a stage mother. She said that we made her proud.

My father must have felt pride too, because he paid for a choreographer[6] to put together our sister act: "The World-Famous Lee Sisters," fifteen minutes of song and dance, real vaudeville[7] stuff. We joked about that a lot, "Yeah, the Lee Sisters—Ug-Lee and

---

6. **choreographer.** Arranger of dance to music
7. **vaudeville.** Song, dance, and comedy acts

---

words for everyday use

bar • rage (bə räzh') *n.*, outpouring of many things at once. *A <u>barrage</u> of protests followed Principal Slinter's announcement that the field trip was cancelled.*

ex • ca • vate (ek' skə vāt) *v.*, dig out and remove. *The archeologists <u>excavated</u> the ruins of a temple in a jungle in Cambodia.* **excavated,** *adj.*

1. They went there to drink the water that collected on top of the tar, but then when they wandered in they got stuck and died.
2. When her older sister was told she was too tall for a part, she replied that she had a younger sister, who got the part instead. The narrator was three at the time.

LITERARY NOTE

ANALOGY. An **analogy** is a comparison of things that are alike in some ways but different in others. Share the definition of *analogy* with students and encourage them to discuss whether there is any analogy to the narrator's situation present in the nonfiction in italic type on this page. In other words, how is the situation of the young animals similar to the situation of the narrator and child actors like her? *Answers.* Students may suggest that young animals were drawn to the water holes not knowing about the trap that lay underneath, just as young people are attracted to the fame and glamour of Hollywood and being child stars, unaware of the trap that lies underneath—futile hopeless auditioning and Hollywood's fickle attitude toward who is in and who is out. In both cases, "innocence [is] trapped by ignorance."

Quotables

"Love of fame is the last thing even learned men can bear to be parted from."

—Tacitus (A.D. 55–120)

1. It worked for several years because of their age and height difference. People thought they were cute and liked their corny jokes. They were a success until the younger sister grew too tall and they didn't seem cute anymore.
2. Only soft cartilage connects the bones, and this dissolves quickly after death and the bones are no longer connected.
3. She was small for her age—at nine she could pass for five or six, yet she could read and memorize parts a five-year-old couldn't.

CULTURAL NOTE

In this story, the narrator's father gambles while he is Las Vegas. Discourage students from engaging in any type of gambling. The odds of winning are slim, and gambling can be addictive. People have destroyed their own lives and those of their family as well by becoming addicted to gambling.

ADDITIONAL QUESTIONS AND ACTIVITIES

A **stereotype** is an unexamined, false idea about a type of person or group of people. Encourage students to read the Language Arts Survey. "Avoiding False Arguments and Propaganda: Stereotypes," and "Communicating with Others: being Considerate of Other Cultures." Then encourage a class discussion on whether students would want to be in the "Oriental Holiday" show if they were Asian American. Why might it be offensive to some Asian Americans?
Answers. Students may suggest that Asian Americans might find the show's attitude toward Asian Americans and its depiction of them as patronizing as its is described on this page, unless it is very carefully written and done.

Home-Lee," but we definitely had a good time. So did our parents. Our father especially liked our getting booked into Las Vegas at the New Frontier Hotel on the Strip. He liked to gamble there, though he said the craps tables in that hotel were "cold," not like the casinos in downtown Las Vegas, where all the "hot" action took place.

In Las Vegas our sister act was part of a show called "Oriental Holiday." The show was about a Hollywood producer going to the Far East, finding undiscovered talent, and bringing it back to the U.S. We did two shows a night in the main showroom, one at eight and one at twelve, and on weekends a third show at two in the morning. It ran the entire summer, often to standing-room-only audiences—a thousand people a show.

Our sister act worked because of the age and height difference. My sister then was fourteen and

> **GUIDED READING**
> Was the sister act a success? Why, or why not?

nearly five foot two; I was seven and very small for my age—people thought we were cute. We had song-and-dance routines to old tunes like "Ma, He's Making Eyes at Me," "Together," and "I'm Following You," and my father hired a writer to adapt the lyrics to "I Enjoy Being a Girl," which came out "We Enjoy Being Chinese." We also told corny jokes, but the Las Vegas audience seemed to enjoy it. Here we were, two kids, staying up late and jumping around, and getting paid besides. To me the applause sometimes sounded like static, sometimes like distant waves. It always amazed me when people applauded. The owner of the hotel liked us so much, he invited us back to perform in shows for three summers in a row. That was before I grew too tall and the sister act didn't seem so cute anymore.

Many of the skeletons in the tar pits are found incomplete—particularly the skeletons of the young, which have only soft cartilage[8] connecting the bones.

In life the soft tissue allows for growth, but in death it dissolves quickly. Thus the skeletons of young animals are more apt to be scattered, especially the vertebrae protecting the spinal cord. In the tar pits,

> **GUIDED READING**
> Why are skeletons of the young more apt to be scattered?

the central ends of many vertebrae are found unconnected to any skeleton. Such bone fragments are shaped like valentines, disks that are slightly lobed—heart-shaped shields that have lost their connection to what they were meant to protect.

I never felt my mother pushed me to do something I didn't want to do. But I always knew if something I did pleased her. She was generous with her praise, and I was sensitive when she withheld it. I didn't like to disappoint her.

I took to performing easily, and since I had started out so young, making movies or doing shows didn't feel like anything special. It was a part of my childhood—like going to the dentist one morning or going to school the next. I didn't wonder if I wanted a particular role or wanted to be in a show or how I would feel if I didn't get in. Until I was fifteen, it never occurred to me that one day I wouldn't get parts or that I might not "have what it takes."

When I was younger, I got a lot of roles because I was so small for my age. When I was nine years old, I could pass for five or six. I was really short. I was always teased about it when I was in elementary school, but I

> **GUIDED READING**
> Why did the narrator get so many roles when she was younger?

didn't mind because my height got me movie jobs. I could read and memorize lines that actual five-year-olds couldn't. My mother told people she made me sleep in a drawer so I wouldn't grow any bigger.

8. **cartilage.** Skeletal tissue

Grauman's Chinese Theatre, Hollywood, 1989. Nik Wheeler.

But when I turned fifteen, it was as if my body, which hadn't grown for so many years, suddenly made up for lost time. I grew five inches in seven months. My mother was amazed. Even I couldn't get used to it. I kept knocking into things, my clothes didn't fit right, I felt awkward and clumsy when I moved. Dumb things that I had gotten away with, like paying children's prices at the movies instead of junior admission, I couldn't do anymore. I wasn't a shrimp or a small fry any longer. I was suddenly normal.

Before that summer my mother had always claimed she wanted me to be normal. She didn't want me to become spoiled by the attention I received when I was working at the studios. I still had chores to do at home, went to public school when I wasn't working, was punished severely when I behaved badly. She didn't want me to feel I was different just because I was in the movies. When I was

> **GUIDED READING**
> What happened when she turned fifteen?

eight, I was interviewed by a reporter who wanted to know if I thought I had a big head.

"Sure," I said.

"No, you don't," my mother interrupted, which was really unusual, because she generally never said anything. She wanted me to speak for myself.

> **GUIDED READING**
> What does the reporter mean by "big head"? What does the narrator think he means?

I didn't understand the question. My sister had always made fun of my head. She said my body was too tiny for the weight—I looked like a walking Tootsie Pop. I thought the reporter was making the same observation.

"She better not get that way," my mother said fiercely. "She's not any different from anyone else. She's just lucky and small for her age."

The reporter turned to my mother, "Some parents push their children to act. The kids feel like they're used."

"I don't do that—I'm not that way," my mother told the reporter.

1. She grew five inches in seven months, her clothes didn't fit right, she started feeling awkward and clumsy. Suddenly, she was normal.
2. The reporter means having a big ego or being overly self-satisfied. She takes it as literally referring to the size of her head.

CROSS-CURRICULAR ACTIVITIES

MATHEMATICS AND SCIENCES. Encourage students to form groups of four and five in order to research human growth and development. Each group should prepare a brief written report on how the body grows both before birth and after. Students should try to answer questions like the following in their reading: What makes the human body grow? When does the human body grow its most? Are growth spurts unusual? When does the body stop growing in size? What parts of the body continue to grow throughout its life?

Students might also create a personal growth journal, describing how they grow physically over the coming year. They might also share their thoughts and feelings about growing and their changing bodies.

ADDITIONAL QUESTIONS AND ACTIVITIES

Inform students that on this page, a reporter says, "Some parents push their children to act. The kids feel like they're used." The narrator's mother responds, "I don't do that—I'm not that way." Encourage students to evaluate the mother's statement. Is it accurate? How do you think the narrator herself feels about her mother's words? *Answers.* Most students will say that the narrator's mother is not speaking the entire truth—she does push her daughter to act. Students may say that the narrator would concur.

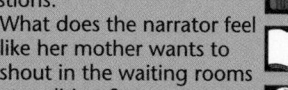
But when she was sitting silently in all those waiting rooms while I was being turned down for one job after another, I could almost feel her wanting to shout, "Use her. Use her. What is wrong with her? Doesn't she have it anymore?" I didn't know what I had had that I didn't seem to have anymore. My mother had told the reporter that I was like everyone else. But when my life was like everyone else's, why was she disappointed?

The churning action of the La Brea Tar Pits makes interpreting the record of past events extremely

difficult. The usual order of deposition[9]—the oldest on the bottom, the youngest on the top—loses all meaning when some of the oldest fossils can be brought to the surface by the movement of natural gas. One must look for an undisturbed spot, a place untouched by the action of underground springs or natural gas or human interference. Complete skeletons become important, because they indicate areas of least disturbance. But such spots of calm are rare. Whole blocks of the tar pit can become displaced, making false sequences of the past, skewing the interpretation for what is the true order of nature.

That year before my sixteenth birthday, my mother seemed to spend a lot of time looking through my old scrapbooks, staring at all the eight-by-ten glossies[10] of the shows that I had done. In the summer we visited with my grandmother often, since I wasn't working and had lots of free time. I would go out to the garden to read or sunbathe, but I could hear my mother and grandmother talking.

"She was so cute back then. She worked with Gene Kelly when she was five years old. She was so smart for her age. I don't know what's wrong with her."

"She's fifteen."

"She's too young to be an ingenue[11] and too old to be cute. The studios forget so quickly. By the time she's old enough to play an ingenue, they won't remember her."

"Does she have to work in the movies? Hand me the scissors."

My grandmother was making false eyelashes using the hair from her hairbrush. When she was young she had incredible hair. I saw an old photograph of her when it flowed beyond her waist like a cascading black waterfall. At seventy, her hair was still black as night, which made her few strands of silver look like shooting stars. But her hair had thinned greatly with age. It sometimes fell out in clumps. She wore it brushed back in a bun with a hairpiece for added fullness. My grandmother had always been proud of her hair, but once she started making false eyelashes from it, she wasn't proud of the way it looked

anymore. She said she was proud of it now because it made her useful.

It was painstaking work—tying knots into strands of hair, then tying them together to form feathery little crescents. Her glamorous false eyelashes were much sought after. Theatrical makeup artists waited months for her work. But my grandmother said what she liked was that she was doing something, making a contribution, and

---

9. **deposition.** Deposit
10. **glossies.** Photographs printed on smooth shiny paper
11. **ingenue.** Actress portraying a naive young woman

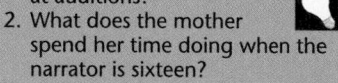

words for everyday use

skew (skyü) v., distort. *Justin was afraid he might skew the survey results if he told people why he was asking the questions.*

cre • scent (kre' sənt) n., curved figure that tapers to two points like a crescent moon. *Nick took one bit of each cookie, leaving a pile of crumbly crescents.*

besides it didn't cost her anything. No overhead. "Till I go bald," she often joked.

She tried to teach me her art that summer, but for some reason strands of my hair wouldn't stay tied in knots.

"Too springy," my grandmother said. "Your hair is still too young." And because I was frustrated then, frustrated with everything about my life, she added, "You have to wait until your hair falls out, like mine. Something to look forward to, oh?" She had laughed and patted my hand.

My mother was going on and on about my lack of work, what might be wrong, that something she couldn't quite put her finger on. I heard my grandmother reply, but I didn't catch it all: "Movies are just make-believe, not real life. Like what I make with my hair that falls out—false. False eyelashes. Not meant to last."

GUIDED READING

What does her grandmother say movies and false eyelashes have in common?

The remains in the La Brea Tar Pits are mostly of <u>carnivorous</u> animals. Very few <u>herbivores</u> are found—the ratio is five to one, a perversion[12] of the natural food chain. The ratio is easy to explain. Thousands of years ago a thirsty animal sought a drink from the pools of water only to find itself trapped by the bottom, gooey with subterranean[13] oil. A shriek of agony from the trapped victim drew flesh-eating predators, which were then trapped themselves by the very same ooze which provided the bait. The cycle repeated itself countless times. The number of victims grew, lured by the image of easy food, the <u>deception</u> of an easy kill. The animals piled on top of one another.

GUIDED READING

Why were so many carnivores attracted to the tar pits?

Le Brea Tarpits, 1991. Alon Reininger.

For over ten thousand years the promise of the place drew animals of all sorts, mostly predators and scavengers—dire[14] wolves, panthers, coyotes, vultures—all hungry for their chance. Most were sucked down against their will in those watering holes destined to be called the La Brea Tar Pits in a place to be named the City of Angels, home of Hollywood movie stars.

12. **perversion.** Abnormal occurence
13. **subterranean.** Underground
14. **dire.** Desperate

words for everyday use

car • ni • vor • ous (kä ni′ və rəs) *adj.,* subsisting on animal tissue. *Dogs and cats are mostly <u>carnivorous</u> animals, but they eat some non-meat food as well.*

her • bi • vore (ər′ bi vōr) *n.,* plant-eating animal. *Most song birds are <u>herbivores</u> and eat mainly seeds, berries, and nuts.*

de • cep • tion (di sep′ shən) *n.,* something that deceives, or tricks. *The magician was a master of <u>deception</u>.*

ANSWERS TO GUIDED READING QUESTIONS

1. They are both just make-believe, not real life, not meant to last.
2. They heard the shrieks of other trapped animals and were lured by the deception of an easy kill, easy food.

LITERARY NOTE

SIMILE. A **simile** is a comparison using *like* or *as.* Have students point to the simile in the words of the grandmother. What two things are being compared. What do these words reveal about the way the grandmother feels about her granddaughter's situation? *Answers.* Students should point to the words, "Movies are just make believes, not real life. Like what I make with my hair that falls out—false. False eyelashes. Not meant to last." The grandmother is comparing fame and the movies to false eyelashes. She seems to feel that her granddaughter's career in movies was not meant to last and never could have lasted because it was fake, not something to be relied on, and was an impermanent career at best. She does not seem upset, but rather accepting.

CROSS-CURRICULAR ACTIVITIES

MATHEMATICS AND SCIENCES. Interested students might research hair loss for extra credit. Why do people lose their hair? Does it affect women as well as men? Students should prepare a brief (no more than a page) report on their findings.

1. She could get really messy and do it with a purpose. She could wear dirty old clothes and filthy sneakers and nobody minded. Dirty clothes were appropriate for the job.
2. Wash, sieve and examine each bucket of sand for any evidence of past life—plant or animal. All of these pieces help tell the entire story of what happened.
3. To work slowly, be observant, and concentrate. She's also learning about time in a different way—over thousands of years—and about what Los Angeles was like long before people lived there.

LITERARY TECHNIQUE

CRISIS. The **crisis,** or **turning point,** is the point in a plot when something happens to determine the future course of events and the eventual fate of the main character. Share this definition with students and ask them the following questions:

- What activity marks a major turning point for the narrator that summer?
- In what way is this activity different and new for the narrator?
- What is the mother's attitude toward the narrator's job?
- What does the narrator tell her mother when she asks whether she would like to go back to a career as an actor? What does she mean by these words?

Answers

- The narrator's discovery of the tar pits and her volunteering to work there marks a turning point for the narrator.
- It is different and new in that people accept her volunteer time, don't turn her away, call her when they say they are going to, and she does not need to be concerned at all about her physical appearance.
- The mother isn't enthusiastic about this interest, but she doesn't discourage her daughter, and she drives her to work.
- The narrator tells her that working as an actor is no longer a "choice." The narrator means that she doesn't have the option of going back to show business—no one wants her, so there is no point in her mother's endless wishing.

I spent a lot of time by myself that summer, wondering what it was that I didn't have anymore. Could I get it back? How could I if I didn't know what it was?

That's when I discovered the La Brea Tar Pits. Hidden behind the County Art Museum on trendy Wilshire Boulevard, I found a job that didn't require me to be small or cute for my age. I didn't have to audition. No one said, "Thank you very much, we'll call you." Or if they did, they meant it. I volunteered my time one afternoon, and my fascination stuck—like tar on the bones of a saber-toothed tiger.

My mother didn't understand what had changed me. I didn't understand it myself. But I liked going to the La Brea Tar Pits. It meant I could get really messy and I was doing it with a purpose. I didn't feel awkward there. I could wear old stained pants. I could wear T-shirts with holes in them.

> **GUIDED READING**
> What does the narrator like about going to the tar pits?

I could wear disgustingly filthy sneakers and it was all perfectly justified. It wasn't a costume for a role in a film or a part in a TV sitcom. My mother didn't mind my dressing like that when she knew I was off to the pits. That was okay so long as I didn't track tar back into the house. I started going to the pits every day, and my mother wondered why. She couldn't believe I would rather be groveling[15] in tar than going on auditions or interviews.

While my mother wasn't proud of the La Brea Tar Pits (she didn't know or care what a fossil was), she didn't discourage me either. She drove me there, the same way she used to drive me to the studios.

"Wouldn't you rather be doing a show in Las Vegas than scrambling around in a pit?" she asked.

"I'm not in a show in Las Vegas, Ma. The Lee Sisters are retired." My older sister had married and was starting a family of her own.

"But if you could choose between…"

"There isn't a choice."

"You really like this tar-pit stuff, or are you just waiting until you can get real work in the movies?"

I didn't answer.

My mother sighed. "You could do it if you wanted, if you really wanted. You still have what it takes."

I didn't know about that. But then, I couldn't explain what drew me to the tar pits either. Maybe it was the bones, finding out what they were, which animal they belonged to, imagining how they got there, how they fell into the trap. I wondered about that a lot.

At the La Brea Tar Pits, everything dug out of the pit is saved—including the sticky sand that covered the bones through the ages. Each bucket of sand is washed, sieved, and examined for pollen grains, insect remains, any evidence of past life. Even the grain size is recorded—the percentage of silt to sand to gravel that reveals the history of deposition, erosion, and disturbance. No single fossil, no one observation, is significant enough to tell the entire story. All the evidence must be weighed before a semblance of truth emerges.

> **GUIDED READING**
> What do people working at the tar pits do with everything they dig out of the pits?

The tar pits had their lessons. I was learning I had to work slowly, become observant, to concentrate. I learned about time in a way that I would never experience—not in hours, days, and months, but in thousands and thousands of years. I imagined what the past must have been like, envisioned Los Angeles as a sweeping basin, perhaps slightly colder and more humid, a time before people and studios arrived. The

> **GUIDED READING**
> What does the narrator learn from the tar pits?

---
15. **groveling.** Crawling

tar pits recorded a warming trend; the kinds of animals found there reflected the changing climate. The ones unadapted disappeared. No trace of their kind was found in the area. The ones adapted to warmer weather left a record of bones in the pit. Amid that collection of ancient skeletons, surrounded by evidence of death, I was finding a secret preserved over thousands and thousands of years. There was something cruel about natural selection and the survival of the fittest[16]. Even those successful individuals that "had what it took" for adaptation still wound up in the pits.

I never found out if I had what it took, not the way my mother meant. But I did adapt to the truth: I wasn't a Chinese Shirley Temple any longer, cute and short for my age. I had grown up. Maybe not on a Hollywood movie set, but in the La Brea Tar Pits. ∎

> **GUIDED READING**
>
> What does she learn about those animals who "had what it took" for adaptation?

---

16. **natural selection...survival of the fittest.** Process in which individuals and groups best adjusted to the environment survive and reproduce.

Respond *to the* SELECTION

How does growing up change your likes, dislikes, and dreams?

About *the* AUTHOR

Cherylene Lee is a Chinese–American writer whose family has been in the United States since the 1850s. Lee was born and raised in Los Angeles, California, and began appearing in television shows and stage plays at a young age. She is the author of stories, poems, and numerous plays including *Carry the Tiger to the Mountain* and *Arthur and Leila*. Lee holds a degree in paleontology from the University of California-Berkeley and a degree in geology from UCLA. Here, Lee responds to some questions about this story and about her writing career.

How did you decide to write this story?
The parallel of Hollywood as a place people are drawn to and the La Brea Tar Pits as a place that animals were drawn to, and my own interest in finding parallels between science, art, and entertainment, are the reasons the story has its peculiar structure. I wrote this story to connect different parts of my life—my interest in per-forming, which seemed very externally driven, and my interest in paleontology which, at the time, seemed like a much more internal quest.

How much of this story is based on your own experiences as a young person?
Most of the feelings are autobiographical, but actual scenes and dialogue are fictionalized.

What type of writing do you most enjoy? Why?
I mostly write plays, and while I believe that preference comes from having to learn dialogue at a very young age, I also know I enjoy the col-laborative process of theater very much. As a playwright, I am one of many artists—along with actors, designers, directors, and produc-ers—who bring words to life on the stage. While I enjoy the creative freedom of working alone (in the imagination, anything is possible), I also enjoy the immediate response of an audience.

"HOLLYWOOD AND THE PITS" **169**

CROSS-CURRICULAR ACTIVITIES

Encourage students to work in groups of two or three to research an animal whose fossils indicate it has changed little over millions of years. Possible subjects include the following: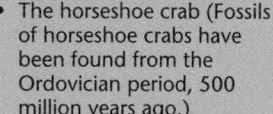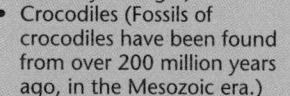
- The horseshoe crab (Fossils of horseshoe crabs have been found from the Ordovician period, 500 million years ago.)
- Crocodiles (Fossils of crocodiles have been found from over 200 million years ago, in the Mesozoic era.)
- The hippopotamus (Fossils have been found from about 2 million years ago.)
- Insects (Fossils have been found of wingless insects from the Debonian period, 400 million years ago.)
- Monitor lizards (These large lizards are the oldest living lizards and are related to a species that lived between 136 and 65 million years ago.)
- Squids, octopuses, and other cephalopods (These ocean creatures first appeared in the Cambrian period about 600 million years ago.)

Students may also choose to research an extinct animal that lived in one of these periods, such as dinosaurs or wooly mammoths. Students should prepare a brief (no more than five-minute) presentation on their animal to the class. They may wish to use visual displays, such as time charts, photographs of living animals, or photographs of fossils to make their presentation more appealing.

GEOLOGIC TIME CHART

ERA	PERIOD	EPOCH	MILLIONS OF YEARS AGO
CENOZOIC	QUATERNARY	HOLOCENE	0.01
		PLEISTOCENE	1.8
	TERTIARY	PLIOCENE	5
		MIOCENE	24
		OLIGOCENE	38
		EOCENE	54
		PALEOCENE	65
MESOZOIC	CRETACEOUS		145
	JURASSIC		210
	TRIASSIC		250
PALEOZOIC	PERMIAN		290
	CARBONIFEROUS PENNSYLVANIAN		365
	CARBONIFEROUS MISSISSIPPIAN		
	DEVONIAN		415
	SILURIAN		465
	ORDOVICIAN		510
	CAMBRIAN		575
PRECAMBRIAN			

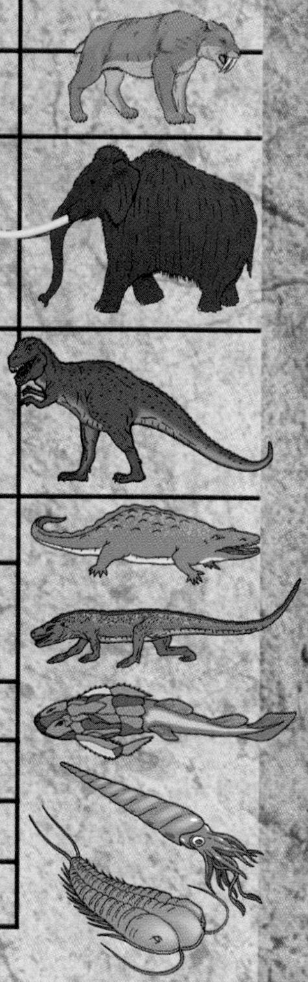

THE PASSAGE OF Time

For thousands of years, the La Brea Tar Pits were important to the early humans who lived in what is now southern California. Indian peoples used the sticky asphalt to bind and mend things together and to glue decorative shells to stone, bone, and wood. Pasted onto baskets and canoes, the tar made these vessels watertight.

Spanish explorers discovered the bubbling swamp in 1769. They noted that this swamp contained enough tar to caulk (seal) many ships. When they built a settlement nearby, they used the tar as a material for waterproofing and for roofing. A century later, workers began mining the asphalt. When they found bones, the miners assumed these remains must be from the cattle and horses people had seen wandering into the pits. In 1875, however, Professor William Denton identified a tooth from the extinct saber-toothed cat. Still, excavation of the tar pits did not begin for another 25 years. Since then, more than one million bones have been removed. Evidence of past life, these fossils began forming when the bones soaked in the asphalt. Then during the rainy season each winter and spring, streams flowed over them. As the sediments—small particles of sand, dirt, and other debris—in the water settled to the bottom, they covered and preserved the bones. Each summer, asphalt from deep underground oozed to the surface, covering the sediment. Over the years, layer upon layer of asphalt and sediment marked the passage of time. Today, the La Brea Tar Pits bustle with activity, as archaeologists continue to remove evidence of past life from the pits.

Many of the larger animals entombed in the pits are now extinct. They needed a cooler, wetter climate to survive. From this finding, scientists have learned that the climate in southern California is warmer and drier than it used to be. Many of the smaller animals and plants found in the pits can still be found in the region. And the process of entrapment continues. About eight to twelve gallons (32 to 48 liters) of asphalt ooze and bubble to the surface each day. The risk of entrapment is highest during the warm summer, when the asphalt is at its gooiest and can easily snare insects, worms, lizards, and some birds and rodents—even an occasional dog.

Critical Thinking

- By what era in geologic history did walking animals appear? By what era did dinosaurs appear? Why do you think the chart has divided the tertiary period and the quaternary period into epochs?
- When did William Denton identify remains of a saber-toothed cat in the La Brea Tar Pits? What time period do you think the cat is from? What assumption did Denton's discovery contradict?
- Why did larger animals trapped in the tar pits die off? Explain how their extinction led scientists to infer that the southern California climate has become warmer and drier?

ANSWERS TO CRITICAL THINKING

- Walking animals appear in the Paleozoic era. Dinosaurs appeared in the Mesozoic era. Students may say that our records of species are more numerous and precise for these eras, and we are aware of more species, so we had to break these periods down to better classify them and make them more manageable.
- William Denton identified the remains in 1875. The cat is from the quaternary period. Denton's discovery contradicted the miners' assumption that the bones were only those of cattle and horses.
- The larger animals died off because they needed a cooler wetter environment, and the environment of Southern California was becoming hot and dry. Scientists inferred this when they learned that creatures who require cool wet environments died out, while ones that could live in a hot, dry environment lived.

ANSWERS TO INVESTIGATE, INQUIRE, IMAGINE

RECALL

1a. The applause sounded sometimes like static, sometimes like distant waves.

2a. She gets very defensive, insisting that her daughter is no different from anyone else.

3a. Each animal that got caught attracted other hungry animals, who were lured by the deception of an easy kill.

4a. She likes being able to wear whatever she wants and get dirty.

INTERPRET

1b. She seems to feel a mixture of disdain (lack of respect) for the audience and happiness with the fun she's having on stage.

2b. While the daughter likes performing, the mother has encouraged her acting career by bringing her to auditions. The mother may feel a bit guilty, not sure if what she's done has been good for her child. She wants her child to be like everyone else, but she also wants her daughter to stand out and make her proud.

3b. The number of child actors keeps growing, as more and more parents hope their children will find fame in Hollywood. Even those who make it will eventually grow up and no longer be child actors. The actors are trapped by the competition to get into Hollywood entertainment just as the animals were trapped in the sticky tar pits.

4b. By wearing whatever she wants and going to the tar pits she is doing what she wants to do for herself, rather than just trying to please others at auditions and interviews.

ANALYZE

5a. *Responses will vary.* For child actors the phrase means luck, being at the right place at the right time. For the main character as a young child it means being small for her age and cute. For the animals in the Tar Pits it means being able to adapt to a changing climate. They still got caught and died in the pits.

SYNTHESIZE

5b. *Responses will vary.* Students may say that the narrator grows up and learns to do what she is interested in rather than acting in ways to please others.

EVALUATE

6a. Time is recorded layer by layer over thousands of years. She gains a sense of it passing in thousands and

---

Recall: GATHERING FACTS

1a. According to the main character, what did the applause she and her sister received for their sister act in Las Vegas sound like?

2a. How does the main character's mother respond when a reporter asks her daughter if she has a big head?

3a. Why did the number of victims at the La Brea Tar Pits keep growing?

4a. Why does the main character like going to the tar pits?

Interpret: FINDING MEANING

1b. Why do you suppose it sounded like this to her? How did she feel about the applause?

2b. Why does the mother interrupt the interview? Why does she respond so defensively? Do you think she pushes her child to act? What expectations does she have for her daughter?

3b. What do you think happens to the child actors in Hollywood? What similarities do you see between Hollywood and the La Brea Tar Pits?

4b. Why would she rather be groveling in tar than going on auditions or interviews? What has changed about her?

Analyze: TAKING THINGS APART

5a. Find references to "having what it takes" in the short story, "Hollywood and the Pits." What does this phrase mean for child actors? for the main character as a young child? for the animals in the La Brea Tar Pits? What happened to animals in the pits who had what it takes?

Synthesize: BRINGING THINGS TOGETHER

5b. What does the narrator learn about herself in this story?

Evaluate: MAKING JUDGMENTS

6a. How is time recorded at the La Brea Tar Pits? What does the main character learn about time from her work at the tar pits? How is this way of looking at time different from how she viewed time in terms of acting?

Extend: CONNECTING IDEAS

6b. How is geologic time different from time as we experience it in our lifetime? How is time measured in a human lifetime? How is it measured in the history of the earth?

ANSWERS TO INVESTIGATE, INQUIRE, IMAGINE (CONT.)

thousands of years, not just in the hours, days, and months that she experiences. It feels much slower because it covers thousands of years instead of time from one audition to the next or one show to the next.

EXTEND

6b. It covers millions of years instead of just minutes, hours, days, months, or years. Time is measured in human terms by years, phases of development, or decades. It is measured by geologic time in eras, which are then broken down into periods and, in turn, epochs.

Understanding *Literature*

FIRST-PERSON POINT OF VIEW. The narrator takes part in the action and refers to himself or herself using the words *I, we, my, mine,* and *our* in a story told from the **first-person point of view**. "Hollywood and the Pits" tells us a lot about what the main character is thinking. What is her personality like? Make a list of character traits based on evidence from the story.

BACKGROUND INFORMATION. In "Hollywood and the Pits," the main story line is broken up several times by paragraphs that gives the reader **background information** about the factual history of the La Brea Tar Pits. Review the italicized passages that refer to the La Brea Tar Pits. How are they inserted in the story? Did their appearance surprise you? Why, or why not? How might these passages be related to other elements of the story?

INTERNAL CONFLICT. Internal conflict is a struggle that takes place inside the mind of a character. Look at the chart you completed that lists signs of inner conflict or struggle for the main character in Hollywood. Compare your list with that of a partner.

Writer's Journal

1. Imagine that you are a young actor who has just finished an audition. Write a **letter** to a friend telling him or her how the audition went and how you feel about it.
2. What would you find if you dug a deep hole in your yard? Write a **log** of items you think you would find, how old the items might be, and any other relevant information about them.
3. Write two **sentences** using the first-person ("I," "we") voice. Then rewrite each sentence using the third-person ("he," "she," "they") voice.

Skill Builders

Speaking and Listening

AUDITIONING. In a small group, select one of your favorite television commercials and pretend you are practicing to audition for a role in the commercial. Act your part with a lot of expression—verbally, facially, and through body language. Listen to others in your group as they practice and give them advice about how they might improve their performance. For more information, see the Language Arts Survey 4.1, "Verbal and Nonverbal Communication."

FIRST-PERSON POINT OF VIEW. Students may say that the narrator is thoughtful, interested in the world around her, modest, and comes to be interested in pleasing herself rather than meeting other people's unrealistic expectations.
BACKGROUND INFORMATION. They are inserted when there is a natural pause in the story and serve to comment on the action or shed some new and interesting light on it. Responses will vary. Students may say that the passages serve to compare the life of a child actor to an animal caught in the Tar Pits.
INTERNAL CONFLICT. Students should compare the list they completed for the Graphic Organizer activity on page 159 with that of a partner.

ANSWERS TO SKILL BUILDERS

Speaking and Listening
AUDITIONING. You may suggest that students can also audition for a commercial of their own invention or for a part that they enjoy from television or film.

Language, Grammar, and Style
WORKING WITH INVERTED SENTENCES.
Responses will vary. Students may say that in the first-person point-of-view that you are limited to seeing directly the thoughts and feelings of one character. Other characters seem to see her as cute when she is little, but as not good for much when she grows. These clues may be colored by the narrator's perception. Most students, however, will feel that the narrator is a reliable one. Mosts students will find that the story is more immediate and more personal when the first-person is used.

Study and Research & Applied English
RESEARCHING AN ARCHAEOLOGICAL SITE. Inform students that their letters should follow the model for a business letter explained in the Language Arts Survey, "Business Letters."

Vocabulary
ADJECTIVES. Students' sentences will vary, but students should use these words as adjectives, not as any other part of speech.

Language, Grammar, and Style
WORKING WITH INVERTED SENTENCES. A sentence is **inverted** when all or part of the complete predicate comes before the verb.

EXAMPLE   After a career in Hollywood, she worked at the La Brea Tar Pits. (The sentence is inverted bec<u>ause</u> <u>After a career in Hollywood</u>, which modifies the verb <u>worked</u>, is in front of the subject <u>we</u>.)

Will you attend the seminar on fossils? (The sentence is inverted because the helping verb <u>will</u>, which is part of the verb <u>will attend</u>, is in front of the subject <u>you</u>.)

Yesterday she starred in her own television show. (The sentence is inverted because <u>Yesterday</u>, which modifies the verb <u>starred</u>, is in front of the subject.

On your own sheet of paper, copy the following sentences. Underline the simple subject once and underline the verb twice. Then write the sentence using regular construction. One example has been done for you. For more information, see the Language Arts Survey 3.23, "Working with Inverted Sentences."

EXAMPLE   When I was younger, <u>I</u> <u>got</u> a lot of roles because I was so small for my age.

Rewritten using regular construction: I got a lot of roles when I was younger because I was so small for my age.

1. Tomorrow she may work as a paleontologist.
2. When I was fifteen, the pit opened its secret to me.
3. Have you ever seen such a wonder?
4. In the La Brea Tar Pits many of the excavated bones belong to juvenile mammals.
5. How could I explain my newfound interest to her?

Study and Research & Applied English
RESEARCHING AN ARCHAEOLOGICAL SITE. Using library resources and/or the Internet, do some preliminary research on the La Brea Tar Pits or on an archaeological site in your state. Then write a letter to the director of the museum or other facility at the site. Express your interest in learning more about the site and ask what programs or activities they have for young teens. Find out what kinds of fossils and/or artifacts have been found there, how old they are, and what this evidence tells us about the past. Keep a research log as you investigate. Share your findings with your class. For more information, see the the Language Arts Survey 5.18, "How to Locate Library Materials," 5.27, "Conducting an Internet Search," and 6.6, "Writing a Business Letter."

Vocabulary
ADJECTIVES. An **adjective** is a word used to modify, or describe, a noun. In the phrase "the blue house," *blue* is an adjective that modifies the noun *house*. Write a sentence for each of the following adjectives.

EXAMPLE   coarse   →   *Jill brushed the horse's* <u>*coarse*</u> *winter fur.*

1. plush
2. semiregular
3. bewildered
4. cascading
5. painstaking
6. glamorous
7. trendy
8. filthy
9. natural
10. ancient

Prereading

"The Serial Garden"
by Joan Aiken

Reader's Resource

- **Homophones** are words that sound alike but are spelled differently and have different meanings. The words *serial* and *cereal* are homophones. So are the words *to*, *too*, and *two*. Such words are also called *homonyms*, although homonym is a more general term that can also refer to words that are spelled alike and sound alike, yet have different meanings. How many more homophones or homonyms can you think of?

- Advertising in print and other media is a multi-billion-dollar industry around the world. One form of advertising is promotional offers, such as the chance to win a prize from a specially marked pacakge. In "The Serial Garden," Mark, the main character, becomes interested in the punch-out garden offered on his cereal box. Another form of advertising is the jingle, a catchy tune written to promote a product. It has a tendency to stick in your head and make you more likely to remember the product being advertised. Can you think of any advertising jingles? Share them with others in your class. Why are jingles effective?

Graphic Organizer

There are two settings in this story: the real world and a fantasy garden. After you read the story, make a cluster chart about the fantasy garden. Begin by copying the chart below onto your own paper. As you read, write details about the garden. Circle the detail and draw a line from the detail to the center circle.

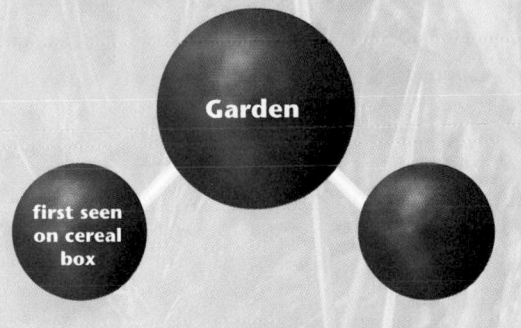

- Garden
- first seen on cereal box

Reader's Journal

Write about the best game, cutout, or prize you have received—or might like to receive—from a cereal box or other package.

Reader's TOOLBOX

FORESHADOWING. Foreshadowing is the act of hinting at events that will happen later in a poem, story, or play. In "The Serial Garden," look for clues about what events might happen.

SETTING. The **setting** of a literary work is the time and place in which it happens. Writers create settings in many different ways. As you read, identify the setting in this story and look for ways in which the author of this selection establishes setting.

ADDITIONAL RESOURCES

UNIT 3 RESOURCE BOOK
- Selection Worksheet 3.2
- Selection Check Test 4.3.3
- Selection Test 4.3.4
- Reading Resource 1.19
- Study and Research Resource 5.3
- Applied English Resource 6.6

READER'S JOURNAL

If students have difficulty thinking of such a game, cutout, or prize, ask them to write about amazing claims or promises they have heard or seen advertisers make.

GRAPHIC ORGANIZER

Students may include the following details in their cluster charts about the garden: Mark tapes the garden together, Brekkfast Brikks song transports Mark to the garden, iron gate, stone wall, flowers not in right proportion, gray fog where garden ends, Mark finds remaining sections of the garden, sundial, paved garden espaliers, huge blue cabbage flowers, grass walk, clipped trees, orchard, lady in white and gold, source of garden is German book of gardens.

GOALS/OBJECTIVES

Studying this lesson will enable students to
- enjoy reading a story with elements of fantasy
- define homophones and point to an example of homophones
- briefly describe some advertising techniques
- define *foreshadowing* and recognize foreshadowing in works they read
- define and identify *setting*
- write a business letter
- collaborate with other students to write a jingle
- understand words created using base words and prefixes

INDIVIDUAL LEARNING STRATEGIES

MOTIVATION
Students may especially enjoy working together to write their own jingles in the Media Literacy and Collaborative Learning exercise on page 195. You may wish to have students write and perform a television commercial that uses their jingle. If possible, videotape the students' commercials to share with other classes.

READING PROFICIENCY
Students may have difficulty with certain British expressions and Mr. Johansen's German expressions. Tell them that when these terms aren't footnotes, they should figure them out from context. Usually, they mean what they sound like. For example, *hullo* is just British for *hello,* while *Gartenbuch* just means garden book, and *natürlich* means naturally. Students will benefit if you create a brief outline of the story for them, highlighting the major events. Check their comprehension by having them write out their answers to the Guided Reading questions.

ENGLISH LANGUAGE LEARNING
Point out the following vocabulary words and expressions:
larder—place in a house where food is kept; pantry
marmalade—jam sometimes containing the sliced rind of a fruit
beastly—disagreeable, unpleasant
scarlet—red
openwork—ornamental, or decorative, with openings in the material
stately—dignified, majestic
Trump of Doom—trumpet which when played is supposed to herald the end of the world
keen—eager, enthusiastic

(Continued on page 177)

Flower Garden, Valley-Field, from "Fragments on the Theory and Practice of Landscape Gardening," 1816. Humphry Repton, Private Collection.

VOCABULARY FROM THE SELECTION

aggrieved	forage	oblige	ventilator
biddable	gaudy	obtain	vigil
booty	grotto	prophesy	vulgar
dessert	hauteur	repulsive	wan
dogged	incalculable	shudder	
etiquette	incantation	susceptible	
ferocious	noisome	tantalizing	

The Serial Garden

Joan Aiken

Cold rice pudding for breakfast?" said

Mark, looking at it with disfavor.

"Don't be fussy," said his mother.

"You're the only one who's complaining."

This was unfair, for she and Mark were

the only members of the family at table,

Harriet having developed measles while

staying with a school friend, while Mr.

Armitage had somehow managed to lock

himself in the larder.[1] Mrs. Armitage

never had anything but toast and

marmalade for breakfast anyway.

---
1. **larder.** Pantry

INDIVIDUAL LEARNING STRATEGIES (CONT.)

SPECIAL NEEDS
Students may benefit from listening to the recording of this selection in the Audio Library. Have them complete the Recall questions in Investigate, Inquire, and Imagine. You may wish to pair students who understand and enjoy the story with special-needs students. Together they can choose a paragraph or two from the story to read aloud or enact for the rest of the class.

ENRICHMENT
Interested students might use their imagination to create their own gardens. Students may create their garden in descriptive writing, in a drawing or painting, or in a diorama or model. Tell students that they can create a realistic garden or a fantastic one. Encourage them to stretch their imaginations, brainstorming different objects, natural and human-made, that might be included in a garden.

HISTORICAL NOTE

Gardens have been popular throughout the world for many centuries. One of the Seven Wonders of the World was the Hanging Gardens of Babylon (modern Iraq). Constructed around 800–600 B.C., the gardens were laid out on layered brick terraces that stretched more than four hundred feet above the ground. The plants were watered with special pumps that brought water from the Euphrates River. For about nine hundred years (from around 400 B.C. to A.D. 500), homes of many rich Romans featured elaborate gardens in courtyards. Outstanding gardens were also developed in Persia and Japan during the sixth century. During the 1400s and 1500s, Italian garden designers created beautiful private gardens near estates. During the next two centuries, French royalty indulged in extravagantly beautiful gardens. The people of

HISTORICAL NOTE (CONT.)

England, with their mild, rainy climate, have long appreciated the joys of gardening. Today, many English gardens that have been cultivated for hundreds of years are open to the public. The colorful and varied flower beds, carefully landscaped trees, artfully clipped hedges, and grand open spaces described in "The Serial Garden" are features common to fine gardens in Europe. Share some of this history of gardens with students so they understand that this story features a grand, decorative garden, not a simple vegetable patch.

HISTORICAL NOTE

Inform students that advertising plays an important role in this story, and share the information in this note with them. Advertising has been around for at least five thousand years. By 3000 B.C., shopkeepers in Babylon were hanging signs outside their stores to let passersby know what was for sale inside. In ancient Egypt, people were hired to walk through town announcing what sort of goods had just arrived by ship at the city port. During the middle ages, such announcers were common in European towns. The invention of the printing presses led to posters announcing sales. Advertising really took off in the Victorian period in England (1837–1901), when many manufactured goods were available. People had exhibitions of manufactured products and advertised them in newspapers, and advertising agencies began to become a big business. Today advertising in print and other media is a multi-billion dollar industry around the world.

Mark went on scowling at the chilly-looking pudding. It had come straight out of the fridge, which was not in the larder.

"If you don't like it," said Mrs. Armitage, "unless you want Daddy to pass you cornflakes through the larder <u>ventilator</u>, flake by flake, you'd better run down to Miss Pride and get a small packet of cereal. She opens at eight; Hickmans doesn't open till nine. It's no use waiting till the blacksmith comes to let your father out; I'm sure he won't be here for hours yet."

There came a gloomy banging from the direction of the larder, just to remind them that Mr. Armitage was alive and suffering in there.

"*You're* all right," shouted Mark heartlessly as he passed the larder door. "There's nothing to stop *you* having cornflakes. Oh, I forgot, the milk's in the fridge. Well, have cheese and pickles then. Or treacle tart."[2]

Even through the zinc grating[3] on the door, he could hear his father <u>shudder</u> at the thought of treacle tart and pickles for breakfast. Mr. Armitage's imprisonment was his own fault, though; he had sworn that he was going to find out where the mouse got

> **GUIDED READING**
> Why is Mark having cold rice pudding for breakfast?

into the larder if it took him all night, watching and waiting. He had shut himself in, so that no member of the family should come bursting in and disturb his <u>vigil.</u> The larder door had a spring catch that sometimes jammed; it was bad luck that this turned out to be one of the times.

Mark ran across the fields to Miss Pride's shop at Sticks Corner and asked if she had any cornflakes.

"Oh, I don't think I

> **GUIDED READING**
> What does Mark hope to buy at Miss Pride's shop?

have any left, dear," Miss Pride said woefully. "I'll have a look. . . . I think I sold the last packet a week ago Tuesday."

"What about the one in the window?"

"That's a dummy, dear."

Miss Pride's shop window was full of nasty, dingy old cardboard cartons with nothing inside them, and several empty display stands that had fallen down and never been propped up again. Inside the shop were a few small, tired-looking tins and jars, which had a worn and scratched appearance as if mice had tried them and given up. Miss Pride herself was

Brekkfast Brikks to start the day
Make you fit in every way.
Children bang their plates with glee
At Brekkfast Brikks for lunch and tea!
Brekkfast Brikks for supper too
Give peaceful sleep the whole night through.

---

2. **treacle tart.** Pastry with a sweet molasses filling
3. **zinc grating.** Metal framework on a door

words for everyday use

ven • ti • la • tor (vənt′ lāt ər) *n.*, device used to bring in fresh air and drive out foul air; fan. *The ventilator in the factory removed the fumes from the air and allowed fresh air to circulate.*

shud • der (shud′ ər) *v.*, shake or tremble suddenly. *When the young boy thought about going into the dark cellar alone, he shuddered.*

vi • gil (vij′ əl) *n.*, watchful staying awake during the usual hours of sleep. *Unlike creatures that sleep at night, the owl keeps a watchful vigil during the nighttime hours.*

small and <u>wan</u>, with yellowish gray hair; she rooted rather hopelessly in a pile of empty boxes. Mark's mother never bought any groceries from Miss Pride's if she could help it, since the day when she had found a label inside the foil wrapping of a cream cheese saying, "This cheese should be eaten before May 11, 1899."

"No cornflakes I'm afraid, dear."

"Any wheat crispies? Puffed corn? Rice nuts?"

"No, dear. Nothing left, only Brekkfast Brikks."

"Never heard of *them*," said Mark doubtfully.

"Or I've a jar of Ovo here. You spread it on bread. That's nice for breakfast," said Miss Pride, with a sudden burst of salesmanship. Mark thought the Ovo looked beastly, like yellow paint, so he took the packet of Brekkfast Brikks. At least it wasn't very big. . . . On the front of the box was a picture of a fat, <u>repulsive</u>, fair-haired boy, rather like the chubby Augustus, banging on his plate with his spoon.

> **GUIDED READING**
>
> What does Mark buy at Miss Pride's shop?

"They look like tiny doormats," said Mrs. Armitage, as Mark shoveled some Brikks into the bowl.

"They taste like them, too. Gosh," said Mark. "I must hurry or I'll be late for school. There's rather a nice cut-out garden on the back of the packet, though; don't throw it away when it's empty, Mother. Goodbye, Daddy," he shouted through the larder door, "hope Mr. Ellis comes soon to let you out." And he dashed off to catch the school bus.

At breakfast next morning Mark had a huge helping of Brekkfast Brikks and persuaded his father to try them.

"They taste just like esparto grass,"[4] said Mr. Armitage fretfully.

"Yes, I know, but do take some more, Daddy. I want to cut out the model garden; it's so lovely."

"Rather pleasant, I must say. It looks like an eighteenth-century German engraving," his father agreed. "It certainly was a stroke of genius putting it on the packet. No one would ever buy these things to eat for pleasure. Pass me the sugar, please. And the cream. And the strawberries."

It was the half-term holiday, so after breakfast Mark was able to take the empty packet away to the playroom and get on with the job of cutting out the stone walls, the row of little trees, the fountain, the yew arch,[5] the two green lawns, and the tiny clumps of brilliant flowers. He knew better than to "stick tabs in slots and secure with paste," as the directions suggested; he had made models from packets before and knew they always fell to pieces unless they were firmly bound together with transparent sticky tape.

It was a long, fiddling, pleasurable job.

Nobody interrupted him. Mrs. Armitage cleaned the playroom only once every six months or so, when she made a <u>ferocious</u> <u>descent</u> on it and tidied up the tape recorders, rollerskates, meteorological sets; and dismantled railway engines; and threw away countless old magazines, stringless tennis rackets, abandoned paintings, and unsuccessful models. There were always bitter complaints from Mark and Harriet; then they forgot and things piled up again till next time.

---

4. **esparto grass.** Coarse grass used to make rope
5. **yew arch.** Gateway in a garden made out of yew branches. A yew is an evergreen bush.

words for everyday use	
wan (wän) *adj.*, pale; sickly. *His <u>wan</u> face revealed that he had been sick all winter.*	
re • pul • sive (ri pul′ siv) *adj.*, disgusting, offensive. *Many people find taking out the garbage to be a <u>repulsive</u> task.*	
fe • ro • cious (fə rō shəs) *adj.*, fierce. *The pride of <u>ferocious</u> lions descended upon the helpless gazelle.*	
des • cent (dē sent′) *n.*, sudden attack or raid. *My younger sister often makes a sudden <u>descent</u> upon my closet and raids it for clothing.*	

1. Mark buys a brand of cereal called Brekkfast Brikks.

CROSS-CURRICULAR ACTIVITIES

APPLIED ARTS. On this page, the narrator describes how Mark enjoys the "long, fiddling, pleasurable job" of putting together a model garden. Encourage students to bring into the classroom an example of a similar type of project they enjoy doing to share with their classmates. For example, students might bring in completed model cars, boats, airplanes, or buildings; carvings; embroidery; or any other type of completed craft item. Each student should then present their creation to the class and tell the other students what their object is, how they created it, how long their object took to make, and how they felt about the project.

Quotables

"The life so short, the craft so long to learn."

—Hippocrates

1. Mark thinks the Brekkfast Brikks
song is ridiculous because he
wouldn't want the cereal for every
meal, as the song suggests.
2. Mark starts singing the song
because the verses keep coming
into his head as he is working on
the garden. He often sings when he
is alone and busy.
3. The cardboard garden suddenly
seems to tower above Mark. He can
enter the garden, and it seems real,
not as if it were made of cardboard.
4. Mark wonders what made the
garden "come alive."

CROSS-CURRICULAR ACTIVITIES

SOCIAL STUDIES. Ask students to
recall various advertising jingles
that they have heard. You
might have them recite these
jingles and write the words of
one or two of them on the
board. Have students read the
Language Arts Survey 5.2,
"Distinguishing Fact from
Opinion" and 5.3, "Avoiding
False Arguments and
Propaganda." Then have
students examine the words of
the jingles written on the
board closely. Ask them the
following questions: What do
the jingles reveal about the products
they advertise? Are the jingles made
up of facts or opinions? How can
you tell whether the statements are
facts or opinions? Do the jingles
include false arguments and
propaganda? Why should people be
skeptical of advertising jingles?

LITERARY TECHNIQUE

FANTASY. A **fantasy** is a very
unrealistic, imaginative story.
Inform students that on this
page elements of a realistic
story are combined with
elements of a fantasy. Ask them
to identify some elements of
realism and some elements of
fantasy on this page.

As Mark worked, his eye was caught by a
verse on the outside of the packet:

"Brekkfast Brikks to start the day
Make you fit in every way.
Children bang their plates with glee
At Brekkfast Brikks for lunch and tea!
Brekkfast Brikks for supper too
Give peaceful sleep the whole night
  through."

"Blimey," thought Mark, sticking a cedar
tree into the middle of
the lawn and then
bending a stone wall
round at dotted lines A,
B, C, and D. "I wouldn't
want anything for breakfast, lunch, tea, and
supper, not even Christmas pudding.
Certainly not Brekkfast Brikks."

> **GUIDED READING**
> What does Mark
> think of the
> Brekkfast Brikks
> song?

He propped a clump of gaudy scarlet flowers
against the wall and stuck them in place.

The words of the rhyme kept coming into
his head as he worked, and presently he found
that they went rather well to a tune that was
running through his mind, and he began to
hum, and then to sing.
Mark often did this when
he was alone and busy.

> **GUIDED READING**
> Why does Mark
> start singing this
> song?

"Brekkfast Brikks to
sta-art the day,
  Ma-ake you fit in every way—

"Blow, where did I put that little bit of
sticky tape? Oh, there it is.

"Children bang their pla-ates with glee
  At Brekkfast Brikks for lunch and tea

"Slit gate with razor-blade, it says; but it'll
have to be a penknife.

"Brekkfast Brikks for supper toohoo
Give peaceful sleep the whole night
  throughoo. . . ."

"Hullo. That's funny,"
said Mark.
  It was funny. The
openwork iron gate he
had just stuck in position now suddenly
towered above him. On either side, to right
and left, ran the high stone wall, stretching
away into foggy distance. Over the top of the
wall he could see tall trees, yews and
cypresses and others he didn't know.

> **GUIDED READING**
> What happens to
> the cardboard
> garden?

"Well, that's the neatest trick I ever saw,"
said Mark. "I wonder if the gate will open."
  He chuckled as he tried it, thinking of the
larder door. The gate did open, and he went
through into the garden.
  One of the things that had already struck
him as he cut them out was that the flowers
were not at all in the right proportions. But
they were all the nicer for that. There were
huge, velvety violets and pansies the size of
saucers; the hollyhocks were as big as
dinnerplates and the turf was sprinkled with
enormous daisies. The roses, on the other
hand, were miniature, no bigger than cuff-
buttons. There were real fish in the fountain,
bright pink.
  "*I* made all this," thought Mark, strolling
along the mossy path to the yew arch. "Won't
Harriet be surprised when she sees it. I wish
she could see it now. I wonder what made it
come alive like that."
  He passed through the yew arch as he said
this, and discovered that
on the other side there
was nothing but gray,
foggy blackness. This, of

> **GUIDED READING**
> What does Mark
> wonder about the
> garden?

> **words for everyday use**
> **gau • dy** (gôd'ē) *adj.*, bright and showy. *The gaudy colors of the advertisement caught my eye.*

LITERARY TECHNIQUE (CONT.)

Answers. Students may point to the following as
examples of realism: Mark realizing that the Brekkfast
Brikks song is silly, Mark realizing he doesn't want
Brekkfast Brikks for every meal, the words and the
rhyme getting stuck in his head, and Mark losing the
tape for a moment. Elements of fantasy include: the
iron gate suddenly towering above Mark, the wall of
the cardboard garden running far into the distance,
Mark being able to open the gate and enter the garden he has made, the flowers being all out of proportion, and the foggy blackness where his garden ends.

course, was where his cardboard garden had ended. He turned through the archway and gazed with pride at a border of huge, scarlet tropical flowers that were perhaps supposed to be geraniums but certainly hadn't turned out that way. "I know! Of course, it was the rhyme, the rhyme on the packet."

He recited it. Nothing happened. "Perhaps you have to sing it," he thought and (feeling a little foolish) he sang it through to the tune that fitted so well. At once, faster than blowing out a match, the garden drew itself together and shrank into its cardboard again, leaving Mark outside.

"What a marvelous hiding place it'll make when I don't want people to come bothering," he thought. He sang the spell once more, just to make sure that it worked; and there was the mossy wall, the stately iron gate, and the treetops. He stepped in and looked back. No playroom to be seen, only gray blankness.

GUIDED READING

How does Mark make the garden shrink?

At that moment he was startled by a tremendous clanging, the sort of sound the Trump of Doom would make if it was a dinner bell. "Blow," he thought. "I suppose that's lunch." He sang the spell for the fourth time; immediately he was in the playroom, and the garden was on the floor beside him, and Agnes was still ringing the dinner bell outside the door.

"All right, I heard," he shouted. "Just coming."

He glanced hurriedly over the remains of the packet to see if it bore any mention of the fact that the cut-out garden had magic properties. It did not. He did, however, learn that this was Section Three of the Beautiful Brekkfast Brikk Garden Series, and that

words for everyday use

ob • tain (əb tān′) *v.*, get possession of. *During the nineteenth century many Americans headed west, hoping to* <u>obtain</u> *good farmland.*

Sections One, Two, Four, Five, and Six would be found on other packets. In case of difficulty in <u>obtaining</u> supplies, please write to Fruhstucksgeschirr-ziegelsteinindustrie (Great Britain), Lily Road, Shepherds Bush.

GUIDED READING

What does Mark learn about the garden by reading the Brekkfast Brikks box?

"Elevenpence a packet," Mark murmured to himself, going to lunch with unwashed hands. "Five elevens are thirty-five. Thirty-five pennies are—no, that's wrong. Fifty-five pence are four-and-seven pence. Father, if I mow the lawn and carry coal every day for a month, can I have four shillings and sevenpence?"

"You don't want to buy another space gun, do you?" said Mr. Armitage looking at him suspiciously. "Because one is quite enough in this family."

"No, it's not for a space gun, I swear."

"Oh, very well."

"And can I have the four-and-seven now?"

Mr. Armitage gave it reluctantly. "But that lawn has to be like velvet, mind," he said. "And if there's any falling off in the coal supply, I shall demand my money back."

"No, no, there won't be," Mark promised in reply. As soon as lunch was over, he dashed down to Miss Pride's. Was there a chance that she would have sections One, Two, Four, Five, and Six? He felt certain that no other shop had even heard of Brekkfast Brikks, so she was his only hope, apart from the address in Shepherds Bush.

"Oh, I don't know, I'm sure," Miss Pride said, sounding very doubtful—and more than a little surprised. "There might just be a couple on the bottom shelf—yes, here we are."

ANSWERS TO GUIDED READING QUESTIONS

1. Mark makes the garden shrink by singing the Brekkfast Brikks song to the same tune again.
2. Mark learns that the garden is part of a series—there are five other sections needed to complete the garden that can be found on other packets of Brekkfast Brikks cereal. He also learns an address to which he can write if he is having trouble obtaining more packets.

ADDITIONAL QUESTIONS AND ACTIVITIES

You might have students discuss whether they think the garden expands so that Mark can enter it, whether Mark shrinks so that the garden seems large, whether Mark has entered a magical world, or whether Mark is imagining entering the garden. Ask why the cardboard garden seems so real to Mark. Is the garden truly magical, or is Mark just very imaginative?

CROSS-CURRICULAR ACTIVITIES

MATHEMATICS AND SCIENCES. Some students might wish to research British currency. Ask them to find out how many pence are in a shilling, how many shillings are in a pound, and how much the pound is worth compared to the dollar. To complete this activity, students should find the latest exchange rates (available at certain banks, newspapers, or on the Internet).

Answers. There are twelve pence in a shilling. There are twenty shillings in a pound. To find how much the pound is worth compared to the dollar, students will have to find a current exchange rate.

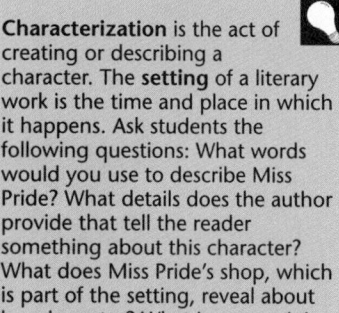
They were sections Four and Five, bent and dusty, but intact, Mark saw with relief. "Don't you suppose you have any more anywhere?" he pleaded.

"I'll look in the cellar but I can't promise. I haven't had deliveries of any of these for a long time. Made by some foreign firm they were; people didn't seem very keen on them," Miss Pride said <u>aggrievedly</u>. She opened a door revealing a flight of damp stone stairs. Mark followed her down them like a bloodhound on the trail.

The cellar was a fearful confusion of mildewed, tattered, and toppling cartons, some full, some empty. Mark was nearly knocked cold by a shower of pilchards[6] in tins, which he dislodged onto himself from the top of a heap of boxes. At last Miss Pride, with a cry of triumph, unearthed a little cache[7] of Brekkfast Brikks, three packets which turned out to be the remaining sections, Six, One, and Two.

"There, isn't that a piece of luck now!" she said, looking quite faint with all the excitement. It was indeed rare for Miss Pride to sell as many as five packets of the same thing at one time.

Mark galloped home with his <u>booty</u> and met his father on the porch. Mr. Armitage let out a groan of dismay.

"I'd almost rather you'd bought a space gun," he said. Mark chanted in reply:

"Brekkfast Brikks for supper too
Give peaceful sleep the whole night through."

"I don't want peaceful sleep," Mr. Armitage said. "I intend to spend tonight mouse-watching again. I'm tired of finding footprints in the Stilton."[8]

During the next few days, Mark's parents watched anxiously to see, Mr. Armitage said, whether Mark would start to sprout esparto grass instead of hair. For he <u>doggedly</u> ate Brekkfast Brikks for lunch, with soup, or sprinkled over his pudding; for tea, with jam; and for supper, lightly fried in dripping; not to mention, of course, the immense helpings he had for breakfast, with sugar and milk. Mr. Armitage, for his part, soon gave out; he said he wouldn't taste another Brekkfast Brikk even if it were wrapped in an inch-thick layer of *paté de foie gras*.[9] Mark regretted that Harriet, who was a handy and uncritical eater, was still away, convalescing from her measles with an aunt.

> **GUIDED READING**
> How often does Mark eat Brekkfast Brikks?

In two days, the second packet was finished (sundial, paved garden, and espaliers).[10] Mark cut it out, fastened it together, and joined it on to Section Three with trembling hands. Would the spell work for this section, too? He sang the rhyme in rather a quavering voice, but luckily the plywood door was shut, and there was no one to hear him. Yes! The gate grew again above him, and when he opened it and ran across the lawn through the yew arch, he found himself in a flagged[11] garden full of flowers like huge blue cabbages.

Mark stood hugging himself with satisfaction, and then began to wander about smelling the flowers, which had a spicy perfume most unlike any flower he could think of. Suddenly he pricked up his ears. Had

---

6. **pilchards.** Small fish
7. **cache.** Secret, hidden supply
8. **Stilton.** Sharp British cheese
9. ***paté de fois gras.*** Puréed goose livers
10. **espaliers.** Trees trained to grow on a trellis
11. **flagged.** Loosely hanging

---

words for everyday use

ag • grieved (ə grēv′ id) *adj.*, troubled or distressed. *The <u>aggrieved</u> hostess cried over the borken dishes.* **aggrievedly,** *adv.*

boo • ty (boot′ ē) *n.*, any gain, prize, or gift. *The pirates hid their stolen <u>booty</u> in a chest and buried it.*

dog • ged (dôg′ id) *adj.*, stubborn; persistent. *Although the celebrity refused to be interviewed, the <u>dogged</u> reporters followed her around.* **doggedly,** *adv.*

The Pheasantry, from "Fragments on the Theory and Practice of Landscape Gardening," 1816.
Humphry Repton. Private Collection.

ART SMART

In the late eighteenth century and early nineteenth century, a movement called Romanticism changed the arts of writing and the visual arts. Romanticism also changed the way people designed gardens. Humphry Repton was one of the most well-known and admired landscape designers of this period. Repton believed a house should be surrounded by formal gardens that gradually gave way to a more natural and untamed landscape. He filled his gardens with reproductions of Roman and Greek ruins and Chinese pagodas. Thomas Jefferson brought the Romantic style of landscaping to the United States when he built his estate at Monticello.

CROSS-CURRICULAR ACTIVITIES

APPLIED ARTS. Encourage students to find other images of famous gardens. Students should go to their school or local library and find some books that show gardens to share with their classmates. Encourage students to explore both European gardens and Japanese gardens, so they might compare the two. Students will note that most European and Japanese gardens are much more elaborate than those commonly found in the United States.

1. Mark hears somebody crying. He
can't see anything but grayness and
mist and a flash of white and gold
draperies.
2. Mark cannot remember the tune
that works the spell to transport
him to the garden.

LITERARY TECHNIQUE

DIALECT. A dialect
is a version of a
language spoken by the people of a
particular place, time, or group. In
this story, Mark's dialect of English
emerges in his interjections ("Oh,
blow" and "Jolly useful") as well as in
phrases such as "Need I go?" instead
of the American equivalent, "Do I
have to go?" Ask students to identify
examples of dialectal speech in this
selection. They should write these
dialectal phrases on one side of a
sheet of paper. On the other side,
they should write down what they
would say instead in their own
dialect. You should point out to
students that, just like Mark, they too
speak a dialect of English particular
to their time and place.

he caught a sound? There! It was like
somebody crying and seemed to come from
the other side of the
hedge. He ran to the next
opening and looked
through. Nothing; only
gray mist and emptiness. But, unless he had
imagined it, just before he got there, he
thought his eye had caught the flash of
white-and-gold draperies swishing past the
gateway.

> **GUIDED READING**
> What sound does
> Mark hear? What
> does he see?

"Do you think Mark's all right?" Mrs.
Armitage said to her husband next day. "He
seems to be in such a dream all the time."

"Boy's gone clean off his rocker, if you ask
me," grumbled Mr. Armitage. "It's all these
doormats he's eating. Can't be good to stuff
your insides with moldy jute.[12] Still, I'm
bound to say he's cut the lawn very decently
and seems to be remembering the coal. I'd
better take a day off from the office and drive
you over to the shore for a picnic; sea air will
do him good."

Mrs. Armitage suggested to Mark that he
should slack off on the Brekkfast Brikks, but
he was so horrified that she had to abandon
the idea. But, she said, he was to run four
times round the garden every morning before
breakfast. Mark almost said, "Which garden?"
but stopped just in time. He had cut out and
completed another large lawn, with a lake and
weeping willows; and on the far side of the
lake he had a <u>tantalizing</u> glimpse of a figure
dressed in white and gold who moved away
and was lost before he could get there.

After munching his way through the fourth
packet, he was able to add on a broad grass
walk bordered by curiously clipped trees. At
the end of the walk, he could see the white-
and-gold person; but when he ran to the spot,

no one was there—the walk ended in the
usual gray mist.

When he had finished and had cut out the
fifth packet (an orchard), a terrible thing
happened to him. For two days he could not
remember the tune that worked the spell. He
tried other tunes, but they
were no use. He sat in the
playroom singing till he
was hoarse or silent with
despair. Suppose he never remembered it
again?

> **GUIDED READING**
> What couldn't Mark
> remember?

His mother shook her head at him that
evening and said he looked as if he needed a
dose. "It's lucky we're going to Shinglemud
Bay for the day tomorrow," she said. "That
ought to do you good."

"Oh, *blow*. I'd forgotten about that," Mark
said. "Need I go?"

His mother stared at him in utter astonishment.

But in the middle of the night he remembered the right tune, leaped out of bed in a
tremendous hurry, and ran down to the
playroom without even waiting to put on his
dressing gown and slippers.

The orchard was most wonderful, for
instead of mere apples, its trees bore oranges,
lemons, limes, and all sorts of tropical fruits
whose names he did not know; and there
were melons and pineapples growing, and
plantains[13] and avocados. Better still, he saw
the lady in her white and gold waiting at the
end of an alley and was able to draw near
enough to speak to her.

"Who are you?" she asked. She seemed
very much astonished at the sight of him.

---

12. **jute.** Strong rope made from plant fibers
13. **plantains.** Banana-like fruit

---

words for everyday use

tan • ta • liz • ing (tan' tə liz' ing) *adj.*, tempting. *Liz knew she shouldn't eat her sister's chocolate, but it looked so tantalizing she had to take a bite.*

"My name's Mark Armitage," he said politely. "Is this your garden?"

Close to, he saw that she was really very grand indeed. Her dress was white satin embroidered with pearls, and swept the ground; she had a gold scarf and her hair, dressed high and powdered, was confined in a small, gold-and-pearl tiara. Her face was rather plain, pink with a long nose, but she had a kind expression and beautiful gray eyes.

"Indeed it is," she announced with <u>hauteur</u>. "I am Princess Sophia Maria Louisa of Saxe-Hoffenpoffen-und-Hamster. What are you doing here, pray?"

"Well," Mark explained cautiously, "it seemed to come about through singing a tune."

"Indeed. That is most interesting. Did the tune, perhaps, go like this?"

The princess hummed a few bars.

"That's it! How did you know?"

"Why, you foolish boy, it was I who put the spell on the garden, to make it come alive when the tune is played or sung."

"I say!" Mark was full of admiration. "Can you do spells as well as being a princess?"

She drew herself up. "Naturally! At the court of Saxe-Hoffenpoffen, where I was educated, all princesses were taught a little magic; not so much as to be <u>vulgar</u>, just enough to get out of social difficulties."

"Jolly useful," Mark said. "How did you work the spell for the garden, then?"

"Why, you see," (the princess was obviously delighted to have somebody to talk to; she sat on a stone seat and patted it, inviting Mark to do likewise) "I had the misfortune to fall in love with Herr Rudolf, the Court Kapellmeister,[14] who taught me music. Oh, he was so kind and handsome! And he was most talented, but my father, of course, would not hear of my marrying him because he was only a common person."

"So what did you do?"

"I arranged to vanish, of course. Rudi had given me a beautiful book with many pictures of gardens. My father kept strict watch to see I did not run away, so I used to slip between the pages of the book when I wanted to be alone. Then, when we decided to marry, I asked my maid to take the book to Rudi. And I sent him a note telling him to play the tune when he received the book. But I believe that spiteful Gertrud must have played me false and never taken the book, for more than fifty years have now passed and I have been here all alone,

waiting in the garden, and Rudi has never come. Oh, Rudi, Rudi," she exclaimed, wringing her hands and crying a little, "where can you be? It is so long—so long!"

"Fifty years," Mark said kindly, reckoning that must make her nearly seventy. "I must say you don't look it."

"Of course I do not, dumbhead. For me, I make it that time does not touch me. But tell me, how did you know the tune that works the spell? It was taught me by dear Rudi."

"I'm not sure where I picked it up," Mark confessed. "For all I know it may be one of the Top Ten. I'll ask my music teacher; he's

---

14. **Kapellmeister.** Conductor of music or of a musical group in Germany

---

hau • teur (hō tur') *n.*, disdainful pride; snobbery. *The king was so full of <u>hauteur</u> that he refused to speak with anyone of low rank.*

vul • gar (vul' gər) *adj.*, crude; distasteful. *Today we think it <u>vulgar</u> to eat with our hands, but that was common practice during medieval banquets.*

ANSWERS TO GUIDED READING QUESTIONS

1. The woman reacts with astonishment to seeing Mark.
2. The princess hums the magic tune that allows Mark to get into the garden.
3. The princess has been in the garden for fifty years.

ADDITIONAL QUESTIONS AND ACTIVITIES

When the princess asks Mark where he heard the tune that works the garden, saying "It was taught me by my dear Rudi," Mark says, "I'll ask my music teacher; he's sure to know. Perhaps he'll have heard of your Rudolf, too." Ask students to predict what will happen when Mark asks Mr. Johansen, his music teacher, about the tune and about Rudolf.

1. Mark plans to ask his music teacher where he might have heard the tune.
2. Mark suddenly thinks that if he should forget the tune while inside the garden, the lonely princess could hold him there.

CROSS-CURRICULAR ACTIVITIES

MATHEMATICS AND SCIENCES AND APPLIED ARTS. On the first day your students begin this selection, show a travel video of famous gardens. On the next day, invite a local gardener or landscape artist to speak with students on how to plant a garden and what might grow best in the soil around the school. With permission from the school, let each class come up with a design for a small garden at school. The students can then plant a small garden. Ask the guest speaker if he or she could donate material to the school (i.e., plants, seeds, and gardening tools) in exchange for a small sign in the garden, such as "Courtesy of Foliage by Flora." As an alternative, have students plant a terrarium. They might keep it in the classroom or donate it to a hospice, daycare center, or nursing home when it is completed.

sure to know. Perhaps he'll have heard of your Rudolf, too."

> **GUIDED READING**
> Whom does Mark plan to ask about the tune?

Privately, Mark feared that Rudolf might very well have died by now, but he did not like to depress Princess Sophia Maria by such a suggestion; so he bade her a polite good night, promising to come back as soon as he could with another section of the garden and any news he could pick up.

He planned to go and see Mr. Johansen, his music teacher, next morning, but he had forgotten the family trip to the beach. There was just time to scribble a hasty post card to the British office of Fruhstucksgeschirrz-iegelsteinindustrie, asking them if they could inform him from what source they had obtained the pictures used on the packets of Brekkfast Brikks. Then Mr. Armitage drove his wife and son to Shinglemud Bay, gloomily <u>prophesying</u> wet weather.

In fact, the weather turned out fine, and Mark found it quite restful to swim and play beach cricket and eat ham sandwiches and lie in the sun. For he had been struck by a horrid thought: suppose he should forget the tune again when he was inside the garden—would he be stuck there, like Father in the larder? It was a lovely

> **GUIDED READING**
> What horrid thought struck Mark?

place to go and wander at will, but somehow he didn't fancy spending the next fifty years there with Princess Sophia Maria. Would she <u>oblige</u> him by singing the spell if he forgot it, or would she be too keen on company to let him go? He was not inclined to take any chances.

It was late when they arrived home, too late, Mark thought, to disturb Mr. Johansen,

who was elderly and kept early hours. Mark ate a huge helping of sardines on Brekkfast Brikks for supper—he was dying to finish Section Six—but did not visit the garden that night.

Next morning's breakfast (Brikks with hot milk for a change) finished the last packet—and just as well, for the larder mouse, which Mr. Armitage still had not caught, was discovered to have nibbled the bottom left-hand corner of the packet, slightly damaging an ornamental <u>grotto</u> in a grove of lime trees. Rather worried about this, Mark decided to make up the last section straightaway, in case the magic had been affected. By now he was becoming very skillful at the tiny, fiddling task of cutting out the little tabs and slipping them into the little slots; the job did not take long to finish. Mark attached Section Six to Section Five and then, drawing a deep breath, sang the <u>incantation</u> once more. With immense relief, he watched the mossy wall and rusty gate grow out of the playroom floor; all was well.

He raced across the lawn, round the lake, along the avenue, through the orchard, and into the lime grove. The scent of the lime flowers was sweeter than a cake baking.

Princess Sophia Maria came towards him from the grotto, looking slightly put out.

"Good morning!" she greeted Mark. "Do you bring me any news?"

"I haven't been to see my music teacher yet," Mark confessed. "I was a bit anxious because there was a hole."

"Ach, yes, a hole in the grotto! I have just been looking. Some wild beast must have made its way in, and I am afraid it may come again. See, it has made tracks like those of a

words for everyday use

proph • e • sy (präf′ ə si′) v., predict. *I <u>prophesied</u> that the class play would be a failure, but instead it was a great success.*

ob • lige (ə blīj′) v., do a favor for. *Because Jorge had done a favor for me, I gladly <u>obliged</u> him when he needed help with his homework.*

grot • to (grät′ ō) n., cavelike house or shrine. *Ancient peoples built <u>grottoes</u> where they would worship their gods.*

in • can • ta • tion (in′ kan tā′ shən) n., magic spell. *The magician sang an <u>incantation</u> and then pulled a rabbit out of his hat.*

big bear." She showed him some enormous footprints in the soft sand of the grotto floor. Mark stopped up the hole with prickly branches and promised to bring a dog when he next came, though he felt fairly sure the mouse would not return.

GUIDED READING

What "wild beast" has made a hole in the grotto?

"I can borrow a dog from my teacher—he has plenty. I'll be back in an hour or so—see you then," he said.

"*Auf Wiedersehen*,[15] my dear friend."

Mark ran along the village street to Mr. Johansen's house, Houndshaven Cottage. He knew better than to knock at the door because Mr. Johansen would be either practicing his violin or out in the barn at the back, and in any case the sound of barking was generally loud enough to drown any noise short of gunfire.

Besides giving music lessons at Mark's school, Mr. Johansen kept a guest house for dogs whose owners were abroad or on holiday. He was extremely kind to the guests and did his best to make them feel at home in every way, finding out from their owners what were their favorite foods, and letting them sleep on his own bed, turn about. He spent all his spare time with them, talking to them and playing either his violin or long playing records of domestic sounds likely to appeal to the canine fancy—such as knives being sharpened, cars starting up, and children playing ball games.

Mark could hear Mr. Johansen playing Brahms' lullaby in the barn, so he went out there; the music was making some of the more <u>susceptible</u> inmates feel homesick: howls, sympathetic moans, and long, shuddering sighs came from the numerous comfortably carpeted cubicles all the way down the barn.

Mr. Johansen reached the end of the piece as Mark entered. He put down his fiddle and smiled welcomingly.

"*Ach, how gut!* It is the young Mark."

"Hullo, sir."

"You know," confided Mr. Johansen, "I play to many audiences in my life all over the world, but never anywhere do I get such a response as from zese dear doggies—it is really remarkable. But come in, come into ze house and have some coffee cake."

Mr. Johansen was a gentle, white-haired, elderly man; he walked slowly with a slight stoop and had a kindly, sad face with large, dark eyes. He looked rather like some sort of dog himself, Mark always thought, perhaps a collie or a long-haired dachshund.

"Sir," Mark said, "if I whistle a tune to you, can you write it down for me?"

"Why, yes, I shall be most happy," Mr. Johansen said, pouring coffee for both of them.

So Mark whistled his tune once more. As he came to the end, he was surprised to see the music master's eyes fill with tears, which slowly began to trickle down his thin cheeks.

"It recalls my youth, zat piece," he explained, wiping the tears away and rapidly scribbling crotchets and minims[16] on a piece of music paper. "Many times I am whistling it myself—it is wissout doubt from me you learn it—but always it is reminding me of how happy I was long ago when I wrote it."

"You *wrote* that tune?" Mark said, much excited.

---

15. *Auf Wiedersehen.* "Goodbye" in German
16. **crochets and minims.** Musical notation

words for everyday use

sus • cep • ti • ble (sə sep' tə bəl) *adj.*, easily affected or influenced. *Once you have had chicken pox, you are no longer <u>susceptible</u> to the disease.*

1. The "wild beast" is actually the mouse that chewed a hole in part of the Brekkfast Brikks box.

LITERARY TECHNIQUE

CHARACTER. A **character** is a person or animal who takes part in the action of a literary work. A **major character** is one who plays an important role in a literary work. A **minor character** is one who plays a lesser role in a literary work. Ask your students the following questions: Is Mark a major character, a minor character, or the main character? What types of characters are his parents, the princess, Miss Pride, and Mr. Johansen? In what ways are the characters of Miss Pride and Mr. Johansen similar? Ask students to explain their answers.

Answers. Mark is the main character. His parents are minor characters, since they do not participate in the major events of the story. The princess should be considered a major character because she plays an important role in the story and participates in the major events. Miss Pride is a minor character, even though she sells the Brekkfast Brikks packages, because she does not participate in the major events of the story. Mr. Johansen is a major character, even though he is introduced late in the story, because he is the princess's long-lost love—a character of central importance to the story. Miss Pride and Mr. Johansen are similar in that they both are portrayed as strange, but likable, characters.

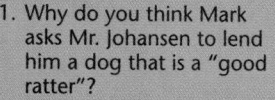 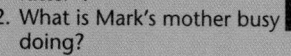
"Why yes. What is so strange in zat? Many, many tunes haf I written."

"Well—" Mark said, "I won't tell you just yet in case I'm mistaken—I'll have to see somebody else first. Do you mind if I dash off right away? Oh, and might I borrow a dog—preferably a good ratter?"

"In zat case, better have my dear Lotta—alzough she is so old she is ze best of zem all," Mr. Johansen said proudly. Lotta was his own dog, an enormous, shaggy, lumbering animal, with a tail like a palm tree and feet the size of electric polishers. She was reputed to be of <u>incalculable</u> age; Mr. Johansen called her his strudel hound. She knew Mark well and came along with him quite <u>biddably</u>, though it was rather like leading a mammoth.

Luckily, his mother, refreshed by her day at the sea, was heavily engaged with Agnes the maid in spring cleaning. Furniture was being shoved about, and everyone was too busy to notice Mark and Lotta slip into the playroom.

A letter addressed to Mark lay among the clutter on the table; he opened and read it while Lotta <u>foraged</u> happily among the piles of magazines and tennis nets and cricket hats and rusting electronic equipment, managing to upset several things and increase the general state of huggermugger in the room.

> Dear Sir, (the letter said—it was from Messrs. Digit, Digit, & Rule, a firm of chartered accountants)—We are in receipt of your inquiry as to the source of pictures on packets of Brekkfast Brikks. We are pleased to inform you that these were reproduced from the illustrations of a little-known 18th-century German work, *Steinbergen's Gartenbuch.* Unfortunately, the only known remaining copy of this book was burnt in the disastrous fire that destroyed the factory and premises of Messrs. Fruhstucks-geschirrziegelsteinindustrie two months ago. The firm has now gone into liquidation and we are winding up their effects.
>
> *Yours faithfully,*
>
> P. J. ZERO, Gen. Sec.

"*Steinbergen's Gartenbuch,*" Mark thought. "That must have been the book that Princess Sophia used for the spell—probably the same copy. Oh, well, since it's burned, it's lucky the pictures were reproduced on the Brekkfast Brikks packets. Come on, Lotta, let's go and find a nice princess then. Good girl! Rats! Chase 'em!"

He sang the spell and Lotta, all enthusiasm, followed him into the garden.

They did not have to go far before they saw the princess—she was sitting sunning herself on the rim of the fountain. But what happened then was unexpected. Lotta let out the most extraordinary cry—whine, bark, and howl all in one—and hurled herself towards the princess like a rocket.

"Hey! Look out! Lotta! *Heel!*" Mark shouted in alarm. But Lotta, with her great paws on the princess' shoulders, had about a yard of salmon-pink tongue out, and was washing the princess' face all over with frantic affection.

The princess was just as excited. "Lotta, Lotta! She knows me. It's dear Lotta; it must

---

words for everyday use

in • cal • cu • la • ble (in kal′ kyə lə bəl) *adj.*, uncertain. *I spent <u>incalculable</u> hours looking for my diary.*

bid • da • ble (bid′ ə bəl) *adj.*, obedient. *The <u>biddable</u> dog followed all of his master's commands.* **biddably,** *adv.*

for • age (fär′ ij) *v.*, rummage; browse for food. *The horse <u>forages</u> in the pasture all summer.*

The Vinery, from "Fragments on the Theory and Practice of Landscape Gardening," 1816.
Humphry Repton. Private Collection.

be! Where did you get her?" she cried to Mark, hugging the enormous dog, whose tail was going round faster than a turbo prop.

"Why, she belongs to my music master, Mr. Johansen, and it's he who made up the tune," Mark said.

The princess turned quite white and had to sit down on the fountain's rim again.

"*Johansen?* Rudolf Johansen? My Rudi! At last! After all these years! Oh, run, run, and fetch him immediately, please! Immediately!"

Mark hesitated a moment.

"Please make haste!" she besought him. "Why do you wait?"

"It's only—Well, you won't be surprised if he's quite *old*, will you? Remember he

hasn't been in a garden keeping young like you."

"All that will change," the princess said confidently. "He has only to eat the fruit of the garden. Why, look at Lotta—when she was a puppy, for a joke I gave her a fig from this tree, and you can see she is a puppy still, though she must be older than any other dog in the world! Oh, please hurry to bring Rudi here."

"Why don't you come with me to his house?"

"That would not be correct <u>etiquette</u>," she said with dignity. "After all, I *am* royal."

"Okay," said Mark. "I'll fetch him. Hope he doesn't think I'm crackers."

words for everyday use

et • i • quette (et' i kit) *n.*, social rules; manners. *It is proper <u>etiquette</u> in Japan to remove one's shoes when entering a home.*

ADDITIONAL QUESTIONS AND ACTIVITIES

Ask students to discuss what they think of the princess's personality. What words would they use to describe her? Why do they think she is this way? Can they see why the music teacher might have loved her? Why do you think the author chose to portray the princess in this way? *Answers.* Students may suggest that the princess is bossy and self-centered. They may suggest that she may be partly this way because she is royalty and spoiled, but she may also have lost some of her manners from being alone for so long. *Responses will vary.* Students may suggest that the author portrayed the princess this way to make the story more humorous.

ART SMART

Encourage students to discuss *The Vinery.* What elements of architecture are used in this part of the garden? What elements of nature are used? *Answers.* Architectural elements include an immense arch that vines can climb across, attached trellises, fences, and statues. Elements of nature include grape vines, flowers, ivy, and potted plants.

1. Mrs. Armitage has burned the
cardboard garden.

LITERARY TECHNIQUE

SUSPENSE AND COMIC RELIEF.
Suspense is a feeling of
anxiousness or curiosity. Writers
create suspense by raising
questions in the reader's mind
and by using details that create
strong emotions. Point out to
students that the author builds
suspense in this scene by having
Mark urge Mr. Johansen to hurry.
Mark and Mr. Johansen are deterred
by having to feed sixty dogs, each of
which requires a different meal. After
this, Mark runs "rings" around old
Mr. Johansen as he walks slowly to
Mark's house. Point out that this
scene is also an example of **comic
relief**—the use of a funny scene in a
serious or suspenseful work to relieve
the intensity felt by the reader or
audience.
Ask students how they feel about this
delay in the action of the story. Did it
heighten their interest, anxiety, or
curiosity? Ask students what they
think will happen. Will Mr. Johansen
arrive in time to be reunited with the
princess, or will something disastrous
occur? Ask students to support their
opinions with reasons.

"Give him this." The princess took off a
locket on a gold chain. It had a miniature of a
romantically handsome young man with dark,
curling hair. "My Rudi," she explained fondly.
Mark could just trace a faint resemblance to
Mr. Johansen.

He took the locket and hurried away. At the
gate, something made him look back; the
princess and Lotta were sitting at the edge of
the fountain, side by side. The princess had
an arm round Lotta's neck; with the other
hand she waved to him, just a little.

"Hurry!" she called again.

Mark made his way out of the house,
through the spring-cleaning chaos, and flew
down the village to Houndshaven Cottage.
Mr. Johansen was in the house this time,
boiling up a <u>noisome</u> mass of meat and
bones for the dogs' dinner. Mark said
nothing at all, just handed him the locket.
He took one look at it and staggered,
putting his hand to his heart; anxiously,
Mark led him to a chair.

"Are you all right, sir?"

"Yes, yes! It was only ze shock. Where did
you get ziss, my boy?"

So Mark told him.

Surprisingly, Mr. Johansen did not find
anything odd about the story; he nodded his
head several times as Mark related the various
points.

"Yes, yes, her letter, I have it still—" he
pulled out a worn little scrap of paper, "but ze
Gartenbuch, it reached me never. Zat wicked
Gertrud must haf sold it to some bookseller
who sold it to Fruhstucksgeschirrziegelstein-
industrie. And so she has been waiting all zis
time! My poor little Sophie!"

"Are you strong enough to come to her
now?" Mark asked.

"*Natürlich!* But first we must give
ze dogs zeir dinner; zey must not go hungry."

So they fed the dogs, which was a long job, as
there were at least sixty and each had a different
diet, including some very odd preferences like
Swiss roll spread with Marmite and yeast pills
wrapped in slices of caramel. Privately, Mark
thought the dogs were a bit spoiled, but Mr.
Johansen was very careful to see that each
visitor had just what it fancied.

"After all, zey are not mine! Must I not take
good care of zem?"

At least two hours had gone by before the
last willow-pattern plate was licked clean and
they were free to go. Mark made rings round
Mr. Johansen all the way up the village. The
music master limped quietly along, smiling a
little. From time to time he said, "Gently, my
friend. We do not run a race. Remember, I
am an old man."

That was just what Mark did remember. He
longed to see Mr. Johansen young and happy
once more.

The chaos in the Armitage house had
changed its location. The front hall was now
clean, tidy, and damp; the rumpus of
vacuuming had shifted to the playroom. With
a black hollow of apprehension in his middle,
Mark ran through the open door and
stopped, aghast. All the toys, tools, weapons,
boxes, magazines, and bits of machinery had
been rammed into the cupboards; the floor
where his garden had been laid out was bare.
Mrs. Armitage was in the playroom taking
down the curtains.

"*Mother!* Where's my Brekkfast Brikks
garden?"

"Oh, darling, you didn't
want it, did you? It was all
dusty; I thought you'd

> **GUIDED READING**
> What has happened
> to the cardboard
> garden?

words for everyday use

noi • some (noi′ səm) *adj.*, offensive to the sense of smell. *The <u>noisome</u> garbage cans made taking out the trash the worst chore of all.*

finished with it. I'm afraid I've burned it in the furnace. Really you *must* try not to let this room get into such a clutter; it's perfectly disgraceful. Why, hullo, Mr. Johansen," she added in embarrassment. "I didn't see you. I'm afraid you've called at the worst possible moment. But I'm sure you'll understand how it is at spring-cleaning time."

She rolled up her bundle of curtains, glancing worriedly at Mr. Johansen; he looked rather odd, she thought. But he gave her his tired, gentle smile, and said, "Why, yes, Mrs. Armitage, I understand, I understand very well. Come, Mark. We have no business here; you can see."

Speechlessly, Mark followed him. What was there to say?

"Never mind," Mrs. Armitage called after Mark. "The Rice Nuts pack has a helicopter on it."

Every week in *The Times* newspaper you will see this advertisement:

> BREKKFAST BRIKKS PACKETS. £100 offered for any in good condition, whether empty or full.

So, if you have any, you know where to send them.

But Mark is growing anxious; none have come in yet, and every day Mr. Johansen seems a little thinner and more elderly. Besides, what will the princess be thinking?

■

Respond *to the* SELECTION

Do you think anybody will ever answer Mark's advertisement? Why, or why not?

About *the* AUTHOR

Born in 1924 in Sussex, England, **Joan Aiken** grew up telling stories. She and her brother exchanged stories about made-up fantasy lands as they walked in the countryside near the family's home. Aiken was fascinated with mysterious places and happenings and loved to read stories by Charles Dickens, an author whose style rubbed off on her, as well as books by Rudyard Kipling, Edgar Allan Poe, and Jane Austen.

Aiken has written more than 40 books for young people and more than 20 books for adults, in addition to numerous short stories. She strives to write material that makes young people think, that treats young people respectfully, and that includes the problems and dilemmas that occur in real life. Aiken says that an "internal monitor" guides her in her writing style. Her two children are her favorite reviewers and critics.

"THE SERIAL GARDEN" **191**

LITERARY NOTE

Achieving (or losing) everlasting life after a long struggle is a common theme in literature. In literature and popular belief, immortality and everlasting youth have been associated with special fruits, plants, and fountains, or with a gift from the gods. Inform students that many cultures have created myths and legends about heroes who struggle for and attain or lose everlasting life. Ask students to compare Mr. Johansen's just missing a chance to eat the fruit of renewed youth with similar events in other stories they know. If they have read the retelling of "The Epic of Gilgamesh," in Unit 7, that tale may come to mind.

Quotables

"'Tis better to have loved and lost Than never to have loved at all."

—Alfred, Lord Tennyson

RESPOND TO THE SELECTION

You might also ask students to discuss what Mr. Johansen might be thinking and feeling about having lost his true love twice.

Checking Your Reading
1. What brand of cereal does Mark buy at Miss Pride's store? **Mark buys Breakfast Brikks.**
2. Why does Mark ask his mother not to throw away the empty cereal carton? **Mark wants to construct the cardboard garden from the empty cereal carton.**
3. What does Mark do to enter the garden? **Mark whistles the theme song for Breakfast Brikks.**
4. Who does Mark meet in the garden? **Mark meets Princess Sophia Maria Louisa.**
5. What happens when Mark's mother cleans the playroom? **Mark's mother destroys the garden.**

Vocabulary in Context
Fill in each blank below with the most appropriate Word for Everyday Use. You may have to change the tense of the word.

> vigil wan repulsive obtain
> doggedly tantalizing susceptible

1. After Joan tumbled down the side of the mountain, the other campers kept a careful **vigil** until help arrived in the morning.
2. Although Ashton said he was feeling better, his **wan** face suggested that he was still ill.
3. Everything served at the fine restaurant was delicious, but Edward couldn't wait to sample the **tantalizing** offerings on the dessert tray.
4. Anita jumped when Mark held the **repulsive** snake toward her.
5. Allan and Kendra stuck **doggedly** to the trail as darkness fell.

Reader's Toolbox
Fill in the blanks using the following terms. You may not use every term, and you may use some terms more than once.

> foreshadowing character allusion
> setting homophone

1. **Foreshadowing** is the act of hinting at events that will happen later in a poem, story, or play.
2. A(n) **homonym** is a word that sounds like another word but is spelled differently and has a different meaning.
3. The **setting** of a literary work is the time and place in which it happens.

Pop Art

Artists—such as the creator of the garden pictures on Mark's Breakfast Brikks boxes—have long been involved in advertising. Many products and their packaging, from cereal boxes to clothing labels, contain art made to help sell the product. Print advertisements in magazines and on billboards also include art. The images associated with the product are intended to evoke a particular feeling or atmosphere—homey, comfortable, cutting edge, or jazzy—to attract potential buyers. As advertising and mass marketing became a driving force in the economy, artists began exploring the art-advertising relationship in what became known as Pop Art.

Pop Art had its real start in London with a 1956 exhibition called "This is Tomorrow." For hundreds of years, art had been about a few geniuses struggling to communicate their inner thoughts through unique masterpieces. But Pop artists were after something fresh, and they responded to what they saw around them—a fast-paced urban world overflowing with cheap, mass-produced goods. In one of the first Pop Art pieces, "Homage to Chrysler Corp," British artist Richard Hamilton showed how cars were being designed not only for performance but also for visual appeal — just like any artwork. His painting focused on the sculptural forms in the fins, bumpers and taillights of new American cars.

Many Pop artists actually came from the advertising world. James Rosenquist was a bill-

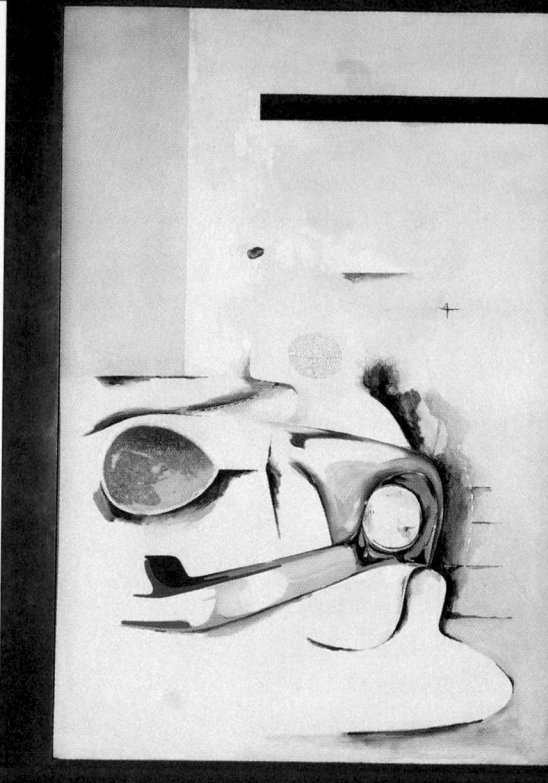

Homage to Chrysler Corp., 1957.
Richard Hamilton. Tate Gallery, London.

board painter, and his art reflects his background. His painting of Marilyn Monroe is billboard size—over seven feet tall. Its fragmented pieces replicate the way we experience images as we speed by billboards or casually glance at the TV. The work is not really a portrait of Marilyn Monroe but a portrait of the image of the movie star.

Andy Warhol began his career illustrating ads for department stores. He called his studio "The Factory" and used mass production methods to manufacture his paintings. The

Two Hundred Campbell's Soup Cans, 1962. Andy Warhol.
Rose Art Museum, Brandeis University, Waltham, Massachusetts.

results were sloppy, garish canvases that resembled newspaper ads and mocked "fine art." His subjects were drawn from his everyday life. He painted rows of Campbell's soup cans, for example, because that is what he had for lunch every day.

Warhol's paintings became instantly famous. He was just as famous for his cool, detached personality. He seemed bored, blank, and empty, as if overwhelmed by popular culture. He summed up Pop Art by saying, "It's about liking things."

Is Pop Art really art? By moving an object that we hardly think of otherwise into an art context, Pop Art makes us think about an object in other ways. For example, what is the difference between a beautiful painting in a museum and a beautiful juice bottle on a store shelf?

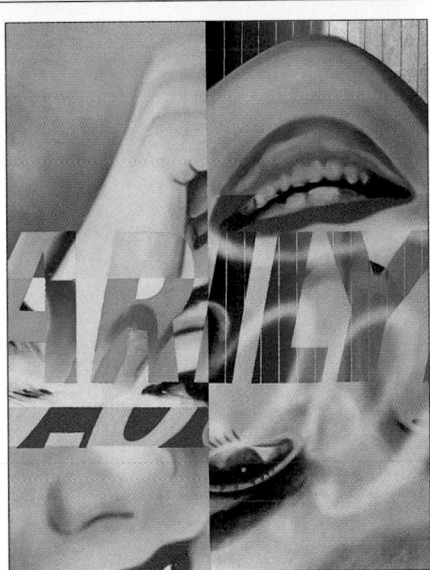

Marilyn Monroe I, 1962. James Rosenquist.
Museum of Modern Art, New York.

"THE SERIAL GARDEN" **193**

RECALL

1a. Mark buys the first box because all the family's cereal is locked in the larder.

2a. When Mark sings the jingle on the side of the box to a catchy tune in his head, the garden becomes life-sized.

3a. Mark meets Princess Sophia Maria Louisa in the garden. She is there by magic to await the arrival of her true but forbidden love, Rudolf.

INTERPRET

1b. Mark is not happy with the new cereal's taste, but he is happy with the cutout garden on the box.

2b. Mark keeps the garden a secret because he thinks it will be a good hiding place.

3b. The story does not provide an explanation of how someone would live in the garden for fifty years. The princess does mention that time does not touch her and that she knows some magic, which is a partial explanation.

ANALYZE

4a. The princess realizes that Rudolf is alive and nearby when she sees Lotta the dog, but she does not go to find him because it would not be proper etiquette. Rudolf realizes that the princess is alive and nearby when he sees her locket, but he does not go to her immediately because he has to feed the dogs he cares for.

SYNTHESIZE

4b. Students may say that both the princess and Rudolf are set in their ways—the princess in her love of old-fashioned etiquette and Rudolf in his life of caring for so many dogs. Students may say the lost opportunity can be blamed on the fact that both characters are set in their ways and don't prioritize immediately reuniting with their long-lost loves above their own routines and rituals. Students may say this casts some doubt on the strength of their love.

EVALUATE

5a. *Responses will vary. A possible response is given.* The story has a stronger ending because it breaks from the traditional "happily ever after" mode and offers an ending that is fresh and surprising.

EXTEND

5b. Students should write their own original happy endings.

Investigate, Inquire, and Imagine

Recall: GATHERING FACTS

1a. What circumstances cause Mark to bring the first box of Brekkfast Brikks into his home?

2a. What action causes Mark's cutout garden to change to a life-sized garden?

3a. Whom does Mark meet inside the garden? Why is she there?

→ Interpret: FINDING MEANING

1b. Is Mark happy with his new cereal? Why, or why not?

2b. Why does Mark keep the garden a secret?

3b. Does the story provide a logical explanation for this person's ability to live in the garden? (For example, does it tell what or how she eats or how she knows that fifty years have passed?) Explain.

Analyze: TAKING THINGS APART

4a. In what ways do Rudolf and the princess themselves prevent their own reunion from occurring?

→ Synthesize: BRINGING THINGS TOGETHER

4b. Why do Rudolf and the princess act as they do? What character traits would you blame for Rudolf and the princess's lost opportunity?

Evaluate: MAKING JUDGMENTS

5a. This story could have ended with Rudolf and the princess living happily ever after in the garden. Do you think the ending it has is stronger or weaker than a happily-ever-after ending?

→ Extend: CONNECTING IDEAS

5b. Write a final segment to "The Serial Garden," giving the story a happy ending.

Understanding Literature

FORESHADOWING. Foreshadowing is the act of hinting at events that will happen later in a poem, story, or play. Early in "The Serial Garden," Mr. Armitage comments that the garden on the cereal box looks like an eighteenth-century German engraving. This comment hints at the later discovery that the source of the drawing no longer exists. More important foreshadowing occurs in three hints about the eventual destruction of the cardboard garden. What hints were given that the garden would be destroyed?

ANSWERS TO UNDERSTANDING LITERATURE

FORESHADOWING. Students may point to the following three hints: the fact that Mark's mother is described as often throwing away items when she cleans the playroom, the fact that the only remaining copies of the illustration were burned in a fire, and the fact that the mouse partially destroyed the garden on the last box.

SETTING. Students may say that the story is set in England in the twentieth century (most likely earlier in the century). Students may point to terms such as *larder, blimey, hullo,* and *jolly useful;* the address of the Brekkfast Brikks company; the fact that pence and shillings are used as monetary units; the fact that cereal costs eleven pence a packet; and the fact that the Armitage family has tea as a meal after lunch each day.

Setting. The **setting** of a literary work is the time and place in which it happens. Writers create settings in many different ways. In fiction, setting is most often revealed by means of descriptions of landscape, scenery, buildings, furniture, clothing, the weather, and the season. It can also be revealed by how characters talk and behave. This story has two settings, the real world and the world of the garden. What time and place do you think the "real world" of this story is set in? What details give clues as to the setting?

Writer's Journal

1. Imagine that you have discovered a secret garden at the back of your closet, or through a special picture of some kind. What would it be like? Write a **paragraph** describing this imaginary garden, and how you discovered it.

2. Imagine that you are Princess Sophia Maria Louisa at the end of "The Serial Garden," and you are wondering why Rudolf has not arrived. Write a **journal entry** from her point of view, going over the possibilities and resigning yourself to a life without true love.

3. Imagine that the princess and Rudolf do reunite. Write the **scene** of their reunion as the script of a play.

Skill Builders

Applied English
Writing a Business Letter. In "The Serial Garden," Mark writes a letter to the factory of Fruhstucksgeschirrziegelstein-industrie, asking about the source of the pictures on the Brekkfast Brikks boxes. Write the letter he would have written, using proper business-letter form, formal tone, and correct spelling, grammar, usage, and punctuation. Refer to the Language Arts Survey 6.6, "Writing a Business Letter."

Media Literacy & Collaborative Learning
Advertising. Form groups of four students and work together to write an advertising jingle like the Brekkfast Brikks song. The jingle should promote a food or product that is generally not considered tasty or exciting. What descriptive words or associations could you use to make the product more appealing to consumers? Describe what advertising techniques you used in your jingle. See the Language Arts Survey 5.3, "Avoiding False Arguments and Propaganda," for ideas. If possible, decide on a tune for the jingle and perform it in front of the class.

ANSWERS TO SKILL BUILDERS

Applied English
Writing a Business Letter. You might wish to have students peer edit and review each other's letters for content, form, and tone. Refer them to the Language Arts Survey 2.37, "Self- and Peer Evaluation." Then have students exchange papers with a partner and review one another's work. Each student should review and incorporate the suggestions of his or her partner, and then turn in both the original and edited versions of the letter.

Media Literacy and Collaborative Learning
Advertising. Encourage students to brainstorm lists of ways they might sell a food they don't particularly like. Students' ideas may range from the practical (for example, pointing out that the food is healthy) to the humorous (for example, suggseting that people can use the food for other things, such as using hard cereal to stuff bean bag chairs). In writing their jingles, students should use false arguments and propaganda as described in the Language Arts Survey 5.3.

(Continued on page 196)

ANSWERS TO
SKILL BUILDERS (CONT.)

Vocabulary

UNDERSTANDING BASE WORDS AND PREFIXES. Student responses should include the following information.

1. preview (*pre-* means "before," so preview means "a viewing held *before*" [the movie's release])
2. reread (*re-* means "again," so reread means "read again")
3. misjudged (*mis-* means "wrong" or "badly," so misjudged means "judged badly"
4. insecurity (*in-*, like *im-*, means "not," so insecurity means "the state of not being secure.")
5. impossible (*im-* means "not," so impossible means "not possible")
6. disembarked (*dis-* means "not" or "opposite," so disembarked means "got off," which is the opposite of embarked)
7. substandard (*sub-* means "below," so substandard means "below standards")
8. retraced (*re-* means again, so retraced means "trace, or go over, again")
9. overqualified (*over-* means "beyond," so overqualified means "beyond qualified")
10. overcome (*over-* means "beyond," so overcome means "to come [or go] beyond" something, like an obstacle)

Vocabulary

UNDERSTANDING BASE WORDS AND PREFIXES. Many words are formed by adding prefixes to a base. Knowing what the prefix or base of a word means may help you figure out the meaning of that word. For example, if you do not know what the word *multilingual* means, but you know that the prefix *multi-* means "many" and the base *lingual* means "of language," you can determine that *multilingual* means "of many languages."

The following chart shows some common prefixes, their meanings, and ways to use them. For other examples see the Language Arts Survey 1.19, "Learning Base Words, Prefixes, and Suffixes."

Prefix	Meaning	Example	Meaning
bi–	two, twice	bicultural	of two cultures
im–	against, not	impossible	not possible
mis–	wrong, badly	misguide	guide badly
pre–	before	preflight	before the flight

Complete each sentence with a word from the following list. Explain why the word you chose makes sense in the sentence, using what you know about prefixes.

dicover	nonbeliever	preview	reread
disembarked	overcome	repay	substandard
impossible	overdo	retraced	uncover
insecurity	overqualified	retried	underqualified
misjudged	preread	review	unwashed

1. Last night the producers and their guests saw the movie before its release to the public. The _____ was well received.
2. Mark read the instructions again. In other words, he _____ them.
3. At first I thought the new student was a snob. But when I saw how friendly he was, I realized I'd _____ him.
4. The modern world doesn't always feel safe and secure. It is full of _____.
5. Mark could not enter the garden now that the models were destroyed. Unless he could find more cereal boxes, it would be _____ to reach the princess.
6. One hour after the airplane landed, the passangers _____.
7. The manufacturer rejected the _____ parts.
8. When I discovered my watch was missing, I _____ my steps through the neighborhood.
9. Lotta's extensive college education made her _____ for the job.
10. Rudi has had to _____ many difficulties in his life.

Prereading

"An Unforgettable Journey"
by Maijue Xiong

Reader's Resource

- **HISTORY CONNECTION.** The Hmong (pronounced muŋ) are an ethnic group from Asia. The Hmong migrated from Mongolia, a region in the north of China, into the Yellow River valley of China around 2500 BC. Around 251 BC, they moved again, traveling southwest to the Yangtze River. In the mid 1800s, they settled in the mountain jungles of Southeast Asia, in what are now the countries of North and South Vietnam, Laos, and Thailand. The Hmong moved so often because they had many conflicts with the Chinese over land and taxes, and were searching for freedom. Freedom is very important to the Hmong people. In fact, some scholars believe the word *Hmong* means "free."

- In 1954, the people of Laos and Vietnam won their independence from France, which had controlled most of Southeast Asia since the 1860s. At the same time Communist groups, who believed that all people should share wealth and resources equally, began fighting to take control of governments in Southeast Asia. The United States entered Vietnam to fight against the Communists, starting a conflict now known as the Vietnam War. The U.S. government also began a war in Laos, organizing thousands of Hmong soldiers to fight against the Lao Communists, or Pathet Lao. However, the government didn't tell the American people about the war in Laos for many years. For this reason, the war in Laos is sometimes called "The Secret War." Thousands of Hmong men and boys fought against the Pathet Lao with the help of aid and supplies from the American Central Intelligence Agency (CIA). In 1975 the Pathet Lao won the war. When they did, all the Hmong who had been fighting with the CIA against the Pathet Lao were in danger. The Pathet Lao killed many Hmong people and destroyed their villages. The Hmong became refugees—people who had to flee their homeland in search of safety. Many of them, such as the family in the selection you are about to read, were eligible to emigrate, or move to, the United States. California, Minnesota, and Wisconsin are home to the majority of Hmong Americans.

Reader's Journal

Write about an unforgettable journey you have taken or an experience you have had that has helped you grow as a person.

Reader's TOOLBOX

AUTOBIOGRAPHY and **POINT OF VIEW.** An **autobiography** is the story of a person's life, written by that person. This selection is an example of autobiography, written by a young Hmong woman living in the United States. Most autobiographies use the first-person **point of view**, in which the narrator uses words such as *I* and *we* and is part of, or witness to, the action. As you read, think of words you would use to describe this and other autobiographical works.

CHRONOLOGICAL ORDER. Events arranged in order of the time when they happened are said to be in **chronological order**. This method of organization is used in most stories, whether they are fiction or nonfiction. The first part of this selection is written entirely in chronological order. In what other ways could a piece of writing be arranged?

GOALS/OBJECTIVES

Studying this lesson will enable students to
- enjoy an autobiography and identify with its narrator
- briefly describe the history of the Hmong and the "Secret War" in Laos
- define *autobiography* and recognize the *point of view* of an autobiography
- define *chronological order* and identify when events are written in this order
- identify and distinguish between prepositions, conjunctions, and interjections
- conduct an interview
- work as part of a group to research southeast Asia

INDIVIDUAL LEARNING STRATEGIES

MOTIVATION
Students may especially enjoy "reading" the storycloth on page 205 and completing its accompanying Critical Thinking activity on page 208. You might encourage students to present a story from their own childhood using a visual medium such as a drawing, painting, sculpture, model, or diorama.

READING PROFICIENCY
Ask students to list the main idea of each paragraph to check their comprehension. This will also provide students with a good summary of the story to aid them in answering the Investigate, Inquire, and Imagine questions.

ENGLISH LANGUAGE LEARNING
Point out the following vocabulary words and expressions:
bamboo shoots—young growth of a woody, sometimes hollow type of grass
ration—fixed portion or share

SPECIAL NEEDS
Tell students to focus on the Guided Reading Questions and the Recall questions in Investigate, Inquire, and Imagine. Students may also benefit from seeing small groups of students enact different scenes from the story. Encourage them to work with other students to enact one of the scenes themselves.

ENRICHMENT
Students may be interested in learning about another southeast Asian country that was tragically affected by the war in Vietnam—Cambodia. Have students research the struggles in Cambodia during the Vietnam War, the reign of the Khmer Rouge under Pol Pot following the Vietnam War, or the Vietnamese takeover of Cambodia.

AN UNFORGETTABLE JOURNEY

Maijue Xiong

I was born in a small village called Muong

Cha in Laos on April 30, 1972. At the time

I was born, my father was a soldier actively

fighting alongside the American Central

Intelligence Agency against the

Communists. Although a war was in

progress, life seemed peaceful. We did not

think of ever leaving Laos, but one day our

lives were changed forever.

CROSS-CURRICULAR CONNECTION

HISTORY. The Central Intelligence Agency (CIA) was founded in 1947 to keep the government informed about foreign activities that might affect the United States in some way. The CIA is in charge of so-called "intelligence activities," meaning the gathering of secret information. The CIA is also in charge of preventing other country's intelligence agencies from gathering important information about the United States.

CROSS-CURRICULAR ACTIVITIES

Encourage students to form their own intelligence groups to research some past activities in which the CIA was involved. Each group should choose one of the subjects below and research it using the Internet, encyclopedias, other reference books, or books about the CIA. Each group should then present their findings to the class in a brief (four- or five-minute) presentation. Possible topics include:

- The activities of the CIA during the Bay of Pigs Crisis in Cuba
- CIA activities during the "Secret War" in Laos during the Vietnam War
- CIA involvement in the effort to sell arms to Iran to support the contra rebels who fought against the Nicaraguan government
- the scandal of Aldrich Ames, former CIA agent

VOCABULARY FROM THE SELECTION

agonizing	rampant
deprivation	refuge
nerve-wracking	refugee
obscure	transition

1. Maijue's family is forced to leave Laos when the country becomes Communist, because her father, who was a commanding officer with the CIA during the "Secret War," is now an enemy of the government and is in danger of being killed.
2. They travel at night and sleep during the day; people drug their children to prevent the Communist soldiers from hearing their cries; parents even abandon those children who won't stop crying.
3. Maijue compares the experience of leaving Laos to a bad dream, of which one only remembers bits and pieces.

CROSS-CURRICULAR CONNECTION

HISTORY. As students may learn if they complete the Enrichment Activity on page 198 of the Teacher's Edition, the people of Cambodia also experienced horrifying times during a Communist takeover. In 1975, Pol Pot and a group of Communist guerillas, or revolutionaries, known as the Khmer Rouge came into power after a civil war. The new Communist government ordered everyone to leave the cities and settled people in agricultural areas, forcing them to labor in the fields to grow rice and other staples. The Khmer Rouge did away with money and education, and killed intellectuals or people they suspected of once having been middle class or state officials. Eventually so many people were killed in these agricultural areas that they became known as "killing fields." Many more people died of hunger, disease, and exhaustion from being overworked. No one knows the exact number of people who were killed or died, but estimates are between two and four million, or about as many people who live in a state like Colorado or South Carolina. Ask students to think about what people do to survive under times of extreme oppression. How might such an experience forever alter a person's perception of the world around him or her?

We found ourselves without a home or a Country and with a need to seek refuge in another country. This period of relocation involved a lot of changes, adjustments, and adaptations. We experienced changes in our language, customs, traditional values, and social status.[1] Some made the transition quickly; others have never fully adjusted. The changes my family and I experienced are the foundation of my identity today.

After Laos became a Communist country in 1975, my family, along with many others, fled in fear of persecution.[2] Because my father had served as a commanding officer for eleven years with the American Central Intelligence Agency in what is known to the American public as the "Secret War," my family had no choice but to leave immediately. My father's life was in danger, along with those of thousands of others. We were forced to leave loved ones behind, including my grandmother who was ill in bed the day we fled our village. For a month, my family walked through the dense tropical jungles and rice fields, along rugged trails through many mountains, and battled the powerful Mekong River.[3] We traveled in silence at night and slept in the daytime. Children were very hard to keep quiet. Many parents feared the Communist soldiers would hear the cries of their young children; therefore, they drugged the children with opium to keep them quiet. Some parents even left those children who would not stop crying behind. Fortunately, whenever my parents told my sisters and me to keep quiet, we listened and obeyed.

> **GUIDED READING**
> Why is Maijue's family forced to leave Laos?

> **GUIDED READING**
> What actions show how desperate people were?

I do not remember much about our flight, but I do have certain memories that have been imprinted in my mind. It is all so unclear— the experience was like a bad dream: when you wake up, you don't remember what it was you had dreamed about but recall only those bits and pieces of the dream that stand out the most. I remember sleeping under tall trees. I was like a little ant placed in a field of tall grass, surrounded by a dense jungle with trees and bushes all around me—right, left, in the back, and in front of me. I also remember that it rained a lot and that it was cold. We took only what we could carry and it was not much. My father carried a sack of rice, which had to last us the whole way. My mother carried one extra change of clothing for each of us, a few personal belongings, and my baby sister on her back. My older sister and I helped carry pots and pans. My stepuncle carried water, dried meat, and his personal belongings.

> **GUIDED READING**
> To what does Maijue compare the experience of leaving Laos?

From the jungles to the open fields, we walked along a path. We came across a trail of red ants and being a stubborn child, I refused to walk over them. I wanted someone to pick me up because I was scared, but my parents kept walking ahead. They kept telling me to hurry up and to step over the ants, but I just stood there and cried. Finally, my father came back and put me on his shoulders, along with the heavy sack of rice he was carrying. My

---

1. **social status.** Position of a person in society, whether high, middle, or lower class
2. **persecution.** Act of injuring others or causing them to suffer, usually because of their beliefs
3. **Mekong River.** River in southeast Asia that forms part of the border between Laos and Thailand

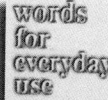

words for everyday use

ref • uge (re′ fyüj) n., shelter or protection from danger. *The hunted fox sought refuge from danger by hiding in its den.*

tran • si • tion (trān si′ shən) n., a passage from one condition or place to another. *Graduation from high school marks a transition into adulthood.*

dad said he carried me on his back practically all the way to Thailand.

I also recall a car accident we had. My father had paid a truckdriver to take my family and relatives to a nearby town. There were about fifteen of us in the truck. My father, along with the driver and my pregnant aunt, sat in front. The rest of us were in the bed of the truck. While going up a steep mountain, the truck got out of control and, instead of going uphill, started sliding downhill and off the road. Everyone was terrified, but with the help of God, the truck was stopped by a tree stump. Everyone panicked and scrambled out, except for my pregnant aunt who was trapped on the passenger's side because the door was jammed. The impact affected her so much that she could not crawl from her seat to the driver's side in order to get out. My father risked his life to save hers. The rest of us stood back and waited breathlessly as he tried to open the jammed door. He managed to free her just as the truck slid down the hill.

Our adventure did not end then—many nights filled with terror were yet to come. After experiencing many cold days and rainy nights, we finally saw Thailand on the other side of the Mekong River. My parents bribed several fishermen to row us across. The fishermen knew we were desperate, yet, instead of helping us,

> *I kept yelling, "We're going to fall out! We're going to fall into the river!"*

they took advantage of us. We had to give them all our valuables: silver bars, silver coins, paper money, and my mother's silver wedding necklace, which had cost a lot of money. When it got dark, the fishermen came back with a small fishing boat and took us across the river. The currents were high and powerful. I remember being very scared. I kept yelling, "We're going to fall out! We're going to fall into the river!" My mom tried to reassure me but I kept screaming in fear. Finally, we got across safely. My family, along with many other families, were picked up by the Thai police and taken to an empty bus station for the night.

After a whole month at this temporary <u>refugee</u> camp set up in the bus station, during which we ate rice, dried fish, roots we dug up, and bamboo shoots we cut down, and drank water from streams, we were in very poor shape due to the lack of nutrition. Our feet were also swollen from walking. We were then taken to a refugee camp in Nongkhai, where disease was <u>rampant</u> and many people got sick. My family suffered a loss: my baby sister, who was only a few months old, died. She had become very skinny from the lack of milk, and there was no medical care available. The memory of her death still burns in my mind like a flame. On the evening she died, my older sister and I were playing with our cousins outside the building where we stayed.

GUIDED READING

How does Maijue's family plan to cross the Mekong?

words for everyday use

ref • u • gee (re' fyoo jē') *n.*, a person who flees, especially someone who flees to a foreign country to escape danger. *The Bosnian <u>refugees</u>, whose homes had been bombed by Serbian planes, escaped their war-torn land by fleeing to other countries.*

ram • pant (ram' pant) *adj.*, wild or unrestrained. *As soon as their teacher left the room, the kindergarteners ran <u>rampant</u>.*

1. Maijue's baby sister dies of starvation and lack of medical care.
2. The Xiong family was prosperous before they were forced to leave Laos. They had enough money and were able to raise all their own food. They had a home, cattle, rice fields, and a garden. In the refugee camps, the family has no money or possessions and barely enough to eat.
3. Maijue's family was able to go to the United States because Maijue's father had been a soldier fighting with the Americans and because Maijue's stepuncle had gone there two years before and could sponsor them.
4. Leaving Thailand is painful for the refugees because they must leave relatives and loved ones behind, knowing they will probably never see these people again.

CROSS-CURRICULAR ACTIVITIES

SOCIAL STUDIES. Encourage students to work in groups of three or four to research the story of a group of refugees. Students should go to their school or local library to research their chosen group of people, using resources including encyclopedias, books, periodicals, and the Internet. Each group should take notes on their chosen group of people trying to find the answer to these essential questions, among other details:

- Why did this group of people have to flee? Was it because of their religious beliefs, their political beliefs, their ethnic background, or some other reason?
- Who or what forced these people to flee and how?
- In what manner did these people move from their old home to their new or temporary one?
- How many refugees died on the journey from one place to another?

Students should then prepare an oral report on their group of refugees, using visual aids if any are available. After giving their oral reports, students should present a

My father came out to tell us the sad news and told us to go find my stepuncle. After we found him, we went inside and saw our mother mourning the baby's death. Fortunately, our family had relatives around to support and comfort us.

GUIDED READING What happens to Maijue's baby sister?

Life in the refugee camp was very difficult. Rice, fish, vegetables, and water were delivered to the camp, but the ration for each family was never enough. Many times, the food my family received did not last until the next delivery. My parents went out to work in the fields to earn a little extra money to buy food. As a child, I did not understand why we had to work so hard and live so poorly.

When I left Laos, I was only three years old. I do not remember much of our life there, but my parents have told me that our family had been quite well off. We had our own house, cattle, rice fields, and a garden where all our vegetables were grown. The money my father received for serving in the army was saved, for there was little need for money. We had enough to eat because we grew our own food. The poor life in the camp is the only life I can remember. I saw my parents' suffering, but I was too young to understand why life was so difficult. Only later did I realize that I and thousands of other young children were victims of a cruel war. Our family remained in Nongkhai for three <u>agonizing</u> years, with our fate uncertain and our future <u>obscure</u>.

GUIDED READING How does the Xiong family's life in the refugee camps compare to their life before their escape?

Our family life in the camp was very unstable, characterized by <u>deprivation</u> and neglect. My older sister and I were left alone for days while my parents were outside the camp trying to earn money to buy extra food. My parents fought a lot during this period, because we were all under such stress. They knew that if we remained in Thailand, there would be no telling what would become of us. We had to find a better life. Some people in the camp were being sponsored to go to the United States. The news spread that anyone who had served in the military with the CIA could apply to go to America. Since my stepuncle had already gone there two years earlier, he sponsored my family. Because my father had been in the military and we had a sponsor, it took only six months to process our papers when usually it took a year or more.

GUIDED READING Why is Maijue's family able to go to the United States?

I can still recall the process of leaving the camp. Our relatives, whom we were leaving behind, walked my family from our house to the bus that was to take us to Bangkok. We boarded the bus with our few belongings. People hung out of the windows to touch loved ones for the last time. They cried, knowing they might never meet again. As the buses slowly made their way through the crowd, people ran after them calling out the names of their relatives. "Have a safe trip to your new home!" they shouted. "Don't forget us who are left behind! Please write and tell us about your new life!" Quickly the camp vanished out of sight . . . forever. The moments filled with laughter and tears shared with close friends and relatives were now just faint memories.

GUIDED READING Why is leaving Thailand so painful for the refugees?

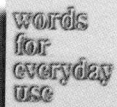

words for everyday use

ag • o • nizing (a' gə niz iŋ) *adj.*, painful. *The pain Moua felt when he broke his arm was <u>agonizing</u>.*

ob • scure (äb skyur') *adj.*, unclear or unknown. *John's understanding of his new job responsibilities was <u>obscure</u>.*

dep • ri • va • tion (de' prə vā' shən) *n.*, the state of being deprived; having something taken away. *The plant I left in the closet died from light <u>deprivation</u>.*

CROSS-CURRICULAR ACTIVITIES (CONT.)

list of their sources. You might suggest that students research one of the following groups or another in which they are interested:
- The boat people who fled from Vietnam
- Afghanistanian refugees who fled to Pakistan
- The refugees of Rwanda
- The Kurds who fled from Turkey
- The people of Kosovo who fled to Albania and neighboring countries

It took a full day to travel to Bangkok, where we stayed for four nights. The building we stayed in was one huge room. It was depressing and <u>nerve-wracking</u>. I especially remember how, when we got off the bus to go into the building, a small child about my age came up to my family to beg for food. I recall the exact words she said to my father, "Uncle, can you give me some food? I am hungry. My parents are dead and I am here alone." My dad gave her a piece of bread that we had packed for our lunch. After she walked away, my family found an empty corner and rolled out our bedding for the

night. That night, the same child came around again, but people chased her away, which made me sad.

In the morning, I ran to get in line for breakfast. Each person received a bowl of rice porridge with a few strips of chicken in it. For four days, we remained in that building, not knowing when we could leave for the United States. Many families had been there for weeks, months, perhaps even years. On the fourth day, my family was notified to be ready early the next morning to be taken to the airport. The plane ride took a long time and I got motion sickness. I threw up a lot. Only when I saw my stepuncle's face after we landed did I know we had come to the end of our journey. We had come in search of a better life in the "land of giants."

On October 2, 1978, my family arrived at Los Angeles International Airport, where my uncle was waiting anxiously. We stayed with my uncle in Los Angeles for two weeks and then settled in Isla Vista because there were already a few Hmong families there. We knew only one family in Isla Vista, but later we met other families whom my parents had known in their village and from villages nearby. It was in Isla Vista that my life really began. My home life was now more stable. My mother gave birth to a boy a month after we arrived in the United States. It was a joyous event because the first three children she had were all girls. (Boys are desired and valued far more than girls in Hmong culture).

I entered kindergarten at Isla Vista Elementary School. The first day was scary

> **GUIDED READING**
>
> What do the refugees call the United States?

> **GUIDED READING**
>
> Why is Maijue's baby brother especially welcomed into the family?

"AN UNFORGETTABLE JOURNEY"   **203**

1. They call the United States the "land of giants."
2. Maijue's brother was the first son born into the family, and boys are more desired and valued than girls in Hmong culture.

ART SMART

Ask students to discuss the photograph on this page. What does the person pictured in the photograph seem to be feeling? What do they think this person's story is? Have students imagine that they took this photograph and entered it into a contest. What would they title their entry?
Answers. Responses will vary, but students should begin their discussion by noting that the person in the photograph is extremely sad and does not want to leave behind the person whose hand she is holding.

CROSS-CURRICULAR CONNECTION

HISTORY/CULTURE. Certain cultures have traditionally valued the birth of male babies more than female babies. In some cultures, notably in China, India, and Sri Lanka, parents have sometimes abandoned or killed unwanted girl babies. Christian churches have condemned the practice, and the Muslim's sacred writing, the Koran, forbids it. Increasingly, cultures that engage in this practice have been forced to abandon it due to condemnation in the world community. The practice, however, does resurface from time to time. Encourage students to discuss what it would be like to grow up female in a culture that values boy children more than girl children. Students may draw on their own experiences as points of comparison and contrast.

ADDITIONAL QUESTIONS AND ACTIVITIES

Ask students the following questions:

1. Why was the first day of school in the United States scary for the narrator? What made the experience easier for her?
2. What shocked the narrator about her classmates? What had the narrator never seen before?
3. What was the narrator introduced to on the first day of school? What object didn't she understand?
4. What does the narrator treasure now that she is older?
5. What attitude do the narrator's parents take toward her education? What have her parents never done themselves?
6. What fills the narrator with a sense of accomplishment?

Answers

1. The first day of school was scary for the narrator because she knew no English. The presence of her cousin made the experience easier for the narrator.
2. The faces of different colors shocked the narrator. She had never seen a blond-haired person before.
3. The narrator was introduced to coloring. She did not know what a crayon was for.
4. The narrator treasures the lessons her parents taught her, which gave her a sense of identity as a Hmong. One thing they taught her is that "nothing comes easy."
5. Her parents are supportive even though they never received an education themselves.
6. The knowledge that she is able to set an example for her younger siblings as the first member of the family to attend college fills her with a sense of accomplishment.

RESPOND TO THE SELECTION

Tell students that their experience need not be one as dramatic as the narrator's. They may recall a time when they were frightened because of worry or anxiety about some future event or because of a near accident. If students find it difficult to talk about their scary experiences, they might write about them in their personal journal instead.

---

because I could not speak any English. Fortunately, my cousin, who had been in the United States for three years and spoke English, was in the same class with me. She led me to the playground where the children were playing. I was shocked to see so many faces of different colors. The Caucasian students shocked me the most. I had never seen people with blond hair before. The sight sent me to a bench, where I sat and watched everyone in amazement. In class, I was introduced to coloring. I did not know how to hold a crayon or what it was for. My teacher had to show me how to color. I also soon learned the alphabet. This was the beginning of my lifelong goal to get an education . . .

Now that I am older, I treasure the long but valuable lessons my parents tried to teach us—lessons that gave me a sense of identity as a Hmong. "Nothing comes easy . . . ," my parents always said. As I attempt to get a college education, I remember how my parents have been really supportive of me throughout my schooling, but because they never had a chance to get an education themselves, they were not able to help me whenever I could not solve a math problem or write an English paper. Although they cannot help me in my schoolwork, I know in my heart that they care about me and want me to be successful so that I can help them when they can no longer help themselves. Therefore, I am determined to do well at the university. I want to become a role model for my younger brother and sisters, for I am the very first member of my family to attend college. I feel a real sense of accomplishment to have set such an example. ■

Respond *to the* SELECTION

What is the scariest experience you have had? How did you handle it?

About *the* AUTHOR

Maijue Xiong got her degrees in sociology and education at the University of California-Santa Barbara, where she also was a cofounder of the Hmong Club. Xiong is a member of the Asian Culture Committee. She lives with her husband in St. Paul, Minnesota, where she teaches at Galtier Magnet Elementary School.

ABOUT THE RELATED READING ➤

The following page shows an example of a Hmong **storycloth**—a pictoral representation of a story—created by **Mee Vang**, a resident of St. Paul, Minnesota. Many Hmong women are skilled at intricate embroidery, used in the ancient Hmong art form *paj ntaub* (pronounced pahn-dow) and in storycloths. Storycloths use pictures to narrate family histories or to tell of events. Until the 1900's, the Hmong people had no written language and passed along stories either orally or through pictures. Vang's storycloth describes her family's flight from Laos to Thailand and to the United States.

Checking Your Reading
1. Why was Maijue's father's life in danger when the Communists took over Laos in 1975? **Maijue's father's life was in danger because he had worked for the CIA against the Communists.**
2. How does the family get across the Mekong River to enter Thailand? **The family pays men to take them across the Mekong River in a boat.**
3. Which of Maijue's close relatives die in the refugee camp? **Maijue's baby sister dies while in the camp.**
4. Where did Maijue's family go after leaving the refugee camp? **Maijue's family emigrated to the United States. They lived in Los Angeles, and later Isla Vista, California.**
5. What is Maijue determined to do, and why? **Maijue is determined to do well in the university because she wants to be successful so she can care for her parents when they are older and also set an example for her younger siblings.**

Vocabulary in Context
Fill in each blank below with the most appropriate Word for Everyday Use.

> transition   refuge   deprivation
> patriarchal   hectic   mentor
> stereotypical

1. Our new neighbors introduced themselves the day we moved in, which helped ease the **transition** to our new home.
2. Many animal species that live in groups are **patriarchal**, but elephants usually live in large communities led by an old female.
3. Despite our attempts to plan well, the holiday season is always **hectic** as we race to shop, cook, and clean before our out-of-town relatives arrive.
4. Babette was not a **stereotypical** Homecoming Queen; she was shy, preferred chess to sports, and had never been a cheerleader.
5. The small hut offered **refuge** to the skiers caught by an unexpected snowstorm.

Reader's Toolbox
1. What is chronological order? **Chronological order is events arranged in order of the time they happened.**
2. From what point of view are autobiographies written? **Autobiographies are written from**

SELECTION CHECK TEST 4.3.5 WITH ANSWERS (CONT.)

the first-person point of view.
3. Is "An Unforgettable Journey" fiction or nonfiction? **"An Unforgettable Journey" is nonfiction.**
4. By about how many years does Maijue age from the beginning to the end of the selection? **Maijue ages about 18 years.**
5. What is the difference between internal and external conflict? **Internal conflict takes place** within a person, in the form of a decision or a choice; external conflict is conflict between a person and an outside force.

RECALL

1a. Maijue's family must leave Laos to escape persecution by the Communist government. They leave behind family and friends, including Maijue's grandmother, who is sick. They flee on foot through dense tropical jungles. They sleep during the day under the tall trees and travel at night.

2a. Life is hard in the refugee camp. Because of a lack of food and medicine, Xiong's baby sister dies. People in the camp don't have enough food to eat and the camp is filled with disease, poverty, and suffering.

3a. For the first time, Maijue is surrounded by English-speakers, people of different colors, and blond-haired children. She uses crayons and learns the alphabet. She is frightened by the language and astonished by seeing people of ethnic backgrounds unfamiliar to her.

INTERPRET

1b. The family risks their lives to escape because they believe that they will be persecuted and even killed under the Communists.

2b. Leaving the camp is difficult, even though the conditions are terrible, because people must part from other members of their family and loved ones. Those who are leaving know that it is unlikely that they will ever see these people again. Leaving is also hard because they are heading toward an uncertain future.

3b. Getting an education is important to Xiong because her parents support her schooling. She says they want her to be successful so she can help them one day when they can no longer help themselves. She also wants to be a role model for her younger siblings.

ANALYZE

4a. They overcome escaping from Laos and the Communists into Thailand; a harsh life and the death of Maijue's baby sister in the refugee camp in Thailand; the waiting list to be accepted into America; awaiting the trip to America in impoverished Bangkok; and the shock of experiencing another culture and language in the United States. *Responses will vary.*

SYNTHESIZE

4b. Xiong's story is about overcoming any obstacle to survive and thrive in the future, and education in

---

Investigate, Inquire, and Imagine

Recall: GATHERING FACTS

1a. Why does Xiong and her family have to flee from their home? Who do they have to leave behind? How do they get away? Where do they hide?

2a. What is life like for Xiong's family in the refugee camp in Thailand?

3a. What new things does Xiong experience in kindergarten? What frightens her? What astonishes her?

→ Interpret: FINDING MEANING

1b. Why are they willing to risk their lives to escape?

2b. Why is leaving the camp so difficult for Xiong's family and other families?

3b. Why is getting an education so important to Xiong?

Analyze: TAKING THINGS APART

4a. What obstacles do Xiong and her family face and overcome? Which of these obstacles are the most difficult to overcome?

→ Synthesize: BRINGING THINGS TOGETHER

4b. How does Xiong's story lead her to the conclusions she makes about the importance of education? How have her experiences shaped the person she has become?

Perspective: LOOKING AT OTHER VIEWS

5a. What event in Maijue Xiong's journey seems to have had the most impact on her? Which experience seems to have been the most frightening? the most gratifying? Explain why you think she felt strongly about these experiences.

→ Empathy: SEEING FROM INSIDE

5b. If you were Maijue Xiong, how would you react to each of the following?
- earning a poor grade
- a younger sibling who shunned his or her cultural heritage
- an insensitive remark about your ethnicity
- a request by your parents to quit school and care for them full time
- a plea by your mother to quit school, get married, and have children

---

ANSWERS TO INVESTIGATE, INQUIRE, IMAGINE (CONT.)

America is an important part of creating a successful future. Students may say her experiences have brought her very close to her family, as she is determined to help support her parents and serve as an example to her siblings.

PERSPECTIVE

5a. Life in the refugee camp and the hunger, disease, and poverty there, as well as the death of her sister,

seem to have made the most impact on Xiong, as she dwells on these experiences for several paragraphs. Being terrified that they would fall out of the boat as they were crossing the Mekong River was also a frightening memory. She seems most gratified about the way her parents support and encourage her education. Xiong may feel strongly

(Continued on page 207)

Understanding *Literature*

AUTOBIOGRAPHY. An **autobiography** is the story of a person's life, written by that person. This selection is an example of autobiography, written by a young Hmong woman living in the United States. Autobiographies are usually told from the *first-person point of view*, in which the narrator uses words such as *I* and *we* and is part of, or witness to, the action. What insight do you gain from reading an autobiography that you might not get from other types of writing? How might this story have been different if someone else had written it about Maijue?

CHRONOLOGICAL ORDER. Events arranged in order of the time when they happened are said to be in **chronological order**. This method of organization is used in most stories, whether they are fiction or nonfiction. The first part of this selection is written in chronological order. What clues signal to you that chronological order is being used? What other methods of organization could have been used in this selection? Explain. Refer to the Language Arts Survey 1.14, "Organizing Ideas," for help.

Writer's Journal

1. Imagine that you are an advice columnist for a children's magazine and that a child writes you asking for advice about how to fit in at a new school and in a new culture. Write an **advice column** containing both the question and a brief answer from you.
2. Make a **list** of the foods mentioned in "An Unforgettable Journey" and another list of the foods you most commonly eat, then compare and contrast the lists.
3. As a newspaper reporter, you have been assigned to write a story about Maijue Xiong. Prepare a list of **interview questions**. Try to ask questions for which you cannot find answers in "Unforgettable Journey."

Graphic *Organizer*

Create a time line like the one below to chart the events in Maijue's story. Begin with the time Maijue was born until the time she entered kindergarten, and include only the major events of the story. Exact dates are not needed.

ANSWERS TO INVESTIGATE, INQUIRE, IMAGINE (CONT.)

about her experiences because they are filled with loss, tragedy, and hope for a better life.

EMPATHY
5b. *Responses will vary. Possible responses are given.*
- Maijue might become determined to master the subject matter and succeed next time.
- She might share stories of their cultural heritage with her sibling to show its importance.
- She might point out that all people are capable of achieving success.
- Maijue might honor her parents' request by working part-time, but continue her education by going to school part-time.
- Maijue might tell her mother she will marry and have a family once she finishes school and establishes her own career.

ANSWERS TO UNDERSTANDING LITERATURE

AUTOBIOGRAPHY and **POINT OF VIEW.** Students might say that an autobiography allows you to know the thoughts of a person, since the person is writing about himself or herself. Maijue's story is told from the first-person point-of-view. If someone else had written the story, we may not have learned as much about Maijue's insights into all the events and situations that shaped her life. Students may say that the story may have lacked some of its dramatic impact and its immediacy.

CHRONOLOGICAL ORDER. Students may say that the use of transitions such as "after," "for a month," "from jungles to the open fields," "our adventure did not end there—many nights filled with terror were yet to come," and "after a whole month" are indications of time passing, and show that the story uses chronological order. Other clues having to do with time include "at the time," "after," "during this period," "in the morning," and "when." Other methods that might have been used include order of importance, by which Maijue could have written first about which life experiences affected her the most and then go on to write about which affected her less, and least. The selection could also have been ordered in spatial order, by which Maijue could have explained in detail the family's journey from point to point on the map.

GRAPHIC ORGANIZER

Students may include the following events on their time charts:

1972—Maijue is born April 30; father is fighting with CIA against Communists
1975—Laos becomes Communist; Xiong family flees
—1 month later, family arrives at Thai temporary refugee camp
—1 month later, the family is taken to another camp at Nongkhai; Maijue's baby sister dies
1978—Family applies for emigration to U.S.
—6 months later, application to go to the U.S. is accepted and family leaves Nongkhai for Bangkok
—October 2: Family arrives at Los Angeles airport
—2 weeks later, the family moves to Isla Vista
—November: Boy born to family
—Maijue starts kindergarten

Language, Grammar, and Style
PREPOSITIONS, CONJUNCTIONS, AND INTERJECTIONS

1. <u>in</u> = preposition; <u>on</u> = preposition
2. <u>behind</u> = preposition
3. <u>and</u> = conjunction; <u>over</u> = preposition; <u>but</u> = conjunction
4. <u>Oh</u> = interjection; <u>into</u> = preposition
5. <u>with</u> = preposition; <u>for</u> = preposition

Speaking and Listening
INTERVIEWING. Have students read the Language Arts Survey 4.7, "Communicating with Another Person," 4.11, "Being Considerate of Other Cultures and Communication Styles," and 4.12, "Overcoming Barriers to Effective Multicultural Communication." Students may wish to ask their interviewee whether he or she minds being tape recorded. Tape-recording will help students to recall their subject's responses exactly, especially if the interview subject speaks with a heavy accent.

Study and Research & Collaborative Learning
LEARNING ABOUT SOUTHEAST ASIA. Refer students to the Language Arts Survey 5.17, "How Library Materials Are Organized" and 5.25, "Using the Internet," for their research. Tell them to document their sources using the information in the Language Arts Survey 5.35, "Documenting Sources," as their guide and to use 5.16, "Taking Notes, Outlining, and Summarizing Information," as guidelines for the note-taking process. Students might also find 2.19, "Working with Time Lines" and 5.22, "Using Almanacs, Yearbooks, and Atlases," helpful for creating time lines and finding maps to use as models, respectively.

Critical Thinking
READING A STORYCLOTH. Responses will vary, but students may note that, like "Unforgettable Journey," the storycloth chronicles Hmong people's journey from villages in Laos to the United States. The storycloth shows Communist soldiers entering a village in Laos and people fleeing to the jungle, where they must camp out in hiding. It shows them traveling by boat across the river to Thailand and the refugee camps there. It shows people applying for emigration to the United States. Vang shows emotions such as fear and terror, when her family is fleeing from the soldiers, relief when crossing the river, and the joy the people feel upon receiving permission to emigrate. She also depicts an

Skill Builders

Language, Grammar, and Style
PREPOSITIONS, CONJUNCTIONS, AND INTERJECTIONS.  Do you know the difference between prepositions, conjunctions, and interjections? Review the Language Arts Survey 2.7, "Prepositions, Conjunctions, and Interjections." Then identify the underlined words in the sentences below as either one of the three.

1. Maijue was born <u>in</u> a small village called Muong Cha in Laos <u>on</u> April 30, 1972.
2. Her family was forced to leave loved ones <u>behind</u> when they left Laos.
3. Maijue needed to hurry <u>and</u> step <u>over</u> the ants, <u>but</u> she just stood there and cried.
4. "<u>Oh</u>, no! We're going to fall <u>into</u> the river!" Maijue thought.
5. The Xiong family stayed <u>with</u> Maijue's uncle <u>for</u> two weeks and then settled in Isla Vista.

Speaking and Listening
INTERVIEWING. Interview an immigrant from another country who is now living in your community to learn about his or her experiences. First, locate a person you could interview. It might be a relative, a neighbor, or someone in your school. Then ask his or her permission for an interview. Before conducting the interview, prepare a list of questions to ask and have your teacher or a peer review the questions for spelling, grammar, and style. You may want to include questions such as the following:

• What cultural differences did you encounter upon coming to the United States?

• What was the most difficult change? What was the most rewarding?

• How are living conditions in the United States different from those in his or her native country? How are they similar?

When you have finished prepare a short biography of your interview subject to share with other members of your class. For more information, see the Language Arts Survey 4.14, "Conducting an Interview."

Study and Research & Collabortive Learning

LEARNING ABOUT SOUTHEAST ASIA. In groups of four or five, research Laos, Vietnam, or Cambodia. Using Internet or library resources, find out about the present political structure of the country you choose, its geography, its population, its major languages and religions, its system of currency, and any other important information. Divide these tasks among the members of your group. For example, one person could research the country's history and create a time line charting major events. Another could draw a map showing the geographical features of the country or research its economy.

Critical Thinking
READING A STORYCLOTH. Look back at the storycloth by Mee Vang on page 205. Scan through the pictures from top to bottom, interpreting Vang's story as you go. How does her story compare to that of Maijue Xiong? How do they differ? What thoughts, emotions, and reflections does Vang show in her storycloth? How does she convey these ideas?

ANSWERS TO SKILL BUILDERS (CONT.)

airplane flying to the people's destination in the United States. Vang conveys thoughts, emotions, and reflections visually through representations of people and places.

Prereading

"The Inn of Lost Time"
by Lensey Namioka

Reader's Resource

- **HISTORY CONNECTION.** In feudal Japan (from the 1100s to the 1800s), the country was broken up into many domains, each held by a feudal lord, or land baron. Fighting between domains was common, and by the 1400s many barons built thick stone walls around their castles. Samurai made up the warrior class—the privileged elite—in feudal Japan. They were the only Japanese who were allowed to carry weapons (usually two swords). Following a special code of conduct, they swore themselves to a feudal lord, whose land they protected in exchange for payment. Masters of the martial arts, the samurai led a life of discipline, self-control, and watchfulness. In addition to samurai, two other classes made up each feudal domain: farmers (or peasants) and artisans (or craftspeople). Gradually, a merchant class also arose and eventually gained wealth and power. Each class led a very separate and distinct lifestyle, with no intermixing among them.

- This story takes place in Japan during the 1700s, when the country experienced famine and civil wars. During this time, Japanese landowners lost money and could not afford to keep debts. Many landowners could no longer afford to keep samurai, and these samurai wandered the countryside looking for work. As the merchant class grew wealthy, merchant families clustered in cities and earned money by trading goods. At the same time, peasants worked hard and still did not have enough to eat. Peasant uprisings were common during this period. While peasants wanted a better life with less suffering, landowners needed money to pay their debts. Meanwhile, merchants wanted to increase their wealth as much as possible, and samurai were looking for opportunities to be paid to defend others.

- "The Inn of Lost Time" draws on Japan's rich oral tradition. An **oral tradition** is a work, idea, or custom passed by word of mouth from generation to generation. The Japanese and many other cultures around the world have a rich tradition of passing stories on by telling them out loud rather than by writing them down. Works found in oral traditions include folk tales, fables, fairy tales, tall tales, nursery rhymes, proverbs, legends, myths, parables, riddles, charms, spells, and ballads. "The Inn of Lost Time" opens with the telling of a traditional Japanese folk tale and then continues with a tale told by Zenta, a wandering samurai.

Reader's Journal

If you were to wake up one morning and find you had slept for fifty years instead of one night, how would you feel? What would you miss the most?

Reader's TOOLBOX

FRAME STORY. A **frame story** opens and closes with the telling of one story, which forms a frame. Within that story another story is told. In this case the story within the story takes up most of the entire piece. The length of each component—the frame and the inner story—can vary. As you read "The Inn of Lost Time," consider why the author chose to use a frame around the inner story. What purpose does the frame serve?

FORESHADOWING. Foreshadowing is the act of hinting at events that will happen later in a literary work. As you read the story, look for places where the author uses foreshadowing and try to predict what will happen.

IRONY OF SITUATION. Irony of situation is an event that contradicts the expectations of the characters or the audience. If you were planning to leave on a camping trip the day your favorite relative unexpectedly arrived for a visit, you would experience irony of situation.

ADDITIONAL RESOURCES

UNIT 3 RESOURCE BOOK
- Selection Worksheet 3.4
- Selection Check Test 4.3.7
- Selection Test 4.3.8

READER'S JOURNAL

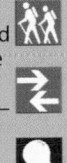

Encourage students to write about people, experiences, and opportunities they would have missed out on. How would they react to such a situation—try to make a new life for themselves, or try to get back to the life they once had?

VOCABULARY FROM THE SELECTION

compensate	inadequacy
decrepit	poignant
delusion	rapt
desolate	ravenous
despised	resemblance
dingy	rueful
escort	tantalizing
gilded	unwary
gruesome	vigorous
idle	

GOALS/OBJECTIVES

Studying this lesson will enable students to
- enjoy a story with an unexpected plot twist
- briefly state what a samurai is and what the situation was like in feudal Japan during the 1700s
- define *frame story* and point to both the frame and the story-within-the story in such works of fiction
- define *foreshadowing* and point to elements of foreshadowing in works that they read
- define *irony of situation* and recognize this type of irony in literary works
- use metaphors
- enact a scene
- research samurai using library materials
- critically view a film featuring samurai

MOTIVATION
Before they read the selection, point out to students that this mysterious story has a surprise ending. Students may be familiar with ghost stories and other stories that end with spooky revelations. Encourage students to sit in a circle and share some of the spooky or mysterious stories they have learned at sleepovers or at camp as part of their own oral tradition.

READING PROFICIENCY
Students may have trouble recognizing the shift from frame tale to the story-within-the story. Inform students that the frame of this story involves the visit of the two samurai to an inn owned by a farmer and his wife. One of the samurai, Zenta, then tells a story from his past, the story about an inn where time was lost. Zenta's story is "the story-within-the story." The action then shifts back to the present and the frame, at which time Zenta reveals something surprising about the inn in which they are staying. Have students create an outline of the main events in the story as they read. Whenever they feel they have "discovered" something about this story, with its many plot twists, they should add this information to their outline.

ENGLISH LANGUAGE LEARNING
Point out the following vocabulary words and expressions:
ronin—samurai without a master
statuettes—small statues
chopsticks—pair of slender sticks held between thumb and forefinger and used as a tool, usually for eating
bizarre—strange or unusual
panel—thin, rectangular piece of material used in a wall or door
basin—bowl
vandalize—damage
depressions—hollows or holes

SPECIAL NEEDS
As sharing stories through the oral tradition is a theme in this story, you might find a storyteller, perhaps an older student with an interest in acting, to read this story aloud to students as expressively as possible. Students might then read "The Inn of Lost Time" on their own, paying close attention to the Guided

The INN of LOST time

Lensey Namioka

Urashima Taro Catching a Turtle, c.1700s. Hatta Koshu. Kyoto National Museum, Japan.

INDIVIDUAL LEARNING STRATEGIES (CONT.)

Reading questions and writing out their answers as they read the story they have just heard.

ENRICHMENT
Inform students that to write this story Lensey Namioka had to research feudal Japan. Creative writers often have to do research to make their writing seem believable and accurate, especially when their writing is set in another place or time. Encourage students to write a brief work of fiction (a poem, description, or very short story) set in another place and time in which they are interested. Students should research this place and time before they write their fictional piece.

"Will you promise to sleep if I tell you a story?" said the father. He pretended to put on a stern expression.

"Yes! Yes!" the three little boys chanted in unison. It sounded like a nightly routine.

The two guests smiled as they listened to the exchange. They were wandering ronin, or unemployed samurai, and they enjoyed watching this cozy family scene.

GUIDED READING

Who was watching the cozy family scene?

The father gave the guests a helpless look. "What can I do? I have to tell them a story, or these little rascals will give us no peace." Clearing his throat, he turned to the boys. "All right. The story tonight is about Urashima Taro."

Instantly the three boys became still. Sitting with their legs tucked under them, the three little boys, aged five, four, and three, looked like a descending row of stone statuettes. Matsuzo, the younger of the two ronin, was reminded of the wayside half-body statues of Jizo, the God of Travelers and Protector of Children.

Behind the boys the farmer's wife took up a pair of iron chopsticks and stirred the ashes of the fire in the charcoal brazier.[1] A momentary glow brightened the room. The lean faces of the two ronin, lit by the fire, suddenly looked fierce and hungry.

The farmer knew that the two ronin were supposed to use their arms in defense of the weak. But in these troubled times, with the country torn apart by civil wars, the samurai didn't always live up to their honorable code.

GUIDED READING

How are the ronin supposed to use their arms? Why do they not always live up to this code of honor?

Then the fire died down again and the subdued red light softened the features of the two ronin. The farmer relaxed and began his story.

The tale of Urashima Taro is familiar to every Japanese. No doubt the three little boys had heard their father tell it before—and more than once. But they listened with rapt attention.

The tale of Urashima Taro is familiar to every Japanese.

Urashima Taro, a fisherman, rescued a turtle from some boys who were battering it with stones. The grateful turtle rewarded Taro by carrying him on his back to the bottom of the sea, where he lived happily with the Princess of the Underseas. But Taro soon became homesick for his native village and asked to go back on land. The princess gave him a box to take with him but warned him not to peek inside.

When Taro went back to his village, he found the place quite changed. In his home he found his parents gone and living there was another old couple. He was stunned to learn that the aged husband was his own son whom he had last seen as a baby. Taro thought he had spent only a pleasant week or two

1. **brazier.** Pan for holding burning coals

words for everyday use

rapt (rapt') adj., mentally engrossed or absorbed. *The rapt fans were silent as the pitcher wound up for the final pitch.*

ANSWERS TO GUIDED READING QUESTIONS

1. Two guests who are wandering ronin are watching.
2. They are supposed to defend the weak, but with the country torn apart by civil wars, they are left without jobs and sometimes use their arms for bad instead of good.

CROSS-CURRICULAR ACTIVITIES

ARTS AND HUMANITIES. The tale of Urashima Taro has been performed in Japanese theater. Encourage students to form groups of five or six to research a tradition form of Japanese theater, such as Noh, Kabuki, or puppet theater. Each member of the group should be in charge of researching a different aspect of the theater, such as the form of the theater or stage itself, the costumes or masks worn (or puppets used), the music of the theater, the types of plays performed, when the type of theater was popular, and so forth. (Students may wish to modify or change this list of aspects depending on the type of theater they choose and the information available in the sources they find.) Each group of students should then present its findings to the class. Encourage students to share visual images or representations of their form of theater. For example if students choose Noh theater, students may wish to bring in a papier mâché Noh mask, a model of a Noh stage, and/or a drawing of a Noh actor.

ADDITIONAL QUESTIONS AND ACTIVITIES

Ask students to think about children's stories they asked to hear over and over again when they were young children, as the farmer's three boys do. Have students compile a short list of such stories and then share their lists with the rest of the class. Are there any similarities? Are there any stories that can be considered class favorites?

1. He discovers that 72 years have passed and his village has changed dramatically. His parents and most of his old friends have died. Living in his parents' home is an old man and his wife. Taro discovers that the old man is actually his son, whom he last saw as a baby.

ART SMART

Utagawa Hiroshige (1797–1858) was a Japanese painter known for his paintings of beautiful landscapes. He was also an expert printmaker, but before he began his career as an artist he was a fire warden, an official whose duty was to fight and prevent fires. He was born Ando Hiroshige, but took the name of his art teacher Utagawa Toyohiro as a sign of respect, changing his name to Utagawa Hiroshige. He was the most popular artist of his day and created more than five thousand prints in his lifetime. Ask students to discuss what words they would use to describe the mood of this image. What emotions does it create in them?

LITERARY TECHNIQUE

FOLK TALE. A **folk tale** is a story passed by word of mouth from generation to generation. Ask students the following questions about this folk tale:
1. Why does the turtle carry Taro to the Princess of the Underseas?
2. What warning does the princess give Taro along with the box?
3. What does Taro find when he returns home?
4. How long did Taro think he had been away? How long was Taro actually away?
5. Why do you think Taro was away for longer than he thought?
6. How does Taro feel when he learns the truth? Why does he feel this way?
7. What happens to Taro when he opens the box?
8. Why do you think Taro decides to open the box?

Answers
1. The turtle carries Taro there because he is grateful to Taro for

Utsu Mountain at Okabe, 1833. Utagawa Hiroshige. Elvehjem Museum of Art, Madison, Wisconsin.

undersea with the princess. On land, seventy-two years had passed! His parents and most of his old friends had long since died.

> **GUIDED READING**
> When Taro returns home, what does he discover? How much time has elapsed?

Desolate, Taro decided to open the box given him by the princess. As soon as he looked inside he changed in an instant from a young man to a decrepit old man of more than ninety.

At the end of the story the boys were close to tears. Even Matsuzo found himself deeply touched. He wondered why the farmer had told his sons such a poignant bedtime story.

Wouldn't they worry all evening instead of going to sleep?

But the boys recovered quickly. They were soon laughing and jostling each other, and they made no objections when their mother shooed them toward bed. Standing in order of age, they bowed politely to the guests, and then lay down on the mattresses spread out for them on the floor. Within minutes the sound of their regular breathing told the guests that they were asleep.

Zenta, the older of the two ronin, sighed as he glanced at the peaceful young faces. "I wish I could fall asleep so quickly. The story of Urashima Taro is one of the saddest that I know among our folk tales."

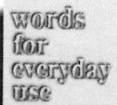

des • o • late (de′ sə lət) *adj.*, lonely, sad. *The desolate bear searched throughout the day for her cubs.*

de • crep • it (di kre′ pət) *adj.*, worn out, weakened from old age. *The roof of the decrepit old shack looked slightly caved in.*

poi • gnant (pói nyənt) *adj.* deeply affecting or touching; somber. *She cried at the poignant sight of the war-torn village.*

LITERARY TECHNIQUE (CONT.)

having rescued him from some boys who were throwing stones at him.
2. The princess tells Taro not to open the box.
3. Taro finds his parents gone and an aged couple, one of whom is his son who he had last seen as a baby, living in the home.
4. Taro thought he was away for a week or two, but he actually was missing for seventy-two years.
5. Students may say that the undersea kingdom

sounds magical, and Taro's sense of time there may have been altered.
6. Taro is desolate because most of his friends and family are long dead.
7. Taro's true age (more than ninety) is restored to him when he opens the box.
8. Students may suggest that Taro opens the box because he is so depressed he feels he has nothing left to lose.

The farmer looked proudly at his sleeping sons. "They're stout lads. Nothing bothers them much."

The farmer's wife poured tea for the guests and apologized. "I'm sorry this is only poor tea made from coarse leaves."

Zenta hastened to reassure her. "It's warm and heartening on a chilly autumn evening."

"You know what I think is the saddest part of the Urashima Taro story?" said Matsuzo, picking up his cup and sipping the tea. "It's that Taro lost not only his family and friends, but a big piece of his life as well. He had lost the most precious thing of all: time."

GUIDED READING

What does Matsuzo think is the saddest part of the Urashima Taro story?

The farmer nodded agreement. "I wouldn't sell even one year of my life for money. As for losing seventy-two years, no amount of gold will make up for that!"

Zenta put his cup down on the floor and looked curiously at the farmer. "It's interesting that you should say that. I had an opportunity once to observe exactly how much gold a person was willing to pay for some lost years of his life." He smiled grimly. "In this case the man went as far as one gold piece for each year he lost."

GUIDED READING

What did Zenta once have the opportunity to observe?

"That's bizarre!" said Matsuzo. "You never told me about it."

"It happened long before I met you," said Zenta. He drank some tea and smiled ruefully. "Besides, I'm not particularly proud of the part I played in that strange affair."

"Let's hear the story!" urged Matsuzo. "You've made us all curious."

The farmer waited expectantly. His wife sat down quietly behind her husband and folded her hands. Her eyes looked intently at Zenta.

"Very well, then," said Zenta. "Actually, my story bears some resemblance to that of Urashima Taro . . ."

> *"He had lost the most precious thing of all: time."*

It happened about seven years ago, when I was a green, inexperienced youngster not quite eighteen years old. But I had had a good training in arms, and I was able to get a job as a bodyguard for a wealthy merchant from Sakai.[2]

As you know, wealthy merchants are relatively new in our country. Traditionally the rich have been noblemen, landowners, and warlords with thousands of followers. Merchants, considered as parasites in our society, are a despised class. But our civil wars have made people unusually mobile and stimulated trade between various parts of the country. The merchants have taken advantage of this to conduct businesses on a scale our fathers could not imagine. Some of them have

GUIDED READING

What do the Japanese think of merchants? How and why has the position of merchants changed?

---

2. **Sakai.** A city in Japan

words for everyday use

rue • ful (rü′ fəl) *adj.*, regretful. *The rueful boy apologized to his sister after stepping on her doll.* **ruefully,** *adv.*

re • sem • blance (rē zem′ bləns) *n.*, likeness, similarity. *Vicki's singing voice had a striking resemblance to that of her grandmother.*

de • spised (di spizd) *adj.*, hated, regarded with dislike and hostility. *This week's school lunch menu includes the despised beef chip surprise.*

ANSWERS TO GUIDED READING QUESTIONS

1. Matsuzo thinks the saddest part is that Taro lost time—the most precious thing of all.
2. Zenta once observed exactly how much a person was willing to pay for some lost years of his life.
3. They are despised and thought to feed off the wealth of others, but civil wars have upset the traditional order of society and people are more able to move up or down the social ladder. The wars have also opened up trade between various parts of the country, and merchants can now conduct much more business than in the past, which has made some of them very wealthy.

ADDITIONAL QUESTIONS AND ACTIVITIES

Ask students to discuss whether they ever wish their time away. For example, do they ever think, "I wish the school year were over and that it could be summer now?" Do they ever think, "I can't wait until I am sixteen and I can drive?" Would they be willing to sell a few months or years of their time for money? Why, or why not?

Quotables

"But at my back I always hear Time's wingèd chariot hurrying near."

—Andrew Marvell, from *"To His Coy Mistress"*

1. It's important to remember that if the need should arise, Tokubei could always write a message home to have money forwarded to him if he needed more.
2. He had heard that the inns there were expensive and he didn't want to spend any more money than he had to.
3. They were hungry, and they were following the mouth-watering smell of freshly cooked rice and the vision of fluffy, freshly aired quilts.

LITERARY TECHNIQUE

NARRATOR AND REPETITION. A **narrator** is a person or character who tells a story. **Repetition** is the use, again, of a sound, word, or group of words. Share these definitions with students and then ask them the following questions:

1. Who is the narrator of the story that begins on page 213 and continues onto these pages?
2. Does the narrator stick to his role of narrating the story, or does he ever address his listeners directly?
3. Who are the narrator's listeners?
4. What example of repetition can you find when the narrator directly addresses his listeners? Why do you think the narrator repeats this sentence?
5. What else does the narrator say directly to his listeners?

Answers

1. Zenta, a ronin, is the narrator of the story.
2. Students should recognize that Zenta addresses his listeners directly from time to time.
3. The listeners are Zenta's companion Matsuzo, the farmer and his wife, as well as the reader of the story.
4. Zenta repeats that he is not proud of the part he played in the story he tells. Students may say that the repetition emphasizes that the story Zenta is about to tells is strange or embarrassing in some way.
5. The narrator says "It's important to remember this," after he says that Tokubei could send home for more money; and "Again, I should have been suspicious," when he reveals that he and Tokubei were the only guests.

---

become more wealthy than a warlord with thousands of samurai under his command.

The man I was <u>escorting</u>, Tokubei, was one of this new breed of wealthy merchants. He was trading not only with outlying provinces but even with the Portuguese from across the sea. On this particular journey he was not carrying much gold with him. If he had, I'm sure he would have hired an older and more experienced bodyguard. But if the need should arise, he could always write a message to his clerks at home and have money forwarded to him. It's important to remember this.

> **GUIDED READING**
>
> What does Zenta say it's important to remember?

The second day of our journey was a particularly grueling one, with several steep hills to climb. As the day was drawing to its close, we began to consider where we should spend the night. I knew that within an hour's walking was a hot-spring resort known to have several attractive inns.

> **GUIDED READING**
>
> Why didn't Tokubei want to go to the hot-spring resort for the night?

But Tokubei, my employer, said he was already very tired and wanted to stop. He had heard of the resort, and knew the inns there were expensive. Wealthy as he was, he did not want to spend more money than he had to.

While we stood talking, a smell reached our noses, a wonderful smell of freshly cooked rice. Suddenly I felt <u>ravenous</u>. From the way Tokubei swallowed, I knew he was feeling just as hungry.

We looked around eagerly, but the area was forested and we could not see very far in any direction. The <u>tantalizing</u> smell seemed to grow and I could feel the saliva filling my mouth.

"There's an inn around here, somewhere," muttered Tokubei. "I'm sure of it."

We followed our noses. We had to leave the well-traveled highway and take a narrow, winding footpath. But the mouth-watering smell of the rice and the vision of fluffy, freshly aired cotton quilts drew us on.

> **GUIDED READING**
>
> Why did they leave the well-traveled highway?

The sun was just beginning to set. We passed a bamboo grove, and in the low evening light the thin leaves turned into little golden knives. I saw a <u>gilded</u> clump of bamboo shoots. The sight made me think of the delicious dish they would make when boiled in soy sauce.

We hurried forward. To our delight we soon came to a clearing with a thatched[3] house standing in the middle. The fragrant smell of rice was now so strong that we were certain a meal was being prepared inside.

Standing in front of the house was a pretty girl beaming at us with a welcoming smile. "Please honor us with your presence," she said, beckoning.

There was something a little unusual about one of her hands, but, being hungry and eager to enter the house, I did not stop to observe closely.

You will say, of course, that it was my duty as a bodyguard to be suspicious and to look out for danger. Youth and inexperience should not have prevented me from wondering why an inn should be found

---

3. **thatched.** Covered with plant material such as straw

---

words for everyday use	
es • cort (es kort′) v., accompany or guide (someone or something). *I will <u>escort</u> you to your car.*
rav • en • ous (ra′ və nəs) adj., very eager for food. *Bill was <u>ravenous</u> after the long hike.*
tan • ta • liz • ing (tan təl iz iŋ) adj., teasingly out of reach. *The <u>tantalizing</u> pie on the windowsill made her stomach rumble.*
gild • ed (gild′ əd) adj., overlayed in golden color; appealing on the surface.

hidden away from the highway. As it was, my stomach growled, and I didn't even hesitate but followed Tokubei to the house.

GUIDED READING

What was odd about the location of the inn? Why wasn't Zenta suspicious?

Before stepping up to enter, we were given basins of water to wash our feet. As the girl handed us towels for drying, I saw what was unusual about her left hand: she had six fingers.

GUIDED READING

What was unusual about the girl's left hand?

Tokubei had noticed it as well. When the girl turned away to empty the basins, he nudged me. "Did you see her left hand? She had—" He broke off in confusion as the girl turned around, but she didn't seem to have heard.

The inn was peaceful and quiet, and we soon discovered the reason why. We were the only guests. Again, I should have been suspicious. I told you that I'm not proud of the part I played.

Tokubei turned to me and grinned. "It seems that there are no other guests. We should be able to get extra service for the same amount of money."

The girl led us to a spacious room which was like the principal chamber of a private residence. Cushions were set out for us on the floor and we began to shed our traveling gear to make ourselves comfortable.

The door opened and a grizzled-haired man entered. Despite his <u>vigorous</u>-looking face his back was a little bent and I guessed his age to be about fifty. After bowing and greeting us he apologized in advance for the service. "We have not always been innkeepers here," he said, "and you may find the accommodations lacking. Our good

intentions must make up for our inexperience. However, to <u>compensate</u> for our <u>inadequacies</u>, we will charge a lower fee than that of an inn with an established reputation."

GUIDED READING

Why did the innkeeper say he will charge a lower fee than other innkeepers?

Tokubei nodded graciously, highly pleased by the words of our host, and the evening began well. It continued well when the girl came back with some flasks of wine, cups, and dishes of salty snacks.

While the girl served the wine, the host looked with interest at my swords. From the few remarks he made, I gathered that he was a former samurai, forced by circumstances to turn his house into an inn.

Having become a bodyguard to a tight-fisted merchant, I was in no position to feel superior to a ronin turned innkeeper. Socially, therefore, we were more or less equal.

We exchanged polite remarks with our host while we drank and tasted the salty snacks. I looked around at the pleasant room. It showed excellent taste, and I especially admired a vase standing in the alcove.[4]

My host caught my eyes on it. "We still have a few good things that we didn't have to sell," he said. His voice held a trace of bitterness. "Please look at the panels of these doors. They were painted by a fine artist."

GUIDED READING

Why did the host's voice have a trace of bitterness?

Tokubei and I looked at the pair of sliding doors. Each panel contained a landscape painting, the right panel depicting a winter scene and the left one the same scene in late

---

4. **alcove.** Nook or small recessed part of a room

words for everyday use

vig • or • ous (vi′ gə rəs) *adj.*, active, lively; energetic. *The <u>vigorous</u> puppies wore me out after an hour of play.*

com • pen • sate (käm′ pən sāt) *v.*, balance, offset; repay. *The restaurant manager gave us a gift certificate to <u>compensate</u> for the poor service we received last night.*

in • ad • e • qua • cy (i na′ di kwə sē) *n.*, the quality or state of not being capable or sufficient. *The receptionist's cheerful personality made up for her <u>inadequacies</u> on the telephone.*

ANSWERS TO GUIDED READING QUESTIONS

1. It was odd that the inn was hidden away from the highway, but he was too hungry to be suspicious.
2. Her hand had six fingers.
3. He was inexperienced at innkeeping, and felt the accommodations might be lacking. The lower fee was meant to compensate for any inadequacies.
4. He regretted that he had to sell so many of his possessions to make ends meet.

LITERARY TECHNIQUE

STEREOTYPE. A **stereotype** is an unexamined, false idea about a type of person or group of people. Share this definition with students and ask them to identify the group of people that is negatively stereotyped in this story. In what way is this group of people negatively characterized? In what way have attitudes toward this group of people changed over time? *Answers.* Students should recognize that merchants are negatively stereotyped. They are characterized as being greedy "parasites in our society, a despised class." Tokubei the merchant is portrayed as materialistic and cheap, overly concerned with his gold. Zenta believes that it lowers his social standing greatly to work for Tokubei. Students may say that now there is no social stigma about being a merchant, and merchants are considered to be no greedier than anyone else.

CROSS-CURRICULAR CONNECTION

HISTORY. Inform students that even though the societies were separated by thousands of miles, there are many similarities between medieval Japan and medieval Europe. Point out to students that both societies had a feudal system, which meant that most of the land was owned by the rich, while a peasant class called serfs had to farm the land for the landowners' profit. In Europe, the wealthiest people were noble lords and ladies, and in Japan, there was a similar class of aristocrats known as

CROSS-CURRICULAR CONNECTION (CONT.)

daimyo. As students have learned, members of the warrior class in Japan were known as *samurai,* and they correspond to the knights of medieval Europe. While Europe had a class of Christian clergy, feudal Europe had a class of Buddhist monks and nuns. At the bottom of the social hierarchy in both places were the commoners, some of whom were free but many of whom were serfs, or slaves. In the late

medieval period of both cultures, a merchant class began to gain power. Merchants came of common background, but were often more wealthy than some nobles. Nobles generally resented the merchant class, and used their rank and birth to sneer at them; however, the merchants' newfound wealth ensured that the nobles could not ignore them.

ADDITIONAL QUESTIONS AND ACTIVITIES

Ask students the following questions: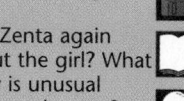
1. What does Zenta again notice about the girl? What does he say is unusual about the way she acts? What does her extra little finger seem to invite?
2. Where does Zenta fall asleep? Where does he wake up?
3. Why does the thought of Tokubei put Zenta into a panic?
4. What does Tokubei say must have happened? Why is he angry?

Answers
1. Zenta notices her sixth finger again. He says while most girls would try to hide a hand with six fingers, she seems to use that hand more than her other one. He says her extra finger invites comment.
2. He falls asleep in the inn, but wakes up outside in the cold.
3. As Tokubei's bodyguard, Zenta is supposed to watch over him, but instead Zenta has fallen asleep and awoken in a strange place.
4. He says they must have been drugged and robbed. He's angry because Zenta failed to protect him.

summer. Our host's words were no <u>idle</u> boast. The pictures were indeed beautiful.

Tokubei rose and approached the screens for a closer look. When he sat down again, his eyes were calculating. No doubt he was trying to estimate what price the paintings would fetch.

After my third drink I began to feel very tired. Perhaps it was the result of drinking on an empty stomach. I was glad when the girl brought in two dinner trays and a lacquered[5] container of rice. Uncovering the rice container, she began filling our bowls.

Again I noticed her strange left hand with its six fingers. Any other girl would have tried to keep that hand hidden, but this girl made no effort to do so. If anything, she seemed to use that hand more than her other one when she served us. The extra little finger always stuck out from the hand, as if inviting comment.

The hand fascinated me so much that I kept my eyes on it, and soon forgot to eat. After a while the hand looked blurry. And then everything else began to look blurry. The last thing I remembered was the sight of Tokubei shaking his head, as if trying to clear it.

When I opened my eyes again, I knew that time had passed, but not how much time. My next thought was that it was cold. It was not only extremely cold but damp.

I rolled over and sat up. I reached immediately for my swords and found them safe on the ground beside me. On the ground? What was I doing on the ground? My last memory was of staying at an inn with a merchant called Tokubei.

> **GUIDED READING**
>
> Where did Zenta find himself when he woke up?

The thought of Tokubei put me into a panic. I was his bodyguard, and instead of watching over him, I had fallen asleep and had awakened in a strange place.

I looked around frantically and saw that he was lying on the ground not far from where I was. Had he been killed?

I got up shakily, and when I stood up my head was swimming. But my sense of urgency gave some strength to my legs. I stumbled over to my employer and to my great relief found him breathing—breathing heavily, in fact.

When I shook his shoulder, he grunted and finally opened his eyes. "Where am I?" he asked thickly.

It was a reasonable question. I looked around and saw that we had been lying in a bamboo grove. By the light I guessed that it was early morning, and the reason I felt cold and damp was because my clothes were wet with dew.

"It's cold!" said Tokubei, shivering and climbing unsteadily to his feet. He looked around slowly, and his eyes became wide with disbelief. "What happened? I thought we were staying at an inn!"

His words came as a relief. One of the possibilities I had considered was that I had gone mad and that the whole episode with the inn was something I had imagined. Now I knew that Tokubei had the same memory of the inn. I had not imagined it.

But why were we out here on the cold ground, instead of on comfortable mattresses in the inn?

> **GUIDED READING**
>
> Why was Zenta relieved when Tokubei asked what happened and said he thought they were staying at an inn?

---

5. **lacquered.** Covered with a shiny coating

words for everyday use   **idle** (i′ dəl) *adj.,* without worth or basis in fact. *Jenny and Sam's idle chatter left me bored.*

The Teahouse at Mariko, 1833. Utagawa Hiroshige. Elvehjem Museum of Art, Madison, Wisconsin.

"They must have drugged us and robbed us," said Tokubei. He turned and looked at me furiously. "A fine bodyguard you are!"

There was nothing I could say to that. But at least we were both alive and unharmed. "Did they take all your money?" I asked.

Tokubei had already taken his wallet out of his sash and was peering inside. "That's funny! My money is still here!"

This was certainly unexpected. What did the innkeeper and his strange daughter intend to do by drugging us and moving us outside?

At least things were not as bad as we had feared. We had not lost anything except a comfortable night's sleep, although from the heaviness in my head I had certainly slept deeply enough—and long enough too. Exactly how much time had elapsed since we drank wine with our host?

All we had to do now was find the highway again and continue our journey. Tokubei suddenly chuckled. "I didn't even have to pay for our night's lodging!"

As we walked from the bamboo grove, I saw the familiar clump of bamboo shoots, and we found ourselves standing in the same clearing again. Before our eyes was the thatched house. Only it was somehow different. Perhaps things looked different in the daylight than at dusk.

But the difference was more than a change of light. As we approached the house slowly, like sleepwalkers, we saw that the thatching was much darker. On the previous evening the thatching had looked fresh and new. Now it was dark with age. Daylight should make things

> **GUIDED READING**
>
> What was different about the house?

LITERARY NOTE

Point out to students the Japanese script in the print by Hiroshige on this page. Inform students that traditionally, Japanese was written vertically from top to bottom or from right to left, although another method goes from left to right like English. In early Japanese history, there was no written language. Later, the Japanese borrowed the writing system of the Chinese, which is known as *kanji* in Japan. Each character in this type of writing began as a picture and has an associated meaning (unlike our phonetic alphabet, where for example, the letter *Q* means nothing on its own). This type of writing is extremely difficult to learn because there are literally thousands of symbols to learn. By 1981, the government had simplified the list from over 10,000 symbols to 1,945, and gave this type of writing the official name *joyo kanji*. Learning these symbols is required of every schoolchild.

The Japanese also have another type of writing called *kana,* which was also developed from Chinese characters, but is phonetic—each character represents a sound, not a meaning.

1. An old woman answered. He panicked when he noticed six fingers on her wrinkled and crooked left hand.
2. He was much younger than the host from the previous night, although there was a strong resemblance between the two.

ADDITIONAL QUESTIONS AND ACTIVITIES

Ask students the following questions:

1. How do both Tokubei and Zenta feel as they approach the strangely altered inn?
2. How does Tokubei think the old woman and the girl with six fingers are related? What does the man at what was once an inn say to contradict this?
3. Why might this news make Tokubei dizzy?
4. What does Zenta say when the man asks him if he shares Tokubei's delusion? In what way can Zenta's words be interpreted? What does this reveal about Zenta?

Answers

1. They both feel frightened.
2. Tokubei thinks that the old woman with six fingers must be the grandmother of the young woman with six fingers. The man says that the only person with six fingers in his family is his mother, the old woman.
3. Tokubei assumes that this news means that the old woman is the young girl who served them, which means that many years must have passed while they slept.
4. Zenta says he won't contradict his elders. His words can be interpreted as meaning he supports either the man or Tokubei, as both are his elders. His words reveal that Zenta is clever.

---

appear brighter, not darker. The plastering of the walls also looked more <u>dingy</u>.

Tokubei and I stopped to look at each other before we went closer. He was pale, and I knew that I looked no less frightened. Something was terribly wrong. I loosened my sword in its scabbard.[6]

We finally gathered the courage to go up to the house. Since Tokubei seemed unable to find his voice, I spoke out. "Is anyone there?"

After a moment we heard shuffling footsteps and the front door slid open. The face of an old woman appeared. "Yes?" she inquired. Her voice was creaky with age.

What set my heart pounding with panic, however, was not her voice. It was the sight of her left hand holding on to the frame of the door. The hand was wrinkled and crooked with the arthritis of old age—and it had six fingers.

> **GUIDED READING**
> Who answered the door? What makes Zenta feel panic?

I heard a gasp beside me and knew that Tokubei had noticed the hand as well.

The door opened wider and a man appeared beside the old woman. At first I thought it was our host of the previous night. But this man was much younger, although the resemblance was strong. He carried himself straighter and his hair was black, while the innkeeper had been grizzled and slightly bent with age.

> **GUIDED READING**
> What was different about the man who comes to the door?

"Please excuse my mother," said the man. "Her hearing is not good. Can we help you in some way?"

Tokubei finally found his voice. "Isn't this the inn where we stayed last night?"

The man stared. "Inn? We are not innkeepers here!"

"Yes, you are!" insisted Tokubei. "Your daughter invited us in and served us with wine. You must have put something in the wine!"

The man frowned. "You are serious? Are you sure you didn't drink too much at your inn and wander off?"

"No, I didn't drink too much!" said Tokubei, almost shouting. "I hardly drank at all! Your daughter, the one with six fingers in her hand, started to pour me a second cup of wine . . ." His voice trailed off, and he stared again at the left hand of the old woman.

"I don't have a daughter," said the man slowly. "My mother here is the one who has six fingers in her left hand, although I hardly think it polite of you to mention it."

"I'm getting dizzy," muttered Tokubei and began to totter.

"I think you'd better come in and rest a bit," the man said to him gruffly. He glanced at me. "Perhaps you wish to join your friend. You don't share his <u>delusion</u> about the inn, I hope?"

"I wouldn't presume to contradict my elders," I said carefully. Since both Tokubei and the owner of the house were my elders, I wasn't committing myself. In truth I didn't know what to believe, but I did want a look at the inside of the house.

The inside was almost the same as it was before but the differences were there when I looked closely. We entered the same room with the alcove and the pair of painted doors. The vase I had admired was no longer there, but the doors showed the same landscapes painted by a master. I peered closely at the pictures and saw that the colors looked faded.

---

6. **scabbard.** Sheath for holding a sword or dagger

words for everyday use

din • gy (din' jē) *adj.*, dirty or discolored; shabby, showing signs of wear or neglect. *The <u>dingy</u> hallways made the building seem old and gloomy.*

de • lu • sion (di loo' zhən) *n.*, an incorrect perception of reality. *Mother says that Aunt Celia's belief in elves is nothing but a <u>delusion</u>.*

What was more, the left panel, the one depicting a winter scene, had a long tear in one corner. It had been painstakingly mended, but the damage was impossible to hide completely.

Tokubei saw what I was staring at and he became even paler. At this stage we had both considered the possibility that a hoax of some sort had been played on us. The torn screen convinced Tokubei that our host had not played a joke: the owner of a valuable painting would never vandalize it for a trivial reason.

GUIDED READING

Why was Tokubei convinced that the host was not just playing a joke?

As for me, I was far more disturbed by the sight of the sixth finger on the old woman's hand. Could the young girl have disguised herself as an old crone?[7] She could put rice powder in her hair to whiten it, but she could not transform her pretty straight fingers into old fingers twisted with arthritis. The woman here with us now was genuinely old, at least fifty years older than the girl.

It was this same old woman who finally gave us our greatest shock. "It's interesting that you should mention an inn, gentlemen," she croaked. "My father used to operate an inn. After he died, my husband and I turned this back into a private residence. We didn't need the income, you see."

"Your . . . your . . . f-father?" stammered Tokubei.

"Yes," replied the old woman. "He was a ronin, forced to go into innkeeping when he lost his position. But he never liked the work. Besides, our inn had begun to acquire an unfortunate reputation. Some of our guests disappeared, you see."

Even before she finished speaking, a horrible suspicion had begun to dawn on me. Her father had been an innkeeper, she said, her father who used to be a ronin. The man who had been our host was a ronin turned innkeeper. Could this mean that this old

woman was actually the same person as the young girl we had seen?

I sat stunned while I tried to absorb the implications. What had happened to us? Was it possible that Tokubei and I had slept while this young girl grew into a mature woman, got married, and bore a son, a son who was now an adult? If that was the case, then we had slept for fifty years!

The old woman's next words confirmed my fears. "I recognize you

GUIDED READING

Why was Zenta stunned by the old woman's words?

now! You are two of the lost guests from our inn! The other lost ones I don't remember so well, but I remember you because your disappearance made me so sad. Such a handsome youth, I thought, what a pity that he should have gone the way of the others!"

"Some of our guests disappeared, you see."

A high wail came from Tokubei, who began to keen[8] and rock himself back and forth. "I've lost fifty years! Fifty years of my life went by while I slept at this accursed inn!"

The inn was indeed accursed. Was the fate of the other guests similar to ours? "Did anyone else return as we did, fifty years later?" I asked.

The old woman looked uncertain and turned to her son. He frowned thoughtfully. "From time to time wild-looking people have come to us with stories similar to

7. **crone.** A withered old woman
8. **keen.** Complain

ANSWERS TO GUIDED READING QUESTIONS

1. One of the painted screens on the door was torn and carefully mended, and Tokubei is sure no one would vandalize a valuable painting just to play a joke.
2. Her words made him wonder whether he and Tokubei had really slept for fifty years, while the young girl got married, raised a son, and grew into the old woman standing before him now.

LITERARY TECHNIQUE

SUSPENSE. **Suspense** is a feeling of anxiousness or curiosity. Writers create suspense by raising questions in the reader's mind and using details that create strong emotions. Encourage students to discuss how the author builds suspense during this encounter between Zenta and Tokubei, and the young man and the old woman. What questions are raised in the reader's mind? *Answers.* Students may say that the suspense is built as more and more "evidence" seems to pile up indicating that Zenta and Tokubei have slept for fifty years, such as seeing that the beautiful paintings have become faded and torn, seeing that the old woman is genuinely old, learning that the old woman's father ran an inn about fifty years ago, and learning that the inn acquired a bad reputation because guests would mysteriously disappear, and then seeing the old woman recognize Zenta and the merchant. Students may say they are questioning whether it is possible that the two men have slipped into the future or slept for fifty years without aging.

1. He had lost his business and his young, beautiful wife.
2. Zenta wanted to find an explanation for the disappearances of guests from the inn, in the hope that they might then be able to reverse the process and regain their lost time.
3. For a large sum of money, she promised to make a spell that would undo the work of an evil spirit. She said this evil spirit dwelled in the bamboo grove and put unwary travelers into a very long sleep.

LITERARY NOTE

Inform students that *carpe diem* is a Latin phrase meaning "seize the day." The *carpe diem* theme in literature told people not to waste time but rather to enjoy themselves while they have a chance because life is short and time passes quickly. This theme was common in English literature of the Renaissance period which lasted from the fifteenth to the early seventeenth century. Share the quotation below with students. Ask students to discuss how this theme relates to the story "The Inn of Lost Time."
Answers. Students may note that the idea that losing years of your life is one of the saddest things that can happen to you reflects the *carpe diem* theme.

Quotables

"Gather ye rosebuds while ye may
Old Time is still a–flying
And this same flower that
  smiles today.
Tomorrow will be dying."

—Robert Herrick

---

yours. Some of them went mad with the shock."

Tokubei wailed again. "I've lost my business! I've lost my wife, my young and beautiful wife! We had been married only a couple of months!"

A <u>gruesome</u> chuckle came from the old woman. "You may not have lost your wife. It's just that she's become an old hag like me!"

> **GUIDED READING**
> What upset Tokubei about losing fifty years?

That did not console Tokubei, whose keening became louder. Although my relationship with my employer had not been characterized by much respect on either side, I did begin to feel very sorry for him. He was right: he had lost his world.

As for me, the loss was less traumatic. I had left home under extremely painful circumstances, and had spent the next three years wandering. I had no friends and no one I could call a relation. The only thing I had was my duty to my employer. Somehow, some way, I had to help him.

"Did no one find an explanation for these disappearances?" I asked. "Perhaps if we knew the reason why, we might find some way to reverse the process."

> **GUIDED READING**
> What did Zenta want to do?

The old woman began to nod eagerly. "The priestess! Tell them about the shrine priestess!"

"Well," said the man, "I'm not sure if it would work in your case . . . ."

"What? What would work?" demanded Tokubei. His eyes were feverish.

"There was a case of one returning guest who consulted the priestess at our local shrine," said the man. "She went into a trance and revealed that there was an evil spirit

dwelling in the bamboo grove here. This spirit would put <u>unwary</u> travelers into a long, unnatural sleep. They would wake up twenty, thirty, or even fifty years later."

"Yes, but you said something worked in his case," said Tokubei.

The man seemed reluctant to go on. "I don't like to see you cheated, so I'm not sure I should be telling you this."

"Tell me! Tell me!" demanded Tokubei. The host's reluctance only made him more impatient.

"The priestess promised to make a spell that would undo the work of the evil spirit," said the man. "But she demanded a large sum of money, for she said that she had to burn some very rare and costly incense[9] before she could begin the spell."

> **GUIDED READING**
> What did the priestess offer to one returning guest who went to her for help?

At the mention of money Tokubei sat back. The hectic flush died down on his face and his eyes narrowed. "How much money?" he asked.

The host shook his head. "In my opinion the priestess is a fraud and makes outrageous claims about her powers. We try to have as little to do with her as possible."

"Yes, but did her spell work?" asked Tokubei. "If it worked, she's no fraud!"

"At least the stranger disappeared again," cackled the old woman. "Maybe he went back to his own time. Maybe he walked into a river."

Tokubei's eyes narrowed further. "How much money did the priestess demand?" he asked again.

---

9. **incense.** Material used to produce a pleasing odor when burned

---

words for everyday use

grue • some (groo′ səm) *adj.*, ghastly; inspiring horror. *The <u>gruesome</u> scene in the haunted house made my heart pound.*
un • wary (ən wār ē) *adj.*, easily fooled. *The <u>unwary</u> ducks were surprised by a hungry fox.*

"I think it was one gold piece for every year lost," said the host. He hurriedly added, "Mind you, I still wouldn't trust the priestess."

"Then it would cost me fifty gold pieces to get back to my own time," muttered Tokubei. He looked up. "I don't carry that much money with me."

GUIDED READING
How much would it cost Tokubei to get back to his own time?

"No, you don't," agreed the host.

Something alerted me about the way he said that. It was as if the host knew already that Tokubei did not carry much money on him.

Meanwhile Tokubei sighed. He had come to a decision. "I do have the means to obtain more money, however. I can send a message to my chief clerk and he will remit[10] the money when he sees my seal."

"Your chief clerk may be dead by now," I reminded him.

"You're right!" moaned Tokubei. "My business will be under a new management and nobody will even remember my name!"

"And your wife will have remarried," said the old woman, with one of her chuckles. I found it hard to believe that the gentle young girl who had served us wine could turn into this dreadful harridan.[11]

"Sending the message may be a waste of time," agreed the host.

"What waste of time!" cried Tokubei. "Why shouldn't I waste time? I've wasted fifty years already! Anyway, I've made up my mind. I'm sending that message."

"I still think you shouldn't trust the priestess," said the host.

That only made Tokubei all the more determined to send for the money. However, he was not quite resigned to the amount. "Fifty gold pieces is a large sum. Surely the priestess can buy incense for less than that amount?"

"Why don't you try giving her thirty gold pieces?" cackled the old woman. "Then the priestess will send you back thirty years, and your wife will only be middle-aged."

While Tokubei was still arguing with himself about the exact sum to send for, I decided to have a look at the bamboo grove. "I'm going for a walk," I announced, rising and picking up my sword from the floor beside me.

The host turned sharply to look at me. For an instant a faint, rueful smile appeared on his lips. Then he looked away.

Outside, I went straight to the clump of shoots in the bamboo grove. On the previous night—or what I perceived as the previous night—I had noticed that clump of bamboo shoots particularly, because I had been so hungry that I pictured them being cut up and boiled.

The clump of bamboo shoots was still in the same place. That in itself

GUIDED READING
Where does Zenta go and what does he find?

proved nothing, since bamboo could spring up anywhere, including the place where a clump had existed fifty years earlier. But what settled the matter in my mind was that the clump looked almost exactly the way it did when I had seen it before, except that every shoot was about an inch taller. That was a reasonable amount for bamboo shoots to grow overnight.

Overnight. Tokubei and I had slept on the ground here overnight. We had not slept here for a period of fifty years.

Once I knew that, I was able to see another inconsistency: the door panels with the painted landscapes. The painting with the winter scene had been on the right last night and it was

GUIDED READING
What other inconsistency did Zenta find?

on the left this morning. It wasn't simply a case of the panels changing places, because the depressions in the panel for the handholds had been reversed. In other words, what I saw just now was not a pair of

10. **remit.** Send (money)
11. **harridan.** Ill-tempered woman

ANSWERS TO GUIDED READING QUESTIONS

1. It would cost fifty gold pieces, one for each year that he had lost.
2. He went straight to the clump of shoots in the bamboo grove and notes that the clump was in the same place as when he had last seen it, that it looked almost exactly the way he had last seen it, and that each shoot had grown about an inch taller—a reasonable amount for bamboo to grow overnight.
3. The painted landscapes on the door panels were not faded and torn by age. They were an entirely different pair of paintings.

ADDITIONAL QUESTIONS AND ACTIVITIES

Inform students that on this page Zenta applies one of the critical thinking skills—analyzing. When you **analyze** something, you break it down into parts and think about how the parts are related to each other and the whole. This ability to think critically is what allows Zenta to solve the mystery of the inn of lost time. Ask students to list the "parts" Zenta breaks the mystery down into. In other words, what clues does Zenta find on these pages? What does he realize when he looks at all these parts together? *Answers.* Clues include Zenta noticing that the host knows that Tokubei doesn't carry fifty pieces of gold with him, Zenta noticing that the patch of bamboo he saw last night is in the same place and seems to only have grown as much as bamboo usually does overnight, the panels that seemingly have aged are an entirely different set of paintings, the young girl and the older woman are actually two different women, each with six fingers, that the roof can be darkened with ashes, and that the young man could have put gray in his hair the previous night to appear older. He realizes that they haven't really lost fifty years of time and that the innkeepers are tricking them to get to Tokubei's money.

ANSWER TO GUIDED READING QUESTION

1. The purpose was to get fifty pieces of gold from Tokubei.

paintings faded and torn by age. They were an entirely different pair of paintings.

But how did the pretty young girl change into an old woman? The answer was that if the screens could be different ones, so could the women. I had seen one woman, a young girl, last night. This morning I saw a different woman, an old hag.

The darkening of the thatched roof? Simply blow ashes over the roof. The grizzled-haired host of last night could be the same man who claimed to be his grandson today. It would be a simple matter for a young man to put gray in his hair and assume a stoop.

And the purpose of the hoax? To make Tokubei send for fifty pieces of gold, of course. It was clever of the man to accuse the shrine priestess

GUIDED READING
What did Zenta figure is the purpose of the hoax?

of fraud and pretend reluctance to let Tokubei send his message.

I couldn't even feel angry toward the man and his daughter—or mother, sister, wife, whatever. He could have killed me and taken my swords, which he clearly admired. Perhaps he was really a ronin and felt sympathetic toward another one.

When I returned to the house, Tokubei was looking resigned. "I've decided to send for the whole fifty gold pieces." He sighed.

"Don't bother," I said. "In fact we should be leaving as soon as possible. We shouldn't even stop here for a drink, especially not of wine."

Tokubei stared. "What do you mean? If I go back home, I'll find everything changed!"

"Nothing will be changed," I told him. "Your wife will be as young and beautiful as ever."

"I don't understand," he said. "Fifty years . . ."

"It's a joke," I said. "The people here have a peculiar sense of humor, and they've played a joke on us."

Tokubei's mouth hung open. Finally he closed it with a snap. He stared at the host,

and his face became first red and then purple. "You—you were trying to swindle me!" He turned furiously to me. "And you let them do this!"

"I'm not letting them," I pointed out. "That's why we're leaving right now."

"Are you going to let them get away with this?" demanded Tokubei. "They might try to swindle someone else!"

"They only went to this much trouble when they heard of the arrival of a fine fat fish like you," I said. I looked deliberately at the host. "I'm sure they won't be tempted to try the same trick again."

"And that's the end of your story?" asked Matsuzo. "You and Tokubei just went away? How did you know the so-called innkeeper wouldn't try the trick on some other luckless traveler?"

Zenta shook his head. "I didn't know. I merely guessed that once the trick was exposed, they wouldn't take the chance of trying it again. Of course I thought about revisiting the place to check if the people there were leading an honest life."

"Why didn't you?" asked Matsuzo. "Maybe we could go together. You've made me curious about that family now."

"Then you can satisfy your curiosity," said Zenta, smiling. He held his cup out for more tea, and the farmer's wife came forward to pour.

Only now she used both hands to hold the pot, and for the first time Matsuzo saw her left hand. He gasped. The hand had six fingers.

"Who was the old woman?" Zenta asked the farmer's wife.

"She was my grandmother," she replied. "Having six fingers is something that runs in my family."

At last Matsuzo found his voice. "You mean this is the very house you visited? This is the inn where time was lost?"

"Where we thought we lost fifty years," said Zenta. "Perhaps I should have warned you first. But I was almost certain that we'd be safe this time. And I see that I was right."

He turned to the woman again. "You and your husband are farmers now, aren't you? What happened to the man who was the host?"

"He's dead," she said quietly. "He was my brother, and he was telling you the truth when he said that he was a ronin. Two years ago he found work with another warlord, but he was killed in battle only a month later."

Matsuzo was peering at the pair of sliding doors, which he hadn't noticed before. "I see that you've put up the faded set of paintings. The winter scene is on the left side."

The woman nodded. "We sold the newer pair of doors. My husband said that we're farmers now and that people in our position don't need valuable paintings. We used the money to buy some new farm implements."

She took up the teapot again. "Would you like another cup of tea?" she asked Matsuzo.

Staring at her left hand, Matsuzo had a sudden qualm. "I—I don't think I want any more."

Everybody laughed. ∎

Respond *to the* SELECTION

If you were Zenta, what would you do when you realized that the innkeeper had tried to trick you? How would you handle the situation?

About *the* AUTHOR

Lensey Namioka was born in Beijing, China. She lives in Seattle, Washington, with her husband, who was raised in Himeji, Japan, and their two daughters. The history of her husband's family led her to write about feudal Japan. Zenta and Matsuzo, the wandering ronin in "The Inn of Lost Time," also appear in several historical mystery novels—*The Samurai and the Long-Nosed Devils, Valley of the Cherry Trees, Village of the Vampire Cat*, and *Island of Ogres*. Namioka has also written *Phantom of Tiger Mountain*, set in historical China, and several contemporary novels, including *Who's Hu?* and *Wormholes*. Namioka and her husband have traveled throughout the world.

"THE INN OF LOST TIME" 223

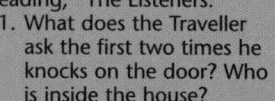
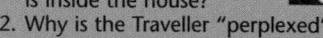
RELATED READING

The Listeners

Walter de la Mare

'Is there anybody there?' said the Traveller,
    Knocking on the moonlit door;
And his horse in the silence champed the grasses
    Of the forest's ferny floor:
And a bird flew up out of the turret,
    Above the Traveller's head:
And he smote upon the door again a second time;
    'Is there anybody there?' he said.
But no one descended to the Traveller;
    No head from the leaf-fringed sill
Leaned over and looked into his grey eyes,
    Where he stood perplexed and still.
But only a host of phantom listeners
    That dwelt in the lone house then
Stood listening in the quiet of the moonlight
    To that voice from the world of men:
Stood thronging the faint moonbeams on the dark stair,
    That goes down to the empty hall,
Hearkening in an air stirred and shaken
    By the lonely Traveller's call.
And he felt in his heart their strangeness,
    Their stillness answering his cry,
While his horse moved, cropping the dark turf,
    'Neath the starred and leafy sky;
For he suddenly smote on the door, even
    Louder, and lifted his head:—
'Tell them I came, and no one answered,
    That I kept my word,' he said.
Never the least stir made the listeners,
    Though every word he spake
Fell echoing through the shadowiness of the still house
    From the one man left awake:
Ay, they heard his foot upon the stirrup,
    And the sound of iron on stone,
And how the silence surged softly backward,
    When the plunging hoofs were gone. ∎

1. **champ.** Chomp
2. **smote.** Banged
3. **perplexed.** Puzzled
4. **thronging.** Crowding
5. **hearkening.** Listening
6. **surged.** Rose

A View from the Mountain Pass Called the Notch of the White Mountains, 1839.
Thomas Cole. National Gallery of Art, Washington, D.C.

ABOUT THE RELATED READING

Born in 1873 in Kent, England, **Walter de la Mare** had a broad writing career. He published novels, essays, plays, poems, short stories, and children's books. He has been considered a master of creepy, ghostly, mysterious poems. Some of de la Mare's best-known works contain haunting images. Other works transform childlike rhymes into magical verses. Many deal with fairies, fantasy, and the shady line between real and unreal. De la Mare died in 1956.

"The Listeners" shows de la Mare's skill at creating a fantastic atmosphere. In the poem, a traveler faces more than what appears on the surface—a seemingly deserted house. The traveler in the poem confronts the mysteries of life and the connection between the living and the dead.

"THE INN OF LOST TIME" 225

RECALL

1a. Zenta and Tokubei note that she has six fingers on her left hand.

2a. The host says the family still has a few good things that they didn't have to sell. His voice holds a trace of bitterness.

3a. Zenta decides to go outside for a walk. The host turns sharply to look at him.

INTERPRET

1b. They want to be sure their guests notice this trait because, since it is so unusual, it will help convince the guests that a long time truly has elapsed. Surely they wouldn't find two different women with six fingers, so it must be true that the girl grew old while they slept.

2b. It sounds like he's not happy about the changes the times have forced him to make. He may feel life has not been fair to him, and he may also feel like other people owe him for his misfortune.

3b. Perhaps he's thinking that Zenta will figure out what really happened when he looks outside.

ANALYZE

4a. Tokubei is very materialistic and preoccupied with his money. For evidence of this, students may point to his unwillingness to travel onward because he has heard that the inns there are expensive, his immediately asking how much gold the other person paid to have the priestess perform the ritual, his inquiring about whether the priestess will perform the ritual to take him back to his own time for thirty gold pieces rather than fifty, and his sighing when he says he is willing to send for the gold.

SYNTHESIZE

4b. Tokubei values money so highly that he is extremely upset when he learns the truth about the inn, accusing the people there of trying to swindle them, telling Zenta that he is responsible for letting them do this, and urging him to do something to the people to prevent them from swindling again. He reacts almost more strongly to almost having been swindled than he does to learning he has slept for fifty years, indicating the value he places on money.

EVALUATE

5a. Students may say that the innkeeper played the trick on Zenta and Tokubei because he is impoverished and was looking for a scheme to get money and thought

---

Investigate, Inquire, and Imagine

Recall: GATHERING FACTS

1a. What do Zenta and Tokubei note is unusual about the girl at the inn?

2a. When Zenta first notices the vase in the alcove, how does the host respond? What does he say? What is his tone of voice?

3a. While Tokubei and the host are arguing about whether he should send for money, what does Zenta decide to do, and how does the host respond?

→ **Interpret:** FINDING MEANING

1b. Why do you suppose the girl, and later the old woman, makes no effort to hide her left hand?

2b. Why does he reply this way? Why does he use this tone of voice?

3b. Why does a faint, rueful smile appear momentarily on the host's lips?

Analyze: TAKING THINGS APART

4a. What words, behaviors, and gestures of Tokubei demonstrate his attitudes about money?

→ **Synthesize:** BRINGING THINGS TOGETHER

4b. How do these attitudes affect his response when he learns about the hoax?

Evaluate: MAKING JUDGMENTS

5a. Evaluate the motives of the innkeeper for playing the trick on Tokubei and Zenta. Why do you think he made up such a scheme? Do you think the innkeeper felt he was justified in trying to swindle the two travelers? Do you think he felt guilty? Explain your answers.

→ **Extend:** CONNECTING IDEAS

5b. In "The Inn of Lost Time," you learn the truth about the swindle and about the supposed lost fifty years by the end of the story. Therefore, you can look at the reasons behind the strange chain of events and at the motives of the people responsible for creating such a mystery. In the poem, "The Listeners," you are left to come to your own conclusions about what is causing the mysterious scene. How does each type of ending affect you?

ANSWERS TO INVESTIGATE, INQUIRE, IMAGINE (CONT.)

that the greedy Tokubei would be a good target. Students may say that the innkeeper feels justified in doing this because he feels wronged in having had to give up the honorable professional of a samurai to turn innkeeper because of the hard financial times. He may feel that the world owes him something, and he doesn't mind taking advantage of a merchant because merchants are part of a newly wealthy but despised class. Students may say he feels guilty about playing the

trick on Zenta, a fellow samurai serving the despised merchant class, because he gives him a rueful smile just before Zenta goes outside and finds evidence of the hoax.

EXTEND

5b. Responses will vary. Students may say that while "The Inn of Lost Time" satisfies their curiosity, "The Listeners" piques it, or makes them even more curious.

Understanding *Literature*

FRAME STORY. A **frame story** opens and closes with the telling of one story, which forms a frame. Within that story another story is told. After reading the entire frame story, go back and examine the frame—the opening and closing. Compare the opening frame with the inner story. What similarities and differences do you see? What similarities do you find strange or surprising? What purpose does the opening frame serve? Look at the closing frame. What purpose does it serve?

FORESHADOWING. **Foreshadowing** is the act of hinting at events that will happen later in a literary work. Zenta foreshadows that something bad may happen by warning that he is not proud of the part he played in the story he tells. What purpose does the foreshadowing serve? How did it affect your interest in the story? How did it help you to predict what would happen?

IRONY OF SITUATION. **Irony of situation** is an event that contradicts the expectations of the characters or the audience. In this story both the characters and the audience experience irony of situation. On several occasions Zenta portrays how Tokubei, though wealthy, wants to spend as little money as possible. Tokubei's greed and the hunger of both Zenta and Tokubei set the two men up for the ultimate irony of situation, when they are tricked into believing they have lost fifty years. They struggle to sort out the difference between how things seem (appearance) and how they really are (reality). As Zenta's tale unfolds, readers also encounter ironies of situation as they struggle to figure out what really happened. Copy the following graphic organizer onto your own paper. Reread or skim the story and note the places where you are surprised by a situation. In your chart, list what you expected in one column and what really happens in another column.

Looking at the entries that come from Zenta's tale, determine which of the highlighted entries in Column 1 (things you thought would happen) might have actually happened if Zenta or Tokubei had made a different choice. Next, examine the entries you listed in Column 2 (things that actually happened). Think about how each event leads to the next, setting Zenta and Tokubei up for the final irony of situation. How might the chain of events have differed if the two men had made different choices? Did the men have any control over the last irony of situation, in which they were tricked? Why, or why not?

Graphic *Organizer*

WHAT I EXPECTED TO HAPPEN	WHAT REALLY HAPPENS
• Farmer expects ronin to use their arms to defend the weak.	• In these troubled times, samurai don't always live up to their honorable code.
• Taro would go back to his village and find it as he left it.	• He finds the place quite changed. They go off the main highway and down a narrow path through a forest to find an inn.
• Tokubei and Zenta would stop at an inn on the main road.	

GRAPHIC ORGANIZER (CONT.)

5. The innkeeper will be a professional innkeeper. / The innkeeper is a former samurai, who is bitter about his fate.
6. They will wake up in the morning in the inn and continue on their journey. / They wake up outside the inn.
7. The innkeeper or the girl with six fingers will explain what happened. / The innkeeper is gone, and the girl seems to have become an old woman

with a son. They say the place hasn't been an inn for a long time and reveal that fifty years have passed since the men slept.

8. Tokubei will have to spend fifty gold pieces to have a priestess reverse the spell. / Zenta figures out that the time travel is a hoax.
9. Zenta will be unable to tell Matsuzo what happened to the inn of lost time. / Zenta reveals that they are staying at the inn of lost time.

FRAME TALE. The folk tale told in the frame is about the same kind of experience that Zenta relays in the inner tale, but the ending of the two tales is different. Readers are surprised that the two tales are about the same thing. The opening frame creates the setting and sets up the irony of situation in that, although the reader does not know it at the time, it introduces the woman who was involved in the hoax of the inner tale. It also introduces a premise for Zenta to tell a story about losing years of one's life. The closing frame provides a resolution and an ironic surprise for both Matsuzo and the reader—who learns that the inn described in the opening and closing frame was the same inn featured in the story Zenta tells.

FORESHADOWING. The foreshadowing lets the reader know that something unusual that may cast dishonor on Zenta as a samurai will take place in the story. Students may say that foreshadowing makes them want to read on and find out what will happen. The foreshadowing gives clues that something mysterious will happened to Zenta and Tokubei in the inn of lost time.

IRONY OF SITUATION. *Responses will vary.* Students may suggest that if Tokubei had not been so greedy and materialistic he would not have been set up for the hoax and that if Zenta had not been so conscientious, observant, and dedicated to his profession, he would have never uncovered the ruse practiced at the inn of lost time. *Responses will vary.*

GRAPHIC ORGANIZER

Responses will vary. Some possible responses are given.
WHAT I EXPECTED TO HAPPEN /WHAT REALLY HAPPENS
1. Farmer expects ronin to use their arms to defend the weak. / In these troubled times, samurai don't always live up to their honorable code.
2. Taro would go back to his village and find it as he left it. / He finds the place quite changed as he has been away for 72 years.
3. Tokubei and Zenta would stop at an inn on the main road. / They go off the main highway and down a narrow path through a forest to find an inn.
4. Tokubei would stop wherever it was convenient, since he was wealthy. / Tokubei wants to find a cheap place to save as much money as possible.

Language, Grammar, and Style
USING METAPHORS. *Responses will vary. Possible responses are given.*
Hew says the leaves turn into little golden knives and the bamboo shoots are in a gilded clump. Zenta is very hungry and seeing the bamboo makes him think of food. The author wants to emphasize the two men's hunger. The golden color also emphasizes their greed—for food (both of them) and for money (Tokubei). For Zenta, wealth is based on simple pleasures such as eating a good meal, while Tokubei is materialistic in a traditional (monetary) sense.
Responses will vary. Possible responses are given.

1. The strawberries—sweet red rosebuds—glistened with sugar and sent out a honeyed smell from the bowl on the table.
2. Chocolate cake is my favorite sin.
3. The smell of hot pepperoni pizza wafting from the pizzeria ovens was a loudspeaker that called hungry people inside the restaurant.
4. Warm bread is a comforting place you call home.
5. Ripe tomato slices—slices of summer—were sprinkled with chopped herbs and a touch of fresh mozzarella.

Speaking and Listening
ACTING. You might have the student who plays each character explain his or her interpretation of the character's motivation and thoughts to the class after the performance.

Study and Research
RESEARCHING. Students may find encyclopedias and books on Japan's history to be their best resources in researching samurai. Students' oral reports should be no more than two or three minutes in length and just point out some basic facts about their chosen samurai's life.

Media Literacy
CRITICAL VIEWING. Students should also try to determine the filmmaker's attitude toward samurai. Was the filmmaker glorifying them? condemning them? What is the overall message the film gives about samurai?

Writer's Journal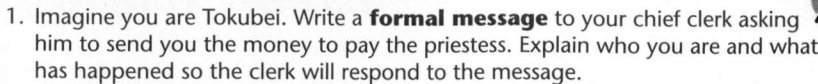

1. Imagine you are Tokubei. Write a **formal message** to your chief clerk asking him to send you the money to pay the priestess. Explain who you are and what has happened so the clerk will respond to the message.

2. Imagine your family has just spent the night in an expensive hotel that had run down, seedy rooms and poor service. Write a **letter of complaint** to the hotel's management, outlining your bad experience and requesting a refund.

3. As a tour guide or escort for young travelers visiting another country, you have been asked to inform parents of the group's travel plans. Write a three-day **itinerary** for the trip, outlining a schedule for each day. Include where you are staying and what activities are planned.

Skill Builders

Language, Grammar, and Style
USING METAPHORS. A *metaphor* is a figure of speech in which one thing  is spoken or written about as if it were another. This figure of speech invites the reader to make a comparison between the two things. When Zenta first approaches the inn, he passes a bamboo grove. What metaphors does he use to describe the grove? Why does he describe the grove in this way? Why would the narrator choose these metaphors? What comparison does this metaphor invite readers to make? Write a sentence including a metaphor for each of the following items, describing the item in words that could sound appetizing to a reader.
example: corn on the cob
The rows of golden pearls glistened with butter.

1. fresh strawberries
2. chocolate cake
3. hot pepperoni pizza
4. warm bread
5. ripe tomato slices

Speaking and Listening
ACTING. In a group of four students, assign parts and act out the scene in which the guests go back into the inn, speak with the man and the old woman, learn about the priestess, and talk about whether to consult her (pages 220–221). After acting out the scene a couple of times, analyze your group's dialogue. What do you think are the thoughts and motives of each character?

Study and Research
RESEARCHING. Research samurai at the library. What can you find out about their lifestyle and beliefs? Gather biographical information on one particular samurai and report about his life to your class.

Media Literacy
CRITICAL VIEWING. At a local  library or video rental store, find movies that feature samurai. Films you may want to look for include: *The Seven Samurai, Musashi Miyamoto, Duel at Ichijoji Temple, Duel at Ganryu Island,* and *Samurai Rebellion.* As you view a film, think about how the samurai and the other characters are represented. Do the characters' words, actions, emotions, thoughts, clothes, and surroundings fit with what you already know about the samurai and about Japanese life in earlier centuries?

for your READING LIST

The Wolves of Willoughby Chase, by Joan Aiken, is the first novel in Aiken's Wolves Chronicles. In this book, the feisty Bonnie Green is joined at Willoughby Chase, the Green family's home, by her orphaned and more timid cousin Sylvia. Lord and Lady Green—Bonnie's parents— go off on a cruise, little knowing that in their absence, the girls' world would be turned upside-down. The girls' well-recommended governess, Miss Slighcarp, reveals her true evil and scheming nature almost the moment the Greens walk out the door; before long Bonnie and Sylvia are spirited away from the once loving home to live in a boarding school that is truly more of a workhouse for orphans. Bonnie and Sylvia face many troubles together: the cruel Miss Slighcarp, the dangerous wolves around Willoughby Chase, betrayal, abandonment, abuse, and near starvation. With spirit, intelligence, and the help of loyal friends, Bonnie and Sylvia manage to keep hope alive in this dark, gothic tale by Joan Aiken.

BOOK REVIEW

Have you ever written a book review? Now is your chance. You can write a book review to post on an Internet site. Many Internet sites devoted to books allow readers to post book reviews. To find them, try using phrases such as "book review" as search terms. One site you may want to use it World of Reading at http://www.worldreading.org/. Ask your librarian or media specialist for other suggestions as well. If you do not have access to the Internet, post your book review in your classroom or library. Some things to consider when creating your own book review:

- You will want to relate part of the story in your review. If someone was considering reading this book, what would he or she want to know about it? Who are the main characters? How would you describe the plot? Remember not to give away the ending!
- Did you like the book? On a scale of 1 to 5, how would you rate it? Why did or didn't you like it?
- Would you recommend this book to others? Who should read it, and why?
- Does this book remind you of other books you have read? In what way?

Other books you may want to read:
Other titles in the Wolves Chronicles, such as ***Black Hearts in Battersea***, ***Nightbirds on Nantucket***, ***The Stolen Lake***, ***The Cuckoo Tree***, and ***Dido and Pa*** by Joan Aiken
Village of the Vampire Cat by Lensey Namioka
The Black Cauldron by Lloyd Alexander
Northanger Abbey by Jane Austen

For Your Reading List
Joan Aiken is considered a master storyteller for young adults. In addition to writing *The Wolves of Willoughby Chase*, Aiken has written hundreds of books and has been awarded a number of honors for her writing. If students want to read more of her work, refer them to the alternate titles at the bottom of page 229, or have them do library or online research for a listing of more titles by her.

Book Review
To get students started on this activity, you may want to have them spend time on the Internet looking at online book reviews other readers have posted. The World of Reading site listed on page 229 is particularly helpful. Students may also be familiar with the Amazon.com home page, which allows users to search for hundreds of books by author, title, and subject area and to both read and post reviews. As students start their reviews, you may want to have them start by recording their responses to the book they are reviewing in their Reader's Journal.

Reflecting

Ask students to brainstorm what makes a good letter. When they have received letters, what parts were the most interesting to read? Have students think of adapting these successful strategies to writing their own personal letter.

GUIDED WRITING
Software

See the Guided Writing Software for an extended version of this lesson that includes printable graphic organizers, extensive student models and student-friendly checklists, and self-, peer, and teacher evaluation features.

Professional Model

In the excerpt below, Dolly Madison describes for her sister the turbulent moments as the British forces near the capital city.

Dear Sister,

My husband left me yesterday morning to join General Winder. He inquired anxiously whether I had courage or firmness to remain in the president's house until his return on the morrow or succeeding day, and on my assurance that I had no fear but for him, and the success of our army, he left, beseeching me to take of myself, and of the Cabinet papers, public and private. I have since received two despatches from him, written with a pencil. The last is alarming, because he desires I should be ready at a moment's notice to enter my carriage, and leave the city; that the enemy seemed stronger than had at first been reported, and it might happen that they would reach the city with the intention of destroying it. I am accordingly ready....

Wednesday morning, twelve o'clock – Since sunrise I have been turning my spy-glass in every direction, and watching with unwearied anxiety, hoping to discover the approach of my dear husband and his friends; but, alas! I can descry only groups of military, wandering in all directions, as if there was

---

Guided Writing

COMPOSING A PERSONAL LETTER

Have you ever visited a place that is very different from where you live? Maria visited the Great Barrier Reef off the coast of Australia. On the way out to the reef, she struggled to control her seasickness as the boat bounced on the huge waves. When she got to the reef, she put on her snorkeling gear, then stepped off the platform into the cold water. It was then that she realized she had just entered a world that was both stunningly beautiful and a little scary.

If you had an experience like Maria's, you might want to share it with a friend. If you weren't able to talk with your friend directly, it could be fun to share your experience in a letter. Writing a letter is one way people can express their observations, thoughts, and feelings about visiting new places or experiencing new situations.

Examining the Model

Dolly Madison, wife of President James Madison, wrote a letter to her sister expressing her feelings and thoughts about a new situation she was experiencing. It was 1814, and the British were nearing the capital city. They believed that if they could capture Washington D.C., they could end the War of 1812. James Madison had already left the White House to help fight against the British. Dolly remained at the house until the very last minute, hoping for her husband's return and arranging for the safe transportation of government papers.

Dolly's concern for her husband and for the government papers is so well expressed that you almost feel as if you are there with Dolly experiencing her observations, feelings, and actions. Phrases such as "inquired anxiously" and "beseeching me" create a sense of urgency about her situation. On your own paper, list several words and phrases that make Dolly's feelings, thoughts, and observations come alive.

Reflecting

Before you plan your letter, think about your own letter-writing habits. How often do you write personal letters? What do you like or dislike about writing them?

What could make writing a letter a worthwhile experience—exchanging notes with a friend at school? corresponding with

---

Examining the Model

Ask students to focus on which questions Dolly Madison is answering that her sister might have. Have students read the Language Arts Survey 2.14, "Questioning: Using the 5 *Ws* and an *H*." Then tell students to fill out a chart similar to the one on page 878. Tell students to read the Language Arts Survey 6.5, "Writing a Personal Letter" and analyze whether or not Dolly Madison meets the established guidelines on page 940.

your grandmother through the mail? sending electronic mail to an overseas pen pal?

When you receive a letter, how do you respond? What makes a letter interesting to read? How do you react when your friends share their views about a place they have been or their observations about a new experience?

Prewriting

WRITING WITH A PLAN. Think about a place that you have visited—a different city or state, a national park, a well-known monument, a new vacation spot, or a different country. You may even think of a new shop, a museum, a zoo, or other place new to you.

Or, what other new situations that you have experienced would you like to tell someone about—trying a different sport or musical instrument? volunteering at an organization? eating strange new foods? going to a new school? Select a new place or new experience that you would like to write about. Rafael visited Florida with his family. He wants to write about some comical experiences he had there. Vickie was riding a horse when she took an unexpected tumble. She plans to write about this experience. Maria generated her ideas about visiting the Great Barrier Reef by filling in the graphic organizer below.

Student Model—Graphic Organizer

What I saw

all sorts of colors in the coral
colorless in places
really big fish
huge waves

What I felt

sick for awhile
scary in some ways
as if I was flying on the boat
exciting

Great Barrier Reef

What I thought

stunningly beautiful
best time of my life

---

a lack of arms, or of spirit to fight for their own fireside.

Three o'clock—Will you believe it, my sister? We have had a battle, or skirmish, near Bladensburg, and here I am still, within sound of the cannon! Mr. Madison comes not. May God protect us! ….And now dear sister, I must leave this house, or the retreating army will make me a prisoner of it by filling up the road I am directed to take. When I shall again write to you, or where I shall be tomorrow, I cannot tell!

Dolly

"Next only to conversation, letters are the most universal and personal form of communication in words. You may never become a published author, but one kind of writing is available to you as long as you live. You can write letters."

—Richard Lederer

GUIDED WRITING **231**

Prewriting

IDENTIFYING YOUR AUDIENCE. Students who cannot think of anyone to write to might find it interesting to start a correspondence with an overseas pen pal. See the Teacher's Note on page 230. Have students read the Language Arts Survey 2.4, "Identifying Your Audience." Students might list their audience on the page with their graphic organizer.

FINDING YOUR VOICE. Have students determine the tone used by Dolly Madison in the Professional Model. Students might list their intended tone on the page with their graphic organizer. Encourage students to read the Language Arts Survey 2.5, "Finding Your Voice," and 3.3, "Register, Tone, and Voice."

Language, Grammar, and Style

Adding Colorful Language to Sentences

LESSON OVERVIEW
In this lesson, students will be asked to do the following:
• Identify Colorful Nouns, Verbs, and Modifiers, 233
• Fix Dull Nouns, Verbs, and Modifiers, 234
• Use Colorful Nouns, Verbs, and Modifiers, 234

INTRODUCING THE SKILL. Remind students that using colorful language will make their letters come alive. Learning to use colorful language can be applied to many assignments in English class and in other classes. Ask students to find examples of colorful language in the Professional Model and in the Student Model.

PREVIEWING THE SKILL. Refer students to the Language Arts Survey 3.37, "Adding Colorful Language to Sentences." You might give students additional examples of sentences using dull language and show students how to make the sentences colorful.

PRACTICING THE SKILL. For additional practice, have students work through the exercise in the following section of the Language, Grammar, and Style Resource located in the Teacher's Resource Kit: 3.37, "Adding Colorful Language to Sentences."

Check to be sure that your letter contains these five parts:
• a heading or return address that includes your street address, city, state, zip code, and the date;
• a greeting or salutation followed by a comma;
• the body of the letter;
• a closing that capitalizes only the first word, for example, *Yours truly*;
• your signature.

You may add a Postscript to your letter after your signature. For more information about writing letters, see the Language Arts Survey 6.5, "Writing a Personal Letter."

 **Language, Grammar, and Style Adding Colorful Language to Sentences.** When you write, use words that tell your reader exactly what you mean. Precise and lively language makes your writing more interesting to your reader.

The **people** made **noise**.

The **mob** made an **uproar**.

Specific verbs also help to create a clear picture in a reader's mind. Use verbs that tell the reader exactly what you mean.

He **took** the pitcher and **drank** the cool water.

Copy the graphic organizer on a piece of paper. Fill in your ideas about places you have visited or situations you have experienced. Then describe your thoughts, feelings, and observations about your experience.

IDENTIFYING YOUR AUDIENCE. If you could write your letter to anyone at all, who would it be? For this letter, the choice is yours. You can write to someone you know, or you can invent your audience for this letter. As you think about the person to whom you are writing, consider which feelings, thoughts, and observations will be most interesting and captivating for that person.

FINDING YOUR VOICE. You can choose the tone of voice for your letter. Tone is the writer's attitude toward the subject or the reader. For example, your tone can be humorous, serious, pretentious, witty, or wise. Rafael, for example, decided to use a humorous tone to express the comical situations that occurred in Florida. Vickie decided to use a lighthearted tone to relate her horse mishap. Maria chose a serious tone to express her appreciation of the reef.

Drafting
Have fun as you begin your rough draft! You do not have to focus on spelling and letter-writing conventions now. You can fix errors later. Just concentrate on telling about the new place or new situation you experienced. Let your readers know your observations, your thoughts, and your reactions to your experience. Share your insights or offer some advice.

You may want to add an occasional question in your letter. Your questions can be direct or rhetorical. A rhetorical question is one that you ask just for effect or to help your reader reflect on something.

You may want to tell about the new place or situation in chronological order. You would tell about what happened first, second, third, and so on. Then you could describe your thoughts about and reactions to your experiences. You might conclude by summarizing your observations or offering advice to your reader.

As another option, you could start by telling your overall impressions about a place or a situation and then list specific events or details to support your impressions. Whichever organization you use, keep a voice that is appropriate for a letter, for your topic, and for your reader.

Peer and Self-Evaluation
After finishing your rough draft, you can do a self-evaluation of your work. If time allows, you may also want to do peer evaluations. For example, you could ask a peer to take on the role of the person to whom the letter was written. For more

---

Drafting

You might want to review chronological order with your students. Events arranged in order of the time when they happened are said to be in chronological order. Encourage students to use their completed Graphic Organizer modeled on page 231 to help them make sure they are including all the pertinent information about the new place or new situation. Have students write a discovery draft in which they do not focus on spelling, grammar, usage, and mechanics. Students might benefit from reading the Language Arts Survey 2.31, "Drafting."

information, see the Language Arts Survey 2.37-2.40, "Self- and Peer Evaluation."

As you evaluate your draft or that of a classmate, ask the following questions:

- Does the letter tell about a new place or situation you have experienced?
- Does the letter describe or explain what the reader should understand about this place or experience?
- Does the letter tell about your emotions, observations, and thoughts in the new place or situation?
- Does the tone work for your audience and your topic? Is the tone maintained throughout the letter?
- Is the organization effective? Does it help make your feelings, thoughts, and observations real and immediate to your reader?
- Which descriptive phrases give a real sense of your experience? Which could be improved to develop a better sense of the experience?
- What adjectives and adverbs could you add to improve your tone of voice?

Student Model—Revised

Rafael, one of Maria's classmates, helped her with a peer evaluation. Her partially revised draft is shown below. After you read Maria's revised draft, revise your own draft.

> Dear Holland,
>   My boat ride out to the Great Barrier Reef was great at first. I was sitting at the front of the boat having the time of my life and making new friends. Then I went inside to get a drink. Everyone was sick! After that, I felt sickly and went back outside. Then I promised myself that I would not go back in there again. Being outside was fun because there were huge waves and every once in a while the boat would quick jump a wave. When it did, I felt like I was flying.
>   When we got out to the reef, the sea had calmed down a lot. We got our snorkeling gear, put it on, and went snorkeling. When I stepped into the water, I was cold at first, then I got used to it. After I did, I stepped off

He **grabbed** the pitcher and **gulped** the cool water.

A modifier is a word that modifies—that is, changes or explains—the meaning of another word. Adjectives and adverbs are modifiers. Colorful modifiers can turn dull reading into dynamic reading.

The **cold** win blew **hard**.

The **frigid** wind blew **furiously**.

Note that of all the words in a sentence, verbs carry the most weight. Often the right verb will demonstrate exactly what you want to say, creating a vivid picture in the reader's mind. Precise nouns are next in importance, and after that come the modifiers—adjectives and adverbs. While colorful modifiers are important, choose them wisely and use them sparingly. Too many can weigh down your writing.

IDENTIFYING COLORFUL NOUNS, VERBS, AND MODIFIERS. Reread Dolly Madison's letter in the Professional Model on pages 230-231. On your own paper, write down at least ten examples of words that Dolly uses that you find especially memorable. Then identify whether each word is a noun, verb, or modifier. Notice especially how Dolly's precise verbs convey her excitement and sense of urgency.

continued on page 234

Peer and Self-Evaluation
Have students use the checklist on page 233 for peer and self-evaluation. See the Guided Writing Resource located in the Teacher's Resource Kit for a blackline master of the checklist. The checklist is intended to act as a student-friendly rubric that should help students identify specific evidence of writing strengths and areas needing improvement. Make sure students provide concrete suggestions for improvement or specific evidence of the effectiveness of their personal letter. Students might benefit from reading the Language Arts Survey 2.37–2.40 for more details about peer and self-evaluation. See the Guided Writing Resource located in the Teacher's Resource Kit for a blackline master of the self- and peer evaluation checklist.

continued from page 233

FIXING DULL NOUNS, VERBS, AND MODIFIERS. Read through the draft of Maria's letter in the Student Model. Where does she use nouns, verbs, and modifiers in a colorful way? What sentences need to be revised to make the language more vivid? On your own piece of paper, rewrite five sentences from Maria's letter, replacing dull words with more colorful language.

USING COLORFUL NOUNS, VERBS, AND MODIFIERS. Look at each sentence in your personal letter. Underline five examples of colorful language and identify whether each example is a noun, verb, or modifier. Replace any dull or vague nouns, verbs, or modifiers with precise and vivid language.

For more information, see the Language Arts Survey 3.37, "Adding Colorful Language to Sentences."

For help in finding precise and colorful language, consult a thesaurus. See the Language Arts Survey 5.21, "Using a Thesaurus."

the platform. I was stunned by the beauty of the reef. My mom and I went out a ways from the platform. I saw all the colors of the rainbow. I felt gratefully to see it.

When we were coming back to the platform, the coral was not as colorfully, there were big fish all around us, I felt a little scared.

On the boat ride home, I stayed outside. I loved the Great Barrier Reef and the big fish. Miss you lots!

Love,
Maria

Revising and Proofreading
Proofread your letter for errors in spelling, grammar, punctuation, capitalization, and other details. For more information, see the Language Arts Survey 2.45, "A Proofreading Checklist."

Publishing and Presenting
You will need a final copy, an address, and a way to deliver your letter to make your letter complete. Write or print your finished copy on stationery. Are there photographs or drawings that you could include with your letter? Before sending your letter in the mail or e-mailing it, have your teacher check the final copy.

Revising and Proofreading
Remind students that revising includes adding or expanding, cutting or condensing, replacing, and moving text. Have students read the Language Arts Survey 2.41, "Revising." A handout of the proofreading checklist found in the Language Arts Survey on page 888 is available in the Teacher's Resource Kit, Guided Writing Resource Book 2.45. Students might be interested in using common proofreader's symbols, which are found in the Language Arts Survey 2.44, "Using Proofreader's Marks."

Publishing and Presenting
Remind students to write the date on their letters. When students receive responses to their letters, they might be interested in sharing in small groups the feedback they received. You might get students to write additional personal letters by awarding extra credit.

UNIT THREE *review*

Review: Words for Everyday Use

Check your knowledge of the following vocabulary words. For each word, write a short sentence that includes the word in context. To review a word, look back to the page number indicated.

- aggrieved (182)
- agonizing (202)
- barrage (163)
- bewilder (162)
- biddable (188)
- booty (182)
- carnivorous (167)
- compensate (215)
- crescent (166)
- deception (167)
- decrepit (212)
- delusion (218)
- deprivation (202)
- descent (179)
- desolate (212)
- despised (213)
- dingy (218)
- dogged (182)
- escort (214)
- etiquette (189)
- excavate (163)

- ferocious (179)
- forage (188)
- gaudy (180)
- gilded (214)
- grotto (186)
- gruesome (220)
- hauteur (185)
- herbivore (167)
- idle (216)
- inadequacy (215)
- incalculable (188)
- incantation (186)
- nerve-wracking (203)
- noisome (190)
- oblige (186)
- obscure (202)
- obsess (162)
- obtain (180)
- poignant (212)
- pore (162)
- prophesy (186)

- rampant (201)
- rapt (211)
- ravenous (214)
- refuge (200)
- refugee (201)
- repulsive (179)
- resemblance, (213)
- rueful (213)
- shudder (178)
- skew (166)
- susceptible (187)
- tantalizing (184, 214)
- transition (200)
- unwary (220)
- ventilator (178)
- vigil (178)
- vigorous (215)
- vulgar (185)
- wan (179)

Review: Literary Tools

Define each of the following terms, giving concrete examples when possible. To review a term, refer to the page number indicated.

- autobiography (197)
- background information (159)
- chronological order (197)
- first-person point of view (159)

- foreshadowing (175, 209)
- frame story (209)
- homophones (175)
- internal conflict (159)
- irony of situation (209)

- point of view (197)
- setting (175)

VOCABULARY DEVELOPMENT. Give students the following exercise.

Read the Language Arts Survey 1.20, "Learning Synonyms, Antonyms, and Homonym" and 5.49, "Synonym and Antonym Questions." Using the vocabulary words on page 235, write a test containing five synonym and antonym questions. Write three answer choices for each problem. When you are done, exchange tests with a partner.

EXAMPLE
Write the letter of the word that is most nearly *opposite* in meaning to the word in capital letters.

1. OBSCURE
(A) unknown
(B) famous
(C) hidden

Answer. (B) famous

The Theme, Genre, and Group Project questions are suitable to assign as essay prompts to help students prepare for the Unit Test. (To evaluate student writing, see the evaluation forms for writing, revising, and proofreading in the Assessment Resource 4.1-4.9.)

The Theme, Genre, and On Your Own questions can also be adapted for use as topics for oral reports or debates. Refer students to the Language Arts Survey 4, Speaking and Listening. (To evaluate these projects, use the Public Speaking Evaluation Form in the Assessment Resource 4.11.)

Reflecting on your reading

Theme

The main characters in each of the selections in this unit are caught between two different worlds. These characters struggle to come to terms with their experience in "another world" (their own past or a fantasy world) and to use that experience to learn something about themselves. In "Hollywood and the Pits," Cherylene Lee's main character, the 15-year-old girl known as the "Chinese Shirley Temple," tries to establish her identity apart from her past as a child celebrity; now that she is no longer sought in Hollywood, she questions whether or not she has "what it takes" to evolve as a person and create a new life and identity for herself. Like many young people, Mark in "The Serial Garden" often feels unable to control his world. Mark is thrilled to find that he can create a magical world for himself, but then he must face the fact that even the garden world he created has a set of rules that must be followed. Maijue Xiong's autobiographical story of her family's "Unforgettable Journey" relates the tragic experience of her flight from another world (Laos) that will always be a part of her, no matter where she goes. And in "The Inn of Lost Time," the samurai Zenta completes a circle in his life by revisiting a scene from his past — a mystical place that makes him question reality and his ability to trust himself. Write about your thoughts on moving from one world to another.

Genre

In this unit, you read short stories, poetry, and nonfiction. You also examined a storycloth and a chart. How does what you see in Mee Vang's storycloth differ from what you read in "Unforgettable Journey? How does the information you find in the Geologic Time Chart differ from the information in "The Passage of Time"? What types of information and ideas are easily conveyed in visual formats? What ideas and information is best read in prose or poetry?

Group Project

Discuss in small groups the experience of living in two different worlds. How do the characters in this unit's selections handle their experiences of living in another world? What did each of the main characters learn about themselves or about life from their experiences? What did they "take" from their other world into their current reality? In your opinion, are the characters from the stories better or worse off because of their experiences?

   Is there such a thing as an ideal world? With the members of your group, write a description of what you agree would be an ideal world. Would any parts of these worlds have a place in your group's ideal world? What would the weather be like? What would the food be like? What would the ideal world look like? How would people spend their days? Is it easy for members of your group to agree on the elements of an ideal world? How different is your group's ideal world from the world you live in? Share your group's version of the ideal world with the class.

Critical Thinking

In the group activity described on the previous page, you will be comparing your impressions of this unit's selections with members of your group. It's always a good idea to think through your own ideas and opinions before you begin a group discussion. The graphic organizer below illustrates one way to organize the details of this unit's selections and your thoughts about their meaning. You can adapt this graphic "world" by adding layers (circles) for each element you want to address.

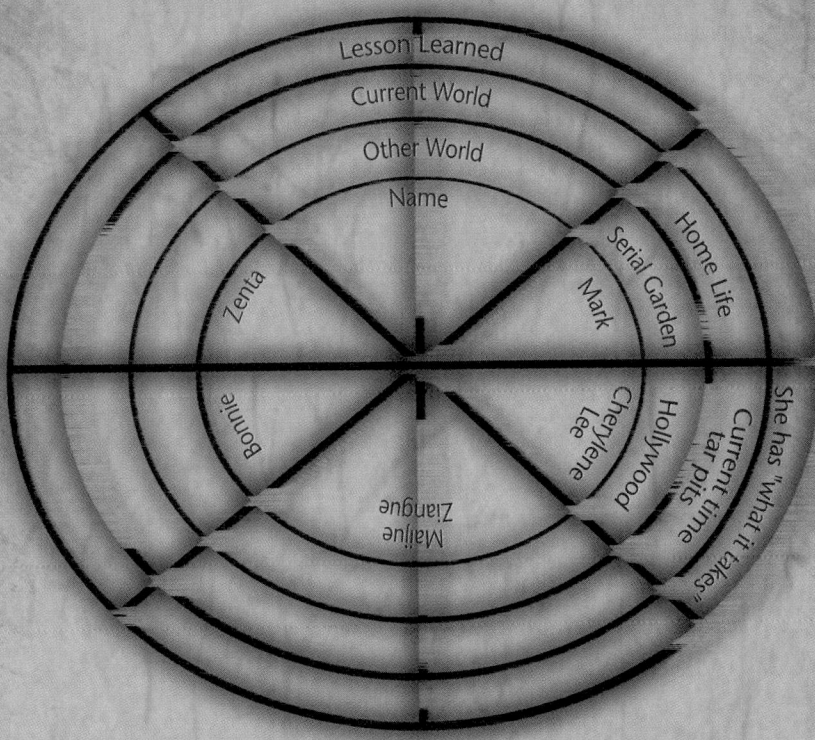

On your Own

Several of this unit's characters experienced another world that existed in their past. Think about your life and what you know of it from the time you were born to now. Create a visual about your life that would read like a storycloth. (Refer to the storycloth created by Mee Vang on page 205). Use simple drawings or symbols, appropriate pictures from magazines, black and white copies of photographs, pieces of fabric—anything that helps tell the story of your personal journey. Once you have finished your storycloth or storyboard, try to look at it with new eyes. Do any themes jump out at you? What experiences are highlighted? Are there any holes in the story? About what would you like to know more? Be prepared to share your storyboard and your findings with the class.

Reflecting on Your Reading
(CONT.)

The Group Project activity can also serve provide an additional or alternate assessment to the Unit 3 Test. Ask students to tie in the insights they have gained from their own journeys to the journeys explored in the literature selections in this unit. (To evaluate group and project work, see the evaluation forms in the Assessment Resource 4.10–4.12.)

Rugby Players, 1920. Andre Lhote. Petite Palais, Geneva, Switzerland.

GOALS/OBJECTIVES

Studying this unit will enable students to
- enjoy fiction, nonfiction, and poems exploring the theme of the sporting life
- define and identify examples of *anecdote, autobiography, concrete poem, description, dialect, memoir, metaphor, personification, point of view, stage directions,* and *tone.*
- engage in a meaningful independent reading experience by reading a sports poem anthology and writing their own related art feature
- write an autobiographical memoir
- demonstrate an ability to use subject-verb agreement

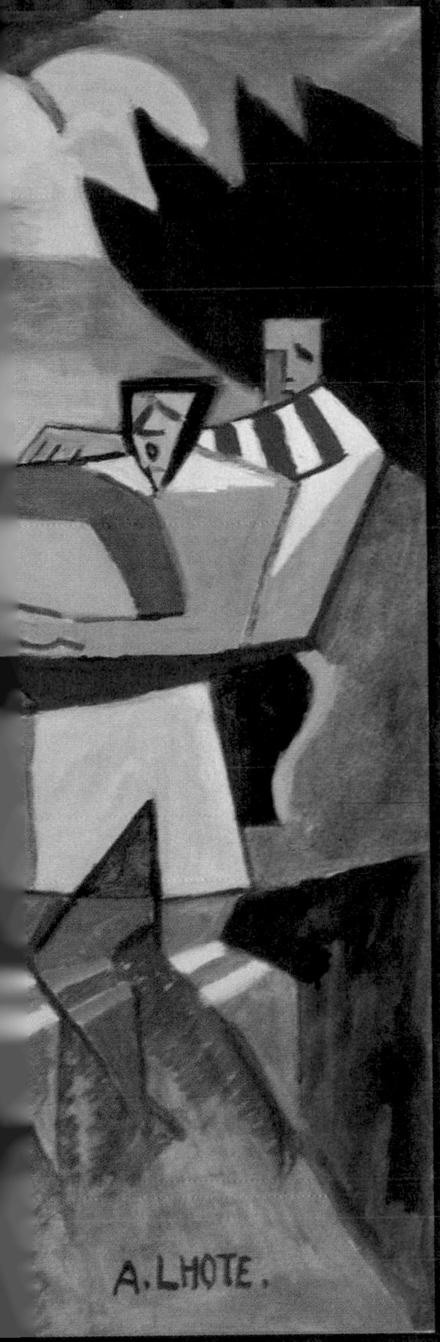

A Sporting LIFE

A. LHOTE.

UNIT FOUR

(Continued on page 240)

Ask students to read the quotes and think about the way sports affect their lives. Then have them choose a quote that reminds them of something that has happened in their own lives. Ask students to write that quote in their journals. Have them write a paragraph beneath the quote that describes the memory they associated with it.

TEACHING THE MULTIPLE INTELLIGENCES (CONT.)

Kinesthetic

Interpersonal

echoes

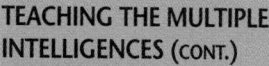

The first thing is to love your sport. Never do it to please someone else. It has to be yours.

—*Peggy Fleming*

The way a team plays as a whole determines its success. You may have the greatest bunch of individual stars in the world, but if they don't play together, the club won't be worth a dime.

—*Babe Ruth*

Be bold. If you're going to make an error, make a doozy, and don't be afraid to hit the ball.

—*Billie Jean King*

Champions aren't made in gyms. Champions are made from something they have deep inside them—a desire, a dream, a vision.

—*Mohammad Ali*

Don't be just like me, be better than me.
—*Florence Griffith Joyner*

Sports do not build character. They reveal it.
—*Heywood Hale Broun*

You don't have to win a medal to feel good about yourself. It's the sense of accomplishment, of doing your best, that makes you a true winner.
—*Shannon Miller*

Talent wins games, but teamwork and intelligence wins championships.
—*Michael Jordan*

240   UNIT FOUR

TEACHING THE MULTIPLE INTELLIGENCES (CONT.)

Prereading

HOW SHE PLAYED THE GAME

by Cynthia L. Cooper

Reader's Resource

- **Eleonora Randolph Sears** was born In 1881. She played a variety of sports—including tennis (winning the national women's doubles championship four times and squash) (winning the first women's national championship). At this time, women were expected to dress in feminine attire while playing sports. Sears began the movement for women to wear practical clothing—such as shorts—when participating in athletic events. She died in 1968.

- **Althea Gibson** was born in 1927. In 1957, she became the first African-American female tennis player to compete and win at Wimbledon and the U.S. Open. That same year she was named Woman Athlete of the Year by the Associated Press. In 1971 Gibson was named to the National Lawn Tennis Hall of Fame.

- **Gertrude Ederle** was born in 1906. After learning to swim as a young child, she went on to win a gold medal in the 400-meter freestyle relay and bronze medals in the 100-meter and 400-meter freestyle races at the 1924 Olympics. In 1926, Ederle swam the English Channel in 14 hours and 31 minutes, breaking the previous record of 16 hours and 23 minutes.

- **Sonja Henie**, born in Norway in 1912, learned to skate and dance as a child. In 1927 she won the first of ten consecutive world ice-skating championships. She also won the gold medal for figure skating at the 1928, 1932, and 1936 Winter Olympics. Henie later became a professional skater and toured in the United States as the star of an ice show. She also made a number of successful movies in the late 1930s and early 1940s. Henie died in 1969.

- **Gretel Bergmann**, a high jumper from Germany, was in her peak form during the 1936 Olympics. Bergmann was asked to leave the German national team, however, because of her Jewish heritage. At this time, Adolf Hitler ruled Germany. The head of the Nazi party, Hitler preached hatred of Jews.

- **Babe Didrikson** was born in 1914 and is considered one of the greatest athletes ever. The Associated Press voted Didrikson the Woman Athlete of the First Half of the Twentieth Century. In addition to being the winner of ten major golf championships, Didrikson excelled in numerous other sports. She broke records in track and field, gained All-American status in basketball, mastered tennis, and was an expert diver. She died of cancer in 1956.

Reader's Journal

What kinds of obstacles have you had to overcome to achieve your dreams?

Reader's TOOLBOX

DIALECT. A **dialect** is a version of a language spoken by people of a particular place, time, or group. Writers often use dialect to give their works a realistic flavor. Notice how the use of dialect helps the reader or audience get to know and understand each character— even when the characters are all played by the same actor.

STAGE DIRECTIONS. Stage directions are notes included in a play to describe how something should look, sound, or be performed. Stage directions describe setting, lighting, music, sound effects, entrances and exits, properties, and the movements of characters. They are usually printed in italics and enclosed in brackets or parentheses. In *How She Played The Game*, stage directions help the reader know what the actor is doing on stage. As you read the play, look for examples of stage directions that describe setting, indicate how something should be performed, and show the movements of characters.

"HOW SHE PLAYED THE GAME" 241

ADDITIONAL RESOURCES

UNIT 4 RESOURCE BOOK
- Selection Worksheet 4.1
- Selection Check Test 4.4.1
- Selection Test 4.4.2
- Language, Grammar, and Style Resource 3.25

READER'S JOURNAL

As an alternate activity, have students write about how they react to those who criticize them unfairly. Does criticism make them want to give up, or does it inspire them to try to prove the person wrong?

GOALS/OBJECTIVES

Studying this lesson will enable students to
- appreciate a play about female athletes
- name some well-known female athletes
- define *dialect* and identify examples of dialect in writing
- define *stage directions* and identify stage directions in a play
- research a sports star
- prepare and deliver a speech
- compare and contrast two articles on an athlete

MOTIVATION

Before students begin reading the play, encourage them to talk about their favorite sports and sports heroes. Encourage them to talk about female athletes they admire, as well as male athletes. Ask them to think about what the best part of being a star athlete is—satisfaction in one's abilities and love of a sport, fame, money, or something else.

READING PROFICIENCY

Have students form pairs and read the play aloud to each other. One student should read the first character's lines while his or her partner listens, and then the two should trade roles for the next character, and so forth.

ENGLISH LANGUAGE LEARNING

Point out the following vocabulary words and expressions
well-bred—showing good breeding; courteous and considerate
frankly—honestly
garb—clothing
ballgirl—girl who retrieves the balls as a tennis match is played
immigrant—person who comes to a new county to settle there
Victrola—old fashioned, wind-up record player
storybook—typical of romantic tales in a book of stories
bristle—irritate, as stiff prickly hairs do
climate—condition of a place or time affecting life or activity

SPECIAL NEEDS

Students would benefit from seeing a videotape of the play enacted or listening to an audiotape of such an enactment.

ENRICHMENT

Encourage students to research the life of another sports figure who overcame adversity and prejudice to succeed as an athlete—Jackie Robinson, the first African American to play major league baseball.

All of the characters in HOW SHE PLAYED THE GAME are real women. As persons from sports history, their very individual stories are dramatized through one actress, who plays all of the roles. The separate stories of the women athletes, are, together, meant to create a collage of the many aspects of personality and character that make a whole. The women, in order of appearance, are:

ALTHEA GIBSON—became the first African-American athlete to break through the barriers of top tennis competition. Although her background as a child of the ghetto made her an unlikely candidate for such a role, her personality did not. We catch up with her on the day she about to win the Wimbeldon tennis match.

ELEONORA RANDOLPH SEARS—one of the century's most versatile sportswomen, Eleo is from Boston, is high-spirited and energetic. Born in the late 1800s, she lived through the 1960s, and serves as the play's "moderator." She introduces and closes the show, and her letters serve as a continuing thread throughout the play.

SONIA HENIE—was the richest athlete in all of history when she died with some forty-two million dollars to her name. Of Norwegian background, she made her fame on ice in the twenties and thirties, and then in movies and her own ice revues. She revolutionized the concept of ice skating by incorporating dance and movement. Her shrewd business skills and a fierce determination combined with her athletic and artistic skills. We see her on ice as her career winds down and she takes stock of her accomplishments and her future.

GERTRUDE EDERLE—was the first woman to swim the English Channel, breaking the records of the five men before her. After her highly publicized Channel swim in the early 1920s, Ederle, an unassuming young woman, seemed to disappear from the public spotlight. We see her forty years after the famous swim, when life has evolved in a different direction.

GRETEL BERGMANN—had the misfortune to be Jewish In Germany at a time when Jews were not welcome. A high jumper, Gretel was added to the German Olympic team of 1936, but when the time to compete came around, Gretel was not in the arena. She relates to us the feelings of all those who find their abilities unfulfilled for reasons beyond themselves.

BABE DIDRIKSON—became famous mostly for her unbelievable skill at golf, but she had a perhaps more extraordinary career in track and field...and tennis...and baseball...and basketball...and....It is no exaggeration to say few athletes ever—male or female—possessed the abilities of Babe Didrikson. While naively rushing forward against the societal forces that wanted women to be everything that she was not, Babe exuded a down-home confidence that pushed her to become a star.

HOW SHE PLAYED THE GAME was first produced Off-Broadway in New York in 1987 by The Women's Project and Productions, Julia Miles, Artistic Director; Suzanne Bennett, Literary Manager. It was produced in a Workshop Production by First Stage, Estelle Richtie Artistic Director; and was originally commissioned by The Playwrights Center, Minneapolis, MN, Gabrielle Cody, Dramaturg. It has played in touring performances in colleges, universities, theatres, special events and festivals.

Cynthia L. Cooper

HOW SHE PLAYED THE GAME

[The actress enters, and takes command of center stage. Playing all the characters and transforming from one to the other from scene to scene, she is now in the character of ELEONORA RANDOLPH SEARS. ELEONORA is a Bostonian, well-bred, energetic, and high-spirited, with more than a bit of verve.[1] Her tone is light, and she has a sense of humor and intelligence about her. SHE whips out a sheet of paper and addresses the audience.]

ELEONORA RANDOLPH SEARS

I want you to listen to this resolution they passed about me:

"Whereas it has been brought to the attention of the Burlingame Mothers Club . . . "

They're out here in California where the United States Polo Team is practicing. Frankly, I had every intention of becoming the first woman on the team.

" . . . that Miss Eleonora Randolph Sears . . . "

That's me…Eleo Sears, great great granddaughter of Thomas Jefferson—the Thomas Jefferson; the Belle of Boston; and voted the Best Dressed Woman of 1910 . . .

" . . . has been parading through our city in the unconventional trousers and clothes of the masculine sex, having bad effects on the sensibilities of our boys and girls; Now be it resolved that we are strongly opposed to this unsightly mannish garb and request that Miss

Sears restrict herself to normal feminine attire.
Signed Mrs. D.S. Harns, the year of 1912."

Naturally, I decided to pay a visit to the Mothers' Club. In trousers!

[ELEONORA speaks as if addressing the Club.]
"Dear women. Mothers! Please sit back down. I have no intention of 'corrupting' you . . . I haven't that much time. This is my unsightly mannish garb. Take a good look, ladies. Because, this is the future staring you straight in the corset![2] Your daughters and their daughters won't stand for being laced up, stowed down, braced against a board! And there's more—women are going to leave these silly parlor meetings and play outdoors! Tennis! Biking! Hiking! Polo! In trousers!

"Ladies, I will make a stand: Women will excel in ways men have not! Not equal. Excel. And to prove it myself, I offer a bet of $200— yes, $200—that I can walk—without stopping—faster and farther than any man has ever done on record. I will walk—from Burlingame to Del Monte, California! One hundred and nine miles! . . . Anyone willing to take my bet?

> **GUIDED READING**
> What does Sears bet?

"Well, then, what a pity . . . Oh . . . Mrs. D.S. Harns, I believe? You accept my bet? Well, what a bully good opportunity. Then, arrange for your monitors . . . I will commence at once!"

---

1. **verve.** Lively enthusiasm
2. **corset.** Tight stiff undergarment worn to support or shape the waist and hips

1. She bets that she can walk, without stopping, faster and farther than any man has ever done on record. She will walk from Burlingame to Del Monte, California, which is a distance of 109 miles.

HISTORICAL NOTE

Inform students that when Sears predicts that women will no longer stand for being "laced up, stowed down, braced against a board" into a corset, she is describing one of the biggest revolutions in fashion in the Western world. For hundreds of years a corset was a staple undergarment for women. They were made of rigid materials, often including whale bone or iron, and women were literally packed and laced into them. They were designed to give women's bodies a very unnatural figure with an extremely tiny waist. One reason why women were once characterized as fainting easily is because corsets made it very difficult to breathe, and when hot or flustered, a woman in a corset might pass out. In the early nineteenth century, as women began to fight for their rights, one of the first things they did as a symbol of their struggle was stop wearing their corsets. For a time, however, traditional, old-fashioned women like the "Mother's Club" described here, as well as most men, condemned women who did not wear and put on bloomers or pants for their then-shocking attire.

CROSS-CURRICULAR ACTIVITIES

SOCIAL STUDIES AND APPLIED ARTS. Interested students may enjoy researching fashion revolutions further and presenting their findings to the class. Encourage students to borrow library books or find and print out images on the Internet related to their chosen topic to use as visual aids. Possible topics include:
- Amelia Jenks Bloomer's fashion revolution
- the fashion revolution Queen Victoria began on her

wedding day
- the introduction of the corset in Renaissance dress
- the transformation in men's clothes in the 1700s from capes to coats
- the popularity of wigs with men of the seventeenth century
- the sudden change in women's fashion following the French Revolution

1. She promises that she will write a little note to every woman trying to make a special mark in sports.

Eleonora Randolph Sears

[ELEONORA *turns as if exiting, begins to strap on her walking shoes, and addresses the audience.*]
One hundred and nine miles is a very long distance. But, I'm no quitter. I'm off.

Five miles. Ten miles. Twenty-five miles. Around about mile 37.1, I'm feeling a little tuckered out. The future of my career as a champion pedestrian doesn't seem too promising.

I promise . . . by George, I promise . . . every time I find out about a woman trying to make a special mark in sports, I will write her a little note. A certain "hey-ho, bully good" congratulations— good luck from me— Eleonora Randolph Sears. I swear to it on this dusty road at mile 37.2 between the cities of Burlingame and Del Monte in the state of California.

[*Conclusion of the opening* ELEONORA *sequence, and the play shifts away from her as the actress transforms into the next character.*]

GUIDED READING

What promise does Sears make?

ALTHEA GIBSON

[The actress takes on the character of ALTHEA GIBSON. Dressed in tennis whites, hair neatly coifed,[3] SHE is strong and tough and carries a tennis racquet with a grip that lets everyone know she intends to use it mercilessly. It is July, 1957, and ALTHEA GIBSON is about to become the first black person—male or female—to win the Wimbeldon championship. When SHE speaks, SHE talks to an off-stage character, Darlene Hard, another tennis player. ALTHEA opens her locker, finds a letter there and reads it.]

"Dear Miss Gibson: Old as I am, I can hardly remember a time when I've been so incensed as I am at the way you've been treated at these so-called tennis tournaments. Well, being the first person—male or female—to break the color barrier is a mighty task. I just want you to know you can count on me rooting my heart out for you whenever you play.

Sincerely: Eleonora Randolph Sears, July, 1957."

That's nice. That's real nice.

[ALTHEA puts the note down. SHE looks up as if someone is signalling her and then calls to Darlene.] What?

Hey there! Fifteen minutes to go, Darlene. The ballgirl just came by. You hear me? The match begins in fifteen minutes!

[ALTHEA picks up the tennis racquet and fiddles with it.]

It's hot out there, Darlene, honey. Real hot. Nearly a hundred degrees of hot. Folks falling out in the stands. It's so hot they ran out and got blocks of ice to keep the Queen cool. To . . . keep . . . the . . . Queen . . . cool. Isn't that something?

GUIDED READING

Who are they trying to keep cool with blocks of ice?

So you take care to splash some cold water on your face before we head out to the court, all right, sugar? I don't want anything happening to you out there today. We got a show to put on for the Queen. Althea Gibson, Darlene Hard . . . two Americans on the grass courts of England.

Me . . . I don't need any cold water. Don't need any ice either. Not today. I'm cool like I've never been. This is the kind of hot we had in Harlem.

Days like today, all of Harlem floats through your memories, pushes out from under your skin like something you can't contain any more. If you listen real close, you can hear the music of Buddy Walker's Harlem Society Orchestra drifting by. And there I am on 143rd Street 'cause in 1939 that's the street the Police Athletic League closed off for us kids to play.

[SHE acts out the next scene.]

"We won! We won! The 143rd Street Club won again!"

"Mr. Walker! Mr. Buddy Walker! Did you see the game? . . . We took the paddle tennis tournament again!"

"Phenomenal? You really thought I played phenomenal? Thanks, Buddy. Will you

---

3. **coifed.** Stylized or arranged

words for everyday use

in • cense (in sens') v., to make very angry. *Coming late to class is the surest way to incense Ms. Porter.*

phe • nom • e • nal (fi nä' mə nəl) adj., remarkable, extraordinary. *Jasper's pitching is phenomenal today.*

ANSWER TO GUIDED READING QUESTION

1. They are trying to keep the Queen of England cool.

CROSS-CURRICULAR ACTIVITIES

APPLIED ARTS. You may have some students in your class who have taken tennis lessons or you may know an adult tennis teacher or expert. Hold a class "Tennis Anyone?" Day, in which students who may never have played tennis are introduced to a new sport. After you have found some individuals who are familiar enough with tennis to teach the sport to others, locate some courts you can use. They may be community courts, or you may have courts at your school or the local high school. See if a local tennis club might donate their courts for a few hours so that a new generation of people can experience the game. See if your school gym, the high school's gym, or a local tennis club will donate used rackets and balls for a few hours. You can then hold a class "Tennis Anyone?" Day, and take an hour or two to show students a few basic tennis rules.

Quotables

"We are merely the stars' tennis-balls, struck and bandied Which way please them."

—John Webster

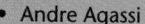
dedicate a song to us tonight?
Right on stage?"

"Why do you ask me a
question like that? I didn't
fight nobody. I didn't have to.
I was winning! And the fact is,
the story going 'round about
me beating up that one boy
on the other team isn't true. I
only did it because he stole
my uncle's five dollars."

"Shoot, Buddy. I don't 'xactly
know *how* I learned to play. I
just did. They didn't teach us
none in school. That's why I
had to quit. And my folks
don't care none. That's why I
had to run away. Now I just
play."

"Would I? Yessir, I would love
to play at the Harlem River
Tennis Courts Club!"

"Yes, sir, I surely do promise."

"Okay, Buddy. I'll say it all the
way through. 'If you take me
to play at the Harlem River
Tennis Courts Club, I . . .
promise . . . not to get into
any fights.' . . . that aren't
absolutely necessary."

I went to the Harlem River Tennis Club,
where the fancy Negro society played. It *was*
different. Everybody was all dressed up in
<u>immaculate</u> white and acted so strange, like it
was a church meeting or something. I just
walked out on the court and played. Pretty
soon all the other players stopped their games and
were watching me. I felt grand. I played hard, just
like I was on 143rd Street.

Althea Gibson at Wimbledon, 1951.

GUIDED READING

How were the
people dressed at
the Harlem River
Tennis Club?

words for everyday use

im • mac • u • late (i ma' kyə lət) *adj.*, perfectly clean. *After Sarah finished cleaning, the kitchen was immaculate.*

But, I guess I kind of had a little slipping in my promise to Buddy.

"What do you mean 'out'? That ball was right on the line! Don't tell me that was out! You tell me to my face that was out!"

[ALTHEA rushes forward like she's going to fight.]

Buddy called me over to the sidelines. "I can't help it, Buddy! The one thing my daddy taught me was how to box. Every time I start to losing, I got to fight the other player."

"I understand," he said. "But you don't really know how to fight. Folks have a different way at the Club. Everyone acts polite. They shake hands. And then they go out and play like tigers and beat the liver and lights—out of the ball."

[Repeating that, gently, as if remembering one of the Ten Commandments.] "Shake hands and beat the liver and lights out of the ball."

Not too long after that the two black doctors saw me play. They thought I was the black tennis player who could play in the white tournaments and win. So, they arranged to take me South, where they were from. I went back to high school. Finished, too. At age 21. Went on to college. And all the while I practiced and worked my tennis game like nobody's business.

GUIDED READING
At what age did Gibson finish high school?

[Looks out as if someone's signalling her.]

What's that? Five more minutes? All right.

Hear that, Darlene? Only five more minutes. Put a washrag to your head. That'll cool you down, doll.

I want to know if you can hear, Darlene? You see, you're white. Harlem's just a name to you. You're still young. About the age I was when I took up tennis. Well, I'm 30 years old, Darlene. That makes me an old lady for tennis.

[As if playing the game.]

Last year, the crowd here at Wimbeldon booed me, and it threw my game. This year, I'm going to serve hard, let the ball jump off the grass. I'm going to rush to the net, cut away the volley. And I won't even notice the heat.

Reason I've been telling you all this, sugar, is, you see, the heat makes me feel right at home. I'm going to win. At last. I've got to, hon. See, I always wanted to be somebody. So what I'm saying, Darlene, is I'm going out there in front of that Queen today, and I'm going to beat the liver and lights out of you. You can understand that, now, can't you, doll?

[Calling.] Yeah. We're ready.

It'll be over soon, hon. Then we'll go back and win the doubles together—you and me. When we go out there, Darlene, I want you to shake my hand. All right, hon?

[SHE grabs the note, sticks it in her bag, and turns, with racquet, as if exiting.]

Yeah. We're ready. We're ready.

— *End of ALTHEA GIBSON* —

ANSWER TO GUIDED READING QUESTION

1. Althea finished high school at twenty-one.

ADDITIONAL QUESTIONS AND ACTIVITIES

Ask students the following questions:
1. What does Althea do when someone tells her that her ball is out?
2. According to Althea, why can't she help this type of behavior?
3. What does Buddy tell Althea about how to "fight" in tennis?
4. Why is Althea especially motivated to win Wimbledon this year?
5. What does Althea tell Darlene she is going to do today?

ANSWERS
1. Althea shouts, contradicts the person, and rushes forward as if she is ready to fight.
2. She says she can't help it because the only thing her father ever taught her was how to box.
3. Buddy says that people fight in a "polite" way at the tennis club: they shake hands politely and then go on the court and "play like tigers and beat the liver and lights—out of the ball."
4. Students may say she is especially motivated because the crowd booed her last year because of her ethnic background.
5. Althea tells Darlene she is going to beat the "liver and lights" out of Darlene in their singles match together and then is going to play with her to win a doubles match.

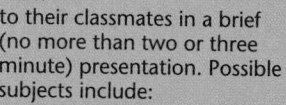

GERTRUDE EDERLE

[Actress takes on the character of GERTRUDE EDERLE, who, in 1926, became the first woman to swim the English Channel. It is 1969 now, and she is 62. GERTRUDE EDERLE is a matronly woman and hardly seems athletic. She is pleasant, and a bit shy. Everything about her seems straightforward, reflecting perhaps her parents' New York-German heritage. She is extremely hard of hearing. In an outfit that indicates swimming—goggles, noseplugs—EDERLE carries a scrapbook, taken from a locker. SHE looks up as if seeing someone.

When SHE first starts speaking, SHE shouts.]

HEY! I REMEMBERED THE SCRAP-BOOK FOR THE CHILDREN. WHAT?

[As if someone has pointed to her ear. The actress quickly puts in a hearing aid.]
I don't mean to blast you out. I take off this silly hearing aid before the swimming class with the deaf children.

[Finishes adjusting hearing aid.]

I'm always afraid of scaring folks off when they find out I'm practically deaf. I told my fiancee back—oh, 40 years ago—back in 1929—I said, "Now that all this channel swimming's made me deaf, sweetheart, I bet you don't want to marry me." Course I was just joking. And he looked at me and moved his lips very slowly, so I could read what he was saying. "I do believe that's the case, Trudy," he said. And you know, I never saw the man again.

[SHE laughs at this.]

Now, then. Here's the photographs. My Olympic medals. Letters.

[A letter falls out.]

Oh, yes, I remember this one.

[SHE half recites the letter. Sound on tape.]

"What a bully[4] accomplishment to be the first woman to swim the English channel! And to beat the records of the five men before you by over two hours! Gertrude Ederle, believe me, I write with my best wishes for your speedy recovery and hope you will not have any regrets."

Ach! Regrets? Can you imagine?

[SHE laughs.] Do I have regrets?

[TRUDY pulls off her hearing aid, puts on a red swimming cap. SHE speaks dreamily, as if stepping into a completely different world.] I wore a red bathing cap. And a black swimsuit, with a silk flag of the United States right on it. It was the same suit I wore at the Olympics in 1924.

[It is the day of the Channel swim. EDERLE talks to William Burgess, who is her trainer.] "Before I start off, I want to thank you for serving as my trainer on the Channel swim, Mr. Burgess. Having somebody who's made the swim gives me courage."

[SHE starts rubbing on jellies, speaking as if a routine chant.] "Olive oil, first. Lanolin[5] second. Then, the special blend of petrolatum[6] and lard."[7]

"But I got something to say, Mr. Burgess. You know, I tried last year and the people in the boat pulled me out before I got across."

"Yes, sir, I know it's bad weather conditions and there's powerful currents . . . and jellyfish . . . and that the water temperature is only 57 degrees."

"I *know* it took you nineteen tries before you made it yourself. But Mr. Burgess . . . my father's a fruit merchant. I couldn't afford coming over on the steamer, or training, or paying for the escort boat. I had to take on a commercial sponsor. You know, that means I won't be able to go to the Olympics again. That's a lot to give up, Mr. Burgess. That's how much I want to swim the Channel."

GUIDED READING

What is Ederle giving up to swim the Channel?

"I know the people in the boat think they're looking out for the swimmer. But, Mr. Burgess, you're not a member of the Women's Swimming Association we have in New York City. You saw the Victrola they installed in the boat? With my favorites—'Yes. We Have No Bananas'—and 'Let Me Call You Sweetheart?' They want me to make it!"

"There. I think I'm all greased up."

[Starts shaking out limbs, making final adjustments.]

"The point is, Mr. Burgess, you're going to be in the boat with the reporters and photographers and I want you to know I am not coming out until I walk on the beach in England. Don't try to pull me out. The Women's Swimming Association is counting on me."

[Re-creating the motion of the swim.]

---

4. **bully.** Excellent; first-rate
5. **lanolin.** Wool grease used in ointments
6. **petrolatum.** Substance made from petroleum oil
7. **lard.** Soft, white fat from hogs

LITERARY TECHNIQUE

DESCRIPTION AND SIMILE. A **description** gives a picture in words of a character, object, or scene. Descriptions make use of sensory details—words and phrases that describe how things look, sound, smell, taste, or feel. A **simile** is a comparison using *like* or *as*. Have students examine the description of swimming in the first paragraph on this page. What does Gertrude say happens when you are in the ocean? What sensory details does she use to create her description of swimming in the ocean? What simile does she use to describe the way the ocean feels? What does she mean by this simile?
Answers. Gertrude says that everything disappears when you are in the ocean and all that's left is what is inside of yourself. Sensory details include sight, sound, and touch: "The eaves crash from the right and the left and the front and the back. Some of them are 18 feet high, seem like they're going to swallow you," and sound: "all you can hear is the roar of the water in every direction." The simile Gertrude uses is, "it feels like it's in you and not that you're in it," meaning that swimming in the ocean feels like the ocean is inside you.

Once you're in the ocean everything else disappears. All of a sudden, there's nothing but what's inside yourself. The water washes over you. The waves crash from the right and the left and from the front and the back. Some of them are 18 feet high, seem like they're going to swallow you. And all you can hear is the roar of the water, in every direction, until it feels like it's in you and not that you're in it. You know then that you're all alone with the ocean . . . just you and it.

Three miles to go. I hear a call over the rush of the water from the boat. Mr. Burgess.

"You've got to give up."

I can hardly believe what he is saying. I let his words roll off me like the waves and I throw myself into the water for more of it.

At 9:40 p.m., on August 6, 1926, I walk out of the ocean in Kingsdown, England with the English Channel swim record.

[SHE laughs.] They were so sure I wouldn't make it that they had already printed an editorial. "In contests on physical skill, speed, and endurance, women must forever remain the weaker sex." Ach!

> **GUIDED READING**
> What did the editorial say about women? What did it assume about Ederle?

[EDERLE laughs, shakes her head, steps back out, puts on her hearing aid. SHE picks up the scrapbook again.]

Oh, there were hard times afterwards. The nervous breakdown. The slip . . . my back was in a cast for four and a half years. And I suppose it's true, Gertrude Ederle is not exactly a household name.

[Looks at letter.]

But do I regret it?

Have you ever heard that song . . . "Let Me Call You Sweetheart?"

[SHE hums, sings it a bit.]

You see, I came back home, and I was the sweetheart of all of New York City. They had the biggest ticker tape parade ever for me . . . Gertrude Ederle, the daughter of a common German immigrant. Two million people filling the streets, flooding it until it looks like the ocean, and cheering for me until it sounds like the roar of the waves. They were throwing confetti from the buildings, and I rode down the street in a brand new car and held my arms out to them. Oh, I suppose it's true they have forgotten me now . . . all those people. But, you see . . . I shall never forget them.

> **GUIDED READING**
> Who will remember Ederle?

Ach. I have to go and start the lessons. You see, once I teach the deaf children how to swim like champions in the ocean ... they shall not forget me.

[SHE folds the letter in half, snaps the book shut, takes off her hearing aid, humming and singing slightly.]

"Let Me Call You Sweetheart . . . "

— *End of GERTRUDE EDERLE* —

SONIA HENIE

[Actress takes on the character of SONIA HENIE. She speaks softly, with a slight Norwegian accent, almost dreamily. SONIA HENIE has an air of confidence, and while somewhat shy, her presence seems to fill the room. It is about 1951. Sonia Henie is 39 years old. SHE whirls around as if skating before the audience.]

My skates shimmer across the ice, turning, turning into the final revolution of the Dying Swan routine. "Revolution." I have hundreds of letters each week and this one with the word revolution comes to my head: "My example has caused a revolution in skating."

I go into the spin. The famous Sonia Henie spin. I push my weight to the tips of my toes, poise my hands very exactly, and I whirl. Around and around. Eighty times around, they say. Suddenly, the whirling, the letter, it all merges into one blur. I begin to think my whole life has been this way—spinning.

I can almost sense the Norwegian woods around me. I am six when I have a gift.

"Mother—these skates are so wonderful! At the river, the men make figure eights on the ice. But I dance! The way I do in ballet! I decided today I want to dance on ice all my life—forever and ever and ever!"

GUIDED READING

What does Henie want to do forever and ever?

Since then, I have never even been a week off skates! I practice and learn, and practice and compete. Now, enough trophies to fill a vault—over 1,400. And my ice <u>extravaganzas</u> and the magazine articles and the dozen movies. And the book—*Wings on My Feet*—that tells the storybook life of Sonia Henie—athlete, ice skating champion, movie star.

I spin yet another time. The girls in the crowd are a rainbow of colors around me. They have collected the Sonia Henie dolls and the Sonia Henie mufflers and mittens and buttons. They have at home the Sonia Henie Pleasure Ice Skates because they want to be like me with a storybook life. They have collected me.

I arch my back into the spin and everything is topsy turvy. My little girl memories are so very different from these girls.

I remember swirling onto the ice at my first Olympics. I am only twelve. They see my short skirt, and gasp. They see my new technique of dancing on ice and gasp again. I finish at the bottom of the list. But, I think, I will be back and win. I am more determined than ever.

I remember Nils Onstad coming to the window as I exercise.

[Actress does ballet exercises, acting out the scene.]

"I should love to join you at the art exhibition, Nils. You are not like the other boys. But, I have my exercises to finish. And then my ballet lesson. And my freestyle practice on ice. I have no time to stop. Ice dancing does not happen of its own accord."

The years run together, like my reflection in the wetness of the ice. Thirty years have spun by, and yet I have not stopped. Nils has called

words for everyday use

ex • trav • a • gan • za *n.,* (ik stra və gan′ zə) spectacular show or event. *The senior banquet was a colorful* <u>extravaganza</u>.

ANSWER TO GUIDED READING QUESTION

1. She wants to dance on ice all her life.

ADDITIONAL QUESTIONS AND ACTIVITIES

Inform students that Sonia Henie helped to create the modern sport of ice skating today in both its use of dance moves and in skaters' costumes. You may wish to bring into class a videotape featuring ice skating so students can see the grace and fluidity of this sport. You might also bring in a clip of a hockey game, so students can see a very different type of skating. Ask students to write in their journals about ice skating and what type of skating appeals to them—the ice skating they see on competition or the type of skating they see in hockey? What appeals to them about this type of skating?

Quotables

"All shod with steel
We hissed along the polished ice,
in games
Confederate."

—William Wordsworth

1. Sonia won't attend the gallery opening because the Hollywood Ice Revue is every night and she has a training schedule.

me this very day, bringing back memories of Oslo.

"Yes, of course I remember you. 'Fame and fortune' would not make me forget."

"So, how exciting! Mr. Nils Onstad, an international art collector! Beautiful things that last through eternity! It is a dream of my own. Someday."

"Why, I should love to join you at the gallery opening. But . . . the Hollywood Ice Revue is every night, and I have a training schedule . . ."

> **GUIDED READING**
> Why won't Henie attend the gallery opening with Mr. Onstad?

"Yes, Nils. I still have a training schedule."

"Yes, yes. Perhaps another time."

The spin says of its own when it is done. The motion slows, the balance becomes more difficult. I lower my arms and kneel into the sit spin.

The spin is over. The applause begins. I smile, I scan the crowd. And, there, for the first time I see the faces—the little girls—red with happiness. The spinning is over and everything is becoming clear: a chapter is missing from the storybook life of Sonia Henie.

I take my bow and make a plan. For the ice melts. The patterns carved on ice are soon gone. The winter has a spring. It is time now for my spring. A springtime in art. A picture is forming in my mind: The Sonia Henie

Sonia Henie at the 1936 Olympics.

Oslo Museum of Art. That will last! "Nils . . . I shall join you."

I sweep the ice one extra time. I reach over the railing and take a button off a little girl's coat, and put it on. A "Skate for Pleasure" button. I have decided. Sonia Henie will spin no more.

— *End of SONIA HENIE* —

MARGARETHE "GRETEL" BERGMANN

[The actress takes on the character of MARGARETHE "GRETEL" BERGMANN. She is rather ordinary-looking with dark hair and eyes, strong legs, and a solemn, but not strident, appearance. SHE speaks with a German accent.]

Sometimes, I think the hardest thing to be an athlete is not to be an athlete. We do not so much choose to be an athlete. It is just what we are. And the times when we are what we are—an athlete— everything comes together—the body and the soul, the heart and the mind—as we race across the dirt of a track, blood rushing, feet flying. And the times when we are not an athlete, when we cannot be an athlete . . . it . . . what shall I say? . . . it bristles against the bones.

GUIDED READING

What does Bergmann think the hardest thing to be an athlete is?

There is no other way to explain. It is like the other things that we are. We are born a woman or a man. We are born with blue eyes or brown. We are born a Gentile or a Jew.

As for me—I was always crazy for sports! When I was growing up in Lauphein, I played on all the boys' teams. In 1930, I won six track and field ribbons. High jump was my best event. I was determined to be a World Class Athlete.

I set my sights on the university in Berlin…to become a teacher of physical education.

[In the next scene, GRETEL speaks to an unseen school administrator:] "*Guten Tag.*[8] I am Fraulein Gretel Bergmann. I have looked over the list of registrants for the university, but I do not find my name."

"Yah. I have my acceptance letter right here."

"I do not understand when you tell me something has changed. My record is good."

"Chancellor Hitler has said not to admit Jews?"

"How long must I wait for the 'climate' to change? I wish to continue sports. Now. In my best years."

"Yah. Yah. I understand there is nothing you can do."

GUIDED READING

Why can't Bergmann find her name on the list of registrants for the university?

I would not give up athletics so easily. I went to England. The London Polytechnic! It was a very good thing: I won the blue ribbon in the high jump, 1934! I was the champion in all of Britain . . . I *was* a World Class Athlete! It was soon after that that my father came to England . . . on a business trip, he said.

[The next sequence is a dialogue between Gretel and her father.]

His eyebrows were tight on his forehead, even as he greeted me.

"Papa . . . why must you be so serious? Look—my new ribbon!"

"Well, yes, I have heard that Hitler is bent on having a <u>fanfare</u> for the Olympics of 1936. It is of no concern to me."

"So, if the Americans say they will not come because of discrimination against the Jews . . .

---

8. **Guten Tag.** German for "good day"

ANSWERS TO GUIDED READING QUESTIONS

1. The hardest thing about being an athlete is not to be an athlete.
2. She can't find her name on the list because Hitler has said not to admit Jews.

HISTORICAL NOTE

Inform students that Adolf Hitler became chancellor of Germany in 1933. Almost immediately he and his political supporters, the Nazis, began persecuting Jews and other minorities. By 1939, Jews were stripped of all their rights and forced to live in closely guarded ghettos. By 1941, Jews were forced to wear yellow Stars of David. Hitler was bent on conquering the world, and soon after he became chancellor, most of the world was involved in a bloody conflict called World War II. Jews in towns Nazis captured during World War II were rounded up, shot, and buried in mass graves. By 1942, the Germans had created their "final solution" to the "Jewish problem." They were sent to extermination camps where those who were fit were forced to labor under horrifying conditions, and those who were too old, too young, too sick, or too starved and mistreated to work were killed in gruesome ways. Over six million Jewish people, and five million other Europeans, were systematically killed by the Germans during this dark period in human history that is known as the Holocaust.

---

words for everyday use

fan • fare (fan' fār) *n.*, a showy outward display. *The parade floats moved down the street amid lots of noise and <u>fanfare</u>.*

ANSWER TO GUIDED
READING QUESTION

1. The Nazis are making threats
against the Jews and against their
families.

HISTORICAL NOTE

The Olympics is a source of great
pride to the nation that hosts this
event. In 1936, this honor fell to
Nazi Germany when the Olympic
games were held in Berlin. Hitler was
excited about these games as he
loved shows of power, and he was
eager to make the games a spectacle
to support German nationalist pride.
Hitler's racist, intolerant attitudes
caused many problems for the
Olympic games in this year. In
addition to the difficulties described
in this play (the United States almost
boycotting the games, the Germans'
false promise to allow Jews to
compete fairly, and the fact that
German athletes were forced to wear
a swastika and salute Hitler), another
scandal occurred at the games. A
United States track star, Jesse Owens,
proved that he was a tremendous
athlete and won four gold medals.
Because he was African American,
however, Hitler refused to
acknowledge him in any way. Many
think this act revealed much about
Hitler's character and the long and
deadly nightmare of racism that was
about to swallow up most of Europe.

Margaret Bergmann at the Women's National A.A.U. championship, 1937.

it is a true thing. A Jew cannot so much as join a track club."

"Come back? It doesn't interest me. I have a future here."

"I don't care if Hitler wants all the German Jewish athletes to try out."

"I don't care if I am the best athlete."

"What? No . . . Papa . . . stop . . . what is it?"

"Threats? They are making threats against me? Who do they threaten?"

"Oh, I see. They make threats against the Jews. And against the families."

> **GUIDED READING**
> Who are the Nazis threatening?

"Yah, papa. I understand. I understand how it is."

I went back to Germany. Twenty-one Jews were "invited" to tryout for the Olympics. Of course, we could not train in the same way as the Aryan athletes . . . but we worked hard all the same. In 1935, only two of us were left on the Olympic team. I was one. The other was Helene Mayer, the fencer, whose grandfather was a Jew. It is so funny that by the religion a Jew is one with a Jewish mother. To the Nazis, anyone with Jewish blood was a Jew.

[As if reading newspaper headlines.] "Miss Bergmann, Jewish high jumper on German team" . . . "Change in Nazi philosophy to admit Jews!" *"U.S. votes to join Olympics!"* "American boys will have their 'birthright of competition.' "And so on and so on. But I was busy . . . working out, running, jumping. In June—only two months before the Olympics—I equalled the high jump

records! Five feet, three inches! Everybody on the team buzzed that I would win.

There was an air of excitement everywhere in Germany about the Olympics that summer. Even the Jewish shopowners were allowed to fly the flag for the Olympics! A big parade was scheduled; the very first Olympic torch was going to be lit. All of Berlin had a spit-polish shine. Soon, the word came: the Americans set sail! The big Games were practically on!

In July—July 16, it was—two weeks before the Olympic Games—I received the letter from the German sports authorities. "Fraulein Bergmann. This letter is to advise you that your achievements have been <u>inadequate</u>, and we have found it necessary to remove you from the German Olympic team. Please depart from the Olympic training grounds immediately."

I was an athlete with no place to compete…no "birthright of competition." I left Germany not long after with ten dollars in my pocket.

So. I have said it is hard to be an athlete and not to be an athlete. But sometimes one must live by another thought, as well. At the medal ceremony in Berlin, all of the German athletes were required to wear a swastika[9] and raise their arms in a Nazi salute. They even said the words, "Heil Hitler." It bristles against the bones. That I could not do. And so, I say to myself, "Margarethe. Perhaps sometimes it is easier on the conscience not to be an athlete, after all."

> **GUIDED READING**
> What are the German athletes required to do at the medal ceremony?

— *End of GRETEL BERGMANN* —

words for everyday use

in • ad • e • quate (i na′ di kwət) *adj.*, not good enough. *The five-dollar bill Mr. Finster gave me was an <u>inadequate</u> payment for mowing his huge lawn.*

ego • tism (ē′ gə ti zəm) *n.*, an overly high opinion of one's own importance. *Charlie's <u>egotism</u> became obvious whenever he began bragging.*

na • ive • ty (nä ē′ və tē) *n.*, simplicity. *The child's remark revealed his <u>naivety</u>.*

BABE DIDRIKSON

[With a musical bridge, the actress takes on the character of Babe Didrikson (also known as Babe Didrikson Zaharis.) Babe Didrikson seems tall, although she is only five feet, six inches. She is angular and has a magnificent body. Her Texas roots show in her voice, as does her homegrown education and a certain kind of <u>naivety</u> mixed with <u>egotism</u>. SHE sits in a bathrobe, picks up a letter, and glances at it.]

What . . . is this one? From Boston. To 'Mildred Didrikson.'

[Tears it in half.]

Don't call me Mildred! It's Babe. Or any of them other names the reporters dreamed up. Like "Muscle Moll." That was one. Or "Texas Tornado." "Terrific Tomboy." Or "Whatta Gal." They got to liking that one. Far as I'm concerned, it's just Babe. Named me Babe right in Beaumont, Texas.

> **GUIDED READING**
> What is Didrikson's first name? What does she prefer to be called?

See, this one day—in 1920 I reckon when I was about nine—I walked out to the baseball diamond where the boys was playing.

[Actress acts out the next scene, as if walking onto a baseball field, grabbing a bat.]

I picked up one of them bats and signalled the fella that was pitching to throw me a few. He didn't really want to and twisted all around on the mound. Well, I whacked that ball good.

---

9. **swastika.** A symbol used by the Nazi Party

ANSWERS TO GUIDED READING QUESTIONS

1. The German athletes are required to wear a swastika and raise their arms in a Nazi salute. They say the words, "Heil Hitler."
2. Didrikson's first name is Mildred, but she prefers to be called Babe.

ADDITIONAL QUESTIONS AND ACTIVITIES

Ask students the following questions:
1. How did Gretel and others feel right before the Olympics?
2. What spoiled Gretel's excitement?
3. What does Gretel do not long after? Why might she have been lucky to make this decision when she did?
4. What does Gretel say "bristles against the bone" at the end of her story?
5. What does she mean when she says, "Perhaps sometimes it is easier on the conscience not to be an athlete, after all"?

Answers
1. Gretel and others were filled with excitement, optimism, and enthusiasm as the games approach and the Americans set sail for Germany.
2. A letter telling Gretel that her achievements are inadequate and that she has been dismissed from the team arrives.
3. Gretel left Germany. She was lucky that she decided to leave in time because not long after she left Jewish people no longer had this option.
4. She says that the fact that the German athletes had to wear swastikas, give a Nazi salute, and say "Heil Hitler" bristles against the bone.
5. Students may suggest that Gretel means that she could not have represented that particular German government in good conscience at the Olympic games because of the racist and intolerant ideas of Germany's ruler.

Babe Didrikson, 1932.

He pitched the next. I whacked that ball even harder. Now he winds up and throws me the best pitch he's got, and I whacked that ball the hardest anyone ever had on that field.

"She hits like Babe Ruth," one of the boys called.

[Signals for more pitches.]

"I might hit like Babe Ruth," I said. "But, I might hit a whole lot better, too."

Gals in Beaumont weren't supposed to be nothing like that. In high school, the girls were mostly in the Miss Purple Club which was something organized to "encourage our boys in athletics to victory." Shoot. I wasn't any Miss Purple, and no Miss Purple was "encouraging" me when I scored 106 points my very self for the girls' basketball championship.

It was about then that I knew Beaumont wasn't enough to hold me. So I went off to Dallas to play basketball for the Golden Cyclones of the Employers Casualty Company. And that's when I found out about track and field.

1932 was about the biggest year for track and field because of the Olympics coming to Los Angeles. The competitors were to be selected at the AAU meet in Illinois. I couldn't hardly sleep the night before. Mrs. Hall, the escort, had to call a doctor out because I had stomach cramps so bad. But in the morning, it was one of those days in an athlete's life when you feel you could fly, you feel you're a feather floating in the air.

At the stadium, I went right up to the man in charge.

[In this sequence, BABE speaks as if she is carrying on a conversation with an invisible person.]

"I'm here to represent the team from Dallas."

"No, sir, there's just me to represent the Dallas team."

"What *event* do I want to enter? *All* the events."

"Well, if the most anyone could possibly do is eight, then that's what I'll do. And the name's Babe, sir. Don't call me Mildred."

I walked out to the stands and Mrs. Hall was the only one I knew. "Cheer for me," I said to her. And while I was warming up, I could hear her: "Go, team, go."

> **GUIDED READING**
>
> What does Didrikson tell Mrs. Hall to do?

[At this point, SHE tries to get the audience to join in a cheer.

BABE does stretches, warm-ups, and then demonstrates each event as she announces the winner.]

The rest of the day went pretty fast. They announced the results over the loudspeaker after each event.

"The hundred yard dash—all winners from the Illinois team. The discus throw, fourth place goes to the Dallas team."

And then finally:

"*Winner* of the shot put: The Dallas team, that is, Mildred—or Babe—Didrikson."

Well, pretty soon, that feeling I had in the morning that nothing could go wrong started a-growing.

"Cheer for me Mrs. Hall," I called.

"The broad jump winner is…Babe Didrikson. First place in the baseball throw with a world's record, Babe Didrikson."

"A new world's record in the javelin with a throw of 139 feet, 3 inches, by Babe Didrikson. Jean Shiley has established a new world's record in the high jump and that's been matched by *Babe Didrikson*! Winner of the 80 meter hurdles in 11.9 seconds, a new world's record by . . . Babe Didrikson."

By the end there I didn't need to be asking anybody to cheer for me…they just did.
   "Go Babe Go."

[Trying to get the audience to cheer.]

I only had me three hours there at the AAU national meet, but when I left, they gave me six gold medals. I broke four world records. And I whupped the other team of 21 women by 30 points to 16.

> **GUIDED READING**
>
> How many world records did Didrikson break?

After I won me three medals at the Olympics, I went back to Beaumont. They had a big parade there for me. And all of the Miss Purple Club was out there a-cheering for me.
You know, folks say I go about winning these athletic games because I have the cooperation thing that has to do with eye, mind and muscle. That sure is a powerful lot of language to use

---

1. Babe tells her to cheer for her.
2. Babe broke four world records.

ADDITIONAL QUESTIONS AND ACTIVITIES

Sports Day. Encourage students to spend some time writing in their journals about what sport or physical activity means the most to them. Students should think about what they feel like when they are doing the sport or activity, the aspects of the sport or activity that appeals to them, and the general knowledge they have about the sport or activity. Interested students might then give a presentation on their favorite sport of physical activity to the class. Students should demonstrate some of their skill at the sport in their presentations. For example, someone who is interested in basketball might take the class outside and show them how to shoot free throws. Someone who enjoys running might show the class some stretches that help you to warm up before a run. A fencer might show others some of the basic stances, and so forth.

CROSS-CURRICULAR ACTIVITIES

Arts and Humanities and Applied Arts. Encourage the class to put on a version of the play "How She Played the game" for another class. Have students divide up all the essential roles of putting on a play. One student should be assigned as the director, another as the stage manager, another as a set designer, another person as a costume designer, and another as the properties manager. Even though this is supposed to be a one-actor play, students may wish to divide up the roles, so that as many students as possible will get to play a part. Students should schedule rehearsals outside of class time. How big and how involved a production this is can be up to you and your students' desired level of involvement. You may wish to create a full production on your school stage with a set and lights, or you may wish to stage a simple production in your own classroom.

1. Babe is diagnosed with cancer.
2. Eleonora promises that she is the future and women will play the game.

RESPOND TO THE SELECTION

Encourage students to discuss both achievements and personal qualities they would like people to associate with their name.

SELECTION CHECK TEST 4.4.1 WITH ANSWERS

Checking Your Reading

1. Which of the athletes broke the color barrier? **Althea Gibson broke the color barrier.**
2. Gertrude Ederle was the first woman to swim across what body of water? **Gertrude Ederle was the first woman to swim across the English Channel.**
3. In the play, which athlete wrote letters to each of the others? **Sears wrote to each of the other athletes in the play.**
4. How many athletes appeared in the play *How She Played the Game*? **There are six athletes in the play: Sears, Gibson, Didrickson, Henie, Bergmann, and Ederle.**

Vocabulary in Context

Fill in each blank below with the most appropriate word from the following *Words for Everyday Use* from "How She Played the Game." You may have to change the tense of the word.

verve phenomenal incense extravaganza egotism revert delirious

1. Jody had hoped for a small wedding and was overwhelmed by her mother's ideas for an expensive _____ for 300 guests. **extravaganza**
2. Joshua was shy when he was introduced to the other members of his acting class, but once he got onstage he played his role with _____. **verve**
3. Even his opponents agreed that cancer survivor Lance Armstrong's victory in the Tour de France was _____. **phenomenal**
4. Jacqui broke curfew even though she knew it would _____ her parents. **incense**

---

about a gal from Texas. All I know is that I can run and I can jump and I can toss things and when they fire a gun or tell me to get busy I just say to myself, "Well, kid, here's where you've got to win another." And I usually do.

I say that even today. To George, my husband. And to Betty, my good friend. Even to the doctors. You see, I done all kinds of sporting events. I won every golf competition they had for women. I was going to enter the U.S. Open, which no woman had ever done, but as soon as the papers printed that, they pretty quick passed a new rule that no woman *could* enter. One time a reporter asked me if there was anything I *didn't* play. "Yeah," I said. "I don't play dolls."

I guess around my 42nd birthday, they come to diagnosing me with cancer or some such thing. But I told those doctors three things. I said, I don't care what it is you call cancer, you just make sure my golf clubs sit over there in the corner of the hospital room as long as I'm here to see them.

> **GUIDED READING**
> What was Didrikson diagnosed with?

And don't be calling me Mildred. The name's Babe.

And you cheer for me, you hear?

— *End of BABE DIDRIKSON* —

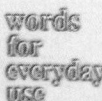**Respond** *to the*
SELECTION

What would you like to be known for after your life is over?

words for everyday use

re • vert (rē vərt') *v.*, return. *The club members voted to revert to the old rules.*

de • lir • i • ous (di lir' ē əs) *adj.*, marked by confusion or wild excitement. *The delirious horse reared and then crashed through the fence.*

ELEONORA

[The actress <u>reverts</u> to the character of ELEONORA RANDOLPH SEARS. She is walking, as in the beginning, clearly exhausted now.]

Eighty miles. Only 29 more to go. Eighty-five. Ninety. I'm walking. Feeling <u>delirious</u>. And, my God, I'm still making promises. Every mile or two. I can't even remember what half of them are anymore. But I'll promise anything if only I can finish.

[Aside.] I'm desperate to win that bet.

Wait! There's something ahead! A dusty old signpost and . . . a horse carriag . . . and a little crowd of people! The hell with promises! I'm in Del Monte!

[SHE yells.] "Ladies of the Mothers' Club! One hundred and nine miles! Nineteen hours and 50 minutes! I made the bully record! Yes indeed! And you ladies look at me. Because I promise you with all the strength of womanhood, one thing: I am the future. We will play the game. And this is how."

> **GUIDED READING**
> What does Sears promise to the Ladies of the Mothers' Club?

[SHE slaps her trousers, music up, strides off stage.]

— *END OF PLAY* —

■

SELECTION CHECK TEST 4.4.1 WITH ANSWERS (CONT.)

5. It wasn't easy to recommend to the board of directors that the best course of action would be to _____ back to the original system. **revert**

Reader's Toolbox

1. What is a dialect? **A dialect is a version of a language spoken by people of a particular place, time, or group. [Writers often use dialect to give their works a realistic flavor.]**
2. What are stage directions? **Stage directions are notes included in a play to describe how something should look, sound, or be performed. [They are usually printed in italics and enclosed in brackets or parentheses.]**

Investigate, Inquire, and Imagine

Recall: GATHERING FACTS

1a. What does Eleonora Randolph Sears say that women will do?

2a. What happens around Gertrude Ederle as she rides in the ticker tape parade?

3a. According to Gretel Bergmann's father, what does Hitler want all the German Jewish athletes to do?

→ **Interpret:** FINDING MEANING

1b. How does she regard the physical strength and abilities of women?

2b. Why will Ederle never forget those people?

3b. What might Hitler gain by achieving this?

Analyze: TAKING THINGS APART

4a. Identify places in the story where women are assumed to be the weaker sex. Using examples from the play, how do the women continue to break this stereotype?

→ **Synthesize:** BRINGING THINGS TOGETHER

4b. What would these women think about women in sports today? What advice might they give to young female athletes?

Evaluate: MAKING JUDGMENTS

5a. Evaluate the effectiveness of using one actor to play all six characters in the play. Would it be more or less effective to use six actors?

→ **Extend:** CONNECTING IDEAS

5b. Find an example of a play in which there is more than one actor. Would this play be effective using only one actor to play all the roles? Why, or why not? What elements would a play require to allow one actor to play all the characters?

Understanding Literature

DIALECT. A **dialect** is a version of a language spoken by people of a particular place, time, or group. Writers often use dialect to give their works a realistic flavor. Notice how the use of dialect helps the reader or audience get to know and understand each character—even when each character is played by the same actor. Give three examples of dialect used by three different characters in the play. What does the dialect tell you about the character?

STAGE DIRECTIONS. Stage directions are notes included in a play to describe how something should look, sound, or be performed. Stage directions describe setting, lighting, music, sound effects, entrances and exits, properties, and the movements of characters. They are usually printed in italics and/or enclosed in brackets or parentheses. In *How She Played the Game*, stage directions help the reader know what the actor is doing on stage.

"HOW SHE PLAYED THE GAME" **259**

ANSWERS TO INVESTIGATE, INQUIRE, IMAGINE

RECALL

1a. She says that women will excel in ways that men have not. She emphasizes that women will not equal but will excel more than men.

2a. Two million people fill the streets of New York and cheer for Gertrude Ederle and throw confetti from the buildings.

3a. Gretel Bergmann's father says that Hitler wants the German Jewish athletes to return to Germany and try out for Germany's Olympic team. He also says that Germany is making threats against the Jews and their families to coerce them into coming back and trying out.

INTERPRET

1b. She believes that women possess great physical strength and abilities and that their abilities surpass those of men.

2b. Ederle will never forget those people because they validate her decision to get a sponsor, give up the Olympics, and swim the English Channel.

3b. Students may say that the United States threat not to attend the 1936 Olympics if Jews are discriminated against would spoil the Olympics Germany is hosting. Thus, Hitler gains the attendance of other nations to the German-hosted Olympics by pretending that he is encouraging Jewish athletes to participate.

ANALYZE

4a. Students may point to Mr. Burgess trying to talk Gertrude Ederle out of the channel swim, the press writing editorials about Ederle's failure and calling women the weaker sex even before she successfully completes her swim, the boys assuming that Babe Didrikson can't play baseball, and the U.S. Open preventing Babe from competing by excluding women. The women break these stereotypes by excelling in athletic competition and breaking records.

SYNTHESIZE

4b. Students may suggest that these women would be pleased to see that women's sports have increased in popularity and level of competition. Women are continually setting and breaking new world's records and challenging preconceived notions about the limits of women's ability. Students may say, however, that the women may be disappointed that women's sports are not given equal coverage or sponsorship in comparison with men's sports. They might encourage female athletes not to be content with the status quo but to keep trying to be

---

ANSWER TO INVESTIGATE, INQUIRE, IMAGINE (CONT.)

the best athletes they can, beat old records, and prove themselves on the fields of competition.

EVALUATE

5a. *Responses will vary.* Some students will like the idea of seeing one actor transform into six very different characters as this proves the actor's skill. Other students may suggest that seeing different actors in each role would be interesting because the director could cast very different physical types to capture the range of different types of women who excel in sports.

EXTEND

5b. Responses will vary, depending on the play students choose. They may note that when there is dialogue between characters, it would be difficult to use only one actor. Using one actor may be best suited for plays that are mostly monologues.

Answers to Understanding Literature can be found on page 260.

TEACHER'S EDITION **259**

Responses will vary. Possible responses are given.
Character: Bostonian, well bred, energetic, and high-spirited, with more than a bit of verve. *How performed:* Her tone is light. *Movement:* The actress enters and takes command of center stage.
Character: Dressed in tennis whites, hair neatly coifed. *How performed:* Repeating that, gently, as if remembering one of the Ten Commandments. *Movement:* Puts the note down. She looks up as if someone is signaling her and then calls to Darlene.
Character: Gertrude Ederle is a matronly woman and hardly seems athletic. *How performed:* When she first starts speaking she shouts. *Movement:* The actress quickly puts in a hearing aid.
Character: Sonia Henie has an air of confidence, and while somewhat shy, her presence seems to fill the room. *How performed:* She speaks softly, with a slight Norwegian accent. *Movement:* Actress does ballet exercises, acting out the scene. *Movement:* n/a
Character: She is rather ordinary looking with dark hair and eyes, strong legs, and a solemn, but not strident appearance. *How performed:* She speaks with a German accent.
Character: She is angular and has a magnificent body. *How performed:* Her Texas roots show in her voice. *Movement:* Tears it [the letter] in half.

Create a chart like the one shown in the graphic organizer below. Give examples of stage directions from *How She Played the Game* that describe character, how something should be performed, and movements of characters. Then get together with a partner. Suppose that each of you is the director of this play, each putting on your own production. Compare your list of stage directions with those of your partner. How do the stage directions force your plays to be the same? What kinds of things are left out of the stage directions that could make your plays different?

Graphic Organizer

Character	How something should be performed	Movements of characters
a Bostonian, well-bred, energetic, and high-spirited	repeating gently	picks up the tennis racket

Writer's Journal

1. Pretend you are Eleonora Randolph Sears. Write a short **note** to your favorite female athlete who tried to make a special mark in sports.

2. Write an additional **paragraph** to the end of Sonia Henie's story. What does she do now that she spins no more?

3. Imagine you have written a play. You are now sitting in the audience and the curtain rises. What does the stage look like? Write the **stage directions** that describe the setting of the opening scene in your play.

ANSWERS TO UNDERSTANDING LITERATURE

DIALECT. *Responses will vary. Possible responses are given.* Students may point to the following examples: Althea Gibson—"Shake hands and beat the liver and lights out of the ball"; Gretel Bergmann—"Guten Tag. I am Fraulein Gretel Bergmann," and Babe Didrikson—"See, this one day—in 1920 I reckon when I was about nine."

STAGE DIRECTIONS. Students should note that the stage directions primarily deal with where characters move, the actions they take, and the way they deliver certain lines. The stage directions, however, only provide an outline for the director and within that outline the director is free to incorporate other actions, gestures, and ways for actors to deliver lines.

Skill Builders

Language, Grammar, and Style

WORKING WITH NEGATIVES. When working with negatives, make sure to use only one negative in each sentence. Check your writing to be sure that you have not used a negative word such *as not, nobody, none, nothing, hardly, barely, can't, doesn't, won't, isn't,* or *aren't* with another negative word. Change double negatives by replacing one of the negative words in the sentence with a positive word. For more information, see the Language Arts Survey 3.25, "Working with Negatives."

   Check each of the sentences below to see whether it uses negatives correctly. Make a numbered list on your own paper. If the sentence is correct, write *Correct* on your paper. If it is incorrect, write the sentence so that it uses negatives correctly.

1. Eleonora Randolph Sears hardly never relaxed or sat still.
2. Nobody could never say nothing to criticize Babe Didrickson's golf game.
3. It didn't make no difference to Gertrude Ederle that the English Channel was so cold.
4. Hardly no one had ever heard of Althea Gibson when she started playing tennis.
5. Sonja Henie wasn't about to let anyone outperform her on the ice.
6. Gretel Bergmann didn't never get to compete in the Olympics in 1936 because she was banned from the German team.
7. There won't be no rematch because of bad weather.
8. Why didn't these athletes never get the recognition they deserved?
9. It amazed me that swimming the Channel wasn't no more exhausting than that.
10. Wouldn't you ever like to take on such a challenge?

Study and Research

RESEARCHING A SPORTS STAR. Using library resources and/or the Internet, research a sports star who has overcome obstacles to reach his or her goals. Compare the athlete's story to one of the characters in the play. How are the two athletes similar? How are they different?

Speaking and Listening

PREPARING A SPEECH. Pretend you are the youngest athlete to win an award or medal in your favorite sport. Write an acceptance speech in which you describe the sacrifices you have had to make in order to dedicate your life to achieving your goal. Write about how it makes you feel and whether or not you would do it again if you could turn back time. If possible, present your speech in class or tape record or videotape your speech to share with the class.

Media Literacy

ANALYZING AN ARTICLE. Find at least two magazine or newspaper articles about an athlete who broke a major record. Compare and contrast the articles. Examine the focus of each article, the points the authors emphasize, the tone of the authors' writing, and the mood the articles create. How do the articles differ? How are they similar? Share your findings with the class.

ANSWERS TO SKILL BUILDERS

Language, Grammar, and Style
WORKING WITH NEGATIVES. Responses may vary, but students' sentences should be similar to the following.

1. Eleonora Randolph Sears hardly ever relaxed or sat still.
2. Nobody could ever say anything to criticize Babe Didrickson's golf game.
3. It didn't make any difference to Gertrude Ederle that the English Channel was so cold.
4. Hardly anyone had ever heard of Althea Gibson when she started playing tennis.
5. *Correct*
6. Gretel Bergmann didn't ever get to compete in the Olympics in 1936 because she was banned from the German team.
7. There won't be a rematch because of bad weather.
8. Why didn't these athletes ever get the recognition they deserved?
9. It amazed me that swimming the Channel wasn't any more exhausting than that.
10. *Correct*

Study and Research
RESEARCHING A SPORTS STAR. Good places for students to look for information on a sports star include encyclopedias, reference books, books of sports heroes for past sports stars, and popular magazines, such as Sports Illustrated, and the Internet for more recent sports stars. Students should then write a brief comparison and contrast essay (no more than a page) comparing their chosen sports star to one of the sports stars featured in the play. Students should make sure that there is a point of comparison between the two when they choose the figures to research and write about.

Speaking and Listening
PREPARING A SPEECH. For information on the verbal and nonverbal cues to use in their speech, refer students to the Language Arts Survey, "Giving a Speech." You may urge students to write "stage directions" along with their speech, or notes about how they will deliver lines and what nonverbal cues such as gestures or facial expressions they will use in their speech.

Media Literacy
ANALAZING AN ARTICLE. Encourage students to think critically about both articles and pay attention to when the author is sharing opinion rather than fact. For more information on how to do this, refer students to the Language Arts Survey, "Discriminating Fact from Opinion."

READER'S JOURNAL

As an alternate activity, students might write about any activity that they would define as their own "first love." What made them decide that they enjoyed this activity? Is it something they still enjoy? Why, or why not?

Reader's Journal

What is your favorite sport to watch or play? Describe what you like most about that sport.

Reader's TOOLBOX

POINT OF VIEW. Point of view is the vantage point from which a poem or story is told. If a poem or story is told from the first-person point of view, the speaker uses the pronouns *I* and *we*. If the speaker uses the pronoun *you*, the writing is in the second-person point of view. In the third-person point of view, the speaker uses words such as *he, she, it,* and *they*. As you read the poems, try to determine the point of view used in each.

TONE. Tone is a writer or speaker's attitude toward the subject. For example, tone can be considered happy, angry, or sad; nostalgic or eager; serious or light. The tone of a piece of writing or of a speech can include one or more of any of the emotions and attitudes that a writer might reveal. As you read these poems, think about the following questions. What attitudes or emotions does the writer reveal in "First Love"? How do the writer's attitudes and emotions differ in "Point Guard"?

Prereading

"FIRST LOVE" by Carl Lindner
and
"Point Guard" by Arnold Adoff

Reader's Resource

- **SPORTS CONNECTION.** James Naismith invented the game of basketball in 1891. As a physical education teacher in Springfield, Massachusetts, Naismith wanted to develop an indoor game that would be fun, easy to learn, and vigorous. At first, Naismith used large peach baskets for the hoops and the game earned the name basketball.

Dr. James Naismith

- As basketball developed further in the 1900s, changes to the rules streamlined the game. Metal hoops took the place of baskets, and standards called for five players per team on the floor at a time. Players began to specialize in specific positions on the floor. Most modern teams have a center, two forwards, and two guards. A guard often specializes as either a point guard—who runs the team's offense—or a shooting guard—who takes more outside shots. The center usually stays near the basket, taking close shots and rebounding. Forwards move around and through the key—the painted free-throw area in front of each basket.

GOALS/OBJECTIVES

Studying this lesson will enable students to
- enjoy two poems about basketball
- briefly explain the history of basketball and some of the positions in modern basketball
- define *point of view* and identify the point of view used in a poem
- define *tone* and recognize the tone of a literary work

- write a sports article using colorful nouns, verbs, and modifiers
- work as a group to create and practice a cheer
- create a timeline of basketball history
- write letters of request and thanks for a sports memorabilia raffle

First

L O V E

Before sixteen
I was fast
enough to fake
my shadow out
and I could read
every crack and ripple
in that patch of asphalt.
I owned
the slanted rim
knew
the dead spot in the
      backboard.
Always the ball came back.

Every day I loved
to sharpen
my shooting
     eye,
waiting
for the touch.
Set shot, jump shot,
layup, hook[1]—
after a while
I could feel
the ball hunger-
ing to clear
the lip of the rim,
the two of us
falling through. ∎

GUIDED READING

What did the speaker love to do?

Carl Lindner

---

1. **Set shot, jump shot, layup, hook.**
Different types of basketball shots

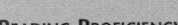
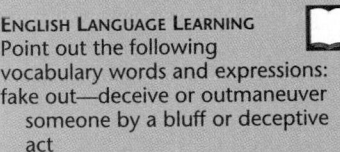

LITERARY TECHNIQUE

Concrete Poem. A **concrete poem,** or **shape poem,** is one printed in a shape that suggests its subject matter. Inform students that the poem "Point Guard" has a unique shape. Ask students to identify how that shape enhances the poem's words. Of what does the shape of the poem remind them?
Answers. Students may suggest that the shape of the poem enhances its subject—basketball—because the shape of the poem reminds them of the zigzagging moves of a basketball player as he or she dribbles and passes the ball down the court.

ADDITIONAL QUESTIONS AND ACTIVITIES

Students may wish to form large groups and attend a school or local basketball game. Tell them to spend some time thinking about the sensory details—the sights, sounds, smells, feels, and tastes of the experience—when they get home. Then, they should each write a few descriptive sentences about the game, incorporating as many concrete sensory details as possible.

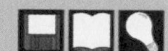

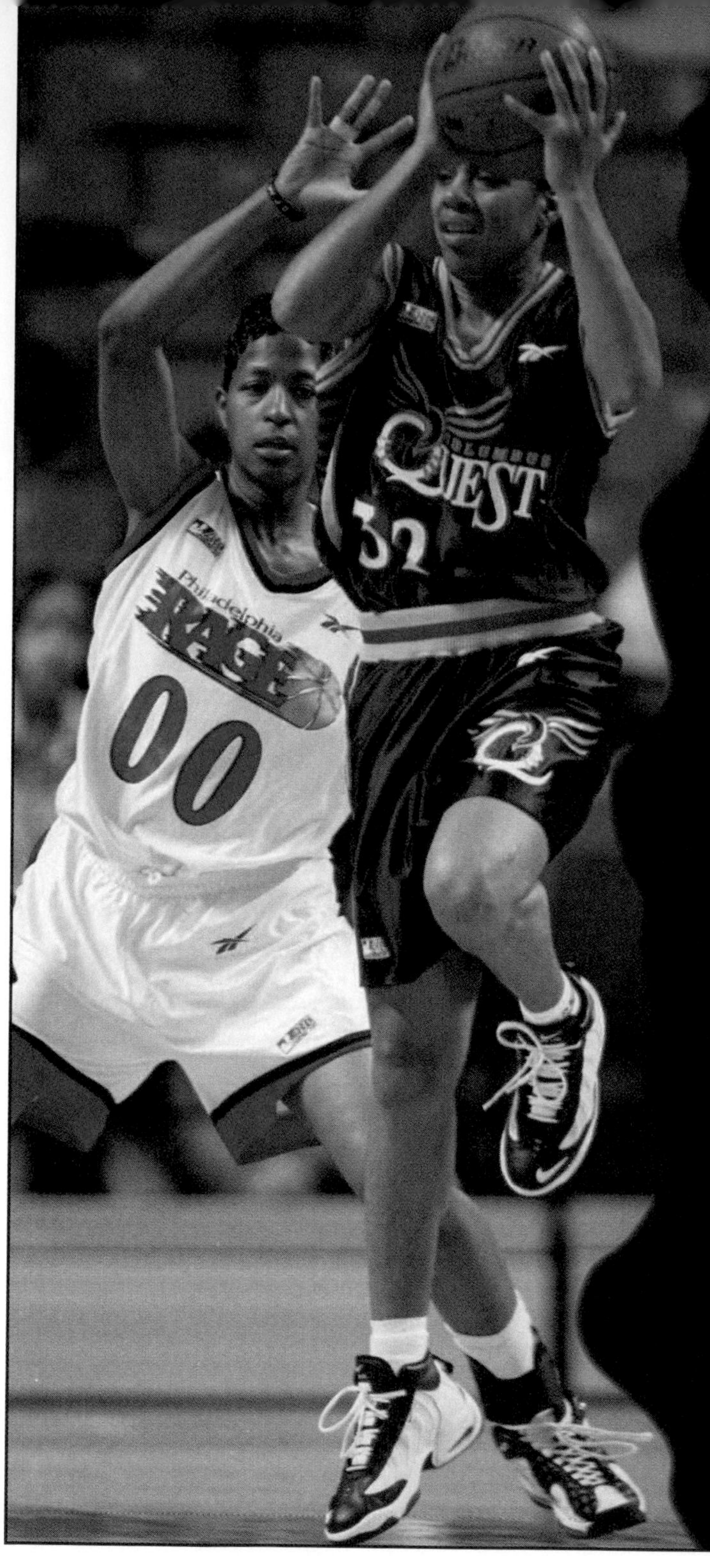

Point Guard

Arnold Adoff

You bring the ball down the court.
The pick[1] is set.
The play is set. The movement of
the ball
is faster
than all
the
defensive
hands and heads,
and you
get free.
You pass into the big girl
at the key. She turns
and
shoots and scores.
The crowd roars. ■

1. **pick.** Strategy in which a player legally blocks the movement of an opponent

Respond *to the* SELECTIONS

Do you prefer quick movements and fast-paced games or slower games that perhaps involve specific strengths or in-depth thought? Explain your answer.

About *the* AUTHORS

Arnold Adoff is a popular poet who has received many awards for his published works, which include the books *Slow Dance Heartbreak Blues, The Basketball Counts,* and *Love Letters.* Adoff lives in Ohio with his wife, Virginia Hamilton.

Adoff grew up listening to stories and poems at home. Poems were to him much like the stories or like little songs. After a 4th-grade teacher showed Adoff the beauty in poetry, he discovered that he wanted to write it himself. He developed a desire to "make something living on the page."

Adoff likes the idea of getting an entire "story" on a single page. He describes two main elements in his poetry—music and meaning. "I like to think of poetry as a mix of saying, or creating meaning, and singing, or creating beautiful sounds," he says. Adoff writes for young people because it is his goal to create an impact on a young person's soul and to make the world a better place. He writes about many subjects. As far as developing ideas to write about, Adoff says you don't have to look far or think of something unusual. "Ideas are as close as your hand in front of your face," he says. He likes to write about sports because sports have always been an important part of his life and his kids' lives.

Carl Lindner, professor of English at the University of Wisconsin–Parkside, has published two books of poems, *Shooting Baskets in a Dark Gymnasium* and *Angling into Light.* Below, Lindner answers a few questions about poetry, sports, and teaching.

What prompted you to write "First Love"?
Basketball was my first great passion. Throughout my teens, I didn't just love to play, I played to live. This poem is about the speaker warming up on the courts, shooting by himself, loosening up as he works on various shots, and then feeling that special connection that comes when shooter, ball and rim are one. That feeling—a combination of unity, sureness, relatedness, clarity, and peace—closely resembles experiencing the bliss of love. It's mystical when you are in this special place or "zone." It's when you know the ball is going in as soon as it leaves your hands, and even before it leaves.

Can you share some thoughts on reading poetry?
Poetry has to be heard before it is seen. I tell my students to "hear" their poems, that poetry enters through the ear and makes its way to the heart; the work of the eye and brain is secondary.

◄ Tonya Edwards looks to pass while being guarded by La'Kesha Frett in a 1998 American Basketball League game.

"FIRST LOVE" AND "POINT GUARD" **265**

RECALL

1a. The speaker says he could fake out his shadow and read every crack and ripple in the asphalt of the court before he was sixteen.

2a. Every day the speaker sharpened his shooting eye by practicing various baseball shots.

3a. The movement of the ball is faster than all the defensive heads and hands.

4a. The big girl shoots and scores a point with the basketball.

INTERPRET

1b. The students may be pointing out that he loved and played basketball from such an early age that it became an essential part of his life and the way he perceived the world around him.

2b. Students may say the speaker practices this every day not only to sharpen his skill, but because it seems to be an activity in which the speaker can focus and find an inner peace and clarity.

3b. The quickness of the point guard's movement and passing leads to a score for the team with the ball.

4b. The big girl might be the center or the shooting guard. The point guard is the "you" in the selection who quickly brings the ball down the court and passes it in the poem.

ANALYZE

5a. Words that describe the speaker's views of his abilities include *fast, could read every crack and ripple, owned the slanted rim,* and *could feel the ball hungering to clear the lip of the rim.* The speaker's views of the abilities of the offensive team are indicated by words such as *is set, faster than all the defensive hands and heads,* and *the crowd roars.*

SYNTHESIZE

5b. In "First Love," the speaker's main idea is his own confidence in his abilities and love for baseball. In "Point Guard," the main idea is the careful planning, quick motion, and team work that lead to scoring a point in baseball.

EVALUATE

6a. *Responses will vary.*

EXTEND

6b. Students may say that "Point Guard" focuses more on describing how an actual basketball play might go on a team, while "First Love" is more focused on a solitary individual practicing the sport. *Responses will vary.*

Investigate, *Inquire,* and Imagine

Recall: GATHERING FACTS

1a. What does the speaker in "First Love" say he could do before he was sixteen?

2a. What did the speaker do every day?

3a. In "Point Guard," what is the movement of the ball faster than?

4a. What does the big girl do?

Interpret: FINDING MEANING

1b. Why might the speaker point out that he could do these things before sixteen?

2b. Why might the speaker have done this every day? What benefits could there have been?

3b. What does this achieve for the team with the ball?

4b. What position might the big girl play? Who is the point guard?

Analyze: TAKING THINGS APART

5a. In "First Love," what words describe the speaker's views about his abilities as a young basketball player? What words indicate the speaker's views on the abilities of the offensive team in "Point Guard"?

Synthesize: BRINGING THINGS TOGETHER

5b. Summarize the speaker's main idea in "First Love." Summarize the speaker's main idea in "Point Guard."

Evaluate: MAKING JUDGMENTS

6a. How well does "First Love" convey the sensations of playing or watching basketball? How well does "Point Guard" achieve the same?

Extend: CONNECTING IDEAS

6b. What different but rewarding aspects of the game does each poem focus on? Which of these two poems most interests you? Why? What is most appealing about the poem you relate to? How does it reflect an experience that you have had?

Understanding Literature

POINT OF VIEW. Point of view is the vantage point from which a poem or story is told. What point of view is used in "First Love"? What point of view is used in "Point Guard"? How does the point of view influence your experience as a reader? How do you experience "First Love"—as a participant or a spectator? How do you experience "Point Guard"?

Answers to Understanding Literature can be found on page 260.

TONE. Tone is a writer or speaker's attitude toward the subject. A writer's emotions and attitudes are reflected in word choice, word order, punctuation, and emphasis. How do you characterize the tone in "First Love"? How is the tone revealed? How would you describe the tone in "Point Guard"? How is that tone revealed? How does each writer's point of view affect the tone of his poem? You may want to use graphic organizers like those shown below to sort your thoughts for each poem. Use direct evidence from the poem to form clues. Describe the tone of each in your own words.

Graphic Organizer

"First Love"	
Clues	I owned the slanted rim, knew the dead spot
Tone	

"Point Guard"	
Clues	The pick is set. / The play is set.
Tone	

Writer's Journal

1. Write a **critique** evaluating a friend's strengths and weaknesses in performing a certain activity.
2. Write a **slogan** persuading other young people to become involved in your favorite sport.
3. Write **directions** for executing one specific skill in a sport of your choice. Imagine you are assisting someone who has never played that sport.

For "First Love" students may list the following clues: before sixteen I was fast enough to fake my shadow out, I owned the slanted rim, knew the dead spot in the backboard, loved to sharpen my shooting eye, I could feel the ball hungering to clear the lip of the rim. They may describe the tone with words such as confident, proud, enthusiastic.

For "Point Guard" students may point to the following clues: the pick is set, the play is set, the movement of the ball is faster than all the defensive hands and heads, shoots and scores, and the crowd roars. Students may say the tone is one of excitement and celebration.

ANSWERS TO UNDERSTANDING LITERATURE

POINT OF VIEW. In "First Love," the point of view is first-person, so the reader can see an individual revealing personal feelings. "Point Guard" uses second-person point of view to help involve the reader in the excitement of a basketball game. Students may say they experience "First Love" as a spectator and "Point Guard" as a participant.

TONE. Students may say that in "First Love" the tone is one of confidence and calm enthusiasm. The tone is revealed through the speaker's confident description of his own ability to play basketball and his seeming ability to "feel" where the ball wants to go. In "Point Guard" students may say the tone is one of active excitement and celebration. The tone is revealed through the triumphant description of the point guard moving the ball faster than defensive heads and hands, the big girl shooting and scoring, and the crowd roaring in applause.

Language, Grammar, and Style & Media Literacy

SPORTS WRITING AND BROADCASTING. Find some professional examples of sports articles in your local metropolitan paper or in a magazine such as *Sports Illustrated*. You may want students to take this activity a step further by having them send their work to a neighborhood or school newspaper or local cable television station. They should include with their work a business letter outlining the project and how they envision it being used. They should also follow up with a phone call.

Collaborative Learning & Speaking and Listening

CREATING A CHEER. If the students' school has a pep squad, talk to them about ideas for cheers. Be careful that when you are teaching this activity, it doesn't evolve into a "cheerleaders are girls, players are boys"–type activity. Emphasize that in universities and many high schools today both men and women are on their school pep or spirit squad and that the squad can root for both boys' and girls' teams.

Study and Research

BASKETBALL PAST AND PRESENT. Students may use the information on the Prereading page of this selection as a starting point for their timelines. Students should be able to find much other information in a good encyclopedia. If students need help in creating time lines, refer them to the Language Arts Survey, "Working with Time Lines."

Applied English

FUNDRAISING. Create a list of possible teams to contact on the board, and assign students' names to these teams so that students aren't all contacting the same team. Be forewarned that professional teams get many such requests, so students may have better feedback from local or college teams.

Skill Builders

Language, Grammar, and Style & Media Literacy

SPORTS WRITING AND BROADCASTING. Both poems you just read use language that is vivid and spare. Vivid language incorporates words that are colorful, active, and creative. Refer to the Language Arts Survey 3.87, "Adding Colorful Language to Sentences" for more information on vivid language. Spare language uses as few words as possible to make a point and avoids unnecessary words and phrases. Many sports writers and broadcasters also use these techniques to create interest and suspense.

By yourself or with a partner, plan to report on a local sporting event, either in print or on video. You may want to start by reviewing articles or sportscasts to see how well they draw in the reader or viewer. What elements of the articles or sportscast would you want to use? On what elements could you improve?

View a local sporting event, taking notes on the progression of the game, meet, or race. Then write a short article or videotape a report of the event. Incorporate vivid language without being wordy. Review your writing or videotape and revise and edit it as needed. When finished, share your work with the class.

Collaborative Learning & Speaking and Listening

CREATING A CHEER. Cheers—rhymed verses to encourage players or spectators at an athletic competition—are often created by individual sports teams, cheerleading teams, or other people involved in the sport. In a small group, brainstorm a short list of cheers you already know. Then write a cheer for an athletic team at your school. Use rhyme and rhythm to cre-ate a cheer that is memorable and easy and fun to recite. Practice chanting your cheer in unison, adding clapping or movement if you wish. Use your cheer at a sporting event.

Study and Research

BASKETBALL PAST AND PRESENT. Research the history of basketball from the 1890s to the present. Look for major changes and developments in the sport. Take notes as you do your research, and verify your findings by using several sources. Then, make a timeline that highlights the developments you investigated. You may want to create your timeline on a large roll of paper or on a series of poster boards so that you can display it in class. You may use the format below to begin.

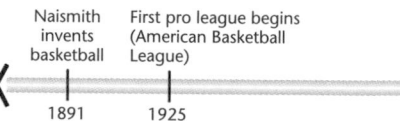

Naismith invents basketball — 1891

First pro league begins (American Basketball League) — 1925

Applied English

FUNDRAISING. Write business letters to several sports teams in your area, requesting any memorabilia—T-shirts, caps, bags, cups, balls, etc.—that they could donate for a raffle to raise money for your school library. Keep track of the responses you get, and follow up on any letters that do not receive a response. Gather the goods you do receive, and with school staff members, plan the raffle. Sell tickets at $1 apiece to students, teachers, and other staff members. On the final day, hold a drawing to determine the winners. Write notes to donors, thanking them for their contributions and reporting the success of the raffle.

Prereading

"400-METER FREE STYLE"

by Maxine Kumin

Reader's TOOLBOX

CONCRETE POEM. A **concrete poem**, or shape poem, is one printed or written in a shape that suggests its subject matter. By using this technique, Kumin makes words and a picture work together to express her impression of a swimming race. How does the shape of the poem create the image of a swimming race? How does the reader's experience parallel that of the swimmer?

METAPHOR AND PERSONIFICATION. Figures of speech are expressions that have more than a literal meaning. Metaphor and personification are two types of figures of speech. A **metaphor** is a figure of speech in which one thing is spoken or written about as if it were another. A metaphor invites the reader to make a comparison between the two things. "Love is a red, red rose" is an example of metaphor. **Personification** is a figure of speech in which an idea, animal, or thing is described as if it were a person. "Love reached out and bit me" is an example of personification. What things are personified in the following poem? Use the graphic organizer shown below to list the things being personified, the descriptions that personify those things, and the meanings of those figures of speech.

Graphic Organizer

- thing being personified

- meaning of the figure of speech

- description

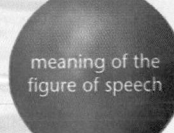

Reader's Journal

What kinds of competition have you experienced? How do you prepare for it?

Reader's Resource

- **SPORTS CONNECTION.** Human beings are not natural swimmers, so swimming techniques—including breathing and arm-leg coordination—must be learned. Swimming is taught in schools and sports centers across the world. In formal lessons, swimmers develop survival techniques and learn one of the most beneficial forms of exercise available. Swimming is also a competitive sport.

- Since the late 1800s, five basic strokes have been developed for training and competition. The most common is the crawl, which is also known as freestyle, because it is the stroke of choice in freestyle competitions. The backstroke, which uses the same basic arm motion as the crawl, was first seen in the Olympics in 1912. The breaststroke is the oldest known swimming stroke. The butterfly was developed in the mid-1900s. The sidestroke used to be used in competition but now is commonly used for recreational swimming and long-distance swimming.

ADDITIONAL RESOURCES

UNIT 4 RESOURCE BOOK
- Selection Worksheet 4.3
- Selection Check Test 4.4.5
- Selection Test 4.4.6
- Language, Grammar, and Style Resource 3.39
- Speaking and Listening Resource 4.19

GRAPHIC ORGANIZER

Under "thing being personified," students might write feet, lungs, and heart. Under "description," students might write "whites of soles of feet salute us on the turns," "his cadent feet tick in the stretch, they know the lessons well," "Lungs know, too," and "plum red heart pumps hard cries hurt." Under meaning of the figure of speech, students might write that the feet of the swimmer seem to be saluting as they rise out of the water, that the speaker has trained so hard that his feet and lungs seem to have learned lessons about swimming too, and that the swimmer's heart is rushing so it might seem as if it is crying "hurt."

READER'S JOURNAL

Students might enjoy illustrating a form of competition they have experienced. Encourage students to display their illustrations and explain what is happening in their pictures.

GOALS/OBJECTIVES

Studying this lesson will enable students to
- have a positive experience reading a concrete poem
- define *concrete poem* and explain how the shape of the poem contributes to its meaning
- define *metaphor* and *personification* and point to the use of these literary techniques in their reading
- view a race critically and analyze elements of the race
- prepare an oral interpretation

ANSWER TO GUIDED READING QUESTION

1. The swimmer moves forward by catching and scooping water and throwing it behind him.

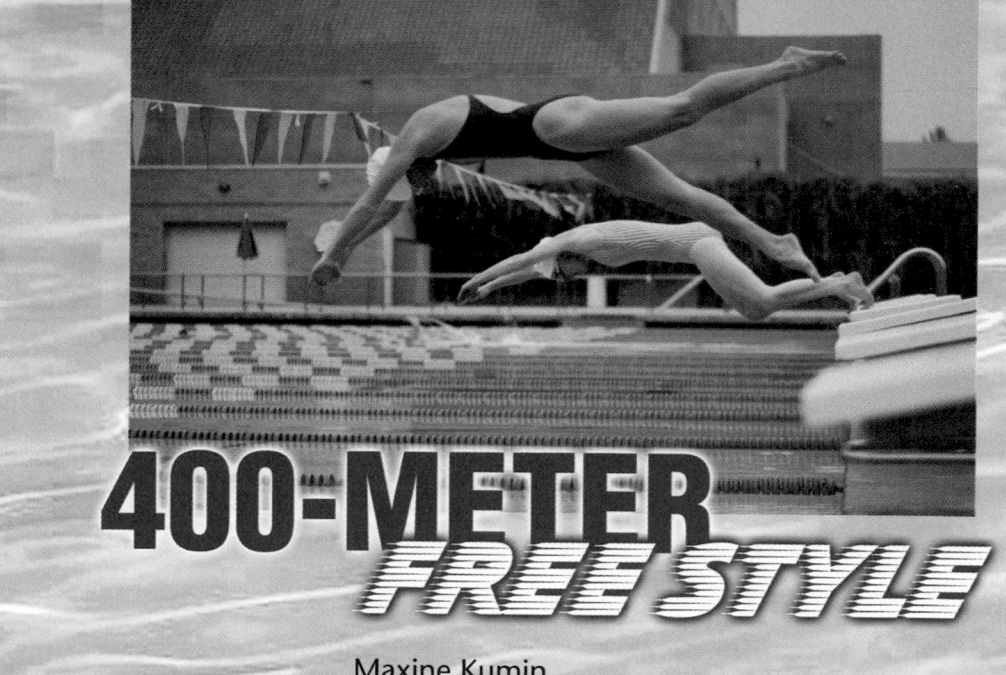

400-METER FREE STYLE

Maxine Kumin

The gun full swing the swimmer catapults and cracks

    s
    i
    x

feet away onto that perfect glass he catches at

a
n
d

throws behind him scoop after scoop cunningly moving

    t
    h
    e

water back to move him forward. <u>Thrift</u> is his wonderful

s
e
c

ret; he has schooled out[1] all <u>extravagance</u>. No muscle

GUIDED READING

How does the swimmer move forward?

---

1. **schooled out.** Trained to eliminate

words for everyday use
thrift (thrift) *n.*, careful management of one's resources. *Her <u>thrift</u> enabled her to save enough money to retire early.*
ex • trav • a • gance (ek strav′ ə gəns) *n.*, unreasonable excess. *The house purchase was such an <u>extravagance</u> that the couple had no money left to buy furniture.*

ples without compensation wrist cock to heel snap to
r
i
p

h
i
s

mobile mouth that siphons in the air that nurtures
h
i
m

at half an inch above sea level so to speak.
T
h
e

astonishing whites of the soles of his feet rise
a
n
d

salute us on the turns. He flips, <u>converts</u>, and is gone
a
l
l

in one. We watch him for signs. His arms are steady at
t
h
e

catch his cadent[2] feet tick in the stretch, they know
t
h
e

lesson well. Lungs know, too; he does not <u>list</u> for
a
i
r

he drives along on little sips carefully <u>expended</u>
b
u
t

that plum red heart pumps hard cries hurt how soon
i
t
s

near one more and makes its final surge   TIME 4:25:9 ■

---

2. **cadent.** Rhythmic

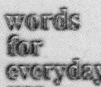

words for everyday use

con • vert (kən vʉrt′) v., turn or change from one form to another. *When water freezes, it <u>converts</u> from a liquid to a solid.*

list (list) v., tilt to one side. *The boat <u>listed</u> from side to side in the rough water.*

ex • pend (ek spend′) v., to use or use up. *I have <u>expended</u> my energy cleaning.*

GUIDED READING

What do the feet know?

RESPOND TO THE SELECTION

As an alternate activity, ask students to imagine they could ask the swimmer in this poem about his sport? What might he say about why he pushes himself to the limit? What rewards does he get from doing so?

SELECTION CHECK TEST 4.4.5 WITH ANSWERS

Checking Your Reading

1. What is the speaker doing? **The speaker is watching a swimming race.**
2. What happens after the gun goes off in the first line of the poem? **The swimmer catapults into the water.**
3. What gets thrown "scoop after scoop"? **Water gets thrown.**
4. Who "flips, converts, and is gone"? **The swimmer "flips, converts, and is gone."**
5. How does the poem end? **The poem ends with the swimmer's race time.**

Vocabulary in Context

Fill in each blank below with the most appropriate word from the following *Words for Everyday Use* from "400-Meter Freestyle." You may have to change the tense of the word.

thrift   convert   list   expend
extravagance

1. Robert wandered around the streets of Paris until the banks opened and he could **convert** his dollars into French francs.
2. "I knew Marie was marrying a rich man," said Estella, "but the **extravagance** of their wedding still surprised me."
3. The expert sailors struggled as the sailboat **listed** dangerously in the high winds.

Reader's Toolbox

1. A figure of speech that compares two things by speaking or writing about one thing as if it were another is known as
   a. personification
   b. metaphor
   c. concrete poem
   d. imagery

In what ways do you push yourself to the limit?

About *the* AUTHOR

Maxine Kumin was born in Philadelphia, Pennsylvania, in 1925. She has written numerous novels, children's books and collections of poetry, short stories, and essays. She received the Pulitzer Prize in 1973 for *Poems of New England* and has received numerous other awards for her writing. Kumin lives in New Hampshire.

Many of Kumin's poems focus on her experiences with family and friends and her observations of nature, animals, the seasons, and life cycles. About her poetry, Kumin says, "I don't think that I fit into any one particular school, and that is all right with me, too. I like being a little bit outside the mainstream."

The poem, "400-Meter Free Style," is in *Our Ground Time Here Will Be Brief: New and Selected Poems,* an anthology published in 1982. Her most recent publication of poems is *Selected Poems 1960–1990,* published in 1997.

272   UNIT FOUR / A SPORTING LIFE

SELECTION CHECK TEST 4.4.5 WITH ANSWERS (CONT.)

2. A figure of speech that describes an idea, animal, or thing as if it were a person is known as
   a. personification
   b. metaphor
   c. concrete poem
   d. imagery

The Women's 400 METERS

Lillian Morrison

Skittish,

they flex knees, drum heels and

shiver at the starting line

waiting the gun

to pour them over the stretch

like a breaking wave.

Bang! they're off

careening down the lanes,

each chased by her own bright tiger. ∎

U.S. sprinter Valerie Brisco wins a
400-meter trial in the 1988
Olympics in Seoul, Korea.

ABOUT THE RELATED READING
Lillian Morrison was born in 1917
in New Jersey. She has worked as a
librarian and as a youth services coordinator. Her fascination with sports
has led her to write collections of
sports poems, including *Sprints and
Distances, Slam Dunk: Basketball
Poems,* and *At the Crack of the Bat:
Baseball Poems.* This poem focuses on
the suspense and anticipation at the
start of a running race. The event,
the 400 Meters, consists of one lap
around a standard track.

LITERARY TECHNIQUE

SIMILE AND METAPHOR. A **simile** is a
comparison using *like* or *as.* A
metaphor is a figure of speech in
which one thing is spoken or written
about as if it were another. Ask
students the following questions:
- What simile is used to describe
  what will happen after the gun
  goes off?
- In what way are the two things
  being compared alike?
- What metaphor is used in the last
  line of the poem?
- What do you think the poet
  means by this line? What might
  the "bright tigers" represent?

Answers
- "To pour them over the
  stretch/like a breaking wave" is
  the simile used.
- The runners are compared to a
  breaking wave as they rush past
  the starting line; the two things
  are alike in that they involve a
  surge of motion.
- "Each chased by her own bright
  tiger" is the metaphor used.
- Students may suggest that the
  poet means that each runner has
  something that inspires her, or
  chases her toward the finish line.
  Students may say that the "bright
  tiger" represents a different goal
  or reason for running to each
  runner.

RECALL

1a. The swimmer is "thrifty" in that no muscle moves without compensation and that every motion is carefully rehearsed and synchronized. The swimmer scoops water just right to draw himself along and moves without wasted motion.

2a. The swimmer's body is confident and his feet and lungs kick and breathe at the right time from hard training. The swimmer is reaching the point of exhaustion, however, as revealed by his heart pumping hard and crying hurt.

INTERPRET

1b. Thrift is important to the swimmer because wasted motion would mean that he would be expending too much energy toward an action that doesn't help to propel the swimmer toward the finish line.

2b. The swimmer remains calm and confident in his body's training, knowing he can take his body to the limit and it will react as he has trained it.

ANALYZE

3a. Students may point to clues such as his arms being steady, the swimmer's not listing for air, and his concern with thrift and not wasting motion.

SYNTHESIZE

3b. The swimmer 's goal is to achieve the best time for swimming 400 meters. He reaches that goal when the stopwatch times him at 4:25:9.

EVALUATE

4a. Students may say that the shape of the poem, imitating a swimmer's laps in a pool, and the vivid description of each motion of the swimmer's body create the experience of witnessing a swimming race. Most students will say that the description of the lessons his body has learned and his heart pumping before the final surge are most effective because they help build suspense and excitement.

EXTEND

4b. The poem creates anticipation and suspense through the description of the skittish women shivering at the starting line, waiting for the gun to go off, so they can surge like a breaking wave. It makes the reader feel like a witness to the events by using the present tense and such action words as "Bang!

274 TEACHER'S EDITION

Investigate, *Inquire,* and Imagine

Recall: GATHERING FACTS

1a. How is the swimmer thrifty in "400-Meter Free Style"?

2a. How does the swimmer's body feel near the end of the race?

→ **Interpret:** FINDING MEANING

1b. Why is thrift important to the swimmer?

2b. How does the swimmer react to the physical pressure?

Analyze: TAKING THINGS APART

3a. What clues in the poem reveal the swimmer's thoughts and emotions?

→ **Synthesize:** BRINGING THINGS TOGETHER

3b. What is the swimmer's goal? How does he reach that goal?

Evaluate: MAKING JUDGMENTS

4a. What elements of "400-Meter Free Style" create the experience of witnessing a swimming race? Which elements are the most effective?

→ **Extend:** CONNECTING IDEAS

4b. How does "The Women's 400 Meters" create a sense of anticipation and suspense? How does it make the reader feel like a witness to the event? How are the feelings of nervousness, suspense, and desire to win conveyed similarly in the two poems? How are they conveyed differently? What elements of "The Women's 400 Meters" mirror elements in "400-Meter Free Style"? What elements of "The Women's 400 Meters" might make the reader think the poem is about swimming?

Understanding *Literature*

CONCRETE POEM. A **concrete poem**, or shape poem, is one printed or written in a shape that suggests its subject matter. As you read "400-Meter Free Style," how did the shape affect your ability to read everything at the same pace? How did that effect make the experience more real? How might you arrange "The Women's 400 Meters" as a concrete poem?

METAPHOR AND PERSONIFICATION. Figures of speech are expressions that have more than a literal meaning. Metaphor and personification are two types of figures of speech. A **metaphor** is a figure of speech in which one thing is spoken or written about as if it were another. A metaphor invites the reader to make a comparison between the two things. What metaphor did you find in "400-Meter Free Style"? **Personificaton** is a figure of speech in which an idea, animal, or

ANSWERS TO INVESTIGATE, INQUIRE, IMAGINE (CONT.)

they're off." Nervousness is conveyed through the skittishness of the women, suspense through them waiting for the gun, and the desire to win through the description of the women careening down the lanes, each chased by her own bright tiger. These emotions are conveyed similarly in both poems through the use of the present tense and active words; they are conveyed differently in that "400-Meter Free Style" focuses more on the swimmer's body, while "The Women's 400 Meters: focuses on what is "chasing" the women—their motivation. Students may say that the description of a breaking wave might make the reader think the poem is about swimming.

Answers to Understanding Literature can be found on page 275.

thing is described as if it were a person. What examples of personification did you find in "400-Meter Free Style"?

Writer's Journal

1. Write a **concrete poem** describing an activity you love.
2. Write a short **news story** describing a race.
3. Write an explanation of the **rules of play** for a newcomer to a particular game or competition you enjoy.

Skill Builders

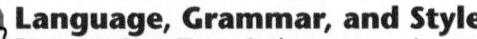

Language, Grammar, and Style

REVIEWING VERB TENSE. Both poems you just read are written in the present tense. What effect does the use of the present tense have on the reader? How would the poems be different if they were written using verbs in the past tense? Choose one of the two poems and rewrite it, changing the verbs from the present to the past tense. Refer to the Language Arts Survey 3.39, "Using Irregular Verbs" to review the past tense of irregular verbs. Which version of the poem do you like better? Why?

Media Literacy

RECORDING A RACE. Make an audiotape or a videotape of a race—running, swimming, biking, or another type of event. Play close attention to the emotions of the race's participants and to the emotions of the spectators. Try to capture these emotions as you record. Also think about the progression of the race. How do people look, sound, and act in the beginning of the race? How do these elements change or shift as the race progresses? How are these elements different at the end of the race? After taping, review your audiotape or videotape. How well did you capture the elements of emotion? How well did you capture the changes in emotion as the race progressed and ended? Evaluate your work, noting what you like best about it and what you would try to improve.

Speaking and Listening

ORAL INTERPRETATION. Form small groups of about four students. Take a moment to reread "400-Meter Free Style." Then, take turns reading the poem aloud to the other members of the group. Focus on recreating the feeling of witnessing a swimming race by varying pace, volume, stress, and emotion. You may choose to do an oral interpretation of "The Women's 400 Meters" in addition to or in place of Maxine Kumin's poem. As you read "The Women's 400 Meters" aloud, try to recreate the feeling of anticipation the runners might feel at the start of the race. Review the Language Arts Survey 4.19, "Oral Interpretation of Poetry" for additional suggestions.

ANSWERS TO SKILL BUILDERS

Language, Grammar, and Style
REVIEWING VERB TENSE. Most students will note that both poems would be less interesting if rewritten in the past tense. The present tense gives the poem suspense and makes the reader feel as if he or she is witnessing the action.

Media Literacy
RECORDING A RACE. Students may also want to interview race participants to ask questions about their thoughts and emotions. They may want to use versions of the following questions. Were you nervous before the race? What went through your mind during the race? How did you feel after the race?

Speaking and Listening
ORAL INTERPRETATION. Tell students that they should occasionally make eye contact with their audience and incorporate nonverbal communications, such as facial expressions and gestures in their interpretations.

ANSWERS TO UNDERSTANDING LITERATURE

CONCRETE POEM. Students may say there were parts they read faster and they read the vertical parts more slowly. Students may say that this made the swimmer's swimming quickly down his lane and then turning in the water seem more real. Students might say the words could be arranged to resemble a race track or a breaking wave.

METAPHOR AND PERSONIFICATION. Students may point to the speakers feet "saluting" as an example of metaphor as his feet are compared to saluting soldiers. Students might point to the following examples of personification: "whites of soles of feet salute us on the turns," "his cadent feet tick in the stretch, they know the lessons well," "Lungs know, too," and "plum red heart pumps hard cries hurt."

READER'S JOURNAL

As an alternate activity, ask students if they have ever come face-to-face with discrimination of any type. How did they handle the situation?

GRAPHIC ORGANIZER

Under "What Ashe learns," students may list the following: how white players treat African American players, never to feel so sorry for another player that you allow him or her to win, that the attention paid to his race indicates that the United States still has a long way to go in creating an equal and tolerant society, and that education is more important in the long term than sports. Under "What Ash teaches," students may say to not let discrimination hold you back from achieving what you can, that on the road to success you need many teachers and much help from others, that it is possible to break out of the shell of shyness, that African Americans should not make sports heroes their only ones, that parents should instill a love of learning in their children, and that education in the long run can take you farther than sports.

AUTOBIOGRAPHY

Reader's Journal

What do you remember as important events or turning points in your childhood? What makes those experiences important?

Reader's TOOLBOX

AUTOBIOGRAPHY. An **autobiography** is the story of a person's life, written by that person. This selection is an excerpt from Arthur Ashe's autobiography *Off the Court*, which was published in 1981. In his autobiography, Ashe shares intimate details about his life and examines his own thoughts, feelings, and reactions to key events in his life. How do these personal details help the reader better understand Ashe as a person?

DESCRIPTION. A **description** gives a picture in words of a character, object, or scene. Many descriptions use sensory details—language that shows how things look, sound, smell, taste, or feel. How does Arthur Ashe use sensory details in this selection? How does he use description to bring the reader into the story?

Prereading

from *Off the Court*
by Arthur Ashe

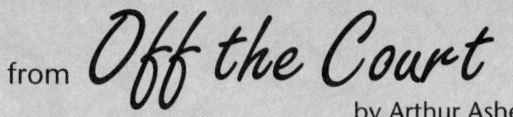

Reader's Resource

- Tennis, which originated in England, began to gain worldwide popularity after the first Wimbledon tournament in 1877. From its earliest days, tennis was a sport played mostly by Britain's wealthiest people. As tennis took hold in the United States, private country clubs cropped up and became the exclusive sites of play. Membership rules at these clubs automatically excluded blacks.

- **HISTORY CONNECTION.** Segregation rules were especially strict in the South, where segregation was commonplace even in the 1940s and 1950s, when Arthur Ashe was a young boy eager to join the sport. African-American tennis players could only play on courts in black sections of town and were often kept out of tournaments in which white athletes played.

- Tennis involves a variety of shots, including the serve, and forehand, backhand, and overhead strokes. Tennis is also played on various surfaces, including grass, clay, and asphalt. Each surface requires different strategies. Competition includes both singles and doubles matches (a match is made up of three to five sets; each set consists of at least six games). Because of the many skills involved, tennis is a difficult sport to master.

Graphic Organizer

In this selection and the related readings that follow, you will learn about many ways in which Arthur Ashe learns about tennis and about life, as well as the insights he shares with others and the ways in which he influences others. Jot down your thoughts in a graphic organizer after finishing your reading.

What Ashe learns	What Ashe teaches
• his own strengths and weaknesses	• to follow your dreams

GOALS/OBJECTIVES

Studying this lesson will enable students to
- appreciate an autobiographical work about the rise of a tennis star despite discrimination
- briefly describe the history and some basic facts about tennis
- define *autobiography* and recognize what the details of an autobiography reveal about the character of its author

- define *description* and understand how sensory detail contributes to description
- use verbs correctly in sentences
- read a statistical chart
- research an unfamiliar sport with a partner

from *Off* the COURT

Arthur Ashe Monument, 1996. Paul Di Pasquale, Richmond, Virginia.

INDIVIDUAL LEARNING STRATEGIES

MOTIVATION
Students may enjoy watching a portion of a recent tennis match on videotape. Ask students to then discuss their reactions to tennis. What makes it exciting? What makes it challenging?

READING PROFICIENCY
Students may have difficulty with the tennis terms in the story. Have them read the Prereading page and footnotes carefully. Tell them that if they run into a term or concept they don't understand they should try to figure it out as much as they can from context. If they are unable to do this, they should jot their question down on a notebook and read on. After students have finished the story, you might have students ask their questions as part of a class discussion and see if you can glean any answers from other students.

ENGLISH LANGUAGE LEARNING
Point out the following vocabulary words and expressions
adept—highly skilled; expert
well-to do—wealthy, rich
agility—quickness and easiness of movement
backboard—vertical board on a tennis court against which it is possible to hit balls
in spades—in an extreme way
maxims—principles or rules of conduct

INDIVIDUAL LEARNING STRATEGIES (CONT.)

SPECIAL NEEDS
Tennis terms and description may make this selection challenging for students. Have them focus on the main events of the story by responding to the Guided Reading questions and answering the Recall questions in the Investigate, Inquire, and Imagine section.

ENRICHMENT
Have students write an autobiographical essay about a challenge in their life and how they reacted to it. Students can compile their essays in a class book titled *Real-Life Challenges*. Students may wish to share their book with other members of the class or with another English class.

ANSWERS TO GUIDED READING QUESTIONS

1. The all-black Richmond Racquet Club and the students at Virginia Union use the Brook Field tennis courts.
2. Ron Charity is one of the best African American tennis players in the country.

You can't compare tennis with baseball, basketball, or football. When Jackie Robinson broke the color line in 1947 with the Brooklyn Dodgers, dozens of good baseball players in the Negro leagues were waiting to follow. When Althea Gibson, the first prominent black in tennis, won national grass-court titles at Forest Hills in 1957 and 1958, there was no <u>reservoir</u> of black talent waiting to walk in if the door ever opened. Blacks had no identification with the sport—on or off the court. Tennis is a difficult game to learn. Very difficult. You have to be a generalist. You can't be a specialist and excel in tennis. You have to become adept in about four or five different sets of exercises, none of which are the same. <u>Physiologically</u>, serving a tennis ball is nothing like hitting a forehand; they're two completely different actions. Hitting a volley is not like hitting an overhead; they too are two completely different functions. You must learn how to do all of them.

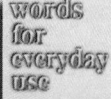

I was too small for any sport but tennis. I learned to swim when I was very young, but I was always a bit afraid of water, even if there was no way to avoid Brook Pool on my doorstep. My father wouldn't let me play football because of my size, which was a disappointment, so I tried to make up for it by working harder in other activities. When I wasn't sitting on the front porch of our house buried in a book, I played baseball, basketball, and tennis.

The four tennis courts just outside our side door were used fairly regularly by a handful of black people in Richmond. The all-black Richmond Racquet Club used Brook Field as its home base. As I grew increasingly sensitive to matters of race and color, I noticed that most of the black tennis players came from the educated, well-to-do segment of our community—principals, doctors, dentists, and lawyers. As a seven-year-old trying to find his niche in a complex, segregated[1] society, I found that significant.

The students at Virginia Union also made good use of the courts in the spring. Their campus was just beyond Brook Field and they had just two courts of their own. They practiced at the playground and played teams from other colleges. Ron Charity spent more time on the courts than anyone else. For hours and hours, he hit balls against the wall or served to an empty court. Even my untrained eye could see an unusual grace in his swing, an agility that surpassed most of his opponents.

> **GUIDED READING**
> Who used the Brook Field tennis courts?

I watched him play against another school one afternoon. He dominated his opponent and won. His name was whispered around the gaggle of girlfriends, relatives, tennis buffs, and curious bystanders who drifted over from the football fields, baseball diamonds, and basketball courts. Ron Charity, they said, was one of the best black players in the country. I was properly impressed.

> **GUIDED READING**
> Who was Ron Charity?

The next afternoon, he was out on the courts again, working on his serve. I watched for a while. Finally, he

---

1. **segregated.** Divided or separated as by race or group

---

words for everyday use

res • er • voir (reˊ zə vwär) *n.*, supply. *This community college is a <u>reservoir</u> of intelligent, educated people.*

phys • i • o • log • i • cal (fi zē ə läˊ ji kəl) *adj.*, relating to bodily function. *There is no <u>physiological</u> difference between identical twins.* **physiologically,** *adv.*

noticed me for the first time.

"What's your name?"

"Arthur Ashe, Junior."

"Your dad runs the playground?"

"Yes, sir."

He nodded and went back to his serve. His wooden racquet flashed high above his head in the late afternoon sun and sliced through the silence. White balls rocketed to the corners of the opposing court. After a while, he stopped and looked at me again.

"You play tennis?"

I shrugged. I had batted some old tennis balls around with the twelve-dollar nylon-strung racquet that had found its way into the wooden equipment box under my bedroom window.

"You want to learn?"

I nodded. At that age, any sport was a challenge I felt I could master. "You got a racquet. Go get it," he said.

Ron Charity was a patient teacher with an understanding of my strengths and limitations. I weighed about fifty pounds. To get a tennis ball across the net and seventy-eight feet down court with a twenty-seven-inch racquet required a firm grip to withstand the torque from off-center hits.

Ron had me use an Eastern forehand grip, like shaking hands with my racquet. This is the best grip for beginners for three reasons: one, the hand is firmly behind the racquet

Arthur Ashe was destined to be a star.

handle at the moment the ball touches the string—a solid support system; two, it allows the best grip for an all-court attack, either down the line, cross-court, or down the middle; three, as I would learn later, it is a good starting point for future experimentation.

Ron stood on the other side of the net and tossed thousands of balls to me in the year that followed. I concentrated on form, my stroke, and getting the ball over the net. When I was alone and couldn't find someone to hit with me, I played against a backboard. Tennis became something I could do by myself, like reading a book, and I soon found myself absorbed in workouts without worrying about friends.

Pound for pound, I was a good little athlete—not a Lynn Swann or Kurt Thomas[2]—but someone with agility, speed, coordination, and a will to win. If all those elements could produce timing, I was on my way. Timing is the most important element in tennis. It separates players into different levels. John McEnroe, Ilie Nastase, and Evonne Goolagong have it in spades. They were born with it. Some good players have good timing with their hands but not with their feet. John

GUIDED READING

What kind of a teacher was Ron Charity?

GUIDED READING

What is the most important element in tennis?

2. **Lynn Swann or Kurt Thomas.** Famous athletes in football and gymnastics, respectively

BIOGRAPHICAL NOTE

John McEnroe (1959–) is an American tennis player who was born in Germany and educated in the United States. He was the youngest player to attend the prestigious Wimbledon competition in 1977, and by 1979 he was ranked third in the world. He is known for his explosive temper on the court. He is also known for a competitive rivalry with another tennis star—Bjorn Borg of Sweden.

Ilie Nastase was a Romanian player who competed in the 1970s with Ashe.

Evonne Goolagong was an Australian female tennis star in the 1970s.

John Newcombe was an Australian tennis star in the 1960s.

Rod Laver (1938–) was an Australian tennis player who became a major star in the 1960s. He won the "grand slam" of tennis twice. (The grand slam is winning the title in Wimbledon and in the United States, French, and Australian championships in the same year.)

Billie Jean King (1943–) was a female American tennis star of the 1960s and 1970s. She was outspoken about equal treatment for female tennis players and beat another male tennis star, Bobby Riggs, in an exhibition match. She won the Wimbledon title ten times.

1. Baseball demands agility rather
than bulk and height and this is in
keeping with Ashe's small frame.
2. The trip was a reminder of the
contradiction between the United
States' democratic slogans about
equality and the reality of the
inequality and segregation in places
such as the District of Columbia.

CROSS-CURRICULAR ACTIVITIES

SOCIAL STUDIES. Inform students for many years in this country schools and other facilities were segregated. This means that these were separate facilities for whites and for African Americans. Before the Civil War, it was illegal in most states to teach reading and writing to slaves. After the Civil War, schools were built for African Americans, but they were seldom equal in terms of their facilities, supplies, and quality of teaching with white schools. Schools were segregated for almost a hundred years, from 1867 until 1954. While segregation was a law in the South, it often happened in the North too, just less openly. In 1954, the Supreme Court made a decision called *Brown versus the Board of Education of Topeka* in which they decided that states could no longer segregate schools because it violated the Fourteenth Amendment of the constitution.

Interested students may wish to work in small groups to research and prepare an oral report on one of the following aspects of the Civil Rights movement in the United States:

- *Brown versus the Board of Education of Topeka*
- the first African American children to attend school in Little Rock, Arkansas, following *Brown v. Board*
- Rosa Parks refusing to give up her bus seat in Montgomery, Alabama
- Martin Luther King, Jr., and the bus boycott in Montgomery
- the 1964 murder of three civil rights workers in Mississippi

---

Newcombe had great hands, but his feet were average. Rod Laver's feet were A+, but his hands rated an "A." Billie Jean King had great hands and feet. I would rate my hands and feet at the "B" level.

The eyes also play a vital role in timing. People are right-eyed and left-eyed, just as they are right-handed, and lefthanded, right-footed and left-footed. When someone focuses on a tennis ball, one eye— and one eye alone—does the focusing. In turning aside during a backswing, the dominant eye can lose contact with the ball momentarily. At 120 miles an hour, a tennis ball can elude the best eyes. From the beginning, I had no trouble waiting for just the right moment. Because of my lack of size and weight, however, I had to develop a semi-lob off the forehand as a form of survival.

I was aware of the limitations of my height and build and soon accepted the fact that basketball and football were not for me. But baseball was a sport that demanded agility and determination rather than bulk or height. The baseball diamond and tennis court became my homes.

> **GUIDED READING**
> Why was baseball a good sport for Ashe?

Baseball had special meaning for all colored boys because of Jackie Robinson. Joe Louis was still a big name in boxing, but he was finishing up his career and most of us only heard about his days of glory as heavyweight champion from our parents. As soon as the Brooklyn Dodgers signed Jackie Robinson, every black man, woman, and child in America became a Dodger fan. The New York Yankees had a farm club in Richmond, the Braves, but they were not very popular with blacks because they were so slow to integrate. In 1978, George Steinbrenner, the Yankee owner, offered me a job on his staff. We talked about it over a hamburger at P. J.'s, but I had to turn it down.

One of the highlights of my summers was the baseball school run by Maxie Robinson, the father of the present ABC-TV anchorman. Even in those days, summer camps and schools were big; Mr. Robinson was the football, basketball, and track coach at Armstrong High School, highly respected and a disciplinarian like Daddy. Every day from nine to twelve-thirty, he taught baseball fundamentals. Later in the summer, the school took a trip to Washington to see the Senators play. I could have cared less if they won. I was a Dodger fan.

The trip was fun. It also was a reminder of our segregated world. Contradictions between the slogans of democracy and equality and our reality were sharpened in the District of Columbia. We could not go to certain places. Even where we were not barred, we were not welcome. I grew up aware that I was a Negro, colored, black, . . . and other less flattering terms.

> **GUIDED READING**
> Of what was the trip a reminder?

Heroes also were few—or so I thought. In the South, black heroes who made waves were discouraged. Booker T. Washington was recognized because he stressed self-help and education, and posed no threat to "the natural order of things." Paul Robeson was moderately popular among blacks. His politics, which we didn't fully understand at the time, made us uneasy. Now, he has been elevated to near deity[3] status. Everybody admired Ralph Bunche, especially after he won the Nobel Peace Prize for his Middle East negotiations. George Washington Carver, who made the peanut fashionable long before Jimmy Carter, was highly regarded. I knew about Maggie Walker, president and founder of Consolidated Bank and Trust, Richmond's first black bank. She was the first woman bank president, black or white, in the country.

---

3. **deity.** Supreme being or god

Like most black children, I held Abe Lincoln in high esteem because I had been taught that he freed the slaves, though for the wrong reasons. My one contemporary white hero was Gene Autry. I liked him because he was the underdog. Roy Rogers was the so-called "king of the cowboys," but Gene Autry was my man. My father took me to see him when I was six years old and I was impressed by the tricks he did with his horse, Champion. Playing cowboys and Indians as a kid, I insisted on being Gene Autry.

In the spring of 1954, Virginia Union hosted the Central Intercollegiate Athletic Association Tennis Tournament. The CIAA was an association of black colleges. I was ten and had been taking lessons from Ron Charity for about three years. During a break in the action, I started hitting some balls on the court that was not in use.

"Somebody wants to meet you," Ron said, approaching the court.

I followed him to a table that was under the tree outside the side door of my house. Seated at the table was the tournament director, recording scores and directing players to the proper courts. Dr. R. W. Johnson was five feet ten inches tall, dark-skinned and handsome, with wavy brown hair and a small scar on his upper lip.

"Dr. Johnson," Ron Charity said, "this is Arthur Ashe, Junior."

He shook my hand and looked me over quizzically. "I understand you're ten years old."

"Yes, sir."

"You've been playing three years."

"Yes, sir."

You like tennis?"

"Yes, sir."

He nodded, asked a few more questions, and dismissed me. I went back to the empty court, but felt him watching me as I played. When I glanced over, he was talking to Ron. Later that day, he talked to my father for a long time.

After the matches, Daddy spoke to me about this Dr. Johnson. "Arthur Junior," he began. I could tell from the form of address that this was to be a serious conversation.

BIOGRAPHICAL NOTE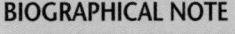

Booker T. Washington (1856–1915) was an African-American educator. He organized a school for African Americans at Tuskegee, Alabama. On September 18, 1895, Washington made a speech, forever known as the "compromise" speech, that drew mixed reactions from African Americans. His position was that African Americans should accept the inferior position they were then given in society and focus on training themselves through job training at places like Tuskegee and by being independent economically. His views made him acceptable to many whites of the day, but African Americans who were more outspoken about equal rights condemned Washington's views and speech.

Paul Robeson (1898–1976) was an African-American singer and actor. He appeared in some of the finest theater of his day, and his singing voice drew crowds. He appeared in eleven motion pictures. In the late 1920s and 1930s Robeson lived in Europe. He returned to the United States as an outspoken admirer of the Soviet Union and a militant civil rights activist.

Ralph Bunche (1904–1971) was an African-American diplomat who had a long and distinguished career in the United Nations. Bunche negotiated an agreement that put an end to the Arab-Israeli War of 1948–1949, and was rewarded in 1950 with the Nobel Peace Prize. He was the first African American to be honored with this award. He was also dedicated to the Civil Rights movements and was a member of the NAACP's board for more than twenty years.

George Washington Carver (1864–1963) was an African-American agricultural expert and an educator. At what is now Tuskegee University (founded by Washington, see note above), Carver began experimenting with different industrial uses for peanuts and other agricultural products.

Jimmy Carter (1924–) was the thirty-ninth president of the United States. He ran his family business—a peanut farm in Plains, Georgia, and from there he launched his political career.

Ashe at the U.S. Open, 1968.

"Dr. Johnson works with young tennis players. He'd like you to come down to his place for a couple of weeks in the summer so you can play against other good players every day. You'll also have a chance to travel to some other tournaments."

If the chance to play against other boys had not been enough, the word "travel" would have done it. Here was a chance to explore the world beyond the pages of my old *National Geographics*. I had been to South Hill in the summer and had traveled to Chicago by train with my grandmother. But Dr. Johnson's offer was almost too good to be true. I had no trouble accepting.

Robert Walter Johnson was born in North Carolina, educated at Lincoln University in Pennsylvania, where he was a black All-American running back. He attended Meharry Medical College in Nashville and was a general practitioner[4] in Lynchburg, Virginia. "Dr. J," as we called him, took up tennis to stay in shape and became a major figure in the American Tennis Association, the black equivalent of the USLTA, until his death in 1971. His obsession was the development of good black junior tennis players.

One year, while driving home from Washington, D.C., he saw a huge sign announcing the "USLTA Inter-Scholastic Championship." He parked his car and watched all those white boys in white tennis uniforms competing against each other. He went to the tournament director and asked if any blacks had ever played. After a long discussion the officials agreed they would accept two black finalists from an all-black qualifying event every year. The first year Dr. Johnson brought players, they lost, 6–0, 6–0, in the first round. He was terribly embarrassed but vowed he would produce a player to win that tournament. I won it in 1961.

Dr. Johnson spent most of his days at his office in the Johnson Medical Building on Fifth Street. He would come home after office hours and play tennis, frequently with some of his cronies[5]. Miss Erdice Creecy, his lifelong secretary and private nurse, supervised his office and three-story house on Pierce Street. The basement of the house was equipped with showers, a recreation room, bar, and a shelf full of books on tennis. I read them all. Dr. Johnson had a tennis court behind his house, a rose garden, and a kennel for his hunting dogs.

Almost all our training and practicing was done in the morning and early afternoon so Dr. Johnson could have the court around five o'clock. I spent only two weeks with him that

---

4. **general practitioner.** Family doctor
5. **crony.** Close friend

first summer but immediately ran into problems. Ron Charity had been my first teacher, and I patterned my game after him. He had worked for a long time with me on my backhand; I felt I could do anything with it. The key was a very long and early backswing. The ball had to be hit way out in front to allow for as much racquet momentum as possible. My timing on my backhand was very good. But I used a standard backhand grip, and that became the source of my troubles.

Dr. Johnson's son, Bobby, who did a lot of the teaching, wanted to change my backhand the first day I was in Lynchburg.

GUIDED READING

What did Bobby want Ashe to do?

"Mr. Charity showed me the other way," I protested. I didn't want to change my grip. I felt I could hit all day and not miss.

"I'm your teacher now and I want to change it," Bobby said firmly. I stood my ground.

"Well, if you want Ron Charity to teach you," Bobby said, "why don't you go home?"

We had reached an <u>impasse</u>. Dr. Johnson called my father. Two hours later, the blue Ford screeched to a stop in the driveway. Daddy listened to the explanations of the problem. He turned to me. "Dr. Johnson is teaching you now, Arthur Junior. You do what they say." Daddy then got in his car and drove back to Richmond.

It was that simple. I always obeyed my father. They had no more trouble with me. But to tell the truth, I didn't really change the grip on my backhand that much.

During those two weeks, Dr. Johnson took me to two tournaments, the Southeastern ATA in Durham, North Carolina, and the Mall Tennis Club tournament in Washington.

I was suddenly exposed to a world of black tennis whose dimensions I had not imagined. There was black tennis in virtually every major city along the East Coast and in the South, the Midwest, and California.

Because I was the youngest player at Dr. Johnson's, I had the dirtiest jobs. I cleaned his doghouse and weeded his rose gardens. Yet I had acquired these skills from my father, who often had a dozen dogs around Brook Field. I swept sidewalks, made beds, washed dishes, and rolled the tennis court. I didn't enjoy these things, but I understood this as my way of paying back, so I did those chores as quickly as I could.

I also had to use the court when nobody else wanted it so the backboard became my challenge. Sometimes the neighbors would complain about my pounding the backboard at 7 a.m. But by the time breakfast came around, I had put in a good forty-five minutes on the board. Those sessions were fantasy times. I imagined that I was Pancho Gonzales or another famous tennis player in a critical situation, at deuce, set point, match point[6]. In practices, Bobby Johnson would make us run patterns. We had to hit so many down the line, so many cross-court, maybe a cross-court then a down-the-line, come to the net and put away the volley. We had daily contests: who could hit the most forehands without an error, the most forehand returns of serve, deep forehand shots, forehand approach shots, forehand passing shots. Then we ran through the whole series for the backhand.

I noticed early that I had more endurance than the older boys. I

GUIDED READING

What did Ashe notice early?

---

6. **deuce, set point, match point.** Scores in a tennis match

ANSWERS TO GUIDED
READING QUESTIONS

1. Bobby wanted Ashe to change his backhand grip.
2. He noticed that he had more endurance than other boys even though he was smaller.

words for everyday use

im • passe (im' pas) n., situation with no escape; deadlock. *The two teams reached an <u>impasse</u>, and all the players were too tired to go on.*

Arthur Ashe at Wimbledon, 1968.

was smaller, couldn't hit as hard or serve as fast, but I could last longer. So I would try to go as long as I could in the practice sessions and against the backboard without missing. I also began to learn the standard tennis principles: on approach shots, go down the line, not cross-court; no drop shots from the baseline; when in doubt, hit a semi-lob deep down the middle; get 70 percent of your first serves in.

There were also maxims meant only for little black Southern boys: when in doubt, call your opponent's shot good; if you're serving the game before the change of ends, pick up the balls on your side and hand them to your opponent during the crossover. Dr. Johnson knew we were going into territory that was often hostile and he wanted our behavior to be beyond reproach. It would be years before I understood the emotional toll of <u>repressing</u> anger and natural frustration.

That summer of '53 was symbolic because it marked the first steps on the road from Richmond. In subsequent years, traveling with Ron Charity and others stressed the importance of <u>camaraderie</u>. Blacks could not eat in restaurants, so we brought our fried chicken, potato salad, and rolls in bags and passed the Thermos around the car. Spending weekends as a guest in someone's house

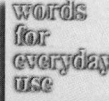

re • press (ri pres´) v., hold in by self-control. *Although Kendra was afraid of dogs, she could <u>repress</u> her fear when near them.*
ca • ma • ra • de • rie (käm rä´ də rē) n., spirit of friendship. *After the school trip, Arnold felt a <u>camaraderie</u> with his class-mates.*

taught me more about social graces than I could have ever learned elsewhere.

I also learned on the court. During a tournament at Barraud Park in Norfolk, I had won the first set against another boy my age and was leading in the second when I started feeling sorry for him. It happens all the time among club players, but not on the prize-money tour anymore. I decided to let my opponent win a few games by making a few intentional errors. I lost the second set, was down, 2–0, in the third, and then began to panic. I tried to come back, but the more I pressed, the more mistakes I made. I lost the third set—and the match. My opponent was elated; I was in tears, angry at myself. It was an important lesson. There would be other occasions when I felt sorry for someone, but I never again let such sympathies affect my game . . .

> **GUIDED READING**
>
> What important lesson did Ashe learn?

My first seventeen years set the stage for the way I view the world. I grew up as an underdog, so I rent from Avis instead of Hertz now. As I played more and more against white juniors, I realized I was fighting assumptions about black inferiorities.

> **GUIDED READING**
>
> What did Ashe realize as he played more against white juniors?

Dr. Johnson tried to combat our insecurities by making "the white boys" the ultimate opponent.

"You're not going to beat those white boys playing like that," he would say. "Hit that to a white boy and you'll go home early," was another of his pet phrases.

Knowing that I would not be admitted to certain tournaments protected me from direct rebuffs. O. H. Parrish and some others I played against were terrific guys—period. Some others were too well-mannered to express racism crudely. No player ever refused to appear on court with me. No official ever called me a name. But the indirect rebuffs and innuendoes left their scars.

The same year that I beat O. H. in the Middle Atlantic Juniors, some kids ransacked the log cabins where we had been housed for the tournament. Officials tried to place the blame on me and phoned Dr. Johnson.

"What do you know about this?" he asked, after I had returned to Lynchburg.

"I don't know anything about it," I said, nervous that I was being implicated and that my future tennis travel could be in jeopardy. "Honest—I don't, Dr. Johnson."

"I believe you, Arthur," he said. "They said they're just investigating, but I wanted to be sure."

Not all of my encounters were harsh. During the National Interscholastics in Charlottesville in 1960, Butch Newman, Cliff Buchholz, and Charlie Pasarell asked me to join them at a movie. I turned them down because I knew I wouldn't get in—but the guys wouldn't take no for an answer. When we got to the theater, the reaction was predictable.

"You can't go in," the woman in the ticket booth said. I wasn't surprised by her statement. But I was slightly elated when Cliff said, "Well, if he can't go in, none of us will go." And all of us left.

That summer, Daddy and Dr. Johnson faced their own decision. I had won a number of important regional

> **GUIDED READING**
>
> How did Ashe's friends react at the theater?

1. He learned to never let his sympathy for another player affect his game.
2. He realizes that he is fighting assumptions about black inferiority as he plays tennis.
3. Ashe's friends leave the theater with him when he is not admitted because of his race.

ADDITIONAL QUESTIONS AND ACTIVITIES

Generate a discussion on Ashe's friends who leave the theater with him when he is not admitted. How would they characterize the actions of Ashe's friends? Ask students to discuss what they have done and would do to support a friend.

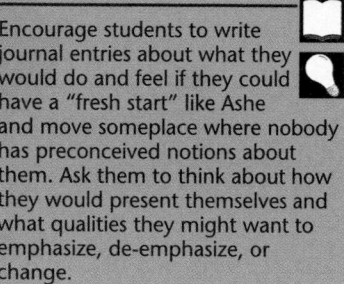
titles and was ranked among the top junior players in the country. Ever the realist, Daddy knew there were few opportunities for a tennis player to make a living from his sport (this was in the days before open tennis). He knew the obstacles I would face as a black tennis player; yet he felt obliged to give me, as the best young black to come along since Althea Gibson, an opportunity to go as far as I could. My peers, the juniors who had become my friends in many cases, would continue to progress, and the Californians could play all year. To keep up with them, I had to be able to play winter tennis. And there were no such opportunities in Richmond.

The solution was to spend my senior year in high school in St. Louis, Missouri, at the home of Richard Hudlin, a good friend of Dr. Johnson and another tennis buff. The move was practical because each summer I had roamed farther and farther away from home. St. Louis would be the final break with Richmond.

GUIDED READING
What was the solution to Ashe's problem?

Everybody goes through stages in life when they wish they could change things about themselves or their circumstances. As a sophomore at Maggie Walker, I had made the varsity baseball team and pitched one inning in our first game that spring. The next morning J. Harry Williams, the principal, called me into his office.

"Arthur Junior," he said bluntly. "I'm kicking you off the baseball team."

I was stunned. "Why, Mr. Williams?"

"Arthur, you've got a great future ahead of you as a tennis player. You've gone further than any other black male, and I don't want to risk you getting hurt."

I was deeply disappointed. But the loss was tempered by his acknowledgement that there was something special about my tennis. Spending my senior year in St. Louis gave me the chance not only to change my tennis game but also my personality.

I was always rather shy and studious. I was good in tennis and baseball, but socially I was shy. I came out of my shell in St. Louis, partly because they made such a fuss over me and nobody knew anything about me. I could be a different person, and nobody would ever know the difference. After growing up in a community where everybody knew who I was, either because of my father or because of my tennis, I could be anything I wanted in St. Louis. Because I had a straight-A average and had already taken subjects in Richmond as a junior that were being taught only to seniors at Sumner High School, I was often allowed to study on my own.

GUIDED READING
What could Ashe do differently in St. Louis?

It amazed me that I had a higher GPA than anybody else in the school. I would have been valedictorian of my senior class at Sumner, with the highest grade-point average, except that I had been in school only one year and didn't qualify. Still, grades aren't everything.

St. Louis was north of the Mason-Dixon Line, so I thought Sumner would have white students. The city had an integrated school system, but Sumner was in an all-black neighborhood. It was a different sort of neighborhood from Richmond's North Side. The kids were more street-wise, and you had to be tougher to survive. There were more kids in the school, and you didn't get that feeling of community that you did at Maggie Walker. People helped one another out in Richmond, even though there was an unwritten feeling that blacks in the public schools in the South were inferior.

Separate-but-equal was the house line for defending dual school systems in Virginia then. It was really separate and unequal. Many black teachers in the southern public schools had only bachelor's degrees. The amount of public money spent on the black schools per pupil was obviously less than the amount of money spent on the white schools per pupil. Many job opportunities were just closed to blacks, so the curriculum at black public schools was often geared toward the jobs that a black graduate could expect to find when he or she graduated, which wasn't very much. You could drive a truck, teach, become a doctor, lawyer, or undertaker, the best blue-collar job was considered that of a mailman.

Mr. Hudlin, his wife, and their son welcomed me into their home. Mr. Hudlin was a teacher at Sumner and his wife Jane was a registered nurse. Mr. Hudlin had been the captain of the tennis team at the University of Chicago in 1924 and had a tennis court in the backyard of his home. His son, Dickie, was a ninth-grader, and we got along fairly well. But I think there was an element of jealousy because of the attention my tennis got from his father. Ironically, Mr. Hudlin wanted nothing more than to have his son become a great player, but Dickie just hated tennis.

My game had evolved considerably from the deep lob that was my main weapon at age seven. Aware that junior tennis depended heavily on consistency, Dr. Johnson's plan for my development concentrated on ground strokes. This theory was a serious mistake— but fortunately, one that was correctable. Dr. J's court at home was clay and few clay-court players, especially juniors, venture to the net. He saw tennis as a game of ground strokes and sound strategy. He believed that a smart player with average strokes could out-think and beat players with better strokes and poor strategy. Up to a point, he was right, and I won more than my share of matches by out-thinking opponents.

Everybody goes through stages in life when they wish they could change things about themselves or their circumstances.

But the appearance of California players, with their upbringing on faster hard courts and the serve-and-volley power game, forced a change in my style. At age sixteen, I had to learn to volley in a hurry and make the jump to the eighteen-and-unders. But once I got to St. Louis, I practiced every day at the St. Louis Armory, on a wooden floor. A wooden floor is fast and slick, balls skid off the floor and accelerate after they bounce. I had to shorten my backswing to play well. With my old round-house backswing, the ball would have been in the back fence before I started moving my racquet forward.

A fast wooden floor also gives a player a false sense of confidence about his serve. Even an average serve seems formidable when it skids off a slick floor. It could have lulled me into accepting the shortcomings on my serve, but Mr. Hudlin and Larry Miller, a white pro, told me to lean forward and put more muscle into my service motion.

I started to return serve differently. Usually, I would stand just behind the baseline and wait for the ball. Now I dropped back a yard and a half or so and charged the ball when my opponent served. I had never been comfortable charging the ball because of my clay-court background, but with my new aggressiveness, I developed new techniques to catch the ball on the rise. In the course of some weight-shifting drills suggested by Larry, I developed a topspin backhand, which worked very well for moving the ball cross-court as I charged forward.

I also changed my grip from the Eastern to the Continental. It is a less secure way of

1. The appearance of Californian players who have been trained on faster hard courts forces Ashe to change his style of play.

1. The offer of a tennis scholarship to
UCLA thrills Ashe.
2. Ashe was expected to assimilate the
history and traditions of tennis.

holding the racquet for the forehand, but it allows you to hit everything—forehand, backhand, volley or serve—with the same grip. The disadvantage is that flat forehands are very difficult to hit with this grip. I began to observe my opponents' grips to figure out what they could and could not do.

In November 1960 I won my first USLTA national title, the National Junior Indoors. At Christmas, on the way back to St. Louis from the Orange Bowl Juniors in Miami Beach, I stopped off in Richmond to visit my family. While I was at home, I got a telephone call one afternoon.

"Arthur, this is J. D. Morgan," the voice on the telephone said. There was a pause. "I'm the tennis coach at UCLA. We're preparing to offer you a scholarship to come out and play for us."

You could have knocked me over with a feather. I was thrilled beyond belief.

> **GUIDED READING**
> What thrilled Ashe?

I said yes even before he finished his offer. I had no idea that UCLA had any interest in me. I would get offers from Michigan, Michigan State, Arizona, and Hampton Institute later, but every junior player knew that UCLA and USC were the schools for tennis.

My father understood my elation but did not understand the significance of UCLA. He supported my decision to go to California, although he was clearly upset at having me move still farther away from the family.

Mr. Hudlin also realized the importance of my UCLA scholarship, and Dr. Johnson was as thrilled as I was. My senior year capped my long career as a junior player. After fulfilling Dr. Johnson's dream of producing a winner in the Interscholastics, I reached the semifinals

of the National Jaycees and the National Juniors. By graduation, I was the fifth-ranked junior in the country and a member of the Junior Davis Cup team that traveled together that summer.

Of course, there was a great deal of fuss about being the "first black" Junior Davis Cup player, the "first black" to get a tennis scholarship to UCLA, the "first black" to win at Charlottesville, etc. Those comments always put me under pressure to justify my accomplishments on racial grounds, as if sports were the cutting edge of our nation's move toward improved race relations. The fact that this kind of accomplishment by a black player got so much attention was an indication that we still had so far to go.

The questions asked in 1960 and 1961 served to remind me of my isolated status in tennis. I played in clubs where the only blacks were waiters, gardeners, and busboys. I knew there was <u>apprehension</u> in some circles about my presence, but I was not about to embarrass myself or anybody else. I was polite, fairly well educated, and I knew which fork to use because I had done some catering with my father.

I was moved into the world of tennis that had little in common with the black experience. The game had a history and tradition I was expected to assimilate,[7] but much of that history and many of those traditions were hostile to me. When I

> **GUIDED READING**
> What was Ashe expected to do?

decided to leave Richmond, I left all that Richmond stood for at the time—its segregation, its conservatism, its parochial[8] thinking, its slow progress toward equality, its lack of opportunity for talented black people. I

---

7. **assimilate.** Absorb into the culture of a group
8. **parochial.** Narrow

words for everyday use   ap • pre • hen • sion (a pri hen' shən) *n.*, suspicion or fear. *Edna felt <u>apprehension</u> every time she remembered the upcoming event.*

had no intention then of coming back. And I really never would, except to see my family, and for a few tournaments and a Davis Cup match years later.

When I got national recognition as a tennis player in my senior year in high school, it was an important step in my personal campaign to overcome assumptions of inequality. But I also knew that no one in Richmond's white tennis establishment had done anything to help me to get where I was. My memories and experiences about Richmond remain firmly rooted in the 1960s. The support I got—from teachers, relatives, and people like Ron Charity and Dr. Johnson—prepared me for the life I would lead outside the South. ■

Respond *to the* SELECTION

What kinds of discrimination have you witnessed or experienced?

About *the* AUTHOR

Arthur Ashe was the first African-American male tennis player to be ranked number one in the world. As a youth, Ashe displayed intelligence, the willingness to work hard, and a determination to win—attributes that led him to become one of the top junior players in the nation. After becoming a top-ranked college player, he won the U.S. Open. In 1975 Ashe won both the Wimbledon and World Championship Tennis men's singles titles.

Ashe's interests extended beyond tennis. He worked to fight prejudice, protested apartheid in South Africa and discrimination in the United States, and involved himself in tennis clinics and educational opportunities for young people. He also wrote a number of books and many articles for newspapers and magazines. Among the books he authored is *A Hard Road to Glory: A History of the African American Athlete*—a three-volume text that remains the only thorough examination of early black athletes in the United States and Canada.

Following an early heart attack in 1979, Ashe underwent quadruple bypass surgery. More than ten years later, Ashe announced to the world that he suffered from AIDS. Doctors had discovered that he had contracted HIV,

the virus that causes AIDS, from a blood transfusion Ashe received after the open-heart surgery. Ashe tirelessly fought the disease and continued to work for the causes he felt strongly about. He died in 1993.

In 1996, a dedication ceremony was held in Ashe's hometown of Richmond, Virginia. A twelve-foot bronze statue of Ashe was unveiled on Monument Avenue to honor him. The following year, a huge crowd in Flushing Meadows, New York, paid tribute to Ashe at the dedication of the new state-of-the-art Arthur Ashe Stadium.

FROM OFF THE COURT **289**

ANSWERS TO CRITICAL THINKING

- Students may say Frank Higgins dedicated this poem to Arthur Ashe because it talks about a father who supports his son's interest in tennis despite the family's difficult financial situation, and it could be a scene out of Ashe's own life in this respect.
- The boy's determination to knock the ball against the building as a way of protesting the discrimination present in society relates to Ashe's own determination to prove people's stereotypes about African Americans false through his work on the tennis court.
- Ashe may have appreciated the boy's ability to release his feelings of frustration through tennis and the father's support of his son.

TENNIS IN THE CITY

for Arthur Ashe   Frank Higgins

He could help us out
selling papers or sacking groceries
but that's what I did growing up.
Every day he's in the alley
knocking that ball against the building.
Whomp   take that   Forest Hills
whomp   whomp   take that   Wimbledon
whomp   whomp   whomp
all   day   long,
the wife tells me so.
Says she watches him from the window
when the bossman has her clean 'em,
says she doesn't know about that boy.
But I know about that boy
and I know this ball's worn
                     and I know this racket's gonna split
no matter how much tape you put on,
so tonight after supper
we're going for new ones, son.
And I want you to start staying
in that alley an hour longer, hear?   ■

ABOUT THE RELATED READING

Frank Higgins has published a poetry collection entitled *Starting from Ellis Island* and a collection of haiku called *Eating Blowfish*. Higgins write drama as well as poetry. His play *Peanutman: A Visit from George Washington Carver* has been produced at youth theaters and schools across the United States. The play *The Sweet By 'n' By* was produced with Gwyneth Paltrow and her mother Blythe Danner.

Critial Thinking

- Why do you think Frank Higgins dedicated this poem to Arthur Ashe?
- What about this poem relates to Ashe's life experiences?
- What might Ashe have appreciated about this poem?

A BLACK ATHLETE LOOKS AT EDUCATION

from *The New York Times*, February 6, 1977

Arthur Ashe

Since my sophomore year at UCLA, I have become convinced that we blacks spend too much time on the playing fields and too little time in the libraries. Consider these facts: for the major professional sports of hockey, football, basketball, baseball, golf, tennis and boxing, there are roughly only 3170 major league positions available (attributing 200 positions to golf, 200 to tennis and 100 to boxing). And the annual turnover is small.

There must be some way to assure that those who try but don't make it to pro sports don't wind up on street corners or in unemployment lines. Unfortunately, our most widely recognized role models are athletes and entertainers—"runnin'" and "jumpin'" and "singin'" and "dancin'."

Our greatest heroes of the century have been athletes—Jack Johnson, Joe Louis, and Muhammad Ali. Racial and economic discrimination forced us to channel our energies into athletics and entertainment. These were the ways out of the ghetto, the ways to get that Cadillac, those regular shoes, that cashmere sport coat.

Somehow, parents must instill a desire for learning alongside the desire to be Walt Frazier. Why not start by sending black professional athletes into high schools to explain the facts of life?

I have often addressed high school audiences and my message is always the same: "For every hour you spend on the athletic field, spend two in the library. Even if you make it as a pro athlete, your career will be over by the time you are 35. You will need that diploma."

Have these pro athletes explain what happens if you break a leg, get a sore arm, have one bad year or don't make the cut for five or six tournaments. Explain to them the star system, wherein for every star earning millions there are six or seven others making $15,000 or $20,000 or $30,000. Invite a bench-warmer or a guy who didn't make it. Ask him if he sleeps every night. Ask him whether he was graduated. Ask him what he would do if he became disabled tomorrow. Ask him where his old high school athletic buddies are.

We have been on the same roads—sports and entertainment—too long. We need to pull over, fill up at the library and speed away to Congress and the Supreme Court, the unions and the business world.

I'll never forget how proud my grandmother was when I graduated from UCLA. Never mind the Davis Cup. Never mind the Wimbledon title. To this day, she still doesn't know what those names mean. What mattered to her was that of her more than thirty children and grandchildren, I was the first to be graduated from college, and a famous college at that. Somehow, that made up for all those floors she scrubbed all those years. ■

ABOUT THE RELATED READING

After his competitive tennis days were over, **Arthur Ashe** expanded his career to include coaching, fundraising, and writing. This editorial was one he wrote for the *New York Times* in 1977. Newspapers and organizations valued Ashe's contributions as an insightful writer and his considerable influence as a sports star.

ADDITIONAL QUESTIONS AND ACTIVITIES

Ask students the following questions:
1. According to Ashe, why should African Americans spend more time in the library?
2. What is Ashe's own message to high school audiences?
3. What does Ashe want pro athletes to explain?
4. What is the "star system"?
5. What roads does Ashe say African Americans have been on too long? What roads does he want to see them on?
6. What makes Ashe's grandmother most proud?

Answers
1. Ashe says that there are only a limited number of careers in sports available and African Americans need a way to support themselves if they are not lucky enough to be one of the few who succeeds in sports.
2. He tells them to spend two hours in the library for every hour on the athletic field because even if you do make it as a pro athlete your career will be over by the time you are 35.
3. Ashe wants pro athletes to explain what happens when an athlete is injured, has a bad year or doesn't make the cut for a tournament.
4. The "star system" means that for every star making a lot of money in sports, there are six or seven other professional athletes making much smaller amounts.
5. He says they have been on the roads of sports and entertainment too long and wants to see them on the road to Congress and the Supreme Court.
6. She is most proud that Ashe graduated from UCLA; she doesn't even know what the Davis Cup and the Wimbledon title mean.

RECALL

1a. Ashe first learned tennis on the courts at Brook Fields, outside his house where the African-American Richmond Racket Club played. Ron Charity, one of the best African-American players in the country, began teaching Ashe to play.

2a. Dr. Johnson's son Bobby, who does much of the tennis teaching, wants to change Bobby's backhand grip. When Ashe won't budge from the grip Ron Charity taught him, Ashe's father is called. Ashe's father drives to the Johnsons' house to tell Ashe to listen to the Johnsons, which resolves the issue because Ashe always obeyed his father.

3a. Ashe came out of his "shell," stopped being so shy, and became more social.

INTERPRET

1b. While Ashe immediately enjoys tennis, at first it only seems to be another sport to try. Later, however, tennis changes Ashe's life and gives him opportunities he might not have otherwise had.

2b. Ashe was willing to challenge any authority other than his father. He learned to show respect to his teachers; however, students may note that Ashe remains headstrong about the way tennis should be played because he notes he didn't change his backhand much at all.

3b. Ashe wanted to make this change because he grew up in a small community where everyone knew everything about him. In St. Louis people don't know anything about him, so he could decide to be whomever and whatever he wanted, which gave him more confidence.

ANALYZE

4a. Ashe got an opportunity to travel to many tournaments and he met many kind coaches and teachers. Through tennis he started a new high school career in St. Louis and he received a scholarship to attend UCLA, so his tennis provided him with the means to afford an education, something Ashe strongly valued. Ashe also came in contact with some white people who subtly discriminated against him, and felt the pressure that came from always having his race mentioned alongside his accomplishments.

SYNTHESIZE

4b. Students may say these experiences strengthened Ashe's love for tennis and made him a more independent, outgoing person. His experiences also made him very aware of racism,

Investigate, *Inquire,* and Imagine

Recall: GATHERING FACTS

1a. Where did Ashe first learn tennis? Who taught him to play?

2a. What dispute did Ashe have with Dr. Johnson's son, Bobby? How was it resolved?

3a. How did Ashe's personality change in St. Louis?

→ **Interpret:** FINDING MEANING

1b. How much did this seem to affect Ashe's life at the time? How much did it seem to affect his future?

2b. How did Ashe react to authority? How might the incident have changed Ashe's perception of authority?

3b. Why did Ashe want to make this change?

Analyze: TAKING THINGS APART

4a. What social experiences did Ashe have as a result of tennis that he otherwise might not have had?

→ **Synthesize:** BRINGING THINGS TOGETHER

4b. How did these experiences help shape Ashe's world view as a youth? How might they have influenced his later ideals, friendships, and work?

Perspective: LOOKING AT OTHER VIEWS →

5a. How does Ashe view the discrimination he experienced and witnessed as a young tennis player?

Empathy: SEEING FROM INSIDE

5b. How might Ashe react to the types of discrimination that exist today?

Understanding *Literature*

AUTOBIOGRAPHY. An **autobiography** is the story of a person's life, written by that person. Although Ashe's book is considered an autobiography, it does contain elements of memoir—a nonfiction narration that focuses on a person's experiences during a particular historical event or time period. Identify parts of this selection that share information about the United States in the 1950s and 1960s. How does Ashe use that information to better portray himself as a person?

DESCRIPTION. A **description** gives a picture in words of a character, object, or scene. What types of descriptions does Ashe offer in this selection? Which characters, objects, or scenes does Ashe describe with the most detail? How does he describe actions? How do the descriptions contribute to the stories Ashe tells about his past?

ANSWER TO INVESTIGATE, INQUIRE, IMAGINE (CONT.)

and the pressure of being an African-American sports star. Students may say his experiences helped shape him into a dedicated tennis player, but they also made him value things other than tennis, such as people who aren't influenced by prejudice.

PERSPECTIVE

5a. Students may say the sly innuendoes of racism on the court Ashe experienced as a youth "left their scars." Later as a professional tennis player, Ashe recognizes that the attention given to his race

indicated that America still had a long way to go in overcoming racism. He also says he sometimes felt isolated among so many white tennis players. He sees his career as an attempt to overcome "assumptions of inequality."

EMPATHY

5b. Students may suggest that Ashe might be pleased about some social improvements, but might still think that the United States has a long way to go in overcoming racism.

Writer's Journal

1. Write an **autobiographical story** about an event in your past that helped shape who you are today.
2. Write the copy for a **promotional poster** to attract interest in a summer tennis clinic for young people.
3. Write a brief **biographical sketch** of Arthur Ashe that could be used as an encyclopedia entry.

Skill Builders

Vocabulary

MASTERING VERBS. The following verbs appear in the selection from *Off the Court* or in "A Black Athlete Looks at Education." Select the sentence that best uses each verb in context, then write a sentence of your own using the verb.

EXAMPLE bar

> (The park rules bar teenagers from camping without supervision.)
>
> The dog bars his teeth when he meets a stranger.
>
> *After Jean failed math, she was barred from playing on the basketball team.*

1. repress
   John repressed his temples, hoping the headache would go away.
   I have to repress my fear of striking out each time I am up to bat.

2. succumb
   I did not want to succumb to the urge to eat another candy bar.
   Our team may succumb the odds and win the game tonight.

3. implicate
   Your muddy footprints may implicate you in the crime.
   Jean implicates that the math test is easy.

4. assimilate
   After spending several summers in Mexico, Alex began to assimilate the customs and language.
   If you do not arrive by 5:00, I will assimilate that you are not coming.

5. instill
   Coach Braxton instills in her players a respect for the game and a sense of pride.
   Amelia asked me to instill the new stereo in her car.

Vocabulary
MASTERING VERBS. Students responses will vary, but make sure students use the chosen words as verbs in sensible sentences.

ANSWERS TO UNDERSTANDING LITERATURE

AUTOBIOGRAPHY. Information students list may include the following: when Jackie Robinson broke baseball's color player he was followed by many African American players, but the same was not true for tennis when Althea Gibson broke the color barrier in the late 1950s; when the speaker grows up Richmond is segregated; Dodgers are popular because they were the first to integrate people of color, but Yankees were slow to integrate; District of Columbia is segregated and Ashe can't go certain places and is called racist names; Gene Autry and Roy Rogers from cowboy films are popular among children; white junior tennis tournament (USLTA) will only accept two African American finalists a year; separate white and African American tournaments; Ashe is taught to be overly polite and subservient to white opponents; African Americans can not eat in restaurants; Ashe experiences "indirect rebuffs and Innuendoes" of racism on tennis courts; Ashe can not get in to movie theaters; some schools are integrated north of the Mason Dixon line; "separate-but-equal" is Virginia's policy but everything is actually not equal; African Americans are taught that the only careers open to them are truck driver, doctor, lawyer, teacher, undertaker, or mailman; much fanfare about She's race along with his talent; and has to go to country clubs where African Americans are only admitted as help. Ashe uses much of this information to show how he develops and thrives despite the racial adversity of his times.
Description. Students may say that Ashe gives particularly vivid descriptions of practicing and playing tennis and the various holds and moves. Ashe also describes the African Americans who taught him and helped make his career as a professional tennis player possible. Students may say the descriptions better enable them to picture the stories about Ashe's past.

Media Literacy
READING STATISTICAL CHARTS. Serena won the second set. Venus won the most total points. Venus had the fastest serve speed, but Serena has the fastest average serve speed. Serena has the higher percentage of break point conversions. Serena approached the net 16 times. Eleven of her attempts at the net were successful. Venus won the point on the second serve 13 times. She won the point on the second serve 50 percent of the time.

Collaborative Learning
& Speaking and Listening
LEARNING AND DEMONSTRATING A SPORT. If students have trouble thinking of such sports, possible choices include fencing, polo, ultimate Frisbee, golf, lacrosse, or synchronized swimming. Inform students that they do not have to learn or present every rule of the sport, but just tell what the basic rules are.

Media Literacy

READING STATISTICAL CHARTS. In March 1999, sisters Venus Williams and Serena Williams faced one another in the Lipton Championships in the first all-sister women's final in 115 years. Venus beat her younger sister in three sets. The match results are shown below.

	set 1	set 2	set 3
Serena Williams	1	6	4
Venus Williams	6	4	6

Match Summary	Serena	Venus
1st serve %	59%	65%
Aces	1	2
Double faults	2	3
Winning % on 1st serve	29 of 52 = 55%	30 of 50 = 60%
Winning % on 2nd serve	15 of 36 = 41%	13 of 26 = 50%
Winners (incl. serves)	21	12
Unforced errors	65	41
Break point conversions	5 of 9 = 55%	7 of 18 = 38%
Net approaches	11 of 16 = 68%	11 of 17 = 64%
Total points won	77	87
Fastest match serve speed	115 mph	118 mph
Average match serve speed	99 mph	96 mph

Which sister won the second set? Who won the most total points? Which sister had the fastest serve speed in the match? Which sister had the fastest average serve speed? Who had a higher percentage of break point conversions? How many times did Serena approach the net? How many of these attempts were successful? How many times did Venus win the point on the second serve? What percentage of the time did she win the point on the second serve?

Collaborative Learning & Speaking and Listening

LEARNING AND DEMONSTRATING A SPORT. With a partner, research a sport that neither of you is familiar with. Use books or information from the Internet to find basic information about the rules of the sport, where it is played, techniques players use, and how the game is won. Prepare a basic overview of the sport to present to your class. If possible, seek permission to use equipment from your school's physical education department to use in your presentation. For more information, see the Language Arts Survey 5.18, "How to Locate Library Materials," 5.27, "Conducting an Internet Search," and 4.18, "Guidelines for Giving a Speech."

Prereading

"Roberto Clemente: *A Bittersweet Memoir*"

by Jerry Izenberg

Reader's Resource

- **HISTORY CONNECTION.** During the early 1900s, the popularity of major-league baseball skyrocketed. The World Series—baseball's championship games—grew to be one of the nation's leading annual sports events. Outstanding players such as Cy Young and Ty Cobb became national stars. Bigger and more modern ballparks were built. In the 1930s, radio broadcasts of baseball games attracted many fans, and the first major-league night games were held, allowing fans to attend games after work.

- In 1939, the National Baseball Hall of Fame and Museum opened in Cooperstown, New York, to display baseball memorabilia and to honor the games greatest players. In 1946, the first major league game was televised, further increasing baseball's popularity.

- Roberto Clemente joined major league baseball in the 1950s and became one of the nation's best-loved players. In 1954, Clemente was drafted by the Pittsburgh Pirates. He led the team to two World Series victories. Clemente was elected to the Baseball Hall of Fame in 1973, a year after his death.

Roberto Clemente grew up in Carolina, Puerto Rico, near the capitol—San Juan. He died while flying supplies to earthquake victims in Nicaragua.

Reader's Journal

Who from the past or present do you most admire, and why?

Reader's TOOLBOX

MEMOIR. A **memoir** is a nonfiction narration that tells a story. A memoir can be autobiographical (about one's own life) or biographical (about someone else's life). Memoirs are based on a person's experiences and reactions to historical events. Biographical memoirs often focus on how the subject of the memoir affected and influenced others and on how other people and events affected and influenced the subject. As you read this memoir, ask yourself these questions: How did Clemente influence or affect other people? How did other people and events influence or affect Clemente?

ANECDOTE. An **anecdote** is a brief story, usually told to make a point. Within the memoir that follows, a number of people who knew Roberto Clemente offer anecdotes about the kind of person he was and the things he did. These anecdotes help create a more complete picture of Clemente, both as a baseball player and as a human being. Which anecdote in the memoir do you find most entertaining? Which do you find most insightful?

295

ADDITIONAL RESOURCES

UNIT4 RESOURCE BOOK
- Selection Worksheet 4.5
- Selection Check Test 4.4.9
- Selection Test 4.4.10

READER'S JOURNAL

Students might expand upon their journal assignment by creating some way to honor this person, such as a speech, a piece of biographical or creative writing, a collage or poster, or a class bulletin board honoring class heroes.

GOALS/OBJECTIVES

Studying this lesson will enable students to
- enjoy a biographical memoir of a baseball player
- define *memoir* and analyze the way the subject of a biographical memoir affected other

- define *anecdote* and recognize anecdotes in their reading
- define *oxymoron* and point to examples of oxymoron
- evaluate Internet sites

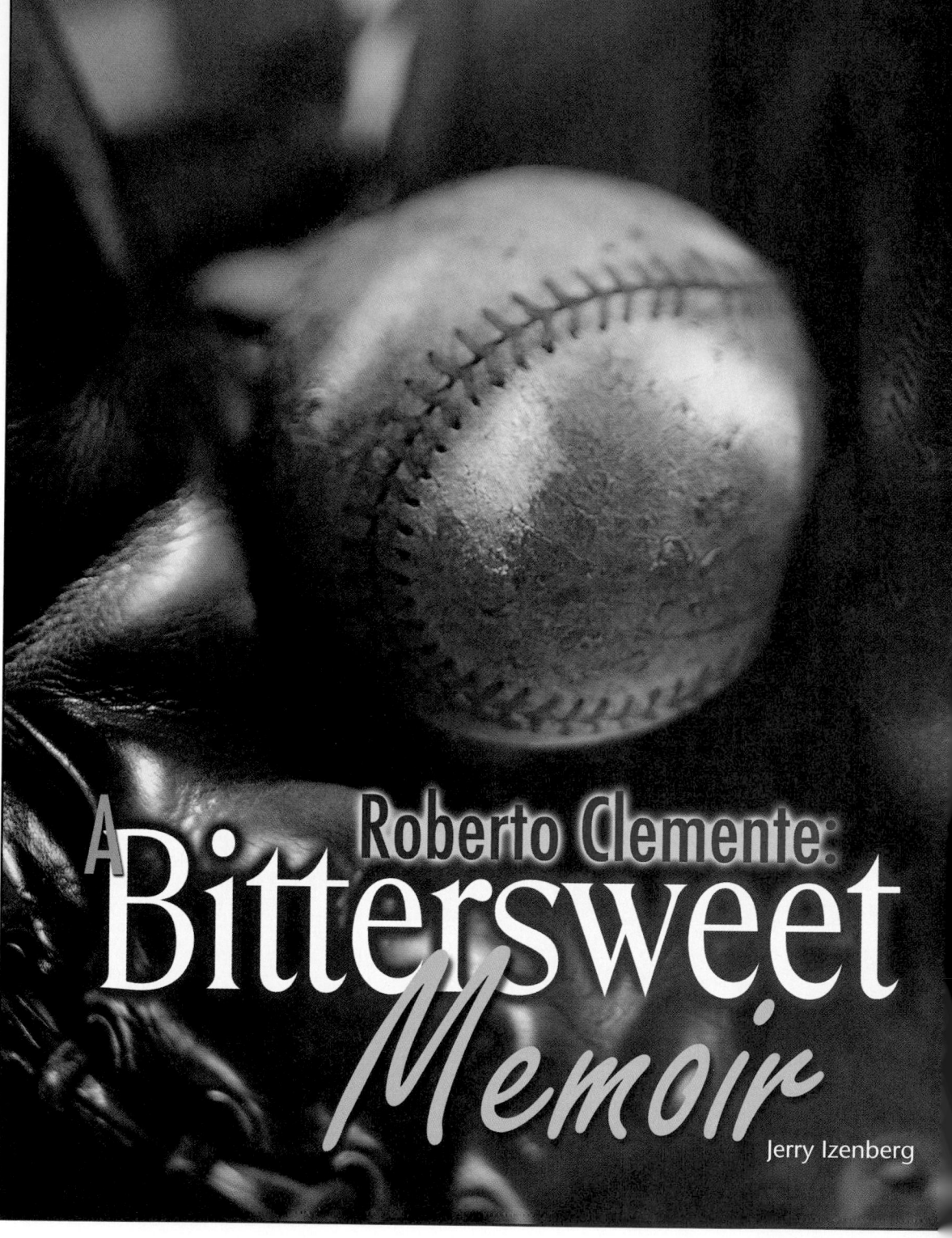

Roberto Clemente: A Bittersweet Memoir

Jerry Izenberg

I saw him play so often. I watched the grace of his movements and the artistry of his reflexes from who knows how many press boxes. None of us really appreciated how pure an athlete he was until he was gone. What follows is a personal retracing of the steps that took Roberto Clemente from the narrow, crowded streets of his native Carolina to the local ball parks in San Juan and on to the major leagues. But it is more. It is a remembrance formed as I stood at the water's edge in Puerto Rico and stared at daybreak into the waves that killed him. It is all the people I met in Puerto Rico who knew him and loved him. It is the way an entire island in the sun and a Pennsylvania city in the smog took his death. . . .

The record book will tell you that Roberto Clemente collected 3,000 hits during his major-league career. It will say that he came to bat 9,454 times, that he drove in 1,305 runs, and played 2,433 games over an eighteen-year span.

But it won't tell you about Carolina, Puerto Rico; and the old square; and the narrow, twisting streets; and the roots that produced him. It won't tell you about the Julio Coronado School and a remarkable woman named María Isabella Casares, whom he called "Teacher" until the day he died and who helped to shape his life in times of despair and depression. It won't tell you about a man named Pedron Zarrilla who found him on a country softball team and put him in the uniform of the Santurce club and who nursed him from promising young athlete to major-league superstar.

And most of all, those cold numbers won't begin to delineate[1] the man Roberto Clemente was. To even begin to understand what this magnificent athlete was all about, you have to work backward. The search begins at the site of its ending.

The car moves easily through the pre-dawn streets of San Juan. A heavy all-night rain has now begun to drive, and there is that post-rain sweetness in the air that holds the promise of a new, fresh, clear dawn. This is a journey to the site of one of Puerto Rico's deepest tragedies. This last says a lot. Tragedy is no stranger to the sensitive emotional people who make this island the human place it is. Shortly before the first rays of sunlight, the car turns down a bumpy secondary road and moves past small shantytowns, where the sounds of the children stirring for the long walk toward school begin to drift out on the morning air. Then there is another turn, between a brace[2] of trees and onto the hardpacked dirt and sand, and although the light has not yet quite begun to break, you can sense the nearness of the ocean. You can hear its waves pounding harshly against the jagged rocks. You can smell its saltiness. The car noses to a stop, and the driver says, "From here you must walk. There is no other way." The place is called Puente Maldonado and the dawn does not slip into this angry place. It

> **None of us really appreciated how pure an athlete he was until he was gone.**

GUIDED READING
What won't the record books tell you?

1. **delineate.** Describe
2. **brace.** Grove that provides shelter from wind

ANSWER TO GUIDED READING QUESTION

1. The record books will not tell you many things about the person Roberto Clemente was and the influences on his life. They will not tell you about where he grew up, about the teacher who had a profound impact on his life, or about Pedron Zarilla who first discovered him as a baseball player.

CROSS-CURRICULAR CONBNECTIONS

HISTORY. Inform students that baseball is one of the oldest and most popular spectator sports. The game as it is known today developed during the 1800s. The first organized baseball club was formed in 1842 by a group of young men in New York City, who named their club the Knickerbocker Baseball Club. They developed a set of twenty rules that later became the foundation of modern baseball. These rules call for two nine-player teams on a well-defined playing field that included a home plate and three bases set apart by specific distances.

The Knickerbockers abolished the practice of plugging, in which fielders could put runners out by throwing the ball at them as they ran between bases. They replaced it with the practice of tagging runners or forcing them out at a base. They also established foul lines, one of the most significant developments in baseball as a sport. In other versions of the game, the ball could be hit in any direction. Foul lines drawn from home plate helped create an area close to the action where spectators could gather and watch the game without interfering.

explodes in a million lights and colors as the large fireball of the sun begins to nose above the horizon.

"This is the nearest place," the driver tells me. "This is where they came by the thousands on that New Year's Eve and New Year's Day. Out there," he says, gesturing with his right hand, "out there, perhaps a mile and a half from where we stand. That's where we think the plane went down."

> **GUIDED READING**
> What happened out in the ocean?

The final hours of Roberto Clemente were like this. Just a month or so before, he had agreed to take a junior-league baseball team to Nicaragua and manage it in an all-star game in Managua. He had met people and made friends there. He was not a man who made friends casually. He had always said that the people you wanted to give your friendship to were the people for whom you had to be willing to give something in return—no matter what the price.

Two weeks after he returned from that trip, Managua, Nicaragua exploded into flames. The earth trembled and people died. It was the worst earthquake anywhere in the Western Hemisphere in a long, long time.

> **GUIDED READING**
> What happened two weeks after Clemente left Nicaragua?

Back in Puerto Rico, a television personality named Luis Vigereaux heard the news and was moved to try to help the victims. He needed someone to whom the people would listen, someone who could say what had to be said and get the work done that had to be done and help the people who had to be helped.

"I knew," Luis Vigereaux said, "Roberto was such a person, perhaps the only such person who would be willing to help."

And so the mercy project, which would eventually claim Roberto's life, began. He appeared on television. But he needed a staging area. The city agreed to give him Sixto Escobar Stadium.

> **GUIDED READING**
> What did Luis Vigereaux know about Clemente's character?

"Bring what you can," he told them. "Bring medicine . . . bring clothes . . . bring food . . . bring shoes . . . bring yourself and help us load. We need so much. Whatever you bring, we will use."

And the people of San Juan came. They walked through the heat and they drove cars and battered little trucks, and the mound of supplies grew and grew. Within two days, the first mercy planes left for Nicaragua.

Meanwhile, a ship had been chartered and loaded. And as it prepared to steam away, unhappy stories began to drift back from Nicaragua. Not all the supplies that had been flown in, it was rumored, were getting through. Puerto Ricans who had flown the planes had no passports, and Nicaragua was in a state of panic.

"We have people there who must be protected. We have black-market types that must not be allowed to get their hands on these supplies," Clemente told Luis Vigereaux. "Someone must make sure—particularly before the ship gets there. I'm going on the next plane."

> **GUIDED READING**
> What was happening to some of the supplies?

The plane they had rented was an old DC-7. It was scheduled to take off at 4:00 P.M. on December 31, 1972. Long before take-off time, it was apparent that the plane needed more work. It had even taxied onto the runway and then turned back. The trouble, a mechanic who was at the airstrip that day <u>conjectured</u>,

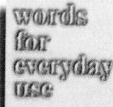

con • jec • ture (kən jek′ chər) v., predict; guess. *Bob <u>conjectures</u> that the Sluggers will win the championship this year.*

had to do with both port [left side] engines. He worked on them most of the afternoon.

The departure time was delayed an hour, and then two, and then three. Across town, a man named Rudy Hernandez, who had been a teammate of Roberto's when they were rookies in the Puerto Rican League and who had later pitched for the Washington Senators, was trying to contact Roberto by telephone. He had just received a five-hundred-dollar donation, and he wanted to know where to send it. He called Roberto's wife, Vera, who told him that Roberto was going on a trip and that he might catch him at the airport. She had been there herself only moments before to pick up some friends who were coming in from the States, and she had left because she was fairly sure that the trouble had cleared and Roberto had probably left already.

"I caught him at the airport and I was surprised," Rudy Hernandez told me. "I said I had this money for Nicaraguan relief and I wanted to know what to do with it. Then I asked him where he was going."

"Nicaragua," Clemente told him.

"It's New Year's Eve, Roberto. Let it wait."

"Who else will go?" Roberto told him. "Someone has to do it."

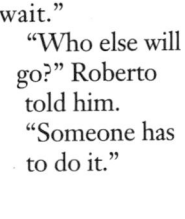

Roberto Clemente, 1962.

At 9 P.M., even as the first stirrings of the annual New Year's Eve celebration were beginning in downtown San Juan, the DC-7 taxied onto the runway, received clearance, rumbled down the narrow concrete strip, and pulled away from the earth. It headed out over the Atlantic and banked toward Nicaragua, and its tiny lights disappeared on the horizon.

GUIDED READING

Why did Clemente believe he had to go to Nicaragua even though it was New Year's Eve?

Just ninety seconds later, the tower at San Juan International Airport received this message from the pilot: "We are coming back around."

Just that.

Nothing more.

And then there was a great silence.

"It was almost midnight," recalls Rudy Hernandez, a former teammate of Roberto's. "We were having this party in my restaurant, and somebody turned on the radio and the announcer was saying that Roberto's plane was feared missing. And then, because my place is on the beach, we saw these giant floodlights crisscrossing the waves, and we heard the sound of the helicopters and the little search planes."

Drawn by a common sadness, the people of San Juan began to make their way toward the beach, toward Puente Maldonado. A cold rain had begun to fall. It washed their faces and blended with the tears.

They came by the thousands and they watched for three days. Towering waves boiled up and made the search virtually impossible. The U.S. Navy sent a team of expert divers into the area, but the battering of the waves defeated them too.

GUIDED READING

What did people begin to do when they heard the news? Why?

ANSWERS TO GUIDED READING QUESTIONS

1. Clemente knew that someone with influence had to go to Nicaragua to take care of the supplies being flown and shipped into the country.
2. People began to go to Puente Maldonado. Drawn by the great tragedy and a common sadness, they gathered together and cried in the rain.

CROSS-CURRICULAR ACTIVITIES

SCIENCE. Have students learn more about the causes of earthquakes and present their information to the class using diagrams or models as aids. Students may also wish to discuss any personal experiences with earthquakes.
SOCIAL STUDIES. Students can research the earthquake in Nicaragua whose victims Clemente was trying to help when he died.

ANSWERS TO GUIDED READING QUESTIONS

1. It was almost impossible to search, but halfway through the week the pilot's body was found. A few days later bits of the cockpit were found, but nothing else turned up.
2. The streets were empty, the radios were silent. Everyone cried and was a "little crazy" that week.
3. The narrator says that it is important to understand that María Isabella Casares is the model of what a teacher should be. She has a rapport based on mutual respect with her students.

ADDITIONAL QUESTIONS AND ACTIVITIES

Discuss with students other tragedies in which a well-known person has died unexpectedly. Ask them to discuss their own reactions to these events as well as mass reactions to the events.

CROSS-CURRICULAR ACTIVITIES

SOCIAL STUDIES. Have students research and present their discoveries on Puerto Rico, Roberto Clemente's home. They can create maps of the island and write descriptions or travel guides to Puerto Rico.

Roberto Clemente, 1972.

Midway through the week, the pilot's body was found in the swift-moving currents to the north. On Saturday bits of the cockpit were sighted.

And then—nothing else.

> **GUIDED READING**
> What were the results of the search?

"I was born in the Dominican Republic," Rudy Hernandez said, "but I've lived on this island for more than twenty years. I have never seen a time or a sadness like that. The streets were empty, the radios silent, except for the constant bulletins about Roberto. Traffic? Forget it. All of us cried. All of us who knew him and even those who didn't, wept that week.

> **GUIDED READING**
> What was unusual about the island after the accident?

"Manny Sanguillen, the Pittsburgh catcher, was down here playing winter ball, and when Manny heard the news he ran to the beach and he tried to jump into the ocean with skin-diving gear. I told him, man, there's sharks there. You can't help. Leave it to the experts. But he kept going back. All of us were a little crazy that week.

"There will never be another like Roberto." Who was he . . . I mean really?

Well, nobody can put together all the pieces of another man's life. But there are so many who want the world to know that it is not as impossible a search as you might think.

He was born in Carolina, Puerto Rico. Today the town has about 125,000 people, but when Roberto was born there in 1934, it was roughly one-sixth its current size.

María Isabella Casares is a schoolteacher. She has taught the children of Carolina for thirty years. Most of her teaching has been done in tenth-grade history classes. Carolina is her home and its children are her children. And among all of those whom she calls her own (who are all the children she taught), Roberto Clemente was something even more special to her.

"His father was an overseer on a sugar plantation. He did not make much money," she explained in an empty classroom at Julio Coronado School. "But then, there are no rich children here. There never have been. Roberto was typical of them. I had known him when he was a small boy because my father had run a grocery store in Carolina, and Roberto's parents used to shop there."

There is this thing that you have to know about María Isabella Casares before we hear more from her. What you have to know is that she is the model of what a teacher should be. Between her and her students even now, as back when Roberto attended her school, there

> **GUIDED READING**
> What does the speaker say it is important to understand about María Isabella Casares?

is this common bond of mutual respect. Earlier in the day, I had watched her teach a class in the history of the Abolition Movement in Puerto Rico. I don't speak much Spanish, but even to me it was clear that this is how a class should be, this is the kind of person who should teach, and these are the kinds of students such a teacher will produce.

With this as a background, what she has to say about Roberto Clemente carries much more impact.

"Each year," she said, "I let my students choose the seats they want to sit in. I remember the first time I saw Roberto. He was a very shy boy and he went straight to the back of the room and chose the very last seat. Most of the time he would sit with his eyes down. He was an average student. But there was something very special about him. We would talk after class for hours. He wanted to be an engineer, you know, and perhaps he could have been. But then he began to play softball, and one day he came to me and said, 'Teacher, I have a problem.'

"He told me that Pedron Zarrilla, who was one of our most prominent baseball people, had seen him play, and that Pedron wanted him to sign a professional contract with the Santurce Crabbers. He asked me what he should do.

"I have thought about that conversation many times. I believe Roberto could have been almost anything, but God gave him a gift that few have, and he chose to use that gift. I remember that on that day I told him, 'This is your chance, Roberto. We are poor

> I believe Roberto could have been almost anything, but God gave him a gift that few have, and he chose to use that gift.

people in this town. This is your chance to do something. But if in your heart you prefer not to try, then Roberto, that will be your problem—and your decision.' "

GUIDED READING
What advice did Clemente's teacher give to him?

There was and there always remained a closeness between this boy-soon-to-be-a-man and his favorite teacher.

"Once, a few years ago, I was sick with a very bad back. Roberto, not knowing this, had driven over from Rio Piedras, where his house was, to see me.

"Where is the teacher?" Roberto asked Mrs. Casares' stepdaughter that afternoon.

"Teacher is sick, Roberto. She is in bed."

"Teacher," Roberto said, pounding on the bedroom door, "get up and put on your clothes. We are going to the doctor whether you want to or not."

"I got dressed," Mrs. Casares told me, "and he picked me up like a baby and carried me in his arms to the car. He came every day for fifteen days, and most days he had to carry me, but I went to the doctor and he treated me. Afterward, I said to the doctor that I wanted to pay the bill.

GUIDED READING
What did Clemente do for his teacher?

"'Mrs. Casares,' he told me, 'please don't start with that Clemente, or he will kill me. He has paid all your bills, and don't you dare tell him I have told you.'

"Well, Roberto was like that. We had been so close. You know, I think I was there the day he met Vera, the girl he later married. She was one of my students, too. I was working

---

ANSWERS TO GUIDED READING QUESTIONS

1. Clemente's teacher told him that playing baseball was his chance to do something, but that if he did not want to try it, that was his problem.
2. Clemente took his teacher to the doctor many times and paid her bills.

ADDITIONAL QUESTIONS AND ACTIVITIES

- Who is María Isabella Casares?
- What impact did she have on Clemente's life?
- Why does the narrator value the opinion of María Isabella Casares?
- What did Clemente want to do?
- What changed his mind?
- What problem did he bring to his teacher?
- Why do you think he asked for her advice?

Answers. María Isabella Casares was Roberto Clemente's teacher. She encouraged him to play baseball, telling him he had been given a gift and he could do great things if he was not afraid to try. The narrator values her opinion because she was a model teacher who shared mutual respect with her students. She had a very close bond with Roberto, so her opinion of him carried some weight. He wanted to be an engineer, but he was offered the opportunity to play baseball. He brought the problem of deciding whether or not to play baseball to his teacher because he respected her opinion.

Quotables

"A teacher affects eternity."
—Henry Adams

Roberto Clemente reaches for a would-be homerun in Game Five of the 1971 World Series.

part-time in the pharmacy and he was already a baseball player by then, and one day Vera came into the store.

"'Teacher,' Roberto asked me, 'who is that girl?'

"'That's one of my students,' I told him. 'Now don't you dare bother her. Go out and get someone to introduce you. Behave yourself.'

"He was so proper, you know. That's just what he did, and that's how he met her, and they were married here in Carolina in the big church on the square."

On the night Roberto Clemente's plane disappeared, Mrs. Casares was at home, and a delivery boy from the pharmacy stopped by and told her to turn on the radio and sit down. "I think something has happened to someone who is very close with you, Teacher, and I want to be here in case you need help."

María Isabella Casares heard the news. She is a brave woman, and months later, standing in front of the empty crypt in the cemetery at Carolina where Roberto Clemente was to have been buried, she said, "He was like a son to me. This is why I want to tell you about him. This is why you must make people—particularly our people, our Puerto Rican children—understand what he was. He was like my son, and he is all our sons in a way. We must make sure that the children never forget how beautiful a man he was."

The next person to touch Roberto Clemente was Pedron Zarrilla, who owned the Santurce club. He was the man who discovered Clemente on the country softball team, and he was the man who signed him for a four-hundred-dollar bonus.

"He was a skinny kid," Pedron Zarrilla recalls, "but even then he had those large powerful hands, which we all noticed right away. He joined us, and he was nervous. But I watched him, and I said to myself, 'this kid can throw and this kid can run, and this kid can hit. We will be patient with him.' The season had been through several games before I finally sent him in to play."

Luis Olmo remembers that game. Luis Olmo had been a major-league outfielder with the Brooklyn Dodgers. He had been a splendid ballplayer. Today he is in the insurance business in San Juan. He sat in his office and recalled very well that first moment when Roberto Clemente stepped up to bat.

"I was managing the other team. They had a man on base and this skinny kid comes out. Well, we had never seen him, so we didn't really know how to pitch to him. I decided to throw him a few bad balls and see if he'd bite.

"He hit the first pitch. It was an outside fast ball, and he never should have been able to reach it. But he hit it down the line for a double. He was the best bad-ball hitter I have ever seen, and if you ask major-league pitchers who are pitching today, they will tell you the same thing. After a while it got so that I just told my pitchers to throw the ball down the middle because he was going to hit it no matter where they put it, and at least if

GUIDED READING

What did Olmo tell his pitchers?

he decided not to swing we'd have a strike on him.

"I played in the big leagues. I know what I am saying. He was the greatest we ever had . . . maybe one of the greatest anyone ever had. Why did he have to die?"

Once Pedron Zarrilla turned him loose, there was no stopping Roberto Clemente. As Clemente's confidence grew, he began to get

better and better. He was the one the crowd came to see out at Sixto Escobar Stadium.

"You know, when Clemente was in the lineup," Pedron Zarrilla says, "there was always this undercurrent of excitement in the ball park. You knew that if he was coming to bat, he would do something spectacular. You knew that if he was on first base, he was going to try to get to second base. You knew that if he was playing right field and there was a man on third base, then that man on third base already knew what a lot of men on third base in the major were going to find out— you don't try to get home against Roberto Clemente's arm."

"I remember the year that Willie Mays came down here to play in the same outfield with him for the winter season. I remember the wonderful things they did and I remember that Roberto still had the best of it.

"Sure I knew we were going to lose him. I knew it was just a matter of time. But I was only grateful that we could have him if only for that little time."

GUIDED READING

What did Pedron Zarrilla know about Clemente?

The major-league scouts began to make their moves. Olmo was then scouting, and he tried to sign him for the Giants. But it was the Dodgers who won the bidding war. The Dodgers had Clemente, but in having him, they had a major problem. He had to be hidden.

This part takes a little explaining. Under the complicated draft rules that baseball used at that time, if the Dodgers were not prepared to bring Clemente up to their major-league team within a year (and because they were winning with proven players, they couldn't), then Clemente could be claimed by another team.

They sent him to Montreal with instructions to the manager to use him as little as possible, to hide him as much as possible, and to tell everyone he had a sore back, a sore

1. He told his pitcher to throw the ball down the middle because Clemente was going to hit it no matter where they put it, and at least if he decided not to swing they might get a strike on him.
2. Zarilla knew he was going to lose Clemente to another baseball team.

BIOGRAPHICAL NOTE

Willie Mays was the third generation of his family to play baseball. Mays played semiprofessional ball at age sixteen, and the next year he joined the Birmingham Black Barons, a team in the Negro National League. He played for the New York Giants. In the 1954 season, the Giants won the World Series, and Mays led the National League in hitting. In 1972, he was traded to the New York Mets. Mays was known for his diving and leaping catches as well as his hitting. Mays retired after the 1973 season and was elected to the Hall of Fame in 1979.

arm, or any other excuse the manager could give. But how do you hide a diamond when he's in the middle of a field of broken soda bottles?

> GUIDED READING
> To what does the speaker compare Clemente?

In the playoffs that year against Syracuse, they had to use Clemente. He hit two doubles and a home run and threw a man out at home the very first try.

The Pittsburgh Pirates had a man who saw it all. They drafted him at the season's end.

And so Roberto Clemente came to Pittsburgh. He was the finest prospect the club had had in a long, long time. But the Pirates of those days were spectacular losers and even Roberto Clemente couldn't turn them around overnight.

> GUIDED READING
> What kind of team were the Pirates when Clemente joined?

"We were bad, all right," recalls Bob Friend, who later became a great Pirate pitcher. "We lost over a hundred games, and it certainly wasn't fun to go to the ball park under those conditions. You couldn't blame the fans for being noisy and impatient. Branch Rickey, our general manager, had promised a winner. He called it his five-year plan. Actually, it took ten."

When Clemente joined the club, it was Friend who made it his business to try to make him feel at home. Roberto was, in truth, a moody man, and the previous season hadn't helped him any.

"I will never forget how fast he became a superstar in this town," says Bob Friend. "Later he would have troubles because he was either hurt or thought he was hurt, and some people would say that he was loafing. But I know he gave it his best shot and he helped make us winners."

The first winning year was 1960, when the Pirates won the pennant and went on to beat the Yankees in the seventh game of the World Series. Whitey Ford, who pitched against him twice in that Series, recalls that Roberto actually made himself look bad on an outside pitch to encourage Whitey to come back with it. "I did," Ford recalls, "and he unloaded. Another thing I remember is the way he ran out a routine ground ball in the last game and when we were a little slow covering, he beat it out. It was something most people forget but it made the Pirates' victory possible."

The season was over. Roberto Clemente had hit safely in every World Series game. He had batted over .300. He had been a superstar. But when they announced the Most Valuable Player Award voting, Roberto had finished a distant third.

"I really don't think he resented the fact that he didn't win it," Bob Friend says. "What hurt—and in this he was right—was how few votes he got. He felt that he simply wasn't being accepted. He brooded about that a lot. I think his attitude became one of 'Well, I'm going to show them from now on so that they will never forget.'

> GUIDED READING
> How did Clemente feel about getting so few votes?

"And you know, he sure did."

Roberto Clemente went home and married Vera. He felt less alone. Now he could go on and prove what it was he had to prove. And he was determined to prove it.

"I know he was driven by thoughts like that," explains Buck Canel, a newspaper writer who covers all sports for most of the hemisphere's Spanish language papers. "He would talk with me often about his feelings. You know, Clemente felt strongly about the fact that he was a Puerto Rican and that he was a black man. In each of these things he had pride.

"On the other hand, because of the early language barriers, I am sure that there were times when he *thought* people were laughing at him when they were not. It is difficult for a Latin-American ballplayer to understand everything said around him when it is said at high speed, if he doesn't speak English that well. But, in any event, he wanted very much to prove to the world that he was a superstar and that he could do things that in his heart he felt he had already proven."

GUIDED READING
What did Clemente want to prove to the world?

In later years, there would be people who would say that Roberto was a hypochondriac (someone who *imagined* he was sick or hurt when he was not). They could have been right, but if they were, it made the things he did even more remarkable. Because I can testify that I saw him throw his body into outfield fences, teeth first, to make remarkable plays. If he thought he was hurt at the time, then the act was even more courageous.

His moment finally came. It took eleven years for the Pirates to win a World Series berth again, and when they did in 1971, it was Roberto Clemente who led the way. I will never forget him as he was during that 1971 series with the Orioles, a Series that the Pirates figured to lose, and in which they, in fact, dropped the first two games down in Baltimore.

When they got back to Pittsburgh for the middle slice of the tournament, Roberto Clemente went to work and led this team. He was a superhero during the five games that followed. He was the big man in the Series. He was the MVP.[2] He was everything he had ever dreamed of being on a ball field.

GUIDED READING
What happened during Clemente's second World Series?

Most important of all, the entire country saw him do it on network television, and never again—even though nobody knew it would end so tragically soon—was anyone ever to doubt his ability.

The following year, Clemente ended the season by collecting his three-thousandth hit. Only ten other men had ever done that in the entire history of baseball.

"It was a funny thing about that hit," Willie Stargell, his closest friend on the Pirates, explains. "He had thought of taking himself out of the lineup and resting for the playoffs, but a couple of us convinced him that there had to be a time when a man had to do something for himself, so he went on and played and got it. I'm thankful that we convinced him, because, you know, as things turned out, that number three thousand was his last hit.

"When I think of Roberto now, I think of the kind of man he was. There was nothing phony about him. He had his own ideas about how life should be lived, and if you didn't see it that way, then he let you know in so many ways, without words, that it was best you each go your separate ways.

"He was a man who chose his friends carefully. His was a friendship worth having. I don't think many people took the time and the trouble to try to understand him, and I'll admit it wasn't easy. But he was worth it.

GUIDED READING
What kind of a friend was Clemente?

"The way he died, you know, I mean on that plane carrying supplies to Nicaraguans who'd been dying in that earthquake, well, I wasn't surprised he'd go out and do something like that. I wasn't surprised he'd go. I just never thought what happened could happen to him."

---

2. **MVP.** Most valuable player

ANSWERS TO GUIDED READING QUESTIONS

1. Clemente wanted to prove to the world that he was a superstar and that he could do things that he felt should have been proven already.
2. Clemente led his team. He was a superhero, the big man in the Series, the MVP. He was everything he ever dreamed of being on the field.
3. Clemente chose his friends carefully, and his friendship was a powerful bond. He believed it was a duty to give as well as receive in friendship.

Quotables

"Never let the fear of striking out get in your way."

—George Herman "Babe" Ruth

ADDITIONAL QUESTIONS AND ACTIVITIES

- In what did Clemente have pride?
- What did people say about Clemente?
- What does the narrator say one can infer about Clemente if what people said was true?

Answers. Clemente had pride in his Puerto Rican heritage and in being a black man. People said he was a hypochondriac, that he only imagined he was sick or hurt. If Clemente was a hypochondriac, he did not let his pains stop him from making remarkable plays. He was willing to push himself to the limit even if he believed he was hurt.

SELECTION CHECK TEST 4.4.9 WITH ANSWERS

Checking Your Reading

1. How did Roberto Clemente die? **Roberto Clemente died in a plane crash.**
2. What project was Clemente working on when he died? **He was flying relief supplies to earthquake victims in Nicaragua.**
3. Who was María Isabella Casares? **She was Clemente's teacher.**
4. Where did Clemente grow up? **Clemente grew up in Carolina, Puerto Rico.**
5. What team did Clemente play for when he won the World Series Most Valuable Player Award? **He played for the Pittsburgh Pirates when named Most Valuable Player.**

Reader's Toolbox

Fill in each blank below with the most appropriate word from the following Words for Everyday Use from "Roberto Clemente." You may have to change the tense of the word.

memoir   anecdote

1. A(n) _____ is nonfiction.
   memoir
2. A(n) _____ may be autobiographical or biographical.
   memoir
3. A(n) _____ is a brief story, usually told to make a point.
   anecdote

"But I know this. He lived a full life. And if he knew at that moment what the Lord had decided, well, I really believe he would have said, 'I'm ready.'"

He was thirty-eight years old when he died. He touched the hearts of Puerto Rico in a way that few people ever could. He touched a lot of other hearts, too. He touched hearts that beat inside people of all colors of skin.

He was one of the proudest of The Proud People.   ∎

Respond *to the* SELECTION

Why do you think Roberto Clemente "touched the hearts" of so many people?

About *the* AUTHOR

Jerry Izenberg is a sportswriter and reporter who writes a syndicated sports column that appears in newspapers around the country. Born in 1930, he graduated from Rutgers University and received his Ph.D. from Harvard University. Izenberg has written a number of books—including *New York Giants: Seventy-Five Years* and *How Many Miles to Camelot: The All-American Sport Myth*—and has written or directed more than thirty television specials. "Roberto Clemente: A Bittersweet Memoir" is taken from his book *Great Latin Sports Figures: Proud People*, which was published in 1976.

Roberto Clemente's career statistics with the Pittsburgh Pirates

Year	G	AB	R	H	2B	3B	HR	RBI	AVG
1955	124	474	48	121	23	11	5	47	.255
1956	147	543	66	169	30	7	7	60	.311
1957	111	451	42	114	17	7	4	30	.253
1958	140	519	69	150	24	10	6	50	.289
1959	105	432	60	128	17	7	4	50	.296
1960	144	570	89	179	22	6	16	94	.314
1961	146	572	100	201	30	10	23	89	*.351
1962	144	538	95	168	28	9	10	74	.312
1963	152	600	77	192	23	8	17	76	.320
1964	155	622	95	*211	40	7	12	87	*.339
1965	152	589	91	194	21	14	10	65	*.329
1966	154	638	105	202	31	11	29	119	.317
1967	147	585	103	*209	26	10	23	110	*.357
1968	132	502	74	146	18	12	18	57	.291
1969	138	507	87	175	20	*12	19	91	.345
1970	108	412	65	145	22	10	14	60	.352
1971	132	522	82	178	29	8	13	86	.341
1972	102	378	68	118	19	7	10	60	.312
Total	**2433**	**9454**	**1416**	**3000**	**440**	**166**	**240**	**1305**	**.317**

G=games played   H=base hits   HR=home runs
AB=official at bats   2B=second-base hits   RBI=runs batted in
R=runs   3B=third-base hits   AVG=batting average
(Batting average is figured by dividing a player's hits by his official at bats. Example: 3000 ÷ 9454 = 0.3173259995769, which rounds off to .317. Batting averages over .300 are considered excellent.)
*=led the National League with this statistic

Critical Thinking

- In which year did Clemente score the most runs?
- During how many years did Clemente have a batting average over .300?
- In his career, Clemente had 3,000 base hits and he played in 2,433 games. During how many years did Clemente play in more games than the number of hits he got the same year?
- During how many years did Clemente get more second-base hits than homeruns?
- Which seem to have been Clemente's best years in baseball? Why?

ANSWERS TO CRITICAL THINKING

1. He scored the most runs in 1966.
2. He had a batting average over .300 during thirteen years.
3. Clemente played in more games than the number of hits he got in only one year, 1955.
4. Clemente got more second base hits than homeruns during seventeen years.
5. Students may say that either 1964 or 1967 seems to be Clemente's best year in baseball because he led the National League with both base hits and his average both years.

Searching for January

W. P. Kinsella

The sand is white as salt but powdery as icing sugar, cool on my bare feet, although if I push my toes down a few inches, yesterday's heat lurks, waiting to surface with the sun.

It is 6:00 A.M. and I am alone on a tropical beach a mile down from our hotel. The calm ocean is a clear, heart-breaking blue. Fifty yards out a few tendrils of sweet, gray fog laze above the water; farther out the mist, water, and pale morning sky merge.

It appears slowly out of the mist, like something from an Arthurian legend, a large, inflatable life raft, the depressing khaki and olive-drab of military camouflage. A man kneeling in front directs the raft with a paddle. He waves when he sees me, stands up and calls out in an urgent voice, but I can't make it out. As the raft drifts closer I can see that the lone occupant is tall and athletic-looking, dark-skinned, with a long jaw and flashing eyes.

"Clemente!" is the first word I hear clearly. "I am Clemente! The baseball player. My plane went down. Days ago! Everyone must think I am dead."

What he says registers slowly. Clemente! It has been fifteen years. Is this some local fisherman playing a cruel joke on a tourist?

"Yes," I call back, after pausing too long, scanning his features again. There is no question: it is Roberto Clemente. "I believe everyone does think you're dead."

"We crashed on New Year's Eve," he said. "I'm the only one who survived."

He steps lithely into the water, pulls the raft up on the beach, tosses the paddle back into the raft.

"Five days I've been out there," he says. "Give or take a day. I sliced up the other paddle with my pocket knife, made a spear. Caught three fish. Never thought I'd enjoy eating raw fish. But I was so hungry they tasted like they were cooked. By the way, where am I?"

I tell him.

He thinks a minute.

"It's possible. We crashed at night on the way to Managua. The plane was carrying three times the weight it should have, but the need was so great. Supplies for the earthquake victims.

"You look so surprised," he says after a pause. "Have they called off the air search already, given us up for dead?" When I remain silent he continues. "Which way is your hotel? I must call my wife, she'll be so worried."

"I am surprised. More than surprised. You are Roberto Clemente, the baseball player?"

"Of course."

"You were lost at sea?"

"Until now."

"There's something not quite right."

"Like what?" says Clemente.

"Like what year do you think this is?"

"When we took off it was 1972, but New Year's Eve. We crashed in the ocean It must be January fifth or sixth, maybe even the seventh, 1973. I haven't been gone so long that I'd lose track of the year."

"What if I told you that it was March 1987?"

"I'd laugh. Look at me! I'd be an old man in 1987. I'd be . . ."

"Fifty two. Fifty three in August."

"How do you know that?"

"I know a little about baseball. I was a fan of yours."

He smiles in spite of himself.

"Thank you. But 1987? Ha! And I don't like the way you said *was*. *Was* a fan of mine." He touches spread fingers to his chest. "These are the clothes I wore the night we crashed. Do I look like I've been wearing them for fifteen years? Is this a fifteen-year growth of beard?" he asks, rubbing a hand across his stubbly chin. "A six day beard would be my guess."

His eyes study me as if I were an umpire who just called an outside pitch strike three: my pale, tourist's skin, the slight stoop as if the weight of paradise is too much for me.

"Say, what are you doing out here alone at dawn?" Clemente says skeptically. "Are you escaped from somewhere? "

"No. But I think you may be. Believe me, it is 1987."

"Can't be. I can tell. I'm thirty-eight years old. I play baseball. See my World Series ring." He thrusts his hand toward me, the gold and diamonds glitter as the sun blushes above the horizon.

I dig frantically in my wallet. "Look!" I cry. "I'm from Seattle. Here's the 1987 Seattle Mariners schedule." I hold the pocket-sized schedule out for him to look at.

"Seattle doesn't have a team."

"They have a new franchise, since 1977. Toronto came in the same year. Read the schedule."

He studies it for a moment.

"It's crazy, man. I've only been gone a few days."

We sit down on the sand, and I show him everything in my wallet: my credit cards, an uncashed check, my driver's license, coins, and bills.

"Try to remember when your plane went down. Maybe there's a clue there."

We walk slowly in the direction of the hotel, but at the edge of the bay, where we would turn inland, Clemente stops. We retrace our steps.

"It was late in the night. The plane was old. It groaned and creaked like a haunted house. I was sitting back with the cargo—bales of clothes, medical supplies—when the pilot started yelling that we were losing altitude. We must have practically been in the water before he noticed. We hit the ocean a few seconds later, and I was buried under boxes and bales as the cargo shifted. A wooden box bounced off my head, and I was out for . . . a few seconds or a few minutes." He rubs the top of his head.

"See, I still got the lump. And I bled some, too." He bends toward me so I can see the small

ADDITIONAL QUESTIONS AND ACTIVITIES

Encourage students to compile a list of evidence for Clemente that he can't have been gone for fifteen years, and then compile a list of evidence for the narrator that Clemente must have been gone for fifteen years.

Encourage students to discuss the
questions Clemente asks the
narrator. What does this reveal about
Clemente's values? Why does
Clemente decide not to return with
the narrator?
Answers. Clemente asks about his
family, his teammates, and his old
team, the Pirates. This reveals the
connection he feels to family and
friends and his passion for baseball.
He decides not to return because he is
afraid if he enters 1987 he may
become an old man and that he
couldn't play baseball in 1987 without
giving away his identity because no
one plays baseball as he does.

swelling, the residue of dried blood clinging around the roots of his sleek, black hair.

"When I woke up I was in front of the emergency door, the cargo had rolled over me and I was snug against the exit. The plane must have been more than half submerged. There was this frightening slurping, gurgling sound. Their I realized my clothes were wet. The raft was on the wall right next to the door. I pulled the door open and the ocean flooded in. I set out the raft, inflated it, and took the paddles and the big water canteen off the wall. I yelled for the others but I don't know if they were alive or if they heard me. There was a mountain of cargo between me and the front of the plane.

"I climbed into the raft, paddled a few yards, and when I looked back the plane was gone. I've been drifting for five or six days, and here I am."

"I don't know where you've been, but you went missing New Year's Eve 1972. They elected you to the Baseball Hall of Fame in 1973, waived the five-year waiting period because you'd died a hero."

"Died?" Clemente begins a laugh, then thinks better of it. "What if I go back with you and call in?"

"You'll create one of the greatest sensations of all time."

"But my wife, my family. Will they all be fifteen years older?"

"I'm afraid so."

"My kids grown up?"

"Yes."

"Maybe my wife has remarried?"

"I don't know, but it's certainly a possibility."

"But, look at me, I'm thirty-eight years old, strong as a bull. The Pirates need me in the outfield."

"I know."

"My teammates?"

"All retired."

"No."

"If I remember right, Bruce Kison was the last to go, retired last year."

"Willie Stargell?"

"Retired in 1982. He's still in baseball but not playing."

"Then I suppose everyone that played at the same time, they're gone too? Marichal? Seaver? Bench? McCovey? Brock? McCarver? Carlton?"

"Carlton's won over three hundred games, but he doesn't know when to quit. He's a marginal player in the American League. So is Don Suttoll, though he's also won three hundred. Jerry Reuss is still hanging on, maybe one or two others. Hank Aaron broke Babe Ruth's home-run record, then a guy from Japan named Sadaharu Oh broke Hank Aaron's record."

"And my Pirates?"

"Gone to hell in a handbasket. They won the World Series in '78, Willie Stargell's last hurrah. They've been doormats for several seasons, will be again this year. Attendance is down to nothing; there's talk of moving the franchise out of Pittsburgh."

"They need Roberto Clemente."

"Indeed they do."

"And Nicaragua? The earthquake?"

"The earth wills out," I said. "The will of the people to survive is so strong . . . . The earthquake is history now."

"And Puerto Rico? Is my home a state yet?"

"Not yet."

He looks longingly toward the path that leads to the hotel and town. We sit for a long time in that sand white as a bridal gown. He studies the artifacts of my life. Finally he speaks.

"If I walk up that path, and if the world is as you say—and I think I believe you—I will become a curiosity. The media will swarm over me unlike anything I've ever known. Religious fanatics will picnic on my blood. If I see one more person, I'll have no choice but to stay here."

"What are your alternatives?"

"I could try to pass as an ordinary citizen who just happens to look like Roberto Clemente did fifteen years ago. But if I become real to the world I may suddenly find myself white-haired and in rags, fifty-three years old. "

"What about baseball?"

"I could never play again, I would give myself away. No one plays the game like Clemente."

"I remember watching you play. When you ran for a fly ball it was like you traveled three feet above the grass, your feet never touching.

'He has invisible pillows of angel hair attached to his feet,' my wife said one night, 'that's how he glides across the outfield.'

"Perhaps you could go to the Mexican Leagues," I suggest. "Remember George Brunet, the pitcher? He's still pitching in the badlands and he's nearly fifty."

"I suffer from greed, my friend, from wanting to claim what is mine: my family, my home, my wealth. My choice is all or nothing."

"The nothing being?"

"To continue the search."

"But how?"

"I've searched a few days and already I've found 1987. Time has tricked me some way. Perhaps if I continue searching for January 1973, I'll find it."

"And if you don't?"

"Something closer then, a time I could accept, that would accept me."

"But what if this is all there is? What if you drift forever? What if you drift until you die?"

"I can't leap ahead in time. It's unnatural. I just can't."

"If you came back to baseball, Three Rivers Stadium would be full every night. You could make Pittsburgh a baseball city again. You'd have to put up with the media, the curious, the fanatics. But perhaps it's what you're destined to do."

"I am destined to be found, maybe even on this beach, but fifteen years in your past. I intend to be found. I'll keep searching for January."

He walked a few steps in the direction of the raft.

"Wait. I'll go and bring you supplies. I can be back in twenty minutes.

"No. I don't want to carry anything away from this time. I have five gallons of water, a bale of blankets to warm me at night, the ingenuity to catch food. Perhaps my footprints in the sand are already too much, who knows?"

He is wading in the clear water, already pushing the raft back into the ocean.

"If you find January . . . if the history I know is suddenly altered, I hope I went to see you play a few times. With you in the line-up the Pirates probably made it into the World Series in '74 and '75. They won their division those years, you know . . . you would have been the difference . . ."

I watch him drift. Trapped. Or am I trapped, here in 1987, while he, through some malfunction of the universe, is borne into timelessness? What if I were to accompany him?

"Wait!" I call. "There's something . . ."

But Clemente has already drifted beyond hearing. I watch as he paddles, his back broad and strong. Just as the mist is about to engulf him, as ocean, fog, and sky merge, he waves his oar once, holding it like a baseball bat, thrusting it at the soft, white sky. ∎

ABOUT THE RELATED READING

W. P. Kinsella was born in 1935 in Edmonton, Alberta, a province in Canada. He graduated from the University of Iowa and was a professor of English from 1978 to 1983 at the University of Calgary in Alberta. Since 1983, Kinsella has written numerous books about baseball and other topics. His book *Shoeless Joe* was made into the motion picture *Field of Dreams*. "Searching for January" is a short story from the book *The Dixon Cornbelt League and Other Baseball Stories*.

ANSWERS TO INVESTIGATE, INQUIRE, IMAGINE

RECALL

1a. He died in a plane crash while bringing aid to earthquake victims in Nicaragua.

2a. María Isabella Casares was Clemente's teacher. She advised him to use his gifts. He brought her to the doctor and paid the bills.

3a. A great achievement was getting three thousand hits. He took pride in his team's World Series victories and in being named MVP in 1971. he brooded about not making MVP in 1960.

INTERPRET

1b. Clemente shows he was caring and unselfish. People gathered together because Clemente was their hero both on and off the baseball field.

2b. Clemente cared for and respected Casares very much. he showed how far he would go to help people.

3b. He was a great baseball player and a person with a strong connection to others and to his roots.

ANALYZE

4a. People who know Clemente think of him as a caring person and a great friend who believes that doing things for others and giving is an important part of human relationships. people who do not know him think of him as a hypochondriac and generally view him more harshly.

SYNTHESIZE

4b. *Responses will vary.* Students may say that Clemente was a great baseball player who was passionate about the sport, but even more than a great baseball player he was a great and giving humanitarian and friend.

EVALUATE

5a. Most students will say that the memoir does an excellent job of portraying Clemente and his impact on the world around him because it focuses on his empathy for others, his close friendships, and his giving nature rather than just his baseball accomplishments.

Investigate, Inquire, and Imagine

Recall: GATHERING FACTS

1a. How did Roberto Clemente die? Where was he traveling? Why was he going there?

2a. Who was María Isabella Casares? What advice did she give Clemente? What did Clemente do for her when she was sick?

3a. What did Clemente achieve in baseball? About what did he brood? In what did he take pride?

Interpret: FINDING MEANING

1b. What did the final actions of Clemente's life reveal about his character? Why did people gather at Puente Maldonado by the thousands?

2b. How do you think Clemente felt about Casares? What do Clemente's interactions with Casares reveal about him?

3b. In what ways was Clemente a role model?

Analyze: TAKING THINGS APART

4a. Examine the kinds of relationships Clemente formed with people. What did friendship mean to him? In what ways do his close friends describe him? How do those descriptions differ from the views of people who did not know him personally?

Synthesize: BRINGING THINGS TOGETHER

4b. Summarize Roberto Clemente's character. In forming your answers, consider the priorities in Clemente's life and what he considered less important. Finally, conclude by considering what aspect of Clemente's character you will remember most after reading about him.

Evaluate: MAKING JUDGMENTS

5a. How well does "Roberto Clemente: A Bittersweet Memoir" achieve the goal of giving readers an understanding about who Clemente was and what his impact on the world was? Explain your answer.

Extend: CONNECTING IDEAS

5b. How does "Searching for January" contribute to your understanding of Clemente? How does the story contribute to your understanding of Clemente's impact on the world? What statement does the story make about the legend Clemente has become?

ANSWERS TO INVESTIGATE, INQUIRE, IMAGINE (CONT.)

EXTEND

5b. Students may say that "Searching for January" again emphasizes the close connection Clemente had with others, especially the earthquake victims and his teammates, as well as his love of, and confidence in his own abilities in, baseball. The story emphasizes that Clemente is gone but not forgotten in the hearts of many people. It is in people's hearts and imaginations that Clemente lives on. The story emphasizes that Clemente is such a legend that people would still like for his fatal accident to be a falsehood because they would love to see him play baseball again.

Understanding *Literature*

MEMOIR. A **memoir** is a nonfiction narration that tells a story. A memoir can be autobiographical (about one's own life) or biographical (about someone else's life). Memoirs are based on a person's experiences and reactions to historical events. Biographical memoirs often focus on how the subject of the memoir affected and influenced others and on how other people and events affected and influenced the subject. How did Clemente's death affect people? How did the opinions of others affect Clemente's goals and decisions?

ANECDOTE. An **anecdote** is a brief story, usually told to make a point. Copy the graphic organizer below to examine the anecdotes in "Roberto Clemente: A Bittersweet Memoir." Fill out a graphic organizer for each individual who offers information about Clemente, and summarize their anecdotes about him. How do the anecdotes complement one another? Which offers the most insight into Clemente the baseball player? Which offers the most insight into Clemente the person?

Graphic *Organizer*

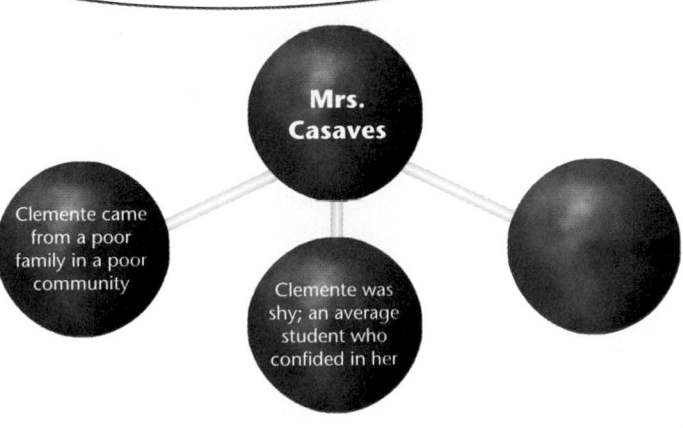

Mrs. Casaves

Clemente came from a poor family in a poor community

Clemente was shy; an average student who confided in her

Writer's Journal

1. Imagine the narrator in "Searching for January" reported his encounter with Clemente to the local press. Write the **headline** for the newspaper story.
2. Write a **trivia question**, and its answer, about one of Roberto Clemente's baseball accomplishments.
3. Write a **tribute** to Roberto Clemente for people visiting the Baseball Hall of Fame and Museum.

MEMOIR. Many people mourned the loss of Clemente as if their hearts were breaking because they admired him on and off the field. Clemente did whatever he could to please and help others, even when it involved some self-sacrifice.

ANECDOTE. Students' organizers may be described as follows: Vigeraux: knows that Clemente will help the earthquake victims; Rudy Hernandez: asked Clemente where he was going on New Year's Eve, Clemente says that he has to go because someone has to help the Nicaraguans, just one message from Clemente's pilot, "We are coming back around," large search for Clemente at midnight, the people drawing together because of their sadness on the beach to mourn Clemente, the streets are silent and radios quiet in Puerto Rico after Clemente's death, Manny Sanguillen a professional catcher keeps trying to go diving to look for Clemente, there will never be another like Roberto; Mrs. Casares: (in addition to the details already listed) asked teacher for advice about playing baseball, she told him to use his gift, Clemente took his teacher to the doctor and paid for her bills, tells him to get someone to introduce him to another one of her students, Vera, whom he later marries, says he is like all our sons in a way; Pedron Zarilla: thought Clemente was a skinny kid, recognized his baseball ability, was patient with him and let him play, says Clemente caused a current of excitement in the ball park and would always do something spectacular at plate, knew that he would lose Clement to another team; Bob Friend: recalls how bad the Pirates once were, tells how Clemente was hurt that he got so few votes for MVP, says he later showed people what he was made of; Buck Canel: says Clemente was concerned people were making fun of him because of the language barrier, Clemente was proud of his heritage; Willie Stargell: had to convince Clemente to go to bat to make what turned out be his three thousandth hit, there was nothing phony about Clemente, he chose friendships carefully and his friendship was worth having, he lived a full life and would have accepted his end. Students may say the anecdotes complement each other because they all work together to portray a great friend and caring individual. Students may say that Bob Friend offers much insight into Clemente as a ball player, but both Mrs. Casares and Willie Stargell offer much insight into Clement as a person.

Language, Grammar, and Style
LOOKING AT OXYMORONS. *Responses will vary, but students may include oxymorons such as the following:*
- tears of happiness (tears are usually associated with sorrow)
- tragicomedy (tragedies are usually about serious or sad events and comedies are about light or happy events)
- slow boil (boiling water moves quickly rather than slowly)
- wet blanket (when people use blankets they are usually dry and warm)
- pretty ugly (the two words mean the exact opposite)

Study and Research & Media Literacy
EVALUATING INTERNET SITES. Students may wish to refer to the Language Arts Survey, "How to Evaluate Internet Web Sites," for more information before they begin this activity.

Vocabulary
VERBS. *Responses will vary.* Students should use each verb in a sentence, using its meaning properly.

Skill Builders

Language, Grammar, and Style

LOOKING AT OXYMORONS. An oxymoron is a combination of contradictory words. Such words or phrases often develop complex meanings despite the fact that their components contradict one another. The word *bittersweet*, which means "pleasant with overtones of sadness," is an oxymoron. Other examples of oxymorons include *freezer burn, definite maybe, deafening silence, act naturally,* and *rush hour.* On your own, create a list of at least five oxymorons not included here. After each item, explain what makes the term an oxymoron.

Study and Research & Media Literacy

EVALUATING INTERNET SITES. Using the Internet, examine the homepage sites of major sports organizations in the United States. Find a site that interests you.

What variety of information does the site offer? What information can you find about individual athletes? teams? championships? How far back in time does the site's information go? How accurate does the information seem to be? How easy is it to navigate in the site?

Some organizations you may want to look for include:
National Baseball Hall of Fame and Museum at http://www.baseballhalloffame.org
Major League Baseball at http://www.majorleaguebaseball.com
National Football League at http://www.nfl.com
Basketball Hall of Fame http://www.hoophall.com
Hockey Hall of Fame http://www.hhof.com
National Track and Field Hall of Fame at http://www.usatf.org
National Softball Hall of Fame and Museum at http://www.softball.org/hall/index.html
International Swimming Hall of Fame at http://www.ishof.com
International Tennis Hall of Fame at http://www.tennisfame.org
International Association of Sports Museums and Halls of Fame at http://www.sportshalls.com

Vocabulary

VERBS. The following verbs appear in "Roberto Clemente: A Bittersweet Memoir" or in "Searching for January." Use each verb in a sentence. If you need help remembering the definition of a particular word, look it up in the dictionary.

EXAMPLE gesture
The bank teller gestured when she was ready to assist me.
1. conjecture
2. defeat
3. recall
4. loaf
5. resent
6. scan
7. retrace
8. swarm
9. suffer
10. drift

for your READING LIST

American Sports Poems is an anthology of poetry about the whole spectrum of sports—from baseball, basketball, and football to fishing, diving, and fencing. Americans are fascinated with the drama of sports competition. But this obsession with sports is more than a love of competition or an appreciation for athletic ability. Sports encompass the full range of human struggle and emotion: hope and disappointment, fear and joy, anticipation and loneliness. These poems capture it all. Even readers who are not sports fans will find something they recognize from their own lives. David Daiches's "To Kate, Skating Better Than Her Date" portrays the desperate excitement of first love in humorous rhyme. Edwards Field's "The Sleeper" deals with the gratitude of a weak, uncoordinated boy for the older boy who believed in him and included him in the game. You may recognize some of the poems, including the words to *Take Me Out to the Ballgame*, the beloved 7th-inning stretch song. Some poems are light-hearted and funny, others are thoughtful and moving. They are all about sports, which some people think are a great metaphor for American life.

WRITE YOUR OWN ARTSMART

Select a poem you particularly enjoy and illustrate it with a piece of art. You may create your own art or choose from a variety of sources, including art books, the Internet, photographs, or magazines. In selecting art, you may find it helpful to think about these questions:

- What is the main idea of this poem?
- What emotions are expressed?
- How have these emotions or ideas played out in my life?
- What images or memories come to mind when I consider this idea or emotion?

Using the ArtSmart features found in your textbook as models, write an ArtSmart feature for your poem and accompanying art or illustration. Your ArtSmart feature should include the following:

- A caption identifying the selection and the artist, even if it is original art you have created. Use the captions in the textbook as models.
- A brief description of the artwork and information about the artist.
- An explanation relating the artwork to the poem selected.

Create a finished presentation, with your poem and ArtSmart feature displayed together.

Other books you may want to read:
The Best American Sports Writing, eds. Glenn Stout and Bill Littlefield
Bat 6, by Virginia Euwer Wolff
A Whole Other Ball Game: Women's Literature on Women's Sports, by Joli Sandoz

For Your Reading List
American Sports Poems, selected by R. R. Knudson and May Swenson, offers a broad range of poems that will appeal to both students who are athletically inclined and those who are not. As alternative reading selections, offer students *The Best American Sports Writing,* edited by Glenn Stout and Bill Littlefield; *Bat 6,* the award-winning novel by Virginia Euwer Wolff; and *A Whole Other Ball Game: Women's Literature on Women's Sports,* by Joli Sandoz. The latter two titles are especially strong works showing women's full participation in what editor Joli Sandoz calls a "fierce love of sport."

Write Your Own ArtSmart
This activity invites students to strengthen their visual literacy skills by tying together literature about sports with fine art, as modeled in the textbook ArtSmart feature. To help guide them, refer them to the Language Arts Survey 1.11, " 'Reading' Art and Photographs" and 6.11, "Displaying Effective Visual Information."

GUIDED WRITING
Software

See the Guided Writing Software for an extended version of this lesson that includes printable graphic organizers, extensive student models and student-friendly checklists, and self-, peer, and teacher evaluation features.

Examining the Model

Point out that Arthur Ashe writes about a simple, personal event that was charged with social significance. Discuss with students the personal qualities of Ashe that are revealed at this time of his life.

Professional Model

In his book *Off the Court*, Arthur Ashe describes his experience as a black tennis player growing up in a racially prejudiced society. His experiences mirror those of many African Americans who lived in the United States in the mid-1950s.

from *Off the Court* by Arthur Ashe, page 285

During the National Inter-scholastics in Charlottesville in 1960, Butch Newman, Cliff Buchholz, and Charlie Pasarell asked me to join them at a movie. I turned them down because I knew I couldn't get in—but the guys wouldn't take no for an answer. When we got to the theater, the reaction was predictable.

"You can't go in," the woman in the ticket booth said. I wasn't surprised by her statement. But I was slightly elated when Cliff said, "Well, if he can't go in, none of us will go." And all of us left.

Guided Writing

WRITING AN AUTOBIOGRAPHICAL MEMOIR

Leanna, a seventh grade student at Oak Street Middle School, never realized that her ideas about the world were important to others—until someone asked. Leanna recalls, "I'll never forget the day my aunt asked me what I thought about the war in Kosovo. I felt terrible about what was happening there. I had already spent several weekends gathering blankets for a relief effort. So, I definitely had an opinion about the war—how it affected me, how I could see it affecting others—but no one had ever asked me for it. Now, she was asking how a thirteen-year-old kid felt about that war."

What about you? When you were younger, events may have happened without you really noticing what they were or the impact they had. But now you relate and respond to many events—from satellite launches, to a skate park closing, to the latest sci-fi movie craze.

You have a unique view of it all. How can you let the world see an event through your eyes? Many people write autobiographical memoirs to share their insights. You can, too.

What is an autobiographical memoir? Like an autobiography, an autobiographical memoir is the story of a person's life written by that person. But an autobiographical memoir is more than personal memories. It tells about a significant event that touched many people besides the writer. It allows the reader to experience that larger event through the writer's unique, personal perspective. An autobiographical memoir is your opportunity to share your thoughts about an event that affects not just you, but an entire community—even a nation.

Examining the Model

The professional model, an excerpt from *Off the Court*, expresses Arthur Ashe's personal feelings and his experience with racism.

Can you feel Ashe's response to the situation? At first, he is resigned to knowing he won't be allowed into the theater. Next, he is elated at having friends who would stick up for him. The reader gains insight into Ashe's thoughts and feelings because Ashe uses his voice to tell his story.

Through this event, Ashe also portrays the effect that racism had on the world around him. The woman in the ticket booth accepted the notion that African Americans couldn't do what other Americans did. Ashe's friends showed the beginnings of change—when some Americans finally said "enough" to racism.

INDIVIDUAL LEARNING STRATEGIES

MOTIVATION
Show a segment of the movie *Angela's Ashes* in class. Then read the excerpt from Frank McCourt's memoir that the film segment was based on. Hold a class discussion on why that excerpt is memorable. Point out to students that personal incidents that might seem insignificant to them might be memorable for others.

READING PROFICIENCY
Before students turn to the Guided Writing lesson on page 316, have them predict what subheadings to expect, based on the previous Guided Writing lessons they have read. Encourage students to predict what the Student Model will be like from reading the Graphic Organizer on page 317.

Prewriting

FINDING YOUR VOICE. You have a natural voice, unique to you. Your voice expresses your feelings, convictions, and insights. How will you tell your story in a way that lets the reader hear you? Use your natural voice.

Practice. For each situation, write a sentence that expresses your immediate response.

- Your hometown football team wins a league title.
- A tornado rips through your town, destroying many homes.
- Your parents announce a family reunion at the lake.

IDENTIFYING YOUR AUDIENCE. Who will read your autobiographical memoir? Since you are expressing your views about a situation that has affected many people, consider that people of all ages will be interested in reading your expressions about an event that affected their lives, too.

WRITING WITH A PLAN. Sometimes a writing topic stands out immediately. Kayla thought about last year's apple harvest festival at her family's farm. Jamal wanted to write about a blizzard that left all of Detroit without mail delivery and electricity for days. Erin wasn't sure what she would write about. She decided to look through her family's scrapbooks, her older brother's yearbooks, and a stack of old magazines. Then she used a graphic organizer to view her ideas and narrow a topic.

Erin filled in this graphic organizer to get ideas for her

Terms to Know
autobiographical memoir
autobiography
chronological order
first-person point of view
subject-verb agreement

> "Sit down right now. Write whatever's running through you... Don't try to control it. Stay present with whatever comes up, and keep your hand moving."
>
> —Natalie Goldberg

Student Model

Events memorable to me
- getting picked for city orchestra
- the blizzard and ice storm ←→
- raft race with Camp Willow
- Broncos winning the Super Bowl
- Cinco de Mayo with Jamie

Events memorable to community
- older people going into space
- the blizzard and ice storm
- Broncos winning the Super Bowl
- the new civic center
- the mayor's resignation

Memorable event I want to write about
Broncos winning the Super Bowl

Why memorable to me
- fun celebrating with friends
- everyone seemed happy

Why memorable to community
- the community was united
- people were proud of the team

Prewriting

FINDING YOUR VOICE. Encourage students to read the Language Arts Survey 2.5, "Finding Your Voice," and 3.3, "Register, Tone, and Voice." Have students analyze Arthur Ashe's voice in the Professional Model and Erin's voice in the Student Model. Tell students to write a description of the voice they plan to use on the same page as the graphic organizer.

IDENTIFYING YOUR AUDIENCE. Have students read the Language Arts Survey 2.4, "Identifying Your Audience." You might have students name their selected audience on the same page with the graphic organizer.

WRITING WITH A PLAN. Have students read the Language Arts Survey 2.12, "Freewriting" and do focused freewriting about their topic.

GRAPHIC ORGANIZER

See the Guided Writing Resource 7.4 for a blackline master of the Graphic Organizer for this lesson. When students turn in their completed memoir, ask them to turn in their graphic organizer with it.

INDIVIDUAL LEARNING STRATEGIES (CONT.)

ENGLISH LANGUAGE LEARNING
See strategies for Reading Proficiency above that will also benefit students who are English language learners. You might encourage non-native speakers to share an experience that happened in their native country that they could then share with the class to make other students more aware of other cultures.

INDIVIDUAL LEARNING STRATEGIES (CONT.)

SPECIAL NEEDS
Students with special needs may need help selecting a topic to write about. You might have an informal discussion with them to generate ideas, or suggest a list of ideas. These students might also need help completing their Graphic Organizer. Pair your special needs students with a proficient student who can help him or her work through the graphic organizer.

ENRICHMENT
Challenge students to read a memoir not excerpted in this unit. Then ask them to write a short review of the memoir on index cards that future students can refer to when selecting a memoir.

Drafting

Encourage students to use their completed Graphic Organizer modeled on page 317 to help them write their draft. Have students write a discovery draft in which they do not focus on spelling, grammar, usage, and mechanics. Students might benefit from reading the Language Arts Survey 2.31, "Drafting."

Reflecting

Students might formulate "one new idea or insight" by freewriting or writing a journal entry in which they reflect on what they have written by responding to the questions on pages 318–319.

Language, Grammar, and Style

Subject-Verb Agreement
LESSON OVERVIEW
In this lesson, students will be asked to do the following:
- Identify Subject-Verb Agreement, 318
- Fix Subject-Verb Agreement Errors, 321
- Use Subject-Verb Agreement, 321

INTRODUCING THE SKILL. Point out some common subject-verb agreement problems. Tell students that using correct subject-verb agreement will make them better writers and that it is a skill that carries over to their work for other classes as well as English.

PREVIEWING THE SKILL. You may want to refer students to the Language Arts Survey 3.38, "Getting Subject and Verb to Agree." You might provide examples of subject-verb agreement errors from students' own writing.

PRACTICING THE SKILL. For additional practice, have students work through the following exercise in the Teacher's Resource Kit: 3.38, "Getting Subject and Verb to Agree."

Strategies for Organizing
Decide on the order in which you will tell about the events. Usually an autobiographical memoir is told in **chronological order**, the order the events happened. If you choose this order, start with the beginning of the event and tell the story from beginning to end. You can number events in your graphic organizer or reorder your cut-up freewrite passages to experiment with different possibilities.

Language, Grammar, and Style
Subject-Verb Agreement

A verb must agree with the subject in **number.** Number refers to whether the subject is singular or plural. Look at the example below from the professional model.

It also (was) a reminder of our segregated world.

The subject *it* is singular. The verb *was* is also singular. The verb and subject agree in number.

IDENTIFYING SUBJECT-VERB AGREEMENT. Read the following example from the professional model. Identify the subject and the verb by underlining the subject and

318 *UNIT FOUR*

---

autobiographical memoir. Copy the graphic organizer on the previous page onto your own paper. Make one list of events that are memorable to you and another list of events that are memorable to your community. Which events appear on both lists? Select one of these events to write about. Then list reasons why the event is important to you and why it's important to a larger community of people.

Next, try **freewriting** about the event you have chosen. This can help you visualize your experience and think about its significance. As you freewrite, you might consider these questions: Who was I when this was happening? What did I think about it then? What do I think about it now? What about me as a person shapes the way I think about this? How did the community respond? What about the community shaped the way it responded to this event?

Drafting
Your goal as you write your autobiographical memoir is to tell how you experienced a significant event or situation that other people also experienced. You will want your readers to see this event through your eyes. You will also want to tell how others reacted. For example, Arthur Ashe described how he, like so many other black people, was barred from certain public places. He also included the reactions of others to this racism.

Write a rough draft of your autobiographical memoir. Concentrate on getting your impressions and ideas down on paper in a fairly logical order. Think about the reasons why the event was memorable to you and to a larger community. Include these reasons as you write. Also think about the questions and ideas you explored in your freewriting. Adding specific details will make your memoir vivid and meaningful for by yourself and your reader.

Do not worry about the mechanics of grammar or spelling. You can go back later and check for errors. At this point, focus on the big picture. By concentrating on how you felt, thought, and perceived things, you can develop a lively, rhythmic, and original piece of writing.

Reflecting
The experience of writing helps you to grow as a writer. It also helps you to grow as a person. One of the values of an autobiographical memoir is that you and the reader have an opportunity to gain great insights. As you reflect on what you have written, ask yourself questions about your writing experience. After considering answers for your questions, add at least one new idea or insight to your draft.

REFLECTING ON YOUR WRITING
- What have I learned about myself through this writing experience?
- What have I learned about the larger community?

- Are these things important to me?
- Will what I have learned through this experience change or shape the way I view myself or the world?
- How will what I have learned through this experience change me as a writer?

Self- and Peer Evaluation

After you finish your first draft, complete a self-evaluation of your writing. If time allows, you may want to get one or two peer evaluations. For more information, see the Language Arts Survey 2.37, "Self- and Peer Evaluation."

As you evaluate your memoir or that of a classmate, answer the following questions:

- Does the memoir clearly identify and describe the event? What details might be added? What details might be deleted?
- Does the memoir explain why this event is significant to the writer and why this event is significant to a larger community?
- What insight or knowledge will the reader gain from reading the memoir?
- Is there a logical order to how the events unfold? If not, at what point does the draft become unclear or confusing? How might this problem be solved?
- Will the memoir appeal to a variety of people? If not, how might word choice and details be modified to have a wider appeal?
- Does the memoir create a picture of how the writer feels and thinks about the event? If not, how might word choice and descriptions be modified to create a clearer picture of the writer's experience?
- What writing conventions—paragraph structure, sentence structure, grammar, punctuation, and capitalization—could be improved to make the memoir easier to read?

Erin did a self-evaluation of her writing, which describes her experience when the team won the Super Bowl. Tony also evaluated Erin's work. The draft is shown below.

Student Model—Draft

Winning the Super Bowl for the second time in a row showed how important the Broncos are to Colorado. The Broncos won and Because they did the voters of Denver decided to them a new statium. The people of Colorado love the Broncos

Why are they so important? Do they make people proud?
—Erin

circling the verb. Then explain why the subject and the verb are in agreement.

> Those comments always put me under pressure to justify my accomplishments on racial grounds.

In the next example from the professional model, the subject and the verb are separated by a prepositional phrase. The subject is *One*. The verb is *was*. Both the subject and the verb are singular.

> One of the highlights of my summers was the baseball school run by Maxie Robinson.

In the next example, the subject and the verb are separated by a prepositional phrase. Identify the subject and the verb. Draw a box around the prepositional phrase between them. Then explain why the subject and the verb are in agreement.

> Contradictions between the slogans of democracy and equality and our reality were sharpened in the District of Columbia.

continued on page 321

Self- and Peer Evaluation

Have students use the checklist on page 319 for self- and peer evaluation. The checklist is intended to act as a student-friendly rubric that should help students identify specific evidence of writing strengths and areas needing improvement. Make sure students provide concrete suggestions for improvement or specific evidence of the effectiveness of their memoir. See the Guided Writing Resource located in the Teacher's Resource Kit for a blackline master of the self- and peer evaluation checklist.

TEACHING NOTE

Have students compare the Student Model—Draft on page 319 with the final version presented on page 321. Have students answer the following questions: How has Erin improved her writing? In what ways can the Student Model—Revised be further improved?

Revising and Proofreading

A handout of the proofreading checklist in the Language Arts Survey is available in the Teacher's Resource Kit, Guided Writing Resource Book 2.45. Remind students that revising includes adding or expanding, cutting or condensing, replacing, and moving text. Have students read the Language Arts Survey 2.41, "Revising." Students may want to use proofreader's symbols, which are found in the Language Arts Survey 2.44, "Using Proofreader's Marks."

What are your neighbors like? Who are they? Can you add details?
—Tony

Can you explain more about why this is important to you?
—Tony

"Trust in yourself. Your perceptions are often far more accurate than you are willing to believe."
—Claudia Black

and the Broncos is a peice of the Culture of Colorado.

Watching the game, I was filled with excitement. The last few minites of the game was intence to watch. Some of us in the living room watching was just holding our breath. As soon as the Broncos ran out the clock, I knew that we had won. Right then and there my neighbors and I went out side as Elway was screaming and reciving the trophy. My neighbors and I were running around, talking about the game, and playing football.

After coming inside, I watched the news. I saw how happy other people were, too. As I was watching the news, people started to get out of hand, so the police had to break up the crowd in down town Denver. The people of Denver loves the Broncos.

Revising and Proofreading

If possible, wait a day before you revise your writing. That way, you will be able to see your writing with "new eyes." Review your self- and peer evaluations. Revise your writing according to these comments. Consider the content, organization, voice, word choice, and readability of your draft. Think about what to take out as well as what to add or reorganize. As you revise, make sure your focus remains clear.

Proofread your revised draft for errors in subject-verb agreement, spelling, grammar, punctuation, capitalization, and other details. A good way to proofread is to read each sentence three times—1) to focus on meaning, 2) to focus on punctuation to make the meaning clear, and 3) to focus on spelling. See the Language Arts Survey 2.45, "A Proofreading Checklist."

Student Model—Revised

    When the Broncos won the Super Bowl
for the second time in a row, all of
Colorado knew just how important the
team was to us. Not only did the
Broncos win, but the voters of Denver
approved a new stadium for them. The
people of Colorado love the Broncos and
consider them part of the culture of
our state.
    Watching the Super Bowl, I was filled
with excitement. The last few minutes
of the game were intense to watch. Some
of us in the living room watching were
just holding our breath. For that
moment, everyone in the neighborhood
and the entire state of Colorado
dreamed and hoped for the same thing.
We were united. As soon as the Broncos
ran out the clock, I knew that we had
won. Elway was screaming and receiving
the trophy. Right then and there my
neighbors and I went outside. Together
we were running around, retelling each
detail about our favorite part of the
game, and playing football all at the
same time. It was a wonderful feeling
to see everyone excited and happy.

Publishing and Presenting

You can rewrite your final copy in ink or
print it from a computer. Consider
adding an illustration or a photograph
to help deliver your meaning. You
can share your work by reading it
to others. Using a computer, you
might develop your writing into
a multimedia report with
illustrations, sounds, and movies.

continued from page 319

Go back to the Professional
Model and identify other
subjects and verbs. Explain
why the subject and the verb
are in agreement.

**FIXING SUBJECT VERB
AGREEMENT ERRORS.** Look at
Erin's autobiographical
memoir. Try to identify and fix
several errors in subject and
verb agreement. Then briefly
explain your editing.

For more help on fixing
subject and verb agreement
errors, see the Language Arts
Survey 3.38. For help on
identifying a subject and a
verb, see the Language Arts
Survey 3.18.

USING SUBJECT-VERB AGREEMENT.
Underline the subject and circle
the verb in each sentence of
your autobiographical memoir.
Check the subject-verb
agreement for number. If any
sentences lack subject-verb
agreement, revise them.
Remember that singular
subjects need a singular verb.
Plural subjects need a plural
verb.

If a prepositional phrase
separates the subject from the
verb, check to see that the
subject agrees with the verb,
not with the object of the
preposition.

Erin found this error with
subject and verb agreement:

The <u>people</u> of Denver
<u>loves</u> the Broncos.

She corrected it like this:

The <u>people</u> of Denver
<u>love</u> the Broncos.

Publishing and Presenting

Before students begin their final
version, they might benefit from
reading the Language Arts Survey
2.46, "Proper Manuscript Form." You
might consider organizing a
conference ("Contemporary Issues as
Reflected in the Memoir") in which
several students from your class read
their memoirs for students in
another class. After the papers are
read, students in the audience could
ask questions and share their
observations.

VOCABULARY DEVELOPMENT. Give students the following exercise.

Using the vocabulary words on page 322, write a test containing five sentence-completion questions. Write three answer choices for each problem. Vary the forms of the words as necessary. When you are done, exchange tests with a classmate.

EXAMPLE

1. He managed his money so carefully that everyone admired him for his great _____.

(A) extravagance
(B) thrift
(C) egotism

Answer: **B**

ADDITIONAL RESOURCES

UNIT 4 RESOURCE BOOK
* Vocabulary Worksheet
* Study Guide: Unit 4 Test
* Unit 4 Test

REFLECTING ON YOUR READING. The Genre, Group Project , and Critical Thinking questions are suitable to assign as essay prompts to help students prepare for the Unit Test. (To evaluate student writing, see the evaluation forms for writing, revising, and proofreading in the Assessment Resource 4.1-4.9.)

The Genre, On Your Own, and Critical Thinking questions can also be adapted for use as topics for oral reports or debates. Refer students to the Language Arts Survey 4, Speaking and Listening. (To evaluate these projects, use the Public Speaking Evaluation Form in the Assessment Resource 4.11.)

UNIT FOUR *review*

Review: Words for Everyday Use

Check your knowledge of the following vocabulary words. For each word, write a short sentence that includes the word in context. To review a word, look back to the page number indicated.

- apprehension (288)
- camaraderie (284)
- conjecture (298)
- convert (271)
- delirious (258)
- egotism (255)
- expend (271)
- extravagance (270)
- extravaganza (251)
- fanfare (253)
- immaculate (246)
- impasse (283)
- implicate (285)
- inadequate (255)
- incense (245)
- innuendo (285)
- list (271)
- naivety (255)
- phenomenal (245)
- physiological (278)
- rebuff (285)
- repress (284)
- reservoir (278)
- revert (258)
- thrift (270)

Review: Literary Tools

Define each of the following terms, giving concrete examples when possible. To review a term, refer to the page number indicated.

- anecdote (295)
- autobiography (276)
- concrete poem (269)
- description (276)
- dialect (241)
- memoir (295)
- metaphor (269)
- personification (269)
- point of view (262)
- stage directions (241)
- tone (262)

Reflecting on the *theme*

Theme

Many of the selections in this unit deal with heroes and heroines in sports history and what drove them to succeed. The play *How She Played the Game* by Cynthia L. Cooper looks at six female personalities from sports history, each of whom was a trend-setter and a record breaker in her chosen sport, but each of whom also faced pressure to back down or to be something else. In "Roberto Clemente: A Bittersweet Memoir" and the Related Reading, "Searching for January," you learn about where the baseball player Roberto Clemente came from, why he was so well-loved, and what drove him to succeed. In the excerpt from *Off the Court*, Arthur Ashe tells about his love of sports and of his struggles against racism as he strove to learn and play professional tennis.

REFLECTING ON YOUR READING. The Group Project activity can also serve provide an additional or alternate assessment to the Unit 4 Test. Ask students to tie in the insights they have gained from inventing their new sport to the types of sports or athletic endeavors explored in the literature selections in this unit. (To evaluate group and project work, see the evaluation forms in the Assessment Resource 4.10–4.12.)

The Group Project activity can also serve provide an additional or alternate assessment to the Unit 5 Test. Ask students to tie in the insights they have gained from their research to the literature selections they have read in this unit. (To evaluate group and project work, see the evaluation forms in the Assessment Resource 4.10–4.12.)

Genre

You have read a play, a short story, poems, autobiography and biography, and an editorial—all of which revolve around the topic of sports in life. How do these different genres uniquely reflect ways humans view and are involved in sports?

Group Project

With members of your group, invent a new sport or athletic pursuit. Will it be an individual or a team activity? Make up rules. Outline what skills would be needed to participate in this sport. What equipment, if any, would be used in this activity? Is this activity competitive? Think about the readings in this unit and the challenges various athletes faced in trying to participate in their chosen sport. Is the athletic pursuit you have invented open to everybody? Would it be harder for some people to participate in this activity than others based on things like age, gender, physical mobility, size, or expense? Be prepared to describe your group's invented "sport" and its limitations with the class.

Critical Thinking

In the play *How She Played the Game*, the German track and field star Gretel Bergmann was not allowed to compete in the 1936 Olympics in Berlin because of discrimination—she was a Jewish person living in Nazi Germany. The graphic organizer shown below will help you to keep track of the various athletes you have studied in this unit and to think about what kinds of hurdles each one faced on the way to achieving his or her goals. Choose an athlete featured in this unit and chart the hurdles this athlete faced.

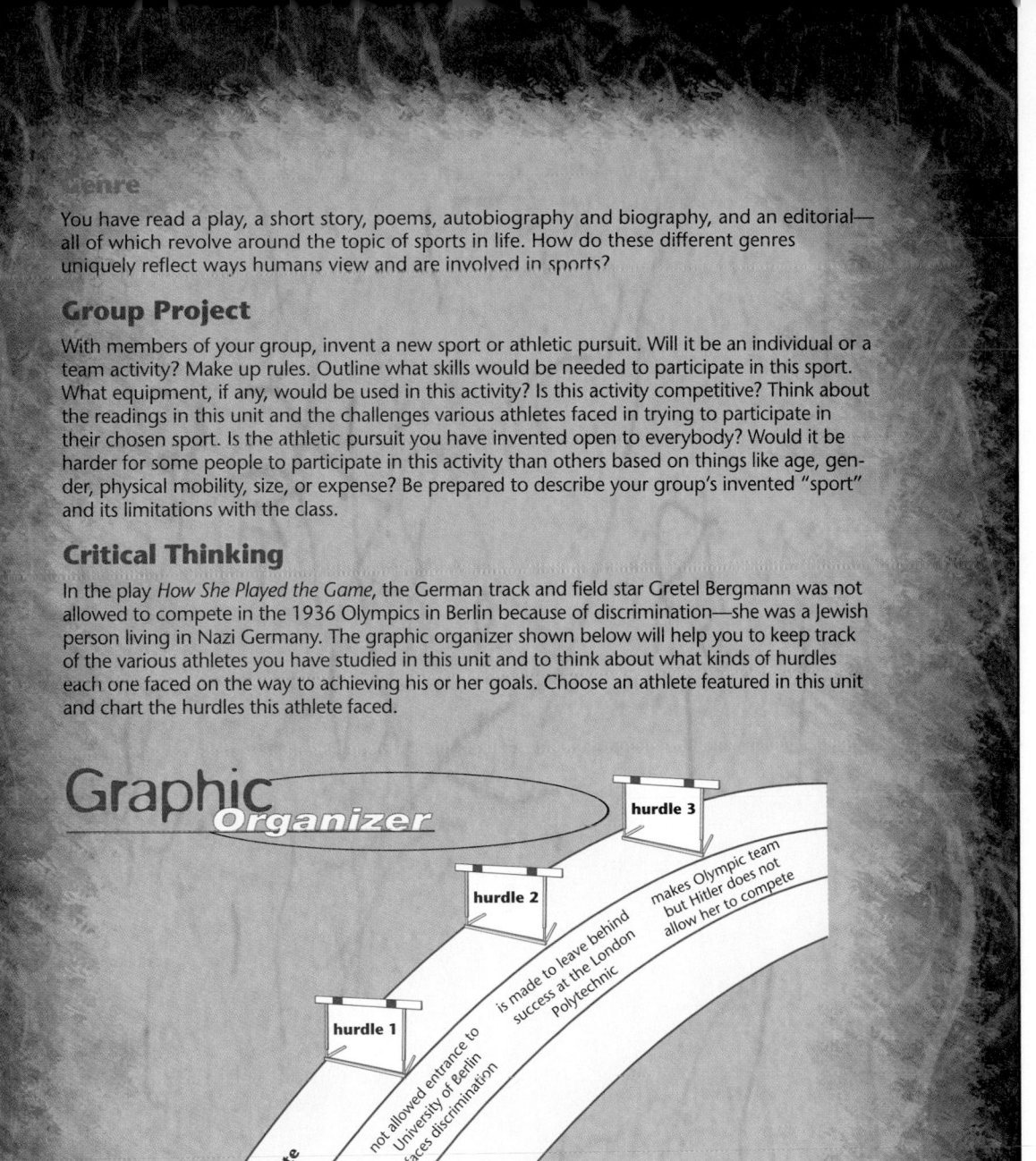

Graphic Organizer

hurdle 3 — makes Olympic team but Hitler does not allow her to compete

hurdle 2 — is made to leave behind success at the London Polytechnic

hurdle 1 — not allowed entrance to University of Berlin faces discrimination

Athlete — Gretel Bergmann

The Race Track (Death on a Pale Horse), c.1896. Albert Pinkham Ryder. Cleveland Museum of Art.

GOALS/OBJECTIVES

Studying this unit will enable students to
- enjoy fiction and poems exploring unusual, scary, and spooky occurrences
- define and identify examples of *aim, antagonist, foreshadowing, mood, motivation, narrator, point of view, protagonist, style,* and *suspense*
- engage in a meaningful independent reading experience by reading a suspense story with a book club
- write a suspenseful setting of their own
- demonstrate an ability to use prepositional phrases effectively

Chills and Thrills

UNIT FIVE

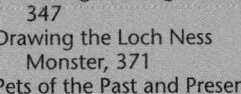

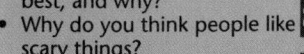

ADDITIONAL QUESTIONS AND ACTIVITIES

Introduce the unit theme by having students read the quotations in the Echoes feature. Ask them the following:

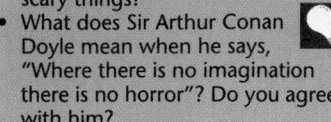

- Which quotations do you like best, and why?
- Why do you think people like scary things?
- What does Sir Arthur Conan Doyle mean when he says, "Where there is no imagination there is no horror"? Do you agree with him?

As an alternate activity, you may want to have students freewrite about one or two of the questions above.

. . . I saw the dull yellow eye of the creature open; it breathed hard, and a convulsive motion agitated its limbs.

—*Mary Shelley,* Frankenstein

Out flew the web and floated wide;
The mirror crack'd from side to side;
"The curse is come upon me," cried
The Lady of Shalott.

—*Alfred, Lord Tennyson*

And so, it is said, you are haunted!
My friend, we are haunted all;
And every homestead holds a ghost
That ever has held a pall.

—*Isabella Banks*

An' the gobble-uns 'll git you
 Ef you
  Don't
   Watch
    Out!

—*James Whitcomb Riley*

The Northern Lights have seen queer sights,
But the queerest they ever did see
Was the night on the marge of Lake Lebarge
I cremated Sam McGee.

—*Robert Service*

There is nothing so delicate, so fragile, as that invisible balance upon which the mind is always trembling . . . Who has not been, or is not to be mad in some lonely hour of life? Who is quite safe from the trembling of the balance?

—*Mary Braddon,* Lady Audley's Secret

By the pricking of my thumbs,
something wicked this way comes.

—*William Shakespeare,* Macbeth

Where there is no imagination there is no horror.

—*Sir Arthur Conan Doyle*

326 *UNIT FIVE*

Prereading

"The 11:59"

by Patricia McKissack

Reader's Resource

- **HISTORY CONNECTION.** From 1880 to the 1960s, trains offered an efficient means of travel for many Americans. The Pullman sleeping car, developed in 1864, provided passengers with comfortable sleeping quarters for overnight trips. By the 1920s, more than 100,000 people slept in Pullman sleeping cars on any given night.

- The men who tended to the sleeping berths, carried luggage, and assisted passengers were Pullman porters. For nearly a century, these porters were almost exclusively African American.

- In their quarters at train stations (called porter houses) and in the backs of trains, porters shared their experiences and told stories such as the story of the "Death Train"—the 11:59.

Graphic Organizer

Element of suspense	What makes it suspenseful
Lester pauses while telling about Daddy Joe	I wondered why he stopped talking and what he would say next

Reader's Journal

Describe a time when you had a feeling something bad was going to happen. Did your feeling turn out to be an accurate prediction?

Reader's TOOLBOX

FORESHADOWING. Foreshadowing is the act of hinting at events that will happen later in a poem, story, or play. Foreshadowing helps create suspense in a story. Look for examples of foreshadowing as you read "The 11:59."

SUSPENSE. Suspense is a feeling of anxiety or curiosity. Writers create **suspense** by raising questions in the reader's mind and by using details that create strong emotions. As you read this story, use the graphic organizer to the left to make a list of ways that the author builds suspense and makes us wonder what will happen to the main character, Lester.

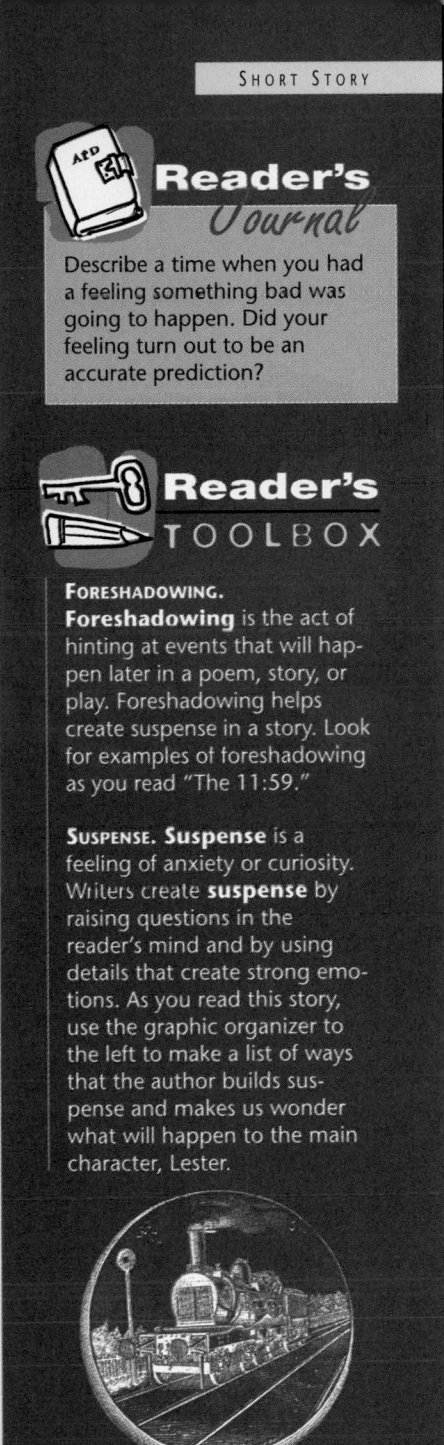

"THE 11:59" 327

ADDITIONAL RESOURCES

UNIT 5 RESOURCE BOOK
- Selection Worksheet 5.1
- Selection Check Test 4.5.1
- Selection Test 4.5.2
- Language, Grammar, and Style Resource 3.69

GRAPHIC ORGANIZER

Responses will vary, but students may include the following elements in their charts:
Element of suspense: Lester says "all us porters got to board that train one day. Ain't no way to escape the final ride on the 11:59"; What makes it suspenseful: I wonder who will be the next porter to have to die, or board that train.
Element of suspense: Lester says "not a living soul" has ever lived to tell about hearing the whistle of the 11:59; What makes it suspenseful: I wonder what it would be like to hear the whistle.
Element of suspense: Lester feels a sharp pain in his chest and hears a train whistle at 11:59. What makes it suspenseful: Does this mean that Lester only has a short time to live? I am worried about what will happen to Lester.
Element of suspense: Lester decides to try to escape the 11:59 by making his house safe; What makes it suspenseful: I wonder if Lester might be able to escape the 11:59 after all.
Element of suspense: *Ticktock, ticktock.* Lester keeps hearing the ticking of a clock. What makes it suspenseful: It seems that time is running out for Lester.

READER'S JOURNAL

As an alternate activity, have students write about how they think they would feel and react to knowing they only had a few more hours to live. What thoughts would run through their minds?

GOALS/OBJECTIVES

Studying this lesson will enable students to
- appreciate a spine-tingling story
- briefly explain a few historical facts about Pullman cars and porters
- define *dialect* and identify dialect in works that they read
- define *suspense* and identify suspenseful elements in a literary work
- compare and contrast modes of travel
- write a classified advertisement
- identify antonyms

VOCABULARY FROM THE SELECTION

chide   specter
meager   worrisome
mesmerize

INDIVIDUAL LEARNING STRATEGIES

MOTIVATION

Ask students to think of examples of when something has come true almost because they have believed in it so strongly. Discuss the idea of "self-fulfilling prophecy" with them.

READING PROFICIENCY

Students may have difficulty understanding Lester's former job and all the language surrounding trains, as most students today are not familiar with train travel. Have them read the Prereading page carefully before they begin reading the selection. It may even be beneficial to have students read the Insights feature on Pullman porters before they begin reading "The 11:59."

ENGLISH LANGUAGE LEARNING

Point out the following vocabulary words and expressions:
yarns—tales, stories
union—association of workers to promote and protect workers' rights
berth—built-in bed or bunk
dig—understand, approve

SPECIAL NEEDS

Students may benefit from hearing the story read aloud on audiotape. This will help to engage them in the suspense of the story.

ENRICHMENT

Interested students might create visual representations of Pullman cars.
Students might create models of these cars or create dioramas depicting their interior. They might also produce sketches, drawings, or paintings of Pullman cars. You might wish to create a Pullman car display to showcase students' creations.

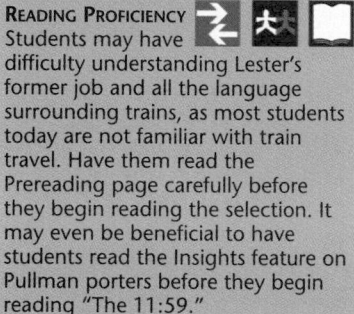

the
11:59

Patricia McKissack

Lester Simmons was a thirty-year retired Pullman car porter—had his gold watch to prove it. "Keeps perfect train time," he often bragged. "Good to the second."

Daily he went down to the St. Louis Union Station and shined shoes to help supplement his <u>meager</u> twenty-four-dollar-a-month Pullman retirement check. He ate his evening meal at the porter house on Compton Avenue and hung around until late at night talking union, playing bid whist[1], and spinning yarns with those who were still "travelin' men." In this way Lester stayed in touch with the only family he'd known since 1920.

There was nothing the young porters liked more than listening to Lester tell true stories about the old days, during the founding of the Brotherhood of Sleeping Car Porters, the first black union in the United States. He knew the president, A. Philip Randolph, personally, and proudly boasted that it was Randolph who'd signed him up as a union man back in 1926. He passed his original card around for inspection. "I knew all the founding brothers. Take Brother E. J. Bradley. We hunted many a day together, not for the sport of it but for something to eat.

"Well, in the end even he couldn't escape the 11:59."

Those were hard times, starting up the union. But we hung in there so you youngsters might have the benefits you enjoy now."

The rookie porters always liked hearing about the thirteen-year struggle between the Brotherhood and the powerful Pullman Company, and how, against all odds, the fledgling[2] union had won recognition and better working conditions.

Everybody enjoyed it too when Lester told tall tales about Daddy Joe, the porters' larger-than-life hero. "Now y'all know the first thing a good Pullman man is expected to do is make up the top and lower berths[3] for the passengers each night."

"Come on, Lester," one of his listeners <u>chided</u>. "You don't need to describe our jobs for us."

"Some of you, maybe not. But some of you, well—" he said, looking over the top of his glasses and raising an eyebrow at a few of the younger porters. "I was just setting the stage." He smiled good-naturedly and went on with his story. "They tell me Daddy Joe could walk flatfooted down the center of the coach and let down berths on both sides of the aisle."

---

1. **bid whist.** Card game played with partners
2. **fledgling.** Inexperienced
3. **berth.** Place for sleeping

words for everyday use

mea • ger (mē′ gər) *adj.*, lacking in quantity or quality. *Jana's meager supper was unsatisfying.*

chide (chīd) *v.*, to express mild disapproval. *Jeff chided Ana when she missed the shot.*

Hearty laughter filled the room, because everyone knew that to accomplish such a feat, Daddy Joe would have to have been superhuman. But that was it: To the men who worked the sleeping cars, Daddy Joe was no less a hero than Paul Bunyan was to the lumberjacks of the Northwestern forests.

"And when the 11:59 pulled up to his door, as big and strong as Daddy Joe was . . ." Lester continued solemnly. "Well, in the end even he couldn't escape the 11:59." The old storyteller eyed one of the rookie porters he knew had never heard the frightening tale about the porters' Death Train. Lester took joy in _mesmerizing_ his young listeners with all the details.

"Any porter who hears the whistle of the 11:59 has got exactly twenty-four hours to clear up earthly matters. He better be ready when the train comes the next night . . ." In his creakiest voice, Lester drove home the point. "All us porters got to board that train one day. Ain't no way to escape the final ride on the 11:59."

> **GUIDED READING**
> What happens when a person hears the whistle of the 11:59?

Silence.

"Lester," a young porter asked, "you know anybody who ever heard the whistle of the 11:59 and lived to tell—"

"Not a living soul!"

Laughter.

"Well," began one of the men, "wonder will we have to make up berths on _that_ train?"

"If it's an overnight trip to heaven, you can best be believing there's bound to be a few of us making up the berths," another answered.

"Shucks," a card player stopped to put in. "They say even up in heaven _we_ the ones gon' be keeping all that gold and silver polished."

"Speaking of gold and silver," Lester said, remembering. "That reminds me of how I gave Tip Sampson his nickname. Y'all know Tip?"

There were plenty of nods and smiles.

The memory made Lester chuckle. He shifted in his seat to find a more comfortable spot. Then he began. "A woman got on board the _Silver Arrow_ in Chicago going to Los Angeles. She was dripping in finery—had on all kinds of gold and diamond jewelry, carried twelve bags. Sampson knocked me down getting to wait on her, figuring she was sure for a big tip. That lady was _worrisome_! Ooowee! 'Come do this. Go do that. Bring me this.' Sampson was running over himself trying to keep that lady happy. When we reached L.A., my passengers all tipped me two or three dollars, as was customary back then.

"When Sampson's Big Money lady got off, she reached into her purse and placed a dime in his outstretched hand. A _dime_! Can you imagine? _Ow!_ You should have seen his face. And I didn't make it no better. Never did let him forget it. I teased him so—went to calling him Tip, and the nickname stuck."

Laughter.

"I haven't heard from ol' Tip in a while. Anybody know anything?"

"You haven't got word, Lester? Tip boarded the 11:59 over in Kansas City about a month ago."

"Sorry to hear that. That just leaves me and Willie Beavers, the last of the old, old-timers here in St. Louis."

> **GUIDED READING**
> What happened to Tip?

Lester looked at his watch—it was a little before midnight. The talkfest had lasted later than usual. He said his good-byes and left,

words for everyday use

mes • mer • ize (mez′ mə rīz) _v._, fascinate; spellbind. _Science fiction movies always_ _mesmerize_ _Cody._

wor • ri • some (wər′ ē səm) _adj._, causing worry. _The_ _worrisome_ _exam made Jolene nervous all week._

1. The person who hears the whistle has 24 hours to live.
2. Tip died a month ago.

ADDITIONAL QUESTIONS AND ACTIVITIES

Ask students the following questions:
1. What is the 11:59?
2. What does it mean to take a "final ride on the 11:59"?
3. What do the porters assume they will have to do in heaven?
4. What does this reveal about the way their lives have been?
5. How did Tip get his name?
6. What does this story reveal about the way that porters were treated?

Answers
1. The 11:59 is the "death train," a train that represents the coming of death to the porters.
2. It means to die.
3. They assume that they will have to make up berths for people on the death train and then polish the gold and silver in heaven.
4. This attitude reveals that the porters have spent much of their lives laboring for others and assume that this will never change, even in death.
5. Tip got his name because of a time when he worked very hard for a wealthy woman who only left him a dime as a tip.
6. The story reveals that porters were treated badly by some customers and sometimes earned very little money for their efforts.

1. Lester feels a sharp pain in his chest and hears the mournful sound of a train whistle.
2. Lester will try to escape the final ride on the 11:59.
3. His arm feels numb.
4. Traveling was Lester's first and only love.

CROSS-CURRICULAR ACTIVITIES

MATHEMATICS AND SCIENCES. Interested students might wish to play the role of doctor or medical examiner and try to determine what is wrong with Lester physically based on the symptoms described here (pain in his chest, numbness in his arm). (Most students should be able to determine that Lester is experiencing a heart attack.) Students should try to find out what causes this condition and how it can be treated. Could Lester have done anything to save himself and escape the 11:59?

taking his usual route across the Eighteenth Street bridge behind the station.

In the darkness, Lester looked over the yard, picking out familiar shapes—the *Hummingbird*, the *Zephyr*. He'd worked on them both. Train travel wasn't anything like it used to be in the old days—not since people had begun to ride airplanes. "Progress," he scoffed. "Those contraptions will never take the place of a train. No sir!"

Suddenly he felt a sharp pain in his chest. At exactly the same moment he heard the mournful sound of a train whistle, which the wind seemed to carry from

> **GUIDED READING**
> What does Lester feel in his chest? What sound does he hear?

some faraway place. Ignoring his pain, Lester looked at the old station. He knew nothing was scheduled to come in or out till early morning. Nervously he lit a match to check the time. 11:59!

"No," he said into the darkness. "I'm not ready. I've got plenty of living yet."

Fear quickened his step. Reaching his small apartment, he hurried up the steps. His heart pounded in his ear, and his left arm tingled. He had an idea, and there wasn't a moment to waste. But his own words haunted him. *Ain't no way to escape the final ride on the 11:59.*

"But I'm gon' try!" Lester spent the rest of the night plotting his escape from fate.

"I won't eat or drink anything all day," he

> **GUIDED READING**
> What is Lester going to try to do?

talked himself through his plan. "That way I can't choke, die of food poisoning, or cause a cooking fire."

Lester shut off the space heater to avoid an explosion, nailed shut all doors and windows to keep out intruders, and unplugged every electrical appliance. Good weather was predicted, but just in case a freak storm came and blew out a window, shooting deadly glass shards in his direction, he moved a straight-

backed chair into a far corner, making sure nothing was overhead to fall on him.

"I'll survive," he said, smiling at the prospect of beating Death. "Won't that be a wonderful story to tell at the porter house?" He rubbed his left arm. It felt numb again.

> **GUIDED READING**
> How does Lester's arm feel?

Lester sat silently in his chair all day, too afraid to move. At noon someone knocked on his door. He couldn't answer it. Footsteps . . . another knock. He didn't answer.

A parade of minutes passed by, equally measured, one behind the other, ticking . . . ticking . . . away . . . The dull pain in his chest returned. He nervously checked his watch every few minutes.

Ticktock, ticktock.

Time had always been on his side. Now it was his enemy. Where had the years gone? Lester reviewed the thirty years he'd spent riding the rails. How different would his life have been if he'd married Louise Henderson and had a gallon of children? What if he'd taken that job at the mill down in Opelika? What if he'd followed his brother to Philly? How different?

Ticktock, ticktock.

So much living had passed so quickly. Lester decided if he had to do it all over again, he'd stand by his choices. His had been a good life. No regrets. No major changes for him.

Ticktock ticktock.

The times he'd had—both good and bad— what memories. His first and only love had been traveling, and she was a jealous companion. Wonder whatever happened to that girl up in Minneapolis? Thinking

> **GUIDED READING**
> What was Lester's first and only love?

about her made him smile. Then he laughed. That girl must be close to seventy years old by now.

ART SMART

Ask students to discuss the image on this page. Does this image match their own thoughts about the way Lester looks? What emotions does Lester seem to be feeling in this image?

"THE 11:59" **333**

ANSWERS TO GUIDED READING QUESTIONS

1. Lester hears a train whistle interrupt the fearful silence.
2. The visitor is the ghost of Tip, a porter who died about a month ago.

ADDITIONAL QUESTIONS AND ACTIVITIES

Encourage students to discuss how Lester's attitude toward his own death changes in the latter part of the story. How does Lester feel when he sees who the porter is? What does Lester say and do when the porter tells him nobody can escape the 11:59? In what manner do Tip and Lester talk? Why do you think Lester's attitude changes toward the end?
Answers. Students might say that Lester feels calmer when he sees his old friend Tip. Lester says "man, I had to try," and chuckles. They talk to each other in a friendly, light, and familiar manner. Students may suggest that Lester realizes he cannot do anything about the situation, so he decides he might as well accept it.

Ticktock, ticktock.

Daylight was fading quickly. Lester drifted off to sleep, then woke from a nightmare in which, like Jonah, he'd been swallowed by an enormous beast.[4] Even awake he could still hear its heart beating . . . *ticktock, ticktock* . . . But then he realized he was hearing his own heartbeat.

Lester couldn't see his watch, but he guessed no more than half an hour had passed. Sleep had overtaken him with such little resistance. Would Death, that shapeless shadow, slip in that easily? Where was he lurking? *Yea, though I walk through the valley of the shadow of death, I will fear no evil . . .* The Twenty-third Psalm was the only prayer Lester knew, and he repeated it over and over, hoping it would comfort him.

Lester rubbed his tingling arm. He could hear the blood rushing past his ear and up the side of his head. He longed to know what time it was, but that meant he had to light a match—too risky. What if there was a gas leak? The match would set off an explosion. "I'm too smart for that, Death," he said.

Ticktock, ticktock.

It was late. He could feel it. Stiffness seized his legs and made them tremble. How much longer? he wondered. Was he close to winning?

Then in the fearful silence he heard a train whistle. His ears strained to identify the sound, making sure it *was* a whistle. No mistake. It came again, the same as the night before. Lester answered it with a groan.

Ticktock, ticktock.

He could hear Time ticking away in his head. Gas leak or not, he had to see his

> **GUIDED READING**
> What noise does Lester hear?

watch. Striking a match, Lester quickly checked the time. 11:57.

Although there was no gas explosion, a tiny explosion erupted in his heart.

Ticktock, ticktock.

Just a little more time. The whistle sounded again. Closer than before. Lester struggled to move, but he felt fastened to the chair. Now he could hear the engine puffing, pulling a heavy load. It was hard for him to breathe, too, and the pain in his chest weighed heavier and heavier.

Ticktock, ticktock.

Time had run out! Lester's mind reached for an explanation that made sense. But reason failed when a glowing phantom dressed in the porters' blue uniform stepped out of the grayness of Lester's confusion.

"It's *your* time, good brother." The specter spoke in a thousand familiar voices.

Freed of any restraint now, Lester stood, bathed in a peaceful calm that had its own glow. "Is that you, Tip?" he asked, squinting to focus on his old friend standing in the strange light.

> **GUIDED READING**
> Who is the visitor?

"It's me, ol' partner. Come to remind you that none of us can escape the last ride on the 11:59."

"I know. I know," Lester said, chuckling. "But man, I had to try."

Tip smiled. "I can dig it. So did I."

"That'll just leave Willie, won't it?"

"Not for long."

"I'm ready."

---

4. **Jonah . . . beast.** Refers to the Biblical story of Jonah and the whale

words for everyday use

spec • ter (spek´ tər) *n.*, spirit or ghost. *The ghostly specter howled from the top of the staircase.*

Lester saw the great beam of the single headlight and heard the deafening whistle blast one last time before the engine tore through the front of the apartment, shattering glass and splintering wood, collapsing everything in its path, including Lester's heart.

When Lester didn't show up at the shoeshine stand two days running, friends went over to his place and found him on the floor. His eyes were fixed on something quite amazing—his gold watch, stopped at exactly 11:59. ■

GUIDED READING

What do Lester's friends find in his apartment two days later?

Respond *to the* SELECTION

How would you want to spend your last 24 hours?

About *the* AUTHOR

Patricia McKissack is an award-winning author of many fiction and nonfiction titles for young readers. She grew up in Nashville, Tennessee, in the 1940s and 1950s, a difficult time in history for Americans of African descent—not until May 7, 1954, did the Supreme Court declare school segregation to be unconstitutional. But of that time, McKissack has said "Nashville's public libraries were not segregated. We could get books. The librarians smiled and treated me like a human being. . . They opened up a world to me I otherwise wouldn't have had."

McKissack went on to earn a degree in English from Tennessee State University. After graduating, she married Frederick McKissack and began teaching. In 1984, Patricia and Frederick collaborated to publish their first book together. Since then, the McKissacks have published many books together and separately. In 1990 they won the Coretta Scott King Award—an award that celebrates literature that promotes unity and peace and inspires young people to strive toward their goals—for *A Long Hard Journey: The Story of the Pullman Porter*. They received this award again in 1993 for *Sojourner Truth: Ain't I a*

Woman and in 1995 for *Christmas in the Big House, Christmas in the Quarters*.

Many of the tales in Patricia's books are based on stories her grandmother told her. *The Dark Thirty: Southern Tales of the Supernatural* grew out of monster stories her brother told her while staying at their grandmother's house.

"THE 11:59"   **335**

INSIGHTS

George Pullman and his "Pullman's Palace"

PULLMAN PORTERS

People traveled by train long before planes and automobiles were invented. In the mid-1800s, however, train travel was uncomfortable. The benches were hard, the cars were full of dust and smoke, and the rough mattresses made it hard to sleep on overnight trips.

After one particularly uncomfortable ride, George Pullman decided to design a railroad car that would make the train ride more comfortable and enjoyable, especially for overnight trips. In 1864, he created a luxury sleeping car. The Pullman car had thick carpeting, beautiful woodwork, curtains, mirrors, chandeliers, and most importantly, porters to meet the needs of the passengers.

Pullman porters delivered first-class service on the Pullman sleeping cars. It was their job to get the sleeping berths ready for the passengers each night. They also cleaned ashtrays and spit-toons, shined shoes, ironed clothes, polished wood, served food, hauled luggage, and did whatever other jobs the passengers desired. They were expected to be diligent and gracious and had to follow a rigid code of behavior.

Many freed slaves who were out of work in the 1860s jumped at the chance to be porters, and they were loyal and hardworking. They were used to long, difficult work and saw the trains as symbols of freedom. The Pullman Company employed African Americans almost exclusively as Pullman porters from 1868 to 1968. Although porters were respected in their communities, the pay was low and the working conditions were difficult. Porters were paid very little and were asked to work 400 hours or 11,000 miles a month, whichever came first. Porters relied on passengers' tips to supplement their meager salaries. If a passenger complained about the service, porters could be fired. Many porters endured racial insults and slurs with a smile to get tips.

After many years of being overworked and underpaid, porters decided to form a union to secure better working conditions. Porters turned to A. Philip Randolph, a well-respected African-American leader and speaker, to guide them, and in August 1925 they formed the Brotherhood of Sleeping Car Porters (BSCP).

Because Pullman was an anti-union company at the time, the BSCP and its members received threats and attacks from the company. After a twelve-year struggle, the Pullman Company finally agreed to a union contract, which was signed on August 25, 1937. This was the first contract ever won by an African-American union. The contract not only made history, but also significantly improved working conditions for Pullman porters. Salaries increased, working hours per month decreased, and porters could not be fired without a hearing. Randolph and the BSCP believed their victory made gains for all African-American workers

Phillip Randolph (back seat) representing Pullman Porters in the 1939 New York Labor Day Parade. Joseph Schwartz.

who were seeking equality and fair working conditions. As Randolph stated, "With a union, black people can approach their employers as proud and upright equals, not as trembling and bowing slaves. Indeed, a solid union contract is, in a very real sense, another Emancipation Proclamation."

INSPECTING THE LINEN-CLOSET.

PREPARING THE DESSERT.

ACROSS THE CONTINENT.—THE FRANK LESLIE EXCURSION TO THE PACIFIC—THE TRIP WESTWARD FROM CHICAGO ON A PULLMAN HOTEL CAR.

Pullman Porters, 1875

"THE 11:59" **337**

RECALL

1a. Lester spends his evenings with the porters, playing cards and telling stories.

2a. He feels a sharp pain in his chest, numbness and tingling in left arm, and stiffness in his legs. Right before he dies, Lester feels an "explosion" in his heart. He then has trouble breathing and feels increased pain, as well as a feeling of a great weight on his chest.

3a. Tip, a fellow porter who died a month ago, is Lester's final visitor.

4a. The watch is stopped at 11:59.

INTERPRET

1b. The porters are his only family; his traveling lifestyle means they were his only friends.

2b. Students may say that Lester is having a heart attack.

3b. Students may say that Tip is the final visitor because he is Lester's friend and he recently died.

4b. Students will say his watch reads that time because that's when Lester died.

ANALYZE

5a. Lester changes from feeling jovial and light-hearted while with his friends to feeling terrified after hearing the whistle of the 11:59. By the end of the story, however, Lester feels calm and accepting of his fate.

SYNTHESIZE

5b. Students may say that Lester knew what was coming and that he couldn't escape it, but he valued his life and so he tried anyway. He felt that he lived the life he wanted to, so he was able to accept death and join his fellow departed porters.

EVALUATE

6a. Students may say the porters formed their own brotherhood or group of closely knit friends because their traveling lifestyle made it hard to form close relationships with other people. They share stories and legends that reinforce their bond.

EXTEND

6b. *Responses will vary.* Students may say it is similar to other groups because it centers on common values and interests and forms a support network. Groups create an identity through their interests and values, and group members usually support and rely on one another.

Investigate, Inquire, and Imagine

Recall: GATHERING FACTS

1a. How does Lester spend evenings now that he has retired?

2a. What physical symptoms does Lester feel during his last day alive?

3a. Who is Lester's final visitor?

4a. What time is on Lester's watch when his friends find him two days later?

Interpret: FINDING MEANING

1b. Why does he spend his evenings in this way?

2b. What do you think is happening to Lester?

3b. Why is he the person to visit Lester?

4b. Why does his watch read that time?

Analyze: TAKING THINGS APART

5a. How does Lester's mood change over the course of the story?

Synthesize: BRINGING THINGS TOGETHER

5b. Do you think Lester knew what would happen at 11:59? In your opinion, did he really think he could escape the "last ride"? How did he feel when the time came?

Evaluate: MAKING JUDGMENTS

6a. How well does this story describe the lives of porters and their relationships with one another? What things did the porters share that enforced their unity? Why would they develop such a strongly bonded group?

Extend: CONNECTING IDEAS

6b. How was the Brotherhood of Sleeping Car Porters like other groups you know or belong to? In what ways do groups create an identity? How do group members interact in a successful organization?

Understanding Literature

SUSPENSE. Suspense is a feeling of anxiousness or curiosity. Writers create **suspense** by raising questions in the reader's mind and by using details that create strong emotions. Look over your list of details and plot events that built suspense in this story. Which were the most effective? Which did you like the best?

FORESHADOWING. Foreshadowing is the act of hinting at events that will happen later in a poem, story, or play. Foreshadowing helps create suspense in a story. Identify an example of foreshadowing in this story. How does foreshadowing affect suspense? How does it complement the plot?

ANSWERS TO UNDERSTANDING LITERATURE

SUSPENSE. *Responses will vary.* Students may say the ticking of a clock (Lester's heartbeat) is especially effective in showing how Lester's life is slipping through his fingers, as he has only hours and then minutes left.

FORESHADOWING. *Responses will vary,* but students may note that suspense builds in the story when even the great Daddy Joe can't escape the "Death Train." The fact that no porter can avoid the fateful *11:59* adds suspense. This is heightened when the reader knows that Lester is about to retire. Such foreshadowing builds suspense and complements the plot by keeping it moving and the reader reading.

Writer's Journal

1. Imagine Lester beat the 11:59. How would he retell the story the next day? Write a **scene** for the story in which Lester describes this experience for the other porters. Consider Lester's dialect, mood, and audience.

2. Imagine that "The 11:59" is made into a major motion picture. Write an **advertisement** that would encourage audiences to see the film.

3. A eulogy is a formal statement of praise made at a funeral. Imagine you are Willie Beavers, one of Lester's coworkers on the Pullman cars. Write a **eulogy**, or tribute, you would deliver at Lester's funeral.

Skill Builders

Critical Thinking & Study and Research

COMPARING AND CONTRASTING MODES OF TRAVEL. Use your library resources to research what travel was like in a Pullman sleeping car. Then, use a Venn Diagram to compare and contrast the Pullman sleeping car with a form of modern transportation such as the automobile or airplane. Which mode of travel would you prefer? Why?

beds for sleeping

food served

seats for sitting and sleeping

Speaking and Listening & Media Literacy

STORYTELLING. Concentrating on Lester's character, analyze what makes him a good storyteller, and make a list of these techniques. Then, practice telling this story—or another story with suspense—using the techniques from your list. Record the story on tape or tell the story using your class as an audience.

Applied English

WRITING A CLASSIFIEDS ADVERTISEMENT.
Inform students that classified ads are usually priced by the number of words or characters, so they should be as concise as possible. Students may find this activity easier if you show them examples of employment ads from your local newspaper.

Vocabulary Development

ANTONYMS
1. a
2. a
3. b
4. a
5. b

Language, Grammar, and Style

WORKING WITH PREPOSITIONS.
1. preposition: to; prepositional phrase: to the St. Louis Station
2. preposition: about; prepositional phrase: about the old days
3. prepositions: of, in; prepositional phrases: of them, in heaven
4. preposition: on; prepositional phrase: on his side
5. prepositions: of, on; prepositional phrases: of dust and smoke, on overnight trips

Applied English

WRITING A CLASSIFIEDS ADVERTISEMENT. Using the Sunday newspaper employment classifieds as examples, create a want ad for the job of porter. Be sure to include as many accurate details as possible. Then imagine you want to apply for the job. Make a list of the skills, experiences, and traits that might help you get the job.

Vocabulary

ANTONYMS. An **antonym** is a word that has the opposite meaning of another word. For example, *loud* is the antonym of *quiet*. Review the Words for Everyday Use from "The 11:59." Then choose the letter of the word that is the antonym of the word in italics.

1. *meager*
   a. excessive
   b. small
2. *fledgling*
   a. experienced
   b. unpopular
3. *chide*
   a. scold

   b. praise
4. *mesmerizing*
   a. boring
   b. scary
5. *worrisome*
   a. distressing
   b. calming

Language, Grammar, and Style

WORKING WITH PREPOSITIONS. A writer uses linkers called **prepositions** to build prepositional phrases. A preposition is used to show how a noun or pronoun is related to other words in the sentence. Prepositional phrases provide specific information to create more specific images in the reader's mind.

EXAMPLE   The 11:59 flew <u>down the tracks</u>.

In the example, the preposition *down* links the noun *11:59* and *tracks*. Note: Sometimes words look like prepositions but are really working as something else. If the word doesn't have an object, it is another part of speech. In the example above, if you ask, "Flew down what?", the answer is "the tracks." The word *down* is a preposition in this sentence. For more information, see the Language Arts Survey 3.69, "Prepositions."

Using your own paper, write out the sentences below. Then circle each preposition and and underline each prepositional phrase.

1. Daily he went down to the St. Louis Union Station.
2. The young porters liked hearing Lester tell stories about the old days.
3. The porters believed there would be at least a few of them in heaven.
4. Time had always been on his side, but now it was his enemy.
5. The old Pullman coaches were full of dust and smoke, and the rough mattresses made it hard to sleep on overnight trips.

Prereading

"Pets"
by Avi

Reader's Resource

- **SCIENCE CONNECTION.** The cats in this story contract a highly contagious, often deadly virus called feline distemper. The illness, found primarily in cats, causes fever, depression, vomiting, diarrhea, and dehydration. Distemper destroys white blood cells, which fight disease, and can cause nervous system damage, other infections, and death. Veterinarians offer a vaccination against the disease and in some cases can also successfully treat the illness with antibiotics as well as other measures for advanced cases.

- Some people believe that the souls of the dead can remain on the earth as ghosts. Scientists have studied evidence that ghosts exist, and ghosts have become a popular subject in literature. No one has ever proven the existence of ghosts, but evidence in photographs, audio recordings, and various unexplained occurrences has led many to believe that ghosts are real. Believers say that certain souls have chosen—for reasons often unknown—to remain on the earth after they have died. Some stay, it is believed, to remain close to family members and loved ones. This story suggests that even pets may stay to be near their owners.

- Many pet owners choose to have their pets buried in pet cemeteries after they die. This tradition has spanned centuries. Researchers have uncovered pet cemeteries used in ancient Greece and in ancient Egypt.

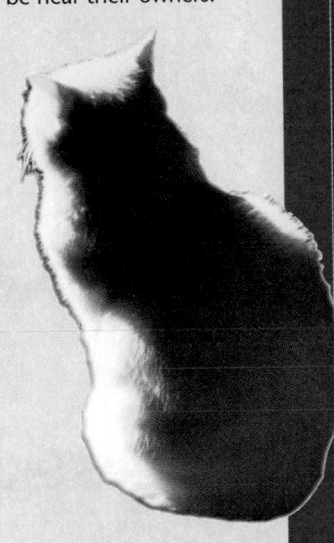

SHORT STORY

Reader's Journal

What is the most remarkable pet you've ever owned or wished to own?

Reader's TOOLBOX

MOOD. Mood, or atmosphere, is the feeling or emotion the writer creates in a literary work. This atmosphere pervades the literary work and causes the reader to expect events in keeping with that mood. Most often several elements of the story contribute to the mood, including the setting, behavior of characters, and events. As you read "Pets," look for these examples of each of these three elements. How would you describe the mood they create?

PROTAGONIST AND ANTAGONIST. A **protagonist** is the main character in a story. The protagonist faces a struggle or conflict. A character who struggles with the main character is called an **antagonist**. As you read "Pets," identify the protagonist. Then determine the antagonist(s) in the story. What is the struggle they face?

"PETS" 341

ADDITIONAL RESOURCES

UNIT 5 RESOURCE BOOK
- Selection Worksheet 5.2
- Selection Check Test 4.5.3
- Selection Test 4.5.4
- Study and Research Resource 5.21, 5.36

READER'S JOURNAL

If students haven't ever owned a pet, tell them to write about pets they have imagined owning.

GOALS/OBJECTIVES

Studying this lesson will enable students to
- enjoy a thrilling story about pets
- define *motif* and recognize motifs in a literary work
- define *protagonist* and *antagonist* and identify both types of characters in a literary work
- research ghosts and think about them critically

INDIVIDUAL LEARNING STRATEGIES

MOTIVATION

Students may especially enjoy the chance to research ghosts and come up with their own theories on ghosts in the Study and Research & Media Literacy activity. Encourage students to be respectful of one another's opinions, even when other students hold viewpoints that are very different from their own.

READING PROFICIENCY

Have students listen to this story read aloud before they begin reading the selection. Encourage them to read the information on distemper on the Prereading page so they know what disease affects the feline and human characters in the story.

ENGLISH LANGUAGE

Point out the following vocabulary words and expressions:
dalmatian—breed of dog that is white with black spots
banister—handrail along a staircase
wing chair—upholstered arm chair with a high back and sides
radiant—shining, reflecting light

SPECIAL NEEDS

Students may benefit from pairing up with a partner and taking turns and reading paragraphs of the story aloud to each other. Each pair should also work together to answer the Guided Reading questions and the Recall questions in the Investigate, Inquire, and Imagine.

ENRICHMENT

Encourage students to make a bulletin board dedicated to pets of the past and the present. Students may want to bring in photographs or draw pictures of their current pets or a pet they like that someone they know owns. Students might also choose to create miniature memorials to pets that have died, by including a photograph or drawing and writing some lines about the pet and its life.

Pets

Avi

Eve Hubbard had a passion for pets. Her entire life had been filled with gerbils, hamsters, a rat, turtles, a dog, a salamander, and most recently, cats.

In the beginning there was Chase. He was the dog Eve's parents got before she was born. A dalmatian, his original name was Clark, but Eve so loved the way he chased other animals, squirrels, birds, cats, other dogs, that she changed his name to Chase.

GUIDED READING
Who was Eve's first pet? What did she name him and why?

When Chase died of old age, Eve was very sad. She insisted they bury him in their backyard. This yard was enclosed by a high brick wall, crowded with trees, shrubs, and flowers. It was a shady, often damp place, where the moss grew thick, while strange-looking mushrooms sprang up overnight, and withered and died just as quickly.

Midgarden was a small, murky pool in which, during the summer, fat goldfish swam. As they darted about the dark water, Eve was reminded of summer heat lightning.

It was in this yard that Chase was laid to rest with a large stone to mark the spot.

Eve's parents decided against another dog. But though her young brother, Jeff, was uninterested in animals, Eve was allowed to have many other pets. None seemed to survive for very long. When they died Eve buried them in the backyard, too. In time there was quite a row of stones, even a cluster of pebbles for departed goldfish.

GUIDED READING
What did Eve do with her pets when they died?

Most recently Eve came to have two kittens. When she got them she made a vow that these pets would survive. One was white with blue eyes and a pink nose. She named her Angel. The black one—a male with yellow eyes and black nose—she called Shadow.

Eve lavished so much care and affection on Angel and Shadow that she was quite certain she loved these pets more than the others. She was equally sure they loved her just as much. There was nothing she would not do for them. She fed them. Washed and groomed them. Talked to them. Petted them. Not only did they thrive, they grew to maturity.

But there were some problems with Angel.

Early on, the two cats had learned that their food was offered at five o'clock. Twenty minutes before the hour, the two could always be found sitting by their bowls, tails twitching as they waited impatiently for Eve to feed them. If Eve was tardy, Angel scolded her loudly. Once, when Eve was twenty minutes late, Angel nipped Eve's hand as their bowls were being filled. That, despite an apology from Eve.

The cats had another eating habit that Eve attributed to a kind of "ladies first" politeness. That is, Shadow always waited for Angel to start before he began to eat.

Once—just as an experiment—Eve held Angel back in order to let Shadow eat first. A furious Angel scratched Eve and butted Shadow aside.

GUIDED READING
What is the problem with Angel?

"I promise I won't do that again," Eve said, sucking the blood from her hand.

Then there was the time Eve purchased a catnip mouse for the cats. It was a Christmas present she bought with her own money. Instead of sharing it, Angel took the stuffed

The Church Cat's Dream II, 1983. Derold Page. Private Collection.

"PETS" **343**

1. Eve bought them a catnip mouse to share, but Angel took the toy into a corner and wouldn't let Shadow play with it.
2. The vet says she has a disease called feline distemper.
3. Angel dies quickly and painlessly in Eve's arms when the vet gives her a shot to put her out of her misery.

LITERARY TECHNIQUE

CHARACTER. A **character** is a person or animal who takes part in the action of a literary work. Encourage students to discuss the character of Angel by asking them the following questions:

- Would you like to have Angel as a pet? Why, or why not?
- What is Angel described as doing in her lifetime? after her death? What do these actions reveal about Angel?
- What words might students use to describe Angel?
- Explain whether *Angel* is a fitting name for this cat.

Answers

- Most students will say they would not want Angel as a pet because she seems mean-tempered and scratches, bites, and tries to trip Eve.
- Angel is described as nipping Eve when she is late serving the cat food, always eating before Shadow, scratching Eve and knocking Shadow aside when Eve tries to let Shadow eat first, not allowing Shadow to play with the toy mouse Eve bought, trying to trip Eve after she takes the toy away, and leaving a dead goldfish on Eve's pillow. Angel hisses and gives Eve a look that seems to mean "Why have you done this to me?" Angel is a mean-tempered, unpleasant cat.
- Students may say that Angel is mean, selfish, bossy, and potentially dangerous.
- Students may say that Angel is not a fitting name because despite the cat's looks, its behavior is not at all angelic.

---

creature into a corner. When Shadow tried to get at it, Angel hissed. Eve—wanting them to share—took the toy away from her and gave it to Shadow.

GUIDED READING
What Christmas present did Eve buy for her two cats and what happened with it?

That night, when Eve was going down the steps, Angel got between her legs. If Eve hadn't managed to grab the banister, she would have fallen. It was almost as if Angel had wanted Eve to hurt herself.

Now and again, Angel caught one of the goldfish in the garden pool. Not that she ate any of them. Instead, she left them by the edge of the pool, as if to warn the other goldfish of her <u>prowess</u>. And twice—when Eve had scolded her about bullying Shadow—she'd carried a dead goldfish into the house and left it on Eve's pillow.

Eve, in her great love for the cats, forgave these excesses.[1]

One late summer day Angel grew ill. She stopped eating, became thin as a rail, developed a dry nose and runny eyes, and mewed continually, as though asking Eve to do something. Despite the special food Eve prepared, despite her tending to Angel every free moment, the cat's legs grew shaky. Her fur, once thick and velvet in its brushed and combed lushness, became scruffy and <u>unkempt</u>.

"I'm afraid it's feline distemper," the veterinarian said in his examining room with the stainless steel tabletop. "I'm sorry to say your friend won't recover. My dear, I think we should put her out of her misery." He looked from Eve to her father. "One injection will do. I promise she won't feel the least bit of pain. As it is, your other cat might catch the same disease. Even humans do, sometimes. What's your cat's name?"

GUIDED READING
What's the matter with Angel?

"Angel."

"I am sorry," he said, and sounded sincere.

Tears trickled from Eve's eyes. There was no arguing with what she could see for herself.

Though the vet—and her father—advised against it, Eve insisted on holding Angel in her arms when the fatal injection was administered. "You don't know how much we love each other," Eve explained softly.

Eve, in her great love for the cats, forgave these excesses.

Angel died quickly and painlessly in Eve's arms, with barely a sound, save for one long, soft hiss and a frightful last look that Eve interpreted as meaning, "Why have you done this to me?"

GUIDED READING
How did Angel die?

The vet—citing[2] local law—said Angel could not be buried in Eve's backyard.

As if all that was not heartbreaking enough, when Eve returned home she felt compelled to explain to Shadow what had happened.

---

1. **excesses.** Extreme indulgences
2. **cite.** Refer to

---

words for everyday use

prow • ess (prō es´) *n.*, extraordinary ability. *Tatia's <u>prowess</u> at the piano impressed the judges.*

un • kempt (ən kemt´) *adj.*, lacking in order or neatness. *Jill and her brothers hurriedly picked up the <u>unkempt</u> house.*

"No more parties for Angel," she told Shadow. "No more dressing her up and pushing her in the baby carriage or pretending she's queen of the house and we, her loyal servants. Oh, Shadow, she's gone. Forever."

Eve's mother offered the gentle suggestion that perhaps Shadow would not understand what had happened to Angel. <u>Indignantly</u>, Eve replied that she was old enough to know her own as well as her cat's mind. "Shadow will understand," she insisted. "And nobody loves her pets so well as I do," she said, midst hot tears.

Within twenty-four hours Eve began to wonder if her mother was right concerning Shadow's capacity to understand. He became edgy and acted strangely. He spent hours searching for the dead Angel. Not only did Shadow keep making the rounds of the white cat's particular haunts, he kept returning to her favorite sleeping spot, the orange seat on the old wing chair in the dark corner of the living room. Though Shadow himself preferred the couch throw pillow, after Angel's death he spent most of his sleeping hours near her spot.

Shadow even had to be encouraged to eat. It was as if he could not accept the notion that Angel was not going to return and feared she would not like it if he ate first.

Two weeks after Angel's death, in the middle of the night, a noise woke Eve. She was in her bed, on the second floor of her house, beneath a feather comforter, with her body snug and warm, her face open to the crisp air. What was it, she wondered, that had woken her? Was it the cry of a cat?

> **GUIDED READING**
> How does Shadow begin to act after Angel's death?

> **GUIDED READING**
> Why does Eve get up in the middle of the night?

In her drowsy state it took her a moment to remember that Angel had died. Usually, the cats lay at the foot of her bed, more often than not with Angel using Shadow as a pillow.

Eve felt about with her toes. There were no cats on her bed. She sat up and looked on the floor.

Shadow was not there, either. Troubled, Eve swung her feet out from under the comforter and walked to the door of her room.

"Shadow!" she called softly.

When there was no reply she called again, louder.

Eve went to the window of her room and looked into the backyard. The night sky was lit up by a three-quarter moon of great brightness. Only a few clouds—like knots of darkness—drifted by. Because of the moonlight, few stars were visible. But there was Shadow, sitting by the edge of the goldfish pool, staring up.

"Shadow!" Eve called.

> **GUIDED READING**
> Where does she find Shadow?

The black cat looked at Eve but—as though <u>summoned</u>—quickly shifted his gaze back to whatever it was that was attracting his attention.

Eve padded downstairs. At the base of the steps she paused to listen. Her parents—she was quite certain—were asleep. So, <u>presumably</u>, was her younger brother, Jeff.

Eve went out the back door, which was open when it should have been closed. Though the cement patio was cold to her bare feet, she continued on.

It took Eve a moment to adjust her eyes to the backyard's gloom, but when she searched

---

words for everyday use

in • dig • nant (in dig' nənt) *adj.*, filled with or expressing anger over something unjust or mean. *The <u>indignant</u> dog walked away from the bowl of cheap dog food.* **indignantly,** *adv.*

sum • mon (su' mən) *v.*, call upon with authority. *The principal <u>summoned</u> me to his office after the hallway scuffle.*

pre • sum • ab • ly (prē zü mə blē) *adv.*, probably; one would assume. *Lunch will be served, <u>presumably</u>, at noon.*

ANSWERS TO GUIDED READING QUESTIONS

1. He becomes edgy and acts strangely. He keeps looking for Angel in her favorite spots.
2. A noise wakes her, and when she realizes Shadow is not in the room with her, she gets up to find him.
3. In the back yard sitting by the edge of the goldfish pool and staring up.

CULTURAL/ HISTORICAL NOTE

Inform students that *thanatology* is a term for the study of death and mourning. People who have worked as counselors with those who are grieving for the death of a loved one have identified a number of stages that the person who is mourning goes through. These stages are denial, anger, bargaining, depression, and acceptance.

Immediately after a death, especially if it was unexpected, people typically cry, have trouble eating and sleeping, and may feel angry about being left by their loved one. People who are close to a person who has died may feel the effect of the death months or even years later.

ADDITIONAL QUESTIONS AND ACTIVITIES

Encourage students to discuss Shadow. What signs can they see that he is mourning Angel? *Answers.* Students may point to Shadow acting edgy, searching for Angel, sleeping on her favorite spots, and being unable to eat.

1. She follows Shadow's gaze and sees a white cat out along a branch in the tree. She thinks it's Angel.
2. She finds a book called *The Truth About Ghosts*. She learns that, if you believe in ghosts, they come back to haunt the living when something from their past feels unfinished. Or maybe they can't bear to be apart from those still living. Or they want something they can't get where they are.

ADDITIONAL QUESTIONS AND ACTIVITIES

Ask students to discuss in small groups whether they believe that Angel is a ghost. What other explanations can they come up with for what Eve and Shadow think they see?

---

about she saw Shadow gazing up just as she had seen him from above. The fur along his black back was standing up. His tail was fluffed out. Eve could see right away that he was very frightened. "Shadow!" Eve whispered. "What is it?"

The black cat swished his tail but did not alter his gaze. Puzzled, Eve sat down on the ground and put her head next to Shadow's head—the better to follow his look—and searched again.

In the tree—out along a branch—was a white cat.

"Angel!" Eve cried.

The white cat hissed and vanished.

Shaken, Eve gathered Shadow in her arms and pressed her face into his thick, sweet-smelling neck. The black cat was trembling.

Eve carried Shadow back to her room and placed him gently on his <u>accustomed</u> sleeping spot at the foot of her bed. The cat flexed his back, walked a tight circle—as if to unwind himself—kneaded the comforter, then plopped down. But he slept, not by Eve's feet, but close to her hands.

"Can animals become ghosts?" Eve asked at the breakfast table the next morning.

Her father lowered his newspaper. "What?"

"When an animal dies, can it become a ghost?"

"What kind of animal?" Jeff asked between mouthfuls of Corn Pops and milk. Jeff was seven.

Eve gave her younger brother a <u>disdainful</u> glance. "Can animals become ghosts?" she asked again.

Her mother, who was reading another part of the newspaper, said, "You have to believe in ghosts first."

> **GUIDED READING**
> What does Eve discover Shadow is looking at?

"Guess what," Jeff interrupted.

"What?"

"Animals can't be ghosts."

Eve looked across the room. Shadow was sitting atop the counter, yellow eyes fixed on her. Eve had no doubt he was paying attention to the conversation. "Shadow believes in ghosts," Eve informed her brother and anyone else who might be listening. "So there," she said and left for school.

In school Eve went to the library and requested a book about ghosts.

"A ghost story?" the librarian asked.

"Not really," Eve explained. "I need to find out some facts about them. What they are. What they want. You see I have one. An animal one."

The librarian looked a little queerly at Eve. But all she said was, "Let me show you what we have." She found a book for Eve titled *The Truth About Ghosts*.

"Cool," Eve said, and worked her way through the pages. What she learned was that ghosts—if you believed in them—came back to haunt the living because during the ghosts' lives something had been left incomplete, undone, or unsaid. Perhaps they could not bear to be apart from those still living. Or they wanted something they could not get where they were.

> **GUIDED READING**
> What book does Eve find in the library, and what does she learn from it?

From the time the cats had been kittens, Eve had tried to train them to lay upon her chest so they could talk out the day before going to sleep. Cats, she knew perfectly well, did not talk. But she was willing to translate their looks into speech. Angel had always refused, but Shadow was willing.

---

words for everyday use

ac • cus • tomed (ə cus′ təmd) *adj.*, often used or practiced. *Dad prefers to rest in his <u>accustomed</u> plaid easy chair.*

dis • dain • ful (dis dān′ fəl) *adj.*, proud or scornful. *The <u>disdainful</u> kids argued in favor of their unusual clothing.*

ART SMART

Ask students to discuss whether this image is how they picture Shadow sitting by the goldfish pool looking up at Angel. What mood is captured in this image? If students had to draw the scene in which Shadow is looking up at Angel by the goldfish pond what elements might they include? What mood would they try to create. Interested students might then create their own artistic interpretations of the scene, using a medium they enjoy, such as painting or making clay models.

Black Cat by a Pond, 1983. Liz Wright. Private Collection.

ANSWERS TO GUIDED READING QUESTIONS

1. Eve believes that Shadow feels that Angel is luring him to join her in death.
2. He has caught the same disease Angel had.

ADDITIONAL QUESTIONS AND ACTIVITIES

Ask students to respond to the following questions about the relationship between Shadow and Angel:

1. In life, which cat was the leader? Which cat was the follower?
2. What does Eve suspect is holding true even after Angels' death?
3. How does Shadow feel about the ghost cat? How can you tell?
4. Explain whether the way Shadow feels about the ghost cat is similar to how he felt about Angel when she was alive.

Answers

1. Angel was the leader and Shadow the follower.
2. Eve suspects that Angel is trying to get Shadow to follow her, and that Shadow is willing to do so, even though Angel is dead.
3. Shadow is both afraid of and entranced by the ghost cat. He shivers and cringes near Eve for protection from the ghost cat, but yet is lured to go see her at night.
4. Students may say that Shadow was intimidated and bullied by Angel in life and this continues after death, but Shadow seems afraid of Angel now that she is dead.

So that evening he sat on her chest, black nose just a few inches from Eve's nose, staring at her with his large yellow eyes and purring like an idling motor.

"Why do you think Angel has come back?" Eve asked. Shadow yawned and turned away.

"Shadow," said Eve, "I think she's haunting you."

"I want you to promise me something," Eve continued. "If you step out to see Angel's ghost again, let me know so I can go with you and tell her to leave you alone. Okay?"

Shadow blinked.

It was two in the morning when Eve woke. Shadow wasn't there. The door was open.

Eve hurried down the steps and into the yard. The moon was bright enough that she could spot Shadow at the edge of the pool, staring into a tree. Angel was in the tree.

"What is it, Angel?" she called gently. "What's the matter? Why can't you rest? What do you want?"

Amid the dark leaves, Angel's body seemed to be shining. Her tail jerked about angrily. Her glare was hostile.

Eve felt something prickly against her leg. Startled, she looked down. It was Shadow, cringing behind her.

"I want you to know," Eve informed Angel with some indignation, "you are scaring Shadow."

The white cat vanished.

The following day Shadow grew sluggish. That evening he did not eat his dinner.

"Shadow," said Eve during their bedtime conversation, "Angel can be very insistent. Remember that time with the catnip mouse?"

"You didn't eat tonight," Eve continued. "That's the way Angel's sickness began. I think you're going to get sick, and die, and go to

her. I believe she wants you where she is so she can have someone to sleep on. Do you think that's so? How can I help you stay?" she asked tearfully. "I'll do anything."

GUIDED READING

What does Eve believe about how Shadow has been feeling?

Shadow, his front paws tucked rather <u>primly</u> under his chest, gazed evenly at Eve with his round yellow eyes. He licked one of his paws and passed the wet paw over his face, as if wiping away tears. Then he got up and walked slowly to the foot of Eve's bed. Instead of doing his usual turn and settling down for the night, he jumped off the bed and crept out of the room, belly low.

"Don't listen to her!" Eve called after him. "Don't!"

She went to the window. The moon was close to being full. As she watched, she saw Shadow walk into the garden and take up his position by the goldfish pond. He was staring into the tree. Eve glanced at the stone that marked Chase's burial spot—and all the other animals' markers—and decided not to go down.

Over the next few days Shadow's health grew worse. Signs of distemper were unmistakable. This time, however, Eve didn't wait quite so long before asking her mother to take the cat to the veterinarian.

He set Shadow on the stainless steel examination table and felt around his ears, looked into his mouth, took his temperature.

"It's what I was afraid of," the vet said sadly, once he had concluded his examination. "He must have gotten the illness from your other cat.

GUIDED READING

What's happening to Shadow?

"But cats," the vet warned, "are a bit like people in regard to illness. Living or dying—

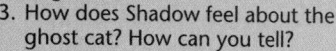

prim (prim') *adj.*, fussy about one's appearance. *Jacob was very <u>prim</u>, while his brother Jordan was messy and unkempt.* **primly**, *adv.*

it can have a lot to do with what they want. Has this fellow been grieving for his partner?"

"He's being haunted by her," Eve said solemnly.

The vet exchanged glances with Eve's mother. To Eve, he said, "Happens that way with humans too, sometimes. Let's hope you caught this illness early enough," he said soothingly and offered Eve a packet of pink pills, as well as instructions on how to give them to Shadow. "Call me if he gets worse."

That night Eve tried talking to Shadow again. His yellow eyes were dull. His nose was dry. "Please tell me what I can do to help you resist Angel," she said to him. "It's not our fault she died. It's not right that she wants to take you with her."

When Shadow made no response, Eve became almost angry. "Shadow," she said, "who picked you out at the ASPCA[3]? Who always fed you and brushed you? Had birthday parties and Christmas with you? Who talks to you every night? Listens to you, lets you sleep on her bed? Please don't forget any of that. Please."

Shadow shut his eyes.

"Oh, Shadow!" Eve cried in frustration. "It's not fair!"

Over the next few days Shadow grew more ill despite the fact that Eve gave him the pills the way the vet had instructed her. She pried the black cat's mouth open, popped a pill deep into his pink throat, then gently held his mouth closed so that he had to swallow.

It was only later that she found a pile of the pink pills—spit up—behind the

> **GUIDED READING**
>
> How does Shadow respond to Eve's pleas?

> **GUIDED READING**
>
> What does Eve later discover happened to the medicine she gives Shadow?

wing chair. Eve feared there was nothing more she could do. Angel had insisted Shadow join her. And he was going.

Even so, Eve kept trying to convince Shadow to stay. She spoke to him about the pleasures of life in their house, with her, the family. "We all love you," she said. Shadow merely listened.

"I'll get you a new friend," Eve pleaded. "I'll go to the ASPCA and find someone this weekend. I'll even look for a white one. A white kitten would be so much fun. Oh, Shadow," she cried, holding the now thin creature close to her heart, "don't go to Angel. Stay with me."

Though he grew sicker, Shadow went out each night and looked up at the tree. Eve, tears running down her cheeks, watched him from her room. How could Angel be so powerful?

"I'm afraid he's doing just as poorly as Angel," Eve's father said Saturday morning.

"He doesn't want to live," Eve informed him.

"You mean, he misses Angel?"

"Dad," Eve said with some bitterness, "Angel is insisting he join her. And Shadow always does what she tells him to do."

"My suggestion," her father said, "is that we take him back to the vet."

That night, when Shadow dragged himself out into the garden, Eve joined him. The black cat sat by the pool, occasionally looking up. Often, in his weakness, he nodded off.

The white cat was in the tree.

"Angel," said Eve, "why must you do this? It wasn't our fault you died. Just because you

---

3. **ASPCA.** American Society for the Prevention of Cruelty to Animals

words for everyday use

sol • emn (sä′ ləm) *adj.*, serious; dignified. *Seymour's* solemn *eyes told us something bad had happened.*

1. Shadow just shuts his eyes.
2. Shadow spit up the medicine behind a chair.

LITERARY TECHNIQUE

ARCHETYPE. Inform students that an **archetype** is an inherited, often unconscious, ancestral memory or motif that recurs throughout history and literature. One archetypal character that appears again and again throughout literature from around the world is the temptress. Eve's namesake from the story of Adam and Eve in the garden of Eden is one of the most well-known examples of a temptress in literature. This Eve tempted Adam to taste the apple from the forbidden tree of knowledge of good and evil. This action led them both to be expelled from the garden of Eden. Generate a class discussion on Angel. In what way is she a temptress? *Answers.* Students may say that Angel is indeed a temptress in that she is trying to get Shadow to follow her into death.

ANSWERS TO GUIDED READING QUESTIONS

1. She thinks about how Angel has betrayed her. She feels hurt and angry.
2. Eve awakes to find both dead cats at her feet on the bed staring at her.
3. She bites Eve's hand.

died doesn't mean everybody else has to. Shadow has a right to his life."

The white cat opened her mouth and hissed.

"And what about me?" Eve cried. "Don't you care about how I feel?"

Angel hissed again.

The next morning Eve and her mother took Shadow to the vet. It was of no use. Shadow died the way Angel had—in Eve's arms.

On the way home, Eve was very silent. All she could think about was that Angel had <u>betrayed</u> her. She was hurt and very angry.

GUIDED READING
What does Eve think about after Shadow dies, and how does she feel?

Eve's mother reached out and touched her. "When you're ready you can get another cat."

Eve said nothing. But she kept asking herself, why was Angel treating her so badly? Had she done something wrong? Had she offended the cats in some way? No, she insisted to herself. It was just the opposite. She had loved them. Given them so much.

The next day a sad Eve put away the cats' bowls, cleaned and stored their litter box, shelved the remaining cans of cat food, and put the cats' collars in a box of mementos she kept at the back of her closet. Her sleep was uninterrupted.

Then, two nights after Shadow died, Eve woke. She turned on her reading lamp and looked toward her feet. Both dead cats, Angel and Shadow, were looking at her, staring with unblinking eyes.

GUIDED READING
What happens two nights after Shadow's death?

Eve was so shocked she drew in her breath sharply. She hardly knew what to do other than to stare back. Suddenly it dawned on her why the cats were there.

"Oh, Shadow, oh Angel," she cried. "You've come back for me, haven't you? You want me to be with you."

The cats stared <u>fixedly</u> at her.

"But why do you want me?" Eve asked. "Is it because you love me so much?"

Eve sat up in bed—arms hugged around her knees—gazing at the cats, waiting for a response. They made not so much as a sound.

After a while Angel stood, arched her back, and crept forward. Approaching Eve, she leaned down and bit her hand.

GUIDED READING
What does Angel do?

"Ow!" Eve cried, snatching her hand away. She sucked at the blood.

Angel sat back on her haunches, licked her lips, and stared at Eve.

Eve suddenly remembered that what Angel did was exactly what she had done that time she thought her food was late. Then, all in rush, Eve understood.

"Is that all I am to you?" she gasped with horror. "Just someone to take care of you? Your servant. Your pet?"

The cats vanished.

The next day Eve told no one of the cats' visit. They didn't believe her before. She knew they wouldn't believe her now. Besides, she was sure she was strong. She would be able to resist the cats' demands.

Four days later the two cats returned. They called to her—soft, <u>plaintive</u> mewing sounds—in her sleep. When she woke she knew they were in the yard.

It was a warm, humid night, the last hot breath of the summer that had been. When Eve stepped onto the patio, she felt almost suffocated by the fragrance that filled the air, the thick, clotted scent of decaying vegetation.

words for everyday use

be • tray (bē trā′) v., violate a trust or act unfaithfully. *Cory <u>betrayed</u> me by revealing my secret to Liz.*
fixed (fikst′) adj., firmly set or with concentration. *Sarah sat with a <u>fixed</u> gaze on the television set.* **fixedly** (fik′ səd lē) adv.
plain • tive (plān′ tiv) adj., mournful, sad; expressing sorrow. *Timmy fell and got up with a <u>plaintive</u> cry.*

The limp leaves on the trees were edged with brown. A heavy dew clung to the plants and shrubbery and weighed them down. Rotting mushrooms glowed faintly and seemed to pulse. A <u>waning</u> moon slipped in and out behind streaks of clouds. In the pool floated a dead goldfish. Its white belly was turned up, a mirror image to the moon in the sky.

The two cats were sitting side by side beneath the tree. Angel seemed to be in bloom. Shadow's ebony fur shimmered. Their tails waved with impatience.

Before the cats were their food bowls. The bowls were empty. Eve understood instantly. The cats were waiting for her to feed them.

Eve stamped her foot. "No," she said. "I will not take care of you anymore. I won't. And there's nothing you can do to make me!"

The cats meowed with aggravation, but faded away.

Over the next few days Eve suffered various visitations. The cats hissed in dark rooms, swiped at her as she went down the hallway. A bleeding scratch appeared on the back of her hand. She tripped over something as she came down the steps. A dead goldfish lay on her pillow. It stank badly.

"I'm not going to join you," Eve told the cats when she saw them next.

Angel spat at her.

Shadow had the decency to look away.

At dinner the following day, Eve said, "I have an important announcement."

"The cats," said Eve, "have come back as ghosts..."

> **GUIDED READING**
>
> What do the cats expect from Eve, and how does she respond?

Her mother, father, and brother looked at her.

"The cats," said Eve, "have come back as ghosts. They are trying to get me to join them."

"Oh yeah, why?" her brother demanded.

"So I can take care of them."

"But they're dead!" her brother protested.

"I just told you, it's their ghosts!"

Eve's mother and father exchanged <u>bemused</u> looks.

"Well," her mother said, "I know they were attached to you."

"And you to them," her father added.

"You think I'm joking, don't you?" said Eve. She left the table sorry she had spoken to them.

The following day Eve became ill. First came <u>fatigue</u>, aching joints, sore throat— then a fever.

Both of Eve's parents worked, so a babysitter had to be brought in to stay with the ailing girl. It was on the third day, when Eve's fever grew high, that Eve's father remained home. When he went to work her mother came home. When his school was out, Jeff sat with her. Eve, however, had eyes for only Angel and Shadow, who either sat or slept at the foot of her bed. They kept gazing at her, mewing, waving their tails. Eve knew they were only waiting for her to die and come take care of them.

> **GUIDED READING**
>
> Who stays at the foot of Eve's bed while she's sick, and why?

> **words for everyday use**
>
> **wane** (wān) *v.*, dwindling; dimming. *Ashley's energy <u>waned</u>, and she fell asleep.* **waning,** *adj.*
>
> **be • muse** (bi myüz′) *v.*, confuse, bewilder. *My jokes always seem to <u>bemuse</u> my mother.* **bemused,** *adj.*
>
> **fa • tigue** (fə tēg′) *n.*, weariness or exhaustion. *After the long day, Evan complained of <u>fatigue</u>.*

1. They're waiting for her to feed them and she refuses.
2. The ghosts of the two cats stay with her. Eve thinks they are waiting for her to die so she can come and take care of them.

ADDITIONAL QUESTIONS AND ACTIVITIES

Ask students the following questions:

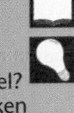

1. How is Eve beginning to feel about her cats, especially Angel?
2. What does Eve suddenly "understand" about Angel? What role reversal has taken place?
3. How does Eve feel about this role reversal? What is she determined not to do?
4. Why do you think Eve gets sick?

Answers

1. Eve is beginning to be angry with her gets, especially Angel, and wants them to leave her alone.
2. When Angel bites her as she did once before when she was late serving food, Even understands that her pets only think of her as their servant, or pet—someone to take care of them—which is why they are returning for her. Eve thought she was the owner, but now she realizes that she is really the pet.
3. Eve isn't happy to realize this, and is determined not to take care of her cats any more or follow them into death.
4. Students may say that Eve gets sick from the disease Angel has when Angel bites her, or if students don't believe in the ghost cat they may say she gets sick from prior exposure to the diseased cats. Other students may say Eve gets sick from the stress of having lost two cats.

"I'm not your pet," she said to them <u>vehemently</u>. "I'm staying here."

"Daddy," she begged, "make them go away."

Her father got a cold compress and laid it over her forehead. "This should help your fever," he said gently.

After the fourth day of high fever, Eve was taken to the hospital. The cats followed her to the sterile white room that almost put Angel's coat to shame. As for Shadow, he looked like a dirty oil spill at the foot of the bed, where they were sitting.

Once, when Eve woke from a deep sleep, she found both cats sitting on her chest. They were side by side, pink and black noses two inches from her face.

"Take care of yourselves!" she cried out angrily. With that she fell into a faint.

That night she was sent home. Her parents and her brother were beside her. They looked sad and whispered among themselves. Sometimes there were tears.

> **GUIDED READING**
> Why was Eve sent home from the hospital? How does her family react?

At the foot of the bed, the two cats, paws folded under their chests, waited patiently.

"Please make the cats go away," Eve said, feebly.

Her family, seeing nothing, could only shake their heads.

That night Eve woke at about two in the morning. Feverish and weak, she crawled out of bed and went to the window. Leaning against the window frame for support, she peered down into the yard. The two cats were there, waiting by their empty bowls. They looked up at Eve and mewed.

A wave of exhaustion washed over the girl. "They need me," she told herself. "They must be very hungry. It must be time to feed them. Only I can do it."

She gazed about the yard until her eyes came to rest on Chase's grave. In the moonlight his marker stone was radiant. Where was he? Why had he never come back to haunt her? Presumably he lay in peace. Eve envied the dog.

With a sigh of resignation,[4] she took up her robe, wrapped it around herself, and went slowly downstairs and into the yard.

Though the night air made her shiver, her forehead felt as if it were burning. Her body was so hot she was sweating. As soon as the cats saw her, they began to mew angrily and swish their tails as if they were whips. Then a thought came to her. Eve stumbled past the cats and into the yard to the area where all her pets had been buried.

The cats, complaining bitterly, darted between her feet, clawing her ankles, nipping at her.

At Chase's grave Eve sank to her knees.

Shadow bit her bare toes. Angel clawed her ankle.

Eve was too far gone to notice these attacks. "Chase," she whispered in a trembling voice, "please come back. I need you badly. I want you to chase these cats away."

> **GUIDED READING**
> Where in the yard does Eve go and why?

So saying, she squeezed her hands together and repeated her words <u>passionately</u>.

Suddenly there was a bark. Eve looked around. It was dim, her vision was fogged, but there before her—unmistakably—was Chase. In her delirium[5] Eve saw him in reverse: where

---

4. **resignation.** Surrender
5. **delirium.** Mental disturbance characterized by confusion and hallucinations

---

words for everyday use

ve • he • ment (vē' ə mənt) *adj.*, marked by forceful energy, emotion, or expression. *Mark made a <u>vehement</u> plea for help.* **vehemently,** *adv.*

pas • sion • ate (pa' shə nət) *adj.*, expressing strong feeling. *Dane was <u>passionate</u> about his desire to travel.* **passionately,** *adv.*

he had been white, he was now black, and his black spots were now white.

Chase paid no attention to her, but was galloping madly toward the cats. Behind him followed a ragged parade of salamanders, turtles, hamsters, gerbils, and many flopping goldfish. All were ghosts.

The cats spun about, hissed, and spat, but as Chase approached, they gave ground quickly. They ran for the wall, scampered up, and disappeared over the top. Chase, panting, stood at the base of the wall and barked furiously. The other ghosts made appropriate noises.

When the cats were gone, Chase trotted over to where Eve was, barked once, twice, then evaporated.

Eve barely made it back to her bed.

But starting the next morning, she became better. Every day that followed she improved, until the doctor declared her cured. He was even heard to say, "And I didn't think she had a ghost of a chance."

In the years that followed, on the anniversary of Chase's death, Eve never failed to leave a large dog biscuit on his burial stone. During that particular night—she always waited up to hear—there <u>invariably</u> was a bark. And in the morning the biscuit was gone.

As for pets, Eve never wanted another. ■

Respond *to the* SELECTION

If you lost a pet or pets the way Eve did, would you ever want to have pets again? Why, or why not?

About *the* AUTHOR

Avi was born in 1937 in Brooklyn, New York. He became interested in writing during his senior year of high school. On writing he has said "I think you become a writer when you stop writing for yourself or your teachers and start thinking about readers." Avi also admits that writing is hard work and that on average, it takes him a year to write a book. He started out writing plays and moved on to writing for young readers once he had children of his own—two sons. Avi has written mystery, adventure, fantasy, and ghost stories. Two of his best-known titles are *The True Confessions of Charlotte Doyle* and *Nothing but the Truth*, both Newbery Honor Award Winners.

words for everyday use

in • vari • able (in ver′ ē ə bəl) *adj.*, not changing. *Every morning, an <u>invariable</u> knock at the door signaled the arrival of our neighbor.* **invariably,** *adv.*

"PETS" **353**

SELECTION CHECK TEST 4.5.3 WITH ANSWERS (CONT.)

1. The **protagonist** is the main character of a story.
2. A(n) **motif** is something that appears repeatedly in one or more works of literature, art, or music.
3. Many things may serve as a(n) **motif**: places, ideas, actions, images, sounds or sights, or activities.
4. A character who struggles with the main character is the **antagonist**.
5. When an author gives a thing, an animal, an emotion, or an idea human characteristics, then he or she is using **personification**.

RESPOND TO THE SELECTION

Ask students whether they think Eve changed her mind about what happened to her once she gets older, and blame the ghost cats she saw on her fever? Or do students think that Eve would stick to her story about what happened?

SELECTION CHECK TEST 4.5.3 WITH ANSWERS

Checking Your Reading

1. Who were Angel and Shadow? **Angel and Shadow were Eve's cats.**
2. Of what disease did Angel die? **Angel died of feline distemper.**
3. What did Shadow do each night after Angel's death? **After Angel's death, Shadow spent each night by the fish pond, looking up at a tree.**
4. What did Eve see that her family didn't? **Eve sees the ghosts of her pets, but the rest of her family cannot.**
5. At the end of the story, what did Chase do for Eve? **Chase chases away the ghosts of the cats that were haunting Eve.**

Vocabulary in Context

Fill in each blank below with the most appropriate word. You may have to change the tense of the word.

wither   prowess   excess   unkempt
disdainful   waning   memento

1. Even though he knew it was getting late, Abe kept shooting baskets in the **waning** sunlight.
2. Martha saw nothing wrong with eating red meat, and was **disdainful** of vegetarian diets.
3. We planted new flowers in the garden, but they soon **withered** in the summer heat.
4. By the young doctor's **unkempt** appearance, I guessed that he hadn't had any sleep all night.

Reader's Toolbox

Fill in the blanks using the following terms. You may use some terms more than once.

motif   personification   antagonist
protagonist

RECALL

1a. He spits it up behind a chair.

2a. She looks at Chase's grave and wonders where he is and why he has never come back to haunt her.

3a. Eve sees him in reverse: where he had been white, he was now black, and his black spots were now white.

INTERPRET

1b. Students may say that Shadow is trying to die so he can join Angel again. Students may point to the way Shadow seems fascinated by Angel as a ghost and is drawn to her.

2b. Eve thinks it's because they want her to keep caring for them. Students may wonder if Eve would have been haunted if she had been able to bury the cats in her backyard along with all the other pets. Then they would have felt taken care of; and they could rest in peace because they would still be a part of Eve's world in her pet cemetery.

3b. The colors may be reversed for a couple of reasons. First, since Chase is now a ghost, his colors might appear the opposite of how they were in life, since death is the opposite of life. Second, because he has come to chase away her problem—the cats—Eve can now reverse her own life from its steady march toward death to a return to life.

ANALYZE

4a. She may have contracted distemper from the cats, either while they were still alive or when the ghost of Angel bites Eve. Or the psychological effect the cats have on her may bring on her illness. Or her family's unwillingness to engage in a discussion of ghosts and what to do about them may bring on her illness.

SYNTHESIZE

4b. *Responses will vary.*

EVALUATE

5a. There's not a lot of exchange. Eve says more than the others, but even that is not a lot. Her brother tries to discount her belief in ghosts. Her parents try to act sympathetic but don't really show much interest in

Investigate, Inquire, and Imagine

Recall: GATHERING FACTS

1a. What does Shadow do with the medicine Eve gives him?

2a. On the night Eve is sent home from the hospital, she once again awakens in the middle of the night. When she looks out the window into the yard, what do her eyes focus on, and what does she ask herself?

3a. When Eve sees Chase, what does he look like?

Interpret: FINDING MEANING

1b. Why do you think Shadow does this? Explain your answer.

2b. Why do you think Chase and all the other pets buried in the backyard haven't come back to haunt Eve? Why do you think it's different with the cats? Why are they haunting her?

3b. Why would Eve see Chase differently from when he was alive? Explain the significance of the change.

Analyze: TAKING THINGS APART

4a. Identify the possible causes of Eve's illness, including what Eve's parents and doctors might believe.

Synthesize: BRINGING THINGS TOGETHER

4b. Based on evidence from the story, create your own explanation for the cause of Eve's illness.

Evaluate: MAKING JUDGMENTS

5a. Evaluate the conversations Eve has with her family. How much exchange is there between people? Who does most of the talking? How do Eve's mother, her father, and her brother each respond to the comments she makes about her cats and ghosts? What effect do you think the reactions of her family have on Eve?

Extend: CONNECTING IDEAS

5b. What are some situations you've experienced in which you felt like a block of communication occurred? How did this affect you? What did you do, or how did you respond?

Understanding *Literature*

MOOD. Mood, or atmosphere, is the feeling or emotion the writer creates in a literary work. The setting, the behavior of characters, and the events that take place in a story work together to create a certain mood. Examine each of these three elements in "Pets" and explain how each contribute to the atmosphere of this story. How would you descibe the mood of the story?

ANSWERS TO INVESTIGATE, INQUIRE, IMAGINE (CONT.)

the topic. Because her family appears unwilling to really listen and help Eve, she just stops talking about the situation. As she grows sicker, her parents seem to attribute her talk about the cats to delusions brought on by her fever. If her family had been able to accept Eve's concerns about ghosts, they may have been able to answer her pleas for help and avoid her illness—and even perhaps Shadow's illness and death—altogether.

EXTEND

5b. *Responses will vary.*

PROTAGONIST AND ANTAGONIST. A **protagonist** is the main character in a story. The protagonist faces a struggle or conflict. A character who struggles with the main character is called an **antagonist**. Eve engages in a long struggle against Angel, and then against Angel and Shadow together. What is the struggle Eve confronts with the cats? How does she resolve this struggle? Who is the protagonist(s)? Who is the antagonist(s)? Label each circle in the Graphic Organizer either protagonist or antagonist.

Graphic *Organizer*

Complete the graphic organizer started below to describe these three characters. Note their individual characteristics in the areas that do not overlap. In the area where the two antagonist circles overlap, note the traits or concerns that those two characters share.

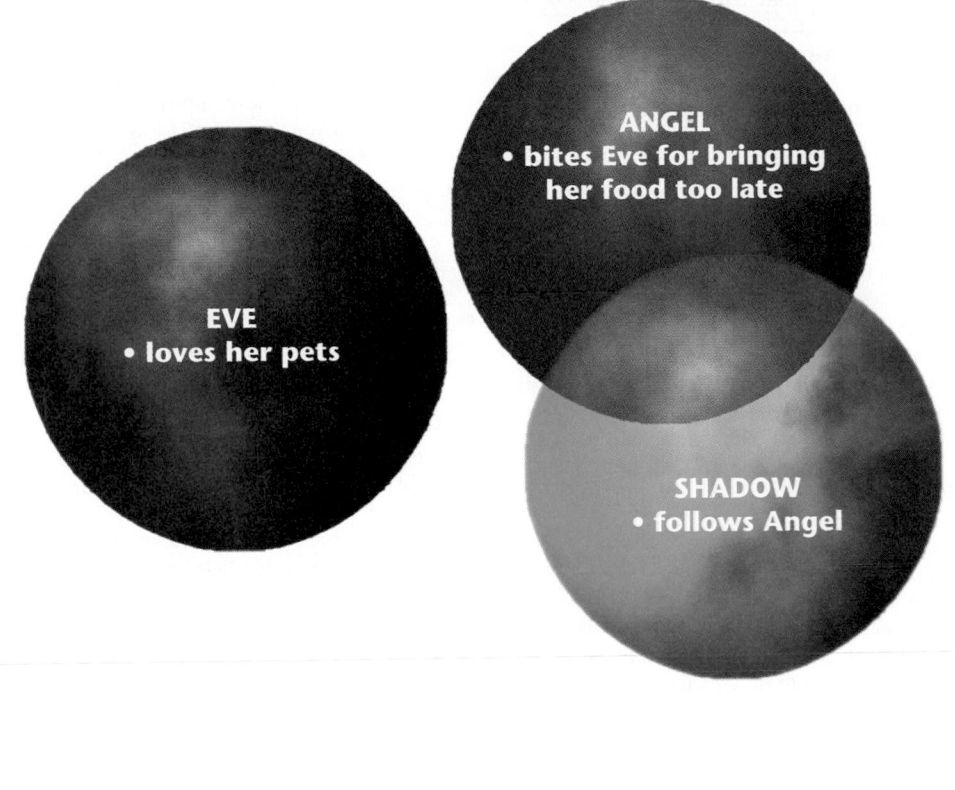

EVE
• loves her pets

ANGEL
• bites Eve for bringing her food too late

SHADOW
• follows Angel

MOTIF. Students may say motifs include Angel's bossing Shadow around, Angel's hissing and being unpleasant, Eve talking to her cats and trying to reason with him, the idea that the dead can come back for you to take them with him, and the pet cemetery and goldfish pond in Eve's backyard. Students may say that Eve's backyard is mostly described at night when strange things are happening so it seems eerie and mysterious. Students may say at first the backyard seems peaceful, even with the pet cemetery, but the setting grows more and more creepy each time the author returns to it. Students may say that they could tell a final confrontation would take place in the backyard.

PROTAGONIST AND ANTAGONIST. Eve confronts the cats about not wanting to follow them into death and take care of them anymore. She resolves this struggle be setting the ghost of her dog (and her other pets) upon the ghosts of her cats.

GRAPHIC ORGANIZER

Students may say that Eve and Angel are similar in that they are female, clever, and determined, but they are different in that Angel is a cat and Eve a human, that Angel dies and Eve doesn't, and that Angel is mean-spirited while Eve is kind and loving. Students may say that Eve and Shadow are similar in their good nature and their both being fascinated by and bullied by Angel. They are different in that Eve is a human and Shadow a cat, that Eve lives and is unwilling to follow Angel while Shadow is willing to follow Angel and dies, and that Eve stands up to Angel while Shadow is too afraid to do so.

Study and Research & Media Literacy
INTERNET RESEARCH. For more information on using Internet sites, refer students to the Language Arts Survey 5.25, "Using the Internet." Students' theories should be based at least in some part on their evidence and how well they are able to support or refute it.

Vocabulary
USING A THESAURUS. You may want to bring several types of print thesauruses into class to allow students to use them in small groups. You may also want to have them use and evaluate computerized thesauruses and have them compare them to print versions.

Media Literacy
ANALYZING AND WRITING NEWS COPY. As students evaluate news articles, have them identify the who, what, why, where, when, and how elements. Refer them to the Language Arts Survey 2.14, "Questioning: Using the 5Ws and an H.

Writer's Journal

1. Write **epitaphs** for Eve to add to the gravestones of Angel, Shadow, and Chase.

2. Imagine that you are Eve and that you have just discovered Shadow for the first time out in the backyard at night looking up in the tree. Write a **diary entry** describing what happened.

3. Write a **short essay** responding to the following question: Do you find Eve's backyard an inviting place? Citing evidence from the story, explain why or why not.

Skill Builders

Study and Research & Media Literacy

INTERNET RESEARCH. Using the library and/or the Internet, research the topic of ghosts to look for answers to the following questions: What are they? Why do they appear? What evidence suggests they are real? What evidence suggests they are imagined?

In your research, did you find consistent answers to each question? Did you find differing answers? Were the explanations you found based on facts? What evidence did sources have to back up their theories? Did you find all the explanations valid? Write your own theories to answer the questions about ghosts based on your research. Refer to the Language Arts Survey 5.36, "Keeping a Research Journal."

Vocabulary

USING A THESAURUS. Think about some of the words that describe the mood of "Pets." Make a list of these words. Using a thesaurus, look each word up and write down a few of its synonyms—pick those that most appeal to you. Once you have a short list of scary words, use them along with at least four Words for Everyday Use, to write a spooky paragraph, poem, or letter. For more information, see the Language Arts Survey 5.21, "Using a Thesaurus."

Media Literacy

ANALYZING AND WRITING NEWS COPY. During the next few evenings, look through your local newspaper and clip articles that cover strange or humorous local, national, or international events. Note the way the articles approach these stories and the facts they choose to provide the reader. Imagine you are a newspaper reporter living next door to Eve. Compose a short list of questions you might ask Eve and members of her family to try to uncover the story beneath the strange goings on in their backyard. Write a short article imitating the style of one of those you clipped from your newspaper. Think carefully about the part of the story you most want to emphasize before writing.

Prereading

"QWERTYUIOP"

by Vivien Alcock

Reader's Resource

- **APPLIED ENGLISH CONNECTION.** This story is about a young woman who has just completed secretarial college. At secretarial college, students learn skills such as typing, shorthand, filing, answering telephones, taking messages, transcribing dictation, composing business letters and memos, and editing and proofreading copy.

- Dictation is an important secretarial skill in which a secretary transcribes, or makes a copy of, material either while someone else is dictating the material live or while listening to a tape recording of the material. The secretary may either write out the copy using shorthand (a method of rapid handwriting that uses abbreviations and symbols in place of full words) or type it using a typewriter or computer. Today, most secretaries are called administrative assistants.

Graphic Organizer

expressive · persuasive · writing aim · literary · informative

Reader's Journal

What would you do if, on the first day of your first job, everything seemed to be working against you?

Reader's TOOLBOX

MOTIVATION. A **motivation** is a force that moves a character to think, feel, or behave in a certain way. As you read "QWERTYUIOP," try to identify what motivations lead Lucy, the main character, to think and act as she does.

AIM. A writer's **aim** is his or her purpose, or goal. People may write to express themselves, to inform others, to persuade others, or to create a literary work. A diary or a personal letter contains expressive writing. A campaign speech relies on persuasive writing. An encyclopedia article or an accident report uses informative writing. Examples of expressive writing include a poem, a play, or a short story. In this story, some of the characters have an aim, or goal, that they try to reach through writing. As you read "QWERTYUIOP," look for examples of different kinds of writing and make a chart like the one to the left to illustrate what you find. Later, go back and expand your diagram with additional examples of writing types you are familiar with. Keep in mind that some writing may have more than one aim.

"QWERTYUIOP" **357**

ADDITIONAL RESOURCES

UNIT 5 RESOURCE BOOK
- Selection Worksheet 5.3
- Selection Check Test 4.5.5
- Selection Test 4.5.6
- Applied English Resource 6.1

GRAPHIC ORGANIZER

Near *expressive,* students may write the letters that Miss Broome writes in the midst of other letters, short stories, personal essays, personal statements of belief. Near *persuasive* students might write debate speeches, letters of application or request, and editorials. Near *informative* students may write the business letters Lucy types, newspaper or magazine articles, and encyclopedia entries. Near *literary,* students might write short stories, novels, dramas, and poems.

READER'S JOURNAL

As an alternate activity, ask students what they would do if they knew someone was determined to see them fail and quit. Would they do so, or would they challenge this person?

GOALS/OBJECTIVES

Studying this lesson will enable students to
- have a positive experience reading a story about a mysterious typewriter
- briefly explain some of the skills required by secretaries
- define *inciting incident* and identify the inciting incident in a work of fiction

- define *aim* and identify the aim of a literary work.
- fill out a job application
- enact a scene from a story

INDIVIDUAL LEARNING STRATEGIES

Motivation
Students may enjoy trying their hands at some of the skills mentioned in this selection. If you have a school business and typing teacher, ask him or her to give your students a lesson in typing and taking dictation.

Reading Proficiency
Students may have trouble with British terms, so tell them to pay careful attention to the footnotes. Students may also benefit from hearing the story read aloud, so you may wish to read the story to them.

English Language Learning
Point out the following vocabulary words and expressions:
kitchenette—small compact kitchen
correcting fluid—white quick-drying paint used to cover mistakes on paper
diploma—certificate issued to a student indicating that the students has graduated
scalded—burned by hot water or steam
swipe—hard sweeping motion
snags—problems
studio apartment—tiny one-room apartment

Special Needs
Have students focus on answering the Guided Reading questions and the Recall questions in the Investigate, Inquire, and Imagine section. Check their comprehension with the check test.

Enrichment
Encourage students to write a personal essay about their career goals. What do they want to be one day? What do they plan on doing to realize this goal?

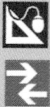

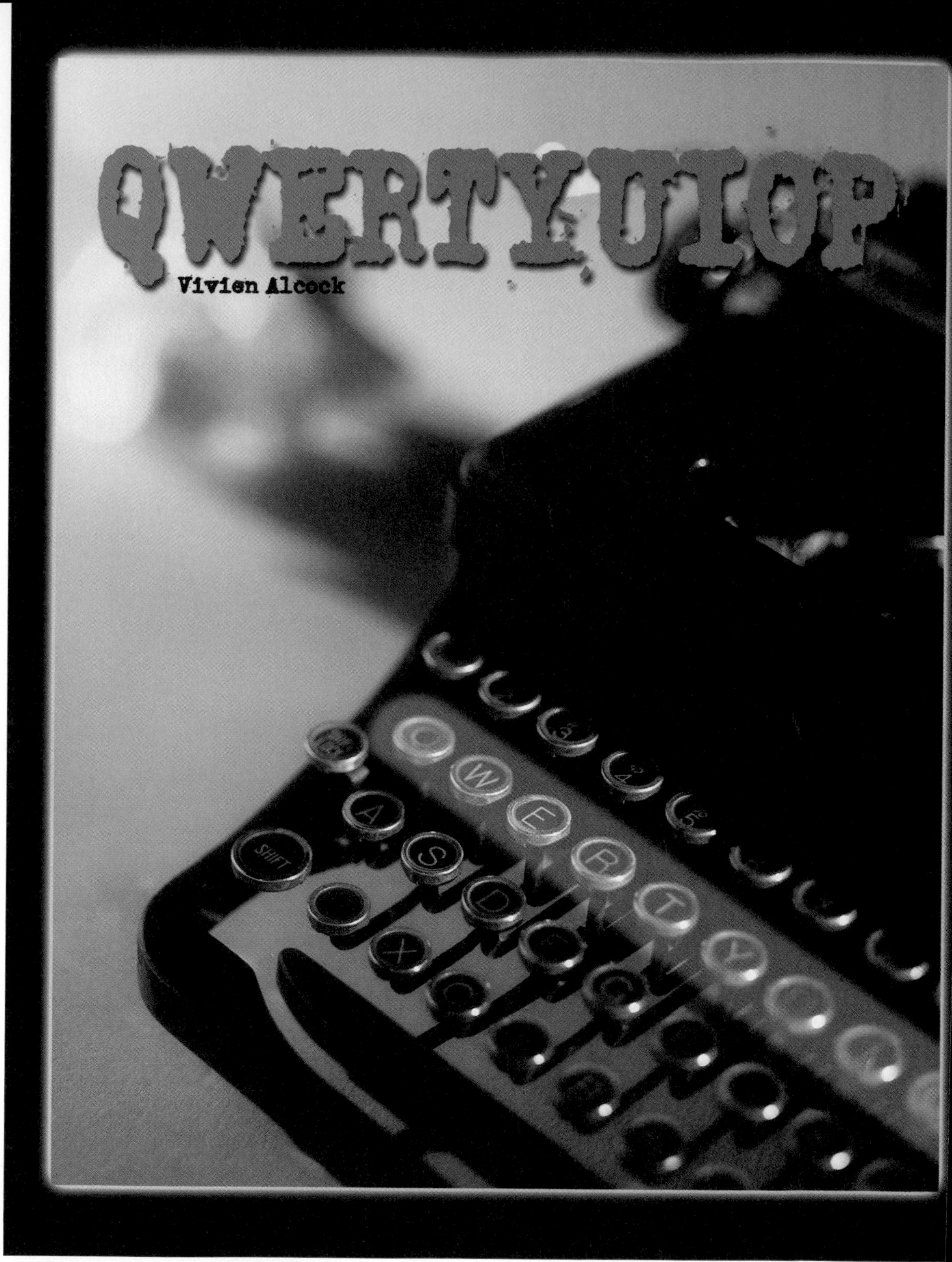
QWERTYUIOP
Vivien Alcock
SHIFT

VOCABULARY FROM THE SELECTION

anxiety
bewilderment
nuisance
pathetic
scald
vacancy
warily

Jobs don't grow on trees, the principal of the Belmont Secretarial College was fond of saying.

"Be positive," Mrs. Price told her departing students, as she shook them by the hand in turn. "Go out into the world and *win!* I have every confidence in you."

When she came to the last student, however, her confidence suddenly <u>evaporated</u>. She looked at Lucy Beck and sighed.

"Good luck, my dear," she said kindly, but rather in the tone of voice of someone wishing a snowman a happy summer.

Lucy Beck was young and small and mouse-colored, easily overlooked. She had a lonely O level[1] and a typing speed that would make a tortoise laugh.

"Whoever will want to employ me?" she had asked Mrs. Price once, and Mrs. Price had been at a loss to answer.

GUIDED READING

Who is Lucy Beck? What does she want and why?

Lucy wanted a job. More than anyone, more than anything, she wanted a job. She was tired of being poor. She was fed up with macaroni and cheese and baked beans. She was sick of secondhand clothes.

"We are jumble sailors on the rough sea of life," her mother would say.

Lucy loved her mother, but could not help wishing she would sometimes lose her temper. Shout. Scream. Throw saucepans at the spinning, grinning head of Uncle Bert.

> "We are jumble sailors on the rough sea of life," her mother would say.

If I get a job, I'm getting out. If I get a job . . . Trouble was that there were hundreds after every <u>vacancy</u>, brighter than Lucy, better qualified than Lucy, wearing strings of O levels round their necks like pearls.

GUIDED READING

Why is Lucy afraid she won't get a job?

Who in their right minds will choose me? Lucy wondered, setting off for her first interview.

So she was astonished to be greeted by Mr. Ross, of Ross and Bannister's, with enormous enthusiasm. She was smiled at, shaken by the hand, given tea and biscuits, and told that her single O level was the very one they had been looking for. Then she was offered the job.

"I hope you will be happy here," Mr. Ross said, showing her out. There was a sudden doubt in his voice, a hint of <u>anxiety</u> behind his smile, but she was too excited to notice.

"I've got the job! I've got the job!" she cried, running into the kitchen at home. "I'm to start on Monday. I'm to be paid on Friday."

Her mother turned to stare at her.

"You never! Fancy that, now! Who'd have thought it!" she said in astonishment.

Lucy was not offended by her mother's surprise. She shared it. They never trusted

---

1. **O level.** Indicates credit for passing one level of training in British school

---

ANSWERS TO GUIDED READING QUESTIONS

1. She is a young, small, mouse-colored girl who has just graduated from secretarial college. More than anything, she wants a job because she is tired of being poor.
2. Hundreds of people apply for every job vacancy, and they are all brighter and more qualified than Lucy.

LITERARY TECHNIQUE

FORESHADOWING. Foreshadowing is the act of hinting at events that will happen later in a poem, story, or play. Share this definition with students and ask them to find hints on this page that all will not be right at Lucy's new job.
Answers. Students may point to the company being so eager to hire Lucy despite her lack of qualification in comparison with others, the hint of anxiety in Mr. Ross's smile, and the doubt in his voice.

luck, but looked at it suspiciously, as if at a stranger coming late to their door.

Ross and Bannister's was a small firm, with a factory just outside the town, making cushions and quilts; and an office on High Street. On Monday morning, at ten to nine, the door to this office was shut and locked.

She was early. She smoothed down her windy hair and waited.

At five past nine an elderly man, with small dark eyes like currants,[2] and a thick icing of white hair, came hobbling up the stairs. He was jingling a bunch of keys.

"Ah," he said, noticing Lucy. "Punctuality is the courtesy of kings—but a hard necessity for new brooms, eh? You *are* the new broom, I suppose? Not an impatient customer waiting to see our new range of sunburst cushions, by any chance?"

"I'm Lucy Beck," she said, adding proudly, "the new secretary."

"Let's hope you stay longer than the other ones," the man said, and unlocked the door. "Come in, come in, Miss Beck. Come into the parlor, said the spider to the fly. I'm Harry Darke, thirty years with Ross and Bannister's, retired with a silver watch, and now come back to haunt the place. Can't keep away, you see." Then he added oddly, half under his breath, "Like someone else I could mention, but won't."

He looked at Lucy, standing shy and awkward, clutching her bag and uncertain what to do. "Poor Miss Beck, you mustn't mind old Harry. Part-time messenger, office boy, tea-maker, mender of fuses. Anything you want, just ask old Harry. Mr. Ross is down at the factory in the morning, but he's left you plenty of work to be getting on with." He pointed to a pile of tapes on the desk. "Letters to be typed, those are. He got behindhand, with the last girl leaving so quick. Left the same day she came. Shot off like a <u>scalded</u> cat!"

"Why?" Lucy asked curiously.

"Hang your coat in the cupboard here," he said, ignoring her question. "Washroom along the passage to the right. Kitchenette to the left. We share it with Lurke and Dare, House Agents, and Mark Tower, Solicitor.[3] No gossiping over the teapots, mind. Most of the young things go to Tom's Cafe for lunch. Put this sign on the door when you leave." He handed her a cardboard notice on a looped string, on which was printed: GONE FOR LUNCH, BACK AT TWO. "Now, is there anything else you want to know before I take off?"

"You're going?" Lucy asked, surprised.

"Yes, my girl. I've errands to do. Not frightened of holding the fort on your own, are you?"

"No, but—"

"You can take a telephone message without getting the names muddled, can't you?"

"Yes, of course."

"Nothing else to it, is there? No need to look like a frightened mouse."

"I'm *not*!"

He looked at her for a long moment, with a strange expression on his face, almost as if he were sorry for her.

"You're very young," he said at last.

"I'm seventeen."

---

2. **currant.** Small seedless raisin
3. **Solicitor.** British lawyer

---

words for everyday use

scald (scäld') *v.*, burn with hot liquid. *Mildred's hot cocoa spilled and <u>scalded</u> her leg.* **scalded,** *adj.*

"Don't look it. Look as if you should be still at school. This your first job?"

"Yes."

He shook his head slowly, still regarding her with that odd pity.

"It's a shame," he said; then, seeing her puzzled face, added briskly, "Well, I'll be off, then. Mr. Ross will be in this afternoon."

Yet still he stood there, looking at her. Embarrassed, Lucy turned away and took the cover off the typewriter.

> **GUIDED READING**
> Why is Lucy embarrassed?

"Just one last thing," the old man said. "That's an electric typewriter."

"I'm used to electric typewriters," Lucy said coldly. She was beginning to be annoyed.

"Not this one. This one's . . . different. You mustn't worry," he said gently, "if it goes a little wrong now and again. Just ignore it. Don't bother to retype the letters. Splash on the old correcting fluid. Look, I got you a big bottle.

> **GUIDED READING**
> What does Harry tell her about the electric typewriter?

Liquid Paper, the things they invent! And if that runs out, cross out the mistakes with a black pen—see, I've put one in your tray. Nice and thick, it is. That should keep her quiet."

"I don't make mistakes," Lucy said; then honesty compelled her to add, "Well, not very many. I've been trained. I've got a diploma."

"Yes. Yes, my dear, so they all had," he said sadly, and left.

After the first moments of strangeness Lucy was glad to be alone. No one breathing down her neck. She looked round the office with pleasure. Hers.

Sunlight streamed through the window. The curtains shifted a little in the spring breeze. There was a small blue-and-green rug on the floor.

I'll have daffodils in a blue vase, Lucy thought. *I can afford flowers now. Or I will be able to, on Friday.*

CULTURAL/HISTORICAL NOTE

Inform students that what is known as the QWERTY keyboard is the one with which most people are familiar. It is named for the first six letters that appear in the top row of alphabetical characters. Another type of keyboard called the Dvorak is considered by some to be more efficient, but people are familiar with the QWERTY so it remains popular.

Better get on with the work. She sat down, switched on the typewriter, inserted paper and carbons,[4] and started the first tape.

"Take a letter to Messrs. Black and Hawkins, Twenty-eight Market Street, Cardington. Dear Sirs . . ." Mr. Ross's voice came clearly and slowly out of the tape deck. Lucy began to type.

She was a touch typist. She did not need to look at the keys. Her fingers kept up their slow, steady rhythm, while her eyes dreamed round the office, out of the window, down into the sunny street.

". . . our new line of sunburst cushions in yellow, orange, and pink," came Mr. Ross's voice.

There was something odd! A sudden wrongness felt by her fingers, a tingling, an icy pricking . . .

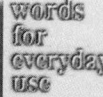

A sudden wrongness felt by her fingers, a tingling, an icy pricking...

She snatched her fingers away and stared at the typewriter. It hummed back at her innocently. What was wrong? There was something . . . Her glance fell on the incompleted letter.

> Dear Sirs,
> I am pleased to inform you that QWERTYUIOP and Bannister's have introduced a new QWERTYUIOP of sunburst cushions in QWERTYUIOP, orange and QWERTYUIOP . . .

She stared at it in horrified <u>bewilderment</u>. What had happened? What had she done?

GUIDED READING

What happens with the first letter Lucy types?

Not even on her first day at the Belmont Secretarial College had she made such ridiculous mistakes. Such strange mistakes—QWERTYUIOP, the top line of letters on a typewriter, repeated over and over again! Thank God there had been no one to notice. They'd think she had gone mad.

She must be more careful. Keep her mind on the job, not allow it to wander out of the window into the sunny shopping street below. Putting fresh paper into the typewriter, she began again.

She was tempted to look at the keyboard . . . "Don't look at the keys! Keep your eyes away!" Mrs. Price was always saying. "No peeping. You'll never make a good typist if you can't do it by touch. Rhythm, it's all rhythm. Play it to music in your head."

So Lucy obediently looked away, and typed to a slow tune in her head, dum diddle dum dee, dum diddle dum dee . . . Why did her fingers feel funny? Why were goose pimples shivering her flesh? Was the typewriter really humming *in tune*?

She sat back, clasping her hands together, and stared at the letter in the machine. It read:

---

4. **carbons.** Papers with colored coating that when placed between two sheets of paper cause pressure from writing to transfer to the bottom sheet

---

words for everyday use

be • wil • der • ment (bi wil' dər mənt) *n.*, state of being confused. *I overslept and woke up in a state of <u>bewilderment</u> over the time shown on the clock.*

Dear Sirs,

YOU ARE SITTING IN MY CHAIR to inform you that GO AWAY a new line of WE DO NOT WANT YOU HERE cushions in yellow, SILLY GIRL and pink. QWERTYUIOP.

She could not believe her eyes. She stared at the extraordinary words and trembled.

"Let's hope you stay longer than the other ones," the old man had said.

Tears came into Lucy's eyes. She tore the sheets out of the typewriter and threw them into the wastepaper basket. Then she put in fresh paper and began again. Grimly, in defiance of⁵ Mrs. Price's teaching, she kept her eyes fixed on the keyboard.

Dear Sirs,

We are pleased to inform you that Ross and Bannister's have introduced a new line of Sunburst cushions . . .

With a rattle the typewriter took over. She felt the keys hitting her fingers from below, leaping up and down like mad children at playtime. She took her hands away and watched.

GUIDED READING

What happens when Lucy takes her hands away from the typewriter?

. . . YOU CAN'T KEEP ME OUT THAT WAY, the typewriter printed. YOU'LL NEVER BE RID OF ME. NEVER. WHY DON'T YOU GO. NO ONE WANTS YOU HERE. NO ONE LIKES YOU. GO AWAY BEFORE

Then it stopped, its threat uncompleted.

Lucy leapt up, overturning her chair, and ran to the door.

"Left the same day she came," the old man had said. "Shot off like a scalded cat!"

"No!" Lucy shouted.

She left the door and went over to the window, looking down at the bright shops. She thought of jumble sales and baked beans.

She thought of pretty new clothes and rump steaks. She might be young and shy and a little slow, but she was not, no, she was *not* a coward!

She went back and sat down in front of the typewriter and glared at it. There it crouched, like a squat, ugly monster, staring at her with its alphabetical eyes.

Lucy typed quickly:

Are you from outer space?

The typewriter rocked, as if with laughter, its keys clicking like badly fitting false teeth.

IDIOT, it wrote.

Who are you? Lucy typed.

MISS BROOME, it answered.

GUIDED READING

Who is Lucy communicating with?

Lucy hesitated. She did not know quite how to reply to this. In the end she typed:

How do you do? I am Miss Beck.

GO AWAY, MISS BECK

Why should I?

I AM SECRETARY HERE, it stated, this time in red letters.

No, you're not! *I* am! Lucy typed angrily.

The machine went mad.

QWERTYUIOP!" / @QWERTYUIOP£—&()*QWERTYUIOP+! it screamed, shaking and snapping its keys like castanets.

Lucy switched it off. She sat for a long time, staring in front of her, her face stubborn. Then she took the cap off the bottle of correcting fluid.

For an hour she battled with the machine. As fast as QWERTYUIOPs and unwanted capitals appeared, she attacked with a loaded brush. The white fluid ran down the typing paper like melting ice cream and dripped thickly into the depths of the typewriter.

---

5. **in defiance of.** Contrary to; despite

ANSWERS TO GUIDED READING QUESTIONS

1. It keeps on typing, printing "You can't keep me out that way. You'll never be rid of me. Never. Why don't you go. No one wants you here. No one likes you."

2. She and the typewriter seem to be having a "conversation" as they type questions and responses back and forth. The typewriter says it is Miss Broome, the company secretary.

ADDITIONAL QUESTIONS AND ACTIVITIES

Ask students to discuss why Lucy shouts "No!" What does this reveal about her character?
Answers. She shouts "no" because while she might be young and shy and a little slow, she was definitely *not* a coward. Some readers may also infer that she's responding to Harry's insinuations that she, like the other secretaries before her, will soon quit her job.

YOU'RE DROWNING ME, it
complained <u>pathetically</u>, and she swiped at
the words with her brush.

HELP!

Another swipe.

PLEASE!

But Lucy showed no mercy. The large
bottle was half empty when she reached the
end of the letter in triumph.

        Yours faithfully,
        George Ross, she typed,
and sat back with a sigh of relief.

The machine began to rattle. Too late,
Lucy snatched the completed letter out of the
typewriter. Across the bottom of the
otherwise faultless page it now said in
large, red capitals:

I HATE YOU!

Furiously she painted the words out.

Mr. Ross came to the
office at four o'clock.
His eyes went to the
corner of the desk
where Lucy had put the completed
letters. If he was surprised to find so
modest a number after a day's work, he
did not say so, but picked them up.

"Any telephone messages?" he asked.

"On your desk, sir," Lucy said, and went
to make him tea.

When she brought it in on a flowered
metal tray, she found Mr. Ross signing the
last letter, his pen skidding awkwardly over
the thick shiny layer of plastic paper. All
the letters were heavily damasked[6] with the
dried fluid, like starched table napkins. He
glanced up at her a little unhappily.

"Did you have trouble with the
machine, Miss Beck?" he asked.

"Yes, sir." (She was afraid to say what
trouble in case he thought she was mad.)

"It's only just come back from being
serviced," he said wearily.

"I'm sorry, sir. It keeps . . . going wrong."

There was a long silence. Then he said with
a sigh, "I see. Well, do what you can. If it's no
better at the end of the week . . ."

He let the sentence hang in the air, so that
she was not certain whether it would be the
typewriter or Lucy Beck who would get the
chop.

---

6. **damasked.** Thickened like a type of fabric

---

words for everyday use

pa • thet • ic (pə thet′ ik) *adj.*, causing pity. *Sonia's pathetic Easter basket contained one measly egg.* **pathetically,** *adv.*

The next morning, Harry Darke raised his eyebrows when he saw Lucy.

GUIDED READING
How does Harry Darke react when he sees Lucy the next morning?

"Still here?" he exclaimed. "Well done, my dear. I never thought I'd be seeing you again. You're braver than you look. Fighting back, eh?"

"Yes," said Lucy briefly. She walked past him and went up to the desk. *Her* desk. Then she took out of her carrier bag a small bunch of daffodils and a blue vase.

"Staking your claim, I see," the old man said, regarding her with admiration. "D'you want me to fill that for you?"

"Thanks."

He came back, carrying a tray.

"Thought I might as well make us tea while I was about it," he said. "Here's your vase."

"Thanks."

"I'll be here till one o'clock today," he said, as she arranged her flowers. "Anything you want to know? Any snags come up I can help you with? Light bulbs changed. Fuses mended. New bottles of correcting fluid handed out . . ."

"Mr. Darke," Lucy said, looking straight into his small, bright eyes, "who is Miss Broome?"

"Wrong question, Miss Beck."

Lucy thought for a moment, then said, "Who *was* Miss Broome?"

He beamed at her approvingly: "You catch on quick, I'll say that for you. In fact, you're not the timid mouse you look, Miss Beck. You're a right little lion. Need to be, if you're going to take on Miss Broome. Tough old devil, she was."

"Tell me about her," Lucy said, as they sat over their tea.

"She was old Mr. Bannister's secretary. Been here forty-three years, girl, woman, and old misery. Sitting there where you're sitting now, her back straight as a ruler, and a chop-your-head-off ruler too! Her stiff old fingers tapping out the letters one by one, with her nose nearly on the keyboard, so shortsighted she'd become by then. None of your touch typing for her! Every letter she stared in the face like it was a criminal and she the judge. You can't wonder she hates you young girls, with your fingers flying over the keys like white butterflies, and your eyes gazing out into the sunshine. They gave her the push, you know."

GUIDED READING
Who was Miss Broome? What happened to her?

"After forty-three years?" Lucy said, shocked into sympathy.

"Well, she was past it, wasn't she? Of course they wrapped it up in tissue paper. Gave her a brass clock and shook her hand and waved her good-bye. She didn't want to go. Didn't have anywhere worth going to—a studio apartment, a gas ring[7] . . . The old bag didn't have any family who'd own her. This place was her home, this job was all she lived for."

Lucy was silent. Her mother had turned Uncle Bert out once, after a row, shouting that she'd had enough of him. Six weeks later, she had asked him to come back. "He looked so lonely, so lost," she had told Lucy. "All by himself in that horrid little room, with the worn linoleum and the curtains all shrunk."

"Sorry for her, are you?" Harry Darke asked, watching her face.

Lucy hardened her heart.

"It's *my* job now," she said. "I need it. She can't have it forever, it's not fair. It's my turn now."

"So it's a fight to the finish, is it, Miss Beck?" he asked, smiling.

"Yes," she said, and unscrewed the cap from the bottle of correcting fluids.

Her mother was working late that night. Lucy, going into the kitchen to get her own supper, was surprised to find the table neatly laid out with ham and salad, apple pie, and a

---

7. **gas ring.** Ring-shaped portable gas burner for cooking

1. He's surprised to see her and says she's braver than she looks.
2. She was Mr. Bannister's secretary. After forty-three years of working for him, she was let go.

ADDITIONAL QUESTIONS AND ACTIVITIES

Encourage students to discuss Miss Broome's situation and their reaction to it. Do they think it was right to make Miss Broome leave after forty-three years? How might she have felt? What does this say about the company's loyalty to employees?

1. She's surprised because she finds that Uncle Bert has neatly laid out the table with dinner and is waiting for her, beaming proudly.
2. He's trying to tell her that she shouldn't judge him because she doesn't know what it's like to not be wanted. She should try being kind instead.
3. Mr. Bannister passed on three years ago and is buried in the cemetery. Miss Broome is also buried there, not far from his grave.

SELECTION CHECK TEST 4.5.5 WITH ANSWERS

Checking Your Reading

1. Why does Lucy Beck want a job so badly? **Lucy Beck wants a job because she is poor.**
2. Why is Lucy afraid no one would hire her? **Lucy was afraid no one would hire her because she was shy and mousy, did not have a really good education, and typed slowly.**
3. What is a touch typist? **A touch typist types by feel, without looking at the keys of the typewriter.**
4. Who was Miss Broome? **Miss Broome had been Mr. Bannister's longtime secretary.**
5. How does Lucy win the battle with Miss Broome? **Lucy wins the battle with Miss Broome by convincing her that Mr. Bannister needs her in heaven.**

Vocabulary in Context

Fill in each blank below with the most appropriate word from the following *Words for Everyday Use* from "Qwertyuiop." You may have to change the tense of the word.

> defiance   pathetically   nuisance
> evaporate   anxiety   scalded
> punctuality

1. Following the unusual sound, Raida found the puppy huddled _____ in the pouring rain.
2. Ms. Reeves believed in _____, and assigned detention to every student who arrived after the tardy bell.
3. Ralph yelped as the stew sloshed out of the pot and _____ his hand.
4. Her junior prom had been a disaster, so thoughts of attending her senior prom filled Terry with _____.
5. Tristan planned a summer barbecue for his birthday, but the mosquitoes were a _____ for his guests.

---

jug of canned milk. Uncle Bert was sitting waiting for her, beaming proudly.

"Thought I'd have your supper ready," he explained, "now that you're a working girl."

"Thanks," she said, but couldn't resist adding nastily, "I don't get paid till Friday, you know. No good trying to borrow money."

He flushed. "You don't think much of me, do you? Who are you to set yourself up as judge and jury? You don't know what it's like . . . not being wanted. A little kindness would help!"

Lucy noticed his hands were shaking. His collapsing face seemed held together in a scarlet net of broken veins. His eyes were miserable.

"Uncle Bert . . . ," she began.

"What?" He looked at her <u>warily</u>.

"I'm sorry. I'm sorry, Uncle Bert."

"I'm sorry, too, Lucy," he said. "I know it's a <u>nuisance</u>, having me here."

"No! No, it isn't! We want you," she said.

They smiled at each other timidly over the kitchen table, each remembering the little girl and the handsome uncle, who had once flown kites together in Waterlow Park.

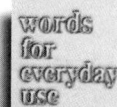
GUIDED READING
What do Uncle Bert and Lucy remember?

Wednesday was Harry Darke's day off. Alone in the office Lucy put a sheet of paper in the typewriter, and typed quickly:

QWERTYUIOP QWERTYUIOP QWERTYUIOP.

The typewriter gave a jerk, as if surprised, and hummed.

Lucy typed:

Dear Miss Broome,
   Mr. Darke told me you used to be secretary to Mr. Bannister—

I AM, interrupted the typewriter.

Lucy went on,

I am sorry to have to tell you that Mr. Bannister [she hesitated, wondering how to put it] . . . passed on three years ago, at the age of eighty-six—

LIAR! I DON'T BELIEVE YOU!

It is true, Miss Broome. I have seen his grave in the cemetery. It is not far from yours. I went along last night and left you flowers—

!!!!!

I did. Mr. Darke is worried about Mr. Bannister. He does not know how he will manage without you—

HE CAN MANAGE WITHOUT ME ALL RIGHT! said the typewriter bitterly, HE TOLD ME TO GO. BRASS CLOCK, WHAT DID I WANT WITH BRASS CLOCKS! I WANTED MY JOB.

They only asked you to go because they were worried about your health. [Lucy typed quickly.] Mr. Darke told me Mr. Bannister was always saying how much he missed you—

? ? ?

Truly. He said Mr. Bannister complained none of the new girls were any good. There was no one like you, he said . . .

The typewriter was silent. Sunlight glittered on its keys, so that they looked wet.

. . . He must miss you. He's probably in an awful muddle up there, mislaying his wings. Losing his harp. He needs someone to look after him . . .

GUIDED READING
Where is Mr. Bannister? Where is Miss Broome?

---

words for everyday use

war • i • ly (war′ ə lē) *adv.*, cautiously. *Warily, she approached the injured animal.*

nui • sance (nü′ sənts) *n.*, something that is annoying or unpleasant. *The customer became a <u>nuisance</u> when he spilled his second glass of water.*

SELECTION CHECK TEST 4.5.5 WITH ANSWERS (CONT.)

Reader's Toolbox
SENTENCE COMPLETION
Fill in the blanks using the following terms. You may use some terms more than once.

> expressive   persuasive   literary   informative

1. Examples of _____ writing include diaries and personal letters. **expressive**
2. Writing that seeks to influence others is _____ writing. **persuasive**
3. If a writer wishes to share facts with others, then his or her aim is to be _____. **informational**
4. Campaign speeches and advertisements are examples of _____ writing. **persuasive**
5. Newspaper articles and accident reports are examples of _____ writing. **informational**

The machine was silent. Lucy waited, but it said nothing more.

So she typed:

GUIDED READING

What is Miss Broome's new job?

Good-bye, Miss Broome. Best of luck in your new job.
Yours sincerely,
Lucy Beck, Secretary

She folded the finished letter into a paper dart and sent it sailing out of the window. The wind caught it and carried it away.

Mr. Ross is delighted now with his new secretary. Harry Darke says she's champion, and gives her chocolate biscuits with her tea.

"However did you do it?" he asked. ■

Respond *to the* SELECTION

If you were Miss Broome, would you have gone back to working for Mr. Bannister? Why, or why not?

About *the* AUTHOR

Vivien Alcock is a commercial artist as well as an award-winning author. She has written many books for young people, including *Stranger at the Window* (1998), *A Kind of Thief* (1992), *The Sylvia Game* (1984), and *The Trial of Anna Cotman* (1990). Many of her books are thrilling mysteries. In *A Kind of Thief*, thirteen-year-old Elinor's father is suddenly arrested and put into prison, and she finds that she must face the truth about him and their way of life. In *The Sylvia Game*, twelve-year-old Emily's artist father takes her on a vacation to the seaside, where she makes friends with a gypsy's son and the young heir to a stately home, who are struck by her resemblance to mysterious, long-dead Sylvia, a girl in a painting by Renoir. The story "QWERTYUIOP" is from a collection of stories about the supernatural, entitled *Ghostly Companions: A Feast of Chilling Tales.* Alcock's writing has been so popular in part because of her spooky and suspenseful plots, but also because her characters are so realistic. As one critic said, "Her characters aren't virtue-mongers spouting classic platitudes, but real teens facing real-life issues and learning from their mistakes and misjudgments."

Vivien was married to another award-winning writer, Leon Garfield (1921–1996). They raised their family in London, where she lives and writes today.

ANSWER TO GUIDED READING QUESTION

1. Her new job is to look after Mr. Bannister up in heaven, helping him keep track of where his wings and his harp are.

RESPOND TO THE SELECTION

As an alternate activity have students discuss what they would do and feel if they were in Miss Broome's situation.

"QWERTYUIOP" **367**

RECALL

1a. Lucy is young and small and mousy, easily overlooked. Mrs. Price has no answer to Lucy's question about who will want to employ her.

2a. They are both surprised, and maybe a little suspicious, too, because they never trusted luck.

3a. She is shocked into sympathy for Miss Broome, and she remembers the time her mother had kicked out Uncle Bert.

INTERPRET

1b. Poverty seems to have had a strong influence on Lucy's character. On the one hand she seems to have low self-esteem and isn't sure how to break the cycle of secondhand clothes and meals of macaroni and cheese and baked beans. Someone with low self-esteem can look mousy and is afraid to assert themselves, and so they are easily overlooked by others. Other people, such as Mrs. Price and Lucy's mother, don't really expect Lucy to get a job, and Lucy herself doesn't quite know how she will ever get a job, either. On the other hand, however, poverty has made Lucy quite determined to overcome her circumstances. She's tired of being poor, and once she gets a lucky break and lands a job, she is determined not to lose that job, no matter what.

2b. For them, luck probably seems to be too little too late when it does come. They are used to Uncle Bert spending any extra money they might accumulate for himself, so luck can never get them any further along the path out of poverty.

3b. She thinks of Uncle Bert because he, too, was kicked out. Both characters are unwanted. Bert, however, is alcoholic, while there is no evidence that Miss Broome is. Another difference is that Miss Broome was employed, while evidence suggests that Bert has no job since Lucy doesn't expect him to be able to pay for things himself. Seeing the similarities between them helps Lucy to feel more sympathetic toward both of them. She seems better able to think of their feelings and the effect she can have on their feelings.

ANALYZE

4a. At first he annoys her with his constant prattle and assumptions about her mousiness. But he also rouses her curiosity with his mysterious comments about previous secretaries not lasting long and challenges readers to predict

Investigate, Inquire, and Imagine

Recall: GATHERING FACTS

1a. What does Lucy look like? What does Mrs. Price say when Lucy asks who will want to employ her?

2a. How do Lucy and her mother react when she gets the job?

3a. How does Lucy react when she learns that Miss Broome was pushed out of her job after forty-three years? Who else does Lucy think of?

→ **Interpret:** FINDING MEANING

1b. How has being poor affected Lucy? What impact has it had on her appearance? on her expectations for herself? on others' expectations for her (for example, the expectations of Mrs. Price and Lucy's mother)?

2b. Why do you think Lucy and her mother react this way? Why would they be suspicious of luck?

3b. Why does she think of this person? What similarities and differences do you see between Miss Broome and that person? How does Lucy's view of each of these characters change when she recognizes their similarities?

Analyze: TAKING THINGS APART

4a. Analyze the role of Harry Darke. Examine what he says and how he responds to Lucy on her first day of work, when she returns the next day, and at the end of the story. How do Darke's comments at these three points in the story influence Lucy?

→ **Synthesize:** BRINGING THINGS TOGETHER

4b. How does he help or hinder her in resolving her problem? Explain your answer.

Evaluate: MAKING JUDGMENTS

5a. What does Lucy learn from Uncle Bert in the story? How does she apply this to her situation with Miss Broome? How effective is Lucy's response to Miss Broome's behavior? What outcomes might other responses have resulted in?

→ **Extend:** CONNECTING IDEAS

5b. Think of a situation in your own life in which someone annoyed you. What was the person doing that you didn't like? Why do you think he or she was acting that way? How did you respond to the situation? In what other ways could you have responded?

368   UNIT FIVE / CHILLS AND THRILLS

ANSWERS TO INVESTIGATE, INQUIRE, AND IMAGINE (CONT.)

what will happen. He annoys her enough to make her all the more determined to do a good job. On her second day, he is clearly surprised and impressed that she is still there. She still seems annoyed by his manner and determined to stake her claim. But he is helpful and informative when she presses him to tell her about Miss Broome, and he gives her high marks for

catching on to Miss Broome so quickly. At each point, he seems to give her enough approval to feed her determination to overcome her struggle with Miss Broome. By the end of the story, he is so impressed that she got rid of the ghost that he treats her like a queen, serving her chocolate biscuits with her tea. Most students will say he helps

(Continued on page 369)

Understanding *Literature*

MOTIVATION. A **motivation** is a force that moves a character to think, feel, or behave in a certain way. What motivates Lucy to react to her problem the way she does? What makes her different from earlier girls who had tried this job? How do her motivations help her become successful?

AIM. A writer's **aim** is his or her purpose, or goal. Look at the graphic organizer you made about the aims used in "QWERTYUIOP." How many different aims did you find? Who used each of the aims you found? Did you list any of the writing examples under more than one aim? If so, which ones, and why?

Writer's Journal

1. Imagine you were also hired to work at Ross and Bannister's, but as a product designer. Make a **product list** for your new spring line of cushions and quilts, emphasizing the line's new colors, styles, patterns, and designs. Be specific in your descriptions.

2. Imagine that Ross and Bannister's planned to completely modernize its modes of operation. Write a **proposal** for the company, offering recommendations for ways to work in a more up-to-date fashion.

3. Write a **greeting card message** that would be appropriate for a person who just accepted his or her first job.

Skill Builders

Applied English

JOB APPLICATIONS. Imagine you are preparing to find your first job. Select a type of work available to young people. You may want to choose from one of the following jobs: office worker, fast-food clerk, lawn-care assistant, house painter, daycare helper. Visit some local businesses to ask a manager for a job application form (you may want to tell him or her that you are doing some preliminary job research). Fill out the job application, wording your responses to fit the job. For more information, see the Language Arts Survey 6.1, "Filling Out Forms."

Collaborative Learning

ACTING. In a group, assign roles and act out the last three scenes of the story (the conversation between Lucy and Harry Darke on her second day at work; the conversation between Lucy and Uncle Bert that evening; the written conversation between Lucy and Miss Broome the next day). Act the scenes out a second time, this time switching roles so that a different person is playing each part. Afterward, discuss the similarities and differences in the way each role was interpreted by the actors.

ANSWERS TO UNDERSTANDING LITERATURE

INCITING INCIDENT. The first letter Lucy tries to type sets off her struggle with Miss Broome, as the ghost of Miss Broome tries to take over the typewriter.

AIM. Students may say that letters Lucy types are informative, with perhaps a hint of persuasiveness (to get people interested in the company's products, while the words Miss Broome interjects into the letters are expressive of her anger and are later informative about who she is and was.

ANSWERS TO SKILL BUILDERS

Applied English
JOB APPLICATION. It may be best if you ask for a job application from a local employer and photocopy it for your classes so that they are all working with the same application.

Collaborative Learning
ACTING. Tell students that they just have to capture the main events and the spirit of the scene. They do not have to memorize lines and can improvise lines if they wish.

ANSWERS TO INVESTIGATE, INQUIRE, AND IMAGINE (CONT.)

her resolve her problem by gradually revealing to her more information about the situation.

SYNTHESIZE
4b. Most students will say he helps her resolve her problem by gradually revealing to her more information about the situation.

EVALUATE
5a. She learns how it feels to be unwanted from Uncle Bert. She applies this by realizing that Miss Broome felt unwanted too. Students may say her behavior was very effective because she got rid of the ghost. *Responses will vary.*

EXTEND
5b. *Responses will vary.*

READER'S JOURNAL

You might encourage students to think about whether people are necessarily lonely when they are alone. Ask students the following questions: At what times in your life have you wanted to be alone? Why did you wish to be alone? Is it possible to be lonely in a crowd? Why might the feeling of loneliness be more painful than the feeling of being alone? When you are lonely, what can you do about your situation?

SHORT STORY

Reader's Journal

What thoughts, ideas, or images make you feel lonely?

Reader's TOOLBOX

STYLE. Style is the manner in which something is said or written. A writer's style depends on many things, including *diction*, or the words the writer chooses, and the way he or she structures sentences. Look for evidence in "The Foghorn" that would help determine the writer's style. What kinds of word choices does Bradbury make? Does the author vary the structure of sentences? How do the writer's choices create a particular style?

MOOD. Mood, or *atmosphere*, is the emotion created in the reader by a piece of writing. A writer creates mood by using concrete details. As you read the story, make a list of the moods you experience as a reader.

Prereading

"THE FOGHORN"

by Ray Bradbury

Reader's Resource

• **SCIENCE CONNECTION.** For thousands of years, eyewitnesses have described a number of unexplainable creatures in various lakes, rivers, and seas around the world. Many of these creatures have become legendary, escaping proof of existence while some people faithfully believe they exist. Those who believe they exist point out that much of the world's underwater territory has never been explored. The oceans are simply too vast to explore completely; lakes where sightings have occurred are typically large, cold, and very deep. In fact, even in modern times new species—or species thought to have become extinct thousands of years ago—have been discovered in remote areas. For example, the coelacanth, a prehistoric fishlike creature that was believed to be extinct for 70 million years, was discovered in 1938 near South Africa. Scientists found the first known giant squid in 1997.

• **HISTORY CONNECTION.** Lighthouses date back to ancient Egypt, where beacon fires were kept lit to guide ships into the Nile River. In 1716, the first U. S. lighthouse was built. Early

lighthouses used candles, fires, oil lamps, and later, gas, to create light. In the 1800s, electricity was first used for light and fog horns, bells, and whistles were introduced. Increased use of radio beams and radar in the 1900s has discontinued the need for conventional lighthouses, in which attendants monitor the lights and horns.

GOALS/OBJECTIVES

Studying this lesson will enable students to
• appreciate a short story that create a definite mood
• explain some of the arguments for and against the existence of the Loch Ness Monster

• define *style* and describe the style in which a work of literature is written
• define *mood* and identify the mood of a literary work
• research underwater creatures

Fog Horns, 1929. Arthur Dove. Colorado Springs Fine Arts Center, Colorado.

THE FOGHORN

Ray Bradbury

INDIVIDUAL LEARNING STRATEGIES

MOTIVATION

Students might enjoy drawing, painting, or making models of the Loch Ness Monster. Encourage students to use the details provided in the Insights feature as well as their own imaginations.

READING PROFICIENCY
Students might find it beneficial to hear the story read aloud as they will better understand the suspenseful action and the mood for them if it is read expressively.

ENGLISH LANGUAGE LEARNING
Point out the following vocabulary words and expressions:
beard of a comet—long tail of melting dust and gas that trails off the main body of a large frozen body that revolves around the sun
duffel—large, cylindrical waterproof bag
brooding—pondering in a troubled way
lament—expression of deep sorrow or grief
reek—stench or smell

SPECIAL NEEDS
Have students work together in small groups to create outlines of the action of the story. This will help students to answer the Guided reading questions and the Investigate, Inquire, and Imagine questions.

ENRICHMENT

Some students might wish to debate the possibility of the continued existence of dinosaur-like creatures. As a class, you might create a large pro and con chart on the board, listing reasons for and against the likelihood of such a creature's existence.

VOCABULARY FROM THE SELECTION

anguished	lament
apparatus	primeval
apparition	projection
ascend	ravel
brood	thresh
concussion	verify
daft	

1. The ocean is full of "a thousand
   shapes and colors, no two alike,"
   just as each snowflake is unique.

LITERARY TECHNIQUE

SIMILE AND METAPHOR. A simile is a comparison using *like* or *as*. A metaphor is a figure of speech in which one thing is spoken or written about as if it were another. Encourage students to identify similes and metaphors on this page. *Answers.* similes: startle the gulls away like decks of scattered cards; all the fish of the seas surface . . . like a big peacock's tail
metaphor: long gray lawn of the sea

ut there in the cold water, far from land, we waited every night for the coming of the fog, and it came, and we oiled the brass machinery and lit the fog light up in the stone tower. Feeling like two birds in the gray sky, McDunn and I sent the light touching out, red, then white, then red again, to eye the lonely ships. If they did not see our light, then there was always our Voice, the great deep cry of our Fog Horn. It shuddered through the rags of mist to startle the gulls away like decks of scattered cards and make the waves turn high and foam.

"It's a lonely life, but you're used to it now, aren't you?" asked McDunn.

"Yes," I said. "You're a good talker, thank the Lord."

"Well, it's your turn on land tomorrow," he said, smiling, "to dance with the ladies."

"What do you think, McDunn, when I leave you out here alone?"

"On the mysteries of the sea." McDunn lit his pipe. It was a quarter past seven on a cold November evening, the heat on, the light switching its tail in two hundred directions, the Fog Horn bumbling in the high throat of the tower. There wasn't a town for a hundred miles down the coast, just a road, which came lonely through dead country to the sea, with few cars on it. Two miles of cold water separated our rock, and rare few ships passed.

"The mysteries of the sea," said McDunn thoughtfully. "You know, the ocean's the biggest snowflake ever? It rolls and swells a thousand shapes and colors, no two alike. Strange. One night, years ago, I was here alone, when all of the fish of the sea surfaced out there. Something made them swim in and lie in

> **GUIDED READING**
>
> What strange event did McDunn witness years ago?

the bay, sort of trembling. They stared up at the tower light going red, white, red, white across them so I could see their funny eyes. I turned cold. They were like a big peacock's tail, moving out there until midnight. Then, without so much as a sound, they slipped away. The million of them was gone. I kind of think maybe, in some sort of way, they came all those miles to worship. Strange. But think how the tower must look to them, standing seventy feet above the water, the God-light flashing out from it, and the tower declaring itself with a monster voice. They never came back, those fish, but don't you think for a little while they thought they were in God's presence?"

I shivered. I looked out at the long gray lawn of the sea stretching away into nothing and nowhere.

"Oh, the sea's full." McDunn puffed his pipe nervously, blinking. He had been nervous all day and hadn't said why. "For all our engines and so-called submarines, it'll be ten thousand centuries before we set foot on the real bottom of the sunken lands, in the fairy kingdoms there, and know real terror. Think of it. It's still the year 300,000 Before Christ down under there. While we've paraded around with trumpets, lopping off each other's countries and heads, they have been living beneath the sea twelve miles deep and cold in a time as old as the beard of a comet."

"Yes, it's an old world."

"Come on. I got something special I been saving up to tell you."

We <u>ascended</u> the eighty steps, talking and taking our time. At the top, McDunn switched off the room lights so there'd be no reflection in the plate glass. The great eye of

words for everyday use

as • cend (ə send') *v.*, climb upward. *We watched the airplane <u>ascend</u> into the clouds.*

the light was humming, turning easily in its oiled socket. The Fog Horn was blowing steadily, once every fifteen seconds.

"Sounds like an animal, don't it?" McDunn nodded to himself. "A big lonely animal crying in the night. Sitting here on the edge of ten billion years calling out to the Deeps, 'I'm here, I'm here, I'm here.' And the Deeps do answer, yes, they do. You been here now for three months, Johnny, so I better prepare you. About this time of year," he said, studying the murk and fog, "something comes to visit the lighthouse."

"The swarms of fish like you said?"

"No, this is something else. I've put off telling you because you might think I'm daft. But tonight's the latest I can put it off, for if my calendar's marked right from last year, tonight's the night it comes. I won't go into detail; you'll have to see it yourself. Just sit down there. If you want, tomorrow you can pack your duffel and take the motorboat into land and get your car parked there at the dinghy pier[1] on the cape. You can drive on back to some little inland town and keep your lights burning nights. I won't question or blame you. It's happened three years now, and this is the only time anyone's been here with me to verify it. You wait and watch."

"You know, the ocean's the biggest snowflake ever?"

GUIDED READING
Like what does the foghorn sound?

GUIDED READING
Why has McDunn not told his secret before now?

Half an hour passed with only a few whispers between us. When we grew tired waiting, McDunn began describing some of his ideas to me. He had some theories about the Fog Horn itself.

"One day many years ago a man walked along and stood in the sound of the ocean on a cold sunless shore and said, 'We need a voice to call across the water, to warn ships; I'll make one. I'll make a voice like all of time and all of the fog that ever was. I'll make a voice that is like an empty bed beside you all night long, and like an empty house when you open the door, and like trees in autumn with no leaves. A sound like the birds flying south, crying, and a sound like November wind and the sea on the hard, cold shore. I'll make a sound that's so alone that no one can miss it, that whoever hears it will weep in their souls. Hearths will seem warmer, and being inside will seem better to all who hear it in the distant towns. I'll make me a sound and an apparatus and they'll call it a Fog Horn. Whoever hears it will know the sadness of eternity and the briefness of life.'"

The Fog Horn blew.

"I made up that story," said McDunn quietly, "to try to explain why this thing keeps coming back to the lighthouse every year. The Fog Horn calls it, I think, and it comes. . . ."

GUIDED READING
To what things does McDunn compare the sound of the foghorn?

---

1. **dinghy pier.** Docking place for small boats

---

words for everyday use

daft (daft) *adj.*, insane; crazy. *Aunt Joan dons a clown suit and pretends to be* <u>daft</u>.

ver • i • fy (ver' ə fi') *v.*, test or check for correctness. *Before writing the article, the reporter was careful to* <u>verify</u> *all the facts.*

ap • pa • ra • tus (ap' ə rat' əs) *n.*, device or machine. *A seismograph is an* <u>apparatus</u> *used to record vibrations within the earth.*

"THE FOGHORN" **373**

ANSWERS TO GUIDED READING QUESTIONS

1. The foghorn sounds like a "big lonely animal crying in the night."
2. McDunn did not tell his secret for fear that the narrator would think he was insane.
3. McDunn compares the foghorn to an empty bed, an empty house, autumn trees with no leaves, the cries of birds flying south, and the sea against a hard, cold shore.

Quotables

"The sea is calm tonight.
The tide is full, the moon lies fair
Upon the straits—"

—Matthew Arnold

LITERARY TECHNIQUE

EXPOSITION, MOOD, AND SUSPENSE. The **exposition** is the part of a plot that introduces the setting and the major characters. **Mood,** or **atmosphere,** is the emotion created in the reader by a piece of writing. **Suspense** is a feeling of anxiousness or curiosity. Ask students the following questions: What does the reader learn about the setting in this story's exposition? What does the reader learn about the major characters introduced? What mood is created in the exposition? What details create a feeling of suspense? About what is the reader anxious or curious? *Answers.* The story is set in a lighthouse on a rocky island far from civilization. The major characters are the narrator, who is new to the lighthouse, and McDunn, who has worked at the lighthouse a long time and is a "great talker." The mood is one of loneliness, mystery, and suspense. The isolation, the repeated use of the word *mysteries,* and McDunn revealing that he has a secret all help create this feeling. The reader is curious to know McDunn's secret and what will happen in this remote place.

1. McDunn says the dinosaurs hid
   away in the "Deep."

LITERARY NOTE

SCIENCE FICTION AND FANTASY. **Science
fiction** is imaginative literature based
on scientific principles, discoveries,
or laws. A **fantasy** is a very
unrealistic or imaginative story.
Science fiction is similar to fantasy in
that both deal with imaginary worlds
but differs from fantasy in having a
scientific basis. Ask students the
following questions: What elements
of this story are realistic? What
elements are not realistic? Do you
think that this story is science fiction,
fantasy, or neither? Support your
answer, using examples from the
text.
Answers. Students may say that the
setting itself and the main characters
are realistic. The sea monster that
appears out of the fog is not realistic.
Responses will vary.

"But—" I said.

"Sssst!" said McDunn. "There!" He nodded
out to the Deeps.

Something was swimming toward the
lighthouse tower.

It was a cold night, as I have said. The high
tower was cold. The light was coming and
going, and the Fog Horn, calling and calling
through the raveling mist. You couldn't see
far and you couldn't see plain, but there was
the deep sea moving on its way about the
night earth, flat and quiet, the color
of gray mud. Here were the two
of us alone in the high tower.
There, far out at first, was a
ripple, followed by a wave,
a rising, a bubble, a bit of
froth. And then, from the
surface of the cold sea
came a head, a large
head, dark-colored, with
immense eyes, and then a
neck. And then—not a
body—but more neck and
more! The head rose a full forty feet
above the water on a slender
and beautiful dark neck. Only then did the
body, like a slender little island of black coral
and shells and crayfish, drip up from the
subterranean. There was a flicker of tail. In
all, from head to tip of tail, I estimated the
monster at ninety or a hundred feet.

I don't know what I said. It seems I said
something.

"Steady, boy," whispered McDunn.

"It's impossible!" I said.

"No, Johnny, we're impossible. It's like it
always was ten million years ago. It hasn't
changed. It's us and the land that've changed,
become impossible. Us!"

*"It's us and the
land that've
changed, become
impossible. Us!"*

It swam slowly and with a great dark
majesty out of the icy waters, far away. The
fog came and went about it, momentarily
erasing its shape. One of the monster eyes
caught and held and flashed back our
immense light, red, white, red, white, like a
disc held high and
sending a message in
primeval code. It was as
silent as the fog through
which it swam.

GUIDED READING

According to
McDunn, what
happened to the
dinosaurs?

"It's a dinosaur of some sort!" I
crouched down holding to the
stair rail.

"Yes, one of the tribe."

"But they died out!"

"No, only hid away in
the Deeps. Deep, deep
down in the deepest
Deeps. Isn't that a word
now, Johnny, a real
word, it says so much:
the Deeps. There's all the
coldness and darkness and
deepness in the world in a
word like that."

"What'll we do?"

"Do? We got our job, we can't leave.
Besides, we're safer here than in any boat
trying to get to land. That thing's as big as a
destroyer and almost as swift."

"But here, why does it come here?"

The next moment I had my answer.

The Fog Horn blew.

And the monster answered.

A cry came across a million years of water
and mist. A cry so anguished and alone that it
shuddered in my head and my body. The
monster cried out at the tower. The Fog
Horn blew. The monster roared again. The

words for everyday use	**ravel** (rav′ əl) v., separate; become thinner. *As the afternoon wore on, thick clouds raveled into streaks of white across a mild blue sky.* **raveling,** *adj.*
	pri • me • val (pri me′ vəl) *adj.,* from the earliest ages. *Remarkably, information about the primeval world often helps us better understand the modern world.*
	an • guished (aŋ′ gwisht) *adj.,* feeling great suffering or pain. *Leroy remained in an anguished state for days after his dog died.*

Fog Horn blew. The monster opened its great toothed mouth and the sound that came from it was the sound of the Fog Horn itself. Lonely and vast and far away. The sound of isolation, a viewless sea, a cold night, apartness. That was the sound.

"Now," whispered McDunn, "do you know why it comes here?"

GUIDED READING

Why does the creature come to this place?

I nodded.

"All year long, Johnny, that poor monster there lying far out, a thousand miles at sea, and twenty miles deep maybe, biding its time. Perhaps it's a million years old, this one creature. Think of it, waiting a million years. Could you wait that long? Maybe it's the last of its kind. I sort of think that's true. Anyway, here come men on land and build this lighthouse, five years ago. And set up their Fog Horn and sound it and sound it out toward the place where you bury yourself in sleep and sea memories of a world where there were thousands like yourself. But now you're alone, all

GUIDED READING

Who is McDunn referring to as "you"?

alone in a world not made for you, a world where you have to hide.

"But the sound of the Fog Horn comes and goes, comes and goes, and you stir from the muddy bottom of the Deeps. And your eyes open like the lenses of two-foot cameras and you move, slow, slow, for you have the ocean sea on your shoulders, heavy. But that Fog Horn comes through a thousand miles of water, faint and familiar. The furnace in your belly stokes up, and you begin to rise, slow, slow. You feed yourself on great slakes of cod and minnow, on rivers of jellyfish, and you rise slow through the autumn months, through September when the fogs started, through October with more fog and the horn still calling you on. And then, late in November, after pressurizing yourself day by day, a few feet higher every hour, you are near the surface

---

2. **saber-tooths.** Prehistoric tigers with large teeth

and still alive. You've got to go slow. If you surfaced all at once you'd explode. So it takes you all of three months to surface, and then a number of days to swim through the cold waters to the lighthouse. And there you are, out there, in the night, Johnny, the biggest monster in creation. And here's the lighthouse calling to you, with a long neck like your neck sticking way up out of the water, and a body like your body, and, most important of all, a voice like your voice. Do you understand now, Johnny, do you understand?"

The Fog Horn blew.

The monster answered.

I saw it all, I knew it all—the million years of waiting alone, for someone to come back who never came back. The million years of isolation at the bottom of the sea, the insanity of time there, while the skies cleared of reptile-birds. The swamps dried on the lands. The sloths and saber-tooths[2] had their day and sank in tar pits, and men ran like white ants upon the hill.

The Fog Horn blew.

"Last year," said McDunn, "that creature swam round and round, round and round, all

ANSWERS TO GUIDED READING QUESTIONS

1. The creature comes to this place because the foghorn sounds like one of its kind, calling to its fellow creatures.
2. He is referring to the strange sea creature as "you."

LITERARY TECHNIQUE

CHARACTERIZATION AND DIALOGUE. Characterization is the act of creating or describing a character. **Dialogue** is conversation involving two or more people or characters. Most of what the reader learns about the two main characters is revealed through their dialogue. What does the narrator's dialogue reveal about him? What does McDunn's dialogue reveal about him? In what way do you envision each character, based upon his dialogue?

Answers. The narrator is a young person who recently became a lighthouse keeper. He is a good listener who keeps an open mind. He is very sympathetic to the plight of the monster. McDunn is older and has been working at the lighthouse longer than the narrator. He is very thoughtful, imaginative, sensitive, and well-spoken. It seems that he himself is very familiar with loneliness, which is why he sympathizes with the monster. *Responses will vary.* Students may say that they envision the narrator as young and McDunn as older.

ANSWERS TO GUIDED READING QUESTIONS

1. Last year the creature swam round and round the lighthouse seeming puzzled, afraid, and angry. Then when the fog lifted it swam away.
2. McDunn says that after a while you want to destroy what you once loved so that it cannot hurt you anymore.

Quotables

"Loneliness is to endure the presence of one who does not understand."

—Elbert Hubbard

HISTORICAL NOTE

The first known lighthouse was the Pharos of Alexandria, in Egypt. Early lighthouses were illuminated by wood fires, candles, and oil lamps. For a time, whale oil was commonly used, a practice which led to the slaughter of many whales. In the nineteenth century, people developed special reflectors that could make the light of an oil lamp as bright as that of a modern car headlight. Because the light was concentrated to a narrow beam, the lamp needed to rotate to be seen easily by boats approaching from different directions. Early lighthouses used cannons and bells as warning signals during bad weather. Lighthouses are still known for their rotating beams of light, although in the twentieth century electric light replaced the oil lamps of the nineteenth century. Sirens and foghorns replaced cannons and bells as warning sounds. Today shipboard technology, including the use of radar and loran, has increased to the extent where lighthouses are not as crucial to navigation, although they are still important aids. Today most lighthouses are automated, so they no longer require resident lighthouse keepers.

night. Not coming too near, puzzled, I say. Afraid, maybe. And a bit angry after coming all this way.

> **GUIDED READING**
> What happened last year?

But the next day, unexpectedly, the fog lifted, the sun came out fresh, the sky was as blue as a painting. And the monster swam off away from the heat and the silence and didn't come back. I suppose it's been <u>brooding</u> for a year now, thinking it over from every which way."

The monster was only a hundred yards off now, it and the Fog Horn crying at each other. As the lights hit them, the monster's eyes were fire and ice, fire and ice.

"That's life for you," said McDunn. "Someone always waiting for someone who never comes home. Always someone loving some thing more than that thing loves them. And after a while you want to destroy whatever that thing is, so it can't hurt you no more."

> **GUIDED READING**
> According to McDunn, what happens when loneliness becomes too great?

The monster was rushing at the lighthouse. The Fog Horn blew.

"Let's see what happens," said McDunn.

He switched the Fog Horn off.

The ensuing minute of silence was so intense that we could hear our hearts pounding in the glassed area of the tower, could hear the slow greased turn of the light.

The monster stopped and froze. Its great lantern eyes blinked. Its mouth gaped. It gave a sort of rumble, like a volcano. It twitched its head this way and that, as if to seek the sound now dwindled off into the fog. It peered at the lighthouse. It rumbled again. Then its eyes caught fire. It reared up, <u>threshed</u> the water, and rushed at the tower, its eyes filled with angry torment.

> **words for everyday use**
> **brood** (brüd) v., to dwell on a gloomy subject, to worry. *Elaine tends to* <u>brood</u> *when something upsets her.*
> **thresh** (thresh) v., beat or strike. *Mee used a broom to* <u>thresh</u> *the dust from the rug.*

The Loch Ness Monster, c.1935. Gino D'Achille. Private Collection.

Quotables

"The fog comes on little cat feet."

—Carl Sandburg

"Unreal City, Under the brown fog of a winter dawn"

—T. S. Eliot

CROSS-CURRICULAR ACTIVITIES

SCIENCE. Fog can form over both land and sea. It severely limits visibility, often making transportation by boat, plane, or car very hazardous. Some students may be interested in researching how fog forms. Such students should research the different weather conditions which make fog likely. Good sources for research include encyclopedias and books about weather and meteorology. Students might then report their findings to the class.

ADDITIONAL QUESTIONS AND ACTIVITIES

To further explore this story, ask students the following questions: Why do McDunn and the narrator feel such sympathy for the monster? Do they identify with the monster in any way? Why, or why not? Do you agree with McDunn's statement about the way living creatures wish to destroy the things that they once loved? What does McDunn mean by the statement, "you can't love anything too much in this world"?

"McDunn!" I cried. "Switch on the horn!"

McDunn fumbled with the switch. But even as he flicked it on, the monster was rearing up. I had a glimpse of its gigantic paws, fishskin glittering in webs between the finger-like projections, clawing at the tower. The huge eye on the right side of its anguished head glittered before me like a cauldron into which I might drop, screaming. The tower shook. The Fog Horn cried, the monster cried. It seized the tower and gnashed at the glass, which shattered in upon us.

> **GUIDED READING**
> How does the creature react to the switching off of the foghorn?

McDunn seized my arm. "Downstairs!"

The tower rocked, trembled, and started to give. The Fog Horn and the monster roared. We stumbled and half fell down the stairs. "Quick!"

We reached the bottom as the tower buckled down toward us. We ducked under the stairs into the small stone cellar. There were a thousand concussions as the rocks rained down. The Fog Horn stopped abruptly. The monster crashed upon the tower. The tower fell. We knelt together, McDunn and I, holding tight, while our world exploded.

Then it was over, and there was nothing but darkness and the wash of the sea on the raw stones.

That and the other sound.

"Listen," said McDunn. "Listen."

We waited a moment. And then I began to hear it. First a great vacuumed sucking of air, and then the lament, the bewilderment, the loneliness of the great monster, folded over and over upon us, above us. The sickening reek of its body filled the air, a stone's thickness away from our cellar. The monster

gasped and cried. The tower was gone. The light was gone. The thing that had called to it across a million years was gone. And the monster was opening its mouth and sending out great sounds. The sounds of a Fog Horn, again and again. And ships far at sea, not finding the light, not seeing anything, but passing and hearing late that night, must've thought: There it is, the lonely sound, the Lonesome Bay horn. All's well. We've rounded the cape.

And so it went for the rest of that night.

The sun was hot and yellow the next afternoon when the rescuers came out to dig us from our stoned-under cellar.

"It fell apart, is all," said Mr. McDunn gravely. "We had a few bad knocks from the waves and it just crumbled." He pinched my arm.

> **GUIDED READING**
> What story does McDunn tell about the destruction of the tower?

There was nothing to see. The ocean was calm, the sky blue. The only thing was a great algaic[3] stink from the green matter that covered the fallen tower stones and the shore rocks. Flies buzzed about. The ocean washed empty on the shore.

The next year they built a new lighthouse, but by that time I had a job in the little town and a wife. I had a good small warm house that glowed yellow on autumn nights, the doors locked, the chimney puffed smoke. As for McDunn, he was master of the new lighthouse, built to his own specifications, out of steel-reinforced concrete. "Just in case," he said.

The new lighthouse was ready in November. I drove down alone one evening

---

3. **algaic.** Made up of algae, or simple water organisms

words for everyday use	**pro · jec · tion** (prō jek′ shən) *n.*, something that sticks out. *A projection from the log caught and snagged her sweater.*
	con · cus · sion (kən kush′ ən) *n.*, violent shaking; shock. *The continuous concussions of the hail hitting the roof woke me.*
	la · ment (lə ment′) *n.*, loud mourning; wailing. *Every time we leave the house, the puppy howls in lament.*

late and parked my car. I looked across the grey waters and listened to the new horn sounding, once, twice, three, four times a minute far out there, by itself.

The monster?

It never came back.

"It's gone away," said McDunn. "It's gone back to the Deeps. It's learned you can't love anything too much in this world. It's gone into the deepest Deeps to wait another million years. Ah, the poor thing! Waiting out there, and waiting out there, while man comes and goes on this pitiful little planet. Waiting and waiting."

GUIDED READING

What has happened to the monster?

I sat in my car, listening. I couldn't see the lighthouse or the light standing out in Lonesome Bay. I could only hear the Horn, the Horn, the Horn. It sounded like the monster calling.

I sat there wishing there was something I could say. ■

Respond *to the* SELECTION

How long would you be willing to wait for what you really wanted in life? Would there come a time at which you would give up?

About *the* AUTHOR

Ray Bradbury is one of the world's most respected writers of science fiction and fantasy. His short stories and novels are lyrical, poetic, and fanciful but address serious themes. Themes that recur in his works include the value of individuality over conformity and modern society's overdependence on machines and technology.

Bradbury was born in Waukegan, Illinois, in 1920. He has published many collections of short stories, including *The Martian Chronicles* and *The Illustrated Man*, and several novels, including *Fahrenheit 451* and *Something Wicked This Way Comes*.

"THE FOGHORN" **379**

ANSWER TO GUIDED READING QUESTION

1. The monster has gone back to the Deep.

RESPOND TO THE SELECTION

As an alternate activity, students might share times in their lives when they were lonely and what they did about the situation.

SELECTION CHECK TEST 4.5.7 WITH ANSWERS

Checking Your Reading

1. What job do the narrator and McDunn share? **They are lighthouse keepers.**
2. What does the sea monster look like? **The sea monster has a large, dark-colored head, a beautiful long dark neck, and immense eyes. It is over ninety feet long.**
3. What lures the sea monster out from the depths of the sea? **It is lonely.**
4. According to McDunn, why does the sea monster not come back? **The sea monster is gone because it has learned " you can't love anything too much in this world."**
5. What are the narrator and McDunn doing at the end of the story? **They are listening to the foghorn.**

Vocabulary in Context
Fill in each blank below with the most appropriate vocabulary word from "The Foghorn." You may have to change the tense of the word.

> verify   ascend   apparatus
> concussion   thresh   anguished
> primeval

1. The viewing towers were over a mile away, but we could still feel the **concussion** from the firing of the space shuttle's huge engines.
2. The tourists were awestruck as they **ascended** the steps of the pyramid.
3. Pauletta could hardly contain her excitement when she discovered evidence of the **primeval** society that had once inhabited the forest.
4. The police detective asked the suspect if anyone could **verify** his alibi for the night of the burglary.
5. As we walked through the meadow, the guide showed us how to use our sticks to **thresh** the tall grass in front of us and scare away .

SELECTION CHECK TEST 4.5.7 WITH ANSWERS (CONT.)

Reader's Toolbox
Fill in the blanks using the following terms. You may use some terms more than once.

> style   mood

1. *Atmosphere* is another word for **mood.**

2. **mood** is the emotion created in the reader by a piece of writing.
3. **style** is influenced by several things, such as diction, grammatical choices, and sentence structure.

The Much Resounding Sea, 1884. Thomas Moran. National Gallery of Art, Washington, DC.

ONCE by the PACIFIC

Robert Frost

The shattered water made a misty din.

Great waves looked over others coming in,

And thought of doing something to the shore

That water never did to land before.

The clouds were low and hairy in the skies,

Like locks blown forward in the gleam of eyes.

You could not tell, and yet it looked as if

The shore was lucky in being backed by cliff,

The cliff in being backed by continent;

It looked as if a night of dark intent

Was coming, and not only a night, an age.

Someone had better be prepared for rage.

There would be more than ocean-water broken

Before God's last *Put out the Light* was spoken. ■

ABOUT THE RELATED READING
Robert Frost (1874–1963) won four Pulitzer Prizes and earned a reputation as one of the world's greatest poets. He also worked as a teacher, a farmer, and an editor. He lived most of his life in New England, where he found inspiration for his poems in the landscape, customs, language, and people of the region.

INSIGHTS

THE WORLD'S MOST FAMOUS UNDERWATER CREATURE

For more than one thousand years, people have reported seeing large, unknown creatures in the Scottish lake known as Loch Ness. The so-called Loch Ness Monster, or Nessie, has been described as being about thirty feet long, with flippers, a humped back, and a long neck. There is no real proof that the Loch Ness Monster exists, but many people throughout history have reported seeing the creature. Some have taken photographs of what seems to be a creature fitting the description.

Several scientific studies have taken place at Loch Ness. In one, sonar equipment—which bounces sound waves off objects and is used to find ships and submarines through water—found no conclusive evidence to prove or disprove Nessie's existence. In the meantime, many tourists flock to Loch Ness each year to try to see for themselves the legendary creature said to live in the lake's depths.

 art smart

One of the most famous photographs of the Loch Ness Monster, thought to have been shot in 1934 by Colonel Robert Wilson, was proved a hoax in 1994. Christian Spurling, stepson of the real photographer, Duke Wetherell, admitted on his deathbed late in 1993 that his stepfather had taken photos of a model monster that Christian assembled from a toy submarine and moldable plastic wood. The photographs were passed along to Wetherell's friend Colonel Wilson, who sold them to the *Daily Mail*. The group never imagined the publicity their stunt would generate, and no one revealed the truth until Spurling's confession nearly sixty years later.

RECALL

1a. McDunn says, "No, Johnny, we're impossible."

2a. The creature is coming to the lighthouse attracted by the sound of its foghorn and its shape, looking for more of its kind.

3a. The sea creature destroys the foghorn and lighthouse.

INTERPRET

1b. McDunn means that the evolution of human society is more unbelievable than the existence of a large, primitive sea creature.

2b. Students may say that the creature returns lured by the false hope of another creature like itself only to be disappointed every year.

3b. The sea creature acts this way because it realizes the foghorn is not another of its kind. Loneliness causes this reaction because the feeling of isolation creates a feeling of desperation.

ANALYZE

4a. Students may say that elements of the story suggesting loneliness include the isolated setting, the job of lighthouse keeper, the description of the sea creature returning every year to cry out to the foghorn, and the description of the sea creature at the end all alone and waiting. *Responses will vary.*

SYNTHESIZE

4b. Students may say that thinking it had found company only to realize that it had been tricked and it would again be lonely filled the creature with rage and despair strong enough to destroy things. Students may say they keep the incident a secret because they know no one will believe their story about the sea creature.

PERSPECTIVE

5a. McDunn thinks that the creature appears because it loves the idea of there being another one of its kind, which the lighthouse represents. These words foreshadow the creature destroying the lighthouse that "betrayed" it.

EMPATHY

5b. Responses will vary, but students may suggest that McDunn has first-hand experience with love and loss.

Investigate, Inquire, and Imagine

Recall: GATHERING FACTS

1a. How does McDunn answer Johnny's exclamation, "It's impossible!"?

2a. Why does the creature come to the lighthouse?

3a. What does the sea creature do to the foghorn and the lighthouse?

Interpret: FINDING MEANING

1b. What does McDunn mean by his response?

2b. Why would the creature return every year, only to leave again?

3b. What do you think causes the sea creature to react in this way?

Analyze: TAKING THINGS APART

4a. What elements of the story suggest loneliness? In which case, if any, does loneliness give way to a happy ending? When does it lead to despair?

Synthesize: BRINGING THINGS TOGETHER

4b. Why might loneliness have led the creature to a desperate action? Why do Johnny and McDunn keep the incident a secret?

Perspective: LOOKING AT OTHER VIEWS

5a. What does McDunn mean by the following passage: "That's life for you. Someone always waiting for someone who never comes home. Always someone loving some thing more than that thing loves them. And after a while you want to destroy whatever that thing is, so it can't hurt you no more."? What does he believe is the reason for the creature's appearance? How does his statement foreshadow the events that follow?

Empathy: SEEING FROM INSIDE

5b. Why may have caused McDunn to make this statement? What in McDunn's own life might have caused him to reflect on love and destruction in this way? How might events in McDunn's life have led him to sympathize with the creature?

Understanding Literature

STYLE. Style is the manner in which something is said or written. A writer's style depends on many things, including his or her *diction*, or the words the writer chooses, and the way he or she forms sentences. Describe how Bradbury chooses and arranges words in the short story. How do these elements form a particular style? How would you describe Bradbury's style in this selection? What, if anything, makes this style unique?

Answers to Understanding Literature can be found on page 383.

Mood. Mood, or atmosphere, is the emotion created in the reader by a piece of writing. A writer creates mood by using concrete details. Using the list of moods you wrote while reading "The Foghorn," complete the graphic organizer below for each mood. As the example shows, write the mood in the center circle. Then go back and reread the story to find examples of concrete details that help create that particular mood, and write each example in a circle connected to the center circle. Do a similar graphic organizer for each mood on your list.

Graphic Organizer

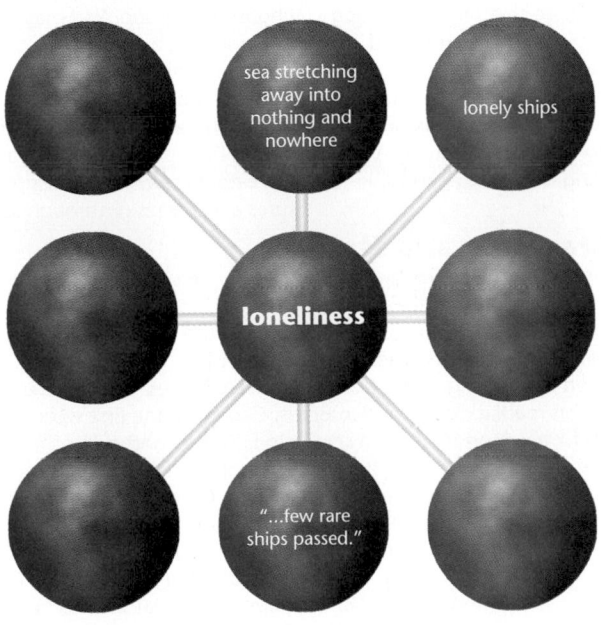

- sea stretching away into nothing and nowhere
- lonely ships
- **loneliness**
- "...few rare ships passed."

Writer's Journal

1. Imagine that as a reporter, you also saw the creature in Lonesome Bay. Write a breaking **news story** about what you witnessed.
2. Since Johnny no longer works at the lighthouse, suppose McDunn needs a new assistant lighthouse keeper. Write a **job description** for the position.
3. Write a **poem** about the sea for a book featuring lighthouse photographs.

STYLE. Students may say that Bradbury chooses very concrete words and uses figurative language to help create a mysterious, lonely, and sad mood. The style is one of sadness and beauty. Students may say the combination of the beauty of the language and the sadness and loneliness of the spell it creates makes his writing style unique.

MOOD. Students may choose the mood of loneliness and add "I'll make a sound that's so alone that no one can miss it, that whoever hears it will weep in their souls," A cry came across a million years of water and mist. A cry so anguished and alone that it shuddered in my head and my body," "I saw it, I knew it all—the million years of waiting alone, for someone to come back who never came back," and "That's life for you. Someone always waiting for someone who never comes home." For suspense, they might write, "Then its eyes caught fire. It reared up, threshed the water, and rushed at the tower, its eyes filled with angry torment," "The huge eye . . . glittered before me like a cauldron into which I might drop, screaming," the glass shattering in upon them, and the men reaching "the bottom as the tower buckled down toward us."

GRAPHIC ORGANIZER

Responses will vary, but students should make sure they fill out several examples for the mood listed in the center circle.

Study and Research
RESEARCHING UNDERWATER CREATURES. For more information on using the Internet, refer students to the Language Arts Survey 5.25, "Using the Internet." Also have students read "How to Evaluate Internet Web Sites" in the Language Arts Survey so they have some guidelines about distinguishing between creditable and unbelievable sites.

Collaborative Learning
INTERPRETING DESCRIPTION. You might wish to have students work in very small groups when they choose to create a drawing or painting and to create a stage scene due to the limited number of characters in the story.

Language, Grammar, and Style
CORRECTING SENTENCE RUN-ONS. Responses will vary, but students should correct run-ons in a similar way.

1. The lighthouse was in a lonely place. Only the bean of the great light itself kept them company.
2. McDunn didn't say much; he was not a talker.
3. Anyone else would have left the lighthouse long ago. McDunn thought it suited him.
4. If I went to Loch Ness, I would wait until I saw Nessie myself. Then I would take his picture. I would be famous if I succeeded.
5. There is no proof that the Loch Ness Monster is real. It would be great if it were true; I think it could happen that a dinosaur could have survived those cold waters.

Skill Builders

Study and Research

RESEARCHING UNDERWATER CREATURES. A number of legendary underwater creatures besides the Loch Ness Monster are reportedly living in lakes, rivers, and seas around the world. Use the Internet to research these creatures. Keep a log with information about each creature. Find information on at least five creatures. Which do you find the most believable? What about that creature makes its existence most believable? For more information, see the Language Arts Survey 5.36, "Keeping a Research Journal."

Collaborative Learning

INTERPRETING DESCRIPTION. In small groups, review "The Foghorn" and discuss the descriptions in the story. Based on the author's descriptions, recreate a scene you choose as a group. You may recreate the scene in a drawing, a painting, a stage scene, or an audio recording. Incorporate as many details from the story as possible. What sights, sounds, sensations, and smells make the author's descriptions effective? How can your group recreate these written descriptions through pictures and scenes or through sound?

Language, Grammar, and Style

CORRECTING SENTENCE RUN-ONS. A **run-on sentence** is made up of two or more sentences that have been run together as if they were one complete thought. Sometimes a run-on will have no punctuation separating the complete thoughts. At other times, it will have a comma where it needs a period.

You can fix a run-on by dividing it into two separate sentences. Mark the end of each idea with a period, question mark, or exclamation point. Capitalize the first word of each new sentence. You can also fix a run-on by using a semicolon. The second part of the sentence is not capitalized. Only use a semicolon to join two sentences if they are very closely related.

RUN-ON	The story about the sea monster coming to crash the lighthouse couldn't really happen Ray Bradbury's story is fiction.
TWO SENTENCES	The story about the sea monster coming to crash the lighthouse couldn't really happen. Ray Bradbury's story is fiction.
RUN-ON	Johnny and McDunn realized the creature was lonely, it was looking for a mate.
SENTENCE WITH SEMICOLON	Johnny and McDunn realized the creature was lonely; it was looking for a mate.

Write the sentences below on your own paper, fixing the run-ons. Decide whether the sentences can be corrected by making two separate sentences or using a semicolon and keeping them as one sentence.

1. The lighthouse was in a lonely place only the beam of the great light itself kept them company.
2. McDunn didn't say much, he was not a talker.
3. Anyone else would have left the lighthouse long ago McDunn thought it suited him.
4. If I went to Loch Ness, I would wait until I saw Nessie myself and I would take his picture I would be famous if I succeeded.
5. There is no proof that the Loch Ness Monster is real, it would be great if it were true, I think it could happen that a dinosaur could have survived those cold waters.

Prereading

"The Tell-Tale Heart"
by Edgar Allan Poe

Reader's T O O L B O X

SUSPENSE. Suspense is a feeling of anxiousness or curiosity. A writer creates suspense by raising questions in the reader's mind and by using details that create strong emotions. How does the author create suspense in "The Tell-Tale Heart"?

NARRATOR. The **narrator** is a person or character who tells a story. The narrator can be a story's main character, a minor character, or an outside observer. A narrator is either reliable or unreliable. A reliable narrator can be trusted by the reader; an unreliable narrator cannot be trusted. Who is the narrator in this story? What do you learn about the narrator as you read? Is the narrator reliable or unreliable? Use the graphic organizer below to list traits of the narrator in the story.

POINT OF VIEW. Point of view is the vantage point from which a story is told. If a story is told from the **first-person point of view**, the narrator uses words such as *I* and *we* and is a part of or a witness to the action. As you read this story, think about how using the first-person point of view influences the mood of the story and about the way information is conveyed in the story.

Graphic Organizer

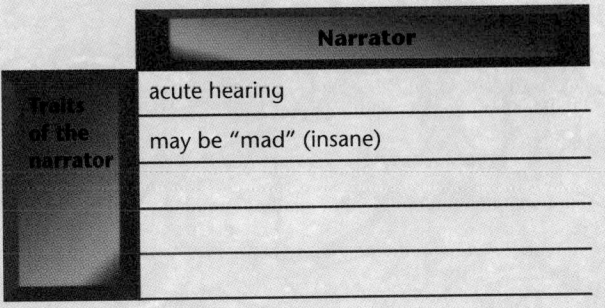

Narrator	
Traits of the narrator	acute hearing
	may be "mad" (insane)

Reader's Journal

Which thing or things in the world around you most frighten or horrify you?

Reader's Resource

- Criminologists are people who investigate the causes of crime and ways in which crimes should be punished and could be prevented. Current methods of criminology focus on a criminal's social environment and psychological condition. While severe mental illnesses sometimes lead to violent behavior, they are rarely the cause of crimes.

- Mental illness is a common and serious health problem in the United States, affecting between twelve and sixteen million people. Mental illness includes schizophrenia, manic depression (bipolar disorder), and severe depression. These serious mental illnesses cause devastating symptoms, both for those who suffer from them and for their families.

ADDITIONAL RESOURCES

UNIT 5 RESOURCE BOOK
- Selection Worksheet 5.5
- Selection Check Test 4.5.9
- Selection Test 4.5.10
- Speaking and Listening Resource 4.20

GRAPHIC ORGANIZER

Responses will vary, but students might fill out their charts with the following:
- narrator's gender is never specified
- speaks clearly
- seems to be aware of what he or she is doing
- able to greet police officers in a calm and rational way
- obsessed with old man's eye and looks in on him every night
- commits a terrible murder in careful and calculated manner
- becomes suddenly quite upset and gives himself away to the officers

READER'S JOURNAL

You might ask students to create a rough sketch of a monster for a chilling tale. Whether the monster is a traditional goblin or ghoul or a person with monstrous inner qualities, the student should try to use vivid details in describing the monster they imagine.

GOALS/OBJECTIVES

Studying this lesson will enable students to
- appreciate a story told by an unreliable narrator
- define *suspense* and identify elements of a story that create suspense
- define *narrator* and distinguish between reliable and unreliable narrators
- define *point of view* and explain the effect point of view can have on a story
- write a letter of advice
- stage a mock trial
- prepare an oral interpretation

MOTIVATION
Students may especially enjoy preparing a dramatic oral interpretation of portions of this story in the Speaking and Listening activity. Encourage students to use elements of verbal and nonverbal communication to make the narrator seem as sane or as insane as they wish, or anywhere in between these two extremes.

READING PROFICIENCY
Students may gain a better understanding of the narrator and his or her mental state if you play them an audiotape of the selection being read aloud. After students have listened to the recording, ask them to discuss what words they would use to describe the narrator. Then ask them to read the selection on their own.

ENGLISH LANGUAGE LEARNING
Point out the following vocabulary words and expressions
chuckled—laughed inwardly or quietly
hearkening—listening
mortal—of, related to, or connected with death
acuteness—sharpness
refrained—held back
foul play—murder, violence
bade—past of bid, meaning to request to come or invite
raved—talked irrationally, as if in a delirium
dissemble—hide under a false appearance

SPECIAL NEEDS
Tell students to focus on the Guided Reading questions and the Recall questions in the Investigate, Inquire, and Imagine section. Students may find the language of this selection difficult to follow, so make sure that they pay attention to the Words for Everyday Use and the footnotes. Also share with them the vocabulary terms above.

The tell-tale HEART

Edgar Allan Poe

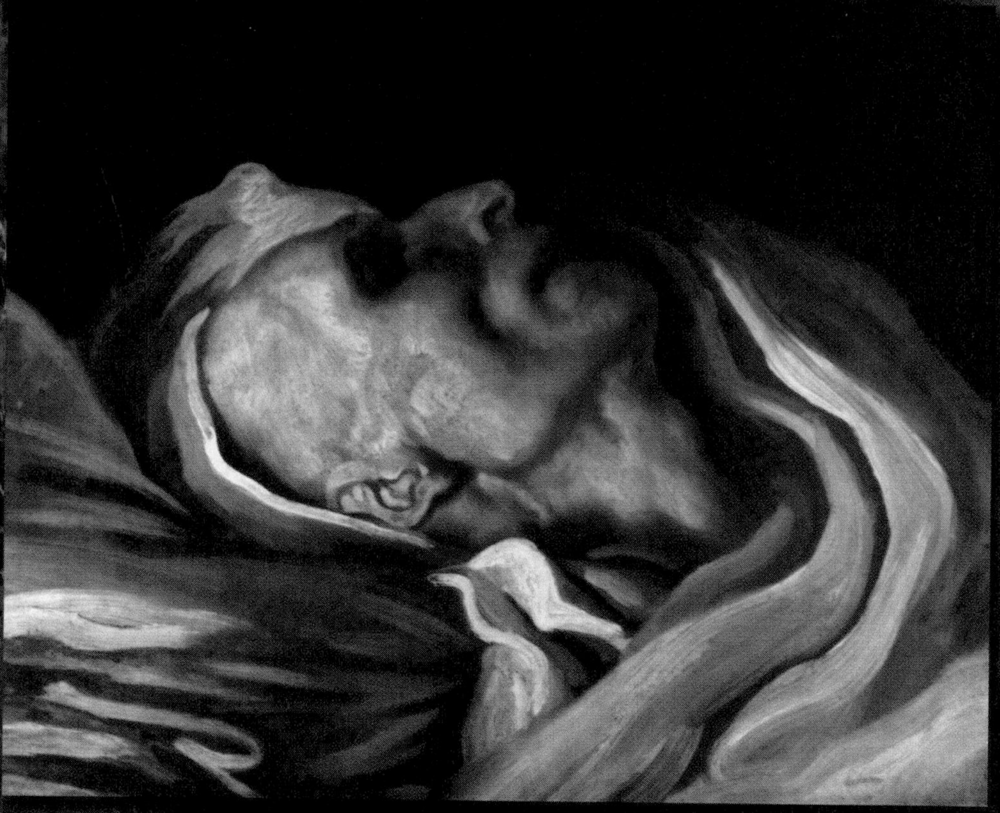

After Death, c.1818. Theodor Gericault. Art Institute of Chicago.

INDIVIDUAL LEARNING STRATEGIES (CONT.)

ENRICHMENT
Encourage students to work in groups to research more about mental illness and how treatment of it has changed over the years. In their research, ask them to  answer the following questions: How have mentally ill people been treated through the ages? In what way has the treatment of mental illness evolved and changed for the better? For the worse?

true!—nervous—very, very dreadfully nervous I had been and am; but why *will* you say that I am mad? The disease had sharpened my senses—not destroyed—not dulled them. Above all was the sense of hearing acute. I heard all things in the heaven and in the earth. I heard many things in hell. How, then, am I mad? Hearken![1] and observe how healthily—how calmly I can tell you the whole story.

It is impossible to say how first the idea entered my brain; but once <u>conceived</u>, it haunted me day and night. Object there was none. Passion there was none. I loved the old man. He had never wronged me. He had never given me insult. For his gold I had no desire. I think it was his eye! Yes, it was this! He had the eye of a vulture—a pale blue eye, with a film over it. Whenever it fell upon me, my blood ran cold; and so by degrees—very gradually—I made up my mind to take the life of the old man, and thus rid myself of the eye forever.

GUIDED READING

What does the speaker dislike about the old man?

Now this is the point. You fancy me mad. Madmen know nothing. But you should have seen *me*. You should have seen how wisely I proceeded—with what caution—with what foresight—with what <u>dissimulation</u> I went to work! I was never kinder to the old man than during the whole week before I killed him. And every night, about midnight, I turned the latch of his door and opened it—oh, so gently! And then, when I had made an opening sufficient for my head, I put in a dark lantern, all closed, closed, so that no light shone out, and then I thrust in my head. Oh, you would have laughed to see how <u>cunningly</u> I thrust it in! I moved it slowly—very, very slowly, so that I might not disturb the old man's sleep. It took me an hour to place my whole head within the opening so far that I could see him as he lay upon his bed. Ha!—would a madman have been so wise as this? And then, when my head was well in the room, I undid the lantern cautiously—oh, so cautiously—cautiously (for the hinges creaked)—I undid it just so much that a single, thin ray fell upon the vulture eye. And this I did for seven long nights—every night just at midnight—but I found the eye always closed; and so it was impossible to do the work; for it was not the old man who vexed me, but his Evil Eye. And every morning, when the day broke, I went boldly into the chamber, and spoke courageously to him, calling him by name in a hearty tone, and inquiring how he had passed the night. So you see he would have been a very profound old man, indeed, to suspect that every night, just at twelve, I looked in upon him while he slept.

GUIDED READING

In what way does the speaker behave toward the old man during the day?

Upon the eighth night I was more than usually cautious in opening the door. A watch's minute hand moves more quickly than did mine. Never, before that night, had I *felt* the extent of my own powers—of my <u>sagacity</u>. I could scarcely contain my feelings of triumph. To think that there I was, opening the door, little by little, and he not even to dream of my secret deeds or thoughts. I fairly chuckled at the idea; and perhaps he heard me; for he moved on the bed suddenly, as if startled. Now you may think that I drew back—but no. His room was as black as pitch with the thick darkness

---

1. **Hearken.** Listen carefully

words for everyday use

con • ceive (kən sēv′) v., form or develop in the mind. *She <u>conceived</u> the idea for the fund-raiser just before she fell asleep.*

dis • sim • u • late (di sim′ yü lāt′) v., act of hiding; pretending. *Susan wore a disguise to <u>dissimulate</u> her identity.* **dissimulation**, n.

cun • ning (kun′ iŋ) adj., skillful or clever. *The <u>cunning</u> quarterback confused the defense with a well executed pass play.* **cunningly**, adv.

sag • ac • i • ty (sə gas′ ə tē) n., wisdom; intelligence. *The youngsters marveled at the <u>sagacity</u> of the old man who had traveled the world.*

ANSWERS TO GUIDED READING QUESTIONS

1. The speaker dislikes the old man's eye.
2. During the day he or she speaks with the man and inquires about how he had passed the night.

CROSS-CURRICULAR CONNECTION

SOCIAL STUDIES. Ask students to research different careers related to the justice system and criminology. Students should go to the library, look up possible careers, and report their information to the class. Students might come across careers such as police officer, lawyer, judge, social worker, and criminologist.

VOCABULARY FROM THE SELECTION

audacity	stealthy
concealment	stifle
conceive	suave
cunning	supposition
derision	vehement
dissimulate	vex
sagacity	

ADDITIONAL QUESTIONS AND ACTIVITIES

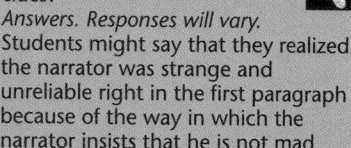

Ask students to discuss the following question:

When did you first begin to realize that the narrator might be strange and unreliable? What was the very first set of clues?

Answers. Responses will vary. Students might say that they realized the narrator was strange and unreliable right in the first paragraph because of the way in which the narrator insists that he is not mad.

Others might say that the first hint of the obsession with the eye of the older man gave them their first clue.

LITERARY TECHNIQUE

Poe has written stories that are ambiguous in that the reader does not know if a tale is about supernatural events told by a sane narrator or about the hallucinations of an insane narrator.

You might tell students that Poe was one of the first writers to use this technique. Today it influences many horror writers.

The story widely considered to be Poe's greatest horror story is "The Black Cat." Like "The Tell-Tale Heart," this story has a murder, a narrator trying to convince a reader of his sanity, the hiding of a body, and the narrator almost convincing the police of his innocence.

(for the shutters were close fastened, through fear of robbers), and so I knew that he could not see the opening of the door, and I kept pushing it on steadily, steadily.

I had my head in, and was about to open the lantern, when my thumb slipped upon the tin fastening, and the old man sprang up in bed, crying out—"Who's there?"

I kept quite still and said nothing. For a whole hour I did not move a muscle, and in the meantime I did not hear him lie down. He was still sitting up in the bed listening; just as I have done, night after night, hearkening to the deathwatches[2] in the wall.

Presently I heard a slight groan, and I knew it was the groan of mortal terror. It was not a groan of pain or grief—oh, no!—it was the low, <u>stifled</u> sound that arises from the bottom of the soul when overcharged with awe. I knew the sound well. Many a night, just at midnight, when all the world slept, it has welled up from my own bosom, deepening, with its dreadful echo, the terrors that distracted me. I say I knew it well. I knew what the old man felt, and pitied him, although I chuckled at heart. I knew that he had been lying awake ever since the first slight noise, when he had turned in the bed. His fears had been ever since growing upon him. He had been trying to fancy them causeless, but could not. He had been saying to himself— "It is nothing but the wind in the chimney— it is only a mouse crossing the floor," or "it is merely a cricket which has made a single chirp." Yes, he has been trying to comfort himself with these <u>suppositions</u>: but he had found all in vain. *All in vain*; because Death, in approaching him, had stalked with his black shadow before him, and enveloped the victim. And it was the mournful influence of the unperceived shadow that caused him to feel—although he neither saw nor heard—to *feel* the presence of my head within the room.

When I had waited a long time, very patiently, without hearing him lie down, I resolved to open a little, a very, very little crevice in the lantern. So I opened it—you cannot imagine how <u>stealthily</u>, stealthily— until at length, a single dim ray, like the thread of the spider, shot from out the crevice and fell upon the vulture eye.

It was open—wide, wide open—and I grew furious as I gazed upon it. I saw it with perfect distinctness—all a dull blue, with a hideous veil over it that chilled the very marrow in my bones; but I could see nothing else of the old man's face or person; for I had directed the ray, as if by instinct, precisely upon the damned spot.

And have I not told you that what you mistake for madness is but over-acuteness of the senses?—now, I say, there

2. **deathwatches.** Wood-boring beetles that make a tapping noise in the wood they invade. They are thought to predict death.

---

words for everyday use

sti • fle (stī fəld) *v.,* hold back; stop, smother. *Val buried her face in her pillow to <u>stifle</u> the sound of her crying.* **stifled,** *adj.*

sup • po • si • tion (sup ə zish' ən) *n.,* something supposed; assumption. *The <u>supposition</u> is that those students with the best records of attendance will do best on the test.*

stealth • y (stel' thē) *adj.,* secret; sneaky. *Quietly, the <u>stealthy</u>, the dog inched toward the scraps in the garbage.* **stealthily,** *adv.*

came to my ears a low, dull, quick sound, such as a watch makes when enveloped in cotton. I knew *that* sound well, too. It was the beating of the old man's heart. It increased my fury, as the beating of a drum stimulates the soldier into courage.

GUIDED READING

What increases the speaker's fury?

But even yet I refrained and kept still. I scarcely breathed. I held the lantern motionless. I tried how steadily I could maintain the ray upon the eye. Meantime the hellish tattoo of the heart increased. It grew quicker and quicker, and louder and louder every instant. The old man's terror *must* have been extreme! It grew louder, I say, louder every moment!—do you mark me well? I have told you that I am nervous; so I am. And now at the dead hour of the night, amid the dreadful silence of that old house, so strange a noise as this excited me to uncontrollable terror. Yet, for some minutes longer I refrained and stood still. But the beating grew louder, louder! I thought the heart must burst. And now a new anxiety seized me—the sound would be heard by a neighbor! The old man's hour had come! With a loud yell, I threw open the lantern and leaped into the room. He shrieked once—once only. In an instant I dragged him to the floor, and pulled the heavy bed over him. I then smiled gaily, to find the deed so far done. But, for many minutes, the heart beat on with a muffled sound. This, however, did not <u>vex</u> me; it would not be heard through the wall. At length it ceased. The old man was dead. I removed the bed and examined the corpse. Yes, he was stone, stone

GUIDED READING

In what way does the speaker behave when he hears the sound?

dead. I placed my hand upon the heart and held it there many minutes. There was no pulsation. He was stone dead. His eye would trouble me no more.

If still you think me mad, you will think so no longer when I describe the wise precautions I took for the <u>concealment</u> of the body. The night waned, and I worked hastily, but in silence. First of all I dismembered the corpse. I cut off the head and the arms and the legs.

I then took up three planks from the flooring of the chamber, and deposited all between the scantlings.[3] I then replaced the boards so cleverly, so cunningly, that no human eye—not even *his*—could have detected anything wrong. There was nothing to wash out—no stain of any kind—no blood spot whatever. I had been too wary for that. A tub had caught all—ha! ha!

When I had made an end of these labors, it was four o'clock—still dark as midnight. As the bell sounded the hour, there came a knocking at the street door. I went down to open it with a light heart,—for what had I *now* to fear? There entered three men, who introduced themselves, with perfect <u>suavity</u>, as officers of the police. A shriek had been heard by a neighbor during the night; suspicion of foul play had been aroused; information had been lodged at the police office, and they (the officers) had been deputed to search the premises.

I smiled,—for *what* had I to fear? I bade the gentlemen welcome. The shriek, I said, was my own in a dream. The old man, I mentioned, was absent in the country. I took my visitors all over the house. I bade them

---

3. **scantlings.** Small beams or timbers

words for everyday use

vex (veks) *v.*, bother; trouble. *She tried not to let the psychic's predictions of doom <u>vex</u> her.*

con • ceal • ment (kən sēl' mənt) *n.*, hiding. *<u>Concealment</u> of the broken lamp was unlikely, as the pieces were scattered across the floor.*

suave (swäv) *adj.*, smooth, graceful; polite. *The <u>suave</u> politician made lots of promises to the community.* **suavity** *n.*

1. The beating of the old man's heart increases the speaker's fury.
2. The speaker begins to panic when he hears the sound.

CROSS-CURRICULAR ACTIVITIES

SOCIAL STUDIES. Mention to students that if the speaker of this story were having a trial today, he probably could make an insanity plea, which would mean he could be found "not guilty by reason of insanity." This means that he would go to a hospital for the treatment of mental illness rather than go to a prison or receive the death penalty.

Students might be interested in learning more about how our judicial system works in these situations. Ask them to go to the library and find out more about trials. Then ask them to make a decision—based on their research—whether or not the speaker of this story might be found insane in a court of law today.

search—search *well*. I led them, at length, to *his* chamber. I showed them his treasures, secure, undisturbed. In the enthusiasm of my confidence, I brought chairs into the room, and desired them *here* to rest from their fatigues, while I myself, in the wild <u>audacity</u> of my perfect triumph, placed my own seat upon the very spot beneath which reposed the corpse of my victim.

The officers were satisfied. My *manner* had convinced them. I was singularly at ease. They sat, and while I answered cheerily, they chatted of familiar things. But, ere long, I felt myself getting pale and wished them gone. My head ached, and I fancied a ringing in my ears: but still they sat and still chatted. The ringing became more distinct;—it continued and became more distinct: I talked more freely to get rid of the feeling; but it continued and gained definitiveness—until, at length, I found that the noise was not within my ears.

No doubt I now grew *very* pale—but I talked more fluently, and with a heightened voice. Yet the sound increased—and what could I do? It was *a low, dull, quick sound—much such a sound as a watch makes when enveloped in cotton.* I gasped for breath—and yet the officers heard it not. I talked more quickly—more <u>vehemently</u>; but the noise steadily increased. I arose and argued about trifles, in a high key and with violent gesticulations;[4] but the noise steadily increased. Why *would* they not be gone? I paced the floor to and fro with heavy strides, as if excited to fury by the observations of the men—but the noise steadily increased. Oh God; what *could* I do? I foamed—I raved—I swore! I swung the chair upon which I had been sitting, and grated it upon the boards, but the noise arose over all, and continually increased. It grew louder—louder—*louder!* And still the men chatted pleasantly, and smiled. Was it possible they heard not? Almighty God!—no, no! They heard!—they suspected!—they *knew!*—they were making a mockery of my horror!—this I thought, and this I think. But anything was better than this agony! Anything was more tolerable than this <u>derision</u>! I could bear those hypocritical smiles no longer! I felt that I must scream or die! and now—again!—hark! louder! louder! louder! *louder!*

"Villains!" I shrieked. "Dissemble no more! I admit the deed!—tear up the planks! here, here!—it is the beating of his hideous heart!" ■

---

4. **gesticulations.** Energetic gestures or movements

Respond *to the* SELECTION

Do you think the old man knew anything about the narrator's thoughts and plans? Why, or why not?

Edgar Allan Poe lived in this house in New York from 1844 until his death.

About the AUTHOR

Edgar Allan Poe (1809–1849) was an American poet, short story writer, and literary critic. Many people consider Poe one of the creators of the modern short story. He is also known for creating the first modern detective story, "Murders in the Rue Morgue," and for developing the psychological horror story in tales such as "The Fall of the House of Usher," "The Black Cat," and "The Tell-Tale Heart." During his lifetime, Poe achieved brief fame for one of his lyric poems, "The Raven." However, it was not until after his death that Poe was hailed as a genius.

"THE TELL-TALE HEART" 391

RECALL

1a. The narrator is planning to kill the old man.

2a. The old man's strange eye bothers the narrator.

3a. The narrator keeps hearing the beating of the old man's heart.

INTERPRET

1b. The narrator feels that he or she must kill the old man because the old man's strange eye bothers him or her.

2b. The narrator is bothered by the eye because of its strange appearance. The narrator describes the eye as "the eye of a vulture—a pale blue eye, with a film over it."

3b. The police officers probably could not hear the sound because they do not seem to be reacting to it. The officers probably believe that the narrator was insane as they watched his or her actions and behavior.

ANALYZE

4a. Students may say that the narrator's clear way of telling the story, the fact that the narrator seems to be aware of his or her actions, and the fact that he or she is able to greet the police officers in a rational way are evidence of sanity. Evidence of insanity includes the narrator's obsession with the old man's eye, the way the narrator looks in on the old man at night, and the narrator being convinced that he or she can hear the beating of the old man's heart even after the murder.

SYNTHESIZE

4b. Students may say that the narrator seems calm and rational at first, but then, by the end of the story, the narrator's mental state is one of panic, paranoia, confusion, and delusion. Students may say that the narrator hasn't changed—he or she was just controlling him or herself more at the beginning of the story and reveals more about his or her true mental state and character as the story progresses.

PERSPECTIVE

5a. Responses will vary. Students may suggest that the old man does seem terrified of the narrator, so he may know who was watching him.

Investigate, Inquire, and Imagine

Recall: GATHERING FACTS

1a. What is the narrator's plan for the old man?

2a. What about the old man bothers the narrator, and why?

3a. What sound does the narrator hear while he is talking to the police officers?

Interpret: FINDING MEANING

1b. Why does he go about his plan in this particular way?

2b. Why might this feature be so troublesome for the narrator?

3b. What do you think the police see and hear while they are with the narrator? What might they conclude from the visit?

Analyze: TAKING THINGS APART

4a. What characteristics of the narrator make him seem sane? What characteristics of the narrator make him or her seem insane?

Synthesize: BRINGING THINGS TOGETHER

4b. What do you think the narrator's mental state is in the beginning of the story? What do you think the narrator's mental state is by the end of the story? Has the narrator changed? Has he remained the same? Explain your answer.

Perspective: LOOKING AT OTHER VIEWS

5a. What could the old man have thought was happening? Do you think he knew who was watching him? Why do you think he reacted the way he did?

Empathy: SEEING FROM INSIDE

5b. What would the old man have thought if he knew how the narrator felt about his eye? How would he have reacted, knowing also that the narrator "loved the old man"?

Understanding Literature

SUSPENSE. Suspense is a feeling of anxiousness or curiosity. A writer creates suspense by raising questions in the reader's mind and by using details that create strong emotions. Which passages in the story create the most suspense for you? Did you try to guess what would happen next? If so, were you correct?

NARRATOR. The **narrator** is a person or character who tells a story. Review your graphic organizer listing the traits of the narrator. Which important details about the narrator are not revealed in the story? Why do you think the author chose not to include those details?

POINT OF VIEW. Point of view is the vantage point from which a story is told. If a story is told in the **first-person point of view**, the narrator uses words such as *I* and *we* and is a part of

---

ANSWERS TO INVESTIGATE, INQUIRE, IMAGINE (CONT.)

Students may say the old man doesn't leave or ask for help before because he tried to excuse what was happening as a trick of his own imagination.

EXTEND

5b. Responses will vary. Students may say that the old man might have tried to distance himself from the narrator but also may have tried to get the narrator mental help.

narrator but also may have tried to get the narrator mental help.

Answers to Understanding Literature can be found on page 393.

or a witness to the action. In the **third-person point of view**, the narrator stands outside the action and uses words such as *he, she, it,* and *they.* Why do you think the author used the first-person point of view in this story? How might the story have differed Poe had used the third-person point-of-view?

Writer's Journal

1. Write a brief **sequel** to the story, featuring a future episode of the narrator's life.
2. From the point of view of the police officers, write a **police report** explaining their findings at the old man's home.
3. Write a **literary review** of "The Tell-Tale Heart," explaining what you liked about the story and/or what you did not like about the story. Either recommend the story to readers or advise them not to read it.

Skill Builders

Applied English

WRITING A LETTER OF ADVICE. Imagine that you are the narrator's lawyer and that a trial is set for the murder of the old man. Write a letter advising your client how to plead (guilty, not guilty, or guilty by reason of insanity). Try to persuade your client by explaining why your advice is the best possible course of action to take.

Cooperative Learning

STAGING A MOCK TRIAL. As a class, try the narrator of "The Tell-Tale Heart" in a mock murder trial. Draw names from a hat to determine who will take on the roles of defendant, defense attorney(s), prosecuting attorney(s), judge, witnesses for the defense, witnesses for the prosecution, bailiff, and jury members. Both the defense and the prosecution should take time to prepare their cases before presenting them to the jury for a verdict on the narrator's innocence or guilt.

Speaking and Listening

ORAL INTERPRETATION. In small groups, divide "The Tell-Tale Heart" into as many sections as people in the group. Take turns among group members, each reading his or her section of the story. Your group may want to begin this activity by reviewing your analysis of the narrator from Investigate, Inquire and Imagine on page 392. Practice reading with emotion, pausing, varying volume and pace, emphasizing certain words and phrases, and using gestures and facial expressions. See the Language Arts Survey 4.20, "Telling a Story" for additional tips.

ANSWERS TO SKILL BUILDERS

Applied English
WRITING A LETTER OF ADVICE. Students' letters should follow the proper form for a business letter. Refer them to the instruction given in The Language Arts Survey, "Business Letters." Inform students that lawyers' letters usually use formal language and that they might wish to emulate this in their own letters.

Cooperative Learning
STAGING A MOCK TRIAL. The defense attorney and the prosecuting attorney will be doing much of the speaking in the mock trial and help shape the course of the trial through their questions, so you may wish to assign all the roles rather than have students pick them from a hat. Choose attorneys who speak well in public and who might ask insightful questions to the witnesses.

Speaking and Listening
ORAL INTERPRETATION. Groups may wish to practice their dramatic interpretations on their own and then present their reading to the class once it has been polished.

ANSWERS TO UNDERSTANDING LITERATURE

SUSPENSE. Students may say the scene when the narrator is standing in the old man's room right before the murder is very suspenseful. Reading this scene, students may have wondered whether the narrator would kill the old man and if the old man would react in time to save himself. Responses will vary.

NARRATOR. The author never reveals the identity or gender of the narrator, which heightens the suspense as the narrator could be anyone. The author also never definitively states whether the narrator is mad or sane, letting the reader judge for him or herself. This engages the reader more in the story.

POINT OF VIEW. The first-person point of view makes the story more frightening and compelling because the reader is essentially seeing through the eyes of a madman. Third-person point of view would have raised fewer questions in the reader's mind about what is true and what is a product of the narrator's madness.

for your READING LIST

The Man Who Was Poe by Avi is a gripping suspense story about a boy named Edmund, whose mother and aunt have mysteriously disappeared. As the story begins, his little sister vanishes as well. All alone, unsure of what to do and fearing they may all be dead, he sets off into the night and meets Auguste Dupin, a dark and troubled stranger that he hopes will help him solve his mystery.

The Man Who Was Poe is historical fiction—that is, fiction written about a true historical character. Avi wondered how the great 19th-century poet and author, Edgar Allan Poe, would have acted if he had found himself in a mystery, in the company of a child. This story, which is every bit as suspenseful and bizarre as one Poe might have written, is Avi's answer. Like all of his books, this one features characters that are neither perfectly good nor completely evil. They are complex and believable. The twists and turns of this story will keep you turning pages long into the night and will leave you thinking about the strange man who was Poe long after you finish.

BOOK CLUB

Before you read this book, review the Language Arts Survey 1.8 "Guidelines for Discussing Literature in a Book Club." Decide, in advance, who will take on each of the roles outlined there. After everyone has finished reading the book, take some time individually to prepare for your role in the discussion.

You may find the following questions helpful in your discussion:
- Was this story believable to you?
- If you found yourself in Edmund's predicament, at the beginning of the story, how would you have acted?
- What aspects of the setting of the story contribute to the suspense and horror?
- What do you think Poe agreed to help Edmund?
- How did Poe's insistence on finishing his story contribute to the suspense?
- Is Poe a sympathetic character? Why, or why not?
- Edmund tells Poe, "You're always talking about death, . . . but it's living you're frightened of." What does Edmund mean by this? Do you agree?
- To whom would you recommend this book? Why?

Other books you may want to read:
18 Best Stories by Edgar Allan Poe
The Stonewalkers by Vivien Alcock

Guided Writing

CREATING A SETTING

A **setting** is the time and place in which the story happens. Writers reveal setting by describing the landscape, scenery, buildings, furniture, clothing, weather, and season. Writers can also reveal setting by describing how characters talk, look, and act.

Your task is to write a setting for a story. One kind of setting you might enjoy writing is the setting for a scary story. Before you write your setting, you need to decide who your audience will be. You will also need to decide what tone and mood would be right for this setting.

In the short story "Pets," Avi describes the yard where Eve's pet dog, Chase, is buried. Most of the story takes place in this yard, including the climax where Chase's ghost comes back to chase away the ghosts of the two cats.

Professional Model

As you read the description of the yard in the short story "Pets," look for words that help set the tone and mood.

from "Pets" by Avi, page 343

When Chase died of old age, Eve was very sad. She insisted they bury him in their backyard. This yard was enclosed by a high brick wall, crowded with trees, shrubs, and flowers. It was a shady, often damp place, where the moss grew thick, while strange-looking mushrooms sprang up overnight, and withered and died just as quickly.

Midgarden was a small, murky pool in which, during the summer, fat goldfish swam. As they darted about the dark water, Eve was reminded of summer heat lightning.

It was in this yard that Chase was laid to rest with a large stone to mark the spot.

Examining the Model

Notice how Avi uses words such as *enclosed, crowded, damp, murky,* and *dark* to set the tone and mood for the story. The author also lets the audience know that in this yard, unusual things can occur: *strange-looking mushrooms sprang up overnight and withered and died just as quickly.*

Reflecting

What is the spookiest story you have ever heard? Where were you when you heard the story? Who told the story? How old were you? Why do you think it sent chills down your spine? What made the story spooky? How important was the setting to the story? Share your ideas with your classmates.

Prewriting

FINDING YOUR VOICE. You will want to use a voice that creates the right tone and mood for your setting. A tone is the writer's attitude toward the subject or the reader. A writer's tone for a spooky story might be mysterious, suspenseful, or serious. A mood is the feeling or emotion the writer creates in a literary work. By working carefully with descriptive language, the writer can evoke emotional responses in the reader such as fear, discomfort, or anticipation.

IDENTIFYING YOUR AUDIENCE. You can write your setting for an audience of younger children, your peers, older students, or adults. Your choice of an audience will affect the description you write as well as the tone and mood you use. Think about what would be appropriate for your audience. For example, would a description of a haunted house be of more interest to a younger audience or to your peers? What audience might like to

continued on page 396

GUIDED WRITING **395**

Reflecting

You might ask students to write a journal entry about a setting that was so well written or so unusual that they still remember it.

GUIDED WRITING
Software

See the Guided Writing Software for an extended version of this lesson that includes printable graphic organizers, extensive student models and student-friendly checklists, and self-, peer, and teacher evaluation features.

Prewriting

FINDING YOUR VOICE. It might be helpful for students to read the Language Arts Survey 2.5, "Finding Your Voice." Have students analyze the voice Avi uses in "Pets" and the voice used by Victoria in the Student Model on page 398.

IDENTIFYING YOUR AUDIENCE. Encourage students to select vocabulary that their audience will know. Have students read the Language Arts Survey 2.4, "Identifying Your Audience." In conjunction with the Teacher's Note Publishing and Presenting on page 398, you might require all students to write for an audience of younger children to whom they can read their completed descriptions.

MOTIVATION
You might show a scene from a scary movie such as *The Haunting* (1999) or a movie set in an exotic location such as *Out of Africa* (1985) for students not interested in writing a scary setting and ask students to describe the setting orally. You might play a tape with different sound effects and ask students to identify the setting. This will prepare students for adding detailed descriptions of the sense of sound in their descriptions.

READING PROFICIENCY
As students are now familiar with the Guided Writing section, ask them to tell you what sections they anticipate seeing in this lesson before they begin reading.

ENGLISH LANGUAGE LEARNING
See strategies for Reading Proficiency above that will also benefit students who are English language learners. You might encourage non-native speakers of English to create a setting in their culture.

SPECIAL NEEDS
Students who find it difficult to write might create a setting on tape and hand in the tape to you. Or, they could prepare a tape and then use the tape to write their description.

ENRICHMENT
Encourage interested students to incorporate their setting into a short story.

Prewriting

WRITING WITH A PLAN. Students will benefit from reading the Language Arts Survey 2.12, "Freewriting." Students who already know what they want to write about can do focused freewriting.

---

hear about a mysterious planet far off in the solar system? You have to gauge what's right for your audience.

WRITING WITH A PLAN. Complete the two **freewriting** exercises below. They will help you get ready to write a setting for a spooky story.

1. Describe an abandoned space station. On your own paper, freewrite for at least three minutes. Incorporate all six of the following words or phrases: *an opened hatch, control settings that had been changed, echoing noise, coldness, steel.* You can add other words to your description.

2. Describe an ancient temple hidden deep in the rainforest. Consider how things look, sound, feel, smell, or taste in the temple. What emotions do you want to evoke in your reader? List three words or phrases on your own paper that you could use to describe the temple. Use those words plus these three words: *dank, whispering, skin-crawling.* Freewrite for at least three minutes using all of the words.

You should now be ready to pick a setting. You can select one of the settings used in your freewriting, or you can use your own. Copy the graphic organizer on this page onto your own paper and fill it in.

Drafting

Encourage students to use their completed Graphic Organizer modeled on page 396 to help them write their draft. Encourage students to write a discovery draft in which they do not focus on spelling, grammar, usage, and mechanics.

Student Model—Graphic Organizer

Setting **Western town**   Audience **younger kids**

Tone and Mood **spooky and scary**

Sight	Sound	Smell	Touch	Taste
tumbleweed blown by wind	wind whistling	musty saloon	sand stinging my face	dust

Place a star next to six words or phrases from your graphic organizer to include in your freewrite. Then freewrite for three minutes on your own paper.

Before you write your draft, you need to decide who will describe the setting. You, as the author, will create the descriptions. But will you act as a narrator—someone outside the story telling the story as it unfolds—and write from a third-person point of view? Or will you act as a character in the setting and describe the setting using the first-person point of view? If you write from the first-person point of view—in which the main character of the story is speaking—you use words like *I, me, my,* and *mine.* If you write from the third person point of view—in which an outside narrator is speaking—you use words like *he, she, it,* and *they.*

You also need to determine how to organize your description. You may want to use **spatial order**, arranging your ideas in the way in which they appear from left to right, from top to bottom, or from foreground to background. The Professional Model from "Pets" uses spatial order, first describing the perimeter of the garden and then describing the middle. Or you may want to arrange your ideas in **order of impression**—the order in which things in the description appear to the narrator. Ray Bradbury's story "The Foghorn" opens on page 372 with a descriptive setting that uses order of impression.

Drafting

Use your graphic organizer and your freewriting notes as you begin your rough draft. Place your narrator or character in your setting, and begin describing what that person sees, hears, touches, smells, and tastes. Focus on creating the mood and tone for your setting. Do not worry about grammar or spelling. You can go back later and check for errors. Your first draft should focus on the big picture instead of the details.

Self- and Peer Evaluation

After you finish your first draft, ask a peer to evaluate your writing. Have your peer draw a picture of the setting that you have described. As you look at the drawing, note the strengths and weaknesses in your description. Then ask your peer to rate your description on a "scariness scale."

As you evaluate your draft or that of a classmate, ask the following questions:

- Is the description appropriate for the intended audience?
- If you were reading this description alone at night by yourself, would you be scared? What details would make it scarier? Which details might be deleted?
- Which descriptions are precise? Which words are vague? How could vague descriptions be improved?
- Which words help set the mood and tone? What words could you change or add to help set the mood and tone?
- What is the most effective part of your description? What is the least effective part of your description? How could you change it to be more effective?
- How does your use of prepositional phrases help you clarify your meaning and add more precise information to your description?

Student Model—Draft

Victoria described a Western ghost town for an audience of younger students.

> "Where am I?" I said. ˇ"I must be ~Use more senses to describe this.~
> dreaming!" Around me it was like the
> (Cap) old <u>west</u>. There was a saloon, a jail,
> even a dirt road. The wind blew a
> ~How did the dust feel?~ tumbleweed from the road and dust flew
> into my face. I started to run when I
> noticed nobody was around. I looked
> around: nobody in sight. But I had this
> ~Add more details here.~ weird feeling someone was watching me.
> I ran inside the saloon. It was empty
> except for a man with a patch over his
> eye in cowboy clothes. ~This doesn't make sense.~

Language, Grammar, and Style

Prepositional Phrases. A **preposition** is used to show how a noun or pronoun is related to other words in the sentence. Examples of common prepositions: *after, among, around, at, behind, beside, for, in, into, on, of, off, over, through, under, until,* and *with.*

A preposition always has an object. The **object** is a noun or pronoun. The preposition and its object (and any words that modify the object) are called a **prepositional phrase**.

IDENTIFYING PREPOSITIONAL PHRASES. Look at the example from "Pets" below. Identify the preposition and its object.

> When Chase died *of old age*, Eve was very sad.

Of is the preposition and *age* is its object. The word *old* modifies the word *age*. The whole prepositional phrase is *of old age*.

A prepositional phrase should be placed next to the word or phrase that it describes. Otherwise, the meaning can be confused. Read the following example.

> Ishmael talked about his vacation in English class.

Does this sentence mean that Ishmael had a vacation in English class or that while he was in English class he talked about his vacation? Placing the

continued on page 398

GUIDED WRITING **397**

Language, Grammar, and Style

Prepositional Phrases
In this lesson, students will be asked to do the following:
- Identify Prepositional Phrases, 397
- Fix Prepositional Phrases, 398
- Use Prepositional Phrases, 398

INTRODUCING THE SKILL. Tell students they already know how to use prepositional phrases, which will make their writing more detailed. This lesson is intended to make them more aware of the benefits of using accurately place prepositional phrases in their writing.

PREVIEWING THE SKILL. Refer students to the Language Arts Survey 3.27, "Identifying Prepositional Phrases," which explains how to identify prepositional phrases.

PRACTICING THE SKILL. For additional practice, have students work through the following exercise in the Teacher's Resource Kit: 3.27, "Identifying Prepositional Phrases."

Self- and Peer Evaluation

You might want to begin by having students review the Language Arts Survey 2.37, "Self- and Peer Evaluation." Then have students use the checklist on page 397 for self- and peer evaluation. The checklist is intended to act as a student-friendly rubric that should help students identify specific evidence of writing strength and areas needing improvement. Make sure they provide concrete suggestions for improvement or specific evidence of why the writing works. A blackline master of the checklist is available in the Guided Writing Resource 7.5. Students critiquing their classmates' work might be interested in using common proofreader's symbols, which are found in the Language Arts Survey 2.44, "Using Proofreader's Marks."

prepositional phrase *in English class* after *talked* makes it clear that Ishmael talked while he was in his English call.

> Ishmael talked in English class about his vacation.

FIXING PREPOSITIONAL PHRASES.
Look at Victoria's revised draft. Identify five prepositional phrases that she used. Decide if each prepositional phrase is effective. If not, what could you do to make it more effective? Find at least one misplaced prepositional phrase. How could you correct the misplacement? Are there any places you could add prepositional phrases?

USING PREPOSITIONAL PHRASES.
As you write your descriptive setting, use several prepositional phrases. The phrases will help you to add more specific information to your setting. Look at your final draft. Identify the prepositional phrases. Correct any that are misplaced. Add prepositional phrases where needed to make your writing more precise and descriptive.

Revising and Proofreading

Read your first draft out loud, listening to the mood it creates and picturing the description in your mind. Then review your self- and peer evaluation comments. Which comments focus on problems you recognize as you read your setting out loud? How will you modify these problem areas? Which comments help you identify other areas that could be improved? How will you improve these areas? Revise your writing based on your answers to these questions. Then proofread your draft for errors in spelling, grammar, punctuation, capitalization, and other details. See the Language Arts Survey 2.45 for a proofreading checklist.

Part of Victoria's revised draft is shown below.

Student Model—Revised

> "Where am I?" I said while getting up from the dirt road. "I must be dreaming!" Around me it was like the old West. I saw a saloon with swinging, creaking doors, a jail, even a dusty, dirt road with pot holes big enough to fit your foot into. The wind blew a dusty tumbleweed from the road. A cloud of dust leaped up, the sand stinging my face. I started to run to the nearest building and that's when I noticed nobody was around, not even a wagon on the road. I looked around: nobody in sight. But I had this weird feeling someone was watching me. I ran inside the saloon. It smelled of dust, mold, and old sarsaparilla. Behind the piano, a man in cowboy clothes with a patch over his eye blinked at me.

Publishing and Presenting

Write or print a final copy of your descriptive setting. You and your classmates may want to share your descriptions by reading them to each other in your classroom. You can turn off the classroom lights, pull the shades, and use a flashlight as you read your description. Or, you could create a poster of your setting and use it as a backdrop for your writing. Display it on a class bulletin board.

UNIT FIVE *review*

Review: Words for Everyday Use

Check your knowledge of the following vocabulary words. For each word, write a short sentence that includes the word in context. To review a word, look back to the page number indicated.

- accustomed (346)
- anguished (374)
- anxiety (359)
- apparatus (373)
- ascend (372)
- audacity (390)
- bemuse (351)
- betray (350)
- bewilderment (362)
- brood (376)
- chide (330)
- concealment (389)
- conceive (387)
- concussion (378)
- cunningly (387)
- daft (373)
- derision (390)
- disdainful (346)

- dissimulation (387)
- indignant (345)
- invariable (353)
- fatigue (351)
- fixed (350)
- lament (378)
- meager (330)
- mesmerize (331)
- nuisance (366)
- passionate (352)
- pathetic (364)
- plaintive (350)
- presumably (345)
- prim (348)
- primeval (374)
- projection (378)
- prowess (344)
- raveling (374)

- sagacity (387)
- scald (360)
- solemn (349)
- specter (334)
- stealthy (388)
- stifled (388)
- suave (389)
- summon (345)
- supposition (388)
- thresh (376)
- unkempt (344)
- vacancy (359)
- vehement (352, 390)
- verify (373)
- vex (389)
- wane (351)
- warily (366)
- worrisome (331)

Review: Literary Tools

Define each of the following terms, giving concrete examples when possible. To review a term, refer to the page number indicated.

- aim (357)
- antagonist (341)
- first-person point of view (385)
- foreshadowing (327)

- mood (341)
- motivation (357)
- narrator (385)
- point of view (385)
- protagonist (341)

- style (370)
- suspense (327)
- third-person point of view (385)

VOCABULARY DEVELOPMENT. Give students the following exercise.

Write a short story using as many of the Words for Everyday Use on page 399 as possible. As an added challenge, try using the words in alphabetical order and see if you can still have your story make sense. The words must be used with their correct definitions, but you may change the tense or form of the word. For example, instead of ascend, you could use *ascended* or *ascending*.

ADDITIONAL RESOURCES

UNIT 5 RESOURCE BOOK
- Vocabulary Worksheet
- Study Guide: Unit 5 Test
- Unit 5 Test

Reflecting
on your reading

Genre & Theme

All the main selections in this unit are short stories—part of the fiction genre. Although genre is most often used to refer to main categories of literature, such as fiction, poetry, and drama, it is also used to refer to describe literary works that focus on particular themes or topics—such as western, romance, travel, or horror. Besides all fitting into the Horror genre category, what else do the stories in this unit have in common? What comparisons can you make among the stories? Think about these questions in terms of character, setting, and plot.

Group Project

Break into small groups and discuss your ideas about unexplained phenomena or events. Do you believe in ghosts? extra-terrestrial life? the ability to see the future or read someone's mind? Have you ever had a strange experience that you cannot explain? In recent years you may have noticed an increase in public interest in scary or unexplainable events—on television, in the movies, in books, in music, and elsewhere. Why do you think people would be more interested in these mysteries now than, say, ten or twenty years ago? Do you think people will continue to be interested in unexplainable events in the future?

Choose a region of the United States or a single state and research what unexplained events are part of its folklore, history, or news. As a class, you could cover most of the country: one small group researching events in the Southeast, another the Pacific Northwest, a third the Eastern Seaboard, and so on. You can search the Internet for information or go to your school or local library. Prepare a short report about the strange phenomena and present the report to the class. Tell where you found your information and discuss how reliable the sources might be. If you have the time and resources, make a poster to go along with your report, highlighting the unexplained events you learned about. You may want to discuss as a class how unexplained events from different parts of the country are similar and how they are different. In what ways do the phenomena reflect the region from which they come in terms of climate, culture, history, or natural resources?

 ## Critical Thinking

This unit presents many diverse ideas worth thinking about critically, especially because many of these ideas are not based in scientific fact, but came from a writer's imagination. Although the stories in this unit are fiction, how do the events they describe resemble stories we have heard or read about elsewhere? On your own paper, complete the Graphic Organizer below to help you keep track of the unexplained events in the various stories in this unit.

Graphic *Organizer*

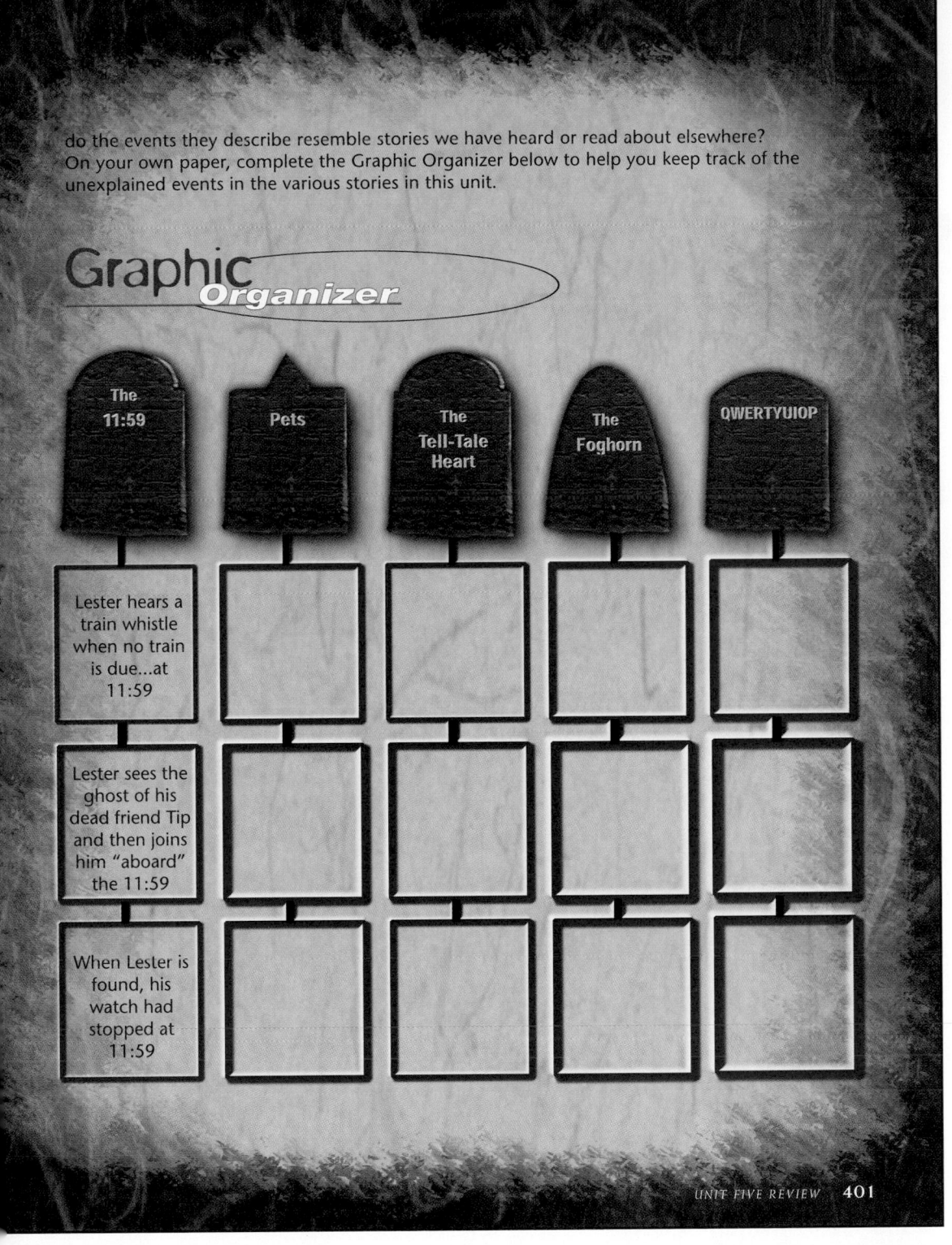

The 11:59	Pets	The Tell-Tale Heart	The Foghorn	QWERTYUIOP
Lester hears a train whistle when no train is due...at 11:59				
Lester sees the ghost of his dead friend Tip and then joins him "aboard" the 11:59				
When Lester is found, his watch had stopped at 11:59				

UNIT SKILLS OUTLINE

Literary Skills and Concepts

Writing Skills and Concepts

Language, Grammar, and Style

GOALS/OBJECTIVES

Studying this unit will enable students to
- appreciate fiction, nonfiction, and poetry exploring the theme of taking flight
- define and identify examples of *climax, diction, free verse, lyric poem, personal essay, point of view, setting, stanza, style,* and *tone*

- read independently to understand aviation; learn to use books as research tools
- write a narrative research paper
- document sources

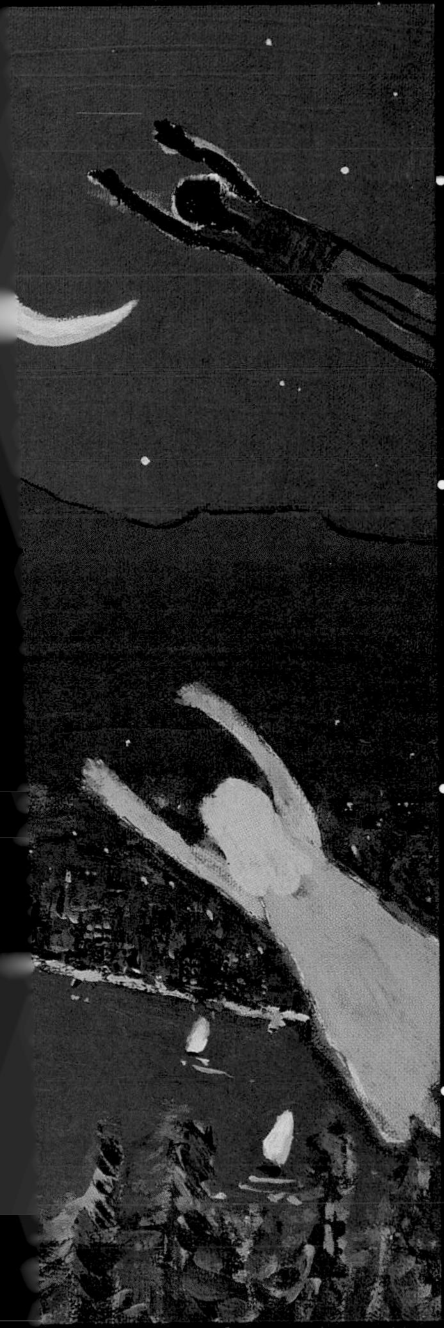

Taking Flight

People Flying. Peter Sycles. Private Collection.

UNIT SIX

(Continued on page 404)

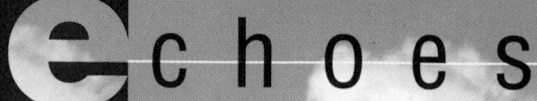

ADDITIONAL QUESTIONS AND ACTIVITIES

Ask students to identify some main themes that two or more of these quotations share. Students might also write a brief personal essay about one of the quotations on this page, reflecting on the meaning of the quotation and its applicability to contemporary life.

"The *Guide* says that there is an art to flying," said Ford, "or rather a knack. The knack lies in learning how to throw yourself at the ground and miss."

—*Douglas Adams from* Life, the Universe and Everything

This is Seagull. I see the horizon. A light blue, a blue band. This is the Earth. How beautiful it is!

—*Valentina Tereshkova, cosmonaut (first woman to orbit Earth)*

There really is not anything amazing in liking to fly. The amazing thing is that so few women, seeing what sport men are having in the air, are doing it themselves.

—*Amelia Earhart*

No bird soars too high if he soars with his own wings.

—*William Blake*

When once you have tasted flight, you will forever walk the earth with your eyes turned skyward, for there you have been, and there you will always long to return.

—*Leonardo da Vinci*

The sky is the only place where there is no prejudice. Up there, everyone is equal. Everyone is free.

—*Bessie Coleman*

Yes, we're off—we're rising. The engine smoothed out into a long sigh, like a person breathing easily, almost like someone singing, ecstatically.

—*Anne Morrow Lindbergh*

Success. Four flights Thursday morning. All against twenty-one-mile wind.

—*Orville and Wilbur Wright, telegram, December 17, 1903*

404 UNIT SIX

TEACHING THE MULTIPLE INTELLIGENCES (CONT.)

Prereading

"The Hummingbird That Lived through Winter"
— by William Saroyan

Reader's T O O L B O X

POINT OF VIEW. Point of view is the vantage point from which a story is told. A story is told from a **first-person point of view** if the narrator of the story is also a character in the story. Just as you would use the pronouns *I* or *we* to tell about something you saw or were involved in, the narrator using first-person point of view uses *I* or *we* to relay the events he or she is witnessing or is part of. A narrator who uses pronouns such as *he, she, it,* and *they,* and avoids using *I* and *we,* does not directly participate in the action, and tells the story from the **third-person point of view**. As you read, identify the point of view from which this story is told. Look for evidence to support your answer.

SETTING. The **setting** of a story is the time and place in which it happens. Authors reveal setting in many ways—by describing landscape, the weather, or the details of a room, neighborhood, or city, for example. As you read, pay attention to changes in time and place. Using a two-column chart like the one below, list the main details of each setting in the story in a box in the left column. In the box to the right of each setting, list one or more details about the hummingbird at the same point in the story.

Graphic *Organizer*

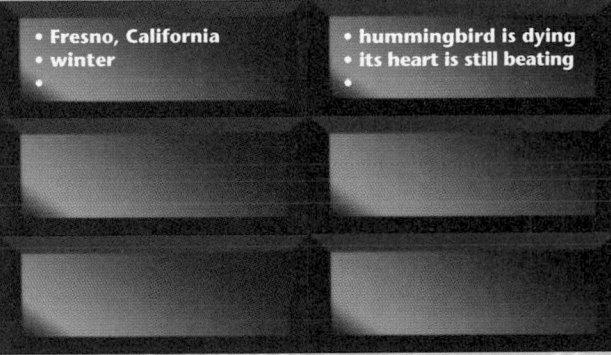

Settings	Details about hummingbird
• Fresno, California • winter	• hummingbird is dying • its heart is still beating

SHORT STORY

Reader's Journal

What would you do if you found a sick or injured animal?

Reader's Resource

- **SCIENCE CONNECTION.** This short story tells about an old man and a hummingbird in the middle of winter in California. Normally, hummingbirds from the United States and Canada migrate to Mexico, Central America, or South America to spend the winter. Hummingbirds live only in the Americas, and just 16 of more than 300 species appear in the United States. More than 150 species are commonly seen near the equator.

- Named for the humming sound of their wings in motion, hummingbirds are the smallest birds on the planet and the only birds able to fly up, down, forward, backward, and sideways. Known for their bold nature, various species of this tiny bird migrate thousands of miles to their winter homes.

405

GRAPHIC ORGANIZER

Students' charts may resemble the following:
Setting: Fresno, California; poor neighborhood; freezing Sunday in the dead of winter; standing in the middle of the street; kitchen of old Dikran's house; the following summer, outside
Details about Hummingbird: hummingbird is dying; its heart is still beating; helpless and heartbreaking; old Dikran blows warm breath on it; hummingbird begins to show signs of fresh life warmth of room, vapor of honey, and the love of the old man cause a change in the bird; bird begins to take dabs of honey; bird suddenly shoots out of hand, suspends itself in space, and spins about the kitchen; old Dikran has narrator open the window so hummingbird can fly away; narrator asks old man if hummingbird lived; old man points to hummingbirds around them and says each of them is their bird.

READER'S JOURNAL

Inform students that it can be extremely dangerous to help sick or injured animals. Even domesticated animals when confused by extreme pain can turn on humans. Tell students it is best to have an adult help them with the animal or call an animal rescue league.

GOALS/OBJECTIVES

Studying this lesson will enable students to
- enjoy a story about a hummingbird
- briefly describe some facts about hummingbirds
- define *point of view* and identify the point of view of a literary work
- define *setting* and point out the settings portrayed in a literary work
- research hummingbird myths and legends
- write an informational advertisement for a wildlife rehabilitation center
- use quotation marks correctly

INDIVIDUAL LEARNING STRATEGIES

Motivation
Locate a videotape of a nature documentary featuring hummingbirds to share with students. This will help students understand their small size and the quickness with which they beat their wings.

Reading Proficiency
Students may benefit from listening to this selection on audiocassette. Have students follow along with the text of the story as they listen.

English Language Learning
Inform students that the characters in this story speak in short, clipped fragments, most likely because English is not their native language but also because people tend to speak in fragment, imperatives, and other short sentences in casual conversation. Inform students that while it is perfectly fine to speak in fragments such as "The little bird. You know, the one that comes in summer and stands in the air and then shoots away," in casual speech and in dialogue in stories, they should avoid this type of language in forms of writing such as essays and test answers.

Special Needs
Students may benefit from seeing or participating in a role-playing session in which a pair of students enacts the actions and then recite the dialogue of this story. The story is brief enough that most students can comfortably enact the whole story, but if students prefer, they may choose just a portion of the story.

Enrichment
Ask students to research the hummingbird, using library or Internet resources. They should learn the migration, mating, and nesting habits of the tiny birds as well as any other interesting facts. One good book on the subject of hummingbirds is *Hummingbirds of North America* by Paul Johnsgard (2nd edition, 1997). Students should then prepare brief written reports on hummingbirds (no more than a page or two).

The Hummingbird that lived through WINTER

William Saroyan

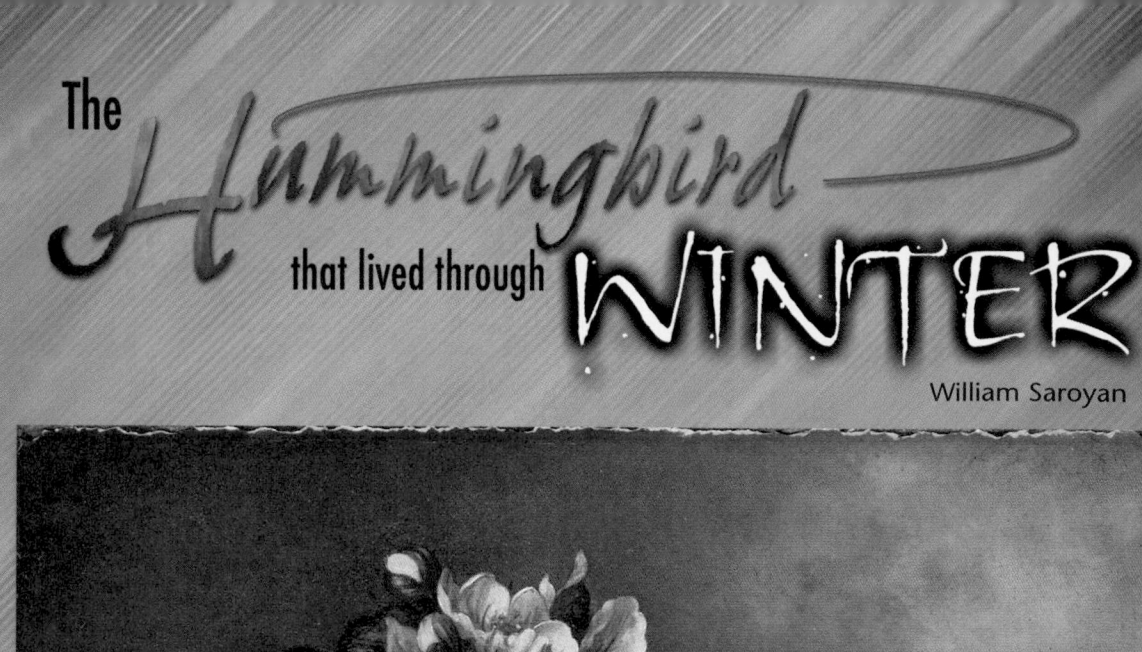

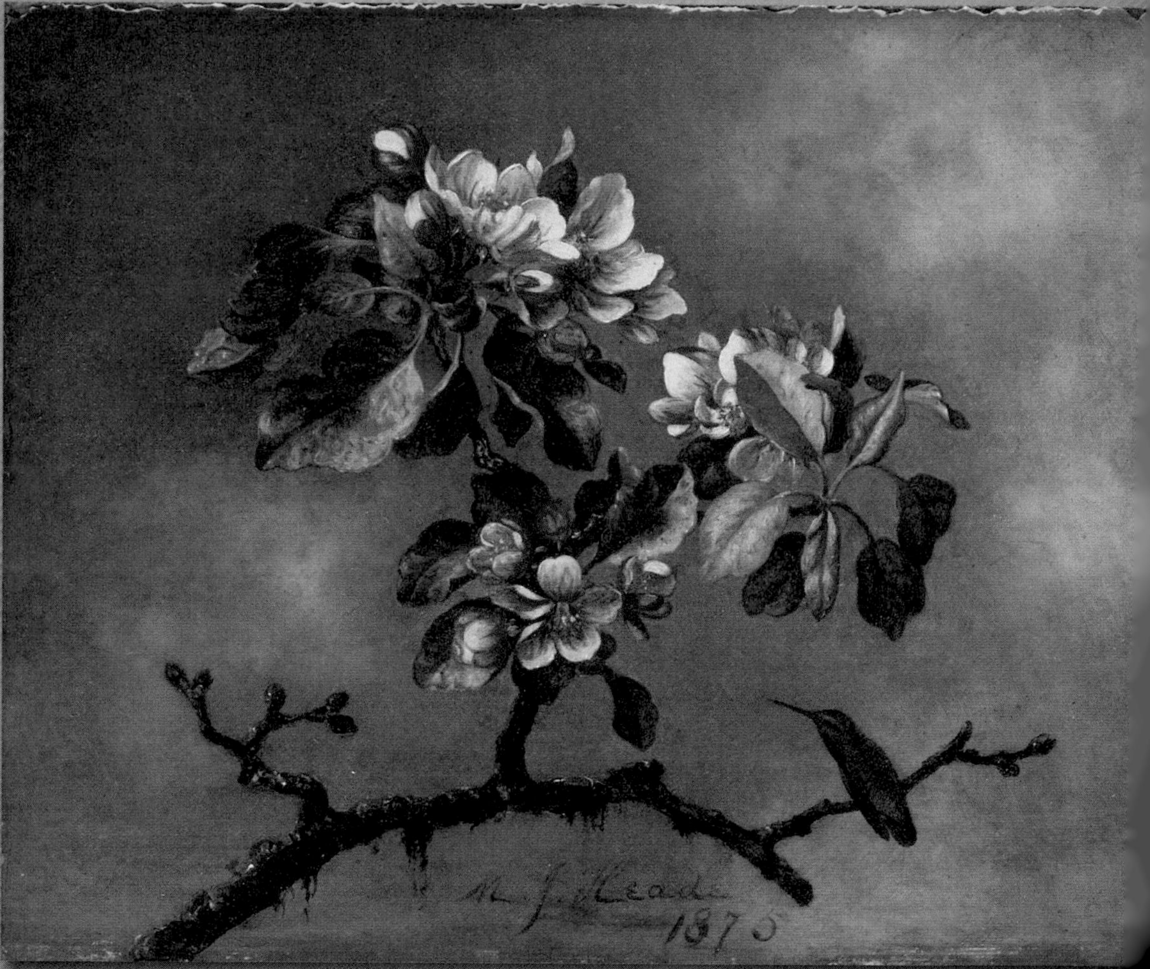

Apple Blossoms and a Hummingbird, 1875. Martin Johnson Heade. Private Collection.

There was a hummingbird once which in the wintertime did not leave our neighborhood in Fresno, California. I'll tell you about it.

Across the street lived old Dikran, who was almost blind. He was past eighty and his wife was only a few years younger. They had a little house that was as neat inside as it was ordinary outside—except for old Dikran's garden, which was the best thing of its kind in the world. Plants, bushes, trees—all strong, in sweet black moist earth whose <u>guardian</u> was old Dikran. All things from the sky loved this spot in our poor neighborhood, and old Dikran loved *them*.

> **GUIDED READING**
> Who loves old Dikran's garden?

One freezing Sunday, in the dead of winter, as I came home from Sunday School I saw old Dikran standing in the middle of the street trying to <u>distinguish</u> what was in his hand. Instead of going into our house to the fire, as I had wanted to do, I stood on the steps of the front porch and watched the old man. He would turn around and look upward at his trees and then back to the palm of his hand. He stood in the street at

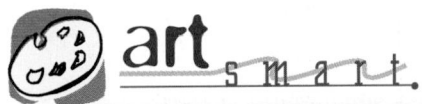
art smart.

Apple Blossoms and a Hummingbird, 1875.
Martin Johnson Heade. Private Collection.

Martin Johnson Heade (1819–1904) belonged to a group of American artists called the Luminists, known for the soft, glowing light effects in their landscape paintings. Hummingbirds as a subject, he said, became for him "an all-absorbing craze." Why do you think the artist depicted the hummingbird sitting on a branch instead of flying?

least two minutes and then at last he came to me. He held his hand out, and in Armenian[1] he said, "What is this in my hand?"

I looked.

"It is a hummingbird," I said half in English and half in Armenian. Hummingbird I said in English because I didn't know its name in Armenian.

"What is that?" old Dikran asked.

"The little bird," I said. "You know. The one that comes in the summer and stands in the air and then shoots away. The one with the wings that beat so fast you can't see them. It's in your hand. It's dying."

> **GUIDED READING**
> What is in old Dikran's hand?

"Come with me," the old man said. "I can't see, and the wife's at church. I can feel its heart beating. Is it in a bad way? Look again once."

I looked again. It was a sad thing to behold. This wonderful little creature of summertime in the big rough hand of the old peasant. Here and pathetic, not suspended in a shaft of summer light, not the most alive thing in the world, but the most helpless and heart-breaking.

"It's dying," I said.

The old man lifted his hand to his mouth and blew warm breath on the little thing in his hand which he could not even see. "Stay now," he said in Armenian. "It is not long till summer. Stay, swift and lovely."

We went into the kitchen of his little house, and while he blew warm breath on the bird he told me what to do.

---

1. **Armenian.** Language spoken by the people dwelling chiefly in Armenia and in neighboring regions of Turkey and Azerbaijan

---

words for everyday use

guard • ian (gär′ dē ən) n., one that guards. *Our puppy is a loyal <u>guardian</u> to our baby sister, barking loudly when anyone new goes near her.*

dis • tin • guish (di stin′ gwish) v., to discern; to detect with the eyes or with other senses. *Because the brothers looked so much alike, from a distance it was difficult to <u>distinguish</u> one from the other.*

1. All things from the sky love old Dikran's garden.
2. A hummingbird is in old Dikran's hand.

SPELLING AND VOCABULARY WORDS

distinguish
guardian
transformation
vapor

ADDITIONAL VOCABULARY

Pronunciations of Proper Nouns and Adjectives
Sa roy an (Sa roy ən) n.
Dik ran (dik ran) n.
Ar me ni an (är mē′nē ən) adj.
Additional Vocabulary
behold—see
dab—a drop
moist—damp, wet
pathetic—sad
restless—unable to rest
stir—move
suspended—hanging
swift—quick

1. The warmth of the room, the vapor of the honey, and the love and will of the old man make the hummingbird feel better.
2. Dikran tells the narrator to open the window to let the bird go because it is alive now and wants to go.
3. Dikran says that each of the hummingbirds is their hummingbird.

CROSS-CURRICULAR ACTIVITIES

SCIENCE AND THE APPLIED ARTS. Inform students that hummingbirds extract nectar from blossoms using their long, narrow bill and tongue, and that when searching for food, they are particularly attracted to the color red. Ask students to research which blossoms attract hummingbirds and when the birds are present in your area. Then, have them create their own hummingbird feeders and fill them with homemade "nectar." Simple feeders can be made using a glass test tube or a pill vial hung at an angle and filled with sugar water. To attract the birds, the students can paint their feeders red or decorate them with a red ribbon or handmade red paper flowers. The feeders should be hung from a branch using floral wire or twist ties fashioned into a harness. Inform students that the feeders must be out of reach of cats! To make the "nectar," mix one part white sugar with four parts water and boil for two minutes. Boiling is important, since it kills mold and bacteria. Allow to cool before placing in the feeder. Never use honey as it can spoil quickly and make the hummingbirds very sick, and do not use red food coloring in the water. The feeder must be cleaned out at least every three days during hot weather. Hummingbirds are very courageous. If students feed them on a regular basis, and if they sit very still, the birds will drink from a feeder held in a student's hand.

SOCIAL STUDIES AND HISTORY. William Saroyan, the author of "Hummingbird in Winter," was very proud of his Armenian heritage and frequently wrote about the experiences of Armenian-American

"Put a tablespoon of honey over the gas fire and pour it into my hand, but be sure it is not too hot."

This was done.

After a moment the hummingbird began to show signs of fresh life. The warmth of the room, the vapor of the warm honey—and, well, the will and love of the old man. Soon the old man could feel the change in his hand, and after a moment or two the hummingbird began to take little dabs of the honey.

"It will live," the old man announced. "Stay and watch."

The transformation was incredible. The old man kept his hand

> **GUIDED READING**
> What makes the hummingbird feel better?

generously open, and I expected the helpless bird to shoot upward out of his hand, suspend itself in space, and scare the life out of me—which is exactly what happened. The new life of the little bird was magnificent. It spun about in the little kitchen, going to the window, coming back to the heat, suspending, circling as if it were summertime and it had never felt better in its whole life.

The old man sat on the plain chair, blind but attentive. He listened carefully and tried to see, but of course he couldn't. He kept asking about the bird, how it seemed to be, whether it showed signs of weakening again, what its spirit was, and whether or not it appeared to be restless; and I kept describing the bird to him.

When the bird was restless and wanted to go, the old man said, "Open the window and let it go."

> **GUIDED READING**
> Why does old Dikran tell the narrator to let the hummingbird go?

"Will it live?" I asked.

"It is alive now and wants to go," he said. "Open the window."

I opened the window, the hummingbird stirred about here and there, feeling the cold from the outside, suspended itself in the area of the open window, stirring this way and that, and then it was gone.

"Close the window," the old man said.

We talked a minute or two and then I went home.

The old man claimed the hummingbird lived through that winter, but I never knew for sure. I saw hummingbirds again when summer came, but I couldn't tell one from the other.

One day in the summer I asked the old man.

"Did it live?"

"The little bird?" he said.

"Yes," I said. "That we gave the honey to. You remember. The little bird that was dying in the winter. Did it live?"

"Look about you," the old man said. "Do you see the bird?"

"I see humming*birds*," I said.

"Each of them is our bird," the old man said. "Each of them, each of them," he said swiftly and gently. ■

> **GUIDED READING**
> What does old Dikran say about the hummingbirds?

---

words for everyday use

va • por (vā' pər) *n.,* scattered matter suspended in the air and clouding it (such as smoke or fog). *Even without hearing the teapot whistle, I knew it was ready by the <u>vapor</u> pouring out of the spout.*

trans • for • ma • tion (trans fər mā' shən) *n.,* change in composition, structure, or outward form and appearance. *After the addition of the new paint, furniture, carpet, and curtains, the <u>transformation</u> of the room was complete.*

CROSS-CURRICULAR ACTIVITIES (CONT.)

people. Show students a map of Eastern Europe and point out the country of Armenia. Ask students to research Armenia, its history, its people and their culture, and to write a brief report telling what they learned. They should include a bibliography of the sources they consulted in their research.

Respond *to the* SELECTION

Do you think the hummingbird lived? Why, or why not?

Most hummingbird photographers set up their camera equipment next to a feeder. Photographers use one or more light systems that flash when the shutter is released on the camera. The camera stands on a tripod. The lights and the camera are connected by a long cable to a push-button shutter release, which the photographer presses to shoot the picture. This enables the photographer to remain hidden from the skittish hummingbirds. If high-speed photography had been available in 1875, how might Martin Johnson Heade have painted the hummingbird (on page 406) differently?

About *the* AUTHOR

William Stonehill Saroyan (1908–1981) wrote more than 60 books during his lifetime. He published his first, *The Daring Young Man on the Flying Trapeze*, at the age of 26. Born in Fresno, California, to Armenian parents, Saroyan attributed much of his inspiration for writing to his Armenian heritage. In his last published book he wrote, "My work is writing, but my real work is being." Much of his "real work of being" was spent cultivating a worldwide understanding of the Armenian culture. About his people, Saroyan said, "For when two of them meet anywhere in the world, see if they will not create a New Armenia."

"THE HUMMINGBIRD THAT LIVED THROUGH WINTER" **409**

RESPOND TO THE SELECTION

Also encourage students to discuss why it was so important to old Dikran to save the hummingbird.

ART SMART

In his painting Heade depicted the hummingbird on a branch. He would not have been able to see the flight of the hummingbird frozen in time; only high speech photography would have enabled that.

SELECTION CHECK TEST 4.6.1 WITH ANSWERS

Checking Your Reading
1. What is special about Dikran's property? **Dikran takes great care of and pride in his garden.**
2. What is the weather like the day Dikran finds the hummingbird? **The weather is cold.**
3. What do Dikran and the narrator feed to the hummingbird? **Dikran and the narrator feed the hummingbird honey.**
4. What does the hummingbird do after it is fed? **The hummingbird recovers, flying around the room and out of the window.**
5. In what season does the story end? **The story ends in summer.**

Vocabulary in Context
Fill in each blank below with the most appropriate word from the following *Words for Everyday Use* from "The Hummingbird That Lived Through Winter." You may have to change the tense of the word.

> vapor   transformation   guardian
>   distinguish

1. "Be careful," the scientist warned the visiting students. "The **vapor** from that chemical is poisonous."
2. Asala had undergone such a **transformation** since he'd last seen her that Quint barely recognized her.
3. It took the archaeologist hours of careful, painstaking brushing before she could **distinguish** the pattern in the ancient clay.

Reader's Toolbox
Fill in the blanks using these terms.

> first person   third person
>   setting   point of view

SELECTION CHECK TEST 4.6.1 WITH ANSWERS (CONT.)

1. If the narrator uses pronouns such as *I* and *we*, then the story is told in the **first person** perspective.
2. A(n) **third person** narrator does not participate in the action.
3. The vantage point from which a story is told is its **point of view**.
4. "The Hummingbird that Lived Through Winter" is told by a character in the story, and is told from the **first person** perspective.
5. Descriptions of Dikran's house, the hummingbird, and the passing of seasons help the reader understand the **setting** of the story.

Mute Dancers: How to Watch a Hummingbird

Diane Ackerman

A lot of hummingbirds die in their sleep. Like a small fury of iridescence, a hummingbird spends the day at high speed, darting and swiveling among thousands of nectar-rich blossoms. Hummingbirds have huge hearts and need colossal amounts of energy to fuel their flights, so they live in a perpetual mania to find food. They tend to prefer red, trumpet-shaped flowers, in which nectar thickly oozes, and eat every 15 minutes or so. A hummingbird drinks with a W-shaped tongue, licking nectar up as a cat might (but faster). Like a tiny drum roll, its heart beats at 500 times a minute. Frighten a hummingbird and its heart can race to over 1,200 times a minute. Feasting and flying, courting and dueling, hummingbirds consume life at a fever pitch. No warm-blooded animal on earth uses more energy, for its size. But that puts them at great peril. By day's end, wrung-out and exhausted, a hummingbird rests near collapse.

In the dark night of the hummingbird, it can sink into a zombielike state of torpor; its breathing grows shallow and its wild heart slows to only 36 beats a minute. When dawn breaks on the fuchsia and columbine, hummingbirds must jump-start their hearts and fire up their flight muscles to raise their body temperature for another all-or-nothing day. That demands a colossal effort, which some can't manage. So a lot of hummingbirds die in their sleep.

But most do bestir themselves. This is why, in American Indian myths and legends, hummingbirds are often depicted as resurrection birds, which seem to die and be reborn on another day or in another season. The Aztec god of war was named Huitzilopochtli, a compound word meaning "shining one with weapon like cactus thorn," and "sorcerer that spits fire." Aztec warriors fought, knowing that if they fell in battle they would be reincarnated as glittery, thuglike hummingbirds. The male birds were lionized for their ferocity in battle. And their feathers flashed in the sun like jewel-encrusted shields. Aztec rulers donned ceremonial robes of hummingbird feathers. As they walked, colors danced across their shoulders and bathed them in a supernatural light show.

While most birds are busy singing a small operetta of who and what and where, hummingbirds are virtually mute. Such small voices don't carry far, so they don't bother much with song. But if they can't serenade a mate, or yell war cries at a rival, how can they perform the essential dramas of their lives? They dance. Using body language, they spell out their intentions and moods just as bees, fireflies or hula dancers do. That means elaborate aerial ballets in which males twirl, joust, sideswipe and somersault. Brazen and fierce, they will take on large adversaries—even cats, dogs or humans.

The Aztec God Quetzalcoatl with a Hummingbird, c.1500. Aztec artist.
Biblioteca Nazionale Centrale, Florence, Italy.

My neighbor Persis once told me how she'd been needled by hummingbirds. When Persis lived in San Francisco, hummingbirds often attacked her outside her apartment building. From their perspective she was on *their* property, not the other way round, and they flew circles around her to vex her away. My encounters with hummingbirds have been altogether more benign. Whenever I've walked through South American rain forests, with my hair braided and secured by a waterproof red ribbon, hummingbirds have assumed my ribbon to be a succulent flower and have probed my hair repeatedly, searching for nectar. Their touch was as delicate as a sweat bee's. But it was their purring by my ear that made me twitch. In time, they would leave unfed, but for a while I felt like a character in a Li'l Abner cartoon who could be named something like "Hummer." In Portuguese, the word for hummingbird (*Beija flora*) means "flower kisser." It was the American colonists who first imagined the birds humming as they went about their chores.

Last summer, the historical novelist Jeanne Mackin winced to see her cat, Beltane, drag in voles, birds and even baby rabbits. Few things can compete with the blood lust of a tabby cat. But one day Beltane dragged in something rare and shimmery—a struggling hummingbird. The feathers were ruffled and there was a bit of blood on the breast, but the bird still looked perky and alive. So Jeanne fashioned a nest for it out of a small wire basket lined in gauze, and fed it sugar water from an eye dropper. To her

ART SMART

Inform students that the god portrayed in this image is Quetzalcoatl, another god who was depicted as a feathered serpent, not Huitzilopochtli, the hummingbird god mentioned in the essay.

HISTORICAL NOTE

Inform students that according to Aztec tradition, their original home was a place called Aztlan, or "place of the herons," probably located in northern Mexico. Huitzilopochtli, the hummingbird god, god of war, and the patron god of the Aztecs, ordered the Aztecs to leave their homeland, and they began to migrate southward, probably in the twelfth century A.D. The Aztecs believed that while their ancestors journeyed Huitzilopochtli gave them a new name, calling them "Mexica," from which comes the name later given to the nation of Mexico. Thus, according to legend, the god of hummingbirds named a modern nation.

amazement, as she watched, "it miscarried a little pearl." Hummingbird eggs are the size of coffee beans, and females usually carry two. So Jeanne knew one might still be safe inside. After a quiet night, the hummingbird seemed stronger, and when she set the basket outside at dawn, the tiny assault victim flew away.

It was a ruby-throated hummingbird that she nursed, the only one native to the East Coast. In the winter they migrate thousands of miles over mountains and open water to Mexico and South America. She may well have been visited by a species known to the Aztecs. Altogether, there are 16 species of hummingbirds in North America, and many dozens in South America, especially near the equator, where they can feed on a buffet of blossoms. The tiniest—the Cuban bee hummingbird—is the smallest warm-blooded animal in the world. About two and one-eighth inches long from beak to tail, it is smaller than the toe of an eagle, and its eggs are like seeds.

Hummingbirds are a New World phenomenon. So, too, is vanilla, and their stories are linked. When the early explorers returned home with the riches of the West, they found it impossible, to their deep frustration, to grow vanilla beans. It took ages before they discovered why—that hummingbirds were a key pollinator of vanilla orchids—and devised beaklike splinters of bamboo to do the work of birds.

Now that summer has come at last, lucky days may be spent watching the antics of hummingbirds. The best way to behold them is to stand with the light behind you, so that the bird faces the sun. Most of the trembling colors aren't true pigments, but the result of light staggering through clear cells that act as prisms. Hummingbirds are iridescent for the same reason soap bubbles are. Each feather contains tiny air bubbles separated by dark spaces. Light bounces off the air bubbles at different angles, and that makes blazing colors seem to swarm and leap. All is vanity in the end. The male's shimmer draws a female to mate. But that doesn't matter much to gardeners, watching hummingbirds patrol the impatiens as if the northern lights had suddenly fallen to earth. ∎

ABOUT THE RELATED READING ⋀
Diane Ackerman is a naturalist and a writer of poetry, nonfiction essays, and books. *The Rarest of the Rare* and *The Moon by Whale Light* are just two of numerous nonfiction works by Ackerman that delve into the mysteries of the natural world. "Mute Dancers: How to Watch a Hummingbird" was originally published in 1994 in *The New York Times Magazine.*

ABOUT THE RELATED READING ➤
As soon as she was able to write, **Felice Holman** was writing poetry. "Humming Bird" comes from *The Song in My Head,* a collection of her poems published in 1990. Holman takes an active interest in young readers and is also the author of *Real* and *Slake's Limbo,* both books for young people.

Humming BIRD

Felice Holman

Whirring as wound wires whir.
Glistened green and brightened blur.
Bird a flower dreamed upon.
A moment fanning, and then gone. ∎

ADDITIONAL QUESTIONS AND ACTIVITIES

Ask students the following questions:
1. How does the hummingbird whir?
2. What does the hummingbird look like?
3. Upon what does the hummingbird "dream"?

Answers
1. It whirs as wound wires whir.
2. It is a glistened green and a brightened blur.
3. The hummingbird "dreams" upon a flower.

LITERARY TECHNIQUE

ALLITERATION AND DESCRIPTION.
Alliteration is the repetition of consonant sounds at the beginning of syllables, as in *hang onto your hat*. A **description** gives a picture in words of a character, object, or scene. Ask students to point to examples of alliteration in the poem. What is the effect of the use of alliteration on the poem as a whole? Ask students what description is provided of the hummingbird. What is unusual about this description? What does this description make you think of the hummingbird?
Answers. Students may point to examples such as "whirring as wound wires whir," "glistened green," and "brightened blur./ Bird." Students may say the use of alliteration gives the poem a musical quality. Students should point to the line "Bird a flower dreamed upon." Students may say this is unusual because they would think that if anything the bird would be dreaming about the flower. Students may say the description of a flower dreaming upon the bird emphasizes the dreamy beauty of the hummingbird, as well as the essential role it plays in pollinating flowers.

RECALL

1a. Old Dikran is the guardian of the plants, bushes, and trees of his garden. Dikran loves "all things from the sky."

2a. Students may say that the obstacles are that Dikran is losing his vision and his native language is Armenian and the narrator can't think of the Armenian word for hummingbird. The narrator describes the actions, appearance, and habits of the hummingbird to Dikran to make him understand the type of bird it is.

3a. They bring the hummingbird into the warm kitchen and heat honey for the hummingbird. Dikran gives the instructions and the narrator carries them out.

4a. The narrator asks old Dikran whether the hummingbird lived through the winter. Dikran says that each of the hummingbirds they now see is their bird.

INTERPRET

1b. Students may say that Dikran enjoys the physical activity of gardening, the garden's beauty, and the fact that his garden draws beautiful living creatures, such as birds.

2b. The narrator becomes involved in the attempt to save the hummingbird's life.

3b. Students may say that the narrator feels that the scene is "incredible," surprising, and "magnificent." He is clearly enthused about the hummingbird's return to life.

4b. Students may suggest that in helping that one bird, whether it lived or died, they formed a close bond with all the hummingbirds.

ANALYZE

5a. Students may point to the following as evidence of Dikran's love for nature and its creatures: Dikran's gardening and loving the creatures of the sky, Dikran's eager concern for the narrator to look at the bird and examine its condition, his blowing on the bird to keep it warm, his bringing it inside, his knowledge about what to do to bring it back to life, and his willingness to let the hummingbird free again.

SYNTHESIZE

5b. Students may say he sees or senses the life of that hummingbird in the other hummingbirds. Students may say that Dikran sees nature and its creatures as being very interconnected.

EVALUATE

6a. Students may say that the story

Investigate, Inquire, and Imagine

Recall: GATHERING FACTS

1a. Of what is old Dikran the guardian? Who does Dikran love?

2a. What two obstacles at first make it hard for old Dikran to know what he is holding? How does he find out what it is?

3a. What do Dikran and the narrator do with the hummingbird? Who gives the instructions and who carries them out?

4a. What does the narrator ask old Dikran at the end of the story? What does old Dikran say about the hummingbirds they see that summer and the bird they found the winter before?

Interpret: FINDING MEANING

1b. In what ways might old Dikran get pleasure from his garden?

2b. How does the narrator's role change at this point?

3b. How does the narrator feel as the hummingbird begins to show signs of energy?

4b. What might old Dikran mean when he says, "Each of them is our bird"?

Analyze: TAKING THINGS APART

5a. What evidence do you find that old Dikran values nature and its creatures?

Synthesize: BRINGING THINGS TOGETHER

5b. How does old Dikran think the hummingbird he helped relates to the hummingbirds he sees the following spring? What does this say about Dikran's attitude toward life?

Evaluate: MAKING JUDGMENTS

6a. How well does William Saroyan's story create a strong image of a hummingbird? Why do you think Saroyan made Dikran blind? How does that detail impact the story? In what way does this story relate to Saroyan's comment that his "real work is being"?

Extend: CONNECTING IDEAS

6b. Compare the hummingbird in the short story with descriptions of hummingbirds shared in the essay by Diane Ackerman. How do the details from the story differ from those in the essay? Does any information appear in both? Review Felice Holman's poem "Humming Bird." What about hummingbirds does this poem capture? How does the information each author chooses to share signal his or her purposes for writing? How do the purposes of each author differ? How are they the same?

ANSWERS TO INVESTIGATE, INQUIRE, IMAGINE (CONT.)

creates a strong image of hummingbirds, as well as passing on information about their habits.

EXTEND

6b. Students may say the story portrays the hummingbirds as more hardy after a period of weakness than does Ackerman in her essay. The essay also provides a lot more facts about hummingbirds, including their heart rate, their sleeping habits, how they communicate with other birds, and their cultural significance among groups of humans.

Information that is repeated is their small size, the quickness with which they beat their wings, their migration patterns, and their seeming ability to resurrect. Students may say the poem captures the physical beauty and the lightning quick wing beats of hummingbirds. Students may say this indicates that the poet is writing to express the hummingbird's beauty. This is similar to Saroyan's purpose, but Saroyan goes farther in showing the connections between people, an individual hummingbird, and hummingbirds as a group.

Understanding *Literature*

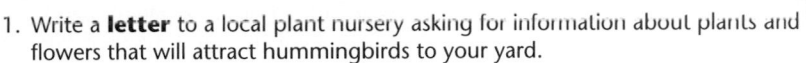

SETTING. The **setting** of a story is the time and place in which it happens. Review the chart you created on setting as you read the story. Why is setting, especially the season, so important in this story? What details of the setting remain the same throughout the story?

POINT OF VIEW. Point of view is the vantage point from which a story is told. In William Saroyan's "The Hummingbird That Lived through Winter," the narrator is a character directly involved in the events of the story. As in any story, the narrator is the source of information for the reader, but in this story the narrator is also a source of information for old Dikran. Look back to the story to find an example of the narrator directly addressing the reader. Locate one or more instances in the story when the narrator provides information for old Dikran.

Writer's Journal

1. Write a **letter** to a local plant nursery asking for information about plants and flowers that will attract hummingbirds to your yard.

2. Write a short **poem** about your favorite animal or bird. Send the poem to a friend or family member who appreciates wildlife.

3. Use **dialogue** to write the conversation that old Dikran might have with his wife when she returns home about finding, helping, and releasing the hummingbird. Focus Dikran's dialogue on details that describe sound, smell, touch, and the way the experience might have made him feel.

Skill Builders

Collaborative Learning & Critical Thinking

DISCUSSING THE STORY. Form small groups. Within your group, share opinions on the fate of the hummingbird. Does everyone share the same opinion? What evidence does the story provide that the hummingbird lived or died? What does old Dikran think happened to the bird? What does the narrator think? Discuss how it can be possible for readers to draw different conclusions about the same story. What unique personal traits might decide how a reader interprets a story or whether a reader likes a story? Decide as a group whether there must always be one right answer to a question or whether there can be more than one answer to some questions. As a group, determine a concrete example of a question or situation that has no obvious right or wrong answer to discuss as a class.

ANSWERS TO UNDERSTANDING LITERATURE

SETTING. Students may say the setting—a freezing time in winter in a poor neighborhood of Fresno California is important because it emphasizes how much the hummingbird's life is at risk. The setting of the neighborhood in Fresno remains the same, although the seasons change.

POINT OF VIEW. For examples of the narrator directly addressing the reader, students may point to the following: "I'll tell you about it." For an example of the narrator providing information for old Dikran, students may point to the following: "The little bird. You know. The one that comes in summer and stands in the air and then shoots away. The one with wings that beat so fast you can't see them. It's in your hand. It's dying."

Collaborative Learning & Critical Thinking

Students may be divided about whether the hummingbird lived or died. Old Dikran thinks that the bird may have died but it lives on in the spirits of the other birds. The narrator does not express a definite opinion, but he too probably thinks that the hummingbird died in the cold weather. Students may say that people read things differently depending on their own experiences, personalities, and the knowledge they bring to the work they read. Students may list a variety of personal traits that can affect an interpretation. Students may say that as long as a response is based on evidence and is supported, there is no right or wrong answer to some questions. Encourage students to generate a long list of open-ended questions.

Study and Research & Speaking and Listening

Refer students to the Language Arts Survey, "How Library Materials Are Organized," and "Using the Internet," for help and added instruction. Tell students that their retellings should remain faithful to the main events in the myth or legend they locate.

Media Literacy

Inform students that their ads will be shaped by the medium they choose. For example, a radio ad is totally dependent on words, while TV, Internet, or print ads can make use of visual images too. If students choose the latter options, encourage them to think about what images would be effective in portraying the organization, as well as the ratio of words to images they wish to include.

Language, Grammar, and Style

1. B
2. C
3. A
4. A
5. C

Study and Research & Speaking and Listening
HUMMINGBIRD MYTHS AND LEGENDS.

Diane Ackerman's nonfiction essay "Mute Dancers: How to Watch a Hummingbird" says that hummingbirds were depicted in various ways in American Indian myths and legends. The Hopi, the Cherokee, and the Aztec are just a few Native American groups that have included hummingbirds in their myths and legends. Form small groups to research this subject. Use the library, the Internet, or both to find a myth or legend that depicts hummingbirds. With your group members, decide on a way to retell the myth or legend. You may want to rewrite the story in your own words and read it to the class, or you may choose to act out the myth or legend.

Media Literacy
WILDLIFE REHABILITATION CENTERS.

If you find a wild animal in need of care, you should contact a professional who knows how to handle the animal and knows what kind of care it needs. You can contact your state's Department of Natural Resources (DNR) or Game, Fish and Parks Department to find the wildlife rehabilitation center closest to you. As a class, collect some basic information on the rehabilitation center from the Internet, from printed literature offered by the center, or by talking to an employee at the center. Then write an informational advertisement to educate people in your community about the rehabilitation center and the services it provides. Think about your likely audience and which medium will best reach them: radio, TV, the Internet, or print. Think about which facts will most likely persuade people to contact the organization if they do find an injured animal. For more information on writing a public service announcement, see the Language Arts Survey 6.10, "Writing a Public Service Announcement."

Language, Grammar, and Style
USING QUOTATION MARKS.

Review the following rules for using quotation marks. Then read the examples below and label each with the letter of the rule that applies to it.

RULES

A. Enclose the words of a direct quotation in quotation marks. When you use a person's exact words in your writing, you are using a direct quotation.

B. Use quotation marks to enclose the titles of short works such as short stories, poems, songs, articles, and parts of books.

C. Use quotation marks or parentheses to enclose the definition of a foreign word or phrase.

EXAMPLES

1. I was fascinated by what I learned about hummingbirds from reading Diane Ackerman's nonfiction essay "Mute Dancers: How to Watch a Hummingbird."

2. The Aztec god of war was named Huitzilopochtli, a compound word meaning "shining one with weapon like cactus thorn," and "sorcerer that spits fire."

3. According to Ackerman, "there are 16 species of hummingbirds in North America, and many dozens in South America."

4. "Each of them is our bird," the old man said.

5. In Portuguese, the word for hummingbird (Beija flor) means "flower kisser."

For more information on how to use quotation marks correctly, refer to the Language Arts Survey 3.86, "Quotation Marks."

Prereading

"Sympathy" and "Caged bird"

by Paul Laurence Dunbar   by Maya Angelou

Reader's Resource

- "Sympathy" was published in 1899 in *Lyrics of the Hearthside*, a collection of poems by Paul Laurence Dunbar. Written during a time in America when a well-paying job and a college education were luxuries unavailable to most African Americans, it echoes the frustration of a talented young black poet. Credited for capturing the true voice of the African American in his poetry, Dunbar set the stage for the emergence of black artists and writers living in Harlem in the 1920s and 1930s, an era known as the Harlem Renaissance. Although best known for his poems written in black folk language, Dunbar also wrote poems like "Sympathy," demonstrating his mastery of standard English verse.

- Maya Angelou's poem "Caged Bird" was published 84 years after "Sympathy" in a poetry collection titled *Shaker, Why Don't You Sing?* She chose the title *I Know Why the Caged Bird Sings* for the first book in her five-book collection of autobiographical works, which shares her experiences of growing up black in the American South in the 1930s and beyond.

Tuskegee History Class, 1902. Frances Benjamin Johnston. Library of Congress.

Reader's TOOLBOX

STANZA. A stanza is a group of lines in a poem. Stanzas are usually separated by spaces from other groups of lines. As you read, note the number and arrangement of stanzas in each poem. With what does each stanza begin and end?

TONE. In a literary work, **tone** is the writer's or speaker's emotional attitude toward the subject or the reader. Examples of the different tones that a writer might create include familiar, playful, sarcastic, serious, and sincere. As you read, think about the attitudes the authors of the poems may reveal. What words and phrases in these poems reveal the authors' tone? How would you describe the tone of each poem in your own words?

Reader's Journal

Write about a time in your life when you didn't feel free to be yourself in words or actions. How did this make you feel? What did you do?

GOALS/OBJECTIVES

Studying this lesson will enable students to
- have a positive experience reading two poems on the same subject—caged birds
- define *stanza* and analyze stanzas of a poem
- define *tone* and identify the tone of a literary work
- write lyrics on freedom
- research human or animal rights issues
- distinguish between the active and the passive voice

READER'S JOURNAL

Ask students to consider what it would be like to spend many years of your life deprived of freedom. What emotions might it create in you? How might extended lack of freedom affect your personality, your hopes, and your dreams?

ANSWERS TO READER'S TOOLBOX

STANZA. Dunbar's poem contains three stanzas. His stanzas are arranged so that each begins with and ends with a personal revelation about how he identifies with the caged bird: I know what the caged bird feels; I know why he beats his wing; I know why the caged bird sings. Angelou's poem contains six stanzas. The stanzas are arranged so that each describes either the free bird or the caged bird. Each of Angelou's stanzas is complete in the description of an action and the surrounding scenery of either the free bird or the caged bird. Each stanza begins with description of an action of the free bird or the caged bird: "A free bird leaps," "But a bird that stalks." Unlike Dunbar's, Angelou's first and last lines of each stanza do not repeat, but each last line does describe an action of either bird, like each first line.

TONE. The authors of these poems are expressing their feelings about the subject of their poems: the caged bird literally, freedom, metaphorically. In "Caged Bird," Maya Angelou laments the fate of the caged bird and celebrates the free bird. Her attitude toward the caged bird is sympathetic, understanding, but not to the degree that Dunbar is sympathetic and understanding. Portions of the Angelou's poem could be interpreted to suggest that in some cases, the caged bird might be in

(Continued on page 418)

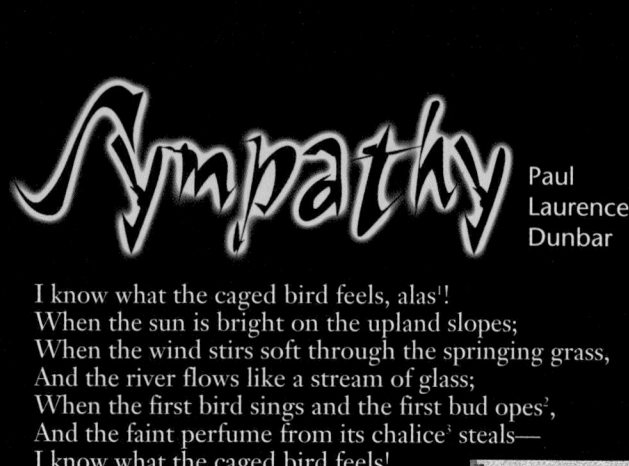

Sympathy
Paul Laurence Dunbar

I know what the caged bird feels, alas[1]!
When the sun is bright on the upland slopes;
When the wind stirs soft through the springing grass,
And the river flows like a stream of glass;
When the first bird sings and the first bud opes[2],
And the faint perfume from its chalice[3] steals—
I know what the caged bird feels!

I know why the caged bird beats his wing
Till its blood is red on the cruel bars;
For he must fly back to his perch and cling
When he fain[4] would be on the bough a-swing[5];
And a pain still throbs in the old, old scars
And they pulse again with a <u>keener</u> sting—
I know why he beats his wing!

I know why the caged bird sings, ah me,
When his wing is bruised and his
  bosom sore,—
When he beats his bars and he would
  be free;
It is not a carol of joy or glee,
But a prayer that he
  sends from his
    heart's deep core,
But a plea, that
    upward to Heaven he flings—
I know why the caged bird sings!

> **GUIDED READING**
> Why does the caged bird beat his wing?

> **GUIDED READING**
> What is the caged bird's song?

1. **alas.** Word used to express unhappiness, pity, or concern
2. **opes.** Opens
3. **chalice.** Cup-shaped interior of a flower
4. **fain.** With pleasure, gladly; by desire; by preference
5. **a-swing.** Swinging

The Conquest of the Air, 1938. Roland Penrose. Southhampton City Art Gallery, England.

words for everyday use
keen (kēn′) *adj.*, sharp, intense. *When the pain from the bee sting began to grow <u>keener</u>, I decided to try coating it with mud.*
keener, *adj.*

ANSWERS TO GUIDED READING QUESTIONS

1. He beats his wing because he has to sit on a perch in his cage when he desperately wants to perch on the bough of a tree.
2. The caged bird's song is a prayer from the core of his being that he sends up to heaven.

ANSWERS TO READER'S TOOLBOX (CONT.)

a cage of his own making. Angelou also relates to the free bird. Dunbar's attitude toward the caged bird is one of complete understanding and sympathy. He uses first-person point to view to express the personal connections he feels to the caged bird. Angelou is more objective and uses third-person point of view.

Caged bird

Maya Angelou

A free bird leaps
on the back of the wind
and floats downstream
till the current ends
and dips his wing
in the orange sun rays
and dares to claim the sky.

But a bird that stalks
down his narrow cage
can <u>seldom</u> see through
his bars of rage
his wings are clipped and
his feet are tied
so he opens his throat to sing.

GUIDED READING

What has happened to the caged bird's wings? his feet?

The caged bird sings
with a fearful <u>trill</u>
of things unknown
but longed for still
and his tune is heard
on the distant hill
for the caged bird
sings of freedom.

The free bird thinks of another breeze
and the trade winds[1] soft through the
    sighing rees
and the fat worms waiting
on a dawn-bright lawn
and he names the sky his
own.

GUIDED READING

What does the free bird think about?

But a caged bird stands on the grave of
    dreams
his shadow shouts on a nightmare scream
his wings are clipped and his feet are tied
so he opens his throat to sing.

The caged bird sings
with a fearful trill
of things unknown
but longed for still
and his tune is heard
on the distant hill
for the caged bird
sings of freedom.

---

1. **trade winds.** Winds blowing almost constantly in one direction; especially a wind blowing almost continually toward the equator from the northeast or from the southeast

words for everyday use

sel • dom (sel' dəm) *adv.*, rarely, infrequently. *They <u>seldom</u> go to the movies, but this film is one that must be seen on the big screen.*

trill (tril) *n.*, a trembling, vibrating sound. *The whistle gave out a high-pitched <u>trill</u> that made my dog stop and raise his ears.*

"SYMPATHY" AND "CAGED BIRD" **419**

ANSWERS TO GUIDED READING QUESTIONS

1. The caged bird's wings are clipped and his feet are tied.
2. The free bird thinks about the next breeze and the trade winds blowing through the trees, and the fat worms it will eat the next morning and because he knows no boundaries, the sky is his. He doesn't have to think about freedom because he has it.

LITERARY TECHNIQUE

SYMBOL. A **symbol** is a thing that stands for or represents both itself and something else. Encourage students to discuss the symbolism in both poems. Ask them what the caged birds might represent in the human world? What might the cage represent? What might the bird's song represent in the human world? *Answers.* Responses will vary, but students may suggest that the caged bird represents the plight of African Americans who earlier in the twentieth century were deprived of much of their civil rights and the same privileges as white Americans. The cage might represent hundreds of years of oppression and intolerance. The bird's song might represent the freedom and quality that African Americans longed for.

SELECTION CHECK TEST 4.6.3 WITH ANSWERS

Checking Your Reading

1. In "Sympathy," what does the poet profess to know? **The poet claims to know what the caged bird feels.**
2. In "Caged Bird," what does the free bird claim? **The free bird claims the sky.**
3. According to both poems, about what do caged birds sing? **The caged bird sings of freedom.**

Vocabulary in Context

Fill in each blank below with the most appropriate word from the following *Words for Everyday Use* from "Sympathy" and "Caged Bird." You may have to change the tense of the word.

> keener   bough   seldom
> glee   trill

1. The band's sound had been loud already, but the new amplifier made it even **keener**.
2. I was hoping for a few more hours of sleep, but the birds' **trill** woke me at dawn.
3. Despite their best intentions, Ralph and Janice **seldom** show up to volunteer.

Reader's Toolbox

Fill in the blanks using the following terms. You may not use every term, and you may use some terms more than once.

> tone   stanza

1. A **stanza** is a group of lines in a poem.
2. A **tone** might be familiar, playful, sincere, humorous, or sarcastic.
3. A **stanza** is usually separated from others by a space.

Respond *to the* SELECTION

If the caged bird of either poem were freed, would its behavior differ from that of a bird that was always free? How? Why?

About *the* AUTHORS

Born Marguerite Johnson in St. Louis in 1928, **Maya Angelou** was raised by her grandmother in segregated Arkansas from the ages of three to seven. Angelou was influenced at an early age by the work of writers like Shakespeare and Paul Laurence Dunbar. In the 1960s she was sought out by Dr. Martin Luther King, Jr. to be the northern coordinator for the Southern Christian Leadership Conference, an organization dedicated to using non-violent protest to end racism and achieve civil rights for African Americans. In 1993, at the request of President Clinton, she wrote and read a poem for his inauguration. Angelou says the basic message in that poem is fundamental to all her work: "What I try to say is that as human beings we are more alike than we are unalike."

Paul Laurence Dunbar was born in Dayton, Ohio, in 1872 to Matilda and Joshua Dunbar. His mother was a former slave. His father escaped slavery by way of the Underground Railroad and joined the Union army in the Civil War. Encouraged by his mother's love of poetry, Dunbar was writing and reciting poems by the age of six. His father's heroism in the Civil War was the inspiration for several of Dunbar's later poems and stories. Dunbar published his first collection of poems, *Oak and Ivy,* in 1892 and sold copies of the book for a dollar each at the first World's Fair. He went on to publish 12 books of poetry, four books of short stories, a play, and five novels before his death on February 9, 1906.

Investigate, Inquire, and Imagine

Recall: GATHERING FACTS

1a. In "Sympathy," what pain becomes sharper for the caged bird?

2a. From where does Dunbar's caged bird summon his prayer?

3a. In "Caged Bird," what does a free bird dare to do?

4a. Of what things does Angelou's caged bird sing?

→ Interpret: FINDING MEANING

1b. Why does this happen?

2b. Why might the speaker of the poem think this?

3b. What does this suggest about the free bird?

4b. What statement does this make about freedom?

Analyze: TAKING THINGS APART

5a. Look back at stanzas 2 and 3 in "Sympathy." Collect details about the bird's imprisonment and his reaction to being caged. List details about the bird's song. Then refer to stanzas 2 and 5 of "Caged Bird." List the details about the imprisonment of that bird and his reaction to being caged. Look at stanza 3 and note the details of the bird's song.

→ Synthesize: BRINGING THINGS TOGETHER

5b. What is significant about the cage of each bird? How does the song of each bird relate to his longing for freedom?

Evaluate: MAKING JUDGMENTS

6a. How can the speaker's images of freedom and imprisonment be interpreted in human terms? Explain your answer.

→ Extend: CONNECTING IDEAS

6b. Choose either Dunbar's or Angelou's poem and, in your mind, recreate the author's caged bird as a person. Consider the circumstances surrounding his or her lack of freedom. Then write a few lines of the song this person might sing.

Understanding Literature

STANZA. A **stanza** is a group of lines in a poem. Stanzas are usually separated by spaces from other groups of lines. What do you notice about the first line of each stanza in Dunbar's poem? What do stanzas 1 and 4 have in common in "Caged Bird"? Why might Angelou have chosen to repeat stanza 3? What things do you think Angelou and Dunbar considered in organizing the stanzas of their poems?

RECALL

1a. The throbbing of the birds "old, old scars" "pulse again with a keener sting."

2a. Dunbar's bird summons his prayer "from his heart's deep core."

3a. A free bird dares to claim the sky.

4a. The caged bird sings "of things unknown but longed for still...the caged bird sings of freedom."

INTERPRET

1b. *Responses will vary.* Some students will say that the bird continues to beat his wings against the bars of the cage and reinjures himself. Other students may say this pain also symbolizes the emotional suffering of long-term captivity that grows sharper the longer the bird is caged.

2b. *Responses will vary.* The speaker identifies with this caged creature; the title of the poem is "Sympathy," and he interprets the caged bird's longing for freedom based on how precious he believes freedom is. The speaker might think this because of what he knows of how slavery affects human beings.

3b. This suggests that the free bird is confident and recognizes no boundaries to its flight.

4b. Even a creature who has never experienced freedom can long for it. The desire for freedom is inborn in all creatures.

ANALYZE

5a. Students may list the following details about imprisonment for "Sympathy": stanza 2—cruel bars, must fly back to his perch when he would rather perch on the bough of a tree. Students may list the following reactions to being caged in "Sympathy": stanza 2— beats his wing until it bleeds; he has been doing this for a long while because he has old scars and new pain; stanza 3—he has a bruised wing and sore breast from beating on the bars of his cage. For "Sympathy," students might list the following details about the bird's song: stanza 3—his song is not a carol of joy or glee, it is a prayer from his heart's deep core that he flings to heaven.
Students may list the following details about imprisonment for "Caged Bird": stanza 2—narrow cage, bars of rage, wings are clipped and feet are tied; stanza 5—grave of dreams, wings are clipped and feet are tied. Students may list the following reactions to

ANSWERS TO INVESTIGATE, INQUIRE, IMAGINE (CONT.)

being caged in "Caged Bird": stanza 2—stalks his cage, can't see through bars of rage, opens his throat to sing; stanza 5—shouts on a nightmare scream. For "Caged Bird," students might say that the bird sings with a fearful trill of things he doesn't know but still longs for; his tune carries to a distant hill; he sings of freedom.

SYNTHESIZE

5b. *Responses will vary.* Dunbar's poem gives few details

about the bird's cage. He describes an actual cage with bars and a perch. He calls the bars cruel. Angelou gives more description of the cage and the bird's physical imprisonment. "Bars of rage," (stanza 2) could be interpreted to mean the cage is not a physical structure, that other things can imprison a creature such as rage or the death of dreams (stanza 5). Angelou's bird has clipped

(Continued on page 422)

STANZA. The first line of each stanza shares something the speaker knows about the caged bird. They both address the free bird. *Responses will vary.* Some students may say that Angelou chooses to repeat this stanza to increase the impact the caged bird has on the reader, to resemble the chorus of a song, or to express the futility of the caged bird's longing for freedom (it keeps singing the same song over and over).

TONE. Dunbar tells the reader he understands the feelings, song, and behavior of the caged bird; he identifies with the caged bird. The image he paints of the bird—bruised and sore and bloody—is sad. Frequent use of exclamation points expresses the overwhelming frustration of the author. By describing the joy, strength, confidence and contentment of the free bird, Angelou's caged bird seems all the more tragic as the reader knows exactly what that bird is missing. Dunbar identifies so closely with the bird that the reader senses he too is familiar with feelings of powerlessness, oppression, and the persistent anger that can accompany it. The tone of Angelou's poem is less grief stricken and more hopeful because of her description of the free bird and because she allows the caged bird's song to carry to the distant hill.

TONE. In a literary work, **tone** is the writer's or speaker's emotional attitude toward the subject or the reader. While someone telling a story can express tone in several ways—choice of words, tone of voice, eye contact, and body language—the writer has only words on the page to create tone. What are some of the ways Dunbar expresses his feelings about the caged bird and about freedom in general? How do Angelou's descriptions of the free bird's experience help express her feelings about the caged bird's experience? How is tone the same in these poems? How is it different?

Writer's Journal

1. Imagine that you meet the person who has caged the bird in "Sympathy." Write a short **persuasive speech** to convince that person to free the bird.

2. Write a **letter** that Maya Angelou might write to Paul Dunbar, telling him of change in our society for African Americans since he wrote his poem.

3. Without looking in the dictionary, create your own personal **definition** of freedom for someone who has never heard of the word. Provide brief examples of freedom and imprisonment.

Skill Builders

Speaking and Listening & Collaborative Learning

WRITING LYRICS. In small groups, brainstorm with classmates about what freedom means. Develop a broad list of ideas about freedom. Your list could include words, phrases, quotes, names of people, or activities. Use the ideas from your list to write song lyrics. Make sure the lyrics include ideas from all the members in your group. Then set your lyrics to music using the melody of an existing song, or make up your own melody. As a group, perform your song for the class or make a recording.

Study and Research

RESEARCHING AN ISSUE. Use library sources, newspaper or magazine articles, and/or the Internet to research both sides of a current or past struggle for human or animal rights. Once you've collected enough information to understand the issue, summarize the struggle in your own words and offer your opinion. Submit your summary, copies of your background materials, and statement of opinion to your teacher for review.

Language, Grammar, and Style

ACTIVE AND PASSIVE VOICE. A verb is in the active voice when the subject of the verb performs the action. A verb is in the passive voice when the subject of the verb receives the action. See the Language Arts Survey 3.58, "Action Verbs and State of Being Verbs," for more information on verbs.

EXAMPLES

Active: Paul Laurence Dunbar **wrote** *Oak and Ivy* in 1892.
Passive: *Oak and Ivy* **was written** in 1892.

ANSWERS TO INVESTIGATE, INQUIRE, IMAGINE (CONT.)

wings and tied feet. Each of these phrases might be interpreted literally or figuratively. Dunbar's bird's song beseeches God in heaven to grant it freedom. Its song is a tragic plea seeming to rise from despair and powerlessness. In stanzas 2 and 6, Angelou follows "his wings are clipped and his feet are tied" with "so he opens his throat to sing." Using the words "so he opens his throat" suggests that the bird sings because it can't do anything else. In this way, the bird's song is an act of freedom. Angelou's bird's song heard on the distant hill is a more hopeful image than the plea Dunbar's bird sends from his heart's deep core. Both songs result from being deprived of freedom.

(Continuied on page 423)

Use the active voice for stronger, more exciting writing and so your readers know who is performing the action. Which of the sentences below best describes the event? Which is in the active voice?

The football was thrown far down the field for the game-winning touchdown.
Byron Lindon, the Spartan quarterback, threw the football down the field for the game-winning touchdown.

Sometimes the passive voice is more appropriate. For example, if you do not know who performed the action, you may use the passive voice to describe what happened. When you want the focus to be on the receiver of the action, you may want to use the passive voice. These two sentences are written in the passive voice.

A mysterious package was left on our front steps.
The five-year-old girl was struck by a car.

Fill out a chart like the one shown below, using the following sentences. After copying the sentence into the left column, determine the subject and the verb. Use an A for active voice and a P for passive voice. In the last column, rewrite passive sentences in the active voice, using a different verb if necessary. If the sentence already uses the active voice, leave the last column blank. Follow the examples already in the chart.

1. Many poems were written by Paul Lawrence Dunbar.
2. Maya Angelou wrote many poems about the African-American experience.
3. Dunbar is considered by many critics to be the first professional black poet.
4. Angelou speaks English, Italian, French, Spanish, and West African Fanti.
5. Dunbar was encouraged by his mother's love of poetry.

Graphic Organizer

Example	Subject	Verb	Active or Passive	Rewrite
Maya Angelou was influenced by Shakespeare and Dunbar.	Maya Angelou	was influenced	P	Shakespeare and Dunbar influenced Maya Angelou.
Dunbar wrote poetry by the age of six.	Dunbar	wrote	A	

Speaking and Listening & Collaborative Learning
Tell students that they may wish to include a simple rhyme scheme in their lyrics to give their song a musical quality. You may wish to play students some patriotic songs as a starting point for their ideas.

Study and Research
Give students the following list of possible topics to choose from:
• using animals for testing in laboratories
• the struggle to overturn school segregation
• Rosa Parks and the Montgomery Bus Boycott
• the struggle for women's suffrage

Language, Grammar, and Style Graphic Organizer
Students' charts may resemble the following:
• Example: Paul Laurence Dunbar was born to Matilda and Joshua Dunbar in 1872.
  Subject: Paul Laurence Dunbar; Verb: was born; Active or Passive: P
  Revised: In 1872, Matilda and Joshua Dunbar became parents to Paul Lawrence Dunbar.
• Example: Maya Angelou wrote many poems about the African-American experience.
  Subject: Maya Angelou; Verb: wrote; Active or Passive: A
• Example: Dunbar is considered by many critics to be the first professional black poet.
  Subject: Dunbar; Verb: is considered; Active or Passive: P
  Revised: Many critics consider Dunbar to be the first professional black poet.
• Example: Angelou speaks English, French, Spanish, and West African Fanti.
  Subject: Angelou; Verb: speaks; Active or Passive: A
• Example: Dunbar was encouraged by his mother's love of poetry.
  Subject: Dunbar Verb: was encouraged; Active or Passive: A
  Revised: His mother's love of poetry encouraged Dunbar.

ANSWERS TO INVESTIGATE, INQUIRE, IMAGINE (CONT.)

EVALUATE
6a. *Responses will vary.* Students may talk about different types of freedom and confinement, but they should make the connection that the struggle to obtain, maintain, or regain freedom is an instinct in all creatures. You may choose to bring the backgrounds of each author into this discussion.

EXTEND
6b. *Responses will vary.*

READER'S JOURNAL

Ask students to share national or worldwide tragedies they have learned of. Which of these tragedies have had the greatest impact on them? Ask students what they felt when they learned of the tragedy? What do they remember most about the incident?

INDIVIDUAL LEARNING STRATEGIES

MOTIVATION
Students may especially enjoy the Collaborative Learning activity in which they get an opportunity to brainstorm about the future. You might expand this into a class activity in which you list students' ideas on the board and talk as a class about which ideas they believe are most likely.

READING PROFICIENCY
Students may benefit from seeing a videotape of Reagan delivering this speech. If you cannot find one in your school or local media library, you might have someone in your school who is known for speaking ability deliver the speech for students, perhaps a guest teacher. Then ask students to go back and read the speech on their own, answering the Guided Reading questions and using the Words for Everyday Use, footnotes, and the vocabulary listed above as tools.

(Continued on page 425)

SPEECH

Reader's Journal

If a national tragedy occurred, would you want to talk about it with your family and friends? Why, or why not?

Reader's TOOLBOX

STYLE. Style is the manner in which something is said or written. Style is commonly broken down into three levels: *high style* for formal occasions or lofty subjects; *middle style* for ordinary occasions or subjects; and *low style* for extremely informal occasions or subjects. Factors that influence style include sentence structure and diction.

DICTION. Diction, when applied to writing, refers to word choice. Diction can be formal or informal, simple or complex, ordinary or unusual. Writers can modify style and diction to match a particular purpose or audience. As you read "The *Challenger* Disaster," think about the diction and style of the speech. Does the speaker use formal or informal language? Are the speaker's points and ideas concrete or abstract? How complex are the speaker's sentences?

Prereading

"The *Challenger* Disaster"

by Peggy Noonan

Reader's Resource

- **HISTORY CONNECTION.** On January 28, 1986, an explosion destroyed the space shuttle *Challenger* less than two minutes after liftoff. Six astronauts and teacher Christa McAuliffe, the first observer aboard a shuttle launch, were killed in the disaster. Classrooms in many schools aired live coverage of the takeoff, and thousands of young people watched as the shuttle exploded in midair. The disaster was the most serious accident ever in the history of the U.S. space program. A later study showed that defective rubber seals on booster rockets caused the explosion. Shortly after this tragedy, President Ronald Reagan delivered this speech.

- Speeches, unlike most kinds of writing, are rarely associated with the writer. Instead, speeches are most often associated with the speaker. Peggy Noonan took credit for the speeches she wrote, an uncommon practice for speech writers.

- **SCIENCE CONNECTION.** Following the tragic explosion of the *Challenger*, families of the shuttle's crew members founded the Challenger Center for Space Science Education, an organization focused on forging interest in math, science, and technology among American young people. More than 35 Challenger Learning Centers across the nation provide students and teachers with the opportunity to fly in simulated space missions and take part in a variety of other activities. Students and teachers can explore the Challenger Center Internet site at www.challenger.org.

GOALS/OBJECTIVES

Studying this lesson will enable students to
- appreciate the importance of the *Challenger* disaster
- define *style* and identify the style in which a speech is written
- define *diction* and examine a writer's diction
- research the Challenger Centers for Space Science Education
- use the dictionary to define words
- write and deliver a speech
- think about possible future space accomplishments

The Challenger DISASTER

Peggy Noonan

Nineteen years ago, almost to the day, we lost three astronauts in a terrible accident on the ground.[1] But we've never lost an astronaut in flight; we've never had a tragedy like this. And perhaps we've forgotten the courage it took for the crew of the shuttle; but they, the *Challenger* Seven, were aware of the dangers, but overcame them and did their jobs brilliantly. We mourn seven heroes: Michael Smith, Dick Scobee, Judith Resnik, Ronald McNair, Ellison Onizuka, Gregory Jarvis, and Christa McAuliffe. We mourn their loss as a nation together.

For the families of the seven, we cannot bear, as you do, the full impact of this tragedy. But we feel the loss, and we're thinking about you so very much. Your loved ones were daring and brave, and they had that special

> **GUIDED READING**
>
> What should we remember about the crew members of the *Challenger?*

1. **lost three astronauts . . . on the ground.** On January 27, 1967, a flash fire occurred on Apollo I during a launch pad test. All three crew members died.

"THE CHALLENGER DISASTER" **425**

ENGLISH LANGUAGE LEARNING
Point out the following
vocabulary words and expressions
brilliantly—in a manner that shows
    great intelligence, talent, and skill
daring—having or showing a bold
    willingness to take risks
pioneers—person who goes before,
    preparing the way for others
fainthearted—cowardly, timidly, shy
coincidence—an accidental and
    remarkable occurrence of events
    or ideas at the same time,
    suggesting but lacking a causal
    relationship
frontiers—an undeveloped
    unexplored region
surly—haughty, arrogant; hostile

SPECIAL NEEDS
Students may benefit from a
discussion about the difference
between speech writing and speech
making. Remind them that the
president who delivered the speech
did not write it, but had it written for
him. Similarly, the writer of this
speech never delivered it to the
public. After students have read the
speech, have them focus on
responding to the Recall questions in
the Investigate, Inquire, and Imagine
section.

ENRICHMENT
Encourage students to
research famous American
speeches made by presidents
following major events. What is
the historical significance of the
speeches? What are some
memorable lines and images
from them? How are they
similar to or different from the
speech written by Peggy Noonan for
President Reagan? How were the
speeches received by their intended
audiences? Students may want to
bring copies of the speeches to class
and read meaningful excerpts aloud.

ANSWER TO GUIDED READING QUESTION

1. We had forgotten that we have only just begun exploring space. We should remember that the crew members were pioneers.

ADDITIONAL QUESTIONS AND ACTIVITIES

At the beginning of the speech, the president states, "Nineteen years ago, almost to the day, we lost three astronauts in a terrible accident on the ground." Is this an effective opening for this speech? Why, or why not? What specific information does the president give in the first paragraph of the speech?

Answers
The opening of the speech is highly effective because it provides an immediate contrast to the Challenger disaster and a contest to the risks of the space program. The specific information the president provides in the first paragraph is the name of the shuttle—*Challenger*—and the names of the seven astronauts who died in the explosion.

CROSS-CURRICULAR CONNECTION

HISTORY. The space program began in 1957, led by the Soviet Union and the United States. The first flights were by unmanned vehicles. Manned flight was begn by the Soviets in 1961. During the 1970s and early 1980s, the United States launched its space shuttle program by building four shuttles. They were named for famous oceangoing ships: *Columbia, Challenger, Discovery,* and *Atlantis.*

RESPOND TO THE SELECTION

Ask students whether they have ever heard of the saying, "Sometimes bad things happen to good people." Have they ever witnessed this kind of occurrence or experienced it themselves? If so, what were the circumstances? How does this saying relate to the speech and the circumstances of the *Challenger* disaster.

SELECTION CHECK TEST 4.6.5 WITH ANSWERS

Checking Your Reading
1. What event is Noonan writing about? **She is writing about the crash of the space shuttle *Challenger.***
2. What, according to Noonan, happened to Sir Francis Drake exactly 390 years before she wrote this speech? **He died at sea, on board his ship.**
3. Whom does Noonan describe as "daring and brave"? **Noonan describes the seven *Challenger* astronauts as daring and brave.**
4. Who is the audience for this speech? **The American public, especially school children, are the audience for this speech.**
5. Who delivered this speech?

grace, that special spirit that says, "Give me a challenge and I'll meet it with joy." They had a hunger to explore the universe and discover its truths. They wished to serve, and they did. They served all of us.

> **GUIDED READING**
> For what did the crew members hunger?

We've grown used to wonders in this century. It's hard to dazzle us. But for twenty-five years the United States space program has been doing just that. We've grown used to the idea of space, and perhaps we forget that we've only just begun. We're still pioneers. They, the members of the *Challenger* crew, were pioneers.

And I want to say something to the schoolchildren of America who were watching the live coverage of the shuttle's takeoff. I know it is hard to understand, but sometimes painful things like this happen. It's all part of the process of exploration and discovery. It's all part of taking a chance and expanding man's horizons. The future doesn't belong to the fainthearted; it belongs to the brave. The *Challenger* crew was pulling us into the future, and we'll continue to follow them. . . .

There's a coincidence today. On this day 390 years ago, the great explorer Sir Francis Drake[2] died aboard ship off the coast of Panama. In his lifetime the great frontiers were the oceans, and a historian later said, "He lived by the sea, died on it, and was buried in it." Well, today we can say of the *Challenger* crew: Their dedication was, like Drake's, complete.

> **GUIDED READING**
> What frontier did Drake face? What frontier did the *Challenger* crew members face? In what ways were they similar?

The crew of the space shuttle *Challenger* honored us by the manner in which they lived their lives. We will never forget them, nor the last time we saw them, this morning, as they prepared for the journey and waved goodbye and "slipped the surly bonds of earth" to "touch the face of God."[3] ∎

---

2. **Sir Francis Drake.** English admiral (*circa* 1540–1596); first Englishman to sail around the world
3. **slipped the surly bonds . . . face of God.** Lines from John Magee's poem "High Flight"

Respond *to the* SELECTION

What might you have said to comfort the families of the crew members?

About *the* AUTHOR

Peggy Noonan was born in 1950 in Brooklyn, New York. After attending college, she worked as a news and editorial writer and then as a broadcast writer and producer. In 1984, Noonan became a special assistant to President Ronald Reagan. During the next two years, she wrote speeches for him on a number of occasions. She later worked with George Bush, writing the speech for his inauguration as president. Her political experiences in

Washington, D.C., provided material for her memoir, *What I Saw at the Revolution: A Political Life in the Reagan Era.*

SELECTION CHECK TEST 4.6.5 WITH ANSWERS (CONT.)

President Ronald Reagan delivered this speech.
Reader's Toolbox
Fill in the blanks using the following terms. You may not use every term, and you may use some terms more than once.

style	high style	middle style
low style	diction	audience

1. _____ is the manner in which something is said or written. **Diction**
2. _____ is often used for formal occasions or formal subjects. **High style**
3. In writing, _____ is often thought of as word choice. **Diction**
4. Factors that influence _____ include grammar and word choice. **style**
5. Writers adjust style to fit the _____ of a piece. **audience**

The Associated Press

January 28, 1986, Tuesday, PM cycle

SECTION: Domestic News

LENGTH: 324 words

HEADLINE: Something Dreadfully Wrong In What Appeared to Be Picture-Perfect Launch

BYLINE: By IKE FLORES, Associated Press Writer

DATELINE: CAPE CANAVERAL, Fla.

BODY:

The liftoff and first few seconds of flight were a beautiful sight as Challenger arced into the bright sunlight to the cheers of hundreds of space center workers watching excitedly outside the building where the shuttle is assembled.

Suddenly, something was dreadfully wrong in what appeared to be a picture-perfect launch.

To those on the ground, the spacecraft riding the towering column of pure white smoke appeared to burst into orange flame, briefly, against the clear, blue sky.

Almost immediately, there was an incredibly big, bright-orange explosion, with a lot of dirty gray smoke surrounding it.

Following that, Challenger's twin solid rocket boosters appeared to separate from the orbiter, one spiraling off to the right and the other to the left.

Hundreds of pieces of debris burst out of the exploding mass and plummeted toward the Atlantic Ocean about 18 miles southeast of the launch pad.

"It's too soon. It's too soon. It can't be separation (of the boosters)," said one bearded worker holding a transistor radio.

"I can't believe it," said a young woman, starting to cry at the sight.

"I can't see the orbiter. I can't see it," said a youth wearing a Lockheed jacket.

There was total confusion. Some of the people were muttering quietly and shaking their heads. Then there was total quiet.

Shock had set in among the engineers, technicians and others who painstakingly assemble the shuttle's three primary components—the orbiter, two solid-fuel rockets and large mustard-colored external fuel tank—at the vehicle assembly building just before it goes to the launch pad aboard a mobile platform.

They had bundled up and come out into the freezing, sunny day to watch with pride what they thought would be their 25th successful shuttle launch.

They quickly broke up into small bunches, not quite believing what they had seen and drifted off into the huge, 52-story building, returning quietly to work.

LANGUAGE: ENGLISH

ABOUT THE RELATED READING

The Associated Press released this newswire report on the day of the Challenger accident.

LITERARY TECHNIQUE

POINT-OF-VIEW. **Point of View** is the vantage point from which a story is told. Inform students that with the exception of editorials, newspaper articles are usually written from the **third-person point of view**, in which the narrator stands outside the action and uses words such as *he, she, it,* and *they.* The writer of the article, however, can try to capture the perspective and points of views of others by observing or inter-;viewing them. Ask students the following questions: Whose point of view does the writer of the articles try to capture? Why might this be an interesting perspective from which to view the *Challenger* disaster? How do these people seem to feel about the disaster?

Answers. Students may say the writer explores the point of view of the people who helped to build the space shuttle *Challenger.* Students may say that it is interesting because these people have such an interest in making sure that their work is sound and that accidents like this do not happen. Students may say these people seem especially devastated and confused by what happened.

ADDITIONAL QUESTIONS AND ACTIVITIES

Ask students the following questions: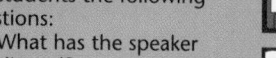

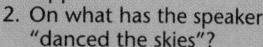

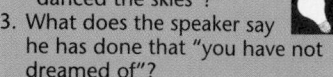

1. What has the speaker slipped?
2. On what has the speaker "danced the skies"?
3. What does the speaker say he has done that "you have not dreamed of"?
4. What has the speaker flung through footless halls of air?
5. In what manner is the speaker flying? How can you tell?
6. What does the speaker say he has done in the sanctity of space?
7. What do you think the speaker means by the last line?

Answers
1. The speaker has slipped the surly bonds of earth.
2. The speaker has "danced the skies on laughter-silvered wings."
3. The speaker says he has "wheeled and soared and swung/High in the sunlit silence."
4. The speaker has flung his eager craft through these halls.
5. Students should recognize that the speaker is flying in an airplane. As evidence they may point to the "wings" and the "craft."
6. The speaker says he has put out his hand and touched the face of God.
7. *Responses will vary.* Students may suggest that the speaker means that flying is a spiritual experience for him.

John Gillespie Magee, Jr.

The poem "High Flight" appears on a memorial for Michael Smith, captain of the *Challenger,* at the waterfront in Beaufort, North Carolina.

ABOUT THE RELATED READING

Born in 1922 in China, where his parents were missionaries, **John Gillespie Magee, Jr.** moved to the United States in 1939. In 1940 Magee enlisted in the Royal Canadian Air Force and became a pilot. He was sent to England in 1941—during World War II—where he flew Spitfires, one of the most famous fighter planes of the war. Magee wrote "High Flight" while flying one day and sent it to his parents with the note, "I am enclosing a verse I wrote the other day. It started at 30,000 feet and was finished soon after I landed." Three months later, Magee was killed when his Spitfire collided with another plane inside a cloud during the Battle of Britain. "High Flight" is the official poem of the Royal Canadian Air Force and the Royal Air Force of Britain. In Beaufort, North Carolina, a memorial for Captain Michael John Smith, the pilot of the space shuttle *Challenger,* bears the words of Magee's poem.

Investigate, Inquire, and Imagine

Recall: GATHERING FACTS

1a. What did the speaker say to comfort the families of the crew members?

2a. What had the U.S. space program been doing for twenty-five years?

3a. How were the crew members like Sir Francis Drake?

Interpret: FINDING MEANING

1b. How might these words have comforted the families?

2b. What could the space program's activities have left people thinking?

3b. How did the mentality of the crew members set them apart from others?

Analyze: TAKING THINGS APART

4a. What words does the speaker use to describe the crew members throughout the speech?

Synthesize: BRINGING THINGS TOGETHER

4b. How do these descriptions help form the speaker's main message? What is the speaker's main message?

Evaluate: MAKING JUDGMENTS

5a. How well does the speaker get across the main message? How well do you think the speaker's words echoed the thoughts of the American public? In what ways might the speaker's message have been different from the thoughts of the American public?

Extend: CONNECTING IDEAS

5b. Does the message sent by the speech parallel that of the newswire text of the same day? Does the message of the speech parallel that of "High Flight"? Explain your answer.

Understanding *Literature*

DICTION AND STYLE. Diction, when applied to writing, refers to word choice. Diction can be formal or informal, simple or complex, ordinary or unusual. Writers can modify style and diction to match a particular purpose or audience. **Style** is the manner in which something is said or written. Factors that influence style include sentence structure and diction.

What type of occasion or subject best describes the context of this speech? How did the intended audience and the intent of the speech affect the diction? How did the diction affect the style of the speech?

"THE CHALLENGER DISASTER" **429**

GRAPHIC ORGANIZER

Students' charts may resemble the following:

The *Challenger* Disaster
- focus on tragedy
- emotional
- focuses on the point of view of the explorers and the feelings of the American people
- avoids focusing on the details of the tragic flight
- tries to explain the tragedy

High Flight
- focus on the wonders of flight
- emotional
- focuses on the speaker's own thoughts and emotions about flight
- focuses on the details of the flight
- tries to explain the joys of flight

newswire
- focus on tragedy
- informational
- focuses on the reactions of the people who made the shuttle that exploded
- focuses on the details of the flight and the ensuing explosion
- offers fact not explanations of the writer's own ideas

Graphic *Organizer*

Create a graphic organizer like the one below to compare and contrast "The *Challenger* Disaster," "High Flight," and the Associated Press newswire text reporting the disaster. As you fill out the columns, consider elements such as style, tone, and point-of-view. Use the graphic organizer for reference as you discuss the selections and their differences in class. What does your graphic organizer indicate about different types of writing?

The *Challenger* Disaster	High Flight	newswire
• focus on tragedy • emotional • • •	• focus on the wonders of flight • emotional • • •	• focus on tragedy • informational • • •

Writer's Journal

1. Write **newswire copy** about a newsworthy event you have witnessed or imagined to send to your local newspaper.

2. Based on the information you have learned about the *Challenger*, its crew, and the explosion, write a ten-question true/false **test** for a parent, teacher, or other person who remembers the event.

3. Write a **caption** for the photograph of the space shuttle *Challenger* on page 425.

Skill Builders

Media Literacy

COMPUTER RESEARCH. Using a computer with an Internet connection, look up information on the Challenger Center for Space Science Education, a national organization that promotes learning about math, science, and technology. Using a search engine, try entering keywords such as "Challenger Center" to find the sites of some of the 35 Challenger Learning Centers. Look for answers to the following questions. Why was the Challenger Center originally founded? Who founded the organization? What happens at the Challenger Learning Centers? Is there a Challenger Learning Center in your state? Where is the closest one to your school? How can students benefit from long-distance Challenger Center programs? How can you get more information?

ANSWERS TO UNDERSTANDING LITERATURE

STYLE AND DICTION. The occasion was a tragic yet formal one. The style should have been a high style because the president of the United States was speaking about a serious topic. The intended audience—the families of the deceased, the schoolchildren who witnessed the explosion, and other Americans—and the intent of the speech affect the president's diction in that he uses simple, clear words and sentences. His diction is straightforward and simple despite the formal seriousness of the subject. The diction affected the style of the speech in that it could be classified as middle style, while the topic of the speech was high style. This made for a compelling speech with a clear message that was easily stated and understood.

Vocabulary

REVIEWING NEW WORDS. The following words appear either in "High Flight" or in the Associated Press newswire. Look up each word in the dictionary. Then write a short definition for each word, and use each word in a sentence.

EXAMPLE *primarily* mainly; chiefly; for the most part. *The old fire truck is used <u>primarily</u> in parades.*

1. surly
2. mirth
3. delirious
4. sanctity
5. trod
6. debris
7. bureau
8. module
9. aerodynamic
10. external

Study and Research & Speaking and Listening

SPEAKING OUT ABOUT THE NEWS. Find a current topic in the national or international news that interests you. Gather information on your topic from newspapers and news magazines, consulting at least three sources.

As you examine what you have found, look for differences among your sources. Does any source omit information found in another source? How do the sources differ in content and focus? Do the sources reveal any biases or opinions about the subject? Do the sources simply offer information, or do they try to persuade the reader to think a certain way? Take notes on what you have learned about

your topic and how sources have reported it. You may want to review the Language Arts Survey 4.28, "Evaluating Information and Media Sources," for more help.

After analyzing the information you have found, write a short speech about your topic. Decide if your speech is to be informational or persuasive. After doing your research, have you made any conclusions about the topic that you feel strongly about? If so, you may want to write a persuasive speech to deliver your opinions about the facts. If not, you may want to write an informational speech to simply report what you have learned. As you write, consider the style and diction that best fit your topic, purpose, and audience. See the Language Arts Survey 4.15, "Giving a Speech," for more help with speeches. Deliver your speech in class.

Collaborative Learning

THINKING ABOUT THE FUTURE. In small groups of about five students, discuss the possibilities that exist in the 21st century for new accomplishments in space exploration. First think about what has already been done in space. Check an encyclopedia for this information, and jot down a few of the space missions that have already taken place.

Now consider the future. Write down at least five possible achievements that your group envisions. Be imaginative as you brainstorm—accomplishments in space in the 21st century could include possibilities we have not yet dreamed of. In the early 20th century, when airplanes were still experimental, no one would have believed that people would travel in space only decades later.

Media Literacy
Have students refer to the Language Arts Survey, "Using the Internet," if students are not familiar with using this research tool. You may wish to bring your students to your school library or computer lab and conduct this as a group activity and a lesson on Internet searches.

Vocabulary
Responses will vary. Possible responses are given.

1. *surly* bad tempered, sullenly rude. *The horse gave me a surly glare as if to say, "Don't even think about trying to ride me, or I'll throw you right off!"*
2. *mirth* joyfulness or merriment, especially when characterized by laughter. *George enjoyed the mirth that characterized his family's dinner table; they would sit for hours telling stories and laughing.*
3. *delirious* wildly excited. *The children tore open their presents in a delirious holiday flurry of motion.*
4. *sanctity* anything held sacred. *We were disgusted that someone would dare commit a crime in the sanctity of the temple.*
5. *trod* walked on. *Leia grimaced in pain when Eric trod on her toe.*
6. *debris* rough broken bits of material after a destruction. *The divers searched the sea bottom looking for debris from long-sunken pirate ships.*
7. *bureau* agency for collecting and giving information and other services. *When she found she wasn't qualified to take out a loan, Rhonda contacted her credit bureau to find out why.*
8. *module* any of a set of units designed to be arranged or joined in a variety of ways. *Without a propulsion module, spacecraft would never leave the ground.*
9. *aerodynamic* built to efficiently move through the air. *The very first cars were boxy, but they gradually became more aerodynamic.*
10. *external* outside, exterior. *Tim's smile was only external and the product of shock; on the inside, he was deeply saddened.*

Study and Research & Speaking and Listening
Students may find the Language Arts Survey, "Determining Messages in the Media," and "How to Analyze a Newspaper or Newsmagazine," helpful in completing the first part of this activity. Tell students that they should try to prepare an extemporaneous speech, one delivered using the help of

ANSWERS TO SKILL BUILDERS (CONT.)

note cards, rather that simply reading their written speech. Students should practice their speech thoroughly at home before they deliver it to their classmates.

Collaborative Learning
Encourage students to think about possibilities such as the following: exploring other planets in the solar

system, learning more about black holes, finding other life forms in the universe, and learning how to travel faster than the speed of light.

UNIT 6 RESOURCE BOOK
• Selection Worksheet 6.4
• Selection Check Test 4.6.7
• Selection Test 4.6.8
• Language, Grammar, and Style Resource 3.15
• Speaking and Listening Resource 4.1

GRAPHIC ORGANIZER

Students may list details such as the following in their charts after "Reeve's brother tried parachute jumping": father disapproves of jumping out of "perfectly good" airplanes, Reeve doesn't like loud noises, father disapproves of cotton balls and wants children to get used to the plane's sound, mother shares her love of being a glider pilot, Reeve sits in the back and watches how her father operates the controls, being in the plane with her father is "self-sufficient" and removed from the world but "monotonous," one Sunday something different happens, there is a jerking sensation and the plane's engine cuts off, Reeve notices her father's sudden alertness as he looks and listens and then calls Stanley to let him know what is going on, Reeve remembers being excited because something different was happening rather than feeling scared, father decides to land plane in cow pasture, Reeve ducks and her father lands the plane successfully, they return home without talking much about the incident, Reeve has learned why her father loves flying—because he becomes the plane.

READER'S JOURNAL

As an alternate activity, ask students if they have ever been in a dangerous situation and only learned how dangerous it was afterward. How did they feel looking back at the situation and what might have happened to them?

Reader's TOOLBOX

PERSONAL ESSAY. A **personal essay** is a short nonfiction work on a single topic related to the life of the writer. A personal essay is written from the author's point of view using the pronouns *I* and *me*. As you read, pay attention to the details the author shares that give the reader a more intimate look at the people involved in the story. Briefly note one or two details that help give a personal feeling to the essay.

CLIMAX. The **climax** is the point of highest interest and suspense in a literary work. As you read, look for the point in the story that signals the coming of the climax in the essay. Then find the highest point of suspense. At what point do you know the climax is over and that all has been resolved? To help keep track of the progression of events, you may want to use a sequence chart like the one to the right. Write in the events that Reeve discusses in the order she presents them. Then go back and identify the climax of the essay. Looking at the boxes in front of the climax, can you find hints that the climax is about to come?

Facing page photo:
Charles, Jon, and Reeve Lindbergh

Prereading

"Flying" by Reeve Lindbergh

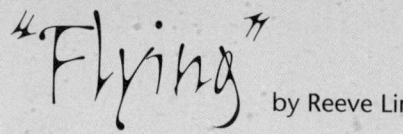

Reader's Resource

• "Flying" is an essay written by Reeve Lindbergh, the youngest daughter of the famous aviator Charles Lindbergh.

• **HISTORY CONNECTION.** After Orville and Wilbur Wright made the first successful airplane flight in 1903, developments in aviation occurred at a rapid pace. By World War I (1914–1918), airplanes were used for transport, attack, and other military purposes. Pilots were making longer and longer flights, and larger airplanes were built to carry more passengers and cargo. By World War II, airplanes and pilots were highly specialized, and aviation technology began to take the shape it continues to build on today.

Graphic Organizer

Reeve and her brothers and sister flew with their father on Saturdays.

Reeve's sister was taught weightlessness.

Reeve's brother tried parachute jumping.

Reader's Journal

Write about a time when you learned something that surprised you about yourself or someone else.

GOALS/OBJECTIVES

Studying this lesson will enable students to
• enjoy a personal essay about flying with a famous aviator
• define *personal essay* and explain what such an essay reveals about the writer and his or her relationships
• define *climax* and identify the climax in a work of nonfiction literature

• examine media articles on Charles Lindbergh
• write a story with a climax
• write a paragraph using vocabulary words
• identify the four types of sentences

Flying

Reeve Lindbergh

PERSONAL ESSAY. Students should note examples such as Reeve stuffing cotton in her ears and hoping her father wouldn't notice and Reeve's lightly teasing way of talking about the horror stories her father told about people who were careless around propellers losing limbs. Some students may choose to dig a little deeper and may point to examples at the end of the story where Reeve shares with the reader the revelation she had about her father and why he flew.

CLIMAX. Students should identify *"And then, one Saturday afternoon, we didn't."* as the sentence that signals the oncoming climax. Some students may say the sentence following that—*"I don't remember now exactly what made me understand there was something wrong with the airplane."*—makes the climax apparent. Reeve talks in the paragraph before about how flying with her father could be monotonous, how he said and did the same things over and over, and how they just "droned along." She then follows with *"And then one Saturday afternoon, we didn't,* and immediately the interest of the reader is peaked, and the climax begins to build in the very next sentence. *"Hold on!" my father said* is the highest point of action. Reeve has told the reader what her father has to do to land the plane safely, and now her father is going to try to do it. At this point the reader doesn't know what will happen. At *"Then we took off our seatbelts and opened the doors and got out,"* the climax has been resolved.

1. The speaker assumed that her father took his family flying to share with them his love of flying, the same way Dads who love sports take their children to ballgames.
2. The speaker knew that starting the propeller was dangerous because her father had warned her about it many times and told her stories of how other people lost limbs due to being careless around propellers.
3. He made the plane climb steeply and then dove sharply.

INDIVIDUAL LEARNING STRATEGIES

MOTIVATION
Ask students if they have ever seen or even ridden in a small plane. Ask them to imagine what this experience might be like. Then have students form pairs and role-play scenes from the story, focusing especially on the crash scene. They should try to capture the emotions and attitudes of the narrator and her father.

READING PROFICIENCY
Students may have difficulty with all the aviation terms. Tell them to pay careful attention to the Words for Everyday Use and the footnotes and share with them the vocabulary above. Tell students to answer the Guided Reading questions as they read and then check their comprehension with the Check Test.

ENGLISH LANGUAGE LEARNING
Point out the following vocabulary words and expressions
cockpit—space in a small plane for the pilot and sometimes the passengers
pier—structure built out over the water and supported by pillars or piles, used as a landing place
propeller—two or more blades that rotate to move a plane
jackhammers—portable type of mechanical hammer used for breaking up rocks; known for being extremely loud
rudder—movable piece attached to the vertical stabilizer of an aircraft used to move the craft to the right or left
banks—long mounds or heaps
sanctuary—holy place, such as a building set aside for worship

(Continued on page 435)

When I was your age, I was flying. I wasn't flying all the time, of course, and I didn't fly by myself, but there I was, nonetheless, on Saturday afternoons in the 1950s, several thousand feet in the air over the state of Connecticut, which is where I grew up. I sat in the back cockpit of a small airplane and looked down at the forests and the fields and the houses and the roads below me from an intense, vibrating height and hoped that my father, in the front cockpit, would not notice that I had cotton balls stuffed in my ears.

I always flew with my father, who had been a pioneer aviator in the 1920s and '30s. I think that he wanted to share his love for the air and for airplanes with his growing family, the way sports-minded fathers took their children to ball games on Saturdays and taught them to play catch afterward. My father took his children to the airport instead and taught them to fly.

> **GUIDED READING**
> Why does the author think her father took his children flying on Saturdays?

Though he was the pilot on these flights, he did not own the airplane. It was a sixty-five-horsepower Aeronca, with tandem cockpits, that he rented from a former bomber pilot[1] whose name was Stanley. Stanley managed the airport, including the huge loaf-shaped hangar that served as a garage for repairs and maintenance to the aircraft, and he leased out the group of small planes tethered near the building like a fleet of fishing boats clustered around a pier.

It was Stanley, most often, who stood in front of the airplane and waited for my father to shout "ConTACT!" from the cockpit window, at which time, Stanley gave the propeller a hefty downward shove that sent it spinning into action and started the plane shaking and shuddering on its way. The job of starting the propeller was simple but perilous. My father had warned us many times about the danger of standing anywhere near a propeller in action. We could list almost as well as he did the limbs that had been severed from the bodies of careless individuals "in a split second" by a propeller's whirling force. Therefore, each time that Stanley started the propeller, I would peer through its blinding whir to catch a glimpse of any pieces of him that might be flying through the air. Each time, I saw only Stanley, whole and smiling, waving us onto the asphalt runway with his cap in his hand and his hair blowing in the wind of our passing—"the propwash" my father called it.

> **GUIDED READING**
> How did Reeve know that starting the propeller is dangerous?

My sister and my three brothers flew on Saturdays too. The older ones were taught to land and take off, to bank and dip, and even to turn the plane over in midair, although my second-oldest brother confessed that he hated this—it made him feel so dizzy. The youngest of my three brothers, only a few years older than me, remembers my father instructing him to "lean into the curve" as the plane made a steep sideways dive toward the ground. My brother was already off balance, leaning away from the curve, and hanging on for dear life. For my sister, our father demonstrated "weightlessness" by having the plane climb so steeply and then dive so sharply that for a moment

> **GUIDED READING**
> What did Reeve's father do to demonstrate weightlessness to her sister?

---

1. **bomber pilot.** Pilot of a wartime airplane designed for bombing

words for everyday use

tan • dem (tan' dəm) *adj.*, having parts arranged one behind the other. *The four of us rented two tandem bicycles and rode around the lake.*

teth • er (te' thər) *v.*, fasten. *I tethered the rowboat to the end of the dock with a long rope.* **tethered**, *adj.*

per • i • lous (per' ə ləs) *adj.*, dangerous. *The lone duck succeeded in making the perilous cross-country journey.*

she could feel her body straining upward against her seatbelt, trying to fight free, while our father shouted out from the front seat that one of his gloves was actually floating in midair.

"See the glove? See the glove?" He called to her over the engine noise and explained that if this state of weightlessness could continue, everything inside the plane would go up in the air. My sister nodded, not speaking, because, she told me later, everything in her stomach was going up in the air, too, and she did not dare open her mouth.

My oldest brother took to flying immediately and eventually got a pilot's license, though he ended up joining the navy and becoming a "frogman," spending as much time underwater with an aqualung[2] and wetsuit[3] as he ever had spent in the air. What he secretly yearned to do during the flying years, though, was to jump right out of an airplane altogether, with a parachute. Finally, many years later, he had his chance and told me about it afterward. He stood at the open door of the airplane, with the parachute strapped to his back, wobbling back and forth at first, like a baby bird afraid to leave the nest. Then he jumped, fell about a hundred feet through the air, and only then pulled the cord that caused the chute to blossom around him like a great circular sail. Swaying under it, he floated toward the ground until he landed, fairly hard. I listened with astonishment; my brother's daring thrilled me to the bone.

My father on the other hand, along with most of the early aviators, was not impressed by the growing enthusiasm for parachute jumping as a sport. Young daredevils like my brother could call it "sky-diving" if they wanted to, but the aviation pioneers referred to it disgustedly as "jumping out of a perfectly good airplane." In their day, a pilot only

GUIDED READING

What did aviation pioneers say about sky-diving?

jumped when he had to: if it was absolutely certain that the airplane was headed for a crash and the parachute was his only hope for survival.

I was considered too young for aerial adventures when I flew, so I did not get dizzy or sick or worry about whether my parachute would open. It was only the noise that gave me trouble. I have never shared other people's enthusiasm for loudness. I don't like sudden sounds

GUIDED READING

What part of flying doesn't Reeve like?

> Then he jumped, fell about a hundred feet through the air, and only then pulled the cord that caused the chute to blossom around him like a great circular sail.

that make you jump with alarm, like the noises of fireworks or guns, or endless sounds that pound in your head so hard you can't think about anything else, like the commotion made by jackhammers and the engines of small airplanes. My sister felt exactly the same way. In fact, she was the one who showed me how to stuff cotton balls in my ears, secretly, for takeoff—when the engine noise was loudest—and for as long during the flight as we could get away with it.

Our father frowned upon the cotton balls. If he saw them, he would make us remove them. He claimed that they diminished the experience of flying and were in any case

2. **aqualung.** Aqua-Lung is a trademarked name of an underwater breathing apparatus
3. **wetsuit.** Close-fitting suit worn by divers to keep warm

---

ANSWERS TO GUIDED READING QUESTIONS

1. He and the other aviation pioneers called it "jumping out of a perfectly good airplane."
2. She doesn't like the loud noise of the engine.

INDIVIDUAL LEARNING STRATEGIES (CONT.)

droned—made a continuous humming or buzzing sound
pastures—fields where grass grows and animals graze
flaps—hinged section on a wing that can be lowered to increase an airplane's lift or raised to increase its drag and slow it down
bobsled—metal sled with steering apparatus and a brake that is raced at very high speeds as a winter sport

SPECIAL NEEDS
Students may find it very useful to complete the Graphic Organizer as they read. This will provide them with a useful outline of the story that will aid them in responding to the Investigate, Inquire, and Imagine questions. If students have difficulty preparing such an outline on their own, you may wish to share the sample responses to the Graphic Organizer activity with them as an aid to comprehension.

ENRICHMENT
Encourage students to work in pairs to research the lives of other famous aviators. Possible choices include Amelia Earhart, Italo Balbo, Floyd Bennet, Louis Blériot, Richard Evelyn Byrd, Claire Lee Chennault, John Glenn, Howard Robard Hughes, Wiley Post, Antoine Saint-Exupéry, or Sir Frank Whittle. After finding information about the aviation and taking notes and locating any visual aids, students should prepare brief (two- to three-minute) oral reports on their chosen aviator.

CROSS-CURRICULAR ACTIVITIES

SOCIAL STUDIES. Interested students might be interested in researching the roles and responsibilities of different branches of the United States military, such as the Navy, the Army, the Air Force, and the Marine Corps. Students may wish to narrow their topic to a particular aspect of their chosen branch, such as career options in this branch, its history, or its role in a particular war. Students should take notes on their research, document their sources, and prepare a brief oral report for the class using visual aids if applicable. Students should then present you with a list of their sources.

Charles Lindbergh speaks at a Lindbergh Day gathering in Springfield, Vermont, in 1927.
Photograph by Hayes Bigelow. Library of Congress.

unnecessary: The engine noise was not so terribly loud that one couldn't get used to it; he certainly had done so. But my sister and I agreed that the only reason he and the other early aviators had "gotten used to" the noise of airplane engines close to their ears was that they had been deafened early on. We were not about to let this happen to us!

My mother, who had also flown back in the early days, always told us that she had loved her experience as a glider pilot[4] best, because there was such extraordinary quiet all around her. In the absence of the usual aircraft engine noise, she could hear the songs of birds and sometimes even the trilling of insects, crickets or cicadas, on the grassy hillsides below. She said that because there was no noise, she could actually feel the power of air, the way it could push up under the wings of a glider and keep it afloat— like a boat on water—with the strength of unseen currents. She talked about "columns of air," stretching like massive tree trunks between earth and sky. "Just because you can't see the air doesn't mean there's nothing to it," she said. "Most of the really important things in our lives are invisible, anyway."

When it was my turn to fly with my father, I sat in the back cockpit and enjoyed the view all around me while he, in the front cockpit, flew the plane. I had a duplicate set of controls in back, with rudder pedals, a stick,

> **GUIDED READING**
>
> What had Reeve's mother loved best about flying?

and instruments, so that if I had been a true student pilot, I could have flown the plane myself, if called upon to do so. But since I was too young to understand or even to reach most of the controls in my cockpit, I just watched them move as if by magic, with no help from me at all, in response to my father's direction and will.

It looked easy. The stick in front of me, exactly like the one in front of my father in the forward cockpit, looked like the gearshift on our car. If it moved backward suddenly (toward me), it meant that my father had decided we were going up. There would be a rushing in my ears, in spite of the cotton, and as I looked over my father's head, through the front window of the aircraft, I would imagine that we were forcing our way right into heaven, higher and higher through ever more brilliantly white banks of cloud. I sometimes daydreamed of bumping into angels, assembled on one of these cloud banks with their halos and their harps, or startling St. Peter at the pearly gates, or God himself in his sanctuary.

> **GUIDED READING**
>
> Where did the author sometimes imagine she was going when she flew with her father?

But then, as I watched, my stick would point forward again, toward what I could see, over the front pilot seat, of the back of my father's neck, with its trim fringe of gray hair

---

4. **glider pilot.** Pilot of an aircraft without an engine

and a khaki shirt collar. Then the airplane would nose down, giving a cockeyed view on all sides of blue sky and wooded hillsides and little tiny roads with buglike cars creeping along them, so very slowly. When we were flying, I was struck always by the <u>insignificance</u> of the world we had left behind. Nothing on the ground had speed, compared to us. Nothing looked real. Once I had climbed into the airplane, all of life seemed concentrated inside the loud space of it, shaking but steady, with my father's own hand on the controls. We were completely self-sufficient, completely safe, rock-solid in the center of the sky.

> **GUIDED READING**
>
> What impressions did Reeve have of things on the ground when she was flying?

It was also a bit <u>monotonous</u>. My father did the same things and said the same things, loudly, over and over. I knew by heart that a pilot had to fly with a steady hand, with no sudden or jerky movements, just a little throttle here, a little wing dip there, always a light, even touch, always a calm approach. I knew all the stories about student pilots—those not already dismembered by propellers—who "froze" to the stick in a panic and could not let go, forcing the plane into a

tragic nosedive. There was no room in my father's lessons with me, his youngest and least experienced child, for soaring like the birds—no wind in the hair, no swooping and circling. We just droned along, my father and me.

And then, one Saturday afternoon, we didn't. I don't remember now exactly what made me understand there was something wrong with the airplane. I think there may have been a jerking sensation that repeated itself over and over. And I think too that there was a huge stillness in the air, a silence so enormous that it took me a moment to realize that it was actually the opposite of noise and not noise itself. The silence was there because the engine had stalled. Perhaps the most <u>profound</u> moment of silence occurred when my father realized that it was not going to start again—no matter what he did. We were in the middle of the sky, on a sunny Saturday afternoon over Connecticut, in a plane without an engine.

> **GUIDED READING**
>
> What alerted Reeve to the fact that something was wrong with the plane?

I don't think there was any drop in altitude, not at first. What I noticed was my father's sudden alertness, as if he had opened a million eyes and ears in every direction. I heard him say something sharp on the

---

words for everyday use

in • sig • nif • i • cance (in sig ni' fi kəns) *n.*, unimportance; smallness in size, weight, number, or influence. *Gazing up at the starry sky above the endless lake in the middle of the vast wilderness, I thought about my <u>insignificance</u>.*

mo • not • o • nous (mə nä' tən əs) *adj.*, characterized by boredom due to the same thing happening again and again. *Making the dumplings was a <u>monotonous</u> task, fill and fold, again and again.*

pro • found (prə faund') *adj.*, all encompassing, complete. *The loud noise woke me and threw me into a <u>profound</u> state of panic.*

ANSWERS TO GUIDED READING QUESTIONS

1. When she was in the air, she had the impression that things taking place on the ground were insignificant and weren't real.
2. A repeated jerking sensation, a huge stillness in the air, and silence.

CROSS-CURRICULAR ACTIVITIES

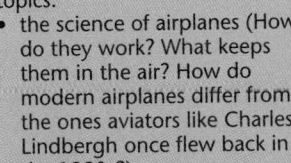

MATHEMATICS AND SCIENCES. Interested students might wish to work in small groups to research and prepare oral reports on one of the following topics:

- the science of airplanes (How do they work? What keeps them in the air? How do modern airplanes differ from the ones aviators like Charles Lindbergh once flew back in the 1920s?)
- airplane travel and safety statistics (How many people travel by plane in the Unites States each year? What are the statistical odds of experiencing a plane crash?)

SOCIAL STUDIES. Other students might wish to research and prepare oral reports on the history of flight by focusing on the Wright brothers achievements. These students should work in pairs to present a brief (no more than five minutes) presentation on the Wright brothers and their contribution to flight.

APPLIED ARTS. Some students might enjoy working in pairs to create a model of a historical aircraft based on research. For example, students might create a model of the type of plane the Wright brothers first flew, the type of plane Lindbergh flew across the Atlantic, or any other type of plane that interests them. Students should share their model and what they learned about this type of plane with their classmates.

1. He had to slip the plane sideways into a pasture surrounded by trees and right it without hitting any of the trees.
2. He was physically and mentally persuading the plane to do the things he needed it to do to land safely, steering it with his whole body, the way one would steer a sled.

Encourage students to discuss whether they ever have felt about anything the way Reeve describes her father feeling about airplanes. Have they ever been involved with an activity they became so much a part of that they seemed to lose their identity? For example, in baseball, do they ever "become" the ball or the bat? Do they love drawing so much that they forget about themselves and become what they are drawing? Encourage students to brainstorm activities that they find as engaging as Lindbergh does flying.

airplanes's two-way radio to Stanley down below, and I could hear the crackle of Stanley's voice coming back. I knew enough not to say very much myself, although my father told friends later that I asked him once, in a conversational way, "Are we going to crash?" And when he told this part of the story, the part where I asked that question, he would laugh.

I don't remember being afraid of crashing. In fact, I don't remember fear at all, but I do remember excitement. At last something different was going to happen! I quickly took the cotton out of my ears because my father was talking. He told me that he was looking for a good place to land. We would have to land, he explained, because the engine wasn't working, and we could not land at the airport, because we were too far away to get there in time. (*In time for what?* I wondered.) He was looking for an open area to put the plane down in, right below us somewhere. We were now over a wooded hillside, dotted here and there with cow pastures: It would have to be a cow pasture. He spotted one that looked possible and circled down toward it.

There was nothing resembling a runway below us and no room to spare. He would have to tip the plane sideways and slip it into the pasture that way, somehow righting it and stopping its movement before it could hit any of the trees at the four edges of the field. We circled lower and lower, barely clearing the treetops, and then he told me to put my head down between my knees.

"Hold on!" my father said.

I didn't see the landing, because my head was down, but I felt it: a tremendous series of bumps, as if we were bouncing on boulders,

> **GUIDED READING**
>
> What does Reeve's father have to do to safely land the plane?

and then the plane shook and rattled to a stop. Then we took off our seatbelts and I opened the doors and got out. I didn't see any cows in the pasture, but there were a bunch of people coming toward us from the road, and it looked as if one of them might be Stanley from the airport. I was careful to stay clear of the propeller.

Nobody could figure out how we had landed safely. They had to take the plane apart to get it out of the pasture, a week or more after that Saturday afternoon. But my father and I got a ride back to the airport with Stanley and drove home in plenty of time for dinner. We didn't talk much on the way home. My father seemed tired, though cheerful, and I was thinking.

I had found out something about him that afternoon, just by watching him work his way down through the air. I held on to the knowledge tightly afterward, and I still hold it to this day. I learned what flying was for my father and for the other early aviators, what happened to him and why he kept taking us up to try flying ourselves. As we came in through the trees, he was concentrating hard, getting the rudder and the flaps set, trying to put us in the best possible position for a forced landing, but he was doing more than that. He was persuading and coaxing and willing the plane to do what he wanted; he was leaning that airplane, like a bobsled, right down to where it could safely land. He could feel its every movement, just as if it were part of his own body. My father wasn't flying the airplane,

> **GUIDED READING**
>
> What does Reeve say her father was doing to the plane as he landed in the pasture?

he was being the airplane. That's how he did it. That's how he had always done it. Now I knew.

∎

Notes from *Reeve Lindbergh*

"In the household where I grew up, writing was a kind of family habit, something the adults around me did every day without thinking too much about it, like taking a walk or brushing their teeth. I can't recall any time during my childhood when one of my parents was not engaged in writing a book. Most often, they were both busy writing books. This made us believe that the best thing you could do with an interesting idea or experience was to write it down. My sister Anne and I caught on to this notion early, and because of it, I think we both became writers before we grew up, though neither of us really believed we were writers until we had published books of our own, when we were parents ourselves.

"I wrote this story about flying with my father because I remember it so clearly after all these years, but I've never told it, from my point of view, until now (though my father used to tell the story and others have too). When I became an adult, I found out how unusual it was to have had a 'forced landing' with Charles Lindbergh, this famous pioneer aviator I was related to, but at the time, it was just a little extra excitement during another Saturday afternoon of flying with my father. I wanted to write the experience down the way it really was, with the sense of excitement and the sense of normal everyday family life mixed up together. I think that's the way life really is."

Respond *to the* SELECTION

Think about an experience you have had with a family member in which you (like Reeve) truly got to know that person better.

About *the* AUTHOR

Photo by Lizzy Brown

Reeve Lindbergh is the youngest daughter of Charles and Anne Morrow Lindbergh and the author of numerous books for children and adults. In 1998, she published *Under a Wing: A Memoir* about growing up in the Lindbergh family.

In *Under a Wing*, as in the essay "Flying," Lindbergh reflects on her father's personality and his influence on her and on others. As a girl, she only gradually came to realize how much of a historical figure her father was. She says, "I grew to realize it through other people and through seeing pictures of him in places where you wouldn't expect to see your father, like your sixth-grade history book. All of a sudden, you're reading and studying and there's your father."

"FLYING" **439**

RESPOND TO THE SELECTION

As an alternate activity (especially if students come from difficult family situations) suggest the following: How would you react to the engine shutting off if you were in the plane instead of Reeve? Explain your response.

SELECTION CHECK TEST 4.6.7 WITH ANSWERS

Checking Your Reading
1. When did Charles Lindbergh typically take his children flying? **Lindbergh took his children flying on Saturday afternoons.**
2. What role did Stanley play when Lindbergh took his children flying? **Stanley spun the propeller to start the plane.**
3. What was the one thing that bothered Reeve Lindbergh about flying? **Reeve didn't like the noise of the flight.**
4. What kind of flying did Reeve's mother, Anne, remember fondly? **Anne Lindbergh liked glider flying.**
5. Where did Charles Lindbergh land the plane when the engine stalled during one of his flights with Reeve? **Lindbergh made his emergency landing in a cow pasture.**

Vocabulary in Context
Fill in each blank below with the most appropriate vocabulary word from "Flying." You may have to change the tense of the word.

tandem   tethered   insignificance
monotonous   profound

1. Dealing with a real tragedy is a reminder of the **insignificance** of the minor difficulties so many of us complain about each day.
2. After teaching Helen Keller, Anne Sullivan wrote, "People seldom see the halting and painful steps by which the most **profound** success is achieved."
3. William had to struggle to stay awake during the **monotonous** lecture.

Reader's Toolbox
1. What is a personal essay? **A personal essay is a short, nonfiction work on a single topic related to the life of the writer.**
2. In a literary work, what is the climax? **The climax is the point of highest interest and suspense in a literary work.**

The Spirit of Charles Lindbergh

Gia Marie Garbinsky

Charles Lindbergh packed into one lifetime enough adventure, excitement, heartbreak, and conflict for ten lifetimes. On May 20, 1927, Lindbergh's famous plane, the *Spirit of St. Louis*, left the ground of Long Island, New York. Less than 34 hours later Lindbergh landed, becoming the first person to fly solo across the Atlantic Ocean from New York to Paris, France. The moment his plane touched down in Paris, he became one of the most famous and popular men of the twentieth century. Waiting for him were huge parades, parties, invitations to visit with kings and presidents, and offers to star in movies. Lindbergh, however, had made the flight for different reasons—a passion and respect for aviation (Lindbergh, *Autobiography* 13–14).

Born on February 4, 1902, in Detroit, Michigan, Charles A. Lindbergh grew up on a farm in Minnesota. Although automobiles and steam engines were in use at that time, horses were still the most common method of transportation. Then in 1903, the Wright brothers changed history by making the first manned airplane flight. Charles saw his first airplane at the age of seven or eight, when one flew right by his house.

From a very young age, Charles loved the outdoors and science. His grandfather was a dentist and an inventor with a laboratory in Detroit. About his grandfather's laboratory, he wrote:

> I was fascinated by the laboratory's magic: the intangible power found in electrified wires, the liquids that could dissolve either metal or stone, the lenses through which one could see the unseeable. Instinctively I was drawn to the farm, intellectually to the laboratory (Lindbergh, *Autobiography* 5).

At the age of 20, Lindbergh enrolled at a flying school in Nebraska. He enlisted in the U.S. Army in 1924, and the next year he became chief pilot on an airmail route between St. Louis, Missouri, and Chicago, Illinois. On one of these flights, he imagined crossing the Atlantic Ocean by air. A few years earlier, a New York hotel owner had offered $25,000 to the person who could complete the first transatlantic flight from New York to Paris. Other pilots had made shorter flights across the Atlantic Ocean. A few men even had tried the flight from New York to Paris—but none had made it (Muha 100). Lindbergh persuaded a group of St. Louis businessmen to invest in his venture. Working with an aircraft company, he designed the *Spirit of St. Louis,* the plane that would carry him across the Atlantic.

The distance was 3,600 miles, and the flight was considered dangerous. Even the takeoff was risky. Just eight months earlier, two airmen had "taxied to a fiery death" just yards from the spot where crew members fueled Lindbergh's plane. As the time neared for takeoff, hundreds of bystanders gathered, and many pressed good luck charms on him. "Several newspapers would report his taking them, but a pilot who had refused to take navigational equipment, had torn unnecessary pages from his notebook, and had trimmed the margins from his maps to save weight was hardly about to stow a cat—to say nothing of rabbits' feet, wishbones, and horseshoes" (Berg 114–115).

At 7:51 A.M. Lindbergh was ready, and at 7:54 A.M. the plane was airborne. He had 5,000 feet of runway to gain the speed and altitude necessary to clear telephone wires at the end of the field—and he cleared those wires by just twenty feet (Berg 116). During the 33½-hour flight Lindbergh's fiercest foe was sleep. In fact, in his book *Autobiography of Values,* he named his lack of sleep his worst enemy. Having heard late the evening before takeoff that a streak of bad weather had unexpectedly cleared, he had not had time to sleep before preparing for the flight. Of his exhaustion, Lindbergh said, "I saw mirages as real as reality had been; I conversed with ghostly forms riding with me in the fuselage; I understood the visions described in ancient myths and sensed elements of man's

existence unknown to me before." He also recounted other obstacles. "A great storm over the ocean almost turned me back. Its icy clouds were a formidable danger. For a time during the night my compasses swung so erratically that I held my course by stars, instead of instruments" (Lindbergh, *Autobiography* 78).

During the hours that Lindbergh traveled alone across the Atlantic, the world waited, desperately hoping. In his nationally syndicated newspaper column on the afternoon of May 20, 1927, Will Rogers wrote:

> No attempt at jokes today. A...slim, tall, bashful, smiling American boy is somewhere over the middle of the Atlantic Ocean, where no lone human being has ever ventured before. He is being prayed for to every kind of Supreme Being that had a following. If he is lost it will be the most universally regretted loss we ever had (Berg 121).

At 10:24 P.M. Paris time, Lindbergh landed. Of the 150,000 people waiting in Paris to greet him, Edwin L. James of *The New York Times* wrote, "Soldiers and police tried for one small moment to stem the tide, then they joined it, rushing as madly as anyone else toward the aviator and his plane" (Berg 129).

Following his successful flight, he toured the nation in the *Spirit of St. Louis,* landing in each state to talk about the promising future of aviation and to promote the building of airports and the establishment of flight routes. He also toured Central and South America. At his first stop in Mexico City, Lindbergh met Anne Morrow, the daughter of the U.S. ambassador to Mexico. Less than twelve months later the two were married. Charles and Anne flew together often. Lindbergh also went on to make other landmark flights—one to China by way of the Great Circle Polar Route and another from West Africa to Brazil. Anne accompanied him and served as radio operator on both flights. (Lindbergh, *Autobiography* 109, 113)

In 1930, the Lindberghs' first child, Charlie, was born. Tragedy hit the family less than two years later. In March of 1932, Charles went upstairs to his son's nursery one night, only to find an open window and a ransom note. Twenty-month old Charlie had been kidnapped.

A few weeks later his body was found close to the woods of their house in New Jersey. The kidnapper was finally caught and convicted more than two years later. During and after this ordeal, the Lindberghs were harassed by the press and the public. No longer feeling safe or comfortable, the Lindberghs—Charles, Anne, and Jon, their second son—moved to England for a while.

In 1935, on behalf of the U.S. government, Lindbergh made the first of several trips to Germany to compile information about the German air force. In 1939, he spoke out against the United States entering World War II, convinced that the Allies could not beat the Germans. The FBI wiretapped Lindbergh's phone, and in 1941, President Franklin Roosevelt condemned him for his opinions, causing Lindbergh to resign from the army.

After the United States entered World War II in 1941, Lindbergh volunteered to serve but was turned down. Instead, Lindbergh went to work as a technical consultant at a plant that made bomber planes for the war. Word of his expertise with planes and flying led an officer in the Marines to suggest that he go undercover—without even the White House knowing—to the South Pacific to train combat pilots.

Soon Lindbergh was flying combat missions. "Approaching the war zones, Lindbergh kept

Charles and Anne Lindbergh in 1927.

refining the duties of his singular job. He flew on dawn patrols and joined rescue missions into the jungle and over the seas; wherever he went, he asked to go to the front lines" (Berg 449). And yet Lindbergh was keenly aware of the results of his efforts in the South Pacific. A journal entry for May 29, 1944—a day on which he dropped a 500-pound bomb on Papua New Guinea, read,

> I don't like this bombing and machine-gunning of unknown targets. You press a button and death flies down. One second the bomb is hanging harmlessly in your racks, completely under your control. The next it is hurtling down through the air, and nothing in your power can revoke what you have done. The cards are dealt. If there is life where that bomb will hit, you have taken it (Berg 449–450).

Lindbergh flew fifty combat flights in all, and the men with whom he flew believed he made an important contribution.

After the war, Lindbergh traveled to Europe and witnessed the damage done by bomber planes. He published a collection of essays and was presented with the Wright Brothers Memorial Trophy for his contributions to aviation and to the nation. In 1953 his book *The Spirit of St. Louis* won the Pulitzer Prize. In 1954 President Dwight D. Eisenhower restored Lindbergh's commission in the Armed Forces. But throughout these events, Lindbergh was questioning his pursuit of technology. He began to long for a simpler way of life.

Of his two lifelong loves, aviation and the outdoors, Lindbergh said:

> Lying under an acacia tree, with the sounds of dawn around me, I realized more clearly, in fact, what man should never overlook: that the construction of an airplane, for instance, is simple when compared with the evolutionary achievement of a bird; that airplanes depend upon advanced civilization; and that where civilization is most advanced, few birds exist.
>
> I realized that if I had to choose, I would rather have birds than airplanes (Mosley 365).

During the last years of his life, Charles Lindbergh became an active and outspoken environmentalist. In the Philippines he worked to save the endangered tamarau, a small, fierce buffalo, and to help preserve the Tasadays, a tribe whose culture dates back to the Stone Age. Lindbergh's conservation work brought him to Africa, Asia, Indonesia, and South America.

After Lindbergh died in 1974, he was buried on the island of Maui, where he and his wife had a simple home surrounded by forest, cliffs, and seashore. He left behind his wife, five children—Jon, Land, Anne, Scott, and Reeve—and a legacy rich in adventure and ideals.

In 1977, a half century after Lindbergh's transatlantic flight, the Charles A. Lindbergh Fund was established. In 1994 the name of the organization became the Charles A. and Anne Morrow Lindbergh Foundation to recognize the "shared vision" and "devoted partnership they formed in pioneering aviation, exploration, conservation, writing, and philosophy." The foundation's mission is to encourage an equal relationship between technological advancement and environmental preservation (Durham n. pag). ■

Charles Lindbergh in Tonga in 1972.

CROSS-CURRICULAR ACTIVITIES

MATHEMATICS AND SCIENCES AND SOCIAL STUDIES. Students may wish to work in small groups to research and present a written report on one of Lindbergh's environmentalist causes. For example, students might prepare a report in the tamarau or the Tasadays. Students should try to present a brief outline of the main facts about this animal or group of people in their report.

Bibliography

Berg, A. Scott. *Lindbergh*. New York: G.P. Putnam's Sons, 1998.

Durham, Dacia. The Charles A. and Anne Morrow Lindbergh Foundation. 24 Oct. 1995, updated 18 June 1999. http://www.mtn.org/lindfdtn/.

Lindbergh, Charles A. *Autobiography of Values.* New York: Harcourt Brace Jovanovich, 1978.

Lindbergh, Charles A. *The Spirit of St. Louis.* New York: Charles Scribner's Sons, 1953.

Mosley, Leonard. *Lindbergh: A Biography.* New York: Doubleday & Company, Inc., 1976.

Muha, Laura. "Revered and Reviled: Charles A. Lindbergh." *Biography Magazine* Dec. 1998: 96+.

ABOUT THE RELATED READING

A native New Yorker, **Gia Marie Garbinsky** lives in Minneapolis, Minnesota, with her husband, Mike, and dog, Digit. She wrote "The Spirit of Charles Lindbergh" to offer young people a short introduction to the life of one of the nation's most famous historical figures.

RECALL

1a. Her mother said "Most of the really important things in our lives are invisible."

2a. She felt that once she climbed into the airplane, whatever happened in there was at the center of everything. She also says she felt completely safe in the plane with her father at the controls.

3a. Her father seemed to be in a good mood, although he was tired.

INTERPRET

1b. *Responses will vary.* Reeve's mother is most likely referring to things like love, respect, confidence, honesty.

2b. *Responses will vary.* Reeve has confidence in her father and that she trusts him. Some students may say that during flights with her father she feels especially close to him, as if only he and she exist in the world.

3b. *Responses will vary.* The fact that her father is tired but cheerful lets the reader know that he wasn't upset or angry about what happened on their flight. He probably feels satisfied with the way he handled the landing.

ANALYZE

4a. Charles Lindbergh took his children flying on Saturday so he could share with them his passion for it. He told his children horror stories to remind them of the danger of being near the propeller. Her father disapproved of sky diving and the cotton balls she and her sister wore in their ears. He claimed the cotton diminished the experience of flying. Reeve tells the reader that flying for her father meant being the airplane, feeling the movements of the plane as if they were part of his own body.

SYNTHESIZE

4b. *Responses will vary.* The stories that Reeve shares within her essay let the reader see Charles Lindbergh in a comfortable and personal setting. Most students will note that Charles Lindbergh was playful and enthusiastic when demonstrating daring stunts to his children. Students may note that he could be stern at times—he would make Reeve and her sister take the cotton balls out of their ears if he saw it. Charles Lindbergh seemed determined to teach Reeve what a good pilot had to do and how dangerous the propeller of a plane could be. Some students may say he had a good sense of humor.

Investigate, Inquire, and Imagine

Recall: GATHERING FACTS

1a. What did Reeve's mother say about the really important things in life?

2a. How does Reeve feel when the engine stops?

3a. What does Reeve say about her father's mood on the drive home?

4a. How does Reeve describe her father's manner of landing the plane?

→ Interpret: FINDING MEANING

1b. What did she mean by this?

2b. What does this tell you about her feelings for her father?

3b. What does this tell you about how he felt after that flight?

4b. What does that description indicate about Charles Lindbergh?

Analyze: TAKING THINGS APART

5a. Reread the essay and make a list of details that Reeve shares about her father's thoughts and feelings on flying.

→ Synthesize: BRINGING THINGS TOGETHER

5b. How does the account Reeve gives of her father's flight experiences with her and her siblings give the reader insight into the personality of Charles Lindbergh? Describe aspects of Charles Lindbergh's personality that are revealed by details Reeve shares about her father.

Perspective: LOOKING AT OTHER VIEWS →

6a. Choose a passage from Reeve's essay and explain how it reveals her thoughts and feelings about her father.

Empathy: SEEING FROM INSIDE

6b. In her notes on this essay, Reeve writes that her father and other people had told the story of the failed engine flight before, but she never had. Imagine that you are Charles Lindbergh and that you landed the plane. How would your telling of the story differ from Reeve's telling of the story? Look for the one detail about her father's telling of the story that Reeve provides in the essay. What does this reveal about her father?

ANSWERS TO INVESTIGATE, INQUIRE, IMAGINE (CONT.)

Students should also note that he was confident as he reacted to the stalled engine and handled the landing.

PERSPECTIVE

5a. *Responses will vary.* Most examples will reveal that Reeve trusts her father, has confidence in him, is slightly in awe of him, and feels great affection for him.

EMPATHY

5b. *Responses will vary.* The most important part of this exercise is that students put themselves in the place of Charles Lindbergh. Charles Lindbergh's telling of this story would differ in several ways: He would have become aware that something was wrong with the plane sooner than Reeve did, and

(Continued on page 445)

Understanding *Literature*

PERSONAL ESSAY. A **personal essay** is a short nonfiction work on a single topic related to the life of the writer. A personal essay is written from the author's point of view using the pronouns *I* and *me*. Review Reeve Lindbergh's notes that follow "Flying." Why does Reeve say she wrote this essay? What fact about her father does Reeve not find out until long after the flight when the engine stalled? Cite an example or two of how Reeve succeeds in capturing "the sense of excitement and the sense of normal everyday family life mixed up together" in her essay. Although she only mentions her mother in one paragraph in the essay, how does Reeve create for the reader a powerful image of her mother?

CLIMAX. The **climax** is the point of highest interest and suspense in a literary work. Look back at the passages you found that lead to, describe, and follow up on the climax in the essay. How does Reeve prepare the reader for the climax in the paragraph that precedes it? Explain. How does the information Reeve provides in the climax of the essay lead to the personal revelation she has about her father? In your own words, summarize the events that create the climax of the essay.

Writer's Journal

1. Create **instructions** for a process or activity that you know how to do well. Assume the instructions are to assist a first-time user or a newcomer to the activity.

2. Write a very brief **essay** about your family that reveals something about your everyday family life and that you could share at a family reunion.

3. Brainstorm a **list** of daring things you would like to do one day. Keep the list and check it from time to time to see if you have tried any of the experiences.

Skill Builders

Study and Research & Media Literacy

EXAMINING THE PRESS. The news media played a large part in the life of Charles Lindbergh. Using library and Internet resources, research how reporters, writers, newscasters, photographers, and other members of the press influenced his life. As you look at information, decide how further to focus your research. You may want to look at his relationships with members of the press or concentrate on the consequences of press coverage of one particular event in his life. You could focus on the role of photographers or on Lindbergh's use of the press to his own benefit. After you have narrowed your topic and gathered information, summarize your findings. Compare and contrast your report with those of your classmates.

PERSONAL ESSAY. Reeve wrote the story because while it had stuck in her mind since it happened, she had never told it from her point of view before. When she became an adult, she found out how unusual it was to have a forced landing with her father. Reeve captures the sense of excitement and the sense of normal everyday family life mixed up together in several places within the essay: Examples include when she tells us that she watches carefully for Stanley's flying body parts whenever he starts the propeller; the stories she tells of her father's daring displays of expertise on the Saturday flights while her sister and brothers silently held on their stomachs—and for dear life; her retelling of her brother's sky-diving adventures and her father's disapproving response; and of course the central anecdote in the essay about the forced landing where she is simply glad for some excitement—her father makes the difficult landing, and they are home in time for dinner.

CLIMAX. A summary of the events of the climax: Reeve was flying with her father when all of sudden she realized that something was wrong. She felt repeated jerks and noticed a huge silence. The engine had stalled and it wasn't going to start again. Her father radioed Stanley and then told Reeve he was looking for a place to land the plane—there wasn't time to get to the airport. Her father would have to land the plane in a small area of pasture enclosed on all sides by trees; there was no room for error. "Hold on!" he said. There were huge bumps as if the plane were bouncing over boulders. Then the plane came to a stop. Reeve sets the climax up in the paragraph preceding the climax by talking about the usual monotony of the flights with her father. The climax of the essay leads to the personal revelation she has about her father. During the flight with the forced landing, Reeve gets to observe her father in a pressure situation and it is then that she fully realizes what flying is about for him and why he is so accomplished at it.

ANSWERS TO INVESTIGATE, INQUIRE, IMAGINE (CONT.)

he would probably tell us how he was going to fix things. The detail that Reeve provides about her father's previous telling: "...although my father told friends later that I asked him once, in a conversational way, 'Are we going to crash?' And when he told this part of the story, the part where I asked that question, he would laugh." Her father's version of the story tells the reader how confident he is in his abilities.

Study and Research & Media Literacy
Students may be particularly interested in researching the press surrounding the Lindbergh kidnapping. Suggest that students try to research newspaper articles from some of the following newspapers that may have covered the story back in 1932: *New York Daily Mirror,* the *New York Journal-American,* the *Chicago Herald-American,* and the *Los Angeles Examiner.*

Collaborative Learning & Speaking and Listening
Students may find it helpful to look at examples of plays or skits in their school library before beginning this activity to see how lines are attributed to characters and how stage directions are used.

Vocabulary Development
Students' paragraphs will vary. Students should use the word in sensible sentences. If students have difficulty using all the words in one paragraph on the same idea, have them write the words in separate sentences in which the meaning of the word is clear from context.

Language, Grammar, and Style
Responses will vary. Possible responses are given.
1. Declarative: "When I was your age, I was flying." *The plane to Jakarta leaves at 2:30.*
2. Imperative: "Lean into the curve.: *Buckle your seatbelts and stow all tray tables in their upright and locked position.*
3. Interrogative: "Are we going to crash?" *Would you like to rent earphones to watch the movie the plane is showing?*
4. Exclamatory: "Hold on!" *I can't believe your flight got in seven hours late!*

Collaborative Learning & Speaking and Listening

CREATING A CLIMAX. Break into small groups of four to five students and review the definition for climax in Understanding Literature. Brainstorm ideas for a suspenseful event to write about as a group. Once you have a list of ideas, decide on one and together write a brief story, describing the events that build to the climax of the suspenseful event. Instead of resolving the climax, however, leave the reader in suspense. Be sure to use the active voice and colorful language in your story. You may want to include dialogue to convey the thoughts and feelings of characters in your writing. When your group has finished, plan how to present your story to the class. Each member in the group should have a role. One person will need to narrate the story. One or more members of the group should act as the story's character or characters. Others will need to manage props, sound effects, and costumes. As you give your presentation, try to convey suspense through words and actions. See the Language Arts Survey 4.1, "Verbal and Nonverbal Communication," for help. After each presentation, discuss possible endings for the stories.

Vocabulary

USING NEW WORDS. Make a list of the Words for Everyday Use found in "Flying" and review their definitions. Write a few paragraphs, including all the words in your writing. When you have finished, exchange your writing with a classmate's work. Check your classmate's work while he or she checks yours. You may refer back to the definitions at any point in this exercise.

Language, Grammar, and Style

TYPES OF SENTENCES. A *sentence* is a group of words that expresses a complete thought. There are four different types of sentences—declarative, imperative, interrogative, and exclamatory.

A *declarative* sentence tells something. It makes a statement and is followed by a period.

EXAMPLE *I was flying when I was your age.*

An *imperative* sentence gives a command or an order or makes a request.

EXAMPLE *Please take that cotton out of your ears.*

An *interrogative* sentence asks a question and ends with a question mark.

EXAMPLE *Are we going to crash?*

An *exclamatory* sentence expresses a strong feeling, such as joy, surprise, excitement, or anger. It ends with an exclamation point.

EXAMPLE *We were not about to let this happen to us!*

Go back to "Flying" and find and copy one more example of each type of sentence. Then, write a sentence of your own for each category. For more information, see the Language Arts Survey 3.15, "Functions of Sentences."

Prereading

"feel like a bird"
by May Swenson

Reader's TOOLBOX

LYRIC POEM. A **lyric poem** is verse that tells the emotions of a speaker and does not tell a story. As you read this poem, think about the following questions. What does this poem reveal about the speaker's emotions? How does the speaker interpret or view the actions of a bird? What about this poem makes it a lyric poem?

FREE VERSE. **Free verse** is poetry that does not use regular rhyme, rhythm, meter, or division into stanzas.

Rhyme is the repetition of sounds at the ends of words. *Rhythm* is the pattern of beats, or stresses, in a poem. *Stanzas* are groups of lines in a poem, separated by spaces from other groups of lines.

Poets who write in free verse sometimes use creative rhyming and rhythm to create imagery. They also may use unconventional word combinations, punctuation, and capitalization. As you read this poem, make some notes in a chart like the one below about the ways in which Swenson uses these literary tools.

Graphic *Organizer*

Rhyme	
Rhythm	
Stanzas	
Word combinations	
Punctuation	
Capitalization	

Reader's Journal

Imagine you are a bird. Describe a flight that you make from home to school.

Reader's Resource

- May Swenson's poems are noted for their vivid imagery and interesting word play. She often wrote about love and about nature. Often in her nature poems, Swenson describes her observations of the movements and everyday activities of birds and other animals.

- Many poems about birds and animals that Swenson and other authors have written appear simple on the surface. But below the surface they commonly have deeper meanings and encourage the reader to think about seemingly simple things in new ways. Look for examples of unique observations that Swenson has made about birds as you read the poem "Feel Like a Bird."

ADDITIONAL RESOURCES

UNIT 6 RESOURCE BOOK
- Selection Worksheet 6.5
- Selection Check Test 4.6.9
- Selection Test 4.6.10
- Language, Grammar, and Style Resource 3.48

GRAPHIC ORGANIZER

Students may note the following in their charts:

RHYME. understand/hand, Wing/thing, coat/boat., Coin/join, Sail/tail, fling/Wing, Heap/leap, Mate/Fate. Students may note that the rhyming pattern is irregular—there is no distinct pattern of rhyme, although there are examples of end rhyme.

RHYTHM. Students may note that the poet uses regular rhyme only sporadically. For example, the first line of the first and second stanza each contain four syllables, but the rhythm is irregular in the other lines.

STANZAS. Students should note the author does use stanzas but they are an irregular blend of three, four, five, and six line stanzas.

WORD COMBINATIONS. Students should notice unusual word combinations such as *star-toes, finger-beak, neat head like/seeds in A Quartered/Apple,* and *sniping at opposites/stereoscope.*

PUNCTUATION. Students should note that there is nor regular punctuation except for an occasional question mark.

CAPITALIZATION. Students should note that the poet capitalizes seemingly random articles, nouns, and modifiers, probably to emphasize them, such as *Coin, A quartered Apple,* and *A Third Sail.*

READER'S JOURNAL

As an alternate activity, ask students would they like to be a bird? Why, or why not? What do you think they would miss about being human?

GOALS/OBJECTIVES

Studying this lesson will enable students to
- have a positive experience reading a free verse poem about a bird
- define *lyric poem* and identify the defining qualities of lyric poems
- define *free verse* and recognize free verse when they read it
- use sources to identify a bird
- form compound words
- correct wordy sentences

1. The beak doesn't a coin in its "feather-pocket."
2. The speaker calls the bird's tail "A Third Sail."

INDIVIDUAL LEARNING STRATEGIES

MOTIVATION
Students may especially enjoy the Study and Research activity in which they are given an opportunity to use their imaginations and consult bird books to determine a species of bird that might be compatible with the bird in the story. Let students know there is no right or wrong answer to this activity.

READING PROFICIENCY
Students may have a difficult time reading this selection on their own due to the unusual combination of words. Play an audiotape of the selection for them or read it to them expressively aloud and tell them to follow along with the words of the poem. You might have students form pairs and then read the poem together and try to come up with a statement of belief explaining what they think the main idea of the poem might be. Pair students who have difficulty reading with students who are stronger readers for this exercise.

ENGLISH LANGUAGE LEARNING
Point out the following vocabulary words and expressions:
sniping—shooting from a hidden position; directing an attack
stereoscope—instrument with two eyepieces in which two photographs of a scene at slightly different angles are presented; the combined image seems to have depth or be three-dimensional to the viewer
giddy—feeling dizzy or unsteady
muffled—wrapped up, as in a shawl, blanket, or cloak

SPECIAL NEEDS
Students may have difficulty comprehending this selection. You may wish to have them only respond to the Guided Reading questions and the Recall questions in the Investigate, Inquire, and Imagine section and leave responding to the rest of the questions as an extra-credit activity for special needs students.

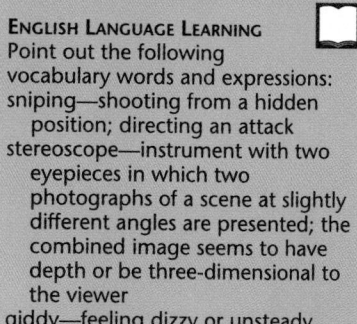

feel
like a
bird

May Swenson

feel like A Bird
understand
he has no hand

instead A Wing
close-lapped
mysterious thing

in sleeveless coat
he halves The Air
skipping there
like water-licked boat

lands on star-toes
finger-beak in
feather-pocket
finds no Coin

GUIDED READING
What doesn't the beak find?

in neat head like
seeds in A Quartered
Apple eyes join
sniping at opposites
stereoscope The Scene
Before

close to floor giddy
no arms to fling
A Third Sail
spreads for calm
his tail

GUIDED READING
What does the speaker call the bird's tail?

hand better
than A Wing?
to gather A Heap
to count
to clasp A Mate?

or leap
lone-free and mount
on muffled shoulders
to span A Fate? ■

Young Rabbit Hawk, 1968. Willard Stone. Heard Museum, Phoenix, Arizona.

INDIVIDUAL LEARNING STRATEGIES (CONT.)

ENRICHMENT
Encourage interested students to write imaginative descriptions of what they think it would be like to be transformed into a bird. Tell students to use concrete details of sight, sound, touch, smell, and taste to make their description of their transformation convincing.

Respond *to the* SELECTION

In what ways is it more convenient to have hands rather than wings?

 art smart

◀ *Young Rabbit Hawk,* 1968. Willard Stone. Heard Museum, Phoenix, Arizona.

Willard Stone (1916–1985) of the Cherokee Nation took an early interest in drawing, but an accident at the age of 13 damaged his drawing hand. His desire to make art could not be discouraged, though, and he found a new outlet in sculpture. Stone developed a deep understanding of the properties of wood and took great care in choosing the right color and grain for his subjects, which included animals and allegories of Cherokee history. His sculpture "Exodus" was chosen as the official symbol of the Cherokee Nation of Oklahoma. What qualities of the wood complement Stone's depiction of a bird? What words in Swenson's poem complement the sculpture?

About *the* AUTHOR

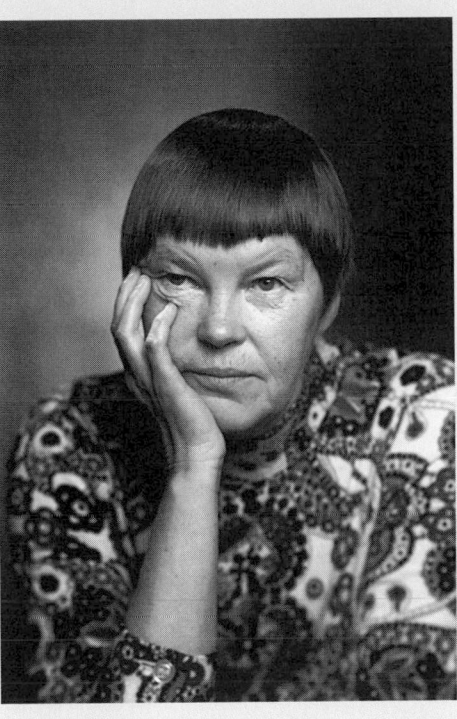

May Swenson was an imaginative American poet, translator, and playwright who lived from 1919 to 1989. Her poetry is characterized by vivid imagery, clever word combinations, and unusual style elements—such as the nontraditional use of capital letters.

Swenson's poems reflect her interest in nature and science. She had a keen eye for observing the world around her and developed a powerful and unique way of describing what she observed.

RESPOND TO THE SELECTION

Ask students to consider this question's opposite, too: In what ways is it better to have wings than hands?

ART SMART

Students should notice how the grain in the wood follows the contours of the bird and simulates feathers.

SELECTION CHECK TEST 4.6.9 WITH ANSWERS

Checking Your Reading

1. According to the poem, what does the bird have instead of a hand? **The bird has a wing instead of a hand.**
2. What does the speaker call "A Third Sail"? **The speaker calls the bird's tail a third sail.**
3. What does the bird fail to find in his "feather-pocket"? **The bird fails to find a coin.**
4. What question does the speaker ask near the end of the poem? **The speaker asks if a hand is better than a wing.**
5. What does the speaker compare to "seeds in A Quartered/Apple"? **The speaker compares the bird's eyes to seeds in an apple.**

Reader's Toolbox

Fill in the blanks using the following terms. You may not use every term, and you may use some terms more than once.

lyric poetry   free verse   rhythm
rhyme   stanza

1. **lyric poetry** is poetry that shares the emotions of the speaker and does not tell a story.
2. **Rhyme** is the repetition of sounds at the ends of words.

freedom

Saadi Youssef, translated by Khaled Mattawa

Alone, now
you
   are free
You pick a sky
and name it
     a sky to live in
     a sky to refuse
But to know that you are
free
and to remain free
you must steady yourself
on a
   foothold of earth
so that the earth may
rise
so that you may give
   wings to all
the children
   of the earth ■

ABOUT THE RELATED READING

Saadi Youssef is a leading Middle Eastern poet whose work is well known throughout the Arab world. Originally from Iraq, Youssef currently lives in Paris, France. Khaled Mattawa has written and translated fiction and poetry.

Investigate, Inquire, and Imagine

Recall: GATHERING FACTS

1a. What does the speaker direct the reader to understand in the first stanza of "Feel Like a Bird"?

2a. In stanza 5, what does the speaker compare to "seeds in A Quartered / Apple"?

3a. What does the speaker ask in the final two stanzas?

→ **Interpret:** FINDING MEANING

1b. Why does the speaker think these instructions are important?

2b. How does this image help the reader envision what the bird is doing in stanza 5?

3b. How might the speaker answer these questions?

Analyze: TAKING THINGS APART

4a. In what ways is the bird unlike a human?

→ **Synthesize:** BRINGING THINGS TOGETHER

4b. How does the bird benefit from freedom more than a human might?

Evaluate: MAKING JUDGMENTS

5a. In "Feel Like a Bird," what insights does the speaker reveal about birds that the average person might not notice? What conclusions about birds does the speaker make based on his or her observations? How well does the speaker voice his or her observations and ideas about birds? Support your answer with evidence from the text.

→ **Extend:** CONNECTING IDEAS

5b. "Feel Like a Bird" and "Freedom" both link the concepts of flight and freedom, and both evoke a response from the reader. How do the poems approach these concepts in different ways? Are there any parallel ideas between the poems? How does your response to "Feel Like a Bird" differ from your response to "Freedom"?

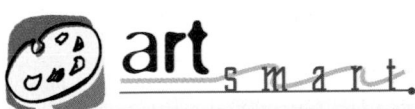 art smart.

◄ **Winged Genius,** c. 900 B.C. Assyrian artist. Museum Deir-ez-Zor, Syria.
The ancient kingdom of Assyria, in what is now Iraq, is one of the oldest known civilizations. Assyrian art depicts many kinds of winged creatures. This stone carving shows a genius (an attendant spirit to the king) with a man's body and an eagle's head and wings. He is performing a purification ritual, sprinkling water from a bucket with a pinecone. Above him is the winged god Ashur. What might a human with birdlike qualities have represented to the Assyrians?

RECALL

1a. The speaker tells the reader to understand that a bird has no hand.

2a. The speaker compares the eyes "sniping at opposites" in the bird's head to "seeds in A Quartered/Apple."

3a. The speaker asks what is better—a hand or a wing.

INTERPRET

1b. Students may suggest that people are so used to experiencing the world through their hands that it is essential for them to imagine what it would be like to have no hand and a wing instead to understand what it would be like to be a bird.

2b. Students may say this helps them see that the speaker is describing what the process of seeing might be like for a bird.

3b. Students may say that the speaker might point out that each has its benefits.

ANALYZE

4a. The bird has wings not hands, star toes, a beak instead of a finger, a sail-like tail, and a different way of seeing. It also can't use coins, gather heaps using hands, or clasp a mate with hands, but it can soar and fly.

SYNTHESIZE

4b. Responses will vary. Students may say that a bird befits more from freedom because it cannot use its wings as hands to do all the activities people do, so it uses them to do what it can do best, leap away into the air.

EVALUATE

5a. Students may say that the speaker reveals how birds use their beaks as fingers as they lack hands, how their far-spread eyes see, how they use their tails as a sail in flight, and how their wings have benefits and drawbacks. Students may say that the speaker concludes that there are wonders of being a bird and free that humans can never know, just as there are humans responsibilities and joys a bird can never know. *Responses will vary.*

ART SMART

Responses will vary, but students may see the human with birdlike qualities as symbolic of transcendence, freedom, or a connection between humans and nature.

ANSWERS TO INVESTIGATE, INQUIRE, IMAGINE (CONT.)

EXTEND

5b. Students may say that both poems associate freedom more with the sky and responsibility more with the world on earth; however, "Feel Like a Bird" makes it clear that birds can only know the freedom of the skies, while "Freedom" implies that people can, too. *Responses will vary.*

LYRIC POEM. *Responses will vary.* Students might say that the bird would seem less strange and inhuman in story form because there would probably be more explanation of the narrator's ideas about the differences between humans and birds. Students might say that in story form you would learn more both about the bird and the speaker, but you might experience less raw emotion.
FREE VERSE. Students may say her unconventional use of rhyme, rhythm, stanzas, word combinations, punctuation, and capitalization helps to emphasize and link certain ideas about birds. As a whole, her use of these techniques help to emphasize to readers how foreign birds are from the human experience and how they must perceive the world much differently than we do. Her use of these tools evoke unusual and startling images of birds.

Understanding *Literature*

LYRIC POEM. A **lyric poem** is verse that tells the emotions of a speaker and does not tell a story. "Feel Like a Bird" is a lyric poem. As the reader, how would you respond differently if this poem were written in story form describing a bird's flight? Would you learn more about the bird? about the speaker? How would your response differ? What emotions does "Freedom" consider?

FREE VERSE. Free verse is poetry that does not use regular rhyme, rhythm, meter, or division into stanzas. In this poem, May Swenson creatively uses free verse, as well as unconventional word combinations, punctuation, and capitalization. With these literary tools, she creates powerful imagery. Look back at your graphic organizer and review the ways in which she uses each technique. What effect do these literary tools have on the poem? on the reader? How does her use of these tools evoke images? Look at the way "Freedom" makes use of some nontraditional stylistic elements. How do these elements contribute to the poem's meaning?

Writer's Journal

1. Write a **free verse poem** for a younger family member, describing for him or her the value of freedom.
2. Imagine that a road project in your town threatens a hawk family, whose nest is in a tree on the planned route. Write a **petition** to the city, asking that the project be delayed until a new suitable habitat is found for the birds.
3. Imagine you had wings instead of hands. What would life be like? Make two **lists**—one of your new limits and one of your new freedoms.

Skill Builders

Study and Research

BIRD IDENTIFICATION. Reread "Feel Like a Bird," and try to picture the bird in your mind. The sculpture shown on page 450 is just one possible representation of the bird. What type of bird do you think the poem describes? What clues lead you to this conclusion? Browse through the pictures and descriptions in a field guide for ideas. Popular field guides you may find in your library include *Birds of North America: A Guide to Field Identification* (Golden Press) and *Field Guide to the Birds of North America* (National Geographic Society). Try drawing the bird you have identified. Use the images from the poem, such as the quartered apple and the sail, to help you create the distinct shapes of the bird's body parts.

Vocabulary

FORMING COMPOUNDS. Compound nouns are nouns (persons, places, things, or ideas) made up of more than one word. Compound adjectives are adjectives (modifiers that describe or limit nouns and pronouns) formed by combining two or more words. Compound nouns and adjectives are sometimes combined as one word. Others are linked with a hyphen. Still others remain open in the form of two words. See the Language Arts Survey 3.48, "Compound Nouns," for more information about compound words.

Compound nouns		Compound adjectives	
belly dancer	push-up	emerald green	roly-poly
safety pin	notebook	poorly written	sunbaked
cocker spaniel	lunchroom	South American	overripe
editor-in-chief	snowflake	quick-tempered	childlike
rock-and-roll		mass-produced	

Examples of compound nouns in "Feel Like a Bird" include *star-toes, finger-beak,* and *feather-pocket.* Compound adjectives in the poem include *close-lapped* and *water-licked.*

Choose an animal with interesting characteristics. Describe the animal in a paragraph, using at least three compound nouns and three compound adjectives. You may use common compounds or you can make up your own as May Swenson did.

Media Literacy & Collaborative Learning

BIRDS IN THE MEDIA. In small groups of about four students, brainstorm and make a list of movies, songs, television programs, poems, and stories that feature birds and flying. What do the birds represent in the examples you found? How many different ideas do birds seem to symbolize? What different emotions do they evoke? Discuss with the group your views on these questions.

Language, Grammar, & Style

CORRECTING WORDY SENTENCES. As you write, you should strive to use only the words and phrases you need to get your point across to the reader. Wordy, complicated sentences can be difficult to read and can create confusion. Edit the sentences below to make them concise.

1. May Swenson was a really good and interesting poet who wrote poems about many different and various subjects and topics such as animals, birds, cats, nature, the environment, her surroundings, and the world.
2. Willard Stone was a Cherokee artist with a lot of artistic talent who became interested in art and sculpture and in creating sculptures in wood, a craft at which he excelled.
3. Saadi Youssef is a Middle Eastern poet who has written many compelling poems and whose popular, interesting, intriguing works are well known and famous throughout much of the Middle East.
4. Assyria was an ancient kingdom from long ago in what is now the nation of Iraq, a country in the Middle East, and was a very old civilization.
5. Poems about flying and being in flight make me feel as if I, too, can fly above the white, fluffy clouds, far above the earth below, and soar like a bird.

Study and Research
Inform students that there is no right or wrong answer to this question, but that they should look to match characteristics of the bird in the poem to a specific species. As starting points students might use the large, wide-set eyes described in the poem and the broad tail.

Vocabulary
Responses will vary, but students should use at least three compound nouns and three compound adjectives. Tell students to be creative and not worry about whether their compound words are in the dictionary for this exercise, but that in more formal activities, such as test answers or essays, they should use standard compound words.

Media Literacy & Collaborative Learning
It might be fun and motivational for students to allow them to bring in clips of videotape, audiotape or CD, and literature featuring birds to share with their classmates. For a different (and less positive) perspective on birds, you may wish to show them a brief clip of Alfred Hitchcock's classic film *The Birds.*

Language, Grammar, and Style
Responses will vary. Possible responses are given.
1. May Swenson used her talent as a poet in exploring subjects in the natural world around her.
2. Willard Stone, a Cherokee, created wooden sculptures that revealed his talent.
3. Saadi Youssef is a poet who has written many compelling works that are well-known in the Middle East, his homeland.
4. Assyria was an ancient Middle Eastern kingdom in what is now modern Iraq.
5. Poems about flying make me feel as if I can fly like a bird above the clouds and the earth.

For Your Reading List

With *Lindbergh* Berg succeeds in surveying the aviator's fascinating life and assessing its historic impact. According to *The New York Times Book Review*, "Berg brings us about as close as I suspect we will ever get to the man himself." Lindbergh's solo flight from New York to Paris captured the imagination of a postwar generation hungry for heroes, and cemented an exalted spot for the twenty-five-year-old pilot from Minnesota in the collective American imagination. Berg's thorough biography suggests that despite the public scrutiny that accompanied his every move until his death in 1974, Lindbergh remained an intensely private man who was painfully shy and emotionally guarded. "Aviation created a brotherhood of casual acquaintances . . . in which he felt comfortable," writes Berg with characteristic perceptiveness.

Books as Research Tools

Students can successfully answer these questions by skimming the book. Have them read the paragraph on skimming in the Language Arts Survey 1.2, "Reading Independently." Refer students to the Language Arts Survey 1.9, "Reading Textbooks" so that they get an overview of the parts of a book. Review with students how to write an effective summary. In addition, you might ask students to research actions and quotations by Lindbergh and then make inferences based on them about his character. Have students read the Language Arts Survey 5.6, "Making Inferences, Predictions, and Hypotheses."

for your READING LIST

LINDBERGH
A. SCOTT BERG

Lindbergh by A. Scott Berg is the Pulitzer Prize-winning biography of one of the most famous men in American history—Charles Lindbergh. While numerous books have been written about Lindbergh, this one is different. In 1989, Berg was approached about writing Lindbergh's biography, but he decided to take the project only with the complete cooperation of the Lindbergh family and access to the Lindbergh archive (never before opened to the public). After almost a year of writing back and forth, Anne Morrow Lindbergh and Berg met in person. After spending a week getting to know each other, Anne granted Berg access to the more than 2,000 boxes of personal papers, letters, and diaries belonging to the family. From Lindbergh's famed 1927 solo flight across the Atlantic to his work in helping to develop the artificial heart, Berg delves into Lindbergh's life in a way no one has ever done before.

BOOKS AS RESEARCH TOOLS

At 628 pages, *Lindbergh* by A. Scott Berg is a challenging book to read. But like other such works, this biography makes a great reference tool. In small groups, evaluate Berg's *Lindbergh* as a research tool. Examine and discuss the following:

- What can you learn about the author and the content by looking at the back cover and reading the jacket flaps? How can this information help you decide whether this book is a reliable reference tool?
- Examine the photographs in the book. What information do the photos and captions offer? How can this information aid you in researching Lindbergh's life?
- Review the table of contents and skim through the first few chapters, looking at their beginnings and endings. How is information in the book organized?
- Examine the index. Have each member of the group choose an index entry and follow it to one of the page references listed. Why is the index an important reference tool? How can you use the index to choose a topic for writing or research?
- Choose a specific event in the life of Lindbergh that all members of your group are interested in and use Berg's book to conduct basic research. Compose a summary of the event to share with your class.

Other books you may want to read:
Under a Wing: A Memoir by Reeve Lindbergh
Going Solo by Roald Dahl
Sky Pioneer: A Photobiography of Amelia Earhart by Corinne Szabo
The Wright Brothers: How They Invented the Airplane by Russell Freedman

Guided Writing

WRITING A NARRATIVE RESEARCH PAPER

Jorge's science teacher showed the class a documentary film about the *Apollo 11* manned lunar landing. Jorge watched as astronaut Neil Armstrong stepped onto the surface of the moon and declared, "That's one small step for man . . . one giant leap for mankind." Afterwards, the teacher told how he, his family, and neighbors had gathered around a small black and white television in 1969 to watch that first historic step onto the moon. Of all the things Jorge had learned during the science unit on space travel, this was the most interesting to him. Jorge decided then that the *Apollo 11* space mission would be the topic for the research paper he had to write for his English class. After class, Jorge went to the library to do some research.

Like Jorge, you may have been assigned a research paper in language arts, science, art, social studies, health, music, or math. While research can be expressed in many ways—through informative, narrative, and persuasive writing—the goal of any research paper is to provide information. For this assignment, you will write a narrative research paper. Unlike an informative research paper that simply supplies information to the reader, a narrative research paper informs by telling a factual story in chronological order about something significant that happened. Biographies of people who have influenced world events, time periods such as the Ice Age or the Roaring Twenties, or events such as the Boston Tea Party or the 1992 Summer Olympics make interesting topics for narrative research papers.

Examining the Model

In the Professional Model, the author narrates the events in chronological order and cites factual information about the flight. The author does not include personal views or extra, unneeded information, but instead focuses on the events surrounding Lindbergh's flight. The specific examples help readers experience the compasses swinging erratically as Lindbergh held his course by the stars and feel the anticipation as the crowds awaited word of Lindbergh's landing.

As in the Professional Model, the first paragraph of a research paper provides an introduction to the story. It starts with a **thesis statement**, which states the main idea in a work of nonfiction. Everything that follows supports that thesis statement.

Note that the author uses direct words from Scott Berg's book,

---

"Research increases your knowledge and understanding of a subject. Sometimes research will confirm your ideas and opinions; sometimes it will challenge and modify them. But almost always it will help to shape your thinking."

—*MLA Handbook for Writers of Research Papers, Fourth Edition*

Professional Model

As you read the excerpt, note how the author narrates the story and provides information.

from "The Spirit of Charles Lindbergh" by Gia Marie Garbinsky, page 440

Charles Lindbergh packed into one lifetime enough adventure, excitement, heartbreak, and conflict for ten lifetimes. On May 20, 1927, Charles Lindbergh's famous plane, the *Spirit of St. Louis*, left the ground of Long Island, New York. Less than 34 hours later Lindbergh landed, becoming the first person to fly solo across the Atlantic Ocean from New York to Paris, France. . . .

The distance was 3,600 miles, and the flight was considered dangerous. Even the takeoff was risky. Just eight months earlier,

continued on page 456

GUIDED WRITING
Software

See the Guided Writing Software for an extended version of this lesson that includes printable graphic organizers, extensive student models and student-friendly checklists, and self-, peer, and teacher evaluation features.

INDIVIDUAL LEARNING STRATEGIES

MOTIVATION
You might show an excerpt from a documentary video on King Tutankhamen's tomb so that students can relate to the student model and get excited about it. Encourage students to brainstorm a list of possible topics that would work for writing a narrative research paper. You might start by writing the examples listed on page 455 on the board.

READING PROFICIENCY
Have students read the Language Arts Survey 1.2, "Reading Independently." Then ask them what type of reading they should practice for this assignment.

ENGLISH LANGUAGE LEARNING
See strategies for Reading Proficiency above that will also benefit students who are English language learners. Students might be interested in choosing a topic from their own culture. To celebrate diversity in your classroom, have non-native English speakers summarize these research papers to the class.

SPECIAL NEEDS
Students with special needs may need help choosing an appropriate topic. You might make a list of possible topics for them to choose from. They might also need help completing their Graphic Organizer. You might pair them with a more proficient student.

ENRICHMENT
Encourage students to prepare visual aids to accompany their research paper. For students interested in making a time line, refer them to the Language Arts Survey 2.19, "Time Lines."

---

two pilots had "taxied to a fiery death" (Berg 114). . . . At 7:51 A.M. Lindbergh was ready, and at 7:54 A.M. the plane was airborne. He had 5,000 feet of runway to gain the speed and altitude necessary to clear telephone wires at the end of the field—and he cleared those wires by twenty feet (Berg 116). During the 33½-hour flight, Lindbergh's fiercest foe was sleep. . . . He also encountered other obstacles. "A great storm over the ocean almost turned me back. Its icy clouds were a formidable danger. For a time during the night my compasses swung so erratically that I held my course by stars, instead of instruments" (Lindbergh, *Autobiography* 78). . . . During the hours that Lindbergh traveled alone across the Atlantic, the world waited, desperately hoping. . . . At 10:24 P.M. Paris time, Lindbergh landed. Of the 150,000 people waiting there to greet him, Edwin L. James of the *New York Times* wrote, "Soldiers and police tried for one small moment to stem the tide, then they joined it, rushing as madly as anyone else toward the aviator and his plane" (Berg 129).

• • •

"The Spirit of St. Louis"
Bibliographic References

Berg, A. Scott. *Lindbergh*. New York: G.P. Putnam's Sons, 1998.

Lindbergh. The author notes Berg's name, and the page number where the words are found, in parentheses after the quotation. The author also makes a reference to Berg's book and the page number where she located the exact number of feet by which the plane cleared the runway. The bibliography following the Professional Model shows the Internet site, the magazine article, and all the books that the author used for research.

IDENTIFYING YOUR AUDIENCE. The audience for your research paper may be your teacher or a panel of teachers and authorities on your topic. Jorge knew that his audience included his language arts, science, and social studies teachers. Before writing, he thought about what each of his teachers would find most interesting about the moon landing, what they might already know, and what unique information might be available about the moon landing. He also thought about what each teacher would look for when evaluating his paper. After you identify your audience, consider these questions.

- What might my audience find most interesting about my topic?
- What they might already know about my topic?
- What background information should they have to appreciate the significance of my topic?
- What unique or new information might interest my audience?

FINDING YOUR VOICE. Voice is the way a writer uses language to reflect his or her unique personality and attitude toward a topic, form, and audience. You express your voice through word choice, tone, and sentence structure.

Look at the two sentences below. Which one uses an interesting voice that could help Jorge narrate the story about the lunar expedition? Why do you prefer it?

Neil Armstrong stepped onto the moon.

The world held its breath as Neil Armstrong stepped onto the lunar surface.

Reflecting

Narrating actual events is an important way to share information with others. Think about interesting news broadcasts, books, and magazine articles that have helped you learn more about actual events. Consider your own experiences narrating actual events. Do you enjoy being able to tell about an event that you think is important? What job opportunities might a good narrator and researcher have?

Prewriting

WRITING WITH A PLAN. You may already have a topic that you would like to write about. Rachel didn't have any topics that she could think of immediately so she carried a notebook and jotted down questions in it for a few days. In math class, she wrote

---

Examining the Model

Students might find it difficult to write a thesis statement. Write a possible thesis statement for some of the topics that students brainstormed in Motivation. The more examples students have, the better their chance of writing a good thesis statement themselves.

questions about how the Greeks discovered geometry. In music class, she wrote questions about how well-known musicians got their start. She was learning about Egypt in her social studies class, so she brainstormed the following questions in her notebook:

> Who built the pyramids?
> What do hieroglyphics mean?
> What roles did women play in ancient Egypt?
> How did the Egyptians build such a great civilization?
> What treasures were in King Tutankhamen's tomb?

Rachel was most interested in learning more about King Tutankhamen. She knew she needed to write her research paper in chronological order, so she wrote this question:

> What led to the discovery of King Tutankhamen's tomb?

If you do not have a topic already in mind, you could carry a notebook with you for a few days, as Rachel did. Brainstorm several questions about what you are learning in each of your classes. Write a question about an idea that you want to investigate, and write it so that it will help you tell a story. Look at the two questions below and decide which question would help you write a narrative research paper in chronological order.

* What happened when Mount St. Helens exploded?
* Where is Mount St. Helens?

Before you begin your research and writing, you may want to do a quick check to see if you have enough resources available at the library. You can also look on the Internet for reliable web sites which can provide both primary and secondary sources of information.

A primary source is a first-hand account of what happened. For example, a NASA Internet web site or a biography that provides an account of the moon mission using Neil Armstrong's, Edwin Aldrin's, and Michael Collins's own words is a primary source of information. If Jorge's science teacher created a bulletin board using information about the lunar landing that he found in other sources, his site would provide secondary source information. Look at the two examples below. Which one is a primary source of information?

* A biography of Sir Edmund Hillary from *Compton's Encyclopedia*
* An interview of Sir Edmund Hillary by James M. Clash, a reporter at *Forbes*

You should try to use at least one primary source. If you do not have three or four good sources of information including at least one primary source, you may need to think of a different question.

After identifying several sources of information, Rachel filled in

Durham, Dacia. The Charles A. and Anne Morrow Lindbergh Foundation. 24 Oct.1995, updated 18 June 1999. <http//www.mtn.org /lindfdth/>.

Lindbergh, Charles A. *Autobiography of Values.* New York: Harcourt Brace Jovanovich, 1978.
Lindbergh, Charles A. *The Spirit of St. Louis.* New York: Charles Scribner's Sons, 1953.

Mosley, Leonard. *Lindbergh: A Biography.* New York: Double-day & Company, Inc., 1976.

Muha, Laura, "Revered and Reviled: Charles A. Lindbergh." *Biography Magazine* Dec. 1998: 96+.

"While planning a work, the writer may and often must think about readers.... Considerations of who will or might read the piece are appropriate and sometimes actively useful in planning it, thinking about it, thinking it out, inviting images."
—Ursula Le Guin

Prewriting

IDENTIFYING YOUR AUDIENCE. Encourage students to read the Language Arts Survey 2.4, "Identifying Your Audience."

FINDING YOUR VOICE. Have students read the Language Arts Survey 2.5, "Finding Your Voice."

Prewriting

WRITING WITH A PLAN. Encourage students who have difficulty thinking of a topic to write a list of things they like. From this list have them write questions like Rachel did to pinpoint possible topics. Again, use the brainstorming list from Motivation to model effective questions that students might ask for those topics; with more models, students will be better equipped to come up with their own questions. If your school library does not have the resources necessary for a student to research their topic, suggest that they visit the local public library. Students having difficulty choosing a topic might want to read the Language Arts Survey 2.7, "Choosing a Topic," and 2.13, "Clustering."

Reflecting

You might put students in small groups and have them narrate an actual event that they participated in or witnessed. This activity will help students realize that narrating is a skill they already know something about. After the narrations have finished, have students write a journal entry about the narrations they heard. Which narration was the most interesting? Why? What did all the narrations have in common? What have they learned about writing a narrative research paper by listening to these narrations?

Language, Grammar, and Style
Documenting

Sources. When you use source materials, you need to give credit to the authors for the information you use in your research. Then readers can verify your research. Crediting authors for their work also protects you against plagiarism. See the Language Arts Survey 5.41, "Avoiding Plagiarism" for more information.

For example, you might want to quote some exact words from Howard Carter as published in *The Discovery of the Tomb of Tutankhamen.* You would need to put his exact words in quotation marks and reference his last name and the page where you found those words:

> According to Carter, "we had almost made up our minds that we were beaten" (Carter xiv).

You would also need to include this source in your bibliography at the end of your paper. Your bibliography entry should read like this:

> Carter, Howard. *The Discovery of the Tomb of Tutankhamen.* New York: Dover Publications, Inc., 1977.

If you use two or more books with the same author, include the author, title of book, and page number in the parenthetical reference.

the graphic organizer below with several *who, what, why, where, when* and *how* questions to help her start her research. For more information on question types, see Language Arts Survey 2.14, "Questioning: Using the 5 *Ws* and an *H.*"

Student Model—Graphic Organizer

```
        Research Paper Topic:
  How was King Tutankhamen's tomb
             discovered?
  WHO      was looking for the tomb?
           was King Tutankhamen?
  WHAT     were they trying to find?
           happened along the way?
           was in the tomb?
           did they do with the treasure?
  WHERE    did they look for the tomb?
           did they find it?
  WHEN     did they find the tomb?
  WHY      were they trying to find it?
           was this an important find?
  HOW      did they find the tomb?
           did they excavate the tomb?
```

Copy the graphic organizer onto your own paper. Fill in your research paper topic by writing a question that you can answer in a story form. Then write *who, what, why, where, when* and *how* questions that will help you do your research.

KEEPING TRACK OF YOUR SOURCES. Take your graphic organizer to the library and collect your source material. Use a separate notecard for each source of information. Write down the title, author, the publishing company, the place and date of publication, the location, and the call number for each book. Write down the addresses of any reliable Internet web sites you plan to use. Record the names of articles in magazines, along with the magazine titles, dates and volume numbers. Give each source you list a number. Write that number next to the source and circle it. When you take notes from the source, include this number on each note card so that you will be able to identify the source of the note later on. You will need your list of sources when you write your bibliography.

TAKING NOTES. Read the questions on your graphic organizer again. Look through each source for answers to your questions. When you find an answer, you can paraphrase, summarize, or quote the information on a piece of paper or on a note card. Do not copy the author's exact words unless you are quoting the author. To copy another person's words without crediting that person as your source is unethical. You want your research paper to reflect your own interesting voice and narrative style. Your notes should be specific, accurate, and brief. You will use your notes later to help you write your draft. See the Language Arts Survey 5.42, "Paraphrasing, Summarizing, and Quoting" for more information.

Use a separate card or piece of paper for each note you write. Include the question you are answering, the number of the source you are using, and the page number where you found the information. You may find that you need to add more *who, what, where, when, why,* and *how* questions to your graphic organizer. Write notes for these questions, too. You will need to reference the source in your paper if you are paraphrasing someone else's ideas in your own words or if you use specific detailed information.

USING QUOTATIONS. Try to include two or three important quotations from authors in your research paper. Write their exact words on a note card and put quotation marks around their words. Use just a few quotations so that the ones you use will be effective. You will need to reference the quotation with the author's last name and the page number in parentheses in your paper. See the Language Arts Survey 5.39 for a sample note card.

ARRANGING THE NOTE CARDS. When Rachel finished her research, she thought about what happened at the beginning, middle, and end of the story. She discarded a few note cards that seemed unimportant. Then she arranged the rest of the cards in chronological order. She numbered the cards so that she could use them later to write her draft. You can follow the same process with your cards or your teacher may want you to use your cards to write an outline. See the Language Arts Survey 2.28 for more information about outlines.

Drafting

WRITING THE THESIS STATEMENT AND THE INTRODUCTION. One way to organize your writing is to identify the main idea of what you want to say. Present this idea in the form of a sentence or two called a thesis statment. A **thesis statement** is simply a sentence that presents the main idea of your paper. To develop ideas for her thesis statement, Rachel reviewed her note cards. What impressed her most was how hard and how long Howard Carter had to work to find King Tutankhamen's tomb. She wrote this thesis statement for her narrative research paper:

Discovering King Tutankhamen's tomb would take a lot of patience, hard work, and determination.

IDENTIFYING PROPER DOCUMENTATION. Read the following exact words from page 255 of John Romer's book, *Valley of the Kings* published by Henry Holt and Company in New York in 1981:

However on the next day—5 November—it became clear to Carter he had found a tomb.

Explain how you would reference this quotation in your paper. Then explain how you would reference this source in your bibliography.

You will also need to reference an author's idea in your paper when you paraphrase it (put it in your own words). Read John Romer's words from page 255 of *Valley of the Kings.* Then paraphrase his ideas:

Finally at the bottom of a stairway of sixteen steep and well-cut steps, Carter's men uncovered a doorway that was still blocked and had its plaster covering intact. It bore the stamp of the royal necropolis, that of Anubis above nine bound captives. Over the years Carter had seen that sealing in almost every Eighteenth Dynasty tomb in the Valley. Now he knew that he had truly found another tomb.

How would you reference this information in your paper?

Continued on page 460

Prewriting (CONT.)

USING QUOTATIONS. For more information on correctly using quotations, have students read the Language Arts Survey 5.42, "Paraphrasing, Summarizing, and Quoting."

ARRANGING THE NOTE CARDS. You might review the definition of chronological order with your students. Students will find the following definition useful. Chronological order is the arrangement of details in order of their occurrence.

Drafting

Encourage students to use their completed Graphic Organizer modeled on page 458 to help them make sure they have answered all their questions. Some students will find it useful to make an outline. Refer them to the Language Arts Survey 2.30, "Formal Outlines." Students might also benefit from reading the Language Arts Survey 2.32, "Drafting an Introduction," 2.33, "Drafting Body Paragraphs," and 2.34, "Drafting a Conclusion."

Language, Grammar, and Style

INTRODUCING THE SKILL. Explain to students that they can use documentation in many of their classes. If they are going on to college, tell them that it is expected that they know this skill.

PREVIEWING THE SKILL. Have students make a chart like that found in the Language Arts Survey on page 935. Ask students to write the Carter quote from page 458 in the top box. Then give them an example of a paraphrase and a summary of the quote. Discuss with students when it is best to use each method.

PRACTICING THE SKILL. For additional practice, have students work through the exercise in the following section of the Study and Research Resource located in the Teacher's Resource Kit: 5.43, "Paraphrasing, Summarizing, and Quoting."

FIXING DOCUMENTATION. You need to document sources correctly. To reference a book in your paper, put the author's last name first and the page number where you found the information:

(Romer 255)

Explain how you would fix the documentation in each example below.

(Carter, 25)

(p.235 Romer)

Donnelly 19)

Look at the reference in the Student Model—Body Paragraph on page 461. Explain whether it is documented correctly. Then read Rachel's revised draft that starts on page 462. What documentation is helpful? Where does Rachel need to include more documentation?

USING DOCUMENTATION CORRECTLY. Read your narrative research paper again. Are there any places that you paraphrased an author's ideas that you need to reference? Are there any exact quotations that you need to reference? Fix any documentation in the body of your paper. Then look at your bibliography. Be sure each source is documented correctly and alphabetized. For more information about documenting sources, see the Language Arts Survey 5.35–5.44.

Rachel planned to use the thesis statement in the introduction to her research paper. She added several sentences to her introduction to identify her topic clearly.

Student Model—Introductory Paragraph

As a young archaeologist in the early 1900s, Howard Carter dreamed of discovering the magnificent tomb of an ancient Egyptian pharaoh. Being the first archaeologist to find a lost tomb might have seemed exciting and fun. However, discovering King Tutankhamen's tomb would take a lot of determination, hard work, and patience. Carter would have to contend with archaeologists who thought all the tombs had been discovered. He also would have to find many people to help him. Would his efforts to find King Tutankhamen's tomb pay off?

Begin your draft with the introductory paragraph, which includes your thesis statement.

WRITING THE BODY. Rachel used her note cards to write the body of her research paper. She described what happened at the beginning, middle, and end of the discovery. As she wrote each sentence, she tried to make sure it supported her thesis statement. She wrote several paragraphs in the body of the paper. Each paragraph had a topic sentence.

Use your ordered note cards or your outline to write the body of the paper. As you draft, include evidence from documented sources to support the ideas you present. This evidence can be paraphrased, summarized, or quoted directly. Write your ideas in chronological order using smooth transitions between your ideas. Use active verbs and precise language. Give specific examples that will make the story interesting to your readers.

While Rachel's introduction was a solid beginning, her body paragraphs needed help. Her self- and peer evaluations included several comments that helped her strengthen her paper.

Student Model—Body Paragraph

This needs a topic sentence.

He went to Egypt when he was 17. He did a lot of work excavating in Egypt before he started looking for King Tutankhamen's tomb. He learned how to speak Arabic. He studied art, *This is interesting, but do I need it?* *Add more transitions?* engineering, and archaeology. Everyone was looking for a king's tomb. He found some other tombs at first. Including the huge tomb of Mentuhotep. He knew a lot about the Valley of the Kings. Carter began to get interested in king Tutankhamen's tomb in 1908. Archaeologists thought all the other tombs had been found. But Carter started working there in 1917 anyway. *This is kind of choppy.* He felt he knew what he was doing and nothing could stop him. Some scientists thought he was foolish.

WRITING THE CONCLUSION. Your paper will need to have a conclusion. Use the conclusion to summarize the main points in your paper and to consider the results of your research. Your conclusion could encourage your readers to discover more about your topic or related topics. Include in your conclusion a summary statement about your thesis and the results of your research.

Student Model—Conclusion Paragraph

Howard Carter worked hard for many years in the Valley of the Kings. Because he was determined and patient, he finally found King Tutankhamen's tomb. Because of Carter's hard work, many people now know his story--and of the rich treasures of one of Egypt's ancient pharaohs.

I like how you end your paper.

Effective conclusion.

"But first you have to get started. The most important thing about writing is, simply, doing it, and like practicing a musical instrument, the more you do it, the more familiar you become with the process, the easier it becomes.

—Patricia Cumming

USING TRANSITIONS. In a narrative research paper, you need to put events in chronological order, or the order in which they occur. Connect events or ideas by using such transition words as *first, second, next, then*, and *finally*.

Review Rachel's revised student model on page 462. Notice the transition words that Rachel has added to her body paragraphs. What words and phrases indicate time passing, or the order in which events occurred?

GUIDED WRITING **461**

Using Transitions

For more information on writing effective transitions, have students read the Language Arts Survey 2.35, "Using Transitions Effectively."

Self- and Peer Evaluation

After finishing your rough draft, you can do a self-evaluation of your work. If time allows, you may also want to do peer evaluations. See the Language Arts Survey 2.37, "Self- and Peer Evaluation," for more details.

As you evaluate your research paper draft or that of a classmate, ask the following questions:

- What true story does the research paper narrate? What is the significance of this story?
- How does the introduction capture the reader's attention? What is its thesis statement?
- Does the body of the research paper use chronological order? How do you know?
- Does the body of the research paper provide enough information about the topic? What information might be added or deleted?
- What transitions help the reader move between ideas? How could transitions be improved?
- Which words are examples of precise language? Which sentences are examples of active voice? Which words and sentences could be improved?
- Does each sentence in the body of the paper support the thesis statement? Which ones need improvement?

Student Model—Revised

Rachel's revised draft is shown below as it appeared in her class research paper anthology. When you hand in your final research paper to your teacher, make sure it is double-spaced and formatted correctly. For more information, see the Language Arts Survey 2.46, "Proper Manuscript Form."

As a young archaeologist in the early 1900s, Howard Carter dreamed of discovering the magnificent tomb of an ancient Egyptian pharoah. Being the first archaeologist to find a lost tomb might have seemed exciting and fun. However, discovering King Tutankhamen's tomb would take a lot of determination, hard work, and patience. Carter would have to contend with archaeologists who thought all the tombs had been discovered. He also would have to find many people to help him. Would his efforts to find King Tutankhamen's tomb pay off?

In the early part of the century, a number of archaeologists were working in the Valley of the Kings where many pharaohs had been buried. They all hoped to find a king's tomb. Howard Carter worked with other archaeologists for a while, and he actually found several tombs, including the huge tomb of Mentuhotep, which had hauntingly beautiful royal statues in it. Eventually, Howard Carter learned all about the Valley of the Kings, and he became determined to find King

Tutankhamen's tomb. This tomb was the only one that hadn't been found.

Some scientists thought that Carter was foolish because all the other tombs had been found. Theodore Davis, an archaeologist, said, "I fear that the Valley of the Kings is now exhausted" (Romer 235). But Carter, who had been interested in King Tutankhamen's tomb since 1908, started working there in 1917 anyway. He felt that he knew what he was doing and nothing could stop him (Edwards 9).

Many people helped Carter to look for the tomb. Lord Carnarvon, an Englishman, gave Carter money for the expedition. Fifty men worked for five years in the Valley of the Kings and they found nothing. They filled baskets with stones and sand. They would carry them off and come back for more. The desert was burning hot and everyone had to look out for snakes and insects. The entire expedition seemed as if it would be a total defeat. Even Carter said, "Season after season had drawn a blank; we had worked for months at a stretch and found nothing, and only an excavator knows how desperately depressing that can be; we had almost made up our minds that we were beaten, and were preparing to leave the Valley" (Carter xiv).

- Is there adequate and accurate documentation in the paper? Does the research paper contain a bibliography? How do the sources support the paper? Are sources documented correctly?
- Does the paper use standard grammar and correct punctuation, capitalization, and proper manuscript format?

"Read, write, and trust your instincts. Listen to good criticism, but pick your critics carefully."
—Paula Danziger

Revising and Proofreading

A handout of the proofreading checklist found in the Language Arts Survey on page 888 is available in the Teacher's Resource Kit, Guided Writing Resource Book 2.45. Students critiquing their classmates' work might be interested in using common proofreader's symbols, which are found in the Language Arts Survey 2.44, "Using Proofreader's Marks."

Revising and Proofreading

Review your self- and peer evaluations. Revise your writing after considering these comments. Think about the story line that you have developed. Take out information that distracts from your story. If there are gaps in the story, go back and fill them in. Check that each paragraph has a topic sentence that is related to your thesis statement. Also check that the details in each paragraph support the topic sentence.

Proofread your revised draft for errors in spelling and grammar. Be sure each source in your paper and in your bibliography is referenced correctly. See the Language Arts Survey 5.35, "Documenting Sources," for more information.

Rachel kept her introduction the same. She revised her next paragraph to include a topic sentence and time order words such as *at that time*, and *eventually*. She took out the facts about Howard Carter learning art and engineering because they did not relate to the paragraph's topic. She revised the third paragraph by adding a quotation to support the idea that other archaeologists did not think the tomb would be found.

However, Carter and his men decided to keep looking. They dug under a stone hut. Then they found a step that was cut right into the rock. There were 16 steps and a sealed door (Romer 255). Carter and his men then had to wait for two more weeks for Lord Carnarvon to get back from England. It was then that they saw the name Tutankhamen on it.

They realized that plunderers had entered the passage in the past, so they weren't sure what they would find. But beyond a second door, where Carter looked into another chamber, he was struck dumb with amazement. Finally, Lord Carnarvon said, "Can you see anything?" All Carter could do was whisper, "Yes, wonderful things" (Carter 96).

Inside the antechamber were life-size statues of kings, alabaster vases, a golden inlaid throne, golden chariots, and gilt couches with their sides carved in the shape of strange animals. This was only the antechamber, not where King Tutankhamen was buried. There were doors to more rooms and they were sealed shut. It took months to discover everything inside the tomb (Heasley n. pag).

Eventually, Carter opened the door and found a golden cabinet. In it were three beautiful coffins; the last one was made all of gold--more than 200 pounds of it. The mummy of King Tutankhamen, covered by a beautiful gold mask, was inside this coffin. The treasures in the tomb were sent to a museum and scientists studied them there. The body of King Tutankhamen himself stays buried in the Valley of the Kings.

Howard Carter worked hard for many years in the Valley of the Kings. Because he was determined and patient, he finally found King Tutankhamen's tomb. Because of Carter's hard work, many people now know his story--and of the rich treasures of one of Egypt's ancient pharaohs.

Bibliography

Carter, Howard. *The Discovery of the Tomb of Tutankhamen*. New York: Dover Publications, Inc., 1977.

Edwards, I. E. S. *The Treasures of Tutankhamen*. New York: Penguin Books, 1976.

Heasley, Michael. Producer. "At the Tomb of Tutankhamen." 1998. <http://www.nationalgeographic.com/egypt>.

Romer, John. *Valley of the Kings*. New York: Henry Holt and Company. 1981.

Publishing and Presenting

Write your final copy neatly in ink or print it from the computer. Prepare a bibliography on a separate sheet of paper and attach it to the back of your paper. Add a title page to the front of the paper that includes the title, your name, class instructor, and date. Include at least one illustration or chart in your research paper. (See the Language Arts Survey 5.19, "Using Reference Works," for more information.) Put your research paper in a folder and display it in the classroom for other students to read. You may want to make an anthology that includes all the research papers your class has done. Plan to read several of your classmates' papers. Tell each student the part of the research paper you enjoyed the most.

Publishing and Presenting

You might have students present their narrative research papers in small groups or in front of the class.

VOCABULARY DEVELOPMENT. Give students the following exercise.

Tell a story in a paragraph in which you use eight of the vocabulary words correctly. You may or may not want to start your story with the example sentence below.

EXAMPLE
Kevin was <u>keen</u> to travel to Africa.

ADDITIONAL RESOURCES

UNIT 6 RESOURCE BOOK
- Vocabulary Worksheet
- Study Guide: Unit 6 Test
- Unit 6 Test

Reflecting on Your Reading

The Genre and Theme questions are suitable to assign as essay prompts to help students prepare for the Unit Test. (To evaluate student writing, see the evaluation forms for writing, revising, and proofreading in the Assessment Resource 4.1–4.9.)

The Genre and Theme questions can also be adapted for use as topics for oral reports or debates. Refer students to the Language Arts Survey 4, Speaking and Listening. (To evaluate these projects, use the Public Speaking Evaluation Form in the Assessment Resource 4.11.)

UNIT SIX *review*

Review: Words for Everyday Use

Check your knowledge of the following vocabulary words. For each word, write a short sentence that includes the word in context. To review a word, look back to the page number indicated.

- distinguish (407)
- guardian (407)
- insignificance (437)
- keen (418)
- perilous (434)

- monotonous (437)
- profound (437)
- seldom (419)
- tandem (434)
- tether (434)

- transformation (408)
- trill (419)
- vapor (408)

Review: Literary Tools

Define each of the following terms, giving concrete examples when possible. To review a term, refer to the page number indicated.

- climax (432)
- diction (424)
- free verse (447)
- lyric poem (447)

- personal essay (432)
- point of view (405)
- setting (405)

- stanza (417)
- style (424)
- tone (417)

Reflecting
on your *reading*

Genre

In this unit, you read a short story, an informational essay, several poems, a speech, a newswire report, and a personal essay. How are each of these pieces of writing different from one another? What makes a short story, for example, different from a personal essay? What makes a newswire report different from an informational essay? What makes a speech unique? How are two poems that treat the same subject still unique?

Theme

The selections in this unit reflect on a number of topics related to flying—birds, airplanes, and space flight. But "Taking Flight" addresses more than just the pure act of flying. The theme of taking flight encompasses different dreams, thoughts, and emotions for different people. How do the following ideas relate to the theme?

- **bravery**
- **freedom**
- **strength**
- **nature**

Media Literacy

Using a computer with an Internet connection, look up the World Wide Web Virtual Library's Aviation site at http://www.db.erau.edu/www_virtual_lib/aviation.html. Choose one of the categories—such as "Helicopters and Gyrocraft"—listed on the home page to research. Read the information supplied when you click on that category and take notes about the topic. Then, use a search engine and type in keywords that describe the topic—"helicopters," for example—to look for additional sites that discuss the topic. Compare the information you got from the WWW Virtual Library with the information in the additional sites. Write a couple of paragraphs about your findings.

Group Project

Divide the class into small groups to discuss the theme of taking flight. Based on your experiences and your reactions to the selections in this unit, try to define what this theme means to the members of your group. You may want to use a graphic organizer like the one below to keep track of your group's ideas. After collecting and discussing these ideas, work together to create a collage on poster board to reflect your group's ideas. You may use written words, magazine clippings, found objects, paint, chalk, and other items for your poster.

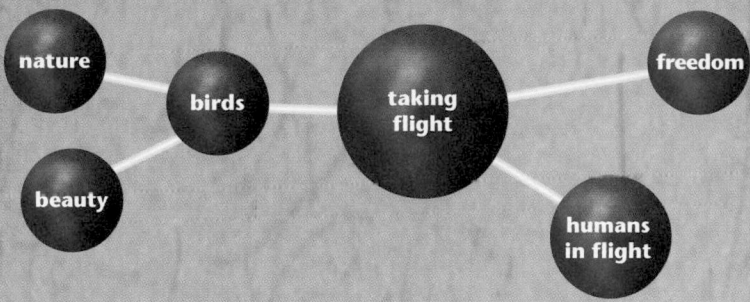

On Your Own

Write a poem that would fit the theme for this unit. Your poem should relate in some way to the theme of taking flight. You may choose to write a lyric poem (which tells your thoughts and emotions) or a narrative poem (which tells a story). To get started, think about what "Taking Flight" means to you. What images come to mind? As you think through your ideas, write down any words or phrases that come to mind. Try to use language that is precise and colorful. Later, read through these words and phrases and try to arrange them in a way that you like. Think about the way the words sound together and about what images the words create. Assembled, do they create images like the ones you first pictured? Do the words describe the specific ideas you want to convey? After finalizing your poem, write it on a poster board to display in your classroom.

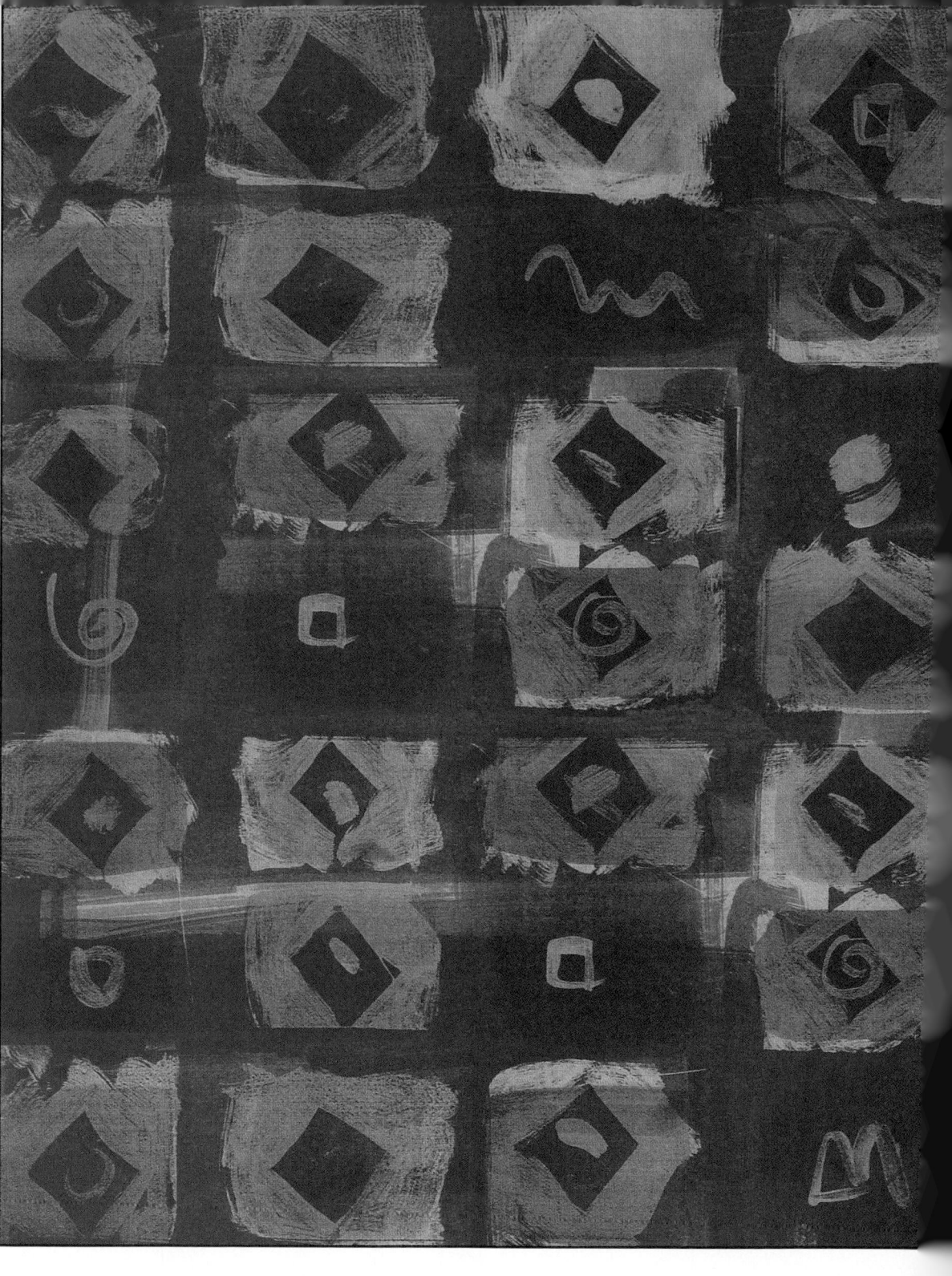

Genres in Literature
PART TWO

GOALS/OBJECTIVES

Studying this lesson will enable students to
- enjoy fiction and nonfiction exploring the theme of passing on the oral tradition
- define and identify examples of *central conflict, characterization, conflict, inciting incident, internal conflict, irony, motive, motive, myth, oral tradition, setting,* and *symbol*
- read independently to explore mythology
- retell a family story
- punctuate dialogue correctly

Pass it On
The Oral Tradition

A Tough Story, 1886. John George Brown.
North Carolina Museum of Art, Raleigh

UNIT SEVEN

Your students can access **The Encyclopedia Mythica** at http://www.pantheon.org/mythica/ for identifications of gods and goddesses, supernatural beings, imaginary lands, and legendary creatures and monsters from around the world. You might have your students use this site to compare and contrast the mythologies of two different cultures. What elements of each are similar? How do they compare to mythologies in our culture?

The Internet site **Myth and Legend from Ancient Times to the Space Age** at http://pibweb.it.nwu.edu/ ~pib/myth.htm helps students discover the difference between folktale, fable and myth and provides links to sites with information about ancient mythology, folklore, and modern myths, like UFOs and urban legends. You might use this site to have students research the significance of monsters and mythical creatures like vampire and why they are still important today.

The Norse Mythology Web Page at http://www.ugcs.caltech.edu/ explores Norse mythology. You might ask students to research Ragnarok, the mythical end of the world. Why did Norse culture have such a myth? Do we have any similar stories in our culture? What did some people think would happen at the millennium?

The Internet site **Myths and Legends** at http://pubpages.unh.edu/ ~cbsiren/myth.html gives access to tales from such far-off places as Korea and Iran, as well as general mythological guides and archives. You might have your students research an animal that frequently appears in mythology, such as the cat or the dragon. What is the significance of these animals in the sories they appear in? What do they represent?

ELEMENTS of THE ORAL TRADITION

Long before people invented writing, they were telling stories, reciting poetry, and singing songs about their beliefs, dreams, and experiences. Many stories were passed down by word of mouth from one generation to the next. The passing of stories, poems, and songs by word of mouth became an important element in forming a group's culture. Together, these works made up what is known as a culture's oral tradition. Eventually many of these stories, poems, and songs were written down and have become an important part of literature. Some of the common forms of traditional oral literature are defined below.

Folk tales are stories passed by word of mouth from generation to generation. Although the term *folk tale* is often used to describe any type of story in the oral tradition, it also refers specifically to stories that could have taken place anywhere and at any time and that are considered anonymous (created by an unknown person). "Hansel and Gretel" and "Little Red Riding Hood" are two well-known folk tales. **Fairy tales** are folk tales that contain supernatural beings, such as fairies, dragons, ogres, and animals with human qualities. Well-known fairy tale characters include Cinderella, Puss in Boots, and Snow White. **Tall tales** are colorful stories that depict the exaggerated wild adventures of North-American folk heroes. Many of these heroes and stories revolve around the American frontier and the Wild West. Some tall tales offer explanations for how certain mountains, lakes, and other geographical features came to exist. Common characters in tall tales include Paul Bunyan, Calamity Jane, Pecos Bill, Davy Crockett, Annie Oakley, and Johnny Appleseed.

Folk songs typically have structured stanzas, a refrain, and a relatively simple melody. They often express a group's shared ideas or feelings. "Yankee Doodle" is an example of a folk song. Narrative folk songs often tell of adventure, war, or everyday life. **Ballads** are short narrative folk songs that are often sung while dancing. They often contain repeated words, lines, or phrases.

Parables are short stories that illustrate a moral or a spiritual truth. Many parables are found in religious writings such as the Christian Bible, the Hebrew Torah, and the Islamic Koran.

Fables are like parables in that they contain a moral. They are also like fairy tales because they have characters that are animals or inanimate objects that speak and act like humans. "The Tortoise and the Hare" is a fable.

Legends are stories that have been passed down through time. These stories are popularly thought of as historical but without evidence to verify that the events occurred. Stories about King Arthur and about Robin Hood are legends.

Myths are traditional stories that explain objects or events in the natural world. These explanations revolve around the actions of supernatural forces, such as gods. Every early culture around the world produced its own myths. This unit contains a variety of myths from around the world. Learning about these myths can help you better understand the cultures from which they stem. Myths also provide a way to compare and contrast the beliefs and attitudes of different traditional cultures. Characters, events, and ideas from myths often appear in contemporary literature. Words derived from mythological characters and places also appear in modern English. Becoming familiar with myths from around the world will help you identify these references in other works and in everyday life.

Prereading

"Persephone and Demeter"

Retold by Ingri and Edgar Parin d' Aulaire

Reader's T O O L B O X

SETTING. The **setting** of a literary work is the time and place in which it happens. Setting is revealed through descriptions of landscape, buildings, scenery, weather, seasons, and other items. What two general areas are the settings of this story? How does one of those settings change over the course of the story?

MYTH. A **myth** is a story that explains the beginnings of things in the natural world. Before the emergence of modern science, people depended on myths to answer basic questions such as what happens to people after they die, what makes plants grow, and why the seasons change. Make a graphic organizer like the one below. As you read, list the questions that the myth answers and the answers it provides.

Graphic Organizer

Questions	Answers
What causes flowers to grow?	Persephone's dancing causes flowers to grow.

Reader's Journal

Which season do you prefer, and why?

Reader's Resource

- In Greek mythology, Demeter, mother of Persephone, was goddess of fertility and of the earth. She was especially associated with grain. Later, the Romans identified her with their goddess of grains, Ceres. The English word *cereal* comes from the Roman name for this goddess.

- Greece has a Mediterranean climate, with mild, wet winters and hot, dry summers. While the weather is quite warm on the islands and coastal regions, in the interior of Greece, the average temperature is only about 72° F in summer and falls below 39° F in winter. Snow covers the mountains and highlands for months at a time.

- **GEOGRAPHY CONNECTION.** Much of Greece is composed of limestone, which is porous and allows surface water to flow down through cracks, forming underground rivers. The descriptions of the underground river Styx and the spring of Lethe are unmistakably similar to the underground rivers found all over Greece. In addition, the idea of Persephone being carried downward through a crack in the earth may also be based on the nature of limestone or possibly on the earthquakes that frequently shake Greece's mountainous lands.

ADDITIONAL RESOURCES

UNIT 7 RESOURCE BOOK
- Selection Worksheet 7.1
- Selection Check Test 4.7.1
- Selection Test 4.7.2
- Reading Resource 1.17

GRAPHIC ORGANIZER

Possible responses may include the following:
Question: What causes nature to bloom?
Answer: Demeter's happiness causes nature to bloom.
Questions: What causes winter?
Answer: Demeter's grief when her daughter has to go to the underworld causes winter.
Question: How did the planting of grain originate?
Answer: It originated when Demeter taught the art to Triptolemus in gratitude for his help.

READER'S JOURNAL

As an alternate activity, students might write their own explanation of what causes winter.

VOCABULARY FROM THE SELECTION

avenge   cleft
barren   root

GOALS/OBJECTIVES

Studying this lesson will enable students to
- appreciate a classical Greek myth
- briefly relate a myth to the geography of Greece
- define *setting* and identify the settings in a myth
- define *myth* and recognize the questions a myth attempts to answer

Demeter, c.500 BC Greek artist. Museo Archaeologico Regionale, Syracuse, Italy.

Persephone and Demeter

Ingri and Edgar Parin d' Aulaire

Persephone grew up on Olympus and her gay laughter rang through the brilliant halls. She was the daughter of Demeter, goddess of the harvest, and her mother loved her so dearly she could not bear to have her out of her sight. When Demeter sat on her golden throne her daughter was always on her lap; when she went down to earth to look after her trees and fields, she took Persephone. Wherever Persephone danced on her light feet, flowers sprang up. She was so lovely and full of grace that even Hades, who saw so little, noticed her and fell in love with her. He wanted her for his queen, but he knew that her mother would never consent to part with her, so he decided to carry her off.

One day as Persephone ran about in the meadow gathering flowers, she strayed away from her mother and the attending nymphs.[1] Suddenly, the ground split open and up from the yawning crevice came a dark chariot drawn by black horses. At the reins stood grim Hades. He seized the terrified girl, turned his horses, and plunged back into the ground. A herd

> **GUIDED READING**
>
> Why does Hades decide to carry off Persephone?

---
1. **nymphs.** Minor nature goddesses

of pigs <u>rooting</u> in the meadow tumbled into the <u>cleft</u>, and Persephone's cries for help died out as the ground closed again as suddenly as it had opened. Up in the field, a little swineherd stood and wept over the pigs he had lost, while Demeter rushed wildly about in the meadow, looking in vain for her daughter, who had vanished without leaving a trace.

With the frightened girl in his arms, Hades raced his snorting horses down away from the sunlit world. Down and down they sped on the dark path to his dismal underground palace. He led weeping Persephone in, seated her beside him on a throne of black marble, and decked her with gold and precious stones. But the jewels brought her no joy. She wanted no cold stones. She longed for warm sunshine and flowers and her golden-tressed[2] mother.

> **GUIDED READING**
>
> How does Persephone feel about Hades's riches?

Dead souls crowded out from cracks and crevices to look at their new queen, while ever more souls came across the Styx[3] and Persephone watched them drink from a spring under dark poplars. It was the spring of Lethe,[4] and those who drank from its waters forgot who they were and what they had done on earth. Rhadamanthus, a judge of the dead, dealt out punishment to the souls of great sinners. They were sentenced to suffer forever under the whips of the <u>avenging</u> Erinyes.[5] Heroes were led to the Elysian fields,[6] where they lived happily forever in never-failing light.

Around the palace of Hades there was a garden where whispering poplars and weeping willows grew. They had no flowers and bore no fruit and no birds sang in their branches. There was only one tree in the whole realm of Hades that bore fruit. That was a little pomegranate[7] tree. The gardener of the underworld offered the tempting pomegranates to the queen, but Persephone refused to touch the food of the dead.

Wordlessly she walked through the garden at silent Hades' side and slowly her heart turned to ice.

Above, on earth, Demeter ran about searching for her lost daughter, and all nature grieved with her. Flowers wilted, trees lost their leaves, and the fields grew <u>barren</u> and cold. In vain did the plow cut through the icy ground; nothing could sprout and nothing could grow while the goddess of the harvest wept. People and animals starved and the gods begged Demeter again to bless the earth. But she refused to let anything grow until she had found her daughter.

> **GUIDED READING**
>
> What effect does Demeter's grief have on nature?

Bent with grief, Demeter turned into a gray old woman. She returned to the meadow where Persephone had vanished and asked the sun if he had seen what had happened, but he said no, dark clouds had hidden his face that day. She wandered around the meadow and after a while she met a youth whose name was Triptolemus. He told her that his brother, a swineherd, had seen his pigs disappear into the ground and had heard the frightened screams of a girl.

Demeter now understood that Hades had kidnapped her daughter, and her grief turned to anger. She called to Zeus and said that she

---

2. **golden-tressed.** Having gold-colored hair
3. **Styx.** River encircling the underworld
4. **Lethe.** River of forgetfulness
5. **Erinyes.** Three female spirits who punish wrongdoers
6. **Elysian fields.** Paradise
7. **pomegranate.** Round, red fruit with many seeds

---

words for everyday use

root (rüt) *vi.*, to dig in the ground, as with the snout. *The dog <u>rooted</u> around, looking for the bone that it had buried.*

cleft (kleft) *n.*, opening. *A spring bubbled up from a <u>cleft</u> in the rock.*

a • venge (ə venj') *v.*, take revenge on. *Robin vowed to <u>avenge</u> Batman's death by tracking down his killer.* **avenging,** *adj.*

bar • ren (bār' ən) *adj.*, producing inferior or scarce vegetation. *The <u>barren</u> garden sat waiting to be planted.*

---

1. Persephone doesn't care about the jewels Hades brings her, which are referred to as "cold stones." She wants to be back on earth in the presence of her mother, the warm sunshine, and the flowers.

2. Demeter's grief causes flowers to wilt, trees to lose their leaves, fields to grow barren and cold, and all growth to stop; as a consequence, people and animals begin to starve.

LITERARY NOTE

Pomegranates figure in much literature from the Mediterranean and the Middle East. Some scholars have suggested that the "apple" that appears in the Genesis story of the Garden of Eden is a pomegranate. Explain to students unfamiliar with pomegranates that these fruits have a thick, bright red skin that covers a thick cluster of tiny seeds, each of which is surrounded by sweet, red flesh.

LITERARY NOTE

According to Greek religion, in order to get into the kingdom of Hades, dead souls had to pay a fee to Charon, the ferryman, who would take them across the river Styx. In Greek myths, the dead are often portrayed as listless and unable to speak. In the *Odyssey*, when Odysseus visits the underworld, he gives the spirits blood to drink, and this animates them, enabling them to speak with him.

HISTORICAL NOTE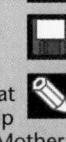

The earliest archaeological remains from the Middle East and from the Mediterranean area contain female figures that are probably related to worship of a fertility goddess or Earth Mother. Most early Middle Eastern and Mediterranean mythologies featured worship of such a deity, variously known as Gaia, Rhea, Demeter,

---

HISTORICAL NOTE (CONT.)

Ishtar, or Cybele. The poet and classics scholar Robert Graves theorized that worship of such a goddess was once widespread from the Middle East through Europe and he wrote a book, *The White Goddess,* on this subject. In recent years, much feminist criticism and research has been produced related to these early Earth goddess religions.

would never again make the earth green if he did not command Hades to return Persephone. Zeus could not let the world perish and he sent Hermes down to Hades, bidding him to let Persephone go. Even Hades had to obey the orders of Zeus, and sadly he said farewell to his queen.

Joyfully, Persephone leaped to her feet, but as she was leaving with Hermes, a hooting laugh came from the garden. There stood the gardener of Hades, grinning. He pointed to a pomegranate from which a few of the kernels were missing. Persephone, lost in thought, had eaten the seeds, he said.

Then dark Hades smiled. He watched Hermes lead Persephone up to the bright world above. He knew that she must return to him, for she had tasted the food of the dead.

> **GUIDED READING**
> Why must Persephone return to Hades?

When Persephone again appeared on earth, Demeter sprang to her feet with a cry of joy and rushed to greet her daughter. No longer was she a sad old woman, but a radiant goddess. Again she blessed her fields and the flowers bloomed anew and the grain ripened.

"Dear child," she said, "never again shall we be parted. Together we shall make all nature bloom." But joy soon was changed to sadness, for Persephone had to admit that she had tasted the food of the dead and must return to Hades. However, Zeus decided that mother and daughter should not be parted forever. He ruled that Persephone had to return to Hades and spend one month in the underworld for each seed she had eaten.

Every year, when Persephone left her, Demeter grieved, nothing grew, and there was winter on earth. But as soon as her daughter's light footsteps were heard, the whole earth burst into bloom. Spring had come. As long as mother and daughter were together, the earth was warm and bore fruit.

Demeter was a kind goddess. She did not want mankind to starve during the cold months of winter when Persephone was away. She lent her chariot, laden with grain, to Triptolemus, the youth who had helped her to find her lost daughter. She told him to scatter her golden grain over the world and teach men how to sow it in spring and reap it in fall and store it away for the long months when again the earth was barren and cold. ∎

Respond to the SELECTION

With which character did you sympathize most: Demeter, Persephone, or Hades? Why?

About the AUTHORS

Ingri d'Aulaire (1904–1980) and **Edgar Parin d'Aulaire** (1898–1986) were authors and illustrators who produced most of their work together. Edgar Parin d'Aulaire was born in Switzerland; he came to the United States in 1929 and became a U.S. citizen in 1939. Ingri Mortenson d'Aulaire was born in

Norway. In 1940, they won the Caldecott Medal for *Abraham Lincoln*. The d'Aulaires also published *D'Aulaires' Book of Greek Myths* and *Norse Gods and Giants*.

The History and Mythology of Ancient Greece

HISTORY. The first of the great Greek civilizations was that of the Minoans, which inhabited the island of Crete between the years 6000 and 1100 BC. They learned to make bronze from copper and tin, thus beginning the Bronze Age.

The culture of Greece from 1600 to 1100 BC is known as Mycenean. In 1250 BC, Mycenean Greeks started the Trojan War. For centuries, people thought that the story of the Trojan War was simply a myth, but in AD 1870, a German named Heinrich Schliemann discovered the ruins of Troy. Later the city was excavated by archaeologists.

During the Archaic Period, from 800 to 500 BC, the first Olympic Games were held, art flourished, and a new Greek script developed. The Greeks of this time also developed a tradition of oral, or spoken, literature performed by professional poets known as bards. The most famous of these bards was Homer, who is credited for two great epic poems, the *Iliad* and the *Odyssey*, which told the fantastic tale of the return of the hero Odysseus from the Trojan War to his home state of Ithaca.

During the sixth century BC, the Ionians, who lived in Greek states in Asia Minor, fell under the rule of the expanding Persian Empire, based in modern-day Iran. After a long series of conflicts, the Persian Wars (492–449 BC), the Greeks defeated the Persians.

The Classical Period began after the Persian Wars and lasted from 479 to 431BC. Greece experienced a golden age, a time when art, philosophy, theater, literature, and trade flourished. Important people of the period included Socrates, Sophocles, Euripides, Herodotus, Thucydides, Pericles, and Hippocrates.

GREEK MYTHOLOGY. The Greeks created their myths by personifying, or giving human attributes to, forces of nature. They believed that at the beginning of time, there was only **Chaos**. Out of Chaos came **Eros**, or love; **Erebos**, or darkness; **Gaia**, the earth; and **Tartaros**, the pit of the earth. The union of Chaos and **Erebos** created **Aether**, the air, and **Hemera**, day. From **Gaia** sprang **Uranos**, the sky, and **Pontos**, the sea. From the union of Gaia and Uranos came the **Titans**, including **Kronos**, or time; **Rheia**, the mother of later gods; **Hyperion**, father of the sun, the moon, and the dawn; **Okeanos**, the ocean; **Mnemosyne**, or memory; **Atlas**, who carried the earth on his shoulders; and **Prometheus**, who created human beings and stole for them the sacred fire of heaven so they could cook and be warm.

Uranos feared the Titans, so he threw them into Tartaros, but Gaia gave her youngest son **Kronos** a sickle, with which he killed Uranos. From the blood of Uranos sprang the **Furies** who torment evildoers. Kronos then ruled. He took Rheia as his wife and they gave birth to the elder Olympian gods.

OLYMPIAN GODS. These are the main Olympian gods. In parentheses are the names the Romans later gave to these gods.

Aphrodite (Venus) was the goddess of love and beauty. According to one myth, she was the daughter of Zeus and Dione.

Apollo was the god of music, poetry, wisdom, light, and truth.

Ares (Mars) was the cruel god of war, who delighted in slaughter.

Artemis (Diana), the sister of Apollo, was the goddess of the woods, the moon, and the hunt.

Athene (Minerva), the goddess of wisdom, justice, war, civilization, and peace, sprang full-grown from the head of her father, Zeus. She was called "tamer of horses."

Demeter (Ceres), was the goddess of corn and the harvest.

Dionysos (Bacchus) was the god of revelry and of the vine.

Hades (Pluto), was the dreaded god of the underworld and the husband of Persephone.

Hebe, the daughter of Zeus and Hera, was the goddess of youth.

Hephaistos (Vulcan) was the god of fire, volcanoes, and the forge.

Hera (Juno) was wife of Zeus and a protector of marriage and the home.

Hermes (Mercury) was the messenger of the gods and the god of mischief.

Hestia (Vesta) was the goddess of chastity and of the hearth.

Persephone (Proserpina) was the goddess of the seasons and the wife of Hades.

Poseidon (Neptune) was the god of the sea.

Zeus (Jupiter) was the leader of the Olympian gods, the god of the sky and of thunder.

RECALL

1a. He believes that Demeter will not give up her daughter to him in marriage.

2a. Sinners are tormented by the Erinyes (or Furies). Heroes go to a pleasant place called the Elysian fields. Average people become lifeless spirits who have forgotten their lives on earth.

3a. Triptolemus tells Demeter that his brother, a swineherd, saw his pigs disappear into the ground and heard the screams of a girl.

INTERPRET

1b. Most students will agree that Hades was not justified because he took Persephone against her will.

2b. Greek myths gave people reason to fear what comes after death—wickedness would be punished, and many people would become listless spirits who cannot remember anything about their former lives on earth.

3b. Demeter's grief is realistic. Few events cause such grief as the loss of a child. The only thing that is not realistic is the way Demeter's grief affects the environment on earth.

ANALYZE

4a. Demeter is basically a kindly goddess who helps provide the world with nature's bounty; however, her state of mind and all of nature are thrown out of balance when she loses her daughter. Persephone seems sweet and kind if a little absentminded; she seems to represent spring. Hades seems grim, silent, and untrustworthy, but he also seems to be lonely. Students may suggest that Hermes plays the role of a messenger or intermediary between those who disagree.

SYNTHESIZE

4b. The gods seem very human in that their moods are very changeable and they seem to make up their minds and act without great consideration of the consequences. Students may suggest this implies that ancient Greeks had to be very concerned about displeasing any of their gods in any way.

EVALUATE

5a. Students will probably not know the rules and regulations common in myths and say that Zeus should have let Persephone return to the earth rather than force her to spend time each year with Hades. Tell students that in Greek myths even

Investigate, Inquire, and Imagine

Recall: GATHERING FACTS

1a. Why does Hades carry off Persephone by force?

2a. According to the myth, what happens to great sinners after their deaths? to heroes? to the average person?

3a. How does Demeter learn what has happened to Persephone?

→ **Interpret:** FINDING MEANING

1b. Do you think Hades is justified in acting as he does? Why, or why not?

2b. If you were an ancient Greek and believed this myth, would you fear what comes after death? Why, or why not?

3b. Is Demeter's grief realistic? Would a real mother react as she does to her daughter's disappearance? Explain.

Analyze: TAKING THINGS APART

4a. Based on the description of the underworld and the other events in the story, analyze the characters of the Greek gods that appear in the myth. What are the main characteristics of each god?

→ **Synthesize:** BRINGING THINGS TOGETHER

4b. What seems to motivate the Greek gods? Describe what you think the people's relationship with their gods was like.

Evaluate: MAKING JUDGMENTS

5a. Does Persephone's schedule at the end of the tale seem fair to you? Explain why or why not.

→ **Extend:** CONNECTING IDEAS

5b. How would you settle the matter if you were Zeus?

Understanding Literature

SETTING. The **setting** of a literary work is the time and place in which it happens. Looking at the two general settings of this story—the world of the living and the world of the dead—explain how the settings are described. What specific objects, elements of time or weather, scenery, or furniture are described? What do they indicate about the time and place of the story?

MYTH. A **myth** is a story that explains the beginnings of things in the natural world. What answers does this myth provide to the following questions: What happens to people after they die? What makes plants such as flowers grow? Why does summer give way to winter? How did people learn to cultivate grain?

ANSWERS TO INVESTIGATE, INQUIRE, IMAGINE (CONT.)

the gods were subject to some forces, such as certain rules, fate, and the necessity of keeping oaths. Thus, even though he is king of the gods, Zeus is powerless to undo the effect that eating the seeds has on Persephone's fate.

EXTEND

5b. Responses will vary, but many students will suggest they would let Persephone return to earth full-time and might even punish Hades for his actions.

Writer's Journal

1. Imagine that you are going to act in a play based on the myth "Persephone and Demeter." Choose a character you would like to play and write a **costume design** for that character. What everyday materials could you use to create your costume?

2. Write a short **persuasive speech** that Demeter might have given to Zeus to convince him that he needed to get Persephone back out of Hades.

3. Imagine that you are babysitting for a young child and want to tell him or her the story of Persephone and Demeter. Write a **retelling** of the myth, using simple language that a child of five or six would understand.

Skill Builders

Study and Research

WORLD MYTHS. Choose an aspect of nature that is explained by the myth "Persephone and Demeter" (such as the nature of life after death, or the origin of grain) and conduct research to find a myth from another culture that explains this phenomenon. For example, you might find a Native American myth, a Babylonian myth, an East Indian myth or a Korean one. Compare the two myths. What are the similarities? What are the differences? Share your findings with the class.

Collaborative Learning

MYTHICAL TALK SHOW. In groups of five or six students, write the script for a show similar to a popular TV talk show, with the characters from the myth acting as guests on the show. Each character should give their perspective on what occurred in the myth "Persephone and Demeter." For example, the student playing Hades could protest that he loves Persephone and that love knows no bounds, while the student playing Demeter could scold him harshly for the pain he has put herself, her daughter, and the mortals through. One student in the group should act as the talk show host, asking questions of each guest and mediating their debate. For fun, another student could act as the guest psychologist or family therapist, giving advice to the other guests on how to resolve their difficulties. When you have finished writing a basic script, put on your show for the rest of the class.

ANSWERS TO UNDERSTANDING LITERATURE

SETTING. The meadow where flowers grow, the golden grain, the sunshine, and the laughter are all part of the description of the world of the living, while the dark underground, cold stones, listless spirits, and sadness are all associated with the world of the dead. Students may say the flower-picking in the field at the beginning of the myth suggests spring, and the dark cold underground suggests winter. Students may say there seems to be an indication that this story took place long ago, before there was any change in the seasons.

MYTH. Heroes got to the Elysian fields after death. Wicked people are punished by the Erinyes. Others drink from the waters of Lethe and forget who they are and what they did in earth. Plants and flowers grow because of Persephone and Demeter. Summer gives way to winter because at that time Persephone has to go into the underworld, and Demeter grieves. People learned to cultivate grain because Demeter taught the skill to Triptolemus.

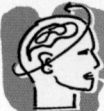

Critical Thinking

UNDERSTANDING SYMBOLS. A symbol is a thing that stands for or represents both itself and something else. For example, a dove is a traditional symbol for peace. After reading this story, what do you think the three pomegranate seeds could symbolize? Think of one or more possible meanings for each of the following traditional symbols.

1. a red rose
2. a lemon
3. a flag
4. a crown
5. a four-leaf clover
6. clouds
7. a mountain
8. a river
9. a band of gold
10. the color black

Media Literacy

GREEK MYTHOLOGY MODERNIZED IN THE MEDIA. Look through magazines and other forms of media for references to gods, heroes, or stories from Greek mythology. One example is Chronos, the Greek god of time, whose name is now a brand name used by a watch manufacturer. Find at least one more example. In what ways could mythological characters and events used to sell products or promote ideas today? How could classical Greek names reflect modern products, services, and ideas? What products might appropriately be named after each of the following: Demeter, Persephone, Hades, Hermes, Zeus, Poseidon, Athena, and Aphrodite?

Language, Grammar, and Style

EXPLORING THE GREEK LANGUAGE. The alphabet used in English comes from the Latin, or Roman, alphabet, which in turn was derived from the Greek. Look at the Greek alphabet on this page. What differences and similarities can you find between it and the English alphabet? Where do you find evidence of the Greek alphabet or its characters in American life? Of the names for Greek characters listed below, what have they come to mean in the English language? Use a dictionary to look up these words and their definitions. On your own paper, list the definition. Then write a sentence using each word. For more information, see the Language Arts Survey 1.17, "Using a Dictionary."

1. alpha
2. beta
3. iota
4. delta
5. omega

The Greek Alphabet

A, α alpha	B, β beta	Γ, γ gamma	Δ, δ delta	E, ε epsilon	Z, ζ zeta
H, η eta	Θ, θ theta	I, ι iota	K, κ kappa	Λ, λ lambda	M, μ mu
N, ν nu	Ξ, ξ xi	O, o omicron	Π, π pi	P, ρ rho	Σ, σ or ς sigma
T, τ tau	Y, υ upsilon	Φ, φ phi	X, χ chi	Ψ, φ psi	Ω, ω omega

Prereading

"The Epic of Gilgamesh"

Retold by Christina Kolb

Reader's Resource

- **HISTORY CONNECTION.** *The Epic of Gilgamesh* originated as stories passed along orally. The stories eventually were written down by Sumerians about 2000 BC. The stories eventually became an epic poem, which was translated into Akkadian and other Mesopotamian languages. The most complete surviving version was written in the Akkadian language on twelve stone tablets. This retelling of the story summarizes the main points of the original epic.

- An epic is a long story, often told in verse, that tells of a culture's heroes and gods. Its length and scope allows it to provide a portrait of an entire culture—its legends, beliefs, values, arts, and ways of life. *The Epic of Gilgamesh* is pessimistic, or dark and gloomy, in its view of the world. Although Gilgamesh is the greatest of heroes, he cannot give the gift of immortality to his fellow mortals and he must accept death as a part of human life.

- Ishtar, or Inanna, as the ancient Mesopotamian people originally called her, was the Queen of Heaven and the goddess of the storehouse, rain, war, love, and the morning and the evening stars. Ishtar sometimes offered fertility and bountiful harvests—and other times brought disaster and war to her people. The Mesopotamians longed for stability. In their mythology, they gradually stripped the unpredictable Ishtar of power and gave more power to benevolent male gods like Anu, Shamash, Enlil, and Ea.

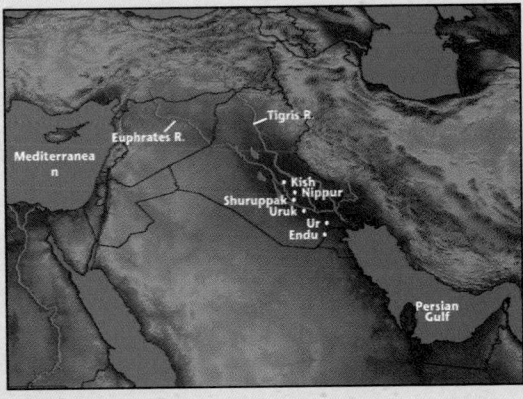

Reader's Journal

Why do you think humans fear aging and death?

Reader's TOOLBOX

CENTRAL CONFLICT. A **central conflict** is the main problem or struggle in the plot of a poem, story, or play. Conflicts can occur in many different ways. A conflict can pit one character against another character or against himself or herself. A character could also come into conflict with society or with nature in a general sense. As you read, try to identify the central conflict of "The Epic of Gilgamesh."

IRONY. Irony is a difference between appearance and reality. An event that contradicts the expectations of the characters, the reader, or the audience of a literary work is an example of **irony of situation**. Which event in this story is an example of irony of situation?

VOCABULARY FROM THE SELECTION

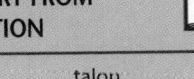

cower	talon
demur	tempestuous
ebb	transgressor
intolerable	vain
oppress	wrest
strew	

ADDITIONAL RESOURCES

UNIT 7 RESOURCE BOOK
- Selection Worksheet 7.2
- Selection Check Test 4.7.3
- Selection Test 4.7.4
- Reading Resource 1.15
- Language, Grammar, and Style Resource 3.86

READER'S JOURNAL

You might ask students to also express their own attitudes, fears, and emotions on death. When did they first become aware of death? What was their reaction?

CROSS-CURRICULAR CONNECTION

HISTORY. Inform students that the Mesopatamians believed in a vast number of gods. Many of these gods were representative of things in the natural world. Mesopotamians believed that natural phenomena such as reeds and salt all had individual personalities and wills. Although there were many gods, the Mesopotamians saw some as being more powerful than others. The most powerful gods met in an assembly to discuss different issues in the universe and to decide upon a course of action. Anu, sky god, was the leader of the assembly and Enlil, second-highest of gods and storm god, often carried out the will of the assembly. Ninhursaga and Enki were third in importance, representing different aspects of the Earth. Early Mesopatamian government was modeled upon this assembly of gods. In early settlements, decisions were made by an assembly of adult freedmen. Gradually, however, city states developed and more power was claimed by one ruler who was at first known as an ensi, or manager of a god's estate, and later as a lugal, or king. Some of the most important gods in Mesopotamian literature are described on page 487.

GOALS/OBJECTIVES

Studying this lesson will enable students to
- appreciate an ancient Mesopotamian story
- define *central conflict* and recognize a central conflict in a literary work
- define and recognize *irony*
- use quotation marks properly
- research and compare and contrast flood stories
- compare and contrast Gilgamesh to a movie or television hero
- research careers in counseling

Gilgamesh. Syrio-Hittite stele.

THE EPIC OF GILGAMESH

Christina Kolb

Gilgamesh, king of Uruk in southern Babylonia, was two-thirds divine and one-third human. He himself built the great city of Uruk. He was like a wild bull—powerful, bold, and able to best any man in combat. Perhaps because he was so very powerful, Gilgamesh was also arrogant. He drove the people of Uruk too hard, <u>oppressing</u> even the weak. Eventually the people of Uruk, weighed down by their heavy burdens, prayed to the gods for relief. The gods granted the people's prayers and created Enkidu.

Enkidu was a wild man, all covered with hair, and he dwelled with the animals. Enkidu was tamed by a priestess who then urged him to strive against Gilgamesh. Enkidu challenged Gilgamesh and

> **GUIDED READING**
> Why do the people of Uruk pray to the gods? For what do they pray?

op • press (ə pres') *v.*, keep down by cruel or unjust use of power. *The cruel tyrant <u>oppressed</u> his people, making them labor long hours without rest.*

ANSWER TO GUIDED READING QUESTION

1. The people of Uruk pray to the gods because Gilgamesh has driven them too hard. They pray for relief from Gilgamesh's oppression.

the two wrestled like bulls. Their fight was long and terrible, but in the end Gilgamesh conquered Enkidu the wild man. From this contest and struggle of bodies emerged the bond of friendship. Together the two brave companions set out seeking adventure. In the cedar forest to the west, they killed Huwawa, a terrible monster who guarded the forest for Enlil, Lord of the Storm.

Ishtar saw Gilgamesh's strength and courage, fell in love with him, and asked him to marry her. Gilgamesh, however, slighted the advances of the <u>tempestuous</u> goddess of love and war, saying that Ishtar was never loyal and faithful to those whom she loved. Enraged, Ishtar flew to the heavens to see her father, Anu. She demanded that Anu make a Bull of Heaven to destroy Gilgamesh. Anu <u>demurred</u>, saying that the Bull of Heaven would cause a seven-year period of drought. Ishtar replied, "If you will not make the Bull of Heaven, I will smash the gates to the underworld, and the dead will devour the living."

Knowing that Ishtar did not make <u>vain</u> threats, Anu created the Bull of Heaven. Ishtar drove the Bull of Heaven down to Uruk. At the river near the city, the bull

> **GUIDED READING**
> Why is Ishtar angry with Gilgamesh?

> **GUIDED READING**
> What does Ishtar threaten to do?

I DREAMED THAT THE GODS WERE IN COUNCIL AND ANU SAID THAT BECAUSE WE TWO HAVE KILLED HUWAWA AND THE BULL OF HEAVEN, ONE OF US MUST DIE.

snorted, and a hole in the earth opened up and swallowed two hundred men. The bull snorted again, and another two hundred men fell into a chasm[1] in the earth. The bull snorted a third time, and Enkidu seized the horns of the Bull of Heaven. Gilgamesh took his sword and struck the Bull of Heaven in the neck. He slew the bull and then made of it an offering to Shamash.

Ishtar mourned the death of the Bull of Heaven and cursed Gilgamesh. Enkidu seized the thigh bone of the bull and threw it in Ishtar's face. Ishtar and the women of her temple gathered to wail over the thigh bone of the Bull of Heaven.[2]

The next day, Enkidu told Gilgamesh that he had a dream. He said, "I dreamed that the gods were in council and Anu said that because we two have killed Huwawa and the Bull of Heaven, one of us must die. Enlil then said, 'Enkidu must die. Gilgamesh shall not die.' Shamash tried to save me, but in vain."

Then Enkidu fell down in sickness. Gilgamesh sat by his sick friend's side. Enkidu's sickness was long. Finally, he told Gilgamesh, "I dreamed Anzu,[3] who has the

> **GUIDED READING**
> Why do the gods decree that one of the heros must die?

---

1. **chasm.** Deep split in the earth
2. **Ishtar . . . Bull of Heaven.** Ishtar was also sometimes portrayed as a goddess of mourning
3. **Anzu.** In Mesopotamian mythology, a terrifying monster

---

words for everyday use

tem • pes • tu • ous (tem pes' chü əs) *adj.,* violent; stormy. *The boat was tossed about by the <u>tempestuous</u> sea.*

de • mur (di mər') *v.,* hesitate because of doubts. *We asked him to state his opinion, but he <u>demurred</u>, saying that he had not yet decided how he felt about the issue.*

vain (vān) *adj.,* without force or effect. *Because Josh did not help Jeremy as he had promised, Jeremy wondered if all Josh's promises were <u>vain</u>.*

1. Ishtar is angry with Gilgamesh because she asked him to marry her and he insulted her.
2. Ishtar threatens to smash the gates to the underworld and allow the dead to devour the living.
3. The gods decree that one of the heroes must die because they have killed Huwawa and the Bull of Heaven.

LITERARY NOTE

Hubris is wanton insolence or arrogance resulting from excessive pride. In ancient literature, a human hero often commits an act of hubris thereby offending the gods who punish the hero and send the hero's fate on a downward spiral. This theme was commonly explored in Greek mythology (in the stories of Niobe and Arachne, for examples) and in Greek tragedy.

You might point out to students that Gilgamesh and Enkidu commit acts of hubris by killing monsters created by the gods. Gilgamesh commits an enormous act of hubris by insulting the goddess Ishtar. Enkidu's death and Gilgamesh's painful and ultimately unsuccessful journey can be seen as punishments for the heroes' acts of hubris. Inform students that tales such as "The Epic of Gilgamesh" pointed out to ancient peoples the importance of accepting, and never striving against, their positions as servants to the gods.

1. Gilgamesh is grieved, enraged, and terrified by Enkidu's death.
2. Gilgamesh is journeying to see Utnapishtim because he wishes to discover how Utnapishtim gained everlasting life.

ADDITIONAL QUESTIONS AND ACTIVITIES

Ask students to discuss Gilgamesh's reaction to Enkidu's death. What is his reaction at first? What does Gilgamesh do after he touches Enkidu's chest and finds that his heart is not beating? What does Gilgamesh do immediately afterward? Why do they think Gilgamesh might be experiencing such a mix of emotions? In what ways do they think that Enkidu's death might be related to Gilgamesh's decision to seek out Utnapishtim?
Answers. Students may say that at first Gilgamesh shows disbelief and confusion, asking Enkidu what "sleep" has seized him and why he cannot hear him. He gently covers Enkidu's face "as if he were a bride." Then Gilgamesh tears his clothes and roars and rages like a madman. Students may say that the death of a loved one causes a range of emotions in people—denial, confusion, tenderness and sentimentality, sadness, and anger. Students may say that Gilgamesh now understands the grim reality of death and hopes to learn how to avoid it by traveling to see Utnapishtim.

---

paws of a lion and the talons of an eagle, seized me and overpowered me. He carried me down to Erkalla's[4] house of darkness, the house where one goes in and never comes back out, the house of death. I won't die gloriously in battle but in sickness and in shame." Soon after this dream, Enkidu died.

Gilgamesh wept over Enkidu. Before this time Gilgamesh had not worried about death, but the passing of Enkidu made death real and terrifying for him. Gilgamesh cried out, "My friend, my younger brother, what sleep is this that has seized you? You have become dark, and you cannot hear me."

GUIDED READING
How does Gilgamesh feel about Enkidu's death?

Gilgamesh touched his friend's heart, but it was still. Gently, Gilgamesh covered his friend's face as if he were a bride. Then Gilgamesh roared with rage, tearing off his finery. Gilgamesh was like a madman in his grief. He wept by Enkidu's side for seven days and nights, but his mourning could not bring Enkidu back to life.

Finally, Gilgamesh got up and began wandering. He longed to speak with Utnapishtim, his ancestor who survived the flood and death itself, Utnapishtim who had been granted eternal life by the gods. Gilgamesh wandered to the mountains where the sun sets, followed the passage between the mountains where the sun travels at night, and came at last to a gate. There stood two terrible scorpions.

One scorpion said to the other, "This one is two-thirds god."

His mate answered, "But one-third man."

The first scorpion asked Gilgamesh, "Why have you journeyed thus far to us?"

Gilgamesh said, "I have come to see my ancestor Utnapishtim. My friend Enkidu has died, the common lot[5] of man has claimed him. Men say that Utnapishtim has found everlasting life."

GUIDED READING
Why is Gilgamesh journeying to see Utnapishtim?

The scorpion said, "No mortal man has journeyed beyond these mountains. There is only death and darkness beyond—you will learn nothing and only come to grief."

"I have already known grief," Gilgamesh said. "I will go on. Open the gate to the mountains!"

The scorpions opened the gate, and Gilgamesh entered the dark. At long last, he came to the valley of the gods. It was lovely, full of fruit and strewn with jewels, and Gilgamesh was overcome by pain, wishing that Enkidu could see what he was seeing. There, Gilgamesh wept, crying "Enkidu, Enkidu."

Shamash came to Gilgamesh and said, "You will never find the eternal life for which you are searching." Gilgamesh, however, would not give up.

Siduri came to Gilgamesh and said, "Gilgamesh, where are you wandering? You will never find the life you seek. When the gods created humans, they let death be man's share and kept life for themselves. Gilgamesh, fill your belly. Make merry. Dance and feast by day and night. Wear fresh clothes and bathe in sweet water. Look at the child who holds your hand, and make your wife happy

---

4. **Erkalla.** Another name for Ereshkigal, the queen of the underworld
5. **lot.** One's fortune in life

words for everyday use

tal • on (tal' ən) n., claw of a bird of prey. *The eagle seized its prey with its talons.*

strew (strü) v., spread by scattering. *The squirrels eat the nuts and strew the shells across the lawn.* **strewn,** adj.

in your embrace. This is the fitting concern of man."

Gilgamesh said, "How can I give up when Enkidu is dust and I too shall die and be laid in the ground?"

Siduri then sent Gilgamesh to Urshanabit, the boatman, who carried Gilgamesh across the sea to Utnapishtim.

"Utnapishtim, my ancestor, I have crossed mountains and seas to see you. In my heart, my friend has died many times, but he still seems alive to me. He became dust so suddenly. Is there something more than death? I am so tired, so very tired."

Utnapishtim touched Gilgamesh's shoulder. "There is nothing everlasting. Houses fall and floods ebb. The sleeping and the dead are alike—death comes to all, master and servant alike. Only the day of a human's death is unknown."

GUIDED READING

What does Utnapishtim say about the fact that he was given eternal life?

Gilgamesh then asked, "If this is so, how did you come to gain eternal life?"

Utnapishtim began his story. "I lived in Shurrupak, on the banks of the Euphrates.[6] The city was old, and its gods grew old— Anu, the father; Enlil; Ishtar; Ea; and the rest. People were numerous, and they raised noise that disturbed the gods. The gods met in council. Enlil, Lord of the Storm, said, 'The noise raised by these humans is intolerable. Sleep is no longer possible.' Enlil planned to release a mighty flood, and the other gods consented.

"Ea could not warn mankind, but he whispered to the reeds of the river, and the reeds whispered to me in my

GUIDED READING

Why do the gods want to cause a flood?

sleep. In my dreams, I heard Ea's voice, saying, 'Tear down your house and build a ship. Into the ship, bring the seed of all living creatures.'

"Who am I to disobey a god? I built an enormous ship, according to Ea's measurements. After six days of working, I completed my ship on the seventh day. I took my family, the seeds of all living animals, and my possessions, and went into the ship. Soon, the tempest roared, and the land was shattered. Even the gods cowered and wept at the storm's fury. Ishtar cried out, 'Why did I cry out for battle in the council of the gods? I have cried out for the destruction of my people, the people to whom I myself gave birth.' The gods sat together and wept, but still the storm raged for six days and seven nights.

"On the seventh day, I opened the window of the ship, and light fell on my face. The world was covered with water, and humanity was dust. There, for a time, I wept. Then I looked for shore. Finally, the ship ran aground against the mountain Nisir. To see if the waters were receding, I sent a dove which returned to me, seeing no place to stand. Then I sent a swallow out to fly. It also returned. Finally, I sent a crow, which saw that the waters had receded and did not return. In gratitude, I made sacrifice to the gods. Ishtar and the other gods approached the offering.

"When Enlil came, he was furious, saying, 'Has life escaped? No humans were to live through this devastation!' Ninurta then blamed Ea for my escape.

---

6. **Euphrates.** River flowing from Turkey southward to Syria and Iraq

words for everyday use

ebb (eb) v., flow back; recede. *When the tide ebbs, we can hunt for shells along the shore.*

in • tol • er • a • ble (in täl' ər ə bəl) adj., unbearable; too severe or painful to be endured. *We thought that Jessica's rudeness to the new students was intolerable.*

cow • er (kou' ər) v., crouch or huddle. *The tiny kitten cowered before the barking dog.*

ANSWERS TO GUIDED READING QUESTIONS

1. Utnapishtim says that all humans must die one day and only that day is unknown.
2. The gods want to cause a flood to rid the land of the noisy humans who disturbed their rest.

Quotables

"Show me a hero and I will write you a tragedy."

—F. Scott Fitzgerald

"We are not now that strength which in old days
Moved earth and heaven, that which we are, we are—
One equal temper of heroic hearts,
Made weak by time and fate, but strong in will
To strive, to seek to find, and not to yield."

—Alfred, Lord Tennyson

CROSS-CURRICULAR CONNECTION

HISTORY. Inform students that the Code of Hammurabi is a collection of two hundred and eight-two legal decisions that Hammurabi made during his reign. The code was written on a stela, or upright stone slab and placed in Babylon's temple to Marduk. The stela also shows a reliaf of Hammurabi and the god Shamash, who was god of the sun and of justice. Many of the laws in the code are based upon much older laws, such as the law that called for an eye for an eye. Penalties in the code varied depending on the social status of the offender with slaves being the class that was punished most harshly for crimes. Despite the code's severity, it did establish some laws protecting widows and orphans. This indicated that rulers were concerned, at least to some degree, with the welfare of less fortunate members of the populace.

ADDITIONAL QUESTIONS AND ACTIVITIES

Encourage students to discuss what they think of Gilgamesh's determination to continue on his journey. Ask them to discuss why he continues on his journey, what is at risk on his journey, and whether or not they would consider Gilgamesh a hero.

LITERARY NOTE

Some students might be
interested in reading the
Mesopotamian creation myth, the
Enuma elish, or "When on High."
This creation myth was written in
Akkadian in the middle of the second
millennium BC. In the Akkadian
version of the text, the hero is
Marduk, the city-god of Babylon,
reflecting Babylon's importance
during that time. A later version of
the text exists in Assyrian, and in this
version the Assyrian god Assur
replaces Marduk as the hero. Some
scholars believe that the *Enuma elish*
was based on an earlier tale in which
Enlil, the storm god, played the
central role. The myth describes how
the basic features of the universe
were formed and how the present
world came to be.

A reading of the *Enuma elish* might
enhance students' readings of "The
Epic of Gilgamesh." In the *Enuma
elish* an older race of gods becomes
disturbed by the clamor of a new
race of gods. The older gods decide
(but fail) to destroy the younger
gods so that their rest will not be
disturbed. This is remarkably similar
to the scene in "The Epic of
Gilgamesh" in which the gods
become disturbed by the noise
raised by humans and decide to
release a terrible flood to wash
humans from the earth. The *Enuma
elish* might also be valuable to
students because in this work many
gods, their domains, and their
relations to other gods are described.

"Ea said, 'You sent the flood senselessly, without thinking it through. You should punish evildoers alone. Let the punishment fit the crime. Do not drive the <u>transgressor</u> too hard. Rather than the flood, you should have let lions, wolves, famine, or plague strike down the people. I did not reveal the secret of our council. Utnapishtim received a vision.'

"Then Enlil picked up my wife and me, touched our foreheads, and blessed us, saying, 'Before now these have been humans. Now, Utnapishtim and his wife are transformed, being like us gods.' Enlil took us away to live here at the source of the rivers.

"So, Gilgamesh," Utnapishtim concluded. "Who will assemble the gods for you, to grant you eternal life? It is not to be repeated."

Gilgamesh bowed his head.

"If you wish," Utnapishtim said, "you may test yourself. Prevail against sleep for six days and nights." While Gilgamesh sat there, sleep immediately drifted over him like wet fog. Utnapishtim laughed to his wife, "Look at this hero who seeks everlasting life! Sleep steals over him like mist even now!"

GUIDED READING

What happens when Gilgamesh tries to keep from sleeping? Why does Utnapishtim laugh?

Each day that Gilgamesh slept, Utnapishtim's wife placed a fresh loaf of bread by his side. On the seventh day, Utnapishtim touched Gilgamesh and he came alive. Gilgamesh protested, "I was barely asleep when you woke me!"

Utnapishtim said, "Come on, Gilgamesh. Count these loaves and discover how many days you have slept. Your first loaf is dry, the second leathery, the third soggy, the fourth white with mold, the fifth gray with mildew, the sixth rotten, and the seventh—you woke."

Gilgamesh said, "What shall I do? Where shall I go? Death is a thief that steals over me. Death is wherever I set my feet."

Utnapishtim took Gilgamesh to Urshanabit, the boatman, to lead him back to his own land. Just as Gilgamesh was leaving, Utnapishtim called out, "You have toiled and worn yourself out, so I will give you a gift to carry back to your own country. I shall reveal to you a great secret. Under the water there grows a plant with deep roots. It will prick your hand like a thorn, but hold on to it. If you succeed in getting that plant, you will have eternal life."

Gilgamesh dove under the waters for the plant and <u>wrested</u> it from the bottom of the sea. Gilgamesh called the plant "The-Old-Man-Will-Be-Made-Young," and he planned to give it to the elders of Uruk and then eat it himself. Once on land, Gilgamesh journeyed for several leagues,[7] making his way toward Uruk. He saw a pool of cool water, and he went down to the water to bathe. A snake smelled the plant and rose out of the water and carried the plant away to eat it. As the snake turned to go back to the water, it shed its skin. Ever since that time, snakes have been able to cast off their skin and become young again, but death has remained the lot of humans.

Gilgamesh cried, "For whom have I labored? For whom has my heart's blood dried? I have not brought a blessing on myself. I did the lowly snake a good service."

Gilgamesh sat down and wept bitter tears. ∎

---

7. **league.** Unit of measure

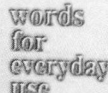

trans • gres • sor (trans gres' sər) *n.,* one who breaks a law or commandment. *The Code of Hammurabi calls for harsh punishments for <u>transgressors</u> of Mesopotamian laws.*

wrest (rest') *v.,* pull or force away violently with a twisting motion. *The small child finally <u>wrested</u> his favorite toy away from the other child.*

Respond to the SELECTION

What do you think of the Mesopotamian gods, as portrayed in this selection? Why do you think they treat humans as they do?

About the AUTHOR

Christina E. Kolb was born in 1972 in Connecticut, where she spent her childhood. At an early age she developed an interest in the literature and culture of many different ancient peoples. She was educated at Harvard College where she studied English and American literature, as well as that of many other cultures. She now lives in Massachusetts and works as an editor and writer.

INSIGHTS — Ancient Mesopotamia

MESOPOTAMIAN HISTORY. Long before the Greeks and Romans developed their influential cultures, the Mesopotamians developed a great civilization in what we now call Iraq. Ancient cities in the region date from 9000 to 7000 B.C. Life in Mesopotamia was made possible by the Tigris and Euphrates Rivers, which carved a narrow, fertile region in the midst of a hot and dry land. This fertile crescent gave rise to small agricultural communities that evolved into powerful city-states (see map on page 481).

MESOPOTAMIAN MYTHOLOGY. Mesopotamians had many different gods—more than two thousand of them. These gods were often associated with a particular city and were said to be the protector of that city. The major gods are listed below.

Anu, the god of the sky and of heaven, was the highest of all the gods.

Dumuzi, also known as Tammuz, was the god of shepherds.

Enki, also known as Ea, was the god of the earth, drinkable water, and crafts, and he frequently helped humans.

Enlil was the god of storms and led the gods in war.

Erishkigal, also known as Erkalla, was the queen of the underworld.

Inanna, also known as Ishtar, was the goddess of love and war and was associated with the evening and morning stars.

Nintu, also known as Ninmah or Ninhursaga, was the queen of the gods and the goddess if the soil and of childbirth.

Sin was the moon god.

Uttu was the goddess of cloth and of weaving.

Utu, also known as Shamash, was the sun god and the god of justice invoked by Hammurabi.

"THE EPIC OF GILGAMESH" **487**

RECALL

1a. Gilgamesh is powerful, bold, strong, and arrogant. Enkidu was created because the people of Uruk prayed for relief from Gilgamesh's oppression. Enkidu is a "wild man" who is covered with hair and lives with the animals.

2a. Ishtar asks Gilgamesh to marry her. Gilgamesh refuses, saying that Ishtar is never faithful or loyal. Ishtar is enraged and flies to her father Anu to ask him to make the Bull of Heaven.

3a. Utnapishtim is Gilgamesh's ancestor who survived the flood. Utnapishtim possesses eternal life. Utnapishtim tells Gilgamesh to prevail against sleep for six days and nights. Gilgamesh fails this test and then Utnapishtim tells Gilgamesh where to gather an underwater plant than can grant eternal life.

INTERPRET

1b. They develop a strong friendship because they are impressed with each other's strength and determination during their wrestling match.

2b. Ishtar is impulsive and easily overcome by feelings of love and hate.

3b. Gilgamesh was unsuccessful at the first test because he fell asleep immediately. He was successful and found the underwater plant but then left it while he bathed and a snake ate it, so he failed in this second attempt to gain eternal life. His failure means that humans must die and cannot know eternal life.

ANALYZE

4a. Gilgamesh's first error is oppressing his people and being a cruel ruler. Gilgamesh also errs in slighting the goddess Ishtar. Enkidu and Gilgamesh kill two creatures of the gods, Huwawa and the Bull of Heaven and even throw the thigh bone of the bull in Ishtar's face. Students should note that most of these errors are committed because of pride and overconfidence. Gilgamesh then fails in his contest against sleep and tries to lie about it. Gilgamesh's final mistake is leaving the plant while he bathes because a snake eats it. These errors are through human weakness and forgetfulness. The consequences of these errors are that the two heroes anger the gods, causing Enkidu's death. The consequence of the later errors is that humans will never know eternal life.

Investigate, Inquire, and Imagine

Recall: GATHERING FACTS

1a. What characteristics does Gilgamesh possess? Why was Enkidu created? What characteristics does Enkidu possess?

2a. What does Ishtar ask Gilgamesh to do? What is his response? What is Ishtar's reaction?

3a. Who is Utnapishtim, and what unusual quality does he have? What two challenges does he give Gilgamesh?

Interpret: FINDING MEANING

1b. Why do Gilgamesh and Enkidu develop such a strong friendship?

2b. What do Ishtar's actions tell you about her character?

3b. How was Gilgamesh successful or unsuccessful? What does his success or failure signify for humans?

Analyze: TAKING THINGS APART

4a. What errors or rash deeds do Gilgamesh and Enkidu commit, and why? What are the consequences?

Synthesize: BRINGING THINGS TOGETHER

4b. What events in nature does this story explain? What view of humans does this story express? What view of the gods does this story express?

Evaluate: MAKING JUDGMENTS

5a. Do you agree with the god Shamash's statement that the "fitting concern of [humans]" is to "fill your belly. Make merry. Dance and feast by day and night. Look at the child who holds your hand, and make your [partner] happy…"? In other words, in your opinion, is the role of humans simply to enjoy life on earth? What other purposes do you think humans should strive to fulfill?

Extend: CONNECTING IDEAS

5b. Medical science has enabled humans to live longer and longer lives. What if humans were someday able to extend their own lives indefinitely due to the use of high technology? Do you think that would be a good thing toward which to strive? Why, or why not? What might society be like if we had eternal life on earth? What might be some of the advantages and disadvantages of eternal life?

Understanding Literature

CENTRAL CONFLICT. A **central conflict** is the main problem or struggle in the plot of a poem, story, or play. What is the central conflict of "The Epic of Gilgamesh"? What did you find to be the most dramatic part of this conflict? What event introduces this conflict? How is this conflict resolved?

ANSWERS TO INVESTIGATE, INQUIRE, IMAGINE (CONT.)

SYNTHESIZE

4b. The story explains why snakes shed their skin. It also explains why humans are fated to die. Humans can accomplish great deeds, but they cannot live forever and must eventually die. The gods are sometimes vengeful and have retained eternal life only for themselves.

EVALUATE

5a. Responses will vary. Most students will say that they disagree and that people also have obligations to better their society and culture.

EXTEND

5b. *Responses will vary.*

IRONY. Irony is a difference between appearance and reality. An event that contradicts the expectations of the characters, the reader, or the audience of a literary work is an example of irony of situation. Although Gilgamesh is not entirely successful in his quest, Utnapishtim directs Gilgamesh to the prize he desires. How is what happens to this prize ironic? Whose expectations are contradicted?

Graphic  Organizer

In Understanding Literature, you identified the central conflict of "The Epic of Gilgamesh." What are some other elements of the story? Read the Language Arts Survey 1.15, "Using Graphic Aids." Then, create a story map like the one below to chart the main elements of "The Epic of Gilgamesh."

Story Map: "The Epic of Gilgamesh"
Setting
Mood
Conflict
Plot
Characters
Themes

Writer's Journal

1. Imagine that you are Ishtar and that you have decided to change your ways. Write a list of New Year's **resolutions**.

2. To help Gilgamesh, write a **petition** to the gods formally requesting eternal life on earth for all humans. Be sure to use formal, polite language, and give several reasons why you believe your request should be granted.

3. Imagine that Gilgamesh had been able to gain eternal life, but only for himself, and were still alive today. Write a **letter** he might have written to his friend Enkidu, explaining whether he is happy with how the world has changed and how he feels now about his "gift" of immortality.

CENTRAL CONFLICT. The central conflict is Gilgamesh's struggle against death to gain eternal life for humans, *Responses will vary.* Enkidu's death introduces the conflict. The conflict is resolved when the snake eats the plant and eternal life is lost for humans.

IRONY. What happens to the prize is ironic because a lowly animal reaps the benefits of Gilgamesh's struggle. Gilgamesh's and the reader's expectations are contradicted.

GRAPHIC ORGANIZER

Students' charts may resemble the following:

SETTING: Uruk in southern Babylonia, then the land beyond where the sun sets, where Gilgamesh finds Utnapishtim across the sea

MOOD: confident and brash, then full of sorrow, loss, and pessimism

Conflict: Gilgamesh's struggle against death and to gain eternal life for humans

PLOT: Enkidu and Gilgamesh become friends and perform heroic adventures together, in the process angering the gods. The gods decree that Enkidu must die. After his friend's death Gilgamesh is filled with grief and tries to find his ancestor Utnapishtim who possesses eternal life. Gilgamesh finds Utnapishtim, hears his story of surviving the flood, and learns that he cannot achieve eternal life in this way. Utnapishtim then offers him a contest to fight off sleep in exchange for eternal life and Gilgamesh fails. Utnapishtim then reveals the location of an underwater plant that can bestow eternal life, but Gilgamesh loses this plant to a snake while bathing.

CHARACTERS: Gilgamesh, Enkidu, Ishtar, and Utnapishtim are major characters; minor characters are Anu, Shamash, two scorpions, Siduri, Ea, Enlil, and a snake.

THEMES: the struggle against death, excessive pride and the fall it leads to, a flood story

Skill Builders

Language, Grammar, and Style

USING QUOTATION MARKS. Use quotation marks in your writing to enclose the exact words spoken by a person or character. For example, quotation marks are used in "The Epic of Gilgamesh" to enclose the words spoken by Gilgamesh, Enkidu, and other characters. You should also use quotation marks to enclose the titles of works such as short stories, poems, songs, articles, and parts of books. Refer to the Language Arts Survey 3.86, "Quotation Marks," for more information. Then, copy the sentences below, adding quotation marks (and capital letters) where needed.

1. The Epic of Gilgamesh is a retelling of a myth from ancient Mesopotamia.
2. Anu said that the Bull of Heaven would cause a seven-year drought.
3. Enkidu told Gilgamesh, I dreamed that Enlil said I would die.
4. Gilgamesh cried, Enkidu, Enkidu.
5. Siduri said, Gilgamesh, you should dance and feast and make merry.
6. Utnapishtim asked, who will grant you eternal life?
7. Gilgamesh said he did not know what to do.
8. Finally, Gilgamesh wrote a poem and called it No Human Is Immortal.

Study and Research & Speaking and Listening

FLOOD STORIES IN THE ORAL TRADITION. Many cultures around the world have flood stories similar to the one in this myth. You may already be familiar with the biblical story of Noah and the flood. Stories of floods also appeared in ancient India, China, Greece, and America. Go to the library and locate other traditional flood stories to bring into class. Then, hold a class reading of these stories and discuss the similarities and differences among these tales. Why do you think flood stories were so common among the ancient peoples of many different lands?

Media Literacy

HERO ON A QUEST. Many popular movies and television shows involve heroes who embark on great quests. As a class, brainstorm some of these movies or shows. Then form groups of four or five and select a movie or show you would like to view and analyze as a group. Watch the movie or show together and then compare its hero and quest with Gilgamesh and his quest. What characteristics does each hero possess, and what motivates each one? Is the goal of the quest achieved, and if so, what must be sacrificed? When you have finished making your comparisons, decide whether "The Epic of Gilgamesh" would make a good television show or movie for today. Why, or why not?

Applied English

RESEARCHING CAREERS. When Gilgamesh loses his best friend Enkidu, he grieves for seven days and nights. When people lose loved ones today, they have counseling options available to help them through the grief. Do some research on jobs in the field of grief counseling. You may use resources such as your school guidance counselor, the local library, or the Internet. Which jobs are available? What personal qualities would a person need to pursue these careers? What training or schooling would be necessary?

Prereading

"The Secret Name of Ra"

Retold by Geraldine Harris

Reader's Resource

- Many gods in Egyptian mythology either die or come close to death—even though they are immortal. In the selection you are about to read, Ra, the sun god, comes close to death.

- **HISTORY CONNECTION.** Ancient Egyptians believed that the sun was born each day as it rose in the east and died each day as it set in the west, traveling into the underworld at night. Accordingly, Egyptians believed that the contrast between day and night was like the contrast between life and death. The Egyptians buried their dead to the west of the Nile, in the land of the setting sun, and believed that the souls of the dead then traveled, like the sun, to the underworld.

- Ancient Egyptians accepted many different explanations of things as equally true and possible. For example, they believed three different explanations of heaven all at the same time: that it was held up by four pillars, that it was actually the goddess Nut who crouched over the earth, and that it was a cow. Similarly, they believed that the pharaoh was the son of Ra. They also believed, however, that he was the living incarnation of Horus, the son of Isis and Osiris. When the pharaoh died, he became the incarnation of Osiris, god of the underworld.

 art smart

Isis, c.1348-1320 BC. Egyptian artist. Tomb of Horemheb, Thebes, Egypt.

Isis, c.1348-1320 BC Egyptian artist.
Ancient Egyptians decorated their tombs with representations of all the things they would need in the next life, including the gods who would help them. The tomb of the Pharaoh Horemheb includes this depiction of Isis, who guaranteed life after death. How is this portrait different from more recent portrait paintings?

 Reader's Journal

Is tricking someone a good way to get something you want? Why, or why not?

 Reader's TOOLBOX

INCITING INCIDENT. The **inciting incident** is the event that introduces the central conflict, or struggle, in a poem, story, or play. As you read, try to pinpoint the inciting incident of "The Secret Name of Ra."

MOTIVE. A **motive** is a reason for acting in a certain way. As you read, determine what motive drives Isis to the action she commits in this story.

ADDITIONAL RESOURCES

UNIT 7 RESOURCE BOOK
- Selection Worksheet 7.3
- Selection Check Test 4.7.5
- Selection Test 4.7.6
- Language, Grammar, and Style Resource 3.86

READER'S JOURNAL

You might ask students to consider how they feel about people who trick others to get what they want. Ask them the following questions: If a person tricks someone to get something from him or her, does this person have a right to what he or she gets? Why, or why not?

VOCABULARY FROM THE SELECTION

abyss	exalt
cunning	quiver
deity	sole
drivel	summon
envoy	virile

ART SMART

Students will probably be more familiar with paintings that use "illusionistic space," which creates the illusion that the picture is 3-dimensional when the surface is, in fact, flat. The Egyptians did know how to create the illusion of perspective (there are examples of that in Egyptian art) but they preferred this look.

GOALS/OBJECTIVES

Studying this lesson will enable students to
- enjoy an Egyptian myth
- explain Egyptian thoughts about the sun and its relationship to life and afterlife
- define *inciting incident* and recognize inciting incidents in works that they read
- define *motive* and identify a character's motives
- analyze the meaning of names
- determine how the geography of Egypt may have affected its people's worldview
- use vocabulary words in sensible sentences

MOTIVATION
You and a social studies teacher may wish to plan a class trip to a museum that has an Egyptian collection so that students can get a valuable glimpse of both high culture and everyday life in ancient Egypt. On students' return ask them to write a personal essay about the Egyptian artifact they liked best, what they liked about it, and what it revealed to them about Egyptian history or culture.

READING PROFICIENCY
Students may find the many names of Egyptian gods confusing. You may wish to share some of the information in the Insights feature with students before they begin reading. Tell students that most of the gods are given a brief description in the story, and that they do not have to remember exactly what each god looks like or is in charge of.

ENGLISH LANGUAGE LEARNING
Point out the following vocabulary words and expressions:
marvelous—causing wonder, surprising, extraordinary
cunning—skillful in deception, sly, crafty
Ennead—group of nine gods
bewildered—confused. puzzled
betray—deliver or expose to an enemy traitorously
wield—exercise; handle and use

SPECIAL NEEDS
Tell students to focus on the Guided Reading questions and the Recall questions in the Investigate, Inquire, and Imagine section.

ENRICHMENT
Encourage students to create artistic representations of Egyptian gods based on their description in the Insights feature on ancient Egypt. Students should choose their favorite medium and then a god and use their imaginations to make the god "come alive" for others through art. Your class might wish to create a display of images of ancient Egyptian gods around your classroom.

Isis, c.1348-1320 B.C. Egyptian artist. Tomb of Horemheb, Thebes, Egypt.

THE SECRET NAME OF RA

Geraldine Harris

Ra, the <u>Sole</u> Creator was visible to the people of Egypt as the disc of the sun, but they knew him in many other forms. He could appear as a crowned man, a falcon or a man with a falcon's head and, as the scarab beetle[1] pushes a round ball of dung in front of it, the Egyptians pictured Ra as a scarab pushing the sun across the sky. In caverns deep below the earth were hidden another seventy-five forms of Ra: mysterious beings with mummified bodies[2] and heads consisting of birds or snakes, feathers or flowers. The names of Ra were as numerous as his forms; he was the Shining One, The Hidden One, The Renewer of the Earth, The Wind in the Souls, The <u>Exalted</u> One, but there was one name of the Sun God which had not been spoken since time began. To know this secret name of Ra was to have power over him and over the world that he had created.

Isis longed for such a power. She had dreamed that one day she would have a marvellous falcon-headed son called Horus and she wanted the throne of Ra to give to her child. Isis was the Mistress of Magic, wiser than millions of men, but she knew that nothing in creation was powerful enough to harm its creator. Her only chance was to turn the power of Ra against himself and at last Isis thought of a cruel and <u>cunning</u> plan. Every day the Sun God walked through his kingdom, attended by a crowd of spirits and lesser <u>deities</u>, but Ra was growing old. His eyes were dim, his step no longer firm and he had even begun to <u>drivel</u>.

One morning Isis mingled with a group of minor goddesses and followed behind the King of the Gods. She watched the face of Ra until she saw his saliva drip onto a clod of earth. When she was sure that no-one was taking any notice of her, she scooped up the earth and carried it away. Isis mixed the earth with the saliva of Ra to form clay and modelled a wicked-looking serpent. Through the hours of darkness she whispered spells over the clay serpent as it lay lifeless in her hands. Then the cunning goddess carried it to a crossroads on the route which the Sun God always took. She hid the serpent in the long grass and returned to her palace.

The next day Ra came walking through his kingdom with the spirits and lesser deities crowding behind him. When he approached the crossroads, the spells of Isis began to work and the clay serpent

TO KNOW THIS SECRET NAME OF RA WAS TO HAVE POWER OVER HIM AND OVER THE WORLD THAT HE HAD CREATED.

> **GUIDED READING**
> Why has Ra kept this one name secret?

> **GUIDED READING**
> Why does Isis want power over Ra?

---

1. **scarab beetle.** Black-winged beetle held sacred by ancient Egyptians
2. **mummified bodies.** Bodies that have been preserved by removing the internal organs and adding a special substance to keep the body from disintegrating

---

words for everyday use

sole (sōl) *adj.*, only. *Fishing was Lucrecia's <u>sole</u> interest.*
ex • alt (eg zôlt') *v.*, praise; glorify; worship. *People in ancient Babylon <u>exalted</u> their city-god Marduk.*
cun • ning (kun' iŋ) *adj.*, clever; sly; crafty. *Foxes are known for their <u>cunning</u> ability to escape from hunters.*
de • i • ty (dē' ə tē) *n.*, god or goddess. *Isis was one of the <u>deities</u> worshiped by the ancient Egyptians.*
driv • el (driv' əl) *v.*, drool. *When our dog knows it is dinnertime, he hungrily <u>drivels</u>.*

ANSWERS TO GUIDED READING QUESTIONS

1. Ra has kept this name a secret because if someone discovers this name, that person will have power over Ra and the world he created.
2. Isis wants power over Ra because she wants to give his throne to the son, Horus, that she dreams she will have.

ADDITIONAL QUESTIONS AND ACTIVITIES

Ask students the following questions: Why does Isis use Ra's saliva to create the serpent? What does Ra say about the thing that has wounded him? What emotions does Ra express about being injured?
Answers
Isis used Ra's saliva because nothing in creation is powerful enough to harm Ra, the creator, so Isis must use Ra's own power against him. Ra says that the thing that has wounded him is deadly, that he knows that he did not create it, and that he does not think any of the gods would do such a thing to him. Ra expresses great surprise.

1. The gods weep and wail with
   concern when their creator is
   injured. Isis pretends to be
   distressed and bewildered.
2. Isis says she needs to know Ra's
   secret name to use in her spells to
   cure him.

CROSS-CURRICULAR CONNECTION

HISTORY. Inform students that the Ennead were the supreme council of gods and the family of the sun god Ra. There were nine members of the Ennead: the sun god and four couples—She, the god of air; Tefnut, goddess of moisture; Geb, the god of earth; Nut, the goddess of the sky; Osiris, god of the underworld and fertility; Isis, goddess of fertility and children: Seth, god of Upper Egypt, deserts, and storms; and Nephthys, Seth's wife.

You might also point out to students that Isis is not always a mischievous, scheming figure in Egyptian mythology. Egyptian gods seldom have consistent roles. For example, while Seth is often depicted as the evil enemy of Osiris and Horus, he also appears as a good god. In other myths, Isis appears as a loving wife who goes to great lengths to save her husband. Just like humans, the Egyptian gods had many different sides to their characters.

quivered into life. As the Sun God passed, it bit him in the ankle and crumbled back into earth. Ra gave a scream that was heard through all creation.

His jaws chattered and his limbs shook as the poison flooded through him like a rising Nile. "I have been wounded by something deadly," whispered Ra. "I know that in my heart, though my eyes cannot see it. Whatever it was, I, the Lord of Creation, did not make it. I am sure that none of you would have done such a terrible thing to me, but I have never felt such pain! How can this have happened to me? I am the Sole Creator, the child of the watery abyss. I am the god with a thousand names, but my secret name was only spoken once, before time began. Then it was hidden in my body so that no-one should ever learn it and be able to work spells against me. Yet as I walked through my kingdom something struck at me and now my heart is on fire and my limbs shake. Send for the Ennead! Send for my children! They are wise in magic and their knowledge pierces heaven."

Messengers hurried to the great gods and from the four pillars of the world came the Ennead: Shu and Tefenet, Geb and Nut, Seth and Osiris, Isis and Nephthys. Envoys traveled the land and the sky and the watery abyss to summon all the deities created by Ra. From the marshes came frog-headed Heket, Wadjet the cobra goddess and the fearsome god, crocodile-headed Sobek. From the deserts came fiery Selkis, the scorpion goddess, Anubis the jackal, the guardian of the dead and Nekhbet the vulture goddess. From the cities of the north came warlike Neith, gentle cat-headed Bastet, fierce lion-headed Sekhmet and Ptah the god of crafts.

From the cities of the south came Onuris, the divine huntsman and ram-headed Khnum with Anukis his wife and Satis his daughter. Cunning Thoth and wise Seshat, goddess of writing; virile Min and snake-headed Renenutet, goddess of the harvest, kindly Meskhenet and monstrous Taweret, goddesses of birth—all of them were summoned to the side of Ra.

The gods and goddesses gathered around the Sun God, weeping and wailing, afraid that he was going to die. Isis stood among them beating her breast and pretending to be as distressed and bewildered as all the other frightened deities.

GUIDED READING
How do the gods and goddesses act when their creator is injured? How does Isis act?

"Father of All," she began, "whatever is the matter? Has some snake bitten you? Has some wretched creature dared to strike at his Creator? Few of the gods can compare with me in wisdom and I am the Mistress of Magic. If you will let me help you, I'm sure that I can cure you."

Ra was grateful to Isis and told her all that had happened. "Now I am colder than water and hotter than fire," complained the Sun God. "My eyes darken. I cannot see the sky and my body is soaked by the sweat of fever."

"Tell me your full name," said cunning Isis. "Then I can use it in my spells. Without that knowledge the greatest of magicians cannot help you."

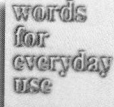
GUIDED READING
Why does Isis say she needs to know Ra's secret name?

"I am the maker of heaven and earth," said Ra. "I made the heights and the depths, I set horizons at east and west and established the gods in their glory. When I open my eyes it is light; when I close them it is dark. The

---

words for everyday use

qui • ver (kwiv′ ər) v., shake or tremble. *The thought of going up to the attic alone made the small child quiver with fear.*

a • byss (ə bis′) n., anything too deep for measurement; ocean depths. *The hole was so deep it seemed a bottomless abyss.*

en • voy (än′ voi′) n., messenger. *The envoy delivered the king's message to the ruler of the distant land.*

sum • mon (sum′ ən) v., call together; order to appear. *The sick man summoned a doctor to his home.*

vir • ile (vir′ əl) adj., having strength; forceful. *Michelangelo's David represents the neoclassic ideal of perfect, virile young manhood.*

mighty Nile floods at my command. The gods do not know my true name but I am the maker of time, the giver of festivals. I spark the fire of life. At dawn I rise as Khepri, the scarab and sail across the sky in the Boat of Millions of Years. At noon I blaze in the heavens as Ra and at evening I am Ra-atum, the setting sun."

"We know all that," said Isis. "If I am to find a spell to drive out this poison, I will have to use your secret name. Say your name and live."

"My secret name was given to me so that I could sit at ease," moaned Ra, "and fear no living creature. How can I give it away?"

Isis said nothing and knelt beside the Sun God while his pain mounted. When it became unbearable, Ra ordered the other gods to stand back while he whispered his secret name to Isis. "Now the power of the secret name has passed from my heart to your heart," said Ra wearily. "In time you can give it to your son, but warn him never to betray the secret!"

Isis nodded and began to chant a great spell that drove the poison out of the limbs of Ra and he rose up stronger than before. The Sun God returned to the Boat of Millions of Years and Isis shouted for joy at the success of her plan. She knew now that one day Horus her son would sit on the throne of Egypt and wield the power of Ra. ∎

> **GUIDED READING**
>
> How does Isis feel about her success? What does she know will happen?

Respond to the SELECTION

How do you feel about the way Isis went about discovering Ra's secret name?

About the AUTHOR

Geraldine Harris has a strong interest in ancient Egypt. She studied Egyptology at Cambridge University in England and has written a book on Egyptian religion. She has written two novels for young people, *White Cranes Castle* and *The Prince of the Godborn*. She has also given lectures on the folklore and mythology of various cultures.

---

1. Isis is filled with joy by her success. She knows that her son Horus will one day sit on the throne of Egypt and wield the power of Ra.

RESPOND TO THE SELECTION

Encourage students to talk about ambition. When is ambition good? When can it lead to wrongdoing?

SELECTION CHECK TEST 4.7.5 WITH ANSWERS

Checking Your Reading
1. What happens to whoever learns the secret name of Ra? **Whoever learns the secret name of Ra has power over him and the world he created.**
2. Who conjures up the snake that bites Ra? **Isis conjures up the snake.**
3. Of what is the snake that bites Ra made? **The snake is made of a clay from dust and Ra's saliva.**
4. For whom does Ra send when he falls ill from the snakebite? **Ra sends for Isis.**
5. Who will one day sit upon the throne of Egypt and wield the power of Ra? **Isis's son Horus will one day sit on the throne of Egypt and wield the power of Ra.**

Vocabulary in Context
Fill in each blank below with the most appropriate word. You may have to change the tense of the word.

> deity   sole   envoy   virile
> summon   abyss   quiver

1. The tiny cat **quivered** with cold until we'd wrapped him up in a towel.
2. The crew barely escaped into the lifeboats before the ship sank into the **abyss**.
3. Laura's kindergarten students love to serve as **envoys** whenever she needs something delivered to the office.
4. This weekend, our **sole** purpose is to enjoy ourselves.
5. James knew he was in trouble as soon as he was **summoned** to the front office.

SELECTION CHECK TEST 4.7.5 WITH ANSWERS (CONT.)

Reader's Toolbox
In each blank above, place the letter of the plot element that fits that position.

a. resolution
b. falling action
c. rising action
d. inciting incident
e. denouement
f. exposition
g. climax
h. crisis

3. g
1. f
2. d
4. a
5. e

CROSS-CURRICULAR CONNECTION

HISTORY. Inform students that the ancient Egyptians also believed that their king was the son of Re, the supreme god, and that the land had been entrusted to the king by Re. However, in Egyptian mythology Re's only son is Shu, god of the air. Tell students that Egyptians were not disturbed by apparent inconsistencies in their system of belief. They believed both that Re only had one son Shu and that the king was the son of Re.

Just as Egyptians willingly accepted more than one explanation of phenomena or occurrences, they also believed that their gods had more than one appearance. Thus Re could appear as a crowned man, a falcon-headed man, a falcon, or a scarab. Students might enjoy drawing or painting some of the Egyptians gods, combining their human and their animal qualities.

CROSS-CURRICULAR CONNECTION

HISTORY. During the period of the Old Kingdom, ancient Egyptians believed that the king became the god Osiris after his death. However, beginning in the Middle Kingdom, ancient Egyptians believed that common people might also continue with their *ka* and become Osiris after death. The ancient Egyptians believed that when a person died, Osiris weighed the person's heart against a symbol of *ma'at.* Those whose good deeds made their heart as light as *ma'at* could pass into the next world and become gods. Those whose hearts were heavier than *ma'at* because of bad deeds would be tortured and destroyed. The gods Re and Anubis were often associated with the judgment of the dead as well.

Located in northeastern Africa, Egypt is a desert country in northeastern Africa. Libya borders Egypt to the west, and Sudan borders Egypt to the south. To the north lies the Mediterranean Sea. The Red Sea and the Sinai Peninsula separate Egypt from Saudi Arabia. The Nile River flows north through the country. Along this great river, the civilization of ancient Egypt flourished for more than 3,000 years.

HISTORY. Egypt began as two separate communities—Lower Egypt and Upper Egypt—around the mid-3000s BC. The two communities joined around 3100 BC. Throughout most of its history, Egypt was ruled by a series of all-powerful kings, or pharaohs. An Egyptian king was believed to be a god. For the first thirty years of his reign, he was identified with the falcon god Horus. After reigning for thirty years, he was identified with the god of fertility and the underworld, Osiris. As the representative of the gods on Earth, the king had the responsibility to establish *ma'at,* or divine order, on earth. Beneath the king was a small class of officials, a very large class of common people, and, especially in later periods, slaves.

The use of writing helped the ancient Egyptians to form and administer a powerful, centralized government. Two forms of writing were invented between 3100 BC and 2575 BC. Hieroglyphs, which combined pictures and representations of sounds, were used for inscriptions on monuments. A simpler cursive form of writing, hieratic, was used for documents. As early as the first dynasty, Egyptians wrote documents on sheets made from the papyrus plant.

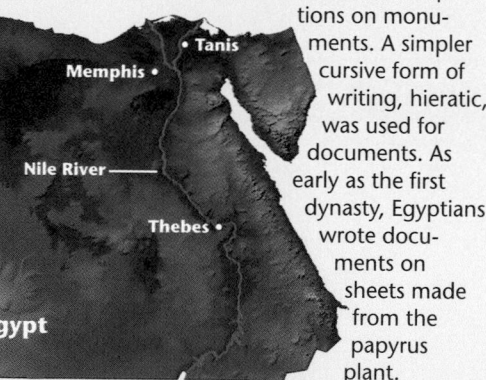

Tanis • Memphis • Nile River Thebes • Egypt

MYTHOLOGY. Like the Mesopotamians, the Egyptians worshiped many gods. Key to Egyptian religion were the concepts of *ma'at* (divine order) and of the *ka,* or soul, which was believed to live on after death. The bodies of royal persons and of some great officials were preserved as mummies so that the *ka* might inhabit the body after death. Great tombs, including the ancient Egyptian pyramids, were built for kings and were stocked with goods for the use of the king's *ka* in the afterlife. These are the major Egyptian gods:

Anubis was a jackal-headed god, associated with mummification, who judged the dead in the underworld.

Geb was the god of earth.

Hathor was the cow-headed goddess of love, dance, and music.

Horus was the falcon-headed son of Isis and Osiris associated with the living king.

Isis, the wife and sister of Osiris, was, among other things, the protector of children.

Nephthys, sister of Isis, Osiris, and Seth, was known as the mistress of the house and was the goddess of the dead.

Nut was the goddess of the sky.

Osiris was a fertility god, the god of the earth, vegetation, the underworld, and the annual rebirth of vegetation following the flooding of the Nile.

Ra, also known as Amon-Re, Re, Atum, and Ra-Horakhty, was the sun god, considered the greatest of all the gods.

Seth was the donkey-headed god of Upper Egypt, deserts, and storms.

Shu was the god of air.

Tefnut was the goddess of moisture.

Thoth was the ibis or baboon-headed god of wisdom and the moon.

Investigate, Inquire, and Imagine

Recall: GATHERING FACTS

1a. What are some of the forms and names Ra took? What is the one thing that could take away this god's power? What is beginning to happen to Ra?

2a. Who is Isis? What dream has she had? What does she want from Ra?

3a. What does Isis create to harm Ra? From what does she create it? What does Isis say Ra must do in order to be cured?

→ **Interpret:** FINDING MEANING

1b. Is Ra a powerful god? Why, or why not?

2b. What does Isis's plan reveal about her character?

3b. What does the fact that the gods work against one another say about them? Which god seems to be the most powerful? most clever?

Analyze: TAKING THINGS APART

4a. The gods and goddesses of ancient Egypt possessed both human and divine qualities. What human qualities do Ra and Isis have? What god-like qualities do they have?

→ **Synthesize:** BRINGING THINGS TOGETHER

4b. What effect do you think seeing a god at his or her weakest, or most human, had on his or her worshippers?

Perspective: LOOKING AT OTHER VIEWS

5a. How do you think Ra feels at the end of the story? Do you think he realizes he has been tricked by Isis? How can you tell? How do you think Ra would have responded if Isis had asked him directly for what she wanted, rather than tricking him? Explain.

→ **Empathy:** SEEING FROM INSIDE

5b. Why did Ra trust Isis? If you were Ra, what would you do next?

Understanding Literature

INCITING INCIDENT. The **inciting incident** is the event that introduces the central conflict, or struggle, in a poem, story, or play. What is the inciting incident in "The Secret Name of Ra"? Does the inciting incident make you sympathize with one character more than another? If so, with which character do you sympathize and why?

MOTIVE. A **motive** is a reason for acting in a certain way. What is Isis's motive for harming Ra? Do you think her motive can be justified? Why, or why not?

ANSWERS TO UNDERSTANDING LITERATURE

INCITING INCIDENT. The inciting incident is Isis's creating a serpent to harm Ra. Students may say this action made them sympathize with Ra because he was the victim of a scheme.

MOTIVE. Isis's motive is to gain power for her son Horus. Students may say that ambition can lead to people harming others, but that this is never justifiable.

ANSWERS TO INVESTIGATE, INQUIRE, IMAGINE

RECALL

1a. Ra took the form of a crowned man, a falcon, a falcon-headed man, and a scarab/ He took the names the Shining One, the Hidden One, The Renewer of the Earth, The Wind in the Souls, and the Exalted One. Knowing Ra's secret name can take away his power. Ra is beginning to grow old.

2a. Isis is the wise Mistress of Magic. She has dreamed that she will have a falcon-headed son called Horus. She wants to know Ra's secret so that she can give the throne of Ra to Horus.

3a. Isis creates a serpent from Ra's saliva and earth. Isis says that Ra must reveal his secret name to her to be cured.

INTERPRET

1b. Students may say that Ra is not that powerful because he is growing old and has a secret weakness.

2b. Students may say that Isis's plan reveals her ambition and her ruthlessness because she is willing to trick Ra and inflict pain on him to get her way.

3b. Students may say that the gods seem similar to ambitious people. Students' responses about the most powerful god will vary. They may say that it seems that Ra was once the most powerful god. Isis seems most clever.

ANALYZE

4a. Ra can grow old and is foolish enough to be tricked, Isis is ruthless and ambitious. They are both far more powerful than humans.

SYNTHESIZE

4b. Students may say that human worshippers could identify with these gods who shared human weaknesses, but that such a view probably did not promote fear or awe of the gods.

PERSPECTIVE

5a. Students may say that Ra knows he has been tricked because he tells Isis she can pass the secret of Ra's name to her son one day. Other students may disagree. Students may say that it is unlikely Ra would want to give up his throne.

EMPATHY

5b. Students may say that he trusted Isis because she was able to convey confusion and concern convincingly. Students might say that Ra should try to secure his throne in some way.

Students may identify the following: *exposition*—Ra has much power and a secret name that gives the knower power over him, while Isis knows she will have a son and wants to give him Ra's power; *Inciting incident*—Isis creates a serpent to harm Ra; *rising action*—Ra is poisoned and falls sick, calling the gods to him, while Isis plays innocent and pretends to be concerned; *climax and crisis*—Isis tells Ra she can heal him if he gives her his secret name; *falling action*—Ra finally shares his secret name with Isis; *resolution*—Isis heals Ra and rejoices as soon as he is alone; *denouement*—Isis knows that Horus will one day wield the power of Ra.

Graphic Organizer

Make a plot pyramid diagram like the one shown below. you have already identified the inciting incident in "The Secret Name of Ra," so you can summarize the incident where it occurs on the pyramid. Try to identify the other elements of plot shown on the pyramid. Refer to the Handbook of Literary Terms to review definitions of any terms. Then, on your plot pyramid diagram, show which events in the story mark the exposition, climax, and other elements.

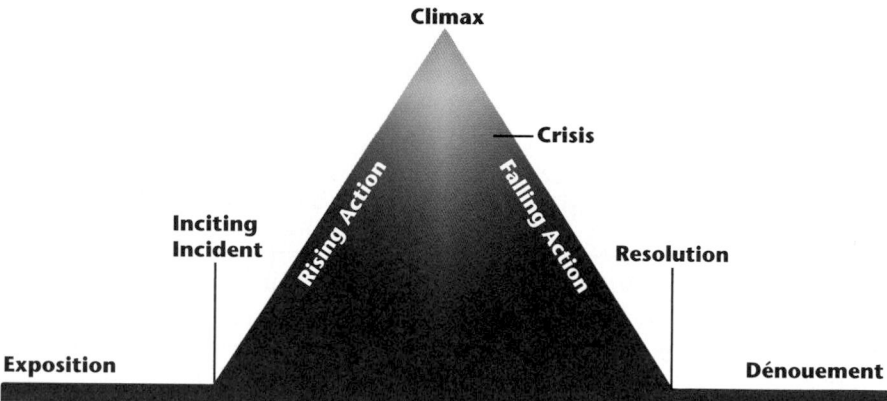

Writer's Journal

1. Imagine that you are Isis and you would like to share with your son how you were able to harm Ra. Write a **recipe** for how to make a clay snake. Refer to a cookbook for the format of a recipe, and make up the quantities of each ingredient.

2. Suppose a friend asked you to explain the main plot of "The Secret Name of Ra." Write a **summary** of the story, including only the most important details. Use informal language.

3. Imagine that Horus has been born and is now set to take power from Ra. Write a brief **continuation** of "The Secret Name of Ra," using your imagination to describe what happens next.

Skill Builders

Collaborative Learning

ANALYZING NAMES. Ra had a secret

name that he could not reveal. We never learn what that secret name was. With a partner, go to the library and find a book that lists names. Select two names that you think would be appropriate for Ra's secret name, based on their meaning or origin. Then, share the names you selected with the class. After everyone has shared their ideas, hold a class vote to choose the name that best suits Ra.

Vocabulary & Speaking and Listening

USING WORDS IN CONTEXT. Write a modern story, using all of the following words from "The Secret Name of Ra." Be creative in integrating all the terms in a way that makes sense. After you have finished your story, read it aloud to the class.

- abyss
- betray
- cavern
- cunning
- deity
- disc
- drivel
- envoy
- exalt
- fiery
- mingle
- quiver
- sole
- summon
- virile
- wail
- wretched

Language, Grammar, and Style.

WORKING WITH QUOTATION MARKS. Review the Language Arts Survey 3.86, "Quotation Marks." Then write each sentence below on your own paper, editing them for errors in use of quotation marks, other punctuation, or capitalization. If the sentence has no errors, write *Correct*.

1. Ra said that she had been wounded by "Something deadly".
2. Geraldine Harris has written a novel called "The Prince of the Godborn".
3. This story about ancient Egypt is called *The Secret Name of Ra.*
4. "Now I am colder than water and hotter than fire," complained the Sun God. "My eyes darken. I cannot see the sky and my body is soaked by the sweat of fever."
5. "My favorite story is "The Secret Name of Ra," Tony said. "Ancient Egypt really interests me".

Study and Research

GEOGRAPHY OF EGYPT. In this selection, Ra points out that he is responsible for flooding the mighty Nile River. Research the Nile River and the geography of Egypt in order to determine how the land itself affected the ancient people who inhabited it. What relationship did ancient Egyptians have with the Nile? What effect did the Nile have on the cycle of life in Egypt? When you have finished your research, write a brief essay to hand in to your teacher. Include any maps or photographs you encounter in your research.

ANSWERS TO SKILL BUILDERS

Collaborative Learning
Possible resources include books for naming children as well as books of names and their meanings. Students should base the name they choose on some element of Ra's character and explain the reasoning behind their choice.

Study and Research
Students might find photographs or illustrations of the Egyptian landscape in encyclopedias, books, magazines, or online resources and bring them in to class to share.

Vocabulary & Speaking and Listening
If students have difficulty with this assignment, have them write individual sentences using one of the vocabulary words in each. Students should make the meaning of the vocabulary word clear from its context.

Language, Grammar, and Style
1. Ra said that she had been wounded by "something deadly."
2. Geraldine Harris has written a novel called *The Prince of the Godborn.*
3. This story about ancient Egypt is called "The Secret Name of Ra."
4. *Correct*
5. "My favorite story is 'The Secret Name of Ra,'" Tony said. "Ancient Egypt really interests me."

READER'S JOURNAL

Examples of greed you might share with students to get them thinking are spending lots of money on luxuries when others are in need, not letting your siblings share in a favorite game, or overcharging people for goods or services.

GRAPHIC ORGANIZER

Students' responses may include the following: *Action:* The people kill the innocent animals that live in the forest and waste the meat. *Result:* The gnomes of the forest warn them. *Action* The hunter wants a cricket in addition to the other game he has taught. *Result:* The hunter is crushed under an elephant. *Action:* Woman cuts off more sky than she can eat. *Result:* The sky is moved far away, and people thereafter have to work to eat.

YORUBA MYTH

Reader's Journal

What does greed mean to you? Write a definition of greed in your journal, and give some examples.

Reader's TOOLBOX

ORAL TRADITION AND MYTH. An **oral tradition** is a work, idea, or custom passed by word of mouth from generation to generation. A **myth** is a story that explains the beginnings of things in the natural world. As you read, determine whether this story is part of the Yoruban oral tradition, whether it is a myth, or whether it is both. How do you know?

MOTIF. A **motif** is anything that appears repeatedly in one or more works of literature, art, or music. Many motifs deal with people's actions and their consequences. One of the most common motifs in the world's mythologies is of a golden age in history ruined by human wickedness. As you read, determine how this motif appears in the story.

Prereading

"Why the Sky is Far Away from the Earth"
Retold by Fitzgerald Iyamabo

Reader's Resource

- **GEOGRAPHY CONNECTION.** After the Ibo, the Yoruba are the largest ethnic group in Nigeria, a West African nation. Most Yoruba live in the southwestern part of the country, and some live in neighboring Benin and Togo. Yoruban towns were traditionally organized around the palace of the local *oba*, or king, which was surrounded by compounds belonging to extended families, each with its own elder male as its leader. The kingdom of Benin, mentioned in this story, was a town that developed into a great Yoruban city-state.

- **ART CONNECTION.** The Yoruba are famed for their magnificent craftsmanship and for their marvelous, complex oral literature. Among the finest products of Yoruban crafts are woven goods, leather goods, carvings in ivory and wood, and works in bronze.

- **CULTURAL CONNECTION.** The Yoruba have some of the most sophisticated and elaborate oral poetry in the world. It includes songs, incantations, works of praise, improvisations, and poetry describing people's ancestries and histories of towns. Like many African peoples, the Yoruba also have many traditional proverbs. One of them is: "If the earthworm does not dance in front of the rooster, he will still be eaten—but at least the rooster cannot say he was provoked."

Graphic Organizer

Actions →	Consequences
people took more of the sky than they needed	sylphs and fairies warned them
people killed innocent animals	

GOALS/OBJECTIVES

Studying this lesson will enable students to
- enjoy a myth from the Yoruban culture of West Africa
- define *oral tradition* and *myth* and give examples of each

- define *motif* and recognize motifs in literature
- research environmental causes
- dramatize a traditional tale

W H Y
the *Sky* is far away
from the earth

Fitzgerald Iyamabo

Doors of the Palace at Ikere-Ekiti, c. 1900. Yoruba artist. British Museum, London.

INDIVIDUAL LEARNING STRATEGIES (CONT.)

Away from the Earth," and read aloud relevant parts of the myth or legend (or the entire myth or legend if it is not too long) with their classmates. Generate a class discussion on the things that are similar in these "Golden Age" stories.

INDIVIDUAL LEARNING STRATEGIES

MOTIVATION
Students may especially enjoy the Speaking and Listening and Collaborative Learning activity in which they are given an opportunity to help transform this myth into a short play. Divide up tasks according to students' interests. Some may lean more toward writing the script, others will enjoy creating props and costumes or the set.

READING PROFICIENCY
Because this story is a part of the oral tradition, it might be especially beneficial for students to hear this story read aloud. Play a videotape of a storyteller telling this story, ask an older student or teacher to act as a storyteller, or play an audiotape of an expressive reading of this myth. Then tell students to reread the story on their own.

ENGLISH LANGUAGE LEARNING
Point out the following vocabulary words and expressions:
croissant—rich flaky bread roll made in the shape of a crescent
sylphs—according to legend a mortal, soulless being that lives in the air
gnomes—according to legend small dwarflike beings that live in the ground and guard its treasures
antelope—grass and leaf-eating creature with hollow unbranched horns that travels in herds on African plains

SPECIAL NEEDS
Students may appreciate the simple language and sentence structure of this myth. Tell students to focus on responding to the Guided Reading questions and Recall questions in the Investigate, Inquire, and Imagine section. Then check their comprehension with the Selection Check Test.

ENRICHMENT
Encourage students to find other myths and legends about a "Golden Age" that ends, often because of people's wickedness. Possibilities include the story of Adam and Eve in the Bible and the ancient Greek myth about the "Five Ages" of the world. Students should compare and contrast the "Golden Age" myth they find to "Why the Sky Is Far

Let me tell you a story my grandfather told me. It is a story his grandfather told him, and his own grandfather before him. Back in those days, in the ancient kingdom of Benin in present-day Nigeria, the sky wasn't far away from the earth. If an adult stood up straight and stretched his hand, he could touch the sky. Why, you ask? Well, the sky was made of the sweetest food you ever imagined. It tasted something like the sweetest croissant with honey baked into it, only better. And it was very light and fluffy.

> **GUIDED READING**
> From whom did the narrator learn this story?

Anyway, people did not need to go looking for food every day because the sky was there, so of course there were no hunters or farmers back then. Then, however, people started to get greedy and wasteful. Often they cut off more of the sky than they needed. The sylphs and fairies that tended the sky warned them not to do so, but no one listened. They warned them that if they kept wasting the food, a day would come when the Owner of the sky would take back His gift. But still no one listened.

> **GUIDED READING**
> Of what do the sylphs and fairies warn the people?

Even worse, people also started to kill the innocent animals that lived in the forest. They had gotten tired of eating the sky every day, and they decided that they wanted meat. The gnomes that worked in the forest were distressed. They warned the people to stop killing Osanobua's[1] creatures, but they continued killing and eating the animals. Worse yet, they also wasted the meat. They would kill an antelope, for instance, eat a little bit of it, and throw the rest away or let it go bad. So the poor creature would lose its life for nothing.

One day a hunter (and there were now hunters among the Binis[2]) was returning from a hunt. Listen to this. He had an elephant on his back, an antelope in his bag, and a rabbit in each hand. When he heard a small cricket chirping in the sand, he wanted that as well! He started digging for it with his big toe. This was too much for Eshu,[3] the mischievous one. He caused the hunter to stumble and fall under the weight of the elephant. He was crushed by the elephant and died immediately. The people were frightened by this, which was a lesson that greed can get you in trouble.

But you see, people forget things quickly. Very soon, they had gone back to their old ways. Osanobua, the patient One, watched sadly as the people continued to disobey Him. But even the patient will one day lose his patience. One day a pregnant woman cut off a large piece of the sky. When she took it into her house, her husband warned her that she might not be able to eat the whole thing, but she reminded him that she was pregnant and eating for two. After a while, she realized that she would not be able to eat everything. She called her husband, and he started to help, but they still couldn't finish it. Frightened, they called their neighbors to help. It seemed that the more food they ate, the more remained. Very soon the whole village was eating, but they soon knew it would be impossible to finish the food.

By this time it was night, so they went into the bush and quietly buried what was left. They thought that in this way they would not be found out, as if you can hide from the all-seeing Eye of Osanobua! Anyway, they woke up the next morning relieved that nothing seemed to have gone wrong. The pregnant woman was the first to go outside her house. Her husband was still inside when he heard her shriek loudly. He rushed outside, and what he saw made his heart start pounding

> **GUIDED READING**
> Why is it ridiculous that the people should try to bury the food?

---

1. **Osanobua.** Almighty God
2. **Binis.** Traditional name for Edo people
3. **Eshu.** Yoruba city

in fear. The sky was no longer there. Then he looked upward, and many, many miles away, he saw the sky. They both started crying loudly, along with the other people who had gathered there, but it was too late.

Then a loud Voice boomed from above: "For years you have enjoyed the many gifts that I gave to you, but you did not think you had to obey my instructions on how to enjoy these gifts. I will still bless you with food, but now you will have to work for it. Because you did the opposite of my will, instead of getting food from above, you will get it from below. You will till the ground until your body aches, before I permit any food to appear. So shall it be from this day forth."

The people cried bitterly, but it was too late. And from that day forth, my friends, the sky has remained far from us, and we have had to depend on the soil for our food. So now you know. Greed will always bring grief, whether it concerns food, riches, attention from others, or anything else. We are allowed only our fair share and no more. ■

> **GUIDED READING**
> What are the consequences of the people's greed?

Respond *to the* SELECTION

Do you feel that the people in this selection get what they deserve? Why, or why not?

About *the* AUTHOR

Fitzgerald Iyamabo was director of Culture of Ife Students' Union in Ile-Ife, Nigeria, where he obtained a degree in English. He later earned a master's degree in business at Boston University. Iyamabo's interests are mainly in history and world cutures. He lives in Boston, Massachusetts.

ANSWER TO GUIDED READING QUESTIONS

1. As a result of their greed, the people have to work the soil in order to eat.

RESPOND TO THE SELECTION

Ask students to discuss why the people might have gotten so greedy.

SELECTION CHECK TEST 4.7.7 WITH ANSWERS

Checking Your Reading
SHORT ANSWER

1. In the beginning of the story, why are there no hunters or farmers in the kingdom of Benin? **There were no hunters or farmers because the people could eat the sky.**
2. Of what do the fairies and sylphs warn the people? **The fairies and sylphs warn the people not to take more of the sky than they needed.**
3. What falls on the hunter and kills him? **An elephant falls on the hunter and kills him.**
4. What do the people do to try and hide their extra food? **They buried the food in the garden.**
5. Why does the pregnant woman shriek when she runs outside her hut? **She shrieks because the sky was no longer within reach.**

READER'S TOOLBOX
Fill in the blanks using the following terms. You may not use every term, and you may use some terms more than once.

point of view   oral tradition
    myth   motif

1. In the days before printing was common, most people could not read so many stories were preserved and passed on through _____. **oral tradition**
2. Stories can make a point about human nature by including one of the many _____ that deal with people's actions and their consequences. **motifs**
3. Many early cultures used _____ to explain things that occurred in the natural world but that they could not understand. **myth**

INSIGHTS

Yoruba Culture and History

The Yoruba are a people numbering over 17 million who live in southwestern Nigeria and in parts of Benin and Togo. They speak Yoruba, live primarily in cities and towns, and are well known for their crafts in wood and metal. In addition to their art, the Yorubans have won praise for their literature. Most notably, the 1986 Nobel Prize for literature was awarded to Wole Soyinka, a Yoruban author.

Archaeologists have found evidence showing that the Yoruba have lived in the area in and around Nigeria since prehistoric times. According to Yoruban mythology, the people were descended from a creator god named Oduduwa, who founded the city of Ife. Ife is still a very important city for the Yoruba. Later the Yoruba controlled a number of large walled cities, and by the 1600s they had a vast empire covering hundreds of miles. In fact, the Yoruban kingdom of Oyo was once the largest and most powerful kingdom in West Africa.

Slavery by Europeans and rule by the British brought down the great kingdoms of the Yoruba. Many Yoruban were taken to Cuba and Brazil as slaves, and Yoruba customs, such as mask-making, ritual dances, and rhythmic music, are still alive in those countries. The British rule of Nigeria ended in 1960.

Today the Yoruba in West Africa live in large cities, and go for part of the year to tend family farms in the rural areas. Some of their staple crops are beans, yams, cassava, bananas,

maize, and palm oil used for making soup. For export, they raise cocoa beans. Although most Yoruban are Christian or Muslim, they also worship the hundreds of Yoruba gods, or orisha, and consult Yoruban herbalists and priests for help with problems.

When a child is born, a diviner, or babalawo, is consulted to determine which orisha the child should follow. Some of the most popular gods are

Yoruba Traditional Lands

Shango, the god of thunder and lightning; **Ifa** (or Orunmila), god of divination; **Eshu**, the messenger and trickster god; and **Ogun**, god of iron and of war. The Yoruba have a rich oral tradition which includes stories about their many gods.

Traditional Yoruban clothing consists of a vest, baggy pants, and a long cloth gown for men. Women wear a wide piece of cloth hanging from the neck to the ankles, with a blouse extending to the waist, and a veil wrapped around the head. However, many Yoruba now wear Western-style clothing.

Investigate, Inquire, and Imagine

Recall: GATHERING FACTS

1a. According to the narrator, how was life different in ancient Benin? What did people do for food?

2a. Who warns the people when they start being wasteful? Who is distressed when the people start killing animals?

3a. What happens to the hunter, and why? What does the woman do after cutting off a large part of the sky? What does she tell her husband? What does she realize? What do the woman, her husband, and her neighbors try to do?

Analyze: TAKING THINGS APART

4a. In what major ways do the people of ancient Benin disobey the will of Osanobua? Order their crimes from least harmful to worst, according to how they are presented in the story.

Evaluate: MAKING JUDGMENTS

5a. Do you agree with the story's interpretation of each crime's seriousness? Which crime do you think is the worst, and why? Explain.

→ Interpret: FINDING MEANING

1b. How do you know that this is a tale out of the oral tradition?

2b. What explanation does this story offer of the origins of hunting? What is particularly shocking about the people's greedy and wasteful ways?

3b. What sort of person is the hunter? How do you know? How does the narrator feel about trying to hide things from Osanobua? How do you know?

→ Synthesize: BRINGING THINGS TOGETHER

4b. What consequences do the people experience? What punishments do they receive for their crimes? What lesson does this story intend to teach?

→ Extend: CONNECTING IDEAS

5b. Do you think the lesson taught in this story is still a valuable one in our society? What modern laws and rules can you think of that are similar to the "laws" or wishes of Osanobua? In your opinion, who are the people most likely to break such laws, and why would they do so?

Understanding Literature

ORAL TRADITION AND MYTH. An **oral tradition** is a work, idea, or custom passed by word of mouth from generation to generation. A **myth** is a story that explains the beginnings of things in the natural world. Myths are common in the oral tradition. What explanation does this myth offer? What aspect of the natural world is explained?

RECALL

1a. In ancient Benin, people did not have to work. They got their food by breaking off pieces of the sky, which was close to the earth.

2a. The sylphs, fairies, and gnomes warn the people when they start being wasteful. The gnomes are distressed about the killing of animals.

3a. The hunter is so greedy he wants a cricket as well, and he is punished when an elephant falls on him and crushes him. The woman takes the pieces home and tries to eat it. She tells her husband she is eating for two. She realizes she cannot possibly eat it all. She, her husband, and the neighbors try to eat it and then try to hide it.

INTERPRET

1b. The story comes from the oral tradition because it has been passed down by word of mouth from grandparent to grandchild.

2b. The story says that people got tired of eating sky every day and decided they wanted meat. It is shocking that the people waste what they kill, causing animals to die for nothing.

3b. The hunter is terribly greedy because he wants the cricket even though he has far more than he can eat. The narrator thinks it is absurd to hide anything from Osanobua and tells the reader or listener so directly.

ANALYZE

4a. The people all act wastefully and greedily, not appreciating Osanobua's gifts. Students may order the crimes as follows: people cut off more of the sky than they need, people kill and waste the meat of animals, hunter wants a cricket in addition to the other animals he caught, woman cuts off too much sky and villagers bury it hoping to conceal their crime. This order is revealed through the level of punishment meted out.

SYNTHESIZE

4b. The people are warned the punished, first singularly (when the elephant falls on the man) and then as a group (when the sky is moved far away from the earth). The story intends to teach that greed always brings grief and people should only take their fair share.

ANSWERS TO INVESTIGATE, INQUIRE, IMAGINE (CONT.)

EVALUATE

5a. Responses will vary. Some students may feel that killing animals needlessly and wasting their flesh is the most serious crime, but there are no right or wrong answers to this question as longs as students explain their reasoning.

EXTEND

5b. *Responses will vary.*

Motif. A **motif** is anything that appears repeatedly in one or more works of literature, art, or music. One of the most common motifs in mythology is of a golden age ruined by human wickedness. What golden age is described in this Yoruban myth? How is the golden age ruined?

Writer's Journal

1. Write a list of **rules** that Osanobua might have written for the people of ancient Benin. Use formal language that you feel is appropriate for a divine set of laws.

2. What is your opinion about people who waste natural resources? Write a **statement of belief** expressing your thoughts about and responses to this issue.

3. Imagine that you want to tell this myth to a friend and continue to pass it on through the oral tradition. Write a **retelling** of the story, using informal language such as you would use in a personal letter or conversation.

Skill Builders

Study and Research
RESEARCHING ENVIRONMENTAL CAUSES.

What is being done to protect the natural resources in Africa? Research an organization such as Greenpeace or an Africa-specific organization that is working to protect natural resources. Ask a librarian for help, or use the Internet. On the Internet, try these Web sites: http://www.greenpeace.org (the homepage for Greenpeace International); http://www.rri.org/nesda.html (Network for Environment and Sustainable Development in Africa); or http://www.saep.org. (Southern Africa Environment Project).

Choose one organization that interests you. What is the mission of this organization? What projects is the organization currently working on? Explain what actions the organization is taking at this time and has taken in the past. Explain which of these environmental causes interests you most. If there are volunteer opportunities with this organization, find out how a person could become involved. When you have finished your research, prepare an oral report to be given to the class.

Speaking and Listening & Collaborative Learning
DRAMATIZING A TRADITIONAL TALE.

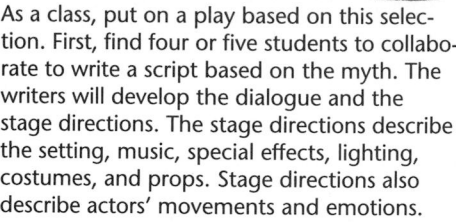

As a class, put on a play based on this selection. First, find four or five students to collaborate to write a script based on the myth. The writers will develop the dialogue and the stage directions. The stage directions describe the setting, music, special effects, lighting, costumes, and props. Stage directions also describe actors' movements and emotions.

While one group writes the script, another group of four or five students should come up with a list of props and simple costume ideas for each character. This group will need to communicate closely with the script writers about costumes and props. A third group of students will design and construct the set.

Depending on the size of the class, possible acting roles include the sylphs and fairies, gnomes, and the villagers. Other students could direct the play, work the lights, create special effects, or videotape the production.

Prereading

"The Instruction of Indra"
Retold by Joseph Campbell (with Bill Moyers)

Reader's Resource

- In this story, the god Indra learns several lessons. These lessons are taken from the ideas of Hinduism, which is the main religion of India. Three Hindu ideas that Inda learns about in this myth are the concepts of detachment, karma, and darma, or duty.

- The Hindu religion teaches that people should work towards detachment from the world and from material things like money and power. The teachings say that all worldly goods and possessions are illusions that will soon pass away.

- Karma, or fate, is an idea that is closely tied with the idea of detachment. Hindus believe that if a person is born into a low caste, or social class, that place in society is simply that person's inescapable fate. Perhaps that person had committed some evil in a past life and now was paying for it in this one. For that reason, in the past, people in India could not rise up in caste by working hard. Those who were poor and needy had to stay poor all their lives and live out their karma.

- Balancing the concepts of karma and detachment is the Hindu idea of darma, or duty. Krishna, in the Hindu holy scripture *Bhagavad-Gita*, taught that a proper life does not involve withdrawal from action in the world. Instead, according to Krishna, one should practice one's darma. One should continue to act in the world, carrying out one's duties, but without expecting to be rewarded for actions on earth.

Graphic Organizer

Make a chart like the one below. As you read, list the lessons Indra learns and what conflict he experiences as a result.

Lesson Learned	Internal Conflict
that there have been Indras before him.	Indra now struggles with his own conceited ideas of himself and must accept that he is not as unique as he thought.

INDIAN MYTH

Reader's Journal

Have you ever known someone who was terribly vain or boastful? If so, how did you feel about this person?

Reader's TOOLBOX

SYMBOL. A **symbol** is something that stands for or represents both itself and something else. In this story, ants appear as a symbol. As you read, try to identify what they symbolize.

INTERNAL CONFLICT. An **internal conflict** is a struggle that takes place inside the mind of the character. In this story, Indra struggles over how best to lead his life. As you read, use the graphic organizer at left to list the struggles that he experiences in this myth.

"THE INSTRUCTION OF INDRA" **507**

GOALS/OBJECTIVES

Studying this lesson will enable students to
- have a positive experience reading an Indian myth
- define *symbol* and identify and explain symbols in a literary work
- define *inner conflict* and recognize this type of struggle in their reading
- investigate word origins
- research and compare and contrast Hinduism and Buddhism

ADDITIONAL RESOURCES

UNIT / RESOURCE BOOK
- Selection Worksheet 7.5
- Selection Check Test 4.7.9
- Selection Test 4.7.10
- Reading Resource 1.17, 1.21

GRAPHIC ORGANIZER

Students may respond as follows:
Lesson Learned: that there have been Indras before him; Internal Conflict: Indra now struggles with his own conceited ideas of himself and must accept that he is not as unique as he thought.
Lesson Learned: As Vishnu sleeps the lotus of the universe grows from his navel and on the lotus sits Brahma the creator. Brahma lives for four-hundred and thirty-two thousand years and as he blinks Indras come in and out of existence. There are also other galaxies, each with its own Brahma, and the Indras are too numerous to count. Internal Conflict: Indra struggles with the knowledge that he is a relatively insignificant part of the universe, and that his rule will end in a blink of Brahma's eye.
Lesson Learned: The ants on the floor are former Indras who rise from the lowest condition to become Indras and then drop down again when they drop a thunderbolt on a monster and think "What a good boy am I." Internal Conflict: Indra realizes that he is doomed to be reborn in a lowly form.

(Continued on page 508)

READER'S JOURNAL

Encourage students to describe their own reactions to vain or boastful people. Ask them to think about a time when they behaved boastfully or vainly. In what way did people react to their behavior? In what way might they behave if they were in the same situation again.

Indra, 967. Hindu artist. Banteay Srei, Angkor, Cambodia.

GRAPHIC ORGANIZER (CONT.)

Lesson Learned: The old man says that every time an Indra dies a world is destroyed, and as half the hairs on his chest have fallen out, in that same amount of time there will be no more Indras. He then says, "Life is short. Why build a house?" Internal Conflict: Indra struggles with the knowledge that there is an end to even great and powerful things and wonders whether it is pointless for him to complete his grand palace given that life is short.

Lesson Learned: After Indra decides to become a yogi, a priest tells him that he has an obligation to fulfill his work as Indra and to love his wife. Internal Conflict: Conflict is resolved as Indra decides to give up his new dream of being a yogi and realizes that even though life is short, he can represent the eternal.

INDIVIDUAL LEARNING STRATEGIES

MOTIVATION
Many characters in this myth are described as having unusual appearances. Students might enjoy working together to create a mural showing scenes from "The Instruction on Indra." Students might tape butcher's paper or other large sheets of paper to a section of wall to use for a mural instead of permanently painting an actual wall.

READING PROFICIENCY
You may wish to play an audiotape of a reading of this selection and have students follow along with the words in their textbook as they listen. Students may benefit from reading the Insights feature on India before reading the myth.

ENGLISH LANGUAGE LEARNING
Point out the following vocabulary words and expressions:
splendid—showy and magnificent
porter—person stationed at the door or gate to admit people entering
shot—reduced to a state of ruin or uselessness

SPECIAL NEEDS
Students may have difficulty understanding some of the concepts in this myth. Have them review the Prereading information carefully, and pay attention to Guided Reading

The *Instruction* of Indra

Joseph Campbell (with Bill Moyers)

INDIVIDUAL LEARNING STRATEGIES (CONT.)

questions as they read. You may wish to have some students focus mostly on the Recall questions in the Investigate, Inquire, and Imagine section, as some of the higher level critical thinking questions will prove too challenging for some students.

ENRICHMENT

Ask students to write two paragraphs. The first should be written from the point of view of a person from a high caste or social group. Students should imagine that they are a member of a very high caste or social group and write about how they feel about karma, or fate, and darma, or duty. The second paragraph should be written from the point of view of a person of the lowest, or "untouchable" caste. Students should imagine that they are members of this less fortunate caste and write about how they feel about fate and their duties.

There is a wonderful story in one of the Upanishads[1] about the god Indra.[2] Now, it happened at this time that a great monster had enclosed all the waters of the earth, so there was a terrible <u>drought</u>, and the world was in a very bad condition. It took Indra quite a while to realize that he had a box of thunderbolts and that all he had to do was drop a thunderbolt on the monster and blow him up. When he did that, the waters flowed, and the world was refreshed and Indra said, "What a great boy am I."

So, thinking, "What a great boy am I," Indra goes up to the <u>cosmic</u> mountain, which is the central mountain of the world, and decides to build a palace worthy of such as he. The main carpenter of the gods goes to work on it, and in very quick order he gets the palace into pretty good condition.

> **GUIDED READING**
> What is Indra's reaction to his success?

But every time Indra comes to inspect it, he has bigger ideas about how splendid and <u>grandiose</u> the palace should be. Finally, the carpenter says, "My god, we are both immortal, and there is no end to his desires. I am caught for <u>eternity</u>." So he decides to go to Brahma, the creator god, and complain.

Brahma sits on a lotus,[3] the symbol of divine energy and divine grace. The lotus grows from the navel of Vishnu, who is the sleeping god, whose dream is the universe. So the carpenter comes to the edge of the great lotus pond of the universe and tells his story to Brahma. Brahma says, "You go home. I will fix this up." Brahma gets off his lotus and kneels down to address sleeping

> **GUIDED READING**
> What is the relationship between Brahma and Vishnu?

Vishnu. Vishnu just makes a gesture and says something like, "Listen, fly, something is going to happen."

Next morning, at the gate of the palace that is being built, there appears a beautiful blue-black boy with a lot of children around him, just admiring his beauty. The porter at the gate of the new palace goes running to Indra, and Indra says, "Well, bring in the boy." The boy is brought in, and Indra, the king god, sitting on his throne, says, "Young man, welcome. And what brings you to my palace?"

"Well," says the boy with a voice like thunder rolling on the horizon, "I have been told that you are building such a palace as no Indra before you ever built."

> **GUIDED READING**
> What does the boy say that surprises Indra?

And Indra says, "Indras before me, young man—what are you talking about?"

The boy says, "Indras before you. I have seen them come and go, come and go. Just think, Vishnu sleeps in the cosmic ocean, and the lotus of the universe grows from his navel. On the lotus sits Brahma, the creator. Brahma opens his eyes, and a world comes into being, governed by an Indra. Brahma closes his eyes, and a world goes out of being. The life of a Brahma is four hundred and thirty-two thousand years. When he dies, the lotus goes back, and another lotus is formed, and another Brahma. Then think of the galaxies beyond galaxies in <u>infinite</u> space, each a lotus, with a Brahma sitting on it, opening

---

1. **Upanishads.** Indian philosophical and religious writings
2. **Indra.** Chief god of the early Aryan religion, later absorbed into Hinduism
3. **lotus.** Pink or white waterlily used as a religious symbol in Hinduism

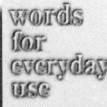

words for everyday use

drought (drout) *n.*, period of dry weather; lack of rain. *There was a period of <u>drought</u> and the crops withered in the sun.*
cos • mic (käz′ mik) *adj.*, relating to the universe as a whole. *In ancient Greek mythology, the <u>cosmic</u> center of the gods was Mt. Olympus.*
gran • di • ose (gran dē ōs′) *adj.*, magnificent; grand. *The eccentric millionaire planned to build a sprawling, <u>grandiose</u> pink mansion.*
e • ter • ni • ty (ē tər′ nə tē) *n.*, time without beginning or end. *The hour spent waiting at the doctor's office seemed to drag on for an <u>eternity</u>.*
in • fi • nite (in′ fə nit) *adj.*, endless. *Some people treat our natural resources as if they were <u>infinite</u>, when in actuality our resources are quite limited.*

ANSWERS TO GUIDED READING QUESTIONS

1. Indra thinks "What a great boy am I," and decides to build a palace worthy of his magnificence.
2. Brahma is the symbol of divine energy and grace who sits on a lotus which comes from the navel of the sleeping god Vishnu who is dreaming of the universe.
3. The boy says, "Indras before you," and Indra was not aware that there were any Indras before him.

ADDITIONAL QUESTIONS AND ACTIVITIES

Ask students the following questions: What does Vishnu say when Brahma tells him about the problem with Indra? Why do you think Vishnu calls Brahma "fly"? What does this comparison indicate about the relationship between Vishnu and Brahma? How long does the life of a Brahma last? *Answers.* Vishnu says, "Listen, fly, something is going to happen." Students may say that Vishnu calls Brahma "fly" because Brahma is insignificant compared to Vishnu. This comparison indicates that a Brahma is just a small part of Vishnu's universe. The life of a Brahma lasts four hundred and thirty-two thousand years.

VOCABULARY FROM THE SELECTION

constellation	infinite
cosmic	manifestation
disillusioned	meditate
drought	mission
eternity	privilege
grandiose	radiantly

his eyes, closing his eyes. And Indras? There may be wise men in your court who would volunteer to count the drops of water in the oceans of the world or the grains of sand on the beaches, but no one would count those Brahmin, let alone those Indras."

While the boy is talking, an army of ants parades across the floor. The boy laughs when he sees them, and Indra's hair stands on end, and he says to the boy, "Why do you laugh?"

The boy answers, "Don't ask unless you are willing to be hurt."

Indra says, "I ask. Teach." (That, by the way, is a good Oriental idea: you don't teach until you are asked. You don't force your <u>mission</u> down people's throats.)

And so the boy points to the ants and says, "Former Indras all. Through many lifetimes they rise from the lowest conditions to highest illumination.[4] And then they drop their thunderbolt on a monster, and they think, 'What a good boy am I.' And down they go again."

> **GUIDED READING**
>
> What does the boy say Indras do throughout many lifetimes?

While the boy is talking, a crotchety old yogi[5] comes into the palace with a banana leaf parasol. He is naked except for a loincloth,[6] and on his chest is a little disk of hair, and half the hairs in the middle have all dropped out.

The boy greets him and asks him just what Indra was about to ask. "Old man, what is your name? Where do you come from? Where is your family? Where is your house?

And what is the meaning of this curious <u>constellation</u> of hair on your chest?"

"Well," says the old fella, "my name is Hairy. I don't have a house. Life is too short for that. I just have this parasol. I don't have a family. I just <u>meditate</u> on Vishnu's feet, and think of eternity, and how passing time is. You know, every time an Indra dies, a world disappears—these things just flash by like that. Every time an Indra dies, one hair drops out of this circle on my chest. Half the hairs are gone now. Pretty soon they will all be gone. Life is short. Why build a house?"

> **GUIDED READING**
>
> Why does the older man say he doesn't have a house?

Then the two disappear. The boy was Vishnu, the Lord Protector,[7] and the old yogi was Shiva, the creator and destroyer of the world, who had just come for the instruction of Indra, who is simply a god of history but thinks he is the whole show.

Indra is sitting there on the throne, and he is completely <u>disillusioned</u>, completely shot. He calls the carpenter and says, "I'm quitting the building of this palace. You are dismissed." So the carpenter got his intention. He is dismissed from the job, and there is no more house building going on.

---

4. **illumination.** Highest spiritual understanding
5. **yogi.** A Hindu holy man, one who practices a spiritual path, or yoga
6. **loincloth.** Cloth worn about the waist and upper thighs
7. **Vishnu, the Lord Protector.** In Hindu belief, one of the appearances of Vishnu on earth was as Krishna, frequently pictured as a beautiful blue-black youth

---

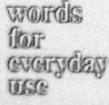

words for everyday use

mis • sion (mish′ ən) *n.,* belief or purpose. *She decided that her <u>mission</u> was to help others, so she joined several volunteer groups.*

con • stel • la • tion (kän′ stə lā′ shən) *n.,* cluster; gathering. *That <u>constellation</u> of stars is known as Orion.*

med • i • tate (med′ ə tāt′) *v.,* spend time in quiet thinking. *Marsh <u>meditates</u> when she has a problem to solve.*

dis • il • lu • sioned (dis′ i lōō′ zhənd) *adj.,* disappointed; dissatisfied. *Mr. Green was shocked and <u>disillusioned</u> by the bad news.*

Indra decides to go out and be a yogi and just meditate on the lotus feet of Vishnu. But he has a beautiful queen named Indrani. And when Indrani hears of Indra's plan, she goes to the priest of the gods and says, "Now he has got the idea in his head of going out to become a yogi."

"Well," says the priest, "come in with me, darling, and we will sit down, and I will fix this up."

So they sit down before the king's throne, and the priest says, "Now, I wrote a book for you many years ago on the art of politics. You are in the position of the king of the gods. You are a manifestation of the mystery of Brahma in the field of time. This is a high privilege. Appreciate it, honor it, and deal with life as though you were what

GUIDED READING
What attitude does the priest say Indra should take toward his position?

you really are. And besides, now I am going to write you a book on the art of love so that you and your wife will know that in the wonderful mystery of the two that are one, the Brahma is radiantly present also."

And with this set of instructions, Indra gives up his idea of going out and becoming a yogi and finds that, in life, he can represent the eternal as a symbol, you might say, of the Brahma.

So each of us is, in a way, the Indra of his own life. You can make a choice, either to throw it all off and go into the forest to meditate, or to stay in the world, both in the life of your job, which is the kingly job of politics and achievement, and in the love life with your wife and family. Now, this is a very nice myth, it seems to me. ∎

GUIDED READING
What lesson is there for all people in this myth?

Respond *to the* SELECTION

Which do you think is the better course for Indra, withdrawing from the world to become a holy man or remaining active in the world? Why?

About *the* AUTHOR

Joseph Campbell (1904–1987) gained an international reputation as a scholar of mythology and comparative religion. As a young man, Campbell became interested in mythology after reading about Native American beliefs. He studied at Columbia University and at universities in Paris, France, and Munich, Germany.

Campbell's wide-ranging scholarship included thorough knowledge of medieval French, the language of much romance literature about knights in shining armor, and of Sanskrit, the language of the religious texts of early India. Campbell's books include a study of hero myths, *The Hero with a Thousand Faces*, and a multivolume comparative study of mythologies around the world, *The Masks of God*. Shortly before Campbell's death, broadcast journalist Bill Moyers interviewed him and followed up by producing a television series and a book based on these interviews called *The Power of Myth*.

words for everyday use

man • i • fes • ta • tion (man′ ə fes tā′ shən) *n.*, example, instance. *Her smile was a manifestation of joy.*

priv • i • lege (priv′ ə lij) *n.*, right or favor. *Because Hannah missed her curfew, her parents took away her phone privileges.*

ra • di • ant • ly (rā′ dē ənt lē) *adv.*, brightly. *The sun shone radiantly upon the sea.*

"*THE INSTRUCTION OF INDRA*" **511**

INSIGHTS
Ancient India

INDIAN HISTORY. Around 2500 BC, in northwestern India, a great civilization developed from a population of farmers on the banks of the Indus River. The Indus Valley Civilization covered a large area and included over seventy villages, as well as the large cities of Mohenjo-Daro and Harappa.

Beginning around 2000 BC, India was invaded from the north, perhaps by people originally from the Steppes region of southern Russia. These people called themselves the Aryans, or "noble ones," and brought with them the Sanskrit language and a religion that developed into Hinduism.

Much of what we know of the Aryans comes from collections of early Sanskrit religious writings called the Vedas. These books describe a people skilled in battle who used horses and chariots, herded cattle, and lived in small agricultural villages. Their society was organized into occupational groups: Brahmans (priests), Kshatriyas (nobles and warriors), Vaisyas (farmers), and Sudras (workers or servants). The Aryans established communities along the Indus River and spread across the whole of northern India, especially along the banks of India's other great river, the Ganges.

INDIAN RELIGION. The early Aryans worshiped many gods, including **Indra**, a sky god associated with war, thunder, and lightning. Eventually the Aryan religion changed into a form of monotheism, or worship of one god, and became known as Hinduism. The Aryans focused their worship on **Brahma** but also worshiped many lesser gods, who were viewed as different forms of the main god. People believed that all things in the universe were part of Brahma, who created the universe and was one with it. The Hindus believed that this universe was sustained by **Vishnu**, the preserver god. Eventually **Shiva**, the destroyer god, would bring the universe to an end, and the cycle of creation would begin again.

In the sixth century BC, a new religion called Buddhism emerged in India and spread into other parts of Asia. Buddhism became a powerful religion in India, although Hinduism later regained its former strength.

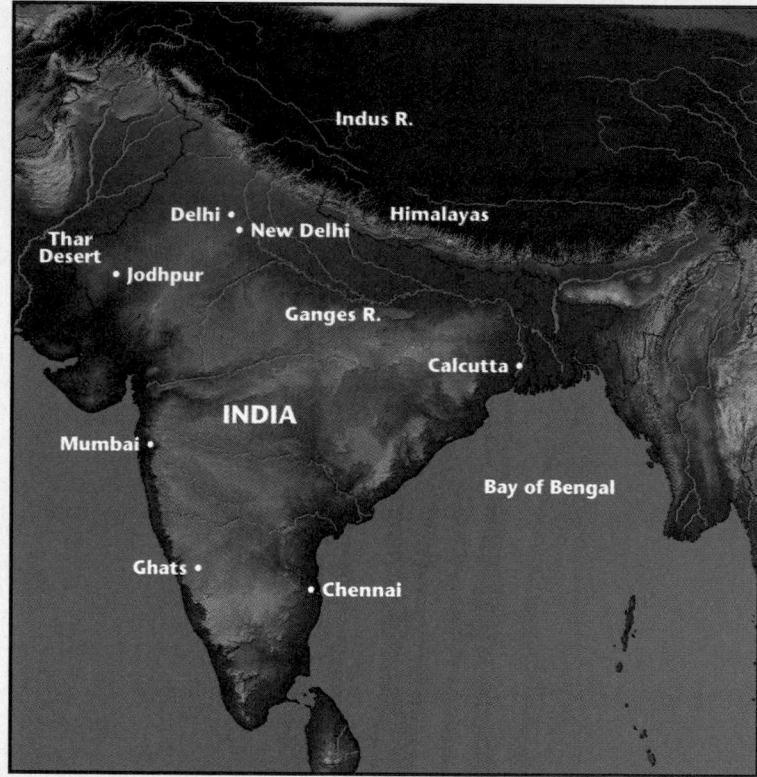

Investigate, Inquire, and Imagine

Recall: GATHERING FACTS

1a. After blowing up the monster, what does Indra think of himself? What does Indra decide to do to demonstrate his greatness?

2a. What does the beautiful blue-black boy tell Indra that surprises him? Who is the blue-black boy, and who is the old yogi? What happens to the old yogi every time an Indra dies?

3a. What does Indra decide to do after giving up plans to finish building his palace?

→ Interpret: FINDING MEANING

1b. How do you feel about Indra at this point in the story?

2b. How does the boy's teaching affect Indra? What does the old yogi mean when he asks Indra, "Why build a house?"

3b. Why does Indrani bring the priest to see Indra? What does Indra learn from the priest?

Analyze: TAKING THINGS APART

4a. In what ways does the story "The Instruction of Indra" reflect Hindu beliefs?

→ Synthesize: BRINGING THINGS TOGETHER

4b. What does this myth teach us about how we should live our lives?

Evaluate: MAKING JUDGMENTS

5a. What do you think about the ideas of detachment and karma? Do you agree that people should work to become detached from worldly goods and power? Do you agree with the idea of karma, or do you believe people should work to improve their lives? Explain, referring to the Prereading if needed.

→ Extend: CONNECTING IDEAS

5b. What role should rich and privileged people play in society? Should they give up their wealth to the poor, or should they just enjoy life, or in what other way do you think the rich should behave? Explain.

Understanding Literature

SYMBOL. A **symbol** is something that stands for or represents both itself and something else. What do the ants in this story symbolize?

INTERNAL CONFLICT. An **internal conflict** is a struggle that takes place inside the mind of the character. In this story, Indra struggles between pridefulness and concern with worldly matters, on the one hand, and humility and concern with spiritual matters, on the other hand. How is the struggle finally ended, or resolved? What middle course does the priest suggest to Indra?

"THE INSTRUCTION OF INDRA" **513**

ANSWERS TO UNDERSTANDING LITERATURE

SYMBOL. Ants symbolize former Indras who have to begin the cycle of rebirth again from the bottom.
INTERNAL CONFLICT. The struggle is resolves by Indra's losing his pride and paying more attention to spiritual matters but still carrying out his worldly duties. The middle course is to find spiritual satisfaction in carrying out one's duties.

ANSWERS TO INVESTIGATE, INQUIRE, IMAGINE

RECALL

1a. Indra thinks very highly of himself. Indra decides to build a palace on the cosmic mountain to demonstrate his greatness.

2a. The boy tells Indra that there have been Indras before him and that there will be Indras after him. The blue-black boy is Vishnu, the Lord Protector. The old yogi is Shiva, the creator and the destroyer of the world. Every time an Indra dies a hair drops out of the circle on the yogi's chest.

3a. Indra decides to become a yogi and meditate on the lotus feet of Vishnu.

INTERPRET

1b. Students may say Indra seems very conceited.

2b. The boy's teaching surprises and humbles Indra. The old yogi means there is no point on focusing your energies on worldly matters because life is so short.

3b. Indrani brings the priest to see Indra because she feels that Indra's decision to turn over his life to meditation is selfish and foolish. Indra learns that his position is a privilege and that he should honor and appreciate it, not retreat from the world.

ANALYZE

4a. The myth tells us that we should accept who we are and carry out our duty in life, The story shows the Hindu belief in rebirth, says that one should accepts one's karma, and stresses that it is important to carry out one's darma.

SYNTHESIZE

4b. The myth shows us that even though we know our lives will end we should not turn away from them but should live them to their fullest and fulfill our duties toward others.

EVALUATE

5a. Responses will vary. Students should support their answers with reasons and relate them to the concepts of detachment and karma.

EXTEND

5b. Responses will vary, but some students will feel that the wealthy do have an obligation to help those who are less fortunate.

Study and Research
Books on Hinduism and Buddhism, unless written for your readers, may be too in depth and difficult for most students. Encourage them to use encyclopedias, other reference books, and periodical articles as sources instead. They may use the Internet, too, but should evaluate their sources to see how reliable they are and avoid using any information from a source that seems unreliable. Refer them to the Language Arts Survey for information on evaluating Internet sites. Students' reports should be brief written reports of no more than two to three pages.

Writer's Journal

1. Suppose you were Indra at the beginning of the story and wanted to build the most magnificent palace for yourself. Write a **design plan** for your palace, describing what rooms your palace will have, and what luxury features you want it to contain.

2. In this story, Indra learns some important lessons. Imagine that you are taking **notes** for him so that he will not forget what he has learned. In your notebook, write some brief notes for him.

3. Imagine that you are an **advice columnist** and Indra writes to you asking for advice about what he should do with his life. Write your advice column, including both Indra's letter and your response.

Skill Builders

Language, Grammar, and Style

INVESTIGATING WORD ORIGINS. In the Hindu religion, the term *karma* means the way in which a person's actions determine that person's fate in the next stage of life. However, the term *karma* has entered the English language in a more simple way, as a synonym for the word *fate* or *destiny*. The study of **word origins** is the investigation of where words come from and how they develop.

Refer to the Language Arts Survey 1.21, "Exploring Word Origins and Word Families," and 1.17, "Using a Dictionary." Then look up the following words in a dictionary. Write the whole etymology, or history, of each word. List all of the abbreviations used in each etymology, along with the meanings of these abbreviations.

EXAMPLE blithe
[ME < OE; ult. < IE base *bhlei-, to shine, gleam]
ME = Middle English; < = derived from; OE = Old English; ult. = ultimately; IE = Indo-European; * = not attested

1. bid   2. insipid   3. cook   4. bodhisattva   5. Seattle

Study and Research

COMPARING HINDUISM AND BUDDHISM. India is the birthplace of two major Eastern religions, Hinduism and Buddhism. How are these two religions similar, and how are they different? With a partner, research the main principles and beliefs of Hinduism and Buddhism, and prepare a report comparing and contrasting the two religions.

Prereading

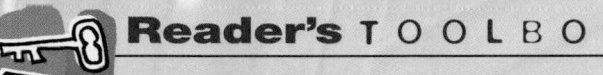

"Amaterasu"

Retold by Carolyn Swift

Reader's T O O L B O X

CONFLICT. A conflict is a struggle between two people or things in a literary work. A plot is formed around this conflict. The conflict can be internal or external. A struggle that takes place between a character and some outside force—such as another character, society, or nature—is an external conflict. A struggle that takes place inside a character is an internal conflict. As you read "Amaterasu," try to determine what type of conflict takes place and which character or characters are involved in the conflict.

CHARACTERIZATION. Characterization is the act of creating a character. Writers create characters by showing what characters say, do, and think; by showing what other characters (and the narrator) say about them, and by showing what physical features, dress, and personality the characters display. As you read, think about how the character of Amaterasu is developed. Use a cluster chart like the one below to keep track of the things you learn about the goddess. What means are used to create the character of Amaterasu? What do you learn about Amaterasu from other characters? What do you learn about her from her actions and her discussion with her brother?

Graphic Organizer

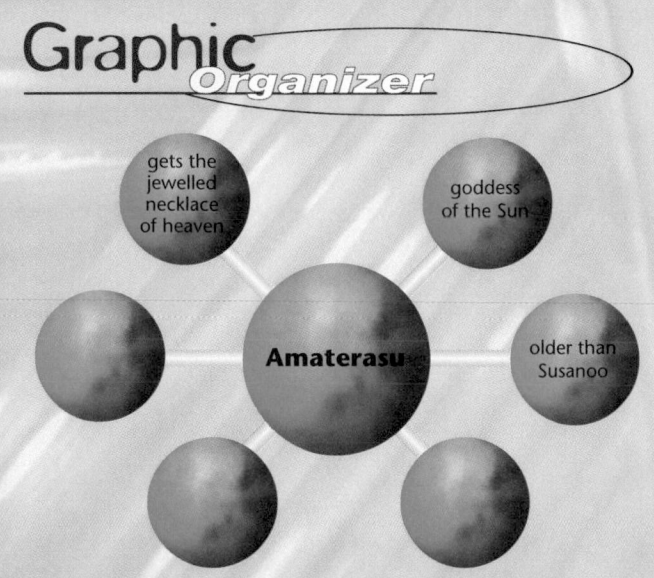

Reader's Journal

When you are upset or afraid, do you like to be alone, or do you prefer to be with others? Explain.

Reader's Resource

- In Shinto, the ancient native religion of Japan, Amaterasu is the goddess of the Sun. Until 1946, all emperors of Japan were considered to be gods descended from Amaterasu. It is said that when the first emperor, Jimmu, took power in 660 B.C., Amaterasu gave him her mirror as proof that he was divine. Today, the mirror is believed to be in Amaterasu's shrine, or place of worship. In this story, you will learn about the origin of this mirror.

- **SCIENCE CONNECTION.** A mirror is a surface that reflects images by diverting light in a certain way. The surface of a mirror must be perfectly smooth. The surface must reflect most of the light that hits it and absorb very little. Early human-made mirrors were polished pieces of bronze, tin, or silver. In Venice in the sixteenth century, people began to attach a thin sheet of metal to glass to create a mirroring surface. New techniques in the nineteenth century allowed mirrors to be created at a lower cost, and the use of mirrors became more common.

"AMATERASU" **515**

GRAPHIC ORGANIZER

Students may include details such as the following in their cluster charts: gets the jeweled necklace of heaven, sister to Susanoo, made goddess of the sun, frightened by loud noise of her brother, able to defend herself as a warrior, able to make a sword (instrument of death) into three daughters (capable of giving new life), argues with her brother as human siblings do, causes rice field to ripen, hides in cave because afraid of brother and the land grows cold and dark, likes looking at her own reflection, likes to hear the cocks crowing in the morning, angry when she believes good spirits have found another sun to replace her, delighted by her reflection and necklaces, was lonely in the cave, gets revenge on brother in the end.

READER'S JOURNAL

As an alternate activity, have students write about how they feel when somebody tricks them. Have them respond to the following questions and prompts: Is it ever pleasant to be tricked? Why, or why not? Write about a specific time when you were tricked. How did it make you feel? What reasons did people have for tricking you?

GOALS/OBJECTIVES

Studying this lesson will enable students to
- enjoy a myth from Japan
- learn about the importance of Amaterasu to Japanese emperors
- define *conflict* and distinguish between internal and external conflicts
- define *characterization* and identify techniques of characterization

INDIVIDUAL LEARNING STRATEGIES

MOTIVATION
Students might enjoy creating their own vision of a sun god or goddess through art. Students might paint, draw, or sculpt how they imagine the sun in human form.

READING PROFICIENCY
The simple sentence structure and diction of this myth make it a good choice for less confident readers. The only trouble students may have is with Japanese names which may be unfamiliar to some. Share pronunciations of these names with students. Tell them to refer to footnotes for unfamiliar terms and share the English Language Learning vocabulary above.

ENGLISH LANGUAGE LEARNING
Point out the following vocabulary words and expressions:
corals—hard bony skeleton of a type of creature that lives and forms reefs in the sea
in vain—fruitlessly, without effect
pigtail—long braid of hair hanging at the back of the head

SPECIAL NEEDS
Students may benefit from hearing the story read aloud on audiotape. Tell students to follow along in their books as they listen. Students might then go back and reread the story. Check their comprehension with the Selection Check test before asking them to move on and respond to the Recall questions in the Investigate, Inquire, and Imagine section. Students might discuss as a group their ideas about the higher level Interpret, Analyze, Synthesize, perspective, and Empathy questions.

ENRICHMENT
Ask students to find and share other myths about sun gods and goddesses. Students might read the myth about Phoebes and Apollo, for example. Students might then discuss the similarities and differences between Apollo and Amaterasu.

Amaterasu

Carolyn Swift

Back in the mists of time there lived a boy called Susanoo. His father and mother were the first people on earth, but then his father became Lord of the Heavens and his mother Lady of the Underworld.

Susanoo himself lived with his brothers and sisters on the bridge which linked heaven and earth, but he was always complaining. He complained about not being able to visit his mother, even though his father explained to him that if he once went to the underworld he would never be able to come back, and he complained even more when his sister Amaterasu was given the jewelled necklace of heaven and made goddess of the sun, while he was given only corals and made god of the sea. Finally his father became sick of his constant moanings and groanings.

"I don't want to see your face around Heaven any more," he told him. "You have the whole earth and sea to play around in so there's no need for you to make all our lives a misery up here."

"Oh, all right," Susanoo grumbled, "but first I must say goodbye to Amaterasu."

So off he stumped to look for her. Being in a bad mood, he shook every mountain he passed so that rocks crashed down the slopes, and he stamped his feet so that the earth quaked. Hearing all the noise, Amaterasu was frightened. She took up her bow and arrow so that, when her younger brother arrived, he found himself facing the drawn bow of a fierce-looking warrior.

"You can put that thing down," he told her. "I come in peace."

"Prove it," she said suspiciously, not taking her eyes off him.

Susanoo handed her his sword. She took it from him and broke it into three pieces. Then, before he could complain, she blew on them and turned them into three beautiful little girls.

"One day these three little daughters of mine will bring new life into the world," she told him, "while your sword could only have brought death."

"I can do better than that!" Susanoo boasted. "Give me the necklaces you're wearing."

So Amaterasu unclasped the five necklaces and gave them to her brother. Then he blew on them and turned them into five little boys.

"Now I have five sons," he said.

"They were made out of my necklaces so they should be my sons!" Amaterasu snapped.

"But your daughters were made from my sword," Susanoo argued.

"That's different!" Amaterasu told him.

At that Susanoo lost his temper. He tore up all the rice fields that Amaterasu had been carefully ripening and caused such destruction that the frightened goddess ran and hid in a cave, blocking the entrance with a large stone.

"AMATERASU" 517

1. Susanoo would probably not be content if he were allowed to go to the underworld. If he were there, he would probably complain about not being able to return. If he rules the sky, he would probably find something else about which to complain. He seems as though he is often unhappy or dissatisfied.

ADDITIONAL QUESTIONS AND ACTIVITIES

- Have students work in pairs in a mirroring activity. Students can take turns mirroring each other's actions. Remind students that if, for example, a students should make a gesture with his or her left hand, the other students should mirror it with his or her right.
- Have students brainstorm a list of ways in which mirrors are used. Some examples might be to aid drivers, by a dentist to examine teeth, for amusement at a fun house, and in stores to create attractive displays for merchandise.

1. Amaterasu thought the people
must have found a new sun to
replace her. She left the cave in
anger to reclaim her position.

LITERARY TECHNIQUE

A **myth** is a story that explains the
beginning of things in the natural
world. What natural events might
the story of Susanoo losing his
temper and Amaterasu hiding in a
cave explain?
Answers. Susanoo's tantrum might
explain a powerful storm that
destroyed the rice fields. Amaterasu's
disappearance might explain an
eclipse, the sun not being seen
because of a storm, or the warmth
and light of the sun being hidden by
heavy covers of smoke and ash from
a volcanic eruption.

Because Amaterasu was the sun goddess, this meant that the world was suddenly plunged into darkness. Without the sun's heat the land became very cold and nothing grew in field or forest. Worse still, the evil spirits took advantage of the darkness to get up to all sorts of wickedness. It was a disaster. Something had to be done, so all the good spirits gathered together in a dry river bed to try to decide what to do.

"We must tempt Amaterasu to come out of the cave," said one.

"And block up the entrance the minute she does, so she can't go back into it again," added another.

"But what would tempt her to come out?" asked a third.

"We must put everything she likes most outside," replied the first.

"And what does she like most?" the third asked.

"Seeing her sunny face reflected in the lake," answered a fourth.

"But we can't bring the lake up to the cave!" objected the third.

"Then we must make something that will reflect her face the way the lake does and put that outside the cave," suggested a fifth.

"I don't know what we could make that would do that," the third grumbled, "and anyway, how will she know it's there unless we can get her to come out of the cave in the first place?"

At that they all looked thoughtful. No one spoke for a while.

"I know!" the second suddenly shouted in triumph. "She always used to come out every morning as soon as she heard the cock crow. We must get all the cocks to crow outside the cave."

So they all put their heads together to try to think what would reflect the sun like the waters of the lake. After trying all sort of things in vain, they finally managed to invent a mirror, or looking-glass. This they hung from the branch of a japonica tree[1] immediately opposite the cave and, knowing Amaterasu's fondness for jewellery, they hung jewelled necklaces from the other branches.

When all was ready, they gathered outside the cave with every cock they could find. First they chanted prayers. Then they gave the signal and all the cocks began to crow. Not satisfied with that, everyone present began to sing and dance, led by the goddess Ama no Uzume[2] doing a tap-dance on an upturned tub.

Wondering what all the noise was about, Amaterasu peeped out of the cave and at once saw her own face reflected in the mirror. She had never seen a looking-glass before, so she thought the people must have found another sun to replace her and ran from the cave in a rage. The others immediately stretched ropes across the mouth of the cave to stop her from going back into it again, but there was no need. By then she had discovered that it was her own shining face looking back at her. She was delighted by this and by the necklaces, as well as the singing and dancing for, truth to tell, she had begun to feel lonely in her cave. So once more the sun's

GUIDED READING

What did
Amaterasu think
when she saw her
reflection? Why
did she leave the
cave?

1. **japonica tree.** Any tree, shrub, or plant associated with the far East
2. **Ama no Uzume.** Goddess of dawn and mirth

bright rays lit the earth and the trees and flowers and rice began to grow again in its heat. Then everyone suddenly remembered the cause of all the trouble.

"If Susanoo had stayed out of heaven when his father told him to, this would never have happened!" they shouted angrily, and went off in a body to look for him. When they found him, they cut off his pigtail as punishment and threw him out of heaven by force. ■

GUIDED READING
Who was blamed for the trouble? Do you think the blame was justly placed? Why, or why not?

Respond *to the* SELECTION

Can you recall a time when you felt you were treated unfairly by your parents or felt that your sibling was favored over you? How did you handle the situation?

About *the* AUTHOR

Carolyn Swift lives in Ireland and has written many books for young people. Her retellings of myths include *Irish Myths and Tales*. She has also written two series of novels known as the Bugsy and Robbers series. Swift has a love for the theater. Before she began writing full time, she worked as an actor and a stage manager.

INSIGHTS .... Ancient Japan

JAPANESE HISTORY. East of China lies the group of islands that make up Japan. The **Jomon** people probably came from mainland Asia around 10,000 BC, displacing the **Ainu**, a native people whose descendants today live on the Japanese island of **Hokkaido**. Japan is a mountainous country, and its geography led to the development of small, independent villages. In the years around AD 150, a priestess named **Himiko** united many of these villages under her rule and established contact and trade with China. This contact had enormous influence on Japan, which eventually adopted Chinese characters for writing the Japanese language. Around AD 200, the Yamato people of central Japan established control over much of the country. The **Yamato** rulers claimed to be descended from the sun goddess, Amaterasu, a claim that Japanese emperors continued into the twentieth century.

JAPANESE RELIGION AND CULTURE. The original religion of Japan, still practiced in much modified form, is called **Shinto**, which means "way of the gods." This religion involved worship of the spirits of nature and departed ancestors. Later the Japanese developed an adapted form of Buddhism known as **Zen Buddhism**. Japanese culture has had enormous influence around the world. Contributions include distinctive styles of poetry, such as **haiku**, varieties of theater known as Noh drama and Kabuki, and a unique, minimalist approach to art and design. The Zen art of flower arranging, known as *ikebana*, is an example of this minimalist approach, as are the sparse and beautiful Japanese gardens.

"AMATERASU" **519**

ANSWERS TO INVESTIGATE, INQUIRE, IMAGINE

RECALL

1a. Susanoo complains that he cannot visit his mother and that he was only given the seas to rule. Susanoo's father tells him to stay out of heaven because all Susanoo does is complain.

2a. Amaterasu breaks Susanoo's sword and makes it into three daughters. Susanoo makes five sons out of her necklace. Susanoo becomes destructive.

3a. Amaterasu is frightened by Susanoo's anger. They will get her attention by having cocks crow outside. They will draw her outside with a mirror.

INTERPRET

1b. Students' responses swill vary. Some may suggest that Susanoo is spoiled and selfish because he doesn't value being given the seas. Students may suggest he is jealous of Amaterasu and acts whiny because he is envious of her.

2b. Susanoo is competitive and has a quick temper. He is destructive when he is angry.

3b. Without the sun, the earth is cold and dark, plants don't grow, and evil spirits cause trouble. Amaterasu is happy about the trick because she was getting lonely inside the cave.

ANALYZE

4a. Susanoo tears up the rice fields Amaterasu had been ripening. The earth grows dark and cold and plants cannot grow. A storm or hurricane could cause the destruction Susanoo creates, and thick clouds covering the sun during such a storm would cause an effect similar to when Amaterasu is in the cave.

SYNTHESIZE

4b. Students may say the story is trying to explain why storms brew and cause destruction and why the sun disappears during such storms.

PERSPECTIVE

5a. Students may say they were not very fond of Susanoo and feared his temper. Students might point to the portrayal of Susanoo as easily upset and angry. Students may be divided on whether this decision was a fair one.

EMPATHY

5b. Responses will vary, but some students may suggest that being god of the sea is hardly a meager position and that Susanoo is trying to cause trouble for very little reason.

Investigate, *Inquire,* and Imagine

Recall: GATHERING FACTS

1a. About what does Susanoo complain? What does Susanoo's father tell him?

2a. What does Amaterasu do with Susanoo's sword? What does he do with her necklaces? What does Susanoo do after their argument?

3a. Why does Amaterasu hide in the cave? What plan do the good spirits develop to draw her out?

→ **Interpret:** FINDING MEANING

1b. Why do you think Susanoo acts this way?

2b. What does this incident indicate about Susanoo's character?

3b. Why are the good spirits concerned about Amaterasu staying in the cave? Does Amaterasu mind being tricked? Why, or why not?

Analyze: TAKING THINGS APART

4a. What does Susanoo do when he is angry? What happens when Amaterasu goes into the cave? What natural occurrences might cause these results?

→ **Synthesize:** BRINGING THINGS TOGETHER

4b. What might this story be trying to explain about the natural world?

Perspective: LOOKING AT OTHER VIEWS →

5a. How do you think the people who first told this story felt about Susanoo? How can you tell? Do you agree with the gods' opinion of Susanoo, and their decision to throw him out of heaven? Why, or why not?

Empathy: SEEING FROM INSIDE

5b. If you were in Susanoo's place, how would you feel about not being able to see your mother and about being chosen as god of the sea rather than god of the sky? In what way would you handle the situation? Explain.

Understanding *Literature*

CHARACTERIZATION. Characterization is the act of creating a character. Writers create characters by direct description, words and actions of the character, and the character's internal states. Create another cluster chart like the one you made for Amaterasu, and fill in information you learn from the story about Susanoo. How does the writer create the character Susanoo?

CONFLICT. A **conflict** is a struggle between two people or things in a literary work. Describe the conflict in "Amaterasu." How does the conflict begin? How is it resolved?

Answers to Understanding Literature can be found on page 521.

for your READING LIST

Heroes and Monsters of Greek Myth, by Bernard and Dorothy Evslin and Ned Hoopes, is a collection of some of the most exciting stories of Greek mythology. The courage and quick thinking of these heroes help them defeat all manner of hideous and terrifying monsters and overcome incredible obstacles to win their rewards—the riches of a kingdom and its throne, the hand of a beautiful princess in marriage, or security from a terrible enemy. Among others, you will read of Perseus and his quest to slay the terrible Medusa, and of Theseus who frees Athens from the burden of sacrificing its young to be devoured by the Minotaur. You will also read about the greed of King Midas and the foolish ambition of Icarus, who tried to fly like the birds. The writing in this collection is as crisp and exciting as the best adventure novel and these stories, thousands of years old, are anything but stale. When you have finished this book, you will understand why they have survived so long and continue to intrigue us.

CREATE A LITERATURE AUDIOTAPE

Books on tape are becoming a very popular way to enjoy literature in our increasingly busy society. For those who are unable to read for themselves, such as the disabled or people with vision problems, audiotaped literature may be the best option. Working with a small group, choose several selections and create an audiotape of the literature.

To begin, decide on your audience. Will you direct your tape towards nursing home shut-ins, young children, struggling readers, or another audience? This decision will help you to choose the literature and will help you determine your reading speed and tone of voice.

Next, review the Language Arts Survey 4.1, "Verbal and Nonverbal Communication," and 3.3, "Register, Tone and Voice." Your verbal clarity and the inflection and expression you use will have a tremendous impact on your listener's experience. Language Arts Survey 4.19, "Oral Interpretation of Poetry" may also be helpful.

Practice your readings several times, aloud, giving each other feedback on such factors as clarity, expression, and volume. Consider having each member of the circle perform one reading in order to introduce some variety.

When you have taped the final product, donate it to an organization which can put it in the hands of the appropriate listeners.

Other books you may want to read:
Adventures of the Greek Heroes by Mollie McLean and Anne Wilseman
Illustrated Book of Mythology: Heros, Heroines and Goddesses from Around the World by Philip Wilkinson and Neil Philip

Heroes and Monsters of Greek Myth introduces young readers to Greek mythology. Students love the interesting and unusual characters contained in the myths, such as courageous Perseus and quick-thinking Theseus. Readers learn a new side of Daedalus, the father of Icarus. The final stories of Atalanta, King Midas, and Pygmalion reveal themes of love and greed that parallel contemporary life. *Adventures of the Greek Heroes* tells the myths of six Greek heroes in a simple, straightforward style. According to the *School Library Journal*, "This is the authors' answer to the need they found in their teaching experience for easy versions of Greek hero tales, and the result is most successful . . . vigorous and appealing. Included are Hercules, Perseus, Theseus, Orpheus, Meleager, and Jason."

Create a Literature Audiotape
Blackline masters are available in the Language, Grammar, and Style Resource for the Language Arts Survey 3.3, "Register, Tone, and Voice" and in the Speaking and Listening Resource for Language Arts Survey 4.1, "Verbal and Nonverbal Communication." Before students make their audiotape, they might pick up successful tips by listening to the selections in the unit recorded in the Audio Library. For their selections, students might pick myths that are not covered in this unit.

ANSWERS TO UNDERSTANDING LITERATURE

CHARACTERIZATION. Students may note details such as the following: always complaining, jealous that Amaterasu is given position of goddess of the sun and the jeweled necklace of heaven, father says "I don't want to see your face around heaven anymore . . . there's no need for you to make all our lives misery up here," made god of the sea and corals, wants to say goodbye to Amaterasu, breaks Amaterasu's necklace into five sons after she breaks his sword, loses his temper and becomes destructive, frightens his sister with his anger, has his pigtail cut off and is thrown out of heaven by force.

ANSWERS TO UNDERSTANDING LITERATURE (CONT.)

CONFLICT. The conflict is between Amaterasu the sun goddess and her brother Susanoo god of the sea because his jealousy and resentment of her leads him to behave destructively frightening Amaterasu into a cave. The conflict begins when Susanoo, in a bad mood, makes the earth shake as he walks, alarming Amaterasu so much that she pulls out a weapon and views her brother with suspicion. It is resolves when the other gods and good spirits lure Amaterasu out of the cave and throw Susanoo from heaven as punishment.

LESSON OVERVIEW

GUIDED WRITING
Software

See the Guided Writing Software for an extended version of this lesson that includes printable graphic organizers, extensive student models and student-friendly checklists, and self-, peer, and teacher evaluation features.

INDIVIDUAL LEARNING STRATEGIES

MOTIVATION
Tell a family story of your own to motivate students. Then discuss with students what makes your story memorable.

READING PROFICIENCY
Have students read the Language Arts Survey 1.9, "Reading Textbooks." Review the parts of a book with students. Then go over the organization of this textbook. Ask students to identify the parts of a unit. Students should realize that Guided Writing is an integral part of each unit.

ENGLISH LANGUAGE LEARNERS
See strategies for Reading Proficiency above that will also benefit students who are English

---

> "Each family, however modest its origin, possesses its own particular tale of the past—a tale which can bewitch us with as great a sense of insistent romance as can ever the traditions of kings."
>
> —Llewelyn Powys

Professional Model

from "Amaterasu" by Geraldine Harris, page 517

Hearing all the noise, Amaterasu was frightened. She took up her bow and arrow so that, when her younger brother arrived, he found himself facing the drawn bow of a fierce-looking warrior.

"You can put that thing down," he told her. "I come in peace."

"Prove it," she said suspiciously, not taking her eyes off him.

Susanoo handed her his sword. She took it from him and broke it into three pieces. Then, before he could complain, she blew on them and turned them into three beautiful little girls.

"One day these three little daughters of mine will bring new life into the world," she told him, "while your sword

---

Guided Writing

RETELLING A FAMILY STORY

One night after dinner, Emil announced that he had to write a story about his family for a class assignment. "But," he lamented, "nothing interesting has ever happened to this family!" His grandma looked at him and said, "Emil, do you know the story of how our family came to America years ago?" Emil nodded; he had heard the story many times. Then his dad added, "Do you remember what happened last year on our camping trip? That would be a story to tell!" Emil nodded again. He realized he not only had family stories that had been passed down for generations, he also had stories from his everyday life.

You, too, may have heard stories that your family tells over and over. They may be the stories handed down over generations or the stories about what happens to you and your brothers and sisters each day. You can preserve one of these stories by writing it down.

Reflecting

Before you begin to write your family story, consider what makes a story worth telling and retelling. Think about the best story you have ever heard. What made that particular story so memorable? What was the mood of the story? How did the storyteller use dialogue to enrich the story? What did the storyteller do to keep your attention? You can use your ideas to help you choose the story you want to preserve.

EXAMINING THE MODEL. In "Amaterasu," Geraldine Harris uses dialogue to create suspense in such a way that the reader wants to know what will happen next. She creates for us exactly what they say, and how they say it. Harris not only gives us the words of Susanoo and Amaterasu, but descriptions of how they speak and what gestures they use.

Read the dialogue in the Professional Model and identify how each character speaks to the other. What does Amaterasu do when she tells Susanoo to "prove it"? At what point does her brother boast? How does Amaterasu respond when Susanoo turns the five necklaces into five sons? Carefully written dialogue not only builds suspense, it also moves the plot forward. Readers want to know what Susanoo and Amaterasu will both do as result of the argument the dialogue reveals.

INDIVIDUAL LEARNING STRATEGIES (CONT.)

language learners. Encourage non-native speakers to share a story that reveals an aspect of their culture. Have students share their stories with the rest of the class. You might pair each English Language Learner with a native speaker who can help the non-native speaker with words and phrases he or she is having trouble with. Ask the advice of your school's ESL teacher for additional ideas.

SPECIAL NEEDS
Students with special needs might need help selecting a family story. You might help them pinpoint a story by talking with them informally. Students may need help completing their Graphic Organizer. Pair them with another student who can help them work through the format by asking relevant questions. (Continued on page 523)

Prewriting

IDENTIFYING YOUR AUDIENCE. The audience for your story is your family, your relatives, and other people you know who may be interested in one of your family's stories. Since you are preserving a part of your family's history, you will want to craft a strong, accurate, and well-written story that your family and others can enjoy reading for years.

FINDING YOUR VOICE. The voice you use to tell your family story should reflect your genuine interest in an authentic story. You will also want your voice to reflect the mood of your story.

To practice finding your voice, think of something funny that happened to your family. On your own paper, write a few sentences to create a lighthearted and upbeat mood.

Try finding your voice again, but think of something serious that happened in your family. Write a few sentences to create a serious or somber mood.

One way you can have some fun finding your voice is to visualize the gestures, posture and expressions you would use as you tell a story to your extended family.

- What would your posture be like as you told your story?
- What room of the house would you be in?
- What expression would others see on your face?
- What expression would you see on your family's faces?

Write a few more sentences to practice finding your voice. Before you begin writing this time, visualize a scary event that your family experienced. Did visualizing your gestures, posture, and expressions help you find the voice for your story?

Writing with a Plan

Perhaps you already have a story in mind that you can write. If you need an idea, close your eyes and tap into a memory you have about your family. The memory can be serious, suspenseful, funny, sad, or joyful. As you visualize the memory, try to recall all the events that were associated with the memory. What was the first event that occurred? What events happened next? What was the last event? Try to recall some lively details about each event.

Next, think about the dialogue that contributed to this story. What did people say that was important? Last, think about how the events have affected your family.

Taj generated ideas about his family story by filling in the graphic organizer on the next page.

Drafting

As you write your rough draft, try visualizing your story as a video playing in your head. For now, you do not have to focus on spelling or mechanics. Instead, concentrate on getting your story down in the order that it happened. Remember to include lively details about each event and add lots of dialogue to move

could only have brought death."

"I can do better than that!" Susanoo boasted. "Give me the necklaces you're wearing."

So Amaterasu unclasped the five necklaces and gave them to her brother. Then he blew on them and turned them into five little boys.

"Now I have five sons," he said.

"They were made out of my necklaces so they should be my sons!" Amaterasu snapped.

"But your daughters were made from my sword," Susanoo argued.

"That's different!" Amaterasu told him.

At that Susanoo lost his temper. He tore up all the rice fields that Amaterasu had been carefully ripening and caused such destruction that the frightened goddess ran and hid in a cave, blocking the entrance with a large stone.

> "Trust that still, small voice that says, 'This might work and I'll try it.'"
> —Diane Mariechild

IDENTIFYING YOUR AUDIENCE. If students are writing for their families, they will not need to supply as much background information as if they are writing for an audience unfamiliar with the characters and the story. Have students read the Language Arts Survey 2.4, "Identifying Your Audience." Encourage students to use vocabulary with which their audience will be familiar. Words and phrases particular to their family will need to be explained.

FINDING YOUR VOICE. Encourage students to read the Language Arts Survey 2.5, "Finding Your Voice," and 3.3, "Register, Tone, and Voice."

WRITING WITH A PLAN. Have students write out any questions they might have about the story they want to tell. Encourage them to talk to family members to get their questions answered and to get their perspective on what happened. Students will benefit from freewriting. Ask them to read the Language Arts Survey 2.12, "Freewriting." Students who have made up their minds about which story they want to tell should do focused freewriting.

Drafting

Encourage students to use their completed Graphic Organizer modeled on page 524 to help them make sure they are including all the pertinent information. Have students write a discovery draft in which they do not focus on spelling, grammar, usage, and mechanics. Students might benefit from reading the Language Arts Survey 2.31, "Drafting."

INDIVIDUAL LEARNING STRATEGIES (CONT.)

ENRICHMENT
In small groups encourage students to verbalize what characteristics come through about their family members in their story and ask them to share what valuable lessons their family members learned from the incident.

Examining the Model

Have students fill out a Character Attribute Chart for Susanoo and Amaterasu. Students should describe the characters' physical appearance, dress, habits/mannerisms/behaviors, relationships with other people, and other information. Then discuss with students how this information makes the characters come alive. Tell students that they can adapt this chart when they reach the prewriting stage.

Reflecting

Encourage students to visualize possible stories they want to tell. They might write a journal entry about one or two stories that have the most potential.

Language, Grammar, and Style

Punctuating Dialogue
LESSON OVERVIEW
In this lesson, students will be asked to do the following:
- Identify Correct Punctuation, 524
- Fix Punctuation Errors, 525
- Use Dialogue Correctly, 525

INTRODUCING THE SKILL. Remind students that using dialogue effectively will help their stories come alive. You might ask students to open their books to any page of any story and ask them to identify what percentage of the story is in dialogue. Students might make a list of tag lines used in the story they picked.

PREVIEWING THE SKILL. Refer students to the Language Arts Survey 3.86, "Quotation Marks." Ask students to alternate reading the examples on page 910 out loud with a partner.

PRACTICING THE SKILL. For additional practice, have students work through the exercise in the following section of the Language, Grammar, and Style Resource located in the Teacher's Resource Kit: 3.86, "Quotation Marks."

Self- and Peer Evaluation
Have students use the checklist on page 525 for self- and peer evaluation. See the Guided Writing Resource located in the Teacher's Resource Kit for a blackline master of the checklist. The checklist is intended to act as a student-friendly rubric that should help students identify specific evidence of writing strengths and areas needing improvement. Make sure students provide concrete suggestions for improvement or specific evidence of the effectiveness of their family story. Students might benefit from reading the Language Arts Survey 2.37-2.40 for more details about self-evaluation and peer evaluation.

Language, Grammar, and Style
Punctuating Dialogue

IDENTIFYING CORRECT PUNCTUATION. When you use a person's exact words in your writing, you are using a direct quotation. Enclose the words of a direct quotation in quotation marks.

EXAMPLES

"Can you punctuate dialogue correctly?" asked the teacher.

"I get mixed up at times," Taj responded.

"I used to get mixed up punctuating dialogue, too. Then I learned a few guidelines that helped me punctuate dialogue correctly," the teacher commented.

A direct quotation should always begin with a capital letter. Separate a direct quotation from the rest of the sentence with a comma, quotation mark, or exclamation point. Do not separate the direct quotation from the rest of the sentence with a period. Sentences of dialogue within the quotation marks are still set off with periods. A punctuation mark that belongs to the direct quotation itself should be placed inside the quotation marks.

Student Model—Graphic Organizer

Family Story
Memory: joining my family

Beginning event
four months old flew from Korea to Minnesota

Middle events
dealing with kids — where's your real mom and dad?
dealing with adults — do you have your own kids?
my parents are real parents
wondering what my birthparents are like
feeling sad and mad
hoping to meet my birthparents someday

Ending event
our family celebrating my adoption

Dialogue to enhance story
Strangers: "Where's your real mom and dad?"
Me: "My parents are about as real as parents get."
Dad: "They just don't know that adoption is a great way to become a family, so we have to educate them!"

Lively details to enhance story
flying from Korea
Mom and Dad excited
grandpa videotaping
feeling like an alien from the moon
Mom getting steamed
my birthparents-- funny and artistic
adoption celebration
Puri
pulgolgi

Why this story is significant for my family
It helps people understand that adoption is a great way to become a family.

your story forward. If you are writing about a story that happened to your family generations ago, you may add the dialogue that you think they might have said. Use the details from your graphic organizer to guide you as you write the rough draft.

Self- and Peer Evaluation
After finishing your rough draft, you can do a self-evaluation of your work. If time allows, you may want to get one or two peer evaluations. See the Language Arts Survey 2.37–2.40 for more details about self-evaluation and peer evaluation. You might also ask someone in your family to help you evaluate your story. As you evaluate your draft, ask yourself these questions:
- What makes this family story memorable?
- What part of the story will engage readers the most? Why?
- How does dialogue enhance your story?
- Where could you add dialogue to move the story forward?
- What is the mood of your story?
- Which details help show the mood of your story?

- What other details could you add to enrich the mood of your story?
- What type of transition words could you add to make your story flow from beginning to end?

Look at Taj's self and peer evaluation of his rough draft, in which he tells about being adopted.

Student Model—Draft

This is plain. Can you make it more interesting?

Families start and grow different ways.

As most of you already know, I'm adopted. I flew all the way from Korea to Minnesota. Mom and Dad were so *How old were you?* excited when the jet pulled into the gate, Then they had to wait until everyone else came off the plane. Finally, I got off the plane. Mom was happy. My grandpa videotaped *Do you have more details about what this was like?* everything.

People don't know much about *Which people?* adoption. I had a friend back in first *Good!* grade who kept asking, "You're adopted?" in a way that made me feel like I was an alien from the moon! Sometimes kids ask me, "Where's your real mom and dad?" Sometimes we're shopping in the grocery store and people say to Mom, "Do you have kids of your own?" You should see

---

Identify the direct quotation in each example below:

"Your golf game has really improved," Avram remarked. "I've never seen anything like it."

Joy asked, "Have you seen my red blouse?"

"He's out at third!" yelled the umpire.

"When I tell my dog to shake, he rolls over. When I tell him to rollover, he sits. He is a silly dog," Katrina said with a laugh.

FIXING PUNCTUATION ERRORS. Look at the examples below. Correct any errors in punctuation and capitalization that you see.

Victor lamented. "I wish Uncle Don were here."

"Did I turn off the iron?" Wondered Mrs. Cameron.

"hey." Allison called, "wait for me!"

Look at the dialogue in Taj's partly revised draft. Try to identify and fix any errors in the punctuation of the dialogue.

USING DIALOGUE CORRECTLY. Examine the dialogue you have used in your family story. Be sure that each quotation begins with a capital letter and is enclosed in quotation marks.

continued on page 526

Teaching Note

Have students compare the Student Model—Draft on page 525 with the final version presented on page 527. What improvements did Taj make? In what ways could the Student Model—Revised be further improved?

Revising and Proofreading
Remind students that revising includes adding or expanding, cutting or condensing, replacing, and moving text. Have students read the Language Arts Survey 2.41, "Revising." A handout of the proofreading checklist found in the Language Arts Survey on page 888 is available in the Teacher's Resource Kit, Guided Writing Resource Book 2.45. Students or family members critiquing the writer's work might be interested in using common proofreader's symbols, which are found in the Language Arts Survey 2.44, "Using Proofreader's Marks."

Next, check to be sure you have used an appropriate tag line for each quotation. In the example below, the tag line goes overboard in an attempt to use vivid language.

"Shall I go now?" Mrs. Marks queried icily.

Last, check to see if your tag lines are believable. In the example below, the tag line is not believable. The dialogue "I guess so" suggests that Adrian is unsure, but the tagline "demanded" says that Adrian is forcing his point.

"I guess so," Adrian demanded.

"Be proud of your written work. Dot the i's and cross the t's. Neatness grows from dotted i's and crossed t's into beautiful pages."
—William Armstrong

Mom! She gets so steamed! Dad tells me "they just don't know that adoption is a great way to become a family, so we have to educate them!" Sometimes I wonder what my birthparents are like.

Why were you adopted?

At times, I feel sad and mad that I don't know more about them. Dad says they are probably funny and artistic— just like me. I hope I meet them someday.

details to add: couldn't take care of baby loved me - made an adoption plan

Each year on November 13ᵗʰ , we celebrate my adoption. We listen to our favorite Korean music cd Puri. Then we eat a meal of pulgolgi and rice and rice candy and a fancy cake. I like being part of my family.

What's this?

Anything you want other people to know?

Revising and Proofreading

As you consider your self-evaluation and your peer and family reviews, think about changes that will make your story more effective. Make the revisions, then proofread your story for errors in spelling, grammar, usage, punctuation, capitalization, and paragraph form. See the Language Arts Survey 2.45, "A Proofreading Checklist," for help.

After reviewing his story and considering his own and his dad's evaluation notes, Taj revised his story.

Student Model—Revised

Families start and grow in different ways. The way my family started is special to me and my parents. I joined our family when I was four months old. I flew all the way from Korea to Minnesota and I was one tired baby when I finally got to the airport. Mom and Dad were so excited when the Northwest Airlines jet pulled into the gate. They had to wait until everyone else came off the plane. Finally, I was carried from the plane. Mom was so happy she cried when she held me for the first time. My grandpa videotaped everything.

Some of my friends don't know much about adoption. I had a friend back in first grade who kept asking, "You're adopted?" in a way that made me feel like I was an alien from the moon! Sometimes kids ask me, "Where's your real mom and dad?" I tell them, "My mom and dad are about as real as parents get!" Sometimes we're shopping in the grocery store and people say to Mom, "Do you have kids of your own?" You should see Mom! She gets so steamed! Dad tells me, "They just don't know that adoption is a great way to become a family, so we have to educate them!"

Sometimes I wonder what my birthparents are like. At times, I feel sad and mad that I don't know more about them. Dad says they are probably funny and artistic just like me. I know they couldn't take care of a baby back then. They loved me though and made an adoption plan for me. I hope I meet them someday.

Each year on November 13th, we celebrate my adoption. We listen to our favorite Korean music CD, *Puri*. Then we eat a meal of pulgolgi (Korean barbecued beef) and rice, and have rice candy and a fancy cake for dessert. I think it's great that I can have cake on my birthday and on my adoption anniversary! The celebration is our way to say that adoption is a great way to become a family.

Publishing and Presenting

Write or print a final copy of your story. Create a cover and add any family pictures that might help illustrate the story. You can read the stories in class or duplicate a copy of the book for each student to take home. If you have access to e-mail, send a copy of your story to family members who may be located in other cities or states or even around the world.

Publishing and Presenting
Have students share their stories orally in small groups. Ask the advisor of your school newspaper if he or she would be interested in printing one of the family stories in the next edition of the paper. Then hold a contest and have students vote on the best story to include. Students might also be interested in printing all the class stories; they could include family photos to accompany the stories.

UNIT SEVEN
review

Review: Words for Everyday Use

Check your knowledge of the following vocabulary words. For each word, write a short sentence that includes the word in context. To review a word, look back to the page number indicated.

- abyss (494)
- avenge (475)
- barren (475)
- cleft (475)
- constellation (510)
- cosmic (509)
- cower (485)
- cunning (493)
- deity (493)
- demur (483)
- disillusioned (510)
- drivel (493)
- drought (509)

- ebb (485)
- envoy (494)
- eternity (509)
- exalt (493)
- grandiose (509)
- infinite (509)
- intolerable (485)
- manifestation (511)
- meditate (510)
- mission (510)
- oppress (482)
- privilege (511)
- quiver (494)

- radiantly (511)
- root (475)
- sole (493)
- strew (484)
- summon (494)
- talon (484)
- tempestuous (483)
- transgressor (486)
- vain (483)
- virile (494)
- wrest (486)

Review: Literary Tools

Define each of the following terms, giving concrete examples when possible. To review a term, refer to the page number indicated.

- central conflict (481)
- characterization (515)
- conflict (515)
- inciting incident (491)

- internal conflict (507)
- irony (481)
- motif (500)
- motive (491)

- myth (473)
- oral tradition (500)
- setting (473)
- symbol (507)

Reflecting *on your* reading

Genre

This unit includes **myths** from various cultures. A myth is a traditional story that explains objects or events in the natural world. These explanations revolve around the actions of supernatural forces, such as gods. Myths were part of the oral tradition in every early culture around the world. An **oral tradition** is a work, idea, or custom passed by word of mouth from generation to generation. Consider carefully for a few minutes how stories of the oral tradition differ from all other genres in literature. What role do you think storytelling played in cultures that carried on the oral tradition? Who do you think told the stories in these culture groups? Why? What effects might the printing of stories have had on the stories themselves and on a culture that had previously passed on its stories orally? What are some of the common traits of mythical characters? What types of obstacles do mythical characters often face?

Theme

A **theme** is a central idea in a literary work. A **motif** is anything that appears repeatedly in one or more works of literature, art, or music. Often, the use of motif contributes to developing and communicating the theme of a work. Reflect on the selections you have read in this unit, and choose a myth that demonstrates use of one of the following motifs: seasonal change, arrogance, greed. Explain how the motif is revealed in the myth and how it relates to possible themes in the myth.

Group Project & Art Smart

In small groups, carefully examine John George Brown's painting, "A Tough Story," on pages 470–471. Brainstorm a list of specific visual details in the painting and then write your ideas about how these details might be interpreted. Choose one or two words that describe the mood of this painting.

On Your Own

Think about some of the stories in your life that are told over and over again. Most likely, you have a collection of favorite stories shared among friends and family members. Choose one of these stories and write it down. Which of the types of oral tradition does your story most resemble? Come up with a title for your story and create a front cover for it that includes the title and any visual elements you choose.

W. J. Aylward

GOALS/OBJECTIVES

Studying this unit will enable students to
- enjoy reading short stories and a novella
- define and identify examples of such literary concepts and techniques as *character, characterization, description, dialogue, first- and third-person point of view, foreshadowing, mood, novella, plot, setting,* and *theme*

- engage in a meaningful independent reading experience by reading a short story anthology and hosting a book review show
- write an informative essay in which they interpret literature
- demonstrate an ability to edit wordy sentences and write in clear and direct sentences

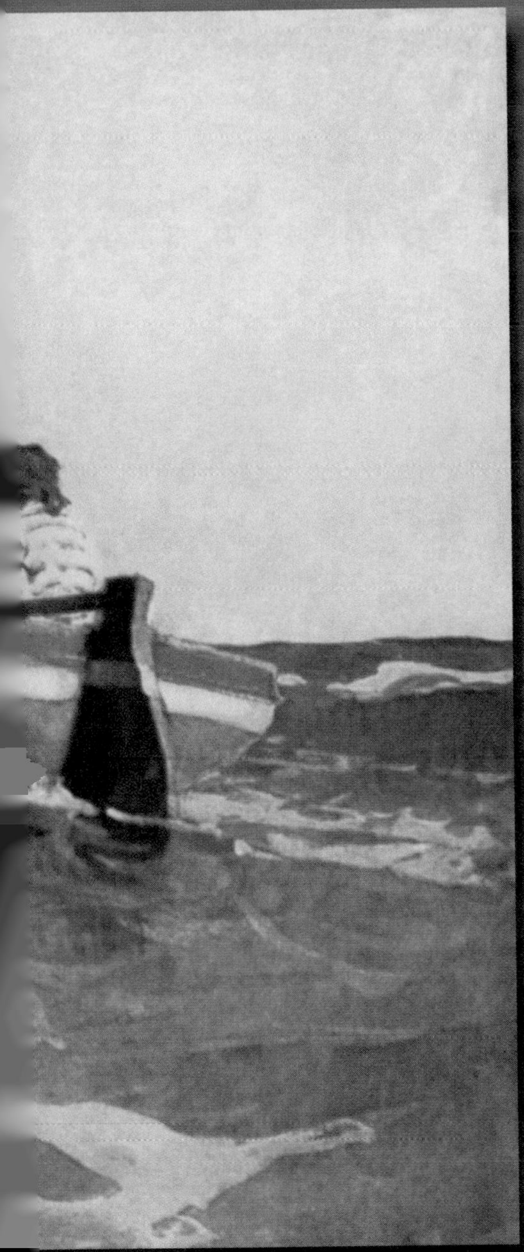

Stories to TELL: FICTION

UNIT EIGHT

(Continued on page 532)

ELEMENTS *of* FICTION

FICTION. Fiction is prose created from the imagination. Prose is writing that uses straightforward language and that differs from poetry in that it doesn't have a rhythmic pattern. Fiction is usually narrative. Narrative writing is that which tells a story. Works of fiction usually contain the elements of character, plot, setting, and theme.

CHARACTER. A **character** is a person (or sometimes an animal) who takes part in the action of a literary work. A *protagonist* is the main character in a story. An *antagonist* is a character who struggles against the main character. A *major character* is one who plays an important role in a literary work. A *minor character* is one who plays a lesser role. A *one-dimensional character*, or flat character, reveals only one quality or character trait. A *three-dimensional character* seems to have all the complexities of an actual human being.

Characters come alive in fiction through **characterization**. Characterization is the act of creating a character. A writer creates characters in three ways—1) by showing what characters say, do, and think; 2) by showing what other characters say about them and 3) by showing what physical features, dress, and personality the characters display.

PLOT. The **plot** of a work of fiction is the series of events or situations related to a *central conflict*, or struggle. The conflict can be internal or external. An *internal conflict* takes place within a character. An *external conflict* is a struggle between a character and an outside force, such as another character, society, or nature.

A plot usually contains the introduction of a conflict, its development, and its eventual resolution. A story may begin with *exposition*—the introduction of the setting and characters. The *inciting incident* is the event that introduces the central conflict. The highest point of suspense in the story is the *climax*. The *crisis*, or turning point, is the point in the story where something happens to decide the future course of events. The *resolution* is the point at which the central conflict ends. The *dénouement* is any final material that finishes the story. Plots are often illustrated using a pyramid.

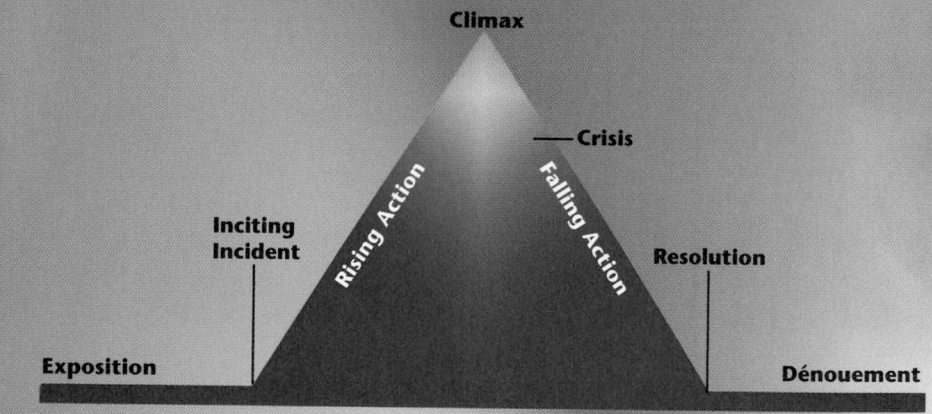

SETTING. The **setting** of a work of fiction (or any other literary work) is the time and place in which it happens. In fiction, the setting is often revealed through the description of the landscape, buildings, rooms, scenery, weather, and season. Setting reveals important information about the time period, geographical location, cultural environment, and physical conditions in which the characters live. These distinctions affect how the reader interprets a character's views and actions. For example, a scene with teenagers dancing in public would seem surprising in 17th-century New England but not in 20th-century Chicago.

THEME. A **theme** of a work of fiction is a central idea. Theme is different from subject. A subject of a work is its topic, such as "horses," "friendship," or "tornadoes." A theme is a broad statement about a topic, such as "animals can be our most loyal companions," "friends are worth more than money," or "tornadoes might destroy buildings but not communities." Many stories share the same subject but have different themes because they make unique statements about that subject.

In identifying a story's theme, keep the following things in mind. A story may have more than one theme. Two readers of the same story may state its theme or themes in different ways, and both may be correct. Describing theme can be a useful means of clarifying your thinking about the story.

OTHER ELEMENTS. Other elements that influence and shape a work of fiction include mood and point of view. *Mood*, or atmosphere, is the emotion created in the reader by a piece of writing. A writer creates a mood by using *concrete details*—words describing how something looks, sounds, smells, tastes, or feels. *Point of view* is the vantage point from which a story is told.

TYPES OF FICTION. Short stories, novels, and novellas are all types of fiction. A **short story** is a brief work of fiction that contains a definite beginning, middle, and end. Although it contains all the main elements of fiction—character, setting, plot, and theme—it may not fully develop each element. A **novel** is a long work of fiction that usually has more complex elements than a short story. Its longer format allows the elements of fiction to be more fully developed. A **novella** is a work of fiction that is longer than a typical short story but shorter than a typical novel. The main elements of fiction are usually more fully developed than in a short story yet not as developed as in a full-length novel.

Some people view fiction in terms of subject matter and define short stories and novels as works of historical fiction, science fiction, westerns, romances, or any of a number of additional categories.

ADDITIONAL RESOURCES

UNIT 8 RESOURCE BOOK
• Selection Worksheet 8.1
• Selection Check Test 4.8.1
• Selection Test 4.8.2

READER'S JOURNAL

Encourage students to explore why they enjoy this place so much and to use sensory details in their journal entries to help capture this place and why it is special.

READER'S TOOLBOX

Setting. Setting is extremely important to this story. The title of the selection foreshadows this. This short piece compares two physical landscapes, and it is through this comparison that the reader gains insight to the character of Leona.
Mood. *Responses will vary.* Some possible responses include: lonely, homesick, melancholy, pensive, wistful, somber. Note: Some students may have difficulty capturing mood with language. Encourage them to come up with a word or two that comes close, then refer them to a thesaurus. Branching out from the words they start with, they should be able to find words that aptly describe their thoughts on the mood of this selection.

Reader's Journal

Think of one of your favorite places to be. In what ways does being there affect your mood? What do you do when you are there?

Reader's TOOLBOX

SETTING. The **setting** of a literary work is the time and place in which it happens. Setting in a literary work is revealed by details that describe the environment in which the story takes place—a particular landscape, season, town, or room, for example. Setting can be used to compare or contrast different experiences or situations. It can also be used to show the passing of time, to create mood, and to develop characters and plot. As you read, consider how important setting is in this story.

MOOD. Mood is the feeling or emotion that the writer creates in a literary work. By working carefully with descriptive language, the writer can evoke in the reader an emotional response such as fear, longing, or anticipation. As you read, think about the mood the author creates in the story and write a word or phrase to describe the mood.

Prereading

"The Ground is Always Damp"
by Luci Tapahonso

Reader's Resource

• **GEOGRAPHY CONNECTION.** Northwestern New Mexico features a dramatic landscape of river valleys, mountain ranges, desert and mesas. At its northwest border New Mexico shares a common point with Colorado, Utah, and Arizona known as the Four Corners. If you stand at this point, you can boast that you are in four states at the same time. The Navajo Nation, with a population of about 200,000 people, is the largest American Indian nation in the United States. Navajo lands span almost 3 million acres across Utah, New Mexico, and Arizona.

• **HISTORY CONNECTION.** The term *Navajo* comes from the Tewa Indian word for "large area of cultivated land." The Navajo people refer to themselves as *Diné,* which means "the people." The Navajo peoples moved into the area that is now New Mexico in the 1300s. They lived as a semi-nomadic group, traveling to hunt and planting corn in established locations. During the 1300s and 1400s, they became known as a band of raiders, attacking the Pueblo Indians and fighting Utes, Comanches, and other local groups. When Spanish *conquistadores* appeared in the area in the mid-1500s, they attempted to move the Native groups into missions and towns and to convert them to Christianity. Some groups complied, but the Navajo violently resisted these changes. Fiercely fighting the Spaniards and their Indian allies, the Navajo remained free and outside Spanish control for 200 years. In the mid- to late 1700s, the Navajo suffered losses due to fighting, and their crops were diminished from drought and destruction. Land grants allowed numerous Spanish settlers to establish ranches on Navajo lands.

• In 1821 Mexico declared its independence from Spain, but less than 30 years later—in 1848—New Mexico and the rest of the region that now makes up the Southwest became part of the United States. U.S. forces built Fort Defiance in Navajo country in 1851. Fighting between the U.S. forces and the Navajo continued until 1864, when the U.S. Army captured more than 8,000 Navajo and marched them 350 miles to Fort Sumner, where they were forced to remain in captivity. When released, the survivors were forced into a resevation that was one-tenth the size of their original lands and contained none of their best grazing lands or water resources.

GOALS/OBJECTIVES

Studying this lesson will enable students to
• enjoy a short story and relate to the narrator's feelings of homesickness
• briefly explain some major events in Navajo history
• define *setting* and recognize how setting contributes to a story

• define *mood* and identify the mood of a short story
• identify and classify sensory details
• use an atlas and the Internet for research
• record and share an oral story

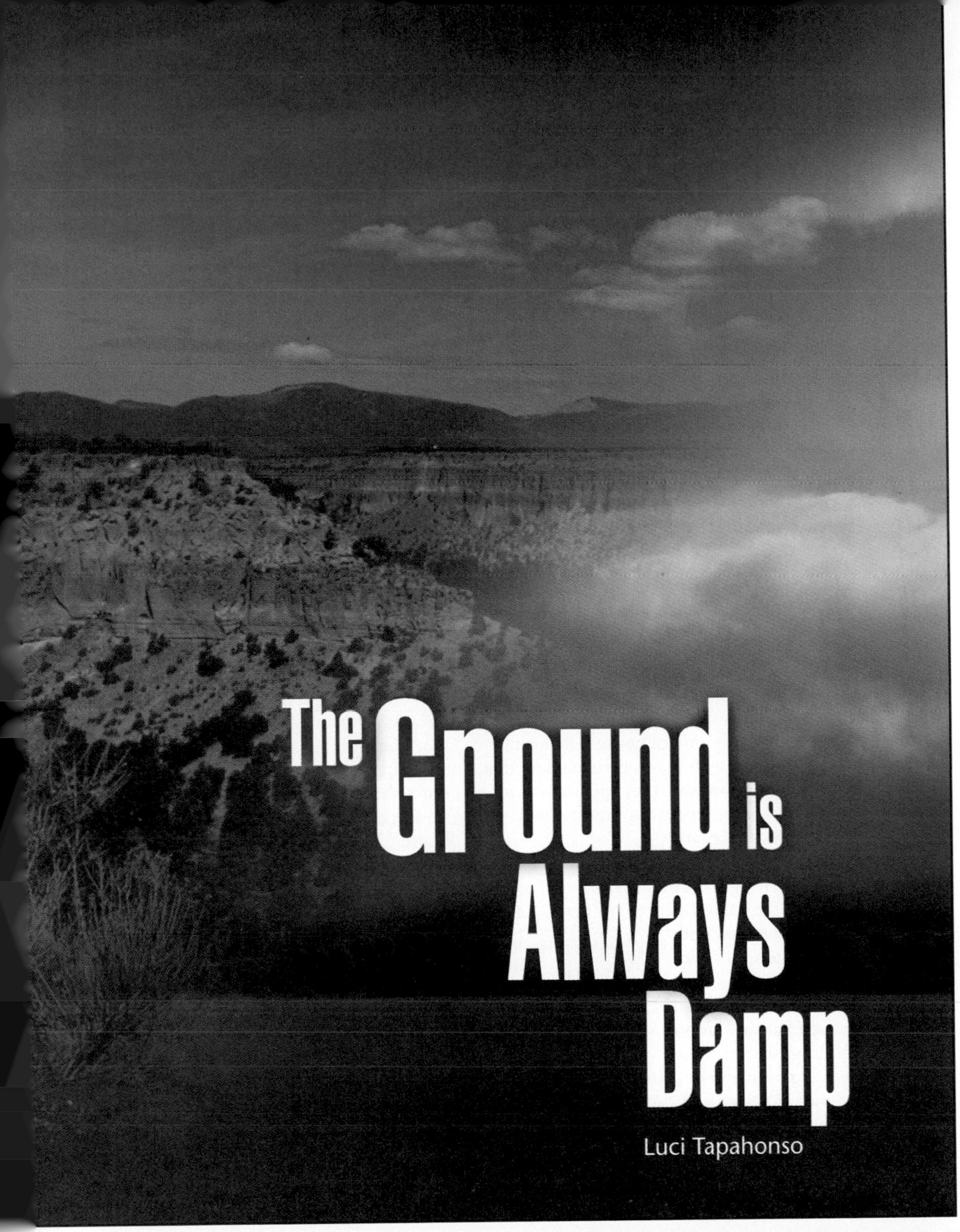

The Ground is Always Damp

Luci Tapahonso

INDIVIDUAL LEARNING STRATEGIES

Motivation
Students, especially those who are not from or have not been to New Mexico, may enjoy seeing photographs of the landscape of Mexico in particular and the Southwest in general. Share photographs, postcards, and brochures featuring the landscape of New Mexico with students.

Reading Proficiency
Some of the place names in this short story will be difficult for students. Share pronunciations with them. Students may benefit from hearing the story read aloud. Have them close their eyes and try to imagine the places and scenes Leona is describing.

English Language Learning
Point out the following vocabulary words and expressions

familiarity—close association
sift—pass through
turquoise—greenish-blue, colored like se semiprecious stone often used in Navajo silver work
dust storms—wind storm that sweeps up clouds of dust when passing along a dry region
horizon—line where the sky seems to meet the earth

Special Needs
Students may have trouble distinguishing the past and where Leona once lived from the present and where she lives now. Tell students to pay attention to introductory phrases such as "In her dreams," and "In contrast," which let the reader know that the writer may be shifting between settings. Tell them to focus on the Guided Reading questions as they read.

Enrichment
Students might work in pairs to research more about the arts and craft Navajo people still practice today. Each pair should choose one of the following topics and present a brief oral report on it:

- Navajo songs and chants (Students should locate a recording; a good place to start is in the world music section of their school, local library, or music store.)
- Navajo pottery (Some students may have access to an example of

INDIVIDUAL LEARNING STRATEGIES (CONT.)

Navajo pottery, as it is popular and collectible; if not, students should find photographs of Navajo pottery to share with others.)

- Navajo baskets (Again students should share images of Navajo baskets. Books on art and Native American vultures may be good sources; students can ask a local museum to point them toward good sources for images.)
- Navajo blankets and rugs (Students should find images of Navajo weaving to share.)
- Navajo silver work (Students should locate an image in one of the sources mentioned above. Magazines and catalogs with a Southwest focus also feature Navajo silver work on occasion.)

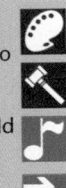

1. Leona dreams she was back at her parents' home.
2. Leona imagines that when she silently talks to her parents, they listen and respond with questions about and explanations of the things she tells and asks them.
3. When Leona dreams, she is always in New Mexico. She is driving to Taos, or watching harvest dances, or selling hay and watermelons with her brothers, and talking and joking in Navajo and English.
4. Where Leona is, the sky is gray.

CROSS-CURRICULAR ACTIVITIES

SOCIAL STUDIES & MATHEMATICS AND SCIENCES. Have students work in groups of four to plan an imaginary two-week Southwestern vacation. Students should begin by researching historical sites, interesting natural features, and other sites in states including New Mexico, Arizona, Utah, and Colorado. The group should vote and decide on a number of places they would like to visit. Students should then research and plan a travel itinerary, including transportation and lodging, keeping track of how much their imaginary trip might cost. Tell students that they must consider how long it takes to get from one place to another in planning their two weeks in the southwest. Students will find travel books (such as Let's Go and Fodor's) helpful. There is also a wealth of travel sites on the Internet that students might explore, and many are focused on specific types of trips, such as Southwestern travel. Inform students that they should not pay for information in their research through travel agents or other sources. (Of course, they should not actually book reservations or flights, either!) Students' final project should include a marked up map, marking the locations of the sites they plan on visiting, connected by lines showing the route they would take. They should provide brief written description of the places they want to see and explain why they think they would enjoy going there. They should also provide an itemized list that provides an estimate of how much their trio might cost, including plane fare, care rentals, lodging, and meal expenses.

One night Leona dreamt that she was sitting outside her parents' home in the bright sunlight. The many trees, the small dusty chickens scratching nearby, and a single cloud above cast sharp dark shadows on the smooth yard. The sudden familiarity of the detailed shadows and clean air startled and awakened her, and later she spoke aloud, addressing her mother who was hundreds of miles away.

> **GUIDED READING**
> What did Leona dream about one night?

"Shimá, my mother, it's cloudy here most of the time. The ground is always damp, and Mom, I don't care to kneel down and sift dirt through my fingers. One day last week, the sun came out for a few hours, and the shadows were soft and furry on the brown grass. That's the way it is here, my mother."

Even though Leona hadn't seen her parents in months, she talked to them silently every day. She imagined that they listened, then responded by explaining things or asking long, detailed questions. Leona did this thoughtfully and felt that they did the same in their daily conversations about her and her children. They wondered what the weather was like and what kind of house Leona and her family lived in. She was certain about this. The difference was that they spoke aloud to each other, or to the various brothers and sisters who lived nearby.

> **GUIDED READING**
> What does Leona imagine?

In her dreams, she was always there in New Mexico, driving the winding roads to Taos, watching the harvest dances at Laguna, or maybe selling hay and watermelons with her brothers. In her dreams, she laughed, talking and joking easily in Navajo and English. She woke herself up sometimes because she had laughed aloud, or said, "Aye-e-e"—that old familiar teasing expression.

> **GUIDED READING**
> When Leona dreams, where is she? What is she doing?

The New Mexico sky is clear and empty. It is a deep blue, almost turquoise, and Leona's family lives surrounded by the Carriso Mountains in the west, the Sleeping Ute Mountains in the north, the La Plata in the east and the Chuska Mountain range to the southwest.[1] They rely on the distance, the thin, clean air, and the mountains to alert them to rain, thunderstorms, dust storms, and intense heat. At various times, her brothers stand looking across the horizon to see what is in store. They can see fifty miles or more in each direction.

In contrast, when Leona looks to the east most mornings, the sky is gray, the air thick with frost, and the wind blows cold dampness.

"My mother, there are no mountains here, and I can't see very far because the air is thick and heavy with a scent I can't recognize. I haven't been able to smell the arrival of snow here, or to distinguish between the different kinds of rain scent. The rain seems all the same here, except in degree, and it is constant. Sometimes it lasts for two days and nights. It pours steadily until brown streams form and drain into the overflowing creek behind the house.

> **GUIDED READING**
> What is the sky like where Leona is?

"Shimá, some nights I just want to walk down the street and smell piñon[2] wood smoke, or stew or beans boiling when I pass a house." In the fall, we talk about the seasonal rituals at home. "Remember," we say, "fresh green chile roasting outside at Farmer's Market or outside of Smith's or Albertson's? When Grandma Acoma baked bread in the outside oven at McCarty's? We all helped. Daddy chopped wood and piled it near the oven. We helped put the oven door back in

---

1. **Carriso, Sleeping Ute, La Plata, Chuska Mountains.** Mountain ranges in northwestern New Mexico, southwestern Colorado, northeastern Arizona
2. **piñon.** Any of various low-growing pines or the edible seed of a pine

place and ran out of the house with potholders and the long poles to bring out the bread. We would help Grandma carry the bread, and she would say, 'Chase the dogs off! They just get in the way!'"

Once Leona's elder daughter said, "Then we didn't know that those times would be memories for us. We didn't know we would leave there. It seemed like it would last and last. The bright afternoons, Grandma's soft strong hands, the smell of bread in the clear blue sky."

Our laughter was different then," she said softly. ■

GUIDED READING
What did Leona's daughter say they didn't know?

Respond *to the* SELECTION

Does the story tell you where Leona is living? Is this important? Why, or why not?

About *the* AUTHOR

Luci Tapahonso, a member of the Navajo Nation, grew up in a family of 11 children in Shiprock, New Mexico. As a child, Tapahonso first learned Navajo, then English. She was writing poetry by the time she was eight or nine. Currently, Tapahonso teaches English, Women's Studies, and American Indian Studies at the University of Kansas. She is the author of *Navajo ABC: A Diné Alphabet Book* and several books of poetry, including *Blue Horses Rush In* and *Sáani Dahataal/The Women Are Singing: Poems and Stories.*

"THE GROUND IS ALWAYS DAMP" **537**

SELECTION CHECK TEST 4.8.1 WITH ANSWERS (CONT.)

1. The **setting** of a literary work is the time and place in which it happens.
2. In "The Ground Is Always Damp," **setting** is used to compare or contrast two different situations.
3. **Mood** is the feeling or emotion that the writer creates in a literary work.
4. By working carefully with **descriptive language,** author Luci Tapahonso evokes a mood of longing.

ANSWER TO GUIDED READING QUESTION

1. Leona's daughter said they didn't know that their times in New Mexico with Grandma would become memories. They didn't know they would leave New Mexico.

RESPOND TO THE SELECTION

Responses will vary. The story does not tell with any certainty where Leona is living. Where Leona is living is not important. What is important is realizing her strong connection to the people and places of New Mexico. The reader might draw the conclusion that no matter where Leona might choose to live, she would also be homesick for New Mexico.

SELECTION CHECK TEST 4.8.1 WITH ANSWERS

Checking Your Reading

1. Who is the main character in this story? Where does she long to be? **The main character is Leona, who longs to be back with her parents in the mountains of New Mexico.**
2. What does Leona tell her mother about her new home? **Leona tells her that in her new home, the ground is always damp, the sky is gray, and that there are no mountains.**
3. When Leona dreams, where is she and what is she doing? **In Leona's dreams, she is in New Mexico driving to Taos or doing things with her family.**
4. Who else misses New Mexico? What does this person say about it? **Leona's elder daughter misses New Mexico. She says that when they lived there, it seemed as if the good times would go on forever.**
5. Where is the place where Leona and her daughter live now? **The place is never identified, but it is very different from New Mexico.**

Reader's Toolbox

Fill in the blanks with the following terms. You may not use every term, and you may use some terms more than once.

theme   setting   mood
descriptive language   conflict

RECALL

1a. A dream of home awakens Leona.

2a. Leona says it is cloudy, that the ground is always damp, that the sky is gray, the air thick with frost, and that it is cold and windy. There are no mountains where she is, and that she can't see into the distance through the thick air.

3a. Leona's daughter says, "Our laughter was different then."

INTERPRET

1b. Some students may say this happened because the Leona's dream seemed so real.

2b. Students should recognize that Leona is not fond of the place where she is living. Her comparisons between her old home and new home make this clear.

3b. *Responses will vary.* Leona's daughter's words, "It seemed like it would last and last. The bright afternoons, Grandma's soft strong hands, the smell of bread in the clear blue sky," make it clear that those times are now cherished memories.

ANALYZE

4a. Students should focus on paragraphs 5, 6, and 7 of the selection for this question. Their responses may include the following: *Landscape of New Mexico:* sky is clear and empty, deep blue, almost turquoise; Leona's family's house is surrounded by mountains. The air is thin and clear, and you can see for many miles in all directions. *Landscape of Leona's new home:* sky is gray; air is thick with frost; there are no mountains; overflowing creek behind her house.

SYNTHESIZE

4b. The landscape of New Mexico provided several things that the landscape of her new home does not. Leona's family's home was surrounded on all sides by mountains, and the thin clear air provides a reliable view in all directions. In New Mexico, the landscape enabled one to predict the weather that was coming, and the mountains must have provided a sense of safety and comfort. Leona laments the lack of mountains in her new landscape and says that she cannot smell the coming weather.

PERSPECTIVE

5a. Most students will say that Leona talks to her mother because she misses her. Talking aloud, even

Investigate, *Inquire,* and Imagine

Recall: GATHERING FACTS

1a. What startles and awakens Leona?

2a. What does Leona tell her mother about the place where she is?

3a. What does Leona's elder daughter say about their laughter during past times spent with Grandma?

→ **Interpret:** FINDING MEANING

1b. Why might this happen to her?

2b. How do you think Leona feels about the place where she is living?

3b. What do you think she means by this?

Analyze: TAKING THINGS APART

4a. Compare and contrast the landscape of Leona's family home in New Mexico with the landscape of the place where Leona is living. List details about each.

→ **Synthesize:** BRINGING THINGS TOGETHER

4b. What did the landscape of New Mexico offer Leona that her new landscape does not? In what ways does Leona define home? Explain your answer.

Perspective: LOOKING AT OTHER VIEWS → **Empathy:** SEEING FROM INSIDE

5a. Why might Leona speak aloud to her mother who is hundreds of miles away?

5b. If you were in Leona's situation—far away from your family and the place where you feel most comfortable—how might you react? What would you do to feel more comfortable in your new home?

Understanding *Literature*

SETTING. The **setting** of a literary work is the time and place in which it happens. Setting in a literary work is revealed by details that describe the environment in which the story takes place—a particular landscape, season, town, or room, for example. Look back to "The Ground is Always Damp" and review the specific descriptions of setting the author provides. How many distinct settings does the author create in the story? What aspects of setting does Tapahonso omit? How do those omissions impact the story?

MOOD. Mood is the feeling or emotion that the writer creates in a literary work. By working carefully with descriptive language, the writer can evoke in the reader an emotional response

---

ANSWERS TO INVESTIGATE, INQUIRE, IMAGINE (CONT.)

though her mother cannot hear her, is a way to connect with her family.

EMPATHY

5b. *Responses will vary.* Students should think about ways they might bring part of their past to their current situation. This question might be painful for students who have recently moved and are not

comfortable yet in their new community. Such students might prefer to write their responses to these questions as a journal entry.

> Answers to Understanding Literature are found on page 539.

such as fear, longing, or anticipation. Choose at least three of your own words that describe the mood of this story. What are some of the ways the author creates mood in the story? Point out parts of the story that you think contribute to creating mood.

Writer's Journal

1. Create a new **title** for "The Ground is Always Damp."
2. Write a one or two paragraph **review** of "The Ground is Always Damp." Point out the story's strengths and/or weaknesses, and state whether you would recommend it to other readers your age.
3. Make a list of **descriptive phrases** that reveal the sights, sounds, and smells of one of your favorite places to someone who has never been there.

Language, Grammar, and Style

WORKING WITH SENSORY DETAILS. A **description** gives a picture in words of a character, object, or scene. Descriptions make use of **sensory details**—words and phrases that describe how things looks, sound, smell, taste, or feel. Look back to "The Ground is Always Damp," and identify words and phrases that appeal to the five senses. Use the chart below to organize your information. If a descriptive phrase addresses more than one of the five senses, include the phrase more than once in the chart. An example is shown.

Graphic Organizer

sight	sound	smell	taste	feel
a single cloud above cast sharp dark shadows on the smooth yard				

After completing the graphic organizer, write five sentences of your own, each describing something that will appeal to each of the five senses.

Language Grammar, and Style
Students' charts may contain the following details:

Sight: "The many trees, the small dusty chickens scratching nearby, and a single cloud above cast dark shadows on the smooth yard"; "One day last week, the sun came out for a few hours, and the shadows were soft and furry on the brown grass"; "It pours steadily until brown streams form and drain into the overflowing creek behind the house"; "The bright afternoons, Grandma's soft strong hands."
Sound: "the small dusty chickens scratching nearby"; "She woke herself up sometimes because she had laughed aloud, or said 'Aye-e-e'"; "the wind blows cold dampness."
Smell: "The air is thick and heavy with a scent I can't recognize. I haven't been able to smell the arrival of snow here, or to distinguish between the different kinds of rain scent."; "small piñon wood smoke, or stew, or beans boiling"; "fresh green chile roasting outside"; "the smell of bread in the clear blue sky."
Taste: Students might note that the sense of taste is included in the description of stew or beans boiling, fresh green chiles roasting, and in the bread the family bakes together.
Feel: "The ground is always damp"; "I don't care to kneel down and sift dirt through my fingers"; "the wind blows cold dampness."

ANSWERS TO UNDERSTANDING LITERATURE

SETTING. The selection alternately describes two main settings: the New Mexico setting and the setting of Leona's new home. These descriptions of Leona's past in New Mexico give the reader insight into Leona and her ties to the Southwest landscape. The selection focuses on the New Mexican setting. The details of Leona's new home only provide insight into Leona's feelings about the place where she grew up. The reader never finds out where Leona's new home is or the time the story is set.

MOOD. Responses will vary, but students may say the mood is lonely, homesick, melancholy, wistful, or somber. Some of the ways the author creates mood include the conversations Leona has with her mother and the imagery of Leona's dreams and memories. Her longing for home is conveyed by her dreams and memories and by the author's choice not to reveal the location of Leona's new home.

Study and Research & Applied English

Refer students to the Language Arts Survey 5.22, "Using Almanacs, Yearbooks, and Atlases," for more information. Students' letters should follow the proper form for a business letter. Refer students to the Language Arts Survey 6.6, "Writing a Business Letter," for more information.

Collaborative Learning & Speaking and Listening

Before students begin this activity, write each student's name on a slip of paper and put them in a container. Students should choose a slip of paper with another student's name. Tell students to listen carefully to the story of the student whose name they have chosen. This encourages students to listen to others outside their circle of friends.

Study and Research and Applied English

USING AN ATLAS AND THE INTERNET FOR RESEARCH. Use the index of an atlas to look up the four mountain ranges mentioned in "The Ground is Always Damp": Carriso (may also be spelled Corrizo), Ute, La Plata, and Chuska. Locate the mountains on the map. Next, identify the following areas on the map: Chaco Canyon National Monument, New Mexico; Window Rock, Arizona; Monument Valley Ruins, Arizona; and Canyon de Chelly National Park, Arizona. Conduct some basic Internet research on the last four sites you located on the map. Choose the site that looks most interesting to you and write a letter to the appropriate chamber of commerce or tourist & visitors' bureau. Your Internet research should lead you to sites that note organizations that you can write to for further information.

Collaborative Learning and Speaking and Listening

RECORDING AND SHARING ORAL STORIES. Form small groups and share the details of a memory that is special to you. It can be a memory of something funny, scary, touching, or strange. Listen carefully to each person's story. After everyone has shared a memory, each person should record the details of someone else's memory. No one should record his or her own story, and each member's story should be recorded. Do the best you can at accurately recording the details, but don't ask the person who shared the story to repeat anything. Once all the stories have been written down, share them with your class. See if your classmates can guess which memories belong to which classmates.

Prereading

"Luke Baldwin's Vow"

by Morley Callaghan

Reader's TOOLBOX

PLOT. A **plot** is a series of events related to a *central conflict*, or struggle. A plot includes the introduction of a conflict, its development, and its resolution. In a short story, the events in the plot usually lead from one to the next. Review the parts of a plot in Elements of Fiction on page 532. As you read "Luke Baldwin's Vow," try to identify the climax—or high point of suspense—in the story.

Graphic *Organizer*

You may want to draw a picture map to help you visualize the plot of the story as you read. Make a series of pictures with short captions to represent the important situations or events within the story. Draw arrows to show the sequence of pictures. The first picture is shown as an example.

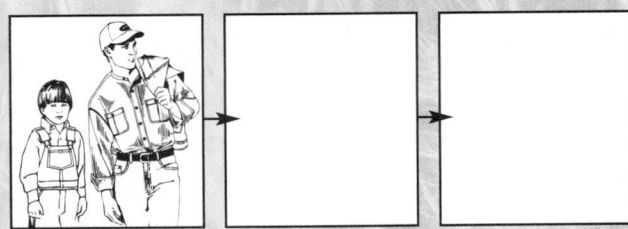

Luke moves in with his Uncle Henry.

CHARACTER. A **character** is a person or animal who takes part in the action of a literary work. **One-dimensional characters** are characters who exhibit a single quality or character trait. **Three-dimensional characters** are characters who seem to have all the complexities of an actual human being. As you read, make a list of the characters in the story. Are there any characters in the story that show only a single quality or character trait? If so, which one(s)?

Reader's Journal

Would you describe yourself as practical, idealistic, or somewhere in between? Explain your answer.

Reader's Resource

- A coming of age story is a tale in which a young person makes a discovery about himself or herself or about the world. In this type of story, the main character is often faced with a challenge. The way in which the character deals with this challenge usually teaches a moral or a value, such as responsibility or honesty. Because of this experience, the main character may also gain maturity.

- A coming of age story also allows different generations to learn from each other. Younger generations may gain wisdom from older generations, while older generations may find new ideas and renewed spirit in learning about younger generations. In "Luke Baldwin's Vow," Luke, the main character, faces a challenge, and the result of his experience helps him decide what kind of person he wants to become.

"LUKE BALDWIN'S VOW" **541**

ADDITIONAL RESOURCES

UNIT 8 RESOURCE BOOK
- Selection Worksheet 8.2
- Selection Check Test 4.8.3
- Selection Test 4.8.4
- Study and Research Resource 5.27

READER'S JOURNAL

Ask students the following questions. Are there times when it is better to be practical than idealistic? Are there times when it is better to be idealistic than practical? Describe some of these times.

READER'S TOOLBOX

Plot. The climax of the story begins when Luke sees Dan in the boat with Sam Carter. The action escalates when Luke cries out to Dan and Sam Carter drops the stone into the river. The climax includes Luke's attempt to save Dan and subsides as the reader learns that Dan is alive. **Character.** Character list: Luke, Uncle Henry, Aunt Helen, Dan, Mr. Kemp, Sam Carter. While Uncle Henry exhibits a single character trait (practicality), Sam Carter is the only true one-dimensional character in the story. Students will analyze the characters more fully in the Understanding Literature section.

GRAPHIC ORGANIZER

Students may create pictures for any of the following events: Luke befriends Dan. Uncle Henry decides to get rid of Dan because he says he isn't worth his keep. Luke disobeys his uncle, and goes to the river. Luke sees Dan in boat with Sam Carter and calls out to Dan. Sam Carter drops a stone attached to a rope attached to Dan in the river. Luke leaps into the water, finds Dan and saves him. Luke decides he can't take Dan back to his Uncle Henry's house. Luke goes to Mr. Kemp for advice and agrees to round up Mr. Kemp's cows for 75 cents a week. Luke makes a proposal to his uncle—he tells him he will pay him 75 cents a week for Dan's keep. Uncle Henry accepts Luke's proposition. Luke makes his vow.

GOALS/OBJECTIVES

Studying this lesson will enable students to
- empathize with a young character who is having a difficult experience
- briefly describe characteristics of a coming-of-age story
- define *plot* and identify the parts of a plot in a story

- define *character* and classify characters as one- or three-dimensional
- brainstorm a slit of valuable things that are not practical
- evaluate Internet sites
- research canine health care

MOTIVATION

Encourage students to have a class discussion on pets they have had strong feelings about. Ask them to describe the pets and explain why they were so meaningful to them.

READING PROFICIENCY

Inform students that this story is set early in the twentieth century and share the English Language Learning vocabulary with them. Then have students form pairs with a reading partner. Students should take turns reading a paragraph or two of the story aloud to each other and then exchange roles, until they have read the entire story aloud. The two should then work on rereading the story and responding to the Guided Reading questions. Tell each pair to list their own questions they have about the story that they could not work out on their own.

ENGLISH LANGUAGE LEARNING

Point out the following vocabulary words and expressions
sawmill—factory where logs are sawed into boards
notations—notes jotted down as reminders or explanations
transaction—business deals or agreements
millpond—pond formed by a dam from which water flows and is used to drive a wheel that moves machinery in a factory
hammock—length of netting suspended by ropes and used as a bed or couch
frantic—wild with anger, pain, or worry
yelp—short sharp cry or bark
sentimental—having or showing tender, gentle, or delicate feelings
hoisting—lifting or pulling up
stupor—state in which the mind or sense are dulled
stumped—puzzled, perplexed
shaver—colloquial term for a boy
exultation—rejoicing, triumph
fervently—with great warmth of feeling

SPECIAL NEEDS

Tell students to focus on responding to the Guided Reading questions and the Recall questions in the Investigate, Inquire, and Imagine section in writing. Students should then form small groups and discuss

Cape Cod Evening, 1939. Edward Hopper. National Gallery of Art.

Luke Baldwin's VOW

That summer when twelve-year-old Luke Baldwin came to live with his Uncle Henry in the house on the stream by the sawmill, he did not forget that he had promised his dying father he would try to learn things from his uncle; so he used to watch him very carefully.

Morley Callaghan

INDIVIDUAL LEARNING STRATEGIES (CONT.)

their ideas about the higher level Interpret, Analyze, Synthesize, Perspective, and Empathy questions. You might the hold a class discussion about these questions and allow special needs students to draw upon their written responses and the small group discussions they have held to aid them in class participation.

ENRICHMENT

Ask students to write a paragraph about a personal coming-of-age experience or the experience of a friend or relative. When everyone has written a paragraph, the pieces can be combined to make a book. Students might want to illustrate the book and create a colorful cover.

Uncle Henry, who was the manager of the sawmill, was a big, <u>burly</u> man weighing more than two hundred and thirty pounds, and he had a rough-skinned, brick-colored face. He looked like a powerful man, but his health was not good. He had aches and pains in his back and shoulders which puzzled the doctor. The first thing Luke learned about Uncle Henry was that everybody had great respect for him. The four men he employed in the sawmill were always polite and attentive when he spoke to them. His wife, Luke's Aunt Helen, a kindly, plump, straightforward woman, never argued with him. "You should try and be like your Uncle Henry," she would say to Luke. "He's so wonderfully practical. He takes care of everything in a sensible, easy way."

Luke used to trail around the sawmill after Uncle Henry not only because he liked the fresh clean smell of the newly cut wood and the big piles of sawdust, but because he was impressed by his uncle's <u>precise</u>, firm tone when he spoke to the men.

Sometimes Uncle Henry would stop and explain to Luke something about a piece of timber. "Always try and learn the essential facts, son," he would say. "If you've got the facts, you know what's useful and what isn't useful, and no one can fool you."

He showed Luke that nothing of value was ever wasted around the mill. Luke used to listen, and wonder if there was another man in the world who knew so well what was needed and what ought to be thrown away.

GUIDED READING
What did Luke promise his father?

GUIDED READING
What do other people think of Uncle Henry?

GUIDED READING
What types of things does Uncle Henry know?

Uncle Henry had known at once that Luke needed a bicycle to ride to his school, which was two miles away in town, and he bought him a good one. He knew that Luke needed good, serviceable clothes. He also knew exactly how much Aunt Helen needed to run the house, the price of everything, and how much a woman should be paid for doing the family washing. In the evenings Luke used to sit in the living room watching his uncle making notations in a black notebook which he always carried in his vest pocket, and he knew that he was <u>assessing</u> the value of the smallest transaction that had taken place during the day.

Luke promised himself that when he grew up he, too, would be admired for his good, sound judgment. But, of course, he couldn't always be watching and learning from his Uncle Henry, for too often when he watched him he thought of his own father; then he was lonely. So he began to build up another secret life for himself around the sawmill, and his companion was the eleven-year-old collie, Dan, a dog blind in one eye and with a slight limp in his left hind leg. Dan was a fat slow-moving old dog. He was very affectionate and his eye was the color of amber.[1] His fur was amber too. When Luke left for school in the morning, the old dog followed him for half a mile down the road, and when he returned in the afternoon, there was Dan waiting at the gate.

Sometimes they would play around the millpond or by the dam, or go down the stream to the lake. Luke was never lonely

GUIDED READING
When is Luke lonely?

---

1. **amber.** Brownish-yellow, translucent fossil resin often used for jewelry

words for everyday use

bur • ly (bər lē) *adj.*, strongly and heavily built. *The <u>burly</u> waiter easily carried the tray filled with dishes.*

pre • cise (prē sīs') *adj.*, exact. *To make good dough, you must use the <u>precise</u> amount of flour.*

as • sess (ə ses') *v.*, evaluate. *We will <u>assess</u> the playground to make sure it is safe.*

ANSWERS TO GUIDED READING QUESTIONS

1. Luke promised his father that he would try to learn things from his Uncle Henry.
2. Everybody had great respect for his uncle. Aunt Helen thinks Uncle Henry is wonderfully practical and sensible.
3. Uncle Henry knows what is needed and what should be discarded. He knows when someone needs something (Luke's bike and good serviceable clothes), how good it should be, and how much it should cost (what it costs to run the household, how much a woman should be paid for washing clothes).
4. Luke is lonely when he thinks of his father.

CROSS-CURRICULAR ACTIVITIES

TEEN LIVING. Ask students to put together a book of original coming-of-age/ rite-of-passage tales. Each student might write a paragraph about a personal experience or the experience of a friend or a relative. When everyone has written a paragraph, the pieces can be combined to make a book. Students might want to illustrate the book and create a colorful cover.

SCIENCE. Ask each student to choose a breed of dog that particularly interests him or her. Students should then research their favorite breeds and present the information to the class. Encourage them to use pictures, diagrams, and other visual aids.

SOCIAL STUDIES. Organize a poll within your school to find out how many people have dogs as pets. Create a flier that can be passed around to everyone. The flier should ask, "Do you have a dog as a pet? If yes, what role does your pet play in your life?" Suggest to students that some people will say that their dogs are friends, companions, or like children or siblings to them. Some people will say that their dogs work as watchdogs or in other practical ways. Students should organize their results and then discuss them.

1. Luke shares with Dan things that he would not say to his aunt and uncle. He shares with the dog things about himself that he might have told his mother and father.
2. Uncle Henry thinks that Dan is no good for anything anymore and just gets in the way.

ADDITIONAL QUESTIONS AND ACTIVITIES

Ask students to answer the following questions:
• In what way does Luke's imagination help ease the pain of his loneliness for his parents?
• Has your own imagination ever gotten you through a difficult time, or helped you to overcome a fear? Have you ever built a world around a favorite pet or toy?

Answers
Students might say that when Luke feels lonely, he turns to the world he's built around his pet Dan. Luke pretends that he and Dan are pirates and hunting tigers. When they round up Mr. Kemp's cows, Luke pretends that they are riding on a range in the Rockies.

Encourage students to freewrite about their own imaginings.

VOCABULARY FROM THE SELECTION

aloof
apprehensive
assess
burley
competent
divert
exultation
furtive
imposing

methodical
ponderous
precise
proposition
resourceful
slow-witted
thwart
wiry

when the dog was with him. There was an old rowboat that they used as a pirate ship in the stream, and they would be pirates together, with Luke shouting instructions to Captain Dan and with the dog seeming to understand and wagging his tail enthusiastically. Its amber eye was alert, intelligent and approving. Then they would plunge into the brush on the other side of the stream, pretending they were hunting tigers. Of course, the old dog was no longer much good for hunting; he was too slow and too lazy. Uncle Henry no longer used him for hunting rabbits or anything else.

When they came out of the brush, they would lie together on the cool, grassy bank being affectionate with each other, with Luke talking earnestly, while the collie, as Luke believed, smiled with the good eye. Lying in the grass, Luke would say things to Dan he could not say to his uncle or his aunt. Not that what he said was important: it was just stuff about himself that he might have told to his own father or mother if they had been alive. Then they would go back to the house for dinner, and after dinner Dan would follow him down the road to Mr. Kemp's house, where they would ask old Mr. Kemp if they could go with him to round up his four cows. The old man was always glad to see them. He seemed to like watching Luke and the collie running around the cows, pretending they were riding on a vast range in the foothills of the Rockies.

Uncle Henry no longer paid much attention to the collie, though once when he tripped over him on the veranda,[2] he shook his

> **GUIDED READING**
> What things does Luke say to Dan?

> **GUIDED READING**
> What does Uncle Henry think of Dan?

head and said thoughtfully, "Poor old fellow, he's through. Can't use him for anything. He just eats and sleeps and gets in the way."

One Sunday during Luke's summer holidays when they had returned from church and had had their lunch, they had all moved out to the veranda where the collie was sleeping. Luke sat down on the steps, his back against the veranda post. Uncle Henry took the rocking chair, and Aunt Helen stretched herself out in the hammock, sighing contentedly. Then Luke, eying the collie, tapped the step with the palm of his hand, giving three little taps like a signal and the old collie, lifting his head, got up stiffly with a slow wagging of the tail as an acknowledgment that the signal had been heard, and began to cross the veranda to Luke. But the dog was sleepy, his bad eye was turned to the rocking chair; in passing, his left front paw went under the rocker. With a frantic yelp, the dog went bounding down the steps and hobbled around the corner of the house, where he stopped, hearing Luke coming after him. All he needed was the touch of Luke's hand. Then he began to lick the hand <u>methodically</u>, as if apologizing.

"Luke," Uncle Henry called sharply, "bring that dog here."

When Luke led the collie back to the veranda, Uncle Henry nodded and said, "Thanks, Luke." Then he took out a cigar, lit it, put his big hands on his knees and began to rock in the chair while he frowned and eyed the dog steadily. Obviously he was making some kind of an important decision about the collie.

"What's the matter, Uncle Henry?" Luke asked nervously.

---

2. **veranda.** An open porch area, usually with a roof

words for everyday use

me • thod • i • cal (mə thä′ di kəl) *adj., arranged in an orderly or systematic fashion. Jan was methodical about tracking every penny she earned, spent, and saved.* **methodically,** *adv.*

"That dog can't see any more," Uncle Henry said.

"Oh, yes, he can," Luke said quickly. "His bad eye got turned to the chair, that's all, Uncle Henry."

"And his teeth are gone, too," Uncle Henry went on, paying no attention to what Luke had said. Turning to the hammock, he called, "Helen, sit up a minute, will you?"

When she got up and stood beside him, he went on. "I was thinking about this old dog the other day, Helen. It's not only that he's just about blind, but did you notice that when we drove up after church he didn't even bark?"

"It's a fact he didn't, Henry."

"No, not much good even as a watchdog now."

"Poor old fellow. It's a pity, isn't it?"

"And no good for hunting either. And he eats a lot, I suppose."

"About as much as he ever did, Henry."

"The plain fact is the old dog isn't worth his keep any more. It's time we got rid of him."

"It's always so hard to know how to get rid of a dog, Henry."

> **GUIDED READING**
> What does Uncle Henry decide about Dan?

"I was thinking about it the other day. Some people think it's best to shoot a dog. I haven't had any shells for that shotgun for over a year. Poisoning is a hard death for a dog. Maybe drowning is the easiest and quickest way. Well, I'll speak to one of the mill hands and have him look after it."

Crouching on the ground, his arms around the old collie's neck, Luke cried out, "Uncle Henry, Dan's a wonderful dog! You don't know how wonderful he is!"

"He's just a very old dog, son," Uncle Henry said calmly. "The time comes when you have to get rid of any old dog. We've got to be practical about it. I'll get you a pup, son. A smart little dog that'll be worth its keep. A pup that will grow up with you."

"I don't want a pup!" Luke cried, turning his face away. Circling around him, the dog began to bark, then flick his long pink tongue at the back of Luke's neck.

> *"Uncle Henry, Dan's a wonderful dog! You don't know how wonderful he is!"*

Aunt Helen, catching her husband's eye, put her finger on her lips, warning him not to go on talking in front of the boy. "An old dog like that often wanders off into the brush and sort of picks a place to die when the time comes. Isn't that so, Henry?"

"Oh sure," he agreed quickly. "In fact, when Dan didn't show up yesterday, I was sure that was what had happened." Then he yawned and seemed to forget about the dog.

But Luke was frightened, for he knew what his uncle was like. He knew that if his uncle had decided that the dog was useless and that it was sane and sensible to get rid of it, he would be ashamed of himself if he were <u>diverted</u> by any sentimental

> **GUIDED READING**
> What does Luke know about his uncle? What does Luke plan to do?

---

words for everyday use

di • vert (də vərt') v., to distract or to turn from one course to another. *The dam <u>diverted</u> river water to the pond.*

---

1. Luke thinks his uncle is trying to get
rid of him so that he can arrange to
have Dan killed.
2. The picture looks wrong to Luke
because it looks lazy and friendly.

HISTORICAL NOTE

The breed of dog known as the collie
was officially established by 1886.
This breed is also known as the
Scotch collie because it is related to
all Scottish breeds of sheep-herding
dogs.

The collie is widely known as a
wonderful and loyal family dog, and
people consider this dog to be a
good companion for children. Many
people associate collies with the
famous fictional dog Lassie, who has
appeared in books, movies, and in
several television series. Lassie was a
friendly and loyal family dog who
often performed heroic acts.

CROSS-CURRICULAR ACTIVITIES

MATHEMATICS AND SCIENCE. Ask
students if they have ever
heard the expression, "It's the
dog days of summer," which
refers to extremely hot, humid
days in the middle of summer. This
expression comes from the star
Sirius, which is part of the
constellation Big Dog. Sirius, the
brightest star in the sky, is high in
the sky during summer months.

• Constellations are random clusters
of stars that people name after
objects, people, or animals. Have
the class form pairs, then assign
each pair one of the constellations
named after animals (see list
below). Each group must go to
the library and look up
information about its constellation
and then create a poster showing
the constellation. Allow students
to use whatever materials they
would like to create their posters.
The following is a list of constellations
named after animals, real and
imaginary:

considerations. Luke knew in his heart that
he couldn't move his uncle. All he could do,
he thought, was keep the dog away from his
uncle, keep him out of the house, feed him
when Uncle Henry wasn't around.

Next day at noontime Luke saw his uncle
walking from the mill toward the house with
old Sam Carter, a mill hand. Sam Carter was
a dull, stooped, <u>slow-witted</u> man of sixty with
an iron-gray beard, who was wearing blue
overalls and a blue shirt. He hardly ever
spoke to anybody. Watching from the
veranda, Luke noticed that his uncle suddenly
gave Sam Carter a cigar, which Sam put in his
pocket. Luke had never seen his uncle give
Sam a cigar or pay much attention to him.

Then, after lunch, Uncle Henry said lazily
that he would like Luke to take his bicycle
and go into town and get him some cigars.

"I'll take Dan," Luke said.

"Better not, son," Uncle Henry said. "It'll
take you all afternoon. I want those cigars.
Get going, Luke."

His uncle's tone was so casual that Luke
tried to believe they were not merely getting
rid of him. Of course he
had to do what he was
told. He had never dared
to refuse to obey an order
from his uncle. But when he had taken his
bicycle and had ridden down the path that
followed the stream to the town road and had
got about a quarter of a mile along the road,
he found that all he could think of was his
uncle handing old Sam Carter the cigar.

Slowing down, sick with worry now, he got
off the bike and stood uncertainly on the
sunlit road. Sam Carter was a gruff, <u>aloof</u> old
man who would have no feeling for a dog.
Then suddenly Luke could go no farther

> **GUIDED READING**
> What does Luke
> think his uncle is
> trying to do?

without getting some assurance that the collie
would not be harmed while he was away.
Across the fields he could see the house.

Leaving the bike in the ditch, he started to
cross the field, intending to get close enough
to the house so Dan could hear him if he
whistled softly. He got about fifty yards away
from the house and whistled and waited, but
there was no sign of the dog, which might be
asleep at the front of the house, he knew, or
over at the saw-mill. With the saws whining,
the dog couldn't hear the soft whistle. For a
few minutes Luke couldn't make up his mind
what to do, then he decided to go back to the
road, get on his bike and go back the way he
had come until he got to the place where the
river path joined the road. There he could
leave his bike, go up the path, then into the
tall grass and get close to the front of the
house and the sawmill without being seen.

He had followed the river path for about a
hundred yards, and when he came to the place
where the river began to bend sharply toward
the house his heart fluttered and his legs felt
paralyzed, for he saw the old rowboat in the
one place where the river was deep, and in the
rowboat was Sam Carter with the collie.

The bearded man in the blue overalls was
smoking the cigar; the dog, with a rope
around its neck, sat contentedly beside him,
its tongue going out in a friendly lick at the
hand holding the rope. It was all like a crazy
dream picture to Luke: all
wrong because it looked
so lazy and friendly, even
the curling smoke from
Sam Carter's cigar. But as Luke cried out,
"Dan, Dan! Come on, boy!" and the dog
jumped at the water, he saw that Sam Carter's
left hand was hanging deep in the water,

> **GUIDED READING**
> What makes this
> picture look
> wrong to Luke?

> **words
> for
> everyday
> use**
>
> **slow-wit • ted** (slō wi′ təd) *adj.*, mentally slow, dull. *Lorna could be <u>slow-witted</u> about certain things, but her humor was
> always sharp.*
>
> **a • loof** (ə lüf′) *adj.*, reserved and cool, distant. *Kara's <u>aloof</u> manner made it hard for her to find friends.*

CROSS-CURRICULAR ACTIVITIES (CONT.)

Giraffe	Ram	Dragon	Hydra (Water
Lion	Little Dog	Bull	Snake)
Hunting Dogs	Lynx	Scorpion	Crow
Little Lion	Crab	Dolphin	Eagle
Swan	Hare	Southern Fish	Goat
Pegasus	Unicorn	Whale	Fishes

holding a foot of rope with a heavy stone at the end. As Luke cried out wildly, "Don't! Please don't!" Carter dropped the stone, for the cry came too late; it was blurred by the screech of the big saws at the mill. But Carter was startled, and he stared stupidly at the riverbank, then he ducked his head and began to row quickly to the bank.

But Luke was watching the collie take what looked like a long, shallow dive, except that the hind legs suddenly kicked up above the surface, then shot down, and while he watched, Luke sobbed and trembled, for it was as if the happy secret part of his life around the sawmill was being torn away from him. But even while he watched, he

> **GUIDED READING**
>
> How does Luke react to seeing Dan disappear into the river?

seemed to be following a plan without knowing it, for he was already fumbling in his pocket for his jackknife, jerking the blade open, pulling off his pants, kicking his shoes off while he muttered fiercely and prayed that Sam Carter would get out of sight.

It hardly took the mill hand a minute to reach the bank and go slinking <u>furtively</u> around the bend as if he felt that the boy was following him. But Luke hadn't taken his eyes off the exact spot in the water where Dan had disappeared. As soon as the mill hand was out of sight, Luke slid down the bank and took a leap at the water, the sun glistening on his slender body, his eyes wild with eagerness as he ran out to the deep place, then arched his back and dived, swimming under water, his open eyes getting used to the greenish-gray haze of the water, the sandy bottom and the embedded rocks.

His lungs began to ache, then he saw the shadow of the collie floating at the end of the taut rope, rock-held in the sand. He slashed at the rope with his knife. He couldn't get much strength in his arm because of the resistance of the water. He grabbed the rope with his left hand, hacking with his knife. The collie suddenly drifted up slowly, like a water-soaked log. Then his own head shot above the surface, and while he was sucking in the air he was drawing in the rope, pulling the collie toward him and treading water. In a few strokes he was away from the deep place and his feet touched the bottom.

Hoisting the collie out of the water, he scrambled toward the bank, lurching and stumbling in fright because the collie felt like a dead weight.

> **GUIDED READING**
>
> Why is Luke frightened?

He went on up the bank and across the path to the tall grass, where he fell flat, hugging the dog and trying to warm him with his own body. But the collie didn't stir, the good amber eye remained closed. Then suddenly Luke wanted to act like a <u>resourceful</u>, <u>competent</u> man. Getting up on his knees, he stretched the dog out on its belly, drew him between his knees, felt with trembling hands for the soft places on the flanks just above the hipbones, and rocked back and forth, pressing with all his weight, then relaxing the pressure as he straightened up. He hoped that he was working the dog's lungs like a bellows.[3] He had read that men who had been thought drowned had been saved in this way.

> **GUIDED READING**
>
> What does Luke do to try to save Dan? How does Luke know how to help Dan?

"Come on, Dan. Come on, old boy," he pleaded softly. As a little water came from the collie's mouth, Luke's heart jumped, and he muttered over and over,

---

3. **bellows.** An instrument that expands to take air in through a valve and contracts to expels it through a tube

---

words for everyday use

fur • tive (fər' tiv) *adj.*, sneaky, underhanded, sly. *Joe fed his broccoli to the furtive dog under the table.* **furtively,** *adv.*

re • source • ful (ri sors' fəl) *adj.*, able to deal effectively with problems and challenges. *Fayed proved himself a resourceful camper by acting confidently when the bear entered our camp.*

com • pe • tent (käm' pə tənt) *adj.*, capable. *Joan can do the project—she is a competent manager.*

ANSWERS TO GUIDED READING QUESTIONS

1. At first he watches, crying and afraid because he feels as though the happy secret part of his life that he created with Dan is being taken away. But then, almost unconsciously, he springs to action and saves Dan.
2. Luke is scared because he thinks that Dan might be dead.
3. Luke presses at intervals on Dan's lungs. He has read that this was a method that has been used to save people who were thought to have drowned.

ADDITIONAL QUESTIONS AND ACTIVITIES

Ask students to answer the following questions:
- Why do you think Luke jumps into the water to save Dan even though he knows that his uncle wants to get rid of the dog? What drives him to save Dan?
- Do you think Luke's actions are brave and admirable, or do you think he should respect his uncle's wishes?

Answers

Responses will vary. Students might say that because Luke shares a friendship with the Dan, he feels a special loyalty toward the dog. Luke depends on the dog during his times of loneliness, so he cannot stand to see this important part of his life taken from him. Students might also say that Luke is responding to his own personal sense of what is right and what is wrong. His uncle believes that getting rid of the dog is the right thing to do, but Luke feels getting rid of the dog is absolutely wrong.

Encourage students to explain their responses to the second question.

LITERARY TECHNIQUE

Mood, or **atmosphere**, is the emotion created in the reader by a piece of writing. A writer can create mood by using certain **images**. An **image** is language that describes something that can be seen, heard, touched, tasted, or smelled.

There is a mood of panic and discomfort when Luke is in the water trying to save Dan. Ask students to identify images such as Luke's aching lungs and his panic as he tries to move his arm against the resistance of the water to slash the rope. Readers can also sense this mood of panic and discomfort in the way that Luke shoots out of the water, sucks in air, and then tries to tread water as he pulls the collie toward him.

After Luke hears his aunt calling him, "the exultation Luke had felt at knowing the collie was safe beside him turned to bewildered despair. . . ." The reader can sense Luke's sadness in the images of his sighing and lying down with the collie for hours. His sadness is also apparent in the long sentences that describe his looking to his house, to the clouds, and to the wide lake for answers to his dilemma.

"You can't be dead, Dan! You can't, you can't! I won't let you die, Dan!" He rocked back and forth tirelessly, applying the pressure to the flanks. More water dribbled from the mouth. In the collie's body he felt a faint tremor. "Oh gee, Dan, you're alive," he whispered. "Come on, boy. Keep it up."

With a cough the collie suddenly jerked his head back, the amber eye opened, and there they were looking at each other. Then the collie, thrusting his legs out stiffly, tried to hoist himself up, staggered, tried again, then stood there in a stupor. Then he shook himself like any other wet dog, turned his head, eyed Luke, and the red tongue came out in a weak flick at Luke's cheek.

"Lie down, Dan," Luke said. As the dog lay down beside him, Luke closed his eyes, buried his head in the wet fur and wondered why all the muscles of his arms and legs began to jerk in a nervous reaction, now that it was all over. "Stay there, Dan," he said softly, and he went back to the path, got his clothes and came back beside Dan and put them on. "I think we'd better get away from this spot, Dan," he said. "Keep down, boy. Come on." And he crawled on through the tall grass till they were about seventy-five yards from the place where he had undressed. There they lay down together.

In a little while he heard his aunt's voice calling, "Luke. Oh, Luke! Come here, Luke!"

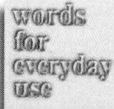

"He's a fine man . . . maybe just a little bit too practical and straightforward."

"Quiet, Dan," Luke whispered. A few minutes passed, and then Uncle Henry called, "Luke, Luke!" and he began to come down the path. They could see him standing there, massive and <u>imposing</u>, his hands on his hips as he looked down the path, then he turned and went back to the house.

As he watched the sunlight shine on the back of his uncle's neck, the <u>exultation</u> Luke had felt at knowing the collie was safe beside him turned to bewildered despair, for he knew that even if he should be forgiven for saving the dog when he saw it drowning, the fact was that his uncle had been <u>thwarted</u>. His mind was made up to get rid of Dan, and in a few days' time, in another way, he would get rid of him, as he got rid of anything around the mill that he believed to be useless or a waste of money.

As he lay back and looked up at the hardly moving clouds, he began to grow frightened. He couldn't go back to the house, nor could he take the collie into the woods and hide him and feed him there unless he tied him up. If he didn't tie him up, Dan would wander back to the house.

"I guess there's just no place to go, Dan," he whispered sadly. "Even if we start off along the road, somebody is sure to see us."

But Dan was watching a butterfly that was circling crazily above them. Raising himself a little, Luke looked through the grass at

> **GUIDED READING**
>
> Why does Luke's joy turn into despair?

---

words for everyday use

im • pos • ing (im pō' ziŋ) *adj.*, impressive in size, bearing, dignity, or grandeur. *My mother, in her evening gown, was an imposing figure as she came down the long staircase to join the party.*

ex • ul • ta • tion (eg' zəl tā shən) *n.*, triumph, excitement, joyousness. *The 4-H team's exultation over winning the fair was obvious.*

thwart (thwart) *v.*, hinder, obstruct; defeat. *Sarah tried, unsuccessfully, to thwart my plans to get a puppy.*

the corner of the house, then he turned and looked the other way to the wide blue lake. With a sigh he lay down again, and for hours they lay there together, until there was no sound from the saws in the mill and the sun moved low in the western sky.

"Well, we can't stay here any longer, Dan," he said at last. "We'll just have to get as far away as we can. Keep down, old boy," and he began to crawl through the grass, going farther away from the house. When he could no longer be seen, he got up and began to trot across the field toward the gravel road leading to town.

On the road, the collie would turn from time to time as if wondering why Luke shuffled along, dragging his feet wearily, his head down. "I'm stumped, that's all Dan," Luke explained. "I can't seem to think of a place to take you."

When they were passing the Kemp place they saw the old man sitting on the veranda, and Luke stopped. All he could think of was that Mr. Kemp had liked them both and it had been a pleasure to help him get the cows in the evening. Dan had always been with them. Staring at the figure of the old man on the veranda, he said in a worried tone, "I wish I could be sure of him, Dan. I wish he was a dumb, stupid man who wouldn't know or care whether you were worth anything. . . . Well, come on." He opened the gate bravely, but he felt shy and unimportant.

> **GUIDED READING**
> What does Luke think about as he comes upon Mr. Kemp's place?

"Hello, son. What's on your mind?" Mr. Kemp called from the veranda. He was a thin, <u>wiry</u> man in a tan-colored shirt. He had a gray, untidy mustache, his skin was wrinkled and leathery, but his eyes were always friendly and amused.

"Could I speak to you, Mr. Kemp?" Luke asked when they were close to the veranda.

"Sure. Go ahead."

"It's about Dan. He's a great dog, but I guess you know that as well as I do. I was wondering if you could keep him here for me."

"Why should I keep Dan here, son?"

"Well, it's like this," Luke said, fumbling the words awkwardly: "My uncle won't let me keep him any more . . . says he's too old." His mouth began to tremble, then he blurted out the story.

"I see, I see," Mr. Kemp said slowly, and he got up and came over to the steps and sat down and began to stroke the collie's head. "Of course, Dan's an old dog, son," he said quietly. "And sooner or later you've got to get rid of an old dog. Your uncle knows that. Maybe it's true that Dan isn't worth his keep."

"He doesn't eat much, Mr. Kemp. Just one meal a day."

> **GUIDED READING**
> What does Mr. Kemp say about Uncle Henry?

"I wouldn't want you to think your uncle was cruel and unfeeling, Luke," Mr. Kemp went on. "He's a fine man . . . maybe just a little bit too practical and straightforward."

"I guess that's right," Luke agreed, but he was really waiting and trusting the expression in the old man's eyes.

"Maybe you should make him a practical <u>proposition</u>."

> **GUIDED READING**
> What does Mr. Kemp suggest to Luke?

"I—I don't know what you mean."

"Well, I sort of like the way you get the cows for me in the evenings," Mr. Kemp said, smiling to himself. "In fact, I don't think you need me to go along with you at all. Now, supposing I gave you seventy-five cents a week. Would you get the cows for me every night?"

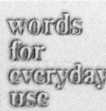
ANSWERS TO GUIDED READING QUESTIONS

1. He thinks about the fact that Mr. Kemp had liked him and Dan, and that he had really enjoyed helping Mr. Kemp round up his cows in the evening.
2. Mr. Kemp says that Luke's uncle isn't a mean man, that he's just a little bit too practical.
3. Mr. Kemp suggests that Luke make his uncle a business proposition. He tells Luke to offer to pay his uncle seventy-five cents a week for Dan's keep.

ADDITIONAL QUESTIONS AND ACTIVITIES

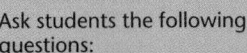

Ask students the following questions:
- Do you like the way Mr. Kemp handles the situation with Luke and Dan? Do you believe his suggestion makes more sense than Luke's original idea? Why, or why not?
- How does Mr. Kemp feel about Luke's uncle?

Answers
Responses will vary. Students might like that Mr. Kemp tries to take an honest approach by encouraging Luke to bargain with his uncle. They might feel that this is a better plan than simply trying to hide the dog at Mr. Kemp's home.

Mr. Kemp feels that Luke's uncle is a good man, but perhaps just a bit too practical. He does not believe that Luke's uncle is cruel or unfeeling.

ANSWER TO GUIDED READING QUESTION

1. Aunt Helen's gentle look boosts Luke's confidence, and he is able to make his proposition to his uncle.

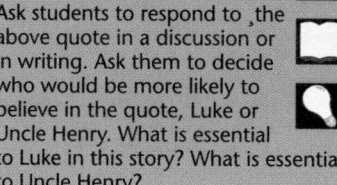

Quotables

"And now here is my secret, a very simple secret. It is only with the heart that one can see rightly; what is essential is invisible to the eye."

—Antoine de Saint Exupéry

ADDITIONAL QUESTIONS AND ACTIVITIES

Ask students to respond to the above quote in a discussion or in writing. Ask them to decide who would be more likely to believe in the quote, Luke or Uncle Henry. What is essential to Luke in this story? What is essential to Uncle Henry?

"Sure I would, Mr. Kemp. I like doing it, anyway."

"All right, son. It's a deal. Now I'll tell you what to do. You go back to your uncle, and before he has a chance to open up on you, you say right out that you've come to him with a business proposition. Say it like a man, just like that. Offer to pay him the seventy-five cents a week for the dog's keep."

"But my uncle doesn't need seventy-five cents, Mr. Kemp," Luke said uneasily.

"Of course not," Mr. Kemp agreed. "It's the principle of the thing. Be confident. Remember that he's got nothing against the dog. Go to it, son. Let me know how you do," he added, with an amused smile. "If I know your uncle at all, I think it'll work."

"I'll try it, Mr. Kemp," Luke said. "Thanks very much." But he didn't have any confidence, for even though he knew that Mr. Kemp was a wise old man who would not deceive him, he couldn't believe that seventy-five cents a week would stop his uncle, who was an important man. "Come on, Dan," he called, and he went slowly and <u>apprehensively</u> back to the house.

When they were going up the path, his aunt cried from the open window, "Henry, Henry, in heaven's name, it's Luke with the dog!"

"Oh. Oh, I see," Uncle Henry said, and gradually the color came back to his face. "You fished him out, eh?" he asked, still looking at the dog uneasily. "Well, you shouldn't have done that. I told Sam Carter to get rid of the dog, you know."

"Just a minute, Uncle Henry," Luke said, trying not to falter. He gained confidence as Aunt Helen came out and stood beside her husband, for

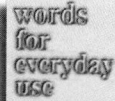
GUIDED READING

What effect does Aunt Helen have on Luke?

her eyes seemed to be gentle, and he went on bravely. "I want to make you a practical proposition, Uncle Henry."

"A what?" Uncle Henry asked, still feeling insecure, and wishing the boy and the dog weren't confronting him.

"A practical proposition," Luke blurted out quickly. "I know Dan isn't worth his keep to you. I guess he isn't worth anything to anybody but me. So I'll pay you seventy-five cents a week for his keep."

"What's this?" Uncle Henry asked, looking bewildered. "Where would you get seventy-five cents a week, Luke?"

"I'm going to get the cows every night for Mr. Kemp."

"Oh, for heaven's sake, Henry," Aunt Helen pleaded, looking distressed, "let him keep the dog!" and she fled into the house.

"None of that kind of talk!" Uncle Henry called after her. "We've got to be sensible about this!" But he was shaken himself, and overwhelmed with a distress that destroyed all his confidence. As he sat down slowly in the rocking chair and stroked the side of his big face, he wanted to say weakly, "All right, keep the dog," but he was ashamed of being so weak and sentimental. He stubbornly refused to yield to this emotion: he was trying desperately to turn his emotion into a bit of good, useful common sense, so he could justify his distress. So he rocked and pondered. At last he smiled. "You're a smart little shaver, Luke," he said slowly. "Imagine you working it out like this. I'm tempted to accept your proposition."

"Gee, thanks, Uncle Henry."

"I'm accepting it because I think you'll learn something out of this," he went on <u>ponderously</u>.

"Yes, Uncle Henry."

---

words for everyday use

ap • pre • hen • sive (ap' rē hen' siv) *adj.,* uneasy, fearful. *I was <u>apprehensive</u> about performing in the big concert.* **apprehensively,** *adv.*

pon • der • ous (pän' dər əs) *adj.,* Heavy, unyielding. *The <u>ponderous</u> problem bothered Jowana day and night.* **ponderously,** *adv.*

"You'll learn that useless luxuries cost the smartest of men hard-earned money."

"I don't mind."

"Well, it's a thing you'll have to learn sometime. I think you'll learn, too, because you certainly seem to have a practical streak in you. It's a streak I like to see in a boy. O.K., son," he said, and he smiled with relief and went into the house.

Turning to Dan, Luke whispered softly, "Well, what do you know about that?"

As he sat down on the step with the collie beside him and listened to Uncle Henry talking to his wife, he began to glow with exultation. Then gradually his exultation

GUIDED READING

What does Uncle Henry think his acceptance of Luke's proposal will teach him?

began to change to a vast wonder that Mr. Kemp should have had such a perfect understanding of Uncle Henry. He began to dream of someday being as wise as old Mr. Kemp and knowing exactly how to handle people. It was possible, too, that he had already learned some of the things about his uncle that his father had wanted him to learn.

Putting his head down on the dog's neck, he vowed to himself fervently that he would always have some money on hand, no matter what became of him, so that he would be able to protect all that was truly valuable from the practical people in the world. ∎

GUIDED READING

What does Luke vow?

Respond *to the* SELECTION

What do you think about the decisions Uncle Henry makes throughout the story? What do you think about Luke's decisions? Explain your answer.

About *the* AUTHOR

Morley Callaghan (1903–1990) was born to Irish parents in Toronto, Ontario, in Canada. In 1923, while working as a reporter at the *Daily Star*—a Toronto newspaper—he met Ernest Hemingway. Hemingway sent some of Callaghan's stories to editors and publishers in Paris. As a result, Callaghan published his first story, "A Girl With Ambition," in 1926. Callaghan was a dedicated writer whose goals were to write well and to keep writing. Like many of his stories, "Luke Baldwin's Vow" deals with the conflict between the demands of the practical world and the spiritual and emotional needs of a character.

"LUKE BALDWIN'S VOW" **551**

SELECTION CHECK TEST WITH ANSWERS (CONT.)

Reader's Toolbox
Fill in the blanks using the following terms.

internal conflict   external conflict   climax
resolution   coming-of-age story
one-dimensional character
three-dimensional character

1. In **coming-of-age stories**, characters of different ages often learn from one another.
2. When a character makes a decision or learns a lesson, he or she experiences **internal conflict**.
3. Characters who exhibit several characteristics and are complex, like real people, are **three-dimensional characters**.
4. In a(n) **coming-of-age story**, a character makes a discovery about himself or herself or about the world.
5. The plot's **resolution** explains how the conflict got solved.

ANSWERS TO GUIDED READING QUESTIONS

1. Uncle Henry says that Luke will learn that "useless luxuries cost the smartest of men hard-earned money."
2. Luke vows to always have money so that he will be able to protect all that is valuable from practical people.

RESPOND TO THE SELECTION

You might also ask students to consider if Uncle Henry should have reacted differently considering that Luke has recently lost his parents. Why, or why not?

SELECTION CHECK TEST WITH ANSWERS

Checking Your Reading
1. Where does Uncle Henry work? **Uncle Henry manages a sawmill.**
2. Why does Uncle Henry want to get rid of Dan? **Uncle Henry wants to get rid of Dan because he is old and can no longer earn his keep.**
3. What did Luke do when he sees Dan go into the water? **Luke jumps into the water to save Dan.**
4. What proposition does Luke make to Uncle Henry? **Luke proposes to pay Uncle Henry for Dan's keep.**
5. What was Luke's vow? **He vows to protect what is truly valuable from the practical people in the world.**

Vocabulary in Context
Fill in each blank below with the most appropriate word from the following Words for Everyday Use.

amber   methodically   aloof
resourceful   imposing   exultation
apprehensively

1. The gem's deep **amber** color sparkled in the sunlight.
2. At 6'3" tall, Lindsay is **imposing** on the tennis court.
3. Tyler proceeded **methodically** through the instructions until he had assembled his new bicycle.
4. I arrived early, but when I walked into the waiting room I noticed several patients already waiting **apprehensively** for their appointments.
5. Serena's **aloof** manner hides her shy nature.

ANSWERS TO INVESTIGATE, INQUIRE, IMAGINE

RECALL

1a. Luke chooses Dan.

2a. Uncle Henry wants to say "All right, keep the dog." He doesn't say it because he thinks it would be shameful to be so emotional. He tells Luke he's a "smart little shaver," and that he accepts his proposal because he thinks Luke will learn something from it.

3a. Luke vows to always have some money on hand to protect the valuable things in life from the practical people in the world.

INTERPRET

1b. *Responses will vary.* Some students might say that Luke chooses Dan because Dan is lonely too. Others may say that Dan makes a good companion for Luke because he is affectionate and always there for Luke. Dan makes a good companion because Luke can tell him things that he might have told his parents.

2b. It gives the reader some insight into Uncle Henry's character by letting the reader know that Uncle Henry does have a sentimental side—he just tries to ignore it.

3b. Luke's vow is emotional. He makes the vow based on how he feels about Dan—and how it felt to almost lose him. Although some students may point out the practicality of keeping money on hand, his vow is an emotional one. Ironically, Uncle Henry expects that Luke will learn that he shouldn't waste money on useless luxuries, but Luke's vow is to save money to protect the things that practical people like his uncle consider useless.

ANALYZE

4a. References to the type of person Luke wants to be when he grows up may include these: "Luke promised himself that when he grew up he, too, would be admired for his good, sound judgement;" "Then suddenly Luke wanted to act like a resourceful, competent man;" "He began to dream of someday being as wise as old Mr. Kemp and knowing exactly how to handle people." Passages that show Luke gaining a better understanding of others include the following: "But Luke was frightened, for he knew what his uncle was like. He knew that if his uncle had decided that the dog was useless and that it was sane and sensible to get rid of it, he would be ashamed of himself if he

Investigate, *Inquire,* and Imagine

Recall: GATHERING FACTS

1a. Who does Luke choose as a companion?

2a. When Luke makes his proposition to Uncle Henry, what does Uncle Henry want to say to Luke? Why doesn't he say it? What does he say instead?

3a. What is Luke's vow?

Interpret: FINDING MEANING

1b. Why might Luke choose this companion?

2b. What does this tell you about Uncle Henry?

3b. Is Luke's vow practical or emotional? How does Luke's vow fit with the lesson Uncle Henry wants him to learn?

Analyze: TAKING THINGS APART

4a. Collect from throughout the story references to the type of person Luke wants to be when he grows up. How do his ideals shift or change as the story progresses? Also, identify passages of the story that show Luke gaining a better understanding of others.

Synthesize: BRINGING THINGS TOGETHER

4b. What does Luke learn about his uncle? What does Luke learn about Mr. Kemp? How does what he learns about each man help him learn about himself? How has Luke kept—or failed to keep—the promise he made to his father?

Perspective: LOOKING AT OTHER VIEWS

5a. View the struggle between Luke and Uncle Henry through the eyes of Aunt Helen. How would she explain why Luke and his uncle acted as they did?

Empathy: SEEING FROM INSIDE

5b. How might Aunt Helen have reacted if Uncle Henry had not accepted Luke's proposition?

Understanding *Literature*

CHARACTER. A **character** is a person or animal who takes part in the action of a literary work. **One-dimensional characters** exhibit a single quality or character trait. **Three-dimensional characters** seem to have all the complexities of an actual human being. Review the story, and make a list of all the characters involved. Make a list of significant details from the story about each character. Reflect on these details and determine which characters in the story are three dimensional and which characters are one dimensional. Which characters, if any, do you find difficult to classify? Write a few sentences on each character briefly explaining why he or she is one dimensional, three dimensional, or difficult to classify.

ANSWERS TO INVESTIGATE, INQUIRE, IMAGINE (CONT.)

were diverted by any sentimental considerations. Luke knew in his heart that he couldn't move his uncle."

SYNTHESIZE

4b. *Responses will vary.* Luke learns from his uncle what it means to know the monetary value of things, but Luke also learns what can happen when a

person is practical to a fault. From Mr. Kemp, Luke learns how valuable understanding others is. From Uncle Henry and Mr. Kemp, Luke learns balance. He also learns that things can be valuable in different ways. He learns that it is dangerous for a person to become so practical that he or she can no longer appreciate the emotional side of life.

(Continued on page 553)

PLOT. A **plot** is a series of events related to a *central conflict*, or struggle. What is the central conflict of the story? A plot includes the introduction of the conflict, its development, and its resolution. Refer back to the Prereading, page 541, and look at your picture map of the plot in "Luke Baldwin's Vow." What point in the story is the climax? Label the picture in your sequence that corresponds with the climax. Then look at the pictures that appear before that point in the sequence. Comparing them to the parts of a plot defined in Elements of Fiction, label the picture that corresponds with *exposition*. Looking at the pictures that follow the climax, label those that correspond with *crisis, resolution,* and *dénouement*.

Writer's Journal

1. Imagine that you are a teacher at Luke's school. Luke has come to you to discuss the fact that Uncle Henry wants to get rid of Dan. Write a **letter** to Uncle Henry explaining why owning Dan is truly valuable to Luke. In your letter, refer to the previous losses that Luke has suffered in his life and to the role that Dan plays in Luke's private life.

2. Write the first **paragraph** of a story that Luke might tell his grandchildren about Dan and his Uncle Henry.

3. A **contract** is a written agreement between two people, companies, or other parties. Write a contract between Luke Baldwin and Uncle Henry stating the terms of the agreement that they come to in the story. Make sure to include details about what happens if either side fails to meet the terms of the agreement.

Skill Builders

Cooperative Learning
BRAINSTORMING ABOUT VALUE. In small groups, reread the last paragraph of "Luke Baldwin's Vow." Then brainstorm a list of things that are, in the opinion of you and your group members, valuable but not practical. How are these things similar to each other? How are they different?

Media Literacy
EVALUATING INTERNET SITES. Using an Internet search engine, look for Internet sites of organizations that promote specific dog breeds. Find at least five organizations' sites by using keywords such as *poodle, husky, rottweiler, spaniel, beagle, collie,* or *chihuahua*. As you work, keep notes about the sites you visit. Indicate what type of information you find at each site, how much information each site offers, and how valuable that information would be for a person deciding what type of dog to adopt. After analyzing the five sites, evaluate each one in a brief paragraph. Consider the following questions. How user-friendly is the site? How much information does it provide? How helpful is that information? Rate the sites in order from best to worst based on your findings. For address of and information on Internet search engines, see the Language Arts Survey 5.27, "Conducting an Internet Search."

"LUKE BALDWIN'S VOW" **553**

ANSWERS TO INVESTIGATE, INQUIRE, IMAGINE (CONT.)

PERSPECTIVE
5a. *Responses will vary.* Aunt Helen would most likely provide a balanced account of the struggle between Luke and his uncle. She would explain Uncle Henry's nature and the fact that Dan was old and not much good for anything, but she would also explain that Luke was just a boy, and that Dan offered him comfort after the death of Luke's parents. She might also say that Uncle Henry

would have liked to just let Luke keep the dog, but that he prided himself on not being swayed by his emotions.

EMPATHY
5b. *Student responses will vary.* Students will probably say that Aunt Helen would be upset with Uncle Henry if he didn't let Luke keep Dan, but that in the end she would abide by Uncle Henry's wishes.

ANSWERS TO UNDERSTANDING LITERATURE

CHARACTER. Students' lists of details will vary, but they should include information on Luke, Uncle Henry, Aunt Helen, Dan, Mr. Kemp, and Sam Carter. Students shouldn't have trouble pointing out that **Luke** and **Mr. Kemp** are three-dimensional characters. The way that Luke is constantly revising his idea of the kind of person he wants to be, his relationship with Dan, and the way he goes against his uncle even though he is usually obedient all serve to present him as a well-rounded character with believable human qualities. Mr. Kemp is old and kind and wise. The way that he understands Uncle Henry and Luke shows that he is both practical and emotional, a well-balanced character with believable human qualities. Students may have more trouble with **Uncle Henry.** Certainly the author uses Uncle Henry to exhibit practicality taken to an extreme, but the author also provides the reader a glimpse into Uncle Henry's sentimental side at the end of the story. Students could make a case for either side of the argument. **Aunt Helen** might be equally difficult for some students to classify. Like Uncle Henry, she seems to delight in what is sensible, and like Uncle Henry, at the end of the story the reader sees her emotional side. **Sam Carter** is described as being quiet and slow-witted. He is the only truly one-dimensional character in the story because he is in the story for one reason, to carry out the act of trying to drown Luke. While it is difficult to classify an animal as one dimensional or three dimensional, a case could be made that the dog **Dan** is a three-dimensional character as he isn't used in the story as a symbol of a singular quality. He is old and lazy and fat, yet he is loyal and affectionate and playful.
PLOT. Students may sum up the parts of a plot as follows:
EXPOSITION: Luke moves in with Uncle Henry
CLIMAX: Dan in the boat, Dan almost drowning, Luke saving him
CRISIS: Luke not knowing what to do and going to Mr. Kemp for advice
RESOLUTION: Uncle Henry accepting Luke's proposition
DÉNOUEMENT: Luke sitting on the porch with Dan, thinking and making his vow.

TEACHER'S EDITION **553**

Cooperative Learning

You may wish to give students the following ideas as prompts to help them generate their own ideas: charity and selflessness, the old teddy bear you had when you were three, and a beautiful painting. Write students ideas on the board as they generate them, so they can look at what has already been said and use these as springboards for further ideas.

Media Literacy

Inform students that they should try to discriminate between facts and opinions. For example, a site that is filled with text such as, "I love border collies. Aren't they cute?" is filled with opinions and may not provide reliable facts. Refer students to the Language Arts Survey 5.2, "Distinguishing Fact from Opinion."

Study and Research

Students might also choose to research illnesses and injuries that affect dogs, such as heartworm, canine distemper, rabies, or hip displaysia. To narrow this assignment, students might wish to limit their list of sources to about five. Tell them that their sources should be of different types—it is not acceptable to only use the Internet or encyclopedias—and that one of their sources must be an interview.

Study and Research

RESEARCHING A VARIETY OF SOURCES. Starting with either a book or an Internet site that provides general information about dogs, create a list of some of the common aspects of canine healthcare. Possible topics include grooming, vaccinations, dental care, spaying and neutering, and aging. Select and investigate a topic that interests you by using a wide variety of source materials. Use library books, the Internet, encyclopedias, magazines, journals, and interviews with experts. Your interviews can include brief question-and-answer sessions with breeders, veterinarians or vet assistants, pet shop owners, groomers, or employees of the Humane Society of the United States or the American Kennel Club.

After you have gathered information on your topic from as many sources as possible, compare and contrast your findings. Do any sources contradict one another? If so, which one do you think offers the correct information? Why? Confirm your ideas by making a follow-up call or consult another reliable source. When you are confident about all the information you have gathered, organize it in a logical way and present your findings to the class. Also report on your sources and your methods of research.

Language, Grammar, and Style

ACTION AND STATE OF BEING VERBS. A verb is a word that expresses action or state of being. Action verbs include words like *sing*, *fly*, *teach*, and *work*. State of being verbs, or linking, verbs include words like *is*, *are*, *am*, *was*, *were*, *be*, *been*, *feel*, *seem*, and *become*. Identify the verbs in the following sentences adapted from "Luke Baldwin's Vow." Tell whether each verb is an action verb or a state of being verb. For more information, see the Language Arts Survey 3.58, "Action Verbs" and 3.59, "State of Being Verbs."

1. Uncle Henry was the manager of the sawmill.
2. He had a rough-skinned, brick-colored face.
3. The four employees were always polite.
4. Luke's Aunt Helen, a kindly, plump, straightforward woman, never argued with Uncle Henry.
5. Luke liked the fresh, clean smell of the newly cut wood.
6. Uncle Henry carried a black notebook in his pocket.
7. They all moved out to the veranda.
8. The dog was sleepy.
9. The dog licked Luke's hand.
10. That dog's teeth are gone.

Prereading

"Getting the Facts of Life"

by Paulette Childress

Reader's TOOLBOX

CHARACTERIZATION, DIALOGUE, AND POINT OF VIEW.
A **character** is a person, or sometimes an animal, who takes part in the action of a literary work. **Characterization** is the act of creating or describing a character. Writers use three major techniques to create character:

- showing what characters say, do, and think;
- showing what other characters say about them;
- showing what physical features, dress, and personality the characters display.

By presenting the words, actions, and thoughts of the character, the writer allows the reader to draw his or her own conclusions about the character based on what the character says, does, thinks, and feels. Revealing the words and thoughts of other characters or of the narrator allows the reader to learn how others perceive the character. Direct descriptions allow the reader to learn about the character's appearance, habits, dress, background, personality, and motivations. As you read "Getting the Facts of Life," think about the character Minerva. In what ways does she change through the course of the story? **Dialogue**—conversation involving two or more people or characters—can be an important part of characterization. Fictional works are made up of dialogue, narration, and description. Through dialogue, the reader hears the character's words and learns about the character's thoughts. In fiction, dialogue is enclosed in quotation marks and usually is accompanied by *tag lines*, words and phrases such as *he said* or *she replied* that tell who is speaking. In "Getting the Facts of Life," watch for dialogue that gives insight into characters. What comments reveal something about the speaker? What do the comments reveal? **Point of view** is the vantage point from which a story is told. If a story is told from the **first-person point of view**, the narrator uses words such as *I* and *we* and is a part of or witness to the action. If a story is told from the **third-person point of view**, the narrator uses words such as *he, she, it,* and *they*. As you read "Getting the Facts of Life," identify the point of view. How does the point of view contribute to characterization in the story?

MOOD. **Mood,** or atmosphere, is the feeling or emotion the writer creates in a literary work. By working carefully with descriptive language, the writer can evoke in the reader an emotional response such as fear, discomfort, longing, or anticipation. What details recur in "Getting the Facts of Life"? What kind of mood do those details help create?

Reader's Journal

What experiences have you had that have forced you to feel more grown-up?

Reader's Resource

- The family in this story is on welfare. Welfare is aid in the form of money or necessities given to families in need. Many different government programs provide this type of aid.

- **HISTORY CONNECTION.** Early welfare programs in the United States were based on the English Poor Laws, a system set up in England in the 1500s and 1600s. Throughout the 1800s, the U.S. welfare system went through numerous reforms but it never disappeared. The Great Depression in the 1930s led to the establishment of the Social Security Act and a variety of programs to fight poverty among elderly people, disabled people, unemployed people, and families with young children. These programs also have gone through many transformations. In the late 1990s, the federal government transferred much of the responsibility for these programs to state goverments.

ADDITIONAL RESOURCES

UNIT 8 RESOURCE BOOK
- Selection Worksheet 8.3
- Selection Check Test 4.8.5
- Selection Test 4.8.6
- Language, Grammar, and Style Resource 3.34

READER'S JOURNAL

Encourage students to write about whether these experiences were positive or negative and how they felt about what happened at the time. How have their feelings changed since the experience?

GOALS/OBJECTIVES

Studying this lesson will enable students to
- identify with the narrator of a short story
- define *characterization, dialogue, and point of view* and recognize how dialogue and point of view contribute to characterization in a short story
- define *mood* and recognize the mood of a short story
- rewrite a scene from a different point of view
- role play a scene involving characters in a short story
- research the welfare system
- compare and contrast a short story to a book or movie

MOTIVATION
Students may especially enjoy the Speaking and Listening activity that presents them with the opportunity to role-play a scene that might take place after the short story ends. Students might like to role-play the scene twice, trying out each role.

READING PROFICIENCY
Tell students that there are some slang terms in this short story that might be unfamiliar to them because this story is set four decades ago. Share the English Language Learning vocabulary with students. Students may benefit from hearing the story read aloud on audiotape. Tell students to follow along with the story's words in their books as they listen to it read aloud.

ENGLISH LANGUAGE LEARNING
Point out the following vocabulary words and expressions:
burner—slang for something that is extremely hot
dog—slang term used as a mild oath
period—exclamation used colloquially to emphasize a completed statement
corralled—rounded up
criminal licks—slang phrase meaning hard spankings
cymbals—brass plates used as musical instruments
pop—any carbonated nonalcoholic beverage; soda pop, soda
pews—benches with backs that are fixed to the floor in rows
regulations—rules
welder—person who heats pieces of metal until they are hot and melted enough to be hammered or pressed together
collards—type of leafy green vegetable
scrub-board—board with ridges used in washing clothes before there were mechanical washing machines

SPECIAL NEEDS
Make sure students focus on the Guided Reading questions and the Recall questions in the Investigate, Inquire, and Imagine section.

ENRICHMENT
Interested students might write personal essays on poverty explaining their thoughts about the best ways to help put an end to poverty. Ask them to think about what tools might help people overcome poverty.

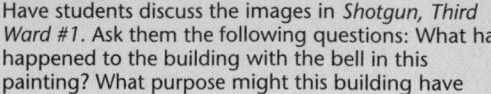

***Shotgun, Third Ward #1**, 1966. John Biggers. National Museum of American Art, Washington, D.C.*

ART SMART

Have students discuss the images in *Shotgun, Third Ward #1*. Ask them the following questions: What has happened to the building with the bell in this painting? What purpose might this building have served? What emotions do the adults in this picture seem to be experiencing? What emotions do the children seem to be experiencing? How do you account for the difference in their emotions?

Getting the FACTS of Life

Paulette Childress

art smart.

John Biggers (b.1924) studied the arts of Africa to see their connections to the culture around him. "Shotgun" in the title of this painting refers to the type of house that Biggers grew up in, which has a hallway that runs its entire length. According to folklore, a shotgun fired through the front door would pass straight through and out the back. However, Biggers discovered that the real origin of the name was the "shogon" house of the Yoruba tribe, an architecture that Africans brought to America. What aspects of this painting match the story "Getting the Facts of Life"? What aspects differ?

VOCABULARY FROM THE SELECTION

comply
convincing
delinquent
eligible
meridian
moderate
notation

partition
repossess
reside
suffocate
surplus
verify
wield

ART SMART

Students may say that the painting seems to depict an earlier time than the one depicted in the story. They may say that the painting and story are similar in that they both reflect poverty. In Biggers's painting, a church has been destroyed by fire and adults gather around talking while children play in the streets. It is clearly summer by the way the children are barefoot and dressed in shorts. You may ask students why they think the woman on the right is looking over her shoulder. Is she fearful or longing to be in another place? In Childress's story, the setting also takes place in summer. The people they pass in the street are not friendly, and the blocks are filled with empty, weedy fields.

1. Minerva has never been to the welfare office; this is her first time.
2. When Stella offered to baby-sit instead of going to the welfare office.
3. Minerva is known as the Witch because she gives hard spankings when she babysits.

LITERARY TECHNIQUE

SETTING

The **setting** of a literary work is the time and place in which it happens. Share this definition with students and ask them the following questions about the setting of this short story:

- What time of year is it when this story takes place? What is the weather like?
- What year is it?
- In what town does the story take place? What urban center is this town near?
- In what specific place in this town does the story begin?
- Where were the narrator and her mother earlier in the story, right after breakfast? What did you learn about the narrator and her family from this setting?
- To what new setting are the narrator and her mother headed? What does this reveal about the narrator's family situation?

Answers

- It is August and the weather is very hot.
- The year is 1961.
- The story takes place in Ecorse, a town right outside of Detroit.
- The story begins with the narrator and her mother walking down the street.
- They were at home, arguing about who would go to the welfare office with the mother. You learn that there are many children in the family and, like in most families, they don't all get along.
- They are headed for the welfare office. This reveals that the family is experiencing financial hardship.

The August morning was ripening into a day that promised to be a burner. By the time we'd walked three blocks, dark patches were showing beneath Momma's arms, and inside tennis shoes thick with white polish, my feet were wet against the cushions. I was beginning to regret how quickly I'd volunteered to go.

"Dog. My feet are getting mushy," I complained.

"You should've wore socks," Momma said, without looking my way or slowing down.

I frowned. In 1961, nobody wore socks with tennis shoes. It was bare legs, Bermuda shorts[1] and a sleeveless blouse. Period.

Momma was chubby but she could really walk. She walked the same way she washed clothes—up-and-down, up-and-down until she was done. She didn't believe in taking breaks.

This was my first time going to the welfare office with Momma. After breakfast, before we'd had time to scatter, she corralled everyone old enough to consider and announced in her serious-business voice that someone was going to the welfare office with her this morning. Cries went up.

GUIDED READING
How many times has Minerva been to the welfare office?

Junior had his papers to do. Stella was going swimming at the high school. Dennis was already pulling the Free Press[2] wagon across town every first Wednesday to get the surplus food—like that.

"You want clothes for school don't you?" That landed. School opened in two weeks.

"I'll go," I said.

"Who's going to baby-sit if Minerva goes?" Momma asked.

Stella smiled and lifted her golden nose. "I will," she said. "I'd rather baby-sit than do that."

That should have warned me. Anything that would make Stella offer to baby-sit had to be bad.

GUIDED READING
What should have warned Minerva that going to the welfare office was bad?

A small cheer probably went up among my younger brothers in the back rooms where I was not too secretly known as "The Witch" because of the criminal licks I'd learned to give on my rise to power. I was twelve, third oldest under Junior and Stella, but I had long established myself as first in command among the kids. I was chief baby-sitter, biscuit-maker and broom-wielder. Unlike Stella, who'd begun her development at ten, I still had my girl's body and wasn't anxious to have that changed. What would it mean but a loss of power? I liked things just the way they were. My interest in bras was even less than my interest in boys, and that was limited to keeping my brothers—who seemed destined for wildness—from taking over completely.

GUIDED READING
Why is Minerva known as "The Witch"?

Even before we left, Stella had Little Stevie Wonder turned up on the radio in the living room, and suspicious jumping-bumping

---

1. **Bermuda shorts.** Short pants that end just above the knee
2. *Free Press.* Newspaper published in Detroit, Michigan

---

words for everyday use

sur • plus (sər' pləs) *adj.*, left-over, excess. *After our team bought uniforms, we used the surplus funds for a pizza party.*

wield (wēld) *v.*, to handle or manage (a tool). *My brother wields a baseball bat like a pro.* **wielder,** *n.*

sounds were beginning in the back. They'll tear the house down, I thought, following Momma out the door.

We turned at Salliotte, the street that would take us straight up to Jefferson Avenue where the welfare office was. Momma's face was pinking in the heat, and I was huffing to keep up. From here, it was seven more blocks on the colored side, the railroad tracks, five blocks on the white side and there you were. We'd be cooked.

"Is the welfare office near the Harbor Show?" I asked. I knew the answer, I just wanted some talk.

"Across the street."

"Umm. Glad it's not way down Jefferson somewhere."

Nothing. Momma didn't talk much when she was outside. I knew that the reason she wanted one of us along when she had far to go was not for company but so she wouldn't have to walk by herself. I could understand that. To me, walking alone was like being naked or deformed— everyone seemed to look at you harder and longer. With Momma, the feeling was probably worse because you knew people were wondering if she were white, Indian maybe or really colored. Having one of us along, brown and clearly hers, probably helped define that. Still, it was like being a little parade, with Momma's pale skin and straight brown hair turning heads like the clang of cymbals. Especially on the colored side.

GUIDED READING

Why does Momma want someone to go with her to the welfare office?

"Well," I said, "here we come to the bad part."

Momma gave a tiny laugh.

Most of Salliotte was a business street, with Old West-looking storefronts and some office places that never seemed to open. Ecorse, hinged onto southwest Detroit like a clothes closet, didn't seem to take

GUIDED READING

Where is Ecorse?

itself seriously. There were lots of empty fields, some of which folks down the residential streets turned into vegetable gardens every summer. And there was this block where the Moonflower Hotel raised itself to three stories over the poolroom and Beaman's drugstore. Here, bad boys and drunks made their noise and did an occasional stabbing. Except for the cars that lined both sides of the block, only one side was busy—the other bordered a field of weeds. We walked on the safe side.

GUIDED READING

What is the safe side of the block?

If you were a woman or a girl over twelve, walking this block—even on the safe side— could be painful. They usually hollered at you and never mind what they said. Today, because it was hot and early, we made it by with only one weak *Hey baby* from a drunk sitting in the poolroom door.

"Hey baby yourself," I said but not too loudly, pushing my flat chest out and stabbing my eyes in his direction.

"Minerva girl, you better watch your mouth with grown men like that," Momma said, her eyes catching me up in real warning though I could see that she was holding down a smile.

"Well, he can't do nothing to me when I'm with you, can he?" I asked, striving to match the rise and fall of her black pumps.

GUIDED READING

Why can't the man do anything to Minerva?

She said nothing. She just walked on, churning away under a sun that clearly meant to melt us. From here to the tracks it was mostly gardens. It felt like the Dixie Peach I'd used to help water-wave[3] my hair was sliding down with the sweat on my face, and my throat was tight with thirst. Boy, did I want a pop. I looked at the last

---

3. **water-wave.** Set hair using a method that requires water

ANSWERS TO GUIDED READING QUESTIONS

1. Momma does not want to walk by herself.
2. Ecorse is located next to southwest Detroit
3. The safe side of the block borders a field of weeds.
4. Minerva feels the man can't do anything to her because she's with her mother.

ADDITIONAL QUESTIONS AND ACTIVITIES

Tell students that segregation is the policy or practice of compelling racial groups to live apart from each other. Ask students to discuss what evidence of racial segregation they see in Minerva's town? What evidence of gender "segregation" they see? How does Minerva seem to feel about this segregation and the "off-limits" sections? How would you feel about this segregation if you were Minerva?

Answers. Students should recognize that the town is described as having a "colored side" and a "white side," separated by railroad tracks. Students may say that the block of Salliote Street near the Moonflower Hotel is gender segregated because dangerous men seem to stay on the side of the street near the hotel, and women walk on the "safe side" near an abandoned field. Minerva seems to feel uncomfortable, angry, and frightened about the segregation; she is uncomfortable when in the white part of town, as evidence by her hurry, and she seems both angry and frightened by the men who make catcalls to passing women. Students may suggest that they would feel similar feelings about such segregation.

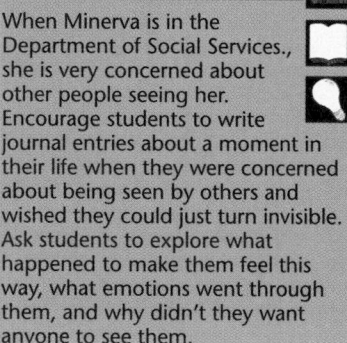

ADDITIONAL QUESTIONS AND ACTIVITIES

When Minerva is in the Department of Social Services., she is very concerned about other people seeing her. Encourage students to write journal entries about a moment in their life when they were concerned about being seen by others and wished they could just turn invisible. Ask students to explore what happened to make them feel this way, what emotions went through them, and why didn't they want anyone to see them.

---

little store before we crossed the tracks without bothering to ask.

Across the tracks, there were no stores and no gardens. It was shady, and the grass was June green. Perfect-looking houses sat in unfenced spaces far back from the street. We walked these five blocks without a word. We just looked and hurried to get through it. I was beginning to worry about the welfare office in earnest. A fool could see that in this part of Ecorse, things got serious.

We had been on welfare for almost a year. I didn't have any strong feelings about it—my life went on pretty much the same. It just meant watching the mail for a check instead of Daddy getting paid, and occasional visits from a social worker that I'd always managed to miss. For Momma and whoever went with her, it meant this walk to the office and whatever went on there that made everyone hate to go. For Daddy, it seemed to bring the most change. For him, it meant staying away from home more than when he was working and a reason not to answer the phone.

> **GUIDED READING**
> What has being on welfare done to Daddy?

At Jefferson, we turned left and there it was, halfway down the block. The Department of Social Services. I discovered some strong feelings. That fine name meant nothing. This was the welfare. The place for poor people. People who couldn't or wouldn't take care of themselves. Now I was going to face it, and suddenly I thought what I knew the others had thought, *What if I see someone I know?* I wanted to run back all those blocks to home.

I looked at Momma for comfort, but her face was closed and her mouth looked locked.

Inside, the place was gray. There were rows of long benches like church pews facing each other across a middle aisle that led to a central desk. Beyond the benches and the desk, four hallways led off to a maze of partitioned offices. In opposite corners, huge fans hung from the ceiling, humming from side to side, blowing the heavy air for a breeze.

Momma walked to the desk, answered some questions, was given a number and told to take a seat. I followed her through, trying not to see the waiting people—as though that would keep them from seeing me.

> **GUIDED READING**
> Why does Minerva try not to see the waiting people?

Gradually, as we waited, I took them all in. There was no one there that I knew, but somehow they all looked familiar. Or maybe I only thought they did, because when your eyes connected with someone's, they didn't quickly look away and they usually smiled. They were mostly women and children, and a few low-looking men Some of them were white, which surprised me. I hadn't expected to see them in there.

Directly in front of the bench where we sat, a little girl with blond curls was trying to handle a bottle of Coke. Now and then, she'd manage to turn herself and the bottle around and watch me with big gray eyes that seemed to know quite well how badly I wanted a pop.

> **GUIDED READING**
> What does the little girl with blond curls seem to know about Minerva?

I thought of asking Momma for fifteen cents so I could get one from the machine in the back but I was afraid she'd still say no so I just kept planning more and more convincing ways to ask. Besides, there was a water fountain near the door if I could make myself rise and walk to it.

---

words for everyday use

par • ti • tion (pär ti′ shən) *v.*, separate or divide as with walls. *Dad will <u>partition</u> the kennel to separate the dogs.* **partitioned,** *adj.*

con • vinc • ing (kən vin′ siŋ) *adj.*, valid; believable. *I thought Albert's argument for buying the house was more <u>convincing</u> than Sue's argument for going to Texas.*

We waited three hours. White ladies dressed like secretaries kept coming out to call numbers, and people on the benches would get up and follow down a hall. Then more people came in to replace them. I drank water from the fountain three times and was ready to put my feet up on the bench before us—the little girl with the Coke and her momma got called—by the time we heard Momma's number.

"You wait here," Momma said as I rose with her.

I sat down with a plop.

The lady with the number looked at me. Her face reminded me of the librarian's at Bunch school. Looked like she never cracked a smile. "Let her come," she said.

"She can wait here," Momma repeated, weakly.

"It's OK. She can come in. Come on," the lady insisted at me.

I hesitated, knowing that Momma's face was telling me to sit.

GUIDED READING

Why does Minerva hesitate when the worker tells her to come in?

"Come on," the woman said.

Momma said nothing.

I got up and followed them into the maze. We came to a small room where there was a desk and three chairs. The woman sat behind the desk and we before it.

For a while, no one spoke. The woman studied a folder open before her, brows drawn together. On the wall behind her there was a calendar with one heavy black line drawn slantwise through each day of August, up to the twenty-first. That was today.

"Mrs. Blue, I have a <u>notation</u> here that Mr. Blue has not reported to the department on his efforts to obtain employment since the sixteenth of June. Before that, it was the tenth of April. You understand that department regulations require that he report monthly to this office, do you not?"

Eyes brown as a wren's belly came up at Momma.

"Yes," Momma

GUIDED READING

What has Mr. Blue failed to do?

answered, sounding as small as I felt.

"Can you explain his failure to do so?"

Pause. "He's been looking. He says he's been looking."

"That may be. However, his failure to report those efforts here is my only concern."

Silence.

"We cannot continue with your case as it now stands if Mr. Blue refuses to <u>comply</u> with departmental regulations. He is still <u>residing</u> with the family, is he not?"

"Yes, he is. I've been reminding him to come in . . . he said he would."

"Well, he hasn't. Regulations are that any able-bodied man, head-of-household and receiving assistance who neglects to report to this office any effort to obtain work for a period of sixty days or more is to be cut off for a minimum of three months, at which time he may reapply. As of this date, Mr. Blue is over

GUIDED READING

What happens to a person who fails to report to the office for 60 days or more?

words for everyday use

no • ta • tion (nō tā′ shən) n., note added to a document. *My mother was unhappy about the <u>notation</u> on my report card about talking in class.*

com • ply (kəm plī′) v., conform to, or follow, a rule. *Safe bicyclists <u>comply</u> with traffic laws.*

re • side (ri zīd′) v., dwell; live permanently in (a home). *My grandmother vacations in Arizona but <u>resides</u> in Alberta, Canada.*

"GETTING THE FACTS OF LIFE"   **561**

ANSWERS TO GUIDED READING QUESTIONS

1. Minerva hesitates because she knows that her mother wants her to sit in the waiting room.
2. He has failed to report to the department regarding his efforts to obtain employment.
3. A person who fails to report is to be cut off for a minimum of three months.

ADDITIONAL QUESTIONS AND ACTIVITIES

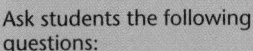
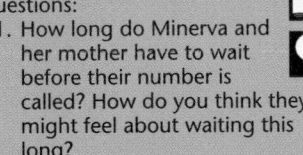

Ask students the following questions:

1. How long do Minerva and her mother have to wait before their number is called? How do you think they might feel about waiting this long?
2. What does Momma tell Minerva to do after the caseworker calls their number? What does the woman tell Minerva to do? Who wins this small argument? What does this reveal about who is in control of the situation?
3. What reasons do you think Momma might have had for wanting Minerva to wait outside?
4. What is Minerva's father doing that jeopardizes her family continuing to receive assistance? Why do you think Mr. Blue is endangering his family by not going to the Department of Social Services? How does this make you feel about Mr. Blue as a character?

Answers

1. They have to wait three hours. They may feel frustrated but helpless to do anything about the situation because they are dependent on the welfare money they are receiving.
2. Momma tells Minerva to wait out in the area with the benches. The caseworker tells Minerva to come with them. The caseworker wins because Momma repeats the order "weakly." while the "lady insisted" that Minerva come with them. This reveals that the caseworker is in control of the situation, while Momma recognizes that she lacks control.

ADDITIONAL QUESTIONS AND ACTIVITIES (CONT.)

3. Students may suggest that Momma wanted to spare Minerva the embarrassment of seeing her mother treated as a charity case and being treated with condescension.
4. Minerva's father, Mr. Blue, has failed to report monthly to the office to discuss his efforts to obtain employment. Students may say that going to the Department of Social Services to do this may injure Mr. Blue's pride, so he tries to avoid going. Students may say they feel sympathy for the embarrassment Mr. Blue feels, but that he is being selfish and irresponsible in not going to the office as schedules because by failing to appear he is endangering his family's well being.

1. She feels bodiless—there is just her face, which won't disappear.
2. She sounds "more and more like Momma should be sorry or ashamed."

ADDITIONAL QUESTIONS AND ACTIVITIES

Ask students to write a journal entry discussing their thoughts on welfare and public assistance. What are its benefits and drawbacks? How might it make the recipients feel to be on public assistance? Do they think people abuse the system or do they think that the majority of people on public assistance are in genuine need? You might have students go back and look at their journal entries after they complete the Study and Research Activity to see if their initial ideas about welfare changed after they researched the topic more.

Teaching Tip: Avoid class or small group discussion about the merits and drawbacks of the welfare system. Students who are receiving public assistance could be made to feel very unconformable and as if they are being criticized for a situation that is beyond their control. Students will also probably want to keep the fact that their family is receiving public assistance private. Any ideas students want to share on this topic should take the form of journal entries seen only by you and the students who wrote them.

---

sixty days <u>delinquent</u>, and officially, I am obliged to close the case and direct you to other sources of aid."

"What is that?"

"Aid to Dependent Children would be the only source available to you. Then, of course, you would not be <u>eligible</u> unless it was <u>verified</u> that Mr. Blue was no longer residing with the family."

Another silence. I stared into the gray steel front of the desk, everything stopped but my heart.

"Well, can you keep the case open until Monday? If he comes in by Monday?"

"According to my records, Mr. Blue failed to come in May and such an agreement was made then. In all, we allowed him a period of seventy days. You must understand that what happens in such cases as this is not wholly my decision." She sighed and watched Momma with hopeless eyes, tapping the soft end of her pencil on the papers before her. "Mrs. Blue, I will speak to my superiors on your behalf. I can allow you until Monday next . . . that's the"—she swung around to the calendar—"twenty-sixth of August, to get him in here."

"Thank you. He'll be in," Momma breathed. "Will I be able to get the clothing order today?"

Hands and eyes searched in the folder for an answer before she cleared her throat and tilted her face at Momma. "We'll see what we can do," she said, finally.

My back touched the chair. Without turning my head, I moved my eyes down to Momma's dusty feet and wondered if she could still feel them; my own were numb. I felt bodiless— there was only my face,

> **GUIDED READING**
> How does Minerva feel listening to the worker talk about their case?

which wouldn't disappear, and behind it, one word pinging against another in a buzz that made no sense. At home, we'd have the house cleaned by now, and I'd be waiting for the daily appearance of my best friend, Bernadine, so we could comb each other's hair or talk about stuck-up Evelyn and Brenda. Maybe Bernadine was already there, and Stella was teaching her to dance the bop.

Then I heard our names and ages—all eight of them—being called off like items in a grocery list.

"Clifford, Junior, age fourteen." She waited. "Yes."

"Born? Give me the month and year."

"October 1946," Momma answered, and I could hear in her voice that she'd been through these questions before.

"Stella, age thirteen."

"Yes."

"Born?"

"November 1947."

"Minerva, age twelve." She looked at me. "This is Minerva?"

"Yes."

No. I thought, no, this is not Minerva. You can write it down if you want to, but Minerva is not here.

"Born?"

"December 1948."

The woman went on down the list, sounding more and more like Momma should be sorry or ashamed, and Momma's answers grew fainter and fainter. So this was welfare. I wondered how many times Momma had had to do this. Once before? Three times? Every time?

> **GUIDED READING**
> How does the worker sound as she reads the list of children?

---

words for everyday use

de • lin • quent (di liŋʸ kwənt) *adj.,* offending by neglect or violation of duty or law; late or overdue. *Mark's school application was <u>delinquent</u> by two weeks.*

el • i • gi • ble (eʹ lə jə bəl) *adj.,* qualified to be chosen or to receive something. *Becky's grades were good enough to make her <u>eligible</u> for the honors society.*

ver • i • fy (verʹ ə fi) *v.,* confirm or demonstrate. *The letter <u>verified</u> that I had completed the necessary work to move up to the next level in archery.*

562   *UNIT EIGHT / STORIES TO TELL: FICTION*

More questions. How many in school? Six. Who needs shoes? Everybody.

"Everybody needs shoes? The youngest two?"

"Well, they don't go to school . . . but they walk."

My head came up to look at Momma and the woman. The woman's mouth was left open. Momma didn't blink.

The brown eyes went down. "Our allowances are based on the <u>median</u> costs for <u>moderately</u> priced clothing at Sears, Roebuck." She figured on paper as she spoke. "That will mean thirty-four dollars for children over ten . . . thirty dollars for children under ten. It comes to one hundred ninety-eight dollars. I can allow eight dollars for two additional pairs of shoes.

"Thank you."

"You will present your clothing order to a salesperson at the store, who will be happy to assist you in your selections. Please be practical as further clothing requests will not be considered for a period of six months. In cases of necessity, however, requests for winter outerwear will be considered beginning November first."

GUIDED READING

Why does the worker tell Momma to be practical when choosing clothes?

Momma said nothing.

The woman rose and left the room.

For the first time, I shifted in the chair. Momma was looking into the calendar as though she could see through the pages to November first. Everybody needed a coat.

I'm never coming here again, I thought. If I do, I'll stay out front. Not coming back in here. Ever again.

She came back and sat behind her desk. "Mrs. Blue, I must make it clear that,

regardless of my feelings, I will be forced to close your case if your husband does not report to this office by Monday, the twenty-sixth. Do you understand?"

GUIDED READING

What will the worker do if Mr. Blue does not report to the office by the twenty-sixth?

"Yes. Thank you. He'll come. I'll see to it."

"Very well." She held a paper out to Momma.

We stood. Momma reached over and took the slip of paper. I moved toward the door.

"Excuse me, Mrs. Blue, but are you pregnant?"

"What?"

"I asked if you were expecting another child."

"Oh. No, I'm not," Momma answered, biting down on her lips.

"Well, I'm sure you'll want to be careful about a thing like that in your present situation."

"Yes."

I looked quickly to Momma's loose white blouse. We'd never known when another baby was coming until it was almost there.

"I suppose that eight children are enough for anyone," the woman said, and for the first time her face broke into a smile.

GUIDED READING

How many children do Mr. and Mrs. Blue have?

Momma didn't answer that. Somehow, we left the room and found our way out onto the street. We stood for a moment as though lost. My eyes followed Momma's up to where the sun was burning high. It was still there, blazing white against a cloudless blue. Slowly, Momma put the clothing order into her purse and snapped it shut. She looked around as if uncertain which way to go. I led the way

words for everyday use

me • di • an (mē′ dē ən) *adj.*, being the exact middle value in a set. *Three years and six months is the <u>median</u> age of the children in that preschool.*

mod • er • ate (mä′ də rət) *adj.*, average; reasonabe. *Uncle Joe's <u>moderate</u> carpenter skills were useful in building the bookshelf.* **moderately,** *adv.*

ANSWERS TO GUIDED READING QUESTIONS

1. She tells Momma to be practical because she will not be able to get help from the office for clothes for six months, except for requests for winter outerwear.
2. She will be forced to close the case.
3. They have eight children.

ADDITIONAL QUESTIONS AND ACTIVITIES

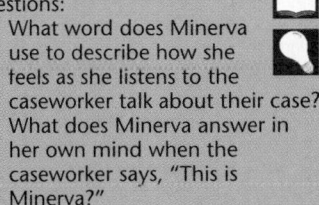

Ask students the following questions:

1. What word does Minerva use to describe how she feels as she listens to the caseworker talk about their case? What does Minerva answer in her own mind when the caseworker says, "This is Minerva?"
2. Why do you think that Minerva feels disconnected from herself and the scene taking place in the caseworker's office?
3. How many children are in the family? What attitude does the caseworker reveal about the number of children in the family?
4. What does the caseworker ask Minerva's mother as she is headed for the door? What is Momma's response? What does the caseworker say about her response. Explain whether or not, in your opinion, the caseworker has any right to ask this questions and respond as she does.

Answers

1. She uses the word *bodyless*. Minerva mentally answers, "No, this is not Minerva. You can write it down if you want to, but Minerva is not here."
2. Students may suggest that Minerva is trying to distance herself from what is a horrifying and humiliating scene for her; she has seen her mother humbled and treated with condescension as a hopeless charity case and has learned that her father is seriously endangering the family's well-being.
3. There are eight children. The caseworker seems to be implying that Momma should be ashamed of herself for having so many children.
4. She asks whether Momma is pregnant, or expecting another child. She bites down on her lip and says that she is not. The caseworker says that she should

ADDITIONAL QUESTIONS AND ACTIVITIES (CONT.)

be careful about having more children in her "present situation." Students may be divided on this question. Some may say that this is a very personal question and none of the caseworker's business. They will say how many children a person has is a private decision. Other students

may say that while they don't approve of the caseworker's approach, as long as the family is on public assistance, the caseworker does have the right to know whether other children are expected because that will affect the amount of assistance the Blue family receives.

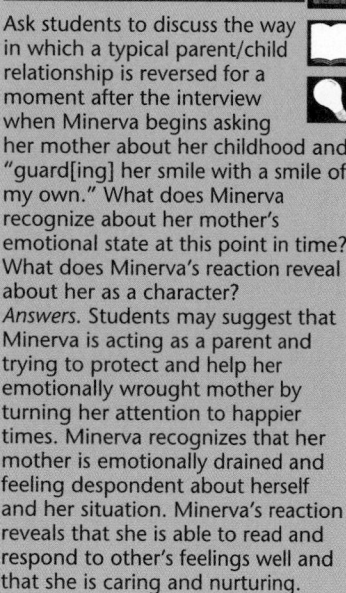
to the corner. We turned. We walked the first five blocks.

I was thinking about how stupid I'd been a year ago, when Daddy lost his job. I'd been happy.

"You all better be thinking about moving to Indianapolis," he announced one day after work, looking like he didn't think much of it himself. He was a welder with the railroad company. He'd worked there for eleven years. But now, "Company's moving to Indianapolis," he said. "Gonna be gone by November. If I want to keep my job, we've got to move with it."

We didn't. Nobody wanted to move to Indianapolis—not even Daddy. Here, we had uncles, aunts and cousins on both sides. Friends. Everybody and everything we knew. Daddy could get another job. First came unemployment compensation.[4] Then came welfare. Thank goodness for welfare, we said, while we waited and waited for that job that hadn't yet come.

> **GUIDED READING**
> Why doesn't anyone in the family want to move to Indianapolis?

The problem was that Daddy couldn't take it. If something got <u>repossessed</u> or somebody took sick or something was broken or another kid was coming, he'd carry on terribly until things got better—by which time things were always worse. He'd always been that way. So when the railroad left, he began to do everything wrong. Stayed out all hours. Drank and drank some more. When he was home, he was so grouchy we were afraid to squeak. Now when we saw him coming, we got lost. Even our friends ran for cover.

At the railroad tracks, we sped up. The tracks were as far across as a block was long. Silently, I counted the rails by the heat of the steel bars through my thin soles. On the other side, I felt something heavy rise up in my chest and I knew that I wanted to cry. I wanted to cry or run or kiss the dusty ground. The little houses with their sun scorched lawns and backyard gardens were mansions in my eyes. "Ohh, Ma . . . look at those collards![5]"

"Umm-hummm," she agreed, and I knew that she saw it too.

"Wonder how they grew so big?"

"Cow dung, probably. Big Poppa used to put cow dung out to fertilize the vegetable plots, and everything just grew like crazy. We used to get tomatoes this big"—she circled with her hands—"and don't talk about squash or melons."

"I bet y'all ate like rich people. Bet y'all had everything you could want."

"We sure did," she said. "We never wanted for anything when it came to food. And when the cash crops were sold, we could get whatever else that was needed. We never wanted for a thing."

"What about the time you and cousin Emma threw out the supper peas?"

"Oh! Did I tell you about that?" she asked. Then she told it all over again. I didn't listen. I watched her face and guarded her smile with a smile of my own.

> **GUIDED READING**
> What is Minerva doing while Momma tells the supper peas story?

We walked together, step for step. The sun was still burning, but we forgot to mind it.

---

4. **unemployment compensation.** Regular payment of money made for a limited time to a worker who has lost a job
5. **collards.** Type of greens like kale

---

 words for everyday use

re • pos • sess (rē pə zes´) *v.*, take back goods from one who fails to make payments on the goods. *My neighbor lost his job, and his sportscar was <u>repossessed</u> the following week.*

suf • fo • cate (sə´ fə kāt) *v.*, deprive of breath; stop the development of. *Toua hoped his family's constant fighting wouldn't <u>suffocate</u> Fayed's gentle nature.* **suffocating,** *v.*

We talked about an Alabama girlhood in a time and place I'd never know. We talked about the wringer washer[6] and how it could be fixed, because washing every day on a scrub-board was something Alabama could keep. We talked about how to get Daddy to the Department of Social Services.

Then we talked about having babies. She began to tell me things I'd never known, and the idea of womanhood blossomed in my mind like some kind of <u>suffocating</u> rose.

"Momma," I said, "I don't think I can be a woman."

> **GUIDED READING**
> What doesn't Minerva think she can be?

"You can," she laughed, "and if you live, you will be. You gotta be some kind of woman."

"But it's hard," I said "sometimes it must be hard."

"Umm-humm," she said, "sometimes it is hard."

When we got to the bad block, we crossed to Beaman's drugstore for two orange crushes. Then we walked right through the groups of men standing in the shadows of the poolroom and the Moonflower Hotel. Not one of them said a word to us. I supposed they could see in the way we walked that we weren't afraid. We'd been to the welfare office and back again. And the facts of life, fixed in our mind like the sun in the sky, were no burning mysteries. ■

---

6. **wringer washer.** Old-fashioned device for laundry that squeezes out the water

Respond *to the* SELECTION

How would you remember the day's events if you were Minerva?

About *the* AUTHOR

Like Minerva Blue, **Paulette Childress** grew up in Ecorse, Michigan. She has written poems and short stories for numerous anthologies and magazines and published *The Watermelon Dress: Portrait of a Woman*, a collection of poetry, in 1983. She is also a painter. Childress currently lives in Dearborn, Michigan.

"GETTING THE FACTS OF LIFE" **565**

SELECTION CHECK TEST WITH ANSWERS (CONT.)

terms. You may not use every term, and you may use some terms more than once.

character   dialogue   characterization   narration
mood   first-person point of view   third person
point of view   setting

1. Fictional works are made up of dialogue, description, and **narration**.

2. If a story is told from the **first-person point of view**, then the narrator is a part of or a witness to the story.

3. Writers use three major techniques for creating a **character:** direct description of actions and speech, portraying behavior, and sharing thoughts and emotions.

RECALL

1a. The weather was hot and sticky.
2a. She thinks to herself that no, this is not Minerva, that Minerva is not here.
3a. They talk about food and about her mother's childhood, about Minerva's father, and about womanhood.

INTERPRET

1b. The heat and bright sun are uncomfortable, just like the visit to the welfare office.
2b. She probably wishes she weren't there at all. She also might feel invisible in the eyes of the welfare office staff.
3b. The mood has become more upbeat. Minerva and her mother are probably relieved that the welfare office visit is over.

ANALYZE

4a. Minerva considers herself as her mother's helper, confidante, and as a more mature young woman. Students may point to the scene in which she tries to shift her mother's mind onto happier topics, guards her mother's smile with her own, and shares her feelings about the difficulties of growing up to be a woman with her mother.

SYNTHESIZE

4b. Students might say that Minerva was a naïve young girl who concerned herself with her siblings, her personal comfort, and her relatively few responsibilities. After the welfare office, Minerva has a more worldly view of life and considers her family's economic welfare, the psychological means by which to convince her father to go to the welfare office, and her mother's well being.

EVALUATE

5a. Students may say that Childress wanted readers to consider the thoughts and feelings of young people and how those thoughts and feelings change or are impacted by a specific event or confrontation. The ideas come across particularly well because the reader learns about Minerva from Minerva herself. By writing the story in the first person point of view with Minerva as the narrator, Childress allows readers into Minerva's mind to see the changes that take place over the course of the story.

EXTEND

5b. *Responses will vary.*

Investigate, Inquire, and Imagine

Recall: GATHERING FACTS

1a. What is the weather like the day Minerva and Momma go to the welfare office?

2a. What does Minerva think when the worker asks her mother if she is twelve-year-old Minerva?

3a. What do Minerva and her mother talk about on the way home?

→ Interpret: FINDING MEANING

1b. How does the weather contribute to Minerva's experience?

2b. Why might she have these thoughts?

3b. How have their moods changed since earlier in the story? Why might they have changed?

Analyze: TAKING THINGS APART

4a. What evidence can you find that Minerva has changed since visiting the welfare office and talking with her mother?

→ Synthesize: BRINGING THINGS TOGETHER

4b. Construct a character sketch of Minerva before the day's events and one of Minerva after the day's events. Then briefly summarize how Minerva has changed due to the day's events.

Evaluate: MAKING JUDGMENTS

5a. What ideas or ideas do you think Paulette Childress wanted to convey through this story? Critique the effectiveness of the story in getting across that message. How effective is the point of view she used? Do you think it would have been more or less effective if told from a different point of view? Explain your answer.

→ Extend: CONNECTING IDEAS

5b. How have you seen people in real life, in books, or in the movies change as a result of a difficult situation? Try to come up with three examples, such as a child, a middle-aged person, and an elderly person, or a poor person, a middle-class person, and a rich person. With whom do you sympathize most? Why?

Understanding Literature

CHARACTERIZATION, DIALOGUE, AND POINT OF VIEW. A **character** is a person or animal who takes part in the action of a literary work. **Characterization** is the act of creating or describing a character. The three major techniques writers use to create character are direct description, portraying characters' speech and behavior, and presenting the thoughts and emotions of characters. What techniques does Paulette Childress White use to develop Minerva's character? Do you think she was effective? Why, or why not? **Dialogue** is conversation involving two or more people or characters. Reread the dialogue between Momma and the worker at the welfare office. What does the dialogue reveal about Momma's character? What does Minerva's reaction to the dialogue reveal about Minerva's character? **Point of view** is the vantage point from which a story is told. If a story is told from the **first-person point of view**, the narrator uses words such as *I* and *we* and is a part of or witness to the action. If a story is told from the **third-person point of view**, the narrator uses words such as *he, she, it,* and *they*. From what point of view is this story told? Whose point of view is it? What would be different about the story if it was told from a different point of view? How would that affect characterization in the story?

Graphic *Organizer*

On a sheet of your own paper, write *Minerva* in an oval in the center of the page. Reread the story and look for words and phrases that characterize Minerva. Write each item in a separate circle and connect the circle to the center oval.

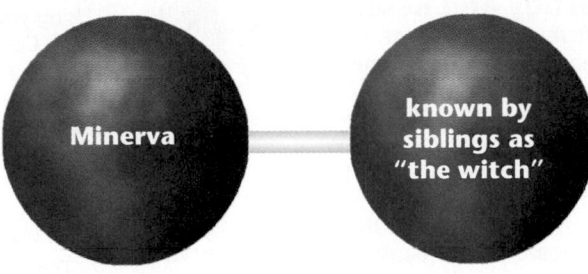

Minerva — known by siblings as "the witch"

When you have finished, find in the circles examples of each of the three techniques of characterization. Do any details correspond to more than one category? Which categories seem to overlap? What does this tell you about the point of view used in this story? What details might you not have learned if the story was told from the third-person point of view?

Writer's Journal

1. Pretend you are Mr. Blue. Write a **paragraph** that describes what you were doing at the time Minerva and her mother are at the welfare office.
2. Imagine you are a politician running for office in Michigan, where this story is set. Write a **position statement** describing your thoughts about the welfare system and your ideas for improving it.
3. Imagine you are Mrs. Blue. Write out the **arguments** you hope to use to persuade your husband, Mr. Blue, to report to the welfare office the following week.

ANSWERS TO
UNDERSTANDING LITERATURE

CHARACTERIZATION, DIALOGUE, AND POINT OF VIEW. The author relies most heavily on the technique of presenting the thoughts and emotions of a character to develop the character of Minerva. There is little dialogue in the selection, and most of the information the reader gets about Minerva, Momma, and the rest of the family is delivered through Minerva's thoughts—which also effectively reveal her emotions. This is an effective technique as Minerva comes off as a very believable character.

The conversation between the worker and Momma reveals that Momma is able to sacrifice her pride to get her family the things they need. It also reveals that Momma, not Daddy, holds the family together. Minerva's reaction to the conversation reveals that she is mature enough to understand what is happening and to be embarrassed by the way the worker treats her mother.

This story is told from the first-person point of view—Minerva's point of view. The story would change significantly if told from a different point of view because Minerva provides a young person's perspective of the experience and the way her mother handles it. Also, because the story deals with an unpleasant, embarrassing situation, the first person point of view gives it more power. The story would lose impact if told by an uninvolved character. Changing the narration would change characterization, not allowing the reader to see Minerva or the other characters through Minerva's eyes. Also, a different narrator would provide a different perspective.

GRAPHIC ORGANIZER

Direct description includes: "It was bare legs, Bermuda shorts and a sleeveless blouse. Period," the name that her siblings give her "The Witch" because of her spankings, the description of her smile guarding her mother's own, and the description of mother and daughter walking right past the group of men on the "bad block" without fear. Examples of portraying characters speech and behavior include Minerva's following the caseworker in rather than remaining on the benches, Minerva leading the way when her mother is uncertain which way to go after leaving the interview, Minerva's asking her mother about her childhood and how they might get Daddy to go to the Department of Social Services, and Minerva revealing her thoughts

GRAPHIC ORGANIZER (CONT.)

about it being hard to be a woman and her fears about growing up to her mother. There are numerous examples of presenting the thoughts and emotions of characters. They include Minerva feeling bodyless and thinking "No . . . Minerva is not here," while she listens to the caseworker; her deciding she will never return to the caseworker's office again; and her remembering the progression of events after her father lost his job. Students may suggest that all three categories overlap in this story because it is presented through the point of view of Minerva's emotions, thoughts, and perceptions. You probably would not have learned as much about thoughts and emotions and would have experienced more direct description if the story were told from the third-person point of view.

Collaborative Learning
Refer students to the Language Arts Survey 2.21, "Pro and Con Charts," for advice on how their charts should be structured and evaluated.

Study and Research
You might encourage students to prepare written reports on their findings rather than oral reports. Students who are on public assistance may feel uncomfortable when discussing this topic, although many will find it valuable. You may also want to enlist the help of a social studies teacher who can present issues related to welfare and other assistance programs.

Media Literacy
Possible books you may wish to encourage students to read include Wilson Rawls's *Where the Red Fern Grows* and Mildred Taylor's *Roll of Thunder, Hear My Cry.* Both these novels are appropriate for this grade level, and the main characters are young people who grow up in poor families and cope with their hardships. You might also have students read sections of or watch a film adaptation of Charles Dickens's classic novel about a poor young orphan, *Oliver Twist.* Students should focus their discussion of how characters are portrayed differently in the two works to how the characters react to and cope with their impoverished state.

Language, Grammar, and Style
Students' sentences will vary, but should be similar to the following.
1. Stella was listening to Little Stevie Wonder singing on the radio.
2. The Blue family had been on welfare for nearly a year.
3. Momma walked to the desk and answered some questions. She was given a number and was told to take a seat.
4. I wanted to run and cry, but I fought my tears.
5. Paulette Childress grew up in Michigan, like the narrator in her story.

Skill Builders

Collaborative Learning

FINDING SOLUTIONS. Imagine Mr. Blue did not report to the welfare office. In small groups of four or five, talk about Mrs. Blue's options. Make a chart that lists the pros and cons to each of her options. Discuss what steps Mrs. Blue would need to take to act upon each of her options. As a group, decide which option offers the best outcome.

Study and Research

RESEARCHING WELFARE. Using library resources and the Internet, research welfare. Answer some of the following questions or come up with your own. What are the benefits of welfare? What are the drawbacks? Can the system be abused? How has the welfare system changed over the years? Has it gotten better or worse? Based on your research, what are you own thoughts about welfare. Use examples from your research to back up your argument. Share your findings with the class.

Media Literacy

ANALYZING A BOOK OR MOVIE. Find a book or movie about a young person whose family is poor. Compare and contrast that person's story with Minerva's story. What was the mood in the book or movie you selected? From what point of view was the story told? What types of things did you learn about the characters? How did the book or movie portray characters differently than those portrayed in "Getting the Facts of Life"? Share your findings with the class.

Language, Grammar, and Style

COMBINING SENTENCES. If you use several short sentences in a paragraph, your writing might sound choppy, and your reader might have trouble understanding how words are connected. You can often combine two sentences that deal with the same main idea. If you are able to combine short sentences, your writing will sound smooth and clear, and the reader will see how ideas are connected to one another.

Using your own paper, rewrite the sentences below. Combine them to make them smooth and clear.

For more information, see the Language Arts Survey 3.34, "Combining and Expanding Sentences."

1. Stella was listening to Little Stevie Wonder. He was singing on the radio.
2. The Blue family had been on welfare. They had been on it for nearly a year.
3. Momma walked to the desk. She answered some questions. She was given a number. She was told to take a seat.
4. I wanted to run. I wanted to cry. I fought my tears.
5. Paulette Childress grew up in Michigan. The narrator of the story grew up in Michigan, too.

Prereading

"A Secret for Two"
by Quentin Reynolds

Reader's TOOLBOX

THEME. A **theme** is a central idea in a literary work. Theme is different from subject or topic. The themes of a literary work are the statements the work makes about life, society, human behavior, or the world. Sometimes the theme of a work is directly stated, but most often, the reader must explore the elements of the literary work—characters, setting, and plot—to discover the theme or themes. Literary works commonly address universal topics that people around the world share—things like love, death, family, friendship. Consider, for example, the Greek myth about King Midas, a king who wishes that everything he touches will turn to gold and whose beloved daughter turns to gold when she hugs him. Possible themes for this story might be: Excessive material wealth can actually make a person poor in other ways; love for one's family is worth more than all the gold in the world. As you read "A Secret for Two," think about what this story says about the universal topics of friendship and familiarity.

FORESHADOWING. Foreshadowing is the act of hinting at events that will happen later in a poem, story, or play. As you read, pay attention to things said by or about Pierre Dupin. Some of these details subtly suggest about Pierre something that the reader doesn't find out until the end of the story. Jot down any hints within the story that cause you to suspect something about Pierre.

Reader's Journal

Identify a routine that you practice daily or weekly. In your journal, describe your routine, how long you've practiced it, how it started, why you do it, and what would happen if you suddenly couldn't keep this routine anymore.

Reader's Resource

- **GEOGRAPHY CONNECTION.** This story is set in Montreal, the largest city in the Canadian province of Quebec. Quebec was settled by the French during the 1600s and 1700s. Even though the territory came under British rule in 1763, few British settled there until after 1800. Even today, about 80 percent of the population of Quebec is French Canadian, and French traditions, language, and customs dominate.

- **HISTORY CONNECTION.** The main character in this story is a milk deliveryman who delivers milk using a horse and wagon. During the late 1800s and early 1900s, even though gas-powered automobiles had been invented, most people still depended on the horse and wagon to get things from one place to another. During those times, milk was delivered daily to each family. In the 1920s, many horse-drawn delivery wagons were replaced by small trucks, and with the change from iceboxes to refrigerators, milk could be delivered twice a week rather than every day. Home delivery of dairy products became much less common in the 1950s with the coming of easy-to-reach supermarkets.

"A SECRET FOR TWO" **569**

ADDITIONAL RESOURCES

UNIT 8 RESOURCE BOOK
- Selection Worksheet 8.4
- Selection Check Test 4.8.7
- Selection Test 4.8.8
- Applied English Resource 6.7

READER'S JOURNAL

As an alternate activity, have students write about an animal they have spent many hours with, such as a pet dog, a horse they learned to ride at camp one summer, or a grasshopper or firefly they caught and kept. What did students get out of the relationship? What, if anything, did the animal get out of the relationship?

GOALS/OBJECTIVES

Studying this lesson will enable students to
- enjoy a short story
- define *theme* and recognize themes in a literary work
- define *foreshadowing* and identify examples of foreshadowing

- research and write an essay on working animals
- write a business memo
- create a news story

ANSWER TO GUIDED READING QUESTION

1. Pierre named his horse after St. Joseph, who was kind, gentle, faithful, and a beautiful spirit, qualities Pierre thought his horse possessed.

INDIVIDUAL LEARNING STRATEGIES

MOTIVATION
Have students find and locate reproductions of photographs, lithographs, paintings or other visual aids that show life in cities and towns during the early 1900s. Students should bring images they find into class by printing them off the internet or borrowing library books. Have students share the images they find with each other. Then ask students to try to imagine what it would have been like to live back then? How might their own lives have been different?

READING PROFICIENCY
The French phrase in this selection may cause students some pause. Tell them to refer to the footnotes where these phrases are explained. make sure students read the Prereading so they understand that in former times milk was delivered to houses by horse-drawn carts each day. Students may better understand the surprise of the secret revealed at the end of the story if you read the story aloud to them expressively. Then have students go back and read this short story through on their own.

ENGLISH LANGUAGE LEARNING
Point out the following vocabulary words and expressions
splendid—worthy of high praise, grand
route—regular course traveled in delivering newspapers, milk, and so forth
foreman—person in charge of a department or group of workers
gaily—happily, showing a good mood
quart, pint—a pint is 16 ounces or two cups, a quart is twice the size of a pint, 32 ounces or a quarter of a gallon
panic-stricken—badly frightened
peak—tapering part of a cap that projects in front of the face

(Continued on page 571)

***Snow in New York**, 1902. Robert Henri. National Gallery of Art, Washington, DC.*

A Secret for Two

Quentin Reynolds

Like many American painters of his generation, Robert Henri (1865–1929) adopted the Impressionist brushstroke. But, while the French Impressionists painted beautiful summer days in the country and the leisure pursuits of the upper classes, Henri and his followers showed the gritty aspects of city life. Critics called the group "The Ashcan School." What reasons might an artist have for using dark, moody colors rather than bright, lively tones?

Montreal is a very large city, but like all cities, it has some very small streets. Streets, for instance, like Prince Edward Street, which is only four blocks long, ending in a cul-de-sac.[1] No one knew Prince Edward Street as well as did Pierre Dupin, for Pierre had delivered milk to the families on the street for thirty years now.

During the past fifteen years the horse which drew the milk wagon used by Pierre was a large white horse named Joseph. In Montreal, especially in that part of Montreal which is very French, the animals, like children, are often given the names of saints. When the big white horse first came to the Provincale Milk Company, he didn't have a name. They told Pierre that he could use the white horse <u>henceforth</u>. Pierre stroked the softness of the horse's neck, he stroked the <u>sheen</u> of its splendid belly, and he looked into the eyes of the horse.

"This is a kind horse, a gentle and a faithful horse," Pierre said, "and I can see a beautiful spirit shining out of the eyes of the horse. I will name him after good St.

GUIDED READING

Why did Pierre name his horse Joseph?

---

1. **cul-de-sac.** Dead-end street

words for everyday use

hence · forth (hens fôrth') *adv.*, from this time on. *Henceforth, we will meet every other week.*

sheen (shēn) *n.*, brightness or shininess. *Mona's long hair had a healthy <u>sheen</u> that people often comment on.*

ART SMART

An artist might use dark, moody colors to portray a grittier, more serious side of reality.

Joseph, who was also kind and gentle and faithful and a beautiful spirit."

Within a year Joseph knew the milk route as well as Pierre. Pierre used to boast that he didn't need reins—he never touched them. Each morning Pierre arrived at the stables of the Provincale Milk Company at five o'clock.

GUIDED READING

About what does Pierre boast?

The wagon would be loaded, and Joseph hitched to it. Pierre would call *"Bonjour, vieil ami"*[2] as he climbed into his seat, and Joseph would turn his head, and the other drivers would smile and say that the horse would smile at Pierre. Then Jacques, the foreman, would say, "All right, Pierre, go on," and Pierre would call softly to Joseph, *"Avance,*[3] *mon ami,"* and this splendid combination would <u>stalk</u> proudly down the street.

The wagon, without any direction from Pierre, would roll three blocks down St. Catherine Street, then turn right two blocks along Roslyn Avenue, then left, for that was Prince Edward Street. The horse would stop at the first house, allow Pierre perhaps thirty seconds to get down from his seat and put a bottle of milk at the front door, and would then go on, skipping two houses and stopping at the third. So down the length of the street. Then Joseph, still without any direction from Pierre, would turn around and come back along the other side. Yes, Joseph was a smart horse.

GUIDED READING

How does Joseph show he is "a smart horse"?

Pierre would boast at the stable of Joseph's skill. "I never touch the reins. He knows just where to stop. Why, a blind man could handle my route with Joseph pulling the wagon."

So it went on for years—always the same. Pierre and Joseph both grew old together, but gradually, not suddenly. Pierre's huge walrus mustache[4] was pure white now, and Joseph didn't lift his knees so high or raise his head quite as much. Jacques, the foreman of the stables, never noticed that they were both getting old until Pierre appeared one morning carrying a heavy walking stick.

"Hey, Pierre," Jacques laughed. "Maybe you got the gout,[5] hey?"

"Mais oui,[6] Jacques," Pierre said a bit uncertainly. "One grows old. One's legs get tired."

"You should teach that horse to carry the milk to the front door for you," Jacques told him. "He does everything else."

He knew every one of the forty families he served on Prince Edward Street. The cooks knew that Pierre could neither read nor write, so instead of following the usual custom of leaving a note in an empty bottle if an additional quart of milk was needed, they would sing out when they heard the rumble of his wagon wheels over the cobbled[7] street, "Bring an extra quart this morning, Pierre."

GUIDED READING

Why did the cooks call out their orders instead of leaving notes?

"So you have company for dinner tonight," he would call back gaily.

Pierre had a remarkable memory. When he arrived at the stable, he'd always remember to tell Jacques, "The Paquins took an extra quart this morning; the Lemoines bought a pint of cream."

---

2. *vieil ami.* (French) Old friend
3. *Avance.* (French) Go ahead
4. **walrus mustache.** Mustache with long, drooping ends like the tusks of a walrus
5. **gout.** A disease characterized by painful swelling of the joints
6. *Mais oui.* (French) But yes
7. **cobbled.** Paved with rounded stones

words for everyday use

stalk (stôk) v., walk in a stiff way. *Members if the marching band <u>stalked</u> by the crowd of spectators at the parade.*

ANSWERS TO GUIDED READING QUESTIONS

1. Pierre boasts that he never has to touch Joseph's reins because Joseph knows the milk route so well.
2. Joseph was a smart horse because he would stop at the first house, pause just long enough for Pierre to deliver the milk, and then move on to the next house where a delivery was required. Joseph was smart enough to skip the houses that didn't get a delivery.
3. The cooks called out their orders because they knew Pierre could not read or write.

INDIVIDUAL LEARNING STRATEGIES (CONT.)

hobbling—walking lamely or awkwardly; limping

SPECIAL NEEDS
Students may not pick up on the elements of foreshadowing in this short story. Tell them to focus on responding to the Guided Reading questions and responding to the Recall questions in the Investigate, Inquire, and Imagine section. Once they understand the main events of the story, they may have an easier time going back and finding clues and hints in the story about there being some secret between Pierre and Joseph.

ENRICHMENT
Have students locate Montreal and the province of Quebec on a map of Canada. Students should identify other provinces and cities as well. Students might then choose a province and research some basic facts about it, such as home many people live there, climate and weather, major industries, and the culture of that province. Students should prepare brief written reports on their chosen provinces. Other students might research the French-Canadian movement in Quebec.

VOCABULARY FROM THE SELECTION

henceforth   stalk
sheen

1. Jacques asks the president if Pierre can be retired with a pension.
2. Jacques tells Pierre that Joseph has died.
3. Jacques sees a dead and lifeless look. He sees the grief that Pierre feels in his heart and soul reflected in his eyes.

ADDITIONAL QUESTIONS AND ACTIVITIES

Students might speak to people who remember a time when home deliveries of groceries and other items was common. Ask students to discuss the advantages and disadvantages of such a system. In what way is the delivery of groceries and other items experiencing renewed popularity today? What communication channel is making this possible. *Answers.* Students' lists of advantages and disadvantages will vary. Students might say it is convenient to have groceries delivered, but you cannot inspect the quality of the items yourself. Students should recognize that home delivery of groceries and other goods is experiencing new popularity due to the increasing number of services offering shopping and delivery on-line, on the Internet.

Jacques would note these things in a little book he always carried. Most of the drivers had to make out the weekly bills and collect the money, but Jacques, liking Pierre, had always excused him from this task. All Pierre had to do was to arrive at five in the morning, walk to his wagon, which was always in the same spot at the curb, and deliver his milk. He returned some two hours later, got down stiffly from his seat, called a cheery "*Au 'voir*"[8] to Jacques, and then limped slowly down the street.

One morning the president of the Provincale Milk Company came to inspect the early morning deliveries. Jacques pointed Pierre out to him and said: "Watch how he talks to that horse. See how the horse listens and how he turns his head toward Pierre? See the look in that horse's eyes? You know, I think those two share a secret. I have often noticed it. It is as though they both sometimes chuckle at us as they go off on their route. Pierre is a good man, Monsieur[9] President, but he gets old. Would it be too bold of me to suggest that he be retired and be given perhaps a small pension?"[10] he added anxiously.

"But of course," the president laughed. "I know his record. He has been on this route now for thirty years, and never once has there been a complaint. Tell him it is time he rested. His salary will go on just the same."

> **GUIDED READING**
> What does Jacques ask the president of the milk company?

But Pierre refused to retire. He was panic-stricken at the thought of not driving Joseph every day. "We are two old men," he said to Jacques. "Let us wear out together. When Joseph is ready to retire—then I, too, will quit."

Jacques, who was a kind man, understood. There was something about Pierre and Joseph which made a man smile tenderly. It was as though each drew some hidden strength from the other. When Pierre was sitting in his seat and when Joseph was hitched to the wagon, neither seemed old.

But when they finished their work, then Pierre would limp down the street slowly, seeming very old indeed, and the horse's head would drop, and he would walk very wearily to his stall.

Then one morning Jacques had dreadful news for Pierre when he arrived. It was a cold morning and still pitch-dark. The air was like iced wine that morning, and the snow which had fallen during the night glistened like a million diamonds piled together.

Jacques said, "Pierre, your horse, Joseph, did not wake up this morning. He was very old. Pierre, he was twenty-five, and that is like being seventy-five for a man."

> **GUIDED READING**
> What dreadful news does Jacques have for Pierre?

"Yes," Pierre said slowly. "Yes. I am seventy-five. And I cannot see Joseph again."

"Of course you can," Jacques soothed. "He is over in his stall, looking very peaceful. Go over and see him."

Pierre took one step forward then turned. "No . . . no . . . you don't understand, Jacques."

Jacques clapped him on the shoulder. "We'll find another horse just as good as Joseph. Why, in a month you'll teach him to know your route as well as Joseph did. We'll . . ."

The look in Pierre's eyes stopped him. For years Pierre had worn a heavy cap, the peak of which came low over his eyes, keeping the bitter morning wind out of them. Now Jacques looked into Pierre's eyes, and he saw something which startled him. He saw a dead, lifeless look in them. The eyes were mirroring the grief that was in Pierre's heart and his soul. It was as though his heart and soul had died.

> **GUIDED READING**
> What does Jacques see in Pierre's eyes?

"Take today off, Pierre," Jacques said, but already Pierre was hobbling off down the street, and had one been near, one would

---

8. *Au 'voir.* (French) Shortened form of "goodbye"
9. *Monsieur.* (French) A title equivalent to Mr. in English
10. **pension.** Regular payment, especially to a retired employee

have seen tears streaming down his cheeks and have heard half-smothered sobs. Pierre walked to the corner and stepped into the street. There was a warning yell from the driver of a huge truck that was coming fast, and there was the scream of brakes, but Pierre apparently heard neither.

Five minutes later an ambulance driver said, "He's dead. Was killed instantly."

Jacques and several of the milk-wagon drivers had arrived, and they looked down at the still figure.

"I couldn't help it," the driver of the truck protested. "He walked right into my truck. He never saw it, I guess. Why, he walked into it as though he were blind."

The ambulance doctor bent down. "Blind? Of course the man was blind. See those cataracts?[11] This man has been blind for five years." He turned to Jacques. "You say he worked for you? Didn't you know he was blind?"

"No . . . no . . ." Jacques said softly. "None of us knew. Only one knew—a friend of his named Joseph. . . . It was a secret, I think, just between those two." ∎

GUIDED READING

What does the ambulance doctor tell Jacques about Pierre?

---

11. **cataracts.** Cloudy areas of the eyes caused by disease

Respond *to the* SELECTION

Do you think Pierre's death was accidental or deliberate? Explain your answer.

About *the* AUTHOR

Quentin Reynolds (1902–1965) was a journalist and author who wrote mostly nonfiction. He was born in New York City and attended Brown University, where he was a star football player and heavyweight boxing champion. He earned a law degree at Brooklyn Law School but soon entered a career in journalism. During World War II (1939–1945), he served as a war correspondent in North Africa, the Middle East, and Europe. He also wrote and narrated two documentaries about World War II. Later he wrote numerous historical and biographical works, including *Custer's Last Stand, The F.B.I., The Life of Saint Patrick, Winston Churchill,* and *With Fire and Sword: Great War Adventures.*

"A SECRET FOR TWO" **573**

ANSWER TO GUIDED READING QUESTION

1. The ambulance doctor tells Jacques that Pierre has been blind for five years.

RESPOND TO THE SELECTION

If students believe Pierre's accident was deliberate, you might wish to warn students about depression and feelings of hopelessness. Emphasize that these feelings pass, and suicide is not an answer.

SELECTION CHECK TEST WITH ANSWERS

Checking Your Reading
1. Where does this story take place? **The story takes place in Montreal, Quebec, Canada.**
2. Who is Joseph? **Joseph is a horse.**
3. What is Pierre's job? **Pierre delivers milk.**
4. What is Pierre's reaction to Jacques' suggestion that he retire? **Pierre refuses to retire.**
5. What is Jacques surprised to discover after Pierre's death? **Jacques is surprised to discover that Pierre was blind.**

Vocabulary in Context
Fill in each blank below with the most appropriate word from the following Words for Everyday Use.

    henceforth   sheen   stalk

1. After numerous violations of the dress code, the school board announced that **henceforth**, students would have to wear uniforms to school.
2. Mary Lou looked in the mirror and admired the **sheen** of her newly washed hair.

Reader's Toolbox
Fill in the blanks using the following terms. You may not use every term, and you may use some terms more than once.

    theme   climax   rising action
    foreshadowing   conflict   resolution
                setting

1. In a story's plot, the **climax** is the high point of the action.
2. A literary work makes a point or points about life, death, human nature, society, or other universal topics through its **theme**.
3. When a literary work contains clues that hint at events that will occur later in a work, the author is using **foreshadowing**.

RECALL
1a. The opening sentence of the story is: "Montreal is a very large city, but like all cities, it has some very small streets."
2a. Pierre is panic-stricken. He asks to be allowed to wait to retire until Joseph retires.
3a. The secret between Pierre and Joseph was that Pierre was blind.

INTERPRET
1b. These words create Pierre's world for us, a small street nestled in the big city—cozy, familiar, safe. By beginning the story with these words, the reader is drawn into Pierre's world.
2b. Pierre's reaction tells the reader that he is dependent on his daily routine and Joseph, that he can't imagine his life without either of them. Some students may say that Pierre doesn't like change.
3b. Pierre was able to keep his blindness a secret for so long because Joseph knew the route so well that he guided Pierre, but also because his customers, knowing that he couldn't read, called special orders out to him, and because Jacques didn't require him to handle the billing of his customers. Also, Pierre's wagon was hitched and ready each morning at the same time and place.

ANALYZE
4a. Details that refer to time and routines being repeated: Pierre delivered milk to families on Prince Edward Street *for thirty years;* Joseph drew the wagon *for fifteen years;* in that part of Montreal, animals and children are *often* named after saints; description of Pierre and Joseph's route, which never varies; "So it went on for years—always the same."; Pierre and Joseph grew old together, *gradually, not suddenly;* Pierre would always remember to tell Jacques about additional orders; Jacques would note them in a book he always carried.

SYNTHESIZE
4b. The author refers to several things that are always same in the story. The reader knows that all these things have been going on for at least 30 years. The author notes a comfortable, familiar setting for Pierre and Joseph. This makes Pierre's loss of Joseph much more devastating.

Investigate, Inquire, and Imagine

Recall: GATHERING FACTS

1a. With what words does the author begin the story?

2a. How does Pierre feel when Jacques suggests he retire? How does Pierre respond?

3a. What was the secret between Pierre and Joseph?

Interpret: FINDING MEANING

1b. What is the effect of this first sentence? Why might the author have begun the story this way?

2b. What does this response tell you about Pierre?

3b. How was Pierre able to keep it a secret for so long?

Analyze: TAKING THINGS APART

4a. Look back to the story and gather words and phrases that refer to time passing and routines being repeated.

Synthesize: BRINGING THINGS TOGETHER

4b. Based on the details you collected, explain in a few sentences how these references add to the impact of the story.

Evaluate: MAKING JUDGMENTS

5a. How successful is the author at creating a believable friendship between Pierre and Joseph? Does the relationship between Pierre and Joseph need to be believable for the story to be effective? Why, or why not? When the author reveals Pierre's secret at the end of the story, how does the reader gain more insight into the relationship between Pierre and Joseph? How does the reader learn more about Pierre's character? How does this detail create a forceful ending to the story?

Extend: CONNECTING IDEAS

5b. Imagine that Pierre had to depend on a person in the same ways that he depended on Joseph. How might things have turned out differently? Why do you think the author chose Joseph, a horse, as Pierre's companion? How does this choice add to or take away from the story?

Understanding Literature

FORESHADOWING. Foreshadowing is the act of hinting at events that will happen later in a poem, story, or play. Throughout "A Secret for Two," the author uses foreshadowing to hint at Pierre's secret. How did you react when you discovered Pierre's secret at the end of the story? Did you guess what it was before the story revealed it? Why do you think the author might have chosen to use foreshadowing in this story? Reread the story and collect as many details as you can find that hint at the secret disclosed at the end of the story.

EVALUATE
5a. Students should provide examples from the story to support their response.

EXTEND
5b. *Responses will vary. Possible responses are given.* Students may suggest that the fact that Joseph is a horse makes it easier for Pierre to keep his secret hidden; had he depended on a human it would be more likely that the human would reveal the secret.

THEME. A **theme** is a central idea in a literary work. Themes often describe aspects of human nature. Thinking about theme as it relates to the topics of friendship and familiarity, reread the story to examine closely the setting, characters, and events that took place. How do these elements contribute to ideas about friendship? about familiarity? Write down your thoughts and impressions as you reread the story. Although themes are linked closely to the ideas the reader takes away from the story, different readers of the same story will express themes differently. Your interpretation of theme must always be supported by evidence from the work. Use the graphic organizer below to develop your statements of theme. After you have written some possible themes, compare your notes with those of your classmates.

Graphic *Organizer*

Use this graphic organizer as a guide for compiling details and recording your ideas about the topic of familiarity and about theme or themes in "A Secret for Two." Some items are given. Fill in others as you work through the activity on your own paper. Then go back and do the same work on the topic of friendship.

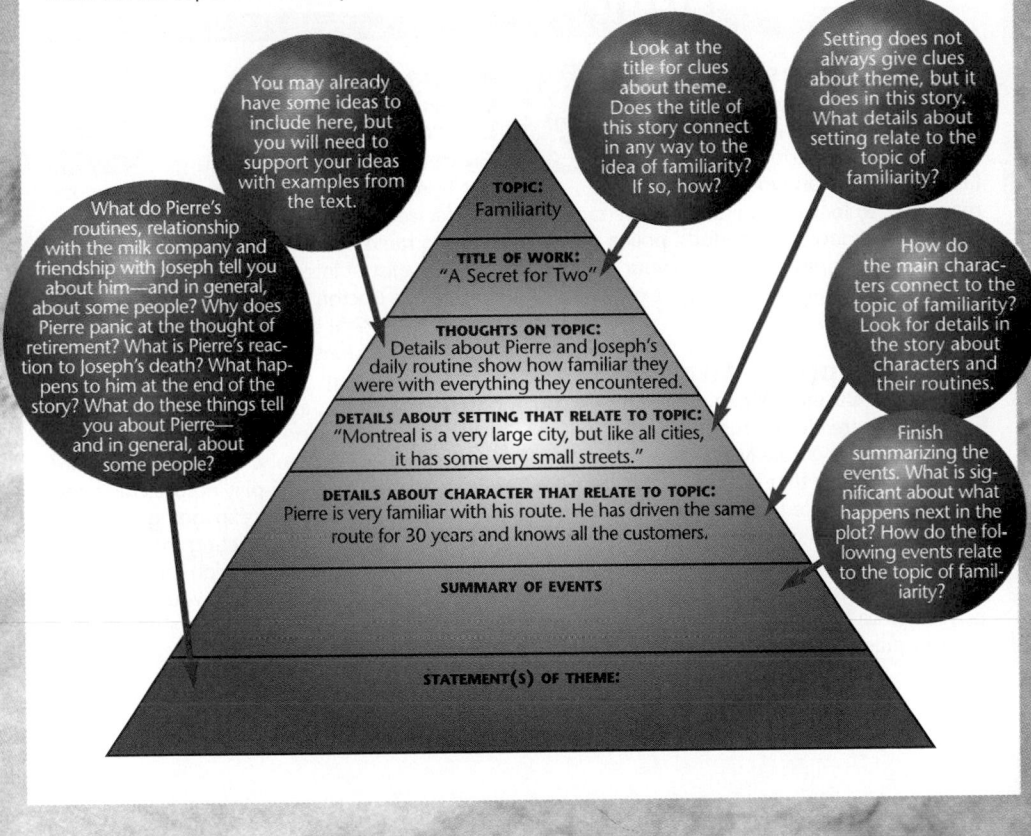

You may already have some ideas to include here, but you will need to support your ideas with examples from the text.

Look at the title for clues about theme. Does the title of this story connect in any way to the idea of familiarity? If so, how?

Setting does not always give clues about theme, but it does in this story. What details about setting relate to the topic of familiarity?

What do Pierre's routines, relationship with the milk company and friendship with Joseph tell you about him—and in general, about some people? Why does Pierre panic at the thought of retirement? What is Pierre's reaction to Joseph's death? What happens to him at the end of the story? What do these things tell you about Pierre—and in general, about some people?

How do the main characters connect to the topic of familiarity? Look for details in the story about characters and their routines.

Finish summarizing the events. What is significant about what happens next in the plot? How do the following events relate to the topic of familiarity?

TOPIC: Familiarity

TITLE OF WORK: "A Secret for Two"

THOUGHTS ON TOPIC: Details about Pierre and Joseph's daily routine show how familiar they were with everything they encountered.

DETAILS ABOUT SETTING THAT RELATE TO TOPIC: "Montreal is a very large city, but like all cities, it has some very small streets."

DETAILS ABOUT CHARACTER THAT RELATE TO TOPIC: Pierre is very familiar with his route. He has driven the same route for 30 years and knows all the customers.

SUMMARY OF EVENTS:

STATEMENT(S) OF THEME:

ANSWERS TO UNDERSTANDING LITERATURE

FORESHADOWING. Some students will say they were surprised by the ending of the story. Others might say they guessed the secret. The use of foreshadowing helps to prepare the reader for the events that happen later in the work. Examples of foreshadowing include: Pierre mentions that a blind man could handle his route with Joseph pulling the wagon; Pierre cannot read or write so customers yell their additional orders out to him; Jacques excuses Pierre from billing and collecting money from his customers; Pierre says he can never see Joseph again; Jacques sees a dead and lifeless look in Pierre's eyes; Pierre steps in front of an oncoming truck.

THEME. One theme has to do with familiarity: When someone depends on certain familiarities for a long time, the loss of them may be more than that person can bear. Another theme involves friendship: A true friend is one you can fully trust, one who keeps your secrets, and one who knows and accepts your imperfections.

Students may provide the following details in each section of their charts:

TOPIC: Familiarity

TITLE OF WORK: "A Secret for Two." Students may note that the title connects to the topic of familiarity, suggesting a special bond of closeness, confidentiality, and trust shared in this case, a man and a horse.

THOUGHTS ON TOPIC: Students may include the following details: Pierre delivered milk to families on Prince Edward Street for thirty years; Joseph drew the wagon for fifteen years; description of Pierre and Joseph's route, which never varies; Pierre would always remember to tell Jacques about additional orders; Jacques would note them in a book he always carried; Pierre couldn't imagine not driving Joseph every day.

DETAILS ABOUT SETTING THAT RELATE TO TOPIC: "Montreal is a very large city, but like all cities, it has some very small streets."; No one knows Prince Edward St. like Pierre. "The wagon, without any direction from Pierre, would roll three blocks down St. Catherine Street, then turn right two blocks along Roslyn Avenue, then left, for that was Prince Edward Street."

DETAILS ABOUT CHARACTERS THAT RELATE TO TOPIC: Pierre was very familiar with his route. He drove the same route for thirty years and knew all the customers. Pierre arrived at the same time every morning. His wagon was always in the same spot at the curb. Joseph knew the route by heart—Pierre never even had to use the reins. Pierre panicked at the thought of retiring, of leaving Joseph and his route. Jacques had his routines too: Pierre would call *'Bonjour, vieil ami'* each morning before Pierre set off.

SUMMARY OF EVENTS: Pierre and Joseph deliver milk together every day. One day Jacques realizes Pierre has gotten old and asks the president of the milk company to let Pierre retire. Pierre refuses, saying he will retire when Joseph retires. Pierre and Joseph continue to deliver milk until one morning when Jacques tells Pierre that Joseph has died. Pierre is grief-stricken. Five minutes later Pierre walks out into traffic and is killed by a truck. The reader finds out that Pierre has been blind for five years.

STATEMENT(S) OF THEME: *Responses will vary.* For some, life means the comfort of familiar things that never change. Sometimes we become so

(Continued on page 576)

Study and Research
Ask students to focus on the discipline and training necessary for their working animal. Possible sources of information for students include encyclopedias, periodicals, books on animals and animal training, Internet resources, and interviews with those who have worked with animals who are trained to work as specific jobs. You may wish to invite a guest speaker to your classroom, such as someone who trains and works with guide dogs.

Applied English
Students should reread parts of the story featuring Pierre's supervisor so that their memos will be in character. Remind students that the supervisor seems to like and admire Pierre, so he would probably not write something as drastic as a suggestion that Pierre be fired. Tell students that business memos should be brief, factual, and very to the point.

**Media Literacy &
Collaborative Learning**
Students might also record the interviews as they are taking place and then edit the tape to find the clips that will work best with their news story. Your school audiovisual department may be able to loan you a camcorder for this assignment. if not, students should prepare their news story on audiotape imagining that it is for a news radio show.

GRAPHIC ORGANIZER (CONT.)

accustomed to certain things that the thought of them being taken away fills us with fear. When someone depends on certain routines, the loss of them may be more than that person can bear. Note: Students should create a similar graphic organizer on the topic of friendship. They may arrive at the theme indicated in the answers to the Understanding Literature questions.

Writer's Journal

1. A **proverb** is a traditional saying. Examples of proverbs include "You can lead a horse to water, but you can't make it drink," or "A friend in need is a friend indeed." Write your own proverb based on the story "A Secret for Two."

2. A diary is a day-to-day record of a person's doings, thoughts, and feelings. Use your imagination to write two **diary entries** for Pierre: one for the day he meets Joseph and one on the day he is told he can retire. Keep in mind the amount of time between the two events.

3. A **eulogy** is a speech or writing in praise of someone, often given upon a person's death. Write a short eulogy for Pierre to be read at his funeral.

Skill Builders

Study and Research
RESEARCH AND WRITING. Use various resources to conduct research on animals that perform specific tasks in the human world. You  may want to focus on animals in entertainment, guide dogs, rescue dogs, police horses, or working elephants. Based on your research, write a short essay about the type of working animal you researched.

Applied English
BUSINESS MEMO. Imagine that you are Pierre's supervisor at the Provincale Milk Company and that you discover that he is blind. Reflect on how to best handle the situation. In the form of a business memo to the president of your company, propose a way to respond to the situation, including the reasons for your proposal. Before beginning this activity, refer to the Language Arts Survey 6.7, "Writing a Memo."

Media Literacy & Collaborative Learning

CREATING A NEWS STORY. Form small groups of four or five students. Suppose that Pierre's death is to be reported on the evening radio news in Montreal. As a group, develop a list of interview questions to ask the ambulance doctor, the truck driver, Jacques, and the president of Provincale Milk Company about the accident and about Pierre's history with the company. Then stage interviews, with one student acting as the reporter and the other students playing the roles of the four characters from the story. As the questions are asked, the students role-playing the characters should create answers by expanding on facts from the story. After completing the interviews, assemble the information into a news story for the evening news. As you write the story, try to focus on a particular angle, such as Pierre's relationship with Joseph, his service to the company, or the secret revealed upon his death. After your writing is completed, record the story on tape.

Prereading

The Snow Goose
by Paul Gallico

Reader's Resource

- **SCIENCE CONNECTION.** The snow goose is a large white goose with black wingtips. The snow goose breeds in summer in the northern reaches of Canada, migrating southward to coastal areas of the United States and southwestern Canada for the winter. In this story, a snow goose is found in England, more than 3,200 miles east of its habitat in Canada.

- **HISTORY CONNECTION.** This story takes place in Essex, a county in southeastern England. It is set between the late 1930s and 1940, at the beginning of World War II (1939–1945). After the Belgian army surrendered to the Germans in 1940, the Allied American, British, and French troops retreated to Dunkirk, a town on the northernmost coast of France, just across the Strait of Dover from England. With German troops advancing, a massive evacuation of Allied forces was necessary. Volunteers in many kinds of vessels, including minesweepers, fishing vessels, yachts, and rowboats, carried soldiers from France to England.

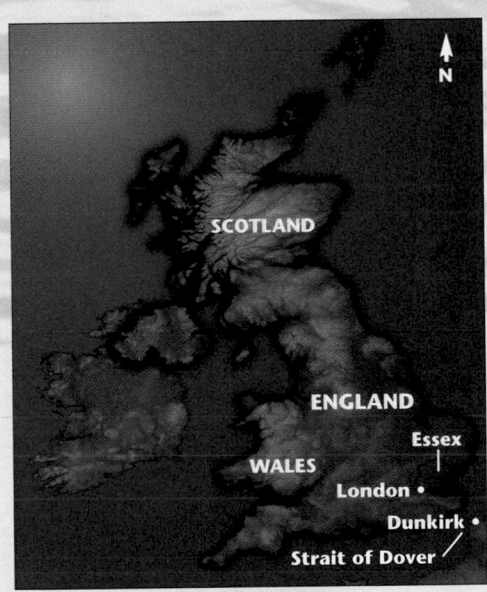

Reader's Journal

What makes a person beautiful?

Reader's TOOLBOX

NOVELLA. A **novella** is a work of fiction that is longer than a short story and shorter than a novel. As you read *The Snow Goose*, try to identify how the main elements of fiction—characterization, plot, setting, and theme—are more fully developed than in a short story.

DESCRIPTION. A **description** gives a picture in words of a character, an object, or a scene. Descriptions make use of *sensory details*—words and phrases that describe how things look, sound, smell, taste, or feel. How does the description of setting in this story create mood, or atmosphere?

THEME. A **theme** is a central idea in a literary work. As you read *The Snow Goose*, write a list of topics that the story addresses. How might these topics relate to a central idea, or theme? What unique ideas does the author offer the reader?

FORESHADOWING. **Foreshadowing** is the act of presenting materials that hint at events to occur later in the story. As you read Part One of the novella, look for hints of events to come in Part Two.

THE SNOW GOOSE **577**

ADDITIONAL RESOURCES

UNIT 8 RESOURCE BOOK
- Selection Worksheet 8.5
- Selection Check Test 4.8.9
- Selection Test 4.8.10

READER'S JOURNAL

You might also share the following prompts with students: What does the saying "beauty is in the eye of the beholder" mean? How can a person learn to see beauty in people and things that are not conventionally beautiful?

GOALS/OBJECTIVES

Studying this lesson will enable students to
- empathize with the feelings of the main characters in this novella
- define *novella* and recognize how elements of fiction are more fully developed in a novella than a short story
- define *description* and identify the mood a description creates
- define *theme* and identify themes in a literary work
- define *foreshadowing* and recognize elements of foreshadowing in their reading
- use and create maps
- study migration patterns of birds
- proofread for spelling errors

INDIVIDUAL LEARNING STRATEGIES

MOTIVATION

Ask students to read the Prereading page carefully in which the evacuation from Dunkirk is described. Tell students to stage their own skit showing what the evacuation from Dunkirk may have been like. Before beginning students may want to read more about this historical event in encyclopedias or history books. Students should then script what action they want to depict and divide up roles among students, assigning some to be American English, and French soldiers, and others to be the captains of the various vessels evacuating them. Students should not narrate the scene, but should try to capture the action, confusion, and noise of such a mass evacuation.

READING PROFICIENCY

Students may benefit from hearing this story read aloud on audiotape. They should follow along with the words on the page as they listen. hearing the story read aloud will help students to understand the passages written in a British dialect. The way the words are pronounce will not throw students off as much as the way they are spelled to capture dialect. Students should then go back and respond to the Guided Reading questions, rereading the story as they respond.

ENGLISH LANGUAGE LEARNING

Inform students that a key part of the story (the soldier's dialogue in Part 2, beginning on page 622) is written in a British dialect. Pair students with English-proficient students and have them work through this difficult passage together. Each pair of students might restate in their own words what the soldier reveals about what happens to Rhyader at Dunkirk. You may also wish to share with students the additional vocabulary listed on the opposite page.

SPECIAL NEEDS

The length of this story will intimidate some students. You may wish to have students read the story by parts to make it more manageable. tell students to focus on responding to Guided Reading questions as they read, as these will point them to important events and passages in the story. You may wish to check students' comprehension

INDIVIDUAL LEARNING STRATEGIES (CONT.)

with a Selection Check Test before asking them to move on to discuss the Investigate, Inquire, and Imagine section.

ENRICHMENT

Interested students might work together on presenting information on the historical context of *The Snow Goose* to their classmates. Students should work together as a group to present an oral report that gives an overview of World War II. Students need not describe every battle of the war, but they should state what began the conflict, what countries were involved, and report some major events of the war, using visual aids to make the war come alive for students.

THE Snow Goose

Paul Gallico

ANSWER TO GUIDED
READING QUESTION

1. Wild geese, gulls, teal, widgeon,
redshanks, curlews, and other wildfowl live in the marsh.

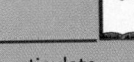

**VOCABULARY FROM
THE SELECTION**

bid	inarticulate
breach	placid
buffet	rebuff
derelict	repel
eerie	rupture
estuary	sanctuary
exertion	sodden
extant	tendril
fragmentary	tousle
garner	tread
harried	turmoil
import	unerring

PART ONE

The great marsh lies on the Essex coast between the village of Chelmsbury and the ancient Saxon[1] oyster-fishing hamlet of Wickaeldroth. It is one of the last of the wild places of England, a low, far-reaching expanse of grass and reeds and half-submerged meadowlands ending in the great saltings and mud flats and tidal pools near the restless sea.

Tidal creeks and <u>estuaries</u> and the crooked, meandering arms of many little rivers whose mouths lap at the edge of the ocean cut through the <u>sodden</u> land that seems to rise and fall and breathe with the recurrence of the daily tides. It is desolate, utterly lonely, and made lonelier by the calls and cries of the wildfowl that make their homes in the marshlands and saltings[2]—the wild geese and the gulls, the teal and

GUIDED READING

Which creatures live in the marsh?

widgeon, the redshanks and curlews that pick their way through the tidal pools. Of human habitants there are none, and none are seen, with the occasional exception of a wildfowler or native oyster- fishermen, who still ply a trade already ancient when the Normans came to Hastings.[3]

Grays and blues and soft greens are the colors, for when the skies are dark in the long winters, the many waters of the beaches and marshes reflect the cold and somber color. But sometimes, with sunrise and sunset, sky and land are aflame with red and golden fire.

Hard by one of the winding arms of the little River Aelder runs the embankment of an old sea wall, smooth and solid, without a

---

1. **Saxon.** Of the Saxons, Germanic people who conquered and then occupied parts of England around AD 500
2. **saltings.** Grassy land regularly flooded by tides
3. **when . . . Hastings.** The narrator means AD 1066, the year the French Normans invaded England and won the Battle of Hastings.

---

words for everyday use

es • tu • ar • y (es′ chə wer ē) *n.,* an inlet of the sea. *The <u>estuary</u> attracts many types of birds and saltwater fish.*

sod • den (säd′ ən) *adj.,* soaked through. *My clothes were <u>sodden</u> after I walked home in the rain.*

◄ *Dungeness, Kent,* 1936. John Piper. Private Collection.

THE SNOW GOOSE **579**

1. The ruins of an abandoned lighthouse stand at low water.
2. They look askance at his misshapen
   body because he is a hunchback
   with a crippled arm.

CROSS-CURRICULAR ACTIVITIES

SOCIAL STUDIES. Inform students
that when this story takes place
many people still had negative
attitudes toward those who were
born with a disability or different
physical appearance, and they
sometimes made the lives of
people who looked different or had a
disability difficult. Interested students
might prepare brief oral reports on
the struggle for equal rights and
fairness that people with disabilities
have undertaken during the twentieth
century and into the twenty-first.
What acts have been passed to help
people with disabilities and how has
life changed for the better for these
people in the United States. What
organizations are dedicated to helping
people with disabilities or ensuring
that they are treated fairly? Other
students might research the way
people with disabilities are treated in
other countries, such as the United
Kingdom, Greece, India, Russia, and
other places around the globe.
Encourage students to discuss how
the United States "measures up"
against other nations in terms of its
attitude toward and treatment of
people with disabilities. Ask them to
think about whether we have father
to go in our attitude toward and
treatment of such people. What are
some of the ways students might help
support persons with disabilities and
ensure fair and equal treatment?

break, a bulwark[4] to the land against the
encroaching sea. Deep into a salting some
three miles from the North Sea it runs, and
there turns north. At that corner its face is
gouged, broken, and shattered. It has been
breached, and at the breach the hungry sea
has already entered and taken for its own the
land, the wall, and all that stood there.

At low water the
blackened and ruptured
stones of the ruins of an
abandoned lighthouse
show above the surface, with here and there,
like buoy markers, the top
of a sagging fencepost.
Once this lighthouse
abutted on the sea and
was a beacon on the
Essex coast. Time
shifted land and water,
and its usefulness
came to an end.

GUIDED READING
What structure
stands at low water?

Lately it served
again as a human
habitation. In it there
lived a lonely man. His body was warped,
but his heart was filled with love for wild and
hunted things. He was ugly to look upon, but
he created great beauty. It is about him, and a
child who came to know him and see beyond
the grotesque form that housed him to what
lay within, that this story is told.

It is not a story that falls easily and
smoothly into sequence. It has been garnered
from many sources and from many people.
Some of it comes in the form of fragments
from men who looked upon strange and
violent scenes. For the sea has claimed its
own and spreads its rippled blanket over the
site, and the great white bird with the

His body was warped, but his heart was filled with love for wild and hunted things.

black-tipped pinions[5] that saw it all from the
beginning to the end has returned to the
dark, frozen silences of the northlands
whence it came.

In the late spring of 1930 Philip Rhayader
came to the abandoned lighthouse at the
mouth of the Aelder. He bought the light and
many acres of marshland and salting
surrounding it.

He lived and worked there alone the year
round. He was a painter of birds and of
nature, who, for reasons, had withdrawn from
all human society. Some of the reasons
were apparent on his fortnightly
visits to the little village of
Chelmsbury for supplies,
where the natives looked
askance[6] at his
misshapen body and
dark visage. For he
was a hunchback and
his left arm was
crippled, thin and bent at
the wrist,
like the claw of a bird.

They soon became used
to his queer figure, small
but powerful, the massive,
dark, bearded head set just slightly below the
mysterious mound on his back, the glowing
eyes and the clawed hand, and marked him
off as "that queer painter chap that lives down
to lighthouse."

GUIDED READING
Why do people in
Chelmsbury look
askance at Rhayader?

Physical deformity often breeds hatred of
humanity in men. Rhayader did not hate; he
loved very greatly, man, the animal kingdom,

---

4. **bulwark.** Defensive wall; breakwater
5. **pinions.** Long feathers at the tip of a wing
6. **askance.** With a side glance

---

words for everyday use

breach (brēch') v., to make a gap by battering; to break. *The soldiers breached the barrier and scrambled through it.*

rup • ture (rup' chər) v., break apart. *The impact of the fall caused the box to rupture.* **ruptured,** adj.

gar • ner (gär' nər) v., gather. *The investigator will garner information from witnesses.*

and all nature. His heart was filled with pity and understanding. He had mastered his handicap, but he could not master the <u>rebuffs</u> he suffered due to his appearance. The thing that drove him into seclusion was his failure to find anywhere a return of the warmth that flowed from him. He <u>repelled</u> women. Men would have warmed to him had they got to know him. But the mere fact that an effort was being made hurt Rhayader and drove him to avoid the person making it.

GUIDED READING

What type of person is Rhayader?

He was twenty-seven when he came to the Great Marsh. He had traveled much and fought valiantly before he made the decision to withdraw from a world in which he could not take part as other men. For all of the artist's sensitivity and woman's tenderness locked in his barrel breast, he was very much a man.

In his retreat he had his birds, his painting, and his boat. He owned a sixteen-footer, which he sailed with wonderful skill. Alone, with no eyes to watch him, he managed well with his deformed hand, and he often used his strong teeth to handle the sheets of his billowing sails in a tricky blow.

GUIDED READING

What does Rhayader have in his retreat?

He would sail the tidal creeks and estuaries and out to sea and would be gone for days at a time, looking for new species of birds to photograph or sketch, and he became adept at netting them to add to his collection of tamed wildfowl in the pen near his studio that formed the nucleus of a <u>sanctuary</u>.

He never shot over a bird, and wildfowlers[7] were not welcome near his premises. He was a friend to all things wild, and the wild things repaid him with their friendship.

Tamed in his enclosures were the geese that came winging down the coast from Iceland and Spitsbergen[8] each October, in great skeins that darkened the sky and filled the air with the rushing noise of their passage—the brown-bodied pink-feet, white-breasted barnacles with their dark necks and clowns' masks, the wild white fronts with black-barred breasts, and many species of wild ducks—widgeon, mallard, pintails, teal, and shovelers.

Some were pinioned,[9] so that they would remain there as a sign and signal to the wild ones that came down at each winter's beginning that here were food and sanctuary.

Many hundreds came and remained with him all through the cold weather from October to the early spring, when they migrated north again to their breeding grounds below the ice rim.

GUIDED READING

How many birds winter with Rhayader?

Rhayader was content in the knowledge that when storms blew, or it was bitter cold and food was scarce, or the big punt guns of the distant bag hunters roared, his birds were safe; that he had gathered to the sanctuary and security of his own arms and heart these many wild and beautiful creatures who knew and trusted him.

They would answer the call of the north in the spring, but in the fall they would come back, barking and whooping and honking in the autumn sky, to circle the landmark of the old light and drop to earth nearby to be his guests again—birds that he

---

7. **wildfowlers.** Hunters
8. **Spitsbergen.** Group of Arctic Ocean islands belonging to Norway
9. **pinioned.** Clipped at the wings or bound

ANSWERS TO GUIDED READING QUESTIONS

1. He is a man who loves man, the animal kingdom, and all nature.
2. He has birds, his painting, and his boat.
3. Hundreds of birds winter with Rhayader.

ADDITIONAL QUESTIONS AND ACTIVITIES

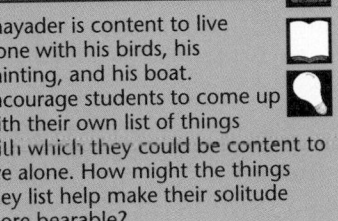

Rhayader is content to live alone with his birds, his painting, and his boat. Encourage students to come up with their own list of things with which they could be content to live alone. How might the things they list help make their solitude more bearable?

words for everyday use

re • buff (ri buf′) *n.*, abrupt refusal. *Mother answered my plea with a loud <u>rebuff</u>.*

re • pel (ri pel′) *v.*, cause distaste or disgust. *The skunk's unique ability to cause a stink <u>repels</u> most humans.*

sanc • tu • ar • y (saŋk′ chə wer′ ē) *n.*, place of refuge or protection. *Dwayne's treehouse in the woods was his <u>sanctuary</u>.*

well remembered and recognized from the previous year.

And this made Rhayader happy, because he knew that implanted somewhere in their beings was the germ knowledge of his existence and his

> **GUIDED READING**
> Why does the birds' return make Rhayader happy?

safe haven, that this knowledge had become a part of them and, with the coming of the gray skies and the winds from the north, would send them <u>unerringly</u> back to him.

For the rest, his heart and soul went into the painting of the country in which he lived and its creatures. There are not many Rhayaders <u>extant</u>. He hoarded them jealously, piling them up in his lighthouse and store-rooms above by the hundreds. He was not satisfied with them, because as an artist he was uncompromising.

But the few that have reached the market are masterpieces, filled with the glow and colors of marsh-reflected light, the feel of flight, the push of birds breasting a mor-ning wind bending the tall flag reeds. He painted the loneliness and the smell of the salt-laden cold, the eternity and agelessness of marshes, the wild, living creatures, dawn flights, and frightened things taking to the air, and winged shadows at night hiding from the moon.

> **GUIDED READING**
> What does Rhayader paint?

One November afternoon, three years after Rhayader had come to the Great Marsh, a child approached the lighthouse studio by means of the sea wall. In her arms she carried a burden.

She was no more than twelve, slender, dirty, nervous and timid as a bird, but beneath the grime as <u>eerily</u> beautiful as a marsh faery. She was pure Saxon, large-boned, fair, and a head to which her body was yet to grow, and deep-set, violet-colored eyes.

She was desperately frightened of the ugly man she had come to see, for legend had already begun to gather about Rhayader, and the native wild-fowlers hated him for interfering with their sport.

But greater than her fear was the need of that which she bore. For locked in her child's heart was the knowledge, picked up somewhere in the swampland, that this ogre who lived in the lighthouse had magic that could heal injured things.

> **GUIDED READING**
> Why does the girl go to Rhayader despite the horrible legend that sur-rounds him?

She had never seen Rhayader before and was close to fleeing in panic at the dark apparition that appeared at the studio door, drawn by her footsteps—the black head and beard, the sinister hump, and the crooked claw.

She stood there staring, poised like a disturbed marsh bird for instant flight.

But his voice was deep and kind when he spoke to her.

"What is it, child?"

She stood her ground and then edged timidly forward. The thing she carried in her arms was a large white bird, and it was quite still. There were stains of blood on its whiteness and on her kirtle[10] where she had held it to her.

The girl placed it in his arms. "I found it, sir. It's hurted. Is it still alive?"

---

10. **kirtle.** Dress or skirt

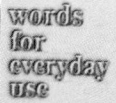

un • err • ing (un er' iŋ) *adj.*, unfailing, faultless. *Jane's <u>unerring</u> arguments helped the debate team to win.* **unerringly,** *adv.*

ex • tant (eks' tənt) *adj.*, still existing. *There are few ocelots <u>extant</u> in South America.*

ee • rie (ir' ē) *adj.*, mysterious; strange. *The howling of the wolves gave me an <u>eerie</u> feeling.* **eerily,** *adv.*

"Yes. Yes, I think so. Come in, child, come in."

Rhayader went inside, bearing the bird, which he placed upon a table, where it moved feebly. Curiosity overcame fear. The girl followed and found herself in a room warmed by a coal fire, shining with many colored pictures that covered the walls, and full of a strange but pleasant smell.

GUIDED READING

What is the room like?

The bird fluttered. With his good hand Rhayader spread one of its immense white pinions. The end was beautifully tipped with black.

Rhayader looked and marveled, and said: "Child, where did you find it?"

"In t' marsh, sir, where fowlers had been. What—what is it, sir?"

"It's a snow goose from Canada. But how in all heaven came it here?"

The name seemed to mean nothing to the little girl. Her deep violet eyes, shining out of the dirt on her thin face, were fixed with concern on the injured bird.

She said: "Can 'ee heal it, sir?"

"Yes, yes," said Rhayader. "We will try. Come, you shall help me."

There were scissors and bandages and splints on a shelf, and he was marvelously deft, even with the crooked claw that managed to hold things.

He said: "Ah, she has been shot, poor thing. Her leg is broken, and the wing tip, but not badly. See, we will clip her primaries,[11] so that we can bandage it, but in the spring the feathers will grow and she will be able to fly again. We'll bandage it close to her body, so that she cannot move it until it has set, and then make a splint for the poor leg."

GUIDED READING

What is wrong with the snow goose?

Her fears forgotten, the child watched, fascinated, as he worked, and all the more so because while he fixed a fine splint to the shattered leg he told her the most wonderful story.

The bird was a young one, no more than a year old. She was born in a northern land far, far across the seas, a land belonging to England.[9] Flying to the south to escape the snow and ice and bitter cold, a great storm had seized her and whirled and <u>buffeted</u> her about. It was a truly terrible storm, stronger than her great wings, stronger than anything. For days and nights it held her in its grip and there was nothing she could do but fly before it. When finally it had blown itself out and her sure instincts took her south again, she was over a different land and surrounded by strange birds that she had never seen before. At last, exhausted by her ordeal, she had sunk to rest in a friendly green marsh, only to be met by the blast from the hunter's gun.

GUIDED READING

What is Rhayader's story?

"A bitter reception for a visiting princess," concluded Rhayader. "We will call her 'La Princesse Perdue,' the Lost Princess. And in a few days she will be feeling better. See?" He reached into his pocket and produced a handful of grain. The snow goose opened its round yellow eyes and nibbled at it.

The child laughed with delight and then suddenly caught her breath with alarm as the full <u>import</u> of where she was pressed in upon her, and without a word she turned and fled out of the door.

GUIDED READING

Why does the girl flee?

---

11. **primaries.** Group of feathers at the end of the wing

12. **land . . . England.** Canada was a dominion of the British Empire until 1982

---

words for everyday use

buf • fet (buf' it) v., strike repeatedly; thrust. *The children <u>buffeted</u> the target with balls.*

im • port (im' pôrt) n., significance. *Fred's minor problems are of little <u>import</u> to me.*

ANSWERS TO GUIDED READING QUESTIONS

1. The room is warmed by a coal fire, shining with many colored pictures that cover the walls, and full of a strange but pleasant smell.
2. She has been shot and her leg and wing tip are broken.
3. His story is about the bird's life and about how she came to England.
4. She suddenly becomes aware of where she is.

ADDITIONAL QUESTIONS AND ACTIVITIES

Ask students the following questions: Explain whether the story Rhayader tells is fiction or fact. How can you tell? Why does Rhayader tell the girl this story.

Answers. Students may say that the story is probably factual, as Rhayader knows a lot about birds and recognizes that this species is not native to England and has been shot, but he is making up the details of the storm and the bird's feelings and reaction to make it more interesting for the girl. Students may say he tells the story to lessen the girl's fear. He also might wish to interest her in the snow goose so she will return to visit.

ANSWERS TO GUIDED READING QUESTIONS

1. The strange white princess from a land far away has captured her imagination.
2. She stops coming when the snow goose leaves. Rhayader experiences loneliness.
3. He paints a picture of a slender, grime-covered child who bore a wounded white bird.

"Wait, wait!" cried Rhayader, and went to the entrance, where he stopped so that it framed his dark bulk. The girl was already fleeing down the sea wall, but she paused at his voice and looked back.

"What is your name, child?"

"Frith."

"Eh?" said Rhayader. "Fritha, I suppose. Where do you live?"

"Wi' t' fisherfolk at Wickaeldroth." She gave the name the old Saxon pronunciation.

"Will you come back tomorrow, or the next day, to see how the Princess is getting along?"

She paused, and again Rhayader must have thought of the wild water birds caught motionless in that split second of alarm before they took to flight.

But her thin voice came back to him: "Ay!"

And then she was gone, with her fair hair streaming out behind her.

The snow goose mended rapidly and by midwinter was already limping about the enclosure with the wild pink-footed geese with which it associated, rather than the barnacles,[13] and had learned to come to be fed at Rhayader's call. And the child, Fritha, or Frith, was a frequent visitor. She had overcome her fear of Rhayader. Her imagination was captured by the presence of this strange white princess from a land far over the

> **GUIDED READING**
> What captures Frith's imagination?

sea, a land that was all pink, as she knew from the map that Rhayader showed her, and on which they traced the stormy path of the lost bird from its home in Canada to the Great Marsh of Essex.

Then one June morning a group of late pink-feet, fat and well fed from the winter at the lighthouse, answered the stronger call of the breeding grounds and rose lazily, climbing into the sky in ever widening circles. With them, her white body and black-tipped pinions shining in the spring sun, was the snow goose. It so happened that Frith was at the lighthouse. Her cry brought Rhayader running from the studio.

"Look! Look! The Princess! Be she going away?"

Rhayader stared into the sky at the climbing specks. "Ay," he said, unconsciously dropping into her manner of speech. "The Princess is going home. Listen! She is bidding us farewell."

Out of the clear sky came the mournful barking of the pink-feet and above it the higher, clearer note of the snow goose. The specks drifted northward, formed into a tiny *v*, diminished, and vanished.

With the departure of the snow goose ended the visits of Frith to the lighthouse. Rhayader learned all over again the meaning of the word

> **GUIDED READING**
> Why does Frith stop going to the lighthouse? How does Rhayader feel when she stops visiting?

loneliness. That summer, out of his memory, he painted a picture of a slender grime-covered child, her fair hair blown by a November storm, who bore in her arms a wounded white bird.

> **GUIDED READING**
> What picture does Rhayader paint from memory?

In mid-October the miracle occurred. Rhayader was in his enclosure, feeding his birds. A gray northeast wind was blowing and the land was sighing beneath the incoming tide. Above the sea and the wind noises he heard a clear, high note. He turned his eyes upward to the

---

13. **barnacles.** Barnacle geese

words for everyday use   **bid** (bid') *v.,* express in leave-taking. *Vanessa bid her grandmother goodbye and ran to the playground.*

evening sky in time to see first an infinite speck, then a black-and-white-pinioned dream that circled the lighthouse once, and finally a reality that dropped to earth in the pen and came waddling forward importantly to be fed, as though she had never been away. It was the snow goose. There was no mistaking her. Tears of joy came to Rhayader's eyes. Where had she been? Surely not home to Canada. No, she must have summered in Greenland or Spitsbergen with the pink-feet. She had remembered and had returned.

When next Rhayader went into Chelmsbury for supplies, he left a message with the postmistress—one that must have caused her much bewilderment. He said: "Tell Frith, who lives with the fisherfolk at Wickaeldroth, that the Lost Princess has returned."

Three days later, Frith, taller, still <u>tousled</u> and unkempt, came shyly to the lighthouse to visit La Princesse Perdue.

Time passed. On the Great Marsh it was marked by the height of the tides, the slow march of the seasons, the passage of the birds,

and, for Rhayader, by the arrival and departure of the snow goose.

GUIDED READING

How is time marked for Rhayader?

The world outside boiled and seethed and rumbled with the eruption that was soon to break forth and come close to marking its destruction. But not yet did it touch upon Rhayader, or, for that matter, Frith. They had fallen into a curious, natural rhythm, even as the child grew older. When the snow goose was at the lighthouse, then she came, too, to visit and learn many things from Rhayader. They sailed together in his speedy boat that he handled so skillfully. They caught wildfowl for the ever increasing colony and built new pens and enclosures for them. From him she learned the lore of every wild bird, from gull to gyrfalcon, that flew the marshes. She cooked for him sometimes and even learned to mix his paints.

GUIDED READING

What does Frith learn from Rhayader?

But when the snow goose returned to its summer home, it was as though some kind of bar was up between them, and she did not come to the lighthouse. One year the bird did not return, and Rhayader was heartbroken. All things seemed to have ended for him. He painted furiously through the winter and the next summer and never once saw the child. But in the fall the familiar cry once more rang from the sky, and the huge white bird, now at its full growth, dropped from the skies as mysteriously as it had departed. Joyously, Rhayader sailed his boat into Chelmsbury and left his message with the postmistress.

Curiously, it was more than a month after he had left the message before Frith reappeared at the lighthouse, and Rhayader, with a shock, realized that she was a child no longer.

After the year in which the bird had remained away, its periods of absence grew shorter and shorter. It had grown so tame that it followed Rhayader about and even came into the studio while he was working.

GUIDED READING

How does the goose act after the year it remained away?

PART TWO

In the spring of 1940 the birds migrated early from the Great Marsh. The world was on fire. The whine and roar of the bombers and the thudding explosions

words for everyday use

tou • sle (tə′ səl) v., rumple, muss. *My father likes to <u>tousle</u> my hair.* **tousled,** *adj.*

ANSWERS TO GUIDED READING QUESTIONS

1. Time is marked by the height of the tides, the march of the seasons, the passage of the birds, and by the arrival and departure of the snow goose.
2. She learns the lore of every wild bird as well as how to mix Rhayader's paints.
3. The goose's periods of absence grew shorter and shorter, and she grew tame.

ADDITIONAL QUESTIONS AND ACTIVITIES

Ask students the following questions: What things do Rhayader and Frith do together? What words does the narrator use to describe the "rhythm" of their relationship? What is happening in the world outside the marsh? To what might the narrator be referring? Has this conflict affected Rhayader and Frith yet?

Answers. They sail, they catch birds for the sanctuary, they build enclosures for the birds, Rhayader tells Frith folklore, and Frith cooks for Rhayader and mixes his paints? The narrator says their relationship had "fallen into a curious, natural rhythm, even as the child grew older." "The world outside boiled and seethed and rumbled with the eruption that was soon to break forth and come close to marking its destruction." Students might say the narrator means that World War II was about to erupt. The increasing political and military conflicts have not yet affected Rhayader and Frith.

CROSS-CURRICULAR ACTIVITIES

APPLIED ARTS. Encourage students to work in groups to create models of the pens and enclosures for birds that Rhayader and Frith might build. Other students might enjoy creating their own bird houses. Students should have adult supervision as they construct their models and birdhouses.

1. Rhayader says the goose will stay.
2. She feels she must leave because she could not understand her relationship with Rhayader.

ADDITIONAL QUESTIONS AND ACTIVITIES

Ask students to discuss the changes that are taking place in the relationship between Frith and Rhayader. How is Rhayader beginning to feel about Frith now that she has grown up? Why doesn't he directly tell her his feelings? Does Frith return his feelings? How does Frith feel about Rhayader?

Answers. Students may say that there is a sense that their friendship is developing toward a more romantic relationship. Rhayader is beginning to feel romantically toward Frith but he doesn't speak about his feelings of love because he feels he must be misshapen and grotesque in her eyes. Students may say that Frith seems confused about her own feelings and she is frightened of Rhayader's strong feelings for her and uncertain what to do about them. The "queer sense of loss" Frith feels may mean that she does have some feelings for Rhayader too but they may not be as strong as Rhayader's feelings of love.

frightened them. The first day of May, Frith and Rhayader stood shoulder to shoulder on the sea wall and watched the last of the unpinioned pink-feet and barnacle geese rise from their sanctuary; she, tall, slender, free as air, and hauntingly beautiful; he, dark, grotesque, his massive bearded head raised to the sky, his glowing dark eyes watching the geese form their flight tracery.

"Look, Philip," Frith said.

Rhayader followed her eyes. The snow goose had taken flight, her giant wings spread, but she was flying low, and once came quite close to them, so that for a moment the spreading black-tipped white pinions seemed to caress them and they felt the rush of the bird's swift passage. Once, twice, she circled the lighthouse, then dropped to earth again in the enclosure with the pinioned geese and commenced to feed.

"She be'ent going," said Frith, with marvel in her voice. The bird in its close passage seemed to have woven a kind of magic about her. "The Princess be goin' t' stay."

"Ay," said Rhayader, and his voice was shaken too. "She'll stay. She will never go away again. The Lost Princess is lost no more. This is her home now—of her own free will."

> **GUIDED READING**
> What does Rhayader say the goose will do?

The spell the bird had girt[14] about her was broken, and Frith was suddenly conscious of the fact that she was frightened, and the things that frightened her were in Rhayader's eyes—the longing and the loneliness and the deep, welling, unspoken things that lay in and behind them as he turned them upon her.

His last words were repeating themselves in her head as though he had said them again: "This is her home now—of her own free will."

The delicate tendrils of her instincts reached to him and carried to her the message of the things he could not speak because of what he felt himself to be, misshapen and grotesque. And where his voice might have soothed her, her fright grew greater and his silence and the power of the unspoken things between them. The woman in her bade her take flight from something that she was not yet capable of understanding.

Frith said: "I—I must go. Goodbye. I be glad the—the Princess will stay. You'll not be so alone now."

> **GUIDED READING**
> Why does Frith feel she must leave?

She turned and walked swiftly away, and his sadly spoken "Goodbye, Frith," was only a half-heard ghost of a sound borne to her ears above the rustling of the marsh grass. She was far away before she dared turn for a backward glance. He was still standing on the sea wall, a dark speck against the sky.

Her fear had stilled now. It had been replaced by something else, a queer sense of loss that made her stand quite still for a moment, so sharp was it. Then, more slowly, she continued on, away from the skyward-pointing finger of the lighthouse and the man beneath it.

It was a little more than three weeks before Frith returned to the lighthouse. May was at its end, and the day, too, in a long golden twilight that was giving way to the silver of the moon already hanging in the eastern sky.

She told herself, as her steps took her thither, that she must know whether the snow goose had really stayed, as Rhayader said it would. Perhaps it had flown away, after all. But her firm tread on the sea wall

---

14. **girt.** Surrounded, encircled.

words for everyday use

ten • dril (ten′ drəl) *n.,* tender shoot. *Tiny tendrils of the ferm poked through the earth.*

tread (tred′) *n.,* act of stepping. *The wooden steps were worn from the tread of visitors.*

was full of eagerness, and sometimes unconsciously she found herself hurrying.

Frith saw the yellow light of Rhayader's lantern down by his little wharf, and she found him there. His sailboat was rocking gently on a flooding tide and he was loading supplies into her—water and food and bottles of brandy, gear and a spare sail. When he turned to the sound of her coming, she saw that he was pale, but that his dark eyes, usually so kind and <u>placid</u>, were glowing with excitement, and he was breathing heavily from his <u>exertions</u>.

> **GUIDED READING**
>
> What changes does Frith see in Rhayader?

Sudden alarm seized Frith. The snow goose was forgotten. "Philip! Ye be goin' away?"

Rhayader paused in his work to greet her, and there was something in his face, a glow and a look, that she had never seen there before.

In the night light she saw the flash of white wings, black-tipped, and the thrust-forward head of the snow goose.

"Frith! I am glad you came. Yes, I must go away. A little trip. I will come back." His usually kindly voice was hoarse with what was suppressed inside him.

Frith asked: "Where must ye go?"

Words came tumbling from Rhayader now. He must go to Dunkirk. A hundred miles across the North Sea. A British army was trapped there on the sands, awaiting destruction at the hands of the advancing Germans. The port was in flames, the position hopeless. He had heard it in the village when he had gone for supplies. Men were putting out from Chelmsbury in answer to the government's call, every tug and fishing boat or power launch that could propel itself was heading across the sea to haul the men off the beaches to the transports and destroyers that could not reach the shallows, to rescue as many as possible from the Germans' fire.

> **GUIDED READING**
>
> Where is Rhayader going?

Frith listened and felt her heart dying within her. He was saying that he would cross the sea in his little boat. It could take six men at a time; in a pinch, seven. He could make many trips from the beaches to the transports.

The girl was young, primitive, <u>inarticulate</u>. She did not understand war, or what had happened in France, or the meaning of the trapped army, but the blood within her told her that here was danger.

> **GUIDED READING**
>
> What do Frith's instincts tell her about Rhayader's trip?

"Philip! Must 'ee go? You'll not come back. Why must it be 'ee?"

The fever seemed to have gone from Rhayader's soul with the first rush of words, and he explained it to her in terms that she could understand.

He said, "Men are huddled on the beaches like hunted birds, Frith, like the wounded and hunted birds we used to find and bring to sanctuary. Over them fly the steel peregrines, hawks and gyrfalcons, and they have no shelter from these iron birds of prey. They are lost and storm-driven and

THE SNOW GOOSE **587**

---

1. She sees that he is pale but that his eyes are glowing with excitement.
2. He is going to rescue British soldiers at Dunkirk.
3. She feels that he will not come back.

LITERARY TECHNIQUE

SIMILE. A **simile** is a comparison using *like* or *as*. Share this definition with students and then ask them the following questions: What simile does Rhayader use to describe the men on the beach at Dunkirk? In what way are then men like these things? Why is this an appropriate simile for Rhayader to use? In what way does this simile help explain why Rhayader is eager to take part in the rescue?

Answers. Rhayader says that men "are huddled on the beach like hunted birds . . . the wounded and hunted birds we used to find and bring to sanctuary." The men are like these things in that they are being hunted, have no means of escape on their own, and are in need of help and rescue. Students might say that this is an appropriate simile for Rhayader to use because of his own and Frith's love of birds, so this simile helps to make his feelings clear to Frith. The simile helps to explain that Rhayader feels the need to care for and rescue helpless things, and that rescuing the soldiers is an extension of the same feelings he has about hunted birds.

<u>harried</u>, like the Princesse Perdue you found and brought to me out of the marshes many years ago, and we healed her. They need help, my dear, as our wild creatures have needed help, and that is why I must go. It is something that I can do. Yes, I can. For once—for once I can be a man and play my part."

Frith stared at Rhayader. He had changed so. For the first time she saw that he was no longer ugly or misshapen or grotesque, but very beautiful. Things were <u>turmoiling</u> in her own soul, crying to be said, and she did not know how to say them.

> **GUIDED READING**
> How does Frith see Rhayader now?

"I'll come with 'ee, Philip."

Rhayader shook his head. "Your place in the boat would cause a soldier to be left behind, and another and another. I must go alone."

He donned rubber coat and boots and took to his boat. He waved and called back: "Goodbye! Will you look after the birds until I return, Frith?"

Frith's hand came up, but only half, to wave too. "God speed you," she said, but gave it the Saxon turn. "I will take care of t' birds. Godspeed, Philip."

It was night now, bright with moon fragment and stars and northern glow. Frith stood on the sea wall and watched the sail gliding down the swollen estuary. Suddenly from the darkness behind her there came a rush of wings, and something swept past her into the air. In the night light she saw the flash of white wings, black-tipped, and the thrust-forward head of the snow goose.

It rose and cruised over the lighthouse once and then headed down the winding creek where

> **GUIDED READING**
> Where does the snow goose go?

Rhayader's sail was slanting in the gaining breeze and flew above him in slow, wide circles.

White sail and white bird were visible for a long time.

"Watch o'er him. Watch o'er him," Fritha whispered. When they were both out of sight at last, she turned and walked slowly, with bent head, back to the empty lighthouse.

Now the story becomes <u>fragmentary</u>, and one of these fragments is in the words of the men on leave who told it in the public room of the Crown and Arrow, an East Chapel pub.

"A goose, a bloomin' goose, so 'elp me," said Private Potton, of His Majesty's London Rifles.

"Garn,"[15] said a bandy-legged artilleryman.

"A goose it was. Jock, 'ere, seed it same as me. It come flyin' down outa the muck an' stink an' smoke of Dunkirk that was over'ead. It was white, wiv black on its wings, an' it circles us like a bloomin' dive bomber. Jock, 'ere, 'e sez: 'We're done for. It's the hangel of death a-come for us.'

" 'Garn,' Hi sez, 'it's a ruddy goose, come over from 'ome wiv a message from Churchill,[16] an' 'ow are we henjoying the bloomin' bathing. It's a omen, that's what it is, a bloody omen. We'll get out of this yet, me lad.'

> **GUIDED READING**
> What do the soldiers think of the snow goose?

"We was roostin' on the beach between Dunkirk an' Lapanny,[17] like a lot o' bloomin' pigeons on Victoria Hembankment, waitin'

---

15. **Garn.** British slang meaning "Go on"
16. **Churchill.** Winston Churchill (1874–1965), Britain's prime minister during World War II
17. **Lapanny.** La Panne, Belgian city on the North Sea near the French border

---

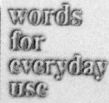

har • ried (har′ ēd) *adj.,* tormented, ravaged. *After ten hours, the <u>harried</u> firefighters finally put out the terrible fire.*

tur • moil (tər′ môil) *n.,* extremely confused or disturbed state. *The fire drill left the school in <u>turmoil</u>.* **turmoil,** *v.*

frag • men • tar • y (frag′ mən ter ē) *adj.,* consisting of disconnected parts. *As I pieced together the <u>fragmentary</u> images from my memory, I began to recall the strange dream.*

for Jerry to pot us.[18] 'E potted us good too. 'E was be'ind us an' flankin' us an' above us. 'E give us shrapnel an' 'e give us H. E., an' 'e peppers us from the bloomin' hatmosphere with Jittersmiths.[19]

"An' offshore is the *Kentish Maid*, a ruddy hexcursion scow[20] wot Hi've taken many a trip on out of Margate in the summer, for two-and-six, waiting to take us off, 'arf a mile out from the bloomin' shallows.

"While we are lyin' there on the beach, done in an' cursin' becos there ain't no way to get out to the boat, a Stuka[21] dives on 'er, an' 'is bombs drop alongside of 'er, throwin' up water like the bloomin' fountains in the palace gardens; a reg'lar display it was.

"Then a destroyer[22] come up an' says: 'No, ye don't,' to the Stuka with ack-acks and pom-poms, but another Jerry dives on the destroyer, an' 'its 'er. Coo, did she go up! She burned before she sunk, an' the smoke an' the stink come driftin' inshore, all yellow an' black, an' out of it comes this bloomin' goose, a-circlin' around us trapped on the beach.

"An' then around a bend 'e comes in a bloody little sailboat, sailing along as cool as you please, like a bloomin' toff[23] out for a pleasure spin on a Sunday hafternoon at 'Enley."[24]

GUIDED READING

How does the sail-boat appear?

"'Oo comes?" inquired a civilian.

"'Im! 'Im that saved a lot of us. 'E sailed clean through a boil of machine gun bullets from a Jerry in a Jittersmith wot was strafin'[25]—Ramsgate motorboat wot 'ad tried to take us off 'ad been sunk there 'arf an hour ago—the water was all frothin' with shell splashes an' bullets, but 'e didn't give it no mind, 'e didn't. 'E didn't 'ave no petrol[26] to burn or hexplode, an' he sailed in between the shells.

"Into the shallows 'e come out of the black smoke of the burnin' destroyer, a little dark man wiv a beard, a bloomin' claw for a 'and, an' a 'ump on 'is back.

"'E 'ad a rope in 'is teeth that was shinin' white out of 'is black beard, 'is good 'and on the tiller[27] an' the crooked one beckonin' to us to come.

"An' over'ead, around and around, flies the ruddy goose.

"Jock, 'ere, says: 'Lawk, it's all over now. It's the bloody devil come for us 'imself. Hi must 'ave been struck an' don't know it.'

"'Garn,' I sez, 'it's more like the good Lord,'e looks to me, than any bloomin' devil.' 'E did, too, like the pictures from the Sunday-school books, wiv 'is white face and dark eyes an' beard an' all, and 'is bloomin' boat.

GUIDED READING

What do the sol-diers call Rhayader?

"'Hi can take seven at a time,' 'e sings out when 'e's in close.

"Our horfficer shouts: 'Good, man! . . . You seven nearest, get in.'

"We waded out to where 'e was. Hi was that weary Hi couldn't clumb over the side, but 'e takes me by the collar of me tunic an' pulls, wiv a 'In ye go, lad. Come on. Next man.'

"An' in Hi went. Coo, 'e was strong, 'e was. Then 'e sets 'is sail, part of wot looks like a bloomin' sieve from machine gun bullets, shouts: 'Keep down in the bottom of the boat, boys, in case we meet any of yer friends,' and we're off, 'im sittin' in the stern wiv 'is rope in 'is teeth, another in 'is crooked claw, an' 'is right 'and on the tiller, a-steerin' an' sailin' through the spray of shells thrown by a land battery[28] somewhere

18. **waitin' . . . us.** Waiting for German soldiers to shoot us
19. **Jittersmiths.** British slang for German combat aircraft
20. **hexcursion scow.** Tourist ferry
21. **Stuka.** German dive bomber
22. **destroyer.** Warship
23. **toff.** Fashionable person
24. **'Enley.** Henley, town in southeastern England, location of an annual rowing race
25. **strafin'.** Strafing; shooting at
26. **petrol.** Gasoline
27. **tiller.** Handle used to turn the rudder of a boat
28. **land battery.** Emplacement for heavy guns and cannons

1. It appears like it is out for a pleasure spin on a Sunday afternoon.
2. Some say he looks like the devil, others say that he looks like the Lord.

ADDITIONAL QUESTIONS AND ACTIVITIES

Encourage students to restate in their own words what the soldier describes seeing Rhayader do at Dunkirk. Students might either retell what happens aloud in their own dialect of English or write a brief summary of the main events. Students should recognize that Rhayader calmly sails to shore and rescues men by transporting them to a larger ship waiting out at sea.

ART SMART

Encourage students to discuss the action pictured in this war memorial. What are the soldiers on shore doing? What are the smaller boats in the sea doing and where are they going? What is happening in the sky above the scene?

HISTORICAL NOTE

Inform students that the memorial depicts only a small part of the scene that took place during the evacuation of Dunkirk. Share with students that more than 335, 000 soldiers were evacuated from the shores of Dunkirk.

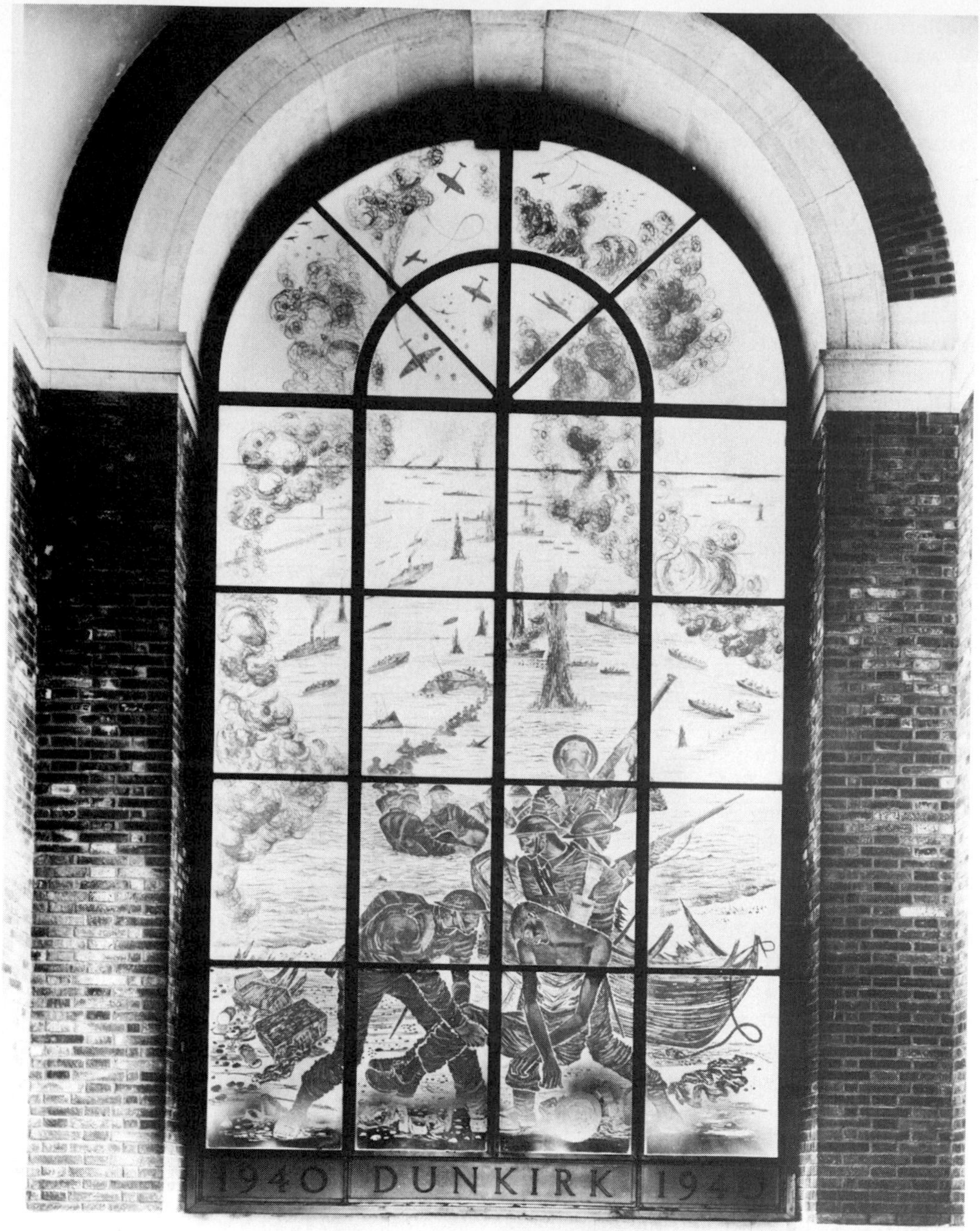

Dunkirk War Memorial, France.

back of the coast. An' the bloomin' goose is flyin' around and around, 'onking above the wind and the row Jerry was making', like a bloomin' Morris autermobile on Winchester by-pass.

" 'Hi told you yon goose was a omen,' Hi sez to Jock. 'Look at 'im there, a bloomin' hangel of mercy.'

" 'Im at the tiller just looks up at the goose, wiv the rope in 'is teeth, an' grins at 'er like 'e knows 'er a lifetime.

GUIDED READING

How does Rhayader look at the goose?

" 'E brung us out to the *Kentish Maid* and turns around and goes back for another load. 'E made trips all afternoon an' all night, too, because the bloody light of Dunkirk burning was bright enough to see by. Hi don't know 'ow many trips 'e made, but 'im an' a nobby[29] Thames Yacht Club motorboat an' a big lifeboat from Poole that come along brought off all there was of us on that particular stretch of hell, without the loss of a man.

"We sailed when the last man was off, an' there was more than seven hunder' of us haboard a boat built to take two hunder'. 'E was still there when we left, an' 'e waved us goodbye and sails off toward Dunkirk, and the bird wiv 'im. Blyme, it was queer to see that ruddy big goose flyin' around 'is boat, lit up by the fires like a white hangel against the smoke.

"A Stuka 'ad another go at us, 'arfway across, but 'e'd been stayin' up late nights, an' missed. By mornin' we was safe 'ome.

"Hi never did find out what become of 'im, or 'oo 'e was—'im wiv the 'ump an' 'is little sailboat. A bloody good man 'e was, that chap."

"Coo," said the artilleryman. "A ruddy big goose. Whatcher know?"

GUIDED READING

What do the soldiers say about Rhayader?

In an officers' club on Brook Street, a retired naval officer, sixty-five years old, Commander Keith Brill-Oudener, was telling of his experiences during the evacuation of Dunkirk. Called out of bed at four o'clock in the morning, he had captained a lopsided Lime-house tug across the Strait of Dover, towing a string of Thames barges, which he brought back four times loaded with soldiers. On his last trip he came in with her funnel shot away and a hole in her side. But he got her back to Dover.

A naval-reserve officer, who had two Brixham trawlers[30] and a Yarmouth drifter[31] blasted out from under him in the last four days of the evacuation, said: "Did you run across that queer sort of legend about a wild goose? It was all up and down the beaches. You know how those things spring up. Some of the men I brought back were talking about it. It was supposed to have appeared at intervals the last days between Dunkirk and La Panne. If you saw it, you were eventually saved. That sort of thing."

"H'm'm'm," said Brill-Oudener, "a wild goose. I saw a tame one. Dashed strange experience. Tragic, in a way, too. And lucky for us. Tell you about it. Third trip back. Toward six o'clock we sighted a derelict small boat. Seemed to be a chap or a body in her. And a bird perched on the rail.

GUIDED READING

What does Brill-Oudener tell the others about a goose?

"We changed our course when we got nearer, and went over for a look-see. By Gad, it was a chap. Or had been, poor fellow. Machine gunned, you know. Badly.

---

29. **nobby.** Stylish
30. **trawlers.** Boats used for fishing
31. **drifter.** Particular type of fishing boat

---

words for everyday use

der • e • lict (der' ə likt) *adj.,* abandoned. *The volunteer group repairs* derelict *housing for homeless people.*

ANSWERS TO GUIDED READING QUESTIONS

1. He grins at her like he has known her a lifetime.
2. They don't know what happened to him. They say that he was a good man.
3. The goose perched on the boat, within which was Rhayader, who had been killed.

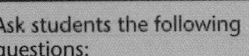
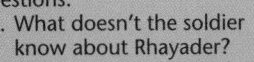
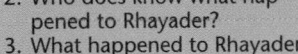

ADDITIONAL QUESTIONS AND ACTIVITIES

Ask students the following questions:

1. What doesn't the soldier know about Rhayader?
2. Who does know what happened to Rhayader?
3. What happened to Rhayader at Dunkirk?
4. In what ways does this part of the story resemble an investigative report in a newspaper or news magazine?

Answers

1. The soldier doesn't know what happened to Rhayader.
2. A retired naval officer, Keith Brill-Oudener knows what happened to Rhayader.
3. Rhayader was killed by machine-gun fire at Dunkirk.
4. Students may say that resembles an investigative report because it seems as if the narrator is interviewing survivors of the Dunkirk evacuation to find out the truth about what happened to Rhayader rather than simply telling the reader what occurred.

1. The goose rises, circles the boat
   three times, and heads west.
2. She sees the snow goose as
   Rhayader.

Face down in the water. Bird was a goose, a tame one.

"We drifted close, but when one of our chaps reached over, the bird hissed at him and struck at him with her wings. Couldn't drive it off. Suddenly young Kettering, who was with me, gave a hail and pointed to starboard. Big mine floating by. One of Jerry's beauties. If we'd kept on our course we'd have piled right into it. Ugh! Head on. We let it get a hundred yards astern[32] of the last barge, and the men blew it up with rifle fire.

"When we turned our attention to the derelict again, she was gone. Sunk. Concussion, you know. Chap with her. He must have been lashed to her. The bird had got up and was circling. Three times, like a plane saluting. Dashed queer feeling. Then she flew off to the west. Lucky thing for us we went over to have a look, eh? Odd that you should mention a goose."

Fritha remained alone at the little lighthouse on the Great Marsh, taking care of the pinioned birds, waiting for she knew not what. The first days she haunted the sea wall, watching, though she knew it was useless. Later she roamed through the storerooms of the lighthouse building with their stacks of canvases on which Rhayader had captured every mood and light of the desolate country and the wondrous graceful, feathered things that inhabited it.

Among them she found the picture that Rhayader had painted of her from memory so many years ago, when she was still a child, and had stood, wind-blown and timid, at his threshold, hugging an injured bird to her.

The picture and the things she saw in it stirred her as nothing ever had before, for much of Rhayader's soul had gone into it. Strangely, it was the only time he had painted the snow goose, the lost wild creature, stormdriven from another land,

> **GUIDED READING**
>
> How does the goose react to the death of Rhayader?

that to each had brought a friend, and which, in the end, returned to her with the message that she would never see him again.

Long before the snow goose had come dropping out of a crimsoned eastern sky to circle the lighthouse in a last farewell, Fritha, from the ancient powers of the blood that was in her, knew that Rhayader would not return.

And so, when one sunset she heard the high-pitched, well-remembered note cried from the heavens, it brought no instant of false hope to her heart. This moment, it seemed, she had lived before many times.

She came running to the sea wall and turned her eyes, not toward the distant sea whence a sail might come, but to the sky from whose flaming arches plummeted the snow goose. Then the sight, the sound, and the solitude surrounding broke the dam within her and released the surging, overwhelming truth of her love, let it well forth in tears.

Wild spirit called to wild spirit, and she seemed to be flying with the great bird, soaring with it in the evening sky, and hearkening to Rhayader's message.

Sky and earth were trembling with it and filled her beyond the bearing of it. "Frith! Fritha! Frith, my love. Goodbye, my love." The white pinions, black-tipped, were beating it out upon her heart, and her heart was answering; "Philip, I love 'ee."

For a moment Frith thought the snow goose was going to land in the old enclosure, as the pinioned geese set up a welcoming gabble. But it only skimmed low, then soared up again, flew in a wide, graceful spiral once around the old light, and then began to climb.

Watching it, Frith saw no longer the snow goose but the soul of Rhayader

> **GUIDED READING**
>
> How does Frith see the snow goose now?

---

32. **astern.** Behind a ship

taking farewell of her before departing forever.

She was no longer flying with it, but earthbound. She stretched her arms up into the sky and stood on tiptoes, reaching, and cried, "Godspeed! Godspeed, Philip!"

Frith's tears were stilled. She stood watching silently long after the goose had vanished. Then she went into the lighthouse and secured the picture that Rhayader had painted of her. Hugging it to her breast, she wended her way homeward along the old sea wall.

Each night, for many weeks there– after, Frith came to the lighthouse

and fed the pinioned birds. Then one early morning a German pilot on a dawn raid mistook the old abandoned lighthouse for an active military objective, dived onto it, a screaming steel hawk, and blew it and all it contained into oblivion.

GUIDED READING
How is Rhayader's sanctuary destroyed?

That evening when Fritha came, the sea had moved in through the breached walls and covered it over. Nothing was left to break the utter desolation. No marsh fowl had dared to return. Only the frightless gulls wheeled and soared and mewed their plaint over the place where it had been. ∎

Respond *to the* SELECTION

To what degree is fate a factor in life? Do things happen because they are simply "meant to be," or can people determine what will happen in their lives?

About *the* AUTHOR

Paul Gallico was born in New York City in 1897. Although his family was very talented in music, Gallico pursued writing and sports. He began his career as a sportswriter for a newspaper. Gallico liked to challenge leading sports figures in contests, which he never won but which gave him interesting material for his writing. In 1936 he began writing fiction. *The Snow Goose*, published in 1940, became a great success. The novella was later made into a screenplay. Gallico continued to write stories and novels, including *The Poseidon Adventure*, and travelled and lived in many places. He died in Monaco in 1976.

THE SNOW GOOSE **593**

SELECTION CHECK TEST WITH ANSWERS (CONT.)

third-person omniscient point of view
first person point of view   novella   setting
theme   motivation   mood

1. Because it is slightly longer, the characters and plot can be more developed in a **novella** than in a short story.
2. Complex, rich descriptions of characters help readers understand the **motivation** behind the actions and choices they make.
3. The details of setting, character and plot create **mood**, or an emotional reaction in the reader.
4. Literary works may have several **themes**, or statements about death, love, nature, or other aspects of human life.
5. World War II and a bleak seaside landscapes are important aspects of the **setting** of *The Snow Goose*.

ANSWER TO GUIDED READING QUESTION

1. Rhayader's sanctuary is destroyed by a German pilot who thought the lighthouse was a military target.

🏃 💾 📖 🔍 🗝 ↪

RESPOND TO THE SELECTION

Ask students to relate these ideas to what happens to Rhayader in this story.

SELECTION CHECK TEST WITH ANSWERS

Checking Your Reading
1. Why does Rhayader move to the lighthouse? **He wants to withdraw from human society because of people's reactions to his physical appearance.**
2. How is the snow goose injured? **The snow goose is shot.**
3. Who brings the snow goose to Rhyader? **Fritha brings the snow goose to Rhyader.**
4. What does Rhyader name the snow goose? **Rhyader names the snow goose The Lost Princess.**
5. Why does Rhyader sail away from the lighthouse? **Rhyader sails away to help British soldiers escape from the Germans.**

Vocabulary in Context
Fill in each blank below with the most appropriate vocabulary word from "The Snow Goose." You may have to change the tense of the word.

sodden   garner   import   extant
placid   derelict   tread

1. The tiny island nation has limited resources and must **import** most of its food.
2. The surface of the lake was **placid** after the storm.
3. Josh, Anthony, and Brett set up a fort in the **derelict** cabin they found in the woods.
4. After walking home in the rain, Evren kicked off his **sodden** shoes by the door of the house.
5. Although he had never taken art lessons, Erich **garnered** much praise for his paintings.

Reader's Toolbox
Fill in the blanks using the following terms. You may not use every term, and you may use some terms more than once.

RECALL

1a. Rhayader lives in an abandoned lighthouse on the Essex coast of southeastern England. He cares for the wild birds and paints pictures.

2a. Frith first visits Rhayader because she finds a wounded bird and has heard that he can do magic to heal things. She is frightened because she has heard bad things about him.

3a. When the goose leaves in spring, Frith stops visiting the lighthouse. The goose marks the passing of time because as she comes and goes with the seasons, so does Frith.

4a. Rhayader leaves to help save the English soldiers at Dunkirk. The goose follows him.

INTERPRET

Responses will vary. possible responses are given.

1b. Rhayader probably chooses to live alone because knowing that he repels people because of his disfiguration causes him pain. Despite his appearance, which frightens people, Rhayader is kind and gentle and full of pity and understanding for living things.

2b. Frith overcomes her fear of Rhayader by becoming involved with saving the snow goose. Her concern for the snow goose and interest in what Rhayader tells her about the goose allows her to become a bit more at ease. At first she is frightened away because of all the bad rumors about Rhayader; later she is frightened away by his growing feelings for her.

3b. The goose's departure means Frith no longer visits, and Rhayader is lonely. The goose seems to bring Frith and Rhayader together. As time passes, Frith becomes more comfortable with Rhayader, until she discovers that very strong feelings are developing between Rhayader and her.

4b. Rhayader leaves to do something meaningful. The soldiers seem to him like the birds that seek shelter with him. He wants to do something to help people and to make a difference. His leaving causes Frith to worry and feel dread. His leaving also makes Frith realize that she too has strong feelings for Rhayader.

ANALYZE

5a. Rhayader demonstrates love, understanding, and kindness in the way he treats the wild birds, in the

Investigate, *Inquire,* and Image

Recall: GATHERING FACTS

1a. Where does Rhayader live? What does he do there?

2a. Why does Frith first visit Rhayader? Why is she frightened?

3a. What happens when the goose leaves in spring? How does the goose mark the passing of time?

4a. What does Rhayader set off to do? What does the goose do?

Interpret: FINDING MEANING

1b. Why has he gone to live alone? What about him makes his appearance deceptive?

2b. How does Frith overcome her fear of Rhayader? What periodically frightens her away again?

3b. How does the goose's departure affect Rhayader? How does the goose affect the relationship between Rhayader and Frith? How do things change between them as time passes?

4b. Why does Rhayader leave? How does his leaving affect Frith?

Analyze: TAKING THINGS APART

5a. In what ways does Rhayader demonstrate love, understanding, and kindness? Mark the points in the story where Frith comes to learn more about the person Rhayader really is.

Synthesize: BRINGING THINGS TOGETHER

5b. How, in Frith's mind, does the snow goose become Rhayader? Why does the snow goose leave? Where does it go?

Perspective: LOOKING AT OTHER VIEWS

6a. What does Rhayader mean to Frith during Part One of the novella? How would she describe her relationship with him? How do her feelings change in Part Two? What does the snow goose mean to Frith? In *The Snow Goose*, the reader knows Frith only in the context of the lighthouse, in the company of Rhayader and the snow goose. How important to her is this part of her life?

Empathy: SEEING FROM INSIDE

6b. Putting yourself in Frith's place, describe what you would do after the destruction of the lighthouse. Where would you live? How would you pass the days? What would be important to you? How would you cope with the changes that occurred? How would you deal with your memories of the snow goose and of Rhayader?

ANSWERS TO INVESTIGATE, INQUIRE, IMAGINE (CONT.)

gentle way he treats Frith, and in the way he seeks to help the soldiers. Frith comes to learn more about Rhayader when she first visits the lighthouse, when she and Rhayader realize the snow goose is going to stay at the lighthouse year round, and when Rhayader sets off to rescue the soldiers.

SYNTHESIZE

5b. Like Rhayader, the snow goose is an outsider that is isolated from other of her kind. The snow goose becomes Rhayader in having bonded so closely with him and then soaring after Rhayader dies. The goose's calls of farewell seem to Frith to be

(Continued on page 595)

Understanding *Literature*

NOVELLA. A **novella** is a work of fiction that is longer than a short story and shorter than a novel. How well does the author create dynamic characters in *The Snow Goose*? How well is the plot developed? How important is the setting, and how does the author use setting as an essential part of the story?

DESCRIPTION. A **description** gives a picture in words of a character, an object, or a scene. Descriptions make use of sensory details—words and phrases that describe how things look, sound, smell, taste, or feel. How does the author's description of setting enhance the story? How does the author's description of the main characters strengthen the story's plot and theme?

THEME. A **theme** is a central idea in a literary work. Look at the list of topics that you created as you read the story. What possible themes from the story can you name? How is the theme (or themes) developed? On what other elements of the story is theme dependent?

FORESHADOWING. **Foreshadowing** is the act of presenting materials that hint at events to occur later in the story. Look back at the story and identify specific passages where foreshadowing occurs. Then find the event that is foreshadowed. You may want to use the following graphic organizer to make a picture of your findings.

Graphic *Organizer*

- The world outside boiled and seethed and rumbled with the eruption that was soon to break forth . . .
- World War II and the evacuation at Dunkirk

Writer's Journal

1. Using the soldiers' accounts of Rhayader's actions during the evacuation of Dunkirk, write a brief **newspaper article** about his role in the event.

2. Write **song lyrics** based on *The Snow Goose*, recreating the novella's mood and theme. Imagine that the song is to be performed during a memorial ceremony for artists, for animal advocates, or for World War II heroes.

3. Write the **message for a memorial plaque** for Rhayader that will stand on the site of the abandoned lighthouse.

ANSWERS TO UNDERSTANDING LITERATURE

NOVELLA. Students might not immediately think that the characters in this novella are dynamic, or that the plot is well-developed because of its refined style and the way the narrator is so removed from the story. However, the third-person omniscient point of view helps reveal the different perspectives of Frith, Rhayader, and the men saved at Dunkirk. You might help students discuss the way Gallico provides a distant, almost timeless narration, and how his technique is largely helped by the austere setting. Setting is so integral to *The Snow Goose* that it almost functions as a character.

DESCRIPTION. The author's description of setting helps convey the sense of alienation and loneliness: "It is desolate, utterly lonely, and made lonelier by the calls and cries of the wildfowl that make their homes in the marshlands and saltings." Character descriptions also help develop the plot and theme. Rhayader is portrayed with physical limitations but with great strength, compassion, and birdlike qualities; Frith is shown as a wild and uncared for child who grows to be a woman and who loves Rhayader and his ability to heal injured things.

THEME. Responses will vary, depending on what themes students named. Some themes might include the value of overcoming alienation; the importance of compassion for those who are different, the possibility of mercy in a flawed world, and self-sacrifice in the face of adversity.

FORESHADOWING. The example sentence given in the Graphic Organizer foreshadows the way the war will disrupt the lives of Rhayader and Frith. Rhayader's death is foreshadowed in the final sentence of the introduction to the novella: "For the sea has claimed its own and spread its rippled blanket over the site, and the great white bird with the black-tipped pinions that saw it all from the beginning to the end has returned to the dark, frozen silences of the northlands whence it came."

ANSWERS TO INVESTIGATE, INQUIRE, IMAGINE (CONT.)

signs from Rhayader. The goose's leaving represents Rhayader's leaving. Her freedom reflects Rhayader's freedom from a life of discomfort.

PERSPECTIVE

6a. To Frith, Rhayader becomes a friend during the first part of the novella. She would probably say that he is a person with whom she likes to visit. In the second part of the novella, Frith begins to realize that Rhayader has strong feelings for her and begins to question her own feelings toward him.

The snow goose, which gives her an excuse to visit the lighthouse, represents her special relationship with Rhayader. Though Rhayader, the snow goose, and the lighthouse are outside Frith's regular life and community, they probably are very important to her.

EMPATHY

6b. Students should recognize that an important part of Frith's life is now gone forever.

Media Literacy
Students may find information about using maps in the Language Arts Survey, "Using Almanacs, Yearbooks, and Atlases." If students have difficulty creating their own maps, let them know that they do not have to capture every physical feature and every town that appears in a map in an atlas. They just have to capture the basic shapes of the regions and some prominent physical features and places. tell students they do not have to worry about drawing their maps to scale.

Collaborative Learning
You might wish to give students the following list of birds as a starting point: the Arctic tern, the snow goose, and the swan. You may want to have students use Living on the Wind: Across the Globe with Migratory Birds by Scott Weidensaul as a resource for this activity. Students might also wish to compare bird migration with that of other creatures that migrate, such as seals, bats, caribou, wildebeests, zebras, and salmon.

Vocabulary
1. recurrence
2. desolate
3. garnered
4. misshapen
5. sanctuary
6. mournful
7. suppressed
8. mysteriously
9. seized
10. fragmentary

Skill Builders

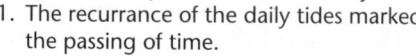

Media Literacy
USING AND CREATING MAPS. Use library resources to locate maps of the Atlantic Ocean, Europe, and England. First, find a map that shows the Atlantic Ocean, with North America to the west and Europe to the east. Make your own map of the region, showing the route that the snow goose may have taken from northern Canada to southeastern England. Next, find a map that shows the coastal area of southeastern England. Create a map of the area showing Essex, a county northeast of London. Finally, using different sources if needed, create a map showing the Essex coast, the North Sea and the Strait of Dover, and Dunkirk in northern France. On this map, trace the possible course of Rhayader.

Collaborative Learning
STUDYING MIGRATION PATTERNS.
Form small groups. With the other members of your group, make a list of eight to ten birds to study. Using encyclopedias, bird-watchers' field guides, and other materials, find information about the migration patterns of the birds on your list. Try to locate answers to the following questions for each type of bird. Where does the bird winter? Where does it spend the summer? Are its habitats broad or limited? What is the average distance it covers when migrating? After compiling this information about each bird, develop a chart as a group. Along the left side of the chart, label each row with the name of one of the birds studied by the group. Along the top, make a column for each of the following: winter habitat, summer habitat, broad or limited habitats, and migration distance. Fill in each cell in the chart. Then compare and contrast the data.
- Which bird travels the longest distance?
- Which bird summers the farthest north?
- Which winters the farthest south?
- Which has the smallest habitats?
- How many birds have similar migration patterns?
- Which has the most unusual migration pattern?

Vocabulary
PROOFREADING FOR SPELLING ERRORS. In each of the following sentences, circle the misspelled word and then spell the word correctly.
1. The recurrance of the daily tides marked the passing of time.
2. The marshland is a lonely, desolite place.
3. The story has been garnerred from many different sources.
4. The man's mishapen body made some people nervous.
5. Many birds returned each year to Rhayader's wildfowl santuary.
6. The moarnful calls of the geese signaled their departure.
7. He surpressed his worries about the dangers ahead.
8. The snow goose mysterously appeared one day.
9. Alarm siezed Frith as she realized what was happening.
10. The fascinating story became fragmentery as it wound to an end.

Getting into Fiction

Merlyn's Pen: The National Magazine of Student Writing began giving young writers a place for their most compelling work in 1985. The magazine, which comes out annually, has published hundreds of short stories, poems, and essays written by students in grades six through twelve. Some of these literary works were later included in the American Teen Writer Series, which includes anthologies of works organized by grade level, genre, and theme. Liana Fredley's story, "Investment in the Future," appears in Getting There: Seventh Grade Writers on Life, School, and the Universe. For information on ordering the magazine or submitting your work, go to the Merlyn's Pen Internet site at

http://www.merlynspen.com

or write to Merlyn's Pen, Inc., P. O. Box 910, East Greenwich, RI 02818.

"Investment in the Future"
by Liana Fredley

Joey counted the money he and his mom had just withdrawn from his savings account. He was almost ten, but he had been saving his money all his life and was waiting for this year, this day, this moment when he would finally come up with $500, enough to buy what he had always wanted: a robot of his very own. He had picked the one that would be his from a Radio Shack catalogue. He was dreaming even now, as he counted up his money, of what he and his robot could do.

Joey heaved a long sigh as he came to the last dollar bill and laid the money down on the seat of his parents' solar car. "What's the matter, Joey?" asked his mother, driving down Lawrence Street into Marietta.

"Oh, Mom, I've got $492! Could you lend me a few? Please?"

"Well, I suppose that could be arranged," said his mother. Then, stealing a glance at her son, she added, "Of course, you'll have to pay it back."

"Great! I just can't wait!" Joey forgot to thank his mom, for he was already thinking of when he could go to Radio Shack to pick up his robot, which he had already named Harold.

"Joey!" his father called from the library in their home. Joey dropped the catalogue he was studying and walked slowly down the stairs, his head drooping low. He knew what was wrong. He had accidentally turned on the dishwasher with only a few dishes in it. His mother had scolded him harshly for that.

"Joey!" his father called again.

"I'm coming!" called Joey as he stepped into the library. The room had a comfortable air to it. Against the far wall a floor-to-ceiling bookcase overflowed with books. Against the other wall was an old desk, on top of which sat an aged

ADDITIONAL QUESTIONS AND ACTIVITIES

1. What does Joey's father question Joey about?
2. How much money has Joey saved?
3. What does Joey's father expect the robot to do? What does Joey want the robot to do?

Answers
1. Joey's father questions him about the robot he is planning to buy.
2. Joey has saved $500 to purchase the robot.
3. Joey's father expects the robot to do something useful, like washing walls or cleaning Joey's room. Joey wants the robot to be his friend.

typewriter still used by the family. Joey wished he felt as comfortable as the room.

"So you are going to buy a robot?" asked his father. "What kind is it? How tall is it? Does it run by batteries? What does it look like? How much does it cost?" Mr. Parker asked this last question rather slowly and after a long pause.

Joey answered all these questions except the last. His father asked again, "How much does it cost?"

"Um...well...about $500...sir!" he stuttered.

"Ahem, well, seeing what it can do and that you do have the money, go ahead and buy it."

"Yeah! Oh, thank you, Dad!"

"Now," said Joey, rubbing his hands together as he had seen the mad scientist on "Big Foot" do so often, "let's dig in!"

"Hold on, kid," replied his father, raising his hand as a policeman would. "We must take nothing out of this box but the instructions. Then we shall read them thoroughly." Mr. Parker pulled out the instructions and read them all to Joey. With Joey's help, Mr. Parker had the robot, Harold, quickly working. Joey's father was so busily and joyously ordering Harold around that he forgot this was Joey's robot.

"C'mon, Dad," cried Joey, as his father sent the loyal robot to surprise Mrs. Parker in the kitchen, "gimme a chance, too." The whirring sound of the robot grew louder as it entered the room, carrying three glasses of cola on ice. Mrs. Parker followed it, aghast.

"Good, Harold!" complimented Joey on the robot's thoughtfulness. "Pretty cool, eh?" he asked, turning to his parents.

"Yeah," grinned Mr. Parker, stealing a glance at Joey's mother. "Pretty cool."

"Now I'm gonna take Harold up to my, I mean, our room to get him acquainted with the house and with me," decided Joey. "I want to get to know him."

All that day and the next, and the next, and the next, Joey stayed out of the hot summer sun and in his room with his friend Harold. He and his robot were becoming quite close and were beginning to talk together in a special way.

"Joey!" called his father one day when he came home from work and found Joey with Harold again. "Why can't you get that robot toy to do something useful, like washing walls for your mom or cleaning your room?

"Dad, are you kidding? Why are you asking this of Harold? He is just like us!" cried Joey, almost in tears at hearing this terrible insult to his best friend.

"OK, OK, have it your way, but make sure you clean up your room today."

"All right, Dad," replied Joey, lowering his voice to speak to Harold. "Come on, Harry. We've gotta clean up our room—now!"

✳ ✳ ✳ ✳ ✳ ✳ ✳ ✳

A month had passed since Joey bought Harold, and it was now time for school again. Joey dreaded this, for he would have to leave his friend alone in the house with only his mother for a whole day! Yet, somehow Joey survived the first day, then rushed home to Harold. He told Harold all about his first day of school.

Later that day, Joey's father came home from working at the lab. His mother was preparing dinner as the afternoon sun filtered through the window. A white truck drove up the driveway and stopped at the Parkers' house. There was green, official-looking lettering on the side of the truck.

Mrs. Parker tool one look and gasped. "John! John! They're here! John!" She dashed through the house calling him.

Mr. Parker knew well who "they" were and why "they" were here. He ran upstairs to Joey's room, where Joey was reading to Harold. "Joey! Joey! They're here! They're here! The scientists! No, we must leave Harold here! Come on, we must go! NOW!

"Dad, no! We're not gonna leave Harold here all alone…NO!" cried Joey, a tear rolling down his red cheek.

"Joey, are you going to risk your freedom for a robot?"

Joey's eyes widened and his mouth gaped open. "How could you?! Have you forgotten?!"

"No, just come on! Please!" cried his father.

Joey slipped something into his pocket, murmured one last work to Harold, the best friend he had ever had, and joined his dad as fast as he could.

"B-but Dan, suppose they are dangerous! I don't like the idea of going in and checking up on a house full of robots!" whispered one of the men from the truck.

"Come on, Ed, I know you're new to this program, but I'm the scientist and you're my assistant. We're supposed to go in and check on the robot Parker family to make sure they are doing OK. You know, check for short circuits and maximum functioning," said the other.

"But they've been out of your power for ten years now. Suppose they like being free, like real humans?"

"I suppose you do have a point there, Ed," Dr. Winthrop agreed, hesitating to open the door of the truck. "But anyway, we have to go, so come on!"

Dr. Winthrop opened the door of the truck and hopped out. Ed followed him. They walked up to the door and gave it a hard rap. They knocked again and again and again. The robot Parker family did not answer.

"They may have forgotten this was the day of their ten-year checkup," suggested Ed. Dr. Winthrop corrected him. "Robots don't forget," he said thoughtfully. Then, after a long pause, he added, "They're probably almost humanized now. We waited too long."

Just as the two scientists were walking away from the house to their truck, the robot Parker family silently slipped out the back door, never to return. The robot Parker family was walking through the woods behind the house when Mrs. Parker sighed and dropped down on her knees. "Oh, it's all my fault," she cried. "I *forgot* this was the day of our ten-year checkup. Does that mean I am now really humanized?"

Joey pulled from his pocket a small, square microchip: Harold's cloned heart. Joey knew he could now create Harold II in his new home, and he would soon have his best friend back. ■

Liana Fredley went to college in Williamsburg, Virginia, and majored in English literature, but her favorite courses were in film. She now lives in the Hell's Kitchen neighborhood of New York City and works as a production editor for a

ADDITIONAL QUESTIONS AND ACTIVITIES

1. Who comes to the house and alarms the Parkers?
2. What is the assignment of the visitors?
3. What do the visitors discover when they enter the house? How do they respond?
4. Where is the Parker family?
5. What does Joey take from his pocket at the end of the story? What will he now be able to do?

Answers

1. Scientists driving a white truck with green, official-looking lettering come to the house.
2. The men are assigned to inspect the robot Parker family; they have been scheduled for a ten-year checkup.
3. The scientists discover that the Parker family is not home. Ed thinks the robots have forgotten, but Dr. Winthrop tells him that robots don't forget, that they have now become humanized.
4. The Parker family is silently slipping out the back door when the scientists leave. They plan never to return.
5. Joey pulls from his pocket a microchip that stores Harold's cloned heart. He will now be able to create Harold II in his new home, and regain his friend.

publisher of scholarly and academic books. She also takes on freelance editing jobs in the evenings—as long as they don't interfere with her moviegoing! Fredley is just starting to learn how to edit movies at the School of Visual Arts and notes that it's actually not that much different from editing books and stories. Eventually, she would like to work as a film editor. Below, she answers a few questions about herself and her story.

What interested you in writing when you were in seventh grade? How did you come to submit your story to Merlyn's Pen?

A couple of my elementary-school teachers were always asking us to write stories, poems, and little plays, which was much more fun than doing worksheets. Then they'd put them all together into booklets of writing by the whole class. (I still have one of those booklets, and I remember my friends in the class every time I read their poems and stories.) Mrs. Rodgers submitted what we'd written to *Merlyn's Pen*.

Are you still a writer? What kind of writing do you like best?

I just write for myself, usually short essays and prose-poetry, the kind of writing that involves a lot of fine-tuning and editing, to keep in practice. Writing is hard work, though, and it would take a strong and determined person to do it day in and day out. I've realized that I'm better at helping other people with their writing.

How did you come up with the idea for your story, "Investment in the Future"?

I don't remember specifically, but I suspect I was reading a lot of O. Henry stories and watching *The Twilight Zone*

around that time and I thought that all stories had to have a shocking, mind-boggling twist at the end.

Did you write the story as it appears, or did you have to go back and edit it? If you ever edited it, how did you go about it?

The first time I edited anything was when I got my first job in publishing after college, and my boss said, "Edit this book." Until then, I had no idea that a story or an essay could be so much improved by reading it over, making changes, rewriting, and then doing it all over again half a dozen times. Now I write just a bit at a time, then go back and work on it sentence by sentence, word by word, until it's close enough to what I want that I can move on to write the next bit.

for your READING LIST

AMERICA STREET
A MULTICULTURAL ANTHOLOGY OF STORIES

Edited by Anne Mazer

America Street, edited by Anne Mazer, is an anthology of short stories by outstanding American authors. The young people you will meet in these pages come from diverse ethnic and cultural backgrounds, yet they all share one important thing in common: they are all trying to find their place in the world.

In Toshio Mori's story, "Business At Eleven," Johnny builds a small and successful business and, thereby, some stability and purpose for himself. Sandra, in "Sixth Grade" by Michelle Wallace, knows she is different from the other kids. She can tell by the way they dress, the way their mothers look and even what they bring in their lunch boxes. But which difference explains the contempt—even hatred—the adults around her seem to feel toward her? In Naomi Shihab Nye's story, "Hamadi," Susan's Palestinian friend may not be up to date on American dress, slang, or customs, but he understands her best friend's grief and knows just what to say. And in "The All-American Slurp" by Lensey Namioka, a young Chinese-American girl learns that, while she and her family struggle to learn American customs, her American friends are just as eager to know about Chinese customs and just as inept at learning them.

HOST A BOOK REVIEW SHOW

Imagine that you and your friends are the production team for a widely viewed public television show about books. On your show, you introduce your viewers to wonderful literature they might not otherwise see, including books by foreign authors, classics, and books from small publishing houses. Prepare and videotape a segment of your show that introduces your viewers to *America Street*. You will want to create a name for your show and a set. You may also want to use theme music to open the program. It may be helpful for each member of the group to take responsibility for some aspect of the production, including set design, theme music, lighting, videotaping, host, and guest author. As you develop your review of the book, consider these questions:

- What makes this book special?
- What sort of reader will find it appealing?
- What are the themes or common threads in this book?
- What highlights would you want to share?
- How did you, as the host, personally respond to the book?
- Are there others books to which you would compare this one?

Another book you may want to read:
Sixteen: Short Stories By Outstanding Writers for Young Adults ed. by Donald R. Gallo

---

For Your Reading List
American Street, edited by Anne Mazer, and Sixteen: *Short Stories by Outstanding Writers for Young Adults,* edited by Donald R. Gallo, provide well-crafted, thought-provoking short stories that students will find especially memorable. In a 1994 review, *The Horn Book* writes about *American Street,* "America's diversity is evident in the carefully selected anthology of fourteen short stories by established contemporary writers of books for both children and adults. A common thread in the tales of immigrant and minority childhood experiences in America is the affirmation of the human spirit. Poignant, humorous, and warm, the brief tales will aid youngsters in understanding themselves and others." *Sixteen: Short Stories by Outstanding Writers for Young Adults* also offers stories based on diverse experiences teen readers will enjoy.

Host a Book Review Show
As students prepare for their role as book review show hosts, have them read the following sections in the Language Arts Survey: 1.3, "Reading Literature: Educating Your Imagination," 1.4, "Educating Your Imagination as an Active Reader," 4.22, "Preparing a Multimedia Presentation," and 6.11, "Displaying Effective Visual Information." See the Assessment Resource 4.10–4.12 for evaluation forms that will help you assess student performance.

LESSON OVERVIEW

Interpreting Literature
Student Model, 602
Examining the Model, 602
Prewriting, 602
Identifying Your Audience, 602
Finding Your Voice, 603
Writing with a Plan, 603
Student Model—Graphic Organizer, 603
Drafting, 604
Self- and Peer Evaluation, 604
Student Model—Draft, 605
Revising and Proofreading, 606
Publishing and Presenting, 606
Reflecting, 607

Language, Grammar, and Style
Editing Wordy Sentences, 604
Identifying Wordy Sentences, 605
Fixing Wordy Sentences, 605
Using Clear and Direct Sentences, 606

Examining the Model

Ask students how Kyra draws the reader's interest into her composition. How does she include the reader in her conclusion?

GUIDED WRITING
Software

See the Guided Writing Software for an extended version of this lesson that includes printable graphic organizers, extensive student models and student-friendly checklists, and self-, peer, and teacher evaluation features.

"... we need to be willing to let our intuition guide us, and then be willing to follow that guidance directly and fearlessly."

—*Shakti Gawain*

EXAMINING THE MODEL. Kyra, a seventh grade student, supports her interpretation of the theme of "Luke Baldwin's Vow" with specific examples from the story. Kyra points out that Luke, Luke's uncle, and Mr. Kemp all have different ideas for solving the problem that Dan presents. Luke's solution does not work for his uncle, and the uncle's solution does not work for Luke. Kyra realizes that Mr. Kemp offers Luke a suggestion from a different angle. Looking from this different angle, Luke finds a solution that works.

Notice that Kyra states the theme of the story in the introductory paragraph. She supports her interpretation of the theme in the next two paragraphs by providing specific examples from the story. Last, she draws a conclusion about the theme in the concluding paragraph.

Prewriting
IDENTIFYING YOUR AUDIENCE.
Before you begin writing, think about your role as a writer and consider your audience. You are like a teacher helping someone

---

Guided Writing

INTERPRETING LITERATURE

Kevin had just read another terrific mystery story. When his friend Ned asked for a synopsis of the story, he replied, "It was about a very clever thief who fooled everyone for a long time. In the end, though, he was caught by an even more clever detective."

"Hmmm," replied Ned. "That sounds like the old 'crime doesn't pay' theme."

As you read the selections in this unit, you examined the **theme**, or central idea of the literature selections. The theme often contains an idea an author wants you to think about. The author develops the theme gradually by carefully arranging the events in the story. The theme is usually not directly stated; instead, readers must discover the theme as they read.

For this assignment, you will write about the theme in one of the selections you read in the unit. You will need to identify a theme in the story and explain how you know it is a theme. You will need to support your interpretation by giving specific examples from the story.

Student Model

from "Different Angles" by Kyra

Have you ever had a problem that you couldn't solve? Then, a friend suggests, "Try this." You try your friend's solution, and it works. This situation is like the theme in "Luke Baldwin's Vow." In this story, Luke cannot find a solution to his problem. Luke learns that it is important to look at different angles of a problem to find the solution that works best for everyone.

Before learning this, Luke doesn't know what to do because his uncle wants to get rid of Dan, Luke's dog. Dan is old and useless to the uncle, but he is Luke's best friend. His uncle already has tried to kill Dan once, but Luke has saved him. Luke knows that even if his uncle forgives him for saving the dog, his uncle's mind is made up. In a few days he will get rid of him in another way. Luke can't take him to the woods and take care of him there because Dan would wander home.

Luke finally asks wise, old Mr. Kemp what to do. Mr. Kemp knows that Luke's uncle wants to get rid of the useless dog. He knows that Luke loves the dog. So he looks for an angle that works

---

for Luke and his uncle. Mr. Kemp suggests, "Why not make a practical proposition to your uncle?" So Luke tells his uncle, "I know Dan's not worth his keep, so I'll pay you seventy five cents a week for his keep." His uncle agrees to his proposition.

By looking at the problem from his uncle's point of view, Luke finds a solution, and he gets to keep his best friend. This shows that looking at several viewpoints is a good way to find a solution. If you have a problem, look at all views before you act. Then you can find a solution.

Student Model—Graphic Organizer

Literature Selection
"Luke Baldwin's Vow"

Freewriting about Resolution
Luke gets to keep Dan. He tells his uncle that he'll pay for Dan's food so that even if he is useless, it doesn't cost his uncle anything to keep Dan.

Freewriting about Conflict
Luke's uncle wants to kill Dan because he's useless; Dan is Luke's best friend. Luke's uncle is practical—doesn't care. Luke knows his uncle won't change his mind.

Freewriting about Theme
Luke can't figure out how to save Dan. He wants to take him someplace safe but he doesn't know where. Mr. Kemp is smart. He knows how the uncle feels and how Luke feels and he knows that their feelings are too far apart from each other to keep Dan alive. So he thinks of something from a different angle that will work for Luke and his uncle.

Theme
If there is a problem, look at all views before you act. Look at different angles to find solutions.

References that support the theme
". . . his [Uncle Henry's] mind was made up to get rid of Dan. (548)

"Luke couldn't take the dog to the woods and take care of him there, because the dog would wander home." (548)

". . . you say right out that you've come with a business proposition." (550)

"'I know Dan isn't worth his keep to you...so I'll pay you seventy-five cents a week for his keep.'" (550)

What else do you want to say about this theme? Explain why the theme is important
If you have a problem that doesn't seem to have a solution, talk to someone. Try to find some other views or angles to base your solution on.

---

understand what you know. Who will benefit from reading your explanation of the story's theme? Consider sharing the insights you have gained with another seventh grade student who has not read the story or with a sixth grade student who is learning how to examine and interpret literature.

FINDING YOUR VOICE. You expect teachers to be reliably informed and able to keep their subjects interesting. Since your audience will read your interpretation of literature, they will expect you to be reliably informed and interesting, too. How can you use language to present an informed and reliable piece of writing that reflects your interesting views and attitude toward the topic? Look at the examples below. Which sentence reflects an informed, reliable, and interesting voice?

Uncle Henry didn't like Dan.

Uncle Henry thought Dan was no longer worth his keep.

WRITING WITH A PLAN. Choose one of the literature selections from the unit that you enjoyed reading. Then copy the graphic organizer onto your own paper. Freewrite about the conflict, resolution, and theme of your story for several minutes. Now, consider the points you made in your freewriting. Use the ideas to write a sentence that states the theme of the story. What ideas in your freewriting

continued on page 604

GUIDED WRITING **603**

GRAPHIC ORGANIZER

See the Guided Writing Resource 7.8 for a blackline master of the Graphic Organizer for this lesson.

IDENTIFYING YOUR AUDIENCE. Have students read the Language Arts Survey 2.4, "Identifying Your Audience." Encourage students to use vocabulary with which their audience will be familiar.

INDIVIDUAL LEARNING STRATEGIES

MOTIVATION
Write several themes on the board such as "the struggle for freedom," "standing together in adversity," "fighting against the odds," and "overcoming obstacles." Then ask students to come up with the names of movies that demonstrate each of those themes.

READING PROFICIENCY
Tell students to read the Language Arts Survey 1.3, "Reading Literature: Educating Your Imagination," and 1.4, "Educating Your Imagination as an Active Reader."

ENGLISH LANGUAGE LEARNING
See strategies for Reading Proficiency above that will also benefit students who are English language learners. Ask non-native speakers if they have read any literature in their native language. Since research shows that students do not transfer reading skills from their native language to their second language, help them to transfer any successful strategies they have to reading literature in English.

SPECIAL NEEDS
Students with special needs might need help understanding theme. You might begin by telling them that subject and theme are different and give an example of each from a story in this unit. These students will also benefit from being guided through the Graphic Organizer. Ask them pointed questions to help them get to the story's theme.

ENRICHMENT
Have students identify the themes for six other stories in the book. Remind students that a story can have more than one theme.

FINDING YOUR VOICE. Encourage students to read the Language Arts Survey 2.5, "Finding Your Voice," and 3.3, "Register, Tone, and Voice." Ask students to identify the voice they intend on using.

WRITING WITH A PLAN. Ask students to read the Language Arts Survey 2.12, "Freewriting." Tell students to do a focused freewrite.

support your theme statement? Underline the ideas that you will use for support. Circle the interesting and lively details in your freewriting that you might use in your draft.

Continue to fill in the graphic organizer with the facts and ideas that support your interpretation of the theme.

Steps to Finding a Story's Theme
- identify the conflict
- consider the resolution
- think it over—what point is the author making by solving the conflict that way?

Discovering Theme
Keep in mind that a story might have more than one theme. Two readers of the same story may state its theme or themes in different ways, and both may be correct.

Language, Grammar, and Style **Editing Wordy Sentences.** As you write, use only words that you need to get your meaning across to a reader. Edit your sentences so that they are not wordy and complicated. Replace complicated or unclear words with simple and clear words. Read the examples on the next page.

Drafting
Use the information on your graphic organizer to guide you as you write the rough draft of your essay. Do not worry at this point about the details of spelling, grammar, usage, and mechanics. Instead, simply concentrate on getting your ideas down on paper.

THE INTRODUCTORY PARAGRAPH. Include an introductory paragraph that states the theme. Write the first sentence so that it captures the attention of your readers. Use a transitional "hook" in the last sentence to move your reader to the next paragraph.

TWO BODY PARAGRAPHS. Provide one idea that supports your theme in each of the next two or three paragraphs. You may want to present your ideas in the order of their importance. Put the most significant example first, then the next most important, and finally, the least important. Go back to your graphic organizer and number the ideas in the order you plan to use them.

THE CONCLUSION. Provide a conclusion in the final paragraph. Restate the theme and summarize your main points of support. Leave your reader thinking about why the theme is important.

Self- and Peer Evaluation
After you finish your first draft, complete a self-evaluation of your writing. If time allows, you may want to get one or two peer evaluations. For more information, see the Language Arts Survey 2.37, "Self- and Peer Evaluation."

As you evaluate your writing, answer the following questions. Take notes on your rough draft to use when you revise your writing.
- How does the writing capture the reader's interest in the first paragraph?
- What is the theme of the story?
- What support for the theme statement is provided? What specific examples from the text are included?
- What additional support and examples might help the reader to understand the theme better?
- Examine the transitions between paragraphs. What could you do to make them more effective?
- How does the concluding paragraph impress the importance of the theme on the reader?
- Which sentences are too wordy? How can the sentences be reworded to be clear and direct?

Notice how Kyra and one of her peers evaluated her first draft.

Student Model—Draft

Have you ever had a problem that you didn't know how to solve? Add an interesting intro—maybe about solving a problem.

The theme of "Luke Baldwin's Vow" is that it is important to look at different angles of a problem to find the solution. That means if you have a

This sentence is confusing. Can you reword?

problem, try and find other views, to find how it would work out best for everyone involved in the problem.

That's what Luke learns in this story.

Before learning this, *transition?*

Luke doesn't know what to do ~~with Dan~~

~~the dog~~ because his uncle wants to get

Dan, Luke's

rid of ~~the~~ dog. His uncle already has

tell why

tried to kill Dan once, but Luke has

saved him. Luke knows that even if he

wordy

should be forgiven for saving the dog,

his uncle's mind is made up ~~to get rid~~

~~of Dan~~. In a few days he will get rid of

him in another way. Luke can't take Dan

to the woods and take care of him there

because Dan will wander home. He finally

asks wise old Mr. Kemp what to do.

Mr. Kemp suggests, "Why not make a

WORDY

I certainly was appreciative of your thoughtful gesture of bringing chicken soup for me to eat when I was sick and didn't feel like getting out of bed.

CLEAR AND DIRECT

Thank you for bringing me chicken soup when I was sick.

IDENTIFYING WORDY SENTENCES.
Look at the two sentences below. Which one is wordy? Which one is clear and direct?

Don't forget to lock the door when you leave.

Make sure that you are very careful not to forget to lock the door to the house when you leave the house.

FIXING WORDY SENTENCES.
Read the following wordy sentence from Kyra's rough draft. Note how she rewrote the sentence to be shorter and cleaner for the final draft.

WORDY

That means if you have a problem, try and find other views, to find how it would work out best for everyone involved in the problem.

CLEAR AND DIRECT

You need to look at several viewpoints and determine what would work best for everyone.

continued on page 606

Drafting

Tell students to use their completed Graphic Organizer modeled on page 603 to help them make sure they are including all the pertinent information. Have students write a discovery draft in which they do not focus on spelling, grammar, usage, and mechanics. Students might benefit from reading the Language Arts Survey 2.31, "Drafting." As students need a transition at the end of the first paragraph, they might want to read the Language Arts Survey 2.35, "Using Transitions Effectively."

Self- and Peer Evaluation

Have students use the checklist on page 604 for self- and peer evaluation. See the Guided Writing Resource located in the Teacher's Resource Kit for a blackline master of the checklist. The checklist is intended to act as a student-friendly rubric that should help students identify specific evidence of writing strengths and areas needing improvement. Make sure students provide concrete suggestions for improvement or specific evidence of the effectiveness of their literary interpretation. Students might benefit from reading the Language Arts Survey 2.37–2.40 for more details about self- and peer evaluation. Students critiquing the writer's work might be interested in using common proofreader's symbols, which are found in the Language Arts Survey 2.44, "Using Proofreader's Marks."

Language, Grammar, and Style

Editing Wordy Sentences
LESSON OVERVIEW
In this lesson, students will be asked to do the following:
• Identify Wordy Sentences, 605
• Fix Wordy Sentences, 605
• Use Clear and Direct Sentences, 606

INTRODUCING THE SKILL. Remind students that using clear and direct sentences will help them become

---

Language, Grammar, and Style

more effective writers and that this skill will help them succeed in classes other than English.

PREVIEWING THE SKILL. Refer students to the Language Arts Survey 3.33, "Correcting Wordy Sentences."

PRACTICING THE SKILL. For additional practice, have students work through the exercise in the following section of the Language, Grammar, and Style Resource located in the Teacher's Resource Kit: 3.33, "Correcting Wordy Sentences." Students maintaining a portfolio might find sentences to edit for wordiness in past assignments.

Kyra wrote the following wordy sentences in her rough draft. Use your own paper to rewrite these sentences, making them shorter and clearer. Then check to see how Kyra changed them in her final draft on page 602.

WORDY
Luke doesn't know what to do with Dan the dog because his uncle wants to get rid of the dog.

WORDY
Luke knew that even if he should be forgiven for saving the dog, his uncle's mind was made up to get rid of Dan.

USING CLEAR AND DIRECT SENTENCES. Look at your own writing and examine each of your sentences. Does each sentence say what you want? Is the sentence direct and clear? Rewrite any wordy sentences so that they are shorter and cleaner.

Reading out loud is a good way to check for wordy sentences. Continue to revise your sentences until they are clear and direct.

For more information, see the Language Arts Survey 3.33, "Correcting Wordy Sentences."

tie this into theme
looks at a differnt angle

practical proposition to your uncle?" *This supports finding a different angle*

(page 550).

So Luke tells his uncle, "I know Dan's not worth his keep, so I'll pay you seventy-five cents a week for his keep" (page 550). His uncle agrees to *This supports finding a different angle*

his proposition.

By looking at the problem from his *Good!*

uncle's point of view, Luke finds a

solution, and he gets to keep his best

friend. *What should this theme mean to us? Looking at several viewpoints helps us find solutions.*

Revising and Proofreading

As you consider your writing, your self-evaluation, and peer reviews, think about the changes that are suggested. Which changes are needed to make your writing about the story's theme clearly understood by your readers? Make revisions according to your decisions.

Next, proofread the copy for errors in spelling, grammar, usage, punctuation, capitalization, and paragraph form. For more information, see the Language Arts Survey 2.45, "A Proofreading Checklist."

Publishing and Presenting

Write or print a final copy of your writing. Use these guidelines to create a literary reference book that includes all of the papers in your class. After collecting the final papers, organize them by putting all of the papers about the same stories together. Then put the papers in the order that the stories are presented in your textbook. Create a table of contents and a binder. Place your reference book in your classroom or school library for use by other students.

Reflecting

A story's theme is usually not directly stated; instead, readers discover the theme as they read the story. Many important ideas are learned the same way—they are not directly stated; they are realized as a situation unfolds. Learning how to consider information that is not directly stated is beneficial in many aspects of student and adult life. How did the process of examining a theme benefit you? How do you feel about your ability to discover the theme in a story? How do you think you will be able to discover other types of information that are not directly stated?

"Since dogs are relatively unimportant in the adult world, it is probably foolish to grieve when they go. But most people do grieve, inconsolably, for a time, and feel restless, lonely, and poor."

—*Brooks Atkinson*

Students might answer the questions in this section in a journal entry. You might ask them to include answers to the following questions. How did the selection you read make you feel? Did the story relate in any way to your own experience? What is the value of literature?

UNIT EIGHT *review*

Review: Words for Everyday Use

Check your knowledge of the following vocabulary words. For each word, write a short sentence that includes the word in context. To review a word, look back to the page number indicated.

- aloof (546)
- apprehensive (550)
- assess (543)
- bid (584)
- breach (580)
- buffet (583)
- burly (543)
- competent (547)
- comply (561)
- convincing (560)
- delinquent (562)
- derelict (591)
- divert (545)
- eerie (582)
- eligible (562)
- estuary (579)
- exertion (587)
- extant (582)
- exultation (548)
- fragmentary (588)

- furtive (548)
- garner (580)
- harried (588)
- henceforth (570)
- import (583)
- imposing (548)
- inarticulate (587)
- median (563)
- methodical (544)
- moderate (563)
- notation (561)
- partition (560)
- placid (587)
- ponderous (550)
- precise (543)
- proposition (549)
- rebuff (581)
- repel (581)
- repossess (564)
- reside (561)

- resourceful (547)
- rupture (580)
- sanctuary (581)
- sheen (570)
- slow-witted (546)
- sodden (579)
- stalk (571)
- suffocate (564)
- surplus (558)
- tendril (586)
- thwart (548)
- tousle (585)
- tread (586
- turmoil (588)
- unerring (582)
- verify (562)
- wield (558)
- wiry (549)

Review: Literary Tools

Define each of the following terms, giving concrete examples when possible. To review a term, refer to the page number indicated.

- character (541)
- characterization (555)
- description (577)
- dialogue (555)
- first-person point of view (555)

- foreshadowing (569)
- mood (534)
- novella (577)
- plot (541)
- point of view (555)

- setting (534)
- theme (569)
- third-person point of view (555)

Reflecting
on your *reading*

Genre

With the exception of *The Snow Goose*, a novella, this unit features short stories. Make a list of the selections you've read in this unit. Next to each selection title, jot down one thing from that selection that stands out in your mind. Look back to Elements of Fiction on pages 532-533 and identify the element of fiction—character, setting, plot, or theme—that most closely addresses what stood out for you in each selection. Which of these elements work to create the effects that most strongly impacted you?

Theme

Look back to Elements of Fiction and review the definition for *theme*. How would you state the theme for each of the selections you read in this unit? If you wish, use the graphic organizer from page 575 to uncover possible themes for these selections. Compare and contrast theme in two selections from this unit.

Group Project

In small groups, each group member should state which story in the unit was his or her favorite, and why. Then, as a group, choose one story. Brainstorm and come up with a creative format in which this story could be presented—for example, a play or a short film—and create the advertising materials that will persuade members of the public to attend the performance.

On Your Own

Write a short story of your own. Choose one of the elements of fiction, and concentrate on developing at least that one element as thoroughly as possible in short-story format. For example, if you choose *setting*, work hard on creating a detailed setting that will make the reader feel as if he or she knows the place. If you decide to focus on *plot*, try to create an interesting and unique plot twist that will surprise readers. After writing a draft of your story, share it with your teacher or a peer to gain his or her input. Then, revise your story and share it with family members and friends. For different ways to publish your story, see the Language Arts Survey 2.49, "Sharing Your Work With Others."

Reflecting on Your Reading

The Genre, Theme, and Group Project questions are suitable to assign as essay prompts to help students prepare for the Unit Test. (To evaluate student writing, see the evaluation forms for writing, revising, and proofreading in the Assessment Resource 4.1–4.9.)

The On Your Own activity can also be used as an additional or alternate assessment to the Unit 8 Test. The effectiveness of the short story students write can help evaluate their understanding of the literary tools listed on page 608. (You may want to use Assessment Resource forms 4.4—4.6 to help students evaluate the effectiveness of their short story.)

Report from Rockport, 1940. Stuart Davis. Private Collection.

GOALS/OBJECTIVES

Studying this unit will enable students to
- appreciate enjoy lyric and narrative poetry
- define and identify techniques in poetry such as imagery, shape, sound, and meaning
- define and identify forms of poetry, including narrative, lyric, and haiku

- engage in a meaningful independent reading experience by reading a poetry anthology on loss and compiling a their own poetry anthology
- write a lyric poem
- demonstrate an ability to use pronoun/antecedent agreement

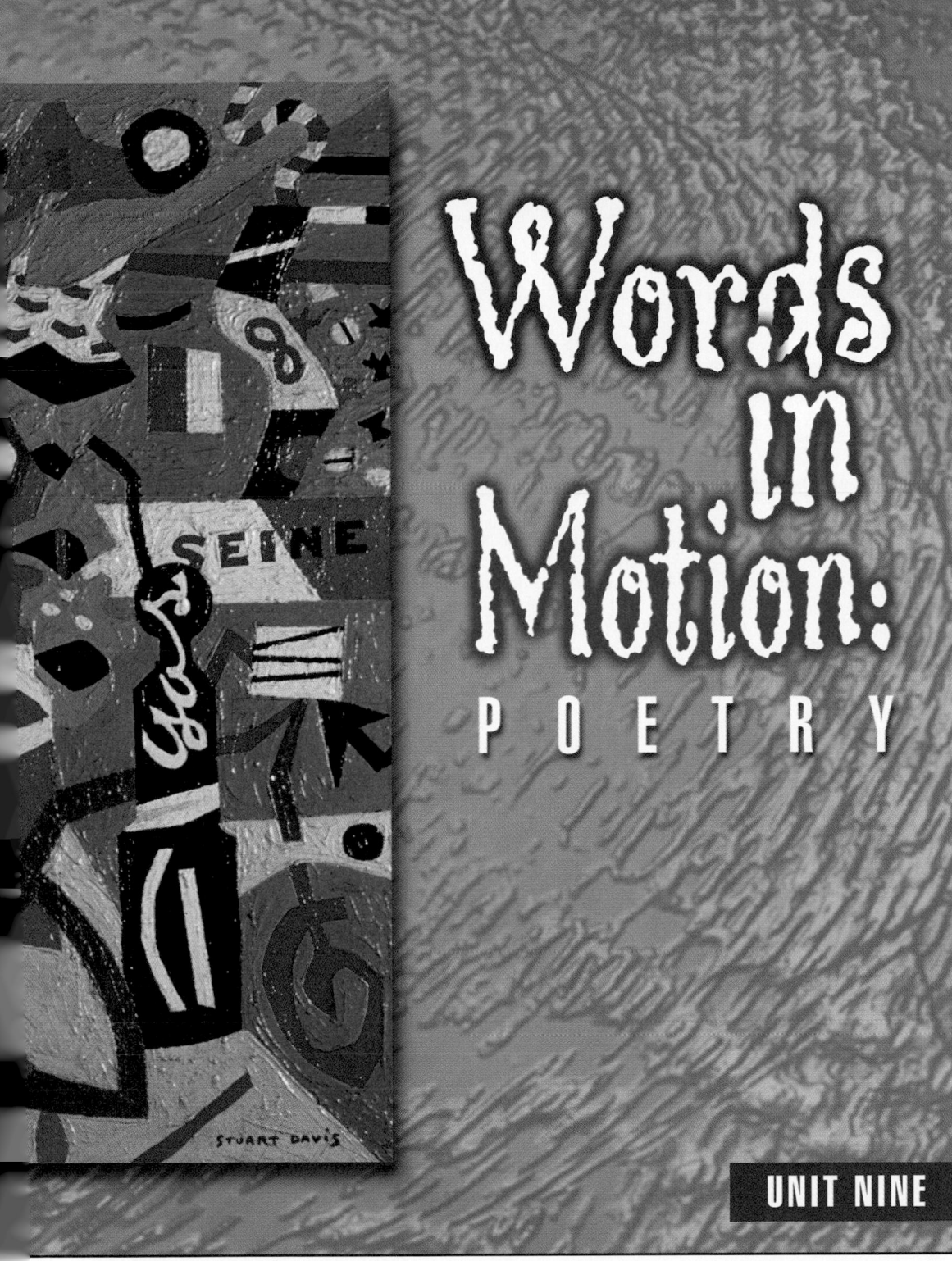

Words in Motion: POETRY

STUART DAVIS

(Continued on page 612)

The Academy of American Poets home page at http://www.poets.org/index.html offers a broad range of information about poetry, a Find-a-Poet link to help students learn more about their favorite poets, activities related to special events, and questions for discussion. This site is an excellent way to help students see what a huge presence poetry has in the United States and beyond.

TEACHING THE MULTIPLE INTELLIGENCES (CONT.)

ELEMENTS *of* POETRY

The main elements of poetry are imagery, shape, sound, and meaning.

IMAGES AND IMAGERY. An **image** is language that creates a concrete representation of an object or an experience. An image is also the vivid mental picture created in the reader's mind by that language. The images in a literary work are referred to, when considered together, as the work's **imagery**. Poets use colorful, vivid language and figures of speech to create imagery. **Colorful language** is precise and lively words and phrases that help to create clear pictures in the reader's mind. A **figure of speech** is language meant to be understood imaginatively instead of literally. Metaphor, simile, and personification are figures of speech. A **metaphor** is a figure of speech in which one thing is spoken or written about as if it were another. A **simile** is a comparison using like or as. **Personification** is describing something not human as if it were human.

SHAPE. The shape of a poem is how it looks on the page. A **concrete poem,** or shape poem, is one with a shape that suggests its subject.

SOUND. The sound of a poem is created through the use of rhyme, rhythm, alliteration, assonance, onomatopoeia, and repetition. **Rhyme** is the repetition of sounds at the ends of words, like *locks, box,* and *socks.* **Rhythm** is the patterns of beats in a line of poetry or prose. **Alliteration** is the repetition of consonant sounds at the beginning of syllables, as in *Peter Piper picked a peck of pickled peppers.* **Assonance** is the repetition of vowel sounds in stressed syllables that end in different consonant sounds, as in *lime light.* **Onomatopoeia** is the use of words or phrases, like *meow* and *beep,* that sound like what they name. **Repetition** is more than one use of a sound, word, or phrase.

MEANING. Meaning in poetry is created in many ways. The use of symbols, appeals to emotion, and techniques such as *dialogue* and *flashback* can add meaning to a poem. A **symbol** is a thing that stands for or represents both itself and something else.

Poetry comes in two main forms: narrative and lyric.

FORMS OF POETRY. A **lyric poem** is highly musical verse that expresses the emotions of a speaker and does not tell a story. Lyric poems focus on ideas. A **narrative poem** is a verse that tells a story. **Haiku** is a highly specialized form of lyric poetry—a traditional Japanese three-line poem. It has five syllables in the first line, seven in the second, and five in the third. Haiku and other poems written in languages besides English must be translated so that people can read them in English.

TEACHING THE MULTIPLE INTELLIGENCES (CONT.)

Prereading

"Poetry" by Nikki Giovanni
and
"How to Eat a Poem" by Eve Merriam

Reader's TOOLBOX

FIGURE OF SPEECH. A **figure of speech** is a statement that has more than a straightforward, literal meaning. Hyperbole, metaphor, personification, and simile are examples of figures of speech. A **metaphor** is a figure of speech in which one thing is spoken or written about as if it were another. A metaphor invites the reader to make a comparison between the two things. Sometimes a metaphor is directly stated: *Love is a red rose.* Other times, a description alone makes the comparison: *That song always leaps from inside me and gallops around in circles, restless and eager.* What metaphors can you find in "Poetry"? What two things does "How to Eat a Poem" compare?

FREE VERSE. **Free verse** is poetry that does not use regular rhyme, rhythm, meter, or division into stanzas. Read both poems out loud. Listen to the rhythm created by natural speech. How would you describe the rhythm of "Poetry"? How would you describe the rhythm of "How to Eat a Poem"?

IMAGE AND IMAGERY. An **image** is language that creates a con-crete representation of an object or experience. An image is also the vivid mental picture created in the reader's mind by that language. The images in a literary work are referred to, when considered all together, as the work's **imagery**. As you read "Poetry," notice the words or phrases that Giovanni uses to describe poetry, poets, and poems. Make a cluster chart like the one shown in the Graphic Organizer below. In the center of your cluster chart write *poetry*. Around it write words or phrases from the poem that describe poetry. Circle the descriptive words or phrases and connect the circles with lines. Make a similar cluster chart for "How to Eat a Poem."

Graphic Organizer

Reader's Journal

What images would you use to describe your favorite poem?

Reader's Resource

- Free verse originated among French poets in the late 1800s. The French poets wanted to use the rhythms found in natural speech. This was achieved by writing lines of different lengths and meter. The lines in these poems usually did not rhyme.

- "Poetry," like poems by many writers, focuses on the poet's craft. "How to Eat a Poem" focuses on the reader of the poem. Successful poets love words and language. Some express their thoughts about language and poetry in a poem, reflecting on how they communicate through their art. Although a good poem may seem natural or simple, most are the end result of writing, crossing out, starting over, scribbling, and rewriting. As poet John Frederick Nims says, "Most writers work hard over their lines to make it seem they have not worked at all."

613

GRAPHIC ORGANIZER

Students may include the following words and phrases from "Poetry": "motion graceful as a fawn"; "gentle as a teardrop"; "strong like the eye"; "poems seek not acceptance but controversy"; "a poem is pure energy/horizontally contained between the mind/of the poet and the ear of the reader"; "poetry is song"; "poetry is joy"; and its message is "life is precious."

Students may include the following words and phrase from "How to Eat a Poem": "It is ready and ripe now, whenever you are"; "no core/or stem/or rind/or pit/or seed/or skin/to throw away."

READER'S JOURNAL

You might expand this assignment by asking students what details of sight, sound, touch, smell, or taste they associate with their favorite piece of writing of any genre. For example, do they like a personal essay they read because it reminds them of the taste of salt in the air by the shore? Do they like a novel they have read because it helps them envision a gritty pirate and his parrot that calls out, "pieces of eight"?

GOALS/OBJECTIVES

Studying this lesson will enable students to
- Have a positive experience reading two poems that explore the speakers' feelings about poetry
- define *figure of speech* and *metaphor* and identify examples of metaphors in poetry
- define and identify examples of *free verse*
- define *image* and *imagery* and identify images in a poem

INDIVIDUAL LEARNING STRATEGIES

MOTIVATION
Encourage students to discuss in small groups foods they consider to be delicious and satisfying to eat. Encourage students to go beyond the taste of the food to discuss what about the experience of eating this food they enjoy. For example, do they enjoy the crunch of biting into one of the fall's first apples? Do they like knowing that it was one of the fall's first apples, and perhaps, that they picked it themselves? Do they enjoy the aroma of Thanksgiving dinner cooking in the oven all day almost more than they enjoy the meal itself?

READING PROFICIENCY
Encourage students to pair up with a reading partner. Have one partner read, "Poetry," as the other closes his or her eyes and listens. The listening partner should then read aloud "How to Eat a Poem," while his or her partner closes his or her eyes and listens. The two should then exchange roles, so each partner gets the benefit of hearing both poems read aloud.

ENGLISH LANGUAGE LEARNING
Point out the following vocabulary words and expressions:
golden—of a high degree of excellence
wariness—quality of being cautious and cunning about detecting and escaping danger
controversy—discussion marked by the expression of opposing views
discard—get rid of
ripe—fully prepared; brought to full flavor or the best state
rind—tough outer layer, such as the peel on a lemon

SPECIAL NEEDS
Students may find "Poetry" to be more challenging that "How to Eat a Poem." Tell students to let the Guided Reading questions point them to important parts of the poem. They may wish to focus their responses to the Investigate, Inquire, and Imagine

Poetry

Nikki Giovanni

poetry is motion graceful
as a fawn
gentle as a teardrop
strong like the eye
finding peace in a crowded room

we poets tend to think our words are golden
though emotion speaks too
loudly to be defined
by silence

> **GUIDED READING**
> According to the speaker, what do poets think their words are?

sometimes after midnight or just
before
the dawn
we sit typewriter in hand
pulling loneliness around us
forgetting our lovers or children who are sleeping
ignoring the weary <u>wariness</u>
of our own logic
to compose a poem
        no one understands it
it never says "love me" for poets are
beyond love
it never says "accept me" for poems seek not
acceptance but controversy
it only says "i am" and therefore
i <u>concede</u> that you are too

> **GUIDED READING**
> Why does a poem never say "accept me"?

a poem is pure energy
horizontally contained between the mind
of the poet and the ear of the reader
if it does not sing discard the ear
for poetry is song
if it does not delight discard
the heart for poetry is joy
if it does not inform then close
off the brain for it is dead
if it cannot heed the <u>insistent</u> message
that life is precious

which is all we poets
wrapped in our loneliness
are trying to say ■

> **GUIDED READING**
> What are all poets trying to say?

> **words for everyday use**
>
> **war • i • ness** (wār′ ē nəs) *n.*, cautiousness, watchfulness. *The cat approached the dog with obvious* <u>wariness</u>.
>
> **con • cede** (kən sēd′) *v.*, to accept as true. *After hearing the same story from several witnesses, the officer* <u>conceded</u> *that the woman had been speeding.*
>
> **in • sis • tent** (in sis′ tənt) *adj.*, persistant, never-tiring. *Jacob sleepily fumbled with the clock to stop the* <u>insistant</u> *beep of the alarm.*

INDIVIDUAL LEARNING STRATEGIES (CONT.)

questions to the Recall questions. They can listen in to the class discussion on higher level questions and participate however much they want, depending on what their comfort level with "Poetry" is.

ENRICHMENT
Encourage interested students to write their own poems about poetry. Tell students not to worry about what their feelings are—the important

thing is that they express them through poetic means. They may wish to include a metaphor in their poem, urging their reader to compare poetry to something, or include vivid images that express their feelings about poetry. Students may experiment with rhyme, rhythm, and meter if they would like, but it might be easier for them to try their hands at writing free verse poems like the two featured here.

How to Eat a POEM

Eve Merriam

Don't be polite.
Bite in.
Pick it up with your fingers and lick the juice
 that may run down your chin.
It is ready and ripe now, whenever you are.
You do not need a knife or fork or spoon
or plate or napkin or tablecloth.
For there is no core
or stem
or rind
or pit
or seed
or skin
to throw away. ■

GUIDED READING
What is there to throw away?

Bitter Next #2: Harlem Renaissance Party, 1988.
Faith Ringgold. The National Museum of American Art,
Washington, DC.

SELECTION CHECK TEST 4.9.1 WITH ANSWERS

Checking Your Reading

1. According to Giovanni, when do poets compose? **Poets compose during the middle of the night: "sometimes after midnight or just/before/the dawn."**

2. According to Giovanni, a poem is pure what? **A poem is pure energy.**

3. According to Giovanni, what is the "insistent message" that poets are trying to say? **The poet's insistent message is that life is precious.**

4. According to Merriam, when is a poem "ready and ripe" to eat? **A poem is ripe and ready to eat "now, whenever you are."**

5. According to Merriam, how should a reader "eat" a poem? **Answers will vary, but could include that readers should eat a poem as one would eat fruit ("Pick it up with your fingers and lick the juice/that may run down your chin"), should eat it completely ("For there is no core/or stem/or rind/or pit/or seed/or skin/to throw away"), and should eat it with gusto ("Don't be polite./ Bite in").**

Vocabulary in Context

Fill in each blank below with the most appropriate word from the following *Words for Everyday Use* from "Poetry" and "How to Eat a Poem." You may have to change the tense of the word.

wariness   concede   insistent

1. After he saw the snake slither into the hole in the wall, Jocelyn approached it with _____. **wariness**

2. Rochelle begged her parents not to make her go to summer school, but they were _____. **insistent**

Reader's Toolbox

Fill in the blanks using the following terms. You may not use every term, and you may use some terms more than once.

metaphor   imagery   free verse
          personification

Respond to the SELECTION

What ideas do you have about poetry and how to enjoy it?

About the AUTHORS

Poet, professor, lecturer, and essayist, **Nikki Giovanni** has never shied away from tackling tough issues in her poetry. In the 1960s, she was one of the most outspoken voices of the Black Rights Movement, much of her work dealing with the political and social struggles of African Americans in a white-dominated culture. Other work by Giovanni focuses on family and relationships. She has also written several books for children. About poetry, Giovanni has commented: "But poetry responds to something. You know, nobody ever got up at a funeral and quoted some novel. Because it doesn't offer comfort. People quote poetry. Nobody ever got married reading the latest rap record. They turn to poetry. So poetry has its place. It offers comfort, it's celebratory and joyful." *Ego-Tripping and Other Poems for Young People,* and *Grand Fathers: Reminiscences, Poems, Recipes and Photos of the Keepers of Our Traditions* are just two of many titles by Nikki Giovanni.

Born on July 19, 1916 in Pennsylvania, **Eve Merriam** pursued her education at four different universities. She lived her adult life in New York City. In the 1940s, she was a copywriter and a writer for radio. Later, she began teaching and lecturing. Merriam published her first book, *Family Circle,* in 1946. Although poetry was always Merriam's first love, she is also a well-known playwright and fiction writer. Eve Merriam died in 1992.

SELECTION CHECK TEST 4.9.1 WITH ANSWERS (CONT.)

1. Much of a work's _____ comes from description that uses sensory details—words and phrases that describe how things look, sound, smell, taste, or feel. **imagery**

2. When one thing is spoken or written about as if it were another, so that the reader can make a comparison between the two things, the author is using _____. **metaphor**

Investigate, *Inquire,* and Imagine

Recall: GATHERING FACTS

1a. According to the speaker in "Poetry," poetry is finding peace in what?

2a. What emotion does the speaker associate with sitting in front of a typewriter?

3a. What is contained between the mind of the poet and the ear of the reader?

4a. What utensils does the speaker In "How to Eat a Poem" say you do not need while reading a poem?

→ **Interpret:** FINDING MEANING

1b. What do you think the speaker means by this?

2b. Why might the poet connect this emotion with writing?

3b. Why might the speaker use this language?

4b. What does not needing special tools or utensils suggest about reading poetry?

Analyze: TAKING THINGS APART

5a. Examine the words and phrases Giovanni uses to describe a poet. What does she say poets do? feel? think? What suggestions does Merriam give to a poetry reader? How do these suggestions about "eating" translate into suggestions about "reading"?

→ **Synthesize:** BRINGING THINGS TOGETHER

5b. How does Giovanni see poets? How do Giovanni's attitudes about poets and poetry reflect on herself as a poet? What does Merriam believe about reading poetry? What might Merriam's attitudes about reading poetry tell you about her likes and dislikes? about her approach to new things?

Evaluate: MAKING JUDGMENTS

6a. Reflect on the ideas that "Poetry" and "How to Eat a Poem" offer the reader. Do you agree with the messages? Why, or why not?

→ **Extend:** CONNECTING IDEAS

6b. How do you view poetry? What does poetry offer you as a reader? What ideas would you want to convey in a poem?

ANSWERS TO INVESTIGATE, INQUIRE, IMAGINE (CONT.)

and that anyone can enjoy it. Her attitude may reveal that Merriam values simplicity and clarity in poetry rather than pretentiousness and deliberate obscurity. Students may say that Merriam seems to be the type of person to jump into new experiences wholeheartedly and feet first.

EVALUATE
6a. *Responses will vary.* Students should recognize the central messages outlined in the response to question 5b, but their thoughts on these ideas will differ.

EXTEND
6b. *Responses will vary.*

ANSWERS TO INVESTIGATE, INQUIRE, IMAGINE

RECALL
1a. Poetry is finding peace in a crowded room.
2a. The speaker associates loneliness and forgetting about others with sitting in front of a typewriter.
3a. Pure energy is contained between the mind of the poet and the ear of the reader.
4a. The speaker says you don't need a knife, fork, spoon, plate, napkin, or tablecloth to read a poem.

INTERPRET
1b. The speaker may mean that poetry is something that can give a personal a private feeling of peace and inner calm in a sometimes crowded and hectic world.
2b. The speaker might connect this feeling with writing because writing is a solitary and private occupation; also the speaker writes best at late hours when everyone else is asleep.
3b. The speaker might use the word energy to describe the strong connection or bond between the writer of the poet and the person who reads it to capture the force and vitality of this invisible link.
4b. Anybody can read a poem at any time without any special equipment.

ANALYZE
5a. Students may say Giovanni uses words like "think our words are golden," "pulling loneliness around us," "forgetting our lovers or children who are sleeping," "ignoring the weary wariness of our own logic," and "poets are beyond love." She suggests that poets place writing as a priority and try to forget the world of obligation and logic to write. She says that poets feel lonely. Merriam suggests that readers "bite in" to poetry, eat it without utensils, and says that there are no parts of poetry to throw away, Students may say this means that readers should begin reading poetry without worrying about whether they have the right tools or are reading the proper way because there is no proper way to read poetry.

SYNTHESIZE
5b. Students may say that Giovanni sees poets as lonely people trying to express to others the preciousness of life. This reveals that Giovanni finds much beauty in the world but sometimes find that her talent separates her from others. Merriam believes that poetry is for everyone

IMAGE AND IMAGERY. The poem describes poems and poetry as motion graceful as a fawn, gentle as a teardrop, strong like they eye finding peace in a crowded room, as seeking controversy, and as pure energy. Images include a graceful fawn, searching for and finding peace among a crowd, writing after everyone has gone to bed, and a link of energy between poet and reader. Students may say the poets used imagery to provide a concrete mental image of something to which readers might compare something as intangible as poetry/ Imagery helps the reader to see poems and poetry as being similar to things in everyday life.

FIGURE OF SPEECH. Metaphors from "Poetry" include "a poem is pure energy," "poetry is song," and poetry is joy" ; metaphors from "How to Eat a Poem" include, "Bite in/Pick it up with your fingers and lick the juice that may run down your chin," "It is ready and ripe now, whenever you are," You do not need a knife," and "there is no core or stem . . . to throw away." The metaphors in "poetry" present an image of poetry as everything that is beautiful and precious in life. The whole of "How to eat a Poem" presents an extended metaphor encouraging the reader to compare reading a poem to eating a piece of fruit. Each metaphor conveys the idea that you do not need special manners or tools to read poetry and that you can take in the whole of a poem. *Responses will vary.*

FREE VERSE. *Responses will vary.* Some students may suggest that they enjoy the lack of predictable rhythm because it seems more like the poem is written in the language of everyday speech and that the poet is having a conversation with them.

Understanding *Literature*

IMAGE AND IMAGERY. An **image** is language that creates a concrete representation of an object or experience. The images in a literary work are referred to, when considered all together, as the work's **imagery**. Look at the cluster charts you made from the model on page 613. In what ways does "Poetry" describe poems and poetry? What images does the poem offer? Why do you think these poets chose to use imagery in their poems? How does the use of imagery help the reader envision a clear picture of what each poet is trying to say?

FIGURE OF SPEECH. Figures of speech are statements that have more than a single literal meaning. Instead, it is a way of expressing or describing one word through another using **metaphors**. A **metaphor** is a figure of speech in which one thing is spoken or written about as if it were another. This figure of speech invites you to compare the two things. Highlight the descriptions in your cluster charts that use metaphor to describe poetry and poems. How do the metaphors in "Poetry" work together to provide a vivid image of poetry? How does metaphor work in "How to Eat a Poem"? What idea does each metaphor convey? What metaphors would you use to describe writing or reading poetry?

FREE VERSE. Free verse is poetry that does not use regular rhyme, rhythm, meter, or division into stanzas. Get together with a partner. Take turns reading "Poetry" and "How to Eat a Poem" out loud. Listen to the rhythm created by natural speech. Then discuss the following questions with your partner. How effective is rhythm in the first poem? Would the speaker's ideas be more strongly conveyed using a traditional form of poetry with predictable rhythms and rhyming patterns? Why, or why not? Answer the same questions for the second poem.

Bitter Next #2: Harlem Renaissance Party, 1988. Faith Ringgold. The National Museum of American Art, Washington, DC.

Faith Ringgold's (b.1930) work combines two traditional artforms: painting and quiltmaking. Quilts have traditionally been used to commemorate important events in an individual's life. Here, Ringgold commemorates writers of the Harlem Renaissance of the 1920s and 1930s, an important period in African-American culture. What handmade objects do you have in your home that commemorate family history? How are they examples of art?

618 *UNIT NINE / POETRY*

Prereading

"Filling Station" by Elizabeth Bishop
and
"A Deserted Barn" by Larry Woiwode

Reader's TOOLBOX

IMAGE AND IMAGERY. An **image** is language that creates a concrete representation of an object or experience. Altogether, the images in a literary work are considered as the work's **imagery**. Specific words and phrases that describe something by engaging one or more of the five senses are called *sensory details*. Which senses does Bishop engage in "Filling Station"? Which senses does Woiwode appeal to in "A Deserted Barn"?

IRONY. Irony is a difference between appearance and reality. Words may say one thing, but they may imply something quite different. Look for examples of irony in "Filling Station." What is ironic about a doily in a filling station?

PERSONIFICATION. Personification is a figure of speech in which something not human is described as if it were human. What is personified in "A Deserted Barn"?

Graphic Organizer

Make a chart like the one shown. As you read the poems, fill in the chart keeping track of irony, personification, and images you encounter.

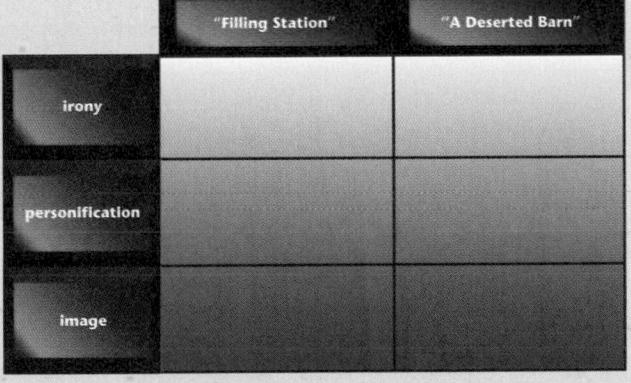

	"Filling Station"	"A Deserted Barn"
irony		
personification		
image		

Reader's Journal

What images would you use to describe your bedroom?

Reader's Resource

- A filling station is a service station for motor vehicles. In the past, filling station attendants pumped gas for customers. Most stations now require patrons to fill their own gas tanks, a change that downsized the number of filling station employees. In addition, many stations now are computerized to allow patrons to pay with a credit card at the tank instead of entering the building to pay a cashier.

- **HISTORY CONNECTION.** As the landmark structure of a family farm, a barn is the symbol of a lifestyle that goes back centuries. Barns symbolize tradition, family, security, and living off the land. They often reflect a local culture through shape, style, and color. As corporate farms and high-tech production facilities take over family farms, traditional barns fall into disrepair or become targets for wrecking balls. A number of organizations, including the National Trust for Historic Preservation "Barn Again!" program, promote the preservation and rehabilitation of historic barns.

619

ADDITIONAL RESOURCES

UNIT 9 RESOURCE BOOK
- Selection Worksheet 9.2
- Selection Check Test 4.9.3
- Selection Test 4.9.4

GRAPHIC ORGANIZER

Students' charts may resemble the following:
"Filling Station"
IRONY: the presence of a flower-embroidered doily on a taboret, or upholstered footstool, and a big begonia amidst the dirt and grease if the filling station
PERSONIFICATION: the cans softly say "ESSO-SO-SO-SO"
IMAGE: dirt, oil, and grease on the station, the people,, and the dog; the big dim doily draping a taboret beside a big hirsute begonia
"A Deserted Barn"
IRONY: the deserted barn fears winter when its tenants leave, even though earlier it described these tenants as "worrying" it
PERSONIFICATION: the barn is the speaker and talks about its feelings
IMAGE: deserted barn with sagging door worried by termites and visted by bids; gray shape at edge of a cedar swamp; the barn under a "cold cloak of snow, and "reflections, at night, from the reflected light of the moon."

READER'S JOURNAL

Encourage students to use sensory details that appeal to sight, sound, touch, taste, and smell to create a vivid picture of their bedrooms.

GOALS/OBJECTIVES

Studying this lesson will enable students to
- appreciate two poems that create vivid images of places
- briefly explain how filling stations and barns have changed in recent years
- define *image* and *imagery* and explain what sensory details images appeal to
- define *irony* and identify irony in a poem
- define *personification* and recognize what is being personified as human

VOCABULARY FROM THE SELECTION

extraneous	saucy
high-strung	translucency

Filling Station, 1935. Walker Evans. Library of Congress.

Filling Station

Elizabeth Bishop

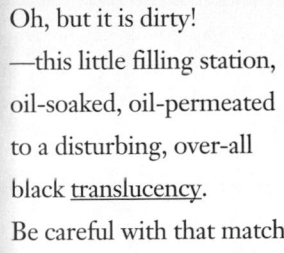

Oh, but it is dirty!
—this little filling station,
oil-soaked, oil-permeated
to a disturbing, over-all
black <u>translucency</u>.
Be careful with that match!

Father wears a dirty,
oil-soaked monkey
   suit

GUIDED READING

What is the father wearing?

that cuts him under the arms,
and several quick and <u>saucy</u>
and greasy sons assist him
(it's a family filling station),
all quite thoroughly dirty.

Do they live in the station?
It has a cement porch
behind the pumps, and on it

a set of crushed and grease-
impregnated[1] wickerwork;
on the wicker sofa
a dirty dog, quite comfy.

Some comic books provide
the only note of color—
of certain color. They lie

upon a big dim doily[2]
draping a taboret[3]
(part of the set),
   beside
a big hirsute begonia.[4]

GUIDED READING

Where are the comic books?

Why the <u>extraneous</u> plant?
Why the taboret?
Why, oh why, the doily?
(Embroidered in daisy stitch
with marguerites,[5] I think,
and heavy with gray crochet.[6])
Somebody embroidered the doily.
Somebody waters the plant,
or oils it, maybe. Somebody
arranges the rows of cans
so that they softly say:
ESSO-SO-SO-SO
to <u>high-strung</u> automobiles.
Somebody loves us all.   ■

---

1. **grease-impregnated.** Being filled or saturated with grease
2. **doily.** Small decorative map
3. **taboret.** Stool
4. **hirsute begonia.** Type of flowering shrub covered with course, stiff hair
5. **marguerites.** Type of flower
6. **crochet.** Needlework formed with a single thread and hooked needle

---

words for everyday use

translucency (trants lū' sənt sē) *n.*, clearness, the quality of being transparent. *The <u>translucency</u> of the water allowed them to see shells and colorful fish.*
saucy (sä' sē) *adj.*, amusingly bold; smart, trim. *Mary's <u>saucy</u> attitude sometimes offends people.*
extraneous (ek strā' nē əs) *adj.*, not forming an essential part. *Alex rewrote his report, editing out all <u>extraneous</u> information.*
high-strung (hī' strəŋ') *adj.*, wound up, unquiet, agitated. *Ben is a <u>high-strung</u> boy, who paces when he is nervous.*

ANSWERS TO GUIDED READING QUESTIONS

1. Father is wearing a dirty, oil-soaked monkey suit that cuts him under the arms.
2. The comic books are on top of a big doily draping a taboret, besides a begonia.

Quotables

"We lived in an old gypsy caravan behind a filling station. My father owned the filling station and the caravan and a small meadow behind, but that was about all he owned in the world. . . . was now a scruffy little boy as you can see, with grease and oil all over me, but that was because I spent all day in the workshop helping my father with the automobiles."

—Roald Dahl, from
Danny the Champion of the World

ADDITIONAL QUESTIONS AND ACTIVITIES

If students like "Filling Station" and the setting described in this poem, you might encourage them to read Roald Dahl's *Danny the Champion of the World* as an independent reading project. This book would be a good choice for less confident readers because the story is told in simple straightforward language, but the story is exciting and moving enough that even more confident readers might enjoy this book.

1. The cattle and horses are gone
   from the barn.
2. The barn fears winter.

ADDITIONAL QUESTIONS AND ACTIVITIES

Ask students the following questions:

1. With what forms of life was the barn filled before it was deserted?
2. With what forms of life is the barn filled during most of the year now that it has been "deserted"?
3. In what ways has the barn's function changed since it has been deserted? In what ways has its function stayed the same?
4. Given what you know about the barn and its function in both the past and during most of the year in the present, why might the barn fear winter? In what way is the barn's function or purpose being taken away in winter?

Answers

1. The barn was filled with horses and cows before it was deserted.
2. The barn is now filled with termites, dung bettles, maggots, rats, flies, starlings, and swallows.
3. The barn is no longer home to the farmer's domesticated animals, but to wild creatures. Its function has stayed the same in that it still provides a home for living creatures.
4. Students may say that barn fears winter because this time of year makes it feel lonely and useless, as if it is dying. In winter the barn is no longer a shelter for living things and is left all alone.

A DESERTED barn

Larry Woiwode

I am a deserted barn—
           my cattle robbed from me,
  My horses gone,
Light leaking in my sides, sun
piercing my tin roof
    Where it's torn.
    I am a deserted barn.

    Dung's still in my gutter.
It shrinks each year as side planks shrink,
Letting in more of the elements,
              and flies.

Worried by termites, dung beetles,
    Maggots, and rats,
    Visited by pigeons and hawks,
No longer able to say what shall enter,
           or what shall not,
    I am a deserted barn.

    I stand in Michigan,
A gray shape at the edge of a cedar swamp.
    Starlings come to my peak,
Dirty, and perch there;
           swallows light on bent
    Lightning rods[1] whose blue
    Globes have gone to

A tenant's son and his .22.
    My door is torn.
It sags from rusted rails it once rolled upon,
    Waiting for a wind to lift it loose;
Then a bigger wind will take out
    My back wall.

    But winter is what I fear,
           when swallows and hawks
Abandon me, when insects and rodents retreat,
    When starlings, like the last of bad thoughts, go off,
    And nothing is left to fill me
Except reflections—
           reflections, at noon,
    From the cold cloak of snow, and
Reflections, at night, from the reflected light of the moon. ■

GUIDED READING
What are gone from the barn?

GUIDED READING
What does the barn fear?

Roadside Barn, 1935. Walker Evans. Library of Congress.

---

1. **lightning rods.** Metallic rods on rooftops that protect a building from lightning

Respond *to the* SELECTION

Describe an old building or another place that has meaning for you.

 **art smart.**

During the Depression, Walker Evans (1903-1975) took photographs in impoverished areas to show the need for relief projects. Although their purpose was to document harsh realities, these photographs have also been praised for their artistic merit. Photographs are often thought to be more truthful than paintings, but even photographers bring their own personal feelings and point of view to their work. What choices can a photographer make that will affect the final picture?

About *the* AUTHORS

Born in Massachusetts in 1911, **Elizabeth Bishop** grew up in New England and Nova Scotia. She graduated from Vassar College in 1934. As a student at Vassar, she worked on the student newspaper and founded a literary magazine. Bishop went on to travel through Europe, and she lived in New York, in Florida, and, for 16 years, in Brazil. During her lifetime, she published only five volumes of poetry—four of them winning major awards, including the Pulitzer Prize for poetry in 1955. Bishop's poetry has long been admired for its pure and precise examination of details in different corners of the world. In addition to writing poetry, Bishop translated a famous Brazilian diary, *The Diary of Helena Morley,* wrote stories for *The New Yorker,* and taught at several important universities before her death in 1979.

Larry Woiwode was born in a small town in North Dakota in 1942. By the mid-1960s, he was living in New York City and publishing stories and poetry in *The New Yorker*. Today, Woiwode is the author of numerous novels and has published fiction and poetry in *The Atlantic, Esquire, Harper's* and *The Paris Review*. In 1978, Woiwode, his wife, and his four children moved back to North Dakota to a 160-acre farm. In 1995, he was named poet laureate of North Dakota, and he received the Award of Merit Medal from the American Academy of Arts & Letters for distinction in the art of the short story.

"FILLING STATION" AND "A DESERTED BARN" **623**

ANSWERS TO INVESTIGATE, INQUIRE, AND IMAGINE (CONT.)

love, tenderness, and care in a place that is so extremely filthy. The last stanza is different because its is filled with an almost desperate loneliness and sadness, where earlier in the poem the abandoned barn was still teeming with life and visitors.

EXTEND

5b. The impact of that poem directly encourage the reader to think about the people who love him or

her and the ways in which they show their feelings through the little details of life. The ending of "A Deserted Barn" is different in that there is no direct appeal to the reader; however, it is similar in that the ending might also cause the reader to think about stages he or she will go through in his or her own life and hope that he or she doesn't end up all alone at the end of his or her life, as does the deserted barn.

SELECTION CHECK TEST 4.9.3 WITH ANSWERS

Check Your Reading
SHORT ANSWER
1. Who is the speaker in "A Deserted Barn"? **The barn is the speaker.**
2. In "A Deserted Barn," in what state is the barn located? **The barn is in Michigan.**
3. In "A Deserted Barn," what fills the barn in winter? **In winter, the barn is filled with reflections.**
4. In "Filling Station," what provides the only note of color? **The only color comes from comic books.**
5. In "Filling Station," on what is the dirty dog lying? **The dirty dog lies on the wicker sofa.**

Vocabulary in Context
SENTENCE COMPLETION
Fill in each blank below with the most appropriate word from the following *Words for Everyday Use* from "Filling Station." You may have to change the tense of the word.

translucency   saucy   extraneous

1. Maris tried to focus her picture through the _____ of the old camera lens. **translucency**
2. Indra packed many _____ items for the trip and then complained about the weight of her suitcase. **extraneous**

Reader's Toolbox
SENTENCE COMPLETION
Fill in the blanks using the following terms. You may not use every term, and you may use some terms more than once.

metaphor   irony   personification   sensory details

1. When something in a literary work appears different than the reader expected, the author may be using _____ . **irony**
2. _____ is a figure of speech in which something that is not human is described with human qualities and traits. **personification**

ANSWERS TO INVESTIGATE, INQUIRE, AND IMAGINE

RECALL
1a. The only note of color is from comic books.
2a. Termites, dung beetles, maggots, and rate "worry" the barn.
3a. Only reflections fill the barn in winter.

INTERPRET
1b. The rest of the station is gray and brown from dirt and grease. Even the doily is gray and the begonia spears to have been oiled rather than watered.
2b. In winter these creatures retreat from the barn, leaving it with a feeling of fear and emptiness.
3b. Students may say that reflection or memories of its past, its former usefulness, and the life it once housed.

ANALYZE
4a. Images of a dirty place include "oil-soaked, oil-permeated to a disturbing, over-all black translucency," "a dirty, oil-soaked monkey suit," "greasy sons," "crushed and grease-impregnated wickerwood," and "dirty dog." The image of a "big dim doily draping over a taboret . . . besides a big hirsute begonia" contrasts with this image. Such details include, "Light leaking in my sides, sun piercing my tin roof," "as side planks shrink/Letting in more of the elements, and flies," "A gray shape at the edge of a cedar swamp./Starlings come to my peak,/Dirty, and perch there," "swallows light on bent/Lightning rods," "My door is torn/It sags from rusted nails it once rolled upon," and "And nothing is left to fill me/Except reflections . . . at noon/From the cold cloak of snow, and . . . at night, from the reflected light of the moon."

SYNTHESIZE
4b. The speaker is pleasantly surprised to see signs of beauty, and of love and caring in the filling station. The speaker in "A Deserted Barn" fears winter because it is left alone then and filled with nothing but reflections of its former life. Reflections off the snow and from the moon fill the barn, but the barn is also filled with reflections, or memories, about its former tenants and usefulness.

EVALUATE
5a. Students may say the contrast comes from the surprising note of

(Continued on page 623)

Investigate, *Inquire,* and Imagine

Recall: GATHERING FACTS

1a. What is the only "note of color" in the filling station?

2a. What creatures "worry" the barn?

3a. What is left to fill the barn in the winter?

→ **Interpret:** FINDING MEANING

1b. How does this note of color compare with the rest of the filling station?

2b. How do those creatures affect the barn later in the poem?

3b. What does the speaker mean by this statement?

Analyze: TAKING THINGS APART

4a. What details in "Filling Station" create an image of a dirty place? What contrasts to this image are offered at the end of the poem? What details in "A Deserted Barn" create an image of a lonely, desolate place?

→ **Synthesize:** BRINGING THINGS TOGETHER

4b. What is the speaker's overall thought about the filling station? Why does the speaker in "A Deserted Barn" fear winter? In what way or ways do reflections fill the barn in winter?

Evaluate: MAKING JUDGMENTS

5a. The last stanza of "Filling Station" provides a contrast to the rest of the poem. Describe that contrast. Similarly, the last stanza of "A Deserted Barn" causes the poem to change directions. How is that stanza different from the rest of the poem?

→ **Extend:** CONNECTING IDEAS

5b. "Filling Station" ends with a passage that could change the reader's perception of the place. How is the impact of that ending different from the impact the ending of "A Deserted Barn" has on the reader? In what way might the two endings be similar?

Understanding *Literature*

IMAGE AND IMAGERY. An **image** is language that creates a concrete representation of an object or an experience. An image is also the vivid mental picture created in the reader's mind by that language. The images in a literary work are referred to, when considered all together, as the work's **imagery**. Draw some of the images that come to your mind as you read each poem. Exchange your pictures with a classmate. Ask him or her to look at your drawings and describe the images he or she sees. How are these descriptions like or unlike the images you meant to represent?

IRONY. **Irony** is a difference between appearance and reality. What examples of irony did you find in "Filling Station"? How does irony affect the impact of the poem? What is ironic about the creatures in "A Deserted Barn"?

PERSONIFICATION. Personification is a figure of speech in which something not human is described as if it were human. Reread "A Deserted Barn." How would the poem change without the use of personification?

ANSWERS TO UNDERSTANDING LITERATURE

IMAGE AND IMAGERY. Students' drawings will vary, but you may wish to have students compare drawings in small groups, so they will have a broader group of pictures to think about when comparing and contrasting their drawings to others.

IRONY. Students may say that the note of care and love in the dirty filling station is ironic because these rather feminine and frilly objects contradict the reader's expectations of what a filthy filling station should be

like. Irony helps the reader to see past the dirt to the feelings these people have about their work and home. Students may say it is ironic that the barn is lonely when the creatures that "worry" it disappear. This contradicts readers' expectations because they might assume the barn would be pleased to rid itself of termites, rats, maggots, and dung beetles.

(Continued on page 625)

Prereading

"the / sky / was"
by E. E. Cummings

Reader's T O O L B O X

CONCRETE POEM. A **concrete poem**, or shape poem, is one with a shape that suggests its subject. Poets develop concrete poems as visual images of the words they contain. Concrete poems can convey powerful images using few words. What image does the shape of "the / sky / was" suggest?

IMAGERY. Taken together, the images in a poem or passage are called its **imagery**. What imagery is in the following poem?

Graphic Organizer

The following are examples of simple concrete poems. Using a simple word or passage, create a concrete poem of your own.

RACE WITH THE WIND DOWN THE HILL

Reader's Journal

How would you complete the following sentence? *The sky was* _____.

Reader's Resource

- E. E. Cummings is famous for breaking the rules of grammar and punctuation. For example, he always spelled his name in all lowercase letters (e. e. cummings). In addition, his titles use only lowercase letters. What other rules does he break in this poem? What does he achieve by doing so?

- **SCIENCE CONNECTION.** Kaleidoscopes are optical devices that use mirrors and brightly colored beads to create colorful patterns. The viewer looks through a hole in one end of a tube and light enters the other end through translucent glass or plastic. The light reflects images—created by a pattern of the beads—off the mirrors inside the tube. As the tube rotates, the beads move and change the pattern. Some kaleidoscopes have transparent glass on the outside of the nonviewing end, allowing the images to be seen from the outside as well.

"THE / SKY / WAS" **625**

ADDITIONAL RESOURCES

UNIT 9 RESOURCE BOOK
- Selection Worksheet 9.3
- Selection Check Test 4.9.5
- Selection Test 4.9.6

GRAPHIC ORGANIZER

Students simple concrete poems will vary. Other possibilities include examples like the following:

Echo . . . echo . . . echo . . . echo . . . echo

or

l st piec s of a puz le
z
o
e

READER'S JOURNAL

Encourage students to go beyond common descriptions such as *blue* or *cloudy* to come up with their own unique statements.

ANSWERS TO UNDERSTANDING LITERATURE (CONT.)

PERSONIFICATION. Without the personification, it would be near impossible for the reader to get insight into the feelings of a deserted barn; the reader would probably get little more than a description without personification and would have to infer the emotion.

VOCABULARY FROM THE SELECTION

luminous

GOALS/OBJECTIVES

Studying this lesson will enable students to
- have a positive experience reading a concrete poem
- define *concrete poem* and explain how shape contributes to the meaning of such a poem
- define *imagery* and identify imagery in a poem
- research an author
- identify the functions of sentences
- read poetry aloud
- interview a poet
- write a business letter
- create imagery through art
- identify synonyms

1. It is spouting "violets."

the sky was

E. E. Cummings

Blaue Reiter Almanac, 1911. Wassily Kandinsky.

```
      the
        sky
          was
    can dy lu
minous
          edible
   spry
        pinks shy
   lemons
   greens coo  l choc
   olate
   s.
       un der,
     a lo
     co
     mo
       tive  s pout
        ing
         vi
          o
          lets  ■
```

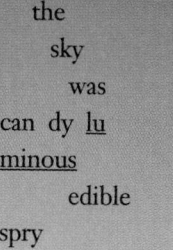

art smart.

Wassilly Kandinsky (1866–1944) was a Russian painter who is credited by many scholars as being the first abstract artist. Abstract art is also called "nonrepresentational art" because it is not meant to represent actual things. In what ways is abstract art like or not like concrete poetry?

GUIDED READING
What is the locomotive spouting?

words for everyday use

lu • mi • nous (lü′ mə nəs) *adj.,* emitting or reflecting steady, glowing light. *The still lake was* luminous *under the sunset.*

Respond _to the_ SELECTION

Describe a clear sky on a summer evening.

About _the_ AUTHOR

Edward Estlin Cummings (1894–1962), the son of a distinguished clergyman, was born in Cambridge, Massachusetts. Cummings attended Harvard College, where he studied literature and classical and modern languages. During World War I, he volunteered to serve as an ambulance driver in France and was imprisoned by French authorities for writing letters that were critical of the war. On his release and return to the United States, he was drafted into the army. His imprisonment in France provided material for his first book, _The Enormous Room,_ published in 1922.

Cummings challenged popular beliefs and habits in his thought and in his style of writing. His unique style is most evident in his breaking of traditional rules of capitalization, punctuation, spelling, and grammar. In keeping with this style, he even signed his name with lowercase letters: ee cummings. In the beginning, critics did not know whether to reject or applaud his work. The most sincere form of flattery is imitation, however, and many poets imitated the work of Cummings. At the time of his death in 1962, Cummings was one of the most popular poets in the nation, second only to Robert Frost. In addition to writing poetry, Cummings was a talented playwright and a well-regarded painter.

RESPOND TO THE SELECTION

You might also ask students to describe the colors they see in the sky and clouds at sunset or at sunrise.

SELECTION CHECK TEST 4.9.5 WITH ANSWERS

Checking Your Reading
SHORT ANSWER
1. What is spouting violets? **A locomotive is spouting violets.**
2. Which color is spry? **The color pink is spry.**
3. What is made of candy? **The sky is made of candy.**

Reader's Toolbox
SHORT ANSWER
1. What is a concrete poem? **A concrete poem is one with a shape that suggests its subject.**
2. What is imagery? **A poem's imagery is the overall picture created by the images in a poem or passage.**

RECALL
1a. The sky appears edible.
2a. A locomotive "spouting violets" is causing the colors.

INTERPRET
1b. The speaker describes the sky as edible because it is filled with the colors of candy.
2b. Students may say the speaker reveals this at the end of the poem to increase the reader's sense of curiosity.

ANALYZE
3a. Such words include *candy, luminous, edible, pinks, shy lemons, greens,* and *cool chocolates.* Students may say that many of them are colors and that many of them describe candy flavors. They differ in that some like *luminous* describe a shining appearance rather than a specific color or taste, while others describe a quality like *shy.* Four of these words are adjectives, and five are nouns.

SYNTHESIZE
3b. *Responses will vary. Possible responses are given.* Students may say something akin to, "The sky looked like candy, shiny and good enough to eat because of the pinks, lemons, greens, and chocolate colors that surround a locomotive's smokestack which is spouting colored smoke."

EVALUATE
4a. Responses will vary. Students may say this poem vividly captures the sky the speaker sees; they may be less sure how well it describes a train's smokestack, especially if they have never seen one.

EXTEND
4b. *Responses will vary.*

Investigate, Inquire, and Imagine

Recall: GATHERING FACTS

1a. What appears *edible*?

2a. What is creating the colors?

Interpret: FINDING MEANING

1b. Why does the speaker describe this thing as edible?

2b. Why does the speaker reveal this at the end of the poem?

Analyze: TAKING THINGS APART

3a. Identify all the words that describe the sky. What do they have in common? How do they differ from one another? How many are adjectives? How many are nouns?

Synthesize: BRINGING THINGS TOGETHER

3b. Paraphrase this poem using simple language and simple sentence structure.

Evaluate: MAKING JUDGMENTS

4a. How well does this poem describe the sky the speaker sees? How well does it describe what a train's smokestack emits?

Extend: CONNECTING IDEAS

4b. Describe the sky as it is today. Include, if you wish, the influences of clouds, sun, rain, snow, smoke, or whatever you think affects the way you see the sky.

Understanding Literature

CONCRETE POEM. A **concrete poem**, or shape poem, is one with a shape that suggests its subject. Poets develop concrete poems as visual images of the words they contain. Concrete poems can convey powerful images using few words. How could you tell what this poem was about before reading it? How might a concrete poem surprise the reader?

IMAGERY. Taken together, the images in a poem or passage are called its **imagery**. How does the shape of the poem influence the poem's imagery?

Writer's Journal

1. Write a short **poem** in free verse for a celebration honoring an historic place or building.
2. Write a **letter** to Nikki Giovanni about "Poetry" or to Eve Merriam about "How to Eat a Poem," sharing your thoughts about the poem you just read.
3. Write **instructions** for an artist who plans to paint a picture of the deserted barn without seeing it or seeing a photo of it. Describe the barn in precise, detailed language.

ANSWERS TO UNDERSTANDING LITERATURE

SHAPE. Students might say that they did not know what the shape of this poem was supposed to represent until the poem's end when it becomes clear that the shape represents the colored smoke rising from the smokestack of a locomotive. This is a sort of surprise for the reader because it explains the shape of the poem to the reader and may answers questions in his or her mind.

IMAGERY. Students may say the shape of the poem creates a visual image of the shape of the smoke and colors the speaker describes in the poem.

Skill Builders

Study and Research

RESEARCHING POETS. Using library resources and the Internet, research the life of one of these poets—Nikki Giovanni, Eve Merriam, Elizabeth Bishop, Larry Woiwode, or E. E. Cummings. Find answers to the following questions. Where did the poet grow up? What was his or her childhood like? What occupations has he or she had? What else has he or she written? Confirm the facts by finding each piece of data in at least two sources. Organize your findings in a brief report.

Language, Grammar, and Style

FUNCTIONS OF SENTENCES. All sentences are one of the following types: declarative, imperative, interrogative, or exclamatory.

A declarative sentence tells something or makes a statement.

> **EXAMPLE** *Joe goes camping with his cousins every weekend.*

An imperative sentence gives a command or makes a request.

> **EXAMPLE** *Pack your own lunch for school.*

An interrogative sentence asks a question and is followed by a question mark.

> **EXAMPLE** *Have you ever seen a dirigible?*

An exclamatory sentence expresses strong emotion and ends with an exclamation point.

> **EXAMPLE** *I can't believe you ate the last piece of pie!*

Look back at the poems in this section. Find examples of each type of sentence, and write them on your own paper. Then read the following passages and modify each sentence as directed.

1. *Change each declarative sentence to an imperative sentence, directing someone else to do the tasks described.*

   At 7:30 I get my bicycle from the garage. I put on my backpack and bike helmet. I ride my bike to the intersection of Third Street and Main. I turn right on Main and go three blocks to James Street. I take a left on James Street, turn into the school parking lot, and lock my bike in the bicycle rack.

2. *Change these declarative sentences to interrogative sentences.*

   You were upset. You either dropped the vase or threw the ball at the vase to break it.

3. *Change these declarative sentences to exclamatory sentences.*

   I am so happy to see you. I love my new shoes. I can't wait to show you around the town.

Speaking and Listening

READING POETRY ALOUD. Find four or five poems written by the same author. Pretend you are that poet giving a reading at a local bookstore. Practice reading your selections to discover how the poem sounds best. Then read your selections to a small group of four or five classmates. If possible, tape record or videotape your session to share with the rest of the class.

Study and Research

Students may use the information contained in the About the Author sections in this book as a starting point for their research. Have students present to you a print-out or a photocopy of the Web site or article they used. They should also present you with a list of their sources. If they are uncertain how to assemble such a list, refer them to the Language Arts Survey, "Documenting Sources."

Language, Grammar, and Style

Students' examples of sentences will vary, but they may include the following:

declarative: A poem is pure energy horizontally contained between the mind of the poet and the ear of the reader.

imperative: Bite in.

interrogative: Why, oh why, the doily?

exclamatory: Oh, but it is dirty!

1. At 7:30 get your bicycle from the garage. Put on your backpack and helmet. Ride your bike to the intersection of Third Street and Main. Turn right on Main and go three blocks to James Street. Take a left on James Street, turn into the school parking lot, and lock your bike in the bicycle rack.

2. Were you upset? Did you drop the vase or throw the ball at the vase to break it?

3. I am so happy to see you! Look at my new shoes! I can't wait to show you around the town!

Speaking and Listening

For information on preparing and delivering readings of poems, refer students to the Language Arts Survey, "Oral Interpretation." You may wish to have students deliver their readings before their classmates rather than on video or audio tape. Tell students that they do not have to memorize the poems, but they should be familiar enough with them to be able to look at their audience. They may find it helpful to write out the poems or make photocopies of them and mark them up with notes about what words to emphasize and how they want to deliver certain lines.

ADDITIONAL RESOURCES

UNIT 9 RESOURCE BOOK
- Selection Worksheet 9.4
- Selection Check Test 4.9.7
- Selection Test 4.9.8

GRAPHIC ORGANIZER

Hope lies to mortals
and most believe her,
But man's deceiver
Was never mine.
The thoughts of others
Were light and fleeting,
Of lovers' meeting
Or luck or fame.
Mine were of trouble,
And mine were steady,
So I was ready
When trouble came.

READER'S JOURNAL

Ask students if they hope to change the way they are to become more optimistic or more pessimistic. Why do they want to make this change?

VOCABULARY FROM THE SELECTION

benign peril

Reader's Journal

Describe yourself as a pessimist or an optimist.

Reader's Resource

- Like many poets, A. E. Housman was interested in appealing to the emotions of the reader, rather than the intellect of the reader, with his poetry. Many of Housman's poems, including "I to My Perils," are pessimistic—assuming that evil outweighs good and emphasizing negative conditions and outcomes.

Prereading

"I to My Perils"

by A. E. Housman

Reader's TOOLBOX

ALLITERATION AND ASSONANCE. Alliteration is the repetition of consonant sounds at the beginnings of syllables, as in *Peter Piper picked a peck of pickled peppers.* **Assonance** is the repetition of vowel sounds in stressed syllables that end in different consonant sounds, as in *down and out* or *asleep under a tree.* Alliteration and assonance help tie together words in a line or in a series of lines. Look for examples of both in this poem.

RHYTHM. Rhythm is the pattern of beats in a line of poetry or prose. The *meter* of a poem is its overall rhythm. Rhythm and meter are determined by the pattern of stresses. *Stress* is the amount of emphasis given to a syllable. *Scanning,* or finding the meter of a poem, is done by marking each strong syllable with a straight mark (/) and each weak syllable with a dipped mark (˘). Read "I to My Perils" aloud several times, focusing on rhythm. Look for a pattern of weak and strong stresses. See the scanned stanza in the Graphic Organizer below. Write down the second stanza of the poem and mark the strong and weak syllables. Is the rhythm pattern the same as the first stanza? Write the remaining stanzas and scan them. Do all the stanzas have the same meter?

Graphic Organizer

/ ˘ ˘ / ˘
I to my pe rils

˘ / ˘ / ˘
Of cheat and char mer

˘ / ˘ / ˘
Came clad in ar mour

˘ / ˘ /
By stars be nign

GOALS/OBJECTIVES

Studying this lesson will enable students to
- identify with a speaker's feelings
- define *alliteration* and *assonance* and identify the use of these techniques in a poem
- define *rhythm* and scan a poem to determine patterns of weakly and strongly stressed syllables

I to My Perils

A. E. Housman

I to my <u>perils</u>
    Of cheat and charmer
Came clad in armour
    By stars <u>benign</u>.
Hope lies to mortals
    And most believe her,
But man's deceiver
    Was never mine.
The thoughts of others
    Were light and fleeting,
Of lovers' meeting
    Or luck or fame.
Mine were of trouble,
    And mine were steady,
So I was ready
    When trouble came. ■

> **GUIDED READING**
> What or whom do most mortals believe?

> **GUIDED READING**
> Of what are the speaker's thoughts?

The Knight, 1513. Albrecht Dürer.

words for everyday use

per • il (per′ əl) *n.*, exposure to the risk of being hurt; danger. *The excitement of mountain climbing outweighs the* <u>perils</u>.

ben • ign (bi nīn′) *adj.*, nonthreatening. *I was scared to go to the new school, but the* <u>benign</u> *atmosphere made it easy to relax and meet people.*

"I TO MY PERILS" **631**

INDIVIDUAL LEARNING STRATEGIES

MOTIVATION
Encourage students to hold an informal class debate on whether the speaker's attitude in this poem makes him or her happy. Divide students into two groups and assign them a position to support in relation to this question. Tell students that they must try to support their assigned position in the debate even if they do not agree with it personally, as this is an exercise in supporting an idea not in personal expression.

READING PROFICIENCY
Students may benefit from listening to an audiotape of this poem being read aloud. (Doing so will also help them to hear the rhythm of the poem.) Have students follow along in their books as they listen.

ENGLISH LANGUAGE LEARNING
Point out the following vocabulary words and expressions:
clad—clothed; dressed
mortals—humans who must eventually die
fleeting—passing swiftly; not lasting

SPECIAL NEEDS
Tell students to focus on the Guided Reading questions and the Recall questions in the Investsigate, Inquire, and Image section. Students may feel more comfortable forming small groups to discuss their answers and thoughts about higher level thinking questions before participating in a whole class discussion.

ENRICHMENT
Encourage students to write an essay in response to the following statement: *Today's youth are very pessimistic about the future.* Students may agree or disagree with this statement, but they should support their opinions with reasons and evidence drawn from their own experiences and observations.

SELECTION CHECK TEST 4.9.7 WITH ANSWERS

Check Your Reading
SHORT ANSWER

1. The speaker comes to his perils clad in what? **The speaker is clad in armour, or armor.**
2. Who lies to mortals? **Hope lies to mortals.**
3. Does the speaker believe the liar? **No, the speaker doesn't believe the liar.**
4. What are the thoughts of others like? **The thoughts of others are light and fleeting.**
5. How are the speaker's thoughts different from the thoughts of others? **The speaker's thoughts are of trouble.**

Vocabulary in Context
SENTENCE COMPLETION

Fill in each blank below with the most appropriate word from the following *Words for Everyday Use* from "I to My Perils." You may have to change the tense of the word.

peril   benign   fleeting

1. Astronauts face great _____ in their quest to explore space. **peril**
2. Alexander appreciated the _____ atmosphere in the doctor's office. **benign**

Reader's Toolbox
MATCHING

a. rhythm   b. meter   c. stress
d. alliteration   e. assonance

_____ 1. the pattern of beats in a line of poetry or prose   **A**

In the following lines of poetry:

> Softly sleeping.
> Sweetly dreaming.

_____ 2. What is demonstrated in the first line?   **D**
_____ 3. What is demonstrated in the second line?   **E**

With what thoughts and emotions do you prepare for a new situation or an important event?

About *the* AUTHOR

Alfred Edward Housman was born in England in 1859, the oldest of seven children in the family. Housman's younger brother Laurence became a famous playwright, his sister Clemence a writer of short stories and novels. Housman became one of the most esteemed classical scholars of his time and a respected poet. He first attended Bromsgrove School, a school that stressed Greek and Latin studies. In 1877, he received a scholarship to St. John's College in Oxford, where he continued his study of the classical languages. Although he was an excellent student while at Oxford, he left without graduating because he failed his final examination. A year later he returned to Oxford to finish his degree. For the next several years, he worked in the London Patent Office, all the while publishing articles for classical journals. In 1892, based on the merit of his published articles, he was appointed Professor of Latin at University College London. He published his first and most famous book of poems, *A Shropshire Lad,* in 1896. The anthology has 63 poems based on difficulties he had faced in life, and the book hasn't been out of print since its publication.

Investigate, *Inquire,* and Imagine

Recall: GATHERING FACTS

1a. What is "man's deceiver"?

2a. What are the thoughts of others like?

→ **Interpret:** FINDING MEANING

1b. Why might the speaker shun this?

2b. How does the speaker view these thoughts?

Analyze: TAKING THINGS APART

3a. Compare the ways in which the speaker describes himself with the ways he or she describes others. What words or phrases tell whether the speaker looks upon himself or herself and others with favor or disfavor?

→ **Synthesize:** BRINGING THINGS TOGETHER

3b. Does the speaker think his or her views are correct, or does he or she think others have the correct perspective? Explain your answer.

Evaluate: MAKING JUDGMENTS

4a. Does the speaker offer valid reasons for his or her beliefs? Why, or why not? What experiences might have led the speaker to embrace his or her way of looking at things?

→ **Extend:** CONNECTING IDEAS

4b. What experiences would lead you to look at things in the same way the speaker does? What experiences would lead you to look at things differently?

Understanding *Literature*

ALLITERATION AND ASSONANCE. Alliteration is the repetition of consonant sounds at the beginnings of syllables. **Assonance** is the repetition of vowel sounds in stressed syllables that end in different consonant sounds. How do alliteration and assonance combine with rhyme to tie together the words and lines in this poem? What effect would eliminating alliteration and assonance have on the poem? Find out for yourself by changing the words in the poem that create these sound patterns.

RHYTHM. Rhythm is the pattern of beats in a line of poetry or prose. The overall rhythm of a poem is its *meter.* Rhythm and meter are determined by the pattern of stresses. *Stress* is the amount of emphasis given to a syllable. Do all the stanzas in "I to My Perils" have the same meter? Look back at your scanning of the poem to determine your answer. What patterns of stresses do you find?

ANSWERS TO UNDERSTANDING LITERATURE (CONT.)

assonance makes the poem seem choppier and less musical.

RHYTHM. Students may say that while every stanza does not match the others perfectly, there is a distinct pattern of rhythm in each stanza. For example, students may say that the first line of every stanza

(with the exception of the first line of the last stanza which carries a slight variation) has a pattern of strongly stressed syllable, followed by two weakly stressed syllables, followed by one strongly and one weakly stressed syllables. The rhythm of other corresponding lines in stanzas is similar as well, with some quite minor exceptions.

RECALL

1a. "Man's deceiver" is hope.

2a. The thoughts of others are "light and fleeting." They think of meeting a lover or achieving luck or fame.

INTERPRET

1b. The speaker might shun hope because hope can sometimes leaf to disappointment when hopes aren't realized.

2b. The speaker seems to feel that hope about loved ones, luck, or fame are doomed to lead to disappointment.

ANALYZE

3a. Students may note the speaker describes his or her pessimism as a positive and noble thing—as a knight's armor. The speaker seems to look down on people who hope and congratulate him- or herself in line such as "man's deceiver/Was never mine," and "I was ready/When trouble came."

SYNTHESIZE

3b. Most students will say that the speaker believes his or her views are correct and that other people are being deceived by false hope.

EVALUATE

4a. Most students will say the speaker does not offer valid reasons in support of his or her beliefs. Students may say the speaker may have once been more hopeful, but was disappointed in one or all of his or her hopes, leading to his or her present pessimism.

EXTEND

4b. *Responses will vary.* Students may say that too many negative experiences might give them an outlook similar to the speaker's, while positive experiences might lead to a viewpoint very different from the speaker's.

ANSWERS TO UNDERSTANDING LITERATURE

ALLITERATION AND ASSONANCE. Students may note that alliteration in lines like "**ch**eat and **ch**armer," and assonance like "**ar**mour/By st**ar**s," make the poem seem to flow together, from one line to the next. These techniques give the poem cohesiveness and a musical quality. Students may say that eliminating the alliteration and

ADDITIONAL RESOURCES

UNIT 9 RESOURCE BOOK
• Selection Worksheet 9.5
• Selection Check Test 4.9.9
• Selection Test 4.9.10

GRAPHIC ORGANIZER

Responses will vary. Possible responses are given. Students may associate fresh vegetables like asparagus with spring. If they are Christian and celebrate Easter, they may associate spring with a meal of ham or lamb. Students may associate summer with foods like fresh fruit, barbecues, cookouts, and ice cream. Students may associate autumn with foods like pumpkin pie, squash, and turkey. Students may associate winter with rich hearty foods like roasts and potatoes. Students responses will definitely depend on their family background and cultural tradition.

READER'S JOURNAL

Also ask students to write about the time of year they associate with this food.

VOCABULARY FROM THE SELECTION

splurge

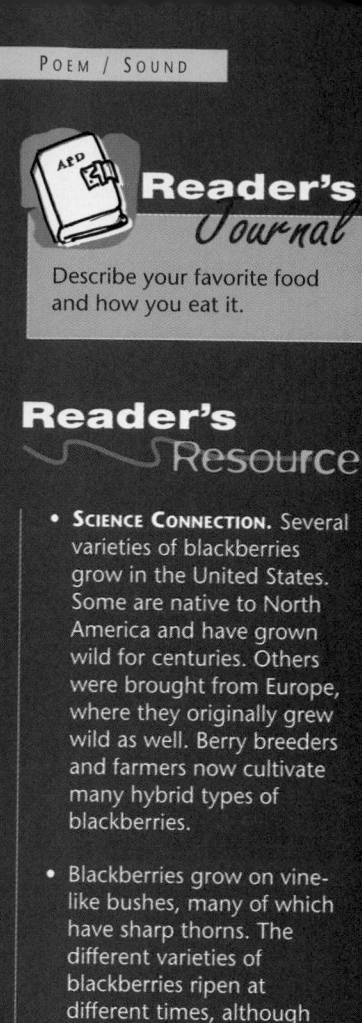

Reader's Journal

Describe your favorite food and how you eat it.

Reader's Resource

• **SCIENCE CONNECTION.** Several varieties of blackberries grow in the United States. Some are native to North America and have grown wild for centuries. Others were brought from Europe, where they originally grew wild as well. Berry breeders and farmers now cultivate many hybrid types of blackberries.

• Blackberries grow on vine-like bushes, many of which have sharp thorns. The different varieties of blackberries ripen at different times, although many are ready to eat in late summer. Berries ripen earlier in southern climates than they do in the north.

Prereading

"Blackberry Eating"

by Galway Kinnell

 ### Reader's TOOLBOX

ONOMATOPOEIA. Onomatopoeia is the use of words or phrases like *meow* or *beep* that sound like what they name. Look for examples of onomatopoeia in "Blackberry Eating."

ALLITERATION. Alliteration is the repetition of consonant sounds at the beginnings of syllables. Tongue twisters demonstrate an exaggerated use of alliteration, as in *She sells seashells by the seashore.* What examples of alliteration can you find in the poem?

Graphic *Organizer*

Think about different foods you associate with certain times of the year, special events, or holidays. Copy this graphic organizer onto your own paper and add your ideas to each season. Be sure to indicate specific holidays or events with which you associate certain foods or meals.

GOALS/OBJECTIVES

Studying this lesson will enable students to
• enjoy a lyric poem that uses sound techniques
• define *onomatopoeia* and recognize examples of this sound technique
• define *alliteration* and identify examples of this technique in a poem

634 TEACHER'S EDITION

BLACKBERRY Eating

Galway Kinnell

I love to go out in late September
among the fat, overripe, icy, black blackberries
to eat blackberries for breakfast,
the stalks very prickly, a penalty
they earn for knowing the
    black art
of blackberry-making; and as I stand among them
lifting the stalks to my mouth, the ripest berries
fall almost unbidden[1] to my tongue,
as words sometimes do, certain
    peculiar words
like *strengths* or *squinched*,
many-lettered, one-syllabled lumps,
which I squeeze, squinch open, and <u>splurge</u> well
in the silent, startled, icy, black language
of blackberry-eating in late September. ∎

---

1. **unbidden.** Not asked or invited

GUIDED READING
For what are the prickly stalks a penalty?

GUIDED READING
What sometimes falls to the speaker's tongue like ripe berries?

words for everyday use

splurge (splərj′) *v.*, to indulge oneself extravagantly or to spend a lot of money. *When Dad got a raise, he <u>splurged</u> and took us all out for a fancy dinner.*

---

1. The prickly stalks are a penalty for the plant's knowing the "black art of blackberry-making."
2. Peculiar words like *strengths* or *squinched* fall to the speaker's tongue like ripe berries.

INDIVIDUAL LEARNING STRATEGIES

MOTIVATION
Students might enjoy talking about and sharing their responses to the Graphic Organizer activity on page 670. Ask students to share their favorite seasonal foods. What different foods does the class enjoy in different seasons? Are there any foods that most students associate with a season?

READING PROFICIENCY
Encourage students to form pairs with a reading partner. They should take turns reading this poem to each other aloud and closing their eyes and listening. Then have students go back and read the poem silently on their own.

ENGLISH LANGUAGE LEARNING
Point out the following vocabulary words and expressions:
stalks—stems of a plant
penalty—punishment, unfortunate consequence as the result of an act or condition
peculiar—particular; unique; special
squinched—puckered or screwed up the face
startled—surprised, frightened

SPECIAL NEEDS
Students who have never picked blackberries or eaten them may have a hard time understanding why the speaker describes the stalks of these plants as a prickly penalty or why the speaker thinks of the word *squinched* when he or she eats this fruit. You might bring in some blackberries for students to sample, or you might let students know that blackberries can be tart and that there are thorns on blackberry bushes. Encourage students to focus on answering the Guided Reading questions and the Recall questions in the Investigate, Inquire, and Image section before discussing the more challenging questions as a group.

INDIVIDUAL LEARNING STRATEGIES (CONT.)

ENRICHMENT
You might encourage interested students to write lyric poems about their favorite foods. You might have them begin this assignment by having them freewrite lists of words or images that come to mind when they think about their favorite food. You might have students compile their poems into an anthology called "Recipes for Happiness" or something similar.

RESPOND TO THE SELECTION

You might also ask students to discuss what seasons they don't like and why.

GRAPHIC ORGANIZER

Under *berries,* students may list the following words: overripe, black, stalks very prickly, black art of blackberry-making, and ripest. Under *words/language* students might list the following words: peculiar, *strengths, squinched,* one-syllabled lumps, silent, startled, icy, black.

SELECTION CHECK TEST 4.9.9 WITH ANSWERS

Checking Your Reading
SHORT ANSWER

1. When does the speaker like to eat blackberries? **The speaker likes to eat blackberries in late September.**
2. What are the stalks like? **The stalks are prickly.**
3. Where is the speaker as he or she eats the blackberries? **The speaker likes to eat blackberries while standing among blackberry bushes.**
4. What types of words "fall almost unbidden to my tongue"? **Peculiar words, "many-lettered, one-syllabled lumps," fall almost unbidden to the speaker's tongue.**
5. What is "silent, startled, icy, black"? **The speaker is describing the language of blackberry eating.**

Reader's Toolbox
MATCHING

a. repetition of consonant sounds
b. words or phrases that sound like what they name
c. repetition of vowel sounds in stressed syllables that end in different consonant sounds
d. pattern of beats in a line of poetry

_____ 1. What is onomatopoeia? **b**
_____ 2. What is alliteration? **a**

Vocabulary
SHORT ANSWER
Write a sentence that correctly illustrates the meaning of the word *splurge. Responses will vary.*

636 TEACHER'S EDITION

Respond *to the* SELECTION

What is your favorite season of the year, and why?

Graphic Organizer

Create a list of descriptive words under the heading *berries* and another under the heading *words/language,* as shown in the example here. Complete the lists.

berries	words/language
fat	many-lettered
icy	black

About *the* AUTHOR

Galway Kinnell was born in Providence, Rhode Island, in 1927. He was educated at Princeton University and at the University of Rochester in New York. Kinnell began publishing poetry in magazines and anthologies in the early 1950s, and his first collection of poems, *What a Kingdom It Was,* was published in 1960. In 1983, he received the Pulitzer Prize for Poetry for *Selected Poems.* About writing poetry, Kinnell has said, " When I found the world of poets, I realized I was not so odd after all. And when, one day, a teacher mentioned that Robert Frost was living and writing on a farm only a few hundred miles north of Pawtucket,

I realized that poetry was not an extinct art, that poets could still exist in the world. And I started to write poetry."

Investigate, *Inquire,* and Imagine

Recall: GATHERING FACTS

1a. What are the blackberries like in late September?

2a. How does the speaker describe "certain peculiar words"? What does the speaker do with those words?

→ **Interpret:** FINDING MEANING

1b. How would the fruit be different earlier in the year? What makes this time of year special for eating blackberries?

2b. How do these words apply to the blackberries?

Analyze: TAKING THINGS APART

3a. Identify the author's descriptive words and phrases in the poem. Use the graphic organizer at left to separate the words that describe the berries from those that describe "certain peculiar words" and the "language of blackberry eating."

→ **Synthesize:** BRINGING THINGS TOGETHER

3b. Examine your graphic organizer. Explain how the descriptions of blackberries could apply to "certain peculiar words" and the "language of blackberry eating" and how the descriptions of those words could apply to blackberries.

Evaluate: MAKING JUDGMENTS

4a. Critique this poem's use of imagery. Explain whether the writer's descriptions capture the essence of "blackberry-eating in late September."

→ **Extend:** CONNECTING IDEAS

4b. How would you use this description to communicate in writing about a favorite food? Write a poem using descriptive language and imagery to show why and how you enjoy a favorite food.

Understanding *Literature*

ONOMATOPOEIA. Onomatopoeia is the use of words or phrases like *meow* or *beep* that sound like what they name. Which words and/or phrases in the poem are examples of onomatopoeia? Which word is both an example of onomatopoeia and a blend, or portmanteau?

ALLITERATION. Alliteration is the repetition of consonant sounds at the beginnings of syllables. Where in the poem did you find alliteration? What consonants are repeated in those words?

"BLACKBERRY EATING" **637**

ANSWERS TO UNDERSTANDING LITERATURE

ONOMATOPOEIA. Students may say that *squinch* and *squinched* are examples of onomatopoeia. Squinch is also an example of a blend of *squint* and *pinch*.
ALLITERATION. Students may note the following examples of alliteration: "**b**lack **b**lackberries . . . breakfast," "**p**rickly, a **p**enalty," "**s**trength or **s**quinched," "**s**queeze, **s**quinch open, and **s**plurge well/in the **s**ilent, **s**tartled . . . **S**eptember." Students may note the consonants *b, p,* and *s* are repeated.

ANSWERS TO INVESTIGATE, INQUIRE, IMAGINE

RECALL
1a. The blackberries are "fat, overripe, icy, black."
2a. The speaker describes "certain peculiar words," like *strengths* or *squinched* as falling unbidden on his or her tongue. The speaker says that he or she "squeeze[s], squinch[es] open, and splurge[s]" these words.

INTERPRET
1b. Students might say that earlier in the year the berries might be very small and underripe or too tart. The berries might also be warm rather than icy and paler in color due to their immaturity. This time of year is special for eating blackberries because the blackberries are at their peak of intense flavor and ripeness.
2b. These words describe the way the speaker eats blackberries and their potent tart flavor and its effect on the eater.

ANALYZE
3a. Students' graphic organizers may resemble that shown on the previous page.

SYNTHESIZE
3b. Students will note that the speaker describes both the blackberries using the same terms he later uses to describe the language of blackberry eating, including *icy* and *black*. Students will note the speaker describes "certain peculiar" words as if these syllable were blackberries falling on his or her tongue. The speaker's description of what he or she does with these words—squeeze, squinch open, and splurge—is also described in terms that could be applied to the eating of blackberries.

EVALUATE
4a. Responses will vary. Most students will say that the speaker does vividly capture the essence of "blackberry-eating in late September." The author does through by using vivid images that appeal to the reader's sense of sight, touch, and taste.

EXTEND
4b. *Responses will vary.* Students should use descriptive language to describe a favorite food.

GRAPHIC ORGANIZER

Responses will vary, but students may list the following examples of alliteration in their charts: **P**ieces out of **p**icture **p**uzzles, **T**wist of **w**ires, **w**orn-out **t**ires, **P**aper **b**ags and **b**roken **b**ricks, **G**atlin' **g**uns, **b**elts that had no **b**uckles, **b**roken **b**ottles, **c**ups with **c**racks, **g**listenin' **g**old, **t**reasure **t**runk, **s**illy **s**ightless. Students may include the following examples of assonance in their charts: b**i**ts of str**i**ng; b**oa**ts that w**ou**ldn't fl**oa**t; r**i**ngs...f**i**ngers; and m**o**dels...b**o**ttles.

READER'S JOURNAL

You might also ask students to write about an item that they treasure which might look worthless to others.

POEMS

Reader's Journal

If you could communicate with any element in nature, what would it be? Why?

Reader's Resource

- "Forgotten Language" and "Hector the Collector" are both from *Where the Sidewalk Ends: The Poems and Drawings of Shel Silverstein*. First published in 1974, the book quickly gained popularity. It is now considered an important— and fun—part of contemporary poetry.

- Many literary works study the theme of communicating with elements in nature, such as animals, plants, and the forces that create weather. Some indigenous groups believe that every animal, plant, and rock has a spirit and that these spirits can communicate with people.

Prereading
"FORGOTTEN LANGUAGE"
and
"Hector the Collector"
by Shel Silverstein

Reader's TOOLBOX

REPETITION. Repetition is more than one use of a sound, word, or group of words. Repetition is a tool that works to create or enhance rhythm. It also gives the sense that the speaker is dwelling on the repeated idea. What words and phrases are repeated in "Forgotten Language"? in "Hector the Collector"?

RHYME. Rhyme is the repetition of sounds at the ends of words. Rhyme can enhance the musical quality of a poem. Many poems reveal a pattern of rhyming words that appear at the ends of lines. These are called *end rhymes*. *Internal rhymes* are rhymes within the line. "Hector the Collector" has both end rhymes and internal rhymes. As you read that poem, identify examples of each type of rhyme.

Graphic Organizer

In addition to rhyme and repetition, "Hector the Collector" (on page 640) has other sound devices. Use this chart to list examples of alliteration and assonance in the poem.

ALLITERATION	ASSONANCE
P̲ieces out of p̲icture p̲uzzles	b̲its of str̲ing
b̲roken b̲ricks	Hector c̲alled to ̲all the people

GOALS/OBJECTIVES

Studying this lesson will enable students to
- enjoy reading two poems that make use of rhyme and repetition
- define *repetition* and identify repeated elements in poems
- define *rhyme* and point to examples of end rhyme and internal rhyme

People at Night, Guided by Phosphorous Traces of Snails, 1940. Joan Miró. Philadelphia Museum of Art.

FORGOTTEN LANGUAGE

Shel Silverstein

Once I spoke the language of the flowers,

Once I understood each word the caterpillar said,

Once I smiled in secret at the gossip of the starlings,

And shared a conversation with the housefly

      in my bed.

Once I heard and answered all the questions

      of the crickets,

And joined the crying of each falling dying

      flake of snow,

Once I spoke the language of the flowers…

      How did it go?

      How did it go? ■

> **GUIDED READING**
> Who did the speaker join in crying?

> **GUIDED READING**
> Whose language did he speak?

INDIVIDUAL LEARNING STRATEGIES

MOTIVATION
Students might enjoy brainstorming a list of "junk" that people usually throw out. You might list students' ideas on the board. Share with them two or three items that Hector collects to get them started.

READING PROFICIENCY
Students may better understand both poems and more easily recognize their rhyme and repetition if they listen to the poems read aloud. Either read both poems aloud expressively to students or play them an audiotape of such a reading. Ask students to follow along with the words of the poems in their books as they listen.

ENGLISH LANGUAGE LEARNING
Point out the following vocabulary words and expressions:
caterpillar—wormlike immature form of a butterfly or moth
gossip—idle talk or rumors, especially about the situations of others
starlings—type of bird with short-tail and long wings

SPECIAL NEEDS
Silverstein's poems are a good choice for special needs students as well as students who say they do not like poetry or who find it difficult. The simple language and the straightforward expression of ideas may help students to grasp these poems more easily than some others. Encourage students who usually find answering higher level questions difficult to discuss their responses to the Investigate, Inquire, and Imagine questions in small groups. You might then hold a whole-class discussion. Encourage students who are usually reluctant to speak out to share their ideas on the Interpret, Analyze, Synthesize, Perspective, and Empathy questions.

INDIVIDUAL LEARNING STRATEGIES (CONT.)

ENRICHMENT
Shel Silverstein is also known for the illustrations he created to accompany many of his poems. Encourage students to draw an illustration for one of the Silverstein poems. If students choose to illustrate "Hector the Collector," tell them that their image should be different from the one that Silverstein produced.

1. The boats leaked and wouldn't
   float. The horns were stopped-up
   and wouldn't toot.
2. Hector loved these things more
   than diamonds and gold.

CROSS-CURRICULAR ACTIVITIES

ARTS AND HUMANITIES. Inform
students that Hector might
enjoy the "found art"
movement. Certain twentieth-
century artists have made
names for themselves by
transforming junk that most
people throw away into works of art.
These artists carefully collect items
like the ones Hector treasures—dolls
with broken heads, bent-up nails and
ice-cream sticks—and transform
them into three-dimensional works
of art, letting the shape of these
objects suggest a new form to them
or assembling the objects in an
abstract manner. Encourage
interested students to create their
own found art by using bits of junk
from around their house to create a
new and precious work of art. Tell
students to check with their families
before using any of the junk they
find. It could just be that a family
member was saving the junk for
some future use him or herself!

Illustration from ***Where the Sidewalk Ends***, 1974. Shel Silverstein

Shel Silverstein

Hector the Collector

Hector the Collector
Collected bits of string,
Collected dolls with broken heads
And rusty bells that would not ring.
Pieces out of picture puzzles,
Bent-up nails and ice-cream sticks,
Twist of wires, worn-out tires,
Paper bags and broken bricks.
Old chipped vases, half shoelaces,
Gatlin' guns[1] that wouldn't shoot,
Leaky boats that wouldn't
    float
And stopped-up horns that
    wouldn't toot.
Butter knives that had no
    handles,
Copper keys that fit no locks,
Rings that were too small for fingers,
Dried-up leaves and patched-up socks.
Worn-out belts that had no buckles.

> **GUIDED READING**
>
> What was wrong
> with the boats and
> the horns?

'Lectric trains that had no tracks.
Airplane models, broken bottles,
Three-legged chairs and cups with cracks.
Hector the Collector
Loved these things with all his soul—
Loved them more than
    shining diamonds,
Loved them more than
    glistenin' gold.
Hector called to all the people,
"Come and share my treasure trunk!"
And all the silly sightless people
Came and looked...and called it junk. ▪

> **GUIDED READING**
>
> Hector loved these
> things more than
> what?

---

1. **Gatlin' guns.** Gatling guns, an early type of machine gun
made in the 1800s

Respond *to the* SELECTION

What things do you treasure? Why are they meaningful to you?

About *the* AUTHOR

"When I was a kid—12, 14, around there—I would much rather have been a good baseball player or a hit with the girls. But I couldn't play ball, I couldn't dance."

Instead, **Shel Silverstein**—author, poet, cartoonist, composer, lyricist, screenwriter, playwright—started writing and drawing at a young age, developing early his unique style and voice. Silverstein was born in Chicago, Illinois in 1932. In the 1950s, he served in the military in Japan and Korea, and he was the cartoonist for the military newsletter. In 1952, he began his professional

career as a magazine writer and cartoonist. Although he is perhaps most widely known for his children's books, Silverstein didn't start out writing for children. One day a friend of his brought him to talk to an editor who convinced him to write for children. He agreed, and went on to publish many books, including *The Giving Tree, A Light in the Attic*, and *Where the Sidewalk Ends*. Shel Silverstein died on May 10, 1999. In a National Public Radio interview on May 11, 1999, children's book critic Leonard Marcus said about Silverstein, "I think you could say that he was the troubadour king of American children's books…I think adults as well as children identify with a lot of his poems, because he was always pointing out what the little, single person, up against a much bigger world, has to contend with."

"FORGOTTEN LANGUAGE" AND "HECTOR THE COLLECTOR" **641**

⚡ 💾 📖 🔍 ➹ ⇄

RESPOND TO THE SELECTION

Ask students to consider whether other people would find these objects as meaningful as they do or whether outsiders might consider their treasures junk. What might these say to someone to explain why their items is a treasure.

SELECTION CHECK TEST 4.9.11 WITH ANSWERS

Check Your Reading
SHORT ANSWER
1. In "Forgotten Language," what language did the speaker once speak? **The speaker once spoke the language of the flowers.**
2. In "Forgotten Language," who gossips? **The starlings gossip.**
3. Name two things that Hector collects. *Responses will vary.*
4. In "Hector the Collector," how does Hector feel about his collection? **He loves it very much.**
5. In "Hector the Collector," what do the people call his collection? **The people call it junk.**

Reader's Toolbox
SENTENCE COMPLETION
Fill in the blanks using the following terms. You may not use every term, and you may use some terms more than once.

repetition   rhyme   end rhyme
internal rhyme   alliteration   assonance

1. _____ is demonstrated in the following line: "and all the silly sightless people." **Alliteration**
2. _____ is demonstrated in the last lines of "Forgotten Language": "How did it go? How did it go?" **Repetition**
3. _____ is demonstrated in the title "Hector the Collector." **Internal rhyme**

RECALL

1a. The speaker used to speak the language of flowers, caterpillars, starlings, houseflies, crickets, and the snow.

2a. All Hector's treasures are broken or useless items that most people would consider to be junk.

3a. Hector calls out to them, "Come and share my treasure trunk!" They call his things junk.

INTERPRET

1b. *Responses will vary.*

2b. Students may say that Hector has fun collecting these items and finds them to be interesting so he places value on them.

3b. Hector may call out to the people because he wants to share with them his love and enthusiasm for these objects. The people respond in this way because they do not share Hector's feelings about his treasures and have different values.

ANALYZE

4a. The speaker communicated with nature by speaking to flowers, understanding the words of the caterpillar, smiling at the gossip of starlings, sharing a conversation with the housefly, answering the questions of crickets, and joining in the crying of falling dying snowflakes.

SYNTHESIZE

4b. The "forgotten" language may signify a close connection to nature and its creatures and an innocence that the speaker has lost as he or she has grown up.

PERSPECTIVE

5a. Students may say that Hector loves his things because they are an expression of his personality and interests; he has spent much time assembling his unique collection of things and he loves them, so to him they are more precious than gold and diamonds.

EMPATHY

5b. Students may say that Hector was probably hurt by the people's response because he may have been hoping they would share his interest and love in his unique collection of junk. Hector might deny that his collection is junk. Hector might change his thinking if people express negative attitudes toward his collection for long enough.

Investigate, Inquire, and Imagine

Recall: GATHERING FACTS

1a. In "Forgotten Language," what language did the speaker used to know?

2a. What do all of Hector's treasures have in common?

3a. What does Hector call to the people? What do they say in response?

Interpret: FINDING MEANING

1b. How might the speaker have forgotten the language?

2b. Why might these things be valuable to Hector?

3b. Why does Hector do this? Why do the people respond this way?

Analyze: TAKING THINGS APART

4a. In what ways did the speaker of "Forgotten Language" once communicate with the different elements in nature?

Synthesize: BRINGING THINGS TOGETHER

4b. What might "forgotten language" signify?

Perspective: LOOKING AT OTHER VIEWS

5a. Why does Hector love his things more than obviously valuable things?

Empathy: SEEING FROM INSIDE

5b. How might Hector have reacted to the people's response? What might he say to the people? How might he one day change his thinking?

Understanding Literature

REPETITION. Repetition is more than one use of a sound, word, or group of words. Repetition is a tool that works to create or enhance rhythm. It also gives the sense that the speaker is "dwelling on" the repeated idea. What does the repetition in "Forgotten Language" indicate about the speaker's focus? What is the speaker dwelling on? Explain whether repetition makes the poem more meaningful. How does repetition enhance the rhythm of "Hector the Collector"?

RHYME. Rhyme is the repetition of sounds at the ends of words. Rhyme can enhance the musical quality of a poem. Many poems reveal a pattern of rhyming words that appear at the ends of lines. These are called *end rhymes. Internal rhymes* are rhymes within the line. How do internal rhymes help tighten the poem "Hector the Collector"? In what ways do end rhymes help weave the poem?

ANSWERS TO UNDERSTANDING LITERATURE

REPETITION. The speaker repeats the lines, "Once I spike the language of the flowers" and "How did it go?" The speaker also repeats the "Once I [verb]" format for the beginnings of many of the lines. This repetition indicates that the speaker is focusing on the loss he or she feels about losing his or her connection to nature. The speaker is dwelling on what he or she could once do and is wondering how he or she lost this ability. Students may say repetition makes this poem more meaningful because it emphasizes the speaker's sadness and sense of loss. Repetition helps give "Hector the Collector" helps give the poem a quick, playful rhythm.

RHYME. Internal rhyme in select lines helps to tighten the poem because the poem is essentially a long list of things. The internal rhyme also provides "surprises" of sound in certain lines to help maintain the reader's interest. End rhymes also help give cohesiveness and help the reader to move with interest through the list of things this poem presents. It also gives this poem a light and playful rhythm.

Writer's Journal

1. Choose one of the poems in this unit and make a **comic strip** to illustrate it. Submit the poem and your comic strip to your school newspaper or to a different publication.

2. Suppose you are writing an editorial about airplane noise in your neighborhood. In your editorial, create an **onomatopoeia** for the sound a low-flying airplane makes.

3. Imagine that you are Hector the Collector as an adult and that you are opening a business to buy and sell antiques and collectors' items. Write a **jingle** advertising your store.

Skill Builders

Language, Grammar, and Style

TECHNIQUES OF SOUND. Write a poem on a subject you find appealing and use at least three of the sound techniques highlighted in this unit. Try to incorporate aspects of rhyme, rhythm, alliteration, assonance, onomatopoeia, and repetition. You may want to begin your poem by freewriting. Write down words and phrases that you like and that create interesting sound combinations. Then work the phrases together into a poem.

Vocabulary

BLENDS. Blends are new words created by joining together two existing words. Look at the following list of words and try to figure out what two words were combined to make each blend. Then, create five new blends of your own. Write them in contextual sentences on the board in your classroom to see if your classmates can guess what two words each blend was derived from.

1. glimmer   3. squiggle   5. mingy
2. smash   4. motel

Study and Research

THESIS STATEMENTS. Choose one of the following topics to research. Then write a thesis about the topic you choose. A thesis is a main idea in a work of nonfiction such as an essay. For example, if your topic is "rhyme in poetry," your thesis might be "rhyme makes poetry more pleasing for most people." After formulating your thesis, use library resources and the Internet to investigate the topic. Find data that supports your thesis and also data that disputes it. After you have exhausted a number of resources, look critically at the information you have pulled together. What can you conclude from your research? Do your findings support or negate your thesis? How would you modify your thesis to fit your findings?

Topics: Rhyme in poetry
Shel Silverstein's poems and pictures
Poetry and song
Uses of alliteration

Speaking and Listening & Collaborative Learning

ORAL INTERPRETATION. Choose a poem from this unit. Practice reading the poem aloud to a partner. Then listen to your partner read aloud the poem he or she selected. Give one another constructive feedback on how to improve your readings. See the Language Arts Survey 4.19, "Oral Interpretation of Poetry," for tips on dramatic reading. When you have perfected your reading, present it to the class.

ANSWERS TO SKILL BUILDERS

Language, Grammar, and Style
TECHNIQUES OF SOUND. Responses will vary, but make sure that students identify their use of the sound techniques listed in the Skill Builder activity on page 643. You may want to challenge students to form teams and write a group poem. The team whose poem includes the most techniques wins.

Vocabulary
BLENDS. For the blends listed, you may need to have students consult a dictionary. See the Language Arts Survey 1.17, "Using a Dictionary." Responses may include the following:

1. glimmer
   blend of *gleam* + *shimmer*

2. smash
   blend of *smack* + *mash*

3. squiggle
   blend of *squirm* + *wiggle*

4. motel
   blend of *motor* + *hotel*

5. mingy
   blend of *mean* + *stingy*

Study and Research
THESIS STATEMENTS. Refer students to the Language Arts Survey 2.25, "Writing a Thesis Statement" and 2.26, "Writing Main Ideas and Supporting Details" for the writing part of this activity. Refer them to the Language Arts Survey, 5.17–5.29, for help in locating and evaluating sources.

Speaking and Listening & Collaborative Learning
ORAL INTERPRETATION. See the Assessment Resource 4.10, "Collaborative Learning Evaluation Form" and 4.11, "Public Speaking Evaluation Form" to evaluate student performance in this activity.

Media Literacy

EVALUATING AN INTERNET SITE. Using a computer with an Internet connection, look up the Poetry Society of America's Poetry in Motion homepage at http://www.poetrysociety.org/motion/homepage.html.

Explore the site and its links and find answers to the following questions:

What is Poetry in Motion? Who started the program?

Where does this program function?

What is the Poetry Society of America? What do members of the society do?

How well does this page and related pages convey information? How well do these pages attract a person's attention?

On a scale of 1-10, with 1 being the lowest rating and 10 being the highest, rate this Internet site. Give solid reasons for your evaluation.

Prereading

"THE LOST PARROT"

by Naomi Shihab Nye

Reader's Resource

- As you read poems such as "The Lost Parrot," you may notice that the author tells a poetic story using much fewer words than in a prose story. The poem may appear simple on the surface, but each word is carefully chosen to suggest deeper meanings. The poet molds and shapes words to describe objects, experiences, and emotions—either from his or her own life or from observation. The poet uses rhythm, rhyme, sound, imagery, and figures of speech to present ideas in a meaningful way and to provoke an emotional response from the reader. No two people will interpret a poem in the same way. Each reader, based on his or her experiences and insights, may come away from the poem with a unique perspective on the poem's meaning, but each perspective has to be justified by the words of the poem.

- **Science Connection.** "The Lost Parrot" is about a boy who is trying to write a poem about a parrot. *Parrot* is the general name for such birds as cockatoos, macaws, and parakeets. Usually, though, the term *parrot* refers to a species of fairly large birds with colorful feathers, strong beaks, and fleshy tongues that enable them to mimic words and even sentences. Some types of parrots have been domesticated as pets, but many species continue to live in tropical rain forests and other natural habitats.

Graphic Organizer

"The Lost Parrot" contains words and phrases that create a feeling of tension, loss, and sadness. As you read, fill in the graphic organizer at right with the words and phrases that you think help create this feeling.

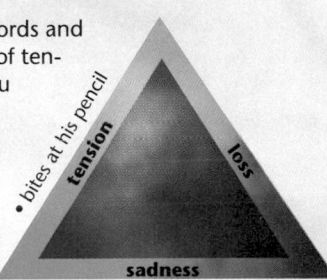

- bites at his pencil

tension

loss

sadness
- frowns

Reader's Journal

Have you ever lost someone or something that you cared about? Describe your experience.

Reader's TOOLBOX

Dialogue. Dialogue is conversation involving two or more people or characters. In fiction, dialogue is enclosed in quotation marks (" ") and is often accompanied by tag lines, which are words and phrases such as *he said* or *she replied* that tell who is speaking. In poetry, however, dialogue is not always indicated by quotation marks or tag lines. As you read "The Lost Parrot," determine whether or not the poem contains dialogue.

Symbol. A **symbol** is something that stands for or represents both itself and something else. In this poem, the lost parrot is a symbol for something else. As you read, think about what the parrot might symbolize.

ADDITIONAL RESOURCES

Unit 9 Resource Book
- Selection Worksheet 9.7
- Selection Check Test 4.9.13
- Selection Test 4.9.14

GRAPHIC ORGANIZER

Near *tension,* students may write bites his pencil, squirms, looks nervous, pencil gripped in fist. Near *sadness* they may write frowning, talks slowly, hunches, stares at the ceiling. Near *loss* they might write "I has a parrot . . .it left," always the same subject for Carlos, I don't know where it went, This time he will guard it carefully, make sure it stays, Before anything else he loves gets away.

READER'S JOURNAL

Encourage students to discuss why it is hard for some people to fully express their feelings when they are sad about a loss.

GOALS/OBJECTIVES

Studying this lesson will enable students to
- identify with the feelings of a character portrayed in a poem
- briefly compare and contrast how a poem tells a story to how a work of prose does
- define *dialogue* and identify dialogue without tag lines or quotation marks in a poem
- define *symbol* and identify a symbol in a poem

INDIVIDUAL LEARNING STRATEGIES

Motivation
You might wish to share with students a documentary film on parrots. Good sources for documentaries include National Geographic-sponsored films, PBS, the Learning Channel, and the Discovery Channel. If you cannot locate a documentary or do not wish to take the class time to show one, you might show students pictures of parrots from books or magazines.

Reading Proficiency
Students may benefit and have an easier time distinguishing dialogue from the rest of the poem if they hear it read aloud on audiotape. You might also let students know ahead of time that dialogue in this poem is indented, but they will have to determine who is speaking based on other details in the poem.

English Language
Point out the following vocabulary words and expressions:
dream-poem—poem based on images from a dream
hunches—draws up the body so as to form a hump or arch
expedition—starting out on a journey for a definite purpose, such as exploration or battle
mangoes—yellow-red tropical fruits, with a hard skin and pit, but flesh that is sweet, juicy, and soft when ripe

Special Needs
Students may benefit from reading the information in the About the Author section before reading the rest of this poem. Doing so will make who Carlos is and who the speaker is clear. This will help students to better attribute the dialogue to the correct character as well as to understand what the poem is about in the poet's own words.

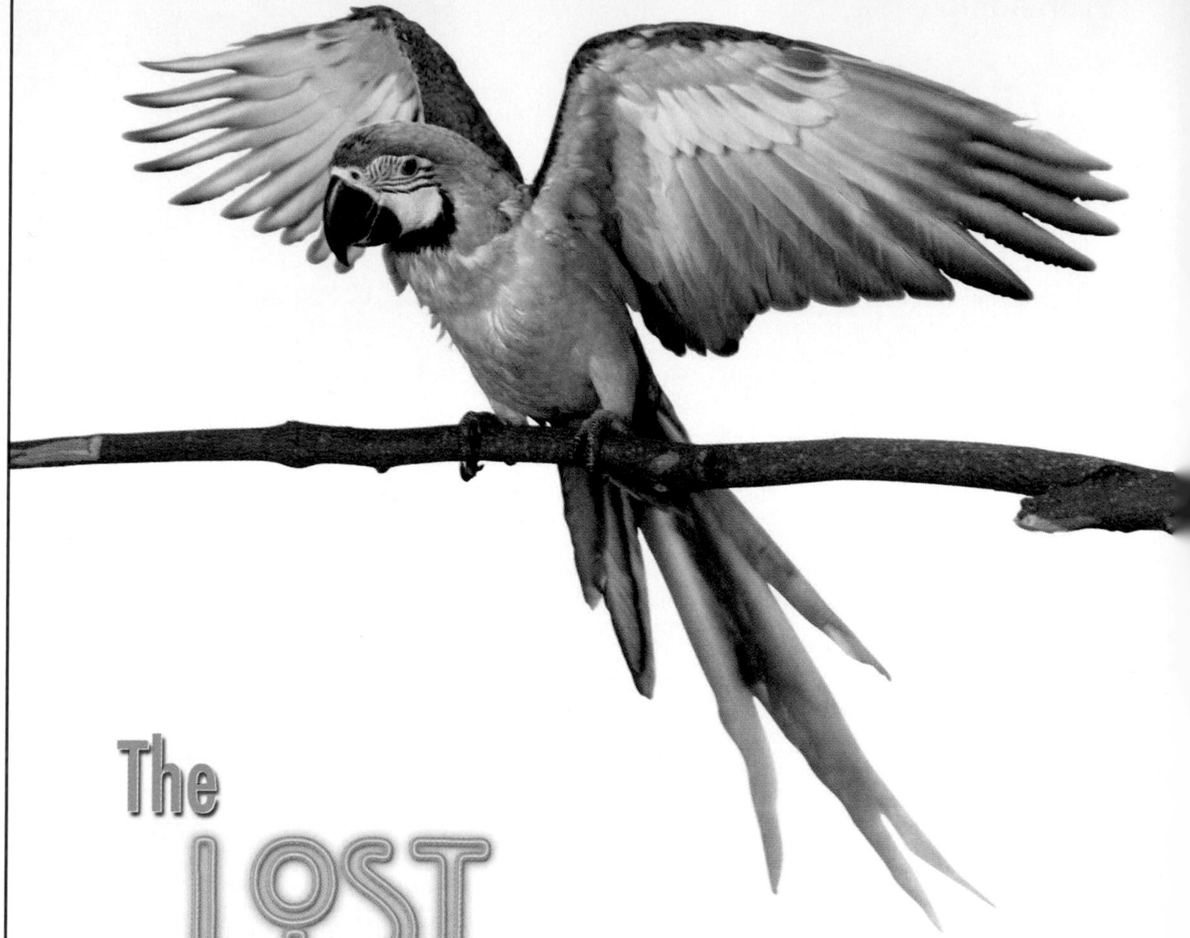

The LOST PARROT

Naomi Shihab Nye

Carlos bites the end of his pencil
He's trying to write a dream-poem, but waves at me, frowning

I had a parrot

INDIVIDUAL LEARNING STRATEGIES (cont.)

Enrichment
Ask interested students to prepare brief written reports on parrots. Students should focus on their natural habitat, their physical characteristics, how long they have been known to live, how they socialize, and parrots in captivity and what they can be trained to do. Ask students to speculate on whether or not a parrot would make a good pet based on what they have learned.

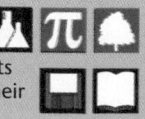

He talks slowly, like his voice travels far
to get out of his body

      A dream-parrot?
      No, a real parrot!
      Write about it

He squirms, looks nervous, everyone else is almost finished
and he hasn't started

      It left
      What left?
      The parrot

GUIDED READING
What happened to the parrot?

He hunches over the table, pencil gripped in fist,
shaping the heavy letters
Days later we will write story-poems, sound-poems,
but always the same subject for Carlos

      It left

He will insist on reading it and the class will look puzzled
The class is tired of the parrot

      Write more, Carlos
      I can't

      Why not?

      I don't know   where   it went

GUIDED READING
Why can't Carlos write more about the parrot?

Each day when I leave he stares at the ceiling
Maybe he is planning an expedition
into the back streets of San Antonio[1]
armed with nets and ripe mangoes
He will find the parrot nesting in a rain gutter
This time he will guard it carefully, make sure it stays

GUIDED READING
What does the speaker think Carlos will do if he finds his parrot?

Before winter comes and his paper goes white
in all directions

Before anything else he loves
gets away   ■

      ————————
      1. **San Antonio.** City in southern Texas

1. The parrot left.
2. Carlos can't write more about the parrot because he doesn't know where it went.
3. The speaker thinks that Carlos will guard the parrot carefully so it won't leave again.

ADDITIONAL QUESTIONS AND ACTIVITIES

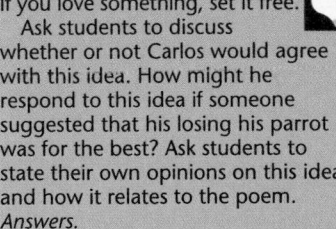

Remind students of the old saying that has been so often repeated it has become cliched: If you love something, set it free.

Ask students to discuss whether or not Carlos would agree with this idea. How might he respond to this idea if someone suggested that his losing his parrot was for the best? Ask students to state their own opinions on this idea and how it relates to the poem.
Answers.
Responses will vary. Students may suggest that Carlos might disagree with this statement because he feels such sadness and loss about his parrot. They may suggest that he will feel differently and may come to agree with this statement in time.
Responses will vary.

SELECTION CHECK TEST 4.9.13 WITH ANSWERS

Checking Your Reading

SHORT ANSWER

1. What is Carlos trying to write? **Carlos is trying to write a dream-poem.**
2. What will Carlos insist on doing in class? **Carlos will insist on reading his poem out loud.**
3. Why does Carlos say he can't write more? **Carlos says he can't write any more because he doesn't know where the parrot went.**
4. To where might Carlos be planning an expedition? **Carlos might be planning to go to the back streets of San Antonio.**
5. Where might Carlos find the parrot? **Carlos might find the parrot in a rain gutter.**

Reader's Toolbox

SENTENCE COMPLETION

Fill in the blanks using the following terms. You may not use every term, and you may use some terms more than once.

dialogue tag lines symbol

1. The words or phrases that tell who is speaking are known as _____. **tag lines**
2. A thing that stands for or represents both itself and something else is called a _____. **symbol**

What would you do if you were Carlos?

About *the* AUTHOR

Naomi Shihab Nye tells about discovering poetry at age six, sharing poetry with young people, and how she came to write "The Lost Parrot."

I started to read poetry at age six, possibly as a refuge from our insulting first-grade textbook—*Come, Jane, come. Look, Jane, look.* I thought, "Were there ever duller people in the world? You have to tell them to look at things? Why weren't they looking to begin with?"

Poets I loved early on: Carl Sandburg, Langston Hughes, Emily Dickinson (very mysterious), William Blake (my second-grade teacher urged us to memorize his "Songs of Innocence"), Walter de la Mare, Rachel Field, Rabindranath Tagore.

I started to write poetry then too, and I sent my first poems to children's magazines by age seven. *Wee Wisdom*, a magazine that still exists, published the first one about my cat Cricket. I got to read the poem over the school intercom, which seemed very space-age in those days.

You could write about anything, which seemed fabulous to me. The field was rich and wide open. Actually, the *process* of writing was much more exciting than the moment of seeing something in print. Writing was another way of thinking, but better, because your thoughts unfolded right there in front of you, and you could go back to them. Often, writing also felt like another kind of friend—a patient companion—you could tell anything to. It would not betray or abandon you.

After college, I worked as a poet-in-the-schools, visiting schools all over my city and state, encouraging students to explore the material of their own lives through words.

"The Lost Parrot" was written for a real boy named Carlos in San Antonio (a third-grader) after I had been working with children and their writing for a few years. A "dream-poem" is a poem in which a writer follows images that first come to him or her through dreaming—whether while sleeping or during a wakeful state. These can be kooky things, impossible things, wished-for things. (Poets think daydreaming is very important.)

I urged students not to write that they had woken up in the last line. 'Stay in the dream,' I said. I urged them to experiment with as many images as they could, describing them so readers could picture them too.

Carlos, however, had only one image and one subject, as the poem suggests.

I couldn't stop thinking of him after I left his classroom. I kept looking for his parrot in the trees. Just recently a woman sent me a poem in which she says she *found* his parrot and raised it for years. I just wish we could find *him* to tell him.

Investigate, Inquire, and Imagine

Recall: GATHERING FACTS

1a. What is Carlos trying to write a poem about? What are the only words Carlos is able to write?

2a. What does the speaker imagine that Carlos is planning?

Analyze: TAKING THINGS APART

3a. Identify the words and phrases that describe Carlos. What does he do? How does he act?

Perspective: LOOKING AT OTHER VIEWS →

4a. Why is the parrot so important to Carlos?

→ **Interpret:** FINDING MEANING

1b. Why is Carlos unable to write more?

2b. Why does the speaker think Carlos wants to do this?

→ **Synthesize:** BRINGING THINGS TOGETHER

3b. Describe Carlos in your own words. What do you think prevents Carlos from writing more?

Empathy: SEEING FROM INSIDE

4b. What do you think will happen to Carlos if he never finds the parrot? How might his teacher and classmates help him?

Understanding Literature

DIALOGUE. "The Lost Parrot" contains **dialogue**, or conversation involving two or more people or characters, but it does not look like the dialogue you normally see in a story. The dialogue in this poem is not separated from the rest of the text by punctuation or by tag lines. Using the dialogue in this poem, rewrite the conversation between the speaker and Carlos, using quotation marks and tag lines to indicate who is speaking. Be creative with your tag lines—for example, instead of writing "he said," write "he whined."

SYMBOL. A **symbol** is something that stands for or represents both itself and something else. What do you think the parrot in this poem might symbolize?

ANSWERS TO UNDERSTANDING LITERATURE

DIALOGUE. *Responses will vary. A possible response is given.*
"I had a parrot," whispered Carlos.
"A dream-parrot?" I asked.
"No, a real parrot!" Carlos insisted.
"Write about it," I suggested.
"It left," was all that Carlos wrote.
"What left?" I inquired.
"The parrot," Carlos sighed.
"Write more, Carlos," I urged him.

"I can't," he mumbled.
I demanded, "Why not?"
In a trembling voice full of long pauses, he breathed, "I don't know where it went."
SYMBOL. Students might say that the parrot symbolizes someone that Carlos has lost, such as a parent or a friend. Students might also say that the parrot symbolizes love, and that Carlos suffers from a lack of love in his life.

ANSWERS TO INVESTIGATE, INQUIRE, IMAGINE

RECALL
1a. Carlos is trying to write a poem about a parrot. The only words Carlos is able to write are "It left."
2a. The speaker imagines that Carlos is planning an expedition to find the parrot.

INTERPRET
1b. Carlos says that he is unable to write more about the parrot because he doesn't know where it went. Students may suggest that Carlos is unable to write more because he is still overcome by sadness and grief and so is unable to put his feelings into words or his experience into perspective.
2b. The speaker thinks that Carlos might want to find the parrot so he can keep it this time.

ANALYZE
3a. Students may point to the words and phrases identified in the answers to the Graphic Organizer activity. Students may say that Carlos seems so focused on the loss of his parrot that he is unable to write about or talk about much else. Students may say that Carlos acts very depressed and forlorn.

SYNTHESIZE
3b. Students may say that Carlos seems devastated to have lost his parrot. He seems very depressed and obsessed with his loss. Students may say Carlos cannot write more because his loss is still too recent and he doesn't have the perspective necessary yet to put his feelings into words.

PERSPECTIVE
4a. *Responses will vary.* Students might say that Carlos has lost someone he loves. They might also say that Carlos seems to be lonely and unhappy and as a result has a hard time in school. Students might say that the parrot is important to Carlos because it represents everything or everyone he has lost.

EMPATHY
4b. Students may say that Carlos will have to slowly learn to cope with his loss and distance himself somewhat from his feelings of loss over time. Students may say that his teacher and classmates can encourage Carlos to talk about his feelings and when he does so keep and open mind, not judge him, and be supportive.

READER'S TOOLBOX

AIM. Students might suggest that the aim may be personal/expressive and imaginative.

FLASHBACK. The flashback begins with the line, "We planted corn one Spring at Acu."

ASSONANCE. Students may point to phrases including "the depth from his thin chest"; "to his son, his song"; "I remember the soft damp sand/in my hand."; "to show me an overturned furrow"; and "tiny alive mice."

READER'S JOURNAL

Encourage students to concentrate on describing one memory that sums up something about the person they have chosen.

VOCABULARY FROM THE SELECTION

clod

POEM / MEANING

Reader's Resource

- Many stories and traditions from southwestern Native American cultures center around corn, often referred to as one of the "three sisters" along with beans and squash. Corn, or maize, is a domesticated plant native to the Americas. Over thousands of years, Native Americans cultivated maize from a wild grass originally growing in southern Mexico to the husked ear of corn with fused kernels found today. Traditionally, corn was an important crop and was eaten at every meal. All parts of the corn plant were used—the husks were braided and woven into masks, moccasins, sleeping mats, baskets, and dolls. After the kernels were removed, the corncobs were used for fuel, ceremonial decorations, and games. Today in the United States, 60 million acres of farmland are used to grow corn, making it the most widespread crop in the country.

- An important theme in the traditions and writings of many Native American cultures is the relationship between humans and nature. Many indigenous people agree that humans should coexist with nature rather than try to control it. This philosophy came into direct conflict with that of white European settlers, who tended to view nature as a resource to be used at will.

Prereading

"My Father's Song"
by Simon Ortiz

Reader's TOOLBOX

AIM. A writer's **aim** is his or her purpose, or goal. People may write to inform (informative/expository writing); to tell a true or invented story (narrative writing); to reflect (personal/expressive writing); to share a perspective meant to entertain, enrich, or enlighten (imaginative writing); or to persuade readers to respond in some way (persuasive/argumentative writing). Many literary works fall under more than one of these categories. For example, an article about water pollution could be both informative and persuasive. A letter could be both narrative and personal/expressive. Based on the title of this poem, what do you think the author's aim, or aims, might be?

FLASHBACK. A **flashback** is a part of a story, poem, or play that presents events that happened prior to the time in which the literary work takes place. Writers use flashbacks in many ways. One common way is to begin a work with a final event or situation and then to go back to the rest of the story or to an event that happened prior to that situation, as a way to explain how that event or situation came about. Another common technique is to begin a story in the middle of the action and then to use a flashback to fill in the events that occurred before the opening of the story. As you read, identify the flashback in the poem.

ASSONANCE. Assonance is the repetition of vowel sounds in stressed syllables that end in different consonant sounds, as with the long *i* sound in *lime light*. Identify phrases in this poem in which assonance is used.

Reader's Journal

Think of someone close to you. What memories come to mind when you think of that person?

GOALS/OBJECTIVES

Studying this lesson will enable students to
- identify with a speaker's feelings about his father
- explain the importance of corn to Native Americans and identify a theme in Native American writing
- define *aim* and identify a poem's aim
- define *flashback* and recognize flashbacks in works of literature

- research Native American or Latino poetry
- use prepositional phrases
- write an advice column
- use precise verbs

My Father's Song
Simon Ortiz

Campesino, 1976.
Daniel Desiga. Collection of
Alfredo Aragon.

Wanting to say things,
I miss my father tonight.
His voice, the slight catch,
the depth from his thin chest,
the tremble of emotion
in something he has just said
to his son, his song:

> We planted corn one Spring at Acu[1]—
> we planted several times
> but this one particular time
> I remember the soft damp sand
> in my hand.
>
> My father had stopped at one point
> to show me an overturned furrow;[2]
> the plowshare[3] had unearthed
> the burrow nest of a mouse
> in the soft moist sand.

GUIDED READING
Whom does the speaker miss?

Very gently, he
scooped tiny pink
  animals
into the palm of his
  hand
and told me to touch them.
We took them to the
  edge
of the field and put
  them in the shade
of a sand moist <u>clod</u>.

I remember the very softness
of cool and warm sand and tiny alive mice
and my father saying things. ■

GUIDED READING
What does the speaker's father find?

GUIDED READING
What does the speaker's father do with his discovery?

1. **Acu.** In Acoma culture, "the place where life happens"
2. **furrow.** Plowed land
3. **plowshare.** Part of the plow that cuts into the earth

words for everyday use
clod (cläd) *n.*, lump or mass of earth. *Clods* of dirt lay scattered around the golf tee.

---

1. The speaker misses his father.
2. The speaker's father finds a mouse's nest.
3. The speaker's father puts the mouse's nest in the shade at the edge of the field.

INDIVIDUAL LEARNING STRATEGIES

MOTIVATION
Ask students to make a list of dishes that use corn as an ingredient. Students might then bring in recipes and together create a corn cookbook. Urge students to prepare some of these dishes for each other to try.

READING PROFICIENCY
Have students form pairs and take turns reading this poem aloud to each other. Students should then read the poems on their own, referring to the Words for Everyday Use, footnotes, and the English Language Learning Vocabulary above to explain any unfamiliar turns.

ENGLISH LANGUAGE LEARNING
Point out the following vocabulary words and expressions:
catch—a break in the voice, caused by emotion
burrow—hole or tunnel dug in the ground by an animal

SPECIAL NEEDS
Some students, especially urban ones, may be confused about what the father and son are doing in the field and why they might find a mouse there. Inform students that land is plowed before it is planted. The plow cuts, breaks up, and overturns the soil. It is often cut into long furrows, or rows. (You might try to locate pictures of a newly plowed field to show students.) Breaking up the soil and loosening its top layer is necessary before planting seeds of corn (as the father and so do in this poem). Mice and other creatures like moles create nests underground for their young. In this poem one of these nests has been broken into by the plow coming through and overturning the soil.

INDIVIDUAL LEARNING STRATEGIES (CONT.)

ENRICHMENT
Ask interested students to write a tribute to a male role model in their own live. Their tribute can take any form they wish—a poem, a personal letter of thanks to the role model, or a speech that might be given to honor this person. In their tributes students should identify what

they learned from this person and why he was or is a role model to them. They may wish to share a memory about one event that is characteristic of the role model's personality.

RESPOND TO THE SELECTION

Also ask students to consider and discuss as a class what the speaker's memory tells you about the character of his father.

SELECTION CHECK TEST 4.9.15 WITH ANSWERS

Checking Your Reading
SHORT ANSWER

1. What does the speaker remember about the sand? **The sand is described as soft, damp, cool and warm.**
2. What does the speaker remember planting? **The speaker remembers planting corn.**
3. What does the plowshare reveal? **The plowshare reveals the nest of a mouse.**
4. What animal does the speaker's father hold in his hand? **The speaker's father holds a mouse in his hand.**
5. What does the speaker do with the animal? **The speaker's father moves the mouse and its family to some shade at the edge of the field.**

Reader's Toolbox
MATCHING

A writer's aim is his or her purpose or goal. Match each aim with its description.

a. informative/expository
b. narrative
c. imaginative
d. personal/expressive
e. persuasive/argumentative

_____ 1. tells a true or invented story **b**
_____ 2. shares a perspective meant to entertain, enrich or enlighten. **c**
_____ 3. convinces readers to respond in some way **e**

Respond *to the* SELECTION

What does the speaker's memory tell you about his relationship with his father?

About *the* AUTHOR

Simon Ortiz knew he loved language at an early age. The language he first spoke was Acoma. A member of the Acoma Pueblo Nation, Ortiz was born in 1941 in Albuquerque, New Mexico. He grew up in the Acoma village of McCartys (Deetseyamah) as a member of the Eagle clan (Dyaanih hanoh). Ortiz says in his book *Woven Stone*, "This early language from birth to six years of age in the Acoma family and community was the basis and source of all I would do later in poetry, short fiction, essay, and other work…"

Ortiz attended the government-run McCartys Day School up to the sixth grade. Students there were required to learn and speak English and were forbidden to speak their native languages. After graduating from high school, Ortiz worked for a year mining uranium in Grants, New Mexico. He went on to college, but quit to join the Army. In 1966, Ortiz went back to school, graduating from the University of New Mexico in Albuquerque. He got his master's degree from the University of Iowa Writers' School. Since then, Simon Ortiz has taught classes in Native American literature and creative writing at several colleges and universities. He has traveled the United States and several countries in Europe sharing his poetry, lecturing, and telling stories. Ortiz is the father of three children. Of his work he has said, "Most of my cultural and literary work continues to focus on issues, concerns, and responsibilities we, as Native Americans, have for our land, culture, and community."

Investigate, *Inquire,* and Imagine

Recall: GATHERING FACTS

1a. Why does the speaker miss his father?

2a. What does the speaker remember about his father?

Analyze: TAKING THINGS APART

3a. In what ways does the speaker describe his father? What does he remember about his father's physical nature? about his mannerisms?

Perspective: LOOKING AT OTHER VIEWS →

4a. What "things" do you think the speaker's father said to his son? What "things" might the speaker want to say to his father?

→ **Interpret:** FINDING MEANING

1b. What do you think has happened to the speaker's father?

2b. Why does the speaker call up this particular memory?

→ **Synthesize:** BRINGING THINGS TOGETHER

3b. This poem is called "My Father's Song," yet there is no singing or music. What is the song in this poem?

Empathy: SEEING FROM INSIDE

4b. What might the speaker do to feel better? How might he choose to celebrate his memories?

Understanding *Literature*

AIM. A writer's **aim** is his or her purpose, or goal. Do you think Ortiz's goal was to inform, persuade, tell a story, reflect, or share his perspectives? What, specifically, was Ortiz trying to convey through this poem? Do you think he accomplished his purpose?

ASSONANCE. Assonance is the repetition of vowel sounds in stressed syllables that end in different consonant sound. Assonance has an effect similar to rhyme. In what way does assonance contribute to the sound of this poem?

FLASHBACK. A **flashback** is a part of a story, poem, or play that presents events that happened prior to the time in which the rest of the literary work takes place. Why do you think the author chose to include a flashback in this poem? What does the flashback contribute to the meaning of the poem?

ANSWERS TO UNDERSTANDING LITERATURE

AIM. Students may say Ortiz's goal was to reflect, tell a story, and/or share his perspective. Students may say Ortiz was trying to convey a little about the character of his father through the story he tells in the poem as well as share the feelings he has about his father and his sense of loss now that his father is gone. Most students will say that Ortiz has accomplished his purpose, but if students have other points of view encourage them to share them and support them with reasons, using examples from the poem as necessary.

ASSONANCE. Assonance helps create a more musical sound to this poem.

FLASHBACK. Students may say that as the speaker's father is dead, he shares a flashback from an early time to share the type of person his father was and help explain why the speaker misses him so much. The flashback shares that the speaker's father was a gentle man who cared for nature and its creatures.

RECALL

1a. The speaker misses his father because he wants to say "things."

2a. The speaker remembers his father saving a mouse's nest and "saying things."

INTERPRET

1b. The speaker's father has died.

2b. Students may say the speaker calls up this particular memory because it shows what kind of character his father possessed—gentle, respectful of the earth's other living creatures, and interested in his son's education in these matters.

ANALYZE

3a. Students may say the speaker remembers his father's voice—the catch in it from emotion and the depth of it. He also remembers his father had a thin chest. He remembers his father stops planting to show him the mouse nest and that he lifts up the animals gently and carefully places them in the shade by the edge of the field.

SYNTHESIZE

3b. Students might say that the song in this poem is the speaker's memory of his father's compassion for the mice they find in the field while planting corn. They might also say that the song is made up of all of the valuable things that the speaker's father taught him.

PERSPECTIVE

4a. Students might say that the speaker's father said things about planting or helping the animals. Students might say that the speaker simply wants to talk to his father about everyday happenings, or perhaps that he would like the chance to tell his father how he feels about him.

EMPATHY

4b. *Responses will vary. Possible responses are given.* Students may suggest that the speaker might share his memories of his father with others and continue to honor his father's memory by sharing what his father taught him about respecting the earth and its creatures with others, perhaps with his own family.

Graphic Organizer

Make a storyboard that shows the action of in this poem chronologically. Recall the major events of the poem, and then illustrate the events in a series of squares.

Writer's Journal

1. Imagine you found Carlos's parrot. Write a lost and found **advertisement** about the parrot for the local newspaper.

2. Write a **note** from Carlos's teacher to Carlos, encouraging him to write his feelings.

3. In "My Father's Song," the speaker's father taught him an important lesson about taking care of animals when he moved the mouse's nest to a safe place. Write five **fortune cookie inserts** that might teach lessons on issues that you think are important in life.

Skill Builders

Study and Research & Collaborative Learning

RESEARCHING POETS. Form a group of three or four students. Using the Internet and library resources, research Native American or Latino poetry. Find out who the most popular writers are and collect samples of their work. Put together a scrapbook of poetry or hold a poetry reading for the rest of your class. Create a bulletin board featuring decorative versions of the poems you have selected, along with information about the authors.

Language, Grammar, and Style

PREPOSITIONAL PHRASES. A **preposition** is used to show how its object is related to other words in the sentence. Common prepositions are *in, on, over, under, before, after, among, at, behind, beside, off, through, until, upon,* and *with*. The preposition begins a phrase that contains the object.

In the sentence below, *under* is the preposition and *the bridge* is the object of the preposition. Note how this **prepositional phrase** gives additional information about where the car drove.

> The car drove *under the bridge.*

Changing the preposition causes the meaning of the sentence to change.

> The car drove *over the bridge.*

Changing the object of the preposition creates a new relationship in the sentence.

> The car drove *under the fallen tree.*

In the sentences above, the prepositional phrase modifies the verb. A prepositional phrase can also modify a noun, an adverb, or an adjective. In the sentence below, the prepositional phrase modifies the noun.

> The boy *in the yellow shirt* is Tom's brother.

Add a prepositional phrase to each of the following sentences to tell something more about the subject or verb.

EXAMPLE My dog barks.

> *My dog barks at the moon.*

1. My house is the small one.
2. Fred and Jeb walked.
3. Sylvia ate a whole pizza.
4. John and Erica laughed.
5. The sun shone.

For more information, see the Language Arts Survey 3.69, "Prepositions."

Applied English

ADVICE COLUMN. Imagine that you are an advice columnist, working for a newspaper. Using one of the poems in this section, write a letter from one of the characters asking for advice, based on the information in the poem. Then write a letter from you to the character, giving the needed advice. If you wish, work in pairs, with each person writing one of the letters.

Vocabulary

USING PRECISE VERBS. The sentences below contain verbs that express meaning but that do not convey precise details about the action in the sentence. Identify the verb in each sentence by underlining it. Then rewrite each sentence, changing the existing verb to a verb that is more specific, more informative, or more creative. See the Language Arts Survey 3.37, "Adding Colorful Language to Sentences" for more help with this activity. Check a thesaurus if you have trouble thinking of new verbs for the sentences. For more information, see the Language Arts Survey 5.21, "Using a Thesaurus."

EXAMPLE I went to the drugstore.

> *I strolled to the drugstore.*

1. Sam quickly wrote directions to his house.
2. Aunt Maud always talks about her little poodle.
3. I will make dessert.
4. The cars move down the road.
5. Jan took a chocolate from the tray.

ADDITIONAL RESOURCES

UNIT 9 RESOURCE BOOK
- Selection Worksheet 9.9
- Selection Check Test 4.9.17
- Selection Test 4.9.18
- Reading Resource 1.20
- Language, Grammar, and Style Resource 3.65
- Speaking and Listening Resource 4.14

GRAPHIC ORGANIZER

Students may include the following information in their completed charts:

SETTING. All in the valley of Death
PROTAGONIST. Rode the six hundred (the Light Brigade)
CONFLICT. Storm'd at with shot and shell / Boldly they rode and well / Into the jaws of Death
RESOLUTION. Then they rode back, but not/Not the six hundred. They that had fought so well / Came through the jaws of death / Back from the mouth of hell / All that was left of them / Left of six hundred.

READER'S JOURNAL

Encourage students to explore whether or not they believe there is a cause important enough for them to sacrifice their lives.

VOCABULARY FROM THE SELECTION

blunder	reel
dismay	sunder
plunge	

Reader's Journal

How would you react if you were required to face a situation that might cost you your life?

Reader's Resource

- **HISTORY CONNECTION.** This poem is based on the Battle of Balaklava, fought on October 25, 1854, during the Crimean War. In the battle, a small force of British soldiers on horseback attacked a strong line of Russian troops armed with heavy artillery (cannons and large guns). Of the 673 British soldiers who fought in the Light Brigade, only 195 survived.

- The Crimean War, which started in 1853 and lasted for three years, was fought between Russia and the Ottoman Empire (modern-day Turkey). The conflict was mainly over control of the Crimea and the vital seaports on the Black Sea. England, France, and Sardinia entered the war on the side of the Turks and fought several bloody battles in an effort to keep Russia from controlling the Black Sea.

Prereading

"The Charge of the Light Brigade"

by Alfred, Lord Tennyson

Reader's TOOLBOX

NARRATIVE POEM. A **narrative poem** is a verse that tells a story. Like most stories, a narrative poem has a setting; a *protagonist*, or main character; a *conflict*, or struggle; and a *resolution*, or final outcome to the conflict. As you read, identify these narrative elements in the poem.

SUSPENSE. Suspense is a feeling of expectation, anxiousness, or curiosity created by questions raised in the mind of the reader or viewer. One way writers create suspense is by using details that create strong emotions. As you read, look for details that create a strong sense of emotion and curiosity about what is happening in the story.

REPETITION. Repetition is more than one use of a sound, word, or phrase. Identify where Tennyson uses repetition in this poem.

Graphic Organizer

Use this graphic organizer to identify evidence in the poem that reveals the setting, protagonist, conflict, and resolution.

Setting	All in the valley of Death
Protagonist	Rode the six hundred
Conflict	
Resolution	

GOALS/OBJECTIVES

Studying this lesson will enable students to
- enjoy a narrative poem
- briefly explain the historical context of "The Charge of the Light Brigade"
- define *narrative poem* and identify parts of the story in such a poem
- define *suspense* and point to elements in a poem that create suspense
- define *repetition* and identify examples of repetition in a poem

The Charge of the Light Brigade

Alfred, Lord Tennyson

"The Charge of the Light Brigade" was set to music by E. T. Paull in the early 1900s.

1

Half a league,[1] half a league,
   Half a league onward,
All in the valley of Death
   Rode the six hundred.
"Forward, the Light Brigade!
"Charge for the guns!" he said:
Into the valley of Death
   Rode the six hundred.

2

"Forward, the Light
   Brigade!"
Was there a man <u>dismay'd</u>?
Not tho' the soldier knew
   Someone had <u>blunder'd</u>:
Theirs not to make reply,
Theirs not to reason why,
Theirs but to do and die:
Into the valley of Death
   Rode the six hundred.

3

Cannon to right of them,
Cannon to left of them,
Cannon in front of them
   Volley'd and thunder'd;
Storm'd at with shot and shell,
Boldly they rode and well,
Into the jaws of Death,
Into the mouth of Hell
   Rode the six hundred.

---

1. **league.** Unit of distance

GUIDED READING
What orders are given to the Light Brigade?

GUIDED READING
How do the soldiers respond to the orders given?

words for everyday use

dis • may (dis mā′) v., unnerve; deter by arousing fear. *The amount of work <u>dismayed</u> Sam, and he gave up.* **dismayed,** *adj.*
blun • der (blun′ dər) v., make a mistake. *I could have scored a goal, but I <u>blundered</u> and shot the puck over the goal.*

"THE CHARGE OF THE LIGHT BRIGADE" **657**

ANSWERS TO GUIDED READING QUESTIONS

1. The orders are to move forward and charge the guns.
2. They follow the order without question.

INDIVIDUAL LEARNING STRATEGIES

MOTIVATION
Ask students to hold a class discussion on their beliefs about war. Is war ever justifiable? If so, when and under what circumstances? Would students be willing to die for their country in a war? Encourage students to be respectful of other students' ideas and opinions.

READING PROFICIENCY
Students may benefit from hearing a dramatic interpretation of this narrative poem before they begin reading. You might encourage an older student who is interested in theater to prepare an interpretation for your class. Then ask students to read through the poem on their own. Tell them to refer to the *Words for Everyday Use* and footnotes in case they come across an unfamiliar word. You might also share with them the English Language Learning vocabulary below.

ENGLISH LANGUAGE LEARNING
Point out the following vocabulary words and expressions:
brigade—large body of troops
cannon—big gun
volley'd—volleyed, meaning propelled or discharged an object into the air
gunners—soldiers who operate or aim guns

SPECIAL NEEDS
Students may have a difficult time visualizing the action of this poem, especially if they are unfamiliar with the way war was fought in the nineteenth century. You may wish to show students a documentary or a scene from a movie about a nineteenth century war, such as the Crimean War.

ENRICHMENT
Encourage interested students to work in small groups to research the Crimean War in

---

INDIVIDUAL LEARNING STRATEGIES (CONT.)

more detail. Students should focus on answering questions such as the following: Why was Russia so interested in controlling the Black Sea? Why were England, France, and Sardinia interested in stopping Russia from doing so? What were some major events in the war? What was the outcome of the war? Students should use a variety of sources for their research. Tell students that they should document their list of sources as they take notes. Groups might then prepare brief oral reports on their findings, using graphic aids as necessary. Students should present you with their lists of sources after they have given their presentation.

RESPOND TO THE SELECTION

You might also encourage students to discuss what they believe should happen to the commander who gave the mistaken order. Should he be punished for this mistake? Why, or why not?

SELECTION CHECK TEST 4.9.17 WITH ANSWERS

Checking Your Reading
SHORT ANSWER
1. How many soldiers are in the group? **There are six hundred soldiers in the group.**
2. Into what valley do the soldiers ride? **The soldiers ride into the valley of Death.**
3. What do the soldiers discover to the left, right, and in front of them? **The soldiers discover that they are surrounded by cannons.**
4. Who are the soldiers attacking? **The soldiers are fighting Cossacks and Russians.**
5. What does all the world do? **All the world wonders.**

Vocabulary in Context
SENTENCE COMPLETION
Fill in each blank below with the most appropriate word from the following *Words for Everyday Use* from "The Charge of the Light Brigade." You may have to change the tense of the word.

dismay	blunder	plunge
	reel	sunder

1. As soon as she'd spoken, Alexandra realized she'd made a terrible _____. **blunder**
2. The water looked very cold, but Heidi took a deep breath and _____ in. **plunged**
3. Richard was _____ when his photos turned out to be blurry. **dismayed**

4

Flash'd all their sabres[2] bare,
Flash'd as they turn'd in air,
Sabring the gunners there,
Charging an army, while
  All the world wonder'd:
<u>Plunged</u> in the battery-smoke
Right thro' the line they broke;
Cossack[3] and Russian
<u>Reel'd</u> from the sabre stroke
  Shatter'd and <u>sunder'd</u>.
Then they rode back, but not
  Not the six hundred.

5

Cannon to right of them,
Cannon to left of them,
Cannon behind them
  Volley'd and thunder'd;

Storm'd at with shot and shell,
While horse and hero fell,
They that had fought so well
Came thro' the jaws of Death
Back from the mouth of Hell,
All that was left of them,
  Left of six hundred.

6

When can their glory fade?
O the wild charge they made!
  All the world wondered.
Honor the charge they made,
Honor the Light Brigade,
  Noble six hundred. ■

> **GUIDED READING**
> What happened as the Light Brigade rode back?

> **GUIDED READING**
> How does the speaker remember the soldiers of the Light Brigade?

---

2. **sabers.** Cavalry swords
3. **cossack.** Member of the Southern Russian cavalry

Respond *to the* SELECTION

What would you have done if you believed your orders to charge had been a mistake?

About *the* AUTHOR

Alfred, Lord Tennyson, born on August 5, 1809, in Somersby, England, was writing poetry by the age of eight. He published his first poems at the age of 18. In 1850 he was named Poet Laureate of England. In 1883 the prime minister of England bestowed the title of "lord" on him. Tennyson continued to produce work throughout his lifetime. He died on October 6, 1892, and was buried in the Poets' Corner of Westminster Abbey. Many consider him to be one of the greatest poets of the 19th century.

> **words for everyday use**
> **plunge** (plunj') v., enter quickly into something. *I <u>plunged</u> into the book as soon as I got home from the library.*
> **reel** (rēl') v., waver or fall back as from a blow. *Glen <u>reeled</u> when the door flew open and hit him.*
> **sunder** (sun' dər) v., break apart or become disunited. *Our group would <u>sunder</u> if we were caught by a violent storm.*

658   *UNIT NINE / POETRY*

SELECTION CHECK TEST 4.9.17 WITH ANSWERS (CONT.)

Reader's Toolbox
SENTENCE COMPLETION
Fill in the blanks using the following terms. You may not use every term, and you may use some terms more than once.

narrative poem	suspense	protagonist
	resolution	conflict

1. The struggle at the heart of a story is known as a _____. **conflict**
2. _____ in a story is the feeling of anxiousness or curiosity created by the story. **suspense**
3. A verse that tells a story is called a _____. **narrative poem**

Investigate, Inquire, and Imagine

Recall: GATHERING FACTS

1a. What does the speaker say about the orders given to the soldiers?

2a. What does the speaker say is a soldier's duty?

3a. What language does the speaker use to describe the valley where the battle takes place?

Analyze: TAKING THINGS APART

4a. Compare and contrast stanzas 4 and 6. What technique is the poet using? Which lines are different, and which lines are the same?

Evaluate: MAKING JUDGMENTS

5a. How well does this poem tell the story of the Battle of Balaklava? What parts of the story could be missing? How well does the poem recreate the setting and mood, or atmosphere, of a horrible battle scene?

→ **Interpret:** FINDING MEANING

1b. Why would the soldiers charge knowing that the command is a mistake?

2b. How do the soldiers' actions demonstrate the sense of duty that the speaker describes?

3b. Explain why these descriptions help you understand what is happening to the Light Brigade.

→ **Synthesize:** BRINGING THINGS TOGETHER

4b. Rewrite in your own words the section of the story found in each of these stanzas. How does the poet's technique emphasize these two parts of the story?

→ **Extend:** CONNECTING IDEAS

5b. Using what you know about war and military capabilities today, explain how a modern battle scene might differ from the battle described in this poem.

Understanding Literature

NARRATIVE POEM. A **narrative poem** is verse that tells a story. Review the graphic organizer you made to identify passages in the poem that reveal information about the setting, the protagonist, the conflict, and the resolution. Create an additional column on the right side of the chart. In it, rewrite in your own words the passages you identified for each category. What is the setting of the poem? Who are the protagonists? What is the conflict? How is the conflict resolved?

SUSPENSE. Suspense is a feeling of expectation, anxiousness, or curiosity. Writers create suspense by raising questions in the reader's mind and by using details that create strong emotions. Review the examples of detail you found in the poem that contribute to the suspense. What adjectives does the author use? What are some of the action verbs? How are these details effective? What details would you use if you were writing a suspenseful narrative about a battle?

REPETITION. Repetition is more than one use of a sound, word, or phrase. How does repetition contribute to the suspense and the mood in this poem?

ANSWERS TO INVESTIGATE, INQUIRE, IMAGINE

RECALL

1a. The speaker says that someone had blundered in giving these orders.

2a. The speaker says that it was not the soldiers' place to "make reply" or to "reason why," but that it was their place to simply "do or die."

3a. The speaker describes it as "the valley of Death," "the jaws of Death," and "the mouth of Hell."

INTERPRET

1b. The soldiers followed orders obediently. They were courageous and sacrificed their safety for their cause.

2b. By charging into the valley and risking death, they show their willingness to "do or die."

3b. The descriptions create a sense of doom, horror, and imminent death. They let the reader know that the light brigade's mission is a doomed one that will claim many lives.

ANALYZE

4a. The poet is using repetition. The lines repeated are "Cannon to right of them / Cannon to left of them / Cannon in front of them / Volley'd and thunder'd / Storm'd at with shot and shell." The remaining lines are different.

SYNTHESIZE

4b. *Responses will vary.* The poet contrasts two like images with two distinct images. The vision of violence and chaos carries over, but the images of the soldiers differ. In stanza 3, they are entering battle ("Into the valley of Death", and in stanza 5 they are retreating from battle ("back from the mouth of hell"). Many of those who "boldly rode" in stanza 3 have fallen in stanza 5, and the survivors ("all that was left of them") flee. Tennyson suggests their slaughter through contrast rather than direct description. The battle hasn't changed, but the soldiers have been changed by the battle. Such an approach suggests the soldiers as fuel for an event much larger than themselves. They are devoured ("jaws of Death") and the refuse is spit out.

ANSWERS TO INVESTIGATE, INQUIRE, IMAGINE (CONT.)

EVALUATE

5a. *Responses may vary.* The poem tells the story with emotion but does not offer many details about the action. The battle is described from beginning to end, but only from one side's point of view. The poem recreates the battle's setting and mood by using vivid imagery of the battle scene.

EXTEND

5b. *Responses will vary.* Students may suggest that horses and cannons would be replaced with more modern means of transport and weapons. Students might also suggest that modern means of communications might also make a misunderstanding about tactical orders less likely (although not impossible).

Answers to Understanding Literature can be found on page 660.

Language, Grammar, and Style
Adverbs include: *well, not, lightly, hurtling, unheeded, bright, there, again.* Antonyms for this set of adverbs includes, respectively: *backward, timidly, badly, definitely, heavily, slowly, heeded, dully, here, once.* If students have difficulty creating a poem using all these adverbs, have them write ten separate sentences, each using a new adverb.

Media Literacy
Students may find it helpful to complete the Enrichment activity for "The Charge of the Light Brigade," so the students being interviewed will have more factual information on which to base their replies.

Vocabulary
Words that end in *'d* include *dismay'd, blunder'd, thunder'd, flash'd, reel'd, shatter'd, sunder'd, volley'd,* and *storm'd.* The word *thro'* is abbreviated for *through.* Past tense verbs in English are formed with an *–ed* ending.

ANSWERS TO UNDERSTANDING LITERATURE

NARRATIVE POEM. *Responses will vary.* Students' rewrites may resemble the following: SETTING: All in a dangerous and deadly place
PROTAGONIST. Rode the six hundred (the Light Brigade) = The six-hundred soldiers rode
CONFLICT. Storm'd at with shot and shell / Boldly they rode and well / Into the jaws of Death = Although the soldiers were showered with shots and shells, they boldly rode toward their almost-certain death.
RESOLUTION. Then they rode back, but not/Not the six hundred. = The surviving soldiers who survived rode back, but there were less than six hundred.
   They that had fought so well / Came through the jaws of death / Back from the mouth of hell / All that was left of them / Left of six hundred. = The soldiers who fought well returned alive from the dangerous battle, but there were few of the original six hundred left.
SUSPENSE. These lines add suspense: "Theirs not to reason why/Theirs but to do and die"; "Cannon to the right of them,/Cannon to the left them,/Cannon in front of them/Volley'd and thunder'd"; "Boldly they rode and well,/Into the jaws of death,/Into the mouth of Hell"; "Then they rode back but not/Not the six hundred"; and "While horse and hero fell." Students may note that the poem uses few

Writer's Journal

1. Make a **list** of words you associate with war. Then write a **short story** using those words.
2. Write a **letter** from a survivor of the Battle of Balaklava to his family at home, telling of the event.
3. Write a **narrative** poem about a conflict you have experienced.

Language, Grammar and Style

ADJECTIVES, ADVERBS, AND ANTONYMS. Make a list of at least adjectives and adverbs in "Charge of the Light Brigade." Find an antonym (a word with the opposite meaning) for each adjective and adverb. Then write a narrative poem of your own, using the new adverbs and adjectives. For more information, see the Language Arts Survey 3.65, "Modifiers," and 1.20, "Learning Synonyms, Antonyms, and Homonyms."

Media Literacy

INTERVIEWING AND REPORTING. Imagine you are a reporter covering the Battle of Balaklava. Interview several classmates, each of whom should respond as a participant in the battle. For example, one student could respond as a soldier in the Light Brigade, another as the officer who gave the orders to charge, and another as a Russian soldier. Write a news story for television, radio, or the newspaper, reporting on the battle and its outcome. If possible, produce the story by videotaping it, making an audio recording, or printing it in newspaper format. See the Language Arts Survey 4.14, "Conducting an Interview," for tips on how to prepare for an interview.

Vocabulary

LOOKING AT WORD FORMATION. Look back at "The Charge of the Light Brigade" and note the shortened words that end in *'d.* What other word is shortened with an apostrophe? Rewrite the words from the poem that contain apostrophes, removing the apostrophes and spelling out the complete words. What letter or letters did you need to add in the past-tense verbs (the words that ended in *'d*)? What rule of grammar lead you to do so?
   What letter or letters did you add to the other shortened word? Why do you think Tennyson shortened these words as he did?

Collaborative Learning

SETTING A POEM TO MUSIC. "The Charge of the Light Brigade" was set to music by E. T. Paull in the early 1900s. In a small group, discuss how you would set the poem to music today. What type of music would best fit the poem? What instruments would the music be for? Would the music be slow-paced or fast-paced? loud or soft? What would the cover of your sheet music look like? Design the cover for the music. On the back cover, write a description of the music that you would favor for the poem.

ANSWERS TO UNDERSTANDING LITERATURE (CONT.)

adjectives, and far more concrete nouns (cannon, jaws, death, mouth, Hell, horse, hero) and vivid verbs (do, die, volleyed, thundered, rode). The action verbs and concrete nouns create a sense of motion and action fitting for a battle scene. *Responses will vary.*

REPETITION. Repeated phrases include "half a league," "valley of Death," "jaws of Death," "mouth of Hell," "theirs not . . . ," "Canon to . . . of them," "Volley'd and thunder'd," "flash'd," "Storm'd at with shot and shell," and "the six hundred."

Prereading

"Corners on the Curving Sky"

Author Unknown

Reader's TOOLBOX

LYRIC POEM. A **lyric poem** is verse that reveals the emotions of a speaker and does not tell a story. Lyric poems are often contrasted with narrative poems, which have telling a story as their main purpose. Many lyric poems stem from poets' observations of themselves, other people, places, things, and situations. What observations does the poet make in "Corners on the Curving Sky"?

SYMBOL. A **symbol** is something that stands for or represents both itself and something else. As you read this poem, look for symbols that represent "different points of view." Use the graphic organizer below to develop your ideas about the poem's symbols.

Graphic Organizer

different points of view

stars in your window

Reader's Journal

What do you think about when you ponder the sky?

Reader's Resource

- Communication between individuals, groups, and even countries always involves points of view. Everyone views the world in a different way based on his or her beliefs, life experiences, emotions, and relationships. When people do not take the unique perspectives of others into account, conflict can arise. Open lines of communication occur when people realize that not everyone shares the same point of view. Accepting, acknowledging, and negotiating different perspectives helps people build relationships based on mutual understanding and respect.

- **SCIENCE CONNECTION.** When you look up at the night sky, what you see depends on where on the earth you are. The moon and stars appear one way to a person on the equator and look totally different to a person at the North Pole. In addition, because the earth rotates around its axis, the stars seem to move across the sky so that each night the sky looks slightly different from the last.

ADDITIONAL RESOURCES

UNIT 9 RESOURCE BOOK
- Selection Worksheet 9.10
- Selection Check Test 4.9.19
- Selection Test 4.9.20

GRAPHIC ORGANIZER

Students may list the following symbols that represent different points of view: round earth, difference in positions, stars in your window, sky burning with light and dark sky, separately cornering universe of our experience.

READER'S JOURNAL

You might ask students whether they think about space and what it may be like up there in space, what other people on earth are doing and thinking about the nighttime sky, or something else. Tell them to list as many thoughts as possible that run through their mind when they look up at the nighttime sky.

GOALS/OBJECTIVES

Studying this lesson will enable students to
- appreciate a lyric poem
- explain briefly why two different people in different places see the night sky differently
- define *lyric poem* and identify the observations a poet makes in a lyric poem
- define *symbol* and identify symbols in a poem

RESPOND TO THE SELECTION

You might ask students to brainstorm a list of issues or situation in which people can differ and both be right. Keep track of their ideas on the chalkboard so that they can play off of other students' ideas to come up with new ones.

ANSWERS TO GUIDED READING QUESTIONS

1. The speaker cannot imagine the stars the other person sees from his or her window.
2. The speaker says our cornering will determine the message of any star and darkness we encounter.

INDIVIDUAL LEARNING STRATEGIES

MOTIVATION
Encourage students to locate books, articles, or Internet sites that depict different constellations. Ask students to choose one constellation and then share with their classmates the name of this constellation, a star map of what it looks like, a description of what the shape is supposed to represent, and some tips for other students on how to recognize the constellation in the nighttime sky.

READING PROFICIENCY
Students may benefit from hearing this poem read aloud on audiotape. Tell students to follow along with the words of the poem as they listen. Have students then read the poem independently.

ENGLISH LANGUAGE LEARNING
Point out the following vocabulary words and expressions:
positions—here means both physical place where a person or thing is and one's opinion or point of view
corner—turn corners
encounter—meet unexpectedly

SPECIAL NEEDS
Students may have difficulty with some of the concepts in this poem. Tell them to concentrate on responding to the Guided Reading questions and the Recall questions.

Extinguished Sun and Moon and Fallen Stars, 1476. Cristoforo de Predis. Biblioteca Real, Turin, Italy.

Corners on the Curving sky

Author Unknown

Our earth is round, and, among other things
That means that you and I can hold
completely different
Points of view and both be right.
The difference of our positions will show
Stars in your window. I cannot even imagine.
Your sky may burn with light,
While mine, at the same moment,
Spreads beautiful to darkness.
Still, we must choose how we separately corner
The circling universe of our experience
Once chosen, our cornering will determine
The message of any star and darkness we
encounter.

GUIDED READING
What is it that the speaker cannot imagine?

GUIDED READING
What does the speaker say "our cornering" will determine?

662 *UNIT NINE / POETRY*

INDIVIDUAL LEARNING STRATEGIES (CONT.)

ENRICHMENT
Encourage interested students to take on an independent research project to explain why the stars in the nighttime sky change over centuries, so that the stars ancient Native Americans saw from the western coast of the Gulf of Mexico are not in the same position as they appear to be to a contemporary Texan living in Corpus Christi today. Have students prepare brief oral reports in response to this question. After students deliver their reports have them give you a list of the sources they used to find an explanation.

Investigate, Inquire, and Imagine

Recall: GATHERING FACTS	**Interpret:** FINDING MEANING
1a. What does the statement, "Our earth is round," mean to the speaker?	1b. What is the connection between this statement and what the speaker says it means?
2a. What is it that the speaker cannot imagine? What does the speaker see in her sky?	2b. Why does the speaker see a different sky than the person he or she addresses sees?
3a. What does the speaker say we must choose?	3b. How does that choice affect each individual?

Analyze: TAKING THINGS APART	**Synthesize:** BRINGING THINGS TOGETHER
4a. What comparisons does the poem make? What contrasts does the poem make?	4b. Explain in your own words what this poem reveals about the idea that people can have "different points of view and both be right."

Evaluate: MAKING JUDGMENTS	**Extend:** CONNECTING IDEAS
5a. To what extent do you agree with the ideas presented in this poem?	5b. What are your thoughts about how people can be different and yet still get along?

Understanding Literature

LYRIC POEM. A **lyric poem** is verse that tells the emotions of a speaker and does not tell a story. Lyric poems are often contrasted with *narrative poems*, which have telling a story as their main purpose. Many lyric poems stem from poets' observations of themselves, other people, places, things, and situations. What emotions are revealed in this lyric poem?

SYMBOL. A **symbol** is something that stands for or represents both itself and something else. How does the poet use the sky to represent his or her ideas? What symbols does he or she use to represent "different points of view"? Go back and finish or modify your graphic organizer to show your final thoughts about symbols. Then identify symbols you might use to represent the different points of view that people might hold.

"CORNERS ON THE CURVING SKY" **663**

ANSWERS TO INVESTIGATE, INQUIRE, IMAGINE (CONT.)

with light with the sky that spreads beautiful to darkness.

SYNTHESIZE
4b. This poem reveals that because of the different places people live and the different experiences people have, they can have ideas and experiences that are both right but different.

EVALUATE
5a. *Responses will vary.* Some students may have difficulty of the notion of there being more than

one right answer or more than one truth. Other students will take readily to this idea. Encourage students to support their views with examples.

EXTEND
5b. *Responses will vary.*

> Answers to Understanding Literature are on page 664.

SELECTION CHECK TEST 4.9.19 WITH ANSWERS

Checking Your Reading
1. What shape is the earth? **The earth is round.**
2. What does the speaker say the reader will see in the window? **The speaker says the reader will see stars in the window.**
3. With what might the sky burn? **The sky might burn with light.**
4. What will our cornering determine? **The cornering will determine the message of any star and darkness we encounter.**

Reader's Toolbox
1. What is the difference between a lyric poem and a narrative poem? **A narrative poem tells a story, while a lyric poem conveys emotion or imagery and does not tell a story.**
2. What is a symbol? **A thing that stands both for itself and something else is a symbol.**

ANSWERS TO INVESTIGATE, INQUIRE, IMAGINE

RECALL
1a. "Our earth is round" means that "you and I can hold/completely different/Points of view and both be right."
2a. The speaker cannot imagine the stars the other person sees from his or her window. The speaker sees the sky "spread beautiful to darkness."
3a. The speaker says we must separately choose how to corner the circling universe of our experience.

INTERPRET
1b. The connection is that from different points on a round earth, things such as the nighttime sky appear differently, and so in describing the sky both people are correct.
2b. The speaker sees a different sky because he or she may be on a different part of the planet, at the opposite end of the earth from the person he or she addresses.
3b. Our choice determines how we will perceive what we see or understand the "message of any star and darkness we/encounter."

ANALYZE
4a. The poem compares the way two different points of view can both be right, stars in two different skies, and understanding the message of two different experiences—stars and darkness. The poem contrasts the points of view (saying they are different) and the sky that burns

GRAPHIC ORGANIZER

For *metaphor*, students might write "emerald hills"; "dark crevice of trunks"; "butterfly's tiny blue hearts/on powdery wings"; "a yellow shrub/furiously sprouts/in a trance of burning stars"; "Branches are suns"; "insects—silver specks."
For *simile*, students might write "Like horses with their swerved necks,/ I concentrate on grass"; "Earthworms insert themselves into the earth/like glossy, pink pins!"; "little, high-pitched, cricketed chirps/rise like tiny bells towards the ageless moon"; "horses trod down the pasture,/disappearing/like an impression of veils."
For *personification*, students might write "apple tree,/knotty with its hollow/belly"; "sun that strokes"; "a crowd of petals close their eyes."

READER'S JOURNAL

Encourage students to explore what they enjoy about the sights, sounds, smells, feelings, and tastes—the sensory details—of this place.

VOCABULARY FROM THE SELECTION

crevice

ANSWERS TO UNDERSTANDING LITERATURE

"CORNERS ON THE CURVING SKY," page 663
LYRIC POEM. The emotions revealed are wonder and acceptance.
SYMBOL. The poet uses the sky to represent the way two different ideas can both be right by showing how the sky will look different in one place than it does in another. She uses differences in positions and the different stars and skies seen to represent different points of view.

LYRIC POEM

Reader's Journal

What is your favorite place to be alone? Explain your answer.

Reader's Resource

- **SCIENCE CONNECTION.** Apple trees belong to the rosaceae, or rose, family. In spring, white flowers that look like tiny roses appear. The flowers are pollinated by birds and insects, causing seeds to grow. The seeds grow into apples in about 140 to 170 days. Apples, like pears, are pomes— fleshy fruits consisting of an outer thickened fleshy layer and a central core with five or more seeds. A healthy apple tree can produce more than 800 pounds of fruit per year.

- In many literary works, the writer creates a microcosm, or "little world." Examples of microcosms in the larger world include dollhouses and aquariums. In literature, a microcosm can represent an author's view of life in the larger world.

Prereading

"Under the Apple Tree"
by Diana Rivera

Reader's TOOLBOX

LYRIC POEM. A **lyric poem** is verse that reveals the emotions of a speaker. Lyric poems are often contrasted with *narrative poems*, which have telling a story as their main purpose. Lyric poems often have songlike qualities. Traditionally, such poems were sung to the music of a lyre (ancient harp). What songlike qualities does "Under the Apple Tree" have?

FIGURE OF SPEECH. A **figure of speech** is a statement or phrase that has more than a straightforward, literal meaning. Metaphor, simile, and personification are all figures of speech. In a **metaphor**, one thing is written about as if it were another, inviting the reader to make a comparison between the two things. A **simile** is a comparison using *like* or *as*. **Personification** describes something not human as if it were human. Try to identify the figures of speech used in "Under the Apple Tree." Use the graphic organizer below to keep track of the figures of speech you find.

Graphic Organizer

Make a Y-shaped grid like this one on your paper. Label the three wedges with *M, S,* and *P,* for each of the figures of speech defined above. Write examples of each in the corresponding spaces.

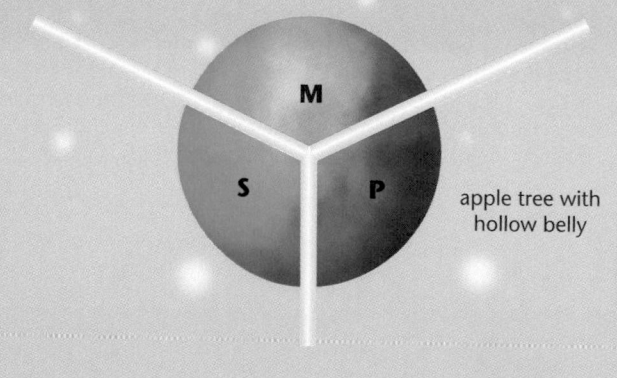

apple tree with hollow belly

GOALS/OBJECTIVES

Studying this lesson will enable students to
- have a positive experience reading a lyric poem
- define *lyric poem* and explain what songlike qualities a lyric poem has
- define *metaphor, simile,* and *personification* and distinguish between these figures of speech

- research astronomy
- stage a poetry reading
- evaluate Internet sites

The Lawrence Tree, 1929. Georgia O'Keeffe. Wadsworth Atheneum, Hartford, Connecticut.

UNDER the Apple Tree

Diana Rivera

I like it here,
under the apple tree,
knotty, with its hollow
belly

here
sitting on its branch
above stone fences that separate pastures,

taking life
here
with the sun that strokes
the sides of trees
casting its shadows on emerald hills.

I like it here,
entering the dark <u>crevice</u> of trunks,
studying the butterfly's tiny blue hearts
on powdery wings.

Like horses with their swerved necks,
I concentrate on grass.
Earthworms insert themselves into the earth
like glossy, pink pins!

> **GUIDED READING**
> What does the sun do?

> **words for everyday use**
> **crev • ice** (krev′ is) *n.*, a narrow opening resulting from a split or crack. *My shoe was caught in the <u>crevice</u> of that rock.*

"UNDER THE APPLE TREE"   **665**

ANSWER TO GUIDED READING QUESTION

1. The sun strokes the sides of trees and casts its shadows on emerald hills.

INDIVIDUAL LEARNING STRATEGIES

MOTIVATION
Students may enjoy the opportunity to display their technical shrewdness and their knowledge about the Web in the Media Literacy activity following this poem. You may wish to form small groups of students, with some students who are very confident with computers and the Internet and others who are less confident. Each group should go to your school library or computer lab to complete this activity, and the students who are more computer-savvy should share what they know with other group members.

READING PROFICIENCY
Have students form pairs with a reading partner. Students should take turns reading aloud the poem to each other and closing their eyes and listening. They then might discuss the images from this poem that created the most vivid pictures in their minds.

ENGLISH LANGUAGE LEARNING
Point out the following vocabulary words and expressions:
knotty—full of hard lumps where branches grow or once grew out
pastures—fields where animals such as cows or horses graze
emerald—green precious jewel; also the color of such a stone
trance—state of altered consciousness, somewhat resembling sleep, in which voluntary movement is lost
glimmer—give a faint flickering light
scraggly—uneven or ragged in growth or form
nestle—settle down comfortably and snugly (in or as in a nest)
trod—walk across
impression—notion, feeling, or recollection

SPECIAL NEEDS
Students may at first find the way ideas are expressed in this lyric poem challenging because there is no narrative, no chronological order

---

INDIVIDUAL LEARNING STRATEGIES (CONT.)

to follow. Share with students the Words for Everyday Use and the English Language Learning. Tell them that as they read they should concentrate on the images produced in their minds as they read and the feelings they associate with these images.

ENRICHMENT
Interested students might research different varieties of apples grown, the difference in the tastes of these apples, and what these apples can be used for. Students might work together to create a chart for a recipe book listing the information they discover on varieties of apples. Ask students to determine if there are more or fewer varieties of apples today that there were fifty years ago.

1. The yellow shrub furiously sprouts
   in a trance of burning stars.
2. At sunset the branch the speaker
   sits on snaps and coils.

RESPOND TO THE SELECTION

You might expand this activity for
urban students to include any
elements of students' surroundings
they notice when they are outside.

SELECTION CHECK TEST 4.9.21
WITH ANSWERS

Checking Your Reading
1. Where does the speaker like to sit?
   **The speaker likes to sit under the
   apple tree or on a branch.**
2. What strokes the sides of trees? **The
   sun strokes the sides of the trees.**
3. What has "tiny blue hearts"?
   Butterflies have tiny blue hearts.
4. What does the blue jay do at
   sunset? **The blue jay disappears at
   sunset.**
5. What creature's sound does the
   speaker hear at night? **The speaker
   hears crickets at night.**

Reader's Toolbox
MATCHING
a. lyric poem   b. figurative language
    c. metaphor   d. simile
        e. personification

_____ 1. describes an animal, a
plant, an idea, a thing, an
emotion, or a thought as if
it were human **e**
_____ 2. compares two things using
"like" or "as" **d**
_____ 3. does not tell a story **a**

ANSWERS TO
UNDERSTANDING LITERATURE

LYRIC POEM. Students may say the poet
shares the emotions of happiness,
contentment, and wonder. We learn
that the speaker likes nature, but we
learn little about his or her dislikes, The
speaker's emotions, mostly repeated in
the phrases, "I like it" and "hear," give
the poem a songlike quality through
the repetition itself. The joyful emotions
are also reminiscent of certain
celebratory songs.

Against the green, a yellow shrub
furiously sprouts
in a trance of burning stars.

> **GUIDED READING**
> What does the yellow shrub do?

Branches are suns
that glimmer from within
taking life
here, under the apple tree,
where a crowd of petals close their eyes,
where scraggly layers of trunk
seem to slowly come apart.

> **GUIDED READING**
> What happens at sunset?

At sunset the branch I sit
on snaps and coils.
The blue jay hastily darts, and disappears.

I like it
here
where birds now nestle and sleep,
where little, high-pitched, cricketed chirps
rise like tiny bells towards the ageless moon.

Here,
where insects,—silver specks—
fly through the glimmering blue.

Oh, but the mouse hides under the hay and
the cracks.
The horses trod down the pasture,
disappearing
like an impression of veils.   ■

Respond *to the* SELECTION

What aspects of nature do you notice most when you are outside?

About *the* AUTHOR

Diana Rivera was born and raised in Puerto
Rico. She has studied art in Rome, Italy, and
currently resides in Upper Grandview, New
York, where she writes and paints. Rivera is the
author of *Bird Language*, a collection of poetry
published in 1994.

ANSWERS TO UNDERSTANDING LITERATURE (CONT.)

FIGURES OF SPEECH. Students may say the examples of
metaphor they identified in their responses to the
Graphic Organizer activity help share the speaker's
unique perspective on the world and the way he or she
sees nature. Students may say the similes they identified
help students to imagine natural scenes by comparing
them to other things they know or can imagine.

Students may say the examples of personification they
identified helps the reader to "see" natural objects in
human terms and so to relate to them better. Students
may say they see human qualities in unexpected places
(petals closing their eyes), which helps them to see the
natural object in a new and unusual way.

Investigate, *Inquire*, and Imagine

Recall: GATHERING FACTS

1a. What does the sun do in the third stanza?

2a. What happens at sunset?

3a. Where do the horses go in the last stanza?

Interpret: FINDING MEANING

1b. How does the speaker regard the sun? What makes you think so?

2b. How does the speaker react? How can you tell?

3b. How does this serve to conclude the poem?

Analyze: TAKING THINGS APART

4a. How many of the speaker's observations describe things? How many of her observations describe actions she witnesses?

Synthesize: BRINGING THINGS TOGETHER

4b. Explain how the speaker's descriptions work together to provide the reader with a vivid picture of the speaker's experience, observations, and reactions to the experience?

Evaluate: MAKING JUDGMENTS

5a. How well does this poem capture and interpret the speaker's experience? What, if anything, does the speaker fail to reveal about her experience?

Extend: CONNECTING IDEAS

5b. In what ways does this poem describe a universal experience that all people could share? In what ways is it more of a personal statement? How would you describe a similar experience in a different way?

Understanding *Literature*

LYRIC POEM. A **lyric poem** is verse that tells the emotions of a speaker and does not tell a story. Lyric poems are often contrasted with *narrative poems*, which have telling a story as their main purpose. Lyric poems often have songlike qualities. What emotions does the speaker share in this poem? What do we learn about the speaker's likes and dislikes? How do the speaker's emotions contribute to the poem's songlike quality?

FIGURES OF SPEECH. A **figure of speech** is a statement or phrase that has more than a straightforward, literal meaning. Metaphor, simile, personification, and hyperbole are all figures of speech. In a *metaphor*, one thing is written about as if it were another, inviting the reader to make a comparison between the two things. A *simile* is a comparison using *like* or *as*. *Personification* describes something not human as if it were human. Look back at your graphic organizer. What examples of metaphor did you find in the poem? What effect do they have on the poem? What similes did you find? How do they impact the poem? What objects in the poem are personified? In what ways does this help the reader "see" an unusual aspect of the object or objects?

"UNDER THE APPLE TREE" 667

EVALUATE

5a. Students may say that this poem does a good job of revealing what the speaker observes and experiences, as well as how the speaker feels about this place. The poem does not, however, reveal much directly about the character of the speaker him or herself or his or her life, other than how much he or she enjoys quietly observing nature from the apple tree.

EXTEND

5b. Students may say that quietly observing nature is an experience all people can share even if they are not observing the exact same scene. Students may say the poem is also a personal statement about a place the speaker loves. *Responses will vary.*

> Answers to Understanding Literature on page 666.

RECALL

1a. The sun strokes the sides of trees and casts shadows on emerald hills.

2a. At sunset the branch the speaker sits on snaps and coils and a blue jay hastily darts away. The speaker then sits longer enjoying the scene even after sunset.

3a. The horses trod down the pasture and disappear in the distance.

INTERPRET

1b. The speaker regards the sun as a good life-giving force. This is evidenced when the speaker mentions "taking life with the sun," and its gently stroking the sides of trees and giving shade to emerald hills.

2b. Students may say the speaker likes the scene as much at night as he or she did during the day. Students may point to the phrase, "I like it here," and the vivid description of night the speaker offers.

3b. Their disappearance concludes the poem because the speaker mentions something leaving his or her range of sight from the apple tree for the first time. The horse are probably heading home, implying that the speaker will soon do the same.

ANALYZE

4a. Students may say that many of the speaker's observations describe things, such as the apple tree itself, the trunks of trees, butterfly wings, and horses' necks. Many more describe actions he or she witnesses such as the sun stroking trees and casting shadows, the earthworms inserting themselves into the earth, the yellow shrub sprouting, the crowd of petals closing their eyes, the layers of trunk seeming to come apart, the blue jay darting away, the birds nestling and sleeping, the insects flying like silver specks, the mouse hiding, and the horses disappearing like veils in the distance.

SYNTHESIZE

4b. *Responses will vary.* Students may say then descriptions help to share the speaker's experiences, observations, and reaction with the reader so the reader feels that he or she too has been to this place and seen these things and can relate to and participate imaginatively in what the speaker describes.

Writer's Journal

1. Imagine that you are a teacher and that your class discussions sometimes result in everyone talking loudly at the same time. Write a **list of ten rules** for group discussion, reminding your students to respect one another's points of view.

2. Write a **lyric poem** describing a secret hideaway that you have or wish to have.

3. Write a "for sale" **classified advertisement** for the property described in "Under the Apple Tree."

Skill Builders

Study and Research

STUDYING ASTRONOMY. Use library resources or the Internet to find information on astronomy. As you research, keep a log to track what information you have found and where you found it. Try to locate answers to the following questions. What stars, constellations, and planets should I be able to see from this geographic location at this time of the year? How can I identify them? Where in the sky should I look? What should I do to get the best view? What unique astronomical objects can be viewed this year that cannot be seen every year? After you have found this information, check your answers by looking at the night sky yourself.

Speaking and Listening

POETRY READING. Stage a reading of "Under the Apple Tree." If you wish, you may use props or other special effects. Try to interpret the poem from the speaker's point of view. As you read, pay particular attention to the voice you use, the emotions you express, your pacing and volume, and your gestures and facial expressions. See the Language Arts Survey 4.19, "Oral Interpretation of Poetry," for more help reading poetry aloud.

Media Literacy

EVALUATING INTERNET SITES. A number of teen and amateur poetry sites and electronic magazines, or e-zines, exist on the Internet. Some are developed and maintained by schools. Others are sponsored by various organizations and Internet publishers. Like books, Internet sites can be reviewed, critiqued, and rated. Develop a list of at least five teen or amateur poetry sites, including a review for each one. Critique each by evaluating its different aspects, such as design, content, and ease of use. Finally, rank each site.

Before searching for the poetry sites, create a list of criteria by which to evaluate them. Then decide which features you believe are most important in a teen or amateur poetry site or e-zine. Use your list to help you evaluate the sites you find. Some site addresses you may wish to start with are listed below. Or, you may want to use a search engine to look for keywords such as *teen, poetry,* and *e-zine.* For more information on Internet research, see the Language Arts Survey 5.25, "Using the Internet"
http://www.cyberteens.com/ezine/
http://www.poetrytodayonline.com/
        TeenPoetry.html
http://members.xoom.com/grnhouse/main.htm
http://www.mightyserver.com/serena/
        teendex.html

Prereading

Haiku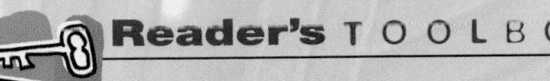

by Matsuo Bashō, Yosa Buson, and Kobayashi Issa; translated by Robert Hass

Reader's TOOLBOX

HAIKU. A **haiku** is a traditional Japanese three-line poem. It has five syllables in the first line, seven in the second line, and five in the third. A traditional haiku presents an image in order to arouse in the reader a specific emotional state. Contemporary poets have adapted the form for other purposes.

IMAGERY. An *image* is language that describes something that can be seen, heard, touched, tasted, or smelled. The images in a literary work are referred to, when considered altogether, as the work's **Imagery**. A haiku usually presents one or more images to capture a moment of reflection. Describe the images in the following haiku. What sensory details create the images? Make a cluster chart for each poem. Write the central image of the poem in a center circle. Around the center circle, add sensory details that contribute to the image.

Graphic Organizer

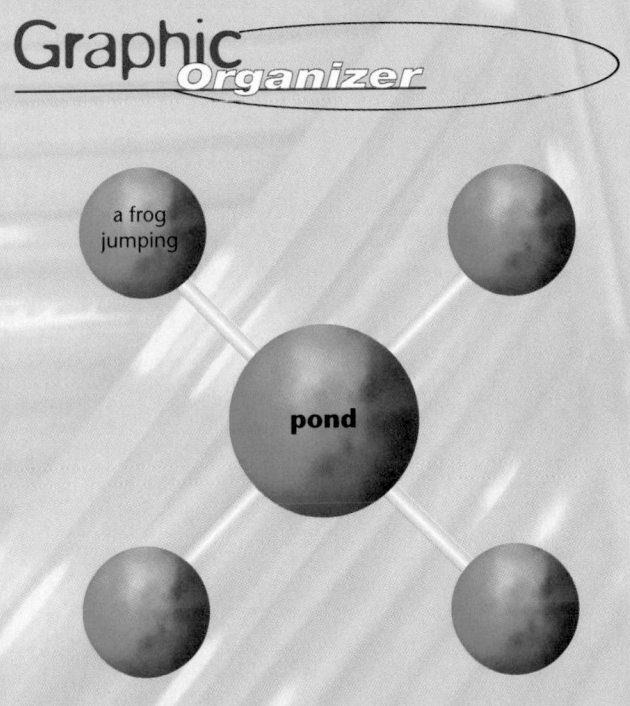

Reader's Journal

What do you hear when you sit perfectly still and listen to everything around you?

Reader's Resource

- Translating poetry is an extremely difficult task. Poetry, even more than prose, is tightly linked to culture and to subtle meanings in language. While some people say that poems should be translated literally, word for word, others feel that the essence of the poem is the important thing. If meaning is the part of a poem that must be translated from one language to another, other aspects of the poem are often lost. The original poem's rhyme and rhythm, for example, may be lost in the translated verse. In these translated haiku, for example, the traditional five-syllable/three-syllable/five syllable lines have been changed.

- Haiku is a poetry form that originated more than five hundred years ago in Japan. The haiku tradition stems from a close observation of nature. The haiku is also characterized by seemingly simple reflections that really offer complex ideas.

ADDITIONAL RESOURCES

UNIT 9 RESOURCE BOOK
- Selection Worksheet 9.12
- Selection Check Test 4.9.23
- Selection Test 4.9.24
- Reading Resource 1.17

GRAPHIC ORGANIZER

Students may include the following information in their cluster charts: pond—old, frog jumps in, sound of water; grasses—misty, quiet waters, evening; night—summer, stars whisper to each other.

READER'S JOURNAL

Encourage students to write about sounds they hear when they are listening carefully that they may not ordinarily notice or might "tune out." Encourage students to notice other sensory details when they sit still and open their senses, such a sights they might not pay attention to ordinarily, smells, and physical feelings. Have students compare their observations in small groups to see what other students picked up on.

GOALS/OBJECTIVES

Studying this lesson will enable students to
- enjoy reading some translated haiku
- define *haiku* and explain the form of a haiku
- define *imagery* and identify the imagery in a poem
- examine different translations
- research the origins of haiku
- identify parts of a dictionary definitions

ANSWERS TO GUIDED READING QUESTIONS

1. The frog jumps into the old pond.
2. The stars are whispering to each other.

INDIVIDUAL LEARNING STRATEGIES

MOTIVATION

Students may find it interesting to see how many Japanese words have entered the English language. Challenge students to use dictionaries, their own knowledge, and the Internet to come up with more Japanese words that have become a part of the English language. Have students bring their lists to class and share them. Compile a list on the chalkboard as students offer suggestions.

READING PROFICIENCY
Students may find the haiku more simple to read than many poems. Let students know, however, that haiku can create complex, detailed, and vivid images in very few words. Read the haiku aloud to students and have them close their eyes and try to picture the scene in each haiku. Students might then discuss in small groups which haiku appealed most to them and which created the most vivid pictures in their minds. Then have students read the haiku independently, slowly and carefully. Ask students to discuss whether their independent reading changed their minds in any way.

ENGLISH LANGUAGE LEARNING
Share with students that in the Japanese language most syllables are given equal stress. Encourage students to try pronouncing the authors' names giving each syllable the same weight or stress.

SPECIAL NEEDS
Encourage students to choose one of the haiku and draw the picture the haiku creates in their mind. Students might then share their drawings with others. Concrete visual images may help some students to better picture the images in these poems.

Haiku

Matsuo Bashō

The old pond—
a frog jumps in,
  sound of water. ■

> **GUIDED READING**
> Into what does the frog jump?

Yosa Buson

  Misty grasses,
quiet waters,
  it's evening. ■

Kobayashi Issa

  Summer night—
even the stars
  are whispering to each other. ■

> **GUIDED READING**
> What are the stars doing?

Sugawara no Michizane Composing a Poem, 1886. Buemon Akiyama Tsukioka Yoshitoshi. Private Collection.

INDIVIDUAL LEARNING STRATEGIES (CONT.)

ENRICHMENT
Encourage students to write their own series of three haiku on the same scene or subject. For example, students might describe a city playground during the night in winter, during the day in summer,  and at night in summer, or students might describe three very different bodies of water. Students who participate might then compile their haiku into a class book of haiku to share with other students.

Respond *to the* SELECTION

If you were a haiku poet, what natural scene would spark your imagination as a potential subject for a haiku?

Sugawara no Michizane Composing a Poem, 1886. Buemon Akiyama Tsukioka Yoshitoshi.

Japanese prints of the Edo period (1603–1867) were called *ukiyo-e*, meaning literally "pictures of the floating world," which evoke a carefree world of beauty and pleasure. Artists specialized in certain subjects, such as travel images, beautiful women, or celebrated poets and actors. Tsukioka Yoshitoshi (1839–1892) is best known for illustrating ghost stories and bizarre folktales, but here he depicts Sugawara no Michizane—a ninth century Japanese statesman who became the shinto god of literature and calligraphy—composing a poem while observing nature. What qualities do *ukiyo-e* prints share with haiku poetry?

About *the* AUTHORS

Matsuo Bashō (1644–1694) was a Japanese haiku master and a teacher of poetry. He also studied Zen Buddhism and practiced meditation. In 1689 he grew unhappy with his role as a teacher, so he sold his house and began to travel. The result was a collection of writings that is his masterpiece, *Narrow Road to the Far North.*

Yosa Buson (1716–1783) was born near Osaka, Japan. He earned his living as a painter but considered himself a poet. Buson produced several books of poems, including *Light from the Snow* (1772) and *A Crow at Dawn* (1773).

Kobayashi Issa (1763–1827) was born in a small village in the mountains of Japan. He was raised by his grandmother. Issa's poetry is filled with images of tiny creatures, especially mice, lice, fleas, and ticks, as a result of his close observations of his natural surroundings.

HAIKU **671**

from *Lost in Translation*

Steven Harvey

Armed with my book of Japanese kana[1] and her calculator-like word-finder, Junko and I sat at the dining room table and translated haiku—at least, we tried. I printed a transliterated[2] version of the haiku on the page in front of us and Junko read through it, her hand opening and closing as she counted off the syllables with her fingers.

"Yes, haiku," she said, when her fingers closed into a fist at the end of the five-syllable last line. She scratched the poison ivy under her eye and began writing English words above the Japanese. Over the word *ana* she wrote "hole" and over *ya* she wrote a colon.

"Haiku very boring," she said, opening her eyes wide as she always does when she is excited. "But if you see in your mind—is okay."

Above the syllable *no* she wrote " 's" but stumbled on the word in front of it. "Shoji," she whispered, "how say that." Eyes wide, she typed quickly into her word-finder. "Shoji like sliding door," she mumbled, "but. . . ." Then she showed me the definition on her machine: "A sliding door with a piece of Japanese paper on a lattice."

"Not good for Sam," she added with a giggle. She brought her hand down in a mock karate chop and said, "Bam."

"That's for sure," I said.

She wrote "sliding door" and the word "then" above the long first word in the first line and "milky way" above the last word in the poem.

"Ama-no-gawa," I said in her language, haltingly, like a child—the word, not a word for me, but a plaything on my tongue.

"Mil-ky way," she answered. "Yes."

After a half hour of poking around at this text, our literal translation of Issa's immortal haiku looked like this:

Then:
Sliding door's hole's
Milky Way.

We both examined the sheet for a while, not sure what to do next — this was our first experiment in translating haiku, and the results seemed, well, meager.

"Words and meaning are very different," she said, apologetically. "You must picture."

Despairing of any verbal solution, she drew a stick figure picture of a person under a window with a hole in the shade. Then she drew several lines from the hole to the man.

"Moonlight," she said, still drawing the lines—as if the figure were bathed in it. "Moonlight."

I looked back at her, puzzled, and pointed out that there was no mention of moon in the poem.

"Always moon in haiku—if night, always moon. I *sure.*" She scratched the poison ivy again just under the rim of her glasses. "Every peoples in Japan know this shoji and this moon," she said. "I *sure.* Must picture moon."

She looked at me and opened her eyes wide again, as if I might look through them and see what she sees. For a moment we shared what is lost in translation. ■

---

1. **kana.** Japanese writing
2. **transliterated.** Written in the characters of a different alphabet

ABOUT THE RELATED READING

This reading is a slice from the book, *Lost in Translation,* a collection of essays in which **Steve Harvey** reflects on language and its importance in everyday life. Harvey is a professor of English at Young Harris College and is also the author of *A Geometry of Lilies: Life and Death in an American Family.*

Investigate, *Inquire,* and Imagine

Recall: GATHERING FACTS

1a. What change does the frog create in the haiku by Bashō?

2a. What time of day does the speaker describe in the haiku by Buson?

3a. What are the stars doing in the haiku by Issa?

→ **Interpret:** FINDING MEANING

1b. How does this change seem either surprising or ordinary?

2b. Why might the speaker use these descriptions for that time of day?

3b. Why does the speaker say "even the stars"?

Analyze: TAKING THINGS APART

4a. Compare and contrast these three haiku. How are they alike? What characteristics do they share? How are they different?

→ **Synthesize:** BRINGING THINGS TOGETHER

4b. What common views might the poets who wrote these haiku share? What values might they have in common?

Evaluate: MAKING JUDGMENTS

5a. Which haiku made the strongest impression on you? What emotions did it evoke in you?

→ **Extend:** CONNECTING IDEAS

5b. How does this haiku relate to you, your life, and your experiences? What similarities exist between it and modern poems you have read, movies you have watched, art you have seen, or scenes you have witnessed?

Understanding *Literature*

HAIKU. A **haiku** is a traditional Japanese three-line poem. It has five syllables in the first line, seven in the second line, and five in the third. A traditional haiku presents an image in order to arouse in the reader a specific emotional state. Why do you think haiku are so short? What does this format contribute to the poem's imagery?

IMAGERY. An *image* is language that describes something that can be seen, heard, touched, tasted, or smelled. The images in a literary work are referred to, when considered altogether, as the work's **imagery**. These images are intended to create a particular emotion in the reader. What generalizations can you make about the imagery in these haiku? What generalizations can you make about the emotions this imagery evokes?

ANSWERS TO INVESTIGATE, INQUIRE, IMAGINE

RECALL

1a. The frog jumps into the pond and makes the sound of water.

2a. The speaker describes evening

3a. The stars are whispering to each other.

INTERPRET

1b. *Responses will vary.* Students may say that the frog's jumping into the pond isn't unusual, but describing the noise the frog makes as the "sound of water" is unusual and surprising because it inspires the reader to think about the sound of water.

2b. Students may say that the speaker is trying to capture the stillness and the coolness of evening with phrases like "misty grasses" and "quiet waters."

3b. The speaker may be trying to imply that others are whispering—perhaps the wind or people.

ANALYZE

4a. Students may say that they are alike in that they all explore natural scenes, and two of them focus in on a specific time of day. They all contain vivid imagery and appeal to sight and sound. Students may say that they are different in that the Basho haiku doesn't mention a specific time of day unlike the others; some of them feature animals, while others do not; some personify nature and others do not.

SYNTHESIZE

4b. Students might suggest that all three poets probably appreciated nature greatly and respected it. It seems they found peace and serenity in quietly observing nature.

EVALUATE

5a. *Responses will vary.*

EXTEND

5b. *Responses will vary.*

ANSWERS TO UNDERSTANDING LITERATURE

HAIKU. Students may suggest that haiku are so short so as to better present the reader with one distinct picture of scene to draw a very specific emotional state related to that scene. The brevity of the poems heightens the intensity of the imagery; they are compact and the reader must pause for a moment to experience them.

IMAGERY. Students may say all the images are related in some way to nature. Students may say that the emotions seem to be related to ways people react to nature—with surprised delight or with pleasure in tranquillity.

Language, Grammar, and Style
It might be easiest for students to comb through these sources to find different translations of the same poems if they work in small groups. You might ask your school or local library to put these books on reserve so that students can examine these books while in the library but cannot check them out. That way no one group can spoil other groups' chances of completing their research.

Study and Research
Refer students to the Language Arts Survey 5.18, "How to Locate Library Materials," before they begin this activity. Students might find reference works, including various literary reference books, to be helpful for this assignment. Anthologies of world literature may also prove helpful, as will books on haiku and the history of Japan.

Vocabulary
1. teriyaki
definition: Japanese dish consisting of meat or fish marinated in spiced soy sauce and broiled, grilled, or barbecued
part of speech: noun
ter ē yä kē
origin: [Jpn < *teri,* nominal form of *teru,* to shine + *yaki,* nominal form of *yaku,* to broil: so called because the sauce makes the meat or fish shiny]
2. kamikaze
definition: pertaining to a suicidal attack by Japanese airplane pilots during World War II
part of speech: adjective
kä mē kä zä
origin: [[Jpn, *lit.,* divine wind *kami,* god + *kaze,* the wind]
3. kimono
definition: robe with wide sleeves and a sash, part of the traditional costume of Japanese men and women
part of speech: noun
kē mō nō
origin: [Jpn *ki (kiru,* to wear) + *mono,* thing]
4. ginkgo
definition: Asiatic tree with fan-shaped leaves and yellow, foul-smelling seeds enclosing a silvery edible inner kernel
part of speech: noun
gēn kyo
origin: [Jpn *ginkyo* < Sino-Jpn *gin,* silver + *kyo,* apricot]
5. kakemono
definition: Japanese silk or paper hanging or scroll with an inscription or picture on it and rollers at the top and bottom
part of speech: noun
kä kä mō nō
origin: [Jpn *kake,* to hang + *mono,* thing]

Writer's Journal

1. Write a **haiku** that reveals something about how you view the world around you. Create this poem for a person who is close to you.
2. Imagine you are compiling a collection of haiku for a book. Write a **promotional blurb** for the back cover of the book, explaining why the book will intrigue poetry readers.
3. Write **instructions** for a photographer whose assignment is to go out and shoot pictures to accompany each of these three haiku on posters. Be as specific as possible.

Skill Builders

Language, Grammar, and Style

EXAMINING TRANSLATIONS. At a local library, search for different collections of translated haiku. The following is a list of some books you may want to find.
The Essential Basho, by Matsuo Bashō, translated by Sam Hamill
The Spring of My Life and Selected Haiku, by Kobayashi Issa, translated by Sam Hamill
The Narrow Road to Oku, by Matsuo Bashō, translated by Donald Keene
The Essential Haiku: Versions of Basho, Buson, and Issa, edited and translated by Robert Hass
Try to find different variations of the same original poems. In what ways do the translations differ from one another? What words generally remain the same? Which translation do you like the best? Why?

Study and Research

ORIGINS OF HAIKU. Using library resources, research early haiku writers. Try to determine the cultural surroundings from which haiku emerged. What was happening in Japanese culture around the same time Japanese poets began writing haiku? How did haiku change through time? Write a short summary of your findings on the history of haiku.

Vocabulary

JAPANESE WORDS. Look up the following words, all of which come from the Japanese language, in a standard English dictionary. Then write out the definition, part of speech, pronunciation, and origin of each word. If you need to review the parts of a dictionary entry, review the Language Arts Survey 1.17, "Using a Dictionary."

1. **teriyaki**
   definition:
   part of speech:
   pronunciation:
   origin:
2. **kamikaze**
   definition:
   part of speech:
   pronunciation:
   origin:
3. **kimono**
   definition:
   part of speech:
   pronunciation:
   origin:
4. **ginkgo**
   definition:
   part of speech:
   pronunciation:
   origin:
5. **kakemono**
   definition:
   part of speech:
   pronunciation:
   origin:
6. **karate**
   definition:
   part of speech:
   pronunciation:
   origin:
7. **dojo**
   definition:
   part of speech:
   pronunciation:
   origin:
8. **karaoke**
   definition:
   part of speech:
   pronunciation:
   origin:

---

6. karate
definition: Japanese system of self-defense characterized chiefly by sharp, quick blows delivered with the hands and feet
part of speech: noun
kä rä tä
origin: [Jpn, lit., prob. *kara,* empty + *te,* hand]

7. dojo
definition: studio or room in which martial arts are taught
part of speech: noun
dō jō
origin: [Jpn]

(Continued on page 675)

for your READING LIST

Loss must be the one truly universal experience. From the moment we are born and must leave the safe, warm and comforting environment of the womb to begin our journey through this life, we experience loss. In her introduction to **What Have You Lost?** Naomi Shihab Nye says that she once walked into the classroom where her "unruly" students waited and said, simply, "What have you lost? Write it down." Her students all picked up pens and pencils and began to fill pages, heads bent, absorbed in the question. It is a question for which we all have a long answer.

What Have You Lost?, edited by Naomi Shihab Nye, is an anthology of poetry about loss—lost toys and lost brothers, lost love, the lost certainty and security of early childhood, the lost familiarity of a grandfather's big car and the scent of his Old Spice cologne, and more. Nye collected these poems for years as she wondered about the way loss affects us, causes us to rethink what we still have, and perhaps helps us to take better care of what remains. The accompanying photographs by Michael Nye, portraits of ordinary people like each of us, remind us that loss is something we all know.

COMPILE YOUR OWN POETRY ANTHOLOGY

Naomi Shihab Nye chose poems for her anthology that held a special meaning for her personally. What poems have you read that made you stop and think? Which ones seemed to express your own feelings? Which ones made you laugh? Which made you cry? Which poems seemed written just for you? Think back over the poetry you have read over the years and compile your own personal poetry anthology. You may want to review your textbooks and other volumes of poetry you have read to select those poems that have touched you in a personal way. If you have written poetry yourself, include some of your own work as well. After selecting several poems, consider the following:

- Is there a theme or a common thread to the poetry I have chosen? What title for my anthology does this suggest?
- How should I write my introduction, explaining when I first read each poem, and why it is significant to me?
- How might I illustrate my anthology? What art or photography would complement and enhance my work?
- How will I bind the anthology? (Consider the use of a notebook or binder that will allow you to add additional poetry in the future.)

Other books you may want to read:
How to Read a Poem and Fall in Love With Poetry by Edward Hirsch
Cool Melons—Turn to Frogs!: The Life and Poems of Issa, ed. by Matthew Gollub

For Your Reading List

What Have You Lost?, edited by Naomi Shihab Nye, offers both humorous and serious poems about loss that will appeal to young adult readers. Hazel Rochman, writing for *Booklist* in April 1999, notes, "as Nye points out in her splendid introduction, one reason why we fuss so much about petty losses is because we cannot bear to face the inevitable larger ones that can never be redeemed or reclaimed." Rochman goes on to say that English teachers will find this an important resource to stimulate students' writing. The alternate selections listed on page 675 include *How to Read a Poem and Fall in Love with Poetry* by Edward Hirsch and *Cool Melons—Turn to Frogs!: The Life and Poems of Issa*, ed. by Matthew Golub. Students will be intrigued by both poetry collections—one which provides a broad overview of poetry and the other which looks at the life of a master of the haiku.

Compile Your Own Poetry Anthology

This activity can serve as an additional or alternate assessment to the preparatory work students will do for the Unit 9 Test. As students prepare to create their own poetry anthology, have them read the following sections in the Language Arts Survey: 1.3, "Reading Literature: Educating Your Imagination," 1.4, "Educating Your Imagination as an Active Reader," 1.5 "Keeping a Reader's Journal," 1.6, "Reading Silently versus Reading Out Loud," 1.7, "Reading with a Book Club or Literature Circle," and 1.8, "Guidelines for Discussing Literature in a Book Club." See the Guided Reading Resource 1.3–1.8 in the Teacher's Resource Kit for blackline masters of worksheets that will help students work these concepts more thoroughly. Refer them also to the Language Arts Survey 4.8, "Communicating in a Small Group" and 4.13, "Collaborative Learning and Communication," if they prepare their anthology as a small group project.

ANSWERS TO SKILL BUILDERS (CONT.)

8. karaoke
origin: [Jpn dō jō, fr. dō, way, art + jō, ground]
definition: a machine that plays the instrumental portion of songs, allowing the user to sing the lyrics into a microphone
part of speech: noun

pronunciation: kä rä ō kä
origin: [Jpn, lit, *kara*, empty + *oke*, shortened from *okesutura*, orchestra: "empty orchestra"]

GUIDED WRITING
Software

See the Guided Writing Software for an extended version of this lesson that includes printable graphic organizers, extensive student models and student-friendly checklists, and self-, peer, and teacher evaluation features.

Examining the Model

You might have students fill out a Sensory Details Chart for the Professional Model to identify the descriptive details used in the poem. Point out the simile "the ripest berries fall almost unbidden to my tongue, as words sometimes do. . . ." Encourage students to use figurative language in their own poem.

Writing poems can be a way of pinning down a dream (almost); capturing a moment, a memory, a happening; and, at the same time, it's a way of sorting out your thoughts and feelings.

—Lillian Morrison

Professional Model

"Blackberry Eating" by Galway Kinnell, page 635.

I love to go out in late
    September
among the fat, overripe, icy,
    black blackberries
to eat blackberries for breakfast,
the stalks very prickly, a penalty
they earn for knowing the
    black art
of blackberry-making; and as I
    stand among them
lifting the stalks to my mouth,
    the ripest berries
fall almost unbidden to my
    tongue,
as words sometimes do, certain
    peculiar words
like strengths or squinched,
many-lettered, one-syllabled
    lumps,
which I squeeze, squinch open,
    and splurge well
in the silent, startled, icy, black
    language
of blackberry-eating in late
    September.

Guided Writing

CREATING A LYRIC POEM

Blundering, backward day
Red clouds and a purple smile
A sigh,
a kite,
a fighting fly
Waiting for the wind to wash us clean

You can almost sing these words, for they hold the imagery, sounds, and rhythm of lyrics. If you have ever written words to a song, you have come close to writing lyric poetry.

A lyric poem is a highly musical verse that expresses the emotions of a speaker. Rather than tell a story, the lyric poem expresses a state of mind, a thought, or a feeling. It captures a moment in time. This form lets you play with language, with the rich sounds and meanings of words.

EXAMINING THE MODEL. In "Blackberry Eating," Kinnell captures a moment in time picking and eating blackberries. Words and phrases like "I love to go out" and "the ripest berries fall almost unbidden to my tongue" express the speaker's thoughts or feelings. But the speaker doesn't stop there. He notices something else. The berries remind him of peculiar words that come to his mouth without thinking, and he compares these words to "one-syllabled lumps" that he squishes in the "icy, black language" of berry eating.

Comparisons and images like these help the reader experience and understand the thoughts Kinnell is describing. And so does the musical language. Read these lines aloud and listen for **alliteration**, or repetition of initial consonant sounds:

blackberries for breakfast
the stalks very prickly, a penalty
which I squeeze, squinch open, and splurge well

What examples of alliteration can you find in Kinnell's poem? If you overuse alliteration, it can take away from the meaning in your poem. But if you use it to emphasize important ideas, it can add a strong, musical element to your writing.

Prewriting

FINDING YOUR VOICE. A lyric poem usually represents the voice of the author, but it can also be the voice of another character. Whether you choose to use your personal voice or that of a fictional speaker, make the voice real and intense so the thoughts and emotions come alive. Since a lyric poem is highly musical, it gives you an opportunity to allow your voice to play with the language through word choice, sound, rhythm, structure, tone, and style.

IDENTIFYING YOUR AUDIENCE. Because a lyric poem expresses the personal thoughts and emotions of you, the author, you might be the most immediate audience for your own poem. Yet the musical nature of a lyric poem invites the poem to be read and shared out loud. Consider your classmates or others who would enjoy your subject as your audience, too.

BRAINSTORMING. Often, when writers describe a general state of being, they find that words like *surprised, confused, annoyed, jealous, sad,* and *happy* will do the job. But to create a more intense experience, you will need to go beyond these vague words and appeal to the reader's senses with specific details.

Pick a feeling and list sensory details for it. Copy the five senses onto your paper and write words and phrases under each that describe your feeling.

Sight: If you could see your word, what color would it be? What shape? What size? List words or phrases comparing your word to something you can see.

Taste: If you could taste your word, what would it taste like?

Touch: If you could touch your word, what would it feel like? What is its texture?

Smell: If you could smell your word, what would it smell like?

Sound: If you could hear your word, what would it sound like? How loud would it be?

Now think back on a moment when you felt your word. Maybe you were riding on a Ferris wheel with your best friend. The rain came and your friend started shrieking. You looked out at the city, through the downpour, wet and shaking, looked at your friend, and you suddenly realized you were glad. Maybe you remember a time you saw a woman pull a tattered wallet from her purse and there was something in that moment that made you feel melancholy.

Write what that moment was like, using descriptions and comparisons that appeal to one or more of the five senses.

WRITING WITH A PLAN. The power of poetry is in its concentrated language. That means explanations and descriptions are condensed into a few words or phrases. For example, in his poem "Blackberry Eating," Galway Kinnell could have said:

> The stalks of blackberries
> are very prickly because
> that's the price they pay
> for being able to do
> something as mysterious
> and amazing as the art of
> making blackberries.

But this explanation lacks the power of Kinnell's concentrated language:

> the stalks very prickly, a
>   penalty
> they earn for knowing the
>   black art
> of blackberry-making...

One way to condense language is to make comparisons, because comparisons offer a quick way to communicate a lot of information. A **simile** is a comparison using *like* or *as*. When you say, "The shortstop's double-play was like a dance," you are using a simile to compare one quality of a double-play to dancing. When you simply say, "The shortstop's double-play was a dance," you create a **metaphor**. A metaphor is a figure of speech in which one thing is spoken or written about as if it were another. In poetry, similes and metaphors are an essential way to communicate fresh and unusual connections in just a few words.

GUIDED WRITING **677**

Prewriting

FINDING YOUR VOICE. Review the definition of speaker with students. The speaker is the voice that speaks, or narrates, a poem. Encourage students to read the Language Arts Survey 2.5, "Finding Your Voice," and 3.3, "Register, Tone, and Voice." Ask students to identify the voice they intend on using and to write it on the same page as their graphic organizer.

IDENTIFYING YOUR AUDIENCE. Have students read the Language Arts Survey 2.4, "Identifying Your Audience." If you plan to have students read their poems to the class upon completion of the assignment, encourage students to think of their peers as their audience. However, to avoid possible self-censoring, which can happen if students worry how their thoughts will be perceived, you may want to give them the option of keeping intensely personal expression private.

BRAINSTORMING. Students might examine additional professional models to get ideas for their Sensory Details Chart. Have them read the Language Arts Survey 2.10, "Learning from Professional Models."

WRITING WITH A PLAN. If you haven't already done so, point out the simile in the Professional Model. Students might benefit from doing a focused freewrite about their selected feeling word and moment when they felt their word. Have students read the Language Arts Survey 2.12, "Freewriting."

INDIVIDUAL LEARNING STRATEGIES

MOTIVATION
Introduce students to The American Academy of Poets Web site at http://www.poets.org. Select a lyric poem in the Listening Booth that you think students will like. Have students listen to the poet read his or her poem while they read along. Then ask students to identify characteristics that make the poem lyrical.

READING PROFICIENCY
Have students read the Language Arts Survey 1.5, "Keeping a Reader's Journal." Ask students to record their reactions to the poem they listened to in Motivation above

INDIVIDUAL LEARNING STRATEGIES (CONT.)

and to the Professional Model. Encourage students to read the Professional Model and Student Model out loud to get a sense of how the language sounds as they work through the lesson. Refer them to the Language Arts Survey 1.6, "Reading Silently versus Reading Out Loud."

ENGLISH LANGUAGE LEARNING
See strategies for Reading Proficiency above that will also benefit students who are English language learners. You might want non-native speakers to bring in a poem in their native language and write a reader's journal entry about it. English language
(Continued on page 679)

Language, Grammar, and Style

Pronoun/Antecendent Agreement

LESSON OVERVIEW

In this lesson, students will be asked to do the following:

- Identify Pronoun/Antecedent Agreement, 678
- Fix Pronoun/Antecedent Agreement, 679
- Use Pronoun/Antecedent Agreement, 680

INTRODUCING THE SKILL. Point out that making pronouns and antecedents agree is something that even adults have to think about. Tell students that readers get confused when the pronoun does not agree with its antecedent. You might need to define "antecedent" for students; the antecedent is the noun that the pronoun references. Tell students that number refers to singular and plural.

PREVIEWING THE SKILL. Refer students to the Language Arts Survey 3.43, "Getting Pronouns and Antecedents to Agree." Have students identify a problem with pronoun/antecedent agreement in the Student Model—Draft.

PRACTICING THE SKILL. For additional practice, have students work through the exercise in the following section of the Language, Grammar, and Style Resource located in the Teacher's Resource Kit: 3.43, "Getting Pronouns and Antecedents to Agree."

"Be proud of your written work. Dot the i's and cross the t's. Neatness grows from dotted i's and crossed t's into beautiful pages."

—William Armstrong

 **Language, Grammar, and Style**

IDENTIFYING PRONOUN/ANTEDEDENT AGREEMENT. Pronouns must always agree with their antecedents. That means pronouns must have the same gender and number as the word or words to which they refer.

GENDER AGREEMENT

- When the antecedent is masculine, the pronoun is masculine:

  <u>Jim</u> got <u>his</u> license today.

- When the antecedent is feminine, the pronoun is feminine:

  The <u>girl</u> found <u>her</u> cat.

- When the antecedent is neutral, use the pronouns *it* or *its*.

  One <u>fish</u> had lost <u>its</u> fin.

- When the antecedent is a word that could stand for both men and women, the masculine pronoun or both the masculine and feminine pronoun can be used:

Aaron, whose word was *contentment* wrote, "Walking in the woods near my home on a hot summer day, through dappled light and sword ferns, the air smells blue." His sentence contains specific images the reader can see. There is also a metaphor comparing the woods to a "blue smell."

Jamel chose *loneliness*. He wrote, "Metallic clouds hung over the November day as I sat alone." Jamel uses a metaphor comparing the clouds to metal. This comparison suggests the qualities of something hard, flat and grey, like loneliness.

Sara chose "baffled" as her feeling and used the graphic organizer below for her prewriting.

Student Model—Graphic Organizer

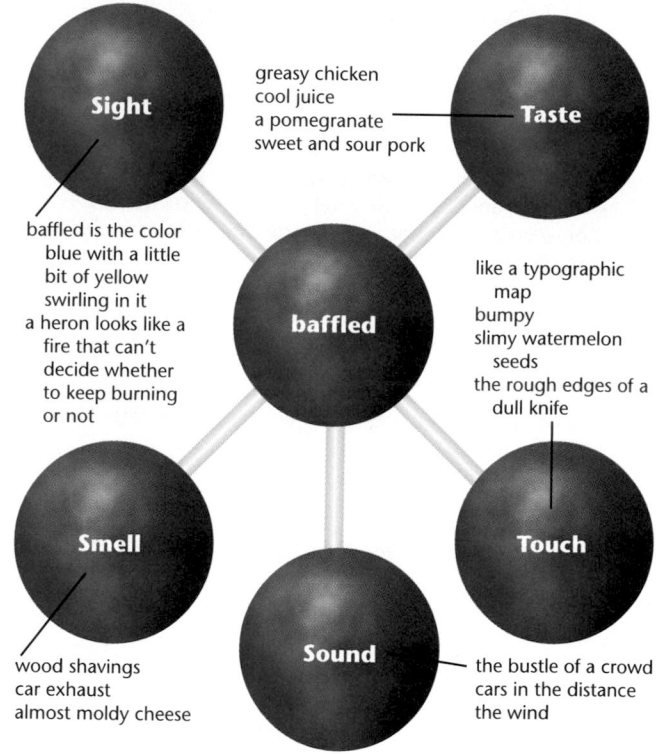

- **Sight**
- **Taste** — greasy chicken, cool juice, a pomegranate, sweet and sour pork
- **baffled**
- Touch — like a typographic map, bumpy, slimy watermelon seeds, the rough edges of a dull knife
- baffled is the color blue with a little bit of yellow swirling in it, a heron looks like a fire that can't decide whether to keep burning or not
- **Smell** — wood shavings, car exhaust, almost moldy cheese
- **Sound** — the bustle of a crowd, cars in the distance, the wind

Drafting

The beginning of a poem is hidden in your prewriting—all you have to do is find it. You can use the sentence or sentences you just wrote to begin your poem or you can think of another time when you experienced your word.

Drafting

Tell students to use their completed Graphic Organizer modeled on page 678. Have students write a discovery draft in which they do not focus on spelling, grammar, usage, and mechanics. Students might benefit from reading the Language Arts Survey 2.31, "Drafting." Point out to students that in writing their poem they are doing descriptive writing. Students might read the Language Arts Survey 2.36, "Writing Description, Dialogue, Narrative, and Exposition."

Whatever moment you pick for your word, you will find many descriptive words and comparisons from your prewriting that you can use in your poem. You will also think of others as you write your first draft.

In every line, put strong images that appeal to the sense of sight, sound, smell, taste, and touch. Expand on some of your metaphors. Instead of saying, "I felt purple," you could say, "I felt purple the way a person feels when he comes home at night and finds nobody there."

Don't focus on line breaks or rhythm at this point. Concentrate on showing your reader what that moment felt like without naming your word. Let your images show the reader what you mean.

Self- and Peer Evaluation

After you have a rough draft of your poem, read it aloud several times. This helps you hear the music of the lines. If you can, get someone else to read it aloud as well. See the Language Arts Survey 2.37 for more details about self- and peer evaluation. As you evaluate your poem, ask yourself these questions:

- What is the moment described in the lyric poem?
- What feelings or thoughts are expressed in the poem? What words communicate this feeling?
- Find images that appeal to the senses. Which images are the strongest? Which are the weakest? Why?
- Which lines or phrases sound musical? Which are lacking in lyrical sound or rhythm? How could these lines be improved?
- Where might the rhythm or meaning benefit from a breaking the line?
- Where has the writer used repetition of sound to emphasize meaning? Where else could the writer repeat sounds or rhythms to emphasize meaning?
- Find any places where the pronoun does not match the antecedent. What word or line changes will fix this problem?

Student Model—Draft

Sarah drafted a poem from her prewriting about a time when she looked at a bird and wondered why things are the way they are. Note that she never used the word *baffled*. Instead, she let her descriptive images and metaphors explain her thoughts.

Based on her self-evaluation comments and comments from one of her classmates, Sarah made changes to her poem.

agreement?

A heron, like all birds, cocks ~~their~~ *its* — Adding a line break would emphasize your thoughts

heads to one side and ‖ I wonder

<u>Anybody</u> who wants to bring <u>his</u> or <u>her</u> own chairs may do so.

<u>Someone</u> lost <u>his</u> jacket after the game.

NUMBER AGREEMENT

- When the antecedent is *plural*, use plural pronouns to refer to it:

<u>Several</u> of the students had to share <u>their</u> books.

- The pronouns *any, some, all,* and *none* may be either singular or plural, depending on how they are used.

Singular: <u>All</u> of the page was marked in <u>its</u> margins.

Plural: <u>All</u> of the riders wore <u>their</u> helmets.

- When an antecedent is singular, no matter if it is followed by a prepositional phrase containing a plural noun, use a singular pronoun:

<u>Everyone</u> in the women's quartets received <u>her</u> letter.

- When two or more singular antecedents are connected by *or* or *nor*, they should be referred to by a singular pronoun:

<u>Neither</u> Sam, Jack, nor Ed has finished <u>his</u> pizza.

FIXING PRONOUN/ANTECEDENT AGREEMENT. Finding and fixing pronoun-antecedent problems in sentences requires that you find the antecedent first and then

continued on page 680

Self- and Peer Evaluation

Have students use the checklist on page 679 for self- and peer evaluation. See the Guided Writing Resource 7.9 located in the Teacher's Resource Kit for a blackline master of the self- and peer evaluation checklist. The checklist is intended to act as a student-friendly rubric that should help students identify specific evidence of writing strengths and areas needing improvement. Make sure students provide concrete suggestions for improvement or specific evidence of the effectiveness of the lyric poem. It might help students to evaluate their peer's poem by reading it out loud. Peer evaluators might be interested in using common proofreader's symbols, which are found in the Language Arts Survey 2.44, "Using Proofreader's Marks."

Teaching Note

Have students compare the Student Model—Draft on page 679 with the final version presented on page 681. Ask students to respond to the following questions: What improvements did Sarah make in her poem? Is there any way the final version could still be improved?

Bibliographic Note

You may be interested in consulting the following works for more ideas about teaching students how to write poetry:

Lehman, David, ed. *Ecstatic Occasions, Expedient Forms: 85 Leading Contemporary Poets Select & Comment on Their Poems.* Ann Arbor: University of Michigan Press.

Oliver, Mary. *A Poetry Handbook.* New York: Harcourt, Brace, & Co.

Padgett, Ron, ed. *Handbook of Poetic Forms.* New York: Teachers & Writers Collaborative.

Tsujimoto, Joseph I. *Teaching Poetry Writing to Adolescents.* NCTE/ERIC.

INDIVIDUAL LEARNING STRATEGIES (CONT.)

learners may need special help understanding the use of figurative language used in poetry, such as the simile used in the Professional Model. These students might be persuaded to share a poem with the class in their native language.

SPECIAL NEEDS

Students with special needs may need help completing their Graphic Organizer. Pair them with a proficient student who can help them work through the cluster chart on page 678.

ENRICHMENT

You might have students find a published poem that centers on one feeling. Have students fill out a Sensory Details Chart to identify the descriptive details used in the poem. Students may wish to work their own poems collaboratively into a performance piece or to prepare their work for publication.

Revising and Proofreading

Remind students that revising includes adding or expanding, cutting or condensing, replacing, and moving text. Have students read the Language Arts Survey 2.41, "Revising." A handout of the proofreading checklist found in the Language Arts Survey on 888 is available in the Teacher's Resource Kit, Guided Writing Resource 2.45.

track down the pronoun referring to it. In poetry, this might mean you have to backtrack through several lines of poetry before you find the antecedent. Then check if they agree in gender and number.

Consider the following sentences. Which pronouns are correct and which need changing?

Nobody expected to find his or her books at the mall.

One of the people at the dance left their coat.

Mary or June will use their own phone to call you back.

Find the pronoun-antecedent problem in Sarah's first draft of her poem. How would you fix it? In poetry, a writer may choose to attach gender qualities to animals and objects. To fix the pronoun-antecedent problem in her poem, Sara could use *it* because *heron* is a neutral word or she could use *he* or *she* to be more personal.

USING PRONOUN/ANTECEDENT AGREEMENT. Read through your poem draft searching for pronouns. Underline them. Now scan backward looking for the words to which they refer. Circle these. Do the pronouns and antecedents agree in gender and number? Correct any problems so that your reader will be able to follow your poem without being confused by disagreement between pronouns and their antecedents.

680   UNIT NINE

Why does a bird fly or does anything

happen at all?

My questions are the sound of a crowd,

a hustle and bustle ———————— good rhythm

the rough edges of a dull knife

~~like~~ the smell of wood shavings mixed

~~with~~ exhaust and ~~like~~ almost-moldy smooth   *this is wordy and not very*

cheese   *slow this down by adding line breaks*   *good alliteration!*

~~sweet~~ and ~~sour~~ ~~pork~~,‖ a pomegranate over   *this would make a good ending*

ripe,

confused‖a fire‖fading   *I like the way you mixed up so many images—They are like your questions—mixed up and confused*

Revising and Proofreading

Based on your self- and peer evaluations, make changes to your draft. Add details, delete extra words, and play with line breaks. What happens when you put a word at the end of a line? Does the word become more or less noticeable? What about the sound of your poem? Trust your ear to tell you when you need a shorter word or a longer line. Change words to fit a rhythm that matches your meaning.

Before you print your final copy, read over your draft for errors in spelling, punctuation, and grammar. In poetry, you are often dealing with lines instead of sentences, so capitalization and punctuation become a matter of choice. However you decide to capitalize or punctuate, stick to a pattern from start to finish so that your format is clear to the reader.

Student Model—Revised

After listening to her poem many times and playing with the language until she was satisfied that the words, sounds, and rhythm in her poem reflected her thoughts, Sarah completed her final draft.

Baffled

A heron cocks his head to one side and
I wonder
Why does a bird fly?
Why does anything happen at all?
My questions are the sound of a crowd,
a hustle and bustle
the rough edges of a dull knife
the smell of wood shavings, exhaust, or
almost-moldy cheese
sweet and sour pork,
a pomegranate
over ripe,
confused
a fire
fading

> A poem must be felt
> to be understood,
> and before it can be
> felt it must be heard.
>
> —*Stanley Kunitz*

> For me poems usually
> begin with "true
> things"—people,
> experiences,
> quotes—but quickly
> ride off into that
> other territory of
> imagination...
>
> —*Naomi Shihab Nye*

Publishing and Presenting

Poetry is best when shared either out loud or as a printed piece of art. To share your poetry out loud, consider reading to a small group of students. Or consider an audio or videotape reading that could be shared over an audio or audiovisual resource at your school. To publish your poem as a work of art, create a small poster by printing the poem in a way that suggests the content and the feeling of the poem. Add art, designs, or colors that also draw out the ideas in the poem. You may want to publish your poem in the school newspaper or literary supplement or to share it.

Reflecting

Poetry asks you to look at and think about things in a unique way. Simile, metaphor, imagery, rhythm, and sound become thinking, viewing, and listening tools for communicating thoughts and emotions. The use of some of these tools may come easily; the use of others may require you to expand your thinking.

How might your thinking develop as you employ simile and metaphor in your thoughts and writing? What growth might occur from focusing on imagery? How might considering the sound and rhythm of your language increase the value of your communication?

As you are speak and write, try little experiments using simile, metaphor, imagery, rhythm, and sound. Then reflect on the changes you see in your communication and the effect these changes have on others.

Publishing and Presenting

You might have students present their poems to the class. Encourage students to practice the poem using the volume, pitch, gestures, and facial expressions they feel best express the meaning of their poem. Some students might want to memorize their poem. Refer students to the Language Arts Survey 4.19, "Oral Interpretation of Poetry." You might suggest that writers of the best poems submit them to a review for publication.

Reflecting

Encourage students to respond to the questions in this section in their journal or to discuss the questions in small groups.

Reflecting on Your Reading

The Genre and Theme questions are suitable to assign as essay prompts to help students prepare for the Unit Test. (To evaluate student writing, see the evaluation forms for writing, revising, and proofreading in the Assessment Resource 4.1–4.9.)

The Genre and Theme questions can also be adapted for use as topics for oral reports or debates. Refer students to the Language Arts Survey 4, Speaking and Listening. (To evaluate these projects, use the Public Speaking Evaluation Form in the Assessment Resource 4.11.)

VOCABULARY DEVELOPMENT. Give students the following exercise.

Write a poem that incororates ten words form the list on page 682. Then, with a partner, practice reading your poems aloud, paying attention to the corrrect pronunciation of the new vocabulary words.

ADDITIONAL RESOURCES

UNIT 9 RESOURCE BOOK
- Vocabulary Worksheet
- Study Guide: Unit 9 Test
- Unit 9 Test

UNIT NINE *review*

Words for Everyday Use

Check your knowledge of the following vocabulary words. Choose ten words that you would like to add to your everyday vocabulary. For each, write a short sentence that includes that word in context. To review a word, look back to the page number indicated.

- benign (631)
- blunder (657)
- clod (651)
- concede (614)
- crevice (665)
- dismay (657)

- extraneous (621)
- high-strung (621)
- insistent (614)
- luminous (626)
- peril (631)
- plunge (658)

- reel (658)
- saucy (621)
- sunder (658)
- translucency (621)
- wariness (614)

Literary Tools

Define each of the following terms, giving concrete examples when possible. To review a term, refer to the page number or page numbers indicated.

- aim (650)
- alliteration (630, 634)
- assonance (630)
- assonance (650)
- dialogue (645)
- figure of speech (613)
- figure of speech (664)
- flashback (650)
- free verse (613)
- haiku (669)

- image (613, 619)
- imagery (613, 619, 625, 669)
- irony (619)
- lyric poem (661, 664)
- metaphor (664)
- narrative poem (656)
- onomatopoeia (634)
- personification (619)
- personification (664)

- repetition (638)
- repetition (656)
- rhyme (638)
- rhythm (630)
- shape (625)
- simile (664)
- suspense (656)
- symbol (645, 661)

Reflecting on your *reading*

Genre

The selections in this unit give you a broad overview of the different forms poetry can take and of the different tools poets use to create certain effects. Look back at the poems in the unit. Which poem or poems do you like the best? What poetic tools do you find most effective? For example, do you appreciate rhyme and rhythm more than other aspects of poetry? Do you like free verse best? Write a brief essay about your favorite poems and why you like them.

Theme

The poems in this unit all highlight unique ideas and all have very different themes. Choose two poems from the unit and reflect on their themes. Begin by asking yourself the following questions:

- What is the poem about? What is its topic or subject?
- How does the title of the poem reflect its subject matter? How does it reflect a main idea, or theme?
- What does the poem say or imply about the subject or topic?

On Your Own

Design a poster for your classroom or hallway, using one of the poems from this unit. Include on the poster the poem written out, the title and name of the author, and images that you feel complement the poem. You may want to use photographs, textures, painting, drawing, or other mediums to create the effect you want.

Group Project

Hold a classroom poetry reading, with each member of your class participating. Each student may choose a poem to recite to the class. To select a poem, you may choose one from this unit, from a book you have at home, or from a library book. Ask the librarian in your school or local library for help if needed. After you have selected your poem, read it aloud several times to learn it well. Then, work on your interpretation of the poem. Rehearse your reading, concentrating on volume, pace, emotion, voice, and body language. For more information, see the Language Arts Survey 4.19, "Oral Interpretation of Poetry."

The Group Project activity can also serve provide an additional or alternate assessment to the Unit 5 Test. Ask students to tie in the insights they have gained from their research to the literature selections they have read in this unit. (To evaluate group and project work, see the evaluation forms in the Assessment Resource 4.10–4.12.)

GOALS/OBJECTIVES

Studying this unit will enable students to
• appreciate a dramatic work about Helen Keller and Annie Sullivan
• define and identify techniques in drama, including *flashback, suspense, stage directions, conflict, resolution, simile, metaphor,* and *characterization*

• engage in a meaningful independent reading experience by reading a collection of short plays and performing them
• write a movie or play review
• recognize dangling and misplaced modifiers and demonstrate an ability to use modifiers correctly

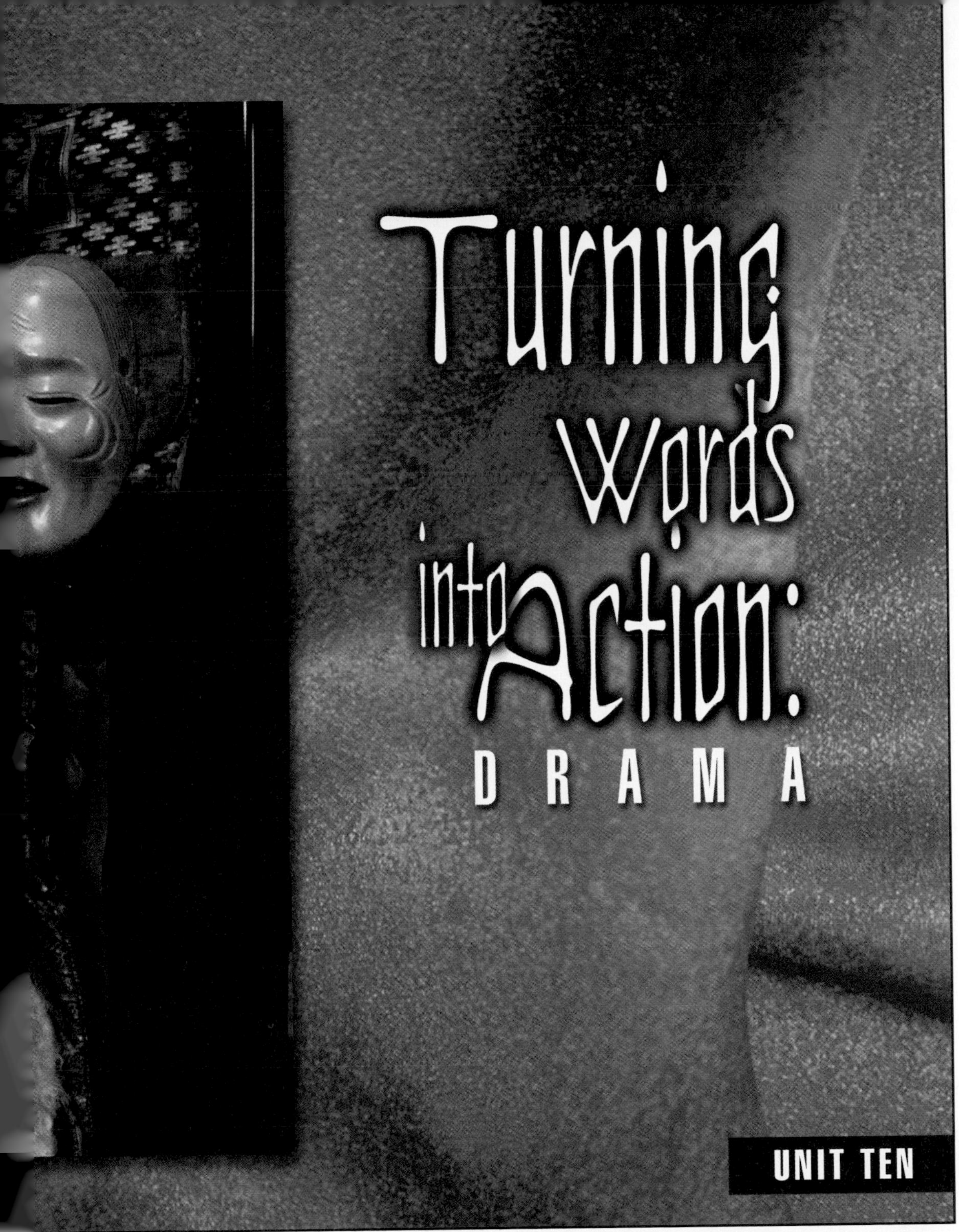

Turning Words into Action: DRAMA

UNIT TEN

TEACHING THE MULTIPLE INTELLIGENCES (CONT.)

Identifying the Miracles in the Story, 750
Inability to Communicate, 688
Oral Reading, 688
Researching the Life of a Social Reformer, 726
Structure of a Play, 689
Volunteering to Help the Blind, 738

CROSS-CURRICULAR CONNECTIONS

Arts and Humanities
Autobiography of Helen Keller, 689
Discussing a Photograph, 723
Discussing Foil, 729
The Miracle Worker Film, 688

Mathematics and Sciences
Causes of Infant Blindness, 690
Guide Dogs for the Blind, 740

Social Studies
Advances in Teaching the Deaf, 718
American Foundation for the Blind, 728
Black Codes, 699
Diseases in the 1880s Oral Report, 690
Education for the Blind, 694
Helen Keller and Equal Rights, 735
Late-Nineteenth-Century Attitudes toward Women, 725
Laws against Corporal Punishment, 717
Life Story of Helen Keller, 746
Life Story of Lon Chaney, 708
Nineteenth-Century Asylums, 693
Other Works of William Gibson, 743
Poorhouses, 697
Prejudices and Unfavorable Terms, 712
Researching the Life of a Social Reformer, 726
The Keller Homestead, 689
Ulysses S. Grant, 714
Working Women in the Nineteenth Century, 701

TEACHING THE MULTIPLE INTELLIGENCES

Logical-Mathematical
Diseases in the 1880s Oral Report, 690

Spatial
Discussing a Photograph, 723
Volunteering to Help the Blind, 738

Kinesthetic
Inability to Communicate, 688
Volunteering to Help the Blind, 738

Interpersonal
American Foundation for the Blind, 728
Diseases in the 1880s Oral Report, 690
Education for the Blind, 694
Guide Dogs for the Blind, 740

Foster students' interest in drama by accessing the following Internet sites:

• **The Dramatic Exchange** at http://www.dramex.org gives students a glimpse of how amateur playwrights can post their own plays on the Internet or find interesting new works to browse and use. This site will appeal to young playwrights, actors, and anyone else interested in theater.

• Teachers can explore ways to bring theater study into their classroom by visiting the **Theatre Education Literature Review** at http://www.aaae.org/theatre/thfront.html.

READER'S TOOLBOX

Responses will vary. Possible responses are given. Note that examples that students may choose are too numerous to be listed. Some examples from the first act of the play are provided. Direct description includes: "The third child is Helen, six and a half years old, quite unkempt, in body a vivacious little person with a fine head, attractive, but noticeably blind, with one eye larger and protruding; her gestures are abrupt, insistent, lacking in human restraint, and her face never smiles." Students may point to the following examples of portraying a character's behavior for Helen: "Helen's hands thrust at their faces in turn, feeling baffledly at the movements of their lips"; "Helen commences to go around, from person to person, tapping for eyes, but no one attends or understands"; "Helen suddenly has come upon the cradle, and unhesitatingly overturns it; the swaddled baby tumbles out." Students may point to the following examples of presenting the thoughts and emotions of Helen: "Helen is scowling, the lips under her fingertips moving in ghostly silence, growing more and more frantic, until in a bizarre rage she bites at her own fingers"; "Helen now has the doll with eyes, and cannot contain herself for joy; she rocks the doll, pats it vigorously, kisses it."

For the character of Annie, students may include this example of direct description: "The chair contains a girl of 20, Annie Sullivan, with a face which in repose is grave and rather obstinate, and when active is impudent, combative, twinkling with all the life that is lacking in Helen's."

ELEMENTS *of* DRAMA

A **drama**, or **play**, is a story told through characters played by actors. Early groups of people around the world enacted ritual scenes related to hunting, warfare, or religion. From these drama arose. Western drama as we know it first began in ancient Greece.

THE PLAYWRIGHT AND THE SCRIPT. The author of a play is the **playwright.** A playwright has limited control in deciding how his or her work is presented. Producers, directors, set designers, and actors all interpret a playwright's work and present their interpretations to the audience.

A **script** is the written text from which a drama is produced. Scripts are made up of stage directions and dialogue. Scripts may be divided into long parts called acts and short parts called scenes.

Stage directions are notes included in a play to describe how something should look, sound, or be performed. Stage directions can describe lighting, costumes, music, sound effects, or other elements of a play. They can also describe entrances and exits, gestures, tone of voice, or other elements related to the acting of a play. Stage directions sometimes provide historical or background information. In stage directions, the parts of the stage are described from the actors' point of view, as shown on the diagram below. As you read the play *The Miracle Worker*, pay attention to the suggestions the playwright has given for the set, the lighting, and props. Also notice the important role that stage directions have throughout this play.

Up Right	Up Center	Up Left
Right Center	Center	Left Center
Down Right	Down Center	Down Left

The speech of the actors in a play is called **dialogue.** A speech given by one character is called a **monologue.** In a play, dialogue appears after the names of characters.

An **act** is a major part of a play. One-act, three-act, and five-act plays are all common. A **scene** is a short section of a literary work, one that happens in a single place and time. There may be any number of scenes in eact act, and the number of scenes may vary from act to act.

THE SPECTACLE. The **spectacle** includes all the elements of the drama that are presented to the audience's senses. The set, props, special effects, lighting, and costumes are part of the spectacle.

READER'S TOOLBOX (CONT.)

Students may point to the following examples of portraying a character's behavior for Annie: "Annie opens the small box he extends, and sees a garnet ring. She looks up, blinking, and down"; "Annie tries to make ladylike small talk, though her energy now and then erupts; she catches herself whenever she hears it."

Students may point to the following examples of presenting the thoughts and emotions of Annie: "Kate is studying her face . . . this is a mutual appraisal . . . and Annie is not quite comfortable under it"; "Annie is amused and talks to her as one might to a kitten"; and "Note she is furious herself."

Prereading

The Miracle Worker by William Gibson

Reader's Resource

- Helen Keller was born June 27, 1880, in Tuscumbia, Alabama. When she was 19 months old, an illness left her blind and deaf. Helen's parents sought the help of Samuel Howe, who had been successful teaching a blind and deaf girl. Kate, Helen's mother, also sought the help of hearing specialist Alexander Graham Bell, who recommended his son-in-law Michael Anagnos. Anagnos was the director of the Perkins Institution for the Blind in Boston. He chose Annie Sullivan to serve as Helen's teacher.

- Annie Sullivan was born in Feeding Hills, Massachusetts. Disease left her nearly blind at age five. After her mother died and she was abandoned by her father, Annie and her brother Jimmie were sent to the state almshouse, or poorhouse, in Tewksbury. Annie was haunted by Jimmie's death, which occurred months after their arrival. Anne partially regained her sight after an operation in 1881. She graduated as valedictorian of her class from Perkins. She had never taught before she was hired to teach Helen Keller.

- Helen and Annie are the main characters in *The Miracle Worker*. Other characters include:
  —Captain Keller, Helen's father, a newspaper publisher and former Confederate Army captain
  —Kate Keller, Helen's mother
  —James, Keller's son and Helen's half-brother
  —Percy, a servant boy
  —Martha, a servant girl
  —Aunt Ev, Keller's sister
  —Anagnos, head of the Perkins School who sends Annie to the Kellers
  —Viney, servant at the Kellers' house
  —students at the Perkins School
  —the doctor who tended to Helen during her illness

Reader's Journal

How do you feel when you are unable to communicate with or express yourself to other people?

Reader's TOOLBOX

- **CHARACTERIZATION.** **Characterization** is the act of creating or describing a character.

- **SUSPENSE. Suspense** is a feeling of anxiousness or curiosity. Writers create suspense by raising questions in the reader's mind and by using details that create strong emotions.

- **STAGE DIRECTIONS. Stage directions** are notes included in a play to describe how something should look, sound, or be performed.

- **FLASHBACK. A flashback** is a part of a story, poem, or play that presents events that happened at an earlier time.

- **CONFLICT AND RESOLUTION.** A **conflict** is a struggle between two people or things in a literary work.

- **SIMILE AND METAPHOR.** A **simile** is a comparison using *like* or *as*. A **metaphor** is a figure of speech in which one thing is spoken or written about as if it were another. These figures of speech invite the reader to make a comparison between the two things.

THE MIRACLE WORKER **687**

ADDITIONAL RESOURCES

UNIT 10 RESOURCE BOOK
- Selection Worksheet 10.1
- Selection Check Test 4.10.1
- Selection Test 4.10.2

Answers to Reader's Toolbox appear on page 686.

VOCABULARY FROM THE SELECTION—ACT 1

benign	inexorable
commence	obstinate
emphatic	placate
facetious	precocious
frantic	steel
impudence	unencumbered
indolent	vitality
indulgent	vivacious

READER'S JOURNAL

If students cannot think of such a time on their own, give them the following prompts: Has there ever been a time when you were trying to speak to someone who spoke no English and so you were unable to communicate? Has there ever been a time when you were too upset or too emotional to explain yourself? Write about how you felt when you were unable to make yourself understood.

GOALS/OBJECTIVES

Studying this lesson will enable students to
- appreciate a play about the education of a deaf and blind girl
- briefly explain who Helen Keller and Annie Sullivan were
- define *characterization* and identify places where the three major techniques of characterization are used in a drama
- define *suspense* and recognize how an author builds suspense in a drama
- define *dialect* and recognize dialect in a drama
- define *stage directions* and point to examples of stage directions in a play
- define *flashback* and poibt to flashbacks in a drama
- define *conflict* and *resolution* and identify these in a drama
- define and recognize *similes* in a play
- prepare a dramatic presentation
- use sign language to spell out a few words

MOTIVATION
Students might enjoy seeing the film version of *The Miracle Worker* (1962) before they begin reading. Patty Duke won an Oscar for her role as Helen Keller, while Anne Bancroft won an Oscar for her portrayal of Annie Sullivan. After students have seen the movie, ask them to discuss the performance and whether they think it was Oscar-worthy.

READING PROFICIENCY
Consider reading this entire play aloud over several days' time. Assign students speaking roles at the beginning of each class and assign one student to narrate the stage directions. (Only the longer explanatory stage directions need be narrated.) As the play is read aloud, the rest of the students should listen and follow along in their textbooks. All students should be given a chance to read lines aloud. After each class period, have students reread the act that they read aloud in class that day. As they reread this part of the play, they should respond to the Guided Reading questions.

ENGLISH LANGUAGE LEARNING
Share with students the following information about the way that plays are structured on paper: Plays are composed of dialogue, or speech, and stage directions, which are the author's instructions about how characters should look, move, and display emotion on stage. Stage directions are traditionally set in italic (slanted) type. Before the dialogue in a play, you will note that there is a name in boldface type. This name is not read aloud, and it is used so that the actors (and readers) know who is delivering each line on stage.

SPECIAL NEEDS
Students may benefit from seeing a version of the play performed before they read it. Otherwise, they may have a hard time making sense of the action and characters from stage directions and dialogue. Tell students to focus on responding to the Guided Reading questions and the Recall questions in the Investigate, Inquire, and Imagine sections as they read.

The *Miracle* Worker

CHARACTERS

A DOCTOR

KATE

KELLER

HELEN

MARTHA

PERCY

AUNT EV

JAMES

ANAGNOS

ANNIE SULLIVAN

BLIND GIRLS

A SERVANT

OFFSTAGE VOICES

A PLAY IN THREE ACTS

"At another time she asked, What is a soul?, 'No one knows,' I replied; 'but we know it is not the body, and it is that part of us which thinks and loves and hopes.... [and] is invisible....' 'But if I write what my soul thinks,' she said, 'then it will be visible, and the words will be its body.' "
—ANNIE SULLIVAN, 1891

THE PLAYING SPACE *is divided into two areas by a more or less diagonal line, which runs from downstage right to upstage left.*

THE AREA *behind this diagonal is on platforms and represents the Keller house; inside we see, down right, a family room, and up center, elevated, a bedroom. On stage level near center, outside a porch, there is a water pump.*

THE OTHER AREA, *in front of the diagonal, is neutral ground; it accommodates various places as designated at various times—the yard before the Keller home, the Perkins Institution for the Blind, the garden house, and so forth.*

THE CONVENTION OF THE STAGING *is one of cutting through time and place, and its essential qualities are fluidity and spatial counterpoint.[1] To this end, the less set there is, the better; in a literal set, the fluidity will seem merely episodic. The stage therefore should be free, airy, underlined by walls. Apart from certain practical items such as the pump, a window to climb out of, doors to be locked—locales should be only skeletal suggestions, and the movement from one to another should be accomplishable by little more than lights.*

---

1. **counterpoint.** Use of contrast

ENRICHMENT
Interested students might enjoy reading Helen Keller's *The Story of My Life* (1903). Students should then write a brief book report, telling

what they learned about Helen Keller and explaining whether they would recommend this book to their classmates.

TIME: *The 1880s.*

PLACE: *In and around the Keller homestead in Tuscumbia, Alabama; also, briefly, the Perkins Institution for the Blind, in Boston*

ACT I

IT IS NIGHT OVER THE KELLER HOMESTEAD.

Inside, three adults in the bedroom are grouped around a crib, in lamplight. They have been through a long vigil,[2] and it shows in their tired bearing and disarranged clothing. One is a young gentlewoman with a sweet girlish face, KATE KELLER; the second is an elderly DOCTOR, stethoscope at neck, thermometer in fingers; the third is a hearty gentleman in his forties with chin whiskers, CAPTAIN ARTHUR KELLER.

DOCTOR: She'll live.

KATE: Thank God.

[The DOCTOR leaves them together over the crib, packs his bag.]

DOCTOR: You're a pair of lucky parents. I can tell you now, I thought she wouldn't.

KELLER: Nonsense, the child's a Keller, she has the constitution[3] of a goat. She'll outlive us all.

DOCTOR [AMIABLY]: Yes, especially if some of you Kellers don't get a night's sleep. I mean you, Mrs. Keller.

KELLER: You hear, Katie?

KATE: I hear.

KELLER: [INDULGENT] I've brought up two of them, but this is my wife's first, she isn't battle-scarred yet.

KATE: Doctor, don't be merely considerate, will my girl be all right?

DOCTOR: Oh, by morning she'll be knocking down Captain Keller's fences again.

KATE: And isn't there anything we should do?

KELLER [JOVIAL]: Put up stronger fencing, ha?

DOCTOR: Just let her get well, she knows how to do it better than we do.

[He is packed, ready to leave.]

Main thing is the fever's gone, these things come and go in infants, never know why. Call it acute congestion of the stomach and brain.

KELLER: I'll see you to your buggy, Doctor.

DOCTOR: I've never seen a baby, more vitality, that's the truth.

[He beams a good night at the baby and KATE, and KELLER leads him downstairs with a lamp. They go down the porch steps, and across the yard, where the DOCTOR goes off left; KELLER stands with the lamp aloft. KATE meanwhile is bent lovingly over the crib, which emits a bleat; her finger is playful with the baby's face.]

KATE: Hush. Don't you cry now, you've been trouble enough. Call it acute congestion, indeed, I don't see what's so cute about a congestion, just because it's yours. We'll have your father run an editorial in his paper, the wonders of modern medicine, they don't know what they're curing even when they cure it. Men, men and their battle scars, we women will have to—

[But she breaks off, puzzled, moves her finger before the baby's eyes.]

---

2. **vigil.** Night watch, especially with the sick
3. **constitution.** Physical makeup

---

words for everyday use

un·en·cum·bered (ən in kəm' bərd) *adj.,* free of impediments. *Lucy left her suitcases at the hotel so she could explore the city unencumbered by their weight.*

in·dul·gent (in dəl' jənt) *adj.,* extremely considerate of another's desires, feelings or overly generous. *Uncle Mickey is indulgent, but Aunt Louise is very strict.*

vi·tal·i·ty (vī ta' lə tē) *n.,* life, liveliness. *At eighty, Norma's vitality matches that of people half her age.*

1. Kate is trying to determine whether the baby can hear.
2. Helen is noticeably blind. She thrusts her hands at the faces of the other children, feeling their mouths move as they talk.

CROSS-CURRICULAR ACTIVITIES

MATHEMATICS AND SCIENCES. Infant blindness can be caused by a number of factors, such as malnutrition, infection by parasites, or disease. Even a disease in a mother can cause blindness in an unborn child; for example, children born to mothers who have had German measles while pregnant are prone to blindness. Inform students that medicine in the 1880s was not as advanced as it is today. Have students form pairs and research diseases that were far more common in the 1880s than they are now. Possibilities include polio, tuberculosis (although that is making a resurgence in some urban areas), and measles. Other students might like to research the state of medicine in the 1880s to discover what medicines, tools, and knowledge doctors had at their disposal. Each pair of students might use encyclopedias, books on history, books on medicine, and Internet resources for their sources. Each pair should document the sources they use, and then prepare and practice an oral report for their classmates. Each pair should present a list of their sources to you after they deliver their oral report.

Will have to—Helen?

[*Now she moves her hand, quickly.*]

Helen.

[*She snaps her fingers at the baby's eyes twice, and her hand falters; after a moment she calls out, loudly.*]

Captain. Captain, will you come—

[*But she stares at the baby, and her next call is directly at her ears.*]

Captain!

[*And now, still staring, KATE screams. KELLER in the yard hears it, and runs with the lamp back to the house. KATE screams again, her look intent on the baby and terrible. KELLER hurries in and up.*]

KELLER: Katie? What's wrong?

KATE: Look.

[*She makes a pass with her hand in the crib, at the baby's eyes.*]

KELLER: What, Katie? She's well, she needs only time to—

KATE: She can't see. Look at her eyes.

[*She takes the lamp from him, moves it before the child's face.*]

She can't *see*!

KELLER [HOARSELY]: Helen.

KATE: Or hear. When I screamed she didn't blink. Not an eyelash—

KELLER: Helen. Helen!

KATE: She can't *hear* you!

KELLER: *Helen!*

[*His face has something like fury in it, crying the*

> **GUIDED READING**
> Why does Kate shout in the baby's ear?

child's name; KATE *almost fainting presses her knuckles to her mouth, to stop her own cry. The room dims out quickly.*

Time, in the form of a slow tune of distant belfry chimes which approaches in a crescendo and then fades, passes; the light comes up again on a day five years later, on three kneeling children and an old dog outside around the pump.

The dog is a setter named BELLE, *and she is sleeping. Two of the children are Negroes,* MARTHA *and* PERCY. *The third child is* HELEN, *six and a half years old, quite unkempt, in body a vivacious little person with a fine head, attractive, but noticeably blind, one eye larger and protruding; her gestures are abrupt, insistent, lacking in human restraint, and her face never smiles. She is flanked by the other two, in a litter of paper-doll cutouts, and while they speak* HELEN'S *hands thrust at their faces in turn, feeling baffledly at the movements of their lips.*]

> **GUIDED READING**
> What is noticeable about Helen? What does she do repeatedly?

MARTHA [SNIPPING]: First I'm gonna cut off this doctor's legs, one, two, now then—

PERCY: Why you cuttin' off that doctor's legs?

MARTHA: I'm gonna give him a operation. Now I'm gonna cut off his arms, one, two. Now I'm gonna fix up—

[*She pushes* HELEN'S *hand away from her mouth.*]

You stop that.

PERCY: Cut off his stomach, that's a good operation.

MARTHA: No, I'm gonna cut off his head first, he got a bad cold.

PERCY: Ain't gonna be much of that doctor left to fix up, time you finish all them opera—

> **words for everyday use**
> vi • va • cious (vī vā shəs) *adj.*, lively in temper or conduct. *The* <u>vivacious</u> *applicant got the job of greeting customers.*

[*But* HELEN *is poking her fingers inside his mouth, to feel his tongue; he bites at them, annoyed, and she jerks them away.* HELEN *now fingers her own lips, moving them in imitation, but soundlessly.*]

MARTHA: What you do, bite her hand?

PERCY: That's how I do, she keep pokin' her fingers in my mouth, I just bite 'em off.

MARTHA: What she tryin' do now?

PERCY: She tryin' *talk.*
She gonna get mad.
Looka her tryin' talk.

GUIDED READING
What is Helen trying to do?

[HELEN *is scowling, the lips under her fingertips moving in ghostly silence, growing more and more* frantic, *until in a bizarre rage she bites at her own fingers. This sends* PERCY *off into laughter, but alarms* MARTHA.]

MARTHA: Hey, you stop now.

[*She pulls* HELEN'S *hand down.*]

You just sit quiet and—

[*But at once* HELEN *topples* MARTHA *on her back, knees pinning her shoulders down, and grabs the scissors.* MARTHA *screams.* PERCY *darts to the bell string on the porch, yanks it, and the bell rings.*

Inside, the lights been gradually coming up on the main room, where we see the family informally gathered, talking, but in pantomime: KATE *sits darning socks near a cradle, occasionally rocking it;* CAPTAIN KELLER *in spectacles is working over newspaper pages at a table; a* benign *visitor in a hat,* AUNT EV, *is sharing the sewing basket, putting the finishing touches on a big shapeless doll made out of towels; an* indolent *young man,* JAMES KELLER, *is at the window watching the children.*

With the ring of the bell, KATE *is instantly on* her feet and out the door onto the porch, to take in the scene; now we see what these five years have done to her, the girlish playfulness is gone, she is a woman* steeled *in grief.*]

KATE [FOR THE THOUSANDTH TIME]:
Helen.

GUIDED READING
What has happened to Kate during the past five years?

[*She is down the steps at once to them, seizing* HELEN'S *wrists and lifting her off* MARTHA; MARTHA *runs off in tears and screams for momma, with* PERCY *after her.*]

Let me have those scissors.

[*Meanwhile the family inside is alerted,* AUNT EV *joining* JAMES *at the window;* CAPTAIN KELLER *resumes work.*]

JAMES [BLANDLY]: She only dug Martha's eyes out. Almost dug. It's always almost, no point worrying till it happens, is there?

[*They gaze out, while* KATE *reaches for the scissors in* HELEN'S *hand. But* HELEN *pulls the scissors back, they struggle for them a moment, then* KATE *gives up, lets* HELEN *keep them. She tries to draw* HELEN *into the house.* HELEN *jerks away.* KATE *next goes down on her knees, takes* HELEN'S *hands gently, and using the scissors like a doll, makes* HELEN *caress and cradle them; she points* HELEN'S *finger housewards.* HELEN'S *whole body now becomes eager; she surrenders the scissors,* KATE *turns her toward the door and gives her a little push.* HELEN *scrambles up and toward the house, and* KATE *rising follows her.*]

GUIDED READING
How does Kate communicate with Helen?

AUNT EV: How does she stand it? Why haven't you seen this Baltimore man? It's not

words for everyday use

fran • tic (fran' tik) *adj.*, emotionally out of control. *Gordon became* frantic *when he realized he had lost Toby.*

be • nign (bi bīn') *adj.*, kindly. *The* benign *stranger helped us find the store.*

in • do • lent (in' dōl lənt) *adj.*, lazy. *The* indolent *worker was fired for his laziness.*

steel (stēəl') *v.*, made hard like steel. *Jules* steeled *himself for the bad news.*

ACT 1 / THE MIRACLE WORKER **691**

ANSWERS TO GUIDED READING QUESTIONS

1. Helen is trying to talk.
2. Kate has been steeled in grief.
3. To communicate with Helen, Kate uses motions that Helen can feel with her hands.

ADDITIONAL QUESTIONS AND ACTIVITIES

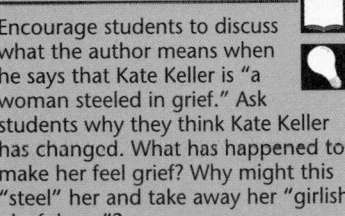

Encourage students to discuss what the author means when he says that Kate Keller is "a woman steeled in grief." Ask students why they think Kate Keller has changed. What has happened to make her feel grief? Why might this "steel" her and take away her "girlish playfulness"?
Answers. Students may suggest that the author means that Kate has become hardened emotionally and is more serious and less able to laugh now. Students should recognize that Kate has changed because of the difficulty of trying to raise and educate Helen when Helen cannot see or hear her. She probably feels grief for Helen because it seems unlikely that she will ever be able to "break through" to Helen on her own. Students may say that the difficulty of her family life has forced Kate to harden her feelings; otherwise she might feel constant pain for Helen's situation.

Quotables

"Although the world is full of suffering, it is also full of the overcoming of it."

—Helen Keller

1. Captain Keller has stopped believing in wonders.
2. Helen is troubled because the doll does not have eyes.
3. Captain Keller does not believe the doctor can help Helen. Kate still holds hope that he can.

ADDITIONAL QUESTIONS AND ACTIVITIES

Ask students the following questions:

1. To whom does Aunt Ev want Captain Keller to write? Why does she want him to write to this person?
2. Why doesn't Captain Keller want to do this? What does he say he has already done?
3. What does Captain Keller ask his wife Kate about doctors? What is her response? What does Kate's response reveal about her as a mother.
4. What upsets Helen about the doll? What does this reveal about Helen? What is nobody able to do at first? How do you think this makes Helen feel? Who eventually notices and helps Helen?

Answers

1. Aunt Ev wants Captain Keller to write to Dr. Chisholm, a famous oculist in Baltimore.
2. Captain Keller doesn't want to do this because he says he has stopped believing in wonders. he says he has already sent Helen to specialists all over Alabama and Tennessee, and he would send her to every "fool doctor in the country" if he thought it would do any good.
3. The captain asks Kate "How many times can you let them break your heart." She says, "Any number of times." Her response reveals her dedication and tenacity—she is determined to find help for Helen.
4. The doll's lack of eyes upsets Helen. This reveals that even though Helen cannot see, she is aware of the features a human face should have. Nobody is able to figure out what Helen wants with the doll. Students may say that Helen feels ignored and frustrated. Her mother understands what Helen wants, and she sews eyes on the doll for her.

---

a thing you can let go on and on, like the weather.

JAMES: The weather here doesn't ask permission of me, Aunt Ev. Speak to my father.

AUNT EV: Arthur. Something ought to be done for that child.

KELLER: A refreshing suggestion. What?

[KATE *entering turns* HELEN *to* AUNT EV, *who gives her the towel doll.*]

AUNT EV: Why, this very famous oculist[4] in Baltimore I wrote you about, what was his name?

KATE: Dr. Chisholm.

AUNT EV: Yes, I heard lots of cases of blindness people thought couldn't be cured he's cured, he just does wonders. Why don't you write to him?

KELLER: I've stopped believing in wonders.

KATE: [ROCKS THE CRADLE]: I think the Captain will write to him soon. Won't you, Captain?

> **GUIDED READING**
> Why hasn't Captain Keller taken Aunt Ev's suggestion?

KELLER: No.

JAMES [LIGHTLY]: Good money after bad, or bad after good. Or bad after bad—

AUNT EV: Well, if it's just a question of money, Arthur, now you're marshal you have this Yankee money. Might as well—

KELLER: Not money. The child's been to specialists all over Alabama and Tennessee, if I thought it would do good I'd have her to every fool doctor in the country.

KATE: I think the Captain will write to him soon.

KELLER: Katie. How many times can you let them break your heart?

KATE: Any number of times.

[HELEN *meanwhile sits on the floor to explore the doll with her fingers, and her hand pauses over the face: this is no face, a blank area of towel, and it troubles*

> **GUIDED READING**
> Why is Helen troubled by the doll?

her. Her hand searches for features, and taps questioningly for eyes, but no one notices. She then yanks at her AUNT'S *dress, and taps again vigorously for eyes.*]

AUNT EV: What, child?

[*Obviously not hearing,* HELEN *commences to go around, from person to person, tapping for eyes, but no one attends or understands.*]

KATE [NO BREAK]: As long as there's the least chance. For her to see. Or hear, or—

KELLER: There isn't. Now I must finish here.

KATE: I think, with your permission, Captain, I'd like to to write.

KELLER: I said no, Katie.

AUNT EV: Why, writing does no harm, Arthur, only a little bitty letter. To see if he can help her.

KELLER: He can't.

KATE: We won't know that to be a fact, Captain, until after you write.

KELLER [RISING, <u>EMPHATIC</u>]: Katie, he can't.

[*He collects his papers.*]

JAMES [<u>FACETIOUSLY</u>]: Father stands up, that makes it a fact.

> **GUIDED READING**
> What difference of opinion do Captain Keller and Kate have?

---

4. **oculist.** Eye doctor

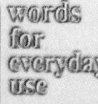

em • pha • tic (im fa′ tik) *adj.*, firm, forceful. *Leon was <u>emphatic</u> about the importance of the players being at practice.*

fa • ce • tious (fə sē′ shəs) *adj.*, witty in a playful but often inappropriate manner. *"I was being <u>facetious</u>," I insisted when Albert became upset by my remark.* **facetiously,** *adv.*

com • mence (kə ments′) *v.*, begin. *The meeting will <u>commence</u> at 3:00 P.M.*

KELLER: You be quiet! I'm badgered enough here by females without your <u>impudence</u>.

[JAMES *shuts up, makes himself scarce.* HELEN *now is groping among things on* KELLER'S *desk, and paws his papers to the floor.* KELLER *is exasperated.*]

Katie.

[KATE *quickly turns* HELEN *away, and retrieves the papers.*]

I might as well try to work in a henyard as in this house—

JAMES [<u>PLACATING</u>]: You really ought to put her away, Father.

KATE: [STARING UP]: What?

JAMES: Some asylum.[5] It's the kindest thing.

AUNT EV: Why, she's your sister, James, not a nobody—

JAMES: Half sister, and half—mentally defective, she can't even keep herself clean. It's not pleasant to see her about all the time.

KATE: Do you dare? Complain of what you *can* see?

GUIDED READING

What does James think of Helen?

KELLER [VERY ANNOYED]: This discussion is at an end! I'll thank you not to broach it again, Ev.

[*Silence descends at once.* HELEN *gropes her way with the doll, and* KELLER *turns back for a final word, explosive.*]

I've done as much as I can bear, I can't give my whole life to it! The house is at sixes and sevens from morning till night over the child, it's time some attention was paid to Mildred here instead!

KATE [GENTLY DRY]: You'll wake her up, Captain.

KELLER: I want some peace in the house, I don't care how, but one way we won't have it is by rushing up and down the country every time someone hears of a new quack. I'm as sensible to this affliction as anyone else, it hurts me to look at the girl.

KATE: It was not our affliction I meant you to write about, Captain.

[HELEN *is back at* AUNT EV, *fingering her dress, and yanks two buttons from it.*]

GUIDED READING

Why is Captain Keller unwilling to continue seeking help for Helen?

AUNT EV: Helen! My buttons.

[HELEN *pushes the buttons into the doll's face.* KATE *now sees, comes swiftly to kneel, lifts* HELEN'S *hand to her own eyes in question.*]

KATE: Eyes?

[HELEN *nods energetically.*]

She wants the doll to have eyes.

[*Another kind of silence now, while* KATE *takes pins and buttons from the sewing basket and attaches them to the doll as eyes.* KELLER *stands, caught, and watches morosely.* AUNT EV *blinks, and conceals her emotion by inspecting her dress.*]

AUNT EV: My goodness me, I'm not decent.

KATE: She doesn't know better, Aunt Ev. I'll sew them on again.

JAMES: Never learn with everyone letting her do anything she takes it into her mind to—

KELLER: You be quiet!

JAMES: What did I say now?

---

5. **asylum.** Institutions for the care of those who are ill or handicapped

---

ANSWERS TO GUIDED READING QUESTIONS

1. James thinks Helen is half mentally defective.
2. Keller says he cannot give up his whole life to finding help, that he no longer has hope for Helen, and that he think they should turn their attention to their new child Mildred.

LITERARY TECHNIQUE

CHARACTER. A **character** is a person or animal who takes part in a literary work. Share this definition with students and ask them the following questions: Who is James and how is he related to Helen? What does he think should be done with Helen? What attitude does he reveal toward Helen? What words would you use to describe James a character so far in the play?
Answers. James is Captain Keller's son and Helen's half-brother. He thinks Helen should be put in an asylum. He doesn't seem to care for Helen every much; he thinks of her as less than human, complains that "she can't even keep herself clean," and says, "It's not pleasant to see her about all the time." James seems to be sarcastic and unfeeling toward others.

CULTURAL/ HISTORICAL NOTE

Inform students that many asylums for those with severe physical, mental, or emotional problems in the nineteenth century were not very nice places. Patients were often simply labeled as hopeless and not given the physical or mental stimulation needed to help them develop. Some of the treatments for patients would be labeled as abusive today. Point out that this makes James's suggestion even more unfeeling.

ANSWERS TO GUIDED READING QUESTIONS

1. James says Helen will never learn while she is allowed to do anything she takes it into her mind to do.
2. Helen wants to talk–she wants to be like everyone else.

CROSS-CURRICULAR ACTIVITIES

HISTORY. Inform students that it was not until the end of the eighteenth century that people began to try to provide education, job training, and books for the blind. Valentin Haüy was the first person to begin a school for the blind; he founded the Institution Nationale in Paris in 1785. John Dix Fisher founded the first school for the blind in the United States in 1829. It was called the Perkins school for the Blind, and the school is still run outside of Boston, Massachusetts. Encourage students to work in small groups to research one of the following topics. Students should then prepare a brief written report on their chosen topic, citing sources such as encyclopedias, books, periodicals, and on-line resources.

- Valentin Haüy's work to help the blind
- John Dix Fisher and the founding of the Perkins School
- other schools for the blind in the United States
- the policy today of integrating blind students in the classroom begun in 1900 in Chicago

---

KELLER: You talk too much.

JAMES: I was agreeing with you!

KELLER: Whatever it was. Deprived child, the least she can have are the little things she wants.

[JAMES, *very wounded, stalks out of the room onto the porch; he remains here, sulking.*]

AUNT EV [INDULGENTLY]: It's worth a couple of buttons, Kate, look.

[HELEN *now has the doll with eyes, and cannot contain herself for joy; she rocks the doll, pats it vigorously, kisses it.*]

This child has more sense than all these men Kellers, if there's ever any way to reach that mind of hers.

[*But* HELEN *suddenly has come upon the cradle, and unhesitatingly overturns it; the swaddled baby tumbles out, and* CAPTAIN KELLER *barely manages to dive and catch it in time.*]

KELLER: *Helen!*

[*All are in commotion, the baby screams, but* HELEN *unperturbed is laying her doll in its place.* KATE *on her knees pulls her hands off the cradle, wringing them;* HELEN *is bewildered.*]

KATE: Helen, Helen, you're not to do such things, how can I make you understand—

KELLER: [HOARSELY]: Katie.

KATE: How can I get it into your head, my darling, my poor—

KELLER: Katie, some way of teaching her an iota of discipline has to be—

KATE [FLARING]: How can you discipline an afflicted child? Is it her fault?

[HELEN'S *fingers have fluttered to her* MOTHER'S *lips, vainly trying to comprehend their movements.*]

KELLER: I didn't say it was her fault.

KATE: Then whose? I don't know what to do! How can I teach her, beat her—until she's black and blue?

KELLER: It's not safe to let her run around loose. Now there must be a way of confining her, somehow, so she can't—

KATE: Where, in a cage? She's a growing child, she has to use her limbs!

KELLER: Answer me one thing, is it fair to Mildred here?

KATE [INEXORABLY]: Are you willing to put her away?

[*Now* HELEN'S *face darkens in the same rage as at herself earlier, and her hand strikes at* KATE'S *lips.* KATE *catches her hand again, and* HELEN *begins to kick, struggle, twist.*]

KELLER: Now what?

KATE: She wants to talk, like—be like you and me.

[*She holds* HELEN *struggling until we hear from the child her first sound so far; an inarticulate weird noise in her throat such as an animal in a trap might make; and* KATE *releases her. The second she is free* HELEN *blunders away, collides violently with a chair; falls, and sits weeping.* KATE *comes to her, embraces, caresses, soothes her, and buries her own face in her hair; until she can control her voice.*]

---

words for everyday use   in • ex • o • ra • ble (i neks' rə bəl) *adj.,* relentless; refusing to be persuaded. *The advancing army was* <u>inexorable</u>: *the only thing to do was flee.* **inexorably,** *adv.*

1. Annie Sullivan is 20. She has a
   grave and obstinate face. She is
   lively and full of impudence.

Every day she slips further away. And I don't know how to call her back.

AUNT EV: Oh, I've a mind to take her up to Baltimore myself. If that doctor can't help her, maybe he'll know who can.

KELLER [PRESENTLY, HEAVILY]: I'll write the man, Katie.

[*He stands with the baby in his clasp, staring at* HELEN'S *head, hanging down on* KATE'S *arm.*

The lights dim out, except the one on KATE *and* HELEN. *In the twilight,* JAMES, AUNT EV, *and* KELLER *move off slowly, formally, in separate directions;* KATE *with* HELEN *in her arms remains, motionless, in an image which overlaps into the next scene and fades only when it is well under way.*

Without pause, from the dark down left we hear a man's voice with a Greek accent speaking:]

ANAGNOS: —who could do nothing for the girl, of course. It was Dr. Bell who thought she might somehow be taught. I have written the family only that a suitable governess, Miss Annie Sullivan, has been found here in Boston—

[*The lights begin to come up, down left, on a long table and chair. The table contains equipment for teaching the blind by touch—a small replica of the human skeleton, stuffed animals, models of flowers and plants, piles of books.*
The chair contains a girl of 20, ANNIE SULLIVAN, *with a face which in repose is*

GUIDED READING
What's Annie
Sullivan like?

1. Annie lacks tact and the ability to bend to others.
2. Annie believes that tantrums indicate that "something" is inside, probably a strong mind.

LITERARY TECHNIQUE

SIMILE. A **simile** is a comparison using *like* or *as*. Share this definition with students and then ask them the following questions:

- What simile does Anagnos use to describe Annie's new student?
- In what ways is Helen like a safe?
- What might the "treasure" inside Helen be?
- What does Annie see as a sign that Helen may not be empty but might have a "treasure" inside?
- Why do you think Annie views Helen's tantrums in this way?

Answers.

- Anagnos says, "She is like a little safe, locked, that no one can open. Perhaps there is a treasure inside."
- Students may suggest that Helen is like a safe because she is deaf, blind, and mute, so she cannot communicate with the outside world, and nobody can reach her to see what she is like inside.
- The "treasure" might be a bright mind hidden inside Helen.
- Annie sees the fact that Helen has tantrums as a sign that she is not empty but might have a treasure inside.
- Students may say that Annie sees Helen's tantrums as a possible sign that there is intelligence inside Helen because her tantrums nay be a means of trying to express herself and make herself understood and are a sign of her frustration at her isolation.

---

grave and rather <u>obstinate</u>, *and when active is impudent, combative, twinkling with all the life that is lacking in* HELEN'S, *and handsome; there is a crude vitality to her. Her suitcase is at her knee.* ANAGNOS, *a stocky bearded man, comes into the light only toward the end of his speech.*]

ANAGNOS: —and will come. It will no doubt be difficult for you there, Annie. But it has been difficult for you at our school too, hm? Gratifying, yes, when you came to us and could not spell your name, to accomplish so much here in a few years, but always an Irish battle. For independence.

[*He studies* ANNIE, *humorously; she does not open her eyes.*]

This is my last time to counsel you, Annie, and you do lack some—by some I mean *all*—what,

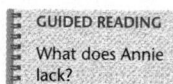

GUIDED READING

What does Annie lack?

tact or talent to bend. To others. And what has saved you on more than one occasion here at Perkins is that there was nowhere to expel you to. Your eyes hurt?

ANNIE: My ears, Mr. Anagnos.

[*And now she has opened her eyes; they are inflamed, vague, slightly crossed, clouded by the granular growth of trachoma,*[6] *and she often keeps them closed to shut out the pain of light.*]

ANAGNOS [SEVERELY]: Nowhere but back to Tewksbury, where children learn to be saucy. Annie, I know how dreadful it was there, but that battle is dead and done with, why not let it stay buried?

ANNIE [CHEERILY]: I think God must owe me a resurrection.

ANAGNOS [A BIT SHOCKED]: What?

ANNIE [TAPS HER BROW]: Well, He keeps digging up that battle!

ANAGNOS: That is not a proper thing to say, Annie. It is what I mean.

ANNIE [MEEKLY]: Yes. But I know what I'm like, what's this child like?

ANAGNOS: Like?

ANNIE: Well— Bright or dull, to start off.

ANAGNOS: No one knows. And if she is dull, you have no patience with this?

ANNIE: Oh, in grownups you have to, Mr. Anagnos. I mean in children it just seems a little—<u>precocious</u>, can I use that word?

ANAGNOS: Only if you can spell it.

ANNIE: Premature. So I hope at least she's a bright one.

ANAGNOS: Deaf, blind, mute—who knows? She is like a little safe, locked, that no one can open. Perhaps there is a treasure inside.

ANNIE: Maybe it's empty, too?

ANAGNOS: Possible. I should warn you, she is much given to tantrums.

ANNIE: Means something is inside. Well, so am I, if I believe all I hear. Maybe you should warn *them*.

GUIDED READING

What do tantrums mean, according to Annie?

ANAGNOS [FROWNS]: Annie. I wrote them no word of your history. You will find yourself among strangers now, who know nothing of it.

ANNIE: Well, we'll keep them in a state of blessed ignorance.

ANAGNOS: Perhaps *you* should tell it?

---

6. **trachoma.** An eye infection caused by bacteria; it can lead to blindness if not treated

---

words for everyday use

ob • sti • nate (äb′ stə nət) *adj.,* stubborn. *We tried to get Marny to change her mind, but she was too* <u>obstinate</u>.

pre • co • cious (pri kō′ sh əs) *adj.,* exceptionally early in development. *The* <u>precocious</u> *child could read by the age of three.*

ANNIE [BRISTLING]: Why? I have enough trouble with people who don't know.

ANAGNOS : So they will understand. When you have trouble.

ANNIE: The only time I have trouble is when I'm right.

[*But she is amused at herself, as is* ANAGNOS.]

Is it my fault it's so often? I won't give them trouble, Mr. Anagnos, I'll be so ladylike they won't notice I've come.

ANAGNOS: Annie, be—humble. It is not as if you have so many offers to pick and choose. You will need their affection, working with this child.

ANNIE [HUMOROUSLY]: I hope I won't need their pity.

ANAGNOS: Oh, we can all use some pity.

[*Crisply*]

So. You are no longer our pupil, we throw you into the world, a teacher. *If* the child can be taught. No one expects you to work miracles, even for twenty-five dollars a month. Now, in this envelope a loan, for the railroad, which you

GUIDED READING

What is not expected of Annie?

will repay me when you have a bank account. But in this box, a gift. With our love.

[ANNIE *opens the small box he extends, and sees a garnet ring. She looks up, blinking, and down.*]

I think other friends are ready to say goodbye.

[*He moves as though to open doors.*]

ANNIE: Mr. Anagnos.

[*Her voice is trembling.*]

Dear Mr. Anagnos, I—

[*But she swallows over getting the ring on her finger, and cannot continue until she finds a woebegone joke.*]

Well, what should I say, I'm an ignorant opinionated girl, and everything I am I owe to you?

ANAGNOS [SMILES]: That is only half true, Annie.

ANNIE: Which half? I crawled in here like a drowned rat, I thought I died when Jimmie died, that I'd never again—come alive. Well, you say with love so easy, and I haven't *loved* a soul since and I never will, I suppose, but this place gave me more than my eyes back. Or taught me how to spell, which I'll never learn anyway, but with all the fights and the trouble I've been here it taught me what help is, and how to live again, and I don't want to say goodbye. Don't open the door, I'm crying.

ANAGNOS [GENTLY]: They will not see.

[*He moves again as though opening doors, and in comes a group of girls, 8-year-olds to 17-year olds; as they walk we see they are blind.* ANAGNOS *shepherds them in with a hand.*]

A CHILD: Annie?

ANNIE [HER VOICE CHEERFUL]: Here, Beatrice.

[*As soon as they locate her voice they throng joyfully to her, speaking all at once;* ANNIE *is down on her knees to the smallest, and the following are the more intelligible fragments in the general hubbub.*]

CHILDREN: There's a present. We brought you a going-away present, Annie!

ANNIE: Oh, now you shouldn't have—

CHILDREN: We did, we did, where's the present?

SMALLEST CHILD [MOURNFULLY]: Don't go, Annie, away.

CHILDREN: Alice has it. Alice! Where's Alice? Here I am! Where? Here!

[*An arm is aloft out of the group, waving a present;* ANNIE *reaches for it.*]

ANNIE: I have it. I have it, everybody, should I open it?

ADDITIONAL QUESTIONS
AND ACTIVITIES

Ask students to discuss Mr. Anagnos's comment that, "No one expects you to work miracles." Why might he tell Annie this before she heads out to her first job? Ask students to predict whether Annie will indeed work miracles. (Tell students to think about this comment in light of the play's title.)
Answers. Students may say Mr. Anagnos tells Annie this so she won't feel so much pressure about her difficult job lying ahead. Students might predict that, given the stories title, Annie will exceed Mr. Anagnos's expectations and work "miracles" with Helen.

CULTURAL/
HISTORICAL NOTE

In the seventeenth, eighteenth, and nineteenth centuries, institutions knows as almshouses or poorhouses were common in Europe and the United States. Here, poor people who could not support themselves, people who got in trouble with the law for debt, petty criminals, and even very young orphans lived and worked in terrible conditions. Increasingly these institutions came under scrutiny in the nineteenth century. Charles Dickens wrote about the horrors of such places in novels such as *Oliver Twist*. In the United States, reformers like Dorothea Dix set about trying to reform and improve such institutions.

1. Annie's gift is a pair of smoked glasses.
2. The children give Annie a doll to give to Helen.
3. Annie promised that she would take care of her brother Jimmy forever and ever.

LITERARY TECHNIQUE

FLASHBACK. A **flashback** is a part of a story, poem, or play that presents events that happened at an earlier time. Share this definition with students and then ask them the following questions: What flashback occurs on this page? Who is the boy with Annie in this flashback? How does Annie feel about the place where they are headed? What promise does Annie make Jimmie? What assessment does the man make of Annie and Jimmie when the arrive? What does he do to Annie and Jimmie? How does Jimmie react to this event? How do you think Annie feels about what has happened? Why do you think Annie recalls this before heading off to take charge of her new pupil?

Answers. Students should recognize that the flashback begins and ends in the second column of page 574 and involves a scene between Annie and a boy named Jimmie when she was younger. The boy is named Jimmie; students who recall the information on the Prereading page will remember that he is Annie's brother. Annie feels "dread" about the place where they are headed. Annie promises Jimmie that she will take care of him "forever and ever." The man says Annie is aged nine and is virtually blind and that Jimmie is aged seven and has a problem with his leg that requires he walk with a crutch. He separates Annie and Jimmie, sending Annie to the women's ward and Jimmie to the men's. Jimmie cries out in terror begging Annie not to let them take him. Annie probably feels helpless to help Jimmie and devastated that she is forced to break her promise to him because of their enforced separation. Students may say that she recalls another time when she feels she has let someone down because she is afraid of letting her new pupil down.

CHILDREN: Open it! Everyone be quiet! Do, Annie! She's opening it. Ssh!

[*A settling of silence while* ANNIE *unwraps it. The present is a pair of smoked glasses, and she stands still.*]

Is it open, Annie?

ANNIE: It's open.

CHILDREN: It's for your eyes, Annie. Put them on, Annie! 'Cause Mrs. Hopkins said your eyes hurt since the operation. And she said you're going where the sun is *fierce*.

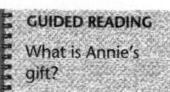
GUIDED READING
What is Annie's gift?

ANNIE: I'm putting them on now.

SMALLEST CHILD [MOURNFULLY]: Don't go, Annie, where the sun is fierce.

CHILDREN: Do they fit all right?

ANNIE: Oh, they fit just fine.

CHILDREN: Did you put them on? Are they pretty, Annie?

ANNIE: Oh, my eyes feel hundreds of per cent better already, and pretty, why, do you know how I look in them? Splendiloquent. Like a race horse!

CHILDREN [DELIGHTED]: There's another present! Beatrice! We have a present for Helen, too! Give it to her, Beatrice. Here, Annie!

[*This present is an elegant doll, with moveable eyelids and a momma sound.*]

It's for Helen. And we took up a collection to buy it. And Laura dressed it.

ANNIE: It's beautiful!

CHILDREN: So don't forget, you be sure to give it to Helen from us, Annie!

GUIDED READING
What present do the children give Annie for Helen?

ANNIE: I promise it will be the first thing I give her. If I don't keep it for myself, that is, you know I can't be trusted with dolls!

SMALLEST CHILD [MOURNFULLY]: Don't go, Annie, to her.

ANNIE [HER ARM AROUND HER]: Sarah, dear. I don't *want* to go.

SMALLEST CHILD: Then why are you going?

ANNIE [GENTLY]: Because I'm a big girl now, and big girls have to earn a living. It's the only way I can. But if you don't smile for me first, what I'll just have to do is—

[*She pauses, inviting it.*]

SMALLEST CHILD: What?

ANNIE: Put *you* in my suitcase, instead of this doll. And take *you* to Helen in Alabama!

[*This strikes the children as very funny, and they begin to laugh and tease the smallest child, who after a moment does smile for* ANNIE.]

ANAGNOS [THEN]: Come, children. We must get the trunk into the carriage and Annie into her train, or no one will go to Alabama. Come, come.

[*He shepherds them out and* ANNIE *is left alone on her knees with the doll in her lap. She reaches for her suitcase, and by a subtle change in the color of the light, we go with her thoughts into another time. We hear a boy's voice whispering; perhaps we see shadowy intimations* [7] *of these speakers in the background.*]

BOY'S VOICE: Where we goin', Annie?

ANNIE [IN DREAD]: Jimmie.

BOY'S VOICE: Where we goin'?

ANNIE: I said—I'm takin' care of you—

GUIDED READING
What did Annie promise at age nine?

BOY'S VOICES: Forever and ever?

MAN'S VOICE [IMPERSONAL]: Annie Sullivan, aged nine, virtually blind. James Sullivan, aged seven—What's the matter with your leg, Sonny?

---

7. **intimations.** Suggestions; hints

ANNIE: Forever and ever.

MAN'S VOICE: Can't he walk without that crutch?

[ANNIE *shakes her head, and does not stop shaking it.*]

Girl goes to the women's ward. Boy to the men's.

BOY'S VOICE [IN TERROR]: Annie! Annie! don't let them take me—Annie!

ANAGNOS [OFFSTAGE]: Annie! Annie?

[*But this voice is real, in the present, and* ANNIE *comes up out of her horror, clearing her head with a final shake; the lights begin to pick out* KATE *in the* KELLER *house, as* ANNIE *in a bright tone calls back.*]

ANNIE: Coming!

[*This word catches* KATE, *who stands half turned and attentive to it, almost as though hearing it.*

Meanwhile ANNIE *turns and hurries out, lugging the suitcase.*

The room dims out; the sound of railroad wheels begins from off left, and maintains itself in a constant rhythm underneath the following scene; the remaining lights have come up on the KELLER *homestead.* JAMES *is lounging on the porch, waiting. In the upper bedroom which is to be* ANNIE'S, HELEN *is alone, puzzledly exploring, fingering and smelling things, the curtains, empty drawers in the bureau, water in the pitcher by the washbasin, fresh towels on the bedstead.*

Downstairs in the family room KATE *turning to a mirror hastily adjusts her bonnet, watched by a Negro servant in an apron,* VINEY.]

> **GUIDED READING**
> What is Helen doing in Annie's room?

VINEY: Let Mr. Jimmy go by hisself, you been pokin' that garden all day, you ought to rest your feet.

KATE: I can't wait to see her, Viney.

VINEY: Maybe she ain't gone be on this train neither.

KATE: Maybe she is.

VINEY: And maybe she ain't.

KATE: And maybe she is. Where's Helen?

VINEY: She upstairs, smellin' around. She know somethin' funny's goin' on.

KATE: Let her have her supper as soon as Mildred's in bed, and tell Captain Keller when he comes that we'll be delayed tonight.

VINEY: Again.

KATE: I don't think we need say *again*. Simply delayed will do.

[*She runs upstairs to* ANNIE'S *room,* VINEY *speaking after her.*]

VINEY: I mean that's what he gone say. "What, again?"

[VINEY *works at setting the table. Upstairs* KATE *stands in the doorway, watching* HELEN'S *groping explorations.*]

KATE: Yes, we're expecting someone. Someone for my Helen.

[HELEN *happens upon her skirt, clutches her leg;* KATE *in a tired dismay kneels to tidy her hair and soiled pinafore.*]

Oh, dear, this was clean not an hour ago.

[HELEN *feels her bonnet, shakes her head darkly, and tugs to get it off.* KATE *retains it with one hand, diverts* HELEN *by opening her other hand under her nose.*]

Here. For while I'm gone.

[HELEN *sniffs, reaches, and pops something into her mouth, while* KATE *speaks a bit guiltily.*]

I don't think one peppermint drop will spoil your supper.

[*She gives* HELEN *a quick kiss, evades her hands, and hurries downstairs again.*

> **GUIDED READING**
> How does Kate appease Helen?

1. Helen is exploring Annie's room, feeling and smelling all of the new things in the room.
2. Kate gives Helen a peppermint drop.

CULTURAL/ HISTORICAL NOTE

Tell students that this story takes place in the South around two decades after the Civil War. Even though African Americans had newly won their freedom, in many places in the South they had won it in name only. Black Codes were instituted in many southern states that made it hard for African Americans to establish themselves economically. Many African Americans were forced to continue on the same roles they had carried out before the Civil War in conditions that were very similar to those that existed under slavery. Many African Americans became sharecroppers, working white farmers' land for a meager share of the crops, or they became domestic servants in homes like the Kellers'.

Meanwhile CAPTAIN KELLER *has entered the yard from around the rear of the house, newspaper under arm, cleaning off and munching on some radishes; he sees* JAMES *lounging at the porch post.*]

KELLER: Jimmie?

JAMES [UNMOVING]: Sir?

KELLER [EYES HIM]: You don't look dressed for anything useful, boy.

JAMES: I'm not. It's for Miss Sullivan.

KELLER: Needn't keep holding up that porch, we have wooden posts for that. I asked you to see that those strawberry plants were moved this evening.

JAMES: I'm moving your—Mrs. Keller, instead. To the station.

KELLER [HEAVILY]: Mrs. Keller. Must you always speak of her as though you haven't met the lady?

[KATE *comes out on the porch, and* JAMES *inclines his head.*]

JAMES [IRONIC]: Mother.

[*He starts off the porch, but sidesteps* KELLER'S *glare like a blow.*]

I said mother!

KATE: Captain.

KELLER: Evening, my dear.

KATE: We're off to meet the train, Captain. Supper will be a trifle delayed tonight.

KELLER: What, again?

KATE [BACKING OUT]: With your permission, Captain?

[*And they are gone.* KELLER *watches them offstage, morosely.*

Upstairs HELEN *meanwhile has groped for her mother, touched her cheek in a meaningful gesture, waited, touched her cheek, waited, then found the open door, and made her way down.*

Now she comes into the family room, touches her cheek again; VINEY *regards her.*]

VINEY: What you want, honey, your momma?

[HELEN *touches her cheek again.* VINEY *goes to the sideboard, gets a tea-cake, gives it into* HELEN'S *hand;* HELEN *pops it into her mouth.*]

Guess one little tea cake ain't gone ruin your appetite.

[*She turns* HELEN *toward the door.* HELEN *wanders out onto the porch, as* KELLER *comes up the steps. Her hands encounter him, and she touches her cheek again, waits.*]

KELLER: She's gone.

[*He is awkward with her; when he puts his hand on her head, she pulls away.* KELLER *stands regarding her, heavily.*]

She's gone, my son and I don't get along, you don't know I'm your father, no one likes me, and supper's delayed.

[HELEN *touches her cheek, waits.* KELLER *fishes in his pocket.*]

Here. I brought you some stick candy, one nibble of sweets can't do any harm.

GUIDED READING

How does Keller appease Helen?

[*He gives her a large stick candy;* HELEN *falls to it.* VINEY *peers out the window.*]

VINEY [REPROACHFULLY]: Cap'n Keller, now how'm I gone get her to eat her supper you fill her up with that trash?

KELLER [ROARS]: Tend to your work!

[VINEY *beats a rapid retreat.* KELLER *thinks better of it, and tries to get the candy away from* HELEN, *but* HELEN *hangs on to it; and when* KELLER *pulls, she gives his leg a kick.* KELLER *hops about,* HELEN *takes refuge with the candy down behind the pump, and* KELLER *then irately flings his newspaper on the porch floor, stamps into the house past* VINEY *and disappears.*]

The lights half dim on the homestead, where VINEY *and* HELEN *going about their business soon find their way off. Meanwhile, the railroad sounds off left have mounted in a crescendo to a climax typical of a depot at arrival time, the lights come up on stage left, and we see a suggestion of a station. Here* ANNIE *in her smoked glasses and disarrayed by travel is waiting with her suitcase, while* JAMES *walks to meet her; she has a battered paper-bound book, which is a Perkins report, under her arm.]*

JAMES [COOLLY]: Miss Sullivan?

ANNIE [CHEERILY]: Here! At last, I've been on trains so many days I thought they must be backing up every time I dozed off—

JAMES: I'm James Keller.

ANNIE: James?

[The name stops her.]

I had a brother Jimmie. Are you Helen's

GUIDED READING

How does James treat Annie?

JAMES: I'm only half a brother. You're to be her governess

ANNIE [LIGHTLY]: Well. Try!

JAMES [EYEING HER]: You look like half a governess.

*[*KATE *enters.* ANNIE *stands moveless, while* JAMES *takes her suitcase.* KATE'S *gaze on her is doubtful, troubled.]*

Mrs. Keller, Miss Sullivan.

*[*KATE *takes her hand.]*

KATE [SIMPLY]: We've met every train for two days.

*[*ANNIE *looks at* KATE'S *face, and her good humor cones back.]*

ANNIE: I changed trains every time they stopped, the man who sold me that ticket ought to be tied to the tracks—

JAMES: You have a trunk, Miss Sullivan?

ANNIE: Yes.

[She passes JAMES *a claim check, and he bears the suitcase out behind them.* ANNIE *holds the battered book.* KATE *is studying her face, and* ANNIE *returns the gaze; this is a mutual appraisal, southern gentlewoman and working-class Irish girl, and* ANNIE *is not quite comfortable under it.]*

You didn't bring Helen, I was hoping you would.

KATE: No, she's home.

[A pause. ANNIE *tries to make ladylike small talk, though her energy now and then erupts; she catches herself up whenever she hears it.]*

ANNIE: You—live far from town, Mrs. Keller?

KATE: Only a mile.

ANNIE: Well. I suppose I can wait one more mile. But don't be surprised if I get out to push the horse!

KATE: Helen's waiting for you, too. There's been such a bustle in the house, she expects something, heaven knows what.

[Now she voices part of her doubt, not as such, but ANNIE *understands it.]*

I expected—a desiccated spinster.[8] You're very young.

ANNIE [RESOLUTELY]: Oh, you should have seen me when I left Boston. I got much older on this trip.

KATE: I mean, to teach anyone as difficult as Helen.

ANNIE: *I* mean to try. They can't put you in jail for trying!

KATE: Is it possible, even? To teach a deaf-blind child *half* of what an ordinary child learns—has that ever been done?

ANNIE: Half?

KATE: A tenth.

GUIDED READING

What remaining hope does Kate lose?

---

8. **dessicated spinster.** Dried-up old woman

ANSWERS TO GUIDED READING QUESTIONS

1. He treats her with some surprise and contempt.
2. Kate's gaze, appraising her, makes Annie slightly uncomfortable.
3. Kate loses hope that Helen will ever be able to learn anywhere as much as a normal child would.

CULTURAL/ HISTORICAL NOTE

Students may be confused by both James's and Kate's cool and snobbish reactions on meeting Annie. Inform students that in the nineteenth century and earlier centuries, people often looked down on women who worked because it meant that their families had no money. Being a governess was considered one of the few "respectable" jobs a poor woman could take, but people with money would often look down on governesses because of their poor background. This would be especially true in the South in the United States because wealthy people in the South had a history of patterning itself after the aristocracy of England.

1. Annie has learned from Dr. Howe's experience, she is young and energetic, and she has been blind.
2. Language is the most important thing.

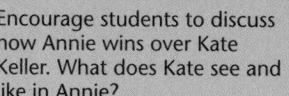

ADDITIONAL QUESTIONS
AND ACTIVITIES

Encourage students to discuss how Annie wins over Kate Keller. What does Kate see and like in Annie? *Answers.* Students should note that Annie wins over Kate with her cheerfulness, confidence, and good humor.

ADDITIONAL QUESTIONS
AND ACTIVITIES

Encourage students to write journal entries about whether they are pessimists or optimists. Do they tend to see the good and possibilities in life or do they see the problems and hardships in life? Ask students whether or not they would be as optimistic as Annie in her situation. Would the define James as an optimist or a pessimist?

ANNIE [RELUCTANTLY]: No.

[KATE'S *face loses its remaining hope, still appraising her youth.*]

Dr. Howe did wonders, but—an ordinary child? No, never. But then I thought when I was going over his reports—

[*She indicates the one in her hand*]

—he never treated them like ordinary children. More like—eggs everyone was afraid would break.

KATE [A PAUSE]: May I ask how old you are?

ANNIE: Well, I'm not in my teens, you know! I'm twenty.

KATE: All of twenty.

[ANNIE *takes the bull by the horns, valiantly.*]

ANNIE: Mrs. Keller, don't lose heart just because I'm not on my last legs. I have three big advantages over Dr. Howe that money couldn't buy for you. One is his work behind me, I've read every word he wrote about it and he wasn't exactly what you'd call a man of few words. Another is to *be* young, why, I've got energy to do anything. The third is, I've been blind.

[*But it costs her something to say this.*]

KATE [QUIETLY]: Advantages.

ANNIE [WRY]: Well, some have the luck of the Irish, some do not.

[KATE *smiles; she likes her.*]

KATE: What will you try to teach her first?

ANNIE: First, last, and—in between, language.

KATE: Language.

ANNIE: Language is to the mind more than light is to the eye. Dr. Howe said that.

KATE: Language.

[*She shakes her head.*]

> **GUIDED READING**
>
> What is the most important thing to teach Helen?

We can't get through to teach her to sit still. You *are* young, despite your years, to have such—confidence. Do you, inside?

[ANNIE *studies her face; she likes her, too.*]

ANNIE: No, to tell you the truth I'm as shaky inside as a baby's rattle!

[*They smile at each other, and* KATE *pats her hand.*]

KATE: Don't be.

[JAMES *returns to usher them off.*]

We'll do all we can to help, and to make you feel at home. Don't think of us as strangers, Miss Annie.

ANNIE [CHEERILY]: Oh, strangers aren't so strange to me. I've known them all my life!

[KATE *smiles again,* ANNIE *smiles back, and they precede* JAMES *offstage.*

The lights dim on them, having simultaneously risen full on the house; VINEY *has already entered the family room, taken a water pitcher, and come out and down to the pump. She pumps real water. As she looks offstage, we hear the clop of hoofs, a carriage stopping, and voices.*]

VINEY: Cap'n Keller! Cap'n Keller, they comin'!

[*She goes back into the house, as* KELLER *comes out on the porch to gaze.*]

She sure 'nuff came, Cap'n.

[KELLER *descends, and crosses toward the carriage; this conversation begins offstage and moves on.*]

KELLER [VERY COURTLY]: Welcome to Ivy Green, Miss Sullivan. I take it you are Miss Sullivan—

KATE: My husband, Miss Annie, Captain Keller.

ANNIE [HER BEST BEHAVIOR]: Captain, how do you do.

KELLER: A pleasure to see you, at last. I trust you had an agreeable journey?

ANNIE: Oh, I had several! When did this country get so big?

JAMES: Where would you like the trunk, father?

KELLER: Where Miss Sullivan can get at it, I imagine.

ANNIE: Yes, please. Where's Helen?

KELLER: In the hall, Jimmie—

KATE: We've put you in the upstairs corner room, Miss Annie, if there's any breeze at all this summer, you'll feel it—

[*In the house the setter* BELLE *flees into the family room, pursued by* HELEN *with groping hands; the dog doubles back out the same door, and* HELEN *still groping for her makes her way out to the porch; she is messy, her hair tumbled, her pinafore now ripped, her shoelaces untied.* KELLER *acquires the suitcase, and* ANNIE *gets her hands on it too, though still endeavoring to live up to the general air of propertied manners.*]

KELLER: *And* the suitcase—

ANNIE [PLEASANTLY]: I'll take the suitcase, thanks.

KELLER: Not at all, I have it, Miss Sullivan.

GUIDED READING

Who struggles with Annie over the suitcase?

ANNIE: I'd like it.

KELLER [GALLANTLY]: I couldn't think of it, Miss Sullivan. You'll find in the south we—

ANNIE: Let me.

KELLER: —view women as the flowers of civiliza—

ANNIE [IMPATIENTLY]: I've got something in it for Helen!

[*She tugs it free;* KELLER *stares.*]

Thank you. When do I see her?

KATE: There. There is Helen.

[ANNIE *turns, and sees* HELEN *on the porch. A moment of silence. Then* ANNIE *begins across the yard to her, lugging her suitcase.*]

KELLER [SOTTO VOCE [9]]: Katie—

[KATE *silences him with a hand on his arm. When* ANNIE *finally reaches the porch steps she stops; contemplating* HELEN *for a last moment before entering her world. Then she drops the suitcase on the porch with intentional heaviness,* HELEN *starts with the jar, and comes to grope over it.* ANNIE *puts forth her hand, and touches* HELEN'S. HELEN *at once grasps it, and commences to explore it, like reading a face. She moves her hand on to* ANNIE'S *forearm, and dress; and* ANNIE *brings her face within reach of* HELEN'S *fingers, which travel over it, quite without timidity, until they encounter and push aside the smoked glasses.* ANNIE'S *gaze is grave, unpitying, very attentive. She puts her hands on* HELEN'S *arms, but* HELEN *at once pulls away, and they confront each other with a distance between. Then* HELEN *returns to the suitcase, tries to open it, cannot.* ANNIE *points* HELEN'S *hand overhead.* HELEN *pulls away, tries to open the suitcase again;* ANNIE *points her hand over her head again.* HELEN *points overhead, a question, and* ANNIE, *drawing* HELEN'S *hand to her own face, nods.* HELEN *now begins tugging the suitcase toward the door; when* ANNIE *tries to take it from her, she fights her off and backs through the doorway with it.* ANNIE *stands a moment, then follows her in, and together they get the suitcase up the steps into* ANNIE'S *room.*]

KATE: Well?

KELLER: She's very rough, Katie.

GUIDED READING

How does Keller describe Annie?

KATE: I like her, Captain.

KELLER: Certainly rear a peculiar kind of young woman in the north. How old is she?

KATE [VAGUELY]: Ohh— Well, she's not in her teens, you know.

KELLER: She's only a child. What's her family like, shipping her off alone this far?

---

9. **sotto voce.** Under the breath, in a private manner

ANSWERS TO GUIDED READING QUESTIONS

1. Helen is messy: her hair is tousled, her pinafore torn, and her shoelaces untied. She is chasing the dog.
2. Keller thinks it is his duty as a gentleman to carry Annie's bag. Annie wants to give Helen a present from the suitcase.
3. Annie wants to get Helen's attention.
4. Annie means the suitcase has to go upstairs.

ADDITIONAL QUESTIONS AND ACTIVITIES

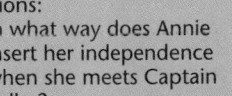

Ask students the following questions:
1. In what way does Annie insert her independence when she meets Captain Keller?
2. What does Captain Keller think of Annie's manners?
3. What else does Captain Keller object to about Annie?
4. Do you think Captain Keller would be pleased immediately with anyone who came to teach Helen? Explain.

Answers
1. Annie inserts her independence by insisting she can carry her own suitcase and refusing to let Captain Keller take it for her.
2. He thinks her manners are "rough" and wonders what type of young women they raise in the north.
3. He objects to her youth and the fact that she is partially blind herself.
4. Students may say Captain Keller has given up hope that anyone can teach Helen, so he would probably find fault with anyone who came to teach her.

ANSWERS TO GUIDED READING QUESTIONS

1. Keller thinks that Annie is too young and that her teaching Helen will be the blind leading the blind.
2. She dresses up in Annie's clothes and stands before a mirror imitating adult actions.
3. Helen wants to know if the doll is for her. Annie says yes.
4. The first word Annie tries to teach Helen is *doll*.

ADDITIONAL QUESTIONS AND ACTIVITIES

Ask students the following questions:

1. What does Helen do that amuses Annie?
2. What does this action reveal about Helen?
3. Does Annie seems to like Helen right away? Explain.
4. How does Annie decide what word to teach Helen first?
5. In what manner does Annie try to teach Helen the word since she cannot see or hear?

Answers

1. Helen dresses up in Annie's clothes and imitates adults' actions.
2. Students may say this action reveals that even though Helen is blind and deaf she has observed enough of adults to imitate them successfully.
3. Students may say that Annie does seem to like Helen right away, attracted by the girl's obvious intelligence.
4. Annie decides to teach Helen *doll* first because Helen is paying attention to the doll.
5. Annie tries signing the letters of the word *doll* in Helen's hand and then pointing to the doll.

KATE: I couldn't learn. She's very close-mouthed about some things.

KELLER: Why does she wear those glasses? I like to see a person's eyes when I talk to—

KATE: For the sun. She was blind.

KELLER: Blind.

KATE: She's had nine operations on her eyes. One just before she left.

KELLER: Blind, good heavens, do they expect one blind child to teach another? Has she experience at least, how long did she teach there?

KATE: She was a pupil.

KELLER [HEAVILY]: Katie, Katie. This is her first position?

KATE [BRIGHT VOICE]: She was valedictorian—

KELLER: Here's a houseful of grownups can't cope with the child, how can an inexperienced half-blind Yankee schoolgirl manage her?

[JAMES *moves in with the trunk on his shoulder.*]

JAMES [EASILY]: Great improvement. Now we have two of them to look after.

KELLER: You look after those strawberry plants!

[JAMES *stops with the trunk.* KELLER *turns from him without another word, and marches off.*]

JAMES: Nothing I say is right.

KATE: Why say anything?

[*She calls.*]

Don't be long, Captain, we'll have supper right away—

[*She goes into the house, and through the rear door of the family room.* JAMES *trudges in with the trunk, takes it up the steps to* ANNIE'S *room, and sets it down outside the door. The lights elsewhere dim somewhat.*

Meanwhile, inside, ANNIE *has given* HELEN *a key; while* ANNIE *removes her bonnet,* HELEN

unlocks and opens the suitcase. The first thing she pulls out is a voluminous shawl. She fingers it until she perceives what it is; then she wraps it around her, and acquiring ANNIE'S *bonnet and smoked glasses as well, dons the lot: the shawl swamps her, and the bonnet settles down upon the glasses, but she stands before a mirror cocking her head to one side, then to the other, in a mockery of adult action.* ANNIE *is amused, and talks to her as one might to a kitten, with no trace of company manners.*]

> GUIDED READING
> What does Helen do upon opening Annie's suitcase?

ANNIE: All the trouble I went to and that's how I look?

[HELEN *then comes back to the suitcase, gropes for more, lifts out a pair of female drawers.*[10]]

Oh, no. Not the drawers!

[*But* HELEN *discarding them comes to the elegant doll. Her fingers explore its features, and when she raises it and finds its eyes open and close, she is at first startled, then delighted. She picks it up, taps its head vigorously, taps her own chest, and nods questioningly.* ANNIE *takes her finger, points it to the doll, points it to* HELEN, *and touching it to her own face, also nods.* HELEN *sits back on her heels, clasps the doll to herself, and rocks it.* ANNIE *studies her, still in bonnet and smoked glasses like a caricature of herself, and addresses her humorously.*]

All right, Miss O'Sullivan. Let's begin with doll.

[*She takes* HELEN'S *hand; in her palm* ANNIE'S *forefinger points, thumb holding her other fingers clenched.*]

D.

[*Her thumb next holds all her fingers clenched, touching* Helen's *palm.*]

> GUIDED READING
> What is Helen's first lesson?

O.

[*Her thumb and forefinger extend.*]

---

10. **drawers.** Underwear

704   UNIT TEN / TURNING WORDS INTO ACTION: DRAMA

704   TEACHER'S EDITION

L.

[*Same contact repeated.*]

L.

[*She puts* HELEN's *hand to the doll.*]

Doll.

JAMES: You spell pretty well.

[ANNIE *in one hurried move gets the drawers swiftly back into the suitcase, the lid banged shut, and her head turned, to see* JAMES *leaning in the doorway.*]

Finding out if she's ticklish? She is.

[ANNIE *regards him stonily, but* HELEN *after a scowling moment tugs at her hand again, imperious.* ANNIE *repeats the letters, and* HELEN *interrupts her fingers in the middle, feeling each of them, puzzled.* ANNIE *touches* HELEN's *hand to the doll, and begins spelling into it again.*]

JAMES: What is it, a game?

ANNIE [CURTLY]: An alphabet.

JAMES: Alphabet?

ANNIE: For the deaf.

[HELEN *now repeats the finger movements in air, exactly, her head cocked to her own hand, and* ANNIE's *eyes suddenly gleam.*]

Ho. How *bright* she is!

JAMES: You think she knows what she's doing?

[*He takes* HELEN's *hand, to throw a meaningless gesture into it; she repeats this one too.*]

She imitates everything, she's a monkey.

ANNIE [VERY PLEASED]: Yes, she's a bright little monkey, all right.

[*She takes the doll from* HELEN, *and reaches for her hand;* HELEN *instantly grabs the doll back.* ANNIE *takes it again, and* HELEN's *hand next, but* HELEN *is incensed now; when* ANNIE *draws her hand to her face to shake her head no, then tries to spell to*

> **GUIDED READING**
> How does Helen react when Annie takes the doll away?

her; HELEN *slaps at* ANNIE's *face.* ANNIE *grasps* HELEN *by both arms, and swings her into a chair, holding her pinned there, kicking, while glasses, doll, bonnet fly in various directions.* JAMES *laughs.*]

JAMES: She wants her doll back.

ANNIE: When she spells it.

JAMES: Spell, she doesn't know the thing has a name, even.

ANNIE: Of course not, who expects her to, now? All I want is her fingers to learn the letters.

JAMES: Won't mean anything to her.

[ANNIE *gives him a look. She then tries to form* HELEN's *fingers into the letters, but* HELEN *swings a haymaker instead, which* ANNIE *barely ducks, at once pinning her down again.*]

Doesn't like that alphabet, Miss Sullivan. You invent it yourself?

[HELEN *is now in a rage, fighting tooth and nail to get out of the chair, and* ANNIE *answers while struggling and dodging her kicks.*]

ANNIE: Spanish monks under a—vow of silence. Which I wish *you'd* take!

[*And suddenly releasing* HELEN's *hands, she comes and shuts the door in* JAMES' *face.* HELEN *drops to the floor, groping around for the doll.* ANNIE *looks around desperately, sees her purse on the bed, rummages in it, and comes up with a battered piece of cake wrapped in newspaper; with her foot she moves the doll deftly out of the the way of* HELEN's *groping, and going on her knee she lets* HELEN *smell the cake. When* HELEN *grabs for it,* ANNIE *removes the cake and spells quickly into the reaching hand.*]

Cake. From Washington up north, it's the best I can do.

[HELEN's *hand waits, baffled.* ANNIE *repeats it.*]

C, a, k, e. Do what my fingers do, never mind what it means.

1. Annie distracts Helen with a piece of cake. When Helen smells the cake, Annie spells *cake.*
2. Helen hits Annie in the face with the doll.
3. Annie realizes it is useless to shout after Helen because Helen cannot hear her.
4. Annie is reminded of her brother Jimmie, the pain he suffered and her promise to take care of him forever.

ADDITIONAL QUESTIONS AND ACTIVITIES

Encourage students to discuss their thoughts about why Helen hits Annie.
Answers. Students may say that Helen is frustrated because she doesn't understand why Annie is making signs into her hands; she only knows that Annie has taken away her doll.

[*She touches the cake briefly to* HELEN's *nose, pats her hand, presents her own hand.* HELEN *spells the letters rapidly back.* ANNIE *pats her hand enthusiastically, and gives her the cake;* HELEN *crams it into her mouth with both hands.* ANNIE *watches her, with humor.*]

Get it down fast, maybe I'll steal that back too. Now.

[*She takes the doll, touches it to* HELEN's *nose, and spells again into her hand.*]

D, o, l, l. Think it over.

[HELEN *thinks it over, while* ANNIE *presents her own hand. Then* HELEN *spells three letters.* ANNIE *waits a second, then completes the word for* HELEN *in her palm.*]

> **GUIDED READING**
> What new tactic does Annie take with Helen?

L.

[*She hands over the doll, and* HELEN *gets a good grip on its leg.*]

Imitate now, understand later. End of the first les—

[*She never finishes, because* HELEN *swings the doll with a furious energy, it hits* ANNIE *squarely in the face, and she falls back with a cry of pain, her knuckles up to her mouth.* HELEN *waits, tensed for further combat. When* ANNIE *lowers her knuckles she looks at blood on them; she works her lips, gets to her feet, finds the mirror, and bares her teeth at herself. Now she is furious herself.*]

You little wretch, no one's taught you *any* manners? I'll—

[*But rounding from the mirror she sees the door slam,* HELEN *and the doll are on the outside, and* HELEN *is turning the key in the lock.* ANNIE *darts over, to pull the knob, the door is locked fast. She yanks it again.*]

> **GUIDED READING**
> Why does Annie stop mid-sentence? What does she realize?

Helen! Helen, let me out of—

[*She bats her brow at the folly of speaking, but* JAMES, *now downstairs, hears her and turns to see* HELEN *with the key and doll groping her way down the steps,* JAMES *takes in the whole situation, makes a move to intercept* HELEN, *but then changes his mind, lets her pass, and amusedly follows her out onto the porch. Upstairs* ANNIE *meanwhile rattles the knob, kneels, peers through the keyhole, gets up. She goes to the window, looks down, frowns.* JAMES *from the yard sings gaily up to her:*]

JAMES:

Buffalo girl, are you coming out tonight,

Coming out tonight,

Coming out—

[*He drifts back into the house.* ANNIE *takes a handkerchief, nurses her mouth, stands in the middle of the room, staring at door and window in turn, and so catches sight of herself in the mirror; her cheek scratched, her hair dishevelled, her handkerchief bloody, her face disgusted with herself. She addresses the mirror, with some irony.*]

ANNIE: Don't worry. They'll find you, you're not lost. Only out of place.

[*But she coughs, spits something into her palm, and stares at it, outraged.*]

And toothless.

[*She winces.*]

Oo! It hurts.

[*She pours some water into the basin, dips the handkerchief, and presses it to her mouth. Standing there, bent over the basin in pain—with the rest of the set dim and unreal, and the lights upon her taking on the subtle color of the past—she hears again, as do we, the faraway voices, and slowly she lifts her head to them; the boy's voice is the same, the others are cracked old crones in a nightmare, and perhaps we see their shadows.*]

BOY'S VOICE: It hurts. Annie, it hurts.

FIRST CRONE'S VOICE: Keep that brat shut up, can't you, girlie, how's a body to get any sleep in this damn ward?

BOY'S VOICE: It hurts. It hurts.

SECOND CRONE'S VOICE: Shut up, you!

BOY'S VOICE: Annie, when are we goin' home? You promised!

ANNIE: Jimmie—

BOY'S VOICE: Forever and ever, you said forever—

[ANNIE *drops the handkerchief, averts to the window, and is arrested there by the next cry.*]

Annie? Annie, you there? Annie! It *hurts*!

THIRD CRONE'S VOICE: Grab him, he's fallin'!

BOY'S VOICE: *Annie!*

DOCTOR'S VOICE [A PAUSE, SLOWLY]: Little girl. Little girl, I must tell you your brother will be going on a—

[*But* ANNIE *claps her hands to her ears, to shut this out, there is instant silence.*

As the lights bring the other areas in again, JAMES *goes to the steps to listen for any sound from upstairs.* KELLER *re-entering from left crosses toward the house; he passes* HELEN *en route to her retreat under the pump.* KATE *re-enters the rear door of the family room, with flowers for the table.*]

KATE: Supper is ready, Jimmie, will you call your father?

JAMES: Certainly.

[*But he calls up the stairs, for* ANNIE'S *benefit:*]

Father! Supper!

KELLER [AT THE DOOR]: No need to shout, I've been cooling my heels for an hour. Sit down.

JAMES: Certainly.

KELLER: Viney!

[VINEY *backs in with a roast, while they get settled around the table.*]

VINEY: Yes, Cap'n, right here.

KATE: Mildred went directly to sleep, Viney?

VINEY: Oh yes, that babe's a angel.

KATE: And Helen had a good supper?

VINEY [VAGUELY]: I dunno, Miss Kate, somehow she didn't have much of a appetite tonight—

KATE: [A BIT GUILTY] Oh. Dear.

KELLER [HASTILY]: Well now. Couldn't say the same for my part, I'm famished. Katie, your plate.

KATE [LOOKING]: But where is Miss Annie?

[*A silence.*]

JAMES [PLEASANTLY]: In her room.

KELLER: In her room? Doesn't she know hot food must be eaten hot? Go bring her down at once, Jimmie.

JAMES [RISES]: Certainly. I'll get a ladder.

KELLER [STARES]: What?

JAMES: I'll need a ladder. Shouldn't take me long.

KATE [STARES]: What shouldn't take you—

KELLER: Jimmie, do as I say! Go upstairs at once and tell Miss Sullivan supper is getting cold—

JAMES: She's locked in her room.

KELLER: Locked in her—

KATE: What on earth are you—

GUIDED READING
What does James finally reveal?

JAMES: Helen locked her in and made off with the key.

KATE: [RISING]: And you sit here and say nothing?

JAMES: Well, everyone's been telling me not to say anything.

[*He goes serenely out and across the yard, whistling.* KELLER *thrusting up from his chair makes for the stairs.*]

1. James finally reveals that Annie is locked in her room.

BIBLIOGRAPHIC NOTE

Encourage your students to read one of the following books on living with a disability:

- Lillian Rosen's *Just Like Everybody Else* (novel)
- James B. Garfield's *Follow My Leader* (novel)
- Jill Krementz's *How It Feels to Live with a Physical Disability*

You also might share with students the following list of famous writers who were blind or near blind: Homer, John Milton, and James Joyce.

1. Annie replies with some annoyance that if there were a key on her side she would not be stuck in the room.
2. Keller acts as though it is Annie's fault that she is locked in the room.

CROSS-CURRICULAR ACTIVITIES

SOCIAL STUDIES. Interested students might research the life story of Lon Chaney. (His parents were deaf mutes, and he later used the skills in pantomime he used to communicate with his parents to begin an acting career on stage and film.) Students should prepare brief (no more than a page) written reports, sharing some of the highlights and accomplishments in Chaney's life.

KATE: Viney, look out in back for Helen. See if she has that key.

VINEY: Yes, Miss Kate.

[VINEY *goes out the rear door.*]

KELLER [CALLING DOWN]: She's out by the pump!

[KATE *goes out on the porch after* HELEN, *while* KELLER *knocks on* ANNIE'S *door, then rattles the knob, imperiously.*]

Miss Sullivan! Are you in there?

ANNIE: Oh, I'm in here, all right.

KELLER: Is there no key on your side?

ANNIE [WITH SOME ASPERITY]: Well, if there was a key in here, *I* wouldn't be in here. Helen took it, the only thing on my side is me.

KELLER: Miss Sullivan. I—

[*He tries, but cannot hold it back.*]

> **GUIDED READING**
>
> How does Annie react to Keller's question?

Not in the house ten minutes, I don't see how you managed it!

[*He stomps downstairs again, while* ANNIE *mutters to herself.*]

ANNIE: And even I'm not on my side.

KELLER [ROARING]: Viney!

VINEY [REAPPEARING]: Yes, Cap'n?

KELLER: Put that meat back in the oven!

[VINEY *bears the roast off again, while* KELLER *strides out onto the porch.* KATE *is with* HELEN *at the pump, opening her hands.*]

KATE: She has no key.

KELLER: Nonsense, she must have the key. Have you searched in her pockets?

KATE: Yes. She doesn't have it.

KELLER: Katie, she must have the key.

KATE: Would you prefer to search her yourself, Captain?

KELLER: No, I would not prefer to search her! She almost took my kneecap off this evening, when I tried merely to—

[JAMES *reappears carrying a long ladder, with* PERCY *running after him to be in on things.*]

Take that ladder back!

JAMES: Certainly.

[*He turns around with it.* MARTHA *comes skipping around the upstage corner of the house to be in on things, accompanied by the setter* BELLE.]

KATE: She could have hidden the key.

KELLER: Where?

KATE: Anywhere. Under a stone. In the flower beds. In the grass—

KELLER: Well, I can't plow up the entire grounds to find a missing key! Jimmie!

JAMES: Sir?

KELLER: Bring me a ladder!

JAMES: Certainly.

[VINEY *comes around the downstage side of the house to be in on things; she has* MILDRED *over her shoulder, bleating.* KELLER *places the ladder against* ANNIE'S *window and mounts.* ANNIE *meanwhile is running about making herself presentable, washing the blood off her mouth, straightening her clothes, tidying her hair. Another Negro servant enters to gaze in wonder, increasing the gathering ring of spectators.*]

KATE [SHARPLY]: What is Mildred doing up?

VINEY: Cap'n woke her, ma'am, all that hollering.

KELLER: Miss Sullivan!

[ANNIE *comes to the window, with as much air of gracious normality as she can manage;* KELLER *is at the window.*]

ANNIE [BRIGHTLY]: Yes, Captain Keller?

KELLER: Come out!

ANNIE: I don't see how I can. There isn't room.

SELECTION CHECK TEST 4.10.1 WITH ANSWERS (CONT.)

4. How does the writer build up suspense about Annie before she actually arrives at the Keller household? **Responses will vary, but could include that the family discusses Annie, we see her meeting with Mr. Anagnos, and the family meets the trains at the station for two days before Annie finally arrives.**

5. The stage directions indicate that the stage is divided into two areas. What is in each area? **Behind the diagonal, in upstage right, sits the Keller's house and, near the center of the stage, a water pump. In front of the diagonal, in downstage left, is a neutral area that accommodates different things at different times—the Perkins Institute for the Blind, the garden house, etc.**

KELLER: I intend to carry you. Climb onto my shoulder and hold tight.

ANNIE: Oh, no. It's—very chivalrous of you, but I'd really prefer to—

KELLER: Miss Sullivan, follow instructions! I will not have you also tumbling out of our windows.

[ANNIE *obeys, with some misgivings.*]

I hope this is not a sample of what we may expect from you. In the way of simplifying the work of looking after Helen.

ANNIE: Captain Keller, I'm perfectly able to go down a ladder under my own—

KELLER: I doubt it, Miss Sullivan. Simply hold onto my neck.

GUIDED READING
How does Annie think she should get down from her room?

[*He begins down with her, while the spectators stand in a wide and somewhat awe-stricken circle, watching.* KELLER *half-misses a rung, and* ANNIE *grabs at his whiskers.*]

My *neck,* Miss Sullivan!

ANNIE: I'm sorry to inconvenience you this way—

KELLER: No inconvenience, other than having that door taken down and the lock replaced, if we fail to find that key.

ANNIE: Oh, I'll look everywhere for it.

KELLER: Thank you. Do not look in any rooms that can be locked. There.

[*He stands her on the, ground.* JAMES *applauds.*]

ANNIE: Thank you very much.

[*She smooths her skirt, looking as composed and ladylike as possible.* KELLER *stares around at the spectators.*]

KELLER: Go, go, back to your work. What are you looking at here? There's nothing here to look at.

[*They break up, move off.*]

Now would it be possible for us to have supper, like other people?

[*He marches into the house.*]

KATE: Viney, serve supper. I'll put Mildred to sleep.

[*They all go in.* JAMES *is the last to leave, murmuring to* ANNIE *with a gesture.*]

JAMES: Might as well leave the l, a, d, d, e, r, hm?

[ANNIE *ignores him, looking at* HELEN; JAMES *goes in too. Imperceptibly the lights commence to narrow down.* ANNIE *and* HELEN *are now alone in the yard,* HELEN *seated at the pump, where she has been oblivious[11] to it all, a battered little savage, playing with the doll in a picture of innocent contentment.* ANNIE *comes near, leans against the house, and taking off her smoked glasses, studies her, not without awe. Presently* HELEN *rises, gropes around to see if anyone is present,* ANNIE *evades her hand, and when* HELEN *is satisfied she is alone, the key suddenly protrudes out of her mouth. She takes it in her fingers, stands thinking, gropes to the pump, lifts a loose board, drops the key into the well, and hugs herself gleefully.* ANNIE *stares. But after a moment she shakes her head to herself, she cannot keep the smile from her lips.*]

ANNIE: You *devil.*

[*Her tone is one of great respect, humor, and acceptance of challenge.*]

GUIDED READING
What does Helen do when she thinks she is alone? How does Annie react to Helen's action?

You think I'm so easily gotten rid of? You have a thing or two to learn, first. I have nothing else to do.

[*She goes up the steps to the porch, but turns for a final word, almost of warning.*]

And nowhere to go.

[*And presently she moves into the house to the others, as the lights dim down and out, except for the small circle upon* HELEN *solitary at the pump, which ends the act.*]

---

11. **oblivious.** Completely unaware

ANSWERS TO GUIDED READING QUESTIONS

1. Annie thinks that she should climb down the ladder. Keller insists on carrying Annie down the ladder.
2. James is making fun of Annie's attempts to teach Helen to spell.
3. Helen pulls the key out of her mouth and drops it down the well. Annie greets Helen's action with respect and amusement.
4. Helen thinks she will be able to drive Annie away. Annie will not be easy to get rid of because she has nothing else to do and no where else to go.

SELECTION CHECK TEST 4.10.1 WITH ANSWERS

Checking Your Reading
1. What caused Helen's blindness and deafness? **Helen's blindness and deafness were caused by an illness she suffered when she was 19 months old.**
2. Which member of the family has to be persuaded to write to the doctor? **Captain Keller has to be persuaded to write to the doctor.**
3. What present do the children give Annie to take to Helen? **The children give Annie a doll to take to Helen.**
4. What does Annie say she will teach Helen first? **Annie says she will teach Helen language first.**
5. What does Helen do with the key to Annie's room? **Helen drops the key to Annie's room down the well.**

Vocabulary in Context
Fill in each blank below with the most appropriate vocabulary word from act 1 of "The Miracle Worker." You may have to change the tense of the word.

facetious   benign   unencumbered
frantic   impudence
emphatic   steel

1. Sheila thought she was prepared for the trip, but the last-minute chores made her _____. **frantic**
2. The weather report warned residents of the beach town to _____ themselves for another storm. **steel**
3. Taylor is smart and enjoys school, but his _____ often lands him in trouble. **impudence**
4. The new principal was _____ as he insisted that everyone attend the opening assembly. **emphatic**
5. The _____ smile of the police officer put the little boy at ease. **benign**

SELECTION CHECK TEST 4.10.1 WITH ANSWERS (CONT.)

Reader's Toolbox
1. In the opening scene, Helen is 19 months old, and the next scene takes place five years later. How do the stage directions indicate the passage of time? **The passage of time is indicated by the lights when dim and then come back up, and by the tolling of a distant bell.**
2. How do the stage directions indicate that Annie is remembering the past when she hears her brother's voice? **The lights change colors to indicate the passage of time.**
3. What are the three major techniques a writer uses to describe a character? **A writer describes a character through direct description, through portraying a character's behavior, and through sharing the character's thoughts and emotions.**

RECALL

1a. She moves her lips, imitating the movement she felt when Percy was speaking. Helen is upset because the doll does not have any eyes.

2a. Kate gives Helen a peppermint drop, Viney gives her a tea-cake and Keller gives her a stick of candy.

3a. Annie has Dr. Howe's work behind her, she is young and energetic, and she has been blind. She will not give up easily because Helen has something to learn and Annie has nothing else to do and no where else to go.

INTERPRET

1b. Helen tries to imitate what she feels others doing. She knows that they move their mouths, but she cannot make sense of moving her own. She is upset that the doll does not have eyes that she feels on people. She recognizes that mouths and eyes are important although they do not have meaning in her world.

2b. Kate, Keller and Viney give Helen these items to keep her calm and happy and because they do not know how else to communicate with her. Helen readily accepts these items, but they do not satisfy her need to communicate with others.

3b. *Responses may vary.* These three things are likely to be beneficial to Annie. She can build upon the work done by somebody else, she will have the energy to keep going in the face of adversity, and she understands what it is like to be blind. Her determination and the fact that she has no where to go if she does not succeed will also be assets.

ANALYZE

4a. Helen tries to communicate by imitating the mouth movements she feels in others, by touching her cheek to show that she wants her mother, and through facial expressions and pointing. Annie communicates with Helen by finger spelling words and trying to connect them to objects or actions.

SYNTHESIZE

4b. Language is the key to allowing Helen to express herself to others and to unlock the door for learning about other things. Helen communicates with great difficulty with occasional signs, but mostly with pointing and motioning. Annie tries to teach Helen a systematic way to communicate by

Investigate, Inquire, and Imagine

Recall: GATHERING FACTS

1a. What does Helen do after poking her fingers in Percy's mouth? What upsets Helen about the doll made by Aunt Ev?

2a. What do Kate, Keller, and Viney give to Helen when Kate goes to get Annie?

3a. What three advantages does Annie say she has over Dr. Howe? At the end of the act, why does Annie say she will not be gotten rid of so easily?

Interpret: FINDING MEANING

1b. Why do the incidents with Percy and with the doll upset Helen? What do these occurrences show about Helen's world?

2b. Why do Kate, Keller, and Viney give Helen these things? Explain whether these gestures satisfy Helen.

3b. Explain whether you think the assets Annie lists will be important to her as she tries to teach Helen.

Analyze: TAKING THINGS APART

4a. Identify three ways in which Helen communicates with other people. Explain how Annie communicates with Helen.

Synthesize: BRINGING THINGS TOGETHER

4b. Annie says that she will teach Helen, "First, last, and—in between, language." Why is learning language so important for Helen? Explain how Annie's method of communicating with Helen differs from the way in which Helen now communicates.

Evaluate: MAKING JUDGEMENTS

5a. Do you think Annie is up to the challenge of teaching Helen? Explain.

Extend: CONNECTING IDEAS

5a. In what ways are Helen's behavior problems similar to those of a typical, sighted and hearing child? Explain whether you think Helen deserves to be treated differently because of her disabilities.

Understanding Literature

CHARACTERIZATION. Review the complete definition of **characterization** in the Handbook of Literary Terms. Choose five words to describe Annie's character. Identify actions, dialogue from other characters or other passages from this act that show you this side of Annie. What are Annie's weaknesses, according to other charactors? What are her strengths?

SUSPENSE. Suspense is a feeling of anxiousness or curiosity. Writers create suspense by raising questions in the reader's mind and using details that create strong emotion. What questions were raised by the events in act 1? When did the events make you feel anxious?

ANSWERS TO INVESTIGATE, INQUIRE, IMAGINE (CONT.)

giving her a way to translate the words the people around her use. The key to Annie's method is for Helen to understand that the finger spelled letters have a meaning.

EVALUATE

5a. Responses will vary, but students should use evidence from the text.

EXTEND

5b. Responses will vary. You might engage students in a discussion about whether some of Helen's problems are caused when her behavior is excused because of her disability.

ACT 2

IT IS EVENING.

The only room visible in the KELLER *house is* ANNIE'S, *where by lamplight* ANNIE *in a shawl is at a desk writing a letter; at her bureau* HELEN *in her customary unkempt state is tucking her doll in the bottom drawer as a cradle, the contents of which she has dumped out, creating as usual a fine disorder.*

ANNIE *mutters each word as she writes her letter, slowly, her eyes close to and almost touching the page, to follow with difficulty her penwork.*
ANNIE: "…and, nobody, here, has, attempted, to, control, her. The, greatest, problem, I, have, is, how, to, disipline, her, without, breaking, her, spirit."

[*Resolute voice*]

"But, I, shall, insist, on, reasonable, obedience, from, the, start—"

GUIDED READING
What is the greatest difficulty Annie faces?

[*At which point* HELEN, *groping about on the desk, knocks over the inkwell.* ANNIE *jumps up, rescues her letter, rights the inkwell, grabs a towel to stem the spillage, and then wipes at* HELEN'S *hands;* HELEN *as always pulls free, but not until* ANNIE *first gets three letters into her palm.*]

Ink.

[HELEN *is enough interested in and puzzled by this spelling that she* proffers *her hand again; so* ANNIE *spells and* impassively *dunks it back in the spillage.*]

GUIDED READING
What does Annie do when Helen spills the ink?

Ink. It has a name.

[*She wipes the hand clean, and leads* HELEN *to her bureau, where she looks for something to engage her. She finds a sewing card, with needle and thread, and going to her knees, shows* HELEN'S *hand how to connect one row of holes.*]

Down. Under. Up. And be careful of the needle—

[HELEN *gets it, and* ANNIE *rises.*]

Fine. You keep out of the ink and perhaps I can keep out of—the soup.

[*She returns to the desk, tidies it, and resumes writing her letter, bent close to the page.*]

"These, blots, are, her, handiwork. I—"

[*She is interrupted by a gasp:* HELEN *has stuck her finger, and sits sucking at it, darkly. Then with* vengeful *resolve she seizes her doll, and is about to dash its brains out on the floor when* ANNIE *diving catches it in one hand, which she at once shakes with hopping pain but otherwise ignores, patiently.*]

All right, let's try temperance.

[*Taking the doll, she kneels, goes through the motion of knocking its head on the floor, spells into* HELEN'S *hand:*]

Bad, girl.

[*She lets* HELEN *feel the grieved expression on her face.* HELEN *imitates it. Next she makes* HELEN *caress the doll and kiss the hurt spot and hold it gently in her arms, then spells into her hand:*]

Good, girl.

[*She lets* HELEN *feel the smile on her face.* HELEN *sits with a scowl, which suddenly clears; she pats the doll, kisses it, wreathes her face in a large artificial smile, and bears the doll to the washstand, where she carefully sits it.* ANNIE *watches, pleased.*]

Very good girl—

WORDS FOR EVERYDAY USE
prof • fer (präf' fər) v., present for acceptance, offer. *The well-trained dog* proffered *its paw to shake.*
im • pas • sive (im pa' siv) adj., giving no sign of emotion. *The man yawned and gave me an* impassive *handshake.* **impassively,** adv.
venge • ful (vənj' fəl) adj., revengeful. *The Count's* vengeful *look showed that he was plotting revenge.*
tem • per • ance (tem' pə rəns) n., moderation in action; restraint. *If you eat too much chocolate, you need to learn* temperance.

ACT 2 / THE MIRACLE WORKER **711**

ANSWERS TO UNDERSTANDING LITERATURE

CHARACTERIZATION. *Responses will vary. Possible responses are given.* Helen is spoiled. Nobody says no to Helen. They give her sweets to avoid bad behavior. Helen is wild and unkempt. When Annie arrives she is messy, her hair is tumbled and her pinafore is ripped. Helen is quick or clever. She almost immediate imitates the symbols Annie spells to her. Helen is angry. When she does not get her way, she hits Annie and locks her in the room.

DIALECT. Some examples include: "I'm gonna cut off his head first, he got a bad cold," "Ain't gonna be much of that doctor left to fix up, time you finish all them oper–," "That's how I do, she keep pokin' her fingers in my mouth, I just bite 'em off," "She tryin' *talk.* She gonna get mad. Looka her tryin' to talk," Let Mr. Jimmy go by hisself, you been pokin' that garden all day," and "She upstairs, smellin' around. She know somethin' funny's goin' on."

ANSWERS TO GUIDED READING QUESTIONS

1. Annie must find a way to discipline Helen without breaking her spirit.
2. Annie spells "ink" into Helen's hand.

VOCABULARY FROM THE SELECTION—ACT 2

apprehensive	irresolute
compel	laborious
compunction	nonplussed
dour	proffer
feigned	protracted
feint	relinquish
impassive	temperance
impertinent	vengeful
incarnate	vexedly
interminable	wry
intractable	zeal

ADDITIONAL QUESTIONS AND ACTIVITIES

Ask students the following questions:

1. What does Annie say that nobody in the Keller house has tried to do? Why might this make Annie's job difficult?
2. What does Annie say Helen needs? What does she say she will insist on?
3. What does Helen do as soon as Annie say she will insist on this? In what way does this action undercut Annie's resolution?

Answers

1. Annie says that nobody in the Keller house has tried to control Helen. Students may say this makes Annie's job difficult because Helen is used to getting her way and being allowed to do whatever she wishes, so she might react negatively to the discipline necessary to teach her.
2. Annie says that Helen needs discipline. She says she will insist on "reasonable obedience, from the start."
3. Helen comes and knocks over the inkwell, indicating that Annie has a difficult task ahead of her in insisting on obedience.

1. Annie spells "bad girl" while making a grieved expression and "good girl" while smiling.
2. Kate is moved, but not overly excited.
3. Helen does not yet know what a word is. She does not connect the words Annie spells to objects, actions or anything else.
4. She compares it to the gibberish and baby talk that anyone speaks to a hearing child.
5. Annie spells "card," but Helen spells "cake."
6. Annie tells Kate that it is only a finger game. Helen has to learn that things have names.

CULTURAL/ HISTORICAL NOTE

Point students to Kate Keller's comment that Helen is "impaired," and Annie's responses, "Ho, there's nothing impaired in that head, it works like a mousetrap!" One of the prejudices people with disabilities have struggled to overcome beginning in the late nineteenth century was the assumption that they lacked the ability to perform the same mental and physical tasks as other people. People with disabilities have come to reject terms like *impaired* and *handicapped* because of the negative ideas they perpetuate; hence, terms like *hearing-challenged* and *sight-challenged* are becoming more commonplace. Many people with disabilities prefer such terms because they imply that their disability is a challenge in their lives but one that they can overcome to live active lives, both mentally and physically.

[*Whereupon* HELEN *elevates the pitcher and dashes it on the floor instead.* ANNIE *leaps to her feet, and stands inarticulate;* HELEN *calmly gropes back to sit to the sewing card and needle.*

ANNIE *manages to achieve self-control. She picks up a fragment or two of the pitcher, sees* HELEN *is puzzling over the card, and resolutely kneels to demonstrate it again. She spells into* HELEN'S *hand.*

KATE *meanwhile coming around the corner with folded sheets on her arm, halts at the doorway and watches them for a moment in silence; she is moved, but level.*]

KATE [PRESENTLY]: What are you saying to her?

[ANNIE *glancing up is a bit embarrassed, and rises from the spelling, to find her company manners.*]

ANNIE: Oh, I was just making conversation. Saying it was a sewing card.

KATE: But does that—

[*She imitates with her fingers*]

—mean that to her?

ANNIE: No. No, she won't know what spelling is till she knows what a word is.

KATE: Yet you keep spelling to her. Why?

ANNIE [CHEERILY]: I like to hear myself talk!

KATE: The Captain says it's like spelling to the fence post.

ANNIE [A PAUSE]: Does he, now.

KATE: Is it?

ANNIE: No, it's how I watch you talk to Mildred.

KATE: Mildred.

ANNIE: Any baby. Gibberish, grown-up gibberish, baby-talk gibberish, do they understand one word of it to start? Somehow they begin to. If they hear it, I'm letting Helen hear it.

KATE: Other children are not—impaired.

ANNIE: Ho, there's nothing impaired in that head, it works like a mousetrap!

KATE [SMILES]: But after a child hears how many words, Miss Annie, a million?

ANNIE: I guess no mother's ever minded enough to count.

GUIDED READING
To what does Annie compare the way she spells to Helen?

[*She drops her eyes to spell into* HELEN'S *hand, again indicating the card;* HELEN *spells back, and* ANNIE *is amused.*]

KATE [TOO QUICKLY]: What did she spell?

ANNIE: I spelt card. She spelt cake!

[*She takes in* KATE'S *quickness, and shakes her head, gently.*]

No, it's only a finger-game to her, Mrs. Keller. What she has to learn first is that things have names.

KATE: And when will she learn?

ANNIE: Maybe after a million and one words.

[*They hold each other's gaze;* KATE *then speaks quietly.*]

KATE: I should like to learn those letters, Miss Annie.

ANNIE [PLEASED]: I'll teach you tomorrow morning. That makes only half a million each!

GUIDED READING
What explanation does Annie give Kate? What does Helen have to learn?

KATE [THEN]: It's her bedtime.

[ANNIE *reaches for the sewing card,* HELEN *objects,* ANNIE *insists, and* HELEN *gets rid of* ANNIE'S *hand by jabbing it with the needle.* ANNIE *gasps, and moves to grip* HELEN'S *wrist; but* KATE *intervenes with a proffered sweet, and*

HELEN *drops the card, crams the sweet into her mouth, and scrambles up to search her mother's hands for more.* ANNIE *nurses her wound, staring after the sweet.*]

I'm sorry, Miss Annie.

ANNIE [INDIGNANTLY]: Why does she get a reward? For stabbing me?

GUIDED READING
How does Kate intervene when Helen stabs Annie with the needle?

KATE: Well—

[*Then, tiredly*]

We catch our flies with honey, I'm afraid. We haven't the heart for much else, and so many times she simply cannot be <u>compelled</u>.

ANNIE [OMINOUS]: Yes. I'm the same way myself.

[KATE *smiles, and leads* HELEN *off around the corner.* ANNIE *alone in her room picks up things and in the act of removing* HELEN'S *doll gives way to unmannerly temptation: she throttles it. She drops it on her bed, and stands pondering. Then she turns back, sits decisively, and writes again, as the lights dim on her.*]

[*Grimly*]

"The, more, I, think, the, more, certain, I, am, that, obedience, is, the, gateway, through, which, knowledge, enters, the, mind, of, the, child—"

GUIDED READING
Of what does Annie become more and more certain?

[*On the word "obedience" a shaft of sunlight hits the water pump outside, while* ANNIE'S *voice ends in the dark, followed by a distant cockcrow; daylight comes up over another corner of the sky, with* VINEY'S *voice heard at once.*]

VINEY: Breakfast ready!

[VINEY *comes down into the sunlight beam, and pumps a pitcherful of water. While the pitcher is brimming we hear conversation from the dark; the light grows to the family room of the house where all are either entering or already seated at breakfast, with* KELLER *and* JAMES *arguing the war.* HELEN *is wandering around the table to explore the contents of the other plates. When* ANNIE *is in her chair, she watches* HELEN. VINEY *re-enters, sets the pitcher on the table;* KATE *lifts the almost empty biscuit plate with an inquiring look,* VINEY *nods and bears it off back, neither of them interrupting the men.* ANNIE *meanwhile sits with fork quiet, watching* HELEN, *who at her mother's plate pokes her hand among some scrambled eggs.* KATE *catches* ANNIE'S *eyes on her; smiles with a* <u>wry</u> *gesture.* HELEN *moves on to* JAMES'S *plate, the male talk continuing,* JAMES *deferential and* KELLER *overriding.*]

GUIDED READING
What does Helen do while the others are sitting at breakfast?

JAMES: —no, but shouldn't we give the devil his due, father? The fact is we lost the South two years earlier when he outthought us behind Vicksburg.[1]

KELLER: Outthought is a peculiar word for a butcher.

JAMES: Harness maker, wasn't he?

KELLER: I said butcher, his only virtue as a soldier was numbers and he led them to slaughter with no more regard than for so many sheep.

JAMES: But even if in that sense he was a butcher, the fact is he—

---

1. **Vicksburg.** City in Western Mississippi, site of a battle and Confederate loss during the Civil War

ANSWERS TO GUIDED READING QUESTIONS

1. Kate gives Helen a sweet.
2. Annie becomes more and more certain that obedience is the gateway through which knowledge enters the mind of the child.
3. Helen walks about taking food off other people's plates.

ADDITIONAL QUESTIONS AND ACTIVITIES

Ask students to discuss what further evidence is presented on this page that nobody has ever tried to discipline Helen before? *Answers.* Students may point to the fact that Kate gives Helen a sweet after she jabs Annie with a needle rather than punishing her. Also, nobody objects when Helen grabs food off their plates.

words for everyday use

com • pel (kəm pel') *v.,* cause to do through excessive pressure. *At first, Judd had to <u>compel</u> the dog to heel by jerking on his leash, but after a few weeks the dog obeyed eagerly.*

wry (rī) *adj.,* ironic or sarcastic; grimly humorous. *"Well, that was fun," was Lester's <u>wry</u> comment after he fell down the stairs.*

1. Keller and James ignore Helen.
Annie removes Helen's hand from
her plate.

BIOGRAPHICAL NOTE

Inform students that many
Southerners felt great resentment
after the Civil War. Here, Captain
Keller and James are discussing one
of the Union's generals, Ulysses S.
Grant (1822–1855). Grant
distinguished himself in the military
during the Mexican War. (Tell
students that the Northerners who
supported the United States
government were known as the
Union forces because they sought to
preserve the union of the United
States of America, while the
Southern soldiers were known as
Confederate soldiers because the
states that broke away tried to form
a new nation called the Confederate
States of America.) When the Civil
War broke out Grant was appointed
colonel and later general of the
Illinois Volunteers. He established his
reputation as a military commander
during the battle of Vicksburg in
1863. (This is the battle that Captain
Keller and his son discuss.) Not long
after Grant captured Vicksburg, he
was made commander of the entire
Union army in 1864. The Civil War
ended when General Robert E. Lee
surrendered to Grant at Appomattox
Court House on April 9, 1865. Grant
later became the eighteenth
president of the United States. His
presidency lasted from 1869–1877.

KELLER: And a drunken one, half the war.

JAMES: Agreed, father. If his own people said
he was I can't argue he—

KELLER: Well, what is it you find to admire
in such a man, Jimmie, the butchery or the
drunkenness?

JAMES: Neither, father, only the fact that he
beat us.

KELLER: He didn't.

JAMES: Is it your contention we won the war,
sir?

KELLER: He didn't beat us at Vicksburg. We
lost Vicksburg because Pemberton gave
Bragg five thousand of his cavalry and
Loring, whom I knew personally for a nin-
compoop before you were born, marched
away from Champion's Hill with enough men
to have held them, we lost Vicksburg by stupidity verging on treason.

JAMES: I would have said we lost Vicksburg
because Grant was one thing no Yankee general was before him—

KELLER: Drunk? I doubt it.

JAMES: Obstinate.

KELLER: Obstinate. Could any of them compare even in that with old Stonewall? If he'd
been there we would still have Vicksburg.

JAMES: Well, the butcher simply wouldn't
give up, he tried four ways of getting around
Vicksburg and on the fifth try he got around.
Anyone else would have pulled north and—

KELLER: He wouldn't have got around if we'd
had a Southerner in command, instead of a
half-breed Yankee traitor like Pemberton—

[*While this background talk is in progress,*
HELEN *is working around the table, ultimately
toward* ANNIE'S *plate. She messes with her
hands in* JAMES'S *plate, then in* KELLER'S, *both
men taking it so for granted they hardly notice.*]

Then HELEN *comes grop-
ing with soiled hands past
her own plate, to* ANNIE'S;
her hand goes to it, and
ANNIE, *who has been waiting, deliberately lifts and
removes her hand.* HELEN *gropes again,*
ANNIE *firmly pins her by the wrist, and
removes her hand from the table.* HELEN
thrusts her hands again, ANNIE *catches them,
and* HELEN *begins to flail and make noises; the
interruption brings* KELLER'S *gaze upon them.*]

GUIDED READING

How do Keller and
James react to
Helen groping
around their
plates? What does
Annie do?

What's the matter there?

KATE: Miss Annie. You see, she's accustomed
to helping herself from our plates to anything
she—

ANNIE [EVENLY]: Yes, but *I'm* not accustomed
to it.

KELLER: No, of course not. Viney!

KATE: Give her something, Jimmie, to quiet
her.

JAMES [BLANDLY]: But her table manners are
the best she has. Well.

[*He pokes across with a chunk of bacon at*
HELEN'S *hand, which* ANNIE *releases; but*
HELEN *knocks the bacon away and stubbornly
thrusts at* ANNIE'S *plate,* ANNIE *grips her wrists
again, the struggle mounts.*]

KELLER: Let her this time, Miss Sullivan, it's
the only way we get any adult conversation. If
my son's half merits that
description.

[*He rises.*]

I'll get you another plate.

GUIDED READING

What excuses do
the Kellers make for
Helen's behavior?

ANNIE [GRIPPING HELEN]: I have a plate,
thank you.

KATE [CALLING]: Viney! I'm afraid what
Captain Keller says is only too true, she'll
persist in this until she gets her own way.

KELLER [AT THE DOOR]: Viney, bring Miss Sullivan another plate—

ANNIE [STONILY]: I have a plate, nothing's wrong with the *plate*, I intend to keep it.

[*Silence for a moment, except for* HELEN'S *noises as she struggles to get loose; the* KELLERS *are a bit* nonplussed, *and* ANNIE *is too darkly intent on* HELEN'S *manners to have any thoughts now of her own.*]

JAMES: Ha. You see why they took Vicksburg?

KELLER [UNCERTAINLY]: Miss Sullivan. One plate or another is hardly a matter to struggle with a deprived child about.

ANNIE: Oh, I'd sooner have a more—

[HELEN *begins to kick,* ANNIE *moves her ankles to the opposite side of the chair.*]

—heroic issue myself, I—

KELLER: No, I really must insist you—

[HELEN *bangs her toe on the chair and sinks to the floor, crying with rage and* feigned *injury;* ANNIE *keeps hold of her wrists, gazing down, while* KATE *rises.*]

Now she's hurt herself.

ANNIE [GRIMLY]: No, she hasn't.

KELLER: Will you please let her hands go?

KATE: Miss Annie, you don't know the child well enough yet, she'll keep—

ANNIE: I know an ordinary tantrum well enough, when I see one, and a badly spoiled child—

JAMES: Hear, hear.

KELLER [VERY ANNOYED]: Miss Sullivan! You would have more understanding of your pupil if you had some pity in you. Now kindly do as I—

ANNIE: Pity?

[*She releases* HELEN *to turn equally annoyed on* KELLER *across the table; instantly* HELEN *scrambles up and dives at* ANNIE'S *plate. This time* ANNIE *intercepts her by pouncing on her wrists like a hawk, and her temper boils.*]

For this *tyrant?* The whole house turns on her whims, is there anything she wants she doesn't get? I'll tell you what I pity, that the sun won't rise and set for her all her life, and every day you're telling her it will, what good will your pity do her when you're under the strawberries, Captain Keller?

KELLER [OUTRAGED]: Kate, for the love of heaven will you—

KATE: Miss Annie, please, I don't think it serves to lose our—

ANNIE: It does you good, that's all. It's less trouble to feel sorry for her than to teach her anything better, isn't it?

KELLER: I fail to see where you have taught her anything yet, Miss Sullivan!

ANNIE: I'll begin this minute, if you'll leave the room, Captain Keller!

KELLER [ASTONISHED]: Leave the—

ANNIE: Everyone, please.

[*She struggles with* HELEN, *while* KELLER *endeavors to control his voice.*]

GUIDED READING

What does Annie recognize in Helen's actions? Who agrees with her?

GUIDED READING

What does Annie pity?

words for everyday use

non • plussed (nän pləst′) *adj.*, at a loss what to say or do. *Jake was* nonplussed *upon meeting the movie star.*
feigned (fānd) *adj.*, faked. *The actor's love for his leading lady was* feigned, *but very convincing.*

1. The Kellers tell Annie that Helen is accustomed to eating off the plates of others and that it is the only way they get any adult conversation.
2. James is referring to his previous point about the winning tactics of being obstinate.
3. Annie recognizes that Helen is a spoiled child having a tantrum. James agrees with her.
4. Annie pities "that the sun won't rise and set for her all her life" and every day Keller tells her that it will.

LITERARY TECHNIQUE

EUPHEMISM AND CONFLICT. A **euphemism** is a less emotionally powerful phrase used in place of one that might be offensive. A **conflict** is a struggle between two people or things in a literary work. Point out to students that when Annie says, "when you're under the strawberries, Captain Keller," she is using a euphemism meaning, "when you are dead and buried, Captain Keller." Death is a part of human life that has inspired many, many euphemisms. Ask students to list some that they may have heard. Is the euphemism Annie uses one that they know? Is it similar to others they know? (They may note it is like "pushing up daisies," euphemism for death.)

Then ask students the following questions about the conflict that takes place on this page: What conflict does Annie decide to have with Helen? Why do you think she decides to make this into a conflict rather than letting Helen have her way? In what way does this erupt into a conflict between Annie and Captain and Kate Keller? What does Annie point out about the lack of conflict that has taken place in this house and its effects? What negative effect does Annie say she sees pity having on Helen?

Answers. Annie decides to refuse to allow Helen to grab food from her plate and grabs her wrists whenever she tries to do so. Students may recognize that Annie thinks that Helen needs to learn discipline and obedience before she can learn anything else, so she is trying to teach Helen a lesson in manners and some discipline. Students may say that Kate and the Captain come to their daughter's defense saying that "one plate or another is hardly a

LITERARY TECHNIQUE (CONT.)

matter to struggle with a deprived child about." They urge her to have pity on their daughter. Annie refuses to pity Helen, saying that Helen is a little tyrant who rules the house through her tantrums. Annie says that the whole house caves in to Helen rather than risking conflict with her. Annie says that pity won't do Helen any good, won't help her take care of herself, after her parents are dead.

1. Annie says that is easier to feel sorrier for Helen than to teach her anything.
2. Annie must unteach Helen six years of pity.
3. Keller is upset that Annie has spoken to him in this manner. He threatens to send her back to Boston.
4. James thinks that what Annie has said is exceptionally intelligent.

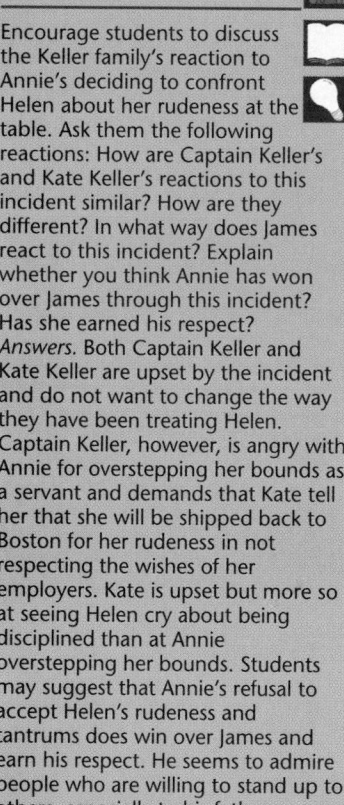

ADDITIONAL QUESTIONS AND ACTIVITIES

Encourage students to discuss the Keller family's reaction to Annie's deciding to confront Helen about her rudeness at the table. Ask them the following reactions: How are Captain Keller's and Kate Keller's reactions to this incident similar? How are they different? In what way does James react to this incident? Explain whether you think Annie has won over James through this incident? Has she earned his respect? *Answers.* Both Captain Keller and Kate Keller are upset by the incident and do not want to change the way they have been treating Helen. Captain Keller, however, is angry with Annie for overstepping her bounds as a servant and demands that Kate tell her that she will be shipped back to Boston for her rudeness in not respecting the wishes of her employers. Kate is upset but more so at seeing Helen cry about being disciplined than at Annie overstepping her bounds. Students may suggest that Annie's refusal to accept Helen's rudeness and tantrums does win over James and earn his respect. He seems to admire people who are willing to stand up to others, especially to his father.

KELLER: Miss Sullivan, you are here only as a paid teacher. Nothing more, and not to lecture—

ANNIE: I can't *un*teach her six years of pity if you can't stand up to one tantrum! Old Stonewall, indeed. Mrs. Keller, you promised me help.

KATE: Indeed I did, we truly want to—

ANNIE: Then leave me alone with her. Now!

KELLER [IN A WRATH]: Katie, will you come outside with me? At once, please.

[*He marches to the front door.* KATE *and* JAMES *follow him. Simultaneously* ANNIE *releases* HELEN'S *wrists, and the child again sinks to the floor, kicking and crying her weird noises;* ANNIE *steps over her to meet* VINEY *coming in the rear doorway with biscuits and a clean plate, surprised at the general commotion.*]

> **GUIDED READING**
> What does Annie demand that everyone do?

VINEY: Heaven sakes—

ANNIE: Out, please.

[*She backs* VINEY *out with one hand, closes the door on her astonished mouth, locks it, and removes the key.* KELLER *meanwhile snatches his hat from a rack, and* KATE *follows him down the porch steps.* JAMES *lingers in the doorway to address* ANNIE *across the room with a bow.*]

JAMES: If it takes all summer, general.

[ANNIE *comes over to his door in turn, removing her glasses grimly; as* KELLER *outside begins speaking,* ANNIE *closes the door on* JAMES, *locks it, removes the key, and turns with her back against the door to stare ominously at* HELEN, *kicking on the floor.*

JAMES *takes his hat from the rack, and going down the porch steps joins* KATE *and* KELLER *talking in the yard,* KELLER *in a sputter of ire.*]

KELLER: This girl, this—cub of a girl—*presumes!* I tell you, I'm of half a mind to ship

her back to Boston before the week is out. You can inform her so from me!

> **GUIDED READING**
> Why is Keller upset? What does he threaten to do?

KATE [EYEBROWS UP]: I, Captain?

KELLER: She's a *hireling!* [2] Now I want it clear, unless there's an apology and complete change of manner she goes back on the next train! Will you make that quite clear?

KATE: Where will you be, Captain, while I am making it quite—

KELLER: At the office!

[*He begins off left, finds his napkin still in his irate hand, is uncertain with it, dabs his lips with dignity, gets rid of it in a toss to* JAMES, *and marches off.* JAMES *turns to eye* KATE.]

JAMES: Will you?

[KATE'S *mouth is set, and* JAMES *studies it lightly.*]

I thought what she said was exceptionally intelligent. I've been saying it for years.

> **GUIDED READING**
> What does James think of what Annie said?

KATE [NOT WITHOUT SCORN]: To his face?

[*She comes to relieve him of the white napkin, but reverts again with it.*]

Or will you take it, Jimmie? As a flag?

[JAMES *stalks out, much offended, and* KATE *turning stares across the yard at the house; the lights narrowing down to the following pantomime in the family room leave her motionless in the dark.*

ANNIE *meanwhile has begun by slapping both keys down on a shelf out of* HELEN'S *reach; she returns to the table, upstage.* HELEN'S *kicking has subsided, and when from the floor her hand finds* ANNIE'S *chair empty she pauses.* ANNIE *clears the table of* KATE'S, JAMES'S, *and* KELLER'S *plates; she gets back to her own across*

---

2. **hireling.** Paid employee

the table just in time to slide it deftly away from HELEN's *pouncing hand. She lifts the hand and moves it to* HELEN's *plate, and after an instant's exploration,* HELEN *sits again on the floor and drums her heels.* ANNIE *comes around the table and resumes her chair. When* HELEN *feels her skirt again, she ceases kicking, waits for whatever is to come, renews some kicking, waits again.* ANNIE *retrieving her plate takes up a forkful of food, stops it halfway to her mouth, gazes at it devoid of appetite, and half-lowers it; but after a look at* HELEN *she sighs, dips the forkful toward* HELEN *in a for-your-sake toast, and puts it in her own mouth to chew, not without an effort.*

HELEN *now gets hold of the chair leg, and half-succeeds in pulling the chair out from under her.* ANNIE *bangs it down with her rear, heavily, and sits with all her weight.* HELEN's *next attempt to topple it is unavailing, so her fingers dive in a pinch at* ANNIE's *flank.* ANNIE *in the middle of her mouthful almost loses it with startle, and she slaps down her fork to round on* HELEN. *The child comes up with curiosity to feel what* ANNIE *is doing, so* ANNIE *resumes eating, letting* HELEN's *hand follow the movement of her fork to her mouth, whereupon* HELEN *at once reaches into* ANNIE's *plate.* ANNIE *firmly removes her hand to her own plate.* HELEN *in reply pinches* ANNIE's *thigh, a good mean pinchful that makes* ANNIE *jump.* ANNIE *sets the fork down, and sits with her mouth tight.* HELEN *digs another pinch into her thigh, and this time* ANNIE *slaps her hand smartly away;* HELEN *retaliates with a*

> **GUIDED READING**
> What does Annie do when Helen tries to find out what she is doing?

> **GUIDED READING**
> What happens when Helen tries to pinch Annie again?

roundhouse fist that catches ANNIE *on the ear, and* ANNIE's *hand leaps at once in a forceful slap across* HELEN's *cheek;* HELEN *is the startled one now.* ANNIE's *hand in* compunction *falters to her own face, but when* HELEN *hits at her again,* ANNIE *deliberately slaps her again.* HELEN *lifts her fist* irresolute *for another roundhouse,* ANNIE *lifts her hand resolute for another slap, and they freeze in this posture, while* HELEN *mulls it over. She thinks better of it, drops her fist, and giving* ANNIE *a wide berth, gropes around to her* MOTHER's *chair, to find it empty; she blunders her way along the table upstage, and encountering the empty chairs and missing plates, she looks bewildered; she gropes back to her* MOTHER's *chair, again touches her cheek and indicates the chair, and waits for the world to answer.*

ANNIE *now reaches over to spell into her hand, but* HELEN *yanks it away; she gropes to the front door, tries the knob, and finds the door locked, with no key. She gropes to the rear door, and finds it locked, with no key. She commences to bang on it.* ANNIE *rises, crosses, takes her wrists, draws her resisting back to the table, seats her, and releases her hands upon her plate; as* ANNIE *herself begins to sit,* HELEN *writhes out of her chair, runs to the front door, and tugs and kicks at it.* ANNIE *rises again, crosses, draws her by one wrist back to the table, seats her, and sits;* HELEN *escapes back to the door, knocking over her* MOTHER's *chair en route.* ANNIE *rises again in pursuit, and this time lifts* HELEN *bodily from behind and bears her kicking to her chair. She deposits her, and once more turns to sit.* HELEN *scrambles out, but as she passes* ANNIE *catches her up again from behind and*

> **GUIDED READING**
> Whom does Helen look for when she gives up fighting with Annie?

ANSWERS TO GUIDED READING QUESTIONS

1. Annie dips it in, almost as a toast to show that she is doing this for Helen.
2. Annie resumes eating.
3. Annie slaps Helen's hand away. Helen punches Annie who slaps her back.
4. Helen looks for her mother.

CULTURAL/ HISTORICAL NOTE

Students may be shocked that when Helen hits Annie, her teacher, Annie, slaps Helen back. Let students know that it was only fairly recently, toward the latter half of the twentieth century, that there was public outcry about corporal punishment against children, such as punishing children by spanking them. Throughout much of history, teachers would cane, paddle, or spank students who misbehaved or slap their wrists or hands with rulers. Today it is illegal to practice corporal punishment in most public schools in the United States.

Tell students that Annie's actions would have seemed much less shocking in their time period; however, the author still intends for Annie's slap to be shocking for both the reader or audience and Helen. Annie is using extreme methods to try to break through to Helen and teach her some discipline and self-control.

ANSWERS TO GUIDED READING QUESTIONS

1. Annie is trying to make Helen sit at the table.
2. Helen finally tries to eat from her own plate.
3. Annie gives a small bow.

CULTURAL/ HISTORICAL NOTE

Inform students that more than twenty million people in the United States have some form of hearing loss. Of these, two million are deaf, having hearing loss so severe that their hearing cannot be helped through hearing aids or other devices. Until the sixteenth century, people believed that it was impossible to teach a deaf person language or educate them in any way. Pedro de Ponce, a Benedictine monk, was one of the first people to try to prove this belief wrong by teaching the deaf. Since that time, great advances have been made in teaching deaf students.

There are two major methods for teaching the deaf language. In one method, the deaf person is taught to read lips and to speak. While you need sight in order to read lips, Helen Keller did learn to speak without sight. The other method involves teaching the deaf students sign language and finger spelling. This is the method Annie Sullivan is using to try to teach Helen.

One problem in teaching the deaf is that they have been deprived of the normal childhood experience of listening to language before they comprehend it. Without language stimulation, it sometimes takes longer for a deaf student to excel academically. When a deaf child, however, is exposed to language at a young age through sign language, however, that child is more likely to be at or ahead of grade level.

Inform students that teaching students who are deaf and blind like Helen is even more challenging because such students cannot be taught to read lips, unless they are feeling a person's lips as they speak. Helen is also an especially challenging student because she has not been able to participate at all in the normal childhood introduction to language. The concept of words is completely unknown to her.

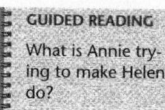

deposits her in the chair; HELEN scrambles out on the other side, for the rear door, but ANNIE at her heels catches her up and deposits her again in the chair. She stands behind it. HELEN scrambles out to her right, and the instant her feet hit the floor ANNIE lifts and deposits her back, she scrambles out to her left, and is at once lifted and deposited back. She tries right again and is deposited back, and tries left again and is deposited back, and now _feints_ ANNIE to the right but is off to her left, and is promptly deposited back. She sits a moment, and then starts straight over the table-top, dishware notwithstanding; ANNIE hauls her in and deposits her back, with her plate spilling in her lap, and she melts to the floor and crawls under the table, _laborious_ among its legs and chairs; but ANNIE is swift around the table and waiting on the other side when she surfaces, immediately bearing her aloft; HELEN clutches at JAMES's chair for anchorage, but it comes with her, and halfway back she abandons it to the floor. ANNIE deposits her in her chair, and waits. HELEN sits tensed motionless. Then she tentatively puts out her left foot and hand, ANNIE interposes her own hand, and at the contact HELEN jerks hers in. She tries her right foot, ANNIE blocks it with her own, and HELEN jerks hers in. Finally, leaning back, she slumps down in her chair, in a sullen biding.

> **GUIDED READING**
> What is Annie trying to make Helen do?

> **GUIDED READING**
> What does Helen finally do?

ANNIE backs off a step, and watches; HELEN offers no move. ANNIE takes a deep breath. Both of them and the room are in considerable disorder, two chairs down and the table a mess, but ANNIE makes no effort to tidy it; she only sits on her own chair, and lets her energy refill. Then she takes up knife and fork,

and resolutely addresses her food. HELEN's hand comes out to explore, and seeing it ANNIE sits without moving, the child's hand goes over her hand and fork, pauses—ANNIE still does not move—and withdraws. Presently it moves for her own plate, slaps about for it, and stops, thwarted. At this, ANNIE again rises, recovers HELEN's plate from the floor and a handful of scattered food from the deranged tablecloth, drops it on the plate, and pushes the plate into contact with HELEN's fist. Neither of them now moves for a pregnant[3] moment—until HELEN suddenly takes a grab of food and wolfs it down. ANNIE permits herself the humor of a minor bow and warming of her hands together; she wanders off a step or two, watching. HELEN cleans up the plate.

> **GUIDED READING**
> How does Annie react when Helen begins to eat from her own plate?

After a glower[4] of indecision, she holds the empty plate out for more. ANNIE accepts it, and crossing to the removed plates, spoons food from them onto it; she stands debating the spoon, tapping it a few times on HELEN's plate; and when she returns with the plate she brings the spoon, too. She puts the spoon first into HELEN's hand, then sets the plate down. HELEN discarding the spoon reaches with her hand, and ANNIE stops it by the wrist; she replaces the spoon in it. HELEN impatiently discards it again, and again ANNIE stops her hand, to replace the spoon in it. This time HELEN throws the spoon on the floor. ANNIE after considering it lifts HELEN bodily out of the chair, and in a wrestling match on the floor closes her fingers upon the

> **GUIDED READING**
> Now that Helen has eaten from her own plate, what does Annie want her to do?

---

3. **pregnant.** Meaningful and having possibilities
4. **glower.** Sullen brooding look of annoyance or anger

words for everyday use

feint (fānt) v., fake to one direction in order to draw attention from the true attack. _Duke feinted left and quickly moved right._
la • bo • ri • ous (lə bōr′ ē əs) adj., involving hard effort. _Inez reached the peak despite the laborious last mile._

spoon, and returns her with it to the chair. HELEN *again throws the spoon on the floor.* ANNIE *lifts her out of the chair again; but in the struggle over the spoon* HELEN *with* ANNIE *on her back sends her sliding over her head;* HELEN *flees back to her chair and scrambles into it. When* ANNIE *comes after her she clutches it for dear life;* ANNIE *pries one hand loose, then the other, then the first again, then the other again, and then lifts* HELEN *by the waist, chair and all, and shakes the chair loose.* HELEN *wrestles to get free, but* ANNIE *pins her to the floor, closes her fingers upon the spoon, and lifts her kicking under one arm; with her other hand she gets the chair in place again, and plunks* HELEN *back on it. When she releases her hand,* HELEN *throws the spoon at her.*

ANNIE *now removes the plate of food.* HELEN *grabbing finds it missing, and commences to bang with her fists on the table.* ANNIE *collects a fistful of spoons and descends with them and the plate on* HELEN; *she lets her smell the plate, at which* HELEN *ceases banging, and* ANNIE *puts the plate down and a spoon in* HELEN'S *hand.* HELEN *throws it on the floor.* ANNIE *puts another spoon in her hand.* HELEN *throws it on the floor.* ANNIE *puts another spoon in her hand.* HELEN *throws it on the floor. When* ANNIE *comes to her last spoon she sits next to* HELEN, *and gripping the spoon in* HELEN'S *hand compels her to take food in it up to her mouth.* HELEN *sits with lips shut.* ANNIE *waits a stolid moment, then lowers* HELEN'S *hand. She tries again;* HELEN'S *lips remain shut.* ANNIE *waits, lowers* HELEN'S *hand. She tries again; this time* HELEN *suddenly opens her mouth and accepts the food.* ANNIE

> **GUIDED READING**
> What does Helen do after finally taking a mouthful from the spoon?

lowers the spoon with a sigh of relief, and HELEN *spews the mouthful out at her face.* ANNIE *sits a* moment with eyes closed, then takes the pitcher and dashes its water into HELEN'S *face, who gasps astonished.* ANNIE *with* HELEN'S *hand takes up another spoonful, and shoves it into her open mouth.* HELEN *swallows involuntarily, and while she is catching her breath* ANNIE *forces her palm open, throws four swift letters into it, then another four, and bows toward her with devastating pleasantness.*]

> **GUIDED READING**
> What does Annie spell to Helen?

ANNIE: Good girl.

[ANNIE *lifts* HELEN'S *hand to feel her face nodding;* HELEN *grabs a fistful of her hair, and yanks. The pain brings* ANNIE *to her knees, and* HELEN *pummels her; they roll under the table, and the lights commence to dim out on them.*

Simultaneously the light at left has been rising, slowly, so slowly that it seems at first we only imagine what is intimated in the yard: a few ghostlike figures, in silence, motionless, waiting. Now the distant belfry chimes commence to toll the hour, also very slowly, almost—it is twelve—interminably; the sense is that of a long time passing. We can identify the figures before the twelfth stroke, all facing the house in a kind of watch: KATE *is standing exactly as before, but now with*

> **GUIDED READING**
> What does the bell indicate?

the baby MILDRED *sleeping in her arms, and placed here and there, unmoving, are* AUNT EV *in her hat with a hanky to her nose, and the two Negro children,* PERCY *and* MARTHA *with necks outstretched eagerly, and* VINEY *with a knotted kerchief on her head and a feather duster in her hand. The chimes cease, and there is silence. For a long moment none of the group moves.*]

VINEY [PRESENTLY]: What am I gone do, Miss Kate? It's noontime, dinner's comin', I didn't get them breakfast dishes out of there yet.

> **words for everyday use**
> in • ter • mi • na • ble (in term ne bel) *adj.,* seeming to have no end. *The bus was delayed and the wait seemed* interminable. **interminably,** *adv.*

1. Aunt Ev means that she thinks the Kellers are better than Annie and shouldn't allow her to take charge of their lives in this way.
2. They are ravaged and undone. Annie looks as though she has fought in a battle.

LITERARY TECHNIQUE

METAPHOR. A **metaphor** is a figure of speech in which one thing is spoken or written about as if it were another. The metaphor invites the listener or reader to make a comparison between the two things. Share this definition with students. Tell them that sometimes an author will choose to extend a metaphor throughout a literary work, repeating it and building on it with each occurrence. Tell students that the author of this play creates an extended metaphor in which Annie, a Northerner, is compared to Ulysses S. Grant who prevailed over the South in the battle of Vicksburg and later accepted the surrender of Robert E. Lee, commander of the Southern Confederate forces, at Appomattox Court House. Ask students to discuss the way that Gibson continues this metaphor on this page after Annie's battle to force Helen to eat properly.
Answers. Gibson continues the metaphor by revealing that the Kellers are cousins to Robert E. Lee, the Southern general who surrendered to Grant and by describing Annie "looking as though she had indeed just taken Vicksburg" after her struggle with Helen, suggesting a connection between Annie and Grant. Annie is also like Grant in that she stubbornly persisted and won. Although the room is a mess, Helen ate at the table and folded her napkin.

[KATE *says nothing, stares at the house.* MARTHA *shifts* HELEN's *doll in her clutch, and it plaintively says momma.*]

KATE [PRESENTLY]: You run along, Martha.

[AUNT EV *blows her nose.*]

AUNT EV [WRETCHEDLY]: I can't wait out here a minute longer, Kate, why, this could go on all afternoon, too.

KATE: I'll tell the captain you called.

VINEY [TO THE CHILDREN]: You hear what Miss Kate say? Never you mind what's going on here.

[*Still no one moves.*]

You run along tend your own bizness.

[*Finally* VINEY *turns on the children with the feather duster.*]

Shoo!

[*The two children divide before her. She chases them off.* AUNT EV *comes to* KATE, *on her dignity.*]

AUNT EV: Say what you like, Kate, but that child is a *Keller.*

[*She opens her parasol,*[5] *preparatory to leaving.*]

I needn't remind you that all the Kellers are cousins to General Robert E. Lee. I don't know *who* that girl is.

[*She waits; but* KATE *staring at the house is without response.*]

The only Sullivan I've heard of—from Boston too, and I'd think twice before locking her up with that kid—is that man John L.[6]

[*And* AUNT EV *departs, with head high. Presently* VINEY *comes to* KATE, *her arms out for the baby.*]

VINEY: You give me her, Miss Kate, I'll sneak her in back, to her crib.

[*But* KATE *is moveless, until* VINEY *starts to take the baby;* KATE *looks down at her before <u>relinquishing her.</u>*]

KATE [SLOWLY]: This child never gives me a minute's worry.

VINEY: Oh yes, this one's the angel of the family, no question bout *that.*

[*She begins off rear with the baby, heading around the house; and* KATE *now turns her back on it, her hand to her eyes. At this moment there is the slamming of a door; and when* KATE *wheels* HELEN *is blundering down the porch steps into the light, like a ruined bat out of hell.* VINEY *halts, and* KATE *runs in;* HELEN *collides with her mother's knees, and reels off and back to clutch them as her savior.* ANNIE *with smoked glasses in hand stands on the porch, also much undone, looking as though she had indeed just taken Vicksburg.* KATE *taking in* HELEN's *ravaged state becomes steely in her gaze up at* ANNIE.]

KATE: What happened?

[ANNIE *meets* KATE's *gaze, and gives a factual report, too exhausted for anything but a flat voice.*]

ANNIE: She ate from her own plate.

[*She thinks a moment.*]

She ate with a spoon. Herself.

[KATE *frowns, uncertain with thought, and glances down at* HELEN.]

---

5. **parasol.** Small umbrella for shading from the sun
6. **only Sullivan . . . John L.** John L. Sullivan was a heavyweight fighter from Boston.

words for everyday use

re • lin • quish (ri lin′ kwish) *vt.*, give up, release. *The dog refused to <u>relinquish</u> the bone.*

And she folded her napkin.

[KATE'S *gaze now wavers, from* HELEN *to* ANNIE, *and back.*]

KATE [SOFTLY]: Folded—her napkin?

ANNIE: The room's a wreck, but her napkin is folded.

[*She pauses, then:*]

I'll be in my room, Mrs. Keller.

[*She moves to re-enter the house, but she stops at* VINEY'S *voice.*]

VINEY [CHEERILY]: Don't be long, Miss Annie. Dinner be ready right away!

[VINEY *carries* MILDRED *around the back of the house.* ANNIE *stands unmoving, takes a deep breath, stares over her shoulder at* KATE *and* HELEN, *then inclines her head graciously, and goes with a slight stagger into the house. The lights in her room above steal up in readiness for her.*

KATE *remains alone with* HELEN *in the yard, standing protectively over her, in a kind of wonder.*]

KATE [SLOWLY]: Folded her napkin.

[*She contemplates the wild head in her thighs, and moves her fingertips over it, with such a tenderness, and something like a fear of its strangeness, that her own eyes close; she whispers, bending to it:*]

My Helen—folded her napkin—

[*And still erect, with only her head in surrender;* KATE *for the first time that we see loses her <u>protracted</u> war with grief; but she will not let a sound escape her, only the grimace of tears comes, and sobs that shake her in a grip of silence. But* HELEN *feels them, and her hand comes up in its own wondering, to interrogate her mother's face,*

GUIDED READING
What does Annie say happened?

until KATE *buries her lips in the child's palm.*

GUIDED READING
How does Kate react to this news?

Upstairs, ANNIE *enters her room, closes the door, and stands back against it; the lights, growing on her with their special color, commence to fade on* KATE *and* HELEN. *Then* ANNIE *goes wearily to her suitcase, and lifts it to take it toward the bed. But it knocks an object to the floor, and she turns back to regard it. A new voice comes in a cultured murmur, hesitant as with the effort of remembering a text:*]

MAN'S VOICE: This—soul—

[ANNIE *puts the suitcase down and kneels to the object: it is the battered Perkins report, and she stands with it in her hand, letting memory try to speak:*]

This—blind, deaf, mute—woman—

[ANNIE *sits on her bed, opens the book, and finding the passage, brings it up an inch from her eyes to read, her face and lips following the overheard words, the voice quite factual now:*]

Can nothing be done to disinter[7] this human soul? The whole neighborhood would rush to save this woman if she were buried alive by the caving in of a pit, and labor with <u>zeal</u> until she were dug out. Now if there were one who had as much patience as zeal, he might awaken her to a consciousness of her immortal—

GUIDED READING
What question does the passage from the Perkins report ask?

[*When the boy's voice comes,* ANNIE *closes her eyes, in pain.*]

BOY'S VOICE: Annie? Annie, you there?

---

7. **disinter.** Take out of the grave; free

ANSWERS TO GUIDED READING QUESTIONS

1. Annie says that Helen ate with a spoon, herself, and folded her napkin.
2. Kate surrenders to her grief for the first time.

ADDITIONAL QUESTIONS AND ACTIVITIES

Ask students the following questions:

1. How would you think that Kate might feel about hearing the news that Helen ate at the table and folded her napkin?
2. How does Kate react to this news? What emotions does she seem to be feeling?
3. Why do you think the news Kate has just heard produced such a strong emotional reaction in her?
4. How does Annie seem to feel after her "lesson," or her battle with Helen?

Answers

1. Students might suggest that they thought that Kate would react with happiness to such news?
2. Kate holds Helen protectively, touches her tenderly, repeats, "My Helen folded her napkin," and submits for once to grief and allows a "grimace of tears" to overcome her for a moment. Kate seems to be overwhelmed with mixed emotions, happiness and grief, and hope and despair fill her at once.
3. Students may say Kate had given up hope that her child would ever do even the most common thing that other children do, so hearing that her wild daughter ate at a table with a spoon and actually folded her napkin fills her with unexpected emotion.
4. Annie seems to feel exhausted but triumphant; she has won a small but important battle.

1. The Perkins report asks, "Can nothing be done to disinter this human soul?" Annie must free Helen's mind or soul, to help her communicate with and interact with the rest of the world.
2. Annie remembers talking to Jimmy about going to school instead of staying to take care of him forever.
3. The voices warn her not to tell anyone where she came from.

ADDITIONAL QUESTIONS AND ACTIVITIES

Ask students the following questions:

1. Why do you think Annie looks back at these words on Helen in her report from the Perkins School? How might she be feeling about the job she has undertaken right now?
2. What memories do the words of the report stir in Annie?
3. In what way does Annie break her promise to Jimmie?
4. What "journey" does Jimmie go on? What happens to Jimmie?
5. What does Annie imagine Jimmie saying from beyond the grave?
6. What does this memory reveal about the way Annie feels about what happened to her brother Jimmie?

Answers

1. Students may say she looks back on these words because she is in need of inspiration and wants to remind herself of the duty she has to dig deep to save Helen's soul from being trapped inside her without means of expression or communication. She might feel she has taken on an impossible job and that she cannot hope to succeed in breaking through to Helen. She may feel like giving up, so she reminds herself of what she has been sent to do.
2. They stir memories of living at the almshouse with her brother.
3. Annie breaks her promise to Jimmie by vowing to go to school when she grows up rather than taking care of Jimmie forever and ever.

ANNIE: Hush.

BOY'S VOICE: Annie, what's that noise?

[ANNIE *tries not to answer; her own voice is drawn out of her, unwilling.*]

ANNIE: Just a cot, Jimmie.

BOY'S VOICE: Where they pushin' it?

ANNIE: To the deadhouse.

BOY'S VOICE: Annie. Does it hurt, to be dead?

[ANNIE *escapes by opening her eyes, her hand works restlessly over her cheek; she retreats into the book again, but the cracked old crones interrupt, whispering.* ANNIE *slowly lowers the book.*]

FIRST CRONE'S VOICE: There is schools.

SECOND CRONE'S VOICE: There is schools outside—

THIRD CRONE'S VOICE: —schools where they teach blind ones, worse'n you—

FIRST CRONE'S VOICE: To read—

SECOND CRONE'S VOICE: To read and write—

THIRD CRONE'S VOICE: There is schools outside where they—

FIRST CRONE'S VOICE: There is schools—

[*Silence.* ANNIE *sits with her eyes shining, her hand almost in a caress over the book. Then:*]

BOY'S VOICE: You ain't goin' to school, are you, Annie?

ANNIE [WHISPERING]: When I grow up.

BOY'S VOICE: You ain't either, Annie. You're goin' to stay here take care of me.

ANNIE: I'm goin' to school when I grow up.

> **GUIDED READING**
> What conversation does Annie remember between herself and Jimmy?

BOY'S VOICE: You said we'll be together, forever and ever and ever—

ANNIE [FIERCE]: I'm goin' to school when I grow up!

DOCTOR'S VOICE [SLOWLY]: Little girl. Little girl, I must tell you. Your brother will be going on a journey, soon.

[ANNIE *sits rigid, in silence. Then the boy's voice pierces it, a shriek of terror.*]

BOY'S VOICE: *Annie!*

[*It goes into* ANNIE *like a sword, she doubles onto it; the book falls to the floor. It takes her a racked moment to find herself and what she was engaged in here; when she sees the suitcase she remembers, and lifts it once again toward the bed. But the voices are with her; as she halts with suitcase in hand.*]

FIRST CRONE'S VOICE: Goodbye, Annie.

DOCTOR'S VOICE: Write me when you learn how.

SECOND CRONE'S VOICE: Don't tell anyone you came from here. Don't tell anyone—

THIRD CRONE'S VOICE: Yeah, don't tell anyone you came from—

FIRST CRONE'S VOICE: Yeah, don't tell anyone—

SECOND CRONE'S VOICE: Don't tell any—

> **GUIDED READING**
> What warning do the voices issue?

[*The echoing voices fade. After a moment* ANNIE *lays the suitcase on the bed; and the last voice comes faintly, from far away.*]

BOY'S VOICE: Annie. It hurts, to be dead. Forever.

[ANNIE *falls to her knees by the bed, stifling her mouth in it. When at last she rolls blindly away from it, her palm comes down on the open report;*

---

words for everyday use

zeal (zēal) *n.,* eagerness, enthusiasm. *Carol's* <u>zeal</u> *for travel led her all around the world.*

ADDITIONAL QUESTIONS AND ACTIVITIES (CONT.)

4. Jimmie goes on a "journey" to the "deadhouse." Jimmie dies.
5. Annie imagines Jimmie saying that it hurts forever to be dead.
6. This memory reveals that Annie feels guilty and responsible for Jimmie's death because she could do nothing to save him and eventually did leave him behind after he died to go to school. She feels guilty about living and thriving, while Jimmie died in the almshouse.

ART SMART

Ask students to identify Helen and
Annie in this photograph. Have them
explain how they could recognize
both characters. What gesture is
Helen making? What does it seem
that she is trying to do?

*she opens her eyes, regards it dully, and then, still
on her knees, takes in the print.*]

MAN'S VOICE [FACTUAL]: —might awaken her
to a consciousness of her immortal nature. The
chance is small indeed; but with a smaller
chance they would have dug desperately for her
in the pit; and is the life of the soul of less
import than that of the body?

[ANNIE *gets to her feet. She drops the book on
the bed, and pauses over her suitcase; after a
moment she unclasps and opens it. Standing
before it, she comes to her decision; she at once
turns to the bureau, and taking her things out
of its drawers, commences to throw them into the
open suitcase.*

*In the darkness down left a hand strikes a
match, and lights a hanging oil lamp. It is*
KELLER'S *hand, and his voice accompanies it,
very angry; the lights rising here before they fade
on* ANNIE *shows* KELLER *and* KATE *inside a*
*suggestion of a garden house, with a bay-window
seat toward center and a door at back.*]

KELLER: Katie, I will not *have* it! Now you
did not see when that girl after supper
tonight went to look for Helen in her
room—

KATE: No.

KELLER: The child practically climbed out of
her window to escape from her! What kind
of teacher *is* she? I thought I had seen her at
her worst this morning, shouting at me, but I
come home to find the entire house disorganized by her—Helen won't stay one second
in the same room, won't come to the table
with her, won't let herself be bathed or
undressed or put to bed by her, or even by
Viney now, and the end result is that *you* have
to do more for the child than before we hired
this girl's services! From the moment she
stepped off the train she's been nothing but a

1. Kate must do more because Helen will not let Annie touch her or even stay in the same room with her. Keller says that since Annie stepped off the train she has been a burden, incompetent, impertinent, ineffectual and immodest.
2. Kate does not agree that Annie has been ineffectual. She points to Annie teaching Helen to fold her napkin.
3. Keller wants Kate to give Annie notice. He does not think Annie will ever be able to teach Helen anything.
4. Keller begins to tell Annie of his dissatisfaction and decision to end her employment.

Quotables

"When one door of happiness closes, another opens; but often we look so long at the closed door that we do not see the one which has been opened for us."

—Helen Keller

ADDITIONAL QUESTIONS AND ACTIVITIES

Encourage students to discuss the above quotation in terms of the situation Helen Keller is facing at this point in the story. Ask students the following questions to guide the discussion: What is Helen used to being able to do in her household? In what way does Annie's arrival close the door on this period in Helen's life? Do you think Helen was happy before Annie came to put an end to this period? Why, or why not? Was it easier? Why, or why not? What words would you use to describe Helen's life before Annie's arrival? What new door that Annie is opening does Helen not yet see?
Answers. Helen is used to getting her way, being able to do anything she wants without punishment or discipline, and never having to behave in a polite, considerate, or civilized manner. Annie's arrival puts an end to this period in Helen's life because she won't stand for Helen's rude, selfish, impolite behavior. Most students will say that although life

burden, incompetent, <u>impertinent</u>, ineffectual, immodest—

KATE: She folded her napkin, Captain.

KELLER: What?

KATE: Not ineffectual. Helen did fold her napkin.

KELLER: What in heaven's name is so extraordinary about folding a napkin?

KATE [WITH SOME HUMOR]: Well. It's more than you did, Captain.

KELLER: Katie. I did not bring you all the way out here to the garden house to be frivolous. Now, how does Miss Sullivan propose to teach a deaf-blind pupil who won't let her even touch her?

KATE [A PAUSE]: I don't know.

KELLER: The fact is, today she scuttled any chance she ever had of getting along with the child. If you can see any point or purpose to her staying on here longer, it's more than—

KATE: What do you wish me to do?

KELLER: I want you to give her notice.

KATE: I can't.

KELLER: Then if you won't, I must. I simply will not—

[*He is interrupted by a knock at the back door.* KELLER *after a glance at* KATE *moves to open the door;* ANNIE *in her smoked glasses is standing outside.* KELLER *contemplates her, heavily.*]

Miss Sullivan.

ANNIE: Captain Keller.

> **GUIDED READING**
> Why must Kate now do more for Helen? What does Keller complain Annie has been since she stepped off the train?

> **GUIDED READING**
> On what point does Kate disagree? What evidence does she use to support her claim?

[*She is nervous, keyed up to seizing the bull by the horns again, and she assumes a cheeriness which is not unshaky.*]

Viney said I'd find you both over here in the garden house. I thought we should—have a talk?

KELLER [RELUCTANTLY]: Yes, I— Well, come in.

[ANNIE *enters, and is interested in this room; she rounds on her heel, anxiously, studying it.* KELLER *turns the matter over to* KATE, *sotto voce.*]

Katie.

KATE [TURNING BACK, COURTEOUSLY]: Captain.

[KELLER *clears his throat, makes ready.*]

KELLER: I, ah—wanted first to make my position clear to Mrs. Keller, in private. I have decided I—am not satisfied—in fact, am deeply dissatisfied—with the manner in which—

> **GUIDED READING**
> What does Keller begin to do?

ANNIE [INTENT]: Excuse me, is this little house ever in use?

KELLER [WITH PATIENCE]: In the hunting season. If you will give me your attention, Miss Sullivan.

[ANNIE *turns her smoked glasses upon him; they hold his unwilling stare.*]

I have tried to make allowances for you because you come from a part of the country where people are—women, I should say—come from who—well, for whom—

[*It begins to elude him.*]

—allowances must—be made. I have decided, nevertheless, to—that is, decided I—

> **words for everyday use**
> **im • per • ti • nent** (im pər' tən ənt) *adj.*, given to rudeness. *Hortense's <u>impertinent</u> remarks gave her a reputation for being rude.*

ADDITIONAL QUESTIONS AND ACTIVITIES (CONT.)

was in some respects easier for Helen, because nobody had any expectations of her, her life was not happy and there was no chance of her being able to grow, learn, and change. Students may say Helen's life was wild, undisciplined, and selfish but also isolated and lonely. Annie is opening a door to a world of communication with others, a way to express herself, that Helen can not yet see.

[Vexedly]

Miss Sullivan, I find it difficult to talk through those glasses.

ANNIE [EAGERLY, REMOVING THEM]: Oh, of course.

KELLER [DOURLY]: Why do you wear them, the sun has been down for an hour.

ANNIE [PLEASANTLY, AT THE LAMP]: Any kind of light hurts my eyes.

[A silence; KELLER ponders her, heavily.]

KELLER: Put them on. Miss Sullivan, I have decided to—give you another chance.

ANNIE [CHEERFULLY]: To do what?

KELLER: To—remain in our employ.

[ANNIE'S eyes widen.]

But on two conditions. I am not accustomed to rudeness in servants or women, and that is the first. If you are to stay, there must be a radical change of manner.

ANNIE [A PAUSE]: Whose?

KELLER [EXPLODING]: Yours, young lady, isn't it obvious? And the second is that you persuade me there's the slightest hope of your teaching a child who flees from you now like the plague, to anyone else she can find in this house.

ANNIE [A PAUSE]: There isn't.

[KATE stops sewing, and fixes her eyes upon ANNIE.]

KATE: What, Miss Annie?

ANNIE: It's hopeless here. I can't teach a child who runs away.

KELLER [NONPLUSSED]: Then—do I understand you—propose—

> **GUIDED READING**
>
> What does Keller announce he has decided? What conditions does he lay out?

ANNIE: Well, if we all agree it's hopeless, the next question is what—

KATE: Miss Annie.

[She is leaning toward ANNIE, in deadly earnest; it commands both ANNIE and KELLER.]

I am not agreed. I think perhaps you—underestimate Helen.

ANNIE: I think everybody else here does.

KATE: She did fold her napkin. She learns, she learns, do you know she began talking when she was six months old? She could say "water." Not really—"wahwah." "Wahwah," but she meant water, she knew what it meant, and only six months old, I never saw a child so—bright, or outgoing—

[Her voice is unsteady, but she gets it level.]

It's still in her, somewhere, isn't it? You should have seen her before her illness, such a good-tempered child—

ANNIE [AGREEABLY]: She's changed.

[A pause, KATE not letting her eyes go; her appeal at last is unconditional, and very quiet.]

KATE: Miss Annie, put up with it. And with us.

KELLER: Us!

KATE: Please? Like the lost lamb in the parable,[7] I love her all the more.

ANNIE: Mrs. Keller, I don't think Helen's worst handicap is deafness or blindness. I think it's your love. And pity.

KELLER: Now what does that mean?

> **GUIDED READING**
>
> According to Annie, what is Helen's worst handicap?

8. **lamb in the parable.** Refers to a Biblical story in which a shepherd loses one lamb and leaves all others to find the one.

---

words for everyday use

vex · ed · ly (vek′ səd lē) *adv.*, with irritation. *The teacher* vexedly *repeated the instructions which she had already given three times.*

dour (douər) *adj.*, harsh, gloomy. *Eeyore's* dour *expression shows that he is a very unhappy person.* **dourly,** *adv.*

---

1. Keller has made allowances because Annie comes from the North.
2. Keller announces that he has decided to give Annie another chance.
3. Keller requires that Annie change her manners and that she persuade him that there is a hope of her teaching Helen.
4. Kate says that at six months old, Helen was speaking, saying "wahwah" for water.

CULTURAL/ HISTORICAL NOTE

Some students may be confused by Captain Keller's condescending attitude toward women, and his saying things like, "I am not accustomed to rudeness in servants and women." Inform students that when this play takes place, toward the close of the nineteenth century, life was very different for most women from life today at the beginning of the twenty-first century. In the nineteenth century, the woman who worked was rare; most women depended on their husbands for financial support. Women had few rights. They could not vote until later in the twentieth century. It was difficult for them to get divorces, so divorce was extremely rare, and when women did divorce they usually lost custody of their children. Married women had few rights; in the eyes of the law the husband was the head of the household and controlled even the assets that women brought with them into the marriage.

By the end of the nineteenth century, more and more women were rejecting the limited role society enforced on them and were fighting for their rights. Tell students that, for the period, Annie Sullivan was very modern, even revolutionary. She worked and was willing to stand up to Captain Keller, suggesting with her innocent sounding question, "Whose?" that if anyone should have a radical change in manner, it should be Captain Keller. Inform students that in general, most, but not all, women who supported the women's rights movement were from the North, so Annie's behavior would be seen as more unusual in the South, where traditional ideas about the role of women in society were perpetuated by Southern men like Captain Keller.

1. Helen's greatest handicap is Kate's love and pity.
2. They considered putting Helen in an institution, but Kate saw people like animals and rats in the hall.
3. Annie wants Helen to be dependent on her for everything. She feels the only person who lets Helen have the things she needs should be her teacher.
4. Her plan will let her get back in touch with Helen and if she is not around Keller, she cannot be rude to him.

CROSS-CURRICULAR ACTIVITIES

HISTORY. Students may be shocked by the terrible conditions in institutions described on this page and the next. Encourage students to work in small groups to research the life and work of either Dorothea Dix or Jane Addams. Both women were contemporaries of Helen Keller and were active reformers, who sought to do away with the old type of institution Kate Keller and Annie Sullivan describe, and begin new social programs. Students might work in groups of two to four students and prepare brief written reports on their chosen reformer's life and work. Students should strive to explain what the legacy of each of these reformers is in their informative essays.

ANNIE: All of you here are so sorry for her you've kept her—like a pet, why, even a dog you housebreak. No wonder she won't let me come near her. It's useless for me to try to teach her language or anything else here. I might as well—

KATE [CUTS IN]: Miss Annie, before you came we spoke of putting her in an asylum.

[ANNIE *turns back to regard her. A pause.*]

ANNIE: What kind of asylum?

KELLER: For mental defectives.

KATE: I visited there. I can't tell you what I saw, people like—animals, with—*rats*, in the halls, and—

[*She shakes her head on her vision.*]

What else are we to do, if you give up?

ANNIE: Give up?

KATE: You said it was hopeless.

ANNIE: Here. Give up, why, I only today saw what has to be done, to begin!

[*She glances from* KATE *to* KELLER, *who stare, waiting; and she makes it as plain and simple as her nervousness permits.*]

I—want complete charge of her.

KELLER: You already have that. It has resulted in—

ANNIE: No, I mean day and night. She has to be dependent on me.

KATE: For what?

ANNIE: Everything. The food she eats, the clothes she wears, fresh—

> **GUIDED READING**
> What had the Kellers considered before Annie came? Why did Kate choose not to follow this course of action?

> **GUIDED READING**
> What does Annie want control of with Helen?

[*She is amused at herself, though very serious.*]

—air, yes, the air she breathes, whatever her body needs is a—primer, to teach her out of. It's the only way, the one who lets her have it should be her teacher.

[*She considers them in turn; they digest it,* KELLER *frowning,* KATE *perplexed.*]

Not anyone who *loves* her, you have so many feelings they fall over each other like feet, you won't use your chances and you won't let me.

KATE: But if she runs from you—*to* us—

ANNIE: Yes, that's the point. I'll have to live with her somewhere else.

KELLER: What!

ANNIE: Till she learns to depend on and listen to me.

KATE [NOT WITHOUT ALARM]: For how long?

ANNIE: As long as it takes.

[*A pause. She takes a breath.*]

I packed half my things already.

KELLER: Miss—Sullivan!

[*But when* ANNIE *attends upon him he is speechless, and she is merely earnest.*]

ANNIE: Captain Keller, it meets both your conditions. It's the one way I can get back in touch with Helen, and I don't see how I can be rude to you again if you're not around to interfere with me.

> **GUIDED READING**
> How does Annie's plan meet both of Keller's conditions?

KELLER [RED-FACED]: And what is your intention if I say no? Pack the other half, for home, and abandon your charge to—to—

ANNIE: The asylum?

[*She waits, appraises* KELLER'S *glare and* KATE'S *uncertainty, and decides to use her weapons.*]

I grew up in such an asylum. The state almshouse.⁹

[KATE'S *head comes up on this, and* KELLER *stares hard;* ANNIE'S *tone is cheerful enough, albeit*¹⁰ *level as gunfire*]

Rats—why, my brother Jimmie and I used to play with the rats because we didn't have toys. Maybe you'd like to know what Helen will find there, not on visiting days? One ward was full of the—old women, crippled, blind, most of them dying, but even if what they had was catching there was nowhere else to move them, and that's where they put us. There were younger ones across the hall, prostitutes mostly, with T.B.,¹¹ and epileptic fits, and a couple of the kind who keep after other girls, especially young ones, and some insane. Some just had the D.T.'s.¹² The youngest were in another ward to have babies they didn't want, they started at thirteen, fourteen. They'd leave afterwards, but the babies stayed and we played with them, too, though a lot of them had—sores all over from diseases you're not supposed to talk about, but not many of them lived. The first year we had eighty, seventy died. The room Jimmie and I played in was the deadhouse, where they kept the bodies till they could dig—

GUIDED READING

What does Annie tell the Keller's about the past? What does she say Helen will experience if they put her in an asylum?

KATE [CLOSES HER EYES]: Oh, my dear—

ANNIE: —the graves.

[*She is immune to* KATE'S *compassion.*]

No, it made me strong. But I don't think you need send Helen there. She's strong enough.

[*She waits again; but when neither offers her a word, she simply concludes.*]

No, I have no conditions, Captain Keller.

KATE [NOT LOOKING UP]: Miss Annie.

ANNIE: Yes.

KATE [A PAUSE]: Where would you—take Helen?

ANNIE: Ohh—

[*Brightly*]

Italy?

KELLER [WHEELING]: What?

ANNIE: Can't have everything, how would this garden house do? Furnish it, bring Helen here after a long ride so she won't recognize it, and you can see her every day. If she doesn't know. Well?

GUIDED READING

Where does Annie suggest she enact her plan? Why is this place ideal?

KATE [A SIGH OF RELIEF]: Is that all?

ANNIE: That's all.

KATE: Captain.

[KELLER *turns his head; and* KATE'S *request is quiet but firm.*]

With your permission?

KELLER [TEETH IN CIGAR]: Why must she depend on you for the food she eats?

ANNIE [A PAUSE]: I want control of it.

KELLER: Why?

ANNIE: It's a way to reach her.

KELLER [STARES]: You intend to *starve* her into letting you touch her?

ANNIE: She won't starve, she'll learn. All's fair in love and war, Captain Keller, you never cut supplies?

KELLER: This is hardly a war!

---

9. **almshouse.** Poorhouse
10. **albeit.** Even though
11. **T.B.** Teberculosis, a contagious infection of the lungs which is deadly if not treated
12. **D.T.'s.** Violent mental confusion and trembling caused by long-term, excessive use of alcohol

ANSWERS TO GUIDED READING QUESTIONS

1. Annie tells the Kellers that she once lived in the state almshouse. If Helen is sent there, she will find old, dying women, prostitutes, the insane, and sick babies.
2. Annie suggests the garden house. It will give her the space and privacy she needs and will give the Kellers the opportunity to see Helen.
3. She compares them to a war or a siege.

ADDITIONAL QUESTIONS AND ACTIVITIES

Ask students the following questions:

1. What does Annie reveal to the Kellers about her past and where she grew up?
2. What type of people were brought together in the women's ward of this place?
3. How many babies were born in the almshouse Annie's first year there? How many died?
4. Where does Annie say she and her brother played?
5. What does Annie say her experience did for her? What suggestion does Annie have for Helen in relation to this place?
6. Explain what you think it costs Annie to talk in a cheerful manner about this experience?

Answers

1. Annie reveals that she grew up in an asylum, a poorhouse, like the one to which the Kellers have considered sending Helen.
2. She says that old dying women, prostitutes with diseases, pregnant women, insane women, and young girls were all brought together there.
3. Annie says that of the eighty babies born, seventy died.
4. She says that she and her brother played in the deadhouse where bodies were stored until they could be buried.
5. Annie says her experience made her strong, but she says that Helen is not strong enough to cope with such a place.
6. Students may say that even though Annie's manner is cheerful, it probably causes her much emotional pain and costs her much strength to talk about her painful experiences growing up.

1. Annie must accomplish a miracle in
   two weeks.
2. Annie shows Kate the first letter of
   the alphabet.

CROSS-CURRICULAR ACTIVITIES

SOCIAL STUDIES. Interested students might do some Internet research on the American Foundation for the Blind. They should find answers to the following questions: When was the American Foundation for the Blind (AFB) founded? Who joined the AFB as Counselor on National and International Relations in 1921? What does the AFB Press do? Whose personal material does the AFB archive? What is the CTIB that AFB maintains? What does the AFB help do before Congress and other government agencies? What are "talking books"?

Answers. The AFB was founded in 1921. Helen Keller joined in this capacity in 1921. The FAB Press publishes a *Journal of Visual Impairment Blindness* as well as books, pamphlets, videos, and periodicals about blindness. The AFB archives Helen Keller's personal material. The AFB maintains the Careers Technology Information Bank (CTIB), a network of blind individuals who use technology to assist them and can mentor others. The AFB represents the interests of blind and visually impaired people before Congress and other government agencies. Talking books are recordings of books in the Library of Congress that blind people may listen to.

ANNIE: Well, it's not love. A siege[13] is a siege.

KELLER [HEAVILY]: Miss Sullivan. Do you *like* the child?

ANNIE [STRAIGHT IN HIS EYES]: Do you?

[*A long pause.*]

KATE: You could have a servant here—

ANNIE [AMUSED]: I'll have enough work without looking after a servant! But that boy Percy could sleep here, run errands—

KATE [ALSO AMUSED]: We can let Percy sleep here, I think, Captain?

ANNIE [EAGERLY]: And some old furniture, all our own—

KATE [ALSO EAGER]: Captain? Do you think that walnut bedstead in the barn would be too—

KELLER: I have not yet consented to Percy! Or to the house, or to the proposal! Or to Miss Sullivan's—staying on when I—

[*But he erupts in an irate surrender.*]

Very well, I consent to everything!

[*He shakes the cigar at* ANNIE.]

For two weeks. I'll give you two weeks in this place, and it will be a miracle if you get the child to tolerate you.

KATE: Two weeks? Miss Annie, can you accomplish anything in two weeks?

KELLER: Anything or not, two weeks, then the child comes back to us. Make up your mind, Miss Sullivan, yes or no?

> **GUIDED READING**
> To what does Annie compare her attempts to reach Helen?

> **GUIDED READING**
> How much time does Keller give Annie?

ANNIE: Two weeks. For only one miracle?

[*She nods at him, nervously.*]

I'll get her to tolerate me.

[KELLER *marches out, and slams the door.* KATE *on her feet regards* ANNIE, *who is facing the door.*]

KATE [THEN]: You can't think as little of love as you said.

[ANNIE *glances questioning.*]

Or you wouldn't stay.

ANNIE [A PAUSE]: I didn't come here for love. I came for money!

[KATE *shakes her head to this, with a smile; after a moment she extends her open hand.* ANNIE *looks at it, but when she puts hers out it is not to shake hands, it is to set her fist in* KATE'S *palm.*]

> **GUIDED READING**
> What does Annie do when Kate extends her hand?

KATE [PUZZLED]: Hm?

ANNIE: A. It's the first of many. Twenty-six!

[KATE *squeezes her fist, squeezes it hard, and hastens out after* KELLER. ANNIE *stands as the door closes behind her, her manner so <u>apprehensive</u> that she finally slaps her brow, holds it, sighs, and, with her eyes closed, crosses herself for luck. The lights dim into a cool silhouette scene around her; the lamp paling out, and now, in formal entrances, persons appear around* ANNIE *with furniture for the room:* PERCY *crosses the stage with a rocking chair and waits;* MARTHA *from another direction bears in a stool,* VINEY *bears in a small table, and the other Negro servant rolls in a bed partway from left; and* ANNIE, *opening her eyes to put her glasses back on, sees them. She turns around in the room once, and goes into action, pointing out loca*

---

13. **siege.** Military blockade to force a city to surrender

---

> **words for everyday use** **ap • pre • hen • sive** (a pri hent' siv) *adj.,* filled with anxiety; fearful. *Everyone was <u>apprehensive</u> before the test.*

tions for each article; the servants place them and leave, and ANNIE then darts around, interchanging them. In the midst of this—while PERCY and MARTHA reappear with a tray of food and a chair, respectively—JAMES comes down from the house with ANNIE'S suitcase, and stands viewing the room and her quizzically; ANNIE halts abruptly under his eyes, embarrassed, then seizes the suitcase from his hand, explaining herself brightly.]

ANNIE: I always wanted to live in a doll's house!

[She sets the suitcase out of the way, and continues; VINEY at left appears to position a rod with drapes for a doorway, and the other servant at center pushes in a wheelbarrow loaded with a couple of boxes of HELEN'S toys and clothes. ANNIE helps lift them into the room, and the servant pushes the wheelbarrow off. In none of this is any heed taken of the imaginary walls of the garden house, the furniture is moved in from every side and itself defines the walls.

ANNIE now drags the box of toys into center, props up the doll conspicuously on top; with the people melted away, except for JAMES, all is again still. The lights turn again without pause, rising warmer.]

JAMES: You don't let go of things easily, do you? How will you—win her hand now, in this place?

ANNIE [CURTLY]: Do I know? I lost my temper, and here we are!

JAMES [LIGHTLY]: No touching, no teaching. Of course, you *are* bigger—

ANNIE: I'm not counting on force, I'm counting on her. That little imp is dying to know.

JAMES: Know what?

ANNIE: Anything. Any and every crumb in God's creation. I'll have to use that appetite too.

GUIDED READING

What does Annie believe will allow her to eventually reach Helen?

[She gives the room a final survey, straightens the bed, arranges the curtains.]

JAMES [A PAUSE]: Maybe she'll teach you.

ANNIE: Of course.

JAMES: That she isn't. That there's such a thing as—dullness of heart. Acceptance. And letting go. Sooner or later we all give up, don't we?

GUIDED READING

What does James suggest Annie should do?

ANNIE: Maybe you all do. It's my idea of the original sin.

JAMES: What is?

ANNIE [WITHERINGLY]: Giving up.

JAMES [NETTLED]: You won't open her. Why can't you let her be? Have some—pity on her, for being what she is—

ANNIE: If I'd ever once thought like that, I'd be dead!

JAMES [PLEASANTLY]: You will be. Why trouble?

[ANNIE turns to glare at him; he is mocking.]

Or will you teach me?

[And with a bow, he drifts off.

Now in the distance there comes the clopping of hoofs, drawing near, and nearer, up to the door; and they halt. ANNIE wheels to face the door. When it opens this time, the KELLERS—KATE in travelling bonnet, KELLER also hatted—are standing there with HELEN between them; she is in a cloak. KATE gently cues her into the room. HELEN comes in groping, baffled, but interested in the new surroundings; ANNIE evades her exploring hand, her gaze not leaving the child.]

ANNIE: Does she know where she is?

KATE [SHAKES HER HEAD]: We rode her out in the country for two hours.

KELLER: For all she knows, she could be in another town—

1. Annie displays Helen's doll prominently, so that Helen will find something familiar when she arrives.
2. Annie depends on Helen's desire to learn.
3. James suggests Annie leave be and show Helen some pity.
4. Helen is interested and curious about her new surroundings.

LITERARY NOTE

Introduce to students the concept of a foil in literature. Share with them that a **foil** is a character whose attributes, or nature, contrast with those of another character. The foil's attributes help emphasize the very different attributes of the other character. For example, in a story about a miser, a spendthrift who spends money constantly might appear as a foil. Ask students to think about the ways in which James is a foil to Annie. In what ways are James's and Annie's attitudes toward Helen different? In what ways does James's attitudes about Helen help emphasize Annie's attitude? *Answers.* Students may suggest that James is a foil to Annie in that he has given up on Helen and thinks she'll never amount to being little more than an animal, while Annie is confident in Helen's intelligence and believes it will be possible to break through to Helen and communicate with her. James's pessimism helps to emphasize how very optimistic Annie is.

1. Helen is pleased, puzzled and then wary.
2. Helen looks for her mother but finds Annie instead.
3. Helen's rage stops when she finds her doll. She drops to the floor in exhaustion.
4. James wants to know how Annie gets whatever she wants from Keller when he can't.

Quotables

"Please don't feel sorry for me, because I am happy. Some people think I can't understand them, so they will talk to my mother or brother instead of to me. Mom is great about letting them know I am smart, and that it is always better when people talk to me rather than acting like I am not there."

—Mikelle Learned

"Having a physical disability does not mean that a person cannot be successful in whatever he or she pursues, being successful in school or career doesn't depend on your physical state, it depends on your mental state."

—Lisa Ferrerio

ADDITIONAL QUESTIONS AND ACTIVITIES

Share the quotation above with students. (They come from the book *Children With Special Needs*.) Ask students to think about theses quotations and then to write a brief journal essay about how they feel that people without disabilities should treat those with disabilities. As if there is something wrong with them? as if they are special? or as if they are the same, in the ways that matter, as everybody else?

[HELEN *stumbles over the box on the floor and in it discovers her doll and other battered toys, is pleased, sits to them, then becomes puzzled and suddenly very wary. She scrambles up and back to her mother's thighs, but* ANNIE *steps in, and it is hers that* HELEN *embraces.* HELEN *recoils, gropes, and touches her cheek instantly.*]

GUIDED READING
How does Helen react to finding her doll and toys?

KATE: That's her sign for me.

ANNIE: I know.

[HELEN *waits, then recommences her groping, more urgently.* KATE *stands indecisive, and takes an abrupt step toward her, but* ANNIE'S *hand is a barrier.*]

In two weeks.

KATE: Miss Annie, I— Please be good to her. These two weeks, try to be very good to her—

ANNIE: I will.

[KATE, *turning then, hurries out. The* KELLERS *cross back of the main house.*

ANNIE *closes the door.* HELEN *starts at the door jar, and rushes it.* ANNIE *holds her off.* HELEN *kicks her, breaks free, and careens around the room like an imprisoned bird, colliding with furniture, groping wildly, repeatedly touching her cheek in a growing panic. When she has covered the room, she commences her weird screaming.* ANNIE *moves to comfort her, but her touch sends* HELEN *into a paroxysm[14] of rage: she tears away, falls over her box of toys, flings its contents in handfuls in* ANNIE'S *direction, flings the box too, reels to her feet, rips curtains from the window, bangs and kicks at the door, sweeps objects off the mantelpiece and shelf, a little tornado* incarnate, *all destruction, until she comes upon her doll and,*

in the act of hurling it, freezes. Then she clutches it to herself, and in exhaustion sinks sobbing to the floor. ANNIE *stands contemplating her, in some awe.*]

GUIDED READING
What stops Helen's destructive rage?

Two weeks.

[*She shakes her head, not without a touch of disgusted bewilderment.*]

What did I get into now?

[*The lights have been dimming throughout, and the garden house is lit only by moonlight now, with* ANNIE *lost in the patches of dark.*

KATE, *now hatless and coatless, enters the family room by the rear door, carrying a lamp.* KELLER, *also hatless, wanders simultaneously around the back of the main house to where* JAMES *has been waiting, in the rising moonlight, on the porch.*]

KELLER: I can't understand it. I had every intention of dismissing that girl, not setting her up like an empress.

JAMES: Yes, what's her secret, sir?

KELLER: Secret?

JAMES [PLEASANTLY]: That enables her to get anything she wants out of you? When I can't.

GUIDED READING
What secret does James want to know?

[JAMES *turns to go into the house, but* KELLER *grasps his wrist, twisting him half to his knees.* KATE *comes from the porch.*]

KELLER [ANGRILY]: She does *not* get anything she—

JAMES [IN PAIN]: Don't—don't—

---

14. **paroxysm.** Fit or outburst

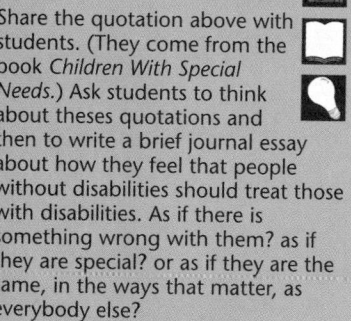

in • car • nate (in kär′ nət) *adj.,* personified, embodied. *Flavia never stops doing good; she is kindness* incarnate.

KATE: Captain.

KELLER: He's afraid.

[*He throws* JAMES *away from him, with contempt.*]

What *does* he want out of me?

JAMES [AN OUTCRY]: My God, don't you know?

[*He gazes from* KELLER *to* KATE.]

Everything you forgot, when you forgot my mother.

GUIDED READING
What does James say he wants from Keller?

KELLER: What!

[JAMES *wheels into the house.* KELLER *takes a stride to the porch, to roar after him.*]

One thing that girl's secret is not, she doesn't fire one shot and disappear!

[KATE *stands rigid, and* KELLER *comes back to her.*]

Katie. Don't mind what he—

KATE: Captain, *I* am proud of you.

KELLER: For what?

KATE: For letting this girl have what she needs.

KELLER: Why can't my son be? He can't bear me, you'd think I treat him as hard as this girl does Helen—

[*He breaks off, as it dawns in him.*]

KATE [GENTLY]: Perhaps you do.

KELLER: But he has to learn some respect!

KATE [A PAUSE, WRYLY]: *Do* you like the child?

[*She turns again to the porch, but pauses, reluctant.*]

How empty the house is, tonight.

[*After a moment she continues on in.* KELLER *stands moveless, as the moonlight dies on him.*]

[*The distant belfry chimes toll, two o'clock, and with them, a moment later, comes the boy's voice on the wind, in a whisper:*]

BOY'S VOICE: Annie. Annie.

[*In her patch of dark* ANNIE, *now in her nightgown, hurls a cup into a corner as though it were her grief, getting rid of its taste through her teeth.*]

ANNIE: No! No pity, I won't have it.

[*She comes to* HELEN, *prone on the floor.*]

On either of us.

[*She goes to her knees, but when she touches* HELEN'S *hand the child starts up awake, recoils, and scrambles away from her under the bed.* ANNIE *stares after her. She strikes her palm on the floor, with passion.*]

GUIDED READING
What happens when Annie touches Helen?

I *will* touch you!

[*She gets to her feet, and paces in a kind of anger around the bed, her hand in her hair, and confronting* HELEN *at each turn.*]

How, how? How do I—

[ANNIE *stops. Then she calls out urgently, loudly.*]

Percy! Percy!

[*She moves swiftly to the drapes, at left.*]

Percy, wake up!

[PERCY'S *voice comes in a thick sleepy mumble, unintelligible.*]

Get out of bed and come in here, I need you.

[ANNIE *darts away, finds and strikes a match, and touches it to the hanging lamp; the lights come up dimly in the room, and* PERCY *stands bare to the waist in torn overalls between the drapes, with eyes closed, swaying.* ANNIE *goes to him, pats his cheeks vigorously.*]

Percy. You awake?

PERCY: No'm.

ANSWERS TO GUIDED
READING QUESTIONS

1. He wants everything Keller forgot when he forgot James's mother.
2. Helen wakes up and scrambles away.
3. Annie makes Percy get up and touch Helen's hand.

LITERARY TECHNIQUE

CONFLICT AND CHARACTER. A **conflict** is a struggle between two people or things in a literary work. A **character** is a person or animal who takes part in a literary work. Share these definitions with students, and then ask them the following questions:

- What conflict is there between James and his father? What does James want out of his father? What does Captain Keller want out of James? Why don't they get along?
- Explain what James's conflict with his father reveals about him as a character. Does it make you more sympathetic to James? Explain why or why not.

Answers

- James fights with his father after he asks him how Annie manages to get whatever she wants out of him when James can't get what he wants out of his father. James wants his old life back, before his mother died, Captain Keller "forgot" his mother, and remarried Kate. Captain Keller wants James to treat him with respect. They don't get along because James doesn't respect his father because he feels he was "forgetting" James's mother by remarrying, and Captain Keller demands respect.
- This conflict reveals that James is nursing some hurt feelings and pain about his mother's death and his father's remarriage. He may feel he is a remainder of an old life that his father is trying to leave behind. Students may say that knowing this does make them more sympathetic to James because it helps explain why he is so unpleasant to Kate Keller and his father's new family.

1. Helen comes out from under the bed and hugs Percy.
2. Helen could talk with her hands if she knew how.
3. Helen spells cake, so Annie gives her cake.
4. Annie spells "milk."

ADDITIONAL QUESTIONS AND ACTIVITIES

Ask students the following questions:
1. What does Annie do with Percy to make Helen curious enough to learn to sign the letters to a new word?
2. What does Annie do when Helen signs the letters to a word like *cake* or *milk*?
3. Why do you think that Annie gives Helen these things? As treats, or for some other reason?
4. Does Annie understand what she is signing yet? How can you tell?

Answers
1. Annie signs letters to Percy, which makes Helen jealous, so she comes over to feel the signs too.
2. Annie gives Helen cake when she signs cake and milk when she signs milk.
3. Students may say that she is trying to get Helen to associate these objects with the words she is teaching her.
4. Helen doesn't understand what she is signing yet; she is just repeating things as if in a game.

ANNIE: How would you like to play a nice game?

PERCY: Whah?

ANNIE: With Helen. She's under the bed. Touch her hand.

[*She kneels* PERCY *down at the bed, thrusting his hand under it to contact* HELEN'S; HELEN *emits an animal sound and crawls to the opposite side, but commences sniffing.* ANNIE *rounds the bed with* PERCY *and thrusts his hand again at* HELEN; *this time* HELEN *clutches it, sniffs in recognition, and comes scrambling out after* PERCY, *to hug him in delight.* PERCY *alarmed struggles, and* HELEN'S *fingers go to his mouth.*]

> **GUIDED READING**
> What does Helen do when she recognizes it is Percy?

PERCY: Lemme go. Lemme go—

[HELEN *fingers her own lips, as before, moving them in dumb imitation.*]

She tryin' talk. She gonna hit me—

ANNIE [GRIMLY]: She *can* talk. If she only knew, I'll show you how. She makes letters.

[*She opens* PERCY'S *other hand, and spells into it:*]

This one is C. C.

[*She hits his palm with it a couple of times, her eyes upon* HELEN *across him;* HELEN *gropes to feel what* PERCY'S *hand is doing, and when she encounters* ANNIE'S *she falls back from them.*]

She's mad at me now, though, she won't play. But she knows lots of letters. Here's another, A. C, a. C, a.

[*But she is watching* HELEN, *who comes groping, consumed with curiosity;* ANNIE *makes the letters in* PERCY'S *hand, and* HELEN *pokes to question what they are up to. Then* HELEN *snatches*

PERCY'S *other hand, and quickly spells four letters into it.* ANNIE *follows them aloud.*]

C, a, k, e! She spells cake, she gets cake.

[*She is swiftly over to the tray of food, to fetch cake and a jug of milk.*]

She doesn't know yet it means this. Isn't it funny she knows how to spell it and doesn't *know* she knows?

[*She breaks the cake in two pieces, and extends one to each;* HELEN *rolls away from her offer.*]

> **GUIDED READING**
> What does Helen spell to Percy? What does Annie do when she sees what Helen spelled?

Well, if she won't play it with me, I'll play it with you. Would you like to learn one she doesn't know?

PERCY: No'm.

[*But* ANNIE *seizes his wrist, and spells to him.*]

M, i, l, k. M is this. I, that's an easy one, just the little finger. L is this—

[*And* HELEN *comes back with her hand, to feel the new word.* ANNIE *brushes her away, and continues spelling aloud to* PERCY.

> **GUIDED READING**
> How does Helen react when Annie spells to Percy?

HELEN'S *hand comes back again, and tries to get in;* ANNIE *brushes it away again.* HELEN'S *hand insists, and* ANNIE *puts it away rudely.*]

No, why should I talk to you? I'm teaching Percy a new word. L. K is this—

[HELEN *now yanks their hands apart; she butts* PERCY *away, and thrusts her palm out insistently.* ANNIE'S *eyes are bright, with glee.*]

Ho, you're *jealous*, are you!

[HELEN'S *hand waits,* <u>intractably</u> *waits.*]

All *right.*

---

words for everyday use

in • trac • ta • ble (in trak′ tə bəl) *adj.,* obstinately. The <u>intractable</u> boy stood at the front of the line despite being told to go to the back. **intractably,** *adv.*

[ANNIE *spells into it, milk; and* HELEN *after a moment spells it back to* ANNIE. ANNIE *takes her hand, with her whole face shining. She gives a great sigh.*]

Good! So I'm finally back to where I can touch you, hm? Touch and go! No love lost, but here we go.

[*She puts the jug of milk into* HELEN'S *hand and squeezes* PERCY'S *shoulder.*]

You can go to bed now, you've earned your sleep. Thank you.

[PERCY *stumbling up weaves his way out through the drapes.* HELEN *finishes drinking, and holds the jug out, for* ANNIE; *when* ANNIE *takes it,* HELEN *crawls onto the bed, and makes for sleep.* ANNIE *stands, looks down at her.*]

Now all I have to teach you is—one word. Everything.

[*She sets the jug down. On the floor now* ANNIE *spies the doll, stoops to pick it up, and*

> **GUIDED READING**
> What does Annie have left to teach Helen?

with it dangling in her hand, turns off the lamp. A shaft of moonlight is left on HELEN *in the bed, and a second shaft on the rocking chair; and* ANNIE, *after putting off her smoked glasses, sits in the rocker with the doll. She is rather happy, and dangles the doll on her knee, and it makes its momma sound.* ANNIE *whispers to it in mock solicitude.*]

Hush, little baby. Don't say a word—

[*She lays it against her shoulder, and begins rocking with it, patting its diminutive behind; she talks the lullaby to it, humorously at first.*]

Momma's gonna buy you—a mockingbird: If that—mockingbird don't sing—

[*The rhythm of the rocking takes her into the tune, softly, and more tenderly.*]

Momma's gonna buy you a diamond ring: If that diamond ring turns to brass—

[*A third shaft of moonlight outside now rises to pick out* JAMES *at the main house, with one foot on the porch step; he turns his body, as if hearing the song.*]

Momma's gonna buy you a looking-glass. If that looking-glass gets broke—

[*In the family room a fourth shaft picks out* KELLER *seated at the table, in thought; and he, too, lifts his head, as if hearing.*]

Momma's gonna buy you a billy goat: If that billy goat won't pull—

[*The fifth shaft is upstairs in* ANNIE'S *room, and picks out* KATE, *pacing there; and she halts, turning her head, too, as if hearing.*]

Momma's gonna buy you a cart and bull: If that cart and bull turns over, Momma's gonna buy you a dog named Rover; If that dog named Rover won't bark—

[*With the shafts of moonlight on* HELEN, *and* JAMES, *and* KELLER, *and* KATE, *all moveless, and* ANNIE *rocking the doll, the curtain ends the act.*]

ACT 2 / THE MIRACLE WORKER **733**

SHORT ANSWER

1. After the Keller family leaves the dining room, what do the stage directions describe happening between Annie and Helen? **The stage directions indicate a terrific struggle between Annie and Helen as Annie forces Helen to use manners at the table.**

2. Flashback is a literary technique in which a character remembers earlier events as if they were happening in the moment. What flashbacks does Annie have? **Annie has flashbacks of her younger brother, who died at the orphanage.**

ANSWER TO GUIDED READING QUESTION

1. Annie has to teach Helen everything.

SELECTION CHECK TEST 4.10.3 WITH ANSWERS

Checking Your Reading

1. What does Kate Keller ask Annie to teach to her? **Kate asks Annie to teach her the finger alphabet she is teaching Helen.**
2. Why does Helen throw a tantrum at the breakfast table? **Helen throws a tantrum because Annie won't allow her to eat off of her plate.**
3. Where does Annie want to take Helen? **Annie wants to take Helen to the garden house.**
4. Kate tells Annie what had been Helen's first word as a baby. What was it? **Helen's first word as a baby had been "water."**

Vocabulary in Context

Fill in each blank below with the most appropriate word from the following *Words for Everyday Use* from act 2 of "The Miracle Worker." You may have to change the tense of the word.

vengeful   proffers   compel   obstinate
feint   protracted   temperance

1. Faced with tables of food, few people can practice **temperance** on Thanksgiving.
2. Jacqueline realizes the dangers of smoking, but she is too **obstinate** to quit.
3. After graduation, we treated ourselves to a **protracted** vacation.
4. After Ben broke up with her, Rosie felt **vengeful** toward him for weeks.
5. The wrestler **feinted** to the left and quickly moved to the right to overpower his opponent.

Reader's Toolbox

Each of the following terms relates to stage directions or character development in Act 2. Fill in each blank below with the letter of the most appropriate word.

a. sunlight   b. a sweet   c. a doll
   d. moonlight   e. a lamp

_____ 1. What does Kate Keller use to calm Helen when she throws a fit of temper? **b**
_____ 2. According to the stage directions, what is used to highlight the pump? **a**
_____ 3. At the end of Act 2, what is used to highlight each of the main characters? **d**

TEACHER'S EDITION   **733**

RECALL

1a. Helen walks about and eats from everyone's plates. The Kellers ignore her. Annie refuses to allow Helen to eat from her plate.

2a. Helen finally sits in her chair, eats with a spoon from her own plate, and folds her napkin.

3a. Annie wants Helen to be dependent on her. She tricks Helen into allowing her to touch her again by talking to Percy, which makes Helen jealous.

INTERPRET

1b. The Kellers find that it is easier to let Helen have her way than to discipline her. Annie insists on treating Helen as she would a child who can see and hear.

2b. These things are not important in and of themselves. They show that Helen is able to learn something and that she responds to discipline. Annie is determined and unwilling to give up on Helen.

3b. Annie is not sure her plan will work, but she is sure that Helen's desire to learn will win out. *Responses will vary.* Students may say that Annie will succeed because of her determination and because she has already begun to teach Helen.

EVALUATE

4a. Annie uses surprise tactics, firm resolve, and in some cases follows Helen's lead. Her methods are unusual, but she is trying to break bad habits that Helen has learned over the course of her life.

EXTEND

4b. Many of Annie's actions, such as slapping Helen, would not be acceptable in a classroom today.

Investigate, Inquire, and Imagine

Recall: GATHERING FACTS

1a. What does Helen do at the breakfast table? How do the Kellers react? How does Annie react?

2a. What does Helen finally do after being in the dining room with Annie all morning?

3a. Why does Annie want to live with Helen in the garden house? How does Annie get Helen to let her touch her again?

Interpret: FINDING MEANING

1b. Why do the Kellers permit Helen's behavior at the table?

2b. Are the specific things that Helen did important? What do her actions signify about her and about Annie?

3b. Is Annie confident her plan will work? Explain why you think it will or will not work.

Analyze: TAKING THINGS APART

4a. Compare Annie's attitude toward and treatment of Helen to that of the Kellers. What conflict arises because of these differences?

Sythesize: BRINGING THINGS TOGETHER

4b. Summarize Annie's philosophy about teaching the disabled.

Evaluate: MAKING JUDGMENTS

5a. Evaluate the tactics Annie uses to teach Helen in the dining room. Are these normal teaching methods? Do you think Annie makes wise choices about teaching Helen?

Extend: CONNECTING IDEAS

5b. What would happen if your teacher used some of the methods Annie Sullivan used with Helen?

Understanding Literature

STAGE DIRECTIONS. Stage Directions are notes included in a play to describe how something should look, sound, or be performed. Stage directions describe setting, lighting, music, sound effects, entrances, exits, props, and the movements of characters. They are usually printed in italics and enclosed in brackets or parentheses. Why does this play rely so heavily on stage directions rather than dialogue? Examine the scene in the dining room. If Helen were a hearing, speaking child being taught manners, how might this scene have been written?

FLASHBACK. A **flashback** is a part of a story, poem, or play that presents event that happened at an earlier time. Find two flashbacks in this act. What do these flashbacks tell you about Annie?

ANSWERS TO UNDERSTANDING LITERATURE

STAGE DIRECTIONS. The play relies so heavily on stage directions because Helen cannot hear or speak; thus, many things must be conveyed through actions. The scene would include more dialogue, possibly yelling. Students might suggest some possible dialogue for the scene.

FLASHBACK. One flashback reminds Annie of her brother Jimmie and her promise to take care of him, while at the same time she was finding about schools where she could learn. Another flashback reminds Annie not to tell anyone where she comes from. These flashbacks reveal that Annie is haunted by her past and feels guilty about her brother who died in the almshouse.

ACT 3

The stage is totally dark, until we see ANNIE *and* HELEN *silhouetted on the bed in the garden house.* ANNIE'S *voice is audible, very patient, and worn; it has been saying this for a long time.*

ANNIE: Water, Helen. This is water. W, a, t, e, r. It has a *name.*

[A silence. Then:]

Egg, e, g, g. It has a *name,* the name stands for the thing. Oh, it's so simple, simple as birth, to explain.

[The lights have commenced to rise, not on the garden house but on the homestead. Then:]

GUIDED READING
What is Annie still trying to get Helen to do?

Helen, Helen, the chick *has* to come out of its shell, sometime. You come out, too.

[In the bedroom upstairs, we see VINEY *unhurriedly washing the window, dusting, turning the mattress, readying the room for use again; then in the family room a diminished group at one end of the table—*KATE, KELLER, JAMES*—finishing up a quiet breakfast; then outside, down right, the other Negro servant on his knees, assisted by* MARTHA *working with a trowel around a new trellis and wheelbarrow. The scene is one of everyday calm, and all are oblivious to* ANNIE'S *voice.]*

There's only one way out, for you, and it's language. To learn that your fingers can talk. And say anything, anything you can name. This is mug. Mug, m, u, g. Helen, it has a *name.* It— has—a—*name*—

GUIDED READING
What is Helen's only way out?

*[*KATE *rises from the table.]*

KELLER [GENTLY]: You haven't eaten, Katie.

KATE [SMILES, SHAKES HER HEAD]: I haven't the appetite. I'm too—restless, I can't sit to it.

KELLER: You should eat, my dear. It will be a long day, waiting.

JAMES [LIGHTLY]: But it's been a short two weeks. I never thought life could be so— noiseless, went much too quickly for me.

*[*KATE *and* KELLER *gaze at him, in silence.* JAMES *becomes uncomfortable.]*

ANNIE: C, a, r, d. Card. C, a—

JAMES: Well, the house has been practically normal, hasn't it?

KELLER [HARSHLY]: Jimmie.

JAMES: Is it wrong to enjoy a quiet breakfast, after five years? And you two even seem to enjoy each other—

GUIDED READING
What does James say about the two weeks without Helen?

KELLER: It could be even more noiseless, Jimmie, without your tongue running every minute. Haven't you enough feeling to imagine what Katie has been undergoing, ever since—

*[*KATE *stops him, with her hand on his arm.]*

KATE: Captain.

[To JAMES.*]*

It's true. The two weeks have been normal, quiet, all you say. But not short. Interminable.

[She rises, and wanders out; she pauses on the porch steps, gazing toward the garden house.]

ANNIE [FADING]: W, a, t, e, r. But it means *this.* W, a, t, e, r. *This.* W, a, t—

JAMES: I only meant that Miss Sullivan is a boon. Of contention, though, it seems.

KELLER [HEAVILY]: If and when you're a parent, Jimmie, you will understand what separation means. A mother loses a—protector.

JAMES [BAFFLED]: Hm?

KELLER: You'll learn, we don't just keep our children safe. They keep us safe.

[He rises, with his empty coffee cup and saucer.]

VOCABULARY FROM THE SELECTION—ACT 3

aversion
consummate

ANSWERS TO GUIDED READING QUESTIONS

1. Annie is till trying to get Helen to understand that things have names.
2. Language is Helen's only way out.
3. James says the two weeks have been short and noiseless.

BIOGRAPHICAL NOTE

Inform students that even though Helen Keller spent many years of her like working to help blind people in organizations such as the American Foundation for the Blind, she once wrote, "My work for the blind has never occupied a center in my personality." Keller did work to support equal rights for groups other than the blind and deaf. She also supported gender and racial equality.

ADDITIONAL QUESTIONS AND ACTIVITIES

Encourage students to discuss the quotation in the above note. Why might Keller have felt the need to focus on causes other than blindness?

1. Helen is clean and neat.
2. Annie needs a teacher as much as Helen.
3. James asks Kate to be his friend.

ADDITIONAL QUESTIONS AND ACTIVITIES

Ask students the following questions:

1. What does Captain Keller say Kate has been living with for five years?
2. What does Captain Keller say another type of separation between parent and child is? What does Captain Keller imply with this statement?
3. What apology does James offer Kate? What does he ask her to be?
4. What does Kate say that James must do with his father?

Answers

1. Captain Keller says that Kate has been living with a type of separation from her daughter for five years.
2. Captain Keller says another type of separation between parents and child is disappointment in a child. The captain is implying he is disappointed in James as a son.
3. James tells Kate that he is sorry about what he said at the table about the peace and quiet and that every time he opens his mouth "frogs jump out." He asks Kate to be a friend to him.
4. Kate says that James must stand up to Captain Keller.

There are of course all kinds of separation, Katie has lived with one kind for five years. And another is disappointment. In a child.

[*He goes with the cup out the rear door.* JAMES *sits for a long moment of stillness. In the garden house the lights commence to come up;* ANNIE, *haggard at the table, is writing a letter; her face again almost in contact with the stationery;* HELEN, *apart on the stool, and for the first time as clean and neat as a button, is quietly crocheting an endless chain of wool, which snakes all around the room.*]

> GUIDED READING
> What is different about Helen?

ANNIE: "I, feel, every, day, more, and, more, in—"

[*She pauses, and turns the pages of a dictionary open before her; her finger descends the words to a full stop. She elevates her eyebrows, then copies the word.*]

"—inadequate."

[*In the main house* JAMES *pushes up, and goes to the front doorway, after* KATE.]

JAMES: Kate?

[KATE *turns her glance.* JAMES *is rather weary.*]

I'm sorry. Open my mouth, like that fairy tale, frogs jump out.

KATE: No. It has been better. For everyone.

[*She starts away, up center.*]

ANNIE [WRITING]: "If, only, there, were, someone, to, help, me, I, need, a, teacher, as, much, as, Helen—"

> GUIDED READING
> What does Annie need?

JAMES: Kate.

[KATE *halts, waits.*]

What does he want from me?

KATE: That's not the question. Stand up to the world, Jimmie, that comes first.

JAMES [A PAUSE, WRYLY]: But the world is him.

KATE: Yes. And no one can do it for you.

JAMES: Kate.

[*His voice is humble.*]

At least we— Could you—be my friend?

> GUIDED READING
> What does James ask of Kate?

KATE: I am.

[KATE *turns to wander, up back of the garden house.* ANNIE'S *murmur comes at once; the lights begin to die on the main house.*]

ANNIE: "—my, mind, is, undisiplined, full, of, skips, and, jumps, and—"

[*She halts, rereads, frowns.*]

Hm.

[ANNIE *puts her nose again in the dictionary, flips back to an earlier page, and fingers down the words;* KATE *presently comes down toward the bay window with a trayful of food.*]

Disinter—disinterested—disjoin—dis—

[*She backtracks, indignant.*]

Disinterested, disjoin— Where's disipline?

[*She goes a page or two back, searching with her finger, muttering.*]

What a dictionary, have to know how to spell it before you can look up how to spell it, disciple, *discipline!* Diskipline.

[*She corrects the word in her letter.*]

Undisciplined.

[*But her eyes are bothering her, she closes them in exhaustion and gently fingers the eyelids.* KATE *watches her through the window.*]

KATE: What are you doing to your eyes?

[ANNIE *glances around; she puts her smoked glasses on, and gets up to come over, assuming a cheerful energy.*]

ANNIE: It's worse on my vanity! I'm learning to spell. It's like a surprise party, the most unexpected characters turn up.

KATE: You're not to overwork your eyes, Miss Annie.

ANNIE: Well.

[*She takes the tray, sets it on her chair, and carries chair and tray to* HELEN.]

Whatever I spell to Helen I'd better spell right.

KATE [ALMOST WISTFUL]: How—serene she is.

ANNIE: She learned this stitch yesterday. Now I can't get her to stop!

GUIDED READING
Why is it important that Annie spell correctly?

[*She disentangles one foot from the wool chain, and sets the chair before* HELEN. HELEN *at its contact with her knee feels the plate, promptly sets her crocheting down, and tucks the napkin in at her neck, but* ANNIE *withholds the spoon; when* HELEN *finds it missing, she folds her hands in her lap, and quietly waits.*

ANNIE *twinkles at* KATE *with mock devoutness.*]

Such a little lady, she'd sooner starve than eat with her fingers.

[*She gives* HELEN *the spoon, and* HELEN *begins to eat, neatly.*]

GUIDED READING
How does Helen react when food is put in front of her?

KATE: You've taught her so much, these two weeks. I would never have—

ANNIE: Not enough.

[*She is suddenly gloomy, shakes her head.*]

Obedience isn't enough. Well, she learned two nouns this morning, key and water, brings her up to eighteen nouns and three verbs.

GUIDED READING
What does Kate think of what Annie has taught Helen? What does Annie think?

KATE [HESITANT]: But—not—

ANNIE: No. Not that they mean things. It's still a finger-game, no meaning.

[*She turns to* KATE, *abruptly.*]

Mrs. Keller—

[*But she defers it; she comes back, to sit in the bay and lift her hand.*]

Shall we play our finger-game?

KATE: How will she learn it?

ANNIE: It will come.

[*She spells a word;* KATE *does not respond.*]

KATE: How?

ANNIE [A PAUSE]: How does a bird learn to fly?

[*She spells again.*]

We're born to use words, like wings, it has to come.

KATE: How?

ANNIE [ANOTHER PAUSE, WEARILY]: All right. I don't know how.

[*She pushes up her glasses, to rub her eyes.*]

I've done everything I could think of. Whatever she's learned here—keeping herself clean, knitting, stringing beads, meals, setting-up exercises each morning, we climb trees, hunt eggs, yesterday a chick was born in her hands—all of it I spell, everything we do, we never stop spelling. I go to bed with—writer's cramp from talking so much!

GUIDED READING
What does Annie never stop doing?

KATE: I worry about you, Miss Annie. You must rest.

ANNIE: Now? She spells back in her *sleep*, her fingers make letters when she doesn't know! In her bones those five fingers know, that hand aches to—speak out, and something in her mind is asleep, how do I—nudge that awake? That's the one question.

KATE: With no answer.

ANNIE [LONG PAUSE]: Except keep at it. Like this.

[*She again begins spelling—I, need—and* KATE'S *brows gather, following the words.*]

ANSWERS TO GUIDED READING QUESTIONS

1. Annie must spell correctly, so she will teach Helen to spell correctly.
2. Helen tucks her napkin in and waits for her spoon.
3. Kate thinks that Annie has taught Helen so much, but Annie does not think that it is enough.
4. Annie spells to Helen, trying to get her to understand a word.

LITERARY TECHNIQUE

SIMILE AND PUN. A **simile** is a comparison using *like* or *as*. A **pun** is a play on words that exploits a double meaning in a word or phrase. Share these definitions with students, and then ask them the following questions:

- What simile does Annie use to describe learning to spell?
- What pun is present in this simile? (If students have difficulty with this question ask them to think about the different meanings you can read into the word *character* in this simile.)
- Now that you have identified the pun in the simile, explain why spelling and a surprise party are alike.

Answers

- Annie uses the simile, "It's like a surprise party, the most unexpected characters turn up."
- The pun is on the word *character*, which in the context of spelling means letters of the alphabet, but in the context of a surprise party it means people or guests.
- Spelling is like a surprise party because unexpected letters turn up in Annie's spelling, just like unexpected people show up at a surprise party.

1. Annie spells "More time?"
2. If Helen ever learns, Kate and Helen will have a lot to say to each other.
3. Annie wants to have her full time to try to reach Helen.
4. Annie is worried that the Kellers are so eager to have Helen back they will spoil her again.
5. She asks for more time.

Quotables

"This was another in a string of tough movies lately. There was lots of laughter in the theater but I was unable to enjoy very little if it. Most of the laughter came from scenes that were almost totally visual. This was difficult. I hate missing a good laugh. My sighted assistant has a difficult time describing things to me during these scenes because they were complex, chaotic, and over in a flash."

—movie review in *Blindspots: Movie Reviews for Visually Impaired People*

ADDITIONAL QUESTIONS AND ACTIVITIES

Share the quote above with students. Tell students that those of them with sight might join a volunteer group to share their eyes with the blind. They might volunteer to attend movies with a blind person to act as a sighted assistant. (Tell students that this is more difficult than its sounds as they must not get too caught up in the movie to forget that there is someone with them who is depending on them to explain visual scenes that may be confusing for those who cannot see them. Also tell students that explaining a visual scene to someone who cannot see is difficult to do and they must be able to explain such scenes quickly, so as not

---

KATE: More—time?

[*She glances at* ANNIE, *who looks her in the eyes, silent.*]

Here?

ANNIE: Spell it.

> **GUIDED READING**
> What does Annie spell to Kate?

[KATE *spells a word—no—shaking her head;* ANNIE *spells two words—why, not—back, with an impatient question in her eyes; and* KATE *moves her head in pain to answer it.*]

KATE: Because I can't—

ANNIE: Spell it! If she ever learns, you'll have a lot to tell each other, start now.

> **GUIDED READING**
> Why does Annie insist that Kate spell everything she says?

[KATE *painstakingly spells in air. In the midst of this the rear door opens, and* KELLER *enters with the setter* BELLE *in tow.*]

KELLER: Miss Sullivan? On my way to the office, I brought Helen a playmate—

ANNIE: Outside please, Captain Keller.

KELLER: My dear child, the two weeks are up today, surely you don't object to—

ANNIE [RISING]: They're not up till six o'clock.

KELLER [INDULGENT]: Oh, now. What difference can a fraction of one day—

ANNIE: An agreement is an agreement. Now you've been very good, I'm sure you can keep it up for a few more hours.

> **GUIDED READING**
> Why won't Annie let Keller in yet?

[*She escorts* KELLER *by the arm over the threshold; he obeys, leaving* BELLE.]

KELLER: Miss Sullivan, you are a tyrant.

ANNIE: Likewise, I'm sure. You can stand there, and close the door if she comes.

KATE: I don't think you know how eager we are to have her back in our arms.

ANNIE: I do know, it's my main worry.

> **GUIDED READING**
> What is Annie's main concern?

KELLER: It's like expecting a new child in the house. Well, she *is*, so—composed, so—

[*Gently*]

Attractive. You've done wonders for her, Miss Sullivan.

ANNIE [NOT A QUESTION]: Have I.

KELLER: If there's anything you want from us in repayment tell us, it will be a privilege to—

ANNIE: I just told Mrs. Keller. I want more time.

> **GUIDED READING**
> What does Annie ask in payment for what she has done with Helen?

KATE: Miss Annie—

ANNIE: Another week.

[HELEN *lifts her head and begins to sniff.*]

KELLER: We miss the child. *I* miss her, I'm glad to say, that's a different debt I owe you—

ANNIE: Pay it to Helen. Give *her* another week.

KATE [GENTLY]: Doesn't she miss us?

KELLER: Of course she does. What a wrench this unexplainable—exile must be to her, can you say it's not?

ANNIE: No. But I—

[HELEN *is off the stool, to grope about the room; when she encounters* BELLE, *she throws her arms around the dog's neck in delight.*]

KATE : Doesn't she need affection too, Miss Annie?

ANNIE [WAVERING]: She—never shows me she needs it, she won't have any—caressing or—

KATE: But you're not her mother.

KELLER: And what would another week accomplish? We are more than satisfied, you've done more than we ever thought possible, taught her constructive—

> **GUIDED READING**
> Why doesn't Keller think Annie needs another week with Helen?

ADDITIONAL QUESTIONS AND ACTIVITIES (CONT.)

to interrupt the flow of the movie.) Students might also volunteer to read aloud to the blind. Sometimes there are books that blind people cannot locate on tape or in Braille immediately, and if they are reading the book for a class, they may need access to the information right away. Students who are confident in their reading ability can be a valuable resource to those without sight in this way.

ANNIE: I can't promise anything. All I can—

KELLER [NO BREAK]: —things to do, to behave like—even look like—a human child, so manageable, contented, cleaner, more—

ANNIE [WITHERING]: Cleaner.

KELLER: Well. We say cleanliness is next to godliness, Miss—

ANNIE: Cleanliness is next to nothing, she has to learn that everything has its name! That words can be her *eyes*, to everything in the world outside her, and inside too, what is she without words? With them she can think, have ideas, be reached, there's not a thought or fact in the world that can't be hers. You publish a newspaper, Captain Keller, do I have to tell you what words are? And she has them already—

KELLER: Miss Sullivan.

ANNIE: —eighteen nouns and three verbs, they're in her fingers now, I need only time to push *one* of them into her mind! One, and everything under the sun will follow. Don't you see what she's learned here is only clearing the way for that? I can't risk her unlearning it, give me more time alone with her, another week to—

KELLER: Look.

[*He points, and* ANNIE *turns.* HELEN *is playing with* BELLE'S *claws; she makes letters with her fingers, shows them to* BELLE, *waits with her palm, then manipulates the dog's claws.*]

What is she spelling?

[*A silence.*]

KATE: Water?

[ANNIE *nods.*]

> **GUIDED READING**
> Why must Helen learn words?

> **GUIDED READING**
> What does Keller see Helen doing with Belle?

KELLER: Teaching a dog to spell.

[*A pause.*]

The dog doesn't know what she means, any more than she knows what you mean, Miss Sullivan. I think you ask too much, of her and yourself. God may not have meant Helen to have the—eyes you speak of.

ANNIE [TONELESS]: I mean her to.

KELLER [CURIOUSLY]: What is it to you?

[ANNIE'S *head comes slowly up.*]

You make us see how we indulge her for our sake. Is the opposite true, for you?

ANNIE [THEN]: Half a week?

KELLER: An agreement *is* an agreement.

ANNIE: Mrs. Keller?

KATE [SIMPLY]: I want her back.

[*A wait;* ANNIE *then lets her hands drop in surrender and nods.*]

KELLER: I'll send Viney over to help you pack.

ANNIE: Not until six o'clock. I have her till six o'clock.

KELLER [CONSENTING]: Six o'clock. Come, Katie.

[KATE *leaving the window joins him around back, while* KELLER *closes the door; they are shut out.*

Only the garden house is daylit now, and the light on it is narrowing down. ANNIE *stands watching* HELEN *work* BELLE'S *claws. Then she settles beside them on her knees, and stops* HELEN'S *hand.*]

ANNIE [GENTLY]: No.

[*She shakes her head, with* HELEN'S *hand to her face, then spells.*]

> **GUIDED READING**
> Who has higher expectations of Helen, Keller or Annie?

1. Helen is spelling water. Annie wants her to spell dog, and to connect the word dog with the dog she is touching.
2. Annie is trying to show Helen what water is. Helen does not understand and imitates Annie by dipping Belle's paw in the water.
3. Annie has housebroken the Kellers' child.
4. She can put the world in Helen's hand.

Quotables

"The most valuable lesson a Seeing Eye dog owner can learn is also the simplest. He must understand that he is blind and that his dog can see. . . . On the other hand, he has the power of reason while his dog has certain powerful irrational instincts. . . . Both have the power to love, which can alone make possible the patience, the concentration, and the self-discipline necessary to weld the two—the man-animal and the dog-animal—into a corporate unit. Through love, they learn to recognize and to forgive both their own and each other's limitations and , therefore, to realize their joint potentialities."

—Peter Putnam, "The Miracle of a blind Man and His Dog"

CROSS-CURRICULAR ACTIVITIES

MATHEMATICS AND SCIENCES. Share the quotation above with students. Encourage interested students to work in small groups to learn more about guide dogs for the blind. Good resources on this topic are available in books, periodicals, and the Internet. Students should use their research to answer questions such as the following in a brief written report: When were guide dogs for the blind first introduced? What types of dogs can become guide dogs? Where are guide dogs trained? In what way are the owner and the dog trained together? What is a guide dog able to do for its owner? What isn't it able to do? Why is it important that sighted people don't try to pet the dog or caress it when it is working?

Dog. D, o, g. Dog.

[*She touches* HELEN'S *hand to* BELLE. HELEN *dutifully pats the dog's head, and resumes spelling to its paw.*]

Not water.

[ANNIE *rolls to her feet, brings a tumbler of water back from the tray, and kneels with it, to seize* HELEN'S *hand and spells.*]

GUIDED READING
What is Annie trying to express to Helen?

Here. Water. *Water.*

[*She thrusts* HELEN'S *hand into the the tumbler.* HELEN *lifts her hand out dripping, wipes it daintily on* BELLE'S *hide, and taking the tumbler from* ANNIE, *endeavors to thrust* BELLE'S *paw into it.* ANNIE *sits watching, wearily.*]

I don't know how to tell you. Not a soul in the world knows how to tell you. Helen, Helen.

[*She bends in compassion to touch her lips to* HELEN'S *temple, and instantly* HELEN *pauses, her hands off the dog, her head slightly averted. The lights are still narrowing, and* BELLE *slinks off. After a moment* ANNIE *sits back.*]

Yes, what's it to me? They're satisfied. Give them back their child and dog, both housebroken, everyone's satisfied. But me, and you.

GUIDED READING
What, according to Annie, has she done for the Kellers?

[HELEN'S *hand comes out into the light, groping.*]

Reach. *Reach!*

[ANNIE *extending her own hand grips* HELEN'S; *the two hands are clasped, tense in the light, the rest of the room changing in shadow.*]

I wanted to teach you—oh, everything the earth is full of, Helen, everything on it that's ours for a wink and it's gone, and what we are on it, the—light we bring to it and leave behind in—words, why, you can see five thousand years back in a light of words,

---

everything we feel, think, know—and share, in words, so not a soul is in darkness, or done with, even in the grave. And I know, I *know,* one word and I can—put the world in your hand—and whatever it is to me, I won't take less! How, how, how do I tell you *this—*

GUIDED READING
What does Annie believe she can do with one word?

[*She spells.*]

—means a *word,* and the word means this *thing,* wool?

[*She thrusts the wool at* HELEN'S *hand;* HELEN *sits, puzzled.* ANNIE *puts the crocheting aside.*]

Or this—s, t, o, o, l,—means this *thing,* stool?

[*She claps* HELEN'S *palm to the stool.* HELEN *waits, uncomprehending.* ANNIE *snatches up her napkin, spells:*]

Napkin!

[*She forces it on* HELEN'S *hand, waits, discards it, lifts a fold of the child's dress, spells:*]

Dress!

[*She lets it drop, spells:*]

F, a, c, e, face!

[*She draws* HELEN'S *hand to her cheek, and pressing it there, staring into the child's responseless eyes, hears the distant belfry begin to toll, slowly: one, two, three, four, five, six.*

On the third stroke the lights stealing in around the garden house show us figures waiting: VINEY, *the other servant,* MARTHA, PERCY *at the drapes, and* JAMES *on the dim porch.* ANNIE *and* HELEN *remain frozen. The chimes die away. Silently* PERCY *moves the draperod back out of sight;* VINEY *steps into the room—not using the doors—and unmakes the bed; the other servant brings the wheelbarrow over, leaves it handy, rolls the bed off;* VINEY *puts the bed linens on top of a waiting boxful of* HELEN'S *toys, and loads the box on the wheelbarrow;* MARTHA *and* PERCY *take out the chairs, with the trayful, then the table; and*

JAMES, *coming down and into the room, lifts* ANNIE'S *suitcase from its corner.* VINEY *and the other servant load the remaining odds and ends on the wheelbarrow, and the servant wheels it off.* VINEY *and the children departing leave only* JAMES *in the room with* ANNIE *and* HELEN. JAMES *studies the two of them, without mockery, and then, quietly going to the door and opening it, bears the suitcase out, and housewards. He leaves the door open.*

KATE *steps into the doorway, and stands.* ANNIE *lifting her gaze from* HELEN *sees her; she takes* HELEN'S *hand from her cheek, and returns it to the child's own, stroking it there twice, her mother-sign, before spelling slowly into it:*]

GUIDED READING
What is the last word Annie signs to Helen before turning her over to Kate?

M, o, t, h, e, r. Mother.

[HELEN *with her hand free strokes her cheek, suddenly forlorn.* ANNIE *takes her hand again.*]

M, o, t, h—

[*But* KATE *is trembling with such impatience that her voice breaks from her, harsh.*]

KATE: Let her come!

[ANNIE *lifts* HELEN *to her feet, with a turn, and gives her a little push. Now* HELEN *begins groping, sensing something, trembling herself; and* KATE *falling one step in onto her knees clasps her, kissing her.* HELEN *clutches her, tight as she can.* KATE *is inarticulate, choked, repeating* HELEN'S *name again and again. She wheels with her in her arms, to stumble away out the doorway;* ANNIE *stands unmoving, while* KATE *in a blind walk carries* HELEN *like a baby behind the main house, out of view.*

ANNIE *is now alone on the stage. She turns, gazing around at the stripped room, bidding it silently farewell, impassively, like a defeated general on the deserted battlefield. All that remains is a stand with a basin of water; and here*

GUIDED READING
How does Annie feel at the end of her two weeks with Helen?

ANNIE *takes up an eyecup, bathes each of her eyes, empties the eyecup, drops it in her purse, and tiredly locates her smoked glasses on the floor. The lights alter subtly; in the act of putting on her glasses* ANNIE *hears something that stops her, with head lifted. We hear it too, the voices out of the past, including her own now, in a whisper:*]

BOY'S VOICE: You said we'd be together, forever— You promised, forever and—*Annie!*

GUIDED READING
What does Annie hear when she is left alone in the garden house?

ANAGNOS' VOICE: But that battle is dead and done with, why not let it stay buried?

ANNIE'S VOICE [WHISPERING]: I think God must owe me a resurrection.

ANAGNOS' VOICE: What?

[*A pause, and* ANNIE *answers it herself, heavily.*]

ANNIE: And I owe God one.

BOY'S VOICE: Forever and ever—

[ANNIE *shakes her head.*]

—forever, and ever, and—

[ANNIE *covers her ears.*]

—forever, and ever, and ever—

[*It pursues* ANNIE; *she flees to snatch up her purse, wheels to the doorway, and* KELLER *is standing in it. The lights have lost their special color.*]

KELLER: Miss—Annie.

[*He has an envelope in his fingers.*]

I've been waiting to give you this.

ANNIE [AFTER A BREATH]: What?

KELLER: Your first month's salary.

[*He puts it in her hand.*]

With many more to come, I trust. It doesn't express what we feel, it doesn't pay our debt. For what you've done.

ANNIE: What have I done?

ANSWERS TO GUIDED READING QUESTIONS

1. Annie signs "mother."
2. Annie is impassive and defeated.
3. Annie hears Jimmie's voice.

ADDITIONAL QUESTIONS AND ACTIVITIES

Ask students the following questions:

1. What does Annie hear the voice of her brother saying after Helen leaves?
2. What does Annie remember saying to Anagnos?
3. What does Annie say she owes to God? What does she mean by this remark?
4. In what ways have Helen and her brother Jimmie become associated in Annie's mind?

Answers

1. She hears Jimmie saying, "You promised we'd be together, forever—You promised, forever and ever."
2. Annie remembers telling Anagnos that God owes her a resurrection.
3. Annie says that she owes God a resurrection. She may mean that she has to save a life to make up for her brother's death, which haunts her.
4. Students may suggest that Annie sees Helen as the child she may be able to save, unlike her brother Jimmie who she was unable to save.

1. Annie has taught Helen to obey.
2. She wanted to teach Helen what language is.
3. He can not undo what Annie has taught Helen.

LITERARY NOTE

Inform students that a **static character** is one who does not change over the course of the action. A **dynamic character** is one who does change. Encourage students to discuss whether Captain Keller, James, and Helen are static or dynamic. Ask students what signs Captain Keller shows of being either a static or dynamic character on page 618? What does James call Annie on page 619? Why does he call her this? What grace does he offer and why? What does this reveal about whether James is static or dynamic? What do Helen's actions on page 619 reveal about her as a static or dynamic character? Explain whether static or dynamic characters appeal to you more in a literary work.

Answers. Students may say that on page 618, Captain Keller reveals that he is a dynamic character. He has changed his attitude toward Annie, is appreciative of what she has done, expresses gratitude, asks her to stay on, and even considers her advice about not spoiling Helen. This is very different from Captain Keller in Acts 1 and 2. James calls Annie general, again comparing her to Ulysses S. Grant, in admiration for her stubborn tenacity that allows her to conquer against the odds. He offers a grace about Jacob wrestling with an angel, and Jacob refuses to let go until the angel blesses him. He then indicates that Helen is the angel and implies that Annie is stubborn Jacob who wrings blessings from the angel. This indicates that James is dynamic because he has become much more appreciative of what Annie is trying to do and has even warmed toward Helen. Students may say that Helen's actions and her new more gentle less unruly behavior reveals that she too is a dynamic character. Students may say that the change dynamic characters undergo makes them more interesting.

KELLER: Taken a wild thing, and given us back a child.

ANNIE [PRESENTLY]: I taught her one thing, no. Don't do this, don't do that—

> **GUIDED READING**
> What has Annie taught Helen?

KELLER: It's more than all of us could, in all the years we—

ANNIE: I wanted to teach her what language is. I wanted to teach her yes.

> **GUIDED READING**
> What did she want to teach Helen?

KELLER: You will have time.

ANNIE: I don't know how. I know without it to do nothing but obey is—no gift, obedience without understanding is a—blindness, too. Is that all I've wished on her?

KELLER [GENTLY]: No, no—

ANNIE: Maybe. I don't know what else to do. Simply go on, keep doing what I've done, and have—faith that inside she's— That inside it's waiting. Like water, underground. All I can do is keep on.

KELLER: It's enough. For us.

ANNIE: You can help, Captain Keller.

KELLER: How?

ANNIE: Even learning no has been at a cost. Of much trouble and pain. Don't undo it.

KELLER: Why would we wish to—

> **GUIDED READING**
> How can Keller help Annie continue to teach Helen?

ANNIE [ABRUPTLY]: The world isn't an easy place for anyone, I don't want her just to obey but to let her have her way in everything is a lie, to *her*; I can't—

[*Her eyes fill, it takes her by surprise, and she laughs through it.*]

And I don't even love her, she's not my child! Well. You've got to stand between that lie and her.

KELLER: We'll try.

ANNIE: Because *I* will. As long as you let me stay, that's one promise I'll keep.

KELLER: Agreed. We've learned something too, I hope.

[*A pause*]

Won't you come now, to supper?

ANNIE: Yes.

[*She wags the envelope, ruefully.*]

Why doesn't God pay His debts each month?

KELLER: I beg your pardon?

ANNIE: Nothing. I used to wonder how I could—

[*The lights are fading on them, simultaneously rising on the family room of the main house, where* VINEY *is polishing glassware at the table set for dinner.*]

—earn a living.

KELLER: Oh, you do.

ANNIE: I really do. Now the question is, can I survive it!

[KELLER *smiles, offers his arm.*]

KELLER: May I?

[ANNIE *takes it, and the lights lose them as he escorts her out.*

Now in the family room the rear door opens, and HELEN *steps in. She stands a moment, then sniffs in one deep grateful breath, and her hands go out vigorously to familiar things, over the door panels, and to the chairs around the table, and over the silverware on the table, until she meets* VINEY; *she pats her flank approvingly.*]

VINEY: Oh, we glad to have you back too, prob'ly.

[HELEN *hurries groping to the front door; opens and closes it, removes its key, opens and closes it again to be sure it is unlocked, gropes back to the rear door and repeats the procedure, removing its*

---

key and hugging herself glee-fully.

AUNT EV *is next in by the rear door, with a relish tray; she bends to kiss* HELEN'S *cheek.* HELEN *finds* KATE *behind her, and thrusts the keys at her.*]

KATE: What? Oh.

[*To* EV]

Keys.

[*She pockets them, lets* HELEN *feel them.*]

Yes, *I'll* keep the keys. I think we've had enough of locked doors, too.

[JAMES, *having earlier put* ANNIE'S *suitcase inside her door upstairs and taken himself out of view around the corner, now reappears and comes down the stairs as* ANNIE *and* KELLER *mount the porch steps. Following them into the family room, he pats* ANNIE'S *hair in passing, rather to her surprise.*]

JAMES: Evening, general.

[*He takes his own chair opposite.*

VINEY *bears the empty water pitcher out to the porch. The remaining suggestion of garden house is gone now, and the water pump is unob-structed;* VINEY *pumps water into the pitcher.*

KATE *surveying the table breaks the silence.*]

KATE: Will you say grace, Jimmie?

[*They bow their heads, except for* HELEN, *who palms her empty plate and then reaches to be sure her mother is there.* JAMES *considers a moment, glances across at* ANNIE, *lowers his head again, and obliges.*]

JAMES [LIGHTLY]: And Jacob was left alone, and wrestled with an angel until the breaking of the day; and the hollow of Jacob's thigh was out of joint, as he wrestled with him; and the angel said, Let me go, for the day breaketh. And Jacob said, I will not let thee go, except thou bless me. Amen.[1]

> **GUIDED READING**
>
> How does Helen feel about being home?

> **GUIDED READING**
>
> What does Helen give to Kate? Why has she removed them from the doors?

[ANNIE *has lifted her eyes suspiciously at* JAMES, *who winks expressionlessly and inclines his head to* HELEN.]

Oh, you angel.

[*The others lift their faces;* VINEY *returns with the pitcher, setting it down near* KATE, *then goes out the rear door; and* ANNIE *puts a napkin around* HELEN.]

AUNT EV: That's a very strange grace, James.

KELLER: Will you start the muffins, Ev?

JAMES: It's from the Good Book, isn't it?

AUNT EV [PASSING A PLATE]: Well, of course it is. Didn't you know?

JAMES: Yes, I knew.

KELLER [SERVING]: Ham, Miss Annie?

ANNIE: Please.

AUNT EV: Then why ask?

JAMES: I meant it *is* from the Good Book, and therefore a fitting grace.

AUNT EV: Well. I don't know about *that.*

KATE [WITH THE PITCHER]: Miss Annie?

ANNIE: Thank you.

AUNT EV: There's an awful *lot* of things in the Good Book that I wouldn't care to hear just before eating.

[*When* ANNIE *reaches for the pitcher,* HELEN *removes her napkin and drops it to the floor.* ANNIE *is filling* HELEN'S *glass when she notices it; she con-siders* HELEN'S *bland expression a moment, then bends, retrieves it, and tucks it around* HELEN'S *neck again.*]

> **GUIDED READING**
>
> What does Helen do as Annie reaches for the pitcher?

JAMES: Well, fitting in the sense that Jacob's thigh was out of joint, and so is this piggie's.

---

1. **And Jacob . . . Amen.** James's blessing references a Biblical story, which he compares lightly to Annie's struggle with Helen.

ANSWERS TO GUIDED READING QUESTIONS

1. Helen is grateful and happy to be home.
2. Helen gives Kate the keys because they have had enough locked doors.
3. James is comparing the struggle with the angel with Annie's struggle with Helen.

BIOGRAPHICAL NOTE

Students may be interested to know that William Gibson, author of this play and its sequel *Monday After the Miracle,* is not only a playwright. Gibson is also a Hugo-award-winning science fiction novelist. His novels are often classified as "cyberpunk" novels because they often deal with characters on the fringes of society in a futuristic, extremely high-tech world and explore concepts such as virtual reality. His novels include *Neuromancer, Count Zero,* and *Virtual Light.* (These novels are above most students' reading levels and some deal with adult themes, so do not suggest these as independent reading projects.) Do ask students if they are surprised to learn that Gibson is a well-known science fiction writer. Why, or why not?

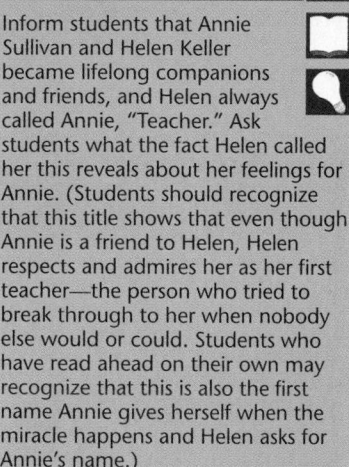

ADDITIONAL QUESTIONS AND ACTIVITIES

Inform students that Annie Sullivan and Helen Keller became lifelong companions and friends, and Helen always called Annie, "Teacher." Ask students what the fact Helen called her this reveals about her feelings for Annie. (Students should recognize that this title shows that even though Annie is a friend to Helen, Helen respects and admires her as her first teacher—the person who tried to break through to her when nobody else would or could. Students who have read ahead on their own may recognize that this is also the first name Annie gives herself when the miracle happens and Helen asks for Annie's name.)

Share with students the excerpt below from one of Helen's letters to Annie. Ask students to discuss what the letter reveals about the difficulties Helen continued to face even after she mastered language and became a successful adult. Which of her senses save her in the excerpt below? What would have happened had Helen not reacted when she did?

AUNT EV: I declare, James—

KATE: Pickles, Aunt Ev?

AUNT EV: Oh, I should say so, you know my opinion of your pickles—

KATE: This is the end of them, I'm afraid. I didn't put up nearly enough last summer, this year I intend to—

[*She interrupts herself, seeing* HELEN *deliberately lift off her napkin and drop it again to the floor. She bends to retrieve it, but* ANNIE *stops her arm.*]

> GUIDED READING
> What does Helen do again?

KELLER [NOT NOTICING]: Reverend looked in at the office today to complain his hens have stopped laying. Poor fellow, *he* was out of joint, all he could—

[*He stops too, to frown down the table at* KATE, HELEN, *and* ANNIE *in turn, all suspended in midmotion.*]

JAMES [NOT NOTICING]: I've always suspected those hens.

AUNT EV: Of what?

JAMES: I think they're Papist. Has he tried—

[*He stops, too, following* KELLER'S *eyes.* ANNIE *now stops to pick the napkin up.*]

AUNT EV: James, now you're pulling my—lower extremity, the first thing you know we'll be—

[*She stops, too, hearing herself in the silence.* ANNIE, *with everyone now watching, for the third time puts the napkin on* HELEN. HELEN *yanks it off, and throws it down.* ANNIE *rises, lifts* HELEN'S *plate, and bears it away.* HELEN, *feeling it gone, slides down and commences to kick up under the table; the dishes jump.* ANNIE *contemplates this for a moment, then coming back takes* HELEN'S *wrists firmly and swings her off the chair.* HELEN

> GUIDED READING
> What does Annie do when Helen drops the napkin for a third time?

struggling gets one hand free, and catches at her mother's skirt; when KATE *takes her by the shoulders,* HELEN *hangs quiet.*]

KATE: Miss Annie.

ANNIE: No.

KATE [A PAUSE]: It's a very special day.

ANNIE [GRIMLY]: It will be, when I give in to that.

[*She tries to disengage* HELEN'S *hand;* KATE *lays hers on* ANNIE'S.]

KATE: Please. I've hardly had a chance to welcome her home—

ANNIE: Captain Keller.

KELLER [EMBARRASSED]: Oh. Katie, we—had a little talk, Miss Annie feels that if we indulge Helen in these—

AUNT EV: But what's the child done?

ANNIE: She's learned not to throw things on the floor and kick. It took us the best part of two weeks and—

AUNT EV: But only a napkin, it's not as if it were breakable!

ANNIE: And everything she's learned *is?* Mrs. Keller, I don't think we should—play tug-of-war for her, either give her to me or you keep her from kicking.

KATE: What do you wish to do?

ANNIE: Let me take her from the table.

AUNT EV: Oh, let her stay, my goodness, she's only a child, she doesn't have to wear a napkin if she doesn't want to her first evening—

> GUIDED READING
> What excuses do Kate and Aunt Ev make for Helen?

ANNIE [LEVEL]: And ask outsiders not to interfere.

AUNT EV [ASTONISHED]: Out—outsi— I'm the child's *aunt!*

KATE [DISTRESSED]: Will once hurt so much, Miss Annie? I've—made all Helen's favorite foods, tonight.

[*A pause*]

KELLER [GENTLY]: It's a homecoming party, Miss Annie.

[ANNIE *after a moment releases* HELEN. *But she cannot accept it, at her own chair she shakes her head and turns back, intent on* KATE.]

ANNIE: She's testing you. You realize?

JAMES [TO ANNIE]: She's testing you.

KELLER: Jimmie, be quiet.

[JAMES *sits, tense.*]

Now she's home, naturally she—

ANNIE: And wants to see what will happen. At your hands. I said it was my main worry, is this what you promised me not half an hour ago?

GUIDED READING

How has Annie's main worry come to pass?

KELLER [REASONABLY]: But she's *not* kicking, now—

ANNIE: And not learning not to. Mrs. Keller, teaching her is bound to be painful, to everyone. I know it hurts to watch, but she'll live up to just what you demand of her, and no more.

JAMES [PALELY]: She's testing *you*.

KELLER [TESTILY]: Jimmie.

JAMES: I have an opinion, I think I should—

KELLER: No one's interested in hearing your opinion.

ANNIE: *I'm* interested, of course she's testing me. Let me keep her to what she's learned and she'll go on learning from me.

GUIDED READING

Why does Annie insist that she be given control of Helen again?

Take her out of my hands and it all comes apart.

[KATE *closes her eyes, digesting it;* ANNIE *sits again, with a brief comment for her.*]

Be bountiful, it's at her expense.

[*She turns to* JAMES, *flatly.*]

Please pass me more of—her favorite foods.

[*Then* KATE *lifts* HELEN'S *hand, and turning her toward* ANNIE, *surrenders her;* HELEN *makes for her own chair.*]

KATE [LOW]: Take her, Miss Annie.

ANNIE [THEN]: Thank you.

[*But the moment* ANNIE *rising reaches for her hand,* HELEN *begins to fight and kick, clutching to the tablecloth, and uttering laments.* ANNIE *again tries to loosen her hand, and* KELLER *rises.*]

ANSWERS TO GUIDED READING QUESTIONS

1. They say that it is a special day and that Helen didn't break anything.
2. Already Helen is testing her new boundaries and the Kellers are giving in to her misbehavior.
3. Annie says that unless she has control of Helen, Helen will not learn anything else from her.

ADDITIONAL QUESTIONS AND ACTIVITIES

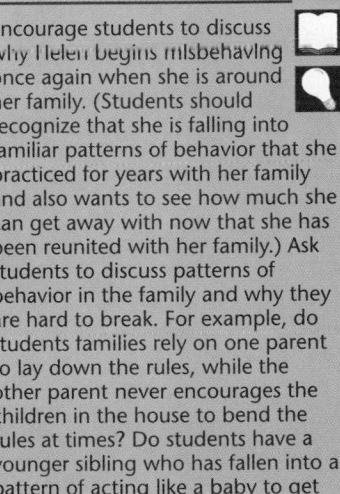

Encourage students to discuss why Helen begins misbehaving once again when she is around her family. (Students should recognize that she is falling into familiar patterns of behavior that she practiced for years with her family and also wants to see how much she can get away with now that she has been reunited with her family.) Ask students to discuss patterns of behavior in the family and why they are hard to break. For example, do students families rely on one parent to lay down the rules, while the other parent never encourages the children in the house to bend the rules at times? Do students have a younger sibling who has fallen into a pattern of acting like a baby to get his or her way?

KELLER [TOLERANT]: I'm afraid you're the difficulty, Miss Annie. Now I'll keep her to what she's learned, you're quite right there—

[*He takes* HELEN'S *hands from* ANNIE, *pats them;* HELEN *quiets down.*]

—but I don't see that we need send her from the table, after all, she's the guest of honor. Bring her plate back.

ANNIE: If she was a seeing child, none of you would tolerate one—

KELLER: Well, she's not, I think some com-promise is called for. Bring her plate, please.

> **GUIDED READING**
> Why do the Kellers accept Helen's behavior?

[ANNIE'S *jaw sets, but she restores the plate, while* KELLER *fastens the napkin around* HELEN'S *neck, she permits it.*]

There. It's not unnatural, most of us take some <u>aversion</u> to our teachers, and occasionally another hand can smooth things out.

[*He puts a fork in* HELEN'S *hand;* HELEN *takes it. Genially:*]

Now. Shall we start all over?

[*He goes back around the table, and sits.* ANNIE *stands watching.* HELEN *is motionless, thinking things through, until with a wicked glee she deliberately flings the fork on the floor. After another moment she plunges her hand into her food, and crams a fistful into her mouth.*]

JAMES [WEARILY]: I think we've started all over—

[KELLER *shoots a glare at him, as* HELEN *plunges her other hand into* ANNIE'S *plate.* ANNIE *at once moves in, to grasp her wrist, and*

HELEN *flinging out a hand encounters the pitcher; she swings with it at* ANNIE; ANNIE *falling back blocks it with an elbow, but the water flies over her dress.* ANNIE *gets her breath, then snatches the pitcher away in one hand, hoists* HELEN *up bodily under the other arm, and starts to carry her out, kicking.* KELLER *stands.*]

ANNIE [SAVAGELY POLITE]: Don't get up!

KELLER: Where are you going?

ANNIE: Don't smooth anything else out for me, don't interfere in any way! I treat her like a seeing child because I *ask* her to see, I *expect* her to see, don't undo what I do!

> **GUIDED READING**
> Why does Annie treat Helen like a seeing child?

KELLER: Where are you taking her?

ANNIE: To make her fill this pitcher again!

[*She thrusts out with* HELEN *under her arm, but* HELEN *escapes up the stairs and* ANNIE *runs after her.* KELLER *stands rigid.* AUNT EV *is astounded.*]

AUNT EV: You let her speak to you like that, Arthur? A creature who *works* for you?

KELLER [ANGRILY]: No. I don't.

[*He is starting after* ANNIE *when* JAMES, *on his feet with shaky resolve, interposes his chair between them in* KELLER'S *path.*]

> **GUIDED READING**
> Who stops Keller from going after Annie?

JAMES: Let her go.

KELLER: What!

JAMES [A SWALLOW]: I said—let her go. She's right.

[KELLER *glares at the chair and him.* JAMES *takes a deep breath, then headlong:*]

words for everyday use

a • ver • sion (ə vər′ zhən) *n.,* dislike; tendency to turn away from. *Nora's* <u>aversion</u> *to green foods does not apply to pistachio ice cream.*

She's right, Kate's right, I'm right, and you're wrong. If you drive her away from here it will be over my dead—chair, has it never occurred to you that on one occasion you might be <u>consummately</u> wrong?

[KELLER's *stare is unbelieving, even a little fascinated.* KATE *rises in trepidation, to mediate.*]

GUIDED READING

How does Keller react to James's outburst?

KATE: Captain.

[KELLER *stops her with his raised hand; his eyes stay on* JAMES'S *pale face, for a long hold. When he finally finds his voice, it is gruff.*]

KELLER: Sit down, everyone.

[*He sits.* KATE *sits.* JAMES *holds onto his chair.* KELLER *speaks mildly.*]

Please sit down, Jimmie.

[JAMES *sits, and a moveless silence prevails;* KELLER'S *eyes do not leave him.*

ANNIE *has pulled* HELEN *downstairs again by one hand, the pitcher in her other hand, down the porch steps, and across the yard to the pump. She puts* HELEN'S *hand on the pump handle, grimly.*]

ANNIE: All right. Pump.

[HELEN *touches her cheek, waits uncertainly.*]

GUIDED READING

Whom does Helen ask for?

No, she's not here. Pump!

[*She forces* HELEN'S *hand to work the handle, then lets go. And* HELEN *obeys. She pumps till the water comes, then* ANNIE *puts the pitcher in her other hand and guides it under the spout, and the water tumbling half into and half around the pitcher douses* HELEN'S *hand.* ANNIE *takes over the handle to keep water coming, and does automatically what she has done so many times before,*

spells into HELEN'S *free palm:*]

Water. W, a, t, e, r. Water. It has a—*name*—

GUIDED READING

What does Annie do as Helen pumps the water?

[*And now the miracle happens.* HELEN *drops the pitcher on the slab under the spout, it shatters. She stands transfixed.* ANNIE *freezes on the pump handle: there is a change in the sundown light, and with it a change in* HELEN'S *face, some light coming into it we have never seen there, some struggle in the depths behind it; and her lips tremble, trying to remember something the muscles around them once knew, till at last it finds its way out, painfully, a baby sound buried under the debris of years of dumbness.*]

GUIDED READING

What miracle happens?

HELEN: Wah. Wah.

[*And again, with great effort*]

Wah. Wah.

[HELEN *plunges her hand into the dwindling water; spells into her own palm. Then she gropes frantically,* ANNIE *reaches for her hand, and* HELEN *spells into* ANNIE'S *hand.*]

ANNIE [WHISPERING]: Yes.

[HELEN *spells it again.*]

Yes!

[HELEN *grabs at the handle, pumps for more water, plunges her hand into its spurt and grabs* ANNIE'S *to spell it again.*]

Yes! Oh, my dear—

[*She falls to her knees to clasp* HELEN'S *hand, but* HELEN *pushes it free, stands almost bewildered, then drops to the ground, pats it swiftly, holds up her palm, imperious.* ANNIE *spells into it:*]

---

words for everyday use

con • sum • mate (känt′ sə mət) *adj.,* perfect; complete. *The luscious dinner capped off a wonderful <u>consummate</u> day.*

ANSWERS TO GUIDED READING QUESTIONS

1. Annie takes Helen to refill the pitcher.
2. James stops him.
3. Keller is unbelieving but fascinated that James is finally standing up to him.
4. Helen is looking for her mother.
5. She spells *water.*
6. Helen connects the word with water and remembers the word. She says wah wah, the baby talk she used to use for water before she lost her hearing.

ADDITIONAL QUESTIONS AND ACTIVITIES

Ask students the following questions:

1. In the stage directions, the writer notes, "And now the miracle happens." What does Helen do when she realizes the connection between the letters she is signing and the water she is pumping?
2. Why is this a miracle?
3. What "miracle" is happening inside at the table while Helen's miracle occurs outside?

Answers

1. Helen is so surprised she drops the pitcher and it shatters. She stands transfixed, the light of understanding comes over her face, and she tries to form a word for the first time since she was six months old.
2. Students may say this is a miracle because Helen, against all odds, will now be able to learn to communicate with others.
3. Students may suggest that this miracle is that James finally stands up to his father and tells him he is wrong about Annie, and the Captain's silence indicates that James may not have only earned his surprise but his respect.

ADDITIONAL QUESTIONS AND ACTIVITIES

Share with students the quotation above. Ask students to discuss how Helen might look back on this scene with Annie in remembering the "story" of her life. Explain how Annie helped to turn Helen's limitation into a privilege. Why might Annie have brought joy into Helen's life? *Answers.* Responses will vary, but students may suggest that Helen might look back and feel grateful because Annie was the person who made it possible for Helen to tell the story of her life and took her out of isolation so she could communicate with others. Students may say Annie transformed Helen's life with the privilege of communication to which she never before had access because of her limitations. Students may say that Annie brought joy into Helen's life by making her part of humanity by teaching her how to communicate with others.

Ground.

[HELEN *spells it back.*]

Yes!

[HELEN *whirls to the pump, pats it, holds up her palm, and* ANNIE *spells into it.*]

Pump.

[HELEN *spells it back.*]

Yes! Yes!

[*Now* HELEN *is in such an excitement she is possessed, wild, trembling, cannot be still, turns, runs, falls on the porch steps, claps it, reaches out her palm, and* ANNIE *is at it instantly to spell:*]

Step.

[HELEN *has no time to spell back now, she whirls groping, to touch anything, encounters the trellis, shakes it, thrusts out her palm, and* ANNIE *while spelling to her cries wildly at the house.*]

> **GUIDED READING**
> What does Helen begin to do after learning the word water?

Trellis. Mrs. Keller! *Mrs. Keller!*

[*Inside,* KATE *starts to her feet.* HELEN *scrambles back onto the porch, groping, and finds the bell string, tugs it; the bell rings, the distant chimes begin tolling the hour, all the bells in town seem to break into speech while* HELEN *reaches out and* ANNIE *spells feverishly into her hand.* KATE *hurries out, with* KELLER *after her;* AUNT EV *is on her feet, to peer out the window; only* JAMES *remains at the table, and with a napkin wipes his damp brow. From up right and left the servants—* VINEY, *the two Negro children, the other servant—run in, and stand watching from a distance as* HELEN, *ringing the bell, with her other hand encounters her mother's skirt; when she throws a hand out,* ANNIE *spells into it:*]

Mother.

[KELLER *now seizes* HELEN'S *hand, she touches him, gestures a hand, and* ANNIE *again spells:*]

Papa— She *knows!*

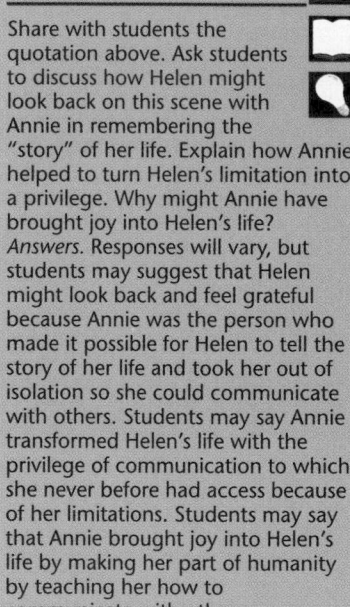

[KATE *and* KELLER *go to their knees, stammering, clutching* HELEN *to them, and* ANNIE *steps unsteadily back to watch the threesome,* HELEN *spelling wildly into* KATE'S *hand, then into* KELLER'S, KATE *spelling back into* HELEN'S; *they cannot keep their hands off her, and rock her in their clasp.*

Then HELEN *gropes, feels nothing, turns all around, pulls free, and comes with both hands groping, to find* ANNIE. *She encounters* ANNIE'S *thighs,* ANNIE *kneels to her;* HELEN'S *hand pats* ANNIE'S *cheek impatiently, points a finger, and waits; and* ANNIE *spells into it:*]

> **GUIDED READING**
> What word does Helen want to know when she pulls away from her parents?

Teacher.

[HELEN *spells it back, slowly;* ANNIE *nods.*]

Teacher.

[*She holds* HELEN'S *hand to her cheek. Presently* HELEN *withdraws it, not jerkily, only with reserve, and retreats a step. She stands thinking it over, then turns again and stumbles back to her parents. They try to embrace her, but she has something else in mind, it is to get the keys, and she hits* KATE'S *pocket until* KATE *digs them out for her.*

ANNIE *with her own load of emotion has retreated, her back turned, toward the pump, to sit;* KATE *moves to* HELEN, *touches her hand questioningly, and* HELEN *spells a word to her.* KATE *comprehends it; their first act of verbal communication, and she can hardly utter the word aloud, in wonder, gratitude, and deprivation; it is a moment in which she simultaneously finds and loses a child.*]

GUIDED READING

What is the first act of verbal communication between Kate and Helen? Why is Kate filled with both gratitude and deprivation?

KATE: Teacher?

[ANNIE *turns; and* KATE, *facing* HELEN *in her direction by the shoulders, holds her back, holds her back, and then relinquishes her.* HELEN *feels her way across the yard, rather shyly, and when her moving hands touch* ANNIE'S *skirt she stops. Then she holds out the keys and places them in* ANNIE'S *hand. For a moment neither of them moves. Then* HELEN *slides into* ANNIE'S *arms, and lifting away her smoked glasses, kisses her on the cheek.* ANNIE *gathers her in.*

KATE *torn both ways turns from this, gestures the servants off, and makes her way into the house, on* KELLER'S *arm. The servants go, in separate directions.*

The lights are half down now, except over the pump. ANNIE *and* HELEN *are here, alone in the yard.* ANNIE *has found* HELEN'S *hand, almost without knowing it, and she spells slowly into it, her voice unsteady, whispering:*]

ANNIE: I, love, Helen.

[*She clutches the child to her, tight this time, not spelling, whispering into her hair.*]

Forever, and—

[*She stops. The lights over the pump are taking on the color of the past, and it brings* ANNIE'S *head up, her eyes opening, in fear; and as slowly as though drawn she rises, to listen, with her hand on* HELEN'S *shoulders. She waits, waits, listening with ears and eyes both, slowly here, slowly there: and hears only silence. There are no voices. The color passes on, and when her eyes come back to* HELEN *she can breathe the end of her phrase without fear:*]

GUIDED READING

What does Annie spell to Helen?

—ever.

[*In the family room* KATE *has stood over the table, staring at* HELEN'S *plate, with* KELLER *at her shoulder; now* JAMES *takes a step to move her chair in, and* KATE *sits, with head erect, and* KELLER *inclines his head to* JAMES; *so it is* AUNT EV, *hesitant, and rather humble, who moves to the door.*

Outside HELEN *tugs at* ANNIE'S *hand, and* ANNIE *comes with it.* HELEN *pulls her toward the house; and hand in hand, they cross the yard, and ascend the porch steps, in the rising lights, to where* AUNT EV *is holding the door open for them.*

The curtain ends the play.]

■

ANSWERS TO GUIDED READING QUESTIONS

1. They fall to their knees, clutching Helen.
2. She wants to know the name for Annie.
3. Helen asks Kate for teacher. Kate is filled with wonder that Helen can communicate, but also with deprivation as her child chooses another.
4. Annie spells "I love Helen. Forever and ever." She waits to hear the voices, but does not.

LITERARY TECHNIQUE

INTERNAL CONFLICT AND RESOLUTION. A struggle that takes place within a character is called an **internal conflict.** The resolution is the point in a poem, story, or play at which the central conflict, or struggle, is ended. Share with students these definitions. Tell them that they will discuss the central conflict and its resolution in the Understanding Literature section, but that this drama also contains an internal conflict in Annie's mind. What is this conflict? In what way is it resolved at the end of the story?

Answers. Students should recognize that the struggle is Annie's struggle to atone for the guilt she feels over not staying with her brother "forever and ever" and his death through her work with Helen. Students should realize that she exorcises the ghosts of her past by breaking through to Helen and telling her that she will love her "forever and ever."

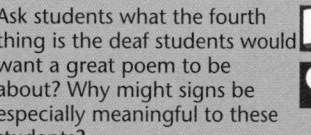
Respond *to the* SELECTION

Explain whether you think Annie Sullivan is a "miracle worker."

About *the* AUTHOR

William Gibson was born in 1914. He grew up in New York City, in an area called the Bronx. As a child, he loved to read and write and hoped to write a novel. His mother encouraged him to aim high, and with her tutoring, Gibson was able to skip a few grades in school. In the end, however, he did not do very well in school. He disliked science, history, and math classes and was not motivated to excel. His main interest was writing. Gibson won several awards for his writing while in high school, and his classmates predicted that he would one day go to Hollywood and write screenplays.

In addition to *The Miracle Worker,* Gibson wrote a popular play called *Two for the Seesaw.*

Both of these were performed on Broadway and made into movies. In 1982, Gibson wrote a sequel to *The Miracle Worker* called *Monday after the Miracle.* This play depicted Helen's life as a college student with Annie Sullivan as her tutor and translator. Gibson has also written poetry, fiction, and an autobiographical book called *A Mass for the Dead.* He now lives in Stockbridge, Massachusetts, where he helped found the Berkshire Theater Festival.

RELATED READING

If you could write one great poem, what would you want it to be about?

(Asked of four student poets at the Illinois Schools for the Deaf and Visually Impaired)

Robert Pinsky

Fire: because it is quick, and can destroy.
Music: place where anger has its place.
Romantic Love—the cold or stupid ask why.
Sign: that it is a language, full of grace,

That it is visible, invisible, dark and clear,
That it is loud and noiseless and is contained
Inside a body and explodes in air
Out of a body to conquer from the mind.

750   *UNIT TEN / TURNING WORDS INTO ACTION: DRAMA*

American Sign Language: The Manual Alphabet

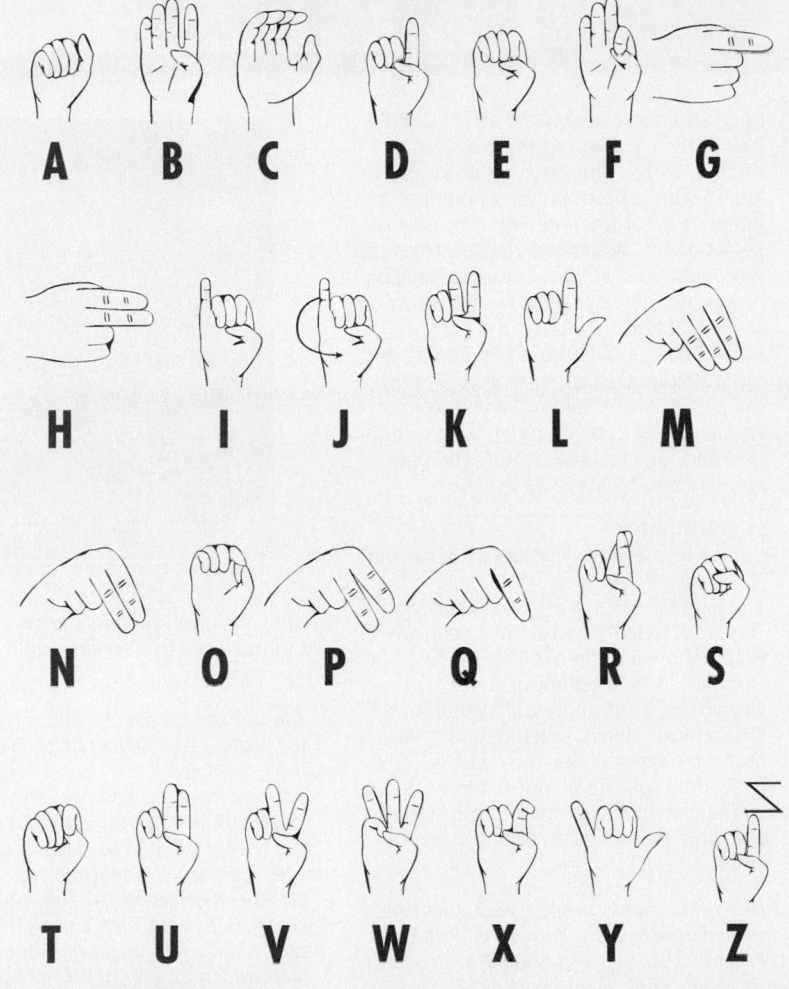

ABOUT THE RELATED READINGS

Robert Pinsky was the Poet Laureate of the United States from 1997 to 2000. He is also the poetry editor of the online journal *Slate* and an instructor at Boston University. Pinsky grew up in a noisy, disorganized household. As a teen he wrote songs and gradually turned to poetry. He plays the saxophone in his free time.

American Sign Language (ASL) is the native language of thousands of deaf people who have deaf parents. It is not based on the English language. It has a unique culture that has developed over generations. ASL is also used by deaf people whose parents were not deaf and by hearing people who communicate with users of sign language.

ACT 3 / *THE MIRACLE WORKER*　**751**

ADDITIONAL QUESTIONS AND ACTIVITIES

Ask students the following questions.

1. What was the most difficult aspect for Laura Mahler as she played the role of Helen Keller?
2. What helped Mahler prepare for the role of Helen?
3. What was the biggest challenge for Mindy Dahlen as she played Annie Sullivan?
4. What physical interactions were involved in playing Annie Sullivan?
5. How does director Steve Barberio regard the role of the audience in a performance.

Answers

1. Mahler says the hardest part was "finding" Helen. She needed to "become" Helen instead of trying simply to act like a girl who was blind, deaf, and mute.
2. Mahler got accustomed to the idea of blindness by wearing a blindfold around the house, taking a bath, and even around a downtown area. The play's director also tried to capture the emotion of not hearing anything by playing loud, banging music.
3. Like Mahler, Dahlen says that the biggest challenge was "becoming" Annie Sullivan instead of just imitating her.
4. Dahlen and Mahler needed to work out timing sequences in scenes that involved struggling and fighting. They would have to gauge the right distance and right moment in scenes involving fighting or slapping, and make sure they didn't flinch.
5. Barberio regards the role of audience as very important. He expects the audience to be open and respectful. He says that if an audience "wants to receive the very best performance possible, they must be ready to participate in the performance by listening quietly, respecting the work of the actors on stage."

Getting Into Drama:
A PRODUCTION OF *THE MIRACLE WORKER*

In October and November 1998, Child's Play Theatre presented the play *The Miracle Worker*. The play was produced by Next Stage, a program incorporating intensive actor training with professional performance. Advanced youth actors work alongside adult mentors to develop professional theater productions. Laura Mahler, at age 15, played the part of Helen Keller, a girl who is blind, deaf, and mute. Mindy Dahlen, who was 17, played the part of Annie Sullivan, a young woman hired to teach Helen to communicate and interact with others. The play was directed by Steve Barberio.

Laura Mahler

Laura Mahler

What was the most difficult part of playing Helen Keller?

The hardest part for me was actually "finding" Helen. I had to find her from inside of me and then let her come through. In the beginning, I was "acting" like a blind, deaf, mute girl instead of "becoming" Helen. I would have to say that the biggest challenge was the blindness, although the deafness and muteness were right up there! I had to get into my own little world and zone out everyone else's.

Helen was a strong-willed, wild, energetic, spoiled, mischievous, curious, difficult child. What aspects of her personality and character were a challenge to portray?

I guess many aspects of her personality came naturally to me, because we have so many similarities. It's just that Helen has to express them differently. For example, when I'm mad, I'll try to talk things out or I'll cool off in my bedroom. When Helen's mad, she will kick and moan and throw tantrums until she gets her way! I had to find the ways that Helen would express her emotions.

How did you prepare for this role? What preparatory experiences helped you "become" Helen?

During rehearsals and away from rehearsals, like at home, I would wear a blindfold. I still had to participate in warm-ups and we blocked my scenes just like [those of] everyone else, but I had to experience everything through the blindfold. What a learning experience it was! I even took a bath with it on. One day the whole cast had to walk through downtown Hopkins (with a rope of course) blindfolded! One rehearsal, the director played loud, banging music to capture the emotion of not hearing anything.

How much preparation time did you have to get ready for this role?

I found out that I was cast as Helen in August. Rehearsals started in September and the show opened in October. From August to September, I read books and researched about Helen. I also got familiar with the script and watched the movie with Anne Bancroft and Patty Duke to get ready for the rehearsals.

How many performances did you do?
We had 26 performances, which was the perfect amount. I'm glad that the run was as long as it was, because all through the run, we were constantly finding new things and improving the show. Almost every show was better than the last one, making closing the best ever!

How did you manage school and work at the same time?
My school was very supportive of the whole process. As long as I kept up with the homework, got the notes that I missed, and kept my grades up, it was okay with them. I had to cut down on the phone and socializing in order to get everything done, but it was worth it.

Mindy Dahlen
What was the most challenging aspect of playing Annie Sullivan?
Probably the most challenging thing I faced when playing Annie Sullivan was making her real. I had to transfer all the head knowledge I had about her into being her. And I had to do it without having to "act" it. I had to find what made it real for me. It was the difference between me imitating what people do when they lost their temper and really losing my temper.

As Annie, which aspects of your interaction with Helen were most difficult?
The physical interaction with Helen-struggling and fighting-actually was not difficult for us. As actors we knew each other very well and were comfortable with it. The most difficult thing came in the actual timing or spacing of an action. For instance,

we didn't feel guilty slapping each other, but we had to each time make sure we were at the right distance so that she could slap me in the face without looking to see where I was. There was also the flinching problem. Sometimes one of us would anticipate a hit or a blow and would involuntarily dodge. We had to focus and stay very "in the moment" so that each event was new, like it was happening for the first time.

What was the most rewarding part of this production?
There are two things that were equally rewarding parts of the production. First, the audience: after every show I saw faces wet with tears and I knew that I had been a part of something that had touched people's hearts and changed them. Second, my own personal growth: I started working on this project not really sure I could do it. I always had this cloud of self-doubt hanging over my head. But on opening night, I realized that I was doing it! And people said I was good! I can't tell you what a realization this was for me.

What kind of training in acting have you had? When did you get started in theater?

Mindy Dahlen

Last year I was in an acting class called Advanced Youth Training Program. We met twice a week and were trained in characterization, scene study, and Shakespeare. That class is what really prepared me for the role of Annie Sullivan, even though I had been involved with theater for 9 years, since I was 8.

What other roles have you played? Which was your favorite?
Some of my most memorable roles have been Beth in *Little Women*, Louanne Pig in two Nancy Carlson plays, an orphan in *Annie*, and a munchkin in *The Wizard of Oz*. My favorite up to this point was Beth March, but now it's definitely Annie Sullivan.

How was your role in The Miracle Worker *different from other roles?*
The role of Annie Sullivan was a complete turn-around from most other roles I've played, with the exception of Beth. In many children's plays, actors portray more of a caricature of reality than a real person. In *The Miracle Worker*, Annie had to be so real. She was a real person and she had to be as believable as any real person can be.

Steve Barberio
What do you look for when you go to a theater performance?
As a director, I take a broad view of a play in performance. The production design is very important. I look at how it fits within the theater space itself and how it serves the play. Are the scenic elements, costumes, properties, and lighting design unified in their service to the play? How well are sound and music integrated into the entire production? How is the casting of the show? Are actors playing with or against their physical/vocal type? What level of training have the actors had and does their training meet the demands of the script?

I also examine how well the director has captured the life of the play. Tempo and rhythm tell a lot about how the director has interpreted the script. Furthermore, his or

Steve Barberio

her stage pictures reveal a conceptual understanding of the relationships among characters. How well does he or she use the space provided? Do the staging patterns visually show us the tensions within the play? How well does he or she build the momentum of the play toward a climax?

If I am attending a play that I already know (i.e. *The Miracle Worker*), I don't spend too much time thinking about the script but look at the whole of the production itself. If it is a new play, I think a lot about the development of the script. Is the writer using a classic structure, or is he or she trying to break the mold in some way? How well does the dialogue reflect the characters in conflict and how does character move the plot?

What do you hope the audience will bring to a performance you direct?
Respect for what they are about to see is at the root of what I expect from an audience. While artists live to serve their audience, the audience must understand that the production and presentation of art is not a science. An audience that is open to the creative and interpretive process will

be ready to receive what the artists have to present. Actors on stage have worked very hard to bring the playwright's words to life. If an audience wants to receive the very best performance possible, they must be ready to participate in the performance process by listening quietly, respecting the work of the actors on stage.

How much time did you spend preparing for this production?
As producing director of the company, I am responsible for play selection and director assignments. Therefore, my work begins when I select the play for production and assign a crew to the show. I begin meeting with designers about four weeks prior to auditions and begin my interpretation of the work about two weeks before that. I rehearse with the actors for about six weeks prior to opening night. In all, I estimate that I spent about 140 hours working on our production of *The Miracle Worker*.

What were the most difficult aspects of putting this production together?
The most difficult aspect of this production was creating an environment that was entirely believable. We used an actor to play the role of Helen Keller who had the use of all of her senses. Therefore, it was most difficult to develop in her a believable portrayal of someone who could not see, speak, nor hear. Furthermore, it was difficult for the other actors who played members of Helen's family to create an atmosphere in which they couldn't communicate with Helen in more conventional ways. Imagine how difficult it would be to communicate with someone who had no ability to see, hear or speak.

Are there any special considerations to address when working with young performers?
It is important to cast kids in roles in which they will excel. While it is often difficult to find plays in which the experience of the characters will be accessible to a young performer, I believe this is an important value to embrace. Another important consideration is to avoid creating an environment in which the "ends will justify the means." By that I mean that when working with young people, one must embrace the value of the process as much as the importance of the end product. Striving to achieve a balance between a healthy creative process and an excellent artistic product is fundamental when working with kids.

How important were the stage preparation and the scenery in this production? Who was responsible for that part of the production? How many people worked behind the scenes?
The scenic elements are very important to any production, whether they are elaborate representations of the world of the play or minimal suggestions of the playwright's concept. We chose to create a naturalistic environment, with very realistic elements such as real food, authentic clothing, and a real dog. The following "behind the scenes" positions were filled by different people: director, stage manager, composer, technical director, set designer, lighting designer, properties designer, costume/makeup designer, assistant stage manager, board operators, and carpenters.

What was the most rewarding part of directing The Miracle Worker*?*
I worked with several excellent actors, both adult and youth. It was a delight to bring a concept to them in rehearsal and watch them entirely embrace that approach. The director's job is so much easier when working with strong actors who are open to new ideas and concepts. Also, I was really happy with the final product. I think it is one of the best plays our audience has seen. I felt throughout the performance run that the quality of the work was excellent. It was very rewarding to be part of such an excellent production.

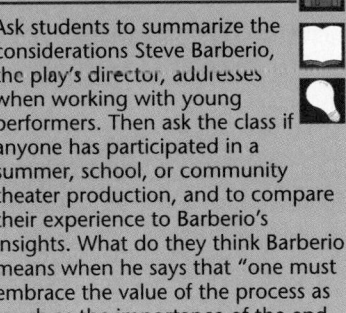

ADDITIONAL QUESTIONS AND ACTIVITIES

Ask students to summarize the considerations Steve Barberio, the play's director, addresses when working with young performers. Then ask the class if anyone has participated in a summer, school, or community theater production, and to compare their experience to Barberio's insights. What do they think Barberio means when he says that "one must embrace the value of the process as much as the importance of the end product." Do they agree?

RECALL

1a. Kate sees Helen crocheting and then sees her eat daintily and neatly. Annie has taught Helen obedience.

2a. Helen drops her napkin repeatedly, drops her fork, eats with her fingers, and spills a pitcher of water.

3a. Helen connects the word *water* with the water running over her hands. She says "wah wah," the word she used to use for water, and understands that things have names. Helen most wants to know what to call Annie. Annie signs "teacher" to her.

INTERPRET

1b. The Kellers are relieved to see that Helen has learned obedience. They didn't think she could be controlled. She now appears more like a "normal" child to them.

2b. The Kellers are not sure how to discipline Helen. They pity her and think that exceptions should be made for her. Annie insists that Helen be treated like a hearing, seeing child, because she has expectations that Helen can learn what a hearing, seeing child could. She also knows that without discipline, it will be impossible to teach Helen anything.

3b. Making the connections that words mean something does open up the door for Helen. She eagerly explores her world, wanting to learn words for everything. It also opens the world of communication to her as she is able to ask questions of her mother and understand the response. Students may say this world is important to her because she now realizes why Annie has been spending so much time with her signing and she is grateful.

ANALYZE

4a. Annie herself has been blind, so she understands some of the challenges Helen faces. Annie also spent time in an institution and knows what it would be like for Helen to live there. Annie is haunted by her past especially by her broken promise to take care of her brother "forever and ever," and is unwilling to give up on Helen.

SYNTHESIZE

4b. Annie is stubborn and determined. She won't give up despite the difficulties Helen places in her path and the conflicts or differences of opinion she has with the Kellers.

Investigate, Inquire, and imagine

Recall: GATHERING FACTS

1a. When Kate visits the garden house at the end of the two weeks, what does she see Helen do? What has Annie taught Helen?

2a. What does Helen do at the dinner table after returning home? Why does she do these things?

3a. What miracle occurs at the pump?

Interpret: FINDING MEANING

1b. Explain why the Kellers are satisfied with what Helen has learned.

2b. Why don't the Kellers discipline Helen? Why is Annie's attitude toward Helen a necessary part of teaching her?

3b. Does this one miracle open the doors Annie thought it would? Why is the word *teacher* so important to Helen?

Analyze: TAKING THINGS APART

4a. Analyze Annie's motivations for teaching Helen. Consider her past, her current options, and the voices she hears.

Synthesize: BRINGING THINGS TOGETHER

4b. In addition to Annie's motivations, what character traits helped her reach Helen? What do you think Annie has learned from Helen?

Evaluate: MAKING JUDGMENTS

5a. Assess whether Annie took the right approach in assuming that the most important thing she could teach Helen was language. What other doors are now open to Helen?

Extend: CONNECTING IDEAS

5b. Look at the description of "sign" in "If You Could Write One Great Poem, What Would You Want It to Be About?" How does sign language do all of these things? Use examples from *The Miracle Worker* or from your own experiences with sign.

ANSWERS TO INVESTIGATE, INQUIRE, IMAGINE (CONT.)

Annie is tenacious and innovative. She is not afraid to suggest a new way of reaching Helen. She tirelessly spells to Helen, wherever they are, whatever they do. Annie has learned some patience herself. She has learned to love Helen and has found some peace from the voices that had haunted her.

EVALUATE

5a. Annie is insistent on teaching Helen language because she believes it is the only way to free Helen from the silent, dark world in which she lives and to give her the key to the rest of the world. Once Helen understands the concept of language, of what a word stands for, she eagerly wants to

(Continued on page 757)

Understanding *Literature*

SUSPENSE. Suspense is a feeling of anxiousness or curiosity. Writers create suspense by raising questions in the reader's mind and by using details that create strong emotion. How is suspense heightened in act 3?

CONFLICT AND RESOLUTION. Review the definitions for **conflict** and **resolution** in the Handbook of Literary Terms. Identify the central conflict in *The Miracle Worker.* How is this conflict resolved? What is the internal conflict Annie experiences? What is the external conflict?

SIMILE AND METAPHOR. A **simile** is a comparison using *like* or *as.* A **metaphor** is a figure of speech in which one thing is spoken or written about as if it were another. Identify a simile or metaphor that describes Helen in each act. Explain what each thing has in common with Helen and/or her situation.

CHARACTERIZATION. Review the definition for **characterization** in the Handbook of Literary Terms. Briefly describe Helen at the beginning of the play, in the middle, and at the end. Identify specific examples from the play that create this character. Next, explain how the character of Annie is developed. What techniques does the playwrite use to develop the characters of Helen and Annie? Explain.

Writer's Journal

1. If you could write one great poem, what would it be about? Write a **four-line stanza** about your subject.
2. More than once during the play, Annie writes letters about her experience with Helen. Write a **letter** from Annie to Anagnos about her latest experience with Helen.
3. Write a **human interest story** to be published in Captain Keller's newspaper about Helen and her teacher.

Skill Builders

Vocabulary

DRAMATIZING VOCABULARY. Many of the stage directions in this play indicate how particular lines of dialogue should be said. For example, on page 689, the doctor says a line "amiably." Test your understanding of the vocabulary used in the stage directions. Form groups of four students and take turns saying the following line from the play: "By morning she'll be knocking down Mr. Keller's fences again." Each student should say the line in one of the following ways: amiably, facetiously, hoarsely, blandly, meekly, mournfully, reluctantly, curtly, vexedly, dourly, wryly, eagerly, witheringly, grimly, and testily. Try saying the line while acting baffled, wistful, emphatic, placating, and jovial. Take turns until you have reached the end of the list. You may need to look up some of the words in the dictionary.

ANSWERS TO UNDERSTANDING LITERATURE (CONT.)

her have her own way and live as she will. Act III: Annie tells Helen that the "chick *has* to come out of its shell. You come, too." Annie is trying to crack open the "shell" of lack of understanding that keeps Helen separated from her world. Annie says that "inside it's waiting. Like water, underground." She is again referring to Helen's potential, the power of her mind if it can find a way out.

CHARACTERIZATION. At the beginning of the play, Helen is wild, uncontrolled, mischievous, and spoiled. She is often unkempt. Helen is unable to communicate
(Continued on page 758)

Answers to Skill Builders is found on page 758.

ANSWERS TO INVESTIGATE, INQUIRE, IMAGINE (CONT.)

learn more about the world, about the people in her life, and so forth. She will now be able to enter into more formal education and have more connection with other people.

EXTEND

5b. *Responses will vary. Possible responses are given.* It is clear that sign is a language. This play shows how it allows the deaf to communicate. It is a language of motion and thus grace. It is visible in that you can see the motion but invisible in the meaning behind the motion. It is explosive in its power to communicate and bubbles out of the speaker. It is the connection between the mind and the world, allowing ideas to come both in and out.

ANSWERS TO UNDERSTANDING LITERATURE

SUSPENSE. Annie's repeated pleas for more time with Helen and the marking of what she has learned add to the suspense that she will break through to Helen. The tolling of the bells mark the end of her time and almost signal defeat. The increasing intensity of Helen's test of Annie's authority adds to the suspense. Suspense peaks when Helen drops the pitcher and stands transfixed; it is clear that she is on the verge of understanding.

CONFLICT AND RESOLUTION. The central conflict is Annie's attempt to break through to Helen by getting her to connect one word with its meaning, which she believes will be the key to Helen learning many other things. The conflict is resolved at the pump, when Helen connects the word Annie spells with water itself.

SIMILE AND METAPHOR. ACT I: Anagnos says that Helen is "like a little safe, locked, that no one can open. Perhaps there is a treasure inside." Anagnos is right that Helen is locked inside herself. Annie does, however, unlock her to release the treasure of her mind. James says, "She's a monkey." He means that Helen is good at imitating, but does not understand. Act II: Annie says that Helen's head "works like a mousetrap." This cliched simile means that Helen has a quick, clever mind. Helen runs from the dining room "like a ruined bat out of hell." She is disheveled, unkempt, and probably exhausted and angry. Annie says that the Kellers have kept Helen "like a pet." Annie means that the Kellers do not treat Helen like a child because it is easier for them to let

for your READING LIST

Thirty Plays From Favorite Stories, edited by Sylvia Kamerman, is a collection of folktales, legends and stories from around the world, presented as short plays. These are complete scripts with stage directions, as well as instructions on properties, set, sound and lighting, and costumes—everything you need to stage a production. You will find many familiar tales, such as "Rumplestiltskin," "The Princess and The Pea," and "Pandora's Box," as well as some that are less familiar. In "The Clever Judge," from an African folktale, a young girl named Maakafi proves she is worthy of going to school when she solves a crime that baffles the judge. In "Scheherazade," from an Arabian legend, a clever Queen finds a way to save her own neck from the king who has executed hundreds of queens before her. In "The Dreadful Dragon of Utrecht," from a Dutch folktale, the Mayor establishes committees for every purpose: the Committee for Clean Canals, the Committee on Creaking Windmills, the Committee to Stop the Clopping of Wooden Shoes, and even the Committee for Getting Rid of the Dreadful Dragon. You will also enjoy "The Tiger and the Brahmin" from an Indian tale in which a wily jackal outsmarts a hungry tiger.

CONDUCT A PERFORMANCE

After everyone has finished reading the book, select one of the plays to perform before an audience. Each participant should volunteer to take on one or more of the jobs—you'll need actors, a director, a stage manager, and costume, set, and lighting designers. In addition to creating the set, props, costumes, and lighting, you will need to rehearse the play several times. You may find that the Language Arts Survey 4.1, "Verbal and Nonverbal Communication" will offer useful ideas. You may want to perform for others in your class, your parents, another class in your school, or for some community organization. Finally, hold a post-production review of your performance, discussing among yourselves the following questions:

- What went well and what did not? Why?
- How did it feel to perform before an audience, or to see the results of my work in preparing a live performance?
- How was my experience of the play as literature different after I participated in a live performance of it?

Other books you may want to read:
The Big Book of Folktale Plays, ed. Sylvia E. Kamerman
Folktale Plays Round the World by Paul T. Nolan

ANSWERS TO UNDERSTANDING LITERATURE (CONT.)

effectually with others and often treats others rudely or even violently. Helen's unacceptable actions include trying to stab Martha, pulling buttons off Aunt Ev's dress, and kicking her father. When Annie arrives, Helen's clothing is torn and rumpled and she is wild and chasing the dog. Kate repeatedly tries to make Helen look neater. In the middle of the play, after Annie has Helen in the garden house, Helen is obedient, neat, and has learned some manners. She is still unable to communicate well with others. Helen sits quietly crocheting. She waits for her fork before beginning to eat. By the end of the play, Helen's spirit and excitement show as she understands a word and has the world opened to her. She is curious and eager as she tries to learn the word for everything right away.

Guided Writing

REVIEWING A MOVIE OR PLAY

Travis couldn't decide whether or not to see the new play at the community theater. Then he saw a review of the play in the school newspaper. The reviewer first gave a short synopsis of the play without giving away the ending. Next, he described how the stage setting had been built to look exactly like a crumbling medieval castle. He described the scary sound effects and the dim lighting that contributed to the spooky mood. The reviewer also praised the performers for their strong portrayals of the aging king and queen. After reading this review, Travis decided to see the play.

Like Travis, you can read a review to help you decide whether or not to see a play or movie. A review can tell you what the movie or play is about and offer an opinion about the quality of the performance. The review might tell you how the play is unique or how an effect was achieved. If the movie or play was *not* well done, the review might persuade you to save your money! In this lesson, you will write a persuasive review to help your peers decide whether or not to see a particular movie or play.

Examining the Models

In the first review, the reviewer states that she expects to tire of seeing another production of *The Miracle Worker*. However, she offers a different opinion. What opinion does she give about the quality of this production of the play? How might her comments persuade readers to see the play?

The reviewer also comments on the acting. She states that Beth Chaplin draws a strong portrait of Annie Sullivan as a scrappy, bare-knuckle fighter. She notes that Rose Dachis does an impressive job as Helen Keller, maintaining a remarkably impassive mask, but keeping Helen's headstrong will and bright spirit just beneath the surface. How might her evaluations of the performers influence a reader's decision to see the play?

In the second review, the reviewer highlights how the director helped the entire cast learn about portraying a blind and deaf person through sensory awareness exercises. How does accentuating information about this technique build a reader's interest in the play?

Both reviews try to persuade the reader to see the play. Sometimes, however, a reviewer tries to persuade readers not to see a play or a movie. In that case, the reviewer needs to give specific information about why the play or movie is not worth viewing.

Professional Models

by Erin Hart, in *Sidewalk*, February 24, 1999

After seeing it more than a half dozen times, I always expect to tire of *The Miracle Worker*. In between, though, I guess I tend to forget what a well-crafted, meaningful and moving play it is. But seeing a fine production such as the current one at Park Square Theatre, makes me happy that it's resurrected so often....

Beth Chaplin draws a strong portrait of Annie Sullivan as a scrappy, bare-knuckle fighter. The gutsy determination and blunt manners that mark her as a survivor of the poorhouse set Sullivan apart from the genteel Kellers. As Helen, Ali Rose Dachis does an impressive job, maintaining a remarkably impassive mask, but keeping Helen's headstrong will and bright spirit just beneath the surface.

Director Janice Stone also gets forceful and keenly felt performances from the rest of the cast, notably Colleen Hennen and Michael Tazla as Helen's loving but exasperated parents. Michael Harris offers a fine reading of Helen's half-brother James, whose mocking hides a desperate need for approval....

Playwright William Gibson is, above all, concerned with isolation and the human need to communicate. Every scene—whether it's between husband and wife, mother and child, father and son, teacher and pupil—revolves

continued on page 760

GUIDED WRITING Software

See the Guided Writing Software for an extended version of this lesson that includes printable graphic organizers, extensive student models and student-friendly checklists, and self-, peer, and teacher evaluation features.

INDIVIDUAL LEARNING STRATEGIES

MOTIVATION
Show a dramatic scene from a movie. (Consider selecting a film with literary merit from the list provided by the Literary Cinema at http://library.thinkquest.org/2847/films.htm.) With the class, write a quick review of that segment of the film. This activity should demonstrate to students that they are capable of writing a review.

READING PROFICIENCY
Based on students' familiarity with earlier Guided Writing lessons, ask students to use their prior knowledge to make predictions about the content of this lesson. What kind of model is going to be presented? Into

INDIVIDUAL LEARNING STRATEGIES (CONT.)

what sections will the lesson be divided? What assignment are students asked to do?

ENGLISH LANGUAGE LEARNING
See strategies for Reading Proficiency above that will also benefit English language learners.

SPECIAL NEEDS
Students may need help writing support

statements for their Graphic Organizer. Pair them with a proficient student who can ask questions to help the student think of appropriate support statements.

ENRICHMENT

You might videotape students as, in pairs, they evaluate current movies à la Siskel and Ebert.

Prewriting

IDENTIFYING YOUR AUDIENCE. Have students read the Language Arts Survey 2.4, "Identifying Your Audience." Encourage students to use vocabulary with which their peers are familiar. Even though they are writing for their peers, students should be reminded to use formal English. Refer students to the Language Arts Survey 3.2, "Formal and Informal English."

FINDING YOUR VOICE. Encourage students to read the Language Arts Survey 2.5, "Finding Your Voice," and 3.3, "Register, Tone, and Voice." Ask students to identify the voice they intend on using.

WRITING WITH A PLAN. Review with students their aim for writing a review. The definition of "aim" is located in the Handbook of Literary Terms on page 944. Students might benefit from doing a focused freewrite once they have selected the movie or play they want to review. Refer students to the Language Arts Survey 2.12, "Freewriting."

Examining the Models

Point out that both professional models are favorable about the play, *The Miracle Worker.* Ask students what they would expect to find in a review critical of the play. What can a reviewer comment on besides the acting?

Professional Models

continued from page 759

around making one's thoughts, feelings and desires known to another. As devastating as it is not to have the tools to communicate, Gibson seems to say, what's worse is having the tools and not making use of them.

....

by Katherine A. Reilly, *Minnesota Sun Publications,* October 13, 1998

Teaching someone without sight or hearing was the task faced by Annie Sullivan, "The Miracle Worker". . .

"I really believe it is the story of her teacher [Sullivan], more than Helen," said Director Steve Barberio who said the story is about the effort Sullivan makes to reconcile her past which she finds through the redemption of teaching Helen.

How does a sighted person convey blindness, or a hearing person convey deafness? These were questions Barberio and his cast had to examine during rehearsals.

In an effort to achieve this, actors participated in several sensory awareness exercises, Barberio said, including one in which the entire cast was blindfolded. The cast also went through the first act with 14-year-old Laura Mahler from Minnetonka, who plays Helen blindfolded. "It really hit home for them as sighted people, how hard it is," Barberio said.

Prewriting

IDENTIFYING YOUR AUDIENCE. When magazines, news-papers, and websites publish reviews, they keep their specific audiences in mind. A review in *The New Yorker* might discuss different points and use a different style than a review in *Seventeen* magazine. For this assign-ment, you will be writing a movie or play review for a school newspaper. Before you write your review, think about the points of discussion and a style that will interest your peers. Your task is to persuade them to see or not to see a particular play or movie.

FINDING YOUR VOICE. Voice is reflected through your personality and attitude toward the movie or play, as well as your choice of words, sentence structure, and style. If you keep this in mind as you state your definite opinion about whether they should see or not see the movie or play, your voice as a reviewer will be informative, persuasive, and engaging. Your voice also needs to be appropriate for a review that could be published in a school newspaper.

Look at the two examples below. Which example would best help persuade one of your peers not to see a particular play? How do the two examples differ in personality, attitude, word choice, sentence structure, and style?

The play is boring.

Watching this play was like being suspended in time. Someone forgot to tell the playwright that the plot needs to move forward!

WRITING WITH A PLAN. Which play or movie should you review? Select one for which you have strong feeling. Persuading others is easier if you have a strong opinion about the movie or play's worth.

You will also want to choose a movie or play that you have either seen very recently or one that you will view especially for this assignment. If you are reviewing a movie or play that you have already seen, try to see it again so you can write about it critically and accurately.

Javier used a graphic organizer to organize his thoughts and rate the 1962 movie version of *"The Miracle Worker."* Copy the graphic organizer onto your own piece of paper. Include a specific detail in the comment that you write that shows how effective or ineffective a part is.

Student Model—Graphic Organizer

Movie or play: *The Miracle Worker*
Production: 1962 movie version directed by Arthur Penn

Synopsis: Helen Keller is blind and deaf and she doesn't know how to talk. She lives like an animal. Annie Sullivan comes to be her tutor. She's the miracle worker because she teaches Helen how to behave and how to talk—sign language—and helps her grow up to be a really smart and good woman.

MAIN CHARACTERS — ACTOR/ACTRESS
Annie Sullivan — Anne Bancroft
Helen Keller — Patty Duke

SUPPORT: The breakfast scene is so good. You'd think Patty Duke is really like this. Anne Bancroft shows she's tougher than Helen but she also shows that she cares.

SUPPORT: At first I was a little mixed up, but then I couldn't quit watching because I kept thinking something wild but good was going to happen.

Setting

1   ②   3   4   DOESN'T APPLY

SUPPORT: Black and white is weird. I guess it was a little boring and a little depressing, but maybe that's good for that kind of movie.

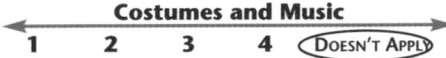

SUPPORT: This wasn't a big part of the movie.

SUPPORT: This is funny, because Helen can't talk, but what Helen and Annie "say" is good. The best "dialogue" is when Helen "says" water.

Special Effects

1   2   3   4   DOESN'T APPLY

SUPPORT: Special effects were not a part of this movie.

OVERALL OPINION: Wow. I wasn't sure because it's an old movie and black and white, but it's a great story it really makes you think about what it would be like but I think the most important thing is that it tells you how cool people can be. Overall rating: 3 out of 4.

WHEN, WHERE, HOW TO VIEW: Rent the video.

> A **synopsis** is a concise statement that summarizes the movie or play.

Drafting

Use the notes on your graphic organizer to guide you as you write the draft of your review. Number the three most important notes on your organizer and write only about those points in your review.

There are two ways you could organize your review. You could organize your notes from the most important reason to see or not see the movie or play to the least important reason. Or, you could start with the least important reason and work your way up to the most important reason.

You may want to begin your review with a synopsis of the movie or play. Then describe each of your reasons for seeing or not seeing the movie or play in the order you have selected. Try to persuade your peers by using interesting and informative examples. Give specific information about why the movie or play was or was not effective. You will also want to give specific information about where and when the movie or play can be seen. End your review with a definite recommendation.

Do not focus on the details of spelling, usage, and mechanics as you write your rough draft. Instead, focus on getting your ideas down on paper.

continued on page 762

GRAPHIC ORGANIZER

See the Guided Writing Resource 7.10 for a blackline master of the Graphic Organizer for this lesson.

Drafting

Remind students not to give away the conclusion of the movie or play. Their synopsis should set the scene and briefly describe the action. Students should use their completed Graphic Organizer modeled on page 761 and any good ideas they detect in their focused freewrite. Have students write a discovery draft in which they do not focus on spelling, grammar, usage, and mechanics. Students might benefit from reading the Language Arts Survey 2.31, "Drafting."

Teaching Note

Have students compare the Student Model—Draft on this page with the final version presented on page 763. Have students answer the following questions. What improvements did Javier make in his final version? What improvements can still be made in the Student Model—Revised?

Peer and Self-Evaluation

Have students use the checklist on page 762 for self- and peer evaluation. See the Guided Writing Resource located in the Teacher's Resource Kit for a blackline master of the checklist. The checklist is intended to act as a student-friendly rubric that should help students identify specific evidence of writing strengths and areas needing improvement. Make sure students provide concrete suggestions for improvement or specific evidence of the effectiveness of their review. Students might benefit from reading the Language Arts Survey 2.37–2.40 for more details about self- and peer evaluation. Students critiquing a peer's review might be interested in using common proofreader's symbols, which are found in the Language Arts Survey 2.44, "Using Proofreader's Marks."

continued from page 761

Peer and Self Evaluation

After you finish your first draft, complete a self-evaluation of your review. If time allows, you may want to get one or two peer evaluations. For more information, see the Language Arts Survey 2.37, "Self- and Peer Evaluation."

As you evaluate your review, answer the following questions. Write notes on your draft to use later when you revise your writing.

- How persuasive is the review? What additional information would help it to be more persuasive?
- Which reasons for seeing or not seeing the movie or play are the most valuable for making a decision? Which reasons, if any, are not valuable for making a decision?
- What support is offered to back up the reasons? How could the support be strengthened?
- How well does the organization of the information work to persuade the reader? What changes could be made to build a stronger case?
- What use of word choice, sentence structure, and style makes the review appropriate for the audience? What changes might improve the review's appeal for the audience?
- What specific information, if any, needs to be added?
- Which sentences have dangling or misplaced modifiers? How would these errors be fixed?

Look at Javier's self-evaluation of his rough draft.

Student Model—Draft

In the beginning of *The Miracle Worker*, a deaf and blind child is born. She runs around, eats, and lives like an animal when she gets a little bit | Sense? older until her parents hire a tutor. Helen the blind and deaf girl learns how to take care of herself, but she also learns to communicate with her family and friends with the deaf alphabet. ⌐ Awkward wording

You should see this movie because of three great points. The first is the dialogue. This may seem funny because Helen can't talk, but the way you see her learn to talk is good⌐ And the *Fix punctuation.* things that Annie "says" to Helen really make you think. *Tell who plays Helen and Annie earlier*

The second reason is the acting is really good. Patty Duke is so good you'd think she's really like this <u>at</u> *misplaced; doesn't make sense* <u>the breakfast scene</u>. Anne Bancroft shows she's tougher than Helen while throwing all the food and stuff around but she also shows how much she cares about Helen.

The third reason is that it's a really good story. It's true‸which

makes it interesting because you want to know what really happened to these people. But it's also exciting because Helen is so wild and Annie is so determined to make her learn all this (stuff). But the best part is that it
Use different word
really makes you think about what it would be like to be like Helen and it
Use different word choice, not slang
tells you how (cool) people can be.

You should rent the movie and watch it.
This needs a more effective conclusion.

Revising and Proofreading

As you consider your self-evaluation and your peer reviews, think about the changes that will make your review more persuasive. Make the revisions. Then proofread your review for errors in spelling, usage, and mechanics. Check your work for dangling and misplaced modifiers.

After considering his self-evaluation notes and the peer evaluation notes, Javier revised his movie review

Student Model—Revised

In the beginning of *The Miracle Worker*, a baby named Helen Keller becomes deaf and blind. As she grows up, she runs around, eats, and lives like an animal until her parents hire a tutor named Annie Sullivan, played by Anne Bancroft. Helen, played by Patty Duke, learns how to take care of herself. She also learns the deaf alphabet so she can communicate with her family and friends.

It may seem funny to say the dialogue is good, because Helen can't talk. But the way you see her learn to talk is a powerful part of the movie. One scene that makes this movie worth

Language, Grammar, and Style
Avoiding Dangling and Misplaced Modifiers

A **dangling modifier** is a modifying phrase or clause that seems to modify a word it is not intended to modify. Sometimes a modifier is too far from the word it is supposed to modify. It is then called a **misplaced modifier**. Look at the examples below.

DANGLING

Valerie drove to the airport while reading my book.

The dangling modifier "while reading my book" seems to modify the word "drove." The writer needs to add a few words to fix this error.

CORRECT

Valerie drove to the airport while I was reading my book.

MISPLACED

Alex played a solo on the cello wearing a white tuxedo.

The misplaced modifier ìwearing a white tuxedoî is too far from the word Alex. It sounds as if the cello was wearing a white tuxedo. The writer needs to reword the sentence.

continued on page 764

Language, Grammar, and Style
Avoiding Dangling and Misplaced Modifiers

LESSON OVERVIEW
In this lesson, students will be asked to do the following:
- Identify Dangling and Misplaced Modifiers, 764
- Fix Dangling and Misplaced Modifiers, 764
- Use Modifiers Correctly, 764

INTRODUCING THE SKILL. Tell students that using dangling and misplaced modifiers can confuse their readers.

PRACTICING THE SKILL. For extra practice, have students work through the exercise in the following section of the Language, Grammar, and Style Resource located in the Teacher's Resource Kit: 3.44, "Recognizing Other Problems with Modifiers."

Revising and Proofreading

Remind students that revising includes adding or expanding, cutting or condensing, replacing, and moving text. Have students read the Language Arts Survey 2.41, "Revising." A handout of the proofreading checklist found in the Language Arts Survey on page 888 is available in the Teacher's Resource Kit, Guided Writing Resource 2.45.

Publishing and Presenting

As students prepare their final copy, refer them to the Language Arts Survey 2.46, "Proper Manuscript Form." If students are maintaining a portfolio, you might have them place their review in it. Students should read the Language Arts Survey 2.48, "Maintaining a Writing Portfolio."

Reflecting

Students might answer the questions in this section in a journal entry.

CORRECT

Wearing a white tuxedo, Alex played a solo on the cello.

or,

Alex, wearing a white tuxedo, played a solo on the cello.

IDENTIFYING DANGLING AND MISPLACED MODIFIERS. Look at this sentence from the Professional Model. Identify the clause that modifies "James." Is the modifier placed correctly in the sentence? How do you know?

Michael Harris offers a fine reading of Helen's half-brother James, whose mocking hides a desperate need for approval.

FIXING DANGLING AND MISPLACED MODIFIERS. Look at the sentences in Javier's rough draft. Fix any dangling and misplaced modifiers by adding words or by rewording the sentence. Then check to see how the writer fixed the sentences in the final copy.

USING MODIFIERS CORRECTLY. Examine each sentence in your movie or play review. Check to see that there are no dangling or misplaced modifiers. Rewrite any sentences that are incorrect.

seeing is when Helen understands her first word—"water." It's really intense. The things that Annie "says" to Helen really make you think, too.

Another reason to see this movie is the acting is really good. At the breakfast scene, Patty Duke is so believable you'd think she's really like this in real life. Anne Bancroft as Annie Sullivan shows she's tougher than Helen when Helen is throwing all the food and dishes around. She also shows how much she cares about Helen.

Finally, *The Miracle Worker* is a really good story. It's true, which makes it interesting because you want to know what really happened to these people. But it's also exciting because Helen is so wild and Annie is so determined to make her learn to communicate and be a real person. But the best part is that it really makes you think about what it would be like to be like Helen. You should rent this movie and watch it because it tells you how incredible people can be. Both Helen and Annie are real miracle workers.

Publishing and Presenting

Write or print a final copy of your review. Submit your review to your school newspaper, or, with your classmates, create a book of movie and play reviews for everyone to use.

Reflecting

Consider how your ability to review a play or movie critically has improved. You should now be more able to offer an opinion and back it up with supporting evidence. You can use that kind of thinking strategy in many other areas of your life.

Consider, too, the kind of information you will now expect others to tell you when you ask them their opinion about a movie or play. Will you be satisfied with a simple statement that the movie was good? What kinds of follow-up questions will you be able to ask your peers? Why is that important?

UNIT TEN *review*

Words for Everyday Use

Check your knowledge of the following vocabulary words. For each word, write a short sentence that includes the word in context. To review a word, look back to the page number indicated.

- apprehensive (728)
- benign (691)
- commence (692)
- compel (713)
- compunction (717)
- dour (725)
- emphatic (692)
- facetious (692)
- feigned (715)
- feint (718)
- frantic (691)
- impassive (711)
- impertinent (724)

- impudence (693)
- incarnate (730)
- indolent (691)
- indulgent (689)
- inexorable (694)
- interminable (719)
- intractable (732)
- irresolute (717)
- laborious (718)
- nonplussed (715)
- obstinate (696)
- placate (693)
- precocious (696)

- proffer (711)
- protracted (721)
- relinquish (720)
- steel (691)
- temperance (711)
- unencumbered (689)
- vengeful (711)
- vexedly (725)
- vitality (689)
- vivacious (690)
- wry (713)
- zeal (722)

Literary Tools

Define each of the following terms, giving concrete examples when possible. To review a term, refer to page 687.

- flashback
- suspense
- stage directions

- conflict
- resolution
- simile

- metaphor
- characterization

Reflecting *on your* *reading*

Genre

How does drama differ from other genres of literature? Discuss the use of set design and lighting in *The Miracle Worker*. Explain how the play, which is restricted to using only dialogue and stage directions, enables the audience to learn the private thoughts and emotions of Annie and to learn about the character of Helen, who cannot speak.

VOCABULARY EXERCISES. Give students the following exercise.

Review the American Sign Language manual alphabet on page 751. Then choose five words from the vocabulary words on page 765 and learn how to finger-spell them. Work in pairs to practice your ability to finger-spell the words you have chosen. As an alternate activity, learn the ASL sign for five vocabulary words by consulting a sign language dictionary or a member of the deaf community. If such resources are not available, invent your own sign for each of five words. See if your partner can guess each word as you sign it. Your partner should choose five different words and have you guess them in the same way. Incorporate gestures in your signs that tie to the definition.

EXAMPLE
apprehension

The sign could show arms extended but fingers clenched in nervousness or fear; this could be accompanied by a frightened facial expression

ADDITIONAL RESOURCES

UNIT 10 RESOURCE BOOK
- Vocabulary Worksheet
- Unit 10 Review
- Unit 10 Test

Reflecting on Your Reading

The question in the Genre section of "Reflecting on Your Reading" can be used to help students prepare for the Unit 10 Test. Have them write a brief essay (of not more than a page) answering this question, using evidence from the text to support their response.

As an alternate question, you may ask students who have seen a production or film version of *The Miracle Worker* to compare and contrast that version with the printed play in their textbook.

The Library, 1960. Jacob Lawrence. National Museum of American Art, Washington, D.C.

GOALS/OBJECTIVES

Studying this unit will enable students to
- enjoy different types of nonfiction
- define and identify concepts and techniques in nonfiction such as *aim, analogy, biography, concrete details, expressive writing, hyperbole, persuasive essay, point of view, scientific writing,* and *unity*
- engage in a meaningful independent reading experience and conduct a creative interview
- write a letter to the editor
- demonstrate an ability to use negatives effectively and avoid double negatives

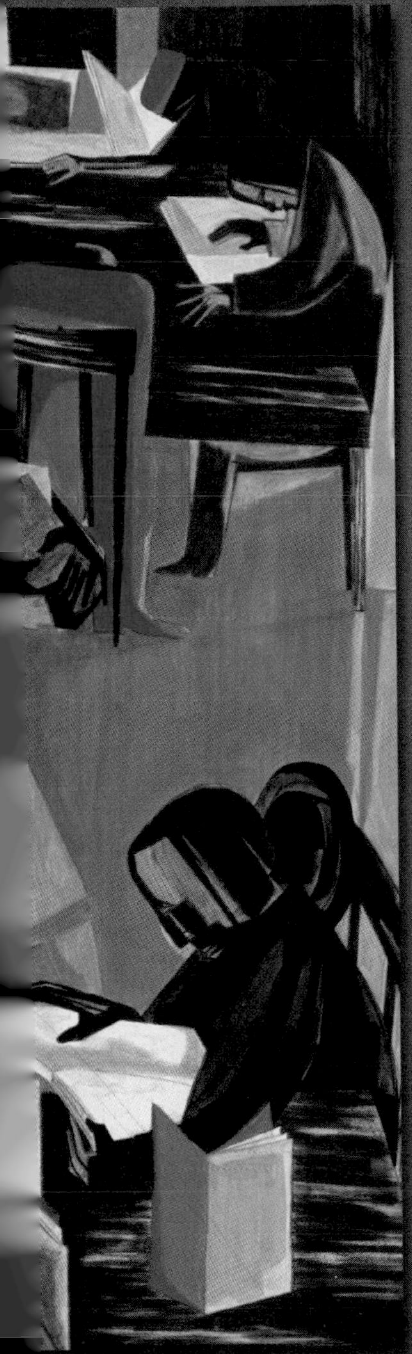

Telling It As It IS

Nonfiction

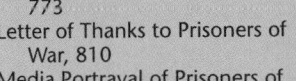

UNIT ELEVEN

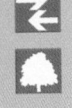

CROSS-CURRICULAR CONNECTIONS

Arts and Humanities
Excerpts from Film *Elizabeth,* 770
Holding an Elizabethan Festival, 773
Letter of Thanks to Prisoners of War, 810
Media Portrayal of Prisoners of War, 810
Persuasive Essay, 792
Using Hyperbole, 781

Mathematics and Sciences
Creating Models of the Atom, 802
Documentary about Space Exploration, 800
Persuasive Essay, 792
Pros and Cons of the Metric System, 800

Social Studies
American Society for the Prevention of Cruelty to Animals, 783
Education of Renaissance Women, 771
Holding an Elizabethan Festival, 773
Power of the Medieval Catholic Church, 774
Roots of the Apartheid, 793
Segregation in the United States, 794
Small-Group Report on the Protestant Reformation, 775
The Divine Right, 772
Vietnam War POWs, 811

Applied Arts
Holding an Elizabethan Festival, 773

TEACHING THE MULTIPLE INTELLIGENCES

Logical-Mathematical
Advertising Tactics, 792
Cats and Dogs Debate, 785
Creating Models of the Atom, 802
Documentary about Space Exploration, 800
Pros and Cons of the Metric System, 800
Royal Family Chart, 770

Spatial
Creating Models of the Atom, 802
Royal Family Chart, 770

Kinesthetic
Admirable Qualities, 769
Do Pet Owners Exaggerate?, 780
Feelings about Prisoners of War, 809
Holding an Elizabethan Festival, 773
Rating the Importance of Clothing, 791
Smallest and Largest Things, 799

TEACHING THE MULTIPLE INTELLIGENCES (CONT.)

Interpersonal
Admirable Qualities, 769
American Society for the Prevention of Cruelty to Animals, 783
Author's Viewpoint, 788
Being a Prisoner of War, 812
Cats and Dogs Debate, 785
Changing Attitudes and Values, 795
Do Pet Owners Exaggerate?, 780
Feelings about Prisoners of War, 809
Holding an Elizabethan Festival, 773

(Continued on page 768)

INTERNET RESOURCES

Voices of Youth, a UNICEF-sponsored Internet site at http://www.unicef.org/voy/, provides for several ways for students to participate online in meaningful activities related to nonfiction. The link to the Meeting Place allows students to learn about and share ideas about world issues. The link to the Learning Place offers problem-solving activities for students to do. A teacher's resource page is also available.

ELEMENTS *of* NONFICITON

NONFICTION. Nonfiction is writing about real people, places, things, and events. Essays, autobiographies, biographies, new stories, speeches, and documentary writing are all types of nonfiction writing.

AIM. Aim is a writer's reason for writing. A writer may write to inform readers or report to them about something that has taken place. This **mode** or type of writing is called **informative writing.** News articles, reports, scientific essays, and speeches are frequently forms of informative writing. A writer may write to entertain, amuse, or enlighten readers. This type of writing is called **imaginative writing**. Poems, short stories, novels, and plays are often examples of imaginative writing. A writer may write to share a story. This type of writing is called **narrative writing.** Biographies and autobiographies are examples of narrative writing. A writer may write to reflect on his or thoughts and emotions about something that is personal to him or her. This type of writing is known as **personal** or **expressive writing.** Diary entries and personal letters are examples of this type of writing. Finally, a writer may want to persuade readers to share his or her view on a particular subject. This type of writing is called **persuasive or argumentative writing,** as the writer's goal is to persuade the reader. Newspaper editorials and petitions are examples of this kind of writing. A writer can have more than one aim in creating a work. A biographical essay, for example, can be both narrative and informative. An essay that offers an opinion about a vacation site may be both expressive, revealing the author's personal reactions to the place, and persuasive, offering arguments for or against visiting the place.

AUTOBIOGRAPHY. An **autobiography** is the story of a person's life told by that person. Autobiographical works are told from the first-person point of view. Personal letters, personal essays, journal entries, and memoirs are all examples of autobiography, along with book-length works of autobiography that tell a complete life story.

BIOGRAPHY. A **biography** is the story of a person's life told by another person. Biographies are told from a third-person point of view, although writers of biography may also include autobiographical excerpts so that the reader may gain some firsthand knowledge about the person whose life story is being told.

ESSAY. An **essay** is a short nonfiction work that expresses a writer's thoughts about a single subject. A well-written essay clearly presents information organized into an introduction, body, and conclusion. There are many types of essays. A *personal or expressive essay,* for example, is a short nonfiction work on a single topic related to the life of the writer. The author of a personal essay may tell a story or an anecdote or reflect on and share thoughts and feelings about something in his or her life. In a *scientific essay,* the writer's main goal is to inform the reader and to communicate specific scientific information.

SPEECH. A **speech** is a public address. Although speeches are delivered orally, most speeches are written first—and many famous historical speeches are passed on through writing. Speeches may be delivered to a wide and varied audience or to a small audience of people with similar interests and experiences. Most speeches address a specific issue or event, although some may encompass several topics. A speech can inform an audience, tell a story, persuade an audience, or reflect on an idea.

DOCUMENTARY WRITING. Documentary writing is writing that records an event in accurate detail. News articles and research reports are both examples of documentary writing.

Prereading

"Elizabeth"

by Milton Meltzer

Reader's T O O L B O X

BIOGRAPHY. A **biography** is the story of a person's life, told by another person. As you read about Elizabeth, note the ways in which author Milton Meltzer creates an image of Elizabeth and her world, even though he never met her or even lived during her time.

CONCRETE DETAILS. Concrete details are specific words that name objects or actions or provide descriptions of those objects or actions. These specific details help the piece of writing to provide clear, conscise, and in-depth information to the reader. As you read, find concrete details in the selection that make the events seem more real or personal. For example, pay attention to the description of Elizabeth's summer festival on page 773. How does the author make that event realistic for the reader?

You might find it helpful to create a time line of Elizabeth's life to see how the pieces fit together.

1533
Elizabeth born

Reader's Journal

Think of a leader you admire. Perhaps this person is the head of a country, president of a company, or someone you know personally. What qualities does this person possess that make him or her an effective leader?

Reader's Resource

- **HISTORY CONNECTION.** From Alfred the Great, in the ninth century, to Elizabeth II today, 56 men and women have reigned as kings or queens of England. Some of these monarchs occupied the throne for only a few months, while others reigned for so long—and so popularly—that their names became linked to entire periods of history. One such ruler was Elizabeth I, who reigned from 1558 until her death In 1603.

- In the long history of the English monarchy, only five women have held the position of sole ruler of England: Mary I (1553–1558), Elizabeth I (1558–1603), Anne (1702–1714), Victoria (1837–1901), and Elizabeth II (1962 to present). Each woman came to the throne because the presiding male ruler or heir had died, or because there was a lack of a male heir altogether.

- Elizabeth not only inherited the crown from her father, King Henry VIII, but also the friction that he created between the monarchy in England and the headquarters of the Catholic Church in Rome.

GRAPHIC ORGANIZER

Students may include the following dates and events from the biography in their time lines: Note that dates are not provided for all events, so where students place events on their timelines may vary slightly.
As a child, Elizabeth loves learning and vows to never marry.
1558—At age 25, Elizabeth becomes queen of England
Appoints Sir William Cecil her principal advisor
Sir Walter Raleigh begins colony of Virginia with Elizabeth's support.
Elizabeth supports Sir Francis Drake's explorations.
1570—Pope Pius V excommunicates Elizabeth
1588—Elizabeth's navy led by Sir Francis Drake defeats the Spanish Armada.
Jesuits persecuted in England.
Plots to kill Elizabeth discovered.
1603—Elizabeth dies

READER'S JOURNAL

You might also ask students to consider what qualities, other than those that contribute to leadership, they admire in this person.

GOALS/OBJECTIVES

Studying this lesson will enable students to
- enjoy a biography of Queen Elizabeth I
- briefly describe some facts about Elizabeth's reign and English monarchy
- define *biography* and note ways in which a biographer creates a vivid image of his or her subject
- define *concrete details* and find examples of concrete details in a biography
- conduct an interview
- discuss the benefits and drawbacks of different governmental systems
- design a coat of arms
- create a public relations poster

Portrait of Queen Elizabeth I, 1500s. English artist. Uffizi, Florence, Italy.

Elizabeth

Milton Meltzer

"Good Queen Bess" her people called her. But "good" is a tame word for one of the most remarkable women who ever lived. Elizabeth I came to the throne of England in 1558 at the age of twenty-five. It was not a happy time for a young woman to take the responsibility for ruling a kingdom. Religious conflicts, a huge government debt, and heavy losses in a war with France had brought England low. But by the time of Elizabeth's death forty-five years later, England had experienced one of the greatest periods in its long history. Under Elizabeth's leadership, England had become united as a nation; its industry and commerce, its arts and sciences had flourished; and it was ranked among the great powers of Europe.

Elizabeth was the daughter of King Henry VIII and his second wife, Anne Boleyn. At the age of two she lost her mother when Henry had Anne's head chopped off. Not a good start for a child. But her father placed her in the care of one lord or lady after another, and the lively little girl with the reddish-gold hair, pale skin, and golden-brown eyes won everyone's affection.

GUIDED READING
Who are Elizabeth's parents? What happens to Elizabeth's mother?

Almost from her infancy Elizabeth was trained to stand in for ruling men, in case the need should arise. So she had to master whatever they were expected to know and do. Her tutors found the child to be an eager student. She learned history, geography, mathematics, and the elements of astronomy and architecture. She mastered four modern languages—French, Italian, Spanish, and Flemish[1]—as well as classic Greek and Latin. She wrote in a beautiful script that was like a work of art. The earliest portrait painted of her—when she was thirteen—shows a girl with innocent eyes holding a book in her long and delicate hands, already confident and queenly in her bearing.

GUIDED READING
What is Elizabeth trained to do, and why?

She was a strong-willed girl who liked to give orders. She loved to be out on horseback, and rode so fast it frightened the men assigned to protect her. She loved dancing too—she never gave it up. Even in her old age she was seen one moonlit night dancing by herself in the garden.

Elizabeth had a half sister, Mary, born of Henry's first wife, Catherine of Aragon. Many years later came Elizabeth, the child of Anne Boleyn, and four years after, her half brother, Edward, the son of Henry's third wife, Jane Seymour. After Henry died, because succession[2] came first through the male, ten-year-old Edward was crowned king. But he lived only another six years. Now Mary took the throne and, soon after, married King Philip II of Spain, a Catholic monarch like herself. He was twenty-seven and she thirty-eight. But they were rarely together, each ruling their own kingdom. Mary died of cancer at the age of forty-two. That made Elizabeth the monarch.

GUIDED READING
Who is ahead of Elizabeth in the line of succession to the throne?

When she came to the throne on November 17, 1558, it was a day to be marked by celebrations, then and long after. As Her Majesty passed down a London street, an astonished housewife exclaimed, "Oh, Lord! The Queen is a woman!" For there were still many who could scarcely believe they were to be ruled by another woman. Elizabeth herself would say with mock modesty that she was "a mere woman." But everyone soon learned she was a very special woman. "Am I not a queen because God has chosen me to be a queen?" she demanded.

As princess and later as queen, Elizabeth lived in various palaces, with much coming and going; each time she moved, she took along her household staff of 120 people. Often the changes were required because there was no sanitation. The smelly palaces had to be emptied so they could be "aired and sweetened."

Even before Elizabeth came of age there was much talk of when she would marry, and whom. Marriages among the nobility and royalty were arranged not for love, but for practical reasons—to add land holdings, to strengthen the <u>prestige</u> and power of

---

1. **Flemish.** Language spoken in Flanders, a region covering a small part of Northern France and Belgium
2. **succession.** Order in which one succeeds to the throne

words for everyday use
pres • tige (pre stēzh′) n., standing or influence in general opinion. *After creating its large central park, the town enjoyed increased prestige in the region.*

---

1. Elizabeth's parents are King Henry VIII and Anne Boleyn. Elizabeth's father had her mother's head chopped off when Elizabeth was only two.
2. Elizabeth is trained to rule others "in case the need should arise."
3. Edward, Henry's son, and then Elizabeth's half-sister Mary are ahead of her in the line of succession to the throne.

CULTURAL/ HISTORICAL NOTE

Inform students that Elizabeth was one of the more fortunate noble women of the Renaissance in terms of her education. Elizabeth was educated as a man of her day would be. In the Renaissance period, most educated men learned several foreign languages well enough to both speak fluently and read widely. They usually learned classic Greek and Latin in addition to several modern European languages. Elizabeth's training in "history, geography, mathematics, and the elements of astronomy and architecture" was also more typical of a male's education than a female's education in that time period.

Most noble women during the Renaissance were given education only in etiquette, dancing, singing, sewing, and making conversation. Some were taught to read, but many others were not. The reasoning behind such a limited education was the thought that a noblewoman's primary duty was to divert and amuse their husbands. Elizabeth was educated more broadly because she might have to rule men one day and so would need to have an education equal to or better than that of most noblemen.

The education of most women who were not of the noble class was even more limited. Some women received no education at all beyond how to do certain menial chores.

Tell students that despite the inequality in education received by people of different genders and classes, there were other exceptions like Elizabeth's. Education of women would become an ideal in certain noble families during the Renaissance. While female education was by no means universal or

---

CULTURAL/HISTORICAL NOTE (CONT.)

necessarily equal to men's, people generally valued a broad education during the Renaissance much more highly than they did in the medieval period and there were more advocates of female education than there had been in the past.

1. Kings claimed that men ruled by divine right, meaning that they believed that God ordered the crown to pass through the male line of descent.
2. She has always said since she was eight years old that she would never marry.
3. Elizabeth wants her people to think well of her.

CULTURAL/ HISTORICAL NOTE

Inform students that the concept of the divine right of kings later paved the way for absolutist monarchies. The central idea of divine right is that a monarch receives the right to rule directly from God and not from the people he or she rules. Encourage students to discuss how the concept of divine right might have led monarchs to act. How might this concept have affected the attitude they took toward their land's common people?

ADDITIONAL QUESTIONS AND ACTIVITIES

Encourage students to discuss the reasons why Elizabeth never married. Students should base their responses on the information contained within this biography as well as their own speculation. What may her personal reasons for never marrying have been? What might her political reasons have been?
Answers. Students may say that her personal reasons for not marrying may stem from witnessing her father's many unsuccessful marriages, which ended in disaster for the women he married (including the beheading of Elizabeth's mother). Her political reasons may have been that she did not want to give away her power to rule to a husband. Also an alliance through marriage with the ruler of one nation might have disastrous consequences for England's political relations with other nations. She also witnesses the resentment her half-sister's marriage to Philip of Spain caused. England had much to gain through manipulating other nations through the hope that Elizabeth would marry the leader of one of their nations.

---

families, to cement an <u>alliance</u> of nations against a common enemy.

And remember, from the most ancient times, kings claimed that they as men were born to rule by divine right. That is, God had ordained that the crown should pass through the male line of descent. But when the king's wife had no male child, it meant trouble. Who then would rule? That crisis often led to civil war as various factions battled for the power to name a king. Many disputed Elizabeth's right to the throne, and as long as she had neither husband nor successor, her life was in danger.

> **GUIDED READING**
> What claim do kings make?

Ever since Elizabeth was eight, however, she had said again and again, "I will never marry." Did marriage look promising to a girl whose father had had six wives, two of whom, including her own mother, he had beheaded? Yet she liked to hear of people who wanted to marry her.

> **GUIDED READING**
> What does Elizabeth say about marrying?

And there was no shortage of suitors.[3] She continued to insist she wished to live unmarried. No matter how often she said it, men did not believe it. Understandably, since she often made a prince or duke who had come to court her believe she was finally ready to give in—only at the last moment to back out. Once, to a delegation from Parliament come to beg her to marry, she declared, "I am already bound unto a husband, which is the Kingdom of England."

And why should she, the absolute ruler of England, allow a man to sit alongside her as king? The power of husbands over wives in that century—and even now, in many places of this world—was so great that a husband might snatch the reins of power from her and leave her with the title but not the authority she loved to exercise.

Was it fun to be queen? As monarch, she commanded great wealth, inherited from her father, and people who wanted favors were always enriching her with lavish presents. She was no spendthrift,[4] however. She hated to see money wasted, whether her own or the kingdom's. Early on she began keeping careful household account books, and later she would do the same with the royal accounts. Always she urged her counselors to carry out orders as inexpensively as possible.

Above everything else, Elizabeth wanted to have her people think well of her. Her deepest desire was to assure them of peace and <u>prosperity</u>. And why not make a grand personal impression upon them at the same time? In her mature years she gave free rein to her love of jewels and staged brilliant displays for the court and the people. Her dresses were decorated with large rubies, emeralds, and diamonds, and she wore jeweled necklaces, bracelets, and rings. In her hair, at her ears, and around her neck she wore pearls—the symbol of virginity.

> **GUIDED READING**
> What does Elizabeth want most?

During her reign she made many great processions through London, the people wild with excitement, crowding the streets—for the English, like most people, loved spectacle. In the first of them, her coronation, she wore gold robes as she was crowned. Trumpets sounded, pipes and drums played, the organ pealed, bells rang. Then came the state banquet in Westminster Hall. It began at 3:00 P.M., and went on till 1:00 A.M.

---

3. **suitors.** Men who court a woman
4. **spendthrift.** Person who spens money wastefully

---

words for everyday use

al • li • ance (ə lī′əns) *n.*, association or unit to benefit members. *The city's Northern neighborhoods formed an <u>alliance</u> to fight crime.*

pros • per • i ty (prä sper′ ə tē) *n.*, condition of being successful or thriving, especially economic well-being. *Fred's store enjoyed <u>prosperity</u> after introducing new merchandise.*

VOCABULARY FROM THE SELECTION

alliance	opposition
directive	prestige
enrage	principal
forfeit	prosperity
gallantry	ruthless
intolerable	translucent
ominous	

Elizabeth was often entertained at house parties. One of them, given by the Earl of Leicester in Kenilworth Castle, lasted for eighteen days in July. Thirty other distinguished guests were invited. The great number of their servants (together with Leicester's) turned the palace into a small town. When darkness fell, candles glittered everywhere, indoors and out, creating a fairyland. Musicians sang and played, the guests danced in the garden, and such a great display of fireworks exploded that the heavens thundered and the castle shook. Then came a pleasure relished in those days: the hideous sport of bear-baiting. A pack of dogs was let loose in an inner courtyard to scratch and bite and tear at thirteen tormented bears. Still, the happy guests retained their appetite for a "most delicious banquet of 300 dishes."

The tremendous festival at Kenilworth was only one of the highlights of Elizabeth's summer festival. She moved from one great house to another all season long, always at the enormous expense of her hosts. They had little to complain of, however, for their wealth was often the product of the queen's generous bestowal of special privileges. In recognition of his high rank and in return for his support, she granted the Duke of Norfolk a license to import carpets from

The Procession of Queen Elizabeth I, c.1500s. English artist. Sherbourne Castle Estates.

So great was the queen's role, however, that her time became known as the Age of Elizabeth.

Turkey free of duty. The Earl of Essex was favored with the profitable right to tax imported sweet wines. Other pets[5] got rich from a monopoly[6] on the importation[7] of or taxation of silks, satins, salt, tobacco, starch.

England was a small nation at that time: less than four million people, about as many as live in Arizona today. But the English were a young people, coming to maturity with new worlds opening up to them, in the mind and

---

5. **pets.** Persons treated with unusual kindness
6. **monopoly.** Exclusive ownership or control
7. **importation.** Practice of bringing in foreign goods

ARTS AND HUMANITIES, SOCIAL STUDIES, AND APPLIED ARTS. Encourage your students to hold an Elizabethan festival to celebrate Elizabethan culture. Divide students into small groups. Each group should research an aspect of Elizabethan culture and present their findings to the class through an oral report and a demonstration. Students should research the topic through library books, reference works, and Internet resources. Possible aspects of Elizabethan culture students might explore include the following:

- Elizabethan drama (Who were the great playwrights of Elizabeth's day? What were the notable theaters? How was theater viewed?) Students might present a brief scene from am Elizabethan play by a playwright such as Ben Jonson, Christopher Marlowe, or William Shakespeare.
- Elizabethan music (What types of music were popular in Elizabeth's day? Who were some well known composers and songwriters? At what different types of events did music play a part?) Students should locate and play an example of one of the many types of Elizabethan music to share with classmates.
- Elizabethan courtly poetry. Inform students that in Elizabeth's day poets passed their poetry around a court, often anonymously. (Who were some of the great poets of Elizabeth's day? What poetic forms and subjects were popular?) Students might read aloud a poem or two from this period to their classmates.
- Elizabethan dance (What were some forms of dancing that were popular? Was there a difference between the dances of courtiers and peasants? If so, how did such dances differ?) Ambitious students may wish to learn a dance to demonstrate to classmates.
- Elizabethan cuisine (What would an Elizabethan banquet such as the one described on this page have been like? What were considered delicacies? What ingredients were used? What ingredients were still rare or unavailable in this period?) Students should research a few Elizabethan recipes and prepare a sample for their classmates.

ANSWERS TO GUIDED READING QUESTIONS

1. The Renaissance is taking place in England.
2. Musicians and writers flower during Elizabeth's reign.
3. Pope Pius V excommunicated Elizabeth and declared that her subjects owed her no allegiance.

CULTURAL/ HISTORICAL NOTE

Some students may be surprised to learn that the Pope would excommunicate Elizabeth, deny her right to rule, and encourage people to assassinate her. Share with students that in the Middle Ages the pope, the head of the Catholic Church, was perhaps the single most powerful leader in Europe, and the Catholic Church was the most powerful governing body. Popes not only directly controlled the politics of Italy, but their power was felt throughout Europe. Thus, when the Pope declared that Elizabeth had no right to rule, there was a very real chance that she might have been overthrown or assassinated. This would almost certainly have been the case if it were not for two events that made the Church slightly less powerful in Europe and especially in England. In 1517, a German monk named Martin Luther began the Protestant Reformation, a movement that rebelled against Catholic authority and launched the establishment of Puritan and Protestant forms of religion. Also, Elizabeth's father, Henry VIII, broke England away from the Church of Rome when the Pope refused to grant him a divorce and established the Church of England, also known as the Anglican Church.

---

across the seas. A rebirth of culture—the Renaissance[8]—had begun in the 1400s. With the revival of interest in the literature of the ancient Greek and Roman worlds came the beginning of a great age of discovery. This period marked the transition from medieval to modern times. The arts and sciences were influenced by changes in economic life. All the nation was swept up in the vast tides of change. Merchants, bankers, the gentry,[9] artisans,[10] seamen, miners—men and women of every class and condition—felt themselves part of the national venture.

> **GUIDED READING**
> What cultural movement is taking place in England?

At the heart of change in England was the queen. But no king or queen rules alone, no matter how authoritative or arrogant they may be. They usually look to others for advice, advice they may follow or reject. Elizabeth appointed ministers to handle the various departments of government, and made Sir William Cecil, then thirty-eight, her principal adviser. He was a brilliant, hardworking master of statecraft, devoted to her and England's well-being, and as ruthless as she and the nation's interests required. When he died in old age, his son Robert replaced him at her side.

So great was the queen's role, however, that her time became known as the Age of Elizabeth. Not only did many fine musicians flower, but writers too, such as Christopher Marlowe and John Donne and Ben Jonson and Edmund Spenser. And above all, the incomparable William Shakespeare, whose plays were sometimes performed at court. Astronomers, naturalists, mathematicians, geographers, and architects pioneered in their fields.

Then, too, there were the daring explorers who pushed English expansion overseas. One of the queen's favorites, Sir Walter Raleigh, planned the colony of Virginia in America and named it for her, the Virgin Queen. The queen herself put money into several of the great voyages, keeping close watch over the plans and their results. She supported Sir Francis Drake on his three-year voyage around the world, profiting mightily from the immense loot he captured from Spanish ships taken in the Pacific.

For Elizabeth, one of the most urgent problems was the question of religion. Her father had broken with the Catholic church and launched the English Reformation, creating the Church of England, with himself at its head. When Elizabeth's older half sister, Mary (who remained Catholic), married the Catholic king of Spain, Philip II, she reconciled England with the Church of Rome. In Mary's brief reign she persecuted those Protestants who refused to conform, executing some 270 of them.

> **GUIDED READING**
> What flourishes during Elizabeth's reign?

When Elizabeth became queen upon Mary's death, she said she hoped religion would not prevent her people from living together in peaceful unity. She did not want to pry into people's souls or question their faith. But in 1570, Pope Pius V excommunicated[11] her, denied her right to the throne, and declared her subjects owed her no allegiance. A directive

> **GUIDED READING**
> What does Pope Pius V decree?

---

8. **Renaissance.** Important cultural period from 1400 to 1700
9. **gentry.** Upper class
10. **artisans.** Artists and craftspeople
11. **excommunicated.** Cast out from a religious community

---

words for everyday use

prin • ci • pal (prin′ sə pəl) *adj.*, most important; cheif. *The principal reason I joined the team was to stay in shape.*

ruth • less (rüth′ ləs) *adj.*, merciless or cruel. *The ruthless sergeant made the soldiers walk for days without food.*

di • rec • tive (də rek′ tiv) *n.*, order or form of guidance. *The police cheif's directive called for all citizens to be on the lookout for the criminal.*

from the pope's office decreed that the assassination of Queen Elizabeth would not be regarded as a sin. The effect of this directive was to turn practicing Catholics—about half of the English, most of them loyal—into potential traitors.

Though Elizabeth had wanted to pursue a middle way of toleration, circumstances threatened to overwhelm her. She had to beware of several Catholic monarchs of Europe who wished to see a Protestant England overthrown. Philip II of Spain sent ambassadors to England to urge Catholics to rise against Elizabeth, put her cousin Mary[12] on the throne, and restore Roman Catholicism as the national faith. The line between power, politics, and religion was becoming very thin.

Missionary priests living abroad were sent into England to stir up <u>opposition</u> to the queen. But the English Catholics as a body never rebelled, nor did they ever intend to. Still, missionary priests such as Edmund Campion were convicted of plotting against Elizabeth and executed.

In 1588 a long-threatened invasion of England by Spain was launched by Philip II. He mistakenly believed that the English Catholics were waiting to welcome him. News of his armada[13] of 130 big ships carrying 17,000 soldiers was terrifying. But the queen did not panic. She supervised the high command personally, meanwhile rallying popular support for the defense of the realm and sending troops to protect the coasts while Sir Francis Drake's ships set out to attack the Spanish fleet.

The Spanish Armada was defeated in three battles, its ships dispersed. When the news came of the tremendous victory, the citizens took to the streets, shouting for joy.

The defeat of the Spanish Armada did not end Spain's aggression against England. The Jesuits[14] in England, who were especially identified with Spain, continued to be persecuted. Richard Topcliffe, a notorious hater of Catholics, was given authority to track down suspects. He examined them under torture to force information about people who had sheltered them. The treatment of them was so vicious and cruel that the victims welcomed death as a release from their agony.

During Elizabeth's reign several plots to assassinate her were uncovered. Elizabeth managed to give the impression that she was not frightened, but those close to her knew she was. When one of the major plots proved to center around Elizabeth's cousin, Mary Queen of Scots, Elizabeth found it almost <u>intolerable</u> to put to death a crowned queen. Yet she ordered the use of torture on Mary's co-conspirators, and in the end, Mary was beheaded. A song composed by William Byrd at the time suggests how <u>ominous</u> the news of a monarch's execution was:

> The noble famous Queen
> who lost her head of late
> Doth show that kings as well as clowns
> Are bound to fortune's fate,
> And that no earthly Prince
> Can so secure his crown
> But fortune with her whirling wheel
> Hath power to pull them down.

GUIDED READING
What is Elizabeth afraid of?

---

12. **Mary.** Mary Stuart (Mary, Queen of Scots, not Elizabeth's half sister.)
13. **armada.** Army
14. **Jesuits.** Members of the Roman Catholic Society of Jesus

words for everyday use

op • po • si • tion (ä pe zi′ shən) *n.*, contrary action or condition. *Opposition* to the plan led the town board to vote it down.

in • tolerable (in tä′ lə rə bəl) *adj.*, unbearable. *My shoes were so tight that the pain was intolerable.*

om • i • nous (ä′ mə nəs) *adj.*, forboding or foreshadowing evil. *The ominous sound of the hurricane alarms caused citizens to panic.*

ANSWER TO GUIDED READING QUESTION

1. Elizabeth is afraid of being assassinated.

CROSS-CURRICULAR ACTIVITIES

Encourage students to work together in small groups to prepare written reports on the Protestant Reformation in Europe. Students should use historical books and documents, encyclopedias, and on-line information as their resources; carefully document their sources and take notes; and then work together to create a written report. Possible topics associated with the Protestant Reformation for students to explore include the following:

- Martin Luther—why he objected to Catholic Church teachings, what he believed, and what he did to ignite a revolution in Europe.
- Henry VIII's motivations for breaking with the Catholic Church and establishing the Church of England.
- Sir Thomas Moore and his execution for failing to recognize Henry as the head of the church.
- John Calvin's contribution to the Protestant Reformation.
- Mary I and the Counter Reformation in England.
- James I attitudes toward Puritanism and Catholicism.

ANSWERS TO GUIDED READING QUESTIONS

1. Elizabeth gets information about conspiracies through spies and secret agents.
2. Public opinion keeps Elizabeth from doing everything she wanted.

ADDITIONAL QUESTIONS AND ACTIVITIES

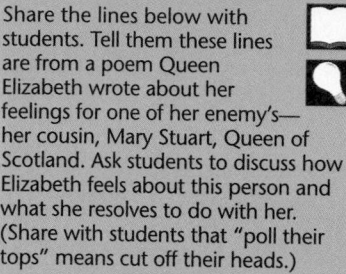

Share the lines below with students. Tell them these lines are from a poem Queen Elizabeth wrote about her feelings for one of her enemy's— her cousin, Mary Stuart, Queen of Scotland. Ask students to discuss how Elizabeth feels about this person and what she resolves to do with her. (Share with students that "poll their tops" means cut off their heads.)

Quotables

"The daughter of debate, that eke discord doth sow
Shall reap no gain where former rule hath taught still peace to grow.
No foreign banished wight shall anchor in this port,
Our realm it brooks no stranger's force, let them elsewhere resort.
Our rusty sword with rest, shall first his edge employ
Ton poll their tops that seek such change and gape for joy."

—Queen Elizabeth I

SELECTION CHECK TEST 4.11.1 WITH ANSWERS

Checking Your Reading

1. Name one thing that Elizabeth enjoyed. **She enjoyed riding horses, dancing, arts and literature, lavish celebrations, and attending house parties.**
2. How many husbands did Elizabeth have in her life? **None. Elizabeth never married.**
3. What did Elizabeth do for Sir Walter Raleigh and for Sir Francis Drake? **She helped both explorers fund their journeys.**
4. Elizabeth was not Catholic. What did Pope Pius V do to her because of this? **The pope excommunicated her, denied her right to the throne, claimed that her subjects owed her no obedience, and**

When two earls combined forces against her, Elizabeth's troops overcame them. The queen was so <u>enraged</u> she ordered that 800 of the mostly poor rebels be hanged. But she spared the lives of their wealthy leaders so that they might enrich her, either by buying their pardons or by <u>forfeiting</u> their lands.

Elizabeth came down hard on writers who criticized her actions. John Stubbs, a zealous Puritan, wrote a pamphlet expressing horror at the possibility the queen might marry a French Catholic. The queen had Stubbs and his publisher tried and convicted for seditious libel.[15] How dare Stubbs say publicly she was too old to marry, and that the much younger French suitor could not possibly be in love with her? Elizabeth was merciless as she invoked the penalty for libel. With a butcher's cleaver, the executioner cut the right hands off Stubbs and his publisher. Not an uncommon punishment.

How did Elizabeth learn of all these plots and conspiracies? How did she know what plans Philip II of Spain was devising to invade her kingdom? Spies and secret agents—they were her eyes and ears. Crucial to the flow of information was Sir Francis Walsingham. Trained as a lawyer, he lived on the Continent[16] for years, mastering the languages and the ins and outs of European affairs. Upon his return home, he was asked by Sir William Cecil, the queen's right arm, to gather information on the doings and plans of foreign governments. Soon he was made chief of England's secret service. He placed over seventy agents and spies in the courts of Europe. And of course he watched closely the activities of people at home suspected of disloyalty. Letters to and from them were secretly opened, to nip plots in the bud.

> **GUIDED READING**
> How does Elizabeth get information about conspiracies?

Monarchs had absolute power. Elizabeth could arrest anyone, including the topmost ranks of the nobility, and imprison them in the Tower of London even if they had not committed any legal offense. The only thing that held her back was her fear of public opinion. It upset her when a crowd gathered at a public execution and was so disgusted by the butchery that they let out roars of disapproval. Still, like all rulers, Elizabeth said she believed that "born a sovereign princess" she enjoyed "the privilege common to all kings" and was "exempt from human jurisdiction[17] and subject only to the judgement of God."

> **GUIDED READING**
> What keeps Elizabeth from doing everything she wanted?

Despite her blazing nervous energy, Elizabeth was often sick. Her ailments were anxiously reported and discussed. For the English believed her survival was their only guarantee of freedom from foreign invasion and civil war. Once, suffering a raging toothache for the first time, the queen feared the pain of having an extraction. She had never had a tooth pulled and was terrified. To reassure her, an old friend, the Bishop of London, had her watch while the dental surgeon pulled out one of the bishop's own good teeth. And then she consented to have her own taken out.

It was commonly believed then that kings and queens had the magical power to cure disease in their subjects. Eager to demonstrate that she too had the sacred power of royalty, Elizabeth prayed intensely before using the royal touch on people with scrofula, a nasty skin disease. Her chaplain said he watched

---

15. **seditious libel.** Crime of creating opposition to authority
16. **Continent.** European continent
17. **jurisdiction.** Legal control

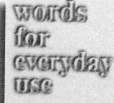

words for everyday use

en • rage (in rāj′) v., fill with rage; anger. *Joan enrages her friends by telling lies about them.* **enraged,** adj.

for • feit (for′ fət) v., lose or lose the right to by some error, offense, or crime. *John forfeited his allowance by failing to mow the lawn.*

SELECTION CHECK TEST 4.11.1 WITH ANSWERS (CONT.)

declared that murdering her would not be considered a sin.

5. How did Elizabeth learn about plots against her by other countries? **Elizabeth employed a wide network of spies, led by Sir Francis Walsingham.**

Vocabulary in Context

Fill in each blank below with the most appropriate word from the following Words for Everyday Use.

ominous   alliance   suitors   enrage   directive
intolerable   prestige

1. The principal's **directive** made it clear that no one was allowed to miss the assembly.

(Continued on page 777)

"her exquisite hands, boldly, and without disgust, pressing the sores and ulcers." In one day it was reported that she healed thirty-eight persons. But if she did not feel divinely inspired, she would not try her touch.

GUIDED READING
What gift does Elizabeth apparently possess?

Even in the last decade of her life, Elizabeth's energy was astonishing. She was as watchful as always over the affairs of state, though sometimes forgetful. But age made her more irritable; she sometimes shouted at her ladies and even boxed their ears. She was less able to control rival factions out for power, and became so fearful of assassins she rarely left her palaces.

A portrait of her done when she was approaching sixty shows her in a great white silk dress studded with aglets[18] of black onyx, coral, and pearl. She wears three ropes of <u>translucent</u> pearls and stands on a map of England, her

England. An ambassador reported that at sixty-three she looked old, but her figure was still beautiful, and her conversation was as brilliant and charming as ever.

There was dancing at court every evening, a pastime she still enjoyed. When it came to displays of <u>gallantry</u> by eager young men, she could act a bit vain and foolish, although never letting any hopeful get out of bounds.

In early 1603 Elizabeth developed a bad cold that led to a serious fever, and then she fell into a stupor[19] for four days. As she lay dying, all of London became strangely silent. On March 24, the life of a rare genius ended. The nation went into mourning.

"Old age came upon me as a surprise, like a frost," she once wrote. ■

---

18. **aglets.** Ornamental pins
19. **stupor.** State of shock or greatly dulled sense

Respond *to the* SELECTION

If you met Elizabeth, do you think you would like her, based on the description given in this biography? Why, or why not?

About *the* AUTHOR

Milton Meltzer has written numerous biographies and books about historical events and eras. Some of his most well-known books are *All Times, All Peoples: A World History of Slavery, Ain't Gonna Study War No More: The Story of America's Peace Seekers,* and *Ten Queens: Portraits of Women of Power*—the book from which this selection was taken. Meltzer has won many awards for his books. He lives with his wife in New York, New York.

---

words for everyday use

trans • lu • cent (trans lü′ sənt) *adj.,* permitting the passage of light. *The <u>translucent</u> curtains let in the morning sun.*

gal • lant • ry (ga′ lən trē) *n.,* show of marked courtesy, amorous attention, or bravery. *The knight's <u>gallantry</u> impressed the princess.*

1. Apparently, Elizabeth has the supposed "scared power of royalty," the ability to heal people of diseases such as scrofula by touching them.

RESPOND TO THE SELECTION

Ask students to discuss whether their opinion of Elizabeth might depend on whether or not they were on the same side as she was. Why, or why not?

SELECTION CHECK TEST 4.11.1 WITH ANSWERS (CONT.)

2. Selena put off going to the dentist until the pain in her tooth became **intolerable**.
3. Everyone in the sailing club was disappointed at the sight of the **ominous** thunderclouds rolling in across the lake.
4. Uakti had not been popular in high school, but she was overwhelmed with **suitors** when she arrived at college.
5. The queen was generous to everyone who served her, but disloyalty **enraged** her.

Reader's Toolbox
1. What is a biography? **A biography is a story about a person written by someone else.**
2. Use concrete details to describe Elizabeth. **Elizabeth had reddish-gold hair, pale skin, exquisite hands and golden-brown eyes; and that she was strong-willed, intelligent, well educated, and energetic.**
3. In what time and place does this selection take place? **The selection takes place in England during what is now known as the Elizabethan era, the sixteenth to early seventeenth centuries.**
4. Use concrete details to describe what daily life might be like in that time and place. **The selection suggests that there was poor sanitation and health care; that people gathered for gruesome public executions and punishments (such as the cutting off of Stubbs' right hand) and for grand processions by royalty; that**

SELECTION CHECK TEST 4.11.1 WITH ANSWERS (CONT.)

entertainment was often grisly (such as bear-baiting) but also could be dignified, as **musicians, playwrights, and poets flourished. Students should use concrete details to describe life under any of these conditions, or others suggested by the text.**

5. Name two other characters who the selection suggests were important to Elizabeth. **Responses will vary, but could include Sir Francis Drake; Sir Francis Walsingham; her sister Mary; Sir William Cecil; Sir Walter Raleigh; her father Henry VIII; Mary, Queen of Scots, the Bishop of London.**

ANSWERS TO INVESTIGATE, INQUIRE, IMAGINE

RECALL

1a. Elizabeth lost her mother Anne Boleyn when Elizabeth's father Henry VIII had her beheaded.

2a. Most people were negative about having a female ruler because they did not like the queen before her because she was sympathetic to Catholics and married a Spanish ruler. Most people also assumed that the divine right of kings had to be passed down on the male side of the family line.

3a. Mary Queen of Scots was the crowned queen of Scotland and Elizabeth's cousin. Elizabeth had her beheaded because she found out that Mary was involved in a plot to have her assassinated.

INTERPRET

1b. *Responses will vary.*

2b. Elizabeth dealt with these attitudes by demanding. "Am I not queen because God has chosen me to be a queen?" thereby implying that her rule was also granted by divine right. Elizabeth also dealt with this attitude by refusing to marry and give up her power to a man.

3b. Students may suggest that Elizabeth found beheading a crowned queen intolerable because she herself is a queen and believes that God gives monarchs their rule, so she may feel it is especially wrong to behead a queen. Other students may suggest that this incident reminds her of another queen who was beheaded—Anne Boleyn, Elizabeth's late mother.

ANALYZE

4a. Students may say that Elizabeth punishes people who go against her will by imprisoning them, torturing them, and having them beheaded. She even prosecuted a writer and publisher who published a criticism of her for libel and punished them by cutting off their rights hands. On the other hand, Elizabeth gave lavish gifts and royal assistance to her supporters.

SYNTHESIZE

4b. Students may suggest that these actions reveal that Elizabeth was a loyal friend but a fearsome enemy. When she came to rule England was in religious and political turmoil. Students may suggest that England seems more stable politically and religiously and seems to have gained status as a European nation; students may suggest, however, that England is still full of spies, plots,

Investigate, Inquire, and Imagine

Recall: GATHERING FACTS

1a. How did Elizabeth lose her mother?

2a. What were people's attitudes about having a female ruler?

3a. Who was Mary Queen of Scots, and why did Elizabeth order her to be beheaded?

→ **Interpret:** FINDING MEANING

1b. How did the death of her mother affect Elizabeth, if at all?

2b. How did Elizabeth deal with these attitudes?

3b. Why did Elizabeth find it "almost intolerable" to put to death a crowned queen?

Analyze: TAKING THINGS APART

4a. Cite examples of Elizabeth's methods of punishing people who went against her will. Make another list of ways in which she benefits her supporters.

→ **Synthesize:** BRINGING THINGS TOGETHER

4b. What do these actions suggest about her personality? What condition was England in when Elizabeth became queen? When she died? What changes did Elizabeth make, and how? Do you think she deserved the title "Good Queen Bess"?

Perspective: LOOKING AT OTHER VIEWS → **Empathy:** SEEING FROM INSIDE

5a. How does Elizabeth view her role as queen? What does she think of the English people?

5b. What might Elizabeth have done in life if she hadn't become queen? Explain your answer.

Understanding Literature

BIOGRAPHY. A **biography** is the story of a person's life, told by another person. Based on this selection, do you think the author admires Elizabeth? Why, or why not? Do you think he wants other people to admire Elizabeth? Explain. Do you think the author is fair in his depiction of Elizabeth? In other words, do you think he tells both sides of the story? Explain your responses.

CONCRETE DETAILS. Concrete details are specific words that name objects or actions or provide descriptions of those objects or actions. What concrete details did "Elizabeth" provide about the life of the queen? How do they help you better understand who she was?

ANSWERS TO INVESTIGATE, INQUIRE, IMAGINE (CONT.)

and political intrigue. Students may say that Elizabeth made changes such as uniting England as a nation, strengthening England's economy and expanding its trade, helping its art and literature to flourish by acting as a generous patron, and making England one of the great powers of Europe. She made these changes by encouraging exploration and supporting naval commanders, quelling plots and insurrections, acting as a generous patron, and through her diplomatic skill. *Responses will vary.*

PERSPECTIVE

5a. Elizabeth takes her role as a queen very seriously, as a duty given her by God, and she relishes the power of her rule. She is, however, very concerned about the English people and wants them to love her. Students may say that this shows she has respect and fondness for the English people.

EMPATHY

5b. *Responses will vary.*

Writer's Journal

1. Imagine that you have been crowned queen (or king) for a day. Write a **schedule** detailing what you would do during a typical day as ruler.

2. Write an imaginary **love letter or poem** from a suitor to Elizabeth. Your letter or poem can be funny, serious, or overly sentimental.

3. Based on the examples from the selection, write a **business letter** to Elizabeth, complaining about a serious issue or praising her for a particular success.

Skill Builders

Speaking and Listening

INTERVIEWING. Working in pairs, with one person acting as a reporter and one acting as Queen Elizabeth, conduct an interview for a morning talk show. You can tape record or videotape the interview, or present it live for the rest of your class. If you wish, you can work in larger groups and create an entire morning talk show. Select people to play the part of other members of Elizabeth's court or family, as well as Elizabeth's opponents and enemies.

Collaborative Learning

GROUP DISCUSSION. As a class, discuss the pros and cons of a constitutional monarchy such as that in England versus the political system in America. Would you want a monarchy in America? Why, or why not?

Study and Research

DESIGNING A COAT-OF-ARMS. Using the Internet or library resources, find examples of coats-of-arms and design one for your family. In creating your family coat-of-arms, consider such things as the meaning of your name, special hobbies or interests that your family has, or where your family is from. If your family has a coat-of-arms already, find out what it means. Write a description or make a picture of your coat-of-arms to display for the entire class.

Applied English & Media Literacy

POSTER DESIGN. Imagine that you work for a public relations firm during the reign of Queen Elizabeth. You have been assigned the task of creating a poster to help improve Elizabeth's image after she makes a disastrous decision and falls out of favor with the public. Select an incident from the selection on which to base your public relations campaign. To get started, analyze public relations advertisements in the media. What do they do to try to control public opinion or to repair the image of an individual, a company, or an organization?

Speaking and Listening
Assign roles for the talk show. The reporter should prepare a list of questions and prompts and share some of these with the guests, so they can begin to think about how the person they are playing might answer. (The reporter may wish to keep some questions as surprises to give the show a spontaneous feel and so that all the answers do not sound rehearsed.) Check with your school to see if you can borrow camcorders or tape recorders to help students in creating their shows.

Collaborative Learning
You may have to ask students to research both political systems first in an encyclopedia so that students will have some points of comparison for the discussion. The class might create a large pro and con chart on the blackboard to keep track of their ideas. For more information on such charts, refer students to the Language Arts Survey, "Creating Pro and Con Charts."

Study and Research
Tell students that while they can model their coats of arms on traditional ones, they can also create highly imaginative and unconventional ones to capture some aspect of their family. You might have students display their coats of arms on a bulletin board.

Applied English & Media Literacy
You might encourage students to look at portraits of Queen Elizabeth (such as the ones that appear in this book) for inspiration. To some extent, such portraits were the public relations posters of Elizabeth's day as they showed her in idealized fashion and often contained symbols of her power and rule over England.

ANSWERS TO UNDERSTANDING LITERATURE

BIOGRAPHY. *Responses will vary. Possible responses are given.* Students may suggest that the author does admire Elizabeth and the effect she had on her England's political stability, the flourishing of the arts in England, England's unification, England's role in world exploration, and England's status as compared with other nations. Students might suggest he wants people to admire Elizabeth but to see her as a whole person—flaws and all.

He is fair in his depiction because he does show a negative side of Elizabeth—the ferocity with which she treated her enemies and those who criticized her.

CONCRETE DETAILS. Responses will vary, but concrete details can include the physical description of Elizabeth, the specific subjects Elizabeth learned, and her love of horseback riding.

GRAPHIC ORGANIZER

Students organizers may include the following phrases and explanations: *I worked in construction, mostly hitting my fingers with a hammer and making serious attempts to cut something off my body with power saws*—Students may say nobody works at hitting themselves or cutting off their own body parts in this way; the author is just exaggerating what a terrible carpenter he is. *This drive has brought me dozens of dogs and cats, a few ducks, some geese, a half dozen guinea pigs, an ocelot, several horses, two cows, a litter of pigs, . . . one hawk . . . one truly evil llama*—students may say the author is exaggerating about how many pets he owned because this number of pets is extremely unlikely. *I was along for the ride, and what a ride it was! We went through three more yards and the back of a bike rental shop and finally slammed into the back doorway of a small café*—it is unlikely that a dog, even a large one, could drag a full grown human this way. *I could fit my head inside his mouth*—it is unlikely that the dog's mouth is this big, and the author is just exaggerating for effect.

READER'S JOURNAL

As an alternate activity, ask students to write about whether pet owners ever exaggerate about their pets or see them differently than others do. For example, have students ever seen a pet owner defend an ugly pet as beautiful, or a mean-tempered pet as sweet?

Reader's Journal

Have you ever had a close relationship with an animal? Why was the animal special to you? If you have never had a pet, what kind would you want, and why?

Reader's Resource

- This short story by Gary Paulson is about a Great Dane named Caesar, whom Paulson adopts when the dog's owner moves to another state.

- Great Danes are large, powerful, and graceful dogs that are often trained for hunting or guard duty. The typical male stands 30 inches high at the shoulder, and both male and female are short-haired and have a sleek coat which can be fawn, black, or white and black; most are fawn-colored. Dogs resembling this type were found in ancient times in Greece, Egypt, China, and England. They were used for hunting wild boars, bears, and wolves in Germany in the 16th century, and were given their present name in that country in 1880.

Prereading

"Caesar"
by Gary Paulsen

Reader's TOOLBOX

POINT OF VIEW. Point of view is the vantage point from which a literary work is told. Works can be written from a first-person point of view in which the narrator uses words such as *I* or *we*. They can also be told from a third-person point of view in which the narrator uses words such as *he, she, it,* and *they* and avoids the use of *I* and *we*. As you read "Caesar," determine whether this selection is told from a first-person or third-person point of view.

HYPERBOLE. A hyperbole is an exaggeration made for effect. An example of hyperbole is the statement "I'm madder than a hornet." As you read "Caesar," look for examples of hyperbole. Create a cluster chart like that shown below to record the examples you find. Each example should have two circles: one in which you write the phrase that uses hyperbole, and the second in which you explain why that phrase is an example of hyperbole.

Graphic Organizer

- hyperbole
- "making serious attempts at cutting something off my body"
- he wouldn't really try to cut off body parts

GOALS/OBJECTIVES

Studying this lesson will enable students to
- enjoy a humorous personal essay
- define *point of view* and distinguish between first- and third-person point of view
- define *hyperbole* and recognize examples of hyperbole

- interview someone who works at an animal shelter
- research a breed of dog
- write a feature story about the cost of owning a Great Dane
- use *I* and *me* correctly

Caesar

Gary Paulsen

The dog was enormous.

We lived in a small cottage in the mountains of Colorado, where I worked in construction, mostly hitting my fingers with a hammer and making serious attempts at cutting something off my body with power saws while I tried to build houses during the day and write at night. I had been looking at the local consumer guide, called *The Shopper's Bulletin*, when I saw an ad:

GUIDED READING

What does the author do for a living? What does he do at night?

EMERGENCY! AM LEAVING FOR HAWAII FOR A CAREER CHANGE. MUST FIND HOME FOR LOVING GREAT DANE NAMED CAESAR AS THEY WON'T ALLOW DOGS IN THE ISLANDS. PLEASE HELP!

GUIDED READING

What is being given away in a newspaper ad?

All right—I know how it sounds. Nobody who lives in a small cottage in the mountains of Colorado with a wife and baby should probably even consider a pet, let alone a dog, let alone a large dog, let alone a *very* large dog—at least nobody with a brain larger than a walnut. But I had once been associated with a female Great Dane named Dad when I was in the army and had ever since had a warm place in my soul for them. The secondary force, the force that kicks in whenever I visit a dog pound, roared into my mind, the force that says, *If you don't take him, who will?* This drive has brought me dozens of dogs and cats, a few ducks, some geese, a half dozen guinea pigs,

GUIDED READING

How does the author respond to the ad?

"CAESAR" 781

ANSWERS TO GUIDED READING QUESTIONS

1. The author works in construction, and at night he writes.
2. A Great Dane named Caesar is being given away in a newspaper ad.
3. The author considers adopting Caesar.

INDIVIDUAL LEARNING STRATEGIES

MOTIVATION
Encourage students to share in small groups funny stories about animals they have known.

READING PROFICIENCY
Students may pick up on the exaggeration and humor in this personal essay more easily if they hear it read aloud expressively. Play an audiotape of a reading of this personal essay for students, and have them follow along in their books as they listen.

ENGLISH LANGUAGE LEARNING
Point out the following vocabulary words and expressions:
consumer—person who buys goods or services
pound—enclosure for confining stray animals until claimed
llama—South American animal that grazes and is used for milk and wool as well as a beast of burden
slobber—saliva
civil—polite
crockery—earthenware pots and jars
outfield—playing area of a baseball field that lies beyond the infield, where the bases are located
grounders—balls that strike the ground and roll or bounce almost immediately

SPECIAL NEEDS
Have students focus on responding to the Guided Reading questions and the Recall questions in the Investigate, Inquire, and Imagine section.

ENRICHMENT
Encourage interested students to write their own personal essay in which they describe an event in their life but make use of hyperbole to exaggerate elements of this event for humorous effect.

VOCABULARY FROM THE SELECTION

aggressive	monosyllabic
commotion	moot
compressed	prolific
dehydrate	quail
disseminate	relative
duplicate	synthetic
emaciate	virtually
lope	

1. The author says that Caesar looks more like a *Tyrannosaurus rex* than a dog and that his measurements are astounding.
2. Caesar's owner leaves quickly.
3. Caesar climbs onto the couch and looks out the window to see where he has gone and then sits down by the front door waiting for his return.

ADDITIONAL QUESTIONS AND ACTIVITIES

Inform students that *Caesar* was the title given to emperors of Rome back when Rome was a powerful empire that ruled much of Europe and parts of Asia and Africa. Ask students to explain why this is a fitting name for the dog. What other names can students come up with that suit this Great Dane?
Answers. Students may say that Caesar is a fitting name because Caesar is a large and powerful dog so the fact that he is named after the ruler of a large and powerful empire is fitting.

---

an ocelot,[1] several horses, two cows, a litter of pigs (followed by more and more litters—my God, they are <u>prolific</u>), one hawk, a blue heron, a large lizard, some dozen or so turtles, a porcupine and God knows how many wounded birds; chipmunks, squirrels and one truly evil llama (am I the *only* person in the world who did not know they can spit dead level for about fifteen yards, hitting your eye every time?).

And so this man brought Caesar, who looked more like a *Tyrannosaurus rex*[2] than a dog, into our small cottage.

His measurements were astounding. He stood forty-one inches at the front shoulder, his head a bit higher, and when he got up on his back legs and put his feet on my shoulders he could drip spit (his favorite hobby seemed to be <u>disseminating</u> spit and slobber) on top of my bald spot.

> **GUIDED READING**
> How does the author describe Caesar?

But size is <u>relative</u>. Had we seen him out in the open, say from half a mile away in the middle of a large field, he would have looked magnificent. Here, in a small room, he overwhelmed the furniture. "Isn't he, you know," my wife said, moving to a position of relative safety in back of the couch, "rather large?"

The man shook his head. "It's just because he's in here. Take him out for a run along side the car and you won't even notice him. Why, just the other day I was talking to my girlfriend and she was saying how Caesar seemed to be getting smaller because he fit into her closet so well, kind of back in the dark"—he moved toward the door as he spoke—"where he likes to make a bed, out of the way back in the dark"—his hand was on

the knob—"why, in a short time you won't even know he's here...."

> **GUIDED READING**
> What does Caesar's owner do when he delivers Caesar to the cottage?

And he was gone. I won't say he ran, but by the time the door was latched he had his car started and was pulling out of the driveway.

It all happened so fast I don't think the dog even knew he was gone. He sat for a moment, staring at me, then out the window; then he climbed on the couch, knocking over the coffee table, two end tables and a lamp. He used his paw to push the drapes aside and saw the car just as it was disappearing and he made a sound like a cross between the closing whistle at a major auto plant and how I imagined the hound of the Baskervilles[3] would sound.

Then he climbed down, moved to the front door and sat.

> **GUIDED READING**
> What does Caesar do when he realizes that his owner has left him?

Staring at the door.
Waiting.

"Well," I said, "that wasn't so bad, was it?"

My wife looked around at the wreckage—when he'd jumped down he'd put his weight on the back of the couch and tipped it over—and sighed. "What do you suppose happens when he has to go to the bathroom?"

It nearly became a <u>moot</u> point. For a time it didn't look as if he would live. I have never seen a dog grieve like Caesar.

His heart was truly broken. He sat by the door all that day and all that first night and when it was apparent his owner was not

---

1. **ocelot.** A medium-sized American wildcat
2. **Tyrannosaurus rex.** A large, meat-eating dinosaur
3. **hound of the Baskervilles.** The large, scary hound from *The Hound of Baskervilles* by Arthur Conan Doyle

---

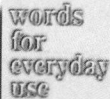
words for everyday use

pro • lif • ic (prə lif' fic) *adj.,* causing abundant growth, generation or reproduction. *A <u>prolific</u> artist, he creates several new paintings and sculptures each year.*

dis • sem • i • nate (di se' mə nāt) *v.,* spread about. *She walked through the crowd <u>disseminating</u> flyers about the upcoming concert.*

rel • a • tive (re' lə tiv) *adj.,* comparative, not independant. *The size of your salary increase is <u>relative</u> to your current salary.*

moot (müt') *adj.,* insignificant; closed to debate. *"Your curfew is a <u>mute</u> point; you're grounded," said my mother.*

782 UNIT ELEVEN / TELLING IT AS IT IS: NONFICTION

coming back right away, he lay down with his nose aimed at the door and waited.

Although he would drink a small amount of water, he would eat nothing. Great Danes are not fat in the best of times—all angles and bones—and within two days he looked positively <u>emaciated</u>. I tried everything. Special dog foods, cooked hamburger, raw liver, bits of bread with honey, fresh steak—he wouldn't touch any of it.

GUIDED READING

What does Caesar refuse to do?

The third day I called a vet.

"Does he drink?"

"Barely."

"How long since he's had food?"

"Two, no, three days."

A long pause. "Well, if he's drinking he's not going to <u>dehydrate</u>. Give him a couple more days and if he doesn't eat then you'll have to bring him in and we'll tube him."

"Tube him?"

"Force a tube down his throat and pump liquid food directly into his stomach."

I looked at Caesar. Even skinny and lying by the door he seemed to block out the light in the room. He was civil enough when we petted him but he mostly ignored us and would pointedly push us out of the way when we came between him and the door. I didn't see how it would be possible to force him to do anything.

It was, in the end, nearly six full days before he came around. I genuinely feared for his life and had decided that if he didn't eat by the morning of the sixth day I would take him in to be force-fed.

GUIDED READING

Of what is the author afraid?

The change came at six in the morning on the sixth day. I was sound asleep—actually close to comatose,[4] as I'd been working on a construction crew pouring cement forms for basements and the work was killing me—and found myself suddenly lying on my side with my eyes open. I didn't remember waking up, but my eyes were open and I was staring directly into the slobbery muzzle of Caesar.

I closed my eyes—lost in sleep for a moment, I did not remember getting the dog—and kept them closed. It was no good. A tongue that seemed to be a foot wide and three feet long slathered spit up the middle of my face and I sat bolt upright and swore.

"Woof."

It was not loud but it was perfect—an exact *woof*—and he looked directly into my eyes when he made the sound. It was so pointed, so decisive and focused, I knew exactly what he wanted.

GUIDED READING

What does Caesar do one morning?

"What was that?" my wife asked without opening her eyes—indeed, she could talk without awakening.

"The dog," I said, "is ready to eat."

GUIDED READING

What does Caesar want?

I rose and made my way to the kitchen, the Great Beast padding along behind me. On the floor were three dishes. One had held canned dog food, a second dry dog food and the third water. They were all empty, licked shiny, and I took the sack of dry food down and filled one of the bowls.

He looked at it, then at me.

"Was I wrong?" I said. "Aren't you hungry?"

He looked at the refrigerator, at the door handle.

"Something in there?"

---

4. **comatose.** Being in a coma

words for everyday use

ema • ci • ate (i mā′ shē āt) v., cause to become very thin. *When Hannah returned from her four-month hiking trek, she was <u>emaciated</u> and dehydrated.* **emaciated,** adj.

de • hyd • rate (de hī′ drāt) v., lose water or body fluids. *It's important to drink water when you're active so you don't <u>dehydrate</u>.*

ANSWERS TO GUIDED READING QUESTIONS

1. Caesar refuses to eat.
2. The author is afraid that Caesar will starve to death.
3. He comes to the side of the author's bed and says, "Woof."
4. Caesar wants to eat.

CROSS-CURRICULAR ACTIVITIES

SOCIAL STUDIES. Inform students that there are so many unwanted animals in shelters that many of them are put to sleep after a short stay there. One of the missions of the American Society for the Prevention of Cruelty to Animals (ASPCA) is to promote spaying, neutering, and animal adoptions so that so many unwanted animals won't have to die each year. The ASPCA was the first organization to undertake this mission in the United States, but there are now many organization dedicated to helping animals. Encourage students to work in small groups to research a group dedicated to helping animals such as the ASPCA, PETA, or another group in which students are interested. Students should not only report on the group, but explain ways in which students can help the group's mission.

ANSWERS TO GUIDED READING QUESTIONS

1. The author is afraid the Caesar will run away.
2. Caesar is wearing a stout nylon leash made from synthetic braid that could withstand a six-thousand-pound test.

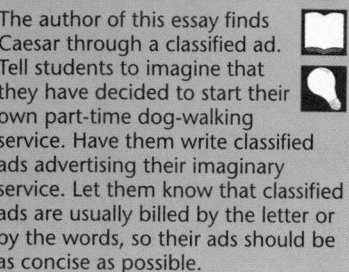

ADDITIONAL QUESTIONS AND ACTIVITIES

The author of this essay finds Caesar through a classified ad. Tell students to imagine that they have decided to start their own part-time dog-walking service. Have them write classified ads advertising their imaginary service. Let them know that classified ads are usually billed by the letter or by the words, so their ads should be as concise as possible.

I swear I saw him nod.

I opened the door and he slid his big head past my leg and studied the shelves for a moment before selecting a leftover chicken, which he swallowed <u>virtually</u> whole, then a cold beef sandwich I'd made for lunch—gone in a bite—and half a lemon meringue pie, before I could catch his collar and pull him back.

"Sit down . . ."

He sat—taking a few seconds to work his bony tail down—and looked at me and belched.

"You're welcome. Do you have to go outside?"

He jumped up and put his paws on my shoulders—his weight <u>compressed</u> my legs a full inch—and then made for the door.

I was in a bit of a dilemma. We lived in the mountains with a great deal of wild country around. The owner had said nothing about whether or not Caesar would run away, but he'd only been with us five nights and I wasn't sure he'd stay. I took his leash and hooked it to his collar and reached for the knob.

GUIDED READING
What is the author afraid that Caesar will do when he gets outside?

I would, I thought, hold him while he did his business (a phrase I've always thought oddly appropriate).

We did not have neighbors within a quarter of a mile so I threw on a pair of sandals sitting by the door, hitched up my boxer shorts—all I was wearing—and opened the door.

I should add here that Caesar's collar was stout nylon and that the leash—which was about six feet long—had a forged-steel snap and was made from woven <u>synthetic</u> braid that would withstand a six-thousand-pound test and that I twisted the loop of the leash tightly around my wrist.

GUIDED READING
What kind of leash is Caesar wearing?

I think—little of it is clear in my memory—I *think* I had the door open an inch before everything went crazy. Later I would piece it together and come up with some of the details—a time-flow of the events leading up to the disaster.

I think—little of it is clear in my memory—I think I had the door open an inch before everything went crazy.

I cracked the door. Caesar got his nose into the opening. He slammed through the door, taking the screen door off its hinges, and headed down the three steps to the gravel drive and across the drive, where I believe he had every intention of stopping to go to the bathroom. For a moment I came close to keeping up but then I lost a sandal—I thought of it later as blowing a tire—and from then on more or less dragged in back of him screaming obscenities and yelling at him to stop. And I think he had every thought to stop, as I said, but my wife's cat, a big tom[5] named Arnie that had been off for days looking for a mate, chose that moment to return home. Arnie, of course, had no knowledge that we'd acquired a dog,

---

5. **tom.** Refers to tomcat, a male domestic cat

---

words for everyday use

vir • tual • ly (vər' chə wə lē) *adv.*, almost entirely. *The house is <u>virtually</u> empty now, except for some boxes and old curtains.*

com • pressed (kəm' prest') *adj.*, reduced in size or volume. *The <u>compressed</u> ball took a long time to inflate.*

syn • thet • ic (sin the' tik) *adj.*, produced artificially. *The wig was made of <u>synthetic</u> hair, not natural hair.*

not just a dog but a house of a dog, a dog to strike terror into a full-size lion, let alone a ten-pound house cat.

GUIDED READING
Who is Arnie? What happens when Caesar sees Arnie?

The effect was immediate. Arnie was a survivor and when he saw Caesar he did what he was best at—he turned and ran. Not up a tree, as one would suppose, but across the road and along a ditch. With a satisfied growl that sounded like thunder, Caesar gave chase.

My tripping feet had nearly caught up with him—I remember the heel of my one sandal slapping so fast it sounded like a motor running—and I was reaching to shorten the leash when Caesar went after Arnie, and I never quite caught up again.

We went through the neighbor's yard at what felt like twenty miles an hour—cat, bounding dog and dragging, underwear-clad human yelling in monosyllabic shrieks. My neighbor was standing in his garage and waved—he may have thought I was waving.

By this time I was just trying to stay alive and couldn't have cared less if Caesar got loose. Indeed I *wanted* him to get loose. But the leash loop was tight around my wrist.

I found to my horror that I was along for the ride, and what a ride it was! We went through three more yards and the back of a bike rental shop along the road and finally slammed into the back doorway of a small cafe where, I learned later, Arnie sometimes went to beg his meals.

Arnie disappeared into the kitchen. Caesar tried to follow him and would have made it except that I became jammed in the door opening and even he could not pull me free.

GUIDED READING
What causes Caesar to stop chasing Arnie?

There was a large woman there holding a very impressive cast-iron frying pan and she looked at me as she might look at a cockroach—looked directly at my head and then at the frying pan, which she hefted professionally. "Who are you?"

"I'm with him," I said, pointing at Caesar while trying to cover my body. My shorts were in tatters and my feet were badly scraped.

"It's wrong to chase cats," she said.

"I'm sorry," I said, and I meant it. Perhaps more than any time in my life I meant it.

"Go away." She pointed to the door with her frying pan. "And take your dog with you."

And so Caesar entered my life.

He became many things to us—friend, entertainer, horror show—but he was never, never boring and his life comes back now in a montage[6] of memories.

There was the Halloween when he greeted a little boy who came to the door in a werewolf costume. There was one moment, priceless, when the two eyed each other, hairy monster-mask to Great Dane muzzle, at exactly the same height. I'm not certain what the little boy expected but he didn't quail—he leaned forward and growled. I'm not sure what Caesar had expected either but it certainly wasn't an angry werewolf. He made a

GUIDED READING
What does the little boy in the werewolf costume do? How does Caesar react?

sound like a train in a tunnel and disappeared into a dark corner of the bedroom closet and would not come out until all the little people stopped coming and the doorbell quit ringing. And it might be noted here that he had a remarkable memory. Every one of the

---

6. **montage.** Rapid succession of images

ANSWERS TO GUIDED READING QUESTIONS

1. Arnie is the author's wife's cat. Caesar chases Arnie.
2. The author can't get loose from Caesar because the leash loop is tight around his wrist.
3. Arnie and Cesar run into the kitchen of a café, but the author gets stuck in the door.
4. The woman in the café tells the author that it is wrong to chase cats.
5. The little boy in the werewolf costume growls at Caesar. Caesar makes a sound like a train in a tunnel and hides in the bedroom closet.

ADDITIONAL QUESTIONS AND ACTIVITIES

It has been said that people are either "dog people" or "cat people," meaning that most people prefer one pet or the other. Encourage your class to hold a debate on which animal makes the better pet. Divide the class into two opposing sides based on students' preferences. Tell students that before the debate they should do some research on dogs and cats, their behavior, their abilities, and how to care for them. Students should use their research as evidence to support their points in the class debate. You should act as the moderator of the debate, calling on different students to give their opinions and preventing the debate from turning into a personal argument.

seven years that he was with us, when the first trick-or-treater came to the door on Halloween, no matter the costume, Caesar went into the bedroom closet, pulled a housecoat over his eyes and would not come out until it was over. He had great heart, but courage against monsters wasn't in him.

Then there was the time I was playing "get the kitty" with him. Arnie wasn't there—usually he was off eating or trying to get married—and I would run around the house yelling at Caesar, "'Get the kitty, get the kitty!" He would <u>lope</u> with me, jumping over furniture and knocking down tables (for obvious reasons I usually played this game only when my wife wasn't there), and I would run and yell and yell until he was so excited he would tear around the house by himself. (I know, I know, but it must be remembered we had no television or other forms of home entertainment.) If it worked well enough I could go and pour a cup of coffee and drink it while Caesar kept galloping, looking for the mystery kitty.

On this one morning I had done it particularly well and he was crazy with excitement, running up and down the stairs, spraying spit (we often had gobbets[7] on the ceilings when he shook his head), bounding through the air with great glee, and just then, at the height of his crazed romp, just then the front doorbell buzzed and without thinking I opened it to see a package-delivery man standing there with a box in his arms.

Caesar went *over* me, through the screen and into the guy at shoulder height. He didn't bite, didn't actually hurt the man at all. In fact when the man was down on his back Caesar licked his face—an experience which I think could be <u>duplicated</u> by sticking your head in a car wash—but the effects were the same as if he'd attacked. The package went up in the air and crashed to the ground with a sound of breaking crockery (it had been a family heirloom vase sent by an aunt—and *had been* would be the correct words). The delivery man wet his pants and in a cloud of dog spit and dust clawed his way free, ran back to the truck and was gone before I knew exactly what had happened. Soon after, we received a polite note saying that that particular company would no longer deliver packages to us.

Caesar never became angry. I never saw him fight or be <u>aggressive</u> to another dog, and while he loved to chase cats, Arnie particularly, when the day was done I would frequently find Arnie curled up on Caesar's back by the stove, the two of them sound asleep. But Caesar would get excited and forget himself when there was food involved, particularly when the food was a hot dog. I think he would have sold his soul for a hot dog. With mustard and relish. When we had hot dogs or went on a picnic he would sit and stare until somebody handed him a wiener and then he would hit like a gator. You had to throw it or he would get your whole hand in his mouth, up to the elbow.

> **GUIDED READING**
> What game does the author play with Caesar?

> **GUIDED READING**
> What happens during this particular game of "get the kitty"?

> **GUIDED READING**
> What causes Caesar to lose control?

---

7. **gobbets.** A small quantity of liquid, drop

---

words for everyday use

lope (lōp′) *v.*, move with a bounding gait. *The puppy excitedly <u>loped</u> over to every newcomer.*

du • pli • cate (dü′ pli kāt) *v.*, repeat, copy. *The young dance students carefully <u>duplicated</u> their teacher's steps.*

ag • gres • sive (ə gre′ siv) *adj.*, forceful; dominating; marked by readiness to attack. *The football team often wins because of their <u>aggressive</u> defense.*

I once was invited to a picnic and softball game in a small town nearby and since it was a nice day I thought it would be fun to bring Caesar. Had I thought a little more I would have remembered two things—that it was a picnic and they would have hot dogs and that Caesar *loved* to play ball—but then had I thought a little more I probably would not have owned Caesar in the first place.

GUIDED READING

What does Caesar love to do?

I brought him out of the back of the truck and people came to see him—one young boy said he looked exactly like a four-legged dinosaur with hair—and after all the oohs and aahs at his size settled down, I left him in the truck with the windows open, told him forcefully, "Stay!" (ha!) and went off to see what was happening.

I had gone about forty yards, saying hello to people and picking up a can of soda, when I met an old friend and stopped to chat. I had my back to the parking area and I suppose heard some of the <u>commotion</u> that was starting but it didn't enter my mind until the man I was speaking to looked over my shoulder and said, "Isn't that Caesar?"

I turned and my heart froze. Caesar was standing next to a small girl—she couldn't have been four—and he towered over her. That wasn't so frightening as what the little girl was doing. She had taken a bite off a hot dog and was holding the remainder out to Caesar.

Images of destruction roared through my mind. He had truly enormous jaws (I could fit my head inside his mouth) and he snapped at his food violently, especially hot

GUIDED READING

What is the little girl about to do? What is the author afraid will happen?

dogs. It was too far for me to run in time and I yelled but it was too late by ages and I wanted to close my eyes but didn't dare and as I watched, Caesar incredibly, with the gentleness of a baby lamb, reached delicately forward and took the hot dog from the girl. He swallowed it in one bite, then licked her face and moved on—though I was calling him—looking for the next child.

They loved him. Kids came from all corners and fed him hot dog after hot dog and he was as careful and gentle as he'd been with the little girl. By this time he had the attention of the crowd and everybody loved him so much I thought they were going to riot when I tried to put him back in the truck.

I let him out when the game started, and he went to work in the outfield. He would sit around center field, in back of the outfielders, and watch the batter. If the ball came long or went between the outfielders he would grab it and run to the nearest player and drop it. I know of two grounders—he shagged to stop a double—I hit both of them and was held at first both times because Caesar stopped the ball when it slithered past both infielders and outfielders.

GUIDED READING

What does Caesar do during the baseball game?

He loved the game and loved the day and when the afternoon was done we went back to the truck and a little girl came running up to me and held out a piece of paper.

Drawn on it in crayon was a picture of a dog, a big dog, with a yellow sun in back of him and stick figures hitting at balls, and scrawled across the bottom was:

WE LOVE YOU SEEZER.

words for everyday use

com • mo • tion (kə mō′ shən) *n.*, noisy confusion. *Someone at the party saw a mouse, and that started a <u>commotion</u>.*

ANSWERS TO GUIDED READING QUESTIONS

1. Caesar loves to play baseball.
2. The little girl is about to feed Caesar a hot dog.
3. Caesar sits in the outfield and stops the balls that the infielders and outfielders miss.

LITERARY TECHNIQUE

SUSPENSE. Suspense is a feeling of anxiousness or curiosity. Writers create suspense by raising questions in the reader's mind and by using details that create strong emotion. Ask students to explain how the author creates suspense in the scene in which the little girl offers Caesar a hot dog. Ask them also to explain whether it is likely that anything bad would happen to the little girl in this essay. Why, or why not? *Answers.* Students may say that the author builds suspense by saying that Caesar loses control over food, especially hot dogs, describing Caesar's enormous jaws which can supposedly fit a person's whole head inside, and by saying that Caesar has been known to snap violently at food. These details make the reader wonder whether Caesar may bite the little girl. Students should recognize, however, that given this essay's humorous subject and lighthearted tone it is unlikely that Caesar will bite the little girl and turn this essay into a more serious story.

ANSWERS TO GUIDED READING QUESTIONS

1. A little girl gives the author a drawing of a big dog with the words, "WE LOVE YOU SEEZER," scrawled across the bottom.
2. The author remembers Caesar on a perfect summer afternoon, eating hot dogs, playing ball, and making friends.

RESPOND TO THE SELECTION

As an alternate activity imagine that Caesar's old owner gave the author a call to ask for his dog back after the owner spent a "perfect summer day" with him. What might the author say?

SELECTION CHECK TEST 4.11.3 WITH ANSWERS

Checking Your Reading

1. Where is Paulsen living when he acquires Caesar? **Paulsen is living in a small cabin in the Colorado mountains.**
2. Why does Paulsen call the veterinarian three days after Caesar comes to live with him? **Paulsen calls the veterinarian because Caesar will not eat.**
3. What scares Caesar on Halloween? **Caesar is scared by a small boy in a werewolf costume.**
4. What is Caesar's favorite food? **Caesar's favorite food is a hot dog.**

Vocabulary in Context

Fill in each blank below with the most appropriate word. You may have to change the tense of the word.

> relative   lope   civil   dilemma
>   tatters   glee   towered

1. Mack realized he had a **dilemma** when his boss asked him to work the night before he had a big test.
2. The babysitter watched her charges chase each other around the playground with **glee**.
3. After they reached the pasture, the riders jumped off and let the horses **lope** to the barn for dinner.
4. Sarah loved her blue dress so much that she wore it until it was in **tatters**.

He is gone now, gone some years from a combination of dysplasia and cancer[8] that was impossible to cure or fix but I still have the drawing in a box somewhere. It shows up from time to time when I am moving or straightening things,

> **GUIDED READING**
> What does a little girl give the author at the end of the day?

and I think of him and the perfect summer afternoon when we ate hot dogs and played ball and made some new friends.

> **GUIDED READING**
> How does the author remember Caesar?

■

---

8. **dysplasia and cancer.** Diseases that affect dogs

Respond *to the* SELECTION

What effects do you think that Caesar had on the author's life? Do you think the author is glad he adopted Caesar? Why, or why not?

About *the* AUTHOR

Gary Paulsen was born in 1939. He had a rough childhood, moving frequently with his parents or into homes of relatives. He was a poor student (he flunked 9th grade). As a teenager, he had to work multiple jobs to support himself.

Paulsen found security at an early age in a small-town library, where a librarian gave him his first library card and introduced him to books. He read constantly, sometimes finishing several books a week.

Paulsen eventually went on to college and began writing. He published his first book, *Special War*, in 1966. Since then, he has published numerous articles and books, ranging from adult how-to plumbing books to westerns, historical fiction, mysteries, and many titles for young people. Paulsen has also been a serious trapper, sailor, and dog-sledder. He has run dog teams in two Iditarod races in Alaska.

Paulsen says he is not like other writers. In an interview in *Booklist,* he explains, "Well, I'm absolutely driven. I simply can't not write. I tried it when I ran dogs, but I ended up writing in longhand by the campfire when the dogs were sleeping…I love it. The hair goes up on the back of my neck when I work, even after 180 books."

788 UNIT ELEVEN / *TELLING IT AS IT IS: NONFICTION*

SELECTION CHECK TEST 4.11.3 WITH ANSWERS (CONT.)

Reader's Toolbox

Fill in the blanks using the following terms. You may not use every term, and you may use some terms more than once.

> point of view   hyperbole   first-person point of view
>   view   third-person point of view

1. **Point of view** is the perspective from which a story is told.
2. When an author uses pronouns such as "I" and "we," he or she is using **first-person point of view**.
3. Sometimes an author uses **hyperbole**, meaning he or she exaggerates to help make a point.

Investigate, Inquire, and Imagine

Recall: GATHERING FACTS

1a. How does the author find out that Caesar needs a new home? What does the author decide to do?

2a. Why does Caesar refuse to eat when he first comes to the author's cottage?

3a. What does Caesar eat at the picnic?

→ Interpret: FINDING MEANING

1b. Why does the author want to adopt Caesar? Is the author convinced that this is a good idea?

2b. What makes Caesar change his mind about eating?

3b. Why are his manners of eating different in this situation?

Analyze: TAKING THINGS APART

4a. Describe Caesar's relationship with Arnie, and give two examples of Caesar's interactions with children.

→ Synthesize: BRINGING THINGS TOGETHER

4b. What do his interactions with Arnie and the children indicate about Caesar's personality?

Evaluate: MAKING JUDGMENTS

5a. How would you describe the author's way of telling this story? Why do you think he writes it this way?

→ Extend: CONNECTING IDEAS

5b. How does this story compare with other pet stories you have heard?

Understanding Literature

POINT OF VIEW. Point of view is the vantage point from which a tory is told. From what point of view is "Caesar" told? Why do you think the author wrote the story from this point of view?

HYPERBOLE. A **hyperbole** is an exaggeration made for effect. Look at your cluster chart of examples of hyperbole from the story. Then discuss the examples with a classmate or small group. Why do you think the author uses hyperbole in the story?

Writer's Journal

1. Write a **postcard** to Caesar's original owner in Hawaii telling him how Caesar is adjusting to his new home.

2. Imagine that you are trying to convince your parents to let you have a dog like Caesar. Write your parents a **letter** telling them all the reasons why a Great Dane would make a good pet.

3. Imagine that you are Caesar and retell an **episode** in this story from his point of view. Try to use hyperbole to make the story interesting and amusing.

"CAESAR" 789

ANSWERS TO UNDERSTANDING LITERATURE

POINT OF VIEW. "Caesar" is told from the first-person point of view. Students might say that the author wrote from the first-person point of view because he is telling about experiences from his own life.

HYPERBOLE. Students might say the author uses hyperbole to make the story interesting and funny.

RECALL

1a. The author reads an ad in the paper that says Caesar needs a new home. The author decides to adopt him.

2a. Caesar refuses to eat because he misses his owner.

3a. Caesar eats the hot dogs children offer him.

INTERPRET

1b. The author wants to adopt Caesar because he was fond of a Great Dane when he was in the army, and he is afraid that if he doesn't take the dog no one else will. The author is not at all sure that this is a good idea because he lives in a very small cottage with his wife and baby, and Great Danes are large dogs.

2b. Students may say Caesar realized his owner wasn't coming back or that he realized that he ended up in a good home and should make the best of it. Students might also suggest that Caesar finally got so hungry he had to either eat or die.

3b. Students may say Cesar eats more gently around the children because he doesn't want to hurt them.

ANALYZE

4a. Caesar chases Arnie, but often at the end of the day Arnie and Caesar will curl up together to sleep. Caesar is scared when a little boy in a werewolf costume growls at him. Caesar gently takes a hot dog a girl offers his at a picnic, when he usually snaps at hot dogs.

SYNTHESIZE

4b. Caesar is playful, gentle, and timid—the type of dog that despite his size would never hurt anyone or anything.

EVALUATE

5a. Students may say the author writes this story with a good sense of humor and with the goal of amusing and entertaining others as well as sharing what a great dog Caesar was.

EXTEND

5b. *Responses will vary.*

Speaking and Listening
You might make this into a collaborative project to ensure that students don't flood a local animal shelter with calls and requests for interviews. Organize students into three or four groups and make sure that they locate and plan to interview different animal shelters. If there is only one local animal shelter, tell students to expand their search to state animal shelters or national organizations dedicated to helping animals.

Study and Research & Media Literacy
Students may also wish to focus on differences in temperament in various breeds of dogs. For example, which dogs are better one-person dogs? Which dogs adjust well to children? Students may also wish to describe what jobs their chosen breeds of dogs were originally used for. Tell students to document the sources they use for research and to present you with this list.

Applied English
Students may have to make some estimates for this assignment. Tell them to assume that the dog needs to be fed at least once a day. They should look up typical weights for a Great Dane and then consult the back of a package of pet food to learn the amount of pet food per day that is appropriate for a dog of this weight. Students may check veterinarians' Web sites to find out how much a check-up at the vet costs. On-line pet stores will be a valuable resource for students in completing this assignment.

Language, Grammar, and Style
1. I
2. I
3. I
4. me
5. me
6. me
7. I
8. me
9. me
10. me

Skill Builders

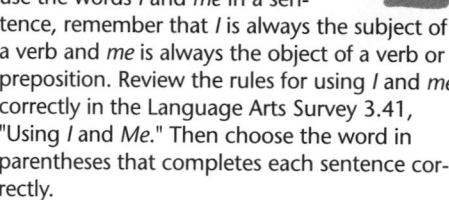

Speaking and Listening

INTERVIEWING. Visit a local animal shelter and interview a staff member to find out how a shelter operates. Prepare a list of questions ahead of time, and ask if you can tape record or videotape the interview. Make sure your questions are open-ended so they will elicit more than a "yes" or "no" answer. If you cannot visit an animal shelter, call and ask your questions over the phone and write up a report to share with the class. For more information, see the Language Arts Survey 4.14, "Conducting an Interview."

Study and Research & Media Literacy

RESEARCHING DOGS. Using the Internet and library resources, research your favorite breed of dog. Find information such as the history of the breed, what activities the dog enjoys, and how to take care of the dog. You might wish to present your findings to the rest of the class using a computer design program, picture displays, videocassettes, or other props.

Applied English

WRITING AN ARTICLE. Write a feature story for a dog magazine about how much per year it would cost to have a Great Dane. Visit the grocery store or pet store to find out how much dog food costs. Also consider items such as a collar, leash, shampoo, toys, and visits to the veterinarian. You might also wish to include in your article information about the best places to shop for pet supplies.

Language, Grammar, and Style

REVIEWING *I* AND *ME*. Before you use the words *I* and *me* in a sentence, remember that *I* is always the subject of a verb and *me* is always the object of a verb or preposition. Review the rules for using *I* and *me* correctly in the Language Arts Survey 3.41, "Using *I* and *Me*." Then choose the word in parentheses that completes each sentence correctly.

1. (I, Me) wish that I could have seen Caesar playing baseball at the picnic.
2. My sister and (I, me) are in charge of feeding and walking our dog, Billy.
3. Sometimes, (I, me) ask my friend Sam to help (I, me) walk my dog.
4. My dog likes to play with other people, but he likes (I, me) best.
5. Between you and (I, me), having a dog is a lot of work, but it's worth it!
6. Mrs. Hathaway always gives birthday presents to my sister and (I, me).
7. My dog and (I, me) like to go for walks in the woods.
8. Arnie, Caesar, and Gary came to visit (I, me).
9. Give the pictures to my friends and (I, me).
10. How did you know where to find (I, me)?

Prereading

"Appearances Are

by Mark Mathabane

Reader's TOOLBOX

PERSUASIVE ESSAY. A **persuasive essay** is a short nonfiction work written to influence the opinion or actions of the reader. To write an effective persuasive essay, the writer carefully considers his or her audience, clearly states his or her position on the subject of the essay, and offers a logical argument with strong reasons and examples that support those reasons.

To develop an argument that is truly persuasive, a writer anticipates any opposition the reader might have and offers information to counter that opposition. He or she writes not to persuade those people that already agree with him or her but to change the minds of readers who don't. As you read, think about the possible audiences Mathabane is writing for. Do you think you are part of the audience he addresses?

Reader's Journal

When have you attempted to persuade someone to do something? What methods of persuasion did you use? Were you successful? Why, or why not?

Reader's Resource

- **SOCIAL STUDIES CONNECTION.** Apartheid is a policy of racial segregation and political and economic discrimination. Under apartheid, a person's race determines what rights he or she has. In South Africa, beginning in 1948, non-whites were forced to endure the conditions of apartheid. During that time, the government forced millions of blacks to live in independent homelands or in separated urban townships. Officials required blacks to carry identification papers and revoked their South African citizenship. Apartheid in South Africa finally ended in 1991.

- "Appearances are Destructive" by Mark Mathabane is an example of persuasive writing, writing that seeks to influence the reader's opinion. In this essay, Mathabane—who grew up under apartheid in South Africa—shares with the reader a glimpse of his sisters' public school experience in America after moving from South Africa. Mathabane uses his sisters' experiences to introduce his position on school dress codes.

READER'S JOURNAL

As an alternate activity, have students write about how important clothing is to them. How high would they rank designer clothing in their list of priorities? What role does peer pressure play in their attitudes toward clothing?

READER'S TOOLBOX

PERSUASIVE ESSAY. Because the persuasive writer writes to convince those readers that disagree with his or her opinion, we know that Mathabane is writing to convince readers that are against school dress codes. This means Mathabane is writing for a broad audience that probably includes a good number of people very involved in education: parents, teachers, administrators, and students. Because the majority of students are probably against dress codes, most students would be part of the audience Mathabane is writing for.

VOCABULARY FROM THE SELECTION

curtail	distraught
derail	infringe
diminution	meretricious

GOALS/OBJECTIVES

Studying this lesson will enable students to
- understand the opinions presented in a persuasive essay
- briefly define apartheid
- define *persuasive essay* and identify how an author tries to persuade his or her readers
- analyze advertisements
- research a fashion designer or company

Appearances are Destructive

Mark Mathabane

As public schools reopen for the new year, strategies to curb school violence will once again be hotly debated. Installing metal detectors and hiring security guards will help, but the experience of my two sisters makes a compelling case for greater use of dress codes as a way to protect students and promote learning.

Shortly after my sisters arrived here from South Africa I enrolled them at the local public school. I had great expectations for their educational experience. Compared with black schools under apartheid, American schools are Shangri-Las,[1] with modern textbooks, school buses, computers, libraries, lunch programs and dedicated teachers.

GUIDED READING
What do American schools have that South African schools don't?

But despite these benefits, which students in many parts of the world only dream about, my sisters' efforts at learning were almost <u>derailed</u>. They were constantly taunted for their homely outfits. A couple of times they came home in tears. In South Africa students were required to wear uniforms, so my sisters had never been preoccupied with clothes and jewelry.

They became so <u>distraught</u> that they insisted on transferring to different schools, despite my reassurances that there was nothing wrong with them because of what they wore.

GUIDED READING
Why were the author's sisters distraught?

I have visited enough public schools around the country to know that my sisters' experiences are not unique. In schools in many areas, Nike, Calvin Klein, Adidas,

---

1. **Shangri-las.** Remote, beautiful, imaginary places where life approaches perfection

words for everyday use

de • rail (dē rāl') v., to hinder or impede the progress of. *Her plans to join the track team were temporarily <u>derailed</u> when she broke her leg.*

dis • traught (dis trät') adj., agitated; troubled. *The bird was <u>distraught</u> over the loss of her nest.*

ANSWERS TO GUIDED READING QUESTIONS

1. American schools have modern textbooks, school buses, computers, libraries, lunch programs, and dedicated teachers.
2. They were distraught because they were ridiculed by other students about the way they dressed.

CULTURAL/HISTORICAL NOTE

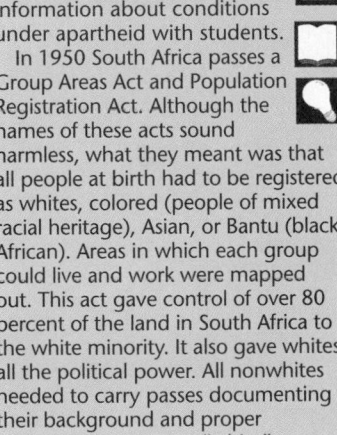

Students might be confused about why the author and his family value education so highly. Share the following information about conditions under apartheid with students.

In 1950 South Africa passes a Group Areas Act and Population Registration Act. Although the names of these acts sound harmless, what they meant was that all people at birth had to be registered as whites, colored (people of mixed racial heritage), Asian, or Bantu (black African). Areas in which each group could live and work were mapped out. This act gave control of over 80 percent of the land in South Africa to the white minority. It also gave whites all the political power. All nonwhites needed to carry passes documenting their background and proper authorization to enter "white" areas.

All nonwhites had to face the humiliation of segregation, separate education, and job restrictions. Bantus were only allowed to work the most menial jobs. Laws passed between 1951 and 1970 in South Africa made conditions even worse for black South Africans. They were made into citizens of different tribal homelands even if they had never set foot on those lands. These laws also forbade black Africans from voting or participating in South African government in any way. While education was free and mandatory for whites, coloreds, and Asians, all Bantu schools charged tuition and required students to buy uniforms and books. This meant that education was a privilege that many black Africans could not afford for their children. Bantu schools were also terribly run down and understaffed. The government also demanded that these schools teach "tribal issues," so students did not receive an education equal with that provided in schools for whites, coloreds, and Asians.

1. Teachers have shared frustrations about students who care more about their hair, shoes, clothing and nails than about learning.
2. They become involved in gangs and peddle drugs to raise the money the need to buy the things they want.

CROSS-CURRICULAR ACTIVITIES

Inform students that South Africa is not the only nation to practice racial segregation. Segregation was also practiced in the United States for much of the twentieth century. Ask students to research segregation in the United States and the events that led to the end of segregation laws. Each student should focus on an aspect of this era in United States history. Possible topics include Jim Crow laws, Rosa Parks and the Montgomery Bus Boycott, the forming of the NAACP, Thurgood Marhsall, Brown vs. the Board of Education, Governor George Wallace and the University of Alabama, Martin Luther King, Jr., and the Civil Rights Act of 1964. Students should share what they learn about their chosen topic with the rest of the class.

SELECTION CHECK TEST 4.11.5 WITH ANSWERS

Checking Your Reading
1. From where did Mathabane's sisters move? **Mathabane's sisters moved from South Africa.**
2. Why did his sisters want to transfer to different schools? **Mathabane's sisters wanted to transfer to different schools because they were teased for wearing unfashionable clothes.**
3. How do many students measure parental love? **Many students measure parental love by how willing their parents are to give them money to buy clothes, shoes, and jewelry.**
4. Rather than skimpy dresses and gaudy looks, what does Mathabane think girls should emphasize to boys? **Mathabane thinks girls should emphasize intelligence and academic excellence.**
5. How do students in other countries who wear uniforms behave differently than American students?

Reebok and Gucci are more familiar names to students than Zora Neale Hurston, Shakespeare and Faulkner.[2] Many students seem to pay more attention to what's on their bodies than in their minds.

Teachers have shared their frustrations with me at being unable to teach those students willing to learn because classes are frequently disrupted by other students ogling themselves in mirrors, painting their fingernails, combing their hair, shining their gigantic shoes or comparing designer labels on jackets, caps and jewelry.

> **GUIDED READING**
> What frustrations have teachers shared with the author?

The fiercest competition among students is often not over academic achievements, but over who dresses most expensively. And many students now measure parental love by how willing their mothers and fathers are to pamper them with money for the latest fads in clothes, sneakers and jewelry.

Those parents without the money to waste on such <u>meretricious</u> extravagances are considered uncaring and cruel. They often watch in dismay and helplessness as their children become involved with gangs and peddle drugs to raise the money.

> **GUIDED READING**
> What does the author say sometimes happens to children whose parents don't buy them the expensive things that other students have?

When students are asked why they attach so much importance to clothing, they frequently reply that it's the cool thing to do, that it gives them status and earns them respect. And clothes are also used to send sexual messages, with girls thinking that the only things that make them attractive to boys are skimpy dresses and gaudy looks, rather than intelligence and academic excellence.

Many students seem to pay more attention to what's on their bodies than in their minds.

The argument by civil libertarians[3] that dress codes <u>infringe</u> on freedom of expression is misleading. We observe dress codes in nearly every aspect of our lives without any <u>diminution</u> of our freedoms—as demonstrated by flight attendants, bus drivers, postal employees, high school bands, military personnel, sports teams, Girl and

---

2. **Zora Neale Hurston, Shakespeare and Faulkner.** All highly acclaimed authors
3. **civil libertarians.** Supporters of freedom from government linterference

words for everyday use

mer • e • tri • cious (mer ə tri′ shəs) *adj.*, falsely attractive, pretentious, superficially significant. *People who don't know Jim well admire him for his <u>meretricious</u> attributes, but I value his kindness and generosity.*

in • fringe (in frinj′) *v.*, to trespass on, intrude on, overstep the bounds of. *Yolanda <u>infringed</u> on her older sister's privacy when she read her sister's diary.*

dim • i • nu • tion (di mə nü′ shən) *n.*, the act or process of diminishing. *At the end of the sale, the shopkeepers were pleased by the <u>diminution</u> of goods.*

SELECTION CHECK TEST 4.11.5 WITH ANSWERS (CONT.)

Students in other countries tend to be neater, less disruptive in class, and more disciplined.

Vocabulary in Context
Fill in each blank below with the most appropriate word. You may have to change the tense of the word.

| meretricious | infringe | diminution | curtail |
| apartheid | derail | civil libertarian | |

1. When the principal censored an article in the school newspaper, the _____ staged a protest. **civil libertarians**

(Continued on page 795)

Boy Scouts, employees of fast-food chains, restaurants hotels.

In many countries where students outperform their American counterparts academically, school dress codes are observed as part of creating the proper learning environment. Their students tend to be neater, less disruptive in class and more disciplined, mainly because their minds are focused more on learning and less on materialism. It's time Americans realized that the benefits of safe and effective schools far outweigh any perceived <u>curtailment</u> of freedom of expression brought on by dress codes. ∎

GUIDED READING
What does the author say Americans should realize?

ANSWER TO GUIDED READING QUESTION

1. The benefits of safe and effective schools outweigh any perceived loss of freedom of personal expression brought on by dress codes.

Respond *to the* SELECTION

How do you think the author's sisters would have been treated at your school? Why?

RESPOND TO THE SELECTION

Encourage students to also discuss whether they might treat the sisters differently if they got to know them and their story about what their family went through in South Africa. What might students learn from the sisters that could change students' own attitudes and values?

About *the* AUTHOR

Mark Mathabane was born on October 18, 1960. The oldest child of seven, Mathabane grew up in extreme poverty in a black township outside Johannesburg, South Africa. Childhood in the poverty-stricken ghetto was difficult. Mathabane's love of books—strongly encouraged by his illiterate but devoted mother—and his dreams of becoming a famous tennis player kept him going. At the age of 18, with the help of former Wimbledon champion Stan Smith, Mathabane left South Africa to attend American University in Washington, D.C., on a tennis scholarship. Mathabane is the author of several books, including *African Women*, but he is best known for *Kaffir Boy*, an autobiography that tells his story of growing up under apartheid in South Africa.

Mathabane with family

SELECTION CHECK TEST 4.11.5 WITH ANSWERS (CONT.)

2. The police force was proud to report a recent _____ in crime. **diminution**
3. Paulette realized she'd have to _____ her socializing and concentrate on studying. **curtail**
4. Too many people focus on such _____ goals as wearing expensive clothes. **meretricious**

Reader's Toolbox
Choose the letter of the phrase that best completes each sentence.
a. who agree with his or her position
b. opinions and/or actions
c. offers information to counter the opposition
d. who disagree with his or her position

1. When considering the audience for a persuasive essay, the author focuses on people _____. **d**
2. A strong persuasive essay anticipates disagreement and _____. **c**
3. The writer of a persuasive essay seeks to influence the reader's _____. **b**

words for everyday use
cur • tail (kər tāl´) v., to make less. *The mayor hoped that more police officers on the streets would help to* <u>curtail</u> *crime.*
curtailment, n.

RECALL

1a. He has great expectations about their education.

2a. They transfer to a new school because they are constantly being ridiculed for the way they dress.

3a. Students say that wearing the right clothes is the cool thing to do and that it earns them status and respect.

INTERPRET

1b. Because he believes American schools are so much better than South African schools. He says American schools are Shangri-las.

2b. The author's sisters might have a particularly difficult time in their first school because school is just one part of their new lives in America where everything is different from South Africa. Also, they lived under apartheid in South Africa where they were treated like outsiders, so in coming to American they are probably desperate to fit in. *Responses will vary.* Some students may say that unless the sisters learn to dress more like American students they will have the same experience in their new school. Other students may point out that the sisters might transfer to a school that has a larger population of students from other countries where they will feel more comfortable. Still other students may say that not all students in all schools value the same things the students the author talks about do, and so they might be treated more kindly in their new school.

3b. *Responses will vary.* Some students may note strong peer pressure and the need to fit in. Others may say that it's a way for students who don't do well in school to gain self-esteem.

ANALYZE

4a. Students from other cultures can be made to feel like outsiders because they don't/can't dress like their American peers. Many students seem to pay more attention to what's on their bodies than what's in their minds. Many students measure parental love buy the things their parents buy for them. We observe dress codes in nearly every aspect of our lives without giving up freedom. Students in schools in other countries that outperform American students observe dress codes.

SYNTHESIZE

4b. *Responses will vary.*

EVALUATE

5a. *Responses will vary.* Many students will probably say that his argument is not effective because he has not

Investigate, *Inquire,* and Imagine

Recall: GATHERING FACTS

1a. What initial expectations does the author have for his sisters' educations?

2a. Why do the author's sisters transfer to another school?

3a. According to this essay, what do students say when they are asked why they attach so much importance to their clothes?

→ **Interpret:** FINDING MEANING

1b. Why does he have these expectations?

2b. Why might the author's sisters have a particularly hard time in their first American school? Do you think their experience in their new school will be different? Why, or why not?

3b. Why might some students feel this way?

Analyze: TAKING THINGS APART

4a. List the five reasons the author gives to support his position on school dress codes. You may want to use the Graphic Organizer shown on page 797 to answer this question.

→ **Synthesize:** BRINGING THINGS TOGETHER

4b. Respond to each of the author's reasons with your own opinion. Then summarize your opinion on school dress code in general.

Evaluate: MAKING JUDGMENTS

5a. Is the author effective in persuading the reader to agree with his point of view on school dress codes? Why, or why not? Which of his reasons most strongly supports his argument? Why? Which of his reasons seems the weakest? Why? How effective do you think this essay would be in persuading parents or teachers to take the author's view on school dress codes?

→ **Extend:** CONNECTING IDEAS

5b. Whether or not you agree with Mathabane's opinion about school dress codes, reflect on some of the individual points he makes in his essay. Which of his observations do you find to be accurate in terms of your school? Does your opinion on the subject change when you consider this issue from the author's point of view?

Understanding *Literature*

PERSUASIVE ESSAY. A persuasive essay is a short nonfiction work written to influence the opinion or actions of the reader. Are you part of the audience Mathabane is addressing in this essay?

In the last paragraph of the essay the author restates his position on school dress codes. What words does he use? Why is this an effective thing to do in a persuasive essay? Can you point out any places in the essay where the author has anticipated and countered the reader's

ANSWERS TO INVESTIGATE, INQUIRE, IMAGINE (CONT.)

changed their minds about dress codes, but they should be encouraged to say why his argument is ineffective by discussing specific points in his argument. Many students may feel that his argument that dress codes make it possible for everyone to fit in more easily is his most effective point. Students may argue that they don't equate parental love with materialism and that this is his

least effective argument. Students may say that parents and teachers might find Mathabane's arguments more persuasive because they are more concerned about ensuring that all students "fit in" in school and focus more on education than clothes.

EXTEND

5b. *Responses will vary.*

response? Use the organizer below to diagram Mathabane's argument in "Appearances Are Destructive." Look back at the essay and to the list of the author's reasons you made for the Analyze question in Investigate, Inquire, and Imagine as you fill in the organizer. Some examples have been filled in to get you started.

Graphic *Organizer*

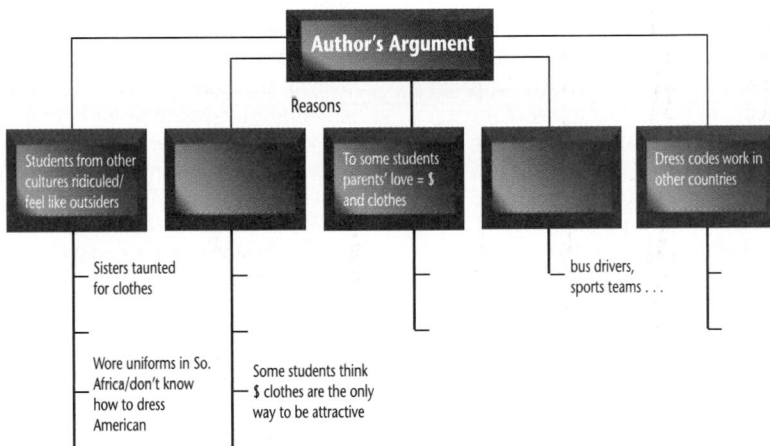

Author's Argument

Reasons

| Students from other cultures ridiculed/ feel like outsiders | | To some students parents' love = $ and clothes | | Dress codes work in other countries |

Sisters taunted for clothes

bus drivers, sports teams . . .

Wore uniforms in So. Africa/don't know how to dress American

Some students think $ clothes are the only way to be attractive

Writer's Journal

1. Write a **letter** to the author's sisters that explains to them why people sometimes act the way the students in their school acted or that tells them it's okay to be different.

2. Imagine that your school has implemented a standard dress code that states that all students are required to wear the same uniform of white shirt and dark pants. Make a **list** of other ways in which you might express your individuality.

3. A motto is a short expression used as a guiding principle such as "if you think you can, you can" or "where there's a will there's a way." Invent a **motto** that expresses something unique about you or that expresses your ideas about individuality and tolerance of people's differences.

Reason 1—Students from other cultures ridiculed/feel like outsiders
Supporting examples—*sisters taunted for clothes*; they come home crying, *wore uniforms in So. Africa/don't know how to dress like Americans*; they transfer schools
Reason 2—Many students care more about what's on their bodies than what's in their minds
Supporting examples—Students know Nike, Calvin Klein, etc. better than Shakespeare, Hurston, Faulkner; teachers' stories of students more interested in hair and clothes than learning; *some students think money and clothes are the only way to be attractive*; fiercest competition is over material goods instead of academics
Reason 3—*To some students parents' love = money and clothes.*
Supporting examples—parents who can't afford material goods are looked down on; kids often join gangs and sell drugs to get money parent's can't/won't give them.
Reason 4—We observe dress codes in nearly every aspect of our lives without giving up freedom.
Supporting examples—*bus drivers, sports teams,* flight attendants, postal employees, Girl and Boy Scouts, military personnel, etc.
Reason 5—Students in schools in other countries that outperform American students observe dress codes.
Supporting examples—dress codes part of learning environment; students are neater, less disruptive, more disciplined; minds focused on learning not materialism.

ANSWERS TO UNDERSTANDING LITERATURE

PERSUASIVE ESSAY. Most students will probably say they are part of Mathabane's audience because they disagree with his stance on dress codes. "It's time Americans realized that the benefits of safe and effective schools far outweigh any perceived curtailment of freedom of expression brought on by dress codes." Restating your argument is an effective way to end a persuasive writing piece because it provides one more opportunity to summarize all your points and put your argument forth. Because Mathabane ends his essay with these words, they are most likely to stay in the reader's mind a little longer. Mathabane anticipates the reader in a few places in this essay: In the introduction he mentions metal

ANSWERS TO UNDERSTANDING LITERATURE (CONT.)

detectors and security guards, acknowledging some common solutions to some common problems in schools today, and he then attaches his proposed solution to those other more widely-employed solutions. He also acknowledges the strongest argument against his dress codes—the argument taken up by civil libertarians and others that enforced dress codes infringe on students' rights to personal expression. He counters this argument by providing

numerous situations in which people wear uniforms and notes that the wearing of the uniforms in no way lessens their sense of freedom. He ends his essay by again mentioning the argument that dress codes infringe on freedom and counters it once again by saying that the benefits brought on by dress codes far outweigh any perceived disadvantages.

**Media Literacy &
Collaborative Learning**
You might choose examples of
advertisements and complete your own
responses to these questions, so
students will have an example on which
they can model their own critical
assessments, Students may find reading
the Language Arts Survey, "How to
Evaluate Advertisements," helpful for
this assignment.

**Study and Research &
Speaking and Listening**
Have students use the research log in
the Study and Research Resource
workbook for this assignment. Tell
students not to base their research only
on promotional material, such as the
company's or designer's own Web site
and literature. Students should also
base their research on more objective
information such as newspaper or
magazine articles.

Skill Builders

Media Literacy & Collaborative Learning

ANALYZING ADVERTISEMENTS. During the next few days collect advertisements for products or companies that are popular with you or your classmates. Look through magazines and newspapers for these advertisements. If you're watching television, make notes about commercials for these designers or companies. Be sure to note the slogans used in the commercials. Once you've collected this material, bring it to class and break into small groups of twos or threes. Share the material you've collected with your group members and discuss the following:

- Make a list of the slogans of the different advertisements and talk about what they mean. How many of the slogans actually make sense to you? How many of them present messages that are positive or relevant to your life? What words are meant to influence you?
- Examine the visual aspects of the advertisements. How many of the advertisements present realistic messages?
- What do you find appealing about the advertisements? What do you find unappealing?
- What audience(s) do you think these advertisements are trying to sell to?

- Which of the advertisements promote products that you own or would like to own? If someone were to offer you the same product made by a designer or company you'd never heard of for half the price, would you buy that instead? Why, or why not?
- Which designers and companies, if any, have such status that people buy their product more for the logo than for the quality of the actual product?
- How does owning products made by well-known designers or companies helps express your individuality? How does it not?

Once you've discussed the questions above with your group, reassemble and discuss your findings as a class. For more information, see the Language Arts Survey 5.3, "Avoiding False Arguments and Propaganda."

Study and Research & Speaking and Listening

RESEARCHING A COMPANY. Using library resources, newspaper and magazine articles, and the Internet, conduct research on a designer or company that you particularly admire. (You may want to talk with the librarian at your school or local library to get advice on where to start looking.) Find out when the company was started and where its headquarters are, whether it operates only in the United States or internationally, what products it manufactures and where the products are made, what charities it sponsors, how many employees it has, and what its profits were for last year. Also include information on any other topics of interest, such as whether the company has been the target of public protest or has been involved in a lawsuit. Compile your findings into a short report to share with the class. Conclude your report by stating whether any of the information you came across in your research changed your opinion about the company or designer, and if so, which information, and why.

Prereading

"The Size of Things"

from *Red Giants and White Dwarfs* by Robert Jastrow

Reader's T O O L B O X

SCIENTIFIC WRITING. Scientific writing aims to communicate scientific concepts, data, or analysis in a concise, straightforward manner. Like any other writer whose purpose is to inform the reader, the science writer sets forth a main idea and builds on it by providing facts or strong examples that support that idea. Sometimes the main purpose of a piece of scientific writing is to advance a *hypothesis*—an unproven theory or assumption. Because scientific concepts are often difficult for the average reader to grasp, the effective science writer is careful to avoid using scientific *jargon*—technical terminology not understood by the average reader—to explain difficult concepts. As you read, determine the main idea of the selection. Is the main idea of the selection scientific fact or an unproven hypothesis?

ANALOGY. An **analogy** is a comparison of things that are alike in some ways but different in others. As you read, keep track of the numerous analogies the author makes throughout the selection. Use the chart below to note the analogies. List those things that are being compared in the left column and the things they are compared to in the right column. The first one has been filled in to get you started.

Graphic *Organizer*

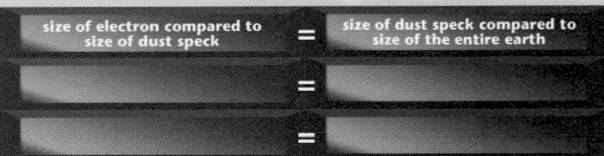

size of electron compared to size of dust speck	=	size of dust speck compared to size of the entire earth
	=	
	=	

Reader's *Journal*

Write about a topic that fascinates you or that you know a lot about. What efforts have you made to discover more about this topic? Why do you find it interesting? What would you most like others to know about it?

SCIENTIFIC ESSAY

Reader's *Resource*

- **MATH CONNECTION.** Measurement is the process of finding the extent or dimensions of something, especially by using a standard unit of measure. Standard units of measure include feet or meters to measure distance; minutes or hours to measure time; pounds or kilograms to measure weight; or degrees Fahrenheit or Celsius to measure temperature.

- **HISTORY CONNECTION.** Ancient peoples developed the first system for measuring length by comparing the length of one thing to the length of another. Many units of measurement were based on parts of the human body. The cubit used by ancient Egyptians, for example, represented the length of a person's forearm from the elbow to the tip of the middle finger. The Romans borrowed many Greek units of measurement, such as the uncia, which was the width of a thumb. The Roman system of measurement was adopted throughout Europe and prevailed until France adopted the metric system in 1795. Today, most countries in the world use the metric system.

ADDITIONAL RESOURCES

UNIT 11 RESOURCE BOOK
- Selection Worksheet 11.4
- Selection Check Test 4.11.7
- Selection Test 4.11.8
- Language, Grammar, and Style Resource 3.97
- Speaking and Listening Resource 4.2, 4.6
- Applied English Resource 6.11

READER'S TOOLBOX

SCIENTIFIC WRITING. The main idea of the selection is that neutrons, protons, and electrons are the basic building blocks of all substances in the universe. This is scientific fact, not an unproven hypothesis.

ANALOGY. Answers to graphic organizer

size of electron compared to size of dust speck = size of dust speck compared to size of Earth

electrons circling around the nucleus = mini solar system

size of the atom = grain of sand on a table 2,000 miles long

the nucleus of the atom = a ping-pong ball placed in the middle of the Houston Astrodome

the size of the sun, the planets, and the distance between them = an orange with grains of sand and cherry pits circling it at distances ranging from 30 feet to several city blocks

the galaxy = a cluster of oranges

the void of space = another orange 2,000 miles away with planetary matter circling it

READER'S JOURNAL

As an alternate activity, ask students what the smallest thing they can imagine is. What is the largest thing they can imagine?

GOALS/OBJECTIVES

Studying this lesson will enable students to
- have a positive experience reading a scientific essay
- briefly explain the development of units of measurement
- define *scientific writing* and identify the main idea in a piece of scientific writing
- define *analogy* and identify analogies in works that they read
- research a scientist
- identify common spelling errors
- create a design for a billboard

The Size of Things

Robert Jastrow

INDIVIDUAL LEARNING STRATEGIES

MOTIVATION
You might wish to show students a documentary video about space exploration to stimulate students' interest in space before they begin reading this selection.

READING PROFICIENCY
Even though this is a fairly straightforward and extremely introductory scientific essay, students who may not be familiar with scientific writing could find it challenging. After students have read the essay on their own, have students form reading groups. Each group should skim through the essay and create a list of main ideas and important concepts that they find. Encourage groups to compare ideas and come up with one class list of main ideas and important concepts from this essay.

ENGLISH LANGUAGE LEARNING
Students may have difficulty understanding all the measurements and numbers in this essay, especially if they come from another country. You might wish to review with students the difference in the United States between thousands, millions, billions, and trillions. In the United States, for example, a billion is a thousand million. In the United Kingdom, on the other hand, a billion is a million millions. Thus a British billionaire has quite a bit more money than his American counterpart. Increasingly, however, people are using the American system where a thousand millions equal a billion.

SPECIAL NEEDS
Special needs students might find some of the concepts introduced in this essay quite challenging. Tell them to focus on answering the Guided Reading questions and the Recall questions in the Investigate, Inquire, and Imagine section. You might wish to treat the higher level questions as extra credit or as discussion questions that do not count against students' grades.

INDIVIDUAL LEARNING STRATEGIES (CONT.)

ENRICHMENT
Encourage students to debate whether or not United States citizens should start using the metric system. Students should state the benefits and drawbacks of using the metric system. Ask students to think about whether the benefits would outweigh the drawbacks or not and how people would react to the conversion. What difficulties might the conversion cause for a time.

You might share with students that scientists almost exclusively use the metric system. For example, a scientist never talks about yards or feet, but measures things in meters.

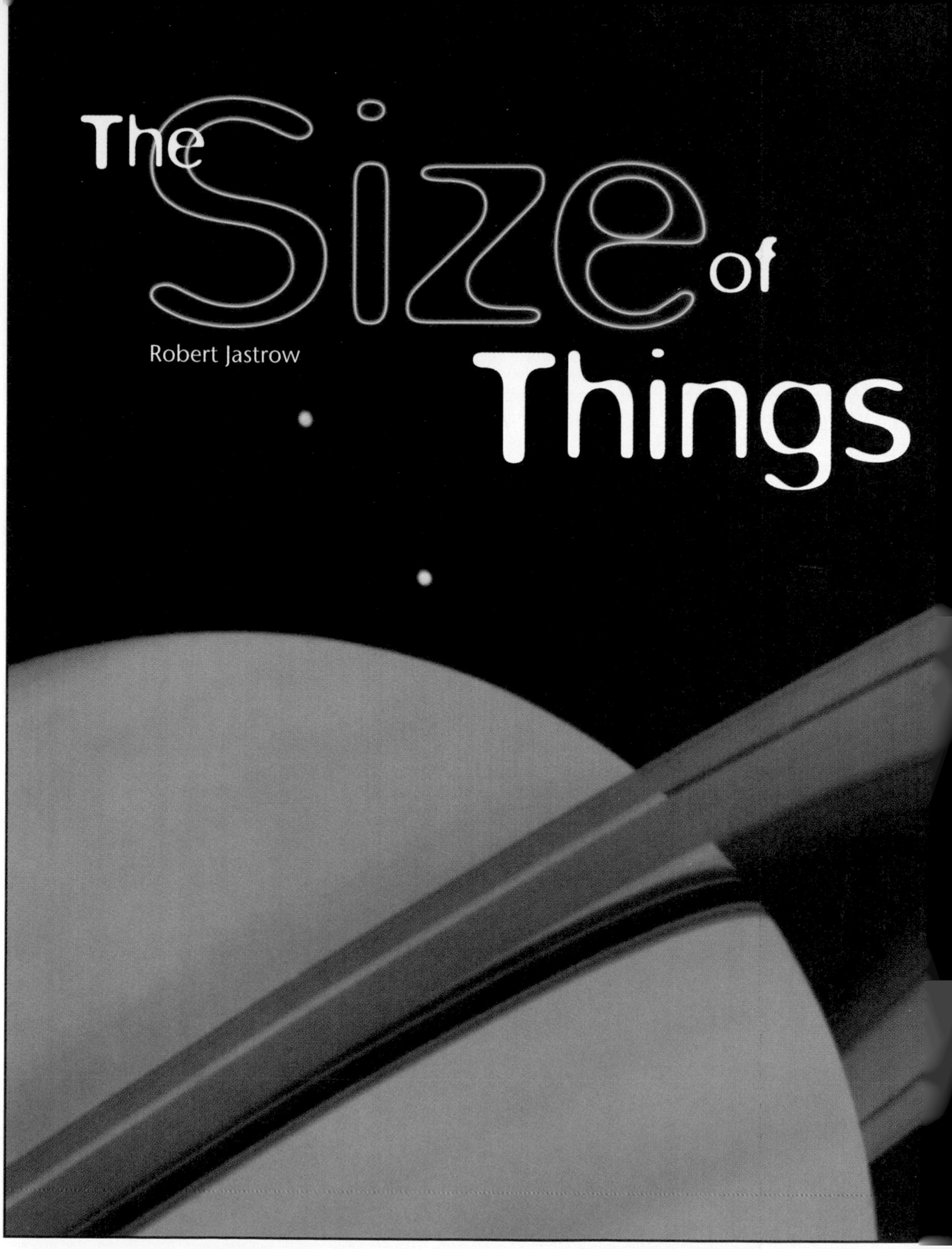

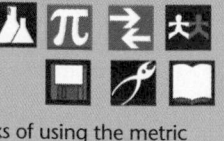

once had occasion to <u>testify</u> before the United States Senate Space and Aeronautics Committee on the scientific background of the space program; my talk dealt with the manner in which all substances in the universe are assembled out of neutrons, protons, and electrons as the basic building blocks. After I left the chamber a senior NASA[1] official continued with a summary of the major space science achievements of the last year. Apparently my scholarly presentation had perplexed the senators, although they were anxious to understand the concepts I had presented. However, the NASA official's relaxed manner reassured them, and someone asked him: "How big is the electron? How much smaller is it than a speck of dust?" The NASA official correctly replied that the size of an electron is to a dust speck as the dust speck is to the entire earth.

> **GUIDED READING**
> What are the basic building blocks of all substances in the universe?

The electron is indeed a tiny object. Its diameter is one 10-trillionth of an inch, a million times smaller than can be seen with the best electron microscope. Its weight is correspondingly small; 10,000 trillion trillion electrons make up one ounce. How can we be certain that such a small object exists? No one has ever picked up an electron with a pair of forceps[2] and said, "Here is one." The evidence for its existence is all indirect. During the 150 years from the late eighteenth century to the beginning of the twentieth century a great variety of experiments were carried out on the flow of electricity through liquids and gases. The existence of the electron was not proved

conclusively by any single one of these experiments. However, the majority of them could be explained most easily if the physicist[3] assumed that the electricity was carried by a stream of small particles, each bearing its own electrical charge. Gradually physicists acquired a feeling, bordering on <u>conviction</u>, that the electron actually exists.

> **GUIDED READING**
> What did physicists assume?

The question now was, how large is the electron, and how much electric charge does each electron carry? The clearest answer to this question came from an American physicist, Robert Millikan, who worked on the problem at the University of Chicago in the first decades of the twentieth century. Millikan arranged a device, clever for its simplicity, in which an atomizer[4] created a mist of very fine droplets of oil just above a small hole in the top of a container. A small number of the droplets fell through the hole and slowly drifted to the bottom of the container. Millikan could see the motions of these droplets very clearly by illuminating them from the side with a strong light so that they appeared as bright spots against a dark background. Millikan discovered that some of these droplets carried a few extra electrons, which had been picked up in the atomizing process. By applying an electrical force to the droplets and studying their motions in response to this force, he could

---

1. **NASA.** National Aeronautics and Space Administration
2. **forceps.** Tongs used most often by doctors and scientists for grasping, compressing, and pulling
3. **physicist.** Specialist in the branch of science that deals with matter, energy, and their interaction
4. **atomizer.** Device used to shoot out a fine spray

---

words for everyday use

tes • ti • fy (tĕs′ tə fī) v., to make a statement based on personal knowledge or belief. *The character witness* <u>testified</u> *in court that during the twenty years he had known the woman on trial, she had never committed an illegal act.*

con • clu • sive (kən klü siv) adj., without a doubt, definitively. *The* <u>conclusive</u> *photos proved that the man had been at the scene of the crime.* **conclusively,** adv.

con • vict • ion (kən vik′ shən) n., a strong and firm belief. *She lives up to her* <u>convictions</u> *about personal responsibility by volunteering several hours per week.*

1. Neutrons, protons, and electrons are the basic building blocks of all substances in the universe.
2. Physicists assumed electricity was carried by a stream of small particles, each bearing its own charge—they assumed that the electron existed.

ADDITIONAL QUESTIONS AND ACTIVITIES

Ask students the following questions: What are the "building blocks" from which all matter in the universe is constructed? What binds these tiny particles together? Of what is a nucleus composed? What do electrons do in relation to the nucleus? What do these particles form?
Answers. Electrons, protons, and neutrons are the building blocks from which all matter in the universe is constructed. A strong force of attraction binds these particles together. A nucleus is composed of neutrons and protons that are attracted to each other. Electrons are attracted to the nucleus and they circle it, much as the planets circle the sun. These particles form an atom.

VOCABULARY FROM THE SELECTION

conclusive   luminous
conviction   testify
deduce   void
diffuse

ANSWERS TO GUIDED READING QUESTIONS

1. Millikan's experiment showed that the charge of the electron is exceedingly minute.
2. Electrons circling a nucleus form a smaller version of the solar system.

CROSS-CURRICULAR ACTIVITIES

SCIENCE. Encourage students to draw two-dimensional or create three-dimensional models of the atom. Students should try to make their models as realistic as possible and to include all the parts of the atom. Materials that could be used to make models include wire, string, beads, gumdrops, marshmallows, or different-colored clay. Students could use smaller objects to represent the electrons and show the nucleus as a much larger object, made up of both protons and neutrons. If they plan to make their atoms solid, using clay or another substance, they should show a cross-section so that the nucleus can be seen. As an example, you might show them the cross-section of a peach and explain that the pit at the center represents the nucleus. Electrons would circle around the nucleus, within the meat of the fruit.

deduce the amount of electric charge carried by the electrons on each droplet. This charge turned out to be exceedingly minute.[5] As a demonstration of its minuteness, it takes an electric current equivalent to a flow of one million trillion electrons every second to light a 10-watt bulb. All this happened rather recently in the history of science. Millikan's first accurate measurements were completed in 1914.

> **GUIDED READING**
> What did Millikan's experiment tell us about the charge of electrons?

The tiny electron, and two sister particles, are the building blocks out of which all matter in the world is constructed. The sister particles to the electron are the proton and the neutron. They were discovered even more recently than the electron; the proton was identified in 1920 and the neutron was first discovered in 1932. These two particles are massive in comparison with the electron—1840 times as heavy—but still inconceivably light by ordinary standards. The three particles combine in an amazingly simple way to form the objects we see and feel. A strong force of attraction binds neutrons and protons together to form a dense, compact body called the nucleus, whose size is somewhat less than one-trillionth of an inch. Electrons are attracted to the nucleus and circle around it as the planets circle around the sun, forming a solar system in miniature.

> **GUIDED READING**
> What do electrons circling a nucleus form a smaller version of?

Together the electrons and the nucleus make up the atom.

The size of a typical atom is one hundred-millionth of an inch. To get a feeling for the smallness of the atom compared to a macroscopic[6] object, imagine that you can see the individual atoms in a kitchen table, and that each atom is the size of a grain of sand. On this scale of enlargement the table will be 2000 miles long.

The comparison of the atom with a grain of sand implies that the atom is a solid object. Actually, the atom consists largely of empty space. Each of the atoms that makes up the surface of a table consists of a number of electrons orbiting around a nucleus. The electrons form a <u>diffuse</u> shell around the nucleus, marking the outer boundary of the atom. The size of the atom is 10,000 times as great as the size of the nucleus at the center. If the outer shell of electrons in the atom were the size of the Astrodome that covers the Houston baseball stadium, the nucleus would be a ping-pong ball in the center of the stadium. That is the emptiness of the atom.

If most of the atom is empty space, why does a tabletop offer resistance when you push it with your finger? The reason is that the surface of the table consists of a wall of electrons, the electrons belonging to the outermost layer of atoms in the tabletop; the surface of your finger also consists of a wall of electrons; where they meet, strong forces of electrical repulsion prevent the electrons in your fingertip from pushing past the outermost electrons in the top of the table into the empty space within each atom. An atomic projectile[7] such as a proton,

---

5. **minute.** Very small, infinitesimal
6. **macroscopic.** Large enough to be observed by the naked eye
7. **projectile.** Body that once shot forth continues on its own

words for everyday use

de • duce (di düs') *adj.,* determine by reason; conclude. *After looking at the evidence, Ginger <u>deduced</u> that her car problems were electrical.*

dif • fuse (di fyüs') *adj.,* not concentrated in one area, spread out. *Populations are highly concentrated in cities, but more <u>diffuse</u> in rural areas.*

accelerated to high speed in a cyclotron,[8] could easily pass through these electrons, which are, after all, rather light and unable to hurl back a fast-moving object. But it would take more force than the pressure of the finger can produce to force them aside and penetrate the inner space of the atom.

The concept of the empty atom is a recent development. Isaac Newton described atoms as "solid, massy, hard, impenetrable, moveable particles." Through the nineteenth century, physicists continued to regard them as small, solid objects. Lord Rutherford, the greatest experimental physicist of his time, once said, "I was brought up to look at the atom as a nice hard fellow, red or grey in color, according to taste." At the beginning of the twentieth century, J. J. Thomson, a British physicist and one of the pioneers in the investigation of the structure of matter, believed that the atom was a spherical plum pudding of positive electric charge in which negatively charged electrons were embedded like raisins. No one knew that the mass of the atom, and its positive charge, were concentrated in a small, dense nucleus at the center, and that the electrons circled around this nucleus at a considerable distance. But in 1911 Rutherford, acting on a hunch, instructed his assistant, Hans Geiger, and a graduate student named Marsden, to fire a beam of alpha particles[9] into a bit of thin gold foil. These alpha particles are extremely fast-moving atomic projectiles which should have penetrated the gold foil and emerged from the other side. Most of them did, but Geiger and Marsden found that in a very few cases the alpha particles came out of the foil on the same side they had entered. Rutherford said later, "It was quite the most incredible event that has ever happened to me in my life. It

> **GUIDED READING**
>
> What were scientists surprised to discover about the atom?

was almost as incredible as if you fired a 15-inch shell at a piece of tissue paper and it came back and hit you."

Later Geiger told the story of the occasion on which Rutherford saw the meaning of the experiment. He relates: "One day [in 1911] Rutherford, obviously in the best of spirits, came into my room and told me that he now knew what the atom looked like and how to explain the large deflections of the alpha particles." What had occurred, Rutherford had decided, was that now and then an alpha particle hit a massive object in the foil, which bounced it straight back. He realized that the massive objects must be very small since the alpha particles hit them so rarely. He concluded that most of the mass of the atom is concentrated in a compact body at its center, which he named the nucleus. Rutherford's discovery opened the door to the nuclear era.

> **GUIDED READING**
>
> What did Rutherford conclude from his experiment?

Let us continue with the description of the manner in which the universe is assembled out of its basic particles. Atoms are joined together in groups to form molecules, such as water, which consists of two atoms of hydrogen joined to one atom of oxygen. Large numbers of atoms or molecules cemented together form solid matter. There are a trillion trillion atoms in a cubic inch of an ordinary solid substance, which is roughly the same as the number of grains of sand in all the oceans of the earth.

The earth itself is an especially large collection of atoms bound together in a ball of rock and iron 8000 miles in diameter, weighing six billion trillion tons. It is one of nine planets, which are bound to the sun by

> **GUIDED READING**
>
> What is the earth?

---

8. **cyclotron.** Accelerator in which charged particles are propelled in spiral paths by the use of a constant magnetic field
9. **alpha particles.** Positively charged particles consisting of two protons and two neutrons each

1. The Milky Way is a luminous band of stars stretching across the sky.
2. No less than 100 billion other galaxies have been observed.
3. If the sun were the size of an orange, the earth would be a grain of sand circling the orange at a distance of thirty feet.

Quotables

"I don't pretend to understand the universe, it is a great deal bigger than I am."

—Thomas Carlyle

"The eternal silence of those infinite spaces terrifies me."

—Blaise Pascal

"Today we can no more predict what use mankind may make of the Moon than could Columbus have imagined the future of the continent he had discovered."

—Arthur C. Clarke

ADDITIONAL QUESTIONS AND ACTIVITIES

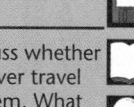

Students might discuss whether or not humans will ever travel to another solar system. What do students think are the chances of discovering life in another solar system? If we discovered life in another solar system, do students think that these forms of life would be similar to those on our planet or completely different?

---

the force of gravity. Together the sun and planets form the solar system. The largest of the planets is Jupiter, whose diameter is 86,000 miles; Mercury, the smallest, is 3100 miles across, one-third the size of the earth, and scarcely larger than the moon. All the planets are dwarfed by the sun, whose diameter is one million miles. The weight of the sun is 700 times greater than the combined weight of the nine planets. Like the atom, the solar system consists of a massive central body—the sun—surrounded by small, light objects—the planets—which revolve about it at great distances.

The sun is only one among 200 billion stars that are bound together by gravity into a large cluster of stars called the galaxy. The stars of the galaxy revolve about its center as the planets revolve about the sun. The sun itself participates in this rotating motion, completing one circuit around the galaxy in 250 million years.

The galaxy is flattened by its rotating motion into the shape of a disk, whose thickness is roughly one-fiftieth of its diameter. Most of the stars in the galaxy are in this disk, although some are located outside it. A relatively small, spherical cluster of stars, called the nucleus of the galaxy, bulges out of the disk at the center. The entire structure resembles a double sombrero[10] with the galactic nucleus as the crown and the disk as the brim. The sun is located in the brim of the sombrero about three-fifths of the way out from the center to the edge. When we look into the sky in the direction of the disk we see so many stars that they are not visible as separate points of light, but blend together into a <u>luminous</u> band

stretching across the sky. This band is called Milky Way.

GUIDED READING
What is the Milky Way?

The stars within the galaxy are separated from one another by an average distance of about 36 trillion miles. In order to avoid the frequent repetition of such awkwardly large numbers, astronomical distances are usually expressed in units of the light year. A light year is defined as the distance covered in one year by a ray of light, which travels at 186,000 miles per second. The distance turns out to be six trillion miles; hence in these units the average distance between stars in the galaxy is five light years, and the diameter of the galaxy is 100,000 light years.

In spite of the enormous size of our galaxy, its boundaries do not mark the edge of the observable universe. The 200-inch telescope on Palomar Mountain has within its range no less than 100 billion other galaxies, each comparable

GUIDED READING
How many other galaxies have been observed?

to our own in size and containing a similar number of stars. The average distance between these galaxies is one million light years. The extent of the visible universe, as it can be seen in the 200-inch telescope, is 15 billion light years.

An analogy will help to clarify the meaning of these enormous distances. Let the sun be the size of an orange; on that scale of sizes the earth is a grain of sand circling in orbit around the sun at a distance of 30 feet; the giant planet Jupiter, 11

GUIDED READING
If the sun were the size of an orange, how big would the earth be and how far would it be from the sun?

---

10. **sombrero.** Tall Mexican hat with a large brim

words for everyday use

lu • mi • nous (lü′ mə nəs) adj., emitting or reflecting light. *The glowing, <u>luminous</u> moon lit my path home last night.*

times larger than the earth, is a cherry pit revolving at a distance of 200 feet or one city block; Saturn is another cherry pit two blocks from the sun; and Pluto, the outermost planet, is still another sand grain at a distance of ten city blocks from the sun.

On the same scale the average distance between the stars is 2000 miles. The sun's nearest neighbor, a star called Alpha Centauri, is 1300 miles away. In the space between the sun and its neighbors there is nothing but a thin distribution of hydrogen atoms, forming a vacuum far better than any ever achieved on earth. The galaxy, on this scale, is a cluster of oranges separated by an average distance of 2000 miles, the entire cluster being 20 million miles in diameter.

An orange, a few grains of sand some feet away, and then some cherry pits circling slowly around the orange at a distance of a city block. Two thousand miles away is another orange, perhaps with a few specks of planetary matter circling around it. That is the <u>void</u> of space. ∎

Respond*to the* SELECTION

Identify something you learned from reading this selection, and describe how it affected you.

About*the* AUTHOR

Robert Jastrow has written several books on astronomy and space. He was one of the first members of NASA as well as the chairperson of NASA's Lunar Exploration Committee. Jastrow is a professor of Earth Sciences at Dartmouth College. He has also appeared on many television programs about astronomy and space exploration.

words for everyday use

void (void′) *n.,* empty space, abyss. *The large tree was uprooted and carried hundreds of feet by the storm, leaving a large <u>void</u> in the earth where it had been.*

"THE SIZE OF THINGS" **805**

SELECTION CHECK TEST 4.11.7 WITH ANSWERS

Checking Your Reading

1. According to Jastrow, comparing the size of an electron to a speck of dust is like comparing the size of a speck of dust to what? **Comparing the size of an electron to a speck of dust is like comparing the size of a speck of dust to the earth.**
2. Which was discovered first, electrons, protons, or neutrons? **Electrons were discovered first.**
3. What makes up most of an atom? **Most of an atom is empty space.**
4. What holds stars together into a galaxy? **Stars are held together into a galaxy by gravity.**
5. The distance covered in one year by a ray of light, which travels at 186,000 miles per second, is known as what? **The distance covered in one year by a ray of light is known as a light-year.**

Vocabulary in Context

Fill in each blank below with the most appropriate word from the following Words for Everyday Use.

> testify minute diffuse void
> sombrero scholarly diameter

1. Outside, the smoke was **diffuse** enough that it didn't bother anyone.
2. Many think that **sombreros** are fashionable, but they also offer good protection from the sun.
3. Gerald had to **testify** in the robber's trial.
4. The first step in our science project was to measure the **diameter** of the container.
5. Skydiving had sounded like fun, but Minerva was terrified as she stared out of the plane's door into the **void**.

Reader's Toolbox

Choose the letter of the phrase that best completes each sentence.

a. things that are alike in some ways but different in others
b. a main idea supported by strong examples
c. to inform the reader
d. unproven theories or assumptions

SELECTION CHECK TEST 4.11.7 WITH ANSWERS (CONT.)

e. technical language that is not understood by the average reader
f. are often difficult for readers to understand
g. scientific concepts, data, or analyses

1. Sometimes scientific writing explains facts, but other times it discusses hypotheses, or _____. **d**

2. The scientific writer's purpose is _____. **c**
3. Science writers write in a straightforward manner, because scientific concepts _____. **f**
4. An analogy is a comparison of _____. **a**
5. Jargon is _____. **e**

RECALL

1a. The topic of the speaker's talk is neutrons, protons, electrons: the basic building blocks of all matter in the universe.

2a. The author says that the size of an electron compared with a speck of dust is equal to comparing the size of a speck of dust to the entire earth.

3a. Rutherford thought the atom was hard. Rutherford's 1911 experiment contradicted his earlier beliefs about the atom by showing that most of the atom's mass was concentrated in a small area in the center, the nucleus.

4a. All the planets are dwarfed by the sun, which weighs 700 times the weight of all the planets combined.

INTERPRET

1b. The speaker probably chose this topic because he believes it is important, because he believes that understanding these concepts is fundamental to understanding everything else—like space.

2b. People might wonder if electrons exist because you can't see them.

3b. He probably believed this because this was the accepted belief at the time. This was what he was brought up to believe and this was what Isaac Newton before him had believed. It would also be logical to believe that the particles that compose solid objects are solid.

4b. The author compares the solar system to the atom because both contain particles that orbit around a central body and great amounts of void. By comparing the atom to the solar system the author is to explain new concepts to the reader by basing them on concepts he has already explained.

ANALYZE

5a. Students may mentions details such as those listed below:
electron: the size of an electron is to a speck of dust as the dust speck is to the entire earth; the electron is a tiny object; the electron's diameter is one 10-trillionth of an inch; 10,000 trillion, trillion electrons make up one ounce; the electron is 1840 times lighter than the neutron or proton
proton: a proton is 1840 times heavier than an electron;
neutron: a neutron is 1840 times heavier than an electron
atom: the size of a typical atom is one-hundred-millionth of an inch; the size of an atom can be

Investigate, *Inquire,* and **Imagine**

Recall: GATHERING FACTS

1a. What is the topic of the talk the speaker gives to the U.S. Senate Space Aeronautics Committee?

2a. What comparison does the author make between an electron, a speck of dust, and the earth?

3a. What did Rutherford at first think about the atom? What did Rutherford find out about the atom in 1911 that contradicted his earlier beliefs?

4a. How large are the planets of the solar system in relation to the size of the sun?

Interpret: FINDING MEANING

1b. Why do you think the speaker chose this topic?

2b. Why might people wonder if electrons exist?

3b. Why might he have had these beliefs? What is surprising about his discovery in 1911?

4b. Why does the author compare the solar system to the atom?

Analyze: TAKING THINGS APART

5a. From the selection, collect one detail about the size of each of the following: an electron, a proton, a neutron, an atom, the nucleus of an atom, earth, the planets, the sun, the galaxy, the universe.

Synthesize: BRINGING THINGS TOGETHER

5b. In your own words, explain how the author uses the concept of size to help the reader understand the ideas he discusses in this selection.

Evaluate: MAKING JUDGMENTS

6a. How effective is the author at clearly explaining the concepts in this selection so that they are understandable to the average reader? Point to specific examples from the selection to support your answer.

Extend: CONNECTING IDEAS

6b. What did reading "The Size of Things" make you think about your size as a human being? In what ways are human beings simultaneously incredibly large and incredibly small?

Understanding *Literature*

SCIENTIFIC WRITING. Scientific writing aims to communicate scientific concepts, data, or analysis in a concise, straightforward manner. Sometimes the main purpose of a piece of scientific writing is to advance a *hypothesis*—an unproven theory or assumption. Briefly review the selection and point out an example of hypothesis. What terms or concepts are difficult to understand? Identify some resources that might provide information to help you better understand these

ANSWERS TO INVESTIGATE, INQUIRE, IMAGINE (CONT.)

compared to the size of a grain of sand on a table 2,000 miles long;
nucleus of an atom: the nucleus of an atom is 10,000 times less than the size of the atom; the nucleus of an atom is less than one-trillionth of an inch; comparing the size of the nucleus with the size of the atom is similar to comparing a ping-pong ball to the Houston Astrodome
Earth: The earth is an especially large collection of

atoms; the earth has a diameter of 8000 miles; the earth weighs six billion trillion tons
planets: the largest of the planets is Jupiter with a diameter of 86,000 miles; the smallest planet is Mercury with a diameter or 3,100 miles; Mercury is one-third the size of the earth and not much larger than the moon; all the planets are dwarfed by the sun

(Continued on page 807)

terms or concepts. Do you think the author is justified in using these terms or concepts, or do you think they are jargon? Explain.

ANALOGY. An **analogy** is a comparison of things that are alike in some ways but different in others. Look back to the list of analogies you made as you read. Go back to the selection if you think you might have missed some and complete your list. Trade lists with the classmate next to you. Which analogies did he or she miss? Which did you miss? Why do you think the author used so many analogies in this selection? Explain.

Writer's Journal

1. *Jargon* is technical terminology specific to a subject that people not involved with that subject don't understand. Make a **list** of words that you think would qualify as jargon. They can be words that only you and your friends know the meanings of, sports terms, computer terms, terms you hear on television or radio, or terms specific to other hobbies you have.

2. An *analogy* is a comparison of things that are alike in some ways but different in others. Create **analogies** that describe the shape of something, the color of something, and the size of something.

3. Imagine that you are a scientist who has just made a remarkable discovery that will change the lives of humans around the world. Write a short **article** for a scientific journal explaining your discovery.

Skill Builders

Study and Research & Collaborative Learning

CONDUCTING RESEARCH FOR PRESENTATION. In a small group, choose one of the scientists mentioned in "The Size of Things," or choose a different scientist. Some scientists you may want to consider include Marie Curie, Rosalind Franklin, Francesco Redi, Emile de Chatelet, Jonas Salk, Caroline Herschel, Margaret Mead, Louis Pasteur, Lise Maitner, and Ivan Pavlov. Using library and Internet sources, conduct research on the scientist you have chosen. Collect information about the scientist's life or about the various ways he contributed to the world of science. If you prefer, gather a mix of interesting facts to present about your scientist. If possible, collect photos and other visuals, too. Then decide as a group how to present your information to your classmates. You may want to create handouts, give an oral presentation that all group members participate in, or create an Internet tour of sites with strong information on your scientist. Whatever format you choose for presenting your information, make sure to keep it interesting and be prepared to answer questions.

ANSWERS TO UNDERSTANDING LITERATURE (CONT.)

ANALOGY. The author is describing things so small—an electron is one 10-trillionth of an inch—and so large— the diameter of our galaxy is 100,000 light years—that we simply can't comprehend the sizes of these things. The reader might be able to think about dividing an inch into 10 parts or even 20, but not into 10 trillion parts. Because readers can't comprehend these extremes of small and large, the author uses analogies that set things to scale using objects we are familiar with or can at least comprehend the size of—an electron compared to a dust speck and a dust speck compared to the earth. By using analogies that set up size relationships between things, the author is better able to create a sense of awe in the reader over the amazing smallness or mammoth vastness of the things he talks about in the selection.

sun: the diameter of the sun is one million miles; the weight of the sun is 799 times greater than the combined weight of the nine planets **galaxy:** the diameter of the galaxy is 100,000 light years (with a light year being equal to 6 trillion miles) **universe:** the universe contains no less than 100 billion other galaxies, each comparable to our own in size—the average distance between these galaxies is one million light years; the extent of the visible universe is 15 billion light years

SYNTHESIZE
5b. The author uses size to organize the information he presents. He begins first with the electron then moves to the proton, the neutron, the nucleus, the atom, and so forth. By organizing information in this manner, the author is also able to develop and move forward his explanations of concepts in the selection because as he moves from miniscule to larger, he makes connections from one thing to the next. By the end of the "The Size of Things" he has created a logical chain of information that connects the electron to the known universe and the void of space, clearly demonstrating his main idea that electrons, protons, and neutrons are the basic building blocks of all existing matter.

EVALUATE
6a. *Responses will vary.*

EXTEND
6b. *Responses will vary.* Some students may point out that reading the selection made them feel large in comparison to things so small their smallness can't be seen or comprehended. Other students may feel small in comparison to things like the earth, the sun, the galaxy, the universe.

ANSWERS TO UNDERSTANDING LITERATURE

SCIENTIFIC WRITING. The main idea is that electrons, protons, and neutrons are the basic building blocks of all substances in the universe. This is scientific fact. Physicists assuming that electrons existed before they had proven their existence is an example of a hypothesis. Responses will vary. Students should point out resources like the dictionary, Internet, science reference books, their science teacher. *Responses will vary.*

Study and Research & Collaborative Learning

You might encourage interested students to research the history and inventors of a scientific invention that has become part of everyday life. Students may be interested in some of the surprising details research into such a topic can uncover. For example, students might research Marchese Guglielmo Marconi and his invention of wireless telegraphy (without Marconi we wouldn't have radios or cellular phones). Students might also find it fascinating to research the history of another invention we take for granted—the facsimile (or fax) machine. Students might be surprised to discover that the fax machine was invented before the telephone, and was originally only used for photographs. Later it was used to deliver scaled-down versions of newspapers to cruise ships.

Language, Grammar, and Style

1. outragous; outrageous
2. enormeous; enormous
3. apparant; apparent
4. fasinating; fascinating
5. tommorow; tomorrow
6. uneccesarry; unnecessary
7. vengance; vengeance
8. none misspelled
9. responsability; responsibility
10. seperate; separate

Media Literacy

Tell students that people passing a billboard do not have time to read much text or carefully examine images for details. Any text students use should be very concise. Images should also be simple and make use of bold and eye-catching designs and colors.

Language, Grammar, and Style

DEVELOPING LANGUAGE SKILLS. Some English words are often misspelled. For a list of 150 commonly misspelled words, turn to the Language Arts Survey 3.97, "Common Spelling Errors." If you master this list, you will avoid many errors in spelling.

Find the misspelled words in the following sentences and rewrite them, spelling them correctly.

1. It is outragous to think how large the sun is in comparison to Earth.
2. The universe seems enormeous to Janine and me.
3. It is apparant that Janine would like to be an astronomer.
4. She finds our lessons in science class fasinating.
5. Tommorow we will be taking a trip to a planetarium to study stars and planets.
6. That amount of research is really uneccesarry at this point.
7. Matilda was so angry, she only wanted to seek vengance on her sister.
8. The sounds I was hearing were very eerie and kind of weird.
9. Taking the dog out for a walk is Sarah's responsability, for which she earns a respectable allowance.
10. The liquids and the solids are supposed to seperate in the test tubes.

Media Literacy

CREATING A BILLBOARD. Imagine that your local science museum is preparing an exhibit on neutrons, protons, and electrons, and on the roles Robert Millikan and Lord Rutherford played in increasing our understanding of what they are and how they work. Write advertising copy for a billboard, and find accompanying visuals to advertise the museum's exhibit. Then create a smaller-sized version of your billboard on posterboard. Your billboard should arouse public interest and provide information about where and when the exhibit will take place. For more information see the Language Arts Survey 6.11, "Displaying Effective Visual Information."

Speaking and Listening

LISTENING FOR COMPREHENSION. Listen to an audio recording of "The Size of Things," taking notes about important points in the selection. Try to pick out the main ideas as you listen, writing your notes in outline form. After listening to the recording, write up a brief summary of what you learned from the recording. For more assistance, review the Language Arts Survey 4.2, "Active versus Passive Listening," and 4.6, "Adapting Listening Skills to Specific Tasks."

Prereading

"The Price of Freedom"

by Cassandra M. Vanhooser

Reader's T O O L B O X

EXPRESSIVE WRITING. A writer's *aim* is his or her purpose, or goal, in a given piece of writing. In an **expressive essay**, a writer's aim is to reflect on an experience, an issue, or an emotion. What does the author of "The Price of Freedom" reflect on? What points does she want to get across to the reader?

UNITY. Unity in a piece of writing is the use of details related to the main idea, or theme. An essay with unity is one in which all the parts help to support the thesis statement, or main idea. What is the main idea in "The Price of Freedom"? In what ways do the other parts of the essay support the main idea? You may want to use a graphic organizer like the one shown below to examine how each paragraph relates to the main idea.

Graphic *Organizer*

	Main Idea	Details Connected to the Main Idea
Paragraph 1	emotions of author →	trying not to cry
Paragraph 2	author's reason for writing →	
Paragraph 3	→	
Paragraph 4	→	
Paragraph 5	→	
Paragraph 6	→	

Reader's Journal

What experiences have you had that were different from your expectations?

Reader's Resource

- **HISTORY CONNECTION.** In 1998, the National Prisoners of War Museum opened in Andersonville, Georgia. The museum is located at the Andersonville National Historic Site, a former Confederate Civil War prison for Union soldiers. In 1970 the U.S. Congress designated the site a memorial for all American prisoners of war (POWs). POWs and other groups began raising the millions of dollars needed to build a museum there. The museum is a tribute to all POWs, from the American Revolution (1775–1783) to the Persian Gulf War (1991).

- An estimated 800,000 American men and women have been held prisoners of war throughout U.S. history. However, by the time the museum opened in 1998 to commemorate their heroism, most of these POWs—many from the Civil War and the World Wars of the early 20th century—had passed away from old age. Only 56,000 POWs remained to hear of the tribute to them. The table on page 813 shows how many POWs were imprisoned during each war and how many died in captivity.

"THE PRICE OF FREEDOM" 809

ADDITIONAL RESOURCES

UNIT 11 RESOURCE BOOK
- Selection Worksheet 11.5
- Selection Check Test 4.11.9
- Selection Test 4.11.10
- Study and Research Resource 5.31

GRAPHIC ORGANIZER

The main idea is that prisoners of war purchased our freedom by sacrificing their own. Paragraph 1 simple states this idea. Paragraph 2 tells that the author is overcome with emotion, which relates to this idea because she is considering the sacrifice the prisoners of war made. Paragraph 3 tells how the author expected the museum to be filled with musty memorabilia but instead she hears the voices and sees the faces of America's POWs, which reveals that this museum honors the sacrifice the POWs made. Paragraph 4 states that the author now understands what American freedom costs, which restates the main idea. Paragraph 5 reveals how many Americans have been held hostage and why the museum site was chosen, emphasizing how many POWs made sacrifices. Paragraph 6 reveals how terrifying even a tiny taste of being a POW is, emphasizing the courage and sacrifice made. Paragraph 7 reveals that the POWs themselves raised the money for the museum, emphasizing the commitment of POWs as well as the authenticity of the museum. Paragraph 8 relays the thoughts of a POW and a museum contributor on why the museum was created—to show people that the world is not all bad, which emphasizes the fact that

(Continued on page 810)

READER'S JOURNAL

As an alternate activity encourage students to express how they feel about prisoners of war. Do they feel sorry for them? Do they think they weren't good soldiers because they were captured? Do they feel gratitude to and admiration of POWs for sacrificing themselves for the good of the United States?

GOALS/OBJECTIVES

Studying this lesson will enable students to
- identify with the feelings the author of an expressive essay reveals
- briefly explain how many people have been held as POWs
- define *expressive essay* and recognize the emotions such an essay conveys
- define *unity* and explain whether an essay has unity
- create descriptive compounds
- interview a veteran
- research Civil War prison camps
- review a film

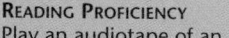

The Price of FREEDOM

Cassandra M. Vanhooser

The nation pays tribute to American prisoners of war who purchased our freedom by sacrificing their own. As hard as I try, I can't stop the hot, salty tears that spill down my cheeks.

I came to the National Prisoner of War Museum in Andersonville, Georgia, expecting to wade through musty memorabilia and obscure statistics. Instead, I hear the voices and see the faces of America's POWs. Now I understand what my freedom—indeed, the independence of every American—truly cost.

From the Revolution to the Gulf War, more than 800,000 men, women, and children have been held captive by enemy forces. Other military museums touch on the subject, but this is the first memorial dedicated <u>solely</u> to the plight of American prisoners of war. Its location—on the very site of the Andersonville Prison Camp where 45,000 Union soldiers were incarcerated[1]—seems fitting.

As I wander through the museum, I get only a tiny taste of <u>indignities</u> prisoners of war endured. I feel gut-wrenching terror when I walk into a darkened room and suddenly face a wall of weapons pointed at me. As I watch interviews with family members, I imagine waiting years for a loved one's return. I look inside the prison door at the simulated Hanoi Hilton[2] and pray I'll never know the mind-numbing experience of being shackled in a tiny cell. In my heart, I bend down to kiss the American soil with each returning soldier.

That I can experience this part of history is in large part thanks to the POWs themselves. The American Ex-Prisoners of War, a veterans group of more than 30,000 members, teamed with the National Park Service to raise the money needed to build the museum. Their influence <u>permeates</u> the project, especially in the commemorative courtyard.

> **GUIDED READING**
> Who raised the money to build the museum?

"The prisoner of war story is cruel," says Bill Fornes, an ex-POW who spent 12 years working on the project. "It's hard. It's emotional. We wanted a place where, after that, visitors could reflect, ease themselves, and realize the world's not all bad." It's here I meet Lloyd Diehl from New Jersey, an ex-POW.

"I'm here to try to heal a little bit from what I experienced and what I still experience," says Lloyd, who was captured on December 19, 1944, in Belgium during the Battle of the Bulge. He spent four months in Stalag 9B, a German prison camp.

"I don't feel shame anymore. I did at first. It's like saying I gave up," he says, his voice quivering with emotion. "You just don't do that. It wasn't in my vocabulary, or I didn't think it was. Then to do it, to surrender—I think we all felt shame.

> **GUIDED READING**
> What emotion did many POWs experience?

"We were reduced to the existence of a dog," he continues. "But we knew that when we got liberated[3]—and we all expected to get liberated—that it was only up from that point."

Lloyd was burying a fellow POW in a prison graveyard when liberation finally came. "An American plane flew over and strafed[4] us, and all we could do was crouch down," he remembers. "He missed us the first time, but he went around and did it again. That time he came in over the top of us and not in front of us, and we waved as he flew by. The third time he went by, he wiggled his wings like he recognized us; then we went out and finished burying this guy."

As Lloyd shares his story, he lays his head on my shoulder and begins to weep, the wounds deep and painful even now, after more than 50 years have passed—I cradle this man—a complete stranger—in my arms and whisper the only words worthy of his sacrifice. ■

> **GUIDED READING**
> What does Lloyd do as he tells his story?

---

1. **incarcerated.** Put in prison
2. **simulated Hanoi Hilton.** Copy of a Vietnamese wartime prison
3. **liberated.** Freed
4. **strafed.** Fired at

---

words for everyday use

sole • ly (sō′ lē) *adv.*, only. *Juana decided to enter the race <u>solely</u> for the fun of it.*

in • dig • ni • ty (in dig′ nə tē) *n.*, insult; humiliating treatment. *We are lucky to have never experienced the <u>indignities</u> that those hostages suffered.*

per • me • ate (par′ mē āt) *v.*, spread through or penetrate something. *The smoke <u>permeated</u> the air.*

1. A group of veterans who were prisoners of war raises the money along with the National Park Service needed to build the museum.
2. Many of them felt ashamed to surrender to their captors.
3. Lloyd weeps as he tells his story.

CROSS-CURRICULAR ACTIVITIES

SOCIAL STUDIES. Encourage students to work in small groups to research the stories of the most recent group of Americans to be held as prisoners of war—the soldiers who were captured and held during the United States' war with Vietnam. Students should prepare brief written reports on their findings. Good resources include newspapers and magazines from that time period, documentaries, historical books, encyclopedias, and on-line resources.

VOCABULARY FROM THE SELECTION

indignity	solely
permeate	

RESPOND TO THE SELECTION

You might also ask students how they think they would react to being made a prisoner of war.

SELECTION CHECK TEST 4.11.9 WITH ANSWERS

Checking Your Reading
SHORT ANSWER

1. What is a prisoner of war? **A prisoner of war is a soldier captured by an enemy country during wartime and put in prison.**
2. What emotions does the author feel when she visits the National Prisoner of War Museum? **Answers will vary, but could include that the author feels sadness, gratitude, empathy, and terror.**
3. Name two things the author sees at the museum. **Answers will vary, but could include the wall of weapons, interviews with family members, a simulation of the Hanoi Hilton, the commemorative courtyard, or prisoners of war.**
4. What was Lloyd Diehl doing when the American pilot spotted him and the other prisoners? **Lloyd Diehl was burying a fellow POW when an American plane flew overhead and spotted the prisoners.**
5. What does the author say to Diehl? **The author says, "Thank you."**

Vocabulary in Context
SENTENCE COMPLETION

Fill in each blank below with the most appropriate word from the following *Words for Everyday Use* from "The Price of Freedom." You may have to change the tense of the word.

liberate	obscure	solely
	indignity	

1. Betty was upset at the _____ of wearing the little paper gown the nurse handed her. **indignity**
2. Tatiana stayed up _____ to watch the late news. **solely**
3. Many artists remain _____ for a long time before becoming famous. **obscure**

Respond *to the* SELECTION

What sacrifices have you made for another person? Why did you make them?

About *the* AUTHOR

Cassandra M. Vanhooser, a travel writer for *Southern Living* magazine, reflects on her work and on her life:

I never actually decided to become a writer. I grew up on a dairy farm in middle Tennessee and had planned to work in the cattle industry. In fact, I received my degree in agriculture from the University of Tennessee.

In many ways, though, I am much more suited to this type of work. I lived the hours I spent as a child sitting on the front porch listening to my grandmother's stories. I have great empathy for people, and I rarely forget a face. And somewhere along the way, I grew to love words.

My favorite stories are about people. I have interviewed famous people, but the ones I really enjoy are everyday people just like you and me. Everybody has a story, and I have a knack for getting people to share their lives with me.

If the fun part is talking to people, the hard part is sitting down to write the story. Writing is a solitary pursuit, and I am a very social person. I have difficulty disciplining myself to sit down and write. I am always glad when I successfully complete a project, though. I love having written.

I currently work as a travel writer for *Southern Living* magazine. Travel writing is exciting because my boss pays me to take vacations and then write about them! It's almost like writing the "What I Did Last Summer" paper that your teacher asks you to write at the beginning of the school year. The trick is to capture a place using all of your senses. I want my readers to feel as if they are standing right beside me when they read my story. Still, I don't give all of the details because there needs to be something for you to discover when you visit.

Museums can be the most dull and boring part of travel writing, but the National Prisoner of War Museum in Andersonville was an exception. The photographer and I arrived bright and early on a Monday morning? "What are our chances of finding an actual POW at this place at 8:00 on a Monday morning," I grumbled as we pulled into a nearly deserted parking lot.

As fate would have it, there had been a meeting of former POWs in Tampa that weekend, and many of them stopped by the museum on their way home. Mr. Diehl, the man I write about in the story, was among the first to arrive. As soon as I met him, I knew I had to tell his story. He was gracious enough to let me do so.

My visit to the POW Museum made me proud to be an American, and I really understood for the first time how much freedom costs. Here was a man who spent months in captivity so I could be free. I wanted every reader to feel the overwhelming sense of gratitude, but it was difficult to reach down inside myself and find the right words to describe those feelings. The hardest part was being honest enough to tell millions of people that I cried broken heartedly in a public place! I wrote and rewrote this story until I felt it honored America's POWs.

My family still operates the dairy in Tennessee, and I travel there often to be with them and to enjoy the country life. I read, cook, garden, and take seriously my role as aunt to five nieces and a nephew. Plus, I am a sports fanatic. I love almost every sport, especially Tennessee football.

SELECTION CHECK TEST 4.11.9 WITH ANSWERS (CONT.)

Reader's Toolbox
SHORT ANSWER

1. What is the author's purpose in writing this essay? **Answers may vary, but could include that the author's purpose is to reflect on her visit to the memorial; to inform readers about the plight of the POW; or to persuade readers to appreciate POWs.**

2. What is the main idea of this essay? **Answers will vary.**

3. What is unity? **Unity is the measure of how well the details in an essay relate to the main idea or theme.**

INSIGHTS

- The largest number of U.S. soldiers were taken prisoner during the Civil War. The fewest were taken during the Spanish-American War. Students may be surprised to learn that the most prisoners of war were taken during a war fellow Americans fought against each other.
- The largest number of prisoners of war died during the Civil War. The largest percentage of U.S. prisoners of war died during the Revolutionary War. Students might say this is because medical conditions were worse back during the Revolutionary War due to the lack of knowledge doctors had about treating wounds and disease.
- There were more U.S. prisoners of war in Europe. More U.S. prisoners of war died, however, on the Pacific front. They might have separated Wold War II in this way because it was fought on two distinct fronts.

American POWs

War	Number of prisoners	POW deaths	Death rate
American Revolution (1775-1783)	20,000	8,500	43%
War of 1812	5,000	252	5%
Spanish-American War (1898)	12	0	0%
Civil War (1861-1865)	346,950	49,102	14%
World War I (1914-1918)	4,120	147	4%
World War II Europe (1939-1945)	95,532	1,124	1%
World War II Pacific (1941-1945)	34,648	12,935	37%
Korean War (1950-1953)	7,140	2,701	38%
Vietnam War (1959-1975)	766	114	15%
Persian Gulf War (1991)	23	0	0%

Data from the National Park Service and the Pentagon

Critical Thinking

- During which war were the largest number of U.S. soldiers taken prisoner? During which war were there the fewest? Do these facts surprise you? Why, or why not?
- During which war did the largest number of U.S. prisoners of war die? During which war did the largest percentage of U.S. prisoners of war die? What reasons might account for this fact?
- This chart divides World War II into two parts—the European front and the Pacific front. Where were there more U.S. prisoners of war? Where did more U.S. prisoners of war die? Why might the developers of this chart have separated World War II this way?

1a. The speaker is at the National Prisoner of War Museum in Andersonville, Georgia.
2a. The speaker sees a wall of weapons and a replica of a prison cell in a Vietnamese POW camp, and she meets POWs and listens to their stories.
3a. Lloyd Diehl was a POW in Stalag 9B, a German prisoner camp, during World War II back in 1944.
4a. The speaker tells Lloyd Diehl, "Thank you."

INTERPRET
1b. The speaker writes about this place because she has been assigned to write a story on it, but is surprised to discover how much this place moves her.
2b. The speaker is frightened when she walks into a darkened room and sees a wall of weapons pointed at her; she is horrified by the tiny cell she sees that replicates a Vietnamese prison; and she is moved by the stories of the POWs she meets there. The speaker is overcome by emotions of sorrow, pity, and gratitude.
3b. He may relate his experiences because being in the museum brings them back to him and he needs to release the emotions he feels to someone.
4b. The speaker thanks him because these are the only words she can think of worthy of his sacrifice.

ANALYZE
5a. The speaker describes sorrow, fear, the hope and hopelessness of waiting for a loved one to return, gratitude, shame, pain, sympathy, appreciation, and admiration.

SYNTHESIZE
5b. These emotions combine to give a sense of the mixed sadness and gratitude the museum inspires in people. These emotions contribute to the message that we should be grateful for the sacrifice made by POWs because they show the pain, fear, and horror of being a POW.

Investigate, Inquire, and Imagine

Recall: GATHERING FACTS

1a. Where is the speaker?

2a. What does the speaker experience as she wanders through the museum?

3a. Where and when had Lloyd Diehl been a prisoner?

4a. What does the speaker tell Lloyd Diehl?

Interpret: FINDING MEANING

1b. Why does she write about this place?

2b. How do these experiences affect her?

3b. Why does the speaker relate his experiences?

4b. Why does she say this?

Analyze: TAKING THINGS APART

5a. Identify all the emotions the speaker describes in the essay.

Synthesize: BRINGING THINGS TOGETHER

5b. How do these emotions combine to give the reader a sense of the speaker's reaction to visiting this place? How do they contribute to the speaker's message?

Evaluate: MAKING JUDGMENTS

6a. In your opinion, how does the speaker view war? prisoners of war? How has this visit affected her? How may her thoughts and viewpoints on these subjects have changed as a result of this visit?

Extend: CONNECTING IDEAS

6b. How might the speaker describe her experience to a visitor from a different country? How would that description be different from or similar to the essay you read?

Understanding Literature

EXPRESSIVE WRITING. A writer's *aim* is his or her purpose, or goal, in a given piece of writing. In an **expressive essay**, a writer's aim is to reflect on an experience, an issue, or an emotion. What reflections does the author share in "The Price of Freedom"? What ideas does she hope the reader becomes aware of? Why might she have these intentions?

UNITY. Unity is the use in a piece of writing of details related to the main idea, or theme. An essay with unity, for example, is one in which all the parts help to support the thesis statement, or main idea. Look back at the outline you made. How does each paragraph relate to the main idea? Does this essay have unity? Why, or why not?

ANSWERS TO INVESTIGATE, INQUIRE, IMAGINE (CONT.)

EVALUATE
6a. *Responses will vary.* Students should recognize, however, that the speaker feels gratitude and admiration for prisoners of war. The visit makes her feel more strongly about POWs and their stories than she thought she would. Students may suggest that where the speaker thought she would find dull historical facts, she encountered people and their stories of fear, sacrifice, and courage.

EXTEND
6b. *Responses will vary.* Students might suggest that the speaker might have a more difficult time conveying her patriotic feelings to someone who is not as familiar with American history.

Answers to Understanding Literature are found on page 815.

Writer's Journal

1. Write a **letter** to Lloyd Diehl, asking him questions about his experiences as a soldier in the Battle of the Bulge and as a POW in Stalag 9B.

2. Write a **proposal** to local officials, outlining your ideas for a new museum. Include in your proposal why the museum is important, how the museum would be funded, and where it might be located.

3. Write a short **recommendation** telling other young people why they should visit the National Prisoner of War Museum.

Skill Builders

Vocabulary
CREATING DESCRIPTIVE COMPOUNDS. In "The Price of Freedom," the author uses terms such as *mind-numbing* and *gut-wrenching* to describe certain experiences. Other such compounds include *stomach-churning*, *tear-jerking*, and *head-spinning*. Write a paragraph describing an experience, real or made up, using several compounds like these. You may borrow from this list as well as create your own compounds.

Speaking and Listening
INTERVIEWING. Consult your teacher, friends, or relatives to find a veteran who was involved in a war and is willing to share his or her thoughts on the subject. Set up a time to meet with that person, and prepare a list of interview questions. You may want to ask the person to describe an event or experience, to tell about the people he or she worked with, or to explain his or her reactions to the war. You may want to make an audio tape of your interview so that you can share it with your class.

Study and Research
RESEARCHING CIVIL WAR PRISON CAMPS. Andersonville Prison Camp—or Camp Sumter, as it was known during the Civil War—housed thousands of Union soldiers captured by the Confederate Army. Many other prison camps existed throughout both Union and Confederate territories during the war. Try to find answers to the following questions about Civil War prison camps.

- How many Union prison camps were there? how many Confederate camps?
- How many captured soldiers did each camp hold? Were any set free before the end of the war? What was life like for the prisoners?
- The chart on page 813 says that more than 49,000 POWs died while in Civil War camps. How many soldiers died on Civil War battle fields?

Media Literacy
REVIEWING A FILM. Search for a videotape of the movie *Andersonville* at your local library or video rental store. After viewing the movie, write a review of it. See the Language Arts Survey 5.31, "How to Evaluate a Film," for more information.

Vocabulary
Students paragraphs will vary, but they should be on a single topic and include a variety of descriptive compounds. If students have difficulty writing such compounds on the same theme, have them list as many such compounds as they can think of.

Speaking and Listening
If students have difficulty finding an interview candidate, have them contact their local VFW (Veterans of Foreign Wars) organization. Forewarn students that they may find it difficult talking to such a veteran about his experiences because of the strong feelings this topic can bring up.

Study and Research
Students may find encyclopedias and history books to be valuable resources in completing this assignment. You may wish to combine the reading of this essay with a lesson on the Civil War taught by the students' history teacher.

Media Literacy
Encourage students to hold small group discussions on what they learned about Andersonville and prisoners of war through this film.

ANSWERS TO UNDERSTANDING LITERATURE

EXPRESSIVE WRITING. The author shares her reflections on the courage and sacrifice of POWs and the debt and gratitude we owe them because of our freedom. She hopes the reader becomes aware that others gave up their freedom to ensure freedom for others. Students may say she is encouraging students to feel the same emotional response she did to meeting and hearing the stories of POWs.

UNITY. Each paragraph expands the main idea that prisoners of war purchased our freedom by sacrificing their own. Students should point to the evidence in their graphic organizers as evidence that this essay does indeed have unity.

for your READING LIST

In virtually every culture, the centuries-old belief has been that women are intellectually inferior to men, and particularly unsuited to wield power. Our modern practice of encouraging leadership roles for women and girls is relatively new in the whole of human history. ***Ten Queens: Portraits of Women in Power*** is a collection of biographies about powerful women in earlier times. Milton Meltzer says that he chose these ten queens because they "ruled in their own right, by themselves. Or if they sat on thrones beside kings, they had as much or more to say about governing than their husbands." From Esther, the 5th-century Jewish queen of the King of Persia, to Elizabeth I of 16th-century England and Catherine the Great of 18th-century Russia, each of these women brought extraordinary courage and intellect to the task of ruling in a world that resisted women in power. Like men who have ruled, some used their power wisely, while others used it cruelly and arrogantly. Meltzer says in his introduction, these queens were not chosen "because they were heroines or saints." They were women who helped shape the history of a world that believed they were incapable of doing so.

INTERVIEW YOUR FAVORITE QUEEN

Working in pairs, conduct a talk show-style interview with a queen whose life interests you. Before you begin, review the Language Arts Survey 4.14, "Conducting an Interview," for guidelines. After reading about the queen you have chosen, develop a list of questions to bring out information of interest to your listeners. The following topics may be helpful to you in developing your questions:

- Culture of the time period in which she reigned
- How she came to the throne
- Significant controversies or conflicts of her reign
- Significant accomplishments of her reign
- Obstacles she had to overcome
- Relationships with her subjects and with other monarchs
- The judgment of history on her reign and on her personal character.

When you have developed your list of questions, decide which of you will portray the queen and which will play the interviewer. If you are the queen, you may want to dress up in appropriate costume and assume the personality of the queen for the interview. Have fun!

Another book you may want to read:
My Life in Dog Years by Gary Paulsen

COMPOSING A LETTER TO THE EDITOR

Have you noticed some things that need fixing in your neighborhood or in your school? One way you can influence others to make changes is by writing a letter to the editor of your school or community newspaper. In your letter, you can define the problem, discuss its causes, and suggest possible solutions for the problem. A letter to the editor needs to be more forceful and persuasive than the movie review you wrote in the previous unit. Your letter to the editor must persuade your readers that the problem you are writing about is important and that they need to take action.

Professional Model

"Appearances Are Destructive" by Mark Mathabane

The fiercest competition among students is often not over academic achievements but over who dresses most expensively. And many students now measure parental love by how willing their mothers and fathers are to pamper them with money for the latest fads in clothes, sneakers, and jewelry.

Those parents without the money to waste on such meretricious extravagances are considered uncaring and cruel. They often watch in dismay and helplessness as their children become involved with gangs and peddle drugs to raise the money. When students are asked why they attach so much importance to clothing, they frequently reply that it's the cool things to do, that it gives them status and earns them respect. And clothes are also used to send sexual messages, with girls thinking that the only things that make them attractive to boys are skimpy dresses and gaudy looks, rather than intelligence and academic excellence…

The argument by civil libertarians that dress codes infringe on freedom of expression is misleading. We observe dress codes in nearly every aspect of our lives without any diminution of our freedoms—as demonstrated by flight attendants, bus drivers, postal employees, high school bands, military personnel, sports teams, Girl and Boy Scouts, employees of fast-food chains, restaurants, hotels.

In many countries where students outperform their American counterparts academically, school dress codes are observed as part of creating the proper learning environment. Their students tend to be neater, less disruptive in class and more disciplined, mainly

"The best way to escape from a problem is to solve it."
—Brendan Francis

Persuasive writing takes many forms. Besides writing a letter to the editor, here are forms that allow you to write persuasively.

- advertisement
- advice column
- book or movie review
- editorial
- petition
- proposal
- recommendation

LESSON OVERVIEW

COMPOSING A LETTER TO THE EDITOR
Professional Model, 817
Examining the Model, 818
Prewriting, 818
Finding Your Voice, 818
Identifying Your Audience, 819
Writing with a Plan, 819
Student Model—Graphic Organizer, 819
Drafting, 819
Self- and Peer Evaluation, 820
Student Model—Draft, 821
Revising and Proofreading, 821
Publishing and Presenting, 822
Student Model—Revised, 822
Reflecting, 823

Language, Grammar, and Style
Avoiding Double Negatives, 818
Identifying Double Negatives, 818
Fixing Double Negatives, 819
Using Double Negatives, 819

GUIDED WRITING *Software*

See the Guided Writing Software for an extended version of this lesson that includes printable graphic organizers, extensive student models and student-friendly checklists, and self-, peer, and teacher evaluation features.

INDIVIDUAL LEARNING STRATEGIES

MOTIVATION
Come into class irate, concerned, or vexed about an issue in your community. Express your position to students. Tell them you feel helpless and ask their advice on what you can do. Write students' suggestions on the board. Someone is bound to suggest writing an editorial. Circle that suggestion and say that that is what you are going to focus on in this unit's Guided Writing lesson.

READING PROFICIENCY
Have students apply the SQ3R method to reading the lesson. Refer students to the Language Arts Survey 1.13, "Strategies for Reading to Learn: SQ3R."

INDIVIDUAL LEARNING STRATEGIES

ENGLISH LANGUAGE LEARNING
See strategies for Reading Proficiency above that will also benefit students who are English language learners. Non-native speakers might be interested in writing a letter to the editor of a newspaper in their native country. Students should be encouraged to share their letters with the class.

SPECIAL NEEDS
Students may need help completing their Graphic Organizer. Pair them with a more proficient student who can help them work through the chart modeled on page 819.

(Continued on page 818)

Examining the Model

Some students will need help with vocabulary presented in the Professional Model. Encourage students to use context clues to estimate word meaning. Refer students to the Language Arts Survey 1.16, "Using Context Clues to Estimate Word Meaning." Words that students cannot guess from context can be looked up in the dictionary. Students might benefit from reading the Language Arts Survey 1.17, "Using a Dictionary."

Prewriting

FINDING YOUR VOICE. Encourage students to read the Language Arts Survey 2.5, "Finding Your Voice," and 3.3, "Register, Tone, and Voice."

Language, Grammar, and Style

Avoiding Double Negatives
LESSON OVERVIEW
In this lesson, students will be asked to do the following:
- Identify Double Negatives, 818
- Fix Double Negatives, 819
- Use Double Negatives, 819

INTRODUCING THE SKILL. Point out that a double negative makes a positive statement. "I don't got no lunch money" means "I have some lunch money." Double negatives are an example of nonstandard English.

PREVIEWING THE SKILL. Refer students to the Language Arts Survey 3.25, "Working with Negatives."

PRACTICING THE SKILL. For additional practice, have students work through the exercise in the following section of the Language, Grammar, and Style Resource located in the Teacher's Resource Kit: 3.25, "Working with Negatives."

"It is often wonderful how putting down on paper a clear statement of a case helps one to see, not perhaps the way out, but the way in."

—C. Benson

Language, Grammar, and Style
Avoiding Double Negatives

A negative is a "no" word. Using two negatives in a sentence when only one is needed is called using a double negative. Some languages, including Spanish, use double negatives. In these languages, using a double negative in a sentence is correct. Standard English, however, does not use a double negative in a given sentence.

Check your writing to be sure that you have not used a negative word such as *not, nobody, nothing, hardly, barely, can't, doesn't, won't, isn't,* or *aren't* with another negative word. Change double negatives by replacing one of the negative words in the sentence with a positive word.

IDENTIFYING DOUBLE NEGATIVES. In the examples below, circle the negatives that appear in each sentence. Identify which sentences are incorrect

818 *UNIT ELEVEN*

because their minds are focused more on learning and less on materialism. It's time Americans realized that the benefits of safe and effective schools far outweigh any perceived curtailment of freedom of expression brought on by dress codes.

Examining the Model
Whether or not a person agrees with Mathabane, it's hard to ignore his argument that schools should have dress codes. Why? Mathabane draws his readers into examining the problem and considering his solution.

Look at the opening statement. Mathabane clearly defines the problem—the competition caused by expensive clothing. His next statement adds a corollary problem caused by the competition—many students measure love by the money their parents spend on them. Do these statements cause a reaction in you? The statements command attention, not because they are flamboyant, but because they are straightforward, recognizable truths.

Next, Mathabane sets out the problem's consequences, serious consequences that are hard to ignore: the perception that parents who are unwilling or unable to spend the money are uncaring, the possibility that students will become involved with gangs and drugs to raise money to buy clothes, the false notion that students become convinced that their status and respect depends on clothing, the way that the emphasis on clothes makes people think physical appearance is more important than intelligence and academic excellence.

Mathabane identifies a major reason why some people are willing to overlook the problem and its consequences—dress codes infringe upon personal freedom. He refutes this with specific, verifiable proof that the reasoning is unfounded. He also identifies the root cause—materialism. Then he offers a solution and supports it with evidence that the solution works.

Prewriting
FINDING YOUR VOICE. Since you are trying to influence others to make changes, you will want to use a compelling voice. Your voice needs to be persuasive, but it must also be reasonable, honest, and straightforward.

Look at the two sentences below. Which one uses a compelling, reasonable, and honest voice?

Students in many countries wear uniforms, and they perform better academically than American students.

Wearing uniforms will definitely make you a great student.

Think about a problem for which you are convinced you know the answer. On your own paper, practice writing several sentences that are compelling, reasonable, and honest statements about the problem and its solution.

INDIVIDUAL LEARNING STRATEGIES

ENRICHMENT
In small groups, have students read several letters to the editor in your local paper and identify the thesis statement in each one. Then students can discuss the problem, consequences, causes, and solutions for each letter. Students might fill out a graphic organizer like the one modeled on page 819 for each letter.

IDENTIFYING YOUR AUDIENCE. Plan on sending your letter to a local or school newspaper. Your readers may be both students and adult members of the community. As you write, think about the information that is appropriate for this audience. What information will your audience need to understand the problem and your solution? What objections might they raise to your solution? What proofs for your solution will be most effective?

WRITING WITH A PLAN. You may already have a problem that you would like to address. Joseph wasn't sure what to write about so he brainstormed a list of ideas with his classmates. He used the three most interesting topics on his brainstorming list to fill in the graphic organizer below. He then decided to write about a problem in his community.

You can use the same process. First, brainstorm a list of topics with your classmates. Next, copy the graphic organizer onto your own paper. Fill in the organizer with the three most interesting topics on your list. List consequences, causes, and best solutions for the problems. Then decide which topic you could write about most persuasively in a letter to the editor.

Student Model—Graphic Organizer

Problem ➜	Consequences ➜	Causes ➜	Solutions
dangerous intersection	someone could get killed	cars speed, run lights	overpass

To write a convincing letter to the editor, Joseph started by writing a thesis statement. A thesis statement is the main idea of the letter. Joseph wrote this thesis statement.

The intersection at I-29 and University needs to be safer for bikers and other people using the crosswalk there.

In the rest of his letter, Joseph continued to define the problem, identified its causes, and suggested two solutions.

Drafting

Use the information in your graphic organizer to guide you as you write your rough draft of your letter. Do not focus at this point on the details of spelling, grammar, usage, and mechanics. Instead, focus on getting your ideas down on paper.

Start by writing your **thesis statement**. Add statements that help to clarify and define the problem. Next, identify the consequences and the causes of the problem. Finally, offer your solution. If part of your solution includes a request for your readers to contact an agency about a problem, provide the

---

because they have double negatives. Then identify the correct sentences that use single negatives.

Pat won't go nowhere without his books.
Pat won't go anywhere without his books.

I don't have no idea.
I don't have any idea.

Jonas can't remember anything about the accident.

Jonas can't remember nothing about the accident.

FIXING DOUBLE NEGATIVES.
Look at the sentences below from Joseph's rough draft. Fix any double negatives by replacing one of the negatives in the sentence with a positive word. You may need to reword the sentence. Then check to see how the writer fixed the sentences in the final copy.

The highway is barely impossible to cross, even with the new traffic signals.

And no police aren't around to enforce the traffic laws.

When a bike meets with a car, it hardly isn't likely that the biker will survive.

USING DOUBLE NEGATIVES.
Examine each sentence in your letter to the editor. Check to see if you have used

continued on page 820

GUIDED WRITING **819**

IDENTIFYING YOUR AUDIENCE. Have students read the Language Arts Survey 2.4, "Identifying Your Audience."

WRITING WITH A PLAN. Some students will have difficulty writing a thesis statement. You might model three topics, filling out a graphic organizer like the one modeled on page 819 and writing a thesis statement for each one. The more examples of thesis statements students see, the more likely they will be able to write one of their own. Once students have identified their topic, have them write a focused freewrite. Refer students to the Language Arts Survey 2.12, "Freewriting."

GRAPHIC ORGANIZER

See the Guided Writing Resource 7.11 for a blackline master of the Graphic Organizer for this lesson.

Drafting

Tell students to use their completed Graphic Organizer modeled on page 819 to help them make sure they incorporate the problem, consequences, causes, and solutions in their draft. Have students write a discovery draft in which they do not focus on spelling grammar, usage, and mechanics. Students might benefit from reading the Language Arts Survey 2.31, "Drafting." Encourage students to use transitions to link their ideas; refer students to the Language Arts Survey 2.35, "Using Transitions Effectively."

---

any double negatives. Change double negatives by replacing one of the negative words in the sentence with a positive word.

....

For help understanding how a thesis statement works, see the Language Arts Survey 2.25, "Writing a Thesis Statement." For help in supporting your ideas, see the Language Arts Survey 2.26, "Writing Main Ideas and Supporting Details."

"My experience of the world is that things left to themselves don't get right."

—*Thomas Henry Huxley*

address and telephone number of that agency. Make it as easy as possible for your readers to respond and help be part of the solution you suggest.

Remember that you are writing for a real newspaper. This is your chance to influence others and bring about change. Express your opinion with a compelling, reasonable, and honest voice and support your ideas by offering facts and listing solutions.

Self- and Peer Evaluation

After you finish your rough draft, complete a self-evaluation of your writing. Since your goal is for others to read your letter and be motivated to make changes because of it, try to get one or two peer reviews.

As you evaluate your letter, answer the following questions. Take notes on your rough draft to use later when you write your final copy.

Letter Content

- How convincing is the letter?
- What improvements might be needed in the thesis statement to more clearly identify and define the problem?
- What consequences are identified? How seriously will the reader view these consequences? What additional consequences might be included?
- What causes are identified? How factual are the causes? What additional causes might be included?
- How does the letter refute other solutions that readers may have to offer?
- Which words and sentences present the most honest, reasonable, and convincing voice? Which words and sentences present the least honest, reasonable, and convincing voice?
- What action to solve the problem does the letter suggest?
- Check each sentence for double negatives. How would the sentences be rewritten correctly?
- Check the letter for a proper heading, inside address, salutation, body, complimentary closing, and signature.

After completing his self-evaluation and considering the comments from a peer's evaluation, Joseph made several changes in his letter to the editor.

Student Model—Draft

```
3608 20th Street South
Fargo, ND  58104

September 27, 1999

[address here]                    I know what you
                                  mean about this
                                  problem!
To the Editor:

    The intersection at I-29 and
University needs to be a safer place
for bikers and other people using the
crosswalk there. A few years ago, it
was easy to cross the highway to get to
the biking trails. But now, with the
way everything is being built up so
quickly, the highway is barely
impossible to cross, even with the new  cars or
traffic signals. No cars are expecting    drivers?
to stop, and sometimes they don't. They
actually run the red light. My friends
and I have seen this happen four times
in the last two weeks. And no police      fix
aren't around to enforce the traffic    no / aren't
laws. If something isn't done, someone
is going to have a serious accident.
When a bike meets with a car, it hardly
isn't likely that the biker will    fix
                                hardly / isn't
survive. Unless something is done soon,
there's going to be a bad accident.       offer
                                          solution
Respectfully,
                        Mention lights
                        and signs.
Joseph Johnson
```

Revising and Proofreading

Look at your self- and peer evaluations. Use your notes and your peers' comments to make decisions about how to revise your letter. If there are any gaps in the letter, go back and fill them in. Take out any information that you feel distracts from the letter. Next, proofread your revised draft for errors in spelling, grammar, usage, and mechanics. Last, try reading your letter aloud. Does it say what you want it to say?

Joseph's final letter corrected some of the problems in his first draft.

"You never know what you can do until you have to do it."
—Betty Ford

TEACHING NOTE

Have students compare the Student Model—Draft on page 821 with the final version presented on page 822. Ask students to answer the following questions. What improvements did Joseph make in the Student Model—Revised? What did he add to his finished product? Why? What ideas do you have for further improving the final version of his letter to the editor?

Revising and Proofreading

Remind students that revising includes adding or expanding, cutting or condensing, replacing, and moving text. Have students read the Language Arts Survey 2.41, "Revising." A handout of the proofreading checklist found in the Language Arts Survey on page 888 is available in the Teacher's Resource Kit, Guided Writing Resource 2.45.

Publishing and Presenting

As students prepare their final copy, refer them to the Language Arts Survey 2.46, "Proper Manuscript Form." If students are maintaining a portfolio, you might have them include a copy of their letter to the editor in it. Students should read the Language Arts Survey 2.48, "Maintaining a Writing Portfolio."

Publishing and Presenting

You can write your final copy in ink or you may print it from a computer. For more information about writing a letter, see the Language Arts Survey 6.6, "Writing a Business Letter." Before you send your letter, check to see that you have included the following information:

- heading
- inside address
- standard salutation
- body
- complimentary closing
- signature

If you are writing a letter to the school newspaper, check to see if your teacher wants you to use your school address, rather than your home address. If you are sending your letter to a local newspaper, address the envelope neatly and include your return address on the upper left-hand corner of the envelope. Add postage and mail your letter promptly.

Student Model—Revised

```
3608 20th Street South
Fargo, ND  58104

September 27, 1999

Fargo Forum
101 5th Street North
Fargo, ND  58102

To the Editor:

     The intersection at I-29 and
University needs to be a safer place
for bikers and other people using the
crosswalk there. A few years ago, it
was easy to cross the highway to get to
the biking trails. But now, with the
way everything is being built up so
quickly, the highway is nearly
impossible to cross, even with the new
traffic signals. Few drivers expect to
stop, and sometimes they don't. My
friends and I have seen cars run the
red light four times in the last two
weeks.
     People complain about the police not
being around to enforce the traffic
laws. But they can't always be there.
Some people have suggested that more
signs could go up reminding drivers
that there is a traffic signal coming
up, and that there is a nearby bike
trail. There are some signs already,
however, and they don't seem to help
much. Other people have said that the
bikers and runners who cross there
should stop doing so. But the crosswalk
at I-29 and University is the only way
to access that part of the bike trail.
The Fargo bike trails are such a great
place to go that it isn't likely that
anyone will stop going there.
     The safest and best solution would
be to build a pedestrian/biker
overpass, where we can actually cross
```

on a bridge over the traffic. This would be expensive, but as the city keeps being developed, more people will use the trail system, not fewer. An overpass would be a long-term solution that would consider our community's growing needs. It would prevent traffic accidents and make the bike trails easier and safer to use. A pedestrian overpass would send a message to everyone that the city wants us to use the recreation system it has made, even as more people continue to move here.

The dangerous intersection at I-29 and University is a problem that won't go away unless we do something about it. If action isn't taken soon, someone is going to have a serious accident. When a bike meets with a car, it isn't likely that the biker will survive.

I would urge the city council and mayor to consider a biker/pedestrian overpass so we can get to our city's great trail system safely. Thank you for considering my suggestion.

Respectfully,

Joseph Johnson
Joseph Johnson

Reflecting

Have you ever met someone who could talk someone else into doing something that really wasn't honest or just? Have you ever watched a television commercial or read an advertisement in a magazine that persuaded you to buy something you didn't need or even want? What do you think the difference is between being good at persuasion and being a good persuader?

What kinds of things do you think someone who is good at persuasion might try to influence you to do? What kind of language might this person use? What kinds of causes might someone who is a good persuader take up? What kind of language might this person use?

• •

For more information about forming truthful statements, see the Language Arts Survey 5.2, "Distinguishing Fact from Opinion" and 5.3, "Avoiding False Arguments and Propaganda."

Reflecting

You might have students answer the questions in this section in a journal entry.

UNIT ELEVEN *review*

Words for Everyday Use

Check your knowledge of the following vocabulary words. Choose ten words that you would like to add to your own daily language. For each word, write a short sentence that includes the word in context. To review a word, look back to the page number indicated.

- aggressive (786)
- alliance (772)
- commotion (787)
- compressed (784)
- conclusive (801)
- conviction (801)
- curtail (795)
- deduce (802)
- dehydrate (783)
- derail (793)
- diffuse (802)
- diminution (794)
- directive (774)
- disseminating (782)
- distraught (793)

- duplicate (786)
- emaciate (783)
- enraged (776)
- forfeiting (776)
- gallantry (777)
- indignity (811)
- infringe (794)
- intolerable (775)
- lope (786)
- luminous (804)
- meretricious (794)
- monosyllabic (785)
- moot (782)
- ominous (775)
- opposition (775)

- permeate (811)
- prestige (771)
- principal (774)
- prolific (782)
- prosperity (772)
- quail (785)
- relative (782)
- ruthless (774)
- solely (811)
- synthetic (784)
- testify (801)
- translucent (777)
- virtually (784)
- void (805)

Literary Tools

Define each of the following terms, giving concrete examples when possible. To review a term, refer to the page number indicated.

- aim (768)
- analogy (799)
- biography (769)
- concrete details (769)

- expressive writing (809)
- hyperbole (780)
- persuasive essay (791)
- point of view (780)

- scientific writing (799)
- unity (809)

Reflecting on your reading

Genre

All the selections in this unit are part of the nonfiction genre. Look back through the unit and make a list of the selections you've read. Enter your list of selections in a chart like the one below. Then complete the other columns in the chart, looking back at the selections as needed. You may also want to review the Elements of Nonfiction on page 768.

Selection Title	Topic	Type of nonfiction	Purpose: what the author wanted to communicate	One thing you've learned
"Elizabeth"				
"Caesar"	adopting a Great Dane			
"Appearances are Destructive"				
"The Size of Things"				
"The Price of Freedom"		expressive essay		

Critical Thinking

Choose one selection in this unit and explain why you think the author chose to write the type of nonfiction he or she did. How is the type of nonfiction suited—or not suited—to the topic the author is writing about? What do you think the author's main purpose for writing is? Identify the mode of writing the author uses in his or her selection. Is the author effective in accomplishing his or her purpose for writing? Why, or why not?

UNIT SKILLS OUTLINE

Literary and Media Skills and Concepts

Writing Skills and Concepts

Language, Grammar, and Style

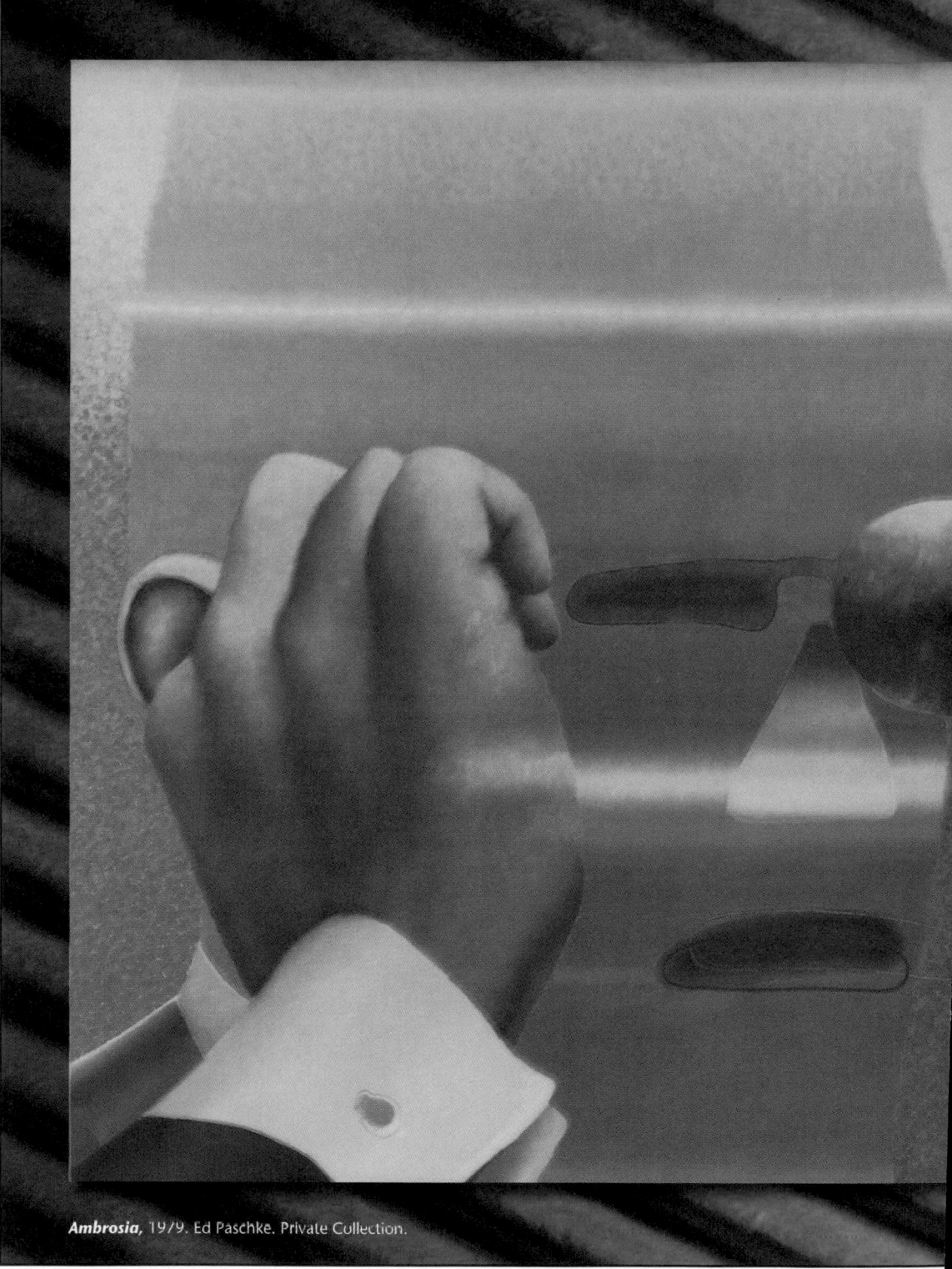

Ambrosia, 1979. Ed Paschke. Private Collection.

GOALS/OBJECTIVES

Studying this unit will enable students to
- enjoy reading informational and visual media and related literature
- define and identify examples of different words related to visual and informational media, such as *caption, graph, key, label,* and *table*
- engage in a meaningful independent reading

experience with a Newbery-award winning book and book club activity
- create a poster in which they provide visual information and analyze cause and effect
- distinguish between active and passive voice, and demonstrate the ability to use active voice effectively

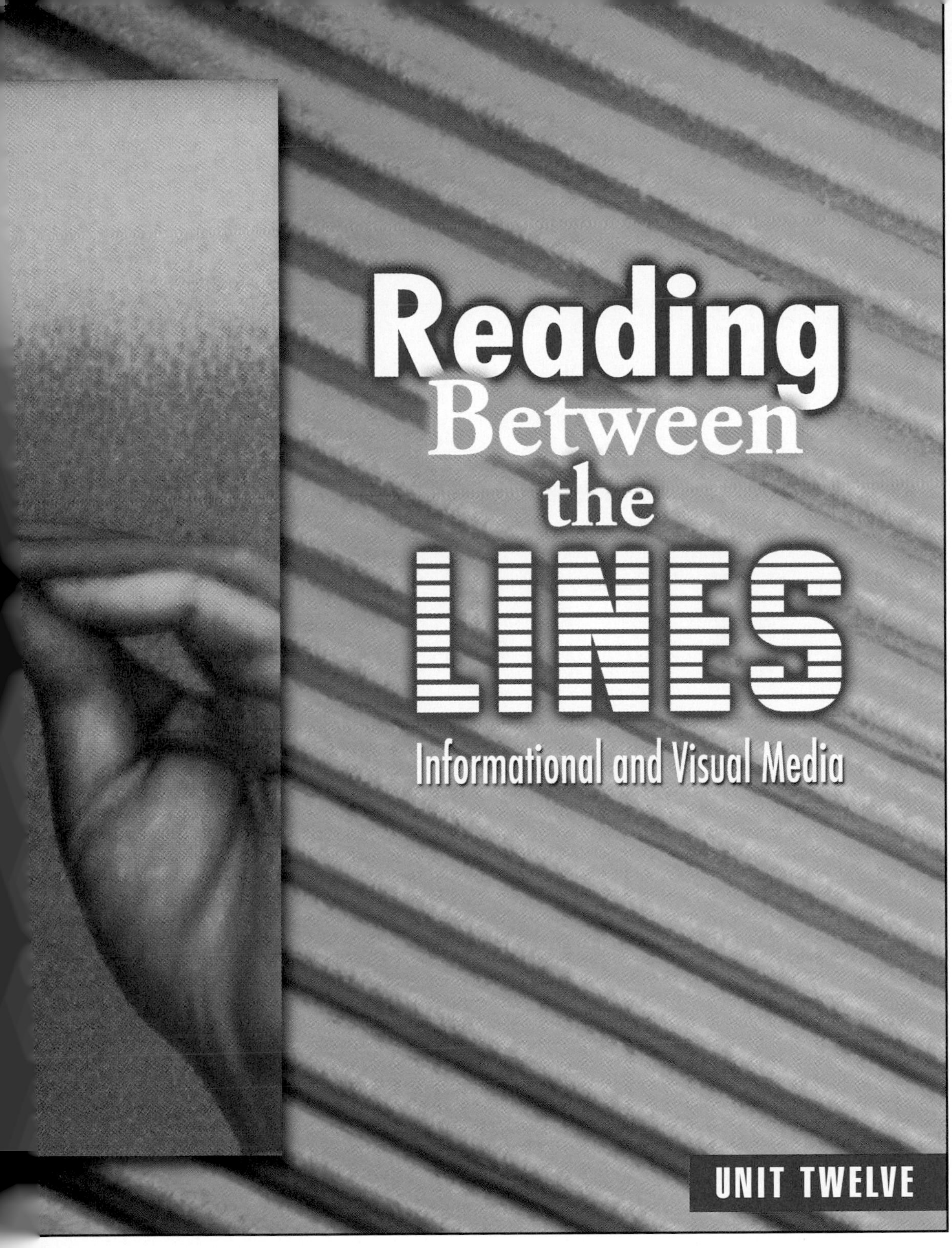

Reading Between the LINES

Informational and Visual Media

UNIT TWELVE

ELEMENTS *of* VISUAL AND INFORMATIONAL MEDIA

CHART. A **chart** is a visual representation of data that is intended to clarify, highlight, or put a certain perspective on the information presented. There are many types of charts each with a different purpose or style. Types include *line charts*, such as a time line; *flow charts*, such as a progress chart; *organizational charts*, such as a bubble chart; *matrix charts or tables, pie charts*, as well as many others, including variations of all of these.

TABLE. A **table** is a type of chart, also called a *matrix chart*, in which data is placed by matching it with vertical and horizontal categories. Before calculators were invented, many people used multiplication tables instead of calculators to multiply numbers. If you were going to multiply 6 and 9, you would look up the horizontal row for 6 and the vertical column for 9. The number at the intersection of the two categories would be the answer for that multiplication.

GRAPH. A **graph** is a rectangular grid—with horizontal and vertical scales of numbers—that demonstrates change in a set of numbers. The horizontal and vertical scales have *axes* (plural of *axis*) that mark the zero value for that scale and thus cross at the point (0,0), called the *origin*. The horizontal axis is usually called the *x-axis*, and the vertical, the *y-axis*. Graphs have a *coordinate system* using numbers to indicate a point on the two axes. For example, a point with x-axis value 7 and y-axis value 3 would be located at the coordinates (7,3). The most common graph has a value scale (such as height) on the y-axis and time on the x-axis. This sort of graph can, for example, show how much a child grows in a year. The vertical column is marked with height in inches or centimeters, and the horizontal row is marked with the time in months. To figure out the height at a certain month, you simply go to that month on the x-axis and follow the column up until you get to the line of the graph. The value there will be the height of the child at that time.

KEY. A **key** is a guide that aids in interpreting and identifying significant marks, especially on a map. Map keys are most often found in boxes in the corners or by the edges of maps. They contain explanations of map symbols and marks, such as boundary lines, roads, types of terrain such as deserts and forests, and other places of significance depending on the map's intended function. Keys can also be included on graphs, charts, diagrams, and tables, serving a similar function as those on maps.

LEGEND. Similar to a key, a **legend** assists the reader in interpreting a map, graph, chart, diagram, or table by giving the title and subject of the graphic and explaining its significant symbols.

MAP. A **map** is a representation, usually on a surface such as paper or a sheet of plastic, of a certain geographic area, showing various significant features of that area, depending on the purpose of the map. There are many different kinds of maps, including world, country, state, local, marine (of a body of water), topographical (of elevation), road, trail, and underwater. Maps can also be made of things other than the land, such as star maps, maps of the body, maps of the brain and other organs, or maps of the inner workings of machinery. Maps often have a key or legend to assist in their interpretation.

ILLUSTRATION. An **illustration** is a photograph, drawing, or diagram that serves to make a concept clearer by providing a visual example. For example, an encyclopedia entry for the wooly mammoth would have a drawn illustration of what scientists think the mammoth looked like, and perhaps a photo illustration of a real fossilized mammoth skeleton.

DIAGRAM. A **diagram** is an illustration that serves to explain a concept or process, including the arrangement and relations of the various parts of the concept, object, or process.

PERSPECTIVE. **Perspective** is the technique of representing, in an image on a flat surface, the size and distance of objects as they might appear to the eye. This technique is achieved by making the lines of the image converge on one or two points to give the effect of depth—the "3-D" effect. Alternately, *perspective* can mean the point of view from which something is seen or understood.

DISTORTION. **Distortion** is the quality or state of having been twisted out of normal, natural, or original shape, or out of true meaning or proportion. For example, photographs can be distorted to emphasize or shrink elements or to make the image fuzzy or broken, among other effects. Computers are sometimes used to distort pictures for dramatic or humorous effect. *Distortion* can also be an altering of the truth of a piece of information, such as exaggerating a fact or a number.

INTERNET. The **Internet** is a vast system of interconnected computer networks. Network administrators cooperate and use certain *protocols*—or codes for working together—in order to allow information to pass among various incompatible systems. One of those protocols is HyperText Transport Protocol (http), which begins the most common site addresses on the Internet.

- *Search Engines* are the tools of choice for navigating the massive, ever-growing Internet. A search engine is a listing of sites, registered in the browser's directory by the site's owner, which can be searched by entering keywords, or topics, pertaining to your subject. Engines can contain tens of millions of sites and are updated constantly.

- *Surfing* is a slang term that simply means browsing through Internet sites. It probably comes from the term *channel surfing*, which originated with the popularity of cable television. Cable gave people so many viewing choices that they would skip from channel to channel, "surfing" the stations for something interesting to watch. The Internet gives an enormous selection of topics and Web sites, and thus people end up "channel surfing" the Internet, much as they do with cable.

INTERNET RESOURCES

The Language Arts Survey at the back of this textbook offers additional resources about the Internet. Refer students to 5.25, "Using the Internet," 5.26, "Browsing versus Searching on the Internet," 5.28, "Using Boolean Search Strategies," 5.29, and "Evaluating Information and Media Sources."

Checking Your Reading

Fill in the blanks using the following terms. You may not use every term, and you may use some terms more than once.

> distortion   map(s)   perspective
> diagram(s)   advertising   table(s)
> key   Internet

1. Most often found in boxes in the corners or by the edges of a document, the **key** is a guide that helps readers interpret and identify significant marks.
2. Before calculators were invented, many people used multiplication **tables** instead of calculators to multiply numbers.
3. **Distortion** causes something to be twisted out of normal, natural, or original shape, or in the case of a piece of information, out of its true meaning.
4. **Diagrams** are similar to illustrations, but they show processes or concepts and help explain how the various parts of a concept or process work together. For instance, a new computer might include one to show how the monitor, keyboard, and CPU should be connected.
5. There are many different kinds of **maps**, including ones that show geographical details of countries, states, bodies of water, planets and stars, or even the brain.

Short Answer

1. Say that on November 1, you planted a tomato plant that was four inches tall, and then you measured it every month for five months. In November, it grew 2 inches; in December, it grew 1 inch; in January, it grew 3 inches; in February, it grew 4 inches; and in March, it grew 3 inches. Make a graph that shows how much the plant grew each month and how tall it would be on April 1. *Responses will vary.*
2. Make a time line that illustrates the major occurrences in your life for the past week. Remember that a time line does not include a great deal of detail but must show the highlights of each day. *Responses will vary.*
3. Draw a simple illustration of your pencil or pen and label the parts. *Responses will vary.*

WEB PAGES. **Web pages** are the basic unit of the World Wide Web, an organizational structure that includes a large part of what is offered on the Internet. World Wide Web page addresses start with http://www.sitename. Their main purpose is to provide information, entertainment, or advertising. These electronic "pages" contain text, pictures, and sometimes animations related to a particular topic. A *web site* is a collection of pages grouped together to organize the information offered by the person, company, or group that owns it.

- The suffix of a web page, indicates what type of person or group owns the page. The suffixes ".com" or ".net" are most often commercial organizations, though they can be private individuals as well. The suffix ".org" is used for not-for-profit organizations; ".gov" indicates a government site, and ".co.uk" uses the code for another country, in this case the United Kingdom.

- Web pages can contain "links," or connections to other pages within the site or completely different sites altogether. These connections are mostly in the form of "hotlinks" or "hyperlinks," which are addresses signaled by underlined blue text.

- Web sites, and their pages, are all collected under a domain, the name of the parent site that they belong to. For instance, rapper/actor Will Smith has his own official web site with its own domain, www.willsmith.net. Geocities, at www.geocities.com, is a domain that houses many web sites and pages under its name.

COMPUTER SOFTWARE. **Computer software** consists of programs and data that allow a computer to perform various functions. The actual physical components of the computer, such as the monitor and computer chips, are called *hardware*, in which "hard" implies that these are physical things that can be touched. Because programs and data are series of electrical impulses with no real physical substance, they are called "soft"ware.

NEWS ARTICLES. **News articles** are informational pieces of writing about a particular topic, issue, event, or series of events. News articles can be found in newspapers, magazines, journals, and Internet sites. Broadcast reporters on the radio and on television verbally present forms of news articles.

ADVERTISING. **Advertising** is the use of media—television, radio, Internet pages, newspapers, magazines, and other publishing formats—to promote a product or service. The intent of advertising is, in most cases, to get a product name out and into the minds of consumers so that they buy the product.

VISUAL ARTS. The **visual arts** include objects that may be two dimensional or three dimensional, stationary or moving. Forms of art included painting, sculpture, drawing, printmaking, collage, photography, video, computer-assisted art, and other forms. Art is a two-part process consisting of the creation by the artist and the interpretation by the viewer. It conveys meaning in ways that draw differing interpretations from different viewers. Concepts and uses of art differ greatly throughout the world and throughout history, but every culture has created objects that have no practical function other than to be visually pleasing and to convey ideas or meaning to viewers.

Prereading

VARIATIONS IN VITAL SIGNS BY AGE
TEMPERATURE CONVERSIONS

Reader's Resource

- **MATH CONNECTION.** The metric system, or International System (SI) was developed in France in the 1700s and has been used around the world ever since. The metric system is considered easy to use because the units of measure are defined as decimals and multiples of ten. The metric system uses degrees Celsius instead of degrees Fahrenheit to measure temperature. Conversely, the commonly used units of measure in the United States—inch, foot, yard, quart, gallon, pound, and degrees Fahrenheit—involve many different computations. The United States is the only industrialized nation that does not regularly use the metric system.

- **SCIENCE CONNECTION.** Vital signs are used to monitor the functions of the body. They include body temperature, pulse, respiration, and blood pressure. Body temperature is the balance between the heat produced by the body and the heat lost by the body. Pulse is a wave of blood created by the contraction of the left ventricle of the heart. In a healthy person, the pulse reflects the heartbeat—the rate of pulse is the same as the rate of contractions in the heart muscle. Respiration is the act of breathing. Resting respirations are measured in breaths per minute. Blood pressure is the measure of the pressure the blood exerts as it moves through the arteries. Systolic pressure is the pressure of the blood as a result of contraction of the ventricles of the heart. Diastolic pressure is the pressure when the ventricles are at rest and is lower than systolic pressure.

Critical Thinking

Look at the table and conversion formula on page 832 to answer these questions.

- A 12-year-old boy has a pulse rate of 107. Does his pulse fall in the normal or abnormal range for his age?
- In your own words, explain what the term "vital signs" means. What does "vital" mean? Rewrite the table name and the column headings to communicate the importance of this information.
- Look at the column called Respiratory rate/minute. Explain "rate/minute" in your own words.
- Why do you think the ratio for our respiratory rate changes as people age?

Reader's Journal

In what situations do you like to work with numbers? When do you find such work difficult?

Reader's TOOLBOX

TABLE. A **table** is a type of chart, also called a matrix chart, in which data is placed by matching it with vertical and horizontal categories. Data in a table is read in rows, which extend horizontally across the table, and columns, which run vertically down the table. The top row (and sometimes the left column) normally has headings that indicate the type of data shown in each corresponding cell, or square that holds data. Before calculators were invented, many people used multiplication tables instead of calculators to multiply numbers. If you were going to multiply 6 and 9, for example, you would look across the horizontal row for 6 and down the vertical column for 9. The number at the intersection of the two categories would be the answer for that multiplication. What do the headings across the top of the Variations in Vital Signs by Age table on page 832 tell you about the information contained in the table?

READER'S JOURNAL

Encourage students to talk or write about their fears and breakthroughs with math. Acknowledging students who are gifted with numbers is a good way to encourage those with logical-mathematical intelligence.

READERS TOOLBOX

Students should say that the headings of the table indicate which vital signs were measured. They also may note that the headings helped clarify what "vital signs" means.

CRITICAL THINKING

- The boy's pulse rate falls outside the normal range for males of age 12.
- Students should say that vital signs are markers of health. They should understand that "vital" means "important" or "major." The rewritten title may be similar to "Changes in Important Health Indicators by Age." The rewritten headings may be similar to the following: How Old; How Warm; Average Heart Beat Rate; Range of Heart Beat Rates; Breathing Rate; Blood Pumping Rate.
- Students may say that "rate/minute" means the number of times a person breathes each minute.
- Students may say that people's breathing slows down as their bodies (and lungs) grow bigger and can work more effectively.

VARIATIONS IN VITAL SIGNS BY AGE

Age	Average temperature	Resting pulse rate/min Average	Resting pulse rate/min Range	Respiratory rate/minute	Mean blood pressure
Newborn	36.1-37.7°C 97.0-100.0°F	125	70-190	30-80	78 systolic 42 diastolic
1 year	37.7°C 99.7°F	120	80-160	20-40	96 systolic 65 diastolic
2 years	37.2°C 98.9°F	110	80-130	20-30	100 systolic 63 diastolic
4 years	37.2°C 98.9°F	100	80-120	20-30	97 systolic 64 diastolic
6 years	37.0°C 98.6°F	100	75-115	20-25	98 systolic 65 diastolic
8 years	37.0°C 98.6°F	90	70-110	20-25	106 systolic 70 diastolic
10 years	37.0°C 98.6°F	90	70-110	17-22	110 systolic 72 diastolic
12 years	37.0°C 98.6°F	male: 85 female: 90	65-105 70-110	17-22	116 systolic 74 diastolic
14 years	37.0°C 98.6°F	male: 80 female: 85	60-100 65-105		120 systolic 76 diastolic
16 years	37.0°C 98.6°F	male: 75 female: 80	55-95 60-100	15-20	123 systolic 76 diastolic
18 years	37.0°C 98.6°F	male: 70 female: 75	50-90 55-95	15-20	126 systolic 79 diastolic
Adult	37.0°C 98.6°F	male: 70 female: 75	50-90 55-95	15-20	120 systolic 80 diastolic
>70 years	36.0°C 96.8°F	male: 70 female: 75	50-90 55-95	15-20	may increase

Data from *Nelson Textbook of Pediatrics, Growth and Development of Children, Pediatrics* (May 1977), National Heart, Lung, and Blood Institute, Task Force on Blood Pressure Control in Children: Report of the Task Force on Blood Pressure Control in Children.

IF YOU KNOW	MULTIPLY BY	TO GET

Temperature Conversions

degrees Fahrenheit —— first subtract 32 then multiply by .56 —— degrees Celsius

degrees Celsius —— first multiply by 1.8 then add 32 —— degrees Fahrenheit

Respond to the SELECTION

Which system of measurement do you think is better—the metric system or the U.S. units of measure? Support your answer with a solid argument.

Ernest Hemingway

A DAY'S *wait*

He came into the room to shut the windows while we were still in bed and I saw he looked ill. He was shivering, his face was white, and he walked slowly as though it ached to move.

"What's the matter, Schatz?"

"I've got a headache."

"You better go back to bed."

"No. I'm all right."

"You go to bed. I'll see you when I'm dressed."

But when I came downstairs he was dressed, sitting by the fire, looking a very sick and miserable boy of nine years. When I put my hand on his forehead I knew he had a fever.

"You go up to bed," I said, "you're sick."

"I'm all right," he said.

When the doctor came he took the boy's temperature.

"What is it?" I asked him.

"One hundred and two."

Downstairs, the doctor left three different medicines in different colored capsules with instructions for giving them. One was to bring down the fever, another a purgative, the third to overcome an acid condition. The germs of influenza can only exist in an acid condition, he explained. He seemed to know all about influenza and said there was nothing to worry about if the fever did not go above one hundred and four degrees. This was a light epidemic of flu and there was no danger if you avoided pneumonia.

Back in the room I wrote the boy's temperature down and made a note of the time to give the various capsules.

"Do you want me to read to you?"

"All right. If you want to," said the boy. His face was very white and there were dark areas under his eyes. He lay still in the bed and seemed very detached from what was going on.

I read aloud from Howard Pyle's *Book of Pirates*; but I could see he was not following what I was reading.

"How do you feel, Schatz?" I asked him.

"Just the same, so far," he said.

I sat at the foot of the bed and read to myself while I waited for it to be time to give another capsule. It would have been natural for him to go to sleep, but when I looked up he was looking at the foot of the bed, looking very strangely.

"Why don't you try to go to sleep? I'll wake you up for the medicine."

"I'd rather stay awake."

After a while he said to me, "You don't have to stay in here with me, Papa, if it bothers you."

"It doesn't bother me."

"No, I mean you don't have to stay if it's going to bother you."

I thought perhaps he was a little lightheaded and after giving him the perscribed capsules at eleven o'clock I went out for a while. It was a bright, cold day, the ground covered with a sleet that had frozen so that it seemed as if all the bare trees, the bushes, the cut brush and all the grass and the bare ground had been varnished with ice. I took the young Irish setter for a little walk up the road and along a frozen creek, but it was difficult to stand or walk on the glassy surface and the red dog slipped and slithered and I fell twice, hard, once dropping my gun and having it slide away over the ice.

We flushed a covey of quail under a high clay bank with overhanging brush and I killed two

Checking Your Reading

1. In the chart of Variations in Vital Signs by Age, what symbols are used to represent Fahrenheit and Celsius? **The C stands for Celsius, and the F stands for Fahrenheit.**
2. What is the average temperature, in Fahrenheit, of people over 6 years old? **The average temperature of people over 6 years old is 98.6 degrees Fahrenheit.**
3. Does a person's resting pulse rate tend to grow faster or slower as they age? **A person's resting pulse rate slows as he or she ages.**
4. In "A Day's Wait," the boy waited all day, expecting what to happen? **The boy expected to die.**
5. What mistake had the boy made that led him to that conclusion? **The boy had confused Celsius with Fahrenheit, and thought his fever would kill him.**

Reader's Toolbox

1. Pretend that you are helping someone learn how to multiply by 1, 2, and 3. Make a chart with 1-3 horizontally across the top and 1-3 vertically down the left side. Then fill each box to show the results of multiplying the numbers. For example, to see the result for multiplying 2 times 3, you should be able to look across the horizontal row for 2 and down the vertical column for 3 and the answer, 6, should occur where the two intersect. **Students' charts should be a multiplication table for the numbers 1, 2, and 3.**
2. When Sylvia and her friends designed a secret language, they used the same alphabet as English, but made each letter correspond to a letter in the alphabet three steps away. So, for example, D = A; O = L; and B = Y. Make yourself a conversion chart to decipher their language, and decode the following phrase: Zhofrph wr wkh foxe! **The answer is "Welcome to the club!"**

---

as they went out of sight over the top of the bank. Some of the covey lit in trees but most of them scattered into brush piles and it was necessary to jump on the ice-coated mounds of brush several times before they would flush. Coming out while you were poised unsteadily on the icy, springy brush they made difficult shooting, and I killed two, missed five and started back pleased to have found a covey close to the house and happy there were so many left to find on another day.

At the house they said the boy had refused to let anyone come into the room.

"You can't come in" he said. "You mustn't get what I have."

I went up to him and found him in exactly the position I had left him, white-faced, but with the tops of his cheeks flushed by the fever, staring still as he had stared at the foot of the bed.

I took his temperature.

"What is it?"

"Something like a hundred," I said. It was one hundred and two and four tenths.

"It was a hundred and two," he said.

"Who said so?"

"The doctor."

"Your temperature is all right," I said. "It's nothing to worry about."

"I don't worry," he said. "but I can't keep from thinking."

"Don't think," I said. "Just take it easy."

"I'm taking it easy," he said and looked straight ahead. He was evidently holding tight on to himself about something.

"Take this with water."

"Do you think it will do any good?"

"Of course it will."

I sat down and opened the *Pirate* book and commenced to read, but I could see he was not following, so I stopped.

"About what time do you think I'm going to die?" he asked.

"What?"

"About how long will it be before I die?"

"You aren't going to die. What's the matter with you?"

"Oh, yes, I am. I heard him say a hundred and two."

"People don't die with a fever of one hundred and two. That's a silly way to talk."

"I know they do. At school in France the boys told me you can't live with forty-four degrees. I've got a hundred and two."

He had been waiting to die all day, ever since nine o'clock in the morning.

"You poor Schatz," I said. "Poor old Schatz. It's like miles and kilometers. You aren't going to die. That's a different thermometer. On that thermometer thirty-seven is normal. On this kind it's ninety-eight."

"Are you sure?"

"Absolutely," I said. "It's like miles and kilometers. You know, like how many kilometers we make when we drive seventy miles in the car?"

"Oh," he said.

But his gaze at the foot of the bed relaxed slowly. The hold over himself relaxed too, finally, and the next day it was very slack and he cried very easily at little things that were of no importance. ∎

ABOUT THE RELATED READING

Ernest Hemingway (1899-1961) wrote a number of short stories and novels and is considered one of the greatest fiction writers of the 20th century. His novels include *The Old Man and the Sea, The Sun Also Rises, A Farewell to Arms,* and *For Whom the Bell Tolls.* Hemingway grew up in Oak Park, Illinois, with his parents and his five siblings. During World War II (1939-1945), an eye problem prevented him from joining the U. S. Army, so he served as an ambulance driver and soldier with the Italian army. Acclaims for Hemingway's work include a Pulitzer Prize in 1953 and a Nobel Prize for literature in 1954.

Investigate, Inquire, and Imagine

Recall: GATHERING FACTS

1a. What do the *C* and the *F* stand for in the Average temperature column?

2a. What column gives you information on the normal range of pulse rates?

3a. What row and column gives you information on the average respiratory rate for a 37-year-old man?

Analyze: TAKING THINGS APART

4a. According to this chart, newborn babies and the elderly are alike in one way and different in another. Explain the way they are alike and the way they are different.

Evaluate: MAKING JUDGMENTS

5a. What do the terms average, normal, and abnormal mean? What does it mean to be out of the average range?

→ Interpret: FINDING MEANING

1b. When Schatz is well, what should his temperature be?

2b. How can you expect your pulse rate to change when you are 16?

3b. For which group is pulse rate generally higher—teenage girls or teenage boys?

→ Synthesize: BRINGING THINGS TOGETHER

4b. In general, does pulse rate and blood pressure follow a similar pattern over the years? Explain your answer.

→ Extend: CONNECTING IDEAS

5b. If Schatz's temperature had reached 44 degrees Fahrenheit, what would that have meant for him? How would you explain to Schatz how doctors and nurses use tables of information?

Understanding Media

TABLE. A **table** is a type of chart, also called a matrix chart, in which data is placed by matching it with vertical and horizontal categories. Data in a table is read in rows, which extend horizontally across the table, and columns, which run vertically down the table. The top row (and sometimes the left column) normally has headings that indicate the type of data shown in each corresponding cell, or square that holds data. In what ways do these tables make it easier to read and interpret the data presented?

ANSWERS TO INVESTIGATE, INQUIRE, IMAGINE

RECALL
1a. The *C* in the Average temperature column stands for Celsius; the *F* stands for Fahrenheit.
2a. The right side of the third column gives information on the normal range of pulse rates.
3a. The fourth column and the twelfth row give the information for the average respiratory rate for a 37-year-old man.

INTERPRET
1b. When Schatz is well, his temperature should be 98.6 degrees Fahrenheit.
2b. Your pulse rate should go down about 5 beats per minute when you are 16.
3b. The pulse rate for teenage girls is generally higher.

ANALYZE
4a. Newborn babies and the elderly are alike in that their temperatures are generally lower than that of people of other ages. They are different in that their pulse rates and respiratory rates differ—newborns have much higher pulse rates and respiratory rates than people over 70.

SYNTHESIZE
4b. In general, pulse rates and blood pressure follow opposite patterns as people age. Pulse rates tend to decrease; blood pressure tends to increase.

EVALUATE
5a. Students may say that "average" and "normal" are similar in this context. "Abnormal" means "not normal." If a person's particular vital sign is outside the average range, that person is different from most people with regards to that particular vital sign. It could mean that the person is simply different or that the person may be ill.

EXTEND
5b. If Schatz's temperature had reached 44 degrees Fahrenheit, he would have been too cold to be alive. Students may say that doctors and nurses use tables of information for quick checks of information they need daily to do their jobs.

ANSWERS TO INVESTIGATE, INQUIRE, IMAGINE (CONT.)

Understanding Media
TABLE. Tables make it easier to read and interpret data because they organize the data in a clear format. The reader doesn't have to sift through words in a paragraph to find the particular number or piece of information that he or she is seeking.

Writer's Journal

1. Create a **chart** for Schatz that shows the Fahrenheit equivalents for at least ten different Celsius temperatures.

2. Write a **product description** for a thermometer that gives readings in both Fahrenheit and Celsius.

3. Write an **editorial article** for a newspaper, stating why a particular U.S. industry should use metric measurements instead of the traditional U.S. measurements.

Skill Builders

Applied English

CREATING A GRAPH. Using the data in the table entitled Variations in Vital Signs by Age, create a graph with a grid like the one shown. On the x-axis, copy the ages from the left-hand column of the table. Label that axis "Ages." Going up from the bottom of the y-axis, write the numbers 0, 5, 10, and so on, in increments of 5, to 80. Label that axis "Respiratory rate/min." Block in the ranges for each age level. What conclusions can you make about how respiratory rates fluctuate throughout life?

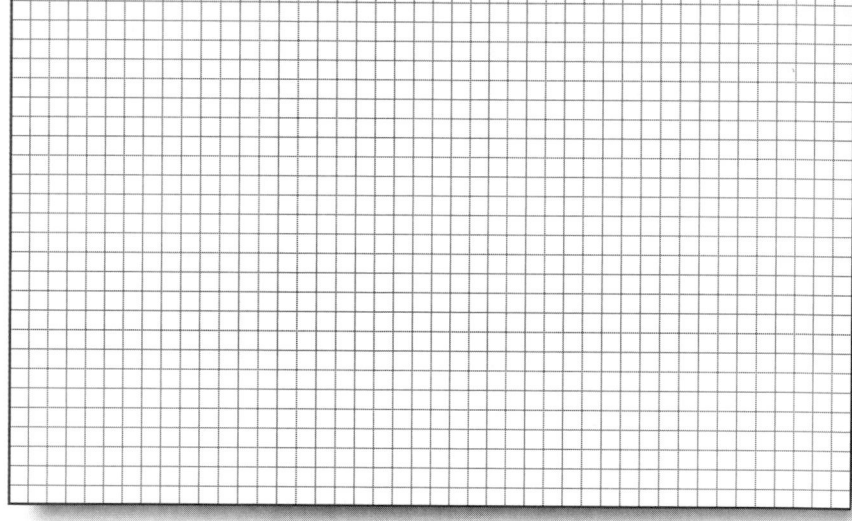

Prereading

Historical Photographs
by Arthur Rothstein

Reader's Resource

- **HISTORY CONNECTION.** During the 1930s, people throughout the United States experienced extreme poverty in what became known as the Great Depression. Because of a stock market crash, banks closed and credit became unavailable. People with little savings were unable to purchase goods. Farmers, could not afford to buy seed to plant crops.

- **SCIENCE CONNECTION.** In large parts of the Midwest, a lack of rain combined with over-farmed fields created a disaster. The drought dried up already scant crops and caused dust storms to take over fields and gardens. In the Oklahoma Dust Bowl, conditions were particularly bad. Cimarron County, in the Oklahoma Panhandle, stood as an example of all that could possibly go wrong in farming the western prairie. Dry dirt blew around sparse fields, blocked doorways, covered gardens, and caused many people to abandon their land.

- The lives of the residents of Cimarron County and other parts of the dust bowl were recorded in photographs during the 1930s. Photographers sent by the Resettlement Administration (1935–1937) and the Farm Security Administration (1937–1942) documented government programs that gave cash loans and helped construct housing. The photographers also recorded the lives of agricultural workers and urban and rural living conditions in the South and in the West.

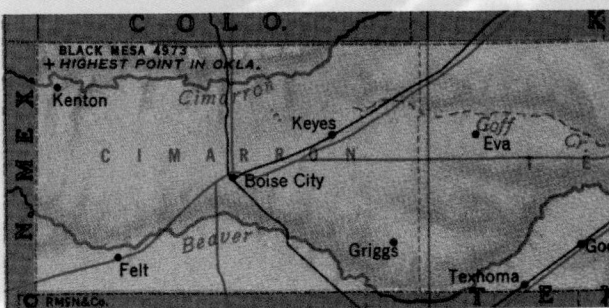

Cimarron County, Oklahoma

Reader's Journal

How do you face difficulties in your life? What strategies do you use?

Reader's TOOLBOX

AIM. In writing, an author's **aim** is his or her purpose or goal. Like writers, many photographers work to achieve a specific purpose. As government employees, Arthur Rothstein and other photographers documented the relief programs of the Farm Security Administration. Rothstein traveled in poor areas of the United States and took pictures of people living in poverty and of relief workers assigned to help them. Although his photographs appear to be unposed images, Rothstein often set them up to achieve a specific effect. What do you think Rothstein wanted these pictures to "say" to viewers? What was Rothstein's aim?

ADDITIONAL RESOURCES

UNIT 12 RESOURCE BOOK
- Selection Worksheet 12.2
- Selection Check Test 4.12.3
- Selection Test 4.12.4

READER'S JOURNAL

Students may want to keep a journal entry on this question private, depending on what they choose to focus on.

READER'S TOOLBOX

Students may say that Rothstein wanted these pictures to tell people how difficult life was in the Oklahoma Dust Bowl. They may say that Rothstein's aim was to show the problems people there faced and to create sympathy among those who saw his pictures.

CROSS-CURRICULAR ACTIVITIES

ARTS AND HUMANITIES. Have students work in pairs or small groups to research the history of photography. Have them explore what it was like to take a photograph—or pose for one—in the early days of photography, and the people who made a name for themselves. Possible early photographers to research include William Henry Fox Talbot, Louis Daguerre, Joseph Niepce, Julia Margaret Cameron, and Margaret Bouke White.

MATHEMATICS AND SCIENCES & APPLIED ARTS. Students can prepare a brief demonstration for the class on how a photographic invention works. Topics might include the darkroom process, different types of lenses, digital camera features, and the differences between color and black and white photography. They may want to compare earlier methods to current high-tech processes and investigate which processes produced the most desirable images. They may also want to investigate health risks of some of the earlier processes, such as working with certain types of chemicals.

Farmer and Sons Walking in the Face of a Dust Storm, 1936. Arthur Rothstein.

Farmer Pumping Water from a Well, 1936. Arthur Rothstein.

Dust Bowl Farmer Raising a Fence to Keep It from Being Buried under Drifting Sand,
1936. Arthur Rothstein.

Historical Photographs Arthur Rothstein

Critical Thinking

- Describe the scene in the top left image. What is happening? Where are the people going? What do you notice about the door?

- What is happening in the bottom left image? What is the man doing? What is he looking at?

- What is the man doing in the above photograph? What is the boy doing? What do you think is buried where the man is digging? How would you describe the photograph?

- In the top left picture, a man and two children are running in front of a building. They seem to be running toward the door of the building. Everywhere there is sandy dust, and the wind seems to be blowing very hard. The dust on the ground is so high that it covers the lower portion of the door. The door probably wouldn't open.
- In the bottom left image, a man is standing by a well. Water is coming out into a bucket and then into a wooden trough. Everywhere there is dust on the ground. The man seems to be waiting and he is looking off into the distance.
- In the top right photo, a man is digging with a big shovel. Dust covers the ground. A boy is sitting nearby and a cow is in the background. The boy seems to be digging with his hands. The man and boy seem to be trying to dig around the fence posts and wire to keep the fence above ground. It seems like a futile job.

CROSS-CURRICULAR ACTIVITIES

SOCIAL STUDIES. Encourage students to bring in different examples of documentary photographs from newspapers, newsmagazines, or online sources. Have them discuss what the news that each photograph conveys, including the who, what, why, where, when, and how of each story. What can the photograph depict that a written report cannot? What written words are needed to help the viewer understand what is happening in the photograph?

RESPOND TO THE SELECTION

As an alternate activity, you may want students to discuss what they think it would have been like living through the Dust Bowl, and what they would have done to survive the harsh circumstances.

SELECTION CHECK TEST 4.12.5 WITH ANSWERS

Checking Your Reading
1. What was Arthur Rothstein's job for the Farm Security Administration? **Rothstein took photographs to show the effects of the relief programs of the Farm Security Administration.**
2. What was happening to the farmers of the Midwest during the time when these photographs were taken? **Responses will vary, but the country was experiencing the Great Depression and, to compound the effects of the Depression, the region was experiencing a drought and farms were failing.**
3. What do the three photographs in this selection depict? *Responses will vary.*
4. What emotions do these photographs make you feel? *Responses will vary.*
5. How might these photographs help you understand these scenes better than a written account might? *Responses will vary.*

Reader's Toolbox
1. What is a writer's aim? **A writer's aim is his or her purpose or goal.**
2. How can a photographer's aim be like a writer's aim? **Responses will vary, but should suggest that photographers can take pictures to achieve a purpose or goal, just like writers can.**
3. Why did Rothstein often set up the photographs he took, rather than taking unposed pictures? **Responses will vary, but students should understand that Rothstein set up his photographs to show a particular effect.**

Respond *to the* SELECTION

What emotions do these photographs evoke? What are your impressions about the people in the photographs?

About *the* PHOTOGRAPHER

Arthur Rothstein was born in New York in 1915. While preparing for medical school, Rothstein ran into tuition problems. In 1935, he left college to join a colleague in what became the Farm Security Administration (FSA). He set up a photo lab and began going out on assignment, taking photographs for the agency. Rothstein's most memorable assignment was a trip in 1936 to the Dust Bowl, where he shot the photographs that appear here.

Rothstein left the FSA in 1940 and went to work for *Look* magazine. During his career, Rothstein served in World War II as a photographer, wrote *Photojournalism: Pictures for Magazines and Newspapers*, and taught college courses. He has also worked as associate editor of *Parade* magazine.

ABOUT THE RELATED READING ➤

This reading is from *Out of the Dust*, a novel written by **Karen Hesse** and published in 1997. The book, which won a Newbery Medal, has been described as a prose poem, because the book is written as a series of dated entries that resemble free-verse poems. Hesse has written a number of books, including *The Music of Dolphins, Phoenix Rising,* and *Letters from Rifka.*

Tested by Dust

While we sat
taking our six-weeks test,
the wind rose
and the sand blew
right through the cracks in the schoolhouse wall,
right through the gaps around the window glass,
and by the time the tests were done,
each and every one of us
was coughing pretty good and we all
needed a bath.

I hope we get bonus points
for testing in a dust storm.

April 1934

Beat Wheat

County Agent Dewey
had some pretty bad news.
One quarter of the wheat is lost:
blown away or withered up.
What remains is little more than
a wisp of what it should be.
And every day we have no rain,
more wheat dies.

County Agent Dewey says, "Soon
there won't be enough wheat
for seed to plant next fall."

The piano is some comfort in all this.
I go to it and I forget the dust for hours,
testing my long fingers on wild rhythms,
but Ma slams around in the kitchen
when I play
and after a while she sends me to the store.
Joe De La Flor doesn't see me pass him by;
he rides his fences, dazed by dust.
I wince at the sight of his rib-thin cattle.
But he's not even seeing them.
I look at Joe and know our future is
drying up
and blowing away with the dust.

April 1934

Banks

Ma says,
everything we lost
when the banks closed
'cause they didn't have enough cash to go
around,
all the money that's ours
is coming back to us in full.

Good.

Now we have money for a doctor
when the baby comes.

April 1934

Give Up on Wheat

Ma says,
"Try putting in a pond, Bayard.
We can fill it off the windmill.
We've got a good well."

Daddy grumbles, "The water'll seep
back into the ground
as fast as I can pump it, Pol.
We'll dry up our well
and then we'll have nothing."

"Plant some other things, then," Ma says.
"Try cotton,
sorghum. If we plant the fields in different
crops,
maybe some will do better,
better than wheat."

Daddy says,
"No.
It has to be wheat.
I've grown it before.
I'll grow it again."

But Ma says, "Can't you see
what's happening, Bayard?
The wheat's not meant to be here."

And Daddy says,
"What about those apple trees of yours, Pol?
You think they are?
Nothing needs more to drink than those two.
But you wouldn't hear of leveling your apples,
would you?"

Ma is bittering. I can see it in her mouth.
"A pond would work," she says,
sounding crusty and stubborn.

And Daddy says, "Look it, Pol, who's the farmer?
You or me?"

Ma says,
"Who pays the bills?"

"No one right now," Daddy says.

Ma starts to quaking but she won't let Daddy see.
Instead, she goes out to the chickens
and
her anger,
simmering over like a pot in an empty kitchen,
boils itself down doing chores.

April 1934

ADDITIONAL QUESTIONS AND ACTIVITIES

1. What happens while the speaker and her classmates are taking their six-weeks test?
2. What bad news does County Agent Dewey have? What is Joe Da La Flor doing when the speaker passes? Why doesn't he "see" anything?
3. What does Ma say about the money the family lost when the banks closed? Do you think she is right?
4. What suggestions does Ma give Pa about getting water and growing crops? Why does he disagree? Why does he think they should plant wheat?

Answers
1. A dust storm rises up during the test.
2. Joe Da La Flor doesn't see anything because he is lost in thoughts about how bad things are.
3. Ma says they are going to get it all back. Responses will vary.
4. She says that they should pump water with the well and that they should try growing a different crop. Pa disagrees because he thinks a well won't work and that nothing will grow any better than the wheat would. He wants to plant wheat because he has always grown wheat and knows how to plant it.

RECALL

1a. The people in the first picture are running.

2a. The man in the second photo is pumping water out, probably for irrigation.

3a. In the third picture, a man and a boy are digging out a fence to keep it from being buried by the blowing dust.

INTERPRET

1b. They seem to be struggling against the wind and running straight into it. They are leaning forward to brace themselves against the wind. The small child seems to be covering his eyes to keep out the blowing dust.

2b. The man seems to be waiting, perhaps for the weather and his circumstances to change. He seems to realize that his work is useless-no amount of water he can pump will keep away the wind and dust.

3b. This action would only provide a temporary solution to the problem.

ANALYZE

4a. The three photos are similar in that they are set in the same time and place and because they all portray people suffering because of their circumstances. They differ in that the first photo shows people running; the other two show people working and trying to fight the dust and its effects.

SYNTHESIZE

4b. The photos all seem to convey a sense of despair and lack of hope due to the Oklahoma Dust Bowl's toll. Students may say the pictures convey sadness, frustration, longing, or desperation.

EVALUATE

5a. Students may say that the photos are very effective in conveying ideas. They may say that the photos speak to the viewer by offering a slice of the life of a person or persons whose experiences are very different from the viewer's.

EXTEND

5b. The photographs convey similar ideas to those in the excerpts from Out of the Dust. The similar themes include poverty, the never-ending blowing dust, the way the blowing dust feels, the lack of rain, the futility of irrigation. Photos give viewers a visual glimpse into the lives of others; written words give readers a mental picture of these lives. Each form provides different details.

Investigate, Inquire, and Imagine

Recall: GATHERING FACTS

1a. What are the people doing in the first photograph?

2a. Describe the man's task in the second image.

3a. What is happening in the third photograph?

→ **Interpret:** FINDING MEANING

1b. How does their movement appear to be a struggle? Why are they leaning forward?

2b. How does the man seem to view his circumstances and his task?

3b. How does this action provide a solution to the problem?

Analyze: TAKING THINGS APART

4a. What do these three images have in common? How do they differ from one another?

→ **Synthesize:** BRINGING THINGS TOGETHER

4b. What message do these photographs have for the viewer? Do they convey hope, anger, fear, happiness, humor, sadness, frustration, or some other emotion? Explain your answer.

Evaluate: MAKING JUDGMENTS

5a. How effective are the photos in conveying an idea? How well do they speak to the viewer? Which of the three is the most powerful? Why?

→ **Extend:** CONNECTING IDEAS

5b. In what ways do the photographs convey the ideas and themes introduced in *Out of the Dust*? How do the two forms—photography and expressive writing—differ in their treatment of the same subject matter? How are they similar?

Understanding Media

AIM. An author's **aim** is his or her purpose or goal. Like writers, many photographers work to achieve specific purposes. Rothstein posed his subjects in many of the photographs he took. What do you think he achieved by asking the people to pose in a certain way? How would the photographs have been different if he had simply taken them while people were working and going about everyday life? What was Rothstein's aim?

ANSWERS TO UNDERSTANDING MEDIA

AIM. Students may say that Rothstein could create even more emotion in photos that he posed. By asking people to move or hold their faces in certain ways, he probably was able to achieve more troubling photos. The photos would have conveyed emotion even if they had not been posed but perhaps not as much. Rothstein's aim was to show people how difficult life was for those living in the Oklahoma Dust Bowl.

Writer's Journal

1. Write a set of **interview questions** that you might ask the subjects in Arthur Rothstein's photographs.

2. Write the copy for a 1930s **public service announcement** that explains the plight of the Dust Bowl farm families and asks for donations. Include a list of the items you think people might need.

3. Write a one-page **short story** based on one or two of Arthur Rothstein's photographs. Imagine the story is for young children who know nothing about this place or time period.

Skill Builders

Study and Research

STUDYING PHOTOGRAPHS. Access the collection "America from the Great Depression to World War II: Photographs from the FSA-OWI 1935–1945" at the Library of Congress Internet site. The collection is located at http://memory.loc.gov/ ammem/fsahtml/ and contains thousands of photographs you can view on a computer screen. Look at photographs from the time period taken by other well-known photographers, such as Dorothea Lange, Walker Evans, Howard Lieberman, Ben Shahn, and Gordon Parks. What is the style of each photographer? Whose photographs seem mostly documentary? Do any photographers take a more artistic approach? Which photographers tend to focus on people? Which focus mainly on places, scenes, or landscapes? What generalizations can you make about each photographer's work?

Applied English

WRITING DIRECTIONS. As an adult, you may have a job that requires you to travel. Imagine you are going on assignment to assess living conditions in the Oklahoma Panhandle region 75 years after the Great Depression. Locate Cimarron County, Oklahoma, on a map. Use road maps of North America or of the United States to find the best route from where you live to Boise City, the county seat of Cimarron County. Write out detailed directions for driving there. Use precise, detailed language in your directions.

Collaborative Learning

RESEARCHING HISTORY. In pairs or small groups, research the migrations caused by the drought and dust storms in the midwestern Dust Bowl. One or two students should examine the migration patterns of people who moved away from the southern part of the Dust Bowl, including Oklahoma, Texas, Kansas, and Colorado. The other student or students should look at the migration patterns of people in the northern midwest—Nebraska, Wyoming, and South Dakota. Compare and contrast your findings. How many people migrated? To where did the northeners migrate? To where did the southerners migrate? How was each group welcomed in its new location? Summarize your findings and your analysis of the research to present to the class.

ANSWERS TO SKILL BUILDERS

Study and Research
STUDYING PHOTOGRAPHS. Responses will vary, depending on the photographs the students choose. They should, however, provide enough details in their responses to be able to generalize about the style of each photographer.

Applied English
WRITING DIRECTIONS. Students may want to start this assignment by consulting the map of Cimarron County on page 837. They should then get a broader perspective of the county's location by locating it on a map of Oklahoma and then the United States. Using a road atlas would be helpful. For more information, see the Language Arts Survey 5.22, "Using Almanacs, Yearbooks, and Atlases."

Collaborative Learning
RESEARCHING HISTORY. Responses will vary, depending on the evidence students uncover. For more information, refer them to the Language Arts Survey 5.17-5.35, "Research Skills." (To evaluate this activity, see the Assessment Resource 4.10, Collaborative Learning Form, and 4.12, Project Evaluation Form.)

READER'S TOOLBOX

COHERENCE. The ideas appear in a progressive, chronological order, which helps the reader understand the process best. The author uses transitions to indicate when the next step is taking place. Some transitions he uses include first-stage valve; second-stage valve; as the diver inhales.

KEYS, CAPTIONS, AND LABELS. The key is at the bottom of the page. The captions are the sections entitled "Breathing In" and "Breathing Out." The labels identify each of the items in the diagrams.

CRITICAL THINKING

• The air in the diver's lungs is at about the same pressure as the water pressure. The air in the cylinder is at a higher pressure.
• The aqualung has a regulator that reduces the pressure of the air in the cylinder.
• As the diver breathes in, the diaphragm allows air to move from the cylinder through the air tubes and to the diver. As the diver breathes out, the diaphragm shuts off the incoming air and a valve opens to let the exhaled air out into the water.

READER'S JOURNAL

Encourage students to talk or write about ways in which they learn best. Are they visual learners? hands-on learners?

DIAGRAM

Reader's Resource

• **TECHNOLOGY CONNECTION.** Like David Macaulay's earlier books, *The New Way Things Work* describes the technology behind a wide array of machines, information systems, and devices that people use. After examining the fundamental concepts on which many technological developments are based, the book offers detailed explanations about how different things operate. The visual format allows these explanations to show cause-and-effect relationships, links among components, and the processes used in different devices and systems.

• **SPORTS CONNECTION.** According to the Professional Association of Dive Instructors, there are about six million active scuba divers worldwide. A person must pass a certification course before taking a dive. Several organizations offer this certification. A course consists of classroom study, hands-on work with gear in a pool or confined area of water, and monitored practice dives. To become certified, students must pass a written test, a swimming test, and four open-water diving tests.

Prereading

"THE AQUALUNG"

by David Macaulay

Reader's TOOLBOX

COHERENCE. Coherence is the logical arrangement of ideas in speech or writing. Writers achieve coherence by presenting their ideas in a logical order and by using transitions to show how their ideas are connected to one another. *Transitions* are words—such as *therefore, consequently,* or *beforehand*—or phrases—such as *as a result* or *in the meantime*—that connect ideas and show relationships between them. Examine how the concepts involved in the workings of an aqualung are presented here. How does the order in which the ideas appear help you understand the process described? Where does the author use transitions? Identify some of the transitions used.

KEYS, CAPTIONS, AND LABELS. A **key** is a guide that aids in interpreting and identifying significant marks, especially on a map. Keys can also be found on graphs, charts, diagrams, and tables. They explain symbols and marks by providing a clear interpretation for each. *Captions* explain a visual item or graphic in writing. *Labels*—simple headers or titles within a graphic that give names to different parts—also assist readers in reading and understanding the graphic. Identify each these guiding tools in the diagram at right.

Critical Thinking
• How does water pressure compare to the pressure of the air in a diver's lungs? How does the air pressure inside the cylinder compare to the water pressure?
• What reduces the pressure of the air coming from the cylinder?
• What happens as the diver breathes in? What happens as the diver breathes out?

Reader's Journal

In what ways have you ever had difficulty understanding an explanation of how something works? What might have helped you to understand it better? In what ways is it difficult to explain how something works?

THE AQUALUNG

With the aid of an aqualung or scuba (Self-Contained Underwater Breathing Apparatus), a diver can stay underwater for long periods. This device does away with the need for a diving suit by supplying air at changing pressures during a dive.

The diver's body is under pressure from the surrounding water, which becomes greater the deeper one dives. The air inside the diver's lungs is at about the same pressure as the water. The air in the cylinder is at high pressure. The aqualung's regulator has two stages that reduce the pressure of the air coming from the cylinder to the same pressure as the water so that the diver can breathe in. The first-stage valve, worked by a spring, opens to admit air at a set pressure always greater than water pressure. The second-stage valve, worked by a lever, opens by suction to admit air at water pressure.

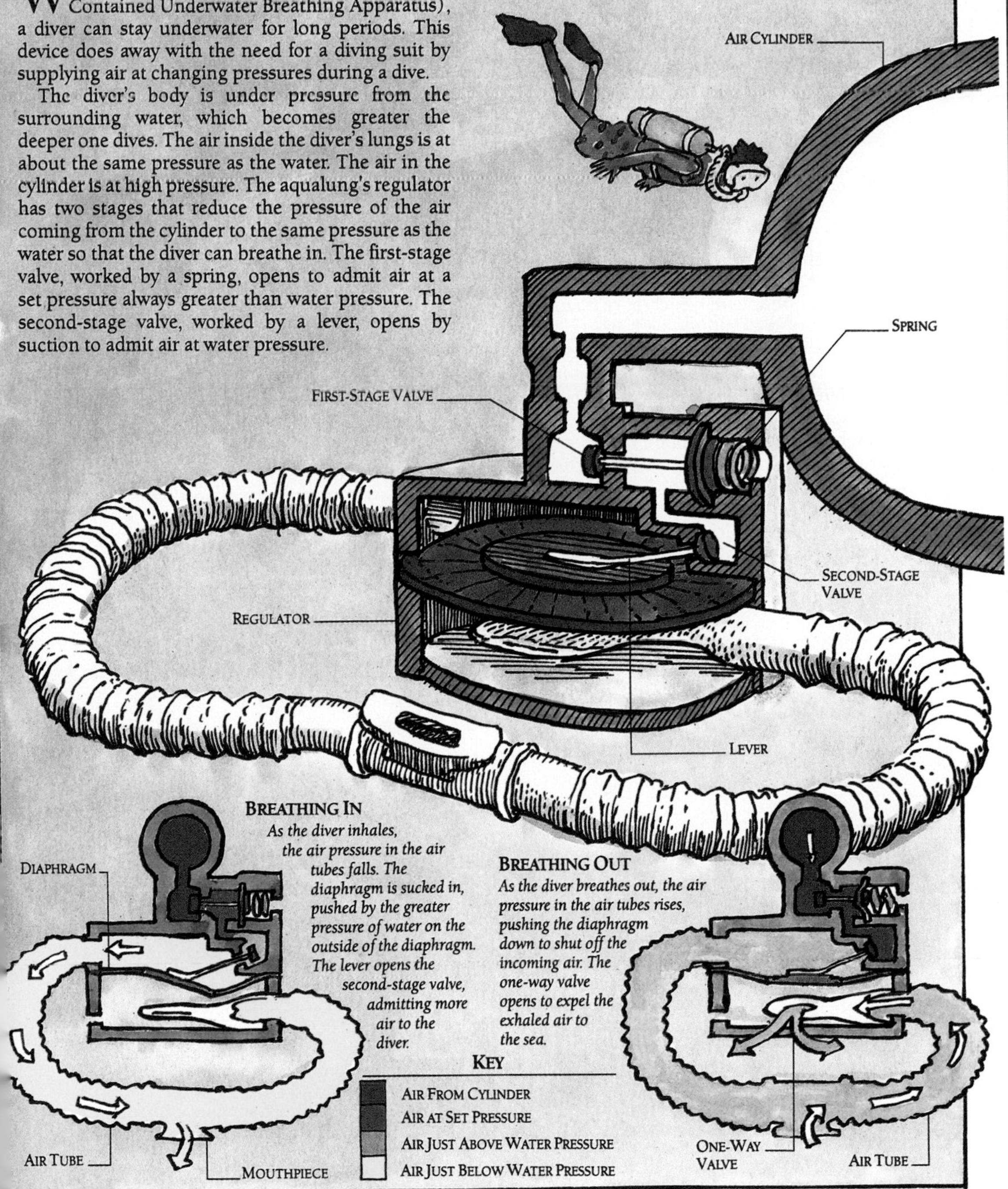

AIR CYLINDER

SPRING

FIRST-STAGE VALVE

SECOND-STAGE VALVE

REGULATOR

LEVER

BREATHING IN
As the diver inhales, the air pressure in the air tubes falls. The diaphragm is sucked in, pushed by the greater pressure of water on the outside of the diaphragm. The lever opens the second-stage valve, admitting more air to the diver.

BREATHING OUT
As the diver breathes out, the air pressure in the air tubes rises, pushing the diaphragm down to shut off the incoming air. The one-way valve opens to expel the exhaled air to the sea.

DIAPHRAGM

AIR TUBE

MOUTHPIECE

ONE-WAY VALVE

AIR TUBE

KEY

AIR FROM CYLINDER
AIR AT SET PRESSURE
AIR JUST ABOVE WATER PRESSURE
AIR JUST BELOW WATER PRESSURE

RESPOND TO THE SELECTION

As an alternate activity, ask students what other high-risk activities they would like to pursue that would require them to depend on technology, such as sky-diving, wind-surfing, and mountain-climbing. Do they enjoy relying on tools and gear? Why, or why not?

SELECTION CHECK TEST 4.12.7 WITH ANSWERS

Checking Your Reading

1. What is another name for an aqualung? **An aqualung is also called a scuba tank, or a Self-Contained Underwater Breathing Apparatus.**
2. What does an aqualung do for a diver? **It supplies air for the diver to breathe.**
3. What happens to the water pressure on a diver's body as he or she goes deeper? **The pressure increases as the diver goes deeper.**
4. What happens to the pressure inside the air tubes when the diver breathes out? **The pressure rises in the air tubes when the diver breahes out.**
5. Where does the diver's expelled air go? **The expelled air goes out into the sea.**

Reader's Toolbox

1. This selection contains a large diagram and two smaller diagrams. What does the diagram depict? **The diagram shows the inside of an aqualung.**
2. The four categories in the key indicate different levels of the pressure of what? **They depict air at different levels of pressure.**
3. Name something that the diagrams especially helped you understand about aqualungs that the written text did not. *Responses will vary.*

Respond *to the* **SELECTION**

Would you ever want to scuba dive? Why, or why not?

About *the* AUTHOR

David Macaulay was born in 1946 in Lancashire, England. As a young boy, he loved to make contraptions—such as miniature cable cars and elevators—with string, tape, boxes, and other simple items. At the age of eleven, Macaulay moved with his family to Bloomfield, New Jersey. As he settled into his new surroundings, he began to draw. By the time he finished high school, Macaulay decided to study design and architecture at the Rhode Island School of Design. After college, he experimented with writing and illustrating books, and in 1973 he published his first book, *Cathedral*. He continued to create books about building—*City* (about the construction of a Roman city), *Pyramid, Castle, Mill*, and others. In 1988, *The Way Things Work* was published. Macaulay revised and updated the award-winning book in 1998, launching *The New Way Things Work*, from which this selection was chosen.

Investigate, Inquire, and Imagine

Recall: GATHERING FACTS

1a. What happens to water pressure as a diver goes into deeper water?

2a. What do the two stages of the aqualung's regulator do?

3a. What happens as the diver inhales?

4a. Where does exhaled air go?

→ **Interpret:** FINDING MEANING

1b. How could that change affect the diver?

2b. Why are two stages necessary?

3b. How does the diaphragm contribute to the process?

4b. Why doesn't the exhaled air return to the cylinder?

Analyze: TAKING THINGS APART

5a. How many main points make up this explanation of how an aqualung works? What are they? How many minor points are under each main point?

→ **Synthesize:** BRINGING THINGS TOGETHER

5b. Explain briefly, in your own words, how an aqualung works.

Evaluate: MAKING JUDGMENTS

6a. How effective is this explanation? How do the visual parts of the explanation contribute to your understanding of the process of breathing with an aqualung?

→ **Extend:** CONNECTING IDEAS

6b. What other concepts, devices, or systems would benefit from an explanation that includes visual components such as this? Why is this format particularly beneficial for the items you list?

Understanding *Media*

COHERENCE. Coherence is the logical arrangement of ideas in speech or writing. Writers achieve coherence by presenting their ideas in a logical order and by using transitions to show how their ideas are connected to one another. *Transitions* are words or phrases that connect ideas and show relationships between them. Examine how the author presents concepts involved in the workings of an aqualung. How does the order in which the ideas appear help you understand the process described? How does the author use transitions and repetition?

KEYS, CAPTIONS, AND LABELS. A **key** is a guide that aids in interpreting and identifying significant marks on maps, graphs, charts, diagrams, and tables. They explain symbols and marks by providing a clear interpretation for each. *Captions* explain a visual item or graphic in writing. *Labels*—simple headers or titles within a graphic that give names to different parts—also assist readers in reading and understanding the graphic. What do you learn from the key in "The Aqualung" diagram? How important is the key in interpreting the diagram? What do you learn from captions? labels? What do they contribute to your understanding?

ANSWERS TO INVESTIGATE, INQUIRE, IMAGINE

RECALL

1a. The deeper a person dives, the greater the water pressure.

2a. The first-stage valve allows high-pressure air to leave the cylinder. The second-stage valve releases the air at water pressure.

3a. As the diver inhales, air moves from the cylinder through the air tubes to the diver. The valves release the air and the diaphragm falls to allow the air to move in this way.

4a. The exhaled air goes into the sea.

INTERPRET

1b. The increase in water pressure could make it harder to breathe without mechanical assistance.

2b. The air needs a place between the two valves to adjust its pressure.

3b. The diaphragm expands and contracts to push air in and out.

4b. The exhaled air isn't as good to breathe again, as it contains less oxygen.

ANALYZE

5a. Two main steps make up the explanation: breathing in and breathing out. Breathing in contains more steps than breathing out. Breathing in consists of the first stage and the second stage valve movements and the diaphragm contraction. Breathing out manipulates the diaphragm.

SYNTHESIZE

5b. Responses may vary. An aqualung has a cylinder with air in it. When the first stage valve opens, high-pressure air is released from the cylinder. When the diaphragm sucks in and the second-stage valve opens, the air enters the air tubes and the diver breathes in. When the diver breathes out, the air is released through a valve into the sea.

EVALUATE

6a. Students may say the explanation is effective because it uses diagrams to demonstrate the process an aqualung uses.

EXTEND

6b. *Responses will vary.*

ANSWERS TO UNDERSTANDING MEDIA

COHERENCE. Students may say that the concepts are addressed in chronological order on the page. They may say that parallel concepts are explained using the same language, making it easier to see the logical progression of events.

KEYS, CAPTIONS, AND LABELS. The key shows what the different colors in the diagrams indicate. The captions explain in detail what happens as the diver breathes in and as the diver breathes out. The labels identify different parts of the aqualung.

Vocabulary
Investigating New Words. Students' contextual sentences will vary. If they are unclear how to write them, have them use the Words for Everyday Use vocabulary feature throughout the textbook as a guide. An example appears on page 804.

Collaborative Learning & Study and Research
Creating a Visual Explanation. To help students as they create their posters, refer them to the Language Arts Survey 6.11, "Displaying Effective Visual Information." (To evaluate student projects, see the Assessment Resource 4.10, Collaborative Learning Evaluation Form, and 4.12, "Project Evaluation Form.")

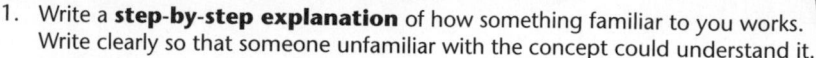

Writer's Journal

1. Write a **step-by-step explanation** of how something familiar to you works. Write clearly so that someone unfamiliar with the concept could understand it.

2. Look around the room for a picture, or think of your surroundings as an image, and write a **caption** for it.

3. Suppose that you are interested in learning more about becoming a certified diver. Write a **request for information** that you might send to a nearby scuba-diving school.

Skill Builders

Vocabulary

INVESTIGATING NEW WORDS. Texts explaining scientific processes often introduce words that seem familiar but that may require additional review to fully understand their meaning in context. Look up the following words from the selection, using a dictionary, encyclopedia, or other reference book. Write a definition for each word, and use each word in a contextual sentence. Try to think of the word in terms of the scientific context in which it is used in the selection. For more information, see the Language Arts Survey 1.17, "Using a Dictionary."

1. pressure
2. regulator
3. stage
4. admit
5. spring
6. lever
7. suction
8. diaphragm
9. valve
10. expel

Collaborative Learning & Study and Research

CREATING A VISUAL EXPLANATION.
Form small groups. With your group members, investigate one of the items below. Each member of the group can try a different resource at the library to learn more about how the chosen item works. Then regroup and discuss what you have learned. After you all understand the workings of the item, plan a poster based on the format of *The New Way Things Work*. Decide what visual elements your explanation will include, where the text should appear, and what labels, keys, and captions you may need. Design your poster as a group and display it in your classroom. Ask your classmates for feedback—does your visual explanation help them to understand the item you have described?

- combination lock
- slide projector
- stapler
- fingernail clipper
- remote-control toy car
- digital clock
- roller coaster
- lawn sprinkler

Language, Grammar, and Style

EDITING TO CLARIFY. When writing to explain cause-and-effect relationships or a process, you may find it helpful to use specific words to clarify your explanation. For example, words like *as, when, before, after, if, then, first, second, finally, because, since, so,* and *therefore* can aid the reader in understanding the relationship or process. Using specific names for parts, and identifying them as the *first, second, left, right, top, bottom, upper,* or *lower* parts, also helps form a clear explanation. Other descriptive words—*short, long, fat, small, tall*—can provide additional information.

On your own paper, write a paragraph using the sequence of events listed below. Show how the steps are linked by combining sentences and inserting words and phrases. Your objective is to clarify the process of catching a mouse in the game *Mousetrap* and to highlight the cause-and-effect relationships among the parts of the mouse-catching contraption. You don't have to know this game before clarifying the directions—in fact, a person unfamiliar with the game is probably even better able to point out confusing directions. You might also find it helpful to draw the steps as you go through the list. For more information, see the Language Arts Survey 6.2, "Following Directions," 6.3, "Giving Directions."

1. Someone turns the crank.
2. A vertical plate with teeth turns a horizontal plate with teeth.
3. The plate has a short bar.
4. The bar presses a long lever.
5. The lever has a rubber band that stretches.
6. The rubber band pulls the lever back.
7. The end of the lever has a stop-sign-like face.
8. The face hits a hanging shoe.
9. The shoe hits a bucket containing a marble.
10. The marble zig-zags down a ramp.
11. It falls into a chute.
12. It rolls down.
13. It hits an upright stick.
14. The stick, with a hand on top, is pushed up.
15. A marble rests on a platform above the hand.
16. The marble falls into a tub.
17. It falls through a hole in the tub.
18. It lands on one end of a teeter-totter-like diving board.
19. The man on the end of the board jumps up.
20. He falls into a washtub.
21. The washtub compresses the platform on which it sits.
22. A cage top is suspended on a stick on the platform.
23. It falls and traps a mouse underneath.

Language, Grammar, and Style

EDITING TO CLARIFY. Students' paragraphs will vary, but they can include the following.

Someone *first* turns the crank, *which causes* a vertical plate with teeth to turn a horizontal plate with teeth. The plate has a short bar, which *then* presses a long lever. *Next,* the lever has a rubber band that stretches *and* pulls the lever back. The end of the lever has a stop-sign-like face, which hits a hanging shoe. The shoe *next* hits a bucket containing a marble. The marble *then* zig-zags down a ramp, falls into a chute, rolls down, and *finally* hits an upright stick. The stick, with a hand on top, is pushed up, *causing* a marble that rests on a platform above the hand to fall into a tub. The marble *first* falls through a hole in the tub and *then* lands on one end of a teeter-totter-like diving board. The man on the end of the board jumps up and falls into a washtub, which compresses the platform on which it sits. *This causes* the cage top, which is suspended on a stick on the platform, to fall and *finally* trap a mouse underneath.

Note: To give students a broader overview of transition words and their purposes, refer them to the Language Arts Survey 2.27, "Choosing a Method of Organization."

ADDITIONAL RESOURCES

UNIT 12 RESOURCE BOOK
- Selection Worksheet 12.2
- Selection Check Test 4.12.7
- Selection Test 4.12.8
- Reading Resource 1.15
- Language, Grammar, and Style Resource 3.17
- Applied English Resource 6.4

READER'S TOOLBOX

CONCRETE LANGUAGE. Examples of concrete language include: hairy roots; forefinger running down one side of the blade; slide the knife down and away

CHRONOLOGICAL ORDER. Students should notice the numbered steps; other indicators include: before you begin; starting at the center; Then; Repeat.

READER'S JOURNAL

Ask students to share their favorite recipe of food made from scratch. They could compile the recipes into a class cookbook and give a copy to each student.

DIRECTIONS

Reader's Resource

- Onions come in many varieties, shapes, sizes, and tastes. Most bulb onions have yellow, white, or reddish skin. Yellow varieties usually are large and very sweet onions. White onions are typically smaller and have a mild flavor. Red onions can be very large and have a sweet flavor. In addition to bulb onions, cooks use green onions, which are small and have long green shoots, and scallions, which resemble green onions but are larger.

- **SCIENCE CONNECTION.** Biochemists have long researched why onions cause people to cry. Many stand by the theory that once an onion's skin is pierced, chemicals within the onion are released. One of these chemicals is thiopropanal-s-oxide, a compound that irritates the eyes. To lessen this effect, experts recommend chilling or soaking the onion before chopping it.

- Using the correct knife can help make chopping easier. Serrated knives have scalloped edges along the blade and work well for slicing tomatoes and crusty bread. Chef's knives have sturdy, flat-edged blades. They work well for chopping almost everything.

850 UNIT TWELVE

Prereading

"How to Chop an Onion in Four Easy Steps" by Ken Haedrich

Still Life with Onions, 1889. Paul Gauguin. ➤

Reader's TOOLBOX

CONCRETE LANGUAGE. A **concrete** word or phrase is one that names or describes something that can be distinguished by one or more of the five senses. The use of concrete, specific words and phrases helps to clarify individual directions and makes the overall process easier to follow. As you read these directions, look for concrete language that helps you to understand the process clearly.

CHRONOLOGICAL ORDER. **Chronological order** is the arrangement of details in order of their occurrence. The use of chronological order is common in writing that describes processes, events, and cause-and-effect relationships. Words such as *first, second, next, then,* and *finally* help to connect individual steps in a process. As you read, look for words that help order the directions.

Graphic Organizer

After reading the process once, go back and reread it, drawing a picture to illustrate each of the four steps.

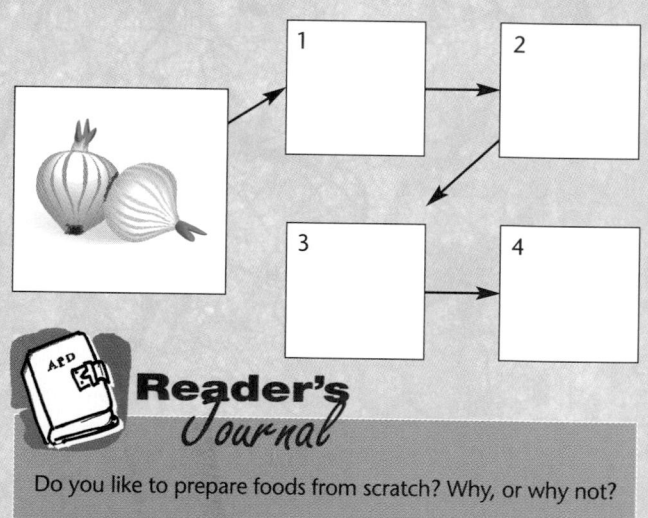

Reader's Journal

Do you like to prepare foods from scratch? Why, or why not?

How to Chop an onion

in Four Easy Steps

Ken Haedrich

1 Select a sharp chef's knife. Before you begin, peel off as many layers of papery skin as you can, the better to make your first cut without your knife <u>glancing</u> off the surface. Pull off any hairy roots, too. They have an unappetizing way of ending up where they shouldn't. Place the onion on its side on a chopping board. Hold your knife comfortably, with your forefinger running down one side of the blade and your thumb pressed against the opposite side. With one fell swoop,[1] slide the knife down and away from you, slicing off the top half inch of the onion. (If your knife isn't particularly sharp, first pierce the surface of the onion with the tip of your knife so the blade has a starting notch.)

> **GUIDED READING**
> Why should you pull off the hairy roots?

2 Turn the onion so it rests on the newly cut flat surface. Starting at the center of the root end, slice the onion in half. Peel off any remaining skin.

3 Rest half the onion on its largest flat surface, root end pointing away from you. Working from the far edge of the onion toward your body, slice down through the onion, leaving about 1/2 inch between each cut. Do not, however, slice through the onion at the root end. (An <u>intact</u> root end keeps the onion from falling apart.)

> **GUIDED READING**
> Which end of the onion should you not slice through?

4 Rotate the onion so the end cut faces your knife blade. Then make 1/2-inch cuts <u>perpendicular</u> to the first set of cuts. The onion will fall apart into neat, 1/2-inch dice. Discard root. Repeat with the other half.

---

1. **one fell swoop.** All at once

---

words for everyday use

glance (glants′) v., to strike awkwardly so as to slide off or be deflected. *The dart glanced the edge of the board and fell to the floor.*

in • tact (in takt′) adj., untouched; entire. *The violent storm ripped the roof from the old cabin but left everything inside intact.*

per • pen • dic • u • lar (pər pən di′ kyə lər) adj., being at right angles to a given line or plane. *Oak Street runs perpendicular to Main Street.*

VOCABULARY FROM THE SELECTION

glance	perpendicular
intact	

RESPOND TO THE SELECTION

As an alternate activity, ask students to describe a process that was hard for them to do at first. What steps did they have to learn to ride a bicycle? learn to water-ski? make a complicated craft project?

SELECTION CHECK TEST 4.12.9 WITH ANSWERS

Checking Your Reading

1. What should you remove from an onion before you chop it? **You should remove as much of the skin as possible, and the hairy roots.**
2. If your knife isn't particularly sharp, what should you do before taking the first slice of the onion? **Pierce the surface of the onion with the tip of the knife.**
3. Why should you leave the root end of the onion intact? **An intact root end keeps the onion from falling apart.**
4. After you have made one set of cuts down the onion, spacing them 1/2-inch apart, how should you position the next set of cuts? **The second set of cuts should be perpendicular to the first set of cuts.**
5. If you follow this procedure, what shape will the chopped onion be in when you are through? **The onion will be in 1/2-inch dices.**

Vocabulary in Context

Fill in each blank below with the most appropriate word from the following Words for Everyday Use. You may have to change the tense of the word.

glance   intact   perpendicular

1. The contractor carefully set the walls in **perpendicular** to the floor.
2. We were relieved to find that the boat was **intact** when the storm was over.
3. I practiced boxing, trying to train my **glancing** blows to land more squarely on the target.

Respond_to the_
SELECTION

Have you ever chopped an onion or other vegetable? Describe the process you used.

About _the_ AUTHOR

Ken Haedrich is a food and travel writer, editor, cooking teacher, and the author of numerous cookbooks and hundreds of food articles. He is also the father of four children, none of whom likes to chop onions—they say it hurts their eyes. Haedrich is a regularly contributing writer to several magazines, including _Bon Appetit_ and _National Geographic Traveler_. In 1992, he won the Julia Child Cookbook Award for _Home for the Holidays_.

RELATED READING

SALSA

The best salsas are those you make to suit your own taste, as hot or as mild as you like. Adjust the amount of onion, pepper, and lime or lemon juice to taste. Serve with corn chips.

- 3 to 4 red-ripe, medium tomatoes, chopped
- 1/4 cup chopped sweet onion or scallions
- 1 to 2 chopped jalapeno or serrano chile peppers
- 1/4 cup chopped fresh cilantro
- 1/2 teaspoon salt
- 1 to 2 tablespoons fresh lime or lemon juice

Combine the tomatoes, onion, peppers, cilantro, salt, and lime juice in a serving dish. Stir well and let sit at room temperature for at least 2 hours before serving. _Serves 4 to 6._ ■

852   *UNIT TWELVE / READING BETWEEN THE LINES*

Investigate, *Inquire,* and Imagine

Recall: GATHERING FACTS

1a. What should you do if your knife is not very sharp?

2a. How do you "rest the onion" before slicing, according to both steps 2 and 3?

→ **Interpret:** FINDING MEANING

1b. How would that help?

2b. What purpose does this serve?

Analyze:

3a. Look at each step of the onion-chopping process. Do any of the four steps contain extra information that you don't need? Could any steps be combined?

→ **Synthesize:**

3b. Summarize, in your own words, Ken Haedrich's steps for chopping an onion.

Evaluate: MAKING JUDGMENTS

4a. Does this process describe the best possible way to chop an onion? Why, or why not?

→ **Extend:** CONNECTING IDEAS

4b. How would you modify the onion-chopping directions so they would apply to chopping another ingredient in the salsa recipe?

Understanding *Media*

CONCRETE LANGUAGE. A **concrete** word or phrase is one that names or describes something that can be distinguished by one or more of the five senses. The use of concrete, specific words and phrases helps to clarify individual directions and makes the overall process easier to follow. How does the use of concrete language clarify the process of chopping an onion in this selection?

CHRONOLOGICAL ORDER. Chronological order is the arrangement of details in order of their occurrence. It is common in writing that describes processes, events, and cause-and-effect relationships. What words does the author use to clarify the order of steps in the process?

Writer's Journal

1. Write **instructions** for slicing an apple. Be as specific as possible, assuming your audience has no idea how to perform the task.
2. Write an **advertisement** for a farmer's market stand that features several varieties of fresh onions.
3. Write **stage directions** describing a person chopping an onion in a play.

Study and Research

ANALYZING A RECIPE. To extend this activity, have students find recipes in newspapers, magazines, or other sources that analyze the nutritional value of a recipe. What categories do the recipes include in their analysis? What are special terms, such as "diabetic exchange," and what do they mean? You may want to arrange for a family and consumer sciences teacher to give a brief presentation on recipe analysis.

Collaborative Learning & Speaking and Listening

WRITING DIRECTIONS. You may want to combine or modify this Skill Builder activity with the Cross-Curricular Activities on page 851.

Language, Grammar, and Style

WRITING IMPERATIVE SENTENCES. Students' sentences will vary, but they should be similar to the following.

1. Katrina, add some salt to the soup.
2. Seymour, help your brother with his math.
3. Plant the flowers after lunch.
4. Children, carefully trace the letters of the alphabet.
5. Jana, drive to town to pick up your father.

Skill Builders

Study and Research

ANALYZING A RECIPE. Find at least two recipes for your favorite food. Analyze each recipe and choose the one that seems closest to your personal taste. Following the recipe you select, prepare the dish with the help of an adult, if needed, and try it. Was it as good as you thought it would be? Why, or why not? Did you modify the recipe in any way? If so, how do you think the change or changes affected the dish?

Collaborative Learning & Speaking and Listening

WRITING DIRECTIONS. In small groups, write directions to prepare a particular entrée (main course). Dishes you may want to consider include spaghetti, tacos, chef salad, or hamburgers. Discuss and come to an agreement on the recipe's ingredients, the quantity of each item, and the method of preparation. If you have access to a kitchen, try out your recipe to see if it creates a palatable entrée. If possible, plan—as a group—a class demonstration of your food preparation. Outline the procedure, indicating which group member is responsible for explaining each step. For more information, refer to the Language Arts Survey 6.4, "Writing a Step by Step Procedure."

Language, Grammar, and Style

WRITING IMPERATIVE SENTENCES. An imperative sentence gives a command or makes a request. Directions are commonly given using imperative sentences. The subject of a command is always *you*, even if it is not stated. Imperative sentences can use a period or, for a stronger command, an exclamation point. Rewrite the following sentences as imperative sentences.

EXAMPLE   John needs to eat his dinner before it gets cold.
John, (you) eat your dinner before it gets cold!

1. Katrina added some salt to the soup.
2. Seymour, could you help your brother with his math?
3. You may plant the flowers after lunch.
4. The children carefully trace the letters of the alphabet.
5. Jana will drive to town to pick up her father.

For more information, see the Language Arts Survey 3.17, "Functions of Sentences."

ADDITIONAL QUESTIONS AND ACTIVITIES

1. How did Dave Schaller and Susan Nagel become involved in designing Web sites?
2. What is their specialty?
3. What do they like best about their work?

Answers

1. They were interested in education for a long time. When the Web began to grow, they realized it could be a great new medium for education. Because they didn't see companies focusing on educational Web development, they formed their own company.
2. Their specialty is developing educational games and simulations for museums, distance learning programs, and corporations.
3. They like learning new things in many different subject areas.

Getting Into Web Development

Web developers **Dave Schaller** and **Susan Nagel**, of **Educational Web Adventures LLP**, have created a variety of interactive Internet sites for young people.

Here they answer a few questions about their work.

How did you become involved in designing Web sites?

We've both been interested in education for a long time, but we worked in different settings—Susan was an art teacher, and Dave was a writer and museum exhibit developer. When the Web appeared in the mid-1990s, we realized that it could be a great new medium for education. We didn't see any companies focusing on educational Web development, so we formed one ourselves. Our specialty is developing educational games and simulations for museums, distance learning programs, and corporations.

What do you like best about your work?

We both like learning new things, and now that's our job! We've done projects about art, history, ecology, space exploration, and many other subjects, and for each one, one of the best parts has been learning about the subject. It's also challenging and fun to make each project take shape.

Web sites are getting more and more complex, and we've got to make sure that all the pieces—the text, graphics, programming, and everything else—fit together just like (or even better than) we'd planned. But watching each site come together is really exciting.

What is the hardest thing about this kind of work?

Neither of us ever expected to run a business, so that part—accounting, marketing, and such—was all new to us. It's been a challenge, but if you love what you're doing, even the hard parts usually feel like fun.

How do you decide what works and what doesn't work so well in a Web site?

Partly, we draw on our previous experience teaching and writing museum exhibits. And we've developed so many games and activities that we have a decent feel for what works and what doesn't. But we still bring in kids to test our projects. We always find things to change and improve after watching them and talking with them. There's nothing better than watching kids grin as they play a game we developed—and nothing more enlightening than watching them frown from frustration or confusion! And, of course, kids and teachers around the world send us their thoughts and suggestions by e-mail!

Here are a few of Dave Schaller and Susan Nagel's recent projects:

FUN ONLINE AT THE CHILDREN'S MUSEUM OF INDIANAPOLIS

Create a puppet show, solve some geo-mysteries, design a space station, and more!
http://www.childrensmuseum.org/

LEONARDO'S WORKSHOP: AN ARTEDVENTURE WITH CARMINE CHAMELEON

Travel back in time to Leonardo da Vinci's workshop to solve this interactive mystery.
http://www.sanford-artedventures.com/

BUILD-A-PRAIRIE

Can you turn a barren plain into a healthy prairie? Choose the right species and watch the prairie come to life!
http://www.umn.edu/bellmuse/mnideals/prairie

FIND THEIR LATEST PROJECTS ON THEIR WEB SITE:

http://www.eduweb.com/adventure.html

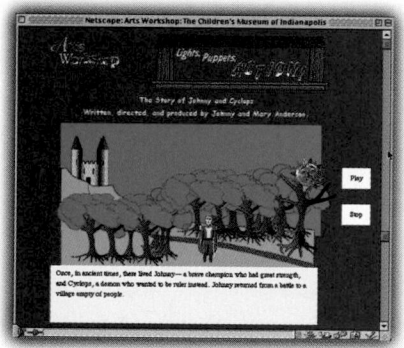

for your READING LIST

KAREN HESSE

"Hard times are about losing spirit, and hope and what happens when dreams dry up."

Out of the Dust by Karen Hesse is the story of Billie Jo, a fourteen-year-old girl growing up in the Oklahoma Dust Bowl during the Great Depression. In a simple, direct voice, she narrates a personal journal of hard times, written in free verse. Year after year, howling winds and blizzards of dust destroy the crops, kill the livestock, and leave a blanket of dirt over everything in sight. Food is scarce and even the air, filled with dust, is thick and choking, unsafe to breathe. The only bright spots in this gray life are Billie Jo's piano and the music teacher who takes her on the road with his band, encouraging her to dream. When a terrible accident happens, it seems that Billi Jo's spirit and hope and dreams will die. But *Out of the Dust* is about a young girl who finds a reason for hope in the midst of this bleak landscape, something permanent despite the winds that blow everything else away. Any reader who has ever felt despair, grief or hopelessness, will find inspiration and comfort in Billie Jo's story.

BOOK CLUB

After everyone in your literature circle has finished reading this book, set a time and place for discussion. You may wish to review the Language Arts Survey 1.8, "Guidelines for Discussing Literature in a Book Club," for more assistance. The following questions may prove helpful:

- What did you learn about the Dust Bowl by reading this book?
- What is Billie Jo's internal conflict? How is the conflict resolved?
- In what ways is Billie Jo like you? In what ways is she unlike you?
- When have you dreamed of a different life? What sort of life do you imagine?
- In resolving her internal conflict, Billie Jo finds her feelings about her life changing. What happens to her that brings about this change?
- Think back over the reading you have done in this course. What kinds of changes have the characters undergone? What kinds of experiences brought about those changes?
- What kinds of changes have you undergone in your life? What kinds of experiences led to those changes?
- What conclusions can you draw about the way our experiences change us?

Other books you may want to read:
The New Way Things Work by David Macaulay
The Old Farmer's Almanac by Robert B. Thomas

For Your Reading List
Karen Hesse's *Out of the Dust* (1997) won the Newbery Award and has received numerous reviews praising it as an innovative literary achievement. *Out of the Dust* uses the experimental form of an extended prose-poem that becomes a novel to chronicle one family's tragic struggle and determination to heal as they experience the Dust Bowl in Depression-era Oklahoma. Students who enjoyed the Related Reading on page 841 will find the novel hard to put down until they have finished reading it. The alternate selections, *The New Way Things Work* by David Macaulay (a selection from this book appears on page 845) and *The Old Farmer's Almanac* by Robert B. Thomas provide students with a reading experience that focuses on visual and informational media. You may want to have students prepare brief written or oral reports in which they choose one entry from either book and explain what they learned and what makes their selection visual or informational rather than literary.

Book Club
As students prepare for their book clubs, have them read the following sections in the Language Arts Survey: 1.3, "Reading Literature: Educating Your Imagination," 1.4, "Educating Your Imagination as an Active Reader," 1.5 "Keeping a Reader's Journal," 1.6, "Reading Silently versus Reading Out Loud," 1.7, "Reading with a Book Club or Literature Circle," and 1.8, "Guidelines for Discussing Literature in a Book Club." See the Guided Reading Resource 1.3–1.8 in the Teacher's Resource Kit for blackline masters of worksheets that will help students work these concepts more thoroughly.

GUIDED WRITING
Software

See the Guided Writing Software for an extended version of this lesson that includes printable graphic organizers, extensive student models and student-friendly checklists, and self-, peer, and teacher evaluation features.

INDIVIDUAL LEARNING STRATEGIES

MOTIVATION
Make overhead transparencies from David Macaulay's book *The New Way Things Work*. Ask students to identify a cause and effect for each diagram.

READING PROFICIENCY
Have students skim the lesson and tell what is different about this assignment. Students, used to seeing long Student Model—Drafts and sometimes even longer final versions, will quickly notice that the written assignment is integrated with a graphic.

ENGLISH LANGUAGE LEARNING
See strategies for Reading Proficiency above that will also benefit students who are English

---

Get to know words that show cause and effect relationships:

> after this
> as a result
> because
> consequently
> if
> in order that
> since
> so
> then
> therefore
> thus
> while

What visuals can you use?
- a sketch, a diagram, or a picture that you draw
- a series of illustrations adapted from a book or Internet source
- an illustration made by using a computer, scanner, or digital camera

If you use a visual that you photocopy or print from your computer, be sure to credit the artist. For more information on crediting sources, see the Language Arts Survey 5.35, "Documenting Sources."

Guided Writing

ANALYZING CAUSE AND EFFECT

Zlata was outside gazing at the sky with her friend Levi. "Looks like the campout might not happen this weekend," Zlata remarked.

"Why do you think that?" Levi asked. "It looks pretty clear to me."

Zlata pointed to the sky. "See those small fluffy clouds? They're fine weather cumulus clouds. It's not even noon, and they're already forming into rows. The weather pattern forming those clouds may cause the weather to change for the worse. Just wait and see. We won't be camping this weekend."

Levi wanted to know how he could predict the weather, too. "Do you know more about weather patterns and clouds?"

"Sure." Zlata got out a paper and pencil and sketched several types of clouds: cirrus cirrostratus, altocumulus, cumulonimbus and cumulus clouds. She labeled the clouds for him and explained the weather patterns that helped form those clouds. Levi studied her picture so he could understand the cause and effect relationship between the weather and the type of clouds. Picture in hand, he left to share the campout news with Mike.

Like Zlata, you may need to explain the process for what caused something else to happen. It is often easier for another person to understand a process if you use a diagram or picture. For this assignment, you will create a poster that combines an explanation of a cause and effect relationship in a process with a picture or diagram.

Professional Model

In *The New Way Things Work*, David Macaulay uses a combination of written explanation and pictures to explain the process of how an aqualung works. Look again at Macaulay's explanation of the aqualung on page 845.

Examining the Model

Much of Macaulay's success as an author comes from his easily understood explanations of how cause and effect relationships work. What techniques does Macaulay use? First, he clearly identifies and explains the cause and effect relationships that make an aqualung work. *When the diver inhales* (the cause), *the pressure on one side of the diaphragm drops* (the effect). *This makes the diaphragm move* (the cause) *which opens the valve that gives air to the diver* (the effect).

INDIVIDUAL LEARNING STRATEGIES (CONT.)

language learners. Non-native speakers may need help understanding the scientific terms chlorophyll and carbon dioxide used in the Graphic Organizer.

SPECIAL NEEDS
Students with special needs may need help thinking of a cause and effect relationship that is appropriate for this assignment. You may need to help these students fill out their Graphic Organizer.

ENRICHMENT
Point out that cause and effect is also visible in human psychology. You might have students list the cause and effect for ten human behaviors. For example, Bill Bradley is driven and disciplined. What caused him to be this way? His mother was demanding and pushed him. Ask students to think of a conflict that could develop from one cause and effect relationship and write a synopsis for a possible short story.

Macaulay presents his ideas in a logical order. He first gives general information about an aqualung. Then he explains that the aqualung's regulator has two stages. He next explains how each stage works. He uses words—such as *because, then*, and *after this*—that show cause and effect relationships.

Macaulay also includes a picture of an aqualung to help readers understand the cause and effect relationships. Note how he labels the important parts of the aqualung and provides a key at the bottom of the page. He also includes a title at the top of the page.

Reflecting

As you look around your classroom and school, you will probably see many diagrams that combine text and pictures. Which diagram in your classroom or school is the most effective one? What makes it catch your eye? How is it different from other displays of information that just use text? Do you think it's true that a picture is worth a thousand words? How does a well-designed diagram affect you?

Prewriting

FINDING YOUR VOICE. Another key to Macaulay's success is his voice. He wants people to enjoy learning how things work. His written work reflects his personality and his light-hearted attitude toward explaining how an aqualung works. He accomplishes this through his word choice, sentence structure, tone, and style.

For example, although Macaulay may use more technical words to identify some parts of the aqualung, he uses simple words—such as *spring, lever*, and *valve*—when possible. He uses similar sentence structure when he describes when and how things happen. And he sets an entertaining yet informative tone with his choice of graphics.

You also want your readers to enjoy learning about your cause and effect relationship. You can do this by allowing your unique personality to shine through, choosing your words carefully, arranging your sentences logically, and using an easy and fun style.

IDENTIFYING YOUR AUDIENCE. Your audience for this assignment will depend on your topic. As you select your topic, determine which audience will benefit from the process you are explaining. After you decide on an audience, consider your audience's needs. For example, if you were going to explain how the seasons change to elementary students, you would use easy words, very short sentences, and a simple diagram. If you were explaining the same process to your peers, you would use precise words, longer sentences, and a more detailed diagram that would be interesting to that particular audience.

How can you tell a cause from an effect?

A cause makes something happen. The effect is what happens.

Turning a radio's volume makes the music louder. *Turning the volume up* is the cause. *The music getting louder* is the effect.

Sometimes an effect becomes a cause. For example, the music getting louder might cause someone to say, "Turn it down!"

As you are arranging text and graphics, consider these guidelines:

- **Use short paragraphs** placed appropriately around your visual.
- **Number the paragraphs** if it makes it easier to understand the process.
- **Include a brief title.** Use lettering that fits the style of your text and picture.
- **Label the parts** of the picture or diagram.
- **Use arrows or numbers** to indicate the flow of the process.
- **Include a key,** if needed, at the bottom of the poster.
- **Balance your text with graphics,** possibly a picture you have drawn or a diagram you have found. Remember to credit all art and graphics that are not your own.

For more information, see the Language Arts Survey 6.11, "Displaying Effective Visual Information."

REFLECTING. Students can consider topics from a variety of fields such as computer technology, history, inventions, cooking, nature, technology, or art.

Prewriting

FINDING YOUR VOICE. Review the definition of tone with students. Tone is a writer's attitude toward the subject or the reader. Encourage students to read the Language Arts Survey 2.5, "Finding Your Voice," and 3.3, "Register, Tone, and voice."

IDENTIFYING YOUR AUDIENCE. Have students read the Language Arts Survey 2.4, "Identifying Your Audience."

 **Language, Grammar, and Style**
Passive and Active Sentences

A verb is in the **active voice** when the subject of the verb performs the action. It is in the **passive voice** when the subject of the verb receives the action.

ACTIVE
> Caroline delivered a powerful speech.

PASSIVE
> A powerful speech was delivered by Caroline.

A common characteristic of poor writing is overuse of the passive voice. Keep your verbs in the active voice unless you have a good reason for using the passive voice. For example, sometimes you may not know who performed the action or it may not be important to identify who performed the action as in the sentence The meeting was adjourned. The active voice makes the writing more natural and interesting.

IDENTIFYING ACTIVE SENTENCES AND PASSIVE SENTENCES.
Identify the sentence below that uses the active voice. Why is the active voice more effective?

> Kaley kicked the football across the parking lot.

> The football was kicked across the parking lot by Kaley.

WRITING WITH A PLAN. Claudia enjoyed learning about geological processes so much that she immediately decided to write about how volcanic islands are formed. She found a diagram in a book that showed the cause and effect relationships. She photocopied the diagram to use as part of her poster.

Gary wasn't sure what to write about, so he thought about the topic that he enjoyed most: music. Next, he tried to think of a process related to music that he could explain. He brainstormed several ideas, then decided to explain how a piano works. He looked inside a piano and saw how the hammers hit the strings when a key is played. He drew a sketch to show the cause and effect relationships among the keys, the hammers, and the strings. He planned to use the sketch on his poster.

If you do not know what to write about, think about topics that you enjoy such as computers, history, inventions, cooking, nature, technology, or art. Then think of a process that you could explain about that topic. You will also need to find or create a visual component that will illustrate the cause and effect relationships in the process.

After selecting photosynthesis as his topic, Dylan used a graphic organizer to list several of the cause and effect relationships in photosynthesis.

Student Model—Graphic Organizer

Process: How Photosynthesis Works

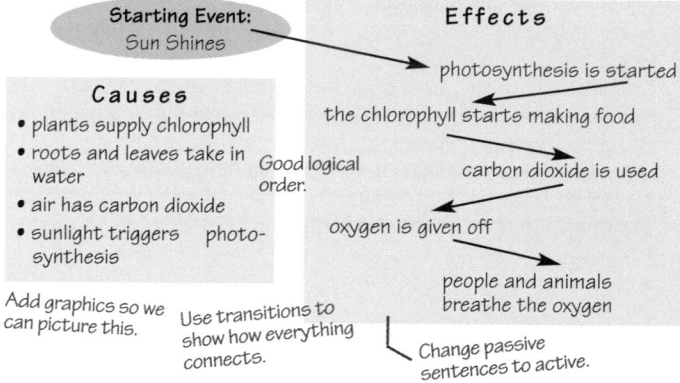

Copy the graphic organizer onto your own paper. Think about the process you are going to explain as well as the sketch, picture, or diagram you are going to use. Then fill in the cause and effect relationships on the graphic organizer.

Drafting
Remember that you will be creating a poster that combines text and a visual component. Look at your picture or diagram as you write. Start by writing about the beginning of the process.

Continue by explaining each of the cause and effect relationships in your process.

Present the cause and effect statements in a brief, but logical way. Try to use specific words to clarify your explanation. For example, words like *as, when, before, after, if, then, first, second, finally, because, since, so,* and *therefore* can help your readers understand a cause and effect relationship.

Using specific names for parts and identifying them as the *first, second, left, right, top, bottom, upper,* or *lower* parts also helps to form a clear explanation. Other descriptive words—*short, long, rough, smooth, fat, small,* and *tall*—help to provide precise information.

After you are satisfied with your text, begin to arrange your text and picture. Keep in mind the size of the poster you are using. Make two copies of your picture or diagram so that you can use a copy on your rough draft. Try several arrangements to see which one best shows the cause and effect relationships.

Macaulay added a diver to his aqualung picture to create an ocean theme. He reinforces this theme by placing a wavy line under the title. The wavy line makes the diver and the aqualung look like they are in the sea. You may want to create a theme for your poster, too. Be careful, however, not to clutter your poster with too much detail.

Self- and Peer Evaluation

After you finish your rough draft, you can do a self-evaluation of your work. If time allows, ask a member of your intended audience to do a review of your work as well. See the Language Arts Survey 2.37 for more details about self-evaluation and peer evaluation. As you evaluate your draft, ask yourself these questions:

- How well does the poster explain the process? Which parts of the process does the poster explain best? Which parts need a clearer or easier explanation?
- Which cause and effect words illustrate the relationships? What additional cause and effect words are needed to show the relationships in the process?
- How clearly does the poster present the order of the steps in the process? How clear is the cause and effect sequence?
- Which specific names for parts are needed to clarify the explanation?
- What descriptive words provide precise information? What descriptive words are still needed to make the information more precise?
- How appealing is the information and the layout design? What changes might make it more interesting and enjoyable?
- Check the poster for passive sentences. What changes are needed to rewrite passive sentences in the active voice?

Look at the peer comments on Dylan's graphic organizer. Then see how he improved his final poster.

FIXING PASSIVE SENTENCES. Each sentence below uses the passive voice. Rewrite each sentence in the active voice.

Many thanks were recently given to several people by city and state officials.

First, Pat was thanked by the fire chief for her bravery.

The fire chief was then thanked by the mayor for his service to the community.

The mayor was also thanked by the governor for coordinating services to the city.

Look at the sentences in Dylan's graphic organizer. Rewrite any passive sentences in the active voice.

USING ACTIVE SENTENCES. Look at your writing and examine each of the sentences. If you have any passive sentences, rewrite them in the active voice. Active sentences will help your explanation be clear and to the point.

Self- and Peer Evaluation

Have students use the checklist on page 861 for self- and peer evaluation. See the Guided Writing Resource 7.12 located in the Teacher's Resource Kit for a blackline master of the checklist. The checklist is intended to act as a student-friendly rubric that should help students identify specific evidence of writing strengths and areas needing improvement. Make sure students provide concrete suggestions for improvement or specific evidence of the effectiveness of their writing. Students might benefit from reading the Language Arts Survey 2.37–2.40 for more details about self- and peer evaluation. Peer reviewers might be interested in using common proofreader's symbols, which are found in the Language Arts Survey 2.44, "Using Proofreader's Marks."

Remind students that revising includes adding or expanding, cutting or condensing, replacing, and moving text. Have students read the Language Arts Survey 2.4.1, "Revising." A handout of the proofreading checklist found in the Language Arts Survey on page 888 is available in the Teacher's Resource Kit, Guided Writing Resource 2.45.

Publishing and Presenting

For better legibility, students might consider printing the text by hand or with a computer. You might have students share their posters with an elementary class in your district. If that is not a realistic option, have students videotape their presentations and give the videotape to the elementary teacher to show his or her class.

Revising and Proofreading

As you consider your self-evaluation and the evaluations from members of your intended audience, think about what will make your poster more effective. Be sure your text clearly explains the cause and effect relationships in a process. Check to see if your text and your visual component work well together. Make all your revisions. Then proofread your writing for errors in spelling, grammar, usage, punctuation, and capitalization. See the Language Arts Survey 2.45, "A Proofreading Checklist" and 6.11, "Displaying Effective Visual Information" for help.

After reviewing his poster and considering all of the evaluation notes, Dylan revised his poster.

Student Model—Revised

Publishing and Presenting

Write or print the final text for your story. Then arrange your text and your picture or diagram on your poster. Include a title, labels, numbers, arrows, and a key as needed.

Display your finished poster in your classroom. Take turns presenting your poster to your classmates. If you have made a poster for a younger audience, tell your peers how that decision influenced your text, your choice of a visual component, and your layout. Then display your poster in a place appropriate for your intended audience.

UNIT TWELVE *review*

Review: Words for Everyday Use

Check your knowledge of the following vocabulary words. Choose ten words that you would like to add to your own daily language. For each word, write a short sentence that includes the word in context. To review a word, look back to the page number indicated.

- glance (851)
- intact (851)
- perpendicular (851)
- aim (837)

- caption (844)
- chronological order (850)
- coherence (844)
- concrete language (850)

- graph (828)
- key (844)
- label (844)
- table (831)

Genre

Review the elements of visual and informational media on pages 828 to 830. Find examples in your school of at least ten of the items defined. How are these items used in your school? What purpose do they serve? How do they convey information?

Media Literacy

Review the Language Arts Survey 5.27, "Conducting an Internet Search." Using a computer with an Internet connection, find a search engine and type in the keywords "media literacy." Explore the sites that the search engine lists, looking at what each has to say about media literacy. Think about these questions as you explore:

- Who is the intended audience of this site? What information does the site offer? What links does it list? What does the term "media literacy" mean to the site authors?

- Which of these sites are for young people? What do these specific sites want kids to learn or know about media literacy? What materials do they offer to young people?

- How do you define media literacy? In what ways are you media literate? What aspects of media literacy would you like to know more about?

ADDITIONAL RESOURCES

UNIT 12 RESOURCE BOOK
- Vocabulary Worksheet
- Study Guide: Unit 12 Test
- Unit 12 Test

VOCABULARY DEVELOPMENT. Have students use the vocabulary in the review of Words for Everyday Use to write contextual sentences. They should underline each vocabulary word used. Students can modify the form of the word as needed.

EXAMPLE

My photo album is so much more meaningful when I include captions that include the date each photograph was taken.

GENRE AND MEDIA LITERARY. The Genre and Media Literacy questions are suitable to assign as essay prompts to help students prepare for the Unit Test. (To evaluate student writing, see the evaluation forms for writing, revising, and proofreading in the Assessment Resource 4.1–4.9.)

MEDIA LITERACY. Students can track their work in the Media Literacy Activity by using the Study and Research Resouce blackline master 5.40, "Documenting and Mapping Internet Research" located in the Teacher's Resource Kit.

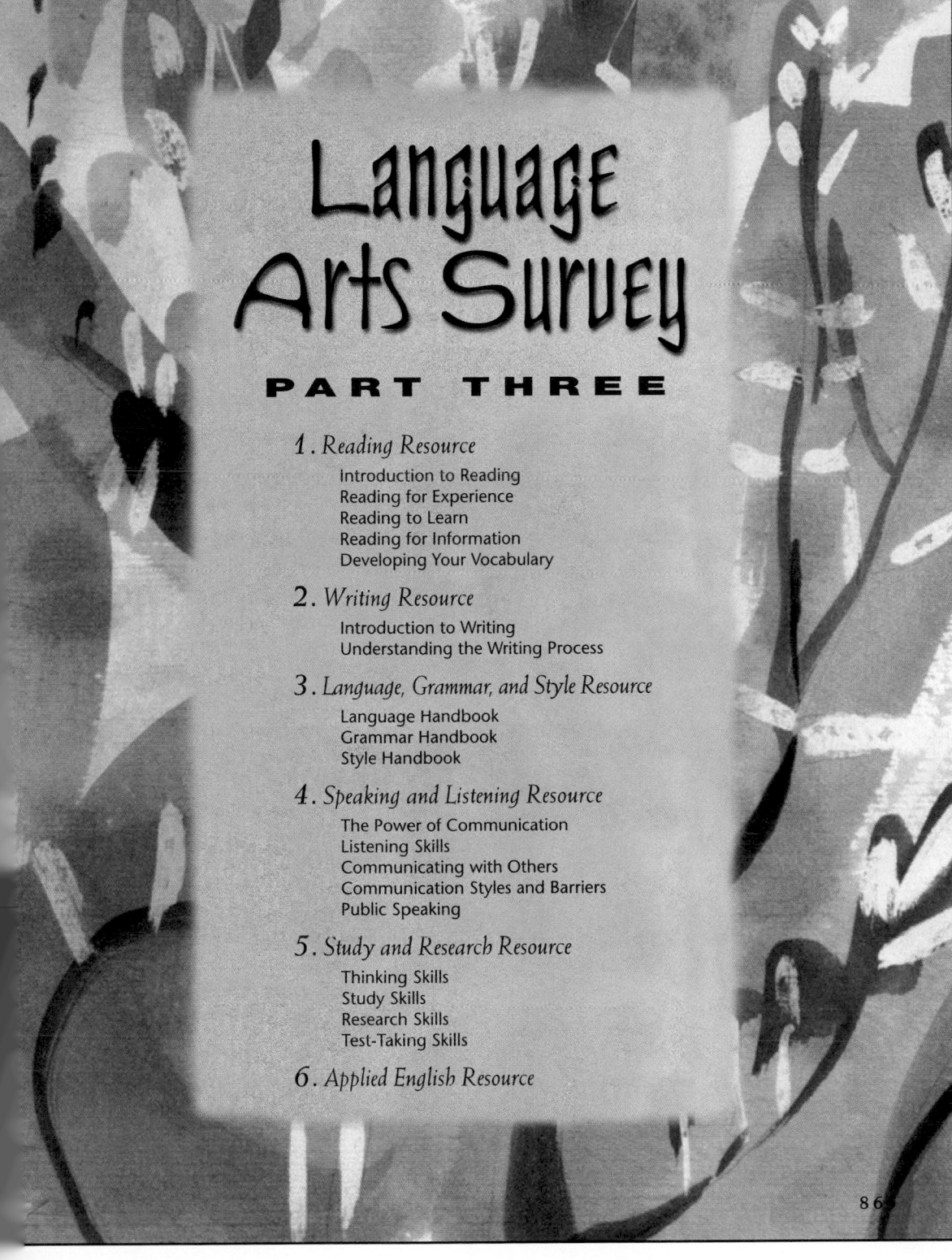

Language Arts Survey

PART THREE

865

READING
Resource

INTRODUCTION TO READING

1.1 Purposes of Reading

You as a reader read for different purposes. You might **read for experience**—for insights into ideas, other people, and the world around you. You can also **read to learn**. This is the kind of reading done most often in school. When you read to learn, you may read textbooks, newspapers and newsmagazines, and visual "texts" such as art and photographs. The purpose of this type of reading is to gain knowledge. Third, you can **read for information** using reference materials, tables, databases, and diagrams.

1.2 Reading Independently

Learning to know and value your own response to what you read to what you read is one of the rewards of becoming an independent reader. Scanning, skimming, and reading slowly and carefully are three different ways of reading.

SCANNING. When you **scan**, you look through written material quickly to locate particular information. To scan, simply run your eye down the page, looking for a key word. When you find the key word, slow down and read carefully.

SKIMMING. When you **skim**, you glance through material quickly to get a general idea of what it is about. Skimming is useful for previewing a chapter in a textbook, for surveying material to see if it contains information that will be useful to you, and for reviewing material for a test or essay. When skimming, look at titles, headings, and words in boldface or colored type. Read topic sentences of paragraphs, first and last paragraphs of sections, and any summaries or conclusions. Glance at illustrations, photographs, charts, maps, or other graphics.

SLOW AND CAREFUL READING. When you **read slowly and carefully**, you look at each sentence, taking the time to absorb its meaning before going on. Slow and careful reading is appropriate when reading for pleasure or when studying a textbook chapter for the first time. If you encounter unfamiliar words, try to figure them out from context or look them up in a dictionary. When reading for school, take notes using a rough outline form. Writing the material will help you to remember it. For more information, see the Language Arts Survey 5.16, "Taking Notes, Outlining, and Summarizing Information."

READING FOR EXPERIENCE

1.3 Reading Literature: Educating Your Imagination

The most important reason to read literature is to educate your imagination. Reading literature will train you to think and feel in new ways.

1.4 Educating Your Imagination as an Active Reader

Reading literature actively means thinking about what you are reading as you are reading it. Here are some important strategies for reading actively:

ASK QUESTIONS AS YOU READ.

- How does what I am reading make me feel?
- What is the setting of this work? How do things look, sound, taste, feel, or smell?
- Do I identify with any of the characters? What would I do if I were in their place?
- Does what I am reading involve a conflict? If so, what is it? How might it be resolved?
- What main images, ideas, symbols, or themes appear in the work?
- What can I learn from the experiences of these characters?

MAKE PREDICTIONS AS YOU READ. Think about what will come next, how situations might turn out, and what characters might do.

SUMMARIZE PARTS AS YOU READ THEM. Especially when reading longer works, stop, perhaps at the end of each chapter or section, to summarize on paper what you have read so far.

1.5 Keeping a Reader's Journal

Keeping a reader's journal will help you get the most out of your experience with literature. A reader's journal can act as a log in which you record the title and author of the selection, along with a brief summary. You might also write about how the literature relates to your life.

1.6 Reading Silently versus Reading Out Loud

When reading independently, you will make the most progress by reading silently. However, you may find it helpful to read difficult passages out loud, even if softly. Hearing the words spoken can help make sense of complex passages. Poetry is also good to read out loud. By speaking the lines, you will hear the rhythm and rhyme. Plays are also intended to be performed. Reading them out loud can be particularly helpful when different people take on the roles of different characters.

1.7 Reading with a Book Club or Literature Circle

No two people are exactly alike. Because of this, the experience that you have when reading a particular story, poem, or play will be different from the experience of each of your classmates. That's what makes discussing literature with other students interesting.

In a classroom literature circle or book club, students form small groups to exchange insights, interpretations, and questions about literature they have read independently. They may discuss a selection and work together to understand it. Or they might read different literary works and meet to compare themes, writing styles of different authors, or different selections by the same author. They can also share personal insights recorded in their reader's journal. The following section give some guidelines to help your book club get started.

1.8 Guidelines for Discussing Literature in a Book Club

BEFORE THE SESSION
- Finish reading the assignment on time.
- Write down ideas in your reader's journal to help yourself get ready for the discussion.
- Mark places in the reading that you don't understand or want to discuss with your group. Also mark passages that you like, disagree with, or find especially worth remembering.
- Bring the literature to school on discussion day.

DURING THE SESSION
- Share your ideas and offer suggestions.
- Speak clearly, loudly, and slowly enough.
- Make eye contact with others.
- Answer questions other people ask.
- Ask questions to help other members clarify or expand on their points.
- Help keep the group on track and focused.
- Encourage others to talk.
- Disagree respectfully when you find it necessary.
- Summarize and repeat your ideas when necessary.
- Give reasons for your opinions.
- Listen politely and ask follow-up questions.
- Try to understand and carry out other members' suggestions.

AFTER THE SESSION
- Evaluate your contribution to the group.
- Evaluate the overall success of your group.
- List ways to improve the next time.

READING TO LEARN

When you are reading to learn, you have two main goals: to expand your knowledge about a topic and to remember the information. When you read to learn, you will often work with textbooks, nonfiction library books, newspapers, journals, newsmagazines, and related art and photographs.

1.9 Reading Textbooks

Textbooks provide a broad overview of a course of study. Textbooks should provide as much material as possible in an objective, factual way.

READER'S JOURNAL. The Reader's Journal questions in the Prereading section of each selection provide students with response questions and writing prompts that they can use to get started writing in their own reading journals. See pages 5, 27, 43, 49, and 61 in Unit 1 for examples.

BOOK CLUB. You might have your students read the books suggested in the For Your Reading List section at the end of each unit and have students conduct a book club in small groups. See pages 145, 229, 394, 454, and 857.

SPEAKING AND LISTENING

Students can apply the guidelines in 1.8, "Guidelines for Discussing Literature in a Book Club" to the Collaborative Learning & Critical Thinking activity on page 415.

MEDIA LITERACY

ART SMART. The Art Smart notes that accompany much of the fine art in this text provide students with an opportunity to critically view and interpret works of art. See the Art Smart notes on pages 10, 26, and 45 in Unit 1 for examples.

THE PARTS OF A BOOK. When previewing book, first glance at all of its parts. Every book will have some or all of the following parts:

THE PARTS OF A BOOK

Title page: Gives the title, author, and publisher

Copyright page: Gives information regarding the publication of the book and the copyrights protecting it from being copied or sold illegally

Table of contents: Lists the units, chapters, and/or subjects of the book and the page numbers where they are found

Preface, introduction, or foreword: Introduces the book

Text: Main part of the book

Afterword or epilogue: Gives conclusion or tells what happened later

Appendix: Gives additional information about subjects covered in the book, often in chart or table form

Glossary: Lists key words used in the book and their definitions

Bibliography: Lists sources used in writing the book or sources for further study

Index: Lists in alphabetical order the subjects mentioned in the book and pages where these subjects are treated

1.10 Reading Newspapers, Journals, and Newsmagazines

Newspapers, journals, and newsmagazines contain an enormous amount of information. Few people have time to read everything that appears in a newspaper each day. Nonetheless, staying aware of the news is important.

To get an overview of a newspaper, journal, or newsmagazine, skim the headlines and leads (the first sentence in a news story that explains the who, what, where, why, and how of the story). Read any news summaries. Then read in depth any stories that seem particularly important or interesting.

When reading news stories and editorials, make sure to distinguish between facts and opinions. **Facts** are statements that can be proved by observation or by consulting a reliable and objective source. **Opinions** are predictions or statements of value or belief. Sound opinions are supported by facts. For more information, see the Language Arts Survey 5.2, "Distinguishing Fact from Opinion."

1.11 "Reading" Art and Photographs

In today's visually stimulating world, books and news media rely on art, photographs, and other visuals as well as the printed word to convey ideas. Being able to understand and interpret graphic images is important. Visual arts offer insights into our world in a different way than print does.

Carefully examining a painting can lead you to discover meaning in it and to compare and contrast the painting's meaning with that of a written work. The same thing happens with photographs. Learning to interpret other graphics or images—drawings, diagrams, charts, and maps—will help you to understand how things work, what things mean, and how things compare.

1.12 Seeking Knowledge as an Active Reader

Reading actively means thinking about what you are reading as you read it. Slow and careful reading—and sometimes rereading—is necessary to understand new and complex material. There are five key skills required for active reading:

- asking questions
- using your prior knowledge to make inferences and predictions about what you are reading
- recognizing what you do not know
- being able to synthesize information or create summaries, and
- knowing when to adapt your reading approach.

ASK QUESTIONS. Questioning allows you to realize what you understand about what you are reading. Before you read, think about your prior knowledge about the subject. Then ask yourself these questions: What is the essential information presented here? How is this new information organized or logically grouped? After reading, think about what you have learned and identify the questions you still have.

BEFORE READING
- What is this going to be about?
- What do I already know about the topic?
- What's my purpose for reading this?

DURING READING
- What does the author want me to know?
- What is the significance of what I am reading?
- What do I need to remember from this material?

AFTER READING
- What have I learned?
- What else do I want to know about this topic?

USE YOUR PRIOR KNOWLEDGE TO MAKE INFERENCES AND PREDICTIONS. While you are reading, use what you already know about the topic to make inferences about what the author is saying. As you read, try to make predictions about the next section.

KNOW WHAT YOU DO NOT KNOW. Recognizing when you do not understand something is as important as knowing that you do understand it. Form questions about the material you do not understand. Reread the text. Explain the topic to another student. Teaching someone else makes you understand the material in deeper ways.

SUMMARIZE OR SYNTHESIZE TEXT. Summarizing what you read helps you understand the main and supporting points in the text and helps you retrieve the information from long-term memory.

ADAPT YOUR READING APPROACH. If you realize that you are not comprehending the material, try another approach. Experiment with different tactics: speed up, slow down, reread, stand up and read, read the same material from another book, read with a dictionary in your lap, or generalize or visualize what you are reading.

1.13 Strategies for Reading to Learn: SQ3R

A five-step reading strategy called SQ3R can help you reduce your study time and increase your ability to understand essential information. The main steps of SQ3R are **S**URVEY, **Q**UESTION, **R**EAD, **R**ECITE, and **R**EVIEW.

SURVEY
- Preview the organization of material.
- Glance at visuals and assess how they contribute

to the meaning of the text.
- Skim headings and introductory paragraphs.
- Notice words in italics, boldface, and other terms that stand out.
- Ask yourself: What is the scope of the reading task? What should I learn from this material?

QUESTION
- Turn chapter titles and headings into questions.
- Ask yourself what the text is offering and what the author is saying.
- Ask yourself what you should know about the material and what you already know about it.
- Question graphics and visual materials. Translate the information they offer into your own words.
- Use words like *who, what, when, where, why,* and *how.*

READ
- Read and interact with the text.
- Underline or copy in your journal the main points.
- Make note of unusual or interesting ideas.
- Jot down words you need to define.
- Write your reactions to what you read.

RECALL
- Condense the major points of the text by writing recall cues.
- Summarize the material you have read. Reread any sections you don't clearly remember.
- Use graphic organizers to visualize or map out the material.
- Reread the text aloud if you need help recalling.

REVIEW
- After you have finished your reading, reread main headings and compare them to your notes.
- Review your notes, summaries, and definitions. Answer any questions you wrote.
- Ask yourself: What do I now understand? What is still confusing?

READING FOR INFORMATION

1.14 Reading Internet Materials, Reference Works, Graphic Aids, and Other Visuals

When you read for information, you are looking for information that answers a specific, immediate question; that teaches you to do something; or

SQ3R. Ask students to apply the SQ3R reading method to the Guided Writing lessons found at the end of each unit.

that will help you make a decision or draw a conclusion. One of the most important tasks for you to learn is how to access, process, and think about the vast amount of information available to you on the Internet and in online and print reference works, graphic aids, and other visuals.

DETERMINE YOUR SPECIFIC PURPOSE FOR READING. State your purpose for reading as clearly as you can. Are you searching the Internet for a review of the movie you're unsure whether to see? Are you learning to operate a computer program? Are you researching data to determine if the cost of a pet?

DETERMINE THE AUTHOR'S PURPOSE. Ask yourself what the writer wants the reader to think, believe, or do after reading this piece. Ask yourself if the author has bias on the topic that is affecting his or her views. If you are on the Internet, ask the following: Who is sponsoring the site? What hyperlinks are embedded in the site? Can you contact the site's author? When was the content written, and how might that affect the information it provides?

DETERMINE HOW THE AUTHOR USES SYMBOLS AND NUMERIC DATA. Work to understand how the author uses symbols, icons, and abbreviated headings on tables. Use any icons as shortcuts for navigating through the text and also for identifying the important material.

USE THE SEARCH APPROACH. Although your reading strategies should vary and relate directly to your purpose for reading, you may find the SEARCH method helpful when you are reading for information. SEARCH stands for **S**CAN, **E**XAMINE, **A**CT, **R**EVIEW, **C**ONNECT, and **H**UNT.

SCAN
- Look over the text and determine how the material is structured.
- Look for a table of contents, a glossary, an index, and other helpful sections.
- On an Internet site, look for a site map.

EXAMINE
- Are there step-by-step directions on diagrams? Do directions reveal exactly what to do or do you need to experiment a little?
- Is there a pattern in headings or icons?

- Are there any references to other sources of information?

ACT
- Explore the procedures you are reading and learn by doing.
- If you are seeking data, take notes about the information. Is it exactly what you were looking for, or do you need to keep looking?

REVIEW
- Revisit the steps of a procedure to make sure you have them clear in your head.
- Compare similar resources and read any additional references or links provided.

CONNECT
- Connect the information to what you previously knew about the topic. How did you build on what you knew?
- Connect text with visual aids. How do the visual aids add to the text?

HUNT
- Look up the meanings of any new words.
- Use the help feature on a computer program to find answers to your questions.
- Make a diagram of a procedure to will help you remember it.

1.15 Using Graphic Aids

Graphic aids are pictures, maps, illustrations, charts, graphs, diagrams, spreadsheets, and other visual materials that present information. Information presented in tables, charts, and graphs can help you find information, see trends, discover facts, and uncover patterns. For a complete description of graphic aids, see "Elements of Visual and Informational Media," on page 828.

Here are guidelines for working with graphics:

BEFORE READING
- Determine the subject of the graphic by reading the title, headings, and other clues.
- Determine how the data is organized, classified, or divided by reading the labels along rows or columns.
- Ask yourself: Why am I reading this document? What do I need to find? Where in this graphic is that information located?

DURING READING
- Survey the data and look for trends.
- Compare columns and rows, noting changes among information fields, look for patterns, or navigate map sections using keys and legends.
- Use legends, keys, and other helpful sections.
- Ask yourself: How does the data I need compare to other data on the graphic? What in this graphic can I skim or skip?

AFTER READING
- Check footnotes or references for additional information about the data and its sources.
- Ask yourself: Did this graphic answer my questions? If so, what are the answers? If not, where do I go to find the answers?

DEVELOPING YOUR VOCABULARY

1.16 Using Context Clues to Estimate Word Meaning

If you come across an unfamiliar word, you can often figure out its meaning by using context clues.

One type of context clue is **restatement**. The author may tell you the meaning of the word by using different words to express the same idea in another sentence.

EXAMPLE

> The dog snarled at Donald malevolently. It looked mean and spiteful.

The restatement provides a context clue that *malevolently* means "maliciously, with intent to do harm."

Another type of context clue is **apposition**. An apposition renames something in different words. Look for a word or phrase in the sentence that clarifies the word you do not know.

EXAMPLE

> Evan's conclusion was based on a fallacy, a false idea about how Maggie felt toward him.

Examples given in a sentence can also be used as context clues.

EXAMPLE

> The words *dad*, *radar*, *noon*, and *tenet* are all palindromes.

1.17 Using a Dictionary

Dictionary entries provide much more information about words than just their spelling and definitions.

The **pronunciation** is given immediately after the entry word. You can find a complete key to pronunciation symbols in the dictionary's table of contents. In some dictionaries, a simplified key is provided at the bottom of each page.

An abbreviation of the **part of speech** usually follows the pronunciation. This label tells the ways in which a word can be used (see the Language Arts Survey, 2.1–2.8, "The Parts of Speech"). If a word can be used in more than one way, definitions are grouped by part of speech.

An **etymology** is the history of a word. In the first entry, the word *pole* can be traced back through Middle English (ME) and Old English (OE) to the Latin (L) word *palus*, which means "stake."

Each **definition** in the entry gives a different meaning of the word. When a word has more than one meaning, the different definitions are numbered. The first definition in an entry is the most common meaning of the word.

Sometimes the entry will include a list of **synonyms**. The entry may also include an illustration of how the word is used.

DICTIONARIES. Students are asked to use their dictionary skills in the Language, Grammar, and Style activity on page 514 and in the Vocabulary activity on page 674.

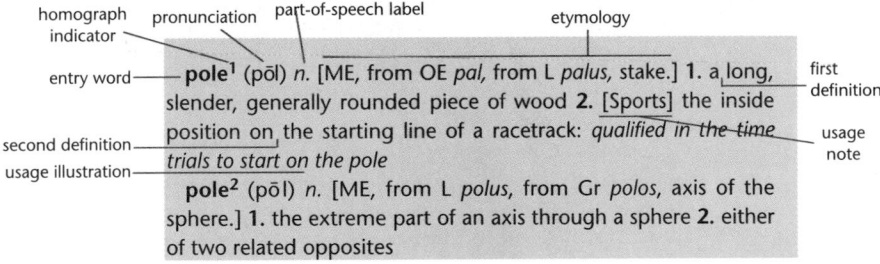

homograph indicator / pronunciation / part-of-speech label / etymology / entry word / first definition / second definition / usage illustration / usage note

pole¹ (pōl) *n.* [ME, from OE *pal*, from L *palus*, stake.] **1.** a long, slender, generally rounded piece of wood **2.** [Sports] the inside position on the starting line of a racetrack: *qualified in the time trials to start on the pole*

pole² (pōl) *n.* [ME, from L *polus*, from Gr *polos*, axis of the sphere.] **1.** the extreme part of an axis through a sphere **2.** either of two related opposites

1.18 Using Glossaries and Footnotes

A **glossary** is an alphabetized list of defined words at the end of an article, chapter, or book. **Footnotes** appear at the foot, or bottom, of a page. Sometimes they cite a source of information. Other times they define annotated words in order of appearance.

1.19 Learning Base Words, Prefixes, and Suffixes

Many words are formed by adding prefixes or suffixes to base words. (See the Language Arts Survey 3.95, "Using Spelling Rules I.") If you are unfamiliar with a word that is formed with a prefix or a suffix, see if you recognize the meaning of the base word and the meaning of its prefix or suffix. See the Prefixes and Suffixes table below.

1.20 Learning Synonyms, Antonyms, and Homonyms

A **synonym** is a word that has the same or nearly the same meaning as another word.

| EXAMPLES | discover, find, locate, pinpoint |

An **antonym** is a word that means the opposite of another word.

EXAMPLES	discover, conceal
	give, take
	success, defeat

A **homonym** is a word that has the same pronunciation as another word but a different meaning, origin, and usually, spelling.

| EXAMPLES | bight, bite, byte |

1.21 Exploring Word Origins and Word Families

The English language gains new words from many different sources. One source is the names of people and places. For example, the hamburger takes its name from the city of Hamburg, Germany. A spoonerism is a slip of the tongue where the beginning sounds of words are switched. It was named after Rev. William A. Spooner, who was noted for such slips. For example, after officiating at a wedding, he told the groom, "It is kisstomary to cuss the bride."

Another source of words in the English language is **acronyms**. Acronyms are words formed from the first letter or letters of the major parts of terms.

| EXAMPLES | sonar, from sound navigation ranging; NATO, from North Atlantic Treaty Organization; NASA, from National Aeronautic and Space Administration |

Some words in the English language are **borrowed** from other languages.

| EXAMPLES | deluxe (French), Gesundheit (German), kayak (Eskimo) |

PREFIXES AND SUFFIXES

prefix	meaning	example	meaning
anti–	"against"	antibacterial	against bacteria
dis–	"not, opposite"	disagreeable	not agreeable
hyper–	"over, excessively"	hyperactive	excessively active
im–, un–	"not"	unusual	not usual
post–	"after"	postseason	after the season
re–	"again"	reprint	print again

suffix	meaning	example	meaning
–er, –or	"one who"	narrator	one who narrates
–ful	"full of"	graceful	full of grace
–ish	"like"	childish	like a child
–ity, –ty	"state of, quality"	captivity	state of being captive
–less	"without"	fearless	without fear
–ment	"act of, state of"	achievement	act of achieving

Many words are formed by **shortening** longer words.

EXAMPLES	ad, from advertisement; auto, from automobile; lab, from laboratory; phone, from telephone

Brand names are often taken into the English language. People begin to use these words as common nouns, even though most of them are still brand names.

EXAMPLES	Scotch tape, Rollerblade, Walkman

1.22 Jargon and Gobbledygook

Jargon is the specialized vocabulary members of a profession use. It tends to be difficult for people outside the profession to understand. A plumber may speak of a "hubless fitting" or a "street elbow" (kinds of pipe). A computer programmer may talk of "ram cache" (part of computer memory).

Jargon is useful to writers who want to authentically describe certain situations. A novel about fighter pilots might feature aviation jargon. A science fiction film might include futuristic jargon about warps in space and energy shields.

Gobbledygook is unclear, wordy jargon used by bureaucrats, government officials, and others. For example, the failure of a program might be called an "incomplete success." A bureaucrat might say, "We are engaged in conducting a study with a view to ascertaining which employees might be assigned to the mobility pool and how we might create revenue enhancement" when he means, "We plan to cut jobs and increase taxes."

1.23 Clichés and Euphemisms

A **cliché** is an expression that has been used so often it has become a cliche. Cliches instantly make writing dull.

EXAMPLES	quick as a wink, pretty as a picture

A **euphemism** is an inoffensive term that substitutes for one considered harsh or offensive.

EXAMPLES	aerial mishap (for "plane crash") building engineer (for "janitor")

1.24 Connotation and Denotation

A **denotation** of a word is its dictionary definition. A **connotation** of a word is all the associations it has in addition to its literal meaning. For example, the words *cheap* and *economical* both denote "inexpensive," but *cheap* connotes shoddy and inferior while *economical* connotes a good value for the money. Writers and speakers should be aware of the connotations as well as the denotations of the words they use. Contrast these denotations and connotations:

EXAMPLES	curious: nosy, snoopy, prying, meddling

The Seven Stages in the Writing Process are developed thoroughly in each of the Guided Writing lessons that appear at the end of each unit. See pages 76-82 at the end of Unit 1 for an example.

PREWRITING. The Parts of a Writing Plan: Purpose, Audience, Form, and Topic, are discussed in depth in each of the Guided Writing lessons that appear at the end of each unit. For examples see pages 76-82, 146-152, 230-234, and 316-321.

WRITING
Resource

INTRODUCTION TO WRITING

2.1 The Writing Process

The most important action that you can take to shape a successful future for yourself is to learn how to write clearly and effectively. Almost anyone can learn to write well by learning the writing process. The writing process is simply the steps that a person takes to put together a piece of writing.

SEVEN STAGES IN THE PROCESS OF WRITING	
STAGE	**TASKS**
1. Prewriting	Plan your writing; choose a topic, audience, purpose, and form; gather ideas; and arrange them logically.
2. Drafting	Get your ideas down on paper.
3. Peer and Self-Evaluation	Evaluate, or judge, the writing piece and suggest ways to improve it. Judging your own writing is called **self-evaluation**. Judging a classmate's writing is called **peer evaluation**.
4. Revising	Work to improve the content, organization, and expression of your ideas.
5. Proofreading	Check your writing for errors in spelling, grammar, capitalization, and punctuation. Correct these errors, make a final copy of your paper, and proofread it again.
6. Publishing and Presenting	Share your work with an audience.
7. Reflecting	Think through the writing process to determine what you learned as a writer, what you accomplished, and what you would like to strengthen the next time you write.

While writing moves through these seven stages, it is also is a continuing cycle. You might need to go back to a previous stage before going on to the next step. Returning to a previous stage will strengthen your final work. Note also that the Reflecting stage can be done between any of the other steps. The more you reflect on your writing, the better your writing will become.

UNDERSTANDING THE WRITING PROCESS

2.2 Prewriting

In the **prewriting** stage of the writing process, you make a writing plan. You decide on a purpose, audience, form, and topic. You also begin to discover your voice and gather and organize ideas.

THE PARTS OF A WRITING PLAN

Purpose	A **purpose**, or **aim**, is the goal that you want your writing to accomplish.
Audience	An **audience** is the person or group of people intended to read what you write.
Form	A **form** is a kind of writing. For example, you might write a paragraph, an essay, a short story, a poem, or a news article.
Topic	A **topic** is simply something to write about. For example, you might write about a sports hero or about a cultural event in your community.

2.3 IDENTIFYING YOUR PURPOSE. A **purpose**, or aim, is the goal that you want your writing to accomplish. For example, you might write to inform, to entertain, to tell a story, to reflect, or to persuade. Your writing might have more than one purpose. For example, a piece of writing might inform about an important event while persuading the audience to respond in a specific way.

MODES AND PURPOSES OF WRITING

MODE	PURPOSE	EXAMPLE
expository/informative writing	to inform	news article, research report
imaginative writing	to entertain, enrich, and enlighten by using a form such as fiction or poetry to share a perspective	poem, short story
narrative writing	to make a point by sharing a story about an event	biography, family history
personal/expressive writing	to reflect	diary entry, personal letter
persuasive/argumentative writing	to persuade readers or listeners to respond in some way, such as to agree with a position, change a view on an issue, reach an agreement, or perform an action	editorial, petition

2.4 IDENTIFYING YOUR AUDIENCE. An **audience** is the person or group of people intended to read what you write. For example, you might write for yourself, for a friend, for a relative, or for your classmates. The best writing usually is intended for a specific audience. Choosing a specific audience beforehand will help you make important decisions about your work. For example, for an audience of young children, you would use simple words and ideas. For an audience of fellow members of a technology club, you would use jargon and other specialized words that the members already know. For more information, see the the Language Arts Survey 3.3, "Register, Tone, and Voice."

THINKING ABOUT YOUR AUDIENCE

- What people would be most interested in my topic?
- How much does the audience that I am considering already know about the topic?
- How much background information do I need to provide?
- What words, phrases, or concepts in my writing will my audience not understand? For which ones will I have to provide clear explanations?
- What can I do at the beginning of my writing to capture my audience's interest?

IDENTIFYING YOUR PURPOSE. Students are asked to identify author's aims in Understanding Literature on pages 369 and 653.

IDENTIFYING YOUR AUDIENCE. The Guided Writing lessons at the end of each unit contain instruction about identifying your audience as part of the prewriting process. For examples, see pages 77, 148, 232, and 317.

Finding Your Voice. Sections on finding your voice are found in each of the Guided Writing lessons at the end of each unit. See pages 77, 148, 232, 317 for examples.

Forms of Writing. Students are asked to use various forms of writing in the Writer's Journal found after each selection. For example, students are asked to write a memo on page 74, a narrative paragraph on page 137, a journal entry on page 195, stage directions on page 260, and a greeting card message on page 369.

Choosing a Topic. Students can learn more about freewriting by reading the Language Arts Survey 2.12, "Freewriting." Students can read more about making a cluster chart in the Language Arts Survey 2.13, "Clustering."

2.5 Finding Your Voice. Voice is the quality of a work that tells you that one person in particular wrote it. Voice makes a person's writing unique. Beginning with the prewriting stage and continuing through the rest of the writing process, a writer discovers his or her own unique voice. For more information, see the section about voice in the Language Arts Survey 3.3, "Register, Tone, and Voice."

2.6 Choosing a Form. Another important decision that a writer needs to make is what form his or her writing will take. A **form** is a kind of writing. For example, you might write a paragraph, an essay, a short story, a poem, or a newspaper article. The following chart lists some forms of writing that you might want to consider.

FORMS OF WRITING

Advertisement	Dialogue	Journal entry	Rap
Adventure	Directions	Letter	Recipe
Advice column	Dream report	Magazine article	Recommendation
Agenda	Editorial	Memorandum	Research report
Apology	Epitaph	Menu	Résumé
Appeal	Essay	Minutes	Schedule
Autobiography	Eulogy	Movie review	Science fiction
Biography	Experiment	Mystery	Short story
Book review	Fable	Myth	Slide show
Brochure	Family history	Narrative	Slogan
Calendar	Fantasy	Newspaper article	Song lyric
Caption	Greeting card	Obituary	Speech
Cartoon	Headline	Parable	Sports story
Character sketch	History	Paraphrase	Statement of belief
Cheer	Human interest story	Petition	Summary
Children's story	Instructions	Play	Tall tale
Comedy	Interview questions	Police/Accident report	Thank-you note
Consumer report	Invitation	Poster	Tour guide
Debate	Itinerary	Proposal	Want ad
Detective story	Joke	Radio or TV spot	Wish list

2.7 Choosing a Topic. A **topic** is simply something to write about. For example, you might write about a sports hero or about a cultural event in your community. Here are some ideas that may help you find interesting writing topics:

WAYS TO FIND A WRITING TOPIC

Check your journal	Search through your journal for ideas that you jotted down in the past. Many professional writers get their ideas from their journals.
Think about your experiences	Think about people, places, or events that affected you strongly. Recall experiences that taught you important lessons or that you felt strongly about.
Look at reference works	Reference works include printed or computerized dictionaries, atlases, almanacs, and encyclopedias.
Browse in a library	Libraries are treasure houses of information and ideas. Simply looking around in the stacks of a library can suggest good writing ideas.

CONTINUED

WAYS TO FIND A WRITING TOPIC

Use the mass media	Newspapers, magazines, radio, television, and films can suggest good writing topics. For example, a glance at listings for public television programs might suggest topics related to the arts, to history, or to nature.
Talk to people	Friends, relatives, teachers, and other people you know make great sources for writing topics.
Do some freewriting	Simply put your pen or pencil down on a piece of paper and write about whatever pops into your mind. Write for two to five minutes without pausing to worry about whether your writing is perfect. Then look back over what you have written to see if you can find any good topics there.
Ask "What if" questions	Ask questions beginning with "What if" to come up with topics for creative writing. For example, you might ask, "What if a kid with a ham radio set received a message from space? Would people believe her?"
Make a cluster chart	Write some general subject such as music or sports in the middle of a piece of paper. Circle this subject. Then, around it, write other ideas that come into your mind as you think about the subject. Circle these and draw lines to connect the outer circles to the inner one.

2.8 FOCUSING A TOPIC. Sometimes a topic is too broad to be treated in a short piece of writing. When you have a topic that is too broad, you must **focus**, or limit, the topic.

WAYS TO FOCUS A WRITING TOPIC

Break the topic into parts	For example, the topic "newspapers" could be broken down into reporting, copyediting, advertising, circulation, and so on.
Ask questions about the topic	Begin your questions with the words *who, what, where, when, why,* and *how.* Then ask what stands out about your topic or what interests you most.
Make a cluster chart or do some freewriting	For information on these techniques, see the Language Arts Survey 1.5, "Finding a Topic."

2.9 Gathering Ideas

Once you have made your writing plan by identifying your purpose, form, audience, and topic, the next step in the prewriting stage is to **gather ideas**. There are many ways to gather ideas for writing. This section will introduce you to some of the most useful ones.

2.10 LEARNING FROM PROFESSIONAL MODELS. Professional models are works by published authors. They can be an excellent way to gather your own ideas. For example, Jamal was impressed by the way Robert Jastrow wrote about size in his essay "The Size of Things" in Unit 11. He analyzed this informative essay and used it as a model when he wrote his own piece on astronomy for a science fair exhibit. For more information, see the way professional models are used in the Guided Writing lessons at the end of each unit in this textbook.

2.11 KEEPING A JOURNAL. A **journal** is a record of your ideas, dreams, wishes, and experiences. Composition books, spiral notebooks, looseleaf binders, and bound books with blank pages all make

LEARNING FROM PROFESSIONAL MODELS. The Guided Writing lessons at the end of each unit contain professional or student writing models as the basis for writing instruction. See examples on pages 76, 146, 230, and 316.

excellent journal books. Some people even keep electronic journals on computers. You may want to use a journal to write thoughts, collect ideas for writing, organize tasks, or keep a learning log.

2.12 FREEWRITING. Freewriting is simply taking a pencil and paper and writing whatever comes into your mind. Try to write for several minutes without stopping and without worrying about spelling, grammar, usage, or mechanics. If you get stuck, just repeat the last few words until something new pops into your mind. To gather ideas about a specific topic, you might want to try **focused freewriting**. In a focused freewrite, you still write nonstop for a few minutes, but you stick with one topic and write whatever comes to mind as you think about that topic.

2.13 CLUSTERING. Another good way to tap what you already know is to make a **cluster chart**. To make a cluster chart, draw a circle in the center of your paper. In it write a topic you want to explore. Draw more circles branching out from your center circle, and fill them with subtopics related to your main topic.

SAMPLE CLUSTER CHART

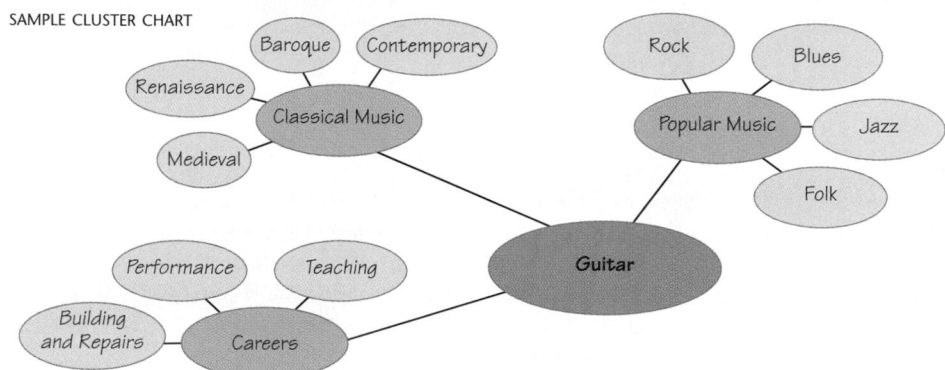

2.14 QUESTIONING: USING THE 5 Ws AND AN H. Using the 5 Ws and an H means asking the **reporting questions** who, what, where, when, why, and how about your topic. This questioning strategy is especially useful for gathering information about an event or for planning a story.

USING QUESTIONING (TOPIC: COWBOY POETRY)	
Who	Cowboy poets from the United States and other parts of the world
What	The Cowboy Poetry Festival, where cowboy poets gather
Where	Elko, Nevada
When	Held annually the last week in January
Why	So cowboys who love performing their songs, poetry, and stories can share them with others
How	This happens because of the huge interest in cowboy poetry and because of the major help from volunteers; the Western Folklife Center in Elko is a major organizer.

2.15 IMAGINING: ASKING WHAT IF QUESTIONS. If you are doing imaginative or creative writing, ask questions that begin with the words what if. "What if" questions can spark your imagination and lead you down unexpected and interesting paths. It can also help you see another side of things and strengthen your own when writing a persuasive piece.

What if I could run school for a week? What changes would I make?

What if I could go back in time to speak with a historical figure?

What if the greenhouse effect melted the polar icecaps and raised the levels of the oceans around the world? How would people respond?

2.16 COMPLETING VENN DIAGRAMS. If you are writing a comparison and contrast essay, one of the best ways to gather ideas is by completing a Venn diagram. A **Venn diagram** shows two slightly overlapping circles. The outer part of each circle shows what aspects of two things are different from each other. The inner, or shared, part of each circle shows what aspects the two things share.

SAMPLE VENN DIAGRAM

"HOLLYWOOD AND THE PITS"
BY CHERYLENE LEE

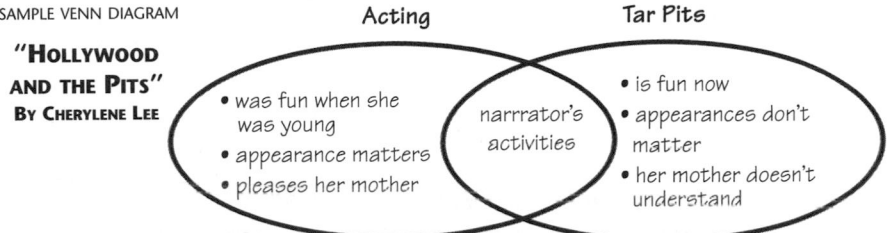

2.17 ANALYZING. To **analyze** is to break something down into its parts and then think about how the parts are related. Analyzing is a way to sort out information about a topic.

2.18 SENSORY DETAIL CHARTS. Most people have the use of five major senses: sight, sound, touch, taste, and smell. The larger the number of these senses you use to observe something, the more you will notice about it. A **sensory detail chart** can help you to collect information about something so that you can describe it thoroughly.

SENSORY DETAILS OF A MARATHON				
SIGHT	**SOUND**	**TOUCH**	**TASTE**	**SMELL**
hundreds of runners of all ages	starting gun	hot, sore feet from standing so long	hot dogs and lemonade from vendor carts	hot asphalt
news reporters and onlookers	crowds clapping			perspiration
running clothes	running shoes slapping on asphalt	stinging face from sun and wind		

2.19 TIME LINES. A **time line** can be useful when you are planning to write a story or a historical account. It gives you an overview of the sequence of events during a particular time period. To make a time line, draw a line on a piece of paper and divide it into equal parts. Label each part with a date or a time. Then add key events at the right places along the time line.

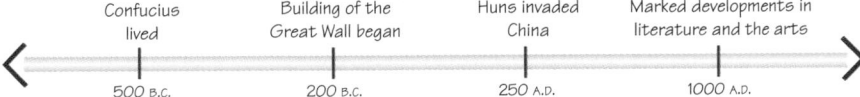

WRITING RESOURCE

2.20 Story Maps. A **story map** is a chart that shows the various parts of a fable, myth, tall tale, legend, short story, or other fictional work. Most story maps include the following elements:

ELEMENTS OF A STORY MAP	
ELEMENT	**DESCRIPTION**
Setting	The time and place in which the story occurs
Mood	The emotion created in the reader by the story
Conflict	A struggle between two forces in the story
Plot	The series of events taking place in the story
Characters	The people (or sometimes animals) who play roles in the story
Theme	The main idea of the story

2.21 Pro and Con Charts. A **pro and con chart** shows arguments for and against taking a particular position on some issue. To create a pro and con chart, begin by writing a statement, called a **proposition**, at the top of a piece of paper. Under the proposition, make two columns, one labeled *Pro* and the other, *Con*. In the pro column, list arguments in favor of the proposition. In the con column, list arguments against the proposition.

PRO AND CON CHART	
Proposition: All students should take an hour of physical education each day.	
Pro	**Con**
—would keep students in good physical condition	—would take time away from academic studies
—improved health would also improve students' ability to think clearly and work hard	—the same ends might be achieved in less time per day

2.22 Interviewing. In an **interview**, you meet with someone and ask him or her questions. Interviewing experts is an excellent way to gain information about a particular topic. When planning an interview, list the questions you would like to ask, including some about the person's background as well as about your topic. Other questions might occur to you as the interview proceeds. See the Language Arts Survey 4.14, "Conducting an Interview."

2.23 Researching for Ideas. No matter what your subject, you can probably find information about it by doing research in reference works. **Reference works** include encyclopedias, dictionaries, almanacs, atlases, indexes, Internet sites, and more. For additional information about reference materials and how to find them, see the Language Arts Survey 5.20, "Using Reference Works" and 5.36, "Keeping a Research Journal."

2.24 Organizing Ideas

After you have gathered ideas for a piece of writing, the next step is to organize these ideas in a useful way. One way is to write a thesis statement and several main ideas with supporting details. Another way to organize ideas is to arrange them in a particular order, as detailed in the Language Arts Survey 2.27, "Choosing a Method of Organization." Finally, an outline can help you organize your writing and prepare it for drafting, the next step in the writing process.

INTERVIEWING. Students are asked to do writing assignments based on interviews in Integrating the Language Arts on pages 125, 208, 576, 660 and 790.

ORGANIZING IDEAS: WRITING WITH A PLAN. For instruction on different types of writing organization, see the Writing with a Plan section of the Guided Writing lessons at the end of each unit. For examples, turn to pages 77, 147, 231, and 317.

2.25 WRITING A THESIS STATEMENT. One way to start organizing your writing, especially if you are writing an informative or persuasive essay, is to identify the main idea of what you want to say. Present this idea in the form of a sentence or two called a thesis statement. A **thesis statement** is simply a sentence that presents the main idea or the position you will take in your essay.

THESIS FOR A PERSUASIVE ESSAY

The development at Rice Creek Farm should be stopped because it will destroy one of the best natural areas near the city.

THESIS FOR AN INFORMATIVE ESSAY

Wilma Rudolph was an athlete who succeeded in the elite sport of tennis before the world was willing to recognize her.

2.26 WRITING MAIN IDEAS AND SUPPORTING DETAILS. Once you have a thesis statement, the next step is to select several main ideas to support your thesis statement. Begin by writing your thesis at the top of a piece of paper. Then list the main points that you will use to support your thesis. For each main idea, list several supporting details—statements, facts, examples, quotes, and illustrations that explain or demonstrate your idea.

THESIS: The development at Rice Creek Farm should be stopped because people will be unable to enjoy the area, a considerable amount of wildlife will be harmed, and an important water resource will be lost.

- People will be unable to enjoy the area
  - Hundreds of people of all ages now bike, run, and swim in the area in the summer and ski in the winter. Last year's recreation survey was completed by 653 people. Eighty-five percent said that they visited Rice Creek Farm at least twice a month.
  - The development of an industrial park would ban people from using the area. It will become a factory site instead of a wooded recreation area. "The industrial park site would be strictly off limits to the public for their own protection," developer Orrin Q. Smedley said in the Rice Creek Times.

- A considerable amount of wildlife will be harmed.
  - The wooded area will be completely eliminated, destroying habitat.
  - The species that will be lost will include deer, fox, racoons, skunks, and wild birds, according to the parks board supervisor.

- An important water resource will be lost.
  - The water resource has many uses, including recreational and agricultural.
  - The quality of our city water supply depends on the preservation of this habitat.

WRITING A THESIS STATEMENT. Students are asked to write a thesis statement in the Guided Writing lessons for Units 6 and 11. See pages 455 and 819.

Choosing a Method of Organization. In the Guided Writing lesson for Unit 1 students are asked to use chronological order to write a personal essay (page 79). In the Guided Writing lesson for Unit 4 students use chronological order to write an autobiographical memoir (page 318). Students use order of importance in the Unit 8 Guided Writing lesson, which asks students to write a composition interpreting literature. The Guided Writing lesson for Unit 12, which asks students to explain a process using a graphic, focuses on cause-and-effect order (page 858).

2.27 Choosing a Method of Organization. Writing can be organized in different ways.

METHOD	DESCRIPTION
Chronological Order	Give events in the order in which they happen or should be done; connect events by using transition words such as *first, second, next, then,* and *finally.* Chronological organization would be a good method for giving a recipe, writing a how-to article on building a bird-feeder, or to describe a process, such as what happens when a volcano erupts.
Spatial Order	Describe parts in order of their location in space, for example, from back to front, left to right, or top to bottom; connect your descriptions with transition words or phrases such as *next to, beside, above, below, beyond,* and *around.* Spatial order would be a useful form for an article describing a kitchen renovation, or a descriptive passage in a science fiction story set in a space station.
Order of Importance	List details from least important to most important or from most important to least important; connect your details with transition phrases such as *more important, less important, most important,* and *least important.* A speech telling voters why they should elect you class president could be organized from the least important reason and build to the most important reason.
Comparison-and-Contrast Order	Details of two subjects are presented in one of two ways. In the first method, the characteristics of one subject are presented, followed by the characteristics of the second subject. This method would be useful to organize an essay that compares and contrasts two fast-food chains. You could use this method to say why one is superior to another. "BurgerWorld has the most restaurants. They broil their hamburgers, and offer a line of low-fat meals. Ma's Burgers has far fewer restaurants, fries their hamburgers, and offers no low-fat choices." In the second method, both subjects are compared and contrasted with regard to one quality, then with regard to a second quality, and so on. An essay organized according to this method could compare the platforms of two political parties, issue by issue: the environment, the economy, and so on. Ideas are connected by transitional words and phrases that indicate similarities or differences, such as *likewise, similarly, in contrast, a different kind,* and *another difference.*
Cause-and-Effect Order	One or more causes are presented followed by one or more effects, or one or more effects are presented followed by one or more causes. A public health announcement warning about the dangers of playing with fire would be usefully organized by cause-and-effect. An essay discussing the outbreak of World War I and the events that led up to it could be organized by effect and causes. Transitional words and phrases that indicate cause and effect include *one cause, another effect, as a result, consequently,* and *therefore.*
Part-by-Part Order	Ideas are presented according to no *overall* organizational pattern. However, each idea is connected logically to the one that precedes it and/or to the one that follows it. A letter to a friend might be organized part by part. One paragraph might discuss a party the writer just attended and the next could focus on the writer's feelings about a person he or she met there. After chronological order, this is the most common method for organizing ideas in writing. Transitional words or phrases include anything that indicates the relationship or connection between the ideas.

2.28 OUTLINING. An **outline** is an excellent framework for highlighting main ideas and supporting details. Rough and formal outlines are the two main types of outlines writers commonly use.

2.29 ROUGH OUTLINES. To create a **rough outline**, simply list your main ideas in some logical order. Under each main idea, list the supporting details set off by dashes.

2.30 FORMAL OUTLINES. A **formal outline** has headings and subheadings identified by numbers and letters. One type of formal outline is the **topic outline**. Such an outline has entries that are words or phrases rather than complete sentences.

2.31 Drafting

After you have gathered your information and organized it, the next step in writing is to produce a draft. A **draft** is simply an early attempt at writing a paper. When working on a draft, keep in mind that you do not have to get everything just right the first time through. You can rework it many times until you are happy with the final product.

Different writers approach drafting in different ways. Some prefer to work slowly and carefully, perfecting each part as they go. Producing such a **careful draft** can be rewarding because you get to see a finished, polished piece emerging part by part. However, many writers find that perfecting each part as they come to it bogs down the process. These writers prefer to write a discovery draft, getting all their ideas down on paper in rough form and then going back over the paper to work it into shape. When writing a **discovery draft**, you do not focus on spelling, grammar, usage, and mechanics. You can take care of those matters during revision.

2.32 DRAFTING AN INTRODUCTION. The purpose of an introduction is to capture your reader's attention and establish what you want to say. An effective introduction can start with a quotation, a question, an anecdote, an intriguing fact, or a description that hooks the reader to keep reading.

OUTLINING. Students are asked to write an outline for a narrative research paper in the Guided Writing lesson for Unit 6. See page 459.

TEACHER'S NOTE

Students are guided through writing an introduction, body paragraphs, and a conclusion for a literature interpretation assignment in the Guided Writing lesson for Unit 8. See page 604.

WRITING DESCRIPTION, DIALOGUE, NARRATIVE, AND EXPOSITION. Students are asked to use description in creating a setting in the Unit 5 Guided Writing lesson on page 395. In the Unit 7 Guided Writing lesson students are asked to incorporate dialogue when retelling a family story (page 522). Students practice narrative writing in the Guided Writing lessons for Units 1, 4, and 6 (pages 76, 316, and 455). Expository writing is the focus of the Unit 11 Guided Writing lesson, which asks students to write a letter to the editor (page 817).

An effective introduction can open with:

A QUOTE

"That's one small step for man, one giant leap for mankind." With these words, Neil Armstrong signaled his success as the first man to set foot on the moon...

A QUESTION

What would it be like if all the birds in the world suddenly stopped their singing?

AN ANECDOTE

When my brother was nineteen, he volunteered in a homeless shelter making sure people had a safe place to spend the night. He told me once that he would never forget the time he met...

A FACT

More than a million new web pages appear each day on the Internet...

A DESCRIPTION

Along the murky bottom of the ocean floor, at the deepest part of the ocean, lies the giant squid, a creature so elusive that few people have ever seen it. For hundreds of years, no one knew it really existed—although tales of sea monsters had long hinted of it.

2.33 DRAFTING BODY PARAGRAPHS. When writing the body of an essay, refer to your outline. Each heading in your outline will become the main idea of one of your paragraphs. To move smoothly from one idea to another, use transitional words or phrases. As you draft, you may want to include evidence from documented sources to support the ideas that you present.

2.34 DRAFTING A CONCLUSION. In the conclusion, bring together the main ideas you included in the body of your essay and create a sense of closure to the issue you raised in your thesis. There is no single right way to conclude a piece of writing. Possibilities include:

- making a generalization
- restating the thesis and major supporting ideas in different words
- summarizing the points made in the rest of the essay
- drawing a lesson or moral
- calling on the reader to adopt a view or take an action
- expanding on your thesis or main idea by connecting it to the reader's own interests
- linking your thesis to a larger issue or concern.

2.35 USING TRANSITIONS EFFECTIVELY. Transitions are words and phrases that help you move smoothly from one idea to the next in your writing. The transition words themselves depend on the method of organization you are using in your paper. For lists of these words and when to use them, see the Language Arts Survey 2.27, "Choosing a Method of Organization."

2.36 WRITING DESCRIPTION, DIALOGUE, NARRATIVE, AND EXPOSITION. Some writing purposes do not require a thesis or a formal outline. They rely on other types of writing to present their ideas effectively. These types include description, dialogue, narration, and exposition. **Narration** tells a story or describes events using time, or **chronological order**, as a way of organization. **Dialogue** presents words as they were actually spoken by people. Quotation marks are usually used to set off direct speech. **Description** portrays a character, an object, or a scene. Descriptions make use of sensory details—words and phrases that describe how things look, sound, taste, or feel. Descriptive writing frequently uses **spatial order** as a way of organization. **Exposition** presents facts or opinions in an organized manner. There are many ways to organize exposition. Among the most common are the following:

- **Analysis** breaks something into its parts and shows how the parts are related.
- **Cause and Effect** identifies and analyzes the causes and effects of something.

- **Classification** involves placing subjects into categories, or classes, according to their properties or characteristics. These groups are then presented, one-by-one, in some reasonable order.
- **Comparison and Contrast Order** is a method of organization in which details about the similarities and differences between two subjects are presented.
- **Definition** explains a concept or idea and examines its qualities.
- **Problem/Solution** writing analyzes a problem and proposes possible solutions. It can be objective or persuasive.
- **Process/How-to** writing presents the steps in a process or gives the reader directions on how to do something.

2.37 Self- and Peer Evaluation

When you evaluate something, you examine it carefully to find its strengths and weaknesses. Evaluating your own writing is called **self-evaluation**. A **peer evaluation** is an evaluation of a piece of writing done by a classmate, or peer.

2.38 How to Evaluate a Piece of Writing. A good evaluation practice is to read through the piece of writing three times:

- First, check for content. If you are evaluating your own writing, make sure that you have said all that you want to say, that you have not left out important details, and that you have not included unimportant or unrelated details. If you are evaluating a peer's writing, make sure the content is clear, that nothing is missing to prevent the work from carrying the reader forward, and that the writer has not included any unrelated details.
- Second, check for organization. Present your ideas in the writing in a reasonable order.
- Third, check the style and language of the piece. Make sure that the language is appropriately formal or informal, that the tone is appropriate, and that the writer has defined any key or unfamiliar terms.

As you check the writing piece, make notes about what the writer needs to revise, or change. See the Language Arts Survey 2.42, "A Revision Checklist," for further information on what to look for as you evaluate your or a peer's writing.

2.39 How to Deliver Helpful Criticism

- Be focused. Concentrate on content, organization, and style. Do not concentrate at this point on proofreading matters such as spelling and punctuation; they can be fixed later.
- Be positive. Let the writer know what he or she has done right. Show how the paper could be improved by making the changes that you are suggesting.
- Be specific. Give the writer concrete ideas for improving his or her work. For example, if you think that two ideas seem unconnected, suggest a way in which they might be connected clearly.
- Be tactful. Consider the other person's feelings, and use a pleasant tone of voice. Do not criticize the writer. Instead, focus on the writing.

2.40 How to Benefit from Helpful Criticism

- Tell your evaluator specific concerns. For example, if you are wondering whether something you have written is clear, ask the evaluator if he or she understands that part of what you have written.
- Ask questions to clarify comments that your evaluator makes.
- Accept your evaluator's comments graciously. Remember that criticisms can be helpful. If you think that a given suggestion will not truly improve your writing, you do not have to follow it.

Self- and Peer Evaluation. Self- and peer evaluation is covered in each of the Guided Writing lessons at the end of the units. See pages 79, 148, 232, and 319 for examples.

2.41 Revising

After identifying weaknesses in a draft through self-evaluation and peer evaluation, the next step is to **revise** the draft. Here are four basic ways to improve meaning and content.

Adding or Expanding. Sometimes writing can be improved by adding details, examples, or transitions to connect ideas. Often a single added adjective, for example, can make a piece of writing clearer or more vivid.

UNREVISED

Wind whistled through the park.

REVISED

A **bone-chilling** wind whistled through the park.

At other times, you will find you will need to add details to back up your main idea.

UNREVISED

Everyone uses the park so its destruction would be a major loss to the community.

REVISED

Of the 653 people who responded to the survey, 85 percent said they would consider the destruction of the park a major loss to the community.

Cutting or Condensing. Often writing can be improved by cutting unnecessary or unrelated material.

UNREVISED

Watson was firmly determined to find the structure of the DNA molecule.

REVISED

Watson was determined to find the structure of the DNA molecule.

Replacing. Sometimes weak writing can be replaced with stronger writing that is more concrete, more vivid, or more precise.

UNREVISED

Chandra lived in a house down the street.

REVISED

Chandra lived in a Garrison colonial down Mulberry Street.

Moving. Often you can improve the organization of your writing by moving part of it so that related ideas appear near one another.

UNREVISED

Mince the garlic in very fine pieces. Then heat a tablespoon of olive oil in a small skillet. Stir it with a wooden spoon and saute just until it starts to brown. Then remove it. Oh— before you put it in the skillet, heat some oil. Use about a tablespoon. Olive oil is best. Use medium low heat.

REVISED

Mince the garlic in very fine pieces. Heat a tablespoon of olive oil in a small skillet at a medium low temperature. When the oil is hot, add the garlic. Stir it with a wooden spoon and saute it just until it starts to brown. Then remove the garlic.

When you mark a piece of writing for revision, use the standard proofreading symbols. The symbols for adding, cutting, replacing, and moving are the first four symbols in the Language Arts Survey 2.44, "Using Proofreader's Marks."

2.42 A REVISION CHECKLIST. The following chart lists some questions to ask yourself whenever you are revising your writing. If you cannot answer *yes* to any of these questions, then you need to revise your work. Continue revising until you can answer *yes*.

REVISION CHECKLIST	
Content	• Does the writing achieve its purpose?
	• Are the main ideas clearly stated and supported by details?
Organization	• Are the ideas arranged in a sensible order?
	• Are the ideas connected to one another within paragraphs and between paragraphs?
Style	• Is the language appropriate to the audience and purpose?
	• Is the mood appropriate to the purpose of the writing?

2.43 Proofreading

When you **proofread** your writing, you read it through to look for errors and mark corrections. When you mark corrections to your writing, use the standard proofreading symbols. With just a little practice you'll find them very easy and convenient.

2.44 USING PROOFREADER'S MARKS. Consult the chart below for standard proofreading marks.

PROOFREADER'S SYMBOLS	
Symbol and Example	**Meaning of Symbol**
The very first time	Delete (cut) this material.
cat cradle	Insert (add) something that is missing.
George	Replace this letter or word.
All the horses king's	Move this word to where the arrow points.
french toast	Capitalize this letter.
the vice-President	Lowercase this letter.
housse	Take out this letter and close up space.
book keeper	Close up space.
gebril	Change the order of these letters.
end. "Watch out," she yelled.	Begin a new paragraph.
Love conquers all	Put a period here.
Welcome friends.	Put a comma here.
Get the stopwatch	Put a space here.
Dear Madam	Put a colon here.
She walked he rode.	Put a semicolon here.
name brand products	Put a hyphen here.
cats meow	Put an apostrophe here.
cat's cradle (stet)	Let it stand. (Leave as it is.)

REVISION CHECKLIST. A blackline master of the Revision Checklist is provided in the Writing Resource 2.42 of the Teacher's Resource Kit.

PROOFREADING. Instruction on revising and proofreading is given in each of the Guided Writing lessons at the end of the units. For examples see pages 81, 150, 234, and 320.

USING PROOFREADER'S MARKS. Encourage students to use proofreader's marks when they do peer evaluations. A blackline master of the Proofreader's Symbols is provided in the Writing Resource 2.44 of the Teacher's Resource Kit.

WRITING RESOURCE

2.45 A PROOFREADING CHECKLIST. After you have revised your draft, make a clean copy of it and proofread it for errors in spelling, grammar, and punctuation. Use the following proofreading checklist.

PROOFREADING CHECKLIST	
Spelling	• Are all words, including names, spelled correctly?
Grammar	• Does each verb agree with its subject?
	• Are verb tenses consistent and correct?
	• Are irregular verbs formed correctly?
	• Are there any sentence fragments or run-ons?
	• Have double negatives been avoided?
	• Have frequently confused words, such as *affect* and *effect*, been used correctly?
Punctuation	• Does every sentence end with an end mark?
	• Are commas used correctly?
	• Do all proper nouns and proper adjectives begin with capital letters?

2.46 PROPER MANUSCRIPT FORM. After proofreading your draft, you will want to prepare your final manuscript. Follow the guidelines given by your teacher or the guidelines given here. After preparing a final manuscript according to these guidelines, proofread it one last time for errors.

• Keyboard your manuscript using a typewriter or word processor, or write it out neatly using blue or black ink.

• Double-space your paper. Leave one blank line between every line of text.

• Use one side of the paper.

• Leave one-inch margins on all sides of the text.

• Indent the first line of each paragraph.

• Make a cover sheet listing the title of the work, your name, the date, and the class.

• In the upper right-hand corner of the first page, put your name, class, and date. On every page after the first, include the page number in the heading, as follows:

EXAMPLE HEADER

Keanna Pérez
English 7
May 3, 2001
p. 2

2.47 Publishing and Presenting Your Work

In the **publishing and presenting stage**, you share your work with an audience.

2.48 MAINTAINING A WRITING PORTFOLIO. A **writing portfolio** is a collection of your writing. Usually, a portfolio is a file folder with your name on it and your writing in it. Your teacher may ask you to keep a complete portfolio, that includes all the pieces that you write, or a selected portfolio

---

PROPER MANUSCRIPT FORM. Encourage students to read the Language Arts Survey 2.46, "Proper Manuscript Form" after they are done revising and proofreading their written assignments.

PUBLISHING AND PRESENTING. Ideas for publishing and presenting student writing are suggested in each of the Guided Writing lessons at the end of the units. For examples, see pages 82, 152, 234, and 321.

MAINTAINING A WRITING PORTFOLIO. You might find additional suggestions for helping students maintain a writing portfolio in *Portfolio Keeping: A Guide for Students* by Nedra Reynolds.

that contains only your very best pieces of writing. From time to time, you and your teacher will evaluate, or examine, your portfolio. You will meet in a student-teacher conference and talk about your pieces of writing. Your teacher will help you to find strengths and weaknesses in your writing. He or she also will help you to make plans for improving your writing in the future.

2.49 SHARING YOUR WORK WITH OTHERS. Some writing is done just for one's self. Journal writing usually falls into that category. Most writing, however, is meant to be shared with others. There are many ways in which to share your work. Here are several ways in which you can publish your writing or present it to others:

- Find a local publication that will accept your work. (A school literary magazine, a school newspaper, or a community newspaper are possibilities.)
- Submit the work to a regional or national publication.
- Enter the work in a contest. Your teacher may be able to tell you about writing contests for students.
- Read your work aloud to classmates, friends, or family members.
- Work with other students to prepare a publication—a brochure, on-line literary magazine, anthology, or newspaper.
- Prepare a poster or bulletin board, perhaps in collaboration with other students, to display your writing.
- Make your own book by typing or word processing the pages and binding them together. Or copy your work into a blank book.
- Hold a reading of student writing as a class or school-wide project.
- Share your writing with other students in a small writers' group.

2.50 Reflecting on Your Writing

In the **reflecting** stage, you think through the writing process to determine what you learned as a writer, what you accomplished, and what skills you would like to strengthen the next time you write. Reflection can be done in a journal, on a self-evaluation form for writing, in small group discussion, or simply in your own thoughts. Here are some questions to ask as you reflect on the writing process and yourself as a writer.

- What have I learned in writing about this topic?
- What have I learned in writing for this purpose?
- What have I learned by using this form?
- How do I perceive my audience? What would I like my audience to gain from my writing?
- What kind of voice does my writing have?
- How have I developed as a writer while writing this piece?
- What strengths have I discovered in my work?
- What aspects of my writing do I want to strengthen? What can I do to strengthen them?

REFLECTING ON YOUR WRITING. Students are asked to reflect on their writing at various stages of the writing process in the Guided Writing lessons at the end of each unit. For examples, turn to pages 76, 152, 230, and 318.

REGISTER, TONE, AND VOICE. Refer students to the Language Arts survey 3.3, "Register, Tone, and Voice" when they are reading the Finding Your Voice section of each Guided Writing lesson. See pages 77, 148, 232, and 317 for examples.

LANGUAGE, GRAMMAR, AND STYLE *Resource*

LANGUAGE HANDBOOK

3.1 Appropriate Uses of English

Language is a powerful and complex tool for conveying meaning. It is also a complex tool. To communicate effectively, you must make choices—whether to use formal or informal English; what tone to use; the effects of irony, sarcasm, and rudeness; and how dialect affects the message.

3.2 Formal and Informal English

Depending on the situation, you might use either formal English or informal English when you speak or write. Formal English is appropriate for school essays, newspaper and magazine articles, some literary works, oral or written reports, and test answers. Informal English is appropriate when speaking with a friend or writing personal letters or notes; it can also be used in some literary works.

Informal English allows grammatical constructions that would not be acceptable in formal English. Many of these constructions will be described in the Grammar Handbook (where they are labeled "nonstandard"). Informal English also uses colloquialisms and slang.

A **colloquialism** is a word or phrase used in everyday conversation.

> EXAMPLES
>
> **You guys** must be sick of doing the same thing day after day.
>
> He was **totally turned off** by the movie.

Slang is a form of speech made up of invented words or old words that are given a new meaning.

> EXAMPLES
>
> You better **chill out** for a while—you're too angry to talk to him now.
>
> She has a real **hang-up** about mushrooms on her pizza.

3.3 Register, Tone, and Voice

To understand the concept of register, imagine that all the different kinds of usage in a language—both formal and informal—form one large set. A **register** is a subset of language usage specific to a particular relationship between people. In talking to a friend, for example, you speak in a register that is casual, warm, and open. In speaking to a young child, you speak in a register that is nonthreatening and simple to understand. In speaking to an official such as a police officer or a government clerk, you speak in a register that is polite but firm—the same register that person should use with you. The words you choose, the grammar you employ to say those words, and your tone of voice will change depending on the register you are using.

People who know how to use the power of language are able to choose the appropriate register for whatever situation they are in. They do not offend strangers by being too familiar or puzzle their friends by being too formal.

Tone is a writer's or speaker's attitude toward a subject. The tone of a message should reflect the speaker's attitude toward the subject and his or her audience. The speaker shapes the tone of a message by carefully choosing words and phrases.

Diction, or choice of words, determines much of a speaker's tone. For instance, when writing a letter of complaint, you could say, "Your new product is so disgusting that I'll never buy anything you make ever again" or "I am concerned with the danger your new product poses to young children." The tone you convey will depend greatly upon word choice.

Voice is the quality of a work that tells you that one person in particular wrote it. Voice makes a spoken or written work unique. The voice of a work can be difficult to define; it may have to do with the way a writer or speaker views people, events, objects, ideas, the passage of time, or even life itself. If this treatment of the subject is consistent throughout, despite variations in tone, register, point of view, and topic, then the writer or speaker has established a voice, or a sense of individuality, in the work. In your own speaking and writing, strive to develop your own voice.

3.4 Irony, Sarcasm, and Rudeness

The standard definition of *rude* means bad-mannered, impolite, or inconsiderate. Interrupting someone else's conversation, cursing, or forgetting to say "please," "thank you," or "excuse me" is being rude. It is easy to confuse sarcasm or irony with rudeness. **Verbal irony** is present when someone says or writes the opposite of what he or she means, either to create humor or to make a point. It can be funny or serious. For example, if someone pushes to the front of a line, and someone else says, "What polite behavior," the speaker is using verbal irony. **Sarcasm** is a specialized kind of irony; the difference is the speaker's intentions. Sarcastic people say the opposite of what they mean in order to criticize, hurt, or humiliate someone. Sarcasm differs from other forms of irony because it is always unkind.

EXAMPLES OF SARCASM

> "Hey, how's that for a smart outfit?" She [Ellen] pointed to the other side of the hall.
>
> The gaudy flowers of Rachel Horton's blouse stood out among the fluffy sweaters and pleated skirts.
>
> —Rona Maynard, "The Fan Club"

3.5 Dialects of English

A **dialect** is a version of a language spoken by people of a particular place, time, or group. Dialects are characterized by differences in pronunciation, word choice, grammar, and accent. They are usually based on regional differences or on social differences (upper class, middle class, and lower class). In the United States, the major regional dialects are northern, southern, midland, and western. Everyone speaks with some type of dialect.

A **standard** dialect exists in the United States and is characterized by traditional words, phrases, and pronunciations. News media, school resources, and government documents usually use this standard form of language.

Consider the way Budge Wilson uses dialect to make her writing more authentic.

> "Always messin' around with animals," complained Mom. "Sometimes I think he's three parts woman and one part child. He's fifteen years old, and last week I caught him bawlin' in the hayloft after we had to shoot that male calf. Couldn't understand why y' can't go on feedin' an animal that'll never produce milk."
>
> —Budge Wilson, "Be-ers and Doers"

Differences in dialect show up especially in the terms people use to refer to things. For example, the generic term for a carbonated beverage is "soda" in Florida and Washington, D.C., "pop" in Ohio and Minnesota, "coke" in Georgia and Tennessee, and "tonic" in Boston.

DIALECTS OF ENGLISH. Students are asked to translate examples of dialect into standard English in Language, Grammar, and Style activities on pages 42 and 125.

IRONY, SARCASM, AND RUDENESS. Students are asked to analyze irony in Understanding Literature on pages 59, 102, 489, 624.

LANGUAGE, GRAMMAR, AND STYLE

GRAMMAR HANDBOOK

In English the basic unit of meaning is the sentence. In this integrated approach, you will examine sentences to determine what they mean. This should help you to be a better reader and more skillful writer. This approach may be new to you, so here are a series of charts and references to help you as you begin. Do not memorize these charts. The more you use them, the less you will need them. With time, you will develop a feeling for the way language works so you will not need them at all.

3.6 Identifying the Parts of Speech

Each word in a sentence has one of four basic functions: it **names**, **modifies**, **expresses**

action or state of being, or **links**. A fifth function is to **interrupt** for effect. English also has words that can work as more than one part of speech. These are called **hybrids**. Following is an overview of the parts of speech. For a more detailed description of what each part of speech does, see the Parts of Speech Summary on page 903.

3.7 Grammar Reference Chart — Parts of Speech Overview

PARTS OF SPEECH	EXAMPLE(S)
NAMERS (nouns and pronouns) are subjects and objects.	
NOUN. A **noun** names a person, place, thing, idea	Adam, journalist, mountain, India, rose, motorcycle, honesty, feeling
PRONOUN. A **pronoun** is used in place of a noun to name a person, place, thing, or idea.	I bought the bricks and used **them** to build a wall. Take Schuyler to the ice cream shop and buy **him** (used in place of Schuyler) a cone.
EXPRESSERS (verbs) name an action or state of being plus the conditions around it.	
VERB. A **verb** expresses action or state of being.	bake, glance, give, build, compose, think, look, feel, am
MODIFIERS (adjectives and adverbs) make other parts of speech more specific.	
ADJECTIVE. An **adjective** modifies, or changes the meaning of, a noun or pronoun.	**gray** skies, **deep** water, **eerie** laughter
ADVERB. An **adverb** modifies, or changes the meaning of, a verb, an adjective, or another adverb.	Leanne gripped the wheel **nervously**. Elliot thought the exam was **extremely** easy. Ray peered over the cliff **very** cautiously.
LINKERS (prepositions and conjunctions) join all the constructions of the English language.	
PREPOSITION. A **preposition** is used to show how a noun or a pronoun is related to other words in the sentence. Common prepositions are *in, after, among, at, behind, beside, off, through, until, upon,* and *with.*	Pablo enjoyed the concert **at** the Wang Center. Theresa squeezed **through** the opening **of** the cave and crawled **into** the narrow passage.
CONJUNCTION. A **conjunction** joins words or groups of words. Common conjunctions are *and, but, for, nor, or, so,* and *yet.*	Wilhelm plays the guitar, **but** Leonard plays drums. Wilhelm **and** Leonard play loudly.
INTERRUPTERS (interjections and other constructions) interrupt a sentence for emphasis.	
INTERJECTION. An **interjection** is a word used to express emotion. Common interjections are *oh, ah, well, say,* and *wow.*	**Hey!** What are you doing in there? **Oh well,** I didn't expect to win the election anyway.

CONTINUED

PARTS OF SPEECH	EXAMPLE(S)
APPOSITIVE. An **appositive** is an interrupter that renames a noun.	My friend **Yang Yardley** did a beautiful project on birds. Mrs. Cokely, **my favorite teacher**, will retire.
NOUN OF DIRECT ADDRESS. A noun of direct **address** says the name of the person or group spoken to and is never the subject of the sentence.	Wait until dark, **Audrey**. **Class**, listen to the instructions. (*Class* is a noun of direct address; the subject of the sentence is *you*; the pronoun *you* is understood.)
HYBRIDS (possessive nouns, pronouns, and verbals) can function as more than one part of speech.	
POSSESSIVE NOUNS AND PRONOUNS. Possessive **nouns** and **pronouns** are nouns and pronouns that function as adjectives.	Angela read **Scott's** essay. (*Scott's* is a possessive noun modifying *essay*.) Angela read **his** essay. (*His* is a possessive pronoun modifying *essay*.)
VERBALS. **Verbals** are verb forms such as participles, gerunds, and infinitives that can function as adjectives, nouns, and adverbs.	I love the **swimming** pool. (*Swimming* is a verbal called a participle, and acts as an *adjective*.) **Swimming** is my favorite sport. (*Swimming* is a verbal called a gerund, and acts as a *noun*.) I like **to swim**. (*To swim* is a verbal called an infinitive.)

To understand how a sentence works, here are other groups of words that you should know about.

3.8 Helping Verbs

A **helping verb** helps a main verb to express action or a state of being. Common helping verbs are *can, could, may, might, must, shall, should, will, would,* and forms of the verb *to be* (am, are, is, was being, been), *to have* (has, have, had) and *to do* (do, does, did).

3.9 The Verb *To Be*

Most languages use the verb *to be* more than any other verb, because its forms have so many uses. To be can be the main verb of a sentence, used to express existence. It can also be a helping verb, one that helps a main verb. Here are some forms of *to be*.

PRESENT
  am, is are

PAST
  was, were, has been, had been

FUTURE
  will be; shall be; will have been; shall have been

OTHER EXPRESSIONS AND FORMS THAT USE BE
  being; can be; could be; could have been; would be; would have been; might be; might have been; must be; must have been

3.10 Linking Verbs

A **linking verb** connects a noun with another noun, a pronoun, or adjective that describes it or identifies it. The most common linking verb is *to be* (*am, are, is, was,* and *been*). Other words that can be used as linking verbs include *seem, look, sound, smell, taste, feel, stay, remain, become,* and *grow*.

3.11 Grammar Reference Chart — Prepositions

These are the most commonly used prepositions. Remember, though, that any word on this list may not always be used as a preposition. If it is a preposition, it will always have an object.

PREPOSITIONS. Students are asked to identify prepositions in the Language, Grammar, and Style activities on pages 208 and 340.

LANGUAGE, GRAMMAR, AND STYLE

aboard	at	concerning	off	until
about	before	down	on	up
above	behind	during	over	upon
across	below	except	past	with
after	beside	for	since	within
against	besides	from	through	without
along	between	in	throughout	
amid	beyond	into	to	
among	but	like	under	
around	by	of	underneath	

3.12 What Is Grammar?

The word *grammar* has two meanings. First, **grammar** is the rules and standards that careful speakers use to write and speak. Second, a **grammar** is the description of a language. Learning about grammar will show you how the rules of the English language are applied.

English is a **syntactic language**. This means that **syntax**, or word order, is the most important factor to understand an English sentence.

3.13 The Importance of Syntax

> Gina walks to work today.

Notice how the words are arranged: the sentence tells who (Gina) and then what that person did (walked to work). But look what happens when the word order is changed:

> To walks Gina today work.
> To work Gina today walks.
> Gina to today work walks.
> Today Gina walks to work.

None of the sentences has the same meaning, or makes much meaning at all, except the last one. But even this isn't the same as "Gina walks to work today," because in English, the most important idea comes first. In "Gina walks to work today," the most important thing in the sentence is Gina. In "Today Gina walks to work," the day is the most important.

3.14 The Sentence: The Basic Building Block of the English Language

From the time you entered school, you have been encouraged to write and speak in sentences, because they are the basic units of meaning. Sometimes a sentence is described as "a group of words that express a complete thought." A sentence is organized to tell 1) *who* or *what* a speaker is talking about, and 2) information about that *who* or *what*.

3.15 Functions of Sentences

Four different kinds of sentences express four different kinds of complete thoughts:

- A **declarative sentence** gives facts. It ends with a period.

- An **interrogative sentence** asks a question. It ends with a question mark.

- An **imperative sentence** gives orders or makes a request. It ends with a period or exclamation mark.

- An **exclamatory sentence** expresses strong feeling. It ends with an exclamation mark.

DECLARATIVE	Tom got a new bicycle.
INTERROGATIVE	Did Tom get a new bicycle?
IMPERATIVE	Get a new bicycle.
EXCLAMATORY	I really want a new bicycle!

FUNCTIONS OF SENTENCES. Students are asked to identify or write declarative, interrogative, imperative, and exclamatory sentences in the Language, Grammar, and Style activities on pages 26, 446, and 629.

3.16 Subjects and Verbs: The Basic Building Blocks in a Sentence

A basic language tool is knowing how to identify the parts of a sentence. The parts of a sentence are the building blocks of meaning.

3.17 Finding the Complete Subject and Complete Predicate in a Sentence

Simple sentences can be divided into two parts: the **subject** and the **predicate**. In the most common English sentences, the first part of the sentence tells us what or who the sentence is about. This is the **complete subject**. Then it gives us information about the subject; this second part of the sentence is called the **complete predicate**. In the following examples, the complete subject is underlined once. The complete predicate is underlined twice.

One of my brothers fixed his own car.
Sharyl and Ken will be presenting Friday's history lesson.
Lala might have been given a wrong classroom number.

NOTE: Every word in every sentence is a part of the complete subject or the complete predicate.

3.18 Finding the Simple Subject and Simple Predicate in a Sentence

Most people find the complete subject and complete predicate too general to be very useful. To find basic meaning, you need to get down to the most basic sentence units—the **simple subject** and the **simple predicate** (more often called the **verb**).

To find the simple subject and verb of a sentence, first find the complete subject and predicate and then remove the extra words until you are left with only the simple subject and verb. What remains is absolutely necessary for basic meaning. The simple subject is the complete subject without any modifiers or linkers—the extra words.

A little fuzzy gray **kitten** walked across our back yard.
I worked for hours on my homework.
Jed's **grandfather** lived by the lake.

The **verb** is the predicate without any complements, linkers, or modifiers. Verbs may have more than one word, and as many as four. Each of the following is one verb:

walked (one word)
is walking (two words)
has been walking (three words)
may have been walking (four words)

3.19 How to Find the Simple Subject and Verb

The following **four-step method** will help you find the simple subject and the verb in a sentence.

SAMPLE SENTENCE

My little sister might not attend school for the rest of the week.

1) Ask, "What is the action of this sentence?" The action is *attend*.

2) Go to the list of helping verbs in 3.9. Check some of the words around the action word. In this sentence, check *might* and *not*. Note that, when you look these words up, *might* is on the list; *not* isn't. Only *might* is a helping verb. The word *not* is actually an adverb, because it describes the action. Therefore, the verb of the sentence is *might attend*.

3) You've found the verb. To find the subject, ask, "Who (or what) did this action?" Ask yourself, "Who might attend?" The answer is *my little sister*.

4) Finally, what words aren't necessary for the simplest meaning? Read the sentence. You can leave out *my*, because *little sister* makes sense. So does just *sister*. You can leave out *little*. *Sister* is the simple subject of the sentence because *my* and *little* are not necessary for basic meaning.

SIMPLE SUBJECTS AND PREDICATES. See the Language, Grammar, and Style activity "Finding the Simple Subject and Verb" in Unit 1 on page 59.

LANGUAGE, GRAMMAR, AND STYLE

DIRECT OBJECTS. Students are asked to identify the direct object in sentences in the Language, Grammar, and Style activity on page 112.

INDIRECT OBJECTS. Students are asked to identify the subject, verb, direct object, and indirect object in sentences in the Language, Grammar, and Style activity on page 126.

INVERTED SENTENCES. Students are asked to change inverted sentences to regular construction in the Language, Grammar, and Style activity on page 174.

COMPOUND NOUNS AND ADJECTIVES. In the Language, Grammar, and Style activity on page 453, students are asked to describe an animal using compound nouns and adjectives.

3.20 Completers for Action Verbs: Direct and Indirect Objects

A sentence must have a subject and a verb, but sometimes a sentence has other parts that complete the meaning. The completers for action verbs are **direct objects** and **indirect objects**.

3.21 DIRECT OBJECTS. Not all sentences have objects. Here are some examples of sentences without objects. In each of these sentences there is no receiver of the action. The verb expresses the total concept.

EXAMPLES

> Birds fly south.
> Work fast.
> I have been walking.

Notice that the following sentences do have receivers of the action. These receivers are called **direct objects**. A **direct object** receives the action in the sentence. In each case, once the verb is found, the direct object answers the question *what*? about the verb.

EXAMPLES

> Birds ate grain. (Birds ate what? *grain*)
> Work the problems fast. (Work what? *problems*)
> I walked the dog. (Walked what? *dog*)

Notice that the last step was to get rid of any modifiers. That tells you what the direct object itself is. Also note: direct object is *never* in a prepositional phrase.

3.22 INDIRECT OBJECTS. Sometimes the direct object is received by someone or something. This receiver is called the **indirect object**. A sentence without a direct object cannot have an indirect object.

EXAMPLE   Mike gave me a red pencil.

> What is the *action* (the verb)? *gave*
> <u>Who</u> gave? (the subject) *Mike*
> <u>What</u> did he give? (the direct object) *pencil*

To find the indirect object, check to see if the direct object had a receiver. Who got the direct object? In this sentence we ask, "Who got the pencil?" The answer is <u>me</u>.

> *Who received* the pencil? (the indirect object) <u>*me*</u>

SUBJECTS AND VERBS: PROBLEM CONSTRUCTIONS

Because we like variety, we English speakers often rearrange our sentences or use different kinds of sentences. Some of these constructions can be very tricky!

3.23 Working with Inverted Sentences

A sentence is **inverted** when all or part of the complete predicate comes before the verb.

EXAMPLES

> Will you walk my dog? (The sentence is inverted because the helping verb *will*, which is part of the verb *will walk*, is in front of the subject *you*.)
> After the dance we went the party. (The sentence is inverted because *after the dance*, which modifies the verb *went*, is in front of the subject <u>we</u>.)
> Tomorrow all of the students will be needing their books. (The sentence is inverted because *Tomorrow*, which modifies the verb *will be needing*, is in front of the subject *all*.)

Notice in the following examples how the complete subject and complete predicate can be pared down to the simple subject and verb.

EXAMPLES

> <u>You</u> <u>will walk</u> my dog.
> <u>You</u> <u>will walk</u>
>
> <u>We</u> <u>went</u> to the party after the dance.
> <u>We</u> <u>went</u>
>
> <u>All</u> of the students <u>will be needing</u> their books.
> <u>All</u> <u>will be needing</u>

3.24 Working with Compound Subjects, Verbs, and Sentences

One way to achieve sentence variety is through compounds— **compound subjects**, **compound verbs**, and **compound sentences**.

Subjects are compound if a sentence has more than one subject.

EXAMPLE

Mike and Harry washed the dishes.

Verbs are compound if a sentence has more than one verb.

EXAMPLE

Harry washed, dried, and put away the dishes.

A sentence can have both a compound subject and a compound verb.

EXAMPLE

Mikka and Juan made and ate their own dinner.

Sentences are compound when two sentences are connected by a semicolon or a by a coordinating conjunction and a comma. Each part of the compound has its own subject and verb.

EXAMPLES

The intermediate swim class practiced front dives; the advanced class practiced back somersaults.

The intermediate swim class practiced front dives, and the advanced class practiced back somersaults.

3.25 Working with Negatives

Negatives such as *not* and *never* frequently affect verbs. They are adverbs, because they add to the meaning of the verb. The verb tells what an action is, and the negative says that the writer or speaker means the opposite of that.

EXAMPLES

I play basketball.

Negative: I do not play basketball.

Make sure to use only one negative in each sentence. Check your writing to be sure that you have not used a negative word such *as not, nobody, none, nothing, hardly, barely, can't, doesn't, won't, isn't,* or *aren't* with another negative word.

DOUBLE NEGATIVE (NONSTANDARD)

I hardly never eat my lunch at school.

Didn't Joyce never go to Chicago?

It doesn't make no difference!

Why wasn't Jerry hurt no worse when the car was destroyed?

CORRECTED SENTENCES (STANDARD)

I hardly ever eat my lunch at school.

Didn't Joyce ever go to Chicago?

It doesn't make any difference!

Why wasn't Jerry hurt any worse when the car was destroyed?

3.26 Using Contractions

Contractions combine two words by shortening and joining them with an apostrophe.

EXAMPLES

isn't, aren't, don't, can't

When you are trying to determine subjects and verbs in a sentence, contractions need to be written out into the two words that they represent. After the contraction is written out, each word should be considered separately. Each of the contractions above contains a negative. Remember that a negative is never part of a verb but is an adverb.

CONTRACTION	WORDS CONTRACTED	PARTS OF SPEECH
isn't	is not	is (verb or helping verb), not (negative; adverb)
aren't	are not	are (verb), not (negative; adverb)
don't	don not	do (verb), not (negative; adverb)
can't	can not	can (helping verb), not (negative; adverb)

3.27 Identifying Prepositional Phrases

No basic part of the sentence is ever in a prepositional phrase, so before determining the subject and verb of a sentence, cross out the prepositional phrases. See 3.11, "Prepositions" for

WORKING WITH NEGATIVES. Students are asked to correct sentences with double negatives in the Language, Grammar, and Style activity on page 261. In Unit 11 the Guided Writing lesson focuses on double negatives.

PREPOSITIONAL PHRASES. In Unit 5 the Guided Writing lesson focuses on prepositional phrases (see page 397). In the Language, Grammar, and Style activity on page 655, students are asked to add prepositional phrases to sentences.

SENTENCE FRAGMENTS. In Unit 1 the Guided Writing lesson focuses on fixing sentence fragments (see page 78).

SENTENCE RUN-ONS. Students are asked to fix sentence run-ons in the Language, Grammar, and Style activity on page 384.

WORDY SENTENCES. Students are asked to edit sentences for wordiness in the Language, Grammar, and Style activity on page 453. The Guided Writing lesson for Unit 8 focuses on editing wordy sentences.

a list of common prepositions. If the word is on the list, find its object. If it has an object, it is a prepositional phrase.

EXAMPLE

She fell off her roller skates.

Is *off her roller skates* a prepositional phrase? Look up *off* on the list in section 3.11. *Off* is on the list. Now ask yourself, "Off what?" The answer is *off her roller skates*. The word off has a *object—roller skates*. Therefore, *off her roller skates* is a prepositional phrase.

3.28 Understood Subjects

Sentences that make requests or give commands frequently have an understood subject. The subject is *you*, but it is not written or spoken.

EXAMPLE

Open your books.

What is meant is *You* open your books. The verb is *open*; the simple subject is *you*.

3.29 *There* Sentences

Frequently *there* is used to begin or serve as one of the first few words in a sentence. It is a modifier, so it will be not part of the simple subject or verb in the sentence. Cross out *there* before determining parts of the sentence.

EXAMPLE

There are six classes scheduled every day.
Classes (simple subject) are *scheduled* (verb)

Have there been any lost coats returned?
Coats (simple subject) *have been returned* (verb)

3.30 Nouns of Direct Address

When you speak to someone, sometimes you say that person's name. This is called a **noun of direct address**. It is not the subject of the sentence; instead, it is an interjection.

EXAMPLES

Kent, take your paper from the pile. (The subject is *you*, not *Kent*.)

Tita, has Sam returned his paper yet? (The subject is *Sam*, not *Tita*.)

WRITER'S WORKSHOP: BUILDING EFFECTIVE SENTENCES

3.31 Correcting Sentence Fragments

A sentence contains a subject and a verb and should express a complete thought. A **sentence fragment** is a phrase or clause that does not express a complete thought but has been punctuated as though it did.

SENTENCE FRAGMENT

Looking for the lost little girl.

COMPLETE SENTENCE

The searchers combed the woods looking for the lost little girl.

3.32 Correcting Sentence Run-ons

A **run-on sentence** is made up of two or more sentences that have been run together as if they were one complete thought. You can fix a run-on by dividing it into two separate sentences. Mark the end of each idea with a period, question mark, or exclamation point. Capitalize the first word of each new sentence.

RUN-ON

Jason tried to jump across the swollen stream he slipped in the mud on the other side.

TWO SENTENCES

Jason tried to jump across the swollen stream. He slipped in the mud on the other side.

3.33 Correcting Wordy Sentences

As you write, use only words necessary to make your meaning clear to a reader. Edit your sentences so that they are not wordy and complicated. Replace complicated or general words with simple and specific words.

WORDY

I certainly am appreciative of your thoughtful gesture of bringing chicken soup for me to eat when I was sick and didn't feel like getting out of bed.

CLEAR AND DIRECT

Thank you for bringing chicken soup when I was sick.

3.34 Combining and Expanding Sentences

If you use several short sentences in a paragraph, your writing might sound choppy, and your reader might have trouble understanding how ideas are connected. **Combining** and **expanding sentences** can bring two sentences together that deal with the same main idea. If you are able to combine short sentences, your writing will sound smooth and clear. The reader will see how ideas are connected to one another.

A good way to combine sentences is to take a word or phrase from one sentence and insert it into another sentence. You might need to change the form of the word.

BORING, SHORT SENTENCES

The thief ducked into the alley. The alley was dark.

COMBINED SENTENCE

The thief ducked into the dark alley.

An effective way to expand sentences is to merge two related sentences into one sentence that states both ideas. Your two sentences can be combined with a comma and a conjunction.

GIVEN SENTENCES

Alex jacked up the car. Margie changed the tire.

COMBINED SENTENCE

After Alex jacked up the car, Margie changed the tire.

3.35 Making Passive Sentences Active

A verb is **active** when the subject of the verb performs the action. It is **passive** when the subject of the verb receives the action.

ACTIVE

Caroline delivered a powerful speech.

PASSIVE

A powerful speech was delivered by Caroline.

Poor writing uses too many passive verbs. Use active verbs unless you have a good reason for using the passive voice. In the examples that follow, note how the active verbs make the writing more natural and interesting.

WITH PASSIVE VERBS

The school was flooded with requests from students for a longer vacation. It was not decided by the school board until later to give them a hearing. The meeting was begun by the student council. The vote was unanimous to extend spring break an extra week. It was considered an unprecedented move favoring all students suffering spring fever.

WITH ACTIVE VERBS

Students flooded the school with requests for a longer vacation. The school board did not decide until later to give them a hearing. The student council began the meeting. Everyone voted to extend spring break an extra week. The unpredecented move favored all students suffering spring fever.

Note that the writer could still combine and expand these sentences to give them more variety. Making such sentences active instead of passive, however, is a good start toward livelier writing.

3.36 Achieving Parallelism

A sentence has **parallelism** when it uses the same grammatical forms to express ideas of equal, or parallel, importance. When you edit your sentences during revision, check to be sure that your parallelism is not faulty.

FAULTY

I really like playing chess, walking my dog, and vacations in Florida.

PARALLEL

I really like playing chess, walking my dog, and taking vacations in Florida.

3.37 Adding Colorful Language to Sentences

When you write, use words that tell your reader exactly what you mean. Precise and lively nouns, verbs, and modifiers make your writing more interesting to your reader.

EXAMPLES

The people made noise.
The mob made an uproar.

COMBINING AND EXPANDING SENTENCES. In the Language, Grammar, and Style activity on page 568 students combine two sentences into one.

MAKING PASSIVE SENTENCES ACTIVE. In the Language, Grammar, and Style activity on page 422 students identify sentences in the active and passive voices and change passive sentences to active ones. In Unit 12 the Guided Writing lesson focuses on changing passive sentences to active sentences (see page 860).

LANGUAGE, GRAMMAR, AND STYLE

He <u>took</u> the pitcher and <u>drank</u> the cool water.

He <u>grabbed</u> the pitcher and <u>gulped</u> the cool water.

The <u>cold</u> wind blew <u>hard</u>.
The <u>frigid</u> wind blew <u>furiously</u>.

EDITING FOR GRAMMAR AND USAGE ERRORS

3.38 Getting Subject and Verb to Agree

A word that describes or stands for *one* person, place, thing, or idea is **singular**. A word that describes or stands for *more than one* person, place, thing, or idea is **plural**.

SINGULAR NOUNS	prize, hand, instrument
PLURAL NOUNS	prizes, children, instruments

In a sentence, a verb must be singular if its subject is singular and plural if its subject is plural. A verb must agree in number with its subject.

SINGULAR AGREEMENT
<u>Charles</u> <u>needs</u> forty more dollars.

PLURAL AGREEMENT
<u>They</u> <u>need</u> forty more dollars.

Some verbs have special forms. The verb forms *is* and *was* are singular. The forms *are* and *were* are plural. The verb form *has* is singular. The verb form *have* is plural.

SINGULAR	<u>Vivian</u> <u>is</u> at the mall.
PLURAL	<u>Vivian and Debbie</u> <u>are</u> at the mall.
SINGULAR	This <u>car</u> <u>has</u> dual airbags.
PLURAL	These <u>cars</u> <u>have</u> dual airbags.

3.39 Using Irregular Verbs

To write about something that happened in the past, use past tense verbs (tense means time in grammar). For regular verbs, add *–ed* or *–d* to the present form of the verb. For more information, see the Language Arts Survey 3.62, "Verb Tenses."

EXAMPLES
The bandit <u>guarded</u> the hideout.
guard (base form) + ed

Carmen <u>gazed</u> at the distant mountains.
gaze (base form) + d

Irregular verbs often have different past tense forms and are formed using a different spelling. The following chart lists some of the most common irregular verbs.

IRREGULAR VERBS			
begin	/ began	grow	/ grew
bring	/ brought	have	/ had
burst	/ burst	hurt	/ hurt
choose	/ chose	know	/ knew
come	/ came	lay	/ laid
cut	/ cut	make	/ made
do	/ did	ride	/ rode
draw	/ drew	run	/ ran
drink	/ drank	see	/ saw
eat	/ ate	sing	/ sang
fall	/ fell	take	/ took
feel	/ felt	teach	/ taught
fly	/ flew	wear	/ wore
give	/ gave	write	/ wrote
go	/ went		

When using irregular verbs in the perfect tense (with *has* or *have*), make sure you do not use the past form instead of the past participle.

NONSTANDARD
I <u>have knew</u> him since I was in middle school.

STANDARD
I <u>have known</u> him since I was in middle school.

Another error to avoid is using the past participle form without a helping verb, or mistaking the past participle for the past.

NONSTANDARD	I <u>flown</u> this plane dozens of times.
STANDARD	I <u>have flown</u> this plane dozens of times.
NONSTANDARD	I <u>done</u> all I could do to convince him.
STANDARD	I <u>did</u> all I could do to convince him.

Finally, do not add *-d* or *-ed* to the past form of an irregular verb.

NONSTANDARD	I <u>ated</u> an apple.
STANDARD	I <u>ate</u> an apple.

3.40 Avoiding Split Infinitives

In the English language, the infinitive is often in the form of two words, *to* and the base word.

EXAMPLES   to catch, to succeed, to entertain

Under traditional rules of grammar, the infinitive should not be "split." In other words, adverbs or other sentence components should not come between *to* and the base word.

NONSTANDARD
Irving begged me to immediately show him the photos.

STANDARD
Irving begged me to show him the photos immediately.

3.41 Using *I* and *Me*

Before you use the words *I* and *me* in a sentence, remember that *I* is always the subject of a verb and *me* is always the object of a verb or of a preposition. *I* is the subject in both of these sentences:

I went sailing in Florida. Amber and I went sailing in Florida.

In both of these sentences, *me* is the object of the verb *helped*.

Lester helped me set up for the party.
Lester helped Brianna and me set up for the party.

If you are not sure which pronoun to use, try each part of your sentence separately.

EXAMPLE
Sam and (I, me) went sledding at the golf course.

After dropping out Sam:
I went sledding at the golf course. OR Me went sledding at the golf course.

Correct: Sam and I went sledding at the golf course.

EXAMPLE
Please apologize for Carol and (I, me).

After dropping out Carol:
Please apologize for me. OR Please apologize for I.

Correct: Please apologize for Carol and me.

3.42 Using *Who* and *Whom*

The pronoun *who* has two different forms. *Who* is used as a subject of a sentence. *Whom* is used as the direct object of a verb or of a preposition.

SUBJECT
Who knows the answer?
Where is the boy who looks after the sheep?

DIRECT OBJECT
Whom did the police arrest?
The plumber whom we called charged a huge fee.

OBJECT OF PREPOSITION
By whom is this painting?
From whom is that gift?

3.43 Getting Pronouns and Antecedents to Agree

Make sure pronouns in your writing agree with their antecedents in number and gender. The **antecedent** is the noun that the pronoun references.

Number refers to singular and plural. If the antecedent is singular, the pronoun must also be singular; if the antecedent is plural, the pronoun must also be plural.

INCORRECT NUMBER
One of the boys need tennis shoes.

CORRECT NUMBER
One of the boys needs tennis shoes.

Gender is the form a pronoun takes to show whether it is masculine, feminine, or neither masculine nor feminine. The pronoun must match its antecedent in terms of gender.

INCORRECT GENDER
Bessie the cow rubbed her head and swished its tail.

CORRECT GENDER
Bessie the cow rubbed her head and swished her tail.

3.44 Recognizing Other Problems with Modifiers

Them is a personal pronoun. *Those* is a demonstrative pronoun, which means it points out a particular person, place, or thing.

Using *I* and *Me*. In the Language, Grammar, and Style activity on page 790, students select either *I* or *me* to complete sentences.

GETTING PRONOUNS AND ANTECEDENTS TO AGREE. In Unit 9 the Guided Writing lesson ask students to identify pronoun/antecedent agreement, fix pronoun/antecedent agreement, and use the correct pronoun in their own writing (see page 678).

NONSTANDARD	Them cars have four-wheel drive.
STANDARD	Those cars have four-wheel drive.

The words *bad* and *badly* often confuse writers. Use *bad* as an adjective, and *badly* as an adverb. The adjective *bad* should follow a linking verb such as *feel, see, smell, sound,* or *taste.*

NONSTANDARD
Reports of the forest fire sounded badly.
STANDARD
Reports of the forest fire sounded bad.
NONSTANDARD
Ricky behaved bad for the babysitter.
STANDARD
Ricky behaved badly for the babysitter.

The words *good* and *well* also tend to confuse writers. *Good* is an adjective used to modify a person, place, thing, or idea, not an action verb. *Well* is an adverb meaning "successfully" or "skillfully" and an adjective meaning "healthy" or "of a satisfactory condition."

NONSTANDARD
Allen swims good.
STANDARD
Allen swims well.
Allen is a good swimmer.
Allen is well now that he is over his cold.

Each modifier has a **positive**, **comparative**, and **superlative** form of comparison. Most one-syllable modifiers and some two-syllable modifiers form comparative and superlative degrees by adding *-er* and *-est.* Other two-syllable modifiers, and all modifiers of more than two syllables, use *more* and *most* to form these degrees.

	POSITIVE	COMPARATIVE	SUPERLATIVE
ADJECTIVES	hungry	hungrier	hungriest
	daring	more daring	most daring
ADVERBS	late	later	latest
	fully	more fully	most fully

To show a decrease in the quality of any modifier, form the comparative and superlative degrees by using *less* and *least.*

EXAMPLES
dense, less dense, least dense
skeptically, less skeptically, least skeptically

Some modifiers form comparative and superlative degrees irregularly. Check the dictionary if you are unsure about the comparison of a modifier.

EXAMPLES
good, better, best
well, better, best
bad, worse, worst

Use the comparative degree when comparing two things. Use the superlative degree when comparing more than two things.

COMPARATIVE
Santha was the **more easily** intimidated of the two sisters.
SUPERLATIVE
The skin is the **largest** organ of the human body.

3.45 Correcting Common Usage Problems

Watch for these words and learn their correct usage as you edit your own writing.

accept, except. To *accept* is to "welcome something" or to "receive something willingly." To *except* is to "exclude or leave something out." *Except* is also used as a preposition meaning "but."

The Tigers *accept* our challenge to a rematch.
I will eat any vegetable *except* collard greens.

advice, advise. *Advice* is a noun meaning "guidance or recommendation regarding a decision." To *advise* is to "recommend or inform."

I took your *advice* about the movie.
I would *advise* you to avoid the sequel.

altogether, all together. *Altogether* is an adverb meaning "thoroughly." Something done *all together* is done as a group or mass.

She was *altogether* frustrated waiting all day.
We were *all together* awaiting news of the surgery.

among, between. Use the word *between* when you are talking about two people or things at a time. Use the word *among* when you are talking about a group of three or more.

Oscar and Lucas had five dollars *between* them.

There was disagreement *among* the team members.

can, may. The word *can* means "able to do something." The word *may* is used to ask or give permission.

Can you swim across Gull Pond?

You *may* go swimming when you finish mowing the lawn.

fewer, less. *Fewer* refers to the number of units of something. *Less* refers to bulk quantity.

I have *fewer* than eight items.

I have *less* energy when it is very humid.

in, into. The preposition *in* indicates location. The preposition *into* indicates direction from the outside to the inside.

The meeting is being held *in* the gym.

The students are going *into* the gym now.

its, it's. The word *its* is a possessive pronoun. The word *it's* is a contraction of it is.

The turtle dug its nest.

The sun will be up by the time it's over.

lay, lie. *Lay* means to "put" or to "place." It always takes a direct object. *Lie* means to "rest" or to "be in a lying position." *Lie* never takes a direct object. (Note, that the past tense of *lie* is *lay*.)

Lay the map on the table.

Gretchen *laid* the map on the table.

Lie down and keep quiet.

Oliver *lay* down and kept quiet.

like, as. *Like* is a preposition meaning "similar to." *Like* usually introduces a phrase. *As* should be used as a conjunction. *As* usually introduces a clause that has a subject and a verb.

NONSTANDARD

The sun came out earlier, just *like* I had hoped.

STANDARD

The sun came out earlier, just *as* I had hoped.

NONSTANDARD

Rodney has been acting *as* a spoiled brat.

STANDARD

Rodney has been acting *like* a spoiled brat.

their, they're, there. These three homonyms (words that sound alike but that have different spellings and meanings) can be very confusing. The word *their* is a possessive pronoun. The word *they're* is the contracted form of they are. The word *there* refers to a place.

Marsupials carry *their* young in a pouch.
They're complaining about the noise.
The lamp should go over *there*.

to, too, two. *To* is a preposition that can mean "in the direction of." *Too* is an adverb that means both "extremely, overly" and "also." *Two* is the spelling for the number 2.

Take the basket *to* Granny's house.
Ivan has *too* many fish in his tank.
Sharon is invited, *too*.
I have *two* wishes left.

your, you're. *Your* is a possessive pronoun. *You're* is the contracted form of you are.

Your mittens are in the dryer.
You're the winner!

PARTS OF SPEECH SUMMARY

As you have seen, the meanings of words often depend upon their positions in a sentence. As their positions change, both meaning and function change. By looking at the relationship of one word to the rest of the words in a sentence, you can determine what the word does.

3.46 Namers — Nouns and Pronouns

Namers are nouns and pronouns. They name people, places, ideas, and things or refer to them; you can tell what they are by what they do. Nouns and pronouns are subjects and objects—direct objects, indirect objects, or objects of prepositions.

3.47 Types of Nouns

A **noun** is a word that names a person, place, thing, or idea.

NOUNS

Cornelius (person), New Orleans (place), wagon (thing), optimism (idea)

3.48 Compound Nouns. A **compound noun** is a noun made up of two or more words. Some compound nouns are written as one word, some as two words, and some as hyphenated words.

COMPOUND NOUNS
porthole, pancake, fire escape, Groundhog Day, mother-in-law

3.49 Common Nouns. A **common noun** names any person, place, thing, or idea.

COMMON NOUNS
plumber, city, bottle, satisfaction

3.50 Proper Nouns. A **proper noun names** a specific person, place, or thing and begins with a capital letter.

PROPER NOUNS
Luke Baldwin, Alaska, Thanksgiving

3.51 Concrete Nouns. A **concrete noun** names a thing that can be touched, seen, heard, smelled, or tasted.

CONCRETE NOUNS
telephone, carpet, peanut butter

3.52 Abstract Nouns. An **abstract noun** names something that cannot be physically sensed.

ABSTRACT NOUNS
excellence, mathematics, despair

3.53 Types of Pronouns

A **pronoun** is used in place of a noun. Sometimes a pronoun refers to a specific person or thing. The most commonly used pronouns are personal pronouns, interrogative pronouns, indefinite pronouns, and relative pronouns. Speakers also use possessive pronouns, but they are hybrids because they have pronoun forms but act as modifiers. Hybrids are discussed in their own section.

3.54 Personal Pronouns. A **personal pronoun** is used in place of the name of a person or thing. The personal pronouns are *I, me, we, us, he, she, it, him, her, you, they,* and *them.* Personal pronouns refer to three groups of speakers: first, second, and third person.

FIRST PERSON	the speaker or speakers talks about themselves: *I, me, we, us*
SECOND PERSON	the speaker talks about the person talked to: *you*
THIRD PERSON	the speaker talks about someone or something else: *he, she, it, they*

All personal pronouns require clear **antecedents**, or nouns that come before the pronoun. That means that the person or thing that the pronoun refers to must be obvious.

EXAMPLE
Have you seen <u>Mary</u>? Yes, I saw <u>her</u> yesterday. (<u>Mary</u> is the antecedent of <u>her</u>.)

3.55 Interrogative Pronouns. An **interrogative pronoun** asks a question. *Who, whose, what, whom,* and *which* are the interrogative pronouns.

EXAMPLES
<u>Which</u> movie would you like to see?
<u>Whose</u> sweater is on the chair?
To <u>whom</u> am I speaking?

3.56 Indefinite Pronouns. An **indefinite pronoun** points out a person, place, or thing, but not a particular one. *Some, someone, somebody, something, any, anyone, anybody, anything, everyone, everybody, everything, other, another, either, neither, all, many, few, each, both, one, none, nobody,* and *nothing* are indefinite pronouns.

INDEFINITE PRONOUNS
<u>Everyone</u> listened attentively to the girl from Thailand.

<u>Something</u> told me that Harold was in trouble.

3.57 Expressers—Verbs

Verbs are the **expressers** of the English language. They work hard to tell whether the action is finished, or continuing, or will happen, and all kinds of conditions for the action. English verbs can be from one to four words long.

EXAMPLES
I <u>study</u> English.
I <u>have studied</u> English.
I <u>could have studied</u> English.
I <u>should have been studying</u> English.

Verbs. On page 59 in the Language, Grammar, and Style activity students are asked to identify the simple subject and verb in a sentence.

Each of the additional words changes the meaning or condition of the action. The same verb may fit into several classes, depending on its use in different sentences.

3.58 ACTION VERBS. Action verbs are the words that refer to actions and to things you can do.

EXAMPLES   have, get, drive, run, get, sleep

3.59 STATE OF BEING VERBS. State of being verbs indicate that something exists. These are all the forms of the verb *to be* that are listed on Grammar Reference Chart 3.11.

3.60 TRANSITIVE VERBS. Transitive verbs are action verbs that have completers. If a verb has a direct object, it is a transitive verb.

EXAMPLE
> The teacher shows movies twice this week.

In this sentence the simple subject is *teacher*; the verb is *has shown*. If you ask the question, *The teacher has shown what?*, the answer is *movies*, so *movies* is a direct object. Because the verb has an object, it is **transitive**.

3.61 INTRANSITIVE VERBS. Intransitive verbs are action verbs that do not have completers.

EXAMPLE   The wind blows all day long.

In this sentence the subject is *wind*, and the verb is *has blown*. When we ask the direct object question, *Wind has blown what?*, there is no answer. *Has blown* is an **intransitive verb**.

3.62 Verb Tenses

Verbs carry a concept of time, called **tense**. The simple tenses express simple past, present, and future. The perfect tenses give information about actions that take place over time.

3.63 SIMPLE TENSES. Present tense shows that something is happening now. **Past tense** verbs talk about something that happened before now, and **future tense** verbs talk about something that will happen in the future:

PRESENT TENSE
> Today I <u>eat</u> chocolate ice cream.
> Today I <u>do eat</u> chocolate ice cream.
> Today I <u>am eating</u> chocolate ice ceam.

Notice that the past tense in English also uses the same three forms as present tense.

PAST TENSE
> Yesterday I <u>ate</u> strawberry ice cream.
> Yesterday I <u>did eat</u> strawberry ice cream.
> Yesterday I <u>was eating</u> strawberry ice cream.

There are only two future tense forms.

FUTURE TENSE
> Tomorrow I <u>will eat</u> vanilla ice cream.
> Tomorrow I <u>will be eating</u> vanilla ice cream.

3.64 PERFECT TENSES. The perfect tenses express past, present and future, but they add information about actions that continued over a period of time and were completed in the past or will be completed in the present or future. All perfect tenses use some form of the helping verb *to have*.

PRESENT PERFECT TENSE
> Today I <u>have worn</u> a sweater. Today I <u>have been wearing</u> a sweater.

PAST PERFECT TENSE
> Yesterday I <u>had worn</u> jeans. Yesturday I <u>had been wearing</u> jeans.

FUTURE TENSE
> Tomorrow I <u>will have worn</u> a sweat shirt. I <u>will have been wearing</u> a sweatshirt.

3.65 Modifiers

Adjectives and adverbs—two kinds of **modifiers**—add meaning to nouns, adjectives, verbs and adverbs. To determine whether the work is an adjective or adverb, follow the following procedure:

1. Look at the word that is modified.

2. Ask yourself, "Is this modified word a noun or pronoun?"

If the answer is yes, the modifier is an adjective. Adjectives modify only nouns and pronouns.

If the answer is no, the modifier is an *adverb*. **Adverbs** modify *verbs*, *adjectives* and other *adverbs*.

3.66 ADJECTIVES. Adjectives modify nouns by telling specific details about them.

NOUN	woman
A LITTLE MORE SPECIFIC	<u>young</u> woman

VERB TENSES. The Unit 2 Guided Writing lesson (page 149) students work on keeping verb tenses consistent in their writing.

ADJECTIVES. In the Language, Grammar, and Style activity on page 26, students add suffixes to verbs to create adjectives. In the Vocabulary activity on page 174 students write sentences incorporating adjectives. In the Language, Grammar, and Style activity on page 660 students identify adjectives in the selection.

ADVERBS. In the Language, Grammar, and Style activity on page 660 students are asked to identify adverbs in the selection.

COORDINATING CONJUNCTIONS. Students are asked to identify coordinating conjunctions in the Language, Grammar, and Style activity on page 208.

| MORE SPECIFIC YET | <u>red-haired</u> <u>young</u> woman |
| EVEN MORE SPECIFIC | smiling, <u>red-headed</u> <u>young</u> woman |

3.67 ADVERBS. Adverbs modify anything that isn't a *namer* (noun or pronoun.) Adverbs can modify verbs, adjectives, and other adverbs. Many times they will tell us where or when; nouns and pronouns tell us who or what.

ADVERBS MODIFY VERBS
Scotty ran home <u>quickly</u>.

Quickly tells how Scotty ran.

ADVERBS MODIFY ADJECTIVES
She wore really new shoes.

New modifies shoes; *really* modifies the modifier, *new*. Since *new* is an adjective, not a noun or pronoun, and *really* modifies *new*, *really* has to be an adverb.

ADVERBS MODIFY OTHER ADVERBS
Scotty ran home <u>really fast</u>.

Fast modifies the verb *ran; really* modifies *fast*. Here one adverb modifies another.

3.68 Linkers

Conjunctions and prepositions are the linkers of the English language. These words join words and phrases to create compound sentences. Because many kinds of links need to be made, there are many kinds of linkers.

3.69 PREPOSITIONS. Prepositions always have objects. Look at the Grammar Reference Chart 3.11, "Prepositions." If you find one of these words in a sentence, find its object. If it has an object, then the preposition and its object(s) form a prepositional phrase.

EXAMPLE
I went t<u>o the store</u> <u>for a loaf</u> <u>of sandwich bread</u>.

In this sentence, three words are on the preposition list: *to, for,* and *of.* Does *to* have an object? Ask, "*to* what?" The answer is *the store. To* has an object, so it is a preposition. *To the store* is a prepositional phrase. After we apply the same test to *for* and *of*, we find that they are both prepositions and that the sample sentence has

three prepositional phrases. These are *to the store, for a loaf,* and *of sandwich bread.*

3.70 COORDINATING CONJUNCTIONS. Coordinating conjunctions join words and groups of words. The most common coordinating conjunctions are *and, or, nor, for, but,* and *so.* Coordinating conjunctions link words or word groups to make them equally important in the sentence.

EXAMPLE
Her morning schedule included math <u>and</u> history <u>and</u> music <u>and</u> home room.

Joining a series of words using coordinating conjunctions between them is perfectly acceptable grammar. Most writers, however, use commas and save multiple conjunctions for sentences with special emphasis. Note that all but the last could be replaced by commas:

EXAMPLE
Her morning schedule included math, history, music, and home room.

When coordinating conjunctions plus commas join two or more complete thoughts that could be separate sentences, the resulting structure is called a **compound sentence**.

EXAMPLE
I wanted to go to movie, but nothing sounded very good.

Here a comma plus *but* joins two short, complete, independent thoughts. Each of the two parts could be a sentence of its own:

EXAMPLE
I wanted to go to a movie. Nothing sounded very good.

3.71 CORRELATIVE CONJUNCTIONS. Correlative conjunctions travel in pairs that belong together. Some of these pairs are *both / and, either / or, neither / nor,* and *not only / but also.*

EXAMPLES
<u>Both</u> her sisters <u>and</u> her brothers had talent.
<u>Neither</u> her mother <u>nor</u> her father had played sports in school.
She <u>either</u> takes drafting <u>or</u> art this semester.
He <u>not only</u> passed French <u>but also</u> aced math.

3.72 Interrupters

Sometimes you will want to interrupt the flow of a sentence and thought by adding an **interrupter**, a word or phrase for emphasis. Most interrupters are set off from the rest of the sentences by commas because they are not basic building blocks of meaning. Interrupters include *interjections, parenthetical expressions, nouns of direct address,* and *appositives.* Another interrupter, *intensifying pronouns,* is discussed in 3.76 "Hybrids."

Interrupters are always set off from other parts of the sentence by commas or, in some cases, dashes or exclamation marks. Interrupters are not basic building blocks of meaning.

3.73 INTERJECTIONS. Interjections are parts of speech that express strong feeling.

EXAMPLES
> <u>Yes</u>, I finally finished my homework.
> <u>Good grief</u>, you did what again?
> <u>Wow</u>! Sam got a new car for his birthday.
> <u>Huh</u>! I don't understand.

Yes, good grief, and *wow* are all interjections. Notice that leaving them out does not affect the meaning of the sentence. Each interjection is set off from the rest of the sentence either by a comma or exclamation point.

3.74 APPOSITIVES. An **appositive** renames a noun. Note that a name, even if it has three or four words, is considered to be one word.

EXAMPLES
> My brother <u>John</u> made the kite for me.
> My friend <u>Yang Yardley</u> did a beautiful project on birds.

John, Yang Yardley and *my favorite teacher,* are appositives. Notice that, like all interrupters, the material in the appositive could be left out without changing the meaning of the sentence.

3.75 Nouns of Direct Address

Nouns of direct address say the name of the person or group spoken to. A noun of direct address is *never* the subject of the sentence. This becomes especially tricky when the subject is understood (not stated), as in commands.

EXAMPLES
> The grass needs to be cut, <u>Jenna</u>, and you must start cutting it now.
>
> <u>Class</u>, listen to the instructions.

3.76 Hybrids

Hybrids are words usually thought of as one part of speech that occasionally function as another. Because word forms are labeled according to what they do, each should be labeled according to what it does in the sentence. Common hybrids include *possessive nouns, possessive pronouns, intensifying pronouns,* and a group of verb forms called *verbals.*

3.77 Possessive Nouns and Pronouns

Possessive nouns are noun forms that modify other words. To form a possessive noun, an apostrophe plus an-*s* is added to a singular noun, and an apostrophe is added to a plural noun. Notice how the possessive noun uses a noun form, but with the suffix, it becomes modifier.

EXAMPLE
> Drew dropped <u>Mary's</u> book.

Mary's modifies *book.* This construction is a hybrid; it looks like a noun, but it functions as an adjective.

Possessive pronouns act much the same way. Many possessive forms look like other pronouns, while a few pronoun forms are uniquely possessive. Forms that are always possessive include *my, mine, your, yours, hers, his, its, our, ours, their,* and *theirs.*

EXAMPLES
> The book is <u>yours</u>.
> This is <u>your</u> book.
> The book is <u>hers</u>.
> Don't lay the book on <u>its</u> side.

Two other possessive forms, *her* and *him,* are not always possessives. They can also serve as nouns, direct objects, and indirect objects.

EXAMPLES
> Give the book to <u>her</u>. (In this sentence, *her* serves as a noun and indirect object.)

INTERJECTIONS. In the Language, Grammar, and Style activity on page 208 students are asked to identify interjections in sentences.

This is her <u>book</u>. (In this sentence, *her* serves as a possessive pronoun and adjective.)

3.78 Verbals

Verbals are verb forms that act as namers or modifiers. There are three different forms of verbals. These include **participles** (*–ing* or *–ed* verb forms that act as modifiers), **gerunds** (*–ing* verb forms that act like nouns), and **infinitives** (*to* verb forms that can act like nouns, adjectives, and adverbs).

Participles are action adjectives.

EXAMPLES
Jana jumped off the **diving** board.
A **watched** pot never boils.

Gerunds are action nouns.

EXAMPLES
Swimming is good exercise.
Mary has improved her **reading**.

Infinitives are formed by adding the word *to* to a verb.

EXAMPLES
I want **to go** home.
Have you ever been given a test **to take**?

STYLE HANDBOOK

3.79 Editing for Punctuation Errors

Several punctuation errors to avoid are the misuse of end marks, commas, and semicolons.

3.80 END MARKS. End marks tell the reader where a sentence ends. They also show the purpose of the sentence. The three end marks are the period, question mark, and exclamation point.

A **declarative sentence** ends with a period.

DECLARATIVE
Friedrich's cousins live in Switzerland.

An **interrogative sentence** ends with a question mark.

INTERROGATIVE
When did World War I begin?

An **exclamatory sentence** ends with an exclamation point.

EXCLAMATORY
The view from the top is breathtaking!

3.81 COMMAS. A **comma** separates words or groups of words within a sentence. Commas tell the reader to pause at certain spots in the sentence. These pauses help keep the reader from running certain words and phrases together when they should be kept apart. You should always use commas to separate items in a series. Three or more words make a series.

EXAMPLE
Choices include <u>carrots</u>, <u>green beans</u>, <u>corn</u>, and <u>asparagus</u>.

Use commas when you combine sentences using *and, but, or, nor, yet, so,* or *for*. Place the comma before these words.

EXAMPLE
Joanna will sing in the talent show, <u>and</u> Margaret will accompany her.

Use a comma to set off words or phrases that interrupt sentences. Use two commas if the word or phrase falls in the middle of the sentence. Use one comma if the word or phrase comes at the beginning or at the end of a sentence.

EXAMPLES
Hercules, <u>a hero of classical mythology</u>, was said to be the strongest man on earth.

<u>After the first quarter</u>, the Knicks dominated the game.

Use commas to separate the parts of a date. Do not use a comma between the month and the year.

EXAMPLES
The Germans surrendered on <u>May 8, 1945</u>.

My appointment is on <u>Wednesday, January 7</u>.

Use commas to separate items in addresses. (Do not put a comma between the state and the ZIP code.)

Francisco was born in Caracas, Venezuela.

They live at 210 Newfield Road, DeWitt, New York 13214.

3.82 SEMICOLONS. You have seen how two related sentences can be combined into one using a conjunction such as *and, but, so,* and *or.* Another way to join two related sentences into one is to use a **semicolon.** The semicolon can be used in place of the comma and the conjunction.

EXAMPLES

A fin was spotted moving through the water, so the bathers scrambled onto the beach.

A fin was spotted moving through the water; the bathers scrambled onto the beach.

3.83 COLONS. Use a **colon** to introduce a list of items.

EXAMPLE

Don't forget the following items for the hike: water bottle, food, first aid kit, extra sweater, and rain gear.

You should also use a colon between numbers that tell hours and minutes.

1:07 p.m.   6:00 a.m.   9:54 p.m.

A colon is often used after the greeting in a business letter.

Dear Sirs: Dear Ms. Flanagan:

3.84 APOSTROPHES. An **apostrophe** is used to form the possessive of nouns. To form the possessive of a singular noun, you should add an apostrophe and an *s* to the end of the word.

EXAMPLES

The Sun's diameter is about 864,000 miles.
(Sun + 's = Sun's)

Isaac's room is plastered with posters of the Pacers.
(Isaac + 's = Isaac's)

EXAMPLES

Moses' staff

Euripedes' tragedies

The possessive of a plural noun is formed two different ways. If the plural noun does not end in *s,* you add an apostrophe and an *s* to the end of

the word. If the plural noun ends with an *s,* add only an apostrophe.

EXAMPLES

The women's volleyball team is undefeated.
(women + 's = women's)

The Vikings' star quarterback is on the injured list.
(Vikings + ' = Vikings')

There are some words that end in s and are singular, such as species or Jesus, that have an irregular possessive form. Form the possessive of these words by adding only an apostrophe.

3.85 UNDERLINING AND ITALICS. **Italics** are a type of slanted printing used to make a word or phrase stand out. In handwritten documents, or in forms of printing in which italics are not available, underlining is used. You should underline or italicize the titles of books, magazines, works of art, movies, and plays.

BOOKS

How the Grinch Stole Christmas
Old Yeller
How the Grinch Stole Christmas
Old Yeller

MAGAZINES

Reader's Digest
Sports Illustrated
Reader's Digest
Sports Illustrated

WORKS OF ART

The Thinker
Starry Night
The Thinker
Starry Night

MOVIES

The Lion King
Dances with Wolves
The Lion King
Dances with Wolves

PLAYS

The Mousetrap
Hamlet
The Mousetrap
Hamlet

3.86 QUOTATION MARKS. When you use a person's exact words in your writing, you are using a **direct quotation**. Enclose the words of a direct quotation in **quotation marks**.

EXAMPLES

"It looks as if thunderclouds are gathering," Sylvia remarked.

Pietro said, "It's good to be back home."

A direct quotation should always begin with a capital letter. Separate a direct quotation from the rest of the sentence with a comma, question mark, or exclamation point. Do not separate the direct quotation from the rest of the sentence with a period. All punctuation marks that belong to the direct quotation itself should be placed inside the quotation marks.

EXAMPLES

"Your golf game has really improved," Avram remarked.

Victor lamented, "I wish Uncle Don were here."

"Did I turn off the iron?" wondered Mrs. Cameron.

Joy asked, "Have you seen my red blouse?"

"He's out at third!" yelled the umpire.

"Hey," Allison called, "Wait for me!"

Use quotation marks to enclose the titles of short works such as short stories, poems, songs, articles, and parts of books.

SHORT STORIES

"The Tell-Tale Heart"
"Be-ers and Doers"

POEMS

"Hummingbird"
"Once by the Pacific"

SONGS

"When Johnny Comes Marching Home"
"Silent Night"

ARTICLES, ESSAYS

"The Size of Things"
"The Power to Decide"

3.87 HYPHENS AND DASHES. A **hyphen** is used to make a compound word.

EXAMPLES

four-year-old boy, great-grandmother, run-of-the-mill, seventh-grade student, three-time winner

A **dash** is used to show a sudden break or change in thought.

EXAMPLE

Juan surprised his teacher—and himself—by getting an *A* on the science test.

3.88 Editing for Capitalization Errors

To avoid capitalization errors, you should know how to capitalize proper nounds and adjectives; geographical names, directions and historical names; and title of art and history books.

3.89 PROPER NOUNS AND ADJECTIVES. Using capital letters is called **capitalization**. Always capitalize proper nouns and adjectives. A proper noun names a specific person, place, or thing. A **proper adjective** is an adjective formed from a proper noun. Make sure to capitalize the many kinds of proper nouns and proper adjectives.

PROPER NOUNS
Lebanon, Queen Elizabeth, Democrat

PROPER ADJECTIVES
Lebanese, Elizabethan, Democratic

There are many different kinds of proper nouns. The chart below should help you to recognize some of them.

TITLES USED WITH NAMES
Dr. Stetson, Ms. Dixon, Mr. Meletiadis

MONTHS, DAYS, HOLIDAYS
January, Wednesday, Labor Day

RELIGIONS
Hinduism, Catholicism, Buddhism

SACRED WRITINGS
the Bible, the Great Spirit, the Koran, the Vedas

CITIES, STATES, COUNTRIES
Seattle, Louisiana, Peru

NATIONALITIES
Danish, Brazilian, Greek

STREETS, BRIDGES
Highland Street, Tappan Zee Bridge

BUILDINGS, MONUMENTS
World Trade Center, USS Arizona Memorial

CLUBS, ORGANIZATIONS, BUSINESSES
Kiwanis Club, National Audubon Society,
Sears Roebuck

3.90 *I* AND FIRST WORDS. Capitalize the first word of every sentence.

EXAMPLES   Did you see that meteor?
The river rose over its banks.

Capitalize the word *I* whenever it appears.

EXAMPLES   Janice and *I* will buy the present.
Whenever *I* see horses, *I* think of
Uncle Sherman.

3.91 FAMILY RELATIONSHIPS AND TITLES OF PERSONS.
A word for a family relation such as *Mom, Dad*, or *Grandpa* should be capitalized if it is used as the name or part of the name of a particular person. Do not capitalize a word for a family relation if a modifier such as *the, a, my*, or *your* comes before it.

CAPITALIZED
When they were children, Dad, Aunt Polly, and
Uncle Richard went down the Grand Canyon on
mules.

NOT CAPITALIZED
My grandma has a cousin who lives in Germany.

Capitalize the official title of a person when it is followed by the person's name or when it is used instead of a name in direct address.

President James Polk, Queen Mary, Sir Winston
Churchill, Pope Paul
"I am honored to meet you, Ambassador."

Do not capitalize references to occupations.

the electrician, the doctor, the sergeant, the judge,
the chef, the editor

Capitalize the official title of a person when it is followed by the person's name or when it is used instead of a name in direct address.

EXAMPLES
President James Polk, Queen Mary, Sir Winston
Churchill, Pope Paul
"I am honored to meet you, Ambassador."

3.92 GEOGRAPHICAL NAMES, DIRECTIONS, AND HISTORICAL NAMES. Capitalize the names of specific places, including terms such as *lake, mountain, river*, or *valley* if they are used as part of a name. Also capitalize historical events, special events, and recognized periods of time.

BODIES OF WATER
Colorado River, Black Sea

CITIES AND TOWNS
Kansas City, Fayetteville

COUNTIES
Cayuga County, Kosciusko County

COUNTRIES
Switzerland, Indonesia

ISLANDS
Ellis Island, Isle of Wight

MOUNTAINS
Pike's Peak, Mount Rainier

STATES
Montana, South Carolina

STREETS AND HIGHWAYS
Erie Boulevard, Route 71

HISTORICAL EVENTS
Continental Congress, Boxer Rebellion

HISTORICAL PERIODS
Paleozoic Era, Industrial Age

SPECIAL EVENTS
Empire State Games, Rose Bowl

Do not capitalize general names for places.

EXAMPLES
The still lake beautifully reflected the white-capped mountain.
Follow this road for two more miles and you will reach a small town.

Capitalize geographical directions if they are part of a specific name or a commonly recognized region. Do not capitalize words such as east(ern), west(ern), north(ern), and south(ern) if they are used only to indicate direction.

CAPITALIZED
<u>Western</u> Samoa, <u>East</u> Africa, <u>South</u> Bend, <u>Northern</u> Ireland

<u>west</u> of Denver, <u>eastern</u> face of the mountain, <u>south</u> side of the city, <u>northern</u> regions

Capitalize historical events, special events, and recognized periods of time.

HISTORICAL EVENTS
Continental Congress, Boxer Rebellion

HISTORICAL PERIODS
Paleozoic Era, Industrial Age

SPECIAL EVENTS
Empire State Games, Rose Bowl

3.93 TITLES OF ART WORKS AND LITERARY WORKS. Apply title capitalization to titles of art works and literary works. In title capitalization, capitalize the first word, the last word, and all other words except articles (a, an, and the) and prepositions.

EXAMPLES

Raphael's *The School of Athens*, Matisse's *Joy of Life*, Jackson Pollock's *Autumn Rhythm*, Shakespeare's *The Taming of the Shrew*, Faulkner's *The Sound and the Fury*, Ray Bradbury's "All Summer in a Day"

3.94 Editing for Spelling Errors

3.95 USING SPELLING RULES I. Always check your writing for spelling errors, and try to recognize the words that give you more trouble than others. Adding prefixes and suffixes often causes spelling errors. A **prefix** is a letter or a group of letters added to the beginning of a word to change its meaning. When adding a prefix, do not change the spelling of the word itself.

EXAMPLES

dis + similar = dissimilar
un + necessary = unnecessary

A **suffix** is a letter or group of letters added to the end of a word to change its meaning. The spelling of most words is not changed when the suffix *–ness* or *–ly* is added.

EXAMPLES

even + ness = evenness
usual + ly = usually

If you are adding a suffix to a word that ends with y, and that y follows a vowel, you should usually leave the y in place. (*Vowels* are the letters a, e, i, o, and u.)

EXAMPLES

employ + ment = employment
stay + ing = staying
destroy + ed = destroyed

If you are adding a suffix to a word that ends with y, and that y follows a consonant, you should usually change the y to i. (Consonants are all letters that are not vowels.)

EXAMPLES

silly + est = silliest
sticky + ness = stickiness
cry + ed = cried
cheery + ly = cheerily

If you are adding a suffix that begins with a vowel to a word that ends with a silent e, you should usually drop the e.

EXAMPLES

shave + ing = shaving
value + able = valuable
rose + y = rosy
take + ing = taking

If you are adding a suffix that begins with a consonant to a word that ends with a silent e, you should usually leave the e in place.

EXAMPLES

tire + less = tireless
sincere + ly = sincerely
fate + ful = fateful
place + ment = placement

3.96 USING SPELLING RULES II. When a word is spelled with the letters i and e and has the long / ē / sound, it is spelled ie except after the letter c.

EXAMPLES

thief, relieve, yield, pierce
ceiling, conceive, receipt, deceive

The only word in the English language that ends in *–sede* is supersede. Only the following three words end in *–ceed: exceed, proceed,* and *succeed.* Every other word that ends with the / sēd / sound is spelled *cede.*

EXAMPLES

precede, recede, concede, accede

Most noun plurals are formed by simply adding *–s* to the end of the word.

stairs, ducklings, kites, rockets

The plurals of nouns that end in *o, s, x, z, ch,* or *sh* should be formed by adding *–es.*

EXAMPLES tomatoes, classes, taxes, topazes, beaches, flashes

An exception to the rule above is that musical terms (and certain other words that end in o) are usually pluralized by adding *–s.*

EXAMPLES pianos, solos, concertos, sopranos, banjos, radios

Form the plurals of nouns that end in y following a vowel by adding *–s.*

EXAMPLES
toy + s = toys
donkey + s = donkeys
Thursday + s = Thursdays
ray + s = rays

Form the plurals of nouns that end in *y* following a consonant by changing the *y* to an *i* and adding *–es.*

EXAMPLES
pony + s = ponies
spy + s = spies
country + s = countries
story + s = stories

3.97 COMMON SPELLING ERRORS. Some English words are often misspelled. Here is a list of 150 commonly misspelled words. If you master this list, you will avoid many errors in your spelling.

COMMONLY MISSPELLED ENGLISH WORDS

absence	catastrophe	guerrilla	noticeable	rhythm
abundant	cellar	hindrance	nucleus	schedule
academically	cemetery	hypocrite	nuisance	seize
accessible	changeable	independent	nutritious	separate
accidentally	clothes	influential	obedience	sergeant
accommodate	colossal	ingenious	occasionally	siege
accurate	column	institution	occurrence	significance
acknowledgment	committee	interference	orchestra	souvenir
acquaintance	conceivable	irrelevant	outrageous	sponsor
adequately	conscientious	irresistible	pageant	succeed
adolescent	conscious	judgment	parallel	surprise
advantageous	consistency	league	pastime	symbol
advisable	deceitful	leisure	peasant	synonymous
ancient	descendant	license	permanent	temperature
annihilate	desirable	lightning	persistent	tomorrow
anonymous	disastrous	liquefy	phenomenon	transparent
answer	discipline	magnificent	physician	twelfth
apparent	efficiency	manageable	pneumonia	undoubtedly
article	eighth	maneuver	prestige	unmistakable
attendance	embarrass	meadow	privilege	unnecessary
bankruptcy	enormous	mediocre	procedure	vacuum
beautiful	enthusiastically	miniature	prophesy	vehicle
beggar	environment	mischievous	prove	vengeance
beginning	exhaust	misspell	receipt	villain
behavior	existence	mortgage	referred	vinegar
biscuit	fascinating	mysterious	rehearsal	weird
breathe	finally	naive	relieve	whistle
business	forfeit	necessity	resistance	withhold
calendar	fulfill	nickel	resources	yacht
camouflage	guidance	niece	responsibility	yield

SPEAKING AND LISTENING *Resource*

THE POWER OF COMMUNICATION

Communication is a form of behavior that fulfills the basic human need to connect and interact with other individuals in society. Because democratic government requires the free exchange of ideas, communication is also fundamental to the political way of life in the United States.

4.1 Verbal and Nonverbal Communication

Human beings use both verbal and nonverbal communication to convey meaning and exchange ideas. When a person expresses meaning through words, he or she is using **verbal communication**. When a person expresses meaning without using words, for example by standing up straight or shaking his or her head, he or she is using **nonverbal communication**. When you speak to another person, you may think that the meaning of what you say comes chiefly from the words you use. However, as much as 60 percent of the meaning of a message may be communicated nonverbally.

ELEMENTS OF VERBAL COMMUNICATION		
ELEMENT	**DESCRIPTION**	**GUIDELINES FOR SPEAKERS**
Volume	loudness or softness	Vary your volume, but make sure that you can be heard.
Melody, Pitch	highness or lowness	Vary your pitch. Avoid speaking in a monotone (at a single pitch).
Pace	speed	Vary the speed of your delivery to suit what you are saying. Excitement, for example, can be communicated by a fast pace, and seriousness can be communicated by slowing down and saying something forcefully.
Tone	emotional quality	Suit your tone to your message, and vary it appropriately as you speak. For example, you might use a light tone for a happy message and a heavier one for a sad message.
Enunciation	clearness with which words are spoken	When speaking before a group, pronounce your words more precisely than you would in ordinary conversation.

continued

INTERNET RESOURCES

Access Teaching Online's *Confidence in Public Speaking* oral language lesson for middle or high school at http://www.teachingonline.org/publicspeaking.html.

ELEMENTS OF NONVERBAL COMMUNICATION

ELEMENT	DESCRIPTION	GUIDELINES FOR SPEAKERS
Eye contact	Looking audience members in the eye	Make eye contact regularly with people in your audience. Include all audience members.
Facial expression	Using your face to show your emotions	Use expressions to emphasize your message—raised eyebrows for a question, pursed lips for concentration, eyebrows lowered for anger, and so on.
Gesture	Meaningful motions of the arms and hands	Use gestures to emphasize points. Be careful, however, not to overuse gestures. Too many can be distracting.
Posture	Position of the body	Keep your spine straight and head high, but avoid appearing stiff. Stand with your arms and legs slightly open, except when adopting other postures to express particular emotions.
Proximity	Distance from audience	Keep the right amount of distance between yourself and the audience. You should be a comfortable distance away, but close enough for the audience to hear you.

LISTENING SKILLS

Learning to listen well is essential for success in personal life, in school, and, later, on the job.

4.2 Active versus Passive Listening

Effective—or active—listening requires skill and concentration. Active listeners focus on what a speaker is trying to communicate. Ineffective listeners view listening as a passive activity, something that simply "happens" without any effort on their part.

4.3 Listening to a Lecture or Demonstration

- Think of creative reasons to listen. Think of reasons why the information is important by asking yourself: How can I use this information?

- As you listen, show the speaker that you are involved. Maintain an attentive posture by sitting up straight, making eye contact, and nodding when you understand.

- Listen for major ideas. Identify the speaker's main points and the facts offered to support them.

You may want to briefly note on paper the major ideas and related details.

- When you do not understand something that the speaker is saying, make a note. Save questions and comments for when the speaker invites questions. Then raise your hand before asking your question or making your comment.

- Do not let yourself become distracted. Avoid daydreaming, focusing on the speaker's delivery, or listening to background noise.

4.4 Listening in Conversations

- Do not monopolize the conversation. Give the other person plenty of opportunities to speak.

- When the other person is speaking, pay attention to what he or she is saying. Show through eye contact, body language, and facial expressions that you are attentive.

- Avoid mentally debating the other person while he or she is speaking. This may distract you from truly hearing what the person has to say. Withhold judgment until the other person has finished.

- Ask the other person questions. Asking questions is a good way to start a conversation, to keep the conversation going, and to show the other person that you are really listening.
- When you speak, respond to what the other person has been saying. Relate what you say to what he or she has said. Take time to think about what the other speaker has said before responding.

4.5 Listening to the Media

- Television, movies, and radio programs can be powerful manipulators. As you watch or listen, think critically and evaluate these messages you see or hear.
- When watching or listening to news programs or commercial advertisements, distinguish facts from opinions. Facts are statements that can be proved by checking a reference work or by making observations. Opinions express personal beliefs. An opinion may express positive or negative attitudes toward a person, object, or idea.
- When watching or listening to an entertainment program, evaluate its quality. Consider the quality of the acting, directing, and writing. Also consider the production qualities—the lighting, sound effects, staging, camera work, costumes, props, and music.
- Think about what idea or message the program is delivering and whether or not you agree with it. Do not assume that just because a program is entertaining, it does not communicate a message.
- Set standards about what you will watch or listen to. Turn off a program if it does not meet your standards.

4.6 Adapting Listening Skills to Specific Tasks

Just as different situations require different types of listening, different tasks or goals may also require different listening strategies and skills.

Listening for comprehension means listening for information or ideas other people communicate. For example, you listen for comprehension when you try to understand directions to a friend's house or your teacher's explanation of how to read a poem. When listening for comprehension, your goal is to understand, so it is important to recognize and remember the key information you hear. Focus on getting the main points of a message.

Listening critically means listening to a message to comprehend and evaluate it. When listening for comprehension, you usually assume that the information presented is true. Critical listening, on the other hand, includes comprehending and judging the arguments and appeals in a message in order to decide whether to accept or reject them. Critical listening is most useful when you encounter a persuasive message such as a sales pitch, advertisement, campaign speech, or news editorial. When evaluating a persuasive message, consider the following: Is the speaker trustworthy and qualified to speak about this subject? Does the speaker present logical arguments supported by solid facts? Does the speaker use unproven assumptions to make a case? Does the speaker use questionable motivational appeals, such as appeals to fear or to prejudice? These questions can help you decide whether or not to be convinced by a persuasive message.

Listening to learn vocabulary involves a very different kind of listening because the focus is on learning new words and how to use them. For instance, if you were to hear a presentation on hip-hop music, the speaker might introduce some of the many terms used in this musical style and explain what they mean. Or you might use a conversation as an opportunity to learn new words. Sometimes it is possible to figure out what an unfamiliar word means based simply on how the word is used in a sentence. Once you learn a new word, try to use it several times so it becomes more familiar and you become comfortable using it. Also look up the word in a dictionary to find out whether it has other meanings or connotations.

Listening for appreciation means listening purely for enjoyment or entertainment. You might listen appreciatively to a singer, a comedian, a storyteller, or a humorous speaker.

COMMUNICATING WITH OTHERS

4.7 Communicating with Another Person

Daily human interactions involve a great deal of **interpersonal communication**, or communication between two individuals. These guidelines will help you to communicate more effectively in such interactions.

- Make eye contact and maintain a relaxed posture.

- Provide feedback as you listen. Smile or nod to show understanding or agreement. Ask questions or make comments. Try not to interrupt or to finish the speaker's sentences for him or her.

- Rephrase what the speaker has said to make sure that you understand him or her. For example, suppose that the speaker says, "Crazy Horse never allowed anyone to take his photograph." You could reflect back, "So, nobody ever photographed Crazy Horse? That's interesting."

- Control your emotions. If you become angry while listening to the speaker, take a deep breath and count to ten. Make sure you haven't misunderstood by rephrasing the statement that angered you. If you can contain your anger, express your objections calmly. If you cannot contain your anger, end your conversation and say that you would like to continue it at another time.

- Distinguish between facts and opinions. Facts are statements that can be proven true, whereas opinions are expressions of personal belief that may or may not be true. Ask if you are unsure whether another person is stating a fact or opinion.

4.8 Communicating in a Small Group

Much human activity takes place in small groups. Although many of the principles of interpersonal communication hold true in small groups, here are additional guidelines to consider when more people are involved.

- Respect group norms and culture. Most organized groups have **norms**, or rules that govern behavior for group members. Groups also have their own culture that may include certain beliefs or rituals.

- Understand group roles. Individual members are likely to fulfill particular roles in a group based on what they do best. Successful group members attempt to fulfill positive and constructive roles within the group and encourage others to do so.

- Take turns participating. Good group members contribute to the discussion but also allow others to participate. If an overly talkative person dominates the discussion, help others join in. You might say, "I've been interested in what you have to say. What do other people think about this issue?"

- Help to foster a positive group climate. **Group climate** refers to the degree of warmth or coldness that group members feel toward each other. Positive or warm group climates are characterized by trust, cooperation, and concern for others. Negative or cold group climates are characterized by suspicion, competition, and selfishness. You can help to create a positive and warm climate by supporting others' ideas, empathizing with others, treating others as equals, and remaining flexible and open to new ideas and information.

- Establish group goals. Some groups have difficulty accomplishing anything because they lack clear-cut goals. Help your group establish clear goals at the beginning and by focusing on these goals whenever the group seems to lose its way.

4.9 Communicating in a Large Group

Generally, the larger the size of the group, the less opportunity there is for each individual to participate. However, there are still principles that can help you communicate in large groups.

- Share group roles. In large groups, many members may have the skills needed for any one role. Sharing roles can allow everyone to contribute.

- Focus on key relationships. It may not be possible to get to know everyone well in a large group. Identify key people in the group with whom you will need to carry out your assignments, and focus on getting to know them well.

SPEAKING AND LISTENING RESOURCE

COMMUNICATING IN A SMALL GROUP. Examples of collaborative learning activities can be found on pages 137, 144, 154, 400, and 431.

COMMUNICATING IN A LARGE GROUP. A group project classroom poetry reading activity is found in the Unit 9 review on page 683.

- Emphasize group identity, norms, and goals. As groups become larger in size, they are likely to become less cohesive. **Cohesiveness** refers to the level of commitment and connnection members feel to each other and the group. Groups that experience low cohesion are usually not productive or successful.

- Stand up when speaking. Make sure that everyone in the room can see and hear you. If there is a microphone available, use it. Speak in a normal tone 4 to 6 inches from the microphone.

- Avoid the pressure to conform. In large groups, individuals are less comfortable speaking out if they disagree with an idea or decision. This can produce "groupthink," where members give in to the pressure to conform and do not critically evaluate information and/or decisions. If you disagree with an expressed idea or decision, speak out and share your reservations.

- Foster responsibility. In large groups, it is relatively easy for individual members to avoid responsibility. Take responsibility yourself, and encourage others in the group to carry out their assigned duties.

4.10 Asking and Answering Questions

In many situations you will find it useful to ask questions of a speaker, or you will be asked questions. Often a formal speech or presentation will be followed by a question-and-answer period. Keep the following guidelines in mind when asking or answering questions.

ASKING QUESTIONS

- Wait to be recognized. In most cases, it is appropriate to raise your hand if you have a question and to wait for the speaker or moderator to call on you.

- Make questions clear and direct. The longer your question, the less chance a speaker will understand it. Make your questions short and to the point.

- Do not debate or argue. If you disagree with a speaker, the question-and-answer period is not the time to hash out an argument. Ask to speak with the speaker privately after the presentation is over, or agree on a later time and place to meet.

- Do not take others' time. Be courteous to other audience members. If you have a follow-up question, ask the speaker if you may proceed with it.

- Do not give a speech. Sometimes audience members are more interested in expressing their own opinion than in asking the speaker a question. Do not give in to the temptation to present a speech of your own.

ANSWERING QUESTIONS

- Come prepared for a question-and-answer period. Although you can never predict the exact questions that people will ask you, you can anticipate many questions that are likely to be asked. Rehearse aloud your answers to the most difficult questions.

- Be patient. Give the audience time to ask questions about your speech. Don't run back to your seat the minute your speech is over.

- Be direct and succinct. Be sure to answer the question directly as it has been asked, and to provide a short but clear answer.

- Rephrase difficult questions. If you are not sure what an audience member's question is, repeat the question back to them to clarify. You may also want to repeat the question if not everyone in the audience could hear it.

- Be courteous. Sometimes audience members will ask a question you have already answered in your speech. Be tactful in such situations. Briefly repeat the information from your speech in case the audience member did not hear or understand you the first time.

- Handle difficult audience members gracefully. Some audience members may hog the stage or try to pick a verbal fight with a speaker. In such situations, keep your cool and gently suggest that the audience member talk to you privately after the presentation so you can discuss the issue with him or her more fully.

COMMUNICATION STYLES AND CULTURAL BARRIERS

4.11 Being Considerate of Other Cultures and Communication Styles

Communication styles and behaviors vary greatly among people of different cultures—even those who live in the same country. There are many possible verbal and nonverbal sources of miscommunication between cultural groups. In some cultures, for example, two people in conversation may stand very close together. In other cultures, standing close is considered an intrusion on personal space. When interacting with a person from another culture, remember to respect the other individual's cultural practices and behaviors.

4.12 Overcoming Barriers to Effective Multicultural Communication

The following guidelines and suggestions will help you to overcome some common barriers and stumbling blocks to communicating with people of different cultural backgrounds.

- Treat people as individuals. Do not assume that everyone is "the same" as you are, or even that people with similar cultural backgrounds are the same. Avoid relying on preconceptions and stereotypes when interacting with someone from another culture.

- Be sensitive to sources of miscommunication. Remember that both verbal and nonverbal behaviors send messages to others, and that both can lead to miscommunication and misunderstanding.

- Seek common ground. People from different cultures may have difficulty communicating if they focus on differences rather than similarities.

- Accept others as they are. Avoid evaluating or judging the behavior, beliefs, feelings, or experiences of others. Instead, learn to accept differences as valid, even if you personally disagree with what someone else thinks or feels.

- Avoid provoking language. Racial, ethnic, or gender slurs or swearing is unacceptable. You-statements ("You are not listening to me," "You should not do that," "You don't know what you're talking about") can feel like an attack, even when they are well intentioned. People often react to you-statements by becoming defensive or hostile. Try to use I-statements instead ("I feel like you aren't listening to me," "I don't think you should do that," "I'm not sure I agree with you").

4.13 Collaborative Learning and Communication

Collaboration is the act of working with one or more other people to achieve a goal. Many common learning situations—such as small group work, tutoring, book clubs, or peer evaluations—involve collaboration.

In collaborative learning situations, remember to listen attentively, be polite, participate, and help keep discussion focused. If you are tutoring someone, find out what the person needs help with and then break the teaching down into small steps. Be patient and supportive. If you are being tutored, explain what you need help with, ask questions, and be patient.

4.14 Conducting an Interview

In an interview, you meet with someone and ask him or her questions. Interviewing experts is an excellent way to gain information about a particular topic. When planning an interview, do some back-ground research on your subject. Write out a list of questions. Other questions might occur to you during the interview.

Set up a time for the interview. Don't just try to work questions into a regular conversation. Be sure the person you are interviewing knows what you want to find out and why you need to know it. This will help him or her to answer your questions in a useful way. Ask open-ended questions. Open-ended questions cannot be answered with a simple "yes" or "no" nor a brief statement of fact. One of the most valuable questions to ask at the end of the interview is, "What would you like to add that I haven't asked about?"

CONDUCTING AN INTERVIEW. For practice, see the interviewing activities in Skill Builders on pages 25, 125, 208, and 576.

SPEAKING AND LISTENING RESOURCE

CONDUCTIING AN INTERVIEW. Additional interviewing activities are found in Skill Builders activities on pages 660, 779, 790, 815, and 816.

GIVING A SPEECH. For practice working on and presenting speeches, see the Speaking and Listening activities on pages 59, 261, and 431.

If possible, tape-record the interview. Be sure to ask the person you are interviewing permission to tape-record the session. Take notes during the interview, whether or not you are also tape-recording it. Write down the main points and key words to help you remember details. Record the person's most important statements word for word. Clarify spelling and get permission for quotes. End the interview on time. The person you are interviewing has been courteous enough to give you his or her time. Thank the person for his or her help. Write up the results of the interview as soon as possible. Over time, what seemed like a very clear note may become unclear.

PUBLIC SPEAKING

4.15 Giving a Speech

The fear of speaking in public, although quite common, can be overcome by preparing a speech thoroughly and by practicing positive thinking and relaxation. Learning how to give a speech is a valuable skill that you will be able to use in the future.

4.16 Types of Speeches

Here are the three main types of speeches:

- **Impromptu speech**. This is a speech given without any advance preparation. If you were surprised by a gift or an award, you might be asked to give a brief, unrehearsed speech.
- **Memorized speech**. This is a speech that has been written out and memorized word for word. Your teacher may ask you to prepare a memorized speech on a topic you are studying at school.
- **Extemporaneous speech**. This is a speech in which the speaker refers to notes occasionally. Most professional speakers prefer to deliver extemporaneous speeches because they combine the liveliness of an impromptu speech with the careful preparation of a memorized speech. The speaker creates an overall plan for the speech, records important points on cards, and rehearses until comfortable with the material. You might give an extemporaneous speech at a city council meeting about school funding.

4.17 Steps in Preparing an Extemporaneous Speech

1. Choose a topic for your speech. Consider the audience, occasion, and your own strengths and weaknesses as a speaker when choosing a topic.

2. Do prewriting to identify what you know or think about the topic. As you write, think about different ways to approach the topic.

3. Research the topic. Use a variety of source materials, including newspapers, magazines, books, interviews, Internet sources, and personal experience.

4. Determine your specific purpose. What are you trying to accomplish in speaking to your audience? Are you trying to demonstrate something to them? Compare and contrast two things or ideas? Strengthen their commitment to something? Spur them to take action?

5. Organize your material. Use a clear, logical, and interesting organizational strategy that suits your specific purpose, audience, and occasion. You may want to stick to three or four main points.

6. Create visual aids. Some material is best presented visually. Visual aids should be neat, attractive, visible from a distance, and relevant to your speech. For more information, see the Language Arts Survey 6.11, "Displaying Effective Visual Information."

7. Prepare note cards. Notecards should be no larger than 4 x 6 inches and should contain as much information as you need to present your speech, but not so much that you are tempted to read from the cards. Write clearly and legibly so you can read your notes at a distance.

8. Rehearse with your note cards. Practice what you will say in front of a live audience or by using a mirror or recording device. Rehearse with visual aids if you are using them.

4.18 Guidelines for Giving a Speech

A speech should always include an introduction, body, and conclusion. The introduction of your speech should spark the audience's interest, present your central idea, and briefly preview your main points. The body of your speech should expand upon each of your main points in order to support the central idea. The conclusion of your speech should be memorable and give your audience a sense of completion.

TIPS FOR SUCCESSFUL PUBLIC SPEAKING

- **Remain confident**. Remember that listeners are generally "for you." To overcome initial nervousness, take two or three deep breaths as you are stepping up to speak.
- **Be sincere and enthusiastic**. Your enthusiasm—or apathy—will spread to your audience.
- **Maintain good but relaxed posture**. Don't slouch or lean. Move around a bit to release normal nervous tension. Keep your hands free to gesture naturally instead of gripping notecards, props, or the podium.
- **Speak slowly**. Spoken words are more difficult than written language and visual images for audiences to process. Practice pausing. Don't be afraid of silence. Focus on communicating with the audience. By looking for feedback, you will pace yourself appropriately.
- **Maintain genuine eye contact**. Treat the audience as individuals, not as a mass of people. Look at individual faces.
- **Speak in a genuine, relaxed tone**. Don't act or stiffen up. Just be yourself.
- **Communicate**. Focus on conveying your message, not "getting through" the speech.

4.19 Oral Interpretation of Poetry

Oral interpretation is the art of presenting a literary work aloud to an audience. In the past, people often entertained one another by reading poems aloud. Oral interpretation can be fun.

After analyzing what the poem is about, make a copy of the poem and mark it to show:

- the emotions that you will express
- places where you will increase or decrease your pace
- places where you will raise or lower your volume
- the gestures and facial expressions that you will use to communicate emotions
- any different voices that you will use when reading (if dramatizing different characters)

When a poem contains more than one voice, such as the voices of a narrator and characters, make each voice sound different from the others.

Excellent ways to differentiate voices when reading include changing your tone (the emotion expressed) and pitch (the highness or lowness of your voice) and looking in a different direction each time you change voices.

To memorize a poem, work line by line. Look at one line. Look away and repeat it. Then check to see that you got it right. Once you get that line right, add a second line. Look away and repeat both lines. Then check them. Continue in this manner until the entire poem is memorized. Have a partner look at a copy of the poem while you recite it out loud. This person can prompt you when you forget a line. Memorize the poem thoroughly before you begin working on the qualities of your reading.

Rehearse your interpretation using a tape recorder or a video recorder. You might also want to rehearse in front of a mirror so that you can view your facial expressions and gestures.

ORAL INTERPRETATION OF POETRY. For activities to provide students experience with oral interpretation of poetry, see pages 94, 521, 643, 668, and 683.

SPEAKING AND LISTENING RESOURCE

TELLING A STORY. Storytelling activities are found in the Speaking and Listening activities on pages 339, 490, and 540. In addition, the Guided Writing lesson at the end of Unit 7 on pages 522–527 asks students to retell a family story.

PARTICIPATING IN A DEBATE. For practice debating see the Speaking and Listening and Collaborative Learning activities on pages 74 and 479.

4.20 Telling a Story

When telling a story, consider these elements:

- Decide on your purpose. Every story has a purpose. Sometimes the purpose is simply to entertain or to share a personal experience, but often there is a moral or lesson that the storyteller hopes listeners will learn from.

- Select a focus. The focus for your story will depend largely on your purpose in telling it. For example, if you were telling the story of Abraham Lincoln's life, and your purpose was to show how someone could rise from humble roots to a position of greatness, you would probably choose a broad focus for the story. You might begin with Lincoln's birth in a Kentucky log cabin and end with his eventual rise to the position of President of the United States and his many accomplishments in office. If your purpose was to show that perseverance is an important virtue, you might choose a narrower focus. Your story could ignore Lincoln's early life and instead focus on his long political career and his many defeats on the way to the presidency.

- Choose your point of view. You can speak in the first person, either as a direct participant in the events or as an observer (real or imagined) who witnessed the event. You can use the third person voice to achieve greater objectivity.

- Determine sequence of events. The **sequence of events** refers to the order in which they are presented. Although it might seem obvious that stories should "begin at the beginning," this is not always the best approach. Some narratives begin with the turning point of the story to create a sense of drama. Others begin at the end of the story and present the events leading up to the point. Wherever you begin your story, your narrative should present events in a logical way and establish a clear sense of direction for your listeners.

- Select details. Carefully chosen details should keep the story focused. A well-constructed story should flow smoothly and not get bogged down by unnecessary details.

- Choose characters. All stories need to include real, believable characters. Provide your listeners with vivid, concrete descriptions of the mental and physical qualities of important characters in the story.

- Create dialogue. Although it is possible to tell a story in which the characters do not speak directly, conversation and dialogue add life to a story. Dialogue should sound authentic, relate to the main action of the story, and advance the plot. When telling a story, you might choose to enact the characters by creating an individual voice for each one.

4.21 Participating in a Debate

A **debate** is a contest in which two people or groups of people defend opposite sides of an issue in an attempt to convince a judge or audience to agree with their views. Debate issues include the following.

EXAMPLES

Whether or not to have year-round schools

Whether imagination is more important than knowledge

Whether or not to prohibit pets from using public parks

The two sides in a debate take opposite stances on the issue. Sometimes you may find that you are defending a side of an issue that you do not personally agree with. For example, you may be asked to support year-round schools, even if you believe the idea is a poor one. Defending a position you do not believe in will allow you to better understand the position of those who disagree with you. Although you may not change your stance, you may come to appreciate why others see the issue differently.

Typically, both sides in a debate are allowed an equal amount of time to prepare for the debate and to state their cases. Sometimes debaters are allowed to cross-examine or ask questions of their opponents during the debate.

Once the debate is finished, the audience or judge considers the arguments of both sides and votes for which side made the more persuasive case. Ideally, judges or audience members will be objective and make their decision based not on their personal views about the issue but on the arguments made by the debaters in the contest.

- **Be prepared.** In a debate, it will never be possible to anticipate all the arguments your opponent might make. However, by carefully researching both sides of the issue, you can prepare for the most likely arguments you will encounter. You can prepare notes on particular issues before the debate to save yourself preparation time during the debate.

- **Be organized.** When attacking or refuting an opponent's argument, or when advancing or defending your own argument, follow a logical organizational pattern to avoid confusing the audience or the other team.

- **Take notes.** Record the main points of each argument and how you can counter it.

- **Be audience centered.** In the heat of the debate, it is easy to become so involved in the argument with your opponent that you forget the goal of the debate: to persuade your audience or judge that your case is correct.

4.22 Preparing a Multimedia Presentation

Whether you use a simple overhead projector and transparencies or create a PowerPoint presentation that incorporates graphics, videoclips, and sound, multimedia technology can add an important visual element to a presentation. Consider the following guidelines when creating a multimedia presentation:

- Ensure that audio-visual elements enhance understanding. The multimedia elements of your presentation should add to the verbal elements, not replace them. Be sure the content of the presentation is easy to understand and that the amount of information—both verbal and visual—will not overwhelm audience members.

- Make sure the presentation is clearly audible and visible. Video clips or graphics may appear blurry on a projection screen, or may not be visible to audience members in the back or at the sides of the room. Audio clips may sound muffled or may echo in a large room. When creating a multimedia presentation, be sure the presentation can be easily and heard from all parts of the room.

- Become familiar with the equipment. Well before the presentation, know how to operate the equipment you will need. Have a backup plan in case the equipment malfunctions. Make sure that you can operate the equipment while speaking at the same time. If you will need to turn the room lights off, make sure you can operate the equipment in the dark and can still see your notecards.

- Be sure the room can accommodate your needs. Once you know where you will make your presentation, be sure the necessary electrical outlets and extension cords are available, that lights can be dimmed or turned off as needed, and that the room can accommodate the equipment you will use.

SPEAKING AND LISTENING RESOURCE

PREPARING A MULTIMEDIA PRESENTATION. See the multimedia activity in which students are asked to host a book review show on page 601.

STUDY AND RESEARCH *Resource*

THINKING SKILLS

This section gives you some tips that can greatly improve your ability to make decisions, to solve problems, and to learn and think critically.

5.1 Making Decisions and Solving Problems

MAKING DECISIONS. When making a decision, you often must weigh several factors. You can compare your options by making a **pros and cons** chart on paper. First make a list of all your options. For each option list the reasons for choosing it (the pros) and the reasons for not choosing it (the cons). Then compare the lists.

PROS AND CONS		
Painting Yearbook Illustration or Drawing It in Pencil		
	Painting	**Drawing in Pencil**
Pros	colorful	easier less expensive
Cons	more expensive more difficult	not colorful

SOLVING PROBLEMS. There are many ways to solve problems. To solve a complex problem, you will probably need to use more than one strategy. Here are two approaches you can try:

Trial and error. Sometimes when you have to solve a problem, you just make a guess and see if it works. In a **trial-and-error approach**, you try one possible solution and if it doesn't work you try

another. If you don't know how to solve a particular math problem, you could guess the answer, plug it back into the problem, and then revise your answer as necessary.

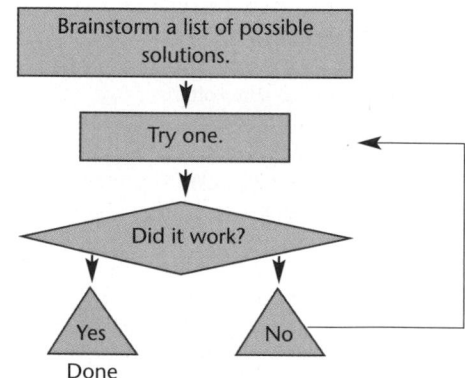

Divide and conquer. Another strategy for problem solving is to divide the problem into parts and then solve each part one at a time in a logical sequence. Here is an example:

PROBLEM
  A friend is coming to stay in your house for a few days and you need to prepare a room for him.

SOLUTION
  Break the job down into small, manageable goals:

STRATEGY
  (1) Move desk and computer from spare room.
  (2) Remove storage boxes from closet and put in basement.
  (3) Clean the room.
  (4) Put cot in room and make bed.

5.2 Distinguishing Fact from Opinion

What is the difference between the following statements?

The language with the greatest number of speakers, over nine hundred million, is Mandarin Chinese.

Mandarin Chinese is the greatest language in the world.

The first statement expresses a **fact**. You can prove this fact by looking in a reference book. The second statement expresses an **opinion**. This statement can be supported but not proved.

A fact is a statement that, at least in principle, could be proved by direct observation. Every statement of fact is either true or false. An opinion is a statement that expresses not a fact about the world but rather an attitude or desire.

An opinion can express an attitude toward something. Such statements often include judgment words such as *good, worthless, valuable, ugly, wonderful, nice,* or *excellent*.

An opinion can also tell not what is but what someone believes should be. Such statements usually include words such as *should, should not, ought to, ought not to, must,* or *must not*.

Some opinions make statements about the future. Because the future is unpredictable, most predictions can be considered opinions.

EXAMPLES

People will live longer in the future.

Tomorrow will be partly cloudy.

EVALUATING FACTS AND OPINIONS. When evaluating a statement, ask yourself whether it can be proved through direct observation or by checking a reliable source such as a reference work or an unbiased expert. An opinion is as good as the facts that support it. The opinion that Mandarin Chinese is the greatest language in the world is supported by such facts as the number of speakers that it has. However, others might argue that English is the greater language because it is spoken more widely around the globe. But no facts would prove or disprove these opinions.

Usually, you can make a stronger case by using facts in place of opinions. For example, instead of saying, "This was a wonderful day," you could say something like, "Today the sun was shining, it was 74 degrees outside, and I got an *A* on my math test. That's what made it a great day." When you express an opinion, especially in writing, include facts to back up or support that opinion.

When reading or listening, be critical about the statements that you encounter. Ask yourself, "Is this a fact or an opinion?" If it is a statement of fact, consider whether it can be proved or seems likely. If it is an opinion, consider whether it is supported by facts.

5.3 Avoiding False Arguments and Propaganda

Another very important thinking skill is learning to use good logic. Not only do you need good facts, but you also need to know how to put those facts together to come up with the right conclusions. Learning how to think clearly will enable you to avoid errors in logic and to arrive at true conclusions. It will also help you to recognize the faulty thinking of others (especially advertisers) who might be trying to persuade you. The intentional use of false arguments to persuade others is called **propaganda**. Here are some of the faulty arguments of which you should be aware:

GLITTERING GENERALITIES AND "SPIN." Glittering generalities are statements given to make something sound more appealing. Such statements can be hard to prove, as they appeal to the emotions.

EXAMPLE

These trading cards are the best ever in this limited-time collection!

ANALYSIS

Nothing in this statement tells the listener why the trading cards are the best ever. Adding "limited-time collection" to the statement vaguely implies that the trading cards will be available for only a short while, and that the listener should buy them quickly before they are unavailable.

Spin is a technique used to slant public perception of the news. Public relations firms and advertisers use this technique to create a favorable perception of a product or organization. Spin can be hard to recognize.

DISTINGUISHING FACT FROM OPINION. Encourage students to distinguish fact from opinion in About the Author sections. Students might make a column listing facts and another column listing opinions. Then ask students to assess the section as being objective or subjective in its approach. Students will generally find that there are more facts than opinions in the About the Author sections.

The accident was a minor incident because only 25 people were injured.

The fact is that 25 people were injured. This does not make it a minor incident; someone is merely interpreting the accident as minor.

STEREOTYPES. An overgeneralization about a group of people is known as a **stereotype**. Stereotypes are one of the most dangerous of all overgeneralizations. Remember that the differences among people within a single group are greater than the average differences between groups. Stereotyping is based on lack of knowledge or experience.

UNSOUND OPINIONS. A sound opinion is one that can be supported by facts. An **unsound opinion** is one that cannot be supported by facts. Be sure that you can back up your opinions with facts.

Miss Rivers won this year's award for excellence in teaching.

Miss Rivers is the best teacher at Adams Middle School.

The statement that "Miss Rivers is the best teacher at Adams Middle School" is someone's personal feeling about her. However, it is probably a sound opinion because it is backed up by the fact that she received the award for excellence in teaching.

CIRCULAR REASONING. **Circular reasoning** is the error of trying to support an opinion by restating it in different words. You can avoid circular reasoning by always backing up your opinions with facts.

That adventure book was exciting because it was full of action.

The "reason" the speaker gives for saying that the book was exciting is really just another way of saying it was exciting. He or she should mention some specific examples to show what makes the story exciting.

LOADED WORDS. In trying to argue for or against something, people will often use **loaded words**, or words that stir up strong feelings, whether positive or negative. Be careful not to let your feelings interfere with your understanding of the facts.

Congressman Philbert is a lazy, good-for-nothing imbecile.

This statement, an emotional attack on the congressman, uses loaded words that will stir up feelings against him. It is not a reasonable evaluation of his policies or actions in office.

BANDWAGON APPEAL. **Bandwagon appeal** plays to your desire to be part of the crowd—to be like everyone else and to do what everyone else is doing. Beware of advertisements or arguments that try to get you to think or act like everyone else. Just because "everybody" believes or does something does not make it good or right for you.

Those who want to be cool wear Star jeans.

This statement suggests that you aren't really part of the "in" crowd unless you wear this brand of jeans. It does not prove, or even say, anything about the quality of the clothing.

5.4 Classifying

One of the many higher-level thinking skills you can develop is the ability to classify. To **classify** is to put into categories. Items in the same category should share one or more characteristics. For example, whales are classified by their method of eating as either baleen or toothed whales. The key step in classifying is choosing categories that fit your purpose. Make sure you clearly define your categories.

5.5 Generalizing

To **generalize** is to make a broad statement based on one or more observations. For example, suppose that you observe that several cats like to stare through windows. You might generalize, based on this discovery, that "cats like to stare through windows." Such generalizations are also called **inferences**. People have learned most of what they know about the world by making generalizations based on their experiences.

Generalizing is an extremely important thinking tool but it is not a perfect one. Generalizations can be proved false by only one exception. Avoid making generalizations based on too little evidence. Keep an open mind and be willing to revise your ideas based on new experiences.

5.6 Making Inferences, Predictions, and Hypotheses

From careful observation, it is possible to make generalizations, or **inferences**, about the world around us. From there it is possible to **predict** what will happen and to form hypotheses. A **hypothesis** is an educated guess about a cause or an effect. A prediction based on a theory is a hypothesis. A possible explanation for an observed event is also a hypothesis. A hypothesis always needs to be tested against experience. Theories and hypotheses can change if a discovery shows that something is otherwise.

5.7 Estimating and Quantifying

To support an argument, you need to provide facts, and often facts are strengthened by numbers or quantities. If you claim, for instance, that too many people are without health insurance, you should **quantify** your claim by stating how many. The numbers you need may be available in reference works. If not, you might be able to **estimate**, or find the approximate quantity. Sometimes you will have only enough knowledge to estimate a range within which the actual number actually falls. If you need to estimate, always make clear that you are doing so.

QUANTIFYING
The science fair had 314 registered participants.

ESTIMATING
The science fair was attended by about 300 students and their parents.

5.8 Analyzing and Synthesizing

When you **analyze** something, you break it down into parts and then think about how the parts are related to each other and to the whole. For example, you might analyze a painting by describing its composition, shapes, lines, colors, and subject. You might analyze a short story by describing its conflict, plot, characters, setting, and theme. You might analyze a movie by describing its acting, directing, writing, settings, and costumes.

When you **synthesize** something, you bring everything that you were considering together into a whole.

5.9 Comparing and Contrasting

Comparing and contrasting are closely related processes. When you **compare** one thing to another, you describe similarities between the two things. When you **contrast** two things, you describe their differences. To compare and contrast, begin by listing the features of each subject. Then go down both lists and check whether each feature is shared or not. You can also show similarities and differences in a Venn diagram. For more information, see the Language Arts Survey 2.16, "Completing Venn Diagrams."

5.10 Evaluating

When you evaluate, you make a judgment about something. You may be asked to compare two things to determine which is more valuable or effective. Evaluate questions use such words as *evaluate, judge, justify, critique, determine whether, decide the effectiveness of,* and *appraise.*

EXAMPLE
In Chaim Potok's story "Zebra," to what degree has John Wilson influenced Zebra? How does this influence compare with the influence of the Vietnam Veterans Memorial on John Wilson?

5.11 Extending

When you extend your knowledge, you connect one experience to another. In the study of literature, you extend your knowledge by making connections between two pieces of literature,

ANALYZING AND SYNTHESIZING. The Analyze and Synthesize question pairs in Inquire, Investigate, and Imagine following each selection provide opportunities for students to develop their analyzing and synthesizing skills.

STUDY AND RESEARCH RESOURCE

EVALUATING AND EXTENDING. The Evaluate and Extend question pairs in Inquire, Investigate, and Imagine following each selection ask students to make judgements about what they have read and to make connections between the selection and other literature, personal experiences, or cultural events.

between the literary work and your own experience, or between a literary work and a cultural or current event. Extend questions use such words as *extend your knowledge, connect, relate,* and *apply.*

EXAMPLE

> How does John Wilson's yearly visit to the Vietnam Veterans Memorial relate to Maya Lin's vision for the memorial?

5.12 Perspective, Empathy, and Self-Understanding

When you are asked to use perspective, empathy, and self-understanding to answer a question, you are exercising an important ability to connect the experience of one person or group to your own. Such thinking allows you to see multiple perspectives, generate alternative viewpoints, and understand another person's feelings and worldview.

STUDY SKILLS

5.13 Developing Good Study Habits

Success in a future career depends largely on success in school. No matter what your experience in school so far, you can improve your performance enormously by developing good study habits.

Homework is best done in a special study area. Choose a quiet location, away from distractions such as conversation, television, or loud music. Choose a place that is well lit and comfortable. Adequate lighting will help you to avoid eyestrain and headaches. Choose a study area that is available at regular times. Set aside a specific time each day for study. Have all the tools that you will need, such as paper, pencils, textbooks, handouts, and reference works, ready and at hand.

Many of your assignments will be due on the following day. Others will be long-term projects. At the end of each school day, make a habit of looking over your assignments. Decide what tasks you need to complete for the following day. Break longer assignments down into specific steps that need to be completed by specific times.

5.14 Keeping an Assignment Notebook

Keeping track of assignments in your head can be dangerous because of the possibility of forgetting important details. Instead, write all your assignments down in an assignment notebook. For each assignment, record:

- The name of the subject
- Details of the assignment, including what, precisely, you need to do
- The date of the assignment
- The date when the assignment is due

5.15 Understanding the Assignment

Understanding an assignment depends on your ability to follow directions.

FOLLOWING SPOKEN DIRECTIONS. Often teachers give assignments orally. When listening to spoken directions, make sure you do the following:

- Listen carefully. Write down the directions as you hear them.
- Notice what steps are involved in the assignment. Also notice the order of these steps.
- Listen for the key word in each step. A key word is one that tells you what to do. Examples are *read, write, organize,* and *memorize.*
- If you do not understand the directions, ask your teacher to explain them.

FOLLOWING WRITTEN DIRECTIONS. Directions for tests usually are written down. Assignment directions also sometimes appear in written form on the board, on overhead transparencies, or on handouts. Make sure to:

- Read all the directions completely before you begin the assignment.
- Ask questions to clarify any points not covered in the directions.
- Divide the assignment into steps. Put these steps in a logical order.
- Decide what materials you will need, and assemble them before you begin.
- Reread each step before you actually do it.

PERSPECTIVE AND EMPATHY. The Perspective and Empathy question pairs in Inquire, Investigate, and Imagine help students to develop insight, self-knowledge, and knowledge of others.

DEVELOPING GOOD STUDY HABITS. Go over the tips in this section at the beginning of every semester with students.

5.16 Taking Notes, Summarizing, and Outlining Information

When **taking notes** in class or while conducting research, you may find it helpful to use a **rough outline**. Write the main ideas, and beneath the main ideas, write related ideas, set off by dashes.

Major Cultures in N. Amer., 1492

- —Eastern woodland (incl. Iroquois & Algonquians)
- —Southeastern (incl. Cherokee & Chicasaw)
- —Plains (incl. Dakota, Pawnee, & Kiowa)
- —Southwestern (incl. Navajo, Hopi, & Apache)
- —Great Basin (incl. Ute & Paiute)
- —Plateau (incl. Nez Perce & Yakima)
- —Northwestern (incl. Chinook & Yurok)
- —California (incl. Shasta, Pomo, & Chumash)

Origins

- —Came to Amer. by land bridge across Bering Strait
- — ~ 35,000 bc
- —May have followed herds, mammoths, musk oxen, etc.

To review the material, you might find it helpful to read over your notes and outline and then **summarize** what you have learned. The act of writing reinforces your memory of what you have learned.

RESEARCH SKILLS

Mastering research skills will help you both in school and in real-life situations outside school. Research is the process of gathering ideas and information. One of the best resources for research is the library.

5.17 How Library Materials Are Organized

Each book in a library is assigned a unique number, called a **call number.** The call number is printed on the **spine** (edge) of each book. The numbers serve to classify books as well as to help the library keep track of them.

Libraries commonly use one of two systems for classifying books. Most school and public libraries use the **Dewey Decimal System.** Most college libraries use the **Library of Congress Classification System** (known as the LC system).

5.18 How to Locate Library Materials

If you know the call number of a book or the subject classification number you want, you can usually go to the bookshelves, or stacks, to obtain the book. Use the signs at the ends of the rows to locate the section you need. Then find the particular shelf that contains call numbers close to yours.

Library collections include many other types of publications besides books, including magazines, newspapers, audio and video recordings, and government documents. Ask a librarian to tell you where to find the materials you need.

To find the call numbers of books that will help you with your research, use the library's catalog. The catalog lists all the books in the library (or group of libraries in a larger system).

COMPUTERIZED CATALOGS. Many libraries today use computerized catalogs. Systems differ from library to library, but most have computer terminals you may use to search through the library's collection. You can usually search by author, title, subject, or key word. To search by author, type the last name first. Type as much of the name as you know.

EXAMPLE

taylor, mildred d

To search by title, omit articles such as a, an, or the at the beginning of titles.

EXAMPLE

red badge of courage

To search by subject, use the subjects provided by the library. To search by key words, use related topics or specific words or names.

EXAMPLE

civil war; racism; great depression; union

A librarian can help you to master system. Here is a sample book entry screen from a computerized catalog.

INTERNET RESOURCES

Let your fingers do the walking and visit the **Internet Public Library** at http://www.ipl.org/. The Internet Public Library is the first public library of the Internet. This site provides library services to the Internet community by finding, evaluating, selecting, organizing, describing, and creating quality information resources; teaches what librarians have to contribute in a digital environment; and promotes the importance of libraries.

RESEARCH SKILLS. For practice applying library research skills, see the Study and Research activities found in the Skill Builders section following each selection.

THE DEWEY DECIMAL SYSTEM. Have students locate a book for each subject and write down its title and call number.

COMPUTERIZED CATALOGS. You might plan to have your school librarian visit your class to explain how to use the computerized catalog in your library. Then give students an assignment sheet and have them use the computerized catalog to list books based on criteria that you provide. For example, students could locate a novel by their favorite author, a book about a topic they are interested in, or a reference book such as a dictionary, thesaurus, or encyclopedia.

Title Cards. Have students make a title card for a book they are interested in.

Using Reference Works. For activities using dictionaries, see the Study and Research activities on pages 480 and 674. For practice using encyclopedias see the Study and Research and Collaborative Learning activities on pages 74 and 596.

Using a Thesaurus. Vocabulary activities using a thesaurus can be found in Skill Builders on pages 356 and 655.

Author	Wallace, David Rains, 1945-
Title	The Quetzal and the Macaw: The story of Costa Rica's National Parks
Publication info.	Sierra Club Books, 1992
No. of pages/size	xvi, 222p. : maps : 24 cm.
ISBN	ISBN 0-87156-585-4
Subjects	National Parks and reserves-Costa Rica-History
	Costa Rica. Servicio de Parques Nacionales-History
	Nature conservation-Costa Rica-History
Dewey call number	333.78

Card Catalogs. Like a computerized catalog, a card catalog contains basic information about each book in the library. In a card catalog the information is typed on paper cards, and the cards are arranged alphabetically in drawers. For each book there is a title card, one author card for each author, and at least one subject card. All of these cards show the book's title, author, and call number, so you can search for a book by title, author, or subject. The following illustration shows a typical title card.

A TITLE CARD

333.78 The Quetzal and the Macaw : the story of
Costa Rica's national parks.
Wallace, David Rains, 1945–
The Quetzal and the Macaw : the story of
Costa Rica's national parks.—San
Francisco: Sierra Club Books, 1992
xvi, 222 p. : maps : 24 cm.
1. National parks and reserves—Costa Rica—
History. 2. Costa Rica. Servicio de
Parques nacionales—History. 3. Nature
conservation—Costa Rica—History. I. Title.
ISBN 0-394-57456-7

Interlibrary Loans. Many libraries are part of larger library networks. In these libraries, the computerized catalog covers the collections of several libraries. If you want a book from a different library, you will need to request the book at the library's request desk or by using its computer. Ask your librarian to help you if you have questions. He or she will be able to tell you when the book will be shipped to your library.

5.19 Using Reference Works

Most libraries have an assortment of reference works in which information is organized so that you can find it easily. Usually, reference works cannot be checked out of the library.

5.20 Types of Dictionaries. You will find many types of dictionaries in the library reference section. The most common is a dictionary of the English language. Examples include *Merriam Webster's Collegiate Dictionary*, *Merriam Webster's New World Dictionary*, and the multi-volume *Oxford English Dictionary*. Other dictionaries focus on slang, abbreviations and acronyms, English/foreign language translation, and spelling. For more information on using a dictionary to look us specific words in English, see the Language Arts Survey 1.17, "Using a Dictionary."

5.21 Using a Thesaurus. A thesaurus is a reference book that groups synonyms, or words with similar meanings. Suppose that you are writing an essay and have a word that means almost but not quite what you want, or perhaps you find yourself using the same word over and over. A thesaurus can give you fresh and precise words to use. For example, if you look up the word sing in a thesaurus, you might find the following synonyms listed:

> sing (v.) carol, chant, croon, hum, vocalize, warble, yodel

5.22 USING ALMANACS, YEARBOOKS, AND ATLASES. **Almanacs and yearbooks** are published each year. An almanac provides statistics and lists, often related to recent events. In an almanac you can find facts about current events, countries of the world, famous people, sports, entertainment, and many other subjects. An overview of the events of the year can be found in a yearbook.

Some of the more widely used almanacs and yearbooks are *The Guinness Book of World Records, World Almanac and Book of Facts,* and *World Book Yearbook of Events.*

An **atlas** is a collection of maps and other geographic information. Some atlases show natural features such as mountains and rivers; others show political features such as countries and cities. If you need to locate a particular feature on a map in an atlas, refer to the gazetteer—an index that lists every item shown on the map.

5.23 USING BIOGRAPHICAL REFERENCES, ENCYCLOPEDIAS, AND PERIODICALS. A **biographical reference** contains information on the lives of famous people. Examples include *Who's Who, Dictionary of American Biography,* and *Contemporary Authors.* Biographical reference books are usually organized in alphabetical order.

Encyclopedias provide a survey of knowledge. General encyclopedias, such as *World Book,* contain information on many different subjects. Specialized encyclopedias, such as the *LaRousse Encyclopedia of Mythology,* contain information on one particular area of knowledge.

The topics in an encyclopedia are treated in articles, which are usually arranged in alphabetical order. If you look up a topic and do not find it, check the index (usually in the last volume). The index will tell you where in the encyclopedia your topic is covered.

An **appendix** provides additional material, often in chart or table form, at the end of a book or other writing. A **glossary** lists key words in a book and their definitions.

5.25 Using the Internet

The **Internet** is a vast collection of computer networks that can provide you with a great wealth of information from libraries, government agencies, high schools and universities, non-profit and educational organizations, museums, user groups, and individuals around the world. The Internet provides a valuable way to do research—if you know how to use it. Here are some guidelines.

5.26 BROWSING VERSUS SEARCHING ON THE INTERNET. **Browsing** means sifting through Internet sites through an Internet browser, or software that connects you to the Internet. **Searching** means conducting focused research by using an Internet search engine. By both browsing and searching, you can gain access to the information you want. Browsing allows you to navigate through different sites, either before or after you have conducted a search. Searching allows you to narrow and expand your research in a focused way to find the particular information you need.

Some of the most popular search engines are: Fast Search: All the Web, All the Time at http://www.alltheweb.com

Altavista at http://www.altavista.digital.com

Infoseek at http://www.infoseek.com

and Yahoo at http://yahoo.com.

When searching, use keywords to narrow or broaden your topic. Browse your results, their links, and links suggested by the search engine. Use different search engines for different results.

To keep track of your Internet research, see the Language Arts Survey 5.40, "Documenting and Mapping Internet Research."

5.28 USING BOOLEAN SEARCH STRATEGIES. Boolean logic refers to the logical relationship among search terms. It is named for the mathematician George Boole. Boolean operators such as AND, OR, NOT, allow you to limit or expand the scope of your topic. Some search engines use other terms or symbols to modify search topics. Refer to each search engine's help feature to learn about these.

5.29 Evaluating Information and Media Sources

To conduct your research efficiently, you need to evaluate your sources and set priorities among

USING AN ALMANAC. You might want to prepare a list of questions that students could find answers for by using an almanac. Have students work with a partner to find answers for the worksheet.

USING THE INTERNET. Internet research activities are found in the Study and Research activities on pages 48, 356, and 540; the Media Literacy activities on pages 430 and 467; and the Group Project on page 400.

EVALUATING MEDIA SOURCES. For practice evaluating media sources see the Media Literacy activities on pages 60, 261, and 445. Activities evaluating Internet sites are provided in the Media Literacy activities on pages 553, 644, and 668.

them. Ideal sources are unbiased, authorative, timely, and written at the right level for you to understand and learn from. Ask these questions when evaluating a source:

- Does the author present the material evenly, acknowledging differing points of view and revealing all sides of an issue? Does he or she have a personal stake in what people think about the subject?

- What is the author's background? What makes him or her an expert on the subject? What kind of reputation does he or she have?

- When was the material published? Is it out of date?

- Is the reading level too high or too low to be helpful to you? Does the source cover the material in too much depth or too superficially?

5.30 How to Read a Newspaper or Newsmagazine. Newspapers and newsmagazines contain an enormous amounts of information. Few people have the time to read all or most of what appears in a newspaper each day. Nonetheless, reading the news is important.

To get the most out of a newspaper, skim the headlines and leads for world, national, state, and local news stories. Read any news summaries included in your paper. Then read in depth any articles, editorials, or features that seem particularly important or interesting.

When reading news stories and editorials, make sure to distinguish between facts and opinions. When you encounter opinions in a newspaper, try to determine whether these opinions are sound. Sound opinions are ones supported by facts. For more information on distinguishing between facts and opinions, see the Language Arts Survey 5.2, "Distinguishing Fact from Opinion."

5.31 How to Evaluate a Film. A great film gives us insight into the lives of others and so expands our understanding and our sympathies. Some films, however, are created solely for the purpose of making money through exploitation of sensational elements or gimmicks. The following guidelines will enable you to become a more discriminating consumer of films.

- **Plan ahead.** Decide in advance which films you would like to see. Don't settle for just any

movie that happens to be playing at your local theater or on television.

- **Listen, watch, and read what the critics have to say.** Take what the critics have to say into consideration to help you decide which movies to see. Once you have seen the movie, decide for yourself whether you agree or disagree with a particular critic. Consider what elements of the movie you liked or disliked, and what could have been altered to make it better. If, after a while, you find one particular critic with whom you tend to agree on a regular basis, use his or her opinion to help you choose which movies to see.

- **Be a critic yourself.** Be critical of dialogue and story lines. Many films recycle conventional story lines and dialogue. Many contain sensational scenes that provoke audiences but forfeit quality in story line, dialogue, and content.

- **Be aware of previews and coming attractions.** These are designed with the help of the production company's marketing and sales departments to motivate you to see their film. Previews can make a film seem more humorous, exciting, and powerful than it really is by showing only the best dialogue and action.

- **Try something new!** Try viewing a film that is much different from the type you usually see. Keep an open mind; you might surprise yourself and enjoy it.

- **Never substitute.** Never see a film adaptation of a literary work as a substitute for reading the work itself. While seeing such an adaptation can be a good introduction to a literary work, you cannot rely on it to capture all the richness of the original work.

5.32 How to Evaluate Radio and Television. Follow the guidelines below to effectively evaluate and control television output:

- **Plan your television and radio time.** Rather than accepting whatever program happens to be on, look at broadcast listings and choose programs that are of interest to you.

- **Be a critic.** Question what you see and hear. What criticisms do you have about a program's quality, message, originality, depth, and reliability?

- **Remember that advertisers pay for most broadcast programs.** They also control the content of the programs they sponsor and pay for your attention because they want to sell you something. Listen to and watch advertisements and programs critically. Read the Language Arts Survey 5.2, "Distinguishing Fact from Opinion," for tips on evaluating information critically.

5.33 How to Evaluate Advertisements.
Advertising messages in the media are everywhere. To sharpen your skills in evaluating them, see the Language Arts Survey 5.2, "Distinguishing Fact from Opinion" and 5.3, "Avoiding False Arguments and Propaganda."

5.34 How to Understand Internet Sites.
Most published print materials have been checked carefully before publication. But anyone can publish something on the Internet—without having to verify facts or guarantee quality. When you use the Internet for research, be careful to evaluate your sources. Here are some guidelines.

- **Consider the resource's domain name.** Documents that end with ".edu" and ".gov" are generally reliable, since they come from educational and governmental organizations. Commercial sites end in ".com." They can be reliable, too, but watch for biases that favor the company's product. Sites ending in ".org" or ".net" can be trusted if they are from a reliable organization, but watch for special interest group sites that slant or "spin" information to their advantage.

- **Evaluate the content.** Examine the content for accuracy. Look for links, source information, and date of publication. Consider the author's reliability and look for a way to contact him or her. Ask yourself whether the information is biased or unbiased.

5.35 Documenting Sources
As you use your research in your writing, you must document your sources of information. Remember to:
- Credit the sources of all ideas and facts that you use.

- Credit original ideas or facts that are expressed in text, tables, charts, and other graphic information.
- Credit all artistic property, including works of literature, song lyrics, and ideas.

5.36 Keeping a Research Journal. Just as a writing journal can help you track your thoughts, experiences, and responses to literature, a research journal can help you track your research. A research journal is a notebook, electronic file, or other means to track the information you find as you conduct research.

5.37 Using Your Research Journal for Documentation. As you conduct your research, rely on your research journal as a place to take notes on the sources you find and your evaluation of them. Keeping a research journal can be an invaluable way to track your research and to take notes.

5.38 Informal and Formal Note-Taking.
Informal Note-taking. Take informal notes when you want information for your own use only, and when you will not need to quote or document your sources. You would take informal notes when preparing materials to use in studying, for instance, as you watch a film or listen to a lecture. Informal note-taking is much like outlining (see 2.29, "Outlining: Rough Outlines"). Use important ideas as headings, and write relevant details below.

Formal Note-taking. Take formal notes when you may need to quote or document your sources. When you are keeping formal notes for a project—for instance, for a debate or a research paper—you should use 4" x 6" index cards.

Preparing Note Cards.
- Identify the source at the top right corner of the card. (Use the source numbers from your bibliography cards.)
- Identify the subject or topic of the note on the top line of the card.
- Use a separate card for each fact or quotation.
- Write the pertinent source page number or numbers after the note.

DOCUMENTING SOURCES. Direct instruction on documenting sources can be found in the Language, Grammar, and Style section of the Guided Writing lesson at the end of Unit 6, pages 458–460.

STUDY AND RESEARCH RESOURCE

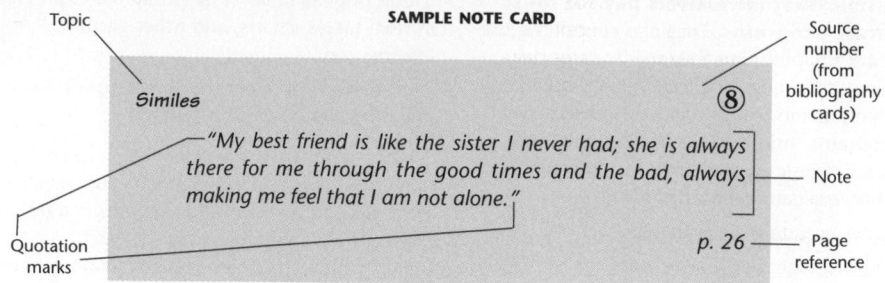

Topic

Similes ⑧

Source number (from bibliography cards)

"My best friend is like the sister I never had; she is always there for me through the good times and the bad, always making me feel that I am not alone."

Note

Quotation marks

p. 26

Page reference

5.39 MAKING BIBLIOGRAPHIES AND BIBLIOGRAPHY CARDS. If you are writing a research paper, your teacher will ask you to include a bibliography to tell where you got your information. A **bibliography** is a list of sources that you used for your writing. A **source** is a book, a magazine, a film, or any other written or audio-visual material that you use to get information. As you work on your paper, you should be writing down on note cards the information for each source that you use. For each source that you use, you should prepare an index card with complete bibliographic information. Include all of the information shown on the sample bibiography card.

Forms for Bibliography Entries.

- **A book**
  Douglass, Frederick. *Escape from Slavery: The Boyhood of Frederick Douglass in His Own Words*. New York: Alfred A. Knopf, 1994.

- **A magazine article**
  Reston, James, Jr. "Orion: Where Stars Are Born." *National Geographic*. December 1995: 90–101.

- **An encyclopedia entry**
  "Lewis and Clark Expedition." *Encyclopedia Americana*. Jackson, Donald. 1995 ed.

- **An interview**
  Campbell, Silas. Personal interview. 6 February 1997.

- **An Internet page**
  Heasley, Michael. Producer. "At the Tomb of Tutankhamen." 1998. <http.//www.nationalgeographic.com/egypt>.

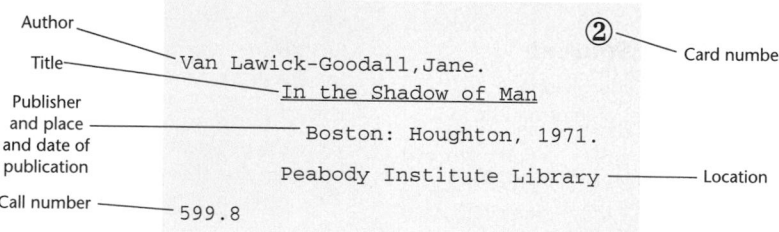

Author

Title

Publisher and place and date of publication

Call number

Van Lawick-Goodall,Jane.

②

Card number

In the Shadow of Man

Boston: Houghton, 1971.

Peabody Institute Library

Location

599.8

5.40 Documenting and Mapping Internet Research. Your research journal is an excellent tool for tracking how you find information, especially for documenting and mapping Internet research. As you browse and search on the Internet, it can be easy to jump from one site to the next and to lose track of how you got from place to place. Here is one way to map your path.

- Write a brief statement of the topic of your research.
- Write key words or phrases that will help you search for this information.
- Note the search engines that you will use.
- As you conduct a search, note how many "hits" or Internet sites the search engine has accessed. Determine whether you need to narrow or expand your search. Write down new key words accordingly, and the results of each new search.
- When you find promising sites, write them down.
- Access each promising site. Evaluate its information using the guidelines in 5.34,

"How to Understand Internet Sites."

- Once you find information to include in your work, document it carefully. For more information on how to document Internet sites, see the Language Arts Survey 5.39, "Making Bibliographies and Bibliography Cards."

5.41 Avoiding Plagiarism. Plagiarism is taking someone else's words or thoughts and pretending that they are your own. Plagiarism is a very serious problem and has been the downfall of many students and even famous people. Whenever you use someone else's writing to help you with a paper or a speech, you must be careful either to put the ideas in your own words or to use quotation marks. In either case, you must give credit to the person whose ideas you are using. Giving such credit to others is called documenting your sources.

5.42 Paraphrasing, Summarizing, and Quoting. As you do research, you notes will include paraphrases, and summaries, and quotations.

Documenting and Mapping Internet Research. Internet research activities are found in the Study and Research activities on pages 48, 356, and 540; the Media Literacy activities on pages 430 and 467; and the Group Project on page 400.

Summarizing. You will find activities that require students to summarize their research in Study and Research on pages 137 and 674.

TYPE OF NOTE	WHEN TO USE	WHAT TO WATCH FOR
Quotation	When the exact wording of a primary source is important to your topic When you are providing a definition	Copy spelling, capitalization, punctuation, and numbers exactly as in the source. Place quotation marks around all direct quotations.
Paraphrase	When the wording of a secondary source is particularly memorable or insightful Most of the time	Record, when appropriate, explanatory background information about the speaker or the context of a quotation. Focus on your main purpose, and note only points related to your topic. Place quotation marks around any quoted words or phrases.
Summary	When the point you are making does not require the detail of a paraphrase	Reread the source after writing your summary to be sure that you have not altered the meaning.

5.43 Parenthetical Documentation. Parenthetical documentation is currently the most widely used form of documentation. To use this method to document the source of a quotation or an idea, place a brief note identifying the source in parentheses immediately after the borrowed material. This type of note is called a **parenthetical citation**, and the act of placing such a note is called **citing a source**. The first part of a parenthetical citation refers the reader to a source in your bibliography. The second part of the citation refers the reader to a specific page or place within the source. If the source is clearly identified in the text, omit it from the citation and give only the page number.

- **For works listed by author or editor, use the author's or editor's last name.**

  Sample bibliographic entry

  McGuinn, Taro. *East Timor: Island in Turmoil.* Minneapolis: Lerner, 1988.

  Sample citation

  "It's unlikely that the problem in East Timor will be solved militarily." (Brown 364).

- **For works listed by title, use the title (abbreviate if necessary).**

  Sample bibliographic entry

  "East Timor." *Encyclopedia Britannica.* 2000 ed.

  Sample citation

  Indonesia's rule over East Timor is disputed by the United Nations. ("East Timor" 632).

- **When the author's name is used in the text, cite only the page number.**

  McGuinn believes that military forces cannot end the problems in East Timor. (80).

5.44 FOOTNOTES AND ENDNOTES. The method of documentation described in Section 5.44 is the most common of many accepted systems. Footnoting and endnoting are two other methods.

Instead of putting citations in parentheses within the text, you can place them at the bottom or foot of the page. These are **footnotes**. In this system, a number or symbol is placed in the text where the parenthetical citation would otherwise be, and a matching number or symbol at the bottom of the page identifies the citation. *Literature and the Language Arts* uses numbered footnotes in the literature selections to define obscure words and to provide background information.

Many books use endnotes instead of footnotes. **Endnotes** are like footnotes in that a number or symbol is placed within the text, but the matching citations are compiled at the end of the book, chapter, or article rather than at the foot of the page.

Footnote and endnote entries begin with the author's (or editor's) name in its usual order (first, then last) and include publication information and a page reference.

A BOOK WITH ONE AUTHOR	[1]Jean Paul-Sartre, *Being and Nothingness* (New York: The Citadel Press, 1966) 149-151.
A BOOK WITH ONE EDITOR AND NO SINGLE AUTHOR	[2]Shannon Ravenel, ed., *New Stories from the South: The Year's Best, 1992* (Chapel Hill, NC: Algonquin Books, 1992) 305.
A MAGAZINE ARTICLE	[3]Andrew Gore, "Road Test: The Apple Powerbook," *MacUser* December 1996: 72.

5.45 Preparing for Tests

Tests are a common part of school life. These guidelines will help you to prepare for and take a test.

PREPARING FOR A TEST

- Know exactly what you will be tested on. If you have questions, ask your teacher.
- Make a study plan to allow yourself time to go over the material. Avoid last-minute cramming.
- Review the subject matter. Use your notes, your SQ3R strategy, and any study questions given by your teacher.
- Make lists of important names, dates, definitions, or events. Ask a friend or family member to quiz you on them.
- Try to predict questions that may be on the test. Make sure you can answer them.
- Get plenty of sleep the night before the test and eat a nutritious breakfast on the morning of the test.

TAKING A TEST

- Survey the test to see how long it is and what types of questions are included.
- Read all directions and questions carefully. Make sure that you know exactly what to do.
- Plan your time. Answer easy questions first. Allow extra time for complicated questions. If a question seems too difficult, skip it and go back to it later. Work quickly, but do not rush.
- Save time for review. Once you have finished, look back over the test. Double-check your answers, but do not change answers too often. Your first ideas are often the correct ones.

5.46 Taking Objective Tests

Objective tests require simple right-or-wrong answers. This chart describes the kinds of questions you may see on objective tests.

QUESTIONS FOUND ON OBJECTIVE TESTS	
Description	**Guidelines**
True/False. You are given a statement and asked to tell whether the statement is true or false.	• If any part of a statement is false, then the statement is false. • Words like *all, always, never,* and *everyone* often appear in false statements. • Words like *some, usually, often,* and *most* often appear in true statements.
Matching. You are asked to match items in one column with items in another column.	• Check the directions. See if each item is used only once. Also check to see if some are not used at all. • Read all items before starting. • Match those you know first. • Cross out items as you match them.
Multiple-choice. You are asked to choose the best answer from a group of answers given.	• Read *all* choices first. • Rule out incorrect answers. • Choose the answer that is most complete or accurate. • Pay particular attention to choices such as *none of the above* or *all of the above.*
Short Answer. You are asked to answer the question with a word, a phrase, or a sentence.	• Read the directions to find out if you are required to answer in complete sentences. • Use correct spelling, grammar, punctuation, and capitalization. • If you cannot think of the answer, move on. Something in another question might remind you of the answer.

STUDY AND RESEARCH RESOURCE

5.47 Strategies for Taking Standardized Tests

Standardized tests are given to many students. You may already have taken a standardized test, such as the Iowa Test of Basic Skills, and you will take more during your school career. Learning how to take standardized tests well can help you to achieve your academic and career goals. When selecting an answer on a standardized test, remember these points.

- If you do not know the answer, try to rule out some choices and then guess from those remaining.
- If a question seems too difficult, skip it and go back to it later. Be aware, however, that most tests allow you to go back to questions only within a section.
- Always follow the instructions of the test monitor.

5.48 ANALOGY QUESTIONS. Analogy questions ask you to find the relationship between a pair of words and then to recognize a similar relationship between another pair of words. In an analogy question, the symbols : and :: mean "is to" and "as," respectively. The example below would be "Mare is to horse as . . ." when read aloud. To answer an analogy question, think of a sentence that relates the two words. For example, you might say "A *mare* is a female *horse*." Then look for another pair of words that would make sense in that sentence: "A *doe* is a female *deer*."

> EXAMPLE **ANALOGY QUESTIONS**
> MARE : HORSE ::
> (A) lamb : sheep
> (B) man : woman
> (C) boy : girl
> (D) bee : wasp
> (E) doe : deer
>
> The answer is E.

5.49 SYNONYM AND ANTONYM QUESTIONS. A synonym or antonym question gives you a word and asks you to select the word that has the same meaning (synonym) or the opposite meaning (antonym). You must select the best answer, even if none is exactly correct. Try all the choices to see which one works best. Always know whether you are looking for a synonym or an antonym, because you will usually find both among the answers.

5.50 SENTENCE COMPLETION QUESTIONS. Sentence-completion questions present you with a sentence that has two words missing. You must select the pair of words that best completes the sentence.

5.51 READING COMPREHENSION QUESTIONS. Reading comprehension questions give you a short piece of writing and then ask you several questions about it. The questions may ask you to figure out something based on information in the passage.

> **STEPS IN ANSWERING READING COMPREHENSION QUESTIONS**
>
> - Read all the questions quickly.
> - Read the passage with the questions in mind.
> - Reread the first question carefully.
> - Scan the passage, looking for key words related to the question. When you find a key word, slow down and read carefully.
> - Answer the first question.
> - Repeat this process to answer the rest of the questions.

5.52 Taking Essay Tests

An **essay** is a short piece of writing that expresses the writer's thoughts about a particular subject. To answer an essay question, follow these guidelines.

- Analyze each question. First, read the *entire* question carefully. Look for key words in the question that tell you what is expected. Underline these words or write them on your own note paper. Then make sure to answer *all* parts of the question.
- Organize Your Answer. Allow time for planning, writing, and reviewing. Before you begin writing, make a rough outline of the main points you will make. Include main points and key details. Later, if you find yourself running out of time, try at least to state your remaining main points and to add a conclusion.
- Write a clear introduction. This will help to keep you on track as you write each paragraph. Your introduction should state the thesis, or main idea, of your essay and should briefly answer the question. In the rest of the essay, you can elaborate on your answer, providing evidence to support it.
- Reviewing your answer. Before you turn in your completed essay, take time to proofread.

APPLIED ENGLISH Resource

THE IMPORTANCE OF APPLIED ENGLISH

Applied English is English in the world of work, or practical English. When you apply English skills to real-world situations, you are using your reading, writing, speaking, and listening abilities for practical reasons.

6.1 Filling Out Forms

Entering a new school, going to a new doctor, registering computer software, applying for a job—these are but a few of the thousands of activities that involve filling out forms. The following guidelines will help you to complete a form in a way that will make a good impression.

GUIDELINES FOR COMPLETING FORMS

- Get an extra copy or make a photocopy of the form so that you can complete a practice form.

- Read through the directions and the form itself before completing it.

- Gather the information you will need to complete the form. This information may include former addresses, dates of events, or a social security number.

- Complete the form neatly. Avoid smudges or cross-outs. Use the writing method requested on the form. Most forms request that you either type or use black or blue ink.

- Do not leave any lines blank. Use N.A. for "not applicable" if a request for information does not apply to you. For example, if you have always lived at the same address, you would write N.A. in the blank following "Previous Addresses."

- Proofread your information for errors in punctuation, spelling, or grammar. Make sure all information is correct.

- Submit the form to the appropriate person or address. Use an envelope or folder to keep the form neat and clean.

- Keep a copy of the form for your own records.

6.2 Following Directions

Every day people all over the world face the challenge of doing something they have never done before. Despite their inexperience, many people are able to succeed because they are able to follow directions. At the same time, someone must be able to give them clear, precise directions. Consider these guidelines before you begin following or giving directions.

GUIDELINES FOR FOLLOWING DIRECTIONS

- If the directions are being given in written form, read them carefully before beginning the procedure. If they are being given in spoken form, take notes as you listen. Ask for clarification if something is confusing.

- Take your time and make sure you have performed each step carefully and accurately before proceeding to the next step.

- If you get stuck following directions, either retrace your steps or reread the step you are on.

6.3 Giving Directions

GUIDELINES FOR GIVING DIRECTIONS

- Think through the directions completely, from start to finish, before you begin.

- Give each step in the correct order and include all necessary steps. Do not assume that your reader or listener already knows any part of the directions unless you are absolutely sure that this is the case.

- Do not include any unnecessary steps.

- Use simple, clear language.

APPLIED ENGLISH

APPLIED ENGLISH RESOURCE **939**

FILLING OUT FORMS. Students are asked to complete a job application form in the Skill Builders Applied English activity on page 369.

WRITING A STEP-BY-STEP PROCEDURE. Students are asked to write a step-by-step explanation of how something works in the Writer's Journal activity on page 848.

WRITING A PERSONAL LETTER. The Language, Grammar, and Style activity in the Guided Writing lesson at the end of Unit 3 gives direct instruction on composing a personal letter, including a student model. See pages 230–234.

- Use transition words such as first, second, third, next, then, and finally to connect your ideas.
- When possible, use a similar sentence structure for each part of the directions.
- When giving directions orally, ask the listener to repeat the directions to you when you have finished. This way you can check to make sure that your directions have been understood.
- If the directions that you are giving are complicated, put them into writing. Number each direction to help you and your reader to keep the steps separate and clear. You may also wish to include a map, diagram, or other illustration. For more information, see the Language Arts Survey 6.11, "Displaying Effective Visual Information."

6.4 Writing a Step-by-Step Procedure

A **step-by-step procedure** is a how-to or process piece that uses directions to teach someone something new. Written procedures include textual information and sometimes graphics. Spoken procedures can include textual and graphic information and other props. Examples of step-by-step procedures include: an oral demonstration of how to saddle a horse, instructions on how to treat a sprained ankle, a video showing how to do the perfect lay-up in basketball, or an interactive Internet site allowing the user to design and send a bouquet of flowers.

To write a step-by-step procedure, review the Language Arts Survey 6.3, "Giving Directions" and 6.11, "Displaying Effective Visual Information." Use these tips:

GUIDELINES FOR A DEMONSTRATION

- If you are showing how to make something, create several different samples to show each step of the procedure. You might also want to have a sample showing a variation.
- Be prepared. The best way to prevent problems is to anticipate and plan for them. Rehearse an oral demonstration several times. If you are preparing the procedure in written form, go through your directions as if you knew nothing about the process. See if you can follow your own directions. Or have a friend work through the procedure and

offer suggestions for improvement.

- Acknowledge mistakes. If you are showing a procedure "live" as an oral demonstration, tell your audience what has gone wrong, and why. Handle the situation in a calm, direct way.
- Know your topic well. The better you know it, the better you will be able to teach others.

6.5 Writing a Personal Letter

One of the easiest and most efficient ways of communicating and practicing your writing skills is to compose personal letters. You may want to write to a friend about your experiences on a vacation, to a relative about a school play or big sports event, or to a pen pal about simple everyday things. Letter writing allows for a lot of creativity. When you write a letter, keep in mind the following points.

GUIDELINES FOR A LETTER

- In addition to descriptions of your topic, include in your letter your reactions and emotions and beliefs about your topic.
- Use concrete, specific language to create the most meaningful and vivid descriptions.
- Consider the recipient of your letter. What background information does he or she need? What does he or she already know about your topic?
- Begin your letter with the date. Under the date, write a salutation, such as "Dear Grandma," or "Dear Julie:" and then follow with your letter. End the letter with your name.

6.6 Writing a Business Letter

A business letter is usually addressed to someone you do not know personally. Therefore, a formal tone is appropriate for such a letter.

Following appropriate form is especially important when writing business letters. If you follow the correct form and avoid errors in spelling, grammar, usage, and mechanics, your letter will sound professional and make a good impression.

A business letter includes the same parts as a personal letter. In addition, an inside address appears above the salutation. The inside address includes the name and title of the person to whom you are writing and the name and address of that person's company or organization (see the model on the following page).

One common form for a business letter is the block form. In the block form, each part of the letter begins at the left margin. The parts are separated by line spaces.

Begin the salutation with the word *Dear*, followed by the courtesy or professional title used in the inside address, such as Ms., Mr., or Dr., and a colon. If you are not writing to a specific person, you may use a general salutation such as *Dear Sir or Madam.*

In the body of your letter, use a polite, formal tone and standard English. Make your points clearly, in as few words as possible.

End with a standard closing such as *Sincerely, Yours truly,* or *Respectfully yours.* Capitalize only the first word of the closing. Type your full name below the closing, leaving three or four blank lines for your signature. Sign your name below the closing in blue or black ink (never in red or green). Proofread your letter before you send it. Poor spelling, grammar, or punctuation can ruin an otherwise well-written business letter.

WRITING A BUSINESS LETTER. Students are asked to write business letters in the Applied English activities on pages 174, 195, 268, 393, 540, and 655; and in the On Your Own activity in the Unit 2 Review on page 154.

498 Blue Key Rd.
Charleston, SC 89943

May 3, 1999

Mr. Davy Jones, Owner
Deep Sea Divers, Inc.
73 Ocean St.
Charleston, SC 89943

Dear Mr. Jones:

Please consider me for a position as a part-time clerk in your store for the coming summer. I understand that in the summer your business increases considerably and that you might have need for a conscientious, reliable, hardworking clerk. I can offer you considerable knowledge of snorkeling and diving equipment and experience working in a retail shop.

I will be available for work three days per week between June 1 and August 12. I am enclosing a resumé and references. Please contact me if you wish to set up an interview.

Sincerely,

Jorge Alvarez
Jorge Alvarez

6.7 Writing a Memo

In businesses, schools, and other organizations, employees, students, and others often communicate by means of memoranda, or memos. For example, the director of a school drama club might write a memo to the editor of the student newspaper announcing tryouts for a new play. Some memos will be more informal than others. If you know the person to whom you are writing well or if the memo has only a social function such as announcing a party, the tone can be fairly informal. Most memos, however, have a fairly formal tone.

A memo begins with a header. Often this header contains the word *memorandum* (the singular form of memoranda) and the following words and abbreviations: TO, FR (meaning from), DT (meaning date), RE (meaning regarding), and C (meaning copy).

APPLIED ENGLISH

APPLIED ENGLISH RESOURCE **941**

WRITING A MEMO. For practice writing a business memo, see the Applied English activity on page 576.

MEMORANDUM

TO: Lisa Lowry
FR: Jack Hart   C: Ms. Wise
RE: Tryouts for the spring production of Oklahoma!
DT: February 12, 1999

Please include the following announcement in the upcoming issue of the Wheaton Crier: Tryouts for the Wheaton Drama Club's spring production of Oklahoma! will be held on Friday, February 26, at 6:00 p.m. in the Wheaton Middle School Auditorium. Students interested in performing in this musical should come to the auditorium at that time prepared to deliver a monologue less than two minutes long and to sing one song from the musical. Copies of the music and lyrics can be obtained from the sponsor of the Wheaton Drama Club, Ms. Wise. For additional information, please contact Ms. Wise or any member of the Drama Club.

Thank you.

WRITING A PROPOSAL. Students are asked to write a fundraising proposal in the Media Literacy and Collaborative Learning activity on page 137.

6.8 Writing a Proposal

A **proposal** outlines a project that a person wants to complete. You would write a proposal if you wanted funding for an art project that would benefit your community, if your friends wanted to help organize a summer program for teens your age, or if your student council wanted to hold a clothing drive for disaster relief. It presents a summary of an idea, the reasons why the idea is important, and an outline of how the project would be carried out. Because the proposal audience is people who can help carry out the proposal, a proposal is both informative and persuasive.

GUIDELINES FOR A PROPOSAL

- Keep the tone positive, courteous, and respectful.

- State your purpose and rationale briefly and clearly.

- Give your audience all necessary information. A proposal with specific details makes it clear what you want approved, and why your audience—often a committee or someone in authority—should approve it.

- Use standard, formal English.

- Format your proposal with headings, lists, and schedules to make your proposed project easy to understand and approve.

6.9 Delivering a Press Release

A **press release** is an informative piece intended for publication in local news media. A press release is usually written to promote an upcoming event or to inform the community of a recent event.

EXAMPLES

a brief notice from the choir director telling the community of the upcoming spring concert

an informative piece by the district public information officer announcing that your school's art instructor has been named Teacher of the Year

DELIVERING A PRESS RELEASE. Students can practice writing a press release in the Applied English activity on page 112.

GUIDELINES FOR A PRESS RELEASE

- Use the 5 Ws and an H—*who, what, where, why, when,* and *how*—questioning strategy to convey the important information at the beginning of the piece. (For help, see the Language Arts Survey 2.14.)

- Keep it brief. Local media are more likely to publish or broadcast your piece if it is short and to the point.

- Include contact information: your name, phone number, and times you can be reached, either for the media representative or, if applicable, for the reading public.

- Type your press release using conventional manuscript form.

- At the top of the press release, type the date.

- Check a previous newspaper for deadline information or call the newspaper office to make sure you get your material there on time. Address the press release to the editor.

6.10 Writing a Public Service Announcement

A **public service announcement**, or PSA, is a brief, informative article intended to be helpful to the community. PSAs are written by non-profit organizations and concerned citizens for print in local newspapers, for broadcast by television and radio stations, and available on the Internet.

EXAMPLES

> an article by the American Cancer Society outlining early warning signs of cancer
>
> an announcement promoting Safety Week
>
> an informative piece telling coastal residents what to do during a hurricane

To write a public service announcement, follow the same guidelines you would for a press release.

6.11 Displaying Effective Visual Information

People frequently learn things best and remember more when information is presented visually. Whenever possible, use charts, tables, pictures, slides, photographs, models, and art to express key points. Depending on their use, visuals can detract from a presentation or enhance it. Before you use a visual, ask yourself:

- Is it attention-grabbing?
- Is it simple and neat?
- Does it serve a real purpose?
- Can I use it easily?
- Does it fit smoothly into the presentation?

GUIDELINES FOR DISPLAYING VISUALS

The success of your presentation will depend on how you display visual information.

- Keep visual information simple. Do not clutter visual display with multiple lettering or font styles, too many small images, or too much textual or graphic information.

- Design your visual display in a way that the viewer's eye will naturally follow.

- Include a title or caption, labels for different parts, and simple, main points when needed.

- Make the visual visible. Type or graphics that are too small can make the best visual presentation useless. If the display is for a speech or exhibit, stand back and see if you can see it from the back of the room or wherever your audience members will be.

- Use bullets or numbering to organize your text. For simple presentations, use either one or the other; don't use both.

- Use color carefully. Color can add visual interest, but it can also be distracting or make a graphic or text area illegible.

- Document all sources of graphic information. The ideas in visual information are someone's intellectual property, just like the ideas in text material. Make sure you give proper credit for all work not your own.

6.12 Working on a Team

Working on a team, or doing collaborative learning, is an essential Applied English skill that depends on a strong ability to communicate. Refer to the Speaking and Listening Resource for more information.

WRITING A PUBLIC SERVICE ANNOUNCEMENT. Students are asked to write a public service announcement in the Media Literacy activity on pages 416 and the Writer's Journal activity 843; and to create a public relations poster in the Applied English and Media Literacy activity on page 779.

DISPLAYING EFFECTIVE VISUAL COMMUNICATION. Students are asked to design a poster or collage in the Applied English activity on page 25 and in the Group Projects on pages 84, 467, and 683; to make a map in the Collaborative Learning and Media Literacy activities on pages 94 and 126; to create a storyboard or story cloth in the On Your Own on page 237; to create a billboard in the Media Literacy activity on page 808; and to analyze historical photographs in the Study and Research activity on page 842.

WORKING ON A TEAM. Collaborative Learning activities follow many of the selections in the Skill Builders section of the Post Reading. Also refer to the Speaking and Listening Resource 4.7–4.13 for more information on group communication and collaborative learning.

APPLIED ENGLISH

ABSTRACT. An **abstract** word, like hope or pride, names something that cannot be directly seen, touched, tasted, heard, or smelled. See *concrete.*

ACRONYM. An **acronym** is a word made from the first letters of a group of words. The word *laser* is an acronym. Many organizations, such as *SADD,* have names that are acronyms.

laser= **L**ight **A**mplication **S**timulated by **E**mission **R**adiation.

SADD = **S**tudents **A**gainst **D**runk **D**riving

ACT. An **act** is a major part of a play. Long plays are often divided into several acts. Sometimes acts are divided into scenes. See *scene.*

ACTOR. An **actor** is someone who plays a character. Actors perform in theater, television, and films. They also do readings and storytelling. Today, the word *actor* is used to speak about both male and female performers.

AIM. A writer's **aim** is his or her purpose, or goal. People may write with the following aims:

- to *inform* (expository/ informational writing);

- to *tell a story,* either true or invented, about an event or sequence of events (narrative writing);
- to *reflect* (personal/expressive writing);
- to *share a perspective* by using an artistic medium, such as fiction or poetry, to entertain, enrich, or enlighten (imaginative writing);
- to *persuade* readers or listeners to respond in some way, such as to agree with a position, change a view on an issue, reach an agreement, or perform an action (persuasive/argumentative writing).

Here are examples of writing that reflect these five aims:

expository/informational
      news article, research report
narrative
      biography, family history
personal/expressive
      diary entry, personal letter
imaginative
      poem, short story

persuasive/argumentative
      editorial, petition

ALLITERATION. **Alliteration** is the repetition of consonant sounds at the beginnings of syllables, as in *bats in the belfry* or *dead as a doornail.* The repetition of the *b* sounds in the following lines are examples of alliteration:

I love to go out in late September
among the fat, overripe, icy, black blackberries
to eat blackberries for breakfast…

—Galway Kinnell, from "Blackberry Eating" (Unit 9)

ANALOGY. An **analogy** is a comparison of things that are alike in some ways but different in others.

ANALYSIS. **Analysis** is the act of dividing a subject into parts and then thinking about how the parts are related. For example, an analysis of a short story might consider these parts: the plot, the setting, the characters, and the theme, or main idea.

ANECDOTE. An **anecdote** is a usually short narrative of an interesting, amusing, or biographical incident. Although anecdotes are often the basis for short stories, an anecdote differs from a short story in that it lacks a complicated plot and relates a single episode.

ANTAGONIST. In a story, a character who struggles with the main character is called an **antagonist.** For example, in "Luke Baldwin's Vow" in Unit 8, Uncle Henry is an antagonist because he wants to get rid of Dan, Luke's dog.

APPOSITION. An **apposition** is a renaming of something in different words. The following sentence includes an apposition:

Annie Sullivan, Helen Keller's teacher, is one of the main characters in The Miracle Worker.

ARTICLE. An **article** is a brief nonfiction work on a specific topic. Encyclopedia entries, newspaper reports, and nonfiction magazine pieces are examples of articles.

ASIDE. An **aside** is a statement made by a character in a play, meant to be heard by the audience but not by the other characters.

ASSONANCE. Assonance is the repetition of vowel sounds in stressed syllables that end in different consonant sounds, as in *lime* *light*.

ATMOSPHERE. See *mood.*

AUTOBIOGRAPHY. An **autobiography** is the story of a person's life, written by that person. "Caesar the Giant," from Gary Paulsen's book *My Life in Dog Years,* in Unit 11, is an example of autobiography.

BACKGROUND INFORMATION. Background information is information provided in a literary work, often at the beginning, to explain the situation to the reader. A writer may include background information to explain the central conflict, the relationships between the characters, the setting, or any other part of his or her work.

BALLAD. A **ballad** is a simple poem that tells a story. Most ballads have four-line stanzas that have the rhyme scheme *abcb*. Sometimes the last line of a stanza is repeated.

BIBLIOGRAPHY. A **bibliography** is a list of books, magazines, or other sources of information. A writer may include a bibliography at the end of his or her work to show where he or she got the information that appears in the work. A complete bibliography entry for a book gives its author, its title, its place of publication, its publisher, and its date of publication:

Lester, Julius. *To Be a Slave.* New York: Scholastic, 1968.

BIOGRAPHY. A **biography** is the story of a person's life, told by another person. Milton Meltzer's "Elizabeth I," from the book *Ten Queens: Portraits of Women in Power,* in Unit 11, is a biography of Queen Elizabeth I.

BLEND. A **blend** is a new word created by joining together two old ones, as in *smog,* from the words *smoke* and *fog;* or *pixel,* which is a dot on a computer screen, from the words *picture* and *element.*

CENTRAL CONFLICT. A **central conflict** is the main problem or struggle in the plot of a poem, story, or play. In Vivien Alcock's "Qwertyuiop" in Unit 5, the central conflict is between the main character and a ghost. See *conflict* and *plot.*

CHARACTER. A **character** is a person or animal who takes part in the action of a literary work. The main character is called the *protagonist.* A character who struggles against the main char-

acter is called an *antagonist.* Characters can also be classified as *major characters* or *minor characters.* Major characters are ones who play important roles in a work. Minor characters are ones who play less important roles. A *one-dimensional character, flat character,* or *caricature* is one who exhibits a single quality, or character trait. A *three-dimensional, full,* or *rounded character* is one who seems to have all the complexities of an actual human being.

CHARACTERIZATION. Characterization is the act of creating or describing a character. Writers use three major techniques to create a character: by showing what characters say, do and think: by showing what other characters say about them; and by showing what physical features, dress, and personality the characters display. See *character.*

CHRONOLOGICAL ORDER. Events arranged in order of the time when they happened are said to be in **chronological order.** This method of organization is used in most stories, whether they are fiction or nonfiction. Chronological order is also used in informative nonfiction writing that describes processes and cause-and-effect relationships.

CLICHÉ. (klē shā') A **cliché** is an overused expression such as *happy as a lark* or *time is money.* Most clichés begin as vivid, colorful expressions but become uninteresting because of overuse.

CLIMAX. The **climax** is the point of highest interest and suspense in a literary work. The climax sometimes signals the turning point of the action in a story or play. See *plot.*

COHERENCE. Coherence is the logical arrangement of ideas in speech or writing. Writers achieve coherence by presenting their ideas in a logical order and by using transitions to show how their ideas are connected to one another. See *transition.*

COINED WORDS. Coined words are ones that are intentionally created, often from already existing words or word parts. Examples of recently coined words include *modem, sitcom,* and *videophone.*

CONCRETE. A **concrete** word, like *cloud* or *airplane,* names something that can be directly seen, tasted, touched, heard, or smelled. Concrete language is particularly effective when it is as specific and detailed as possible. See *abstract.*

CONCRETE POEM. A **concrete poem,** or **shape poem,** is one with a shape that suggests its subject. The following is an example of a concrete poem:

> sky.
> at the
> They point
> what is sacred.
> creeping in to steal
> Stale air cursing intruders
> to the glory of ancient Pharaohs.
> Immense treasure-filled monuments

CONFLICT. A **conflict** is a struggle between two people or things in a literary work. A *plot* is formed around conflict. A conflict can be internal or external. A struggle that takes place between a character and some outside force such as another character, society, or nature is called an *external conflict*. In Vivien Alcock's "Qwertyuiop" in Unit 5, the main character confronts a haunted typewriter, an external force. A struggle that takes place within a character is called an *internal conflict*. In Ji-Li Jiang's "Destroy the Four Olds!" in Unit 1, the main character experiences an internal conflict over whether help get rid of the "old culture," or to oppose this new way of thinking. See *central conflict* and *plot*.

CONNOTATION. A **connotation** is an emotional association attached to a word or statement. For example, the word *unique* has positive emotional associations, while the word *strange* has negative ones, even though the two words denote, or refer to, something highly unusual. See *denotation*.

CONSONANCE. **Consonance** is the use of different vowel sounds followed by the same consonant sound, as in *flim flam*.

CRISIS. The **crisis**, or **turning point**, is the point in a plot when something happens to determine the future course of events and the eventual fate of the main character. See *plot*.

CRITICISM. **Criticism** is the act of explaining or judging a literary work.

DENOTATION. A **denotation** is the basic meaning, or dictionary definition, of a word. See *connotation*.

DESCRIPTION. **Description** is a type of writing that portrays a character, object, or scene. Descriptions make use of *sensory details*—words and phrases that describe how things look, sound, smell, taste, or feel. Effective descriptions contain precise—or concrete—nouns, verbs, adverbs, and adjectives. Descriptions often use imagery and figurative language. Eve Merriam's "How to Eat a Poem," in Unit 9, appeals to the senses of sight, touch, and taste.

DIALECT. A **dialect** is a version of a language spoken by people of a particular place, time, or group. Writers often use dialect to give their works a realistic flavor. The following dialogue from Budge Wilson's "Be-ers and Do-ers" in Unit 1 is written in a dialect spoken in Nova Scotia:

> "The vegetables are comin' along jest fine. No need to shove them more than necessary. It does a man good to look at them hills. You wanta try it sometime. They tell you things."

DIALOGUE. **Dialogue** is conversation involving two or more people or characters. Plays are made up of dialogue and stage directions. Fictional works are made up of dialogue, narration, and description. In a play, dialogue appears after the names of characters:

AUNT EV: Arthur. Something ought to be done for that child.
KELLER: A refreshing suggestion. What?
AUNT EV: Why, this very famous oculist in Baltimore I wrote you about, what was his name?
KATE: Dr. Chisholm.

—William Gibson, from *The Miracle Worker* (Unit 10)

In fiction, dialogue is enclosed in quotation marks (" ") and is often accompanied by tag lines, words and phrases such as *he said* or *she replied* that tell who is speaking:

> "Is the welfare office near the Harbor Show?" I asked. I knew the answer, I just wanted some talk.
> "Across the street."
> "Umm. Glad it's not way down Jefferson somewhere."

—Paulette Childress, from "Getting the Facts of Life" (Unit 8)

DIARY. A **diary** is a day-to-day record of a person's life, thoughts, or feelings.

DRAMA. A **drama**, or play, is a story told through characters played by actors. The script of a drama typically consists of characters' names, dialogue spoken by the characters, and stage directions. Drama is meant to be read or performed before an audience. When a person reads a drama, he or she should imagine what it would be like to see and hear the action. The spectacle of a drama includes everything that the audience sees and hears, such as lighting, costumes, makeup, props, set pieces, music, sound effects, and the movements and expressions of actors. Drama also differs from other types of literature in being a collaborative effort involving the author as well as a director, actors, and others involved in the production. William Gibson's *The Miracle Worker* in Unit 10 is a drama.

DRAMATIC IRONY. **Dramatic irony** happens when something is known by the reader or audience of a literary work but is not known by the characters. An example of dramatic irony occurs in W. P. Kinsella's "Searching for January," in Unit 4. In the story, the narrator and the reader knows that the character of Roberto Clemente has died in a plane crash, but the character himself does not seem to know this.

EDITORIAL. An **editorial** is a short piece of persuasive writing that appears in a newspaper, magazine, or similar work.

ESSAY. An **essay** is a short nonfiction work that expresses a writer's thoughts about a single subject. A good essay develops a single idea, or *thesis*, and is organized into an introduction, a body, and a conclusion. A *personal essay* is a short nonfiction work on a single topic related to the life of the writer. A personal essay is written from the author's point of view using the pronouns *I* and *me*. A *narrative essay* tells a true story to make some point. An *informative* essay is written to communicate facts. A *persuasive essay* is written to advance an opinion. Robert Jastrow's "The Size of Things" in Unit 11 is an informative essay, one written to communicate facts. Al Gore's "Ships In the Desert" in Unit 2, is a narrative and persuasive essay.

EUPHEMISM. A **euphemism** is a less emotionally powerful word or phrase used in place of one that might be offensive. For example, some people use the euphemism *passed away* instead of the more direct and powerful word *dead*. The phrase *pre-owned vehicle*, used in place of *used car*, is an example of a euphemism from advertising.

EXPOSITION. The **exposition** is the part of a plot that introduces the setting and the major characters. Here is part of the exposition from William Saroyan's short story "The Hummingbird That Lived through Winter" from Unit 6:

> There was a hummingbird once which in the wintertime did not leave our neighborhood in Fresno, California. I'll tell you about it.

EXPRESSIVE WRITING. See *aim*.

EXTERNAL CONFLICT. An **external conflict** is a struggle that takes place between a character and something outside that character. The outside force of World War II in Paul Gallico's novella *The Snow Goose* in Unit 8 is an external conflict. See *conflict* and *internal conflict*.

FABLE. A **fable** is a brief story that frequently includes animal characters and a moral.

FAIRY TALE. A **fairy tale** is a type of European folk tale containing supernatural events and often imaginary creatures such as elves, giants, and fairies. "Cinderella" and "The Little Mermaid" are famous examples.

FANTASY. A **fantasy** is a very unrealistic or imaginative story. Fantasy is often contrasted with *science fiction*, in which the unreal elements are given a scientific or pseudoscientific basis. Joan Aiken's "The Serial Garden" in Unit 3 has elements of fantasy. See *science fiction*.

FICTION. **Fiction** is prose writing about imagined events or characters. The primary forms of fiction are the short story, the novella, and the novel. Lensey Namioka's "The Inn of Lost Time" in Unit 3 is an example of a short story. Paul Gallico's *The Snow Goose* in Unit 8 is an example of a novella. Mildred D. Taylor's *Roll of Thunder, Hear My Cry* is a popular contemporary novel. See *novel* and *novella*.

FIGURE OF SPEECH. A **figure of speech** is writing or speech meant to be understood imaginatively instead of literally. Many writers, especially poets, use figures of speech to help readers to see things in new ways. Figures of speech, also called figurative language, includes such literary techniques as *apostrophe*, *hyperbole*, *irony*, *metaphor*, *oxymoron*, *paradox*, *personification*, and *simile*.

FIRST-PERSON POINT OF VIEW. In a story told from the **first-person point of view**, the narrator takes a part in the action and refers to himself or herself using words such as *I* and *we*. See *point of view*.

FLASHBACK. A **flashback** is a part of a story, poem, or play that presents events that happened at an earlier time. Writers use flashbacks for many purposes. One common technique is to begin a work with a final event and then to tell the rest of the story as a flashback that explains how that event came about. Another common technique is to begin a story in the middle of the action and then to use a flashback to fill in the events that occurred before the opening of the story. Lensey Namioka's "The Inn of Lost Time," in Unit 3, includes a flashback, when travellers recall a mystery that happened a long time ago at the same inn.

FOLK SONG. A **folk song** is a traditional or composed song typically made up of *stanzas*, a refrain, and a simple melody. A form of folk literature, folk songs are expressions of commonly shared ideas or feelings and may be narrative or lyric in style. Traditional folk songs are anonymous songs that have been passed down orally. Examples include the ballad "Bonny Barbara Allan," the children's song "Row, Row, Row Your Boat," the railroad song "Casey Jones," and the cowboy song "The Streets of Laredo." Contemporary composers of songs in the folk tradition include Bob Dylan, Joan Baez, Pete Seeger, and Joni Mitchell. See *ballad.*

FOLK TALE. A **folk tale** is a story passed by word of mouth from generation to generation. Famous collections of folk tales include the fairy tales collected by the Brothers Grimm and Zora Neale Hurston's collection of African-American folk tales in *Mules and Men.* An example of a folk tale from this book is Zora Neale Hurston's "How the Snake Got Poison" in Unit 2. See *oral tradition.*

FORESHADOWING. **Foreshadowing** is the act of hinting at events that will happen later in a poem, story, or play. Patricia McKissack's short story "The 11:59" in Unit 5 contains elements of foreshadowing. The main character's fate is hinted at when the reader learns that all retired Pullman car porters meet their deaths in the form of the 11:59 train.

FREE VERSE. **Free verse** is poetry that does not use regular rhyme, rhythm, or division into stanzas. Richard Garcia's poem "The City is So Big" in Unit 2 and Elizabeth Bishop's "Filling Station" in Unit 9 are examples of free verse.

GENRE. A **genre** is a type of literary work. The main types are *drama, fiction, poetry,* and *nonfic-* tion. Some terms used to name literary genres in more specific ways include *autobiography, biography, drama, essay, novel, poetry, short story,* and *tragedy.* Literary works are sometimes classified into genres based on subject matter. Such a classification might describe *detective stories, mysteries, adventure stories, romances, westerns,* and *science fiction* as different genres of fiction.

HAIKU. (hī′ kü′) A **haiku** is a traditional Japanese three-line poem. It has five syllables in the first line, seven in the second, and five in the third. A traditional haiku presents an *image* in order to arouse in the reader a specific emotional state. Unit 9 includes haiku by Matsuo Bashō, Yosa Buson, and Kobayashi Issa.

HYPERBOLE. (hī′ pər′ bə lē) A **hyperbole** is an exaggeration made for effect.

IMAGE. An **image** is language that creates a concrete representation of an object or an experience. An image is also the vivid mental picture created in the reader's mind by that language. The images in a literary work are referred to, when considered altogether, as the work's *imagery.* These lines from Simon Ortiz's "My Father's Song" in Unit 9 contain images of sight, sound, and touch:

> I remember the very softness of cool and warm sand and tiny alive mice and my father saying things.

IMAGERY. Taken together, the images in a poem or passage are called its **imagery**. See *image.*

IMAGINATIVE WRITING. See *aim.*

INCITING INCIDENT. The **inciting incident** is the event that introduces the central conflict, or struggle, in a poem, story, or play. In Joseph Bruchac's short story "Jed's Grandfather" in Unit 2, the bad dream Jed has about his grandfather's illness is the inciting incident. See *plot.*

INFORMATIVE WRITING. See *aim.*

INTERNAL CONFLICT. An **internal conflict** is a struggle that takes place inside the mind of a character. See *conflict.*

IRONY. **Irony** is a difference between appearance and reality. In Rona Maynard's "The Fan Club," in Unit 1, the main character decides to join the "in" group by making fun of another character. It is ironic that the main character does so because earlier in the story she gave a speech about the need to overcome prejudice and to

948   HANDBOOK OF LITERARY TERMS

tolerate others regardless of their differences.

IRONY OF SITUATION. An event that contradicts the expectations of the characters, the reader, or the audience of a literary work is an example of **irony of situation**. In Ernest Hemingway's "A Day's Wait" in Unit 12, Schatz expects to die because he misinterprets his temperature. It is ironic that the boy is preparing himself to die when he has only a mild fever. See *irony*.

JOURNAL. A **journal**, like a *diary*, is a day-to-day record of a person's life, thoughts, or feelings.

LEGEND. A **legend** is a story coming down from the past, often based on important real events or characters. Some people believe that "The Epic of Gilgamesh" in Unit 7 is based upon stories about a real king who lived thousands of years ago in Mesopotamia.

LIGHT VERSE. **Light verse** is poetry meant to be humorous.

LIMERICK. A **limerick** is a five-line light verse. The first, second, and fifth lines end with one rhyme. The third and fourth lines end with another. The rhyme scheme is *aabba*.

> There was an old man who supposed
> That the street door was partially closed;
> But some very large rats
> Ate his coats and his hats,
> While that futile old gentleman dozed.
>
> —Edward Lear

LIMITED POINT OF VIEW. A literary work is written from a **limited point of view** if everything is seen through the eyes of a single character. Ji-li Jiang's autobiographical memoir "Destroy the Four Olds!" in Unit 1, is written from a limited point of view.

LYRIC POEM. A **lyric poem** is highly musical verse that expresses the emotions of a speaker and does not tell a story. Lyric poems are often contrasted with *narrative poems*, which have telling a story as their main purpose. Examples of lyric poems include Carl Sandburg's "Under the Yellow Moon" and "Theme in Yellow," both in Unit 2.

MAIN CHARACTER. A **main character** is the most important figure in a literary work. See *character*.

MAJOR CHARACTER. A **major character** is one who plays an important role in a literary work. See *character*.

MEMOIR. A **memoir** is a nonfiction narration that tells a story. A memoir can be *autobiographical* (about one's own life) or *biographical* (about someone else's life). Memoirs are based on a person's experiences and reactions to historical events. Maijue Xiong's "An Unforgettable Journey" in Unit 3 is an example of a memoir. See *autobiography* and *biography*.

METAPHOR. A **metaphor** is a figure of speech in which one thing is spoken or written about as if it were another. This figure of speech invites the reader to make a comparison between the two things. Eve Merriam's poem "How to Eat a Poem" in Unit 9, describes a poem as if it were a fruit. A metaphor works because the things to be compared have one or more qualities in common. A simile also compares one thing to another, but while using the word *like* or *as*. *My skateboard is a rocket* is a metaphor, while *My skateboard is like a rocket* is a simile.

METER. The **meter** of a poem is its overall rhythm, or pattern of beats. To chart, or scan, the meter of a poem, mark each stressed syllable with a (/) and each unstressed one with a ( ). The following lines from Alfred, Lord Tennyson's "The Charge of the Light Brigade" in Unit 9 have the following pattern of strong and weak beats, or stresses:

> /　⏑　⏑　/　⏑　/
> "For ward, | the Light | Brig ade!"
>
> /　⏑　⏑　/　⏑　/
> "Charge for | the guns!" | he said:

See *stress*.

MOOD. **Mood,** or **atmosphere**, is the feeling or emotion the writer creates in a literary work. By working carefully with descriptive language, the writer can evoke in the reader an emotional response such as fear, discomfort, longing, or anticipation. Notice the uneasy, frightened mood Richard Garcia creates in the first stanza of "The City is So Big" in Unit 2:

> The city is so big,
> Its bridges quake with fear
> I know, I have seen at night

MORAL. A **moral** is a practical or moral lesson, usually relating to the principles of right and wrong, to be drawn from a story or other work of literature.

MOTIF. A **motif** is anything that appears repeatedly in one or more works of literature, art, or music. In Paul Gallico's novella *The Snow Goose,* in Unit 8, the goose is a recurring motif.

MOTIVATION. A **motivation** is a force that moves a character to think, feel, or behave in a certain way.

MOTIVE. A **motive** is a reason for acting in a certain way. For example, in Cherylene Lee's short story "Hollywood and the Pits" in Unit 3, the main character is motivated to study fossils in the LaBrea tar pits in order to move beyond her former career as a child actor.

MYTH. A **myth** is a story that explains objects or events in the natural world. These objects or events are explained as being caused by some supernatural force or being, often a god. The Greek myth "Persephone and Demeter" in Unit 7 explains how the seasons of winter and summer came to be.

NARRATIVE POEM. A **narrative poem** is a verse that tells a story. "The Charge of the Light Brigade" in Unit 9 is an example of a narrative poem. See *ballad.*

NARRATIVE WRITING. See *aim.*

NARRATOR. A **narrator** is a person or character who tells a story. Works of fiction almost always have a narrator. The narrator in a work of fiction may be a major or minor character or simply someone who witnessed or heard about the events being related. In Cherylene Lee's "Hollywood and the Pits" in Unit 3, the narrator is the main character. In Avi's short story "Pets" in Unit 5, the narrator is not a character but an *omniscient,* or all-knowing, observer, who knows everything about the characters and events that take place in the story. See *point of view.*

NONFICTION. **Nonfiction** is writing about real people, places, things, and events. Essays, autobiographies, biographies, and news stories are all types of nonfiction. See *prose.*

NOVEL. A **novel** is a long work of prose fiction. Often novels have involved plots; many characters, both major and minor; and numerous settings.

NOVELLA. A **novella** is a work of fiction shorter than a novel but longer than a short story. Paul Gallico's *The Snow Goose* in Unit 8 is a novella.

OMNISCIENT POINT OF VIEW. A story is written from an **omniscient point of view** if the narrator, or storyteller, knows everything and can see into

the minds of all the characters. Gregorio López y Fuentes's "A Letter to God" in Unit 2 is written from an omniscient point of view. See *point of view* and *narrative.*

ONOMATOPOEIA. **Onomatopoeia** is the use of words or phrases like *meow* or *beep* that sound like what they name.

ORAL TRADITION. An **oral tradition** is works, ideas, or customs of a culture, passed by word of mouth from generation to generation. Works found in the oral traditions of peoples around the world include *folk tales, fables, fairy tales, tall tales, nursery rhymes, proverbs, legends, myths, parables, riddles, charms, spells,* and *ballads.*

OXYMORON. An **oxymoron** is a word or a phrase that contradicts itself, such as *bittersweet, pretty ugly,* or *act natural.*

PARABLE. A **parable** is a story told to communicate a moral.

PARALLELISM. **Parallelism** is the expression of similar ideas in a similar way. Eve Merriam uses parallelism in the closing lines of her poem "How to Eat a Poem" in Unit 9.

PARAPHRASE. A **paraphrase** is a rewriting of a passage in different words. Consider the following example:

> The Hindus worship a number of deities, but all are viewed as manifestations of the one deity named Brahma.

> Paraphrase: The many gods of the Hindu religion are considered aspects of one god called Brahma.

See *summary.*

PERIODICAL. A **periodical** is a newspaper, magazine, or newsletter that is published regularly (once a month, for example).

PERSONAL ESSAY. A **personal essay** is a short nonfiction work on a single topic related to the life of the writer. A personal essay is written from the author's point of view, using the pronouns *I* and *me.* See *essay.*

PERSONAL WRITING. See *aim.*

PERSONIFICATION. **Personification** is a figure of speech in which something not human is described as if it were human. Robert Frost personifies an ocean in his poem "Once by the Pacific," in Unit 5:

The shattered water made a misty din.
Great waves looked over others coming in.
And thought of doing something to the shore
That water never did to land before. . .

PERSUASIVE WRITING. See *aim*.

PLAGIARISM. **Plagiarism** is the act of presenting
someone else's work as if it were your own. To
avoid plagiarism, always give credit to a source
from which you have taken information. In
addition, use quotation marks around material
picked up word for word from a source.

PLOT. A **plot** is a series of events related to a central conflict, or struggle. A plot usually involves
the introduction of a conflict, its development,
and its eventual resolution. The following terms
are used to describe the parts of a plot:

- The **exposition**, or **introduction**, sets the
  tone or mood, introduces the characters and
  the setting, and provides necessary background information.
- The **inciting incident** is the event that introduces the central conflict.
- The **climax** is the high point of interest or
  suspense in the story.
- The **crisis**, or **turning point**, often the same
  event as the climax, is the point in the plot
  where something happens to decide the
  future course of events and the eventual
  working out of the conflict.
- The **resolution** is the point at which the central conflict is ended, or resolved.
- The **dénouement** is any material that follows
  the resolution and that ties up loose ends.

Note that some plots do not contain all of these
parts. See *conflict*.

POETRY. **Poetry** is language used in special ways
so that its sound reflects its meaning more pow-
erfully than in ordinary speech and writing.

POINT OF VIEW. **Point of view** is the vantage
point from which a story is told. If a story is told
from the first-person point of view, the narrator
uses the pronouns *I* and *we* and is a part of or a
witness to the action. Edgar Allan Poe's "The
Tell-Tale Heart" in Unit 5 is told from the *first-
person point of view*:

> True!—nervous—very, very dreadfully nervous
> I had been and am; but why will you say that I
> am mad?

When a story is told from a *third-person point of
view*, the narrator is outside the action; uses
words such as *he, she, it,* and *they*; and avoids
the use of *I* and *we*. Morley Callaghan's story
"Luke Baldwin's Vow" in Unit 8 is told from the
third-person point of view:

> That summer when twelve-year-old Luke
> Baldwin came to live with his Uncle Henry in
> the house on the stream by the sawmill, he
> did not forget that he had promised his dying
> father he would try to learn things from his
> uncle; so he used to watch him very carefully.

PREFACE. A **preface** is a statement made at the
beginning of a literary work that serves as an
introduction.

PROSE. **Prose** is the word used to describe all
writing that is not drama or poetry. Prose
includes fiction and nonfiction. Novels, short
stories, essays, news stories, biographies, autobiographies, and letters are written in prose.

PROTAGONIST. A **protagonist** is the main character in a story. The protagonist faces a struggle
or *conflict*. The protagonist in "The Epic of
Gilgamesh" in Unit 7 is Gilgamesh, King of
Uruk. He struggles against many opponents and
to find everlasting life.

PROVERB. A **proverb**, or **adage**, is a traditional
saying. Examples of proverbs include "Beauty is
only skin deep" and "You can lead a horse to
water, but you can't make it drink." Another
word for proverb is *aphorism*.

PSEUDONYM. (sü' də nim) A **pseudonym** is a
name used by a writer instead of his or her real
name. Lewis Carroll is the pseudonym of
Charles Lutwidge Dodgson.

PUN. A **pun** is a play on words that makes use of
a double meaning.

RAP. A **rap** is an often improvised rhymed verse
that is chanted or sung, often to music.

REALISM. **Realism** is the attempt to present in art
or literature an accurate picture of reality.

REFRAIN. A **refrain** is one or more lines repeated
in a poem or song.

REPETITION. **Repetition** is more than one use of a
sound, word, or group of words.

RESOLUTION. The **resolution** is the point in a poem,
story, or play in which the *central conflict*, or
struggle, ends. In Chaim Potok's short story

"Zebra" in Unit 1, the resolution occurs when Zebra draws a picture for John Wilson, and John Wilson takes it to the Vietnam Veterans Memorial.

REVIEW. A **review** is a piece of writing that describes and judges a work of art, a performance, or a literary work.

RHETORIC. **Rhetoric** is the art of speaking or writing effectively. It involves the study of ways in which speech and writing affect or influence audiences. Rhetoric has also been defined as the art of persuasion.

RHYME. **Rhyme** is the repetition of sounds at the ends of words. Notice the rhyming words that end the second and third lines in A. E. Houseman's "I To My Perils" in Unit 9:

> Hope lies to mortals
> And most <u>believe her</u>,
> But man's <u>deceiver</u>
> Was never mine.

RHYTHM. **Rhythm** is the pattern of beats in a line of poetry or prose. See *meter* and *stress*.

SCENE. A **scene** is a short section of a literary work, one that happens in a single place and time. The first scene in Joan Aiken's story "A Serial Garden" in Unit 3 is set in the Armitage family's kitchen at breakfast time.

SCIENCE FICTION. **Science fiction** is imaginative literature based on scientific principles, discoveries, or laws. It is similar to fantasy in that it deals with imaginary worlds, but differs from fantasy in having a scientific basis. Often science fiction deals with the future, the distant past, or with worlds other than our own. Science fiction stories often take place on distant planets, in parallel universes, or in worlds beneath the ground or the sea. An example of science fiction in this textbook is Ray Bradbury's "The Foghorn" in Unit 5. See *fantasy*.

SET. A **set** is the collection of objects on a stage that create a scene.

SETTING. The **setting** of a literary work is the time and place in which it happens. Writers create settings in many different ways. In drama, the setting is usually made plain by the stage set and the costumes. In fiction, setting is most often revealed by means of descriptions of landscape, scenery, buildings, furniture, clothing, the weather, and the season. It can also be revealed by how characters talk and behave.

Luci Tapahonso's "The Ground Is Always Damp" in Unit 8 contrasts two settings.

SIMILE. A **simile** is a comparison using *like* or *as*. Paul Laurence Dunbar uses a simile in his poem "Sympathy" in Unit 6:

> And the river flows like a stream of glass

SLANT RHYME. A **slant rhyme**, or **half rhyme**, is one that is almost but not completely exact, as in *step* and *stop* or *rot* and *rock*.

SPEAKER. The **speaker** is the voice that speaks, or narrates, a poem. The speaker and the writer of a poem are not necessarily the same person. In Larry Woiwode's poem "A Deserted Barn" in Unit 9, the speaker of the poem is an abandoned barn.

STAGE DIRECTIONS. **Stage directions** are notes included in a play to describe how something should look, sound, or be performed. Stage directions describe setting, lighting, music, sound effects, entrances and exits, properties, and the movements of characters. They are usually printed in italics and enclosed in brackets or parentheses. Here is an example of stage directions from the play *The Miracle Worker* in Unit 10:

> [*She takes the doll, touches it to* HELEN'S *nose, and spells again into her hand.*]

STANZA. A **stanza** is a group of lines in a poem. Stanzas are usually separated by spaces from other groups of lines.

STEREOTYPE. A **stereotype** is an unexamined, false idea about a type of person or group of people. The idea that all teenagers love to shop at malls is a stereotype.

STORYCLOTH. A **storycloth** is an embroidered cloth that represents in pictures a story from the Hmong culture. Until the 1900s, the Hmong people had no written language and passed along stories either orally or through pictures. Storycloths were—and continue to be—an important part of storytelling in the Hmong tradition. A picture of a Hmong storycloth appears in Unit 3.

STRESS. **Stress**, or **accent**, is the amount of emphasis given to a syllable. The pattern of stresses in a poem determines its rhythm. Some syllables are described as being strongly or weakly stressed, and accented or unaccented. When you read a line of poetry, a strongly stressed syllable receives a strong emphasis and a weakly stressed syllable receives a weak one. In the following lines from Shel Silverstein's "Hector the Collector" in Unit 9, the strongly stressed syllables are marked with a slash mark (/).

> / /
> Hec tor the Col lec tor
>
> / /
> Col lec ted bits of string,
>
> / /
> Col lec ted dolls with bro ken heads
>
> / /
> And rus ty bells that would not ring.

SUMMARY. A **summary** is a rewriting of a passage in different and fewer words. See *paraphrase*.

SUSPENSE. **Suspense** is a feeling of anxiousness or curiosity. Writers create suspense by raising questions in the reader's mind and by using details that create strong emotions. In Edgar Allan Poe's short story "The Tell-Tale Heart" in Unit 5, the author builds suspense by causing the reader to wonder whether the police will discover the murderer, who is telling the story.

> No doubt I now grew very pale—but I talked more fluently, and with a heightened voice. Yet the sound increased—and what could I do? It was a *low, dull, quick sound— much such a sound as a watch makes when enveloped in cotton.*

SYMBOL. A **symbol** is a thing that stands for or represents both itself and something else. Some traditional symbols include doves for peace; the color green for jealousy; the color purple for royalty; winter, evening, or night for old age; roses for beauty; roads or paths for the journey through life; and owls for wisdom. In Joseph Bruchac's story "Jed's Grandfather" in Unit 2, birds could be seen as a symbol of freedom from earthly bonds.

TAG LINE. A **tag line** is a phrase like *she said* used in a story to tell who is speaking. See *dialogue*.

TALL TALE. A **tall tale** is a lighthearted or humorous story with many exaggerated elements. There are many tall tales about Paul Bunyan and Pecos Bill.

THEME. A **theme** is a central idea in a literary work.

THESIS. A **thesis** is a main idea in a work of nonfiction such as an essay. The thesis of Robert Jastrow's essay "The Size of Things" in Unit 11 is that it is very difficult to think about something as small as the atom or something as large as the universe.

THIRD-PERSON POINT OF VIEW. In a story told from the **third-person point of view**, the narrator does not take part in the action and tells the story using words such as *he* and *she* and avoiding the use of *I* and *we*. See *point of view*.

TONE. **Tone** is a writer's or speaker's attitude toward the subject or the reader. See *voice*.

TRANSITION. A **transition** is a word, phrase, sentence, or paragraph used to connect ideas and to show relationships between them. Transitions to show chronological order include *at, finally, first, next,* and *then*. Transitions that show spatial order include *above, behind, next to, to the left,* and *on top of*. Transitions that show order of importance are *less important, more important,* and *most importantly*.

UNDERSTATEMENT. An **understatement** is a statement that treats something important as though it were not important. "When George returned home, he was mildly surprised to find his house had burned to the ground," is an understatement.

UNITY. **Unity** is the use in a piece of writing of details related to the main idea, or theme. An essay with unity, for example, is one in which all the parts help to support the thesis statement, or main idea. See *essay*.

VERBAL IRONY. A statement that says one thing but means the opposite is an example of **verbal irony**. For example, if someone pushes to the front of a line, and someone else says, "What polite behavior," that is an example of verbal irony. See *irony*.

VOICE. **Voice** is the way a writer uses language to reflect his or her unique personality and attitude toward topic, form, and audience. A writer expresses voice through tone, word choice, and sentence structure. In "The Instruction of Indra" in Unit 7, Joseph Campbell uses an informal voice, as if he were telling the story to a friend.

> "So the carpenter comes to the edge of the great lotus pond of the universe and tells his story to Brahma. Brahma says, 'You go home. I will fix this up.' Brahma gets off his lotus and kneels down to address sleeping Vishnu. Vishnu just makes a gesture and says something like, 'Listen, fly, something is going to happen.'"

HANDBOOK OF LITERARY TERMS **953**

GLOSSARY
Of Words For Everyday Use

PRONUNCIATION KEY

VOWEL SOUNDS

a	hat	i	sit	o͞o	blue, stew	ə	extra
ā	play	ī	my	oi	boy		under
ä	star			ou	wow		civil
e	then	ō	go	u	up		honor
ē	me	ô	paw, born	ü	blue, stew		bogus
		o͝o	book, put				

CONSONANT SOUNDS

b	but	j	jump	p	pop	th	the
ch	watch	k	brick	r	rod	v	valley
d	do	l	lip	s	see	w	work
f	fudge	m	money	sh	she	y	yell
g	go	n	on	t	sit	z	pleasure
h	hot	ŋ	song, sink	th	with		

a • byss (ə bis′) *n.,* anything too deep for measurement; ocean depths.

ac • cel • er • ate (ik sel′ ə rāt) *v.,* to increase in speed.

ac • cus • tomed (ə cus′ təmd) *adj.,* often used or practiced.

aes • thet • ic (es thet′ ik) *adj.,* referring to beauty.

ag • gres • sive (ə gre′ siv) *adj.,* forceful; dominating; marked by readiness to attack.

ag • gres • sor (ə gres′ ər) *n.,* attacker.

ag • grieved (ə grēv′ id) *adj.,* troubled or distressed. **aggrievedly,** *adv.*

ag • o • nizing (a′ gə niz iŋ) *adj.,* painful.

al • li • ance (ə li′əns) *n.,* association or unit to benefit members.

a • loof (ə lüf′) *adj.,* reserved and cool, distant.

an • guished (aŋ′ gwisht) *adj.,* feeling great suffering or pain.

anx • i • ety (aŋ zi′ ə tē) *n.,* a feeling of uneasiness or fearful concern.

ap • pa • ra • tus (ap′ ə rat′ əs) *n.,* device or machine.

ap • pa • ri • tion (ap′ ə rish′ ən) *n.,* anything that appears unexpectedly or in an extraordinary way; ghost.

ap • pre • hen • sion (a pri hen′ shən) *n.,* suspicion or fear.

ap • pre • hen • sive (a pri hent′ siv) *adj.,* filled with anxiety; fearful.

arc (ärk′) *v.,* to follow a curved course.

as • cend (ə send′) *v.,* move upward, rise. **ascending,** *adj.*

as • sess (ə ses′) *v.,* evaluate.

au • dac • i • ty (ô das′ ə tē) *n.,* bold courage; daring.

aus • pi • cious (ô spi′ shəs) *adj.,* favorable; indicative of future success.

a • venge (ə venj′) *v.,* take revenge on. **avenging,** *adj.*

a • ver • sion (ə vər′ zhən) *n.,* dislike; tendency to turn away from.

bar • rage (bə räzh′) *n.,* outpouring of many things at once.

bar • ren (bär′ ən) *adj.,* producing inferior or scarce vegetation.

bat • ter (bat′ ər) *v.,* wear out, damage, beat. **battered,** *adj.*

be • muse (bi myüz′) *v.,* confuse, bewilder. **bemused,** *adj.*

be • nign (bi bīn′) *adj.,* kindly.

be • tray (bē trā′) *v.,* violate a trust or act unfaithfully.

be • wil • der (bi wil′ dər) *v.,* confuse or puzzle. **bewildered,** *adj.*

be • wil • der • ment (bi wil′ dər mənt) *n.,* state of being confused.

ben • ign (bi nīn′) *adj.,* nonthreatening.

bid (bid′) *v.,* express in leave-taking.

bid • da • ble (bid′ ə bəl) *adj.,* obedient. **biddably,** *adv.*

bil • low (bil′ō) *v.,* surge; swell. **billowing,** *adj.*

bleak (blēk) *adj.,* not promising or hopeful.

blun • der (blun′ dər) *v.,* make a mistake.

boo • ty (boot′ ē) *n.,* any gain, prize, or gift.

breach (brēch′) *v.,* to make a gap by battering; to break.

brood (brüd′) *v.,* to dwell on a gloomy subject, to worry.

buf • fet (buf′ it) *v.,* strike repeatedly; thrust.

bur • ly (burly) *adj.,* strongly and heavily built.

ca • ma • ra • de • rie (käm rä′ də rē) *n.,* spirit of friendship.

car • ni • vor • ous (kä ni′ və rəs) *adj.,* subsisting on animal tissue.

chasm (kaz′ əm) *n.,* deep crack in the earth's surface.

chide (chīd) *v.,* to express mild disapproval.

chor • tle (chôr təl) *v.,* laugh; chuckle.

cleft (kleft) *n.,* opening.

clod (kläd) *n.,* lump or mass of earth.

com • mence (kə ments′) *v.,* begin.

com • mo • tion (kə mō′ shən) *n.,* noisy confustion.

com • pe • tent (käm′ pə tənt) *adj.,* capable.

com • pel (kəm pel′) *v.,* cause to do through excessive pressure.

com • pen • sate (käm′ pən sāt) *v.,* balance, offset; repay.

com • ply (kəm pli′) *v.,* conform to, or follow, a rule.

com • pressed (kəm′ prest′) *adj.,* reduced in size or volume.

com • punc • tion (kəm pəŋk′ shən) *n.,* twinge of regret, anxiety over guilt.

con • ceal • ment (kən sēl′ mənt) *n.,* hiding.

con • cede (kən sēd′) *v.,* to accept as true.

con • ceive (kən sēv′) *v.,* form or develop in the mind.

con • clu • sive (kən klü siv) *adj.,* without a doubt, definitively. **conclusively,** *adv.*

con • cus • sion (kən kush′ ən) *n.,* violent shaking; shock.

con • form (kən fôrm′) *v.,* act obedient or compliant. **conformist,** *n.*

con • jec • ture (kən jek′ chər) *v.,* predict; guess.

con • sum • mate (känt′ sə mət) *adj.,* perfect; complete.

con • tour (kän′ tur) *n.,* the outline of a curve or shape.

con • trar • y (kän′ trer ē) *adj.,* not in agreement with what is usual or expected.

con • vert (kən vərt′) *v.,* turn or change from one form to another.

con • vinc • ing (kən vin′ siŋ) *adj.,* valid; believable.

con • vict • ion (kən vik′ shən) *n.,* a strong and firm belief.

cow • er (kou′ ər) *v.,* crouch or huddle.

cre • scent (kre′ sənt) *n.,* curved figure that tapers to two points like a crescent moon.

crev • ice (krev′ is) *n.,* a narrow opening resulting from a split or crack.

cun • ning (kun′ iŋ) *adj.,* skillful or clever. **cunningly,** *adv.*

cur • tail (kər tāl′) *v.,* to make less. **curtailment,** *n.*

cy • ni • cal (sin′ i kəl) *adj.,* sarcastic; sneering.

daft (daft) *adj.,* insane; crazy.

dap • per (dap ′ər) *adj.,* neat and trim; stylish.

de • cep • tion (di sep′ shən) *n.,* something that deceives, or tricks.

de • crep • it (di kre′ pət) *adj.,* worn out, weakened from old age.

de • duce (di düs′) *adj.,* determine by reason; conclude.

de • hyd • rate (de hī′ drāt) *v.,* lose water or body fluids.

de • i • ty (dē′ ə tē) *n.,* god or goddess.

de • lin • quent (di liŋ′ kwənt) *adj.,* offending by neglect or violation of duty or law; late or overdue.

de • lir • i • ous (di lir′ ē əs) *adj.,* marked by confusion or wild excitement.

de • lu • sion (di loo′ zhən) *n.,* an incorrect perception of reality.

de • mur (di mər′) *v.,* hesitate because of doubts.

dep • ri • va • tion (de′ prə vā′ shən) *n.,* the state of being deprived; having something taken away.

de • rail (dē rāl′) *v.,* to hinder or impede the progress of.

der • e • lict (der′ ə likt) *adj.,* abandoned.

de • ri • sion (di rizh′ ən) *n.,* contempt or ridicule.

des • cent (dē sent′) *n.,* sudden attack or raid.

des • o • late (de′ sə lət) *adj.,* lonely, sad.

de • spised (di spizd) *adj.,* hated, regarded with dislike and hostility.

dif • fuse (di fyüs′) *adj.,* not concentrated in one area, spread out.

dim • i • nu • tion (di mə nü′ shən) *n.,* the act or process of diminishing.

din • gy (din′ jē) *adj.,* dirty or discolored; shabby, showing signs of wear or neglect.

di • rec • tive (də rek′ tiv) *n.,* order or form of guidance.

dis • ci • pli • nar • i • an (dis ə pli ner′ ē ən) *n.,* one who enforces order.

dis • dain • ful (dis dān′ fəl) *adj.,* proud or scornful.

dis • may (dis mā) *v.,* unnerve; deter by arousing fear. **dismayed,** *adj.*

dis • sem • i • nate (di se′ mə nāt) *v.,* spread about.

dis • sim • u • late (di sim′ yü lāt′) *v.,* act of hiding; pretending. **dissimulation,** *n.*

dis • tin • guish (di stin′ gwish) *v.,* to discern; to detect with the eyes or with other senses.

dis • traught (dis trät′) *adj.,* agitated; troubled.

di • vert (də vərt′) *v.,* to distract or to turn from one course to another.

dog • ged (dôg′ id) *adj.,* stubborn; persistent. **doggedly,** *adv.*

dour (douər) *adj.,* harsh, gloomy. **dourly,** *adv.*

driv • el (driv′ əl) *v.,* drool.

du • pli • cate (dü′ pli kāt) *v.,* repeat, copy.

ebb (eb) *v.,* flow back; recede.

ee • rie (ir′ ē) *adj.,* mysterious; strange. **eerily,** *adv.*

ego • tism (ē ′ gə ti zəm) *n.,* an overly high opinion of one's own importance.

el • i • gi • ble (e′ lə jə bəl) *adj.,* qualified to be chosen or to receive something.

ema • ci • ate (i mā′ shē āt) *v.,* cause to become very thin. **emaciated,** *adj.*

em • pha • tic (im fa′ tik) *adj.,* firm, forceful.

en • rage (in rāj′) *v.,* fill with rage; anger. **enraged,** *adj.*

en • voy (än′ voi′) *n.,* messenger.

es • cort (es kort′) *v.,* accompany or guide (someone or something).

es • tu • ar • y (es′ chə wer ē) *n.,* an inlet of the sea.

et • i • quette (et′ i kit) *n.,* social rules; manners.

ex • alt (eg zôlt′) *v.,* praise; glorify; worship.

ex • ca • vate (ek′ skə vāt) *v.,* dig out and remove. **excavated,** *adj.*

ex • er • tion (eg zər′ shən) *n.,* effort.

ex • pend (ek spend′) *v.,* to use or use up.

ex • tant (eks′ tənt) *adj.,* still existing.

ex • tra • neous (ek strā′ nē əs) *adj.,* not forming an essential part.

ex • trav • a • gance (ek strav′ ə gəns) *n.,* unreasonable excess.

ex • trav • a • gan • za *n.,* (ik stra və gan′ zə) spectacular show or event.

ex • u • ber • ant (ig zü′ bə rənt) *adj.,* with joy and enthusiasm. **exuberantly,** *adv.*

ex • ul • ta • tion (eg′ zəl tā shən) *n.,* triumph, excitement, joyousness.

fa • ce • tious (fə sē′ shəs) *adj.,* witty in a playful but often inappropriate manner. **facetiously,** *adv.*

fa • tigue (fə tēg′) *n.,* weariness or exhaustion.

fan • fare (fan′ fār) *n.,* a showy outward display.

fe • ro • cious (fə rō shəs) *adj.,* fierce.

feigned (fānd) *adj.,* faked.

feint (fānt) *v.,* fake to one direction in order to draw attention from the true attack.

fixed (fikst′) *adj.,* firmly set or with concentration. **fixedly** (fik′ səd lē) *adv.*

for • age (fär′ ij) *v.,* rummage; browse for food.

for • feit (for′ fət) *v.,* lose or lose the right to by some error, offesce, or crime.

for • lorn (for lorn′) *adj.,* sad lonely, hopeless.

frag • men • tar • y (frag′ mən ter ē) *adj.,* consisting of disconnected parts.

fran • tic (fran′ tik) *adj.,* emotionally out of control.

fur • tive (fər′ tiv) *adj.,* sneaky, underhanded, sly. **furtively,** *adv.*

gal • lant • ry (ga′ lən trē) *n.,* show of marked courtesy, amorous attention, or bravery.

gar • ner (gär′ nər) *v.,* gather.

gau • dy (gôd′ ē) *adj.,* bright and showy, but lacking in good taste.

gaunt (gant) *adj.,* lean, thin, angular.

ges • ture (jes′chər) *v.,* express or emphasize ideas and emotions with physical movement.

gild • ed (gild′ əd) *adj.,* overlayed in golden color; appealing on the surface.

glance (glants′) *v.,* to strike awkwardly so as to slide off or be deflected.

grot • to (grät′ ō) *n.,* cavelike house or shrine.

grue • some (groo′ səm) *adj.,* ghastly; inspiring horror.

guard • ian (gär′ dē ən) *n.,* one that guards.

har • ried (har′ ēd) *adj.,* tormented, ravaged.

hau • teur (hō tur′) *n.,* disdainful pride; snobbery.

hence • forth (hens fôrth′) *adv.,* from this time on.

her • bi • vores (ər′ bi vor) *n.,* plant-eating animal.

high-strung (hī′ strəŋ′) *adj.,* wound up, unquiet, agitated.

idle (i′ dəl) *adj.,* without worth or basis in fact.

im • mac • u • late (i ma′ kyə lət) *adj.,* perfectly clean.

im • passe (im′ pas) *n.,* situation with no escape; deadlock.

im • pas • sive (im pa′ siv) *adj.,* giving no sign of emotion. **impassively,** *adv.*

im • per • ti • nent (im pər′ tən ənt) *adj.,* given to rudeness.

im • pli • cate (im′ plə kāt) *v.,* show to be connected or involved.

im • port (im′ pôrt) *n.,* significance.

im • pos • ing (im po′ ziŋ) *adj.,* impressive in size, bearing, dignity, or grandeur.

im • pu • dence (im′ pyə dənts) *n.,* cockiness and disregard for others.

in • ad • e • qua • cy (i na′ di kwə sē) *n.,* the quality or state of not being capable or sufficient.

in • ad • e • quate (i na′ di kwət) *adj.,* not good enough.

in • ar • tic • u • late (i när ti′ kyə lət) *adj.,* unable to express ideas well in speech.

in • cal • cu • la • ble (in kal′ kyə lə bəl) *adj.,* uncertain.

in • can • ta • tion (in′ kan tā′ shən) *n.,* magic spell.

in • car • nate (in kär′ nət) *adj.,* personified, embodied.

in • cense (in sens′) *v.,* to make very angry.

in • dict • ment (in dīt′ mənt) *n.,* accusation of wrongdoing, criminal charge.

in • dig • nant (in dig′ nənt) *adj.*, filled with or expressing anger over something unjust or mean. **indignantly,** *adv.*

in • dig • ni • ty (in dig′ nə tē) *n.*, insult; humiliating treatment.

in • do • lent (in′ dōl lənt) *adj.*, lazy.

in • dul • gent (in dəl′ jənt) *adj.*, extremely considerate of another's desires, feelings or overly generous.

in • ex • o • ra • ble (i neks′ rə bəl) *adj.*, relentless; refusing to be pursuaded. **inexorably,** *adv.*

in • fringe (in frinj′) *v.*, to trespass on, intrude on, overstep the bounds of.

in • nu • en • do (in yü en′ dō) *n.*, hint or suggestion, esp. one that hurts someone's reputation.

in • sig • nif • i • cance (in sig ni′ fi kəns) *n.*, unimportance; smallness in size, weight, number, or influence.

in • sis • tent (in sis′ tənt) *adj.*, persistant, never-tiring.

in • tact (in takt′) *adj.*, untouched; entire.

in • ter • mi • na • ble (in term ne bel) *adj.*, seeming to have no end. **interminably,** *adv.*

in • tol • er • a • ble (in täl′ ər ə bəl) *adj.*, unbearable; too severe or painful to be endured.

in • trac • ta • ble (in trak′ tə bəl) *adj.*, obstinately. **intractably,** *adv.*

in • vari • able (in ver′ ē ə bəl) *adj.*, not changing. **invariably,** *adv.*

ir • ra • tion • al (ir rash ´ə nəl) *adj.*, lacking reason; absurd.

ir • res • o • lute (i re′ zə lüt) *adj.*, uncertain how to act.

jaun • ty (jän′ tē) *adj.*, spright, lively. **jauntily,** *adv.*

jos • tle (jäs′l) *v.*, push roughly. **jostling,** *adj.*

keen (kēn′) *adj.*, sharp, intense. **keener,** *adj.*

kin • dling (kin′ liŋ) *n.*, small sticks of wood or other materials used for starting a fire.

la • bo • ri • ous (lə bōr′ ē əs) *adj.*, involving hard effort.

la • den (lād′ ən) *adj.*, carrying a load or burden.

la • ment (lə ment′) *n.*, loud mourning; wailing.

list (list) *v.*, tilt to one side.

lope (lōp′) *v.*, move with a bounding gait.

lu • mi • nous (lü′ mə nəs) *adj.*, emitting or reflecting light.

ma • lev • o • lent (mə le′ və lənt) *adj.*, having or showing hatred.

ma • li • cious (mə li′ shəs) *adj.*, marked by a desire to cause pain or distress.

mal • lea • ble (mal′ ē ə bəl) *adj.*, capable of being shaped or controlled by outside forces.

ma • nip • u • late (mə ni′ pyə lāt) *v.*, to treat or operate with the hands in a skillful manner.

mea • ger (mē′ gər) *adj.*, lacking in quantity or quality.

me • di • an (mē′ dē ən) *adj.*, being the exact middle value in a set.

men • a • ce (men′ əs) *v.*, act threatening. **menacing,** *adj.*

mer • e • tri • cious (mer ə tri′ shəs) *adj.*, falsely attractive, pretentious, superficially significant.

mes • mer • ize (mez′ mə rīz) *v.*, fascinate; spellbind.

me • thod • i • cal (mə thäd′ kəl) *adj.*, *arranged in an* orderly or systematic fashion. **methodically,** *adv.*

mi • ser (mī′ zər) *n.*, a person who is extremely stingy with money.

mod • er • ate (mä′ də rət) *adj.*, average; reasonabe. **moderately,** *adv.*

mono • syl • lab • ic (mä nə sə la′ bik) *adj.*, consisting of one syllable.

mo • not • o • nous (mə nä′ tən əs) *adj.*, characterized by boredom due to the same thing happening again and again.

moot (müt′) *adj.*, insignificant; closed to debate.

mu • ti • late (myü′ təl āt) *v.*, break; ruin; destroy. **mutilated,** *adj.*

na • ive • ty (nä ē′ və tē) *n.*, simplicity.

nerve–wrack • ing (nərv′ ra′ kiŋ) *adj.*, extremely stressful.

noi • some (noi′ səm) *adj.*, offensive to the sense of smell.

non • plussed (nän pləst′) *adj.*, at a loss what to say or do.

no • ta • tion (nō tā′ shən) *n.*, note added to a document.

nui • sance (nü′ sənts) *n.*, something that is annoying or unpleasant.

ob • lige (ə blij′) *v.*, do a favor for.

ob • scure (äb skyur′) *adj.*, unclear or unknown.

ob • sess (əb ses′) *v.*, haunt or preoccupy the mind of. **obsessed,** *adj.*

ob • sti • nate (äb′ stə nət) *adj.*, stubborn.

ob • tain (əb tān′) *v.*, get possession of.

om • i • nous (ä′ mə nəs) *adj.*, forboding or foreshadowing evil.

op • po • si • tion (ä pe zi′ shən) *n.*, contrary action or condition.

op • press (ə pres′) *v.*, keep down by cruel or unjust use of power.

par • ti • tion (pär ti′ shən) *v.*, separate or divide as with walls. **partitioned,** *adj.*

pas • sion • ate (pa′ shə nət) *adj.*, expressing strong feeling. **passionately,** *adv.*

pa • thet • ic (pə the′ tik) *adj.*, causing pity. **pathetically,** *adv.*

peer (pēr′) *v.*, look closely.

per • il (per′ əl) *n.*, danger, exposure to harm.

per • i • lous (per′ ə ləs) *adj.*, dangerous.

per • me • ate (pər′ mē āt) *v.*, spread through or penetrate something.

per • ni • cious (pər ni′ shəs) *adj.*, destructive.

per • pen • dic • u • lar (pər pən dí′ kyə lər) *adj.*, being at right angles to a given line or plane.

phe • nom • e • nal (fi nä′ mə nəl) *adj.*, remarkable, extraordinary.

phe • nom • e • non (fə näm′ ə nən′) *n.*, extremely unusual or extraordinary thing or occurrence.

phys • i • o • log • i • cal (fi zē ə lä′ ji kəl) *adj.*, relating to bodily function. **physiologically,** *adv.*

pity (pi´tē) *v.*, to feel compassion or sympathy for (someone or something).

pla • cate (plā′ cāt) *v.*, to sooth or calm.

plac • id (plas′ id) *adj.*, undisturbed, calm.

plain • tive (plān′ tiv) *adj.*, mournful, sad; expressing sorrow.

plunge (plunj′) *v.*, enter quickly into something.

poi • gnant (pói nyənt) *adj.* deeply affecting or touching; somber.

poised (poizd) *adj.*, composed or ready; marked by balance.

pon • der • ous (pän′ dər əs) *adj.*, Heavy, unyielding. **ponderously,** *adv.*

pore (por′) *v.*, read studiously or attentively.

pre • cise (prē sis′) *adj.*, exact.

pre • co • cious (pri kō′ sh əs) *adj.*, exceptionally early in development.

pre • sum • ab • ly (prē zü mə blē) *adv.*, probably; one would assume.

pres • tige (pre stēzh′) *n.*, standing or influence in general opinion.

prim (prim′) *adj.*, fussy about one's appearance. **primly,** *adv.*

pri • me • val (pri me′ vəl) *adj.*, from the earliest ages.

prin • ci • pal (prin′ sə pəl) *adj.*, most important; cheif.

prism (pri′ zəm) *n.*, a transparent crystal form that distorts light which passes through it.

prof • fer (prä′ fər) *v.*, present for acceptance, offer.

pro • found (prə faund′) *adj.*, all encompassing, complete.

pro • jec • tion (prō jek′ shən) *n.*, something that sticks out.

pro • lif • ic (prə li′ fic) *adj.*, causing abundant growth, generation or reproduction.

proph • e • sy (präf′ ə si′) *v.*, predict.

prop • o • si • tion (prä pə zi′ shən) *n.*, proposal, something offered for consideration or acceptance.

pros • per • i • ty (prä spər′ ə tē) *n.*, economic well-being.

pro • trac • ted (prō trak′ təd) *adj.*, extended.

pro • ver • bi • al (prō vər′ bē əl) *adj.*, well known because commonly referred to.

prow • ess (prō es′) *n.*, extraordinary ability.

quail (kwāal′) *v.*, recoil or cower.

qua • ver (kwā′ vər) *v.*, shake, tremble. **quavery,** *adj.*

quiv • er (kwi′ vər) *v.*, tremble; shake.

ram • pant (ram′ pənt) *adj.*, wild or unrestrained.

rapt (rapt′) *adj.*, mentally engrossed or absorbed.

ravel (rav′ əl iŋ) *v.*, separate; become thinner. **raveling,** *adj.*

rav • en • ous (ra′ və nəs) *adj.*, very eager for food.

re • buff (ri buf′) *n.*, abrupt refusal.

reel (rēl′) *v.*, waver or fall back as from a blow.

ref • uge (re′ fyüj) *n.*, shelter or protection from danger.

ref • u • gee (re′ fyoo jē′) *n.*, a person who flees, especially someone who flees to a foreign country to escape danger.

rel • a • tive (re′ lə tiv) *adj.*, comparative, not independant.

re • lin • quish (ri liŋ′ kwish) *vt.,* give up, release.

ren • dez • vous (rän′ dā vōō′) *n.,* place designated for meeting or assembly.

re • pel (ri pel′) *v.,* cause distaste or disgust.

re • pos • sess (rē pə zes′) *v.,* take back goods from one who fails to make payments on the goods.

re • press (ri pres′) *v.,* hold in by self-control.

re • pul • sive (ri pul′ siv) *adj.,* disgusting, offensive.

re • sem • blance (rē zem′ bləns) *n.,* likeness, similarity.

res • er • voir (re′ zə vwär) *n.,* supply.

re • side (ri zid′) *v.,* dwell; live permanently in (a home).

re • source • ful (ri sors′ fəl) *adj.,* able to deal effectively with problems and challenges.

rev • el (re′ vəl) *v.,* take immense pleasure.

re • vert (rē vərt′) *v.,* return.

root (rüt) *vi.,* to dig in the ground, as with the snout.

rud • dy (rəd′ ē) *adj.,* reddish.

rue • ful (rü′ fəl) *adj.,* regretful. **ruefully,** *adv.*

rup • ture (rup′ chər) *v.,* break apart. **ruptured,** *adj.*

ruth • less (rüth′ ləs) *adj.,* cruel; without mercy. **ruthlessly,** *adv.*

sag • ac • i • ty (sə gas′ ə tē) *n.,* wisdom; intelligence.

sanc • tu • ar • y (saŋk′ chə wer′ ē) *n.,* place of refuge or protection.

saucy (as′ sē) *adj.,* amusingly bold; smart, trim.

scald (scäld′) *v.,* burn with hot liquid. **scalded,** *adj.*

sel • dom (sel′ dəm) *adv.,* rarely, infrequently.

sheen (shēn) *n.,* brightness or shininess.

shud • der (shud′ ər) *v.,* shake or tremble suddenly.

sin • ewy (sin yə wē) *adj.,* strong with cordlike muscles.

skew (skyü′) *v.,* distort.

slow-wit • ted (slō wi′ təd) *adj.,* mentally slow, dull.

so • cial (sō shəl) *n.,* a party or gathering, especially when held by members of a group.

sod • den (säd′ ən) *adj.,* soaked through.

sole (sōl) *adj.,* only.

sole • ly (sō′ lē) *adv.,* only.

sol • emn (sä′ ləm) *adj.,* serious; dignified.

som • ber (säm bər) *adj.,* dark and depressing; gloomy.

spec • ter (spek′ tər) *n.,* spirit or ghost.

spec • u • la • tive (speculative) *adj.,* theoretical, not practical.

splurge (splərj′) *v.,* to indulge oneself extravagantly or to spend a lot of money.

stalk (stôk) *v.,* walk in a stiff way.

stealth • y (stel′ thē) *adj.,* secret; sneaky. **stealthily,** *adv.*

steel (stēəl′) *v.,* made hard like steel.

sti • fle (stī′ fəld) *v.,* hold back; stop, smother. **stifled,** *adj.*

strew (strü′) *v.,* spread by scattering. **strewn,** *adj.*

suave (swäv) *adj.,* smooth, graceful; polite. **suavity,** *n.*

sub • merge (sub mərj′) *v.,* to put or go into or under, as in water.

suf • fo • cate (sə′ fə kāt) *v.,* deprive of breath; stop the development of. **suffocating,** *v.*

sum • mon (su′ mən) *v.,* call upon with authority.

sunder (sun′ dər) *v.,* break apart or become disunited.

sup • po • si • tion (sup ə zish′ ən) *n.,* something supposed; assumption.

sur • plus (sər′ pləs) *adj.,* left-over, excess.

sus • cep • ti • ble (sə sep′ tə bəl) *adj.,* easily affected or influenced.

syn • thet • ic (sin the′ tik) *adj.,* produced artificially.

tal • on (tal′ ən) *n.,* claw of a bird of prey.

tan • dem (tan′ dəm) *adj.,* having parts arranged one behind the other.

tan • ta • liz • ing (tan təl iz iŋ) *adj.,* teasingly out of reach.

taw • ny (tä nē) *adj.,* of a warm sandy color.

tem • per • ance (tem′ pə rəns) *n.,* moderation in action; restraint.

tem • pes • tu • ous (tem pes′ chü əs) *adj.,* violent; stormy.

ten • don (ten′ dən) *n.,* connective tissue attaching muscle to bone.

ten • dril (ten′ drəl) *n.,* tender shoot.

tes • ti • fy (təs′ tə fī) *v.,* to make a statement based on personal knowledge or belief.

teth • er (te′ thər) *v.,* fasten. **tethered,** *adj.*

teth • er (te′ thər) *n.,* a rope, chain, or other restraint used to tie an animal so that it cannot move beyond a certain point.

thresh (thresh′) *v.,* beat or strike.

thrift (thrift) *n.,* careful management of one's resources.

throng (thrôŋ) *v.,* crowd; press upon in large numbers.

thwart (thwärt) *v.,* hinder, obstruct; defeat.

tou • sle (tə′ səl) *v.,* rumple, muss. **tousled,** *adj.*

tran • si • tion (trän si′ shən) *n.,* a passage from one condition or place to another.

trans • for • ma • tion (trans fər mā′ shən) *n.,* change in composition, structure, or outward form and appearance.

trans • gres • sor (trans gres′ sər) *n.,* one who breaks a law or commandment.

trans • lu • cen • cy (trants lü′ sənt sē) *n.,* clearness, the quality of being transparent.

trans • lu • cent (trans lü′ sənt) *adj.,* permitting the passage of light.

tread (tred′) *n.,* act of stepping.

trill (tril) *n.,* a trembling, vibrating sound.

trough (träf′) *n.,* a long shallow container for water or animal feed.

tur • moil (tər′ mòil) *n.,* extremely confused or disturbed state. **turmoil,** *v.*

un • en • cum • bered (ən in kəm′ bərd) *adj.,* free of impediments.

un • err • ing (un er′ iŋ) *adj.,* unfailing, faultless.

un • kempt (ən kemt′) *adj.,* lacking in order or neatness.

un • prec • e • dent • ed (un pres′ ə den′tid) *adj.,* unheard of; new.

un • ruf • fled (un ru′ fəld) *adj.,* poised; cool.

un • wary (ən wär ē) *adj.,* easily fooled.

vac • an • cy (vā′ kənt sē) *n.,* an unoccupied position, site, or piece of property.

va • por (va′ pər) *n.,* scattered matter suspended in the air and clouding it (such as smoke or fog).

vain (vān) *adj.,* without force or effect.

ve • he • ment (vē′ ə mənt) *adj.,* marked by forceful energy, emotion, or expression. **vehemently,** *adv.*

venge • ful (vənj′ fəl) *adj.,* revengeful.

ven • ti • la • tor (vənt′ lāt ər) *n.,* device used to bring in fresh air and drive out foul air; fan.

ver • i • fy (ver′ ə fī′) *v.,* test or check for correctness.

vex (veks) *v.,* bother; trouble.

vex • ed • ly (vek′ səd lē) *adv.,* with irritation.

vi • gil (vij′ əl) *n.,* watchful staying awake during the usual hours of sleep.

vig • or • ous (vi′ gə rəs) *adj.,* active, lively; energetic.

vir • ile (vir′ əl) *adj.,* having strength; forceful.

vir • tual • ly (vər′ chə wə lē) *adv.,* almost entirely.

vi • tal • i • ty (vī tā′ lə tē) *n.,* life, liveliness.

vi • va • cious (vī vā shəs) *adj.,* lively in temper or conduct.

void (void′) *n.,* empty space, abyss.

vul • gar (vul′ gər) *adj.,* crude; distasteful.

wan (wän) *adj.,* pale; sickly.

wane (wān) *v.,* dwindling; dimming. **waning,** *adj.*

war • i • ly (war′ ə lē) *adv.,* cautiously.

war • i • ness (wär′ ē nəs) *n.,* cautiousness, watchfulness.

whee • dling (hwēd liŋ) *adj.,* coaxing; flattering.

wield (wēld) *v.,* to handle or manage (a tool). **wielder,** *n.*

wince (wins) *v.,* flinch, shrink back.

wir • y (wīr′ ē) *adj.,* lean, sinewy, limber.

won • drous (wən′ drəs) *adj.,* extraordinary, remarkable. **wondrously,** *adv.*

wor • ri • some (wər′ ē səm) *adj.,* causing worry.

wrest (rest′) *v.,* pull or force away violently with a twisting motion.

wry (rī) *adj.,* ironic or sarcastic; grimly humorous.

zeal (zeal) *n.,* eagerness, enthusiasm.

INDEX
Of Titles and Authors

INDEX *Of Skills*

READING

advertising, 824
aim, 357, 369, 650, 653, 768, 831, 836
alliteration, 612, 630, 633, 634, 637
analogy, 799, 806
analysis, 849, 854
anecdote, 269, 287
antagonist, 341, 355
argumentative writing, 768
assonance, 612, 630, 633, 650, 653
autobiography, 197, 207, 296, 312, 768
background information, 159, 173
ballads, 472
biography, 768, 769, 778
book clubs, 75, 394, 858, 867
book reviews, 229
captions, 838, 841
central conflict, 481, 488
character, 27, 41, 532, 541, 552, 555, 566
characterization, 113, 125, 515, 520, 532, 555, 566, 687, 710, 757
charts, 314, 822
chronological order, 197, 207, 844, 847
climax, 41, 432, 445
coherence, 838, 841
colorful language, 232-234, 612
computer software, 824
concrete, 125
concrete details, 769, 778
concrete language, 844, 847
concrete poem, 289, 294, 612, 625, 628
conflict, 5, 24, 515, 520, 687, 757
context clues, 871
description, 5, 24, 296, 312, 577, 595
diagram, 823
dialect, 241, 259
dialogue, 61, 74, 555, 567, 645, 649, 686
diction, 424, 429
dictionaries, 514, 674, 871
distortion, 823
documentary writing, 768
drama, 686
essay, 768
expressive essay, 809, 814

expressive writing, 768, 809, 814
external conflict, 5, 24
fables, 472
fairy tales, 472
fiction, 532
figurative language, 127, 137
figure of speech, 612, 613, 618, 664, 667
first-person point of view, 159, 173, 385, 392, 405, 555, 567
flashback, 650, 653, 687, 734
folk songs, 472
folk tales, 472
foreshadowing, 175, 194, 209, 227, 327, 338, 569, 574, 577, 595
For Your Reading List, 75, 145, 229, 315, 394, 454, 521, 601, 675, 758, 816, 858
frame story, 209, 227
free verse, 447, 452, 613, 618
graph, 822
graphic aids, 870
haiku, 612, 669, 673
hyperbole, 780, 789
illustration, 823
image, 43, 47, 612, 613, 618, 619, 624
imagery, 43, 89, 94, 612, 613, 618, 619, 624, 625, 628, 669, 673
imaginative writing, 768
inciting incident, 41, 491, 497
informative writing, 768
internal conflict, 5, 24, 159, 173, 507, 513
Internet, 823, 869
irony, 49, 59, 95, 102, 481, 489, 619, 624
irony of situation, 127, 136, 209, 227, 481
key, 822, 838, 841
labels, 838, 841
legends, 472, 822
lyric poem, 447, 452, 612, 661, 663, 664, 667
map, 823
meaning, 612
memoir, 61, 73, 269, 287
metaphor, 289, 294, 612, 613, 618, 664, 687, 757
mode, 768
monologue, 686
mood, 341, 354, 370, 383, 534,

538, 555
motif, 500, 506
motivation, 357, 369
motive, 61, 74, 491, 497
myths, 472, 473, 478, 500, 505
narrative poem, 612, 656, 659
narrative writing, 768
narrator, 385, 392
news articles, 824, 868
nonfiction, 768
novel, 533
novella, 533, 577, 595
one-dimensional characters, 541, 552
onomatopoeia, 612, 634, 637
oral tradition, 139, 143, 209, 472, 490, 500, 505
parables, 472
personal essay, 432, 445
personal writing, 768
personification, 105, 111, 139, 143, 289, 294, 612, 619, 624, 664
perspective, 823
persuasive essay, 791, 796
persuasive writing, 768
play, 686
playwright, 686
plot, 27, 41, 532, 541, 553
point of view, 197, 262, 266, 385, 392, 405, 415, 555, 567, 780, 789
protagonist, 341, 355
reader's journal, keeping a, 867
reading art, 529, 868
reading photographs, 837, 868
repetition, 612, 638, 642, 656, 659
resolution, 41, 687, 757
rhyme, 612, 638, 642
rhythm, 612, 630, 633
SEARCH, 869
SQ3R, 869
scientific writing, 799, 806
sensory details, 5, 24
setting, 89, 93, 173, 195, 405, 415, 473, 478, 533, 534, 538
shape, 612, 625, 628
short story, 533
simile, 612, 664, 687, 757
sound, 612
speaker, 43, 47
speech, 768
stage directions, 241, 259, 686,

irregular verbs, 295
Japanese words, 674
jargon, 855
language skills, 808
metaphors, 228
misplaced modifiers, 763-764
modifiers, 660
negatives, 261
new words, 431, 446, 842, 871-873
oxymorons, 288
passive voice, 422-423
prefixes, 196
prepositional phrases, 396-398, 655
prepositions, 208, 340
pronoun/antecedent agreement, 678-680
proofreading, 596
proper nouns, 104
punctuation, 424-426
quotation marks, 416, 490, 499
run-on sentences, 384
sensory details, 539
sentence functions, 26, 446, 629
sentence types, 446
simple predicate, 59
simple subject, 59
sound, 643
spelling errors, 596, 808
state of being verbs, 149, 422, 554
subject-verb agreement, 318-321
tense, 150-152
translations, 674
verbs, 59, 149-152, 288, 313, 655
word formation, 660, 872
word origins, 514, 872-873
words in context, 138, 499, 871
wordy sentences, 453, 604-606

SPEAKING AND LISTENING
acting, 173, 228, 369, 393, 479, 506, 855
advertising jingles, 195
asking and answering questions, 25, 125, 208, 479, 576, 815
auditioning, 173
cheers, 268
collaborative learning, 26, 104, 125, 369, 384, 453, 479, 506, 576, 643, 660, 798, 807, 919. See also communication in a small group; discussion groups
communicating in a large group, 683, 917-918
communicating in a small group, 137, 144, 154, 400, 431, 446, 529, 568, 609, 819, 917. See also collaborative learning; discussion groups
debating, 74, 479, 922-923

discussion groups, 84, 236, 415, 467, 779. See also collaborative learning; communicating in a small group
interviewing, 25, 125, 208, 576, 660, 779, 790, 815, 816, 919-920
listening critically, 819, 915-916
listening for comprehension, 125, 540
multicultural communication, 674
multimedia presentations, 601, 848, 923
oral interpretation, 393
oral interpretation of poetry, 94, 295, 521, 643, 668, 683, 921
persuasive speeches, 59
reading poetry aloud, 94, 629, 668, 683
recording, 295, 521, 540
reporting, 125, 660
singing, 144, 195, 422
speeches, 59, 261, 431, 920-921
staging a mock trial, 393, 855
teaching, 314
telling a story, 339, 393, 490, 522-527, 529, 540, 819, 922
verbal and nonverbal communication, 446, 521, 758

STUDY AND RESEARCH
advertisements, 798
almanacs, 112
analyzing, 42, 60, 261, 339, 356, 431, 490, 499, 553, 568, 798, 848
atlases, 540
avoiding false arguments and propaganda, 195, 925-926
biographical references, 228
brainstorming, 431, 453, 490, 529, 553
comparing, 261, 339, 445, 467, 479, 490, 514, 554, 568, 927
computer research. See Internet research
contrasting, 261, 339, 445, 514, 554, 568, 927
designing, 779
dictionaries, 480, 674, 842, 930
documentation, 458-460, 933-936
drafting, 459
encyclopedias, 74, 596, 842, 931
evaluating media sources, 48, 60, 228, 261, 431, 445, 480, 490, 553, 568, 644, 668, 815, 931-933
fact and opinion, distinguishing, 925
field guides, 452

films, 228, 490, 568, 815
index cards, 459
indexes, 540
Internet research, 48, 268, 356, 400, 430, 467, 540, 553, 644, 668, 931
interpreting, 208, 384, 529, 683
inventing a new sport, 323
libraries, 929-930
magazines. See periodicals
maps, 596
narrative papers, 455-465
newspapers or newsmagazines, 261, 356, 445, 932
notes, taking, 459, 929
periodicals, 48, 261, 480
quotations, 459
recording, 295, 521, 540
researching, 25, 42, 48, 94, 104, 126, 137, 144, 174, 208, 261, 499, 506, 554, 568, 576, 629, 654, 790, 798, 807, 815, 837, 929-930
research journals, 356, 384, 668
research papers, 455-465
research tools, 454
sources, 458, 554
statistical charts, 314
summarizing, 137, 445, 674, 837
television, 173, 490, 798
tests 937-938
thesaurus, 356, 655, 930
thesis statement, 455, 459, 643
thinking skills, 924
timelines, 74, 268

APPLIED ENGLISH
advertisements, 112, 340
applications, 369
articles, 125, 790
billboards, 808
business letters, 154, 174, 195, 268, 393, 540, 655, 940-941
directions, 837, 848, 939-940
displaying effective visual material, 25, 84, 94, 112, 126, 237, 467, 683, 779, 808, 842, 943
forms, 369, 939
graphs, 830
memos, 576, 941-942
news copy, 356, 576
personal letter, 230-234, 940
policies, 60
press releases, 112, 137, 942-943
proposals, 942
public service announcements, 416, 779, 943
researching careers, 490
working on a team, 26, 943

INDEX Of Fine Art

INDEX OF FINE ART

INDEX
Of Internet Sites

ACKNOWLEDGMENTS

ART ACKNOWLEDGMENTS

Cover Hiroshige: © Elvehjem Museum of Art, University of Wisconsin-Madison; **Cover** Miro: CORBIS/Philadelphia Museum of Art/© 2000 Artists Rights Society (ARS), New York / ADAGP, Paris; **Cover** Predis: CORBIS/Archivo Iconografico, S.A.; **Cover** Lawrence: Gift of S. C. Johnson & Son, Inc./Art Resource, NY; **viii** Amaterasu Appearing from the Cave, 1882. Taiso Yoshitoshi. Private Collection.CORBIS/Asian Art & Archeology, Inc.; **v** The Patrick Des Jarlait Estate; **vi** The Vinery, from 'Fragments on the Theory and Practice of Landscape Gardening', pub. 1816 (colour litho) by Humphry Repton (1752-1818). Private Collection/The Stapleton Collection/Bridgeman Art Library; **vii** Library of Congress; **viii** Amaterasu Appearing from the Cave, 1882. Taiso Yoshitoshi. Private Collection.CORBIS/Asian Art & Archeology, Inc.; **ix** Campesino, 1976. Daniel Desiga. Collection of Alfredo Aragon; **x** The Procession of Queen Elizabeth I, c.1500s. English artist. Sherbourne Castle Estates. Sherbourne Castle Estates; **xi** Fishermen of the North, 1965. Patrick Des Jarlait. The Patrick Des Jarlait Estate; **xii** "The Miracle Worker". Courtesy of Stages Theatre Company; **2** Planet Art; **10** Courtesy of the artist. Photo by Mel Schockner; **15** Courtesy of the artist. Photo by Mel Schockner; **21** Chiam Potok; **22** © 1995 Larry Powell; **22** AP/David Bookstaver/Wide World Photos; **26** © 1995 Larry Powell; **29** Corel; **33** Corel; **37** Private Collection/Diana Ong/SuperStock; **38** Photo by Elizabeth Eve; **45** Photo courtesy of the artist; **50** Planet Art; **54** Tom Rosenthal/SuperStock; **63** CORBIS/Adam Woolfitt; **71** Photograph © 1996, Elvehjem Museum of Art, University of Wisconsin-Madison. All rights reserved; **72** Allen Nomura; **86** Christina's World, 1948. Andrew Wyeth. Tempera on gesso panel, 321/4x47 3/4". Purchase. Photograph © 1999 The Museum of Modern Art, New York; **92** Lucille Clifton: William Abranowitz/A+C Anthology; **92** Richard Garcia: Dinah Berland; **96** © Greg Smith; **98** Flight of the Swallows (oil on canvas) Giacomo Balla (1871-1958) Private Collection, New York, USA/Peter Willi/Bridgeman Art Library; **100** Joseph Bruchac; **101** Bufo calamita (Natterjack Toad) plate XIII from Part II of 'The Tailless Batrachians of Europe' written by G.A. Boulanger, pub. 1897 (colour litho) by French School (19th century) Natural History Museum, London, UK/Bridgeman Art Library; **106** Simultaneous Contrasts: Sun and Moon, 1912. Robert Delauney. Oil on canvas, 53". The Museum of Modern Art, New York. Photograph 1999 MOMA; **108** Library of Congress; **109** Campesino Sombrero, 1926. Diego Rivera; **114** Danger on the Stairs, 1927. Pierre Roy. Oil on canvas, 36 x 23 5/8". The Museum of Modern Art, New York. Gift of Abby Aldrich Rockefeller. Photograph 1999 MOMA/© 2000 Artists Rights Society (ARS), New York / ADAGP, Paris; **120** Penguin Books; **121** Library of Congress; **123** CORBIS/Hans Georg Roth; **129** © David Turnley/Black Star/PNI; **135** Library of Congress; **140** The Patrick Des Jarlait Estate; **141** The Patrick Des Jarlait Estate; **142** Red Lake Fisherman, Patrick Des Jarlait: The Patrick Des Jarlait Estate; **142** Francis Densmore: CORBIS; **152** PhotoDisc; **156** The False Mirror, 1928. Rene Magritte. Oil on canvas, 21 1/4 x 31 7/8". Purchase. Photograph © 1999 The Museum of Modern Art, New York/© 2000 Charly Herscovici, Brussels / Artists Rights Society (ARS), New York; **160** CORBIS/Craig Aurness; **165** © Nik Wheeler/Black Star/PNI; **167** © Alon Reininger/Contact Press/PNI; **169** Cherylene Lee; **176** Flower Garden, Valley-Field, from 'Fragments on the Theory and Practice of Landscape Gardening', pub. 1816 (colour litho) by Humphry Repton (1752-1818). Private Collection/The Stapleton Collection/Bridgeman Art Library; **183** The Pheasantry, from 'Fragments on the Theory and Practice of Landscape Gardening', pub. 1816 (colour litho) by Humphry Repton (1752-1818). Private Collection/The Stapleton Collection/Bridgeman Art Library; **189** The Vinery, from 'Fragments on the Theory and Practice of Landscape Gardening', pub. 1816 (colour litho) by Humphry Repton (1752-1818). Private Collection/The Stapleton Collection/Bridgeman Art Library; **191** Photo by Rod Aiken; **192** Homage to Chrysler Corp., Richard Hamilton: Tate Gallery, London/Art Resource, NY/© 2000 Artists Rights Society (ARS), New York / DACS, London; **192** Marilyn Monroe I, 1962. James Rosenquist. Oil and spray enamel on canvas, 7' 9" x 6' 1/4". The Sidney and Harriet Janis Collection. Photograph © 1999 The Museum of Modern Art, New York/© James Rosenquist/Licensed by VAGA, New York; **193** CORBIS/Burstein Collection/© 2000 Andy Warhol Foundation for the Visual Arts / Artists Rights Society (ARS), New York/TM Licensed by Campbell's Soup Co. All rights reserved; **198** Hmong portraits: © Scott Takushi; **198** Mountain: CORBIS/Brian Vikander; **203** © Scott Takushi; **204** Storycloth, Mee Vang. Private collection; **210** Kyoto National Museum; **212** Photo © Elvehjem Museum of Art, University of Wisconsin-Madison; **217** Photo © Elvehjem Museum of Art, University of Wisconsin-Madison; **223** Photograph by Don Perkins; **225** Gift of the Avalon Foundation. Photograph © 1999 Board of Trustees, National Gallery of Art, Washington, DC; **238** Rugby Players, 1920 by Andre Lhote (1885-1962). Petite Palais, Geneva, Switzerland/Bridgeman Art Library; **244** Photo courtesy James Patroulis; **246** CORBIS/Bettmann; **248** CORBIS/Bettmann; **252** CORBIS/Bettmann; **254** CORBIS/Bettmann; **256** CORBIS/Bettmann; **262** CORBIS/Bettmann; **263** PhotoDisc; **264** AP/Chris Gardner/Wide World Photos; **265** Courtesy of Carl Lindner; **265** Arnold Adoff; **270** PhotoDisc; **272** AP/Wide World Photos; **273** AP/Wide World Photos; **277** AP/Wide World Photos; **279** Richmond Times-Dispatch; **281** AP/Wide World Photos; **282** AP/Wide World Photos; **284** CORBIS/Jerry Cooke; **289** © Frank Capri/PNI; **290** PhotoDisc; **299** CORBIS/Bettmann; **300** CORBIS/Bettmann; **302** CORBIS/Bettmann; **306** Jerry Izenberg; **316** AP/Wide World Photos; **324** CORBIS/Francis G. Mayer; **328** CORBIS; **333** Drawing by Brian Pinkney. Alfred A. Knopf; **335** Random House; **336** © Culver Pictures/PNI; **337** (bottom) © Culver Pictures/PNI; **337** (top) CORBIS/Joseph Schwartz Collection; **342** The Church Cat's Dream II by Derold Page (contemporary artist). Private Collection/Bridgeman Art Library; **347** Black Cat by a Pond, 1983 (guache) Liz Wright (contemporary artist) Private Collection/Bridgeman Art Library; **353** AP/Wide World Photos; **361** CORBIS/Jack Moebes; **364** CORBIS/Bettmann; **367** Courtesy of John Johnson Ltd; **371** The Colorado Springs Fine Arts Center; **377** The Loch Ness Monster, illustration, c.1935 (litho) by Gino D'Achille (20th century) Private Collection/Bridgeman Art Library; **380** Andrew W. Mellon Fund, Photograph © 1999 Board of Trustees,

National Gallery of Art, Washington, DC; **381** AP/Wide World Photos; **386** CORBIS/Francis G. Mayer; **391** Library of Congress; **402** Peter Sickles/SuperStock; **406** Apple Blossoms and a Hummingbird, 1875 (oil on board) by Martin Johnson Heade. Private Collection/ Christie's Images/Bridgeman Art Library; **409** William Saroyan: Library of Congress; **409** Hummingbird: Corel; **411** Quetzalcoatl, the Toltec and Aztec god; the plumedserpant, god of the wind, learning and priesthood, master of life, creator and civiliser, patron of every art and inventor of metallurgy (manuscript)/Biblioteca Nazionale Centrale, Florence, Italy/Bridgeman Art Library; **413** Corel; **417** Library of Congress; **418** Southhampton City Art Gallery, Hampshire, UK/Bridgeman Art Library; **420** Maya Angelou: CORBIS/Bettman; **420** Paul Laurence Dunbar: Library of Congress; **425** NASA; **426** AP/Al Goldis/Wide World Photos; **428** Photograph by Diane Hardy; **433** Courtesy Reeve Lindbergh; **436** Library of Congress; **439** Photograph by Lizzie Brown; **440** Library of Congress; **442** Library of Congress; **443** CORBIS/Tom Nebbia; **448** Shared Visions Collection, The Heard Museum, Pheonix, Arizona. © Estate of Willard Stone; **449** CORBIS/Oscar White; **450** CORBIS/Gianni Dagli Orti; **470** CORBIS/North Carolina Museum of Art; **474** CORBIS/Mimmo Jodice; **476** Ola d'Aulaire; **477** CORBIS/Archivo Iconografico, S.A.; **482** ET Archive, London; **492** CORBIS/Gianni Dagli Orti; **501** CORBIS/© Werner Forman; **508** CORBIS/Kevin R. Morris; **510** CORBIS/Kevin R. Morris; **516** CORBIS/Asian Art & Archeology, Inc.; **519** Carolyn Swift; **529** CORBIS/North Carolina Museum of Art; **530** PhotoDisc; **542** John Hay Whitney Collection, © 1999 Board of Trustees, National Gallery of Art, Washington; **546** National Museum of American Art, Washington, DC/Art Resource, NY; **548** PhotoDisc; **551** PhotoDisc; **555** Courtesy Paulette Childress; **560** Chester Dale Collection. Board of Trustees, National Gallery of Art, Washington, DC; **563** AP/Wide World Photos; **569** Dungeness, Kent, 1936 (collage and gouache) by John Piper (1903-92) Private Collection/Bridgeman Art Library; **580** CORBIS/Hulton-Deutsh; **583** Library of Congress; **610** CORBIS/Francis G. Mayer/© Estate of Stuart Davis/Licensed by VAGA, New York; **615** © 1988 Faith Ringgold; **616** Eve Merriam: Photo by Bachrach; **616** Nikki Giovanni: Archive Photos; **618** © 1988 Faith Ringgold; **621** Library of Congress; **622** Library of Congress; **623** Elizabeth Bishop: Library of Congress; **623** Larry Woiwode: Basic Books; **626** Plant Art; **627** Library of Congress; **631** CORBIS/Archivo Iconografico, S.A.; **632** Archive Photos; **635** CORBIS/Chinch Gryniewicz; Ecoscene; **636** William Abranowitz/A+C Anthology; **639** CORBIS/Philadelphia Museum of Art/© 2000 Artists Rights Society (ARS), New York/ADAGP, Paris; **640** © 1974 by Evil Eye Music, Inc. Used by permission of HarperCollins Publishers; **641** AP/World Wide Photos; **646** PhotoDisc; **648** Photo by James H. Evans; **651** Campesino, 1976. Daniel Desiga. Collection of Alfredo Aragon; **652** Photo by Alison Freese; **657** Rare Book, Manuscript, and Special Collections Library, Duke University; **658** Library of Congress; **662** CORBIS/Archivo Iconografico, S.A.; **665** Wadsworth Atheneum, Hartford. The Ella Gallup Sumner and Mary Catlin Sumner Collection Fund./ © 2000 The Georgia O'Keeffe Foundation / Artists Rights Society (ARS), New York; **670** CORBIS/Asian Art & Archeology, Inc; **684** CORBIS; **695** Courtesy of Stages Theatre Company; **723** Courtesy of Stages Theatre Company; **733** Courtesy of Stages Theatre Company; **745** Courtesy of Stages Theatre Company; **749** Courtesy of Stages Theatre Company; **750** Robert Pinsky: Photo by Sigrid Estrada © 1998; **750** William Gibson: Library of Congress; **752** Child's Play Theatre; **753** Child's Play Theatre; **754** Child's Play Theatre; **766** Gift of S. C. Johnson & Son, Inc./Art Resource, NY; **770** CORBIS/Archivo Iconografico, S.A.; **773** Sherbourne Castle Estates; **788** Photo by Tim Keating. Courtesy of Random House; **792** © Stuart Cohen/The Image Works; **795** AP/Wide World Photos; **800** CORBIS; **805** Archive Photos; **810** © 1999 Southern Living, Inc. Mark Sandlin, photographer; **812** Photo by Beth Dreiling; **813** PhotoDisc; **826** Ed Paschke/SuperStock; **833** PhotoDisc; **838** Library of Congress; **838** Library of Congress; **839** Library of Congress; **840** Library of Congress; **845** Houghton Mifflin; **846** Photo by Constance Brown; **851** Planet Art; **855** Educational Web Adventures LLP

LITERARY ACKNOWLEDGMENTS

Arcade Publishing. "Name Giveaway" by Phil George. Copyright © 1975, 1993 by Kenneth Rosen. Reprinted from *Voices of the Rainbow* [p. 160], edited by Kenneth Rosen, published by Arcade Publishing, NY, NY. **Arte Público Press.** "Mango Juice" by Pat Mora is reprinted with permission from the publisher of *Borders* (Houston: Arte Público Press—University of Houston, 1986). **The Associated Press.** "Something Dreadfully Wrong in What Appeared to Be Picture-Perfect Launch" reprinted by permission of Associated Press. **Peter Bedrick Books.** "The Secret Name of Ra" from *Gods & Pharaohs from Egyptian Mythology*, by Geraldine Harris. Copyright © 1981 by Eurobook Limited. Reprinted by permission of Peter Bedrick Books, New York. **Bill Berger Associates Inc.** "The Dinner Party" by Mona Gardner, copyright © 1942, 1970 by *Saturday Review*, reprinted by permission of Bill Berger Associates Inc. **BOA Editions, Ltd.** Lucille Clifton: "in the inner city" copyright © 1987 by Lucille Clifton. Reprinted from *Good Woman: Poems and a Memoir* 1969–1980 with the permission of BOA Editions, Ltd. **Brandt & Brandt Literary Agents, Inc.** "The Serial Garden" from *Armitage, Armitage Fly Away Home* by Joan Aiken. Copyright © 1966 by McMillan and Company, Ltd. Copyright renewed © 1994 by Joan Aiken Enterprises, Ltd. Reprinted by permission of Brandt & Brandt Literary Agents, Inc. on behalf of the author. **Walker Brents.** "Hercules", retold by Walker Brents. Copyright © 2000 Walker Brents. Used by permission of Walker Brents. **Bret Adams Limited.** "Hollywood and the Pits" by Cherylene Lee. Copyright © 1992 by Cherylene Lee. Reprinted by permission of Bret Adams Ltd., 448 West 44th St., NY, NY 10036, 212-765-5630. **Candlewick Press Inc.** "Pets" from *What Do Fish Have to Do with Anything?* Text © 1997 Avi Wortis. Cover illustrations by Tracy Mitchell. Reproduced by permission of Candlewick Press Inc., Cambridge, MA. **CDG Books Canada Inc.** From "Luke Baldwin's Vow" as published in *Luke Baldwin's Vow* by Morley Callaghan. Copyright © Morley Callaghan, 1948. Reprinted by permission of Macmillan Canada, an imprint of CDG Books Canada Inc. **Paulette Childress.** "Getting the Facts of Life" by Paulette Childress. Originally published in *Memory of Kin: Stories About Family by Black Writers*. Reprinted by permission of the author. **Ruth Cohen, Inc.** "The Inn of Lost Time", © 1989 by Lensey Namioka, from *Connections: Short Stories by Outstanding Writers For Young Adults*, edited by Donald R. Gallo. Reprinted by permission of Lensey Namioka. All rights are reserved by the Author. **Don Congdon Associates.** "The Foghorn", reprinted by permission of Don Congdon Associates, Inc. Copyright © 1951 by the Curtis Publishing Co., renewed 1979 by Ray Bradbury. **Cynthia Cooper.** "How She Played the Game", copyright 1987 by Cynthia L. Cooper. **The Ecco Press.** "Misty grasses…" by Buson, "The old pond—" by Bashō, "Summer night—" by Issa, from *The Essential Haiku* edited by Robert Hass. Selection and translation copyright © 1994 by Robert Hass. Reprinted by permission of The Ecco Press. **Farrar, Straus & Giroux, LLC.** "A Deserted Barn" from "The End" from *Beyond the Bedroom Wall* by Larry Woiwode. Originally published in *The New Yorker.* Copyright © 1975 by Larry Woiwode. Reprinted by permission of Farrar, Straus & Giroux, LLC. "Filling Station" from *The Complete Poems 1927–1979* by Elizabeth Bishop. Copyright © 1979, 1983 by Alice Helen Methfessel. Reprinted by permission of Farrar, Straus & Giroux, Inc. "The Green Mamba" from *Going Solo* by Roald Dahl. Copyright © 1986 by Roald Dahl. Reprinted by permission of Farrar, Straus & Giroux, Inc. "If You Could Write One Great Poem, What Would You Want It to Be About" from *The Figured Wheel: New and Collected Poems 1966–1996.* Copyright 1996 by Robert Pinsky. Reprinted by permission of Farrar, Straus & Giroux, LLC. **Richard Garcia.** "The City is So Big" by Richard Garcia. Copyright © 1973 by Richard Garcia. **Ken Haedrich.** "How to Chop an Onion in Four Easy Steps" by Ken Haedrich from *Good Cook's Companion.* Reprinted by permission of the author. **Harcourt Brace & Company.** "The Hummingbird That Lived Through Winter" from *My Kind of Crazy, Wonderful People: Seventeen Stories and a Play,* copyright 1944 and renewed 1972 by William Saroyan, reprinted by permission of Harcourt Brace & Company. "Theme in Yellow" and "Under the Harvest Moon" from *Chicago Poems* by Carl Sandburg, copyright 1916 by Holt, Rinehart and Winston and renewed 1944 by Carl Sandburg, reprinted by permission of Harcourt, Inc. **HarperCollins Publishers, Inc.** "Destroy the Four Olds!" from *Red Scarf Girl* by Ji-li Jiang. Copyright © 1997 by Ji li Jiang. Foreword copyright © 1997 by HarperCollins Publishers. Used by permission of HarperCollins Publishers. "Forgotten Language" and "Hector the Collector" from *Where the Sidewalk Ends* by Shel Silverstein. Copyright © 1974 By Evil Eye Music, Inc. Used by permission of HarperCollins Publishers. "How the Snake Got Poison" (pages 105–106) from *Mules and Men* by Zora Neale Hurston. Copyright 1935 by Zora Neale Hurston. Copyright renewed 1963 by John C. Hurston and Joel Hurston. Reprinted by permission of HarperCollins Publishers, Inc. "Point Guard" from *Sports Pages* by Arnold Adoff. Text copyright © 1986 by Arnold Adoff. Used by permission of HarperCollins Publishers. "Searching for January" (pages 111–120) from *The Dixon Cornbelt League and Other Baseball Stories* by W. P. Kinsella. Copyright © 1993 by W. P. Kinsella. Reprinted by permission of HarperCollins Publishers, Inc. **Frank Higgins.** "Tennis in the City; for Arthur Ashe" by Frank Higgins. Reprinted by permission of Frank Higgins, 12500 E. 53rd Terrace, Kansas City, MO 64133. **Henry Holt and Company, LLC.** "I to My Perils" from *The Collected Poems of A. E. Housman.* Copyright 1936 by Barclays Ltd., © 1964 by Robert E. Symons. Reprinted by permission of Henry Holt and Company, LLC. "Once by the Pacific" from *The Poetry of Robert Frost* edited by Edward Connery Lathem. Copyright 1928, © 1969 by Henry Holt and Co., © 1956 by Robert Frost. Reprinted by permission of Henry Holt and Company, LLC. **Holy Cow! Press.** "Jed's Grandfather" from *Turtle Meat and Other Stories* by Joseph Bruchac, copyright © 1992 (Holy Cow! Press). Reprinted by permission of the publisher. **Houghton Mifflin Company.** "Blackberry Eating" from *Three Books* by Galway Kinnell. Copyright © 1993 by Galway Kinnell. Previously published in *Mortal Acts, Mortal Words* (1980). Reprinted by permission of Houghton Mifflin Company. All rights reserved. "Ships in the Desert" from *Earth in the Balance* by Al Gore. Copyright © 1992 by Senator Al Gore. Reprinted by permission of Houghton Mifflin Company. All rights reserved. "Estimated Annual Rate of Species Loss" chart from *Global Ecology Handbook* by Global Tomorrow Coalition. Copyright (c) 1990 by The Global Tomorrow Coalition. Reprinted by permission of Beacon Press, Boston. The Aqua Lung from *The New Way Things Work* by David Macaulay. Text copyright © 1988, 1998 David Macaulay, Neil Ardley. Illustrations copyright © 1988, 1998 David Macaulay. Compilation copyright © 1988, 1998 Dorling Kindersley Limited, London. Reprinted by permission of Houghton Mifflin Company. All rights reserved. "Qwertyuiop" from *Ghostly Companions* © 1984 Vivien Alcock. First published by Methuen Children's Books, an imprint of Egmont Children's Books Limited, London. Reprinted in the United States by permission of John Johnson Limited, London. Reprinted in Canada by permission of Egmont Children's Books Ltd., London. **Alfred A. Knopf, Inc.** "The 11:59" from *The Dark-Thirty: Southern Tales of the Supernatural* by Patricia C. McKissack. Text copyright © 1992 by Patricia C. McKissack. Reprinted by permission of Alfred A. Knopf, Inc. *The Snow Goose* by Paul Gallico. Copyright 1940 by The Curtis Publishing Company. Copyright renewed 1968 by Paul Gallico. Reprinted by permission of Alfred A. Knopf, a division of Random House, Inc. "Zebra" from *Zebra and Other Stories* by Chaim Potok. Copyright © 1998 by Chaim Potok. Reprinted by permission of Alfred A. Knopf, Inc. **Barbara Kouts.** "Birdfoot's Grampa" by Joseph Bruchac from *Entering Onondaga,* © 1978. **Carl Lindner.** "First Love", originally published in *Cottonwood Review 33* (Spring, 1984), copyright by the author. Reprinted by permission of the author. **Liveright Publishing Corporation.** "the/ sky/ was", copyright 1925, 1953, © 1991 by the Trustees for the E .E. Cummings Trust. Copyright © 1976 by George James Firmage. from *Complete Poems: 1904–1962* by E. E. Cummings, edited by George J. Firmage. Reprinted by permission of Liveright Publishing Corporation. **Carol Mann Agency.** "The Size of Things", excerpt from *Red Giants and White Dwarfs* by Robert Jastrow, pages 8–11, 13–15. Copyright © 1979 by Reader's Library, Inc. Reprinted by permission of Carol Mann Agency. **Khaled Mattawa.** "Freedom" by Saadi Youssef, translated by Khaled Mattawa. Reprinted by permission of Khaled Mattawa. **Rona Maynard.** "The Fan Club", copyright by Rona Maynard. **Merlyn's Pen, Inc.** "Investment in the Future" by Liana Fredley from *Merlyn's Pen: Fiction, Essays, and Poems by America's Teens.* Copyright by Merlyn's Pen, Inc. All rights reserved. **The New York Times Company.** "A Black Athlete Looks at Education" by Arthur Ashe, copyright 1977 by the New York Times Co. Reprinted by permission. **Naomi Shihab Nye.** "The Lost Parrot" from *Hugging the Jukebox* by Naomi Shihab Nye. Reprinted by permission of the author. **Simon J. Ortiz.** "Hunger in New York", permission to reprint granted by Simon J. Ortiz. Poem originally published in *Woven Stone,* University of Arizona Press, Tucson, Arizona, 1992. "My Father's Song", permission to reprint granted by Simon J. Ortiz. Poem originally published in *Woven Stone,* University of Arizona Press, Tucson, Arizona, 1992. **Fifi Oscard Agency, Inc.** "Appearances Are Destructive" by Mark Mathabane. Copyright Mark Mathabane. Reprinted by permission of Fifi Oscard Agency, Inc. From *Off the Court* by Arthur Ashe. Copyright Arthur Ashe. Reprinted by permission of Fifi Oscard Agency, Inc. **Penguin Putnam Inc.** "Be-ers and Doers" from *The Leaving and Other Stories* by Budge Wilson. Copyright © 1990 by Budge Wilson, compilation. Used by permission of Philomel Books, a division of Penguin Putnam, Inc. Reprinted in Canada by permission of

House of Anansi Press Limited. "Elizabeth I" from *Ten Queens: Portraits of Women of Power* by Milton Meltzer, copyright © 1998 by Milton Meltzer. Used by permission of Dutton Children's Books, a division of Penguin Putnam Inc. **Poolbeg Press, Ltd.** Excerpt "Amaterasu", from "The Sun, The Looking-Glass, and the Eight-Headed Dragon", retold by Carolyn Swift from *World Myths and Tales*. Copyright © 1993 by Carolyn Swift. Reprinted by permission of Poolbeg Press, Ltd. **Random House, Inc.** "Caesar the Giant" from *My Life in Dog Years* by Gary Paulsen. Copyright ©1998 by Gary Paulsen. Used by permission of Delacorte Press, a division of Random House, Inc. "Caged Bird" from *Shaker, Why Don't You Sing?* by Maya Angelou. Copyright © 1983 by Maya Angelou. Reprinted by permission of Random House, Inc. "The Instruction of Indra", pages 62–64 from *The Power of Myth* by Joseph Campbell & Bill Moyers. Copyright © 1988 by Apostrophe S Productions, Inc. and Bill Moyers and Alfred Van der Marck Editions, Inc. for itself and the estate of Joseph Campbell. Used by permission of Doubleday, a division of Random House, Inc. "Mute Dancers: How to Watch a Hummingbird" is a retitled excerpt from *A Slender Thread* by Diane Ackerman. Copyright © 1996 by Diane Ackerman. Reprinted by permission of Random House, Inc. "Persephone and Demeter" from *D'Aulaire's Book of Greek Myths* by Ingri & Edgar Parin D'Aulaire. Copyright ©1962 by Ingri and Edgar Parin D'Aulaire. Used by permission of Random House Children's Books, a division of Random House, Inc. **Marian Reiner.** "How to Eat a Poem" from *A Sky Full of Poems* by Eve Merriam. Copyright © 1964, 1970, 1973 by Eve Merriam. Copyright renewed 1992 Eve Merriam, 1998 Dee Michel, Guy Michel. Reprinted by permission of Marian Reiner. "The Women's 400 Meters" from *The Sidewalk Racer and Other Poems of Sports and Motion* by Lillian Morrison. Copyright © 1965, 1967, 1968, 1977 by Lillian Morrison. Used by permission of Marian Reiner for the author. "Two People I Want to Be Like" from *If Only I Could Tell You* by Eve Merriam. Copyright 1983 Eve Merriam. Reprinted by permission of Marian Reiner. **Estate of Quentin Reynolds.** "A Secret for Two", by Quentin Reynolds. Copyright 1936 by Crowell-Collier Publishing. Estate of Quentin Reynolds, 35 E. 72nd Street, New York, NY 10021. **Diana Rivera.** "Under the Apple Tree" by Diana Rivera. Copyright © 1996 by Diana Rivera. **Flora Roberts, Inc.** *The Miracle Worker* by William Gibson. Copyright © 1956, 1957 by William Gibson; copyright © 1959, 1960 by Tamarack Productions, Ltd., and George S. Klein and Leo Garel as trustees under three separate deeds of trust; copyright renewed © 1977 by William Gibson. Used by permission of Flora Roberts, Inc. **Scholastic Inc.** "Tested by Dust", "Banks", "Beat Wheat", "Give Up on Wheat" from *Out of the Dust* by Karen Hesse. Published by Scholastic Press, a division of Scholastic Inc. Copyright © 1997 by Karen Hesse. Reprinted by permission. "The Power to Decide" by Kathy Wilmore, published in *Junior Scholastic*, November 3, 1997. Copyright © 1997 by Scholastic Inc. Reprinted by permission. **Simon & Schuster.** "A Day's Wait", reprinted with permission of Scribner, a division of Simon & Schuster, from *The Short Stories of Ernest Hemingway*. Copyright 1933 by Charles Scribner's Sons. Copyright renewed © 1961 by Mary Hemingway. "Feel Like a Bird", reprinted with the permission of Simon & Schuster Books for Young Readers, an imprint of Simon & Schuster Children's Publishing Division from *The Complete Poems to Solve* by May Swenson. Text copyright © 1993 The Literary Estate of May Swenson. "Humming Bird". Reprinted with the permission of Atheneum Books for Young Readers, an imprint of Simon & Schuster Children's

Publishing Division from *The Song in My Head and Other Poems* by Felice Holman. Text copyright © 1985 Felice Holman. **The Society of Authors.** "The Listeners" from *The Complete Poems of Walter de la Mare* by Walter de la Mare. Reprinted by permission of The Literary Trustees of Walter de la Mare, and the Society of Authors as their representative. **Southern Progress Corp.** "The Price of Freedom" by Cassandra Vanhooser. Copyright 1999 Southern Living, Inc. Reprinted with permission. **Temple University Press.** Excerpted and reprinted from "An Unforgettable Journey" by Maijue Xiong, included in *Hmong Means Free: Life in Laos and America* edited by Sucheng Chan, by permission of Temple University Press. © 1994 by Temple University. All rights reserved. **The University of Arizona Press.** "The Ground is Always Damp" from *Blue Horses Rush In* by Luci Tapahonso. Copyright © 1997 Luci Tapahonso. Reprinted by permission of the University of Arizona Press. **The University of Georgia Press.** "American History" from *The Latin Deli: Prose & Poetry* by Judith Ortiz Cofer, published by The University of Georgia Press. Copyright © 1993 Judith Ortiz Cofer. Reprinted by permission of the publisher. "Lost in Translation" from *Lost in Translation* by Steven Harvey, published by The University of Georgia Press. Copyright © 1997 by Steven Harvey. Reprinted by permission of the publisher. **University of Virginia Library.** From *An Indian Boy's Story* by Ah-nen-la-de-ni. Reprinted by permission of Electronic Text Center, University of Virginia Library. **University Press of Virginia.** "Sympathy" from *The Collected Poetry of Paul Laurence Dunbar*. Reprinted by permission of the University Press of Virginia. **Rhoda Weyr.** "Flying" by Reeve Lindbergh. Copyright © 1966 by Reeve Lindbergh. Permission granted by The Rhoda Weyr Agency, New York. **William Morris Agency, Inc.** "Roberto Clemente: A Bittersweet Memoir" from *Great Latin Sports Figures* by Jerry Izenberg. Copyright © 1976 by Jerry Izenberg. Reprinted by permission of William Morris Agency, Inc. on behalf of the Author. **William Morrow & Company, Inc.** "Poetry" from *The Women and the Men* by Nikki Giovanni. Text: Copyright © 1970, 1974 and 1975 by Nikki Giovanni. Reprinted by permission of William Morrow and Company, Inc. **W.W. Norton.** "400-Meter Freestyle", copyright © 1959 and renewed 1987 by Maxine Kumin, from *Selected Poems 1960–1990* by Maxine Kumin. Reprinted by permission of W.W. Norton & Company, Inc. **Yankee Publishing Inc.** Recipe for Salsa. Reprinted from *The Old Farmer's Almanac Guide to Summer's Best Recipes* © 1998, Yankee Publishing Inc., Dublin, NH.

We have made every effort to trace the ownership of all copyrighted material and to secure permission from copyright holders. In the event of any question arising as to the use of any material, we will be pleased to make the necessary corrections in future printings. Thanks are due to the following authors, publishers, and agents for permission to use the materials indicated.